Vending machines have these labels that say "war~m"
on them during the winter. I feel so relaxed when I read
it as "deadlines coming clo~se." In the first chapter, if
Luffy had said "I'll become the Pirate Ki~ng!" it would
have seemed really weird. Time to star~t volume 52!

– *Eiichiro Oda, 2008*

· **AUTHOR BIOGRAPHY** ·

Eiichiro Oda began his manga career in 1992 at the age of 17,
when his one-shot cowboy manga *Wanted!* won second place in
the coveted Tezuka manga awards. Oda went on to work as an
assistant to some of the biggest manga artists in the industry,
including Nobuhiro Watsuki, before winning the Hop Step
Award for new manga artists. His pirate adventure *One Piece*,
which debuted in *Weekly Shonen Jump* magazine in 1997,
quickly became one of the most popular manga in Japan.

ONE PIECE: SABAODY 52-53-54

SHONEN JUMP Manga Omnibus Edition
A compilation of the graphic novel volumes 52–54

STORY & ART BY EIICHIRO ODA

English Adaptation: Megan Bates (graphic novel volume 52),
Lance Caselman (graphic novel volumes 53 and 54)
Translation: Taylor Engel, HC Language Solutions, Inc (graphic novel volumes 52 and 53),
Labaaman, HC Language Solutions, Inc (graphic novel volume 54)
Touch-up Art & Lettering: Hudson Yards (graphic novel volumes 52 and 53),
Vanessa Satone (graphic novel volume 54)
Design: Shawn Carrico (Omnibus edition),
Sean Lee (graphic novel volumes 52 and 54),
Fawn Lau (graphic novel volume 53)
Editor: Megan Bates (Omnibus edition),
Megan Bates and Alexis Kirsch (graphic novel volumes 52 and 53),
Yuki Murashige, John Bae and Alexis Kirsch (graphic novel volume 54)

Printed in the U.S.A.

Published by VIZ Media, LLC
P.O. Box 77010
San Francisco, CA 94107

10 9 8 7 6 5 4 3 2 1
Omnibus edition first printing, December 2016

www.viz.com

www.shonenjump.com

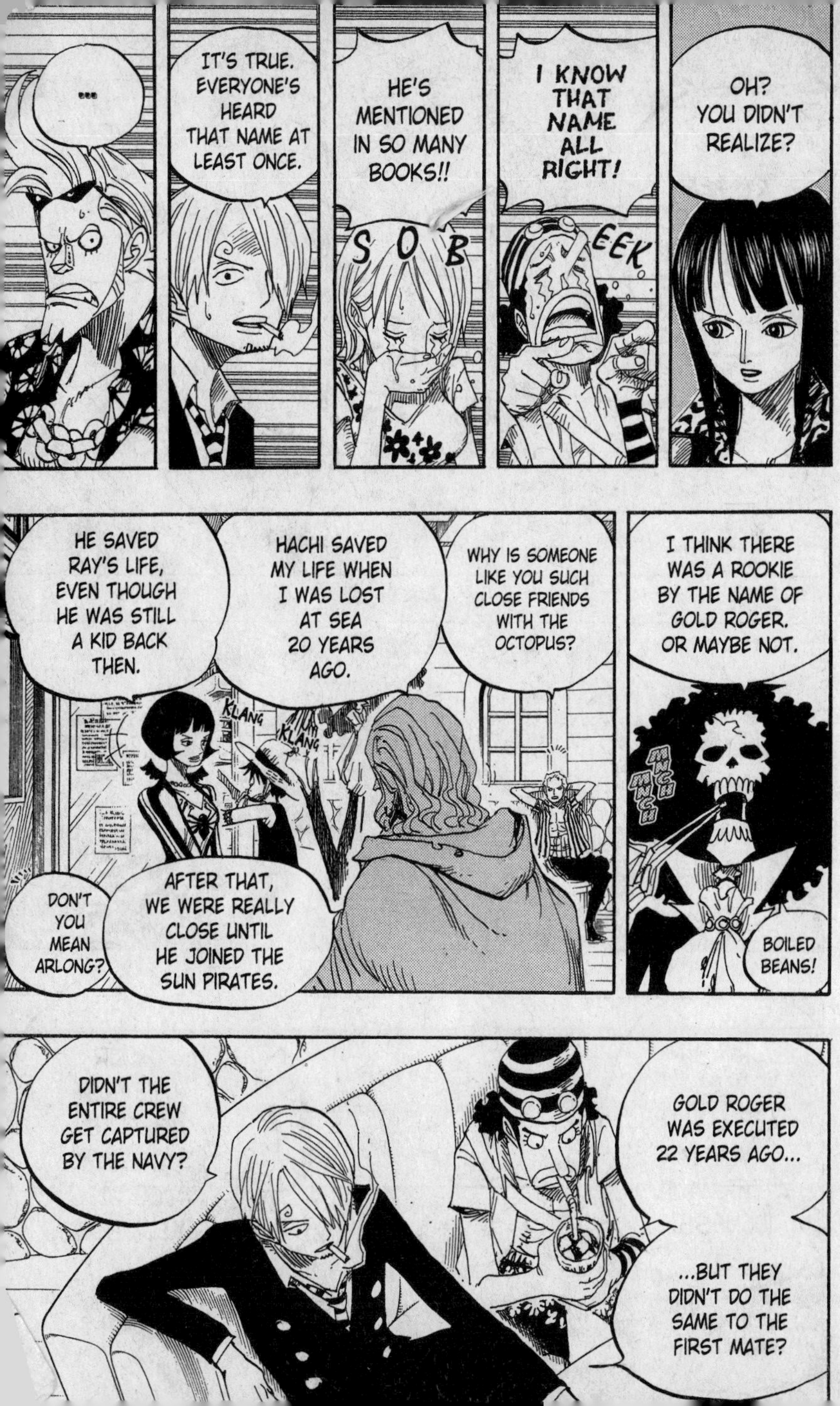

OH? YOU DIDN'T REALIZE?
I KNOW THAT NAME ALL RIGHT!
EEK
HE'S MENTIONED IN SO MANY BOOKS!!
SOB
IT'S TRUE. EVERYONE'S HEARD THAT NAME AT LEAST ONCE.
...
I THINK THERE WAS A ROOKIE BY THE NAME OF GOLD ROGER. OR MAYBE NOT.
BOILED BEANS!
WHY IS SOMEONE LIKE YOU SUCH CLOSE FRIENDS WITH THE OCTOPUS?
HACHI SAVED MY LIFE WHEN I WAS LOST AT SEA 20 YEARS AGO.
HE SAVED RAY'S LIFE, EVEN THOUGH HE WAS STILL A KID BACK THEN.
KLANG
KLANG
AFTER THAT, WE WERE REALLY CLOSE UNTIL HE JOINED THE SUN PIRATES.
DON'T YOU MEAN ARLONG?
GOLD ROGER WAS EXECUTED 22 YEARS AGO...
...BUT THEY DIDN'T DO THE SAME TO THE FIRST MATE?
DIDN'T THE ENTIRE CREW GET CAPTURED BY THE NAVY?

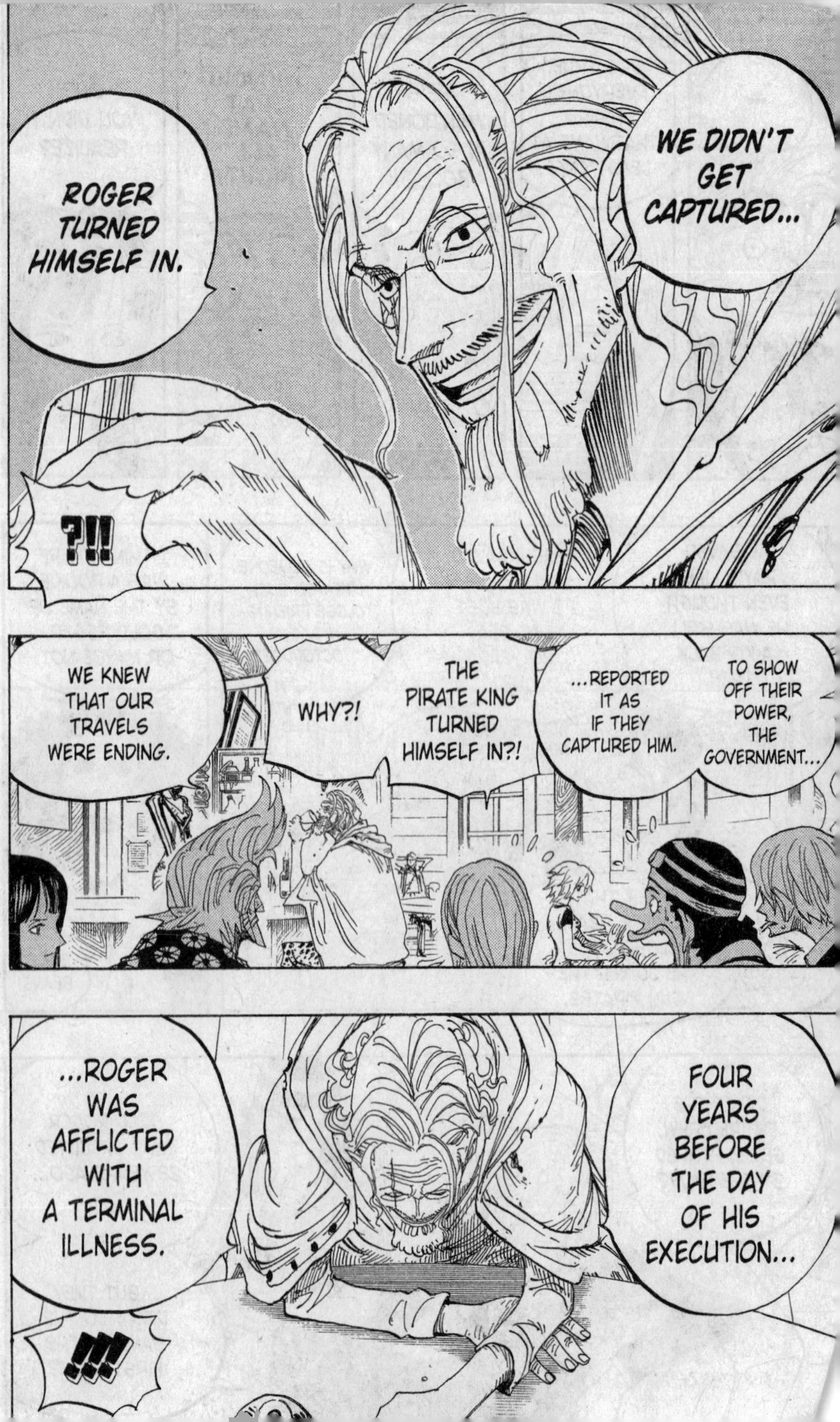
WE DIDN'T GET CAPTURED...
ROGER TURNED HIMSELF IN.
?!!
TO SHOW OFF THEIR POWER, THE GOVERNMENT...
...REPORTED IT AS IF THEY CAPTURED HIM.
THE PIRATE KING TURNED HIMSELF IN?!
WHY?!
WE KNEW THAT OUR TRAVELS WERE ENDING.
FOUR YEARS BEFORE THE DAY OF HIS EXECUTION...
...ROGER WAS AFFLICTED WITH A TERMINAL ILLNESS.
!!!

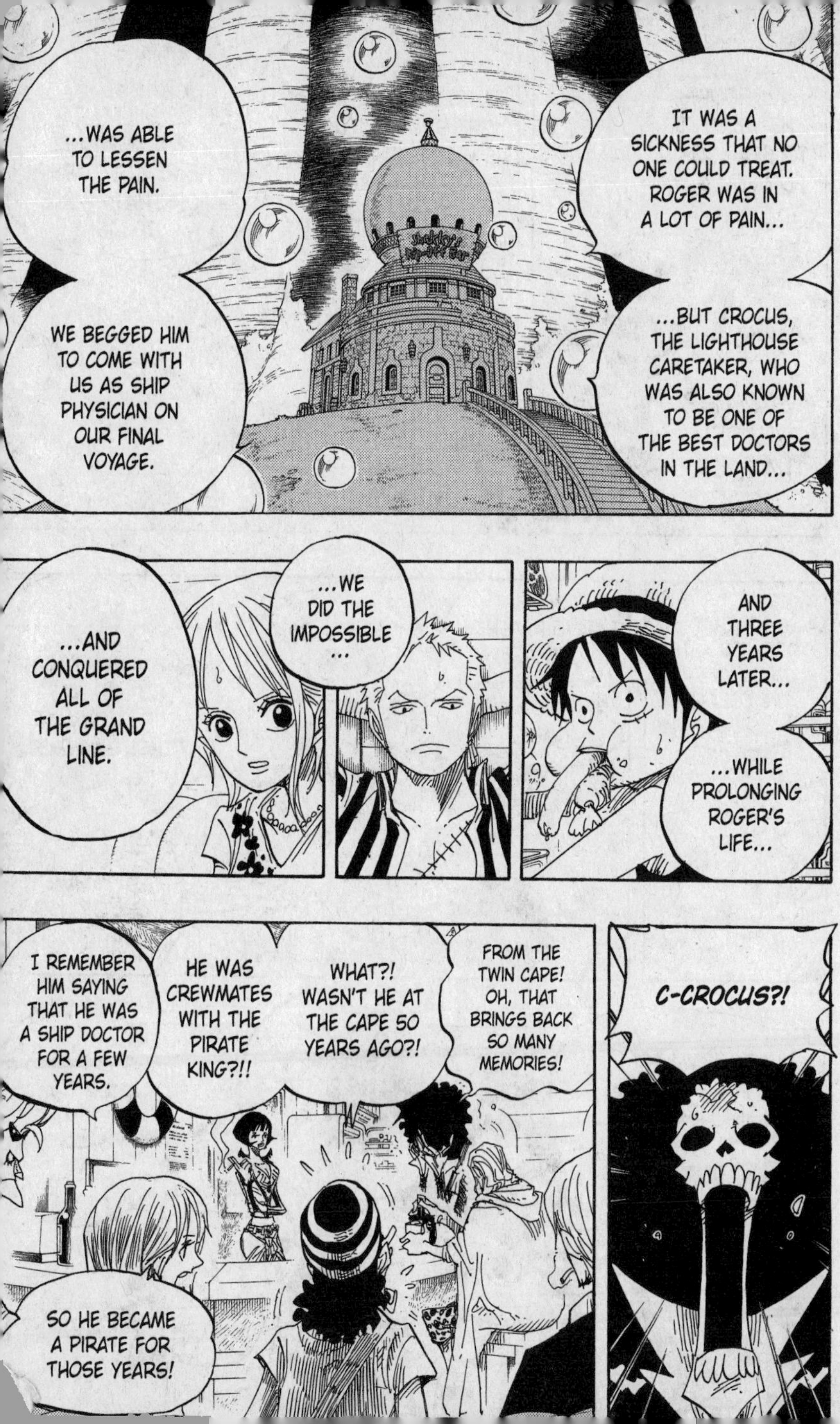
IT WAS A SICKNESS THAT NO ONE COULD TREAT. ROGER WAS IN A LOT OF PAIN...
...BUT CROCUS, THE LIGHTHOUSE CARETAKER, WHO WAS ALSO KNOWN TO BE ONE OF THE BEST DOCTORS IN THE LAND...
...WAS ABLE TO LESSEN THE PAIN.
WE BEGGED HIM TO COME WITH US AS SHIP PHYSICIAN ON OUR FINAL VOYAGE.
AND THREE YEARS LATER...
...WHILE PROLONGING ROGER'S LIFE...
...WE DID THE IMPOSSIBLE...
...AND CONQUERED ALL OF THE GRAND LINE.
C-CROCUS?!
FROM THE TWIN CAPE! OH, THAT BRINGS BACK SO MANY MEMORIES!
WHAT?! WASN'T HE AT THE CAPE 50 YEARS AGO?!
HE WAS CREWMATES WITH THE PIRATE KING?!!
I REMEMBER HIM SAYING THAT HE WAS A SHIP DOCTOR FOR A FEW YEARS.
SO HE BECAME A PIRATE FOR THOSE YEARS!

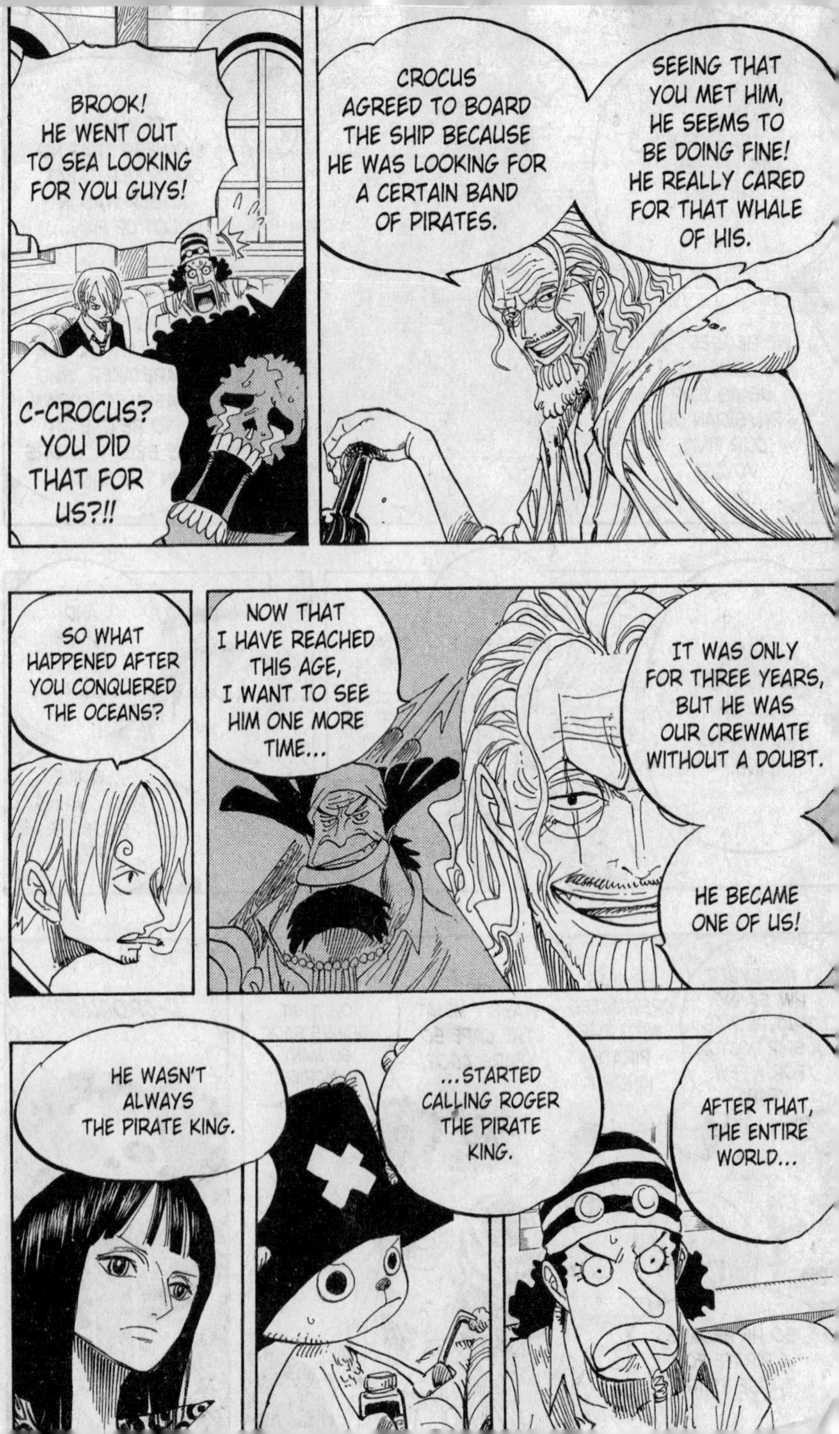
SEEING THAT YOU MET HIM, HE SEEMS TO BE DOING FINE! HE REALLY CARED FOR THAT WHALE OF HIS.
CROCUS AGREED TO BOARD THE SHIP BECAUSE HE WAS LOOKING FOR A CERTAIN BAND OF PIRATES.
BROOK! HE WENT OUT TO SEA LOOKING FOR YOU GUYS!
C-CROCUS? YOU DID THAT FOR US?!!
IT WAS ONLY FOR THREE YEARS, BUT HE WAS OUR CREWMATE WITHOUT A DOUBT.
HE BECAME ONE OF US!
NOW THAT I HAVE REACHED THIS AGE, I WANT TO SEE HIM ONE MORE TIME...
SO WHAT HAPPENED AFTER YOU CONQUERED THE OCEANS?
AFTER THAT, THE ENTIRE WORLD...
...STARTED CALLING ROGER THE PIRATE KING.
HE WASN'T ALWAYS THE PIRATE KING.

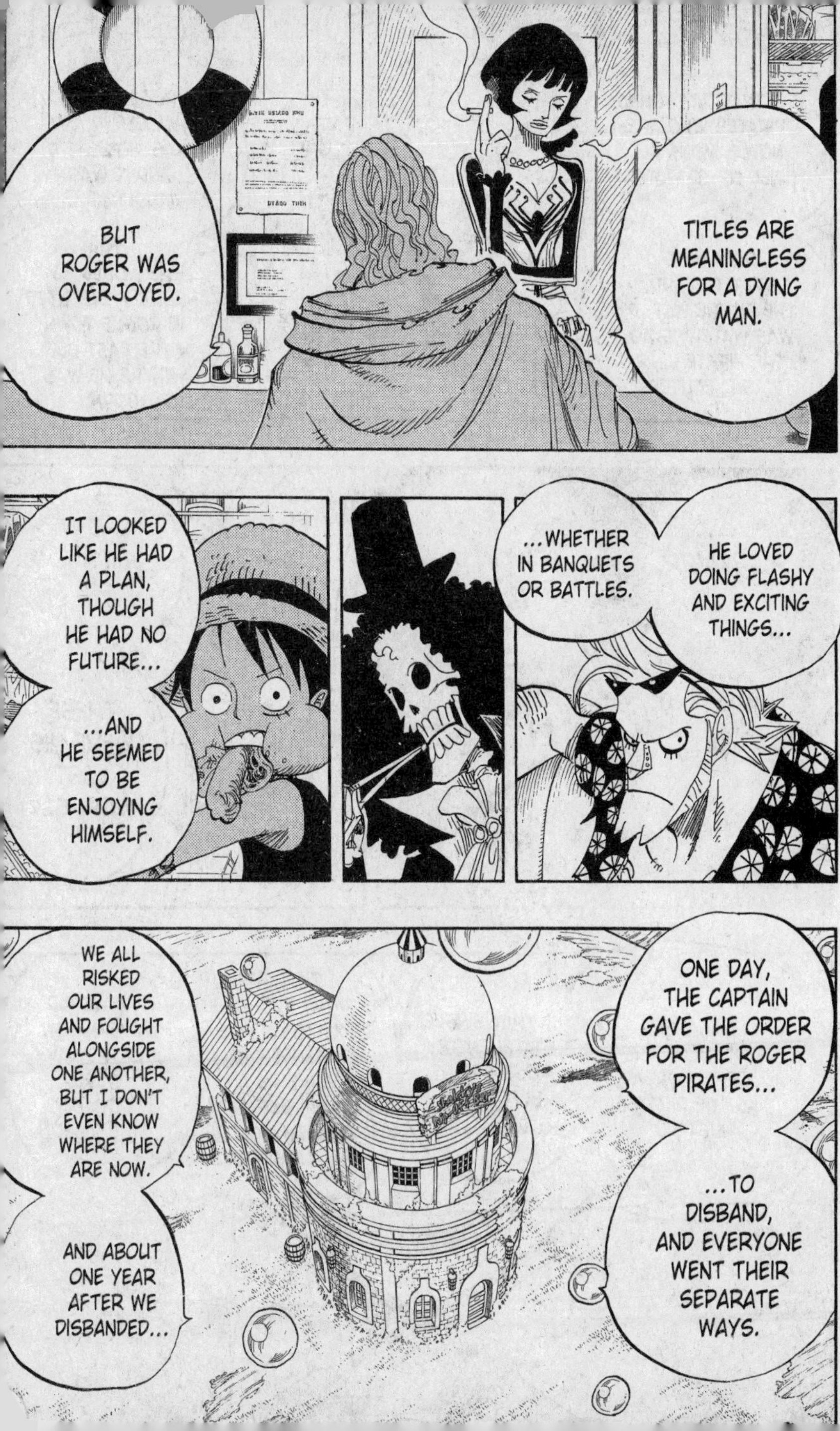
TITLES ARE MEANINGLESS FOR A DYING MAN.
BUT ROGER WAS OVERJOYED.
HE LOVED DOING FLASHY AND EXCITING THINGS...
...WHETHER IN BANQUETS OR BATTLES.
IT LOOKED LIKE HE HAD A PLAN, THOUGH HE HAD NO FUTURE...
...AND HE SEEMED TO BE ENJOYING HIMSELF.
ONE DAY, THE CAPTAIN GAVE THE ORDER FOR THE ROGER PIRATES...
...TO DISBAND, AND EVERYONE WENT THEIR SEPARATE WAYS.
WE ALL RISKED OUR LIVES AND FOUGHT ALONGSIDE ONE ANOTHER, BUT I DON'T EVEN KNOW WHERE THEY ARE NOW.
AND ABOUT ONE YEAR AFTER WE DISBANDED...

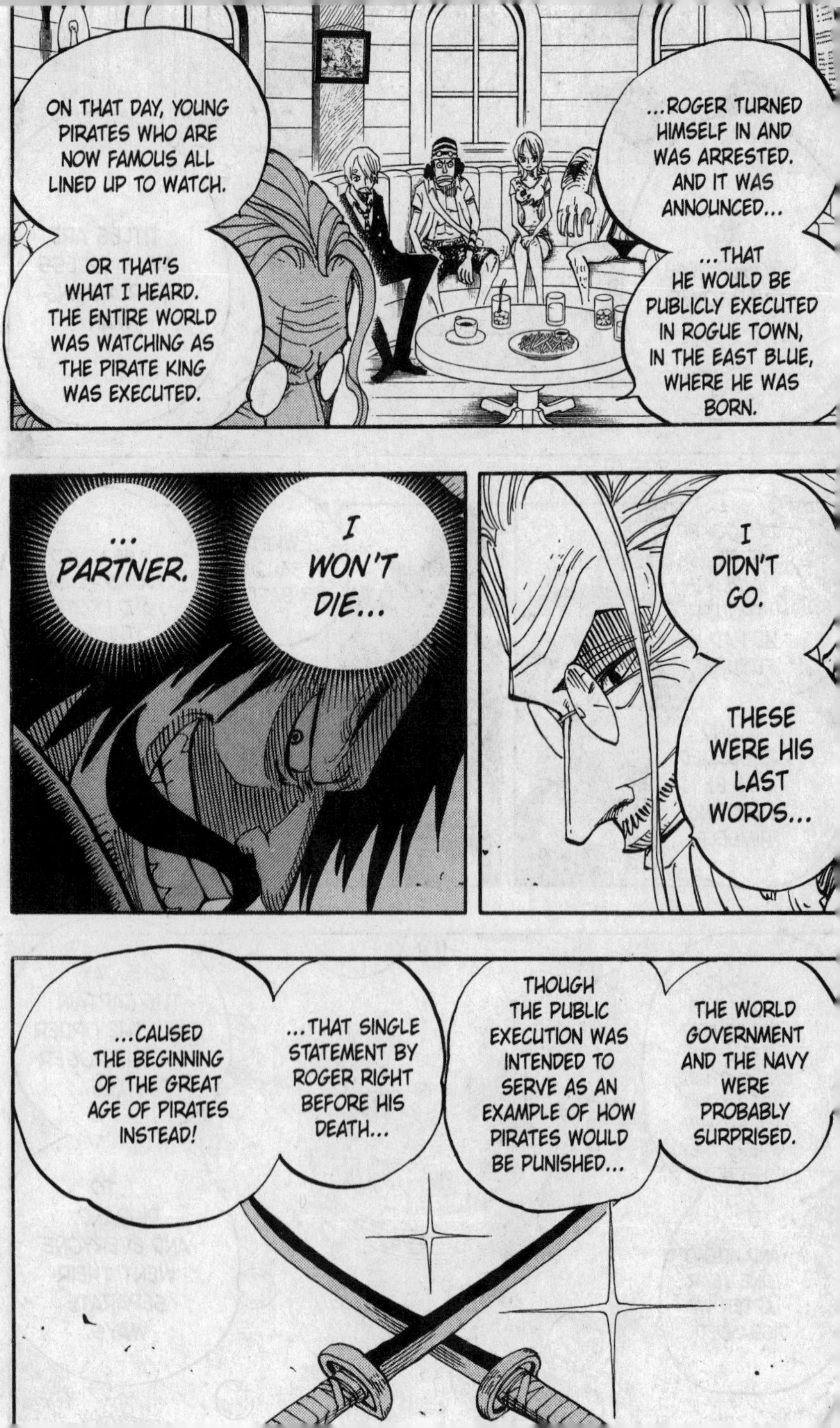
...ROGER TURNED HIMSELF IN AND WAS ARRESTED. AND IT WAS ANNOUNCED...
...THAT HE WOULD BE PUBLICLY EXECUTED IN ROGUE TOWN, IN THE EAST BLUE, WHERE HE WAS BORN.
ON THAT DAY, YOUNG PIRATES WHO ARE NOW FAMOUS ALL LINED UP TO WATCH.
OR THAT'S WHAT I HEARD. THE ENTIRE WORLD WAS WATCHING AS THE PIRATE KING WAS EXECUTED.
I DIDN'T GO.
THESE WERE HIS LAST WORDS...
I WON'T DIE...
... PARTNER.
THE WORLD GOVERNMENT AND THE NAVY WERE PROBABLY SURPRISED.
THOUGH THE PUBLIC EXECUTION WAS INTENDED TO SERVE AS AN EXAMPLE OF HOW PIRATES WOULD BE PUNISHED...
...THAT SINGLE STATEMENT BY ROGER RIGHT BEFORE HIS DEATH...
...CAUSED THE BEGINNING OF THE GREAT AGE OF PIRATES INSTEAD!

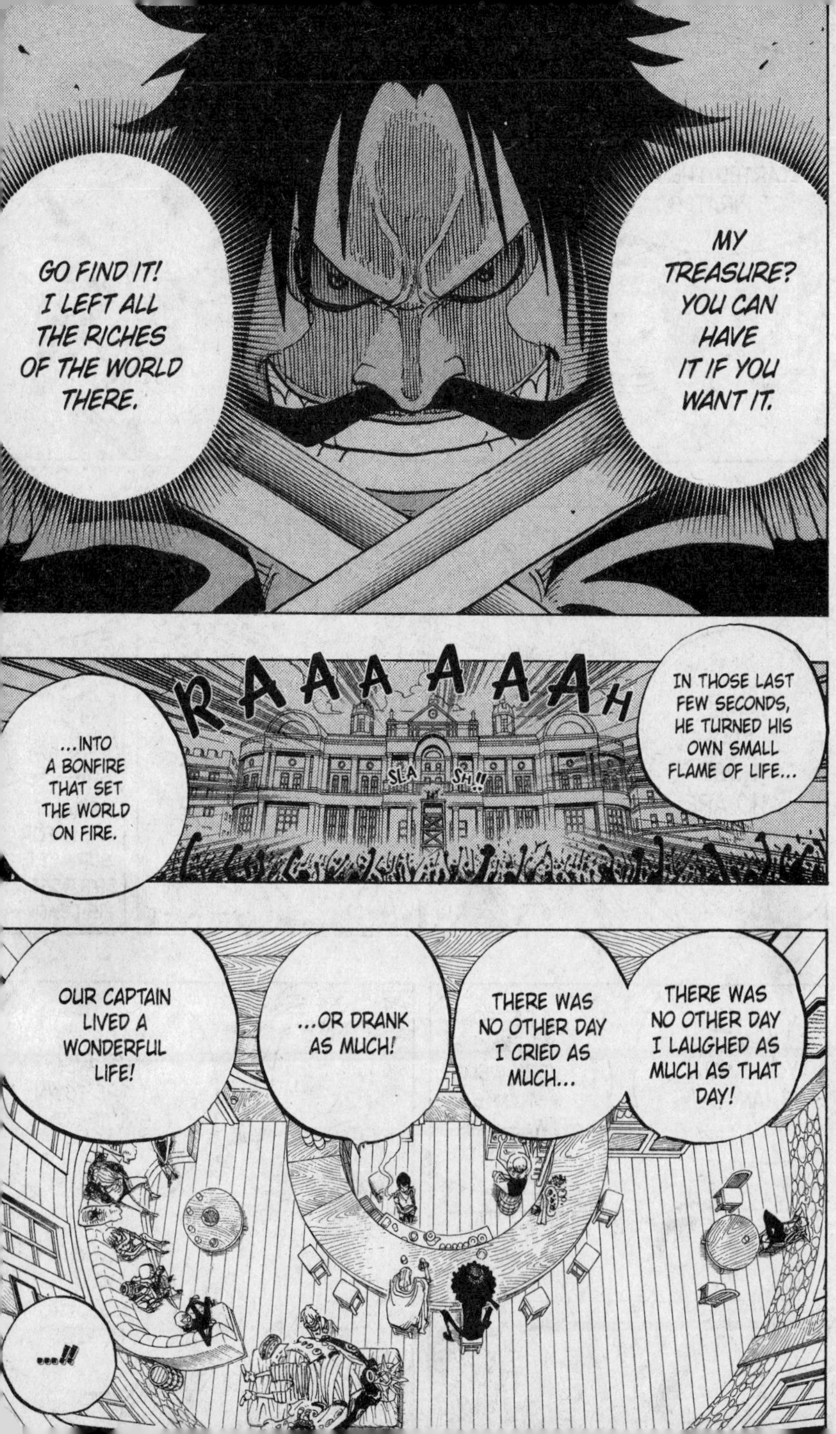
MY TREASURE? YOU CAN HAVE IT IF YOU WANT IT.
GO FIND IT! I LEFT ALL THE RICHES OF THE WORLD THERE.
IN THOSE LAST FEW SECONDS, HE TURNED HIS OWN SMALL FLAME OF LIFE...
RAAAAAAH
SLASH!!
...INTO A BONFIRE THAT SET THE WORLD ON FIRE.
THERE WAS NO OTHER DAY I LAUGHED AS MUCH AS THAT DAY!
THERE WAS NO OTHER DAY I CRIED AS MUCH...
...OR DRANK AS MUCH!
OUR CAPTAIN LIVED A WONDERFUL LIFE!
...!!

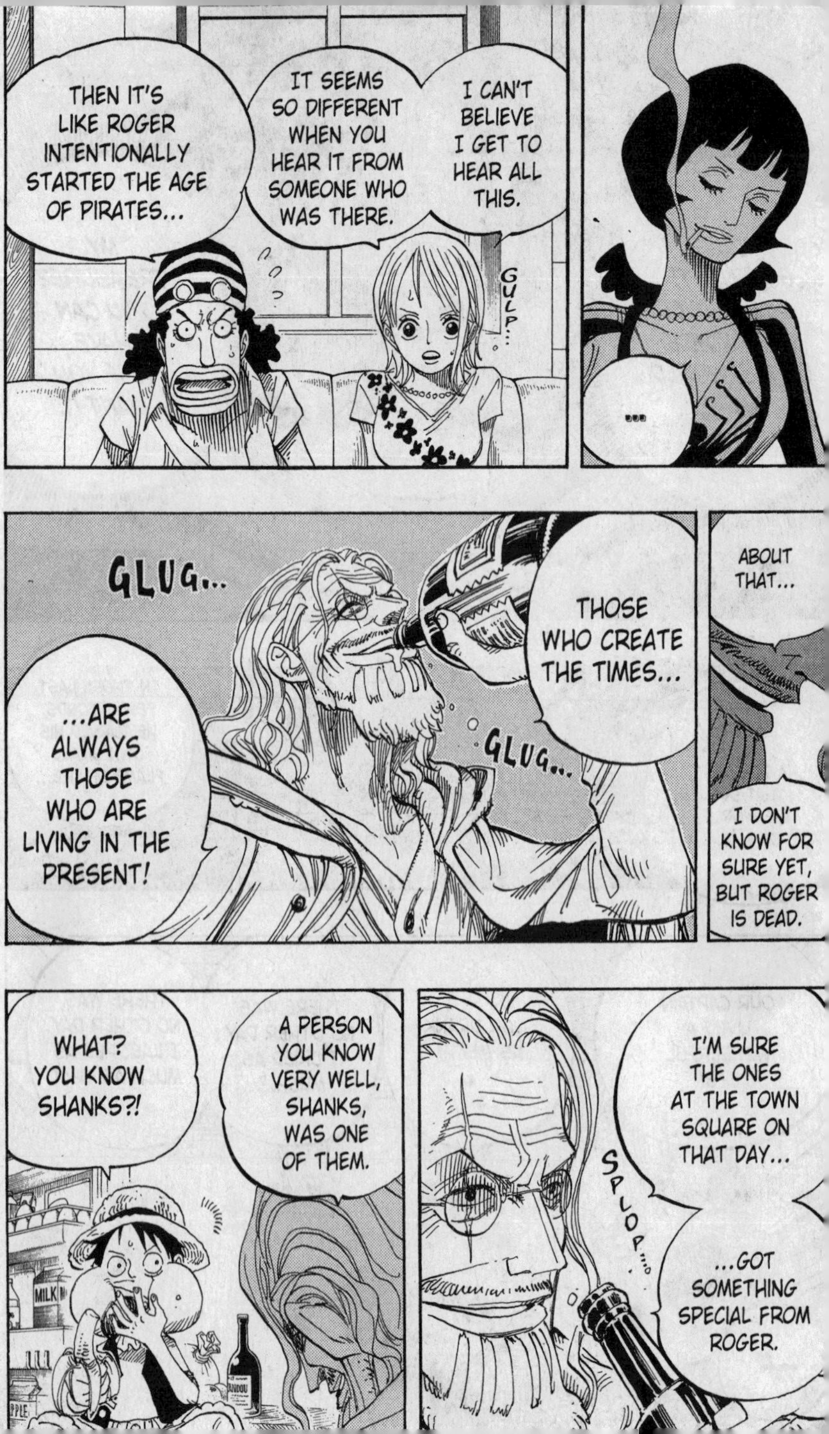
...
I CAN'T BELIEVE I GET TO HEAR ALL THIS.
IT SEEMS SO DIFFERENT WHEN YOU HEAR IT FROM SOMEONE WHO WAS THERE.
THEN IT'S LIKE ROGER INTENTIONALLY STARTED THE AGE OF PIRATES...
GULP...
ABOUT THAT...
I DON'T KNOW FOR SURE YET, BUT ROGER IS DEAD.
THOSE WHO CREATE THE TIMES...
GLUG...
GLUG...
...ARE ALWAYS THOSE WHO ARE LIVING IN THE PRESENT!
I'M SURE THE ONES AT THE TOWN SQUARE ON THAT DAY...
...GOT SOMETHING SPECIAL FROM ROGER.
SPLOP...
A PERSON YOU KNOW VERY WELL, SHANKS, WAS ONE OF THEM.
WHAT? YOU KNOW SHANKS?!
MILK

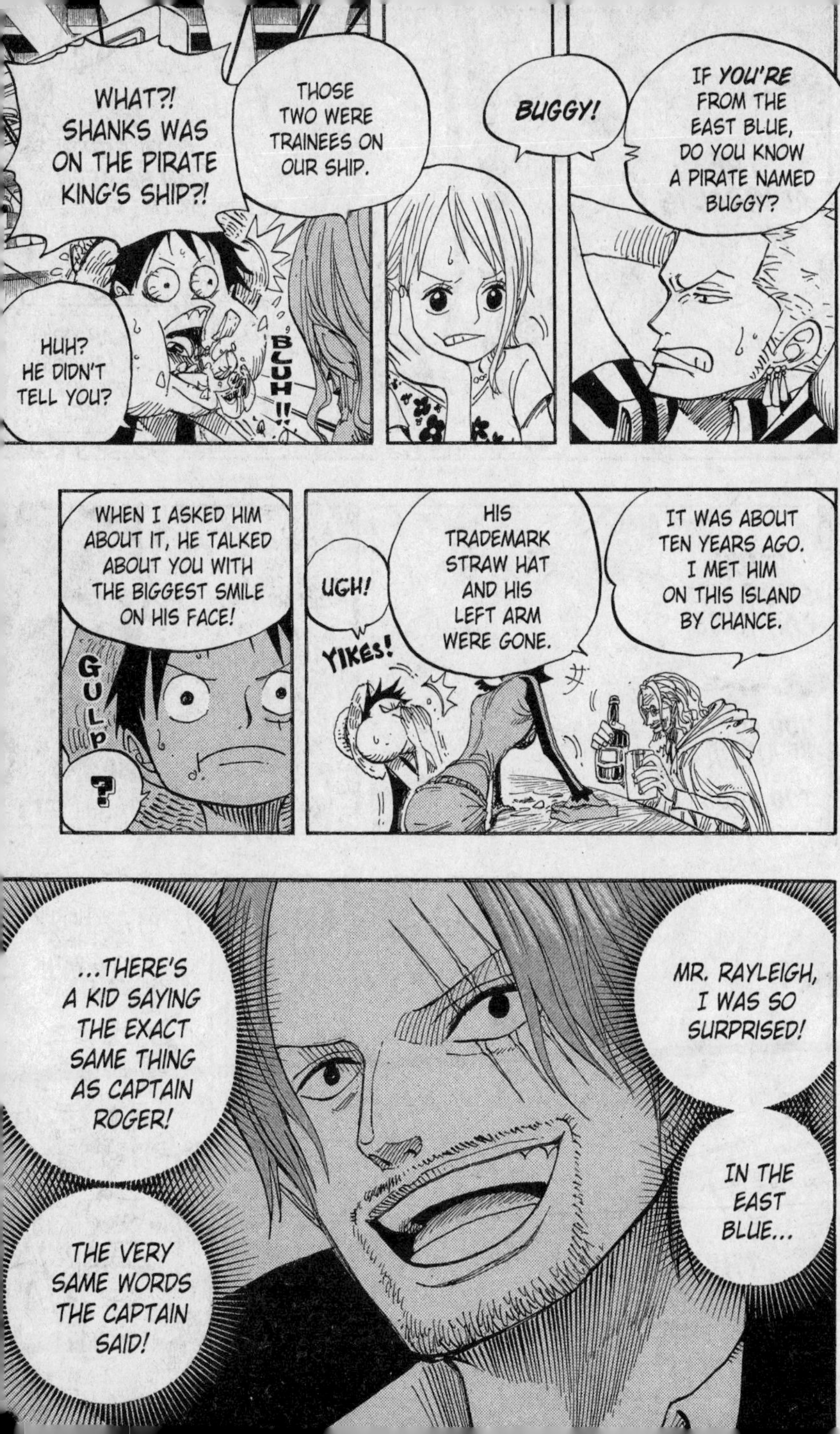
IF YOU'RE FROM THE EAST BLUE, DO YOU KNOW A PIRATE NAMED BUGGY?
BUGGY!
THOSE TWO WERE TRAINEES ON OUR SHIP.
WHAT?! SHANKS WAS ON THE PIRATE KING'S SHIP?!
BLUH!!
HUH? HE DIDN'T TELL YOU?
IT WAS ABOUT TEN YEARS AGO. I MET HIM ON THIS ISLAND BY CHANCE.
HIS TRADEMARK STRAW HAT AND HIS LEFT ARM WERE GONE.
UGH!
YIKES!
WHEN I ASKED HIM ABOUT IT, HE TALKED ABOUT YOU WITH THE BIGGEST SMILE ON HIS FACE!
GULP
?
MR. RAYLEIGH, I WAS SO SURPRISED!
IN THE EAST BLUE...
...THERE'S A KID SAYING THE EXACT SAME THING AS CAPTAIN ROGER!
THE VERY SAME WORDS THE CAPTAIN SAID!

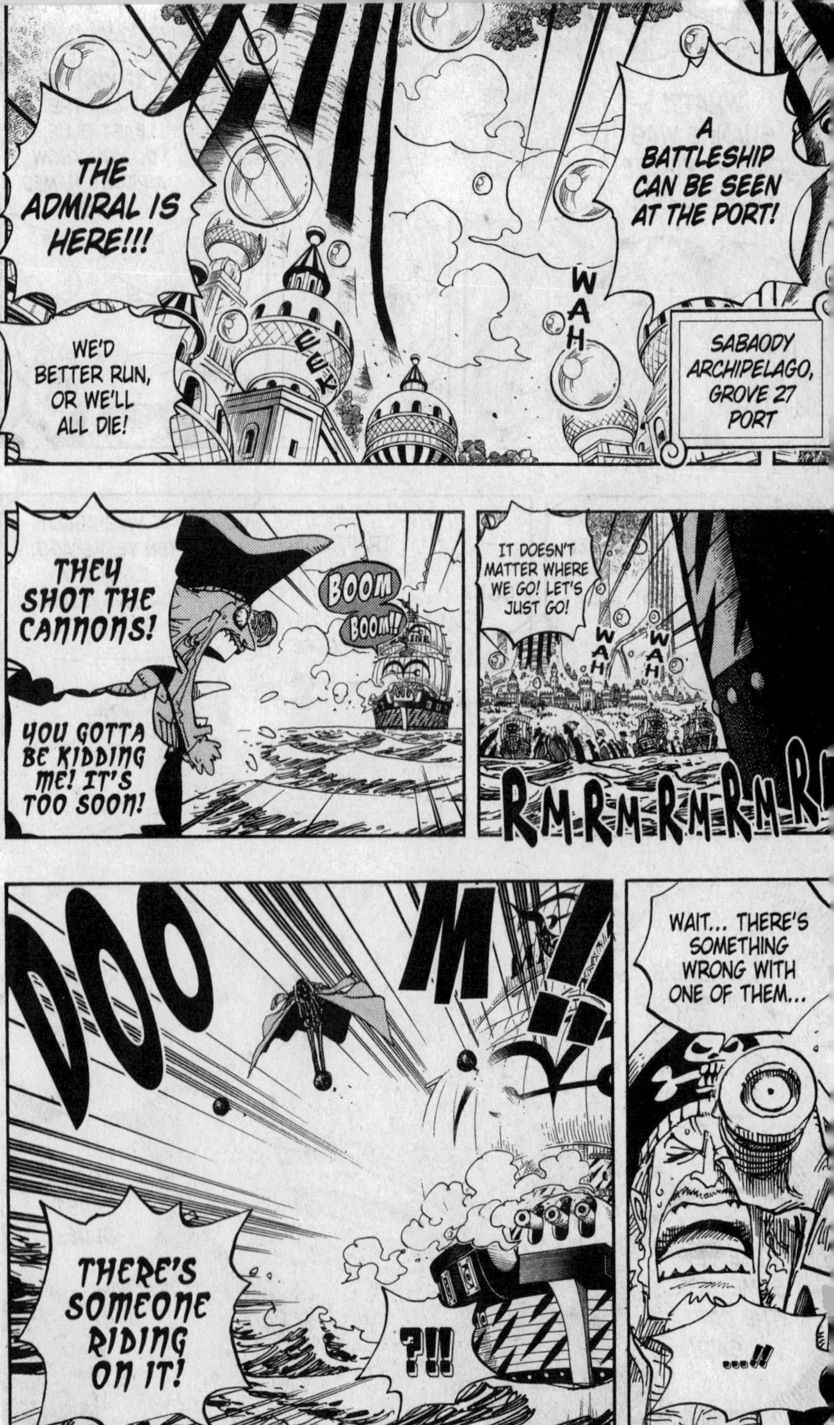
A BATTLESHIP CAN BE SEEN AT THE PORT!
SABAODY ARCHIPELAGO, GROVE 27 PORT
WAH
EEK
THE ADMIRAL IS HERE!!!
WE'D BETTER RUN, OR WE'LL ALL DIE!
IT DOESN'T MATTER WHERE WE GO! LET'S JUST GO!
WAH
WAH
RMRMRMRMRMR
BOOM
BOOM!!
THEY SHOT THE CANNONS!
YOU GOTTA BE KIDDING ME! IT'S TOO SOON!
WAIT... THERE'S SOMETHING WRONG WITH ONE OF THEM...
...!!
DOOM!!
?!!
THERE'S SOMEONE RIDING ON IT!

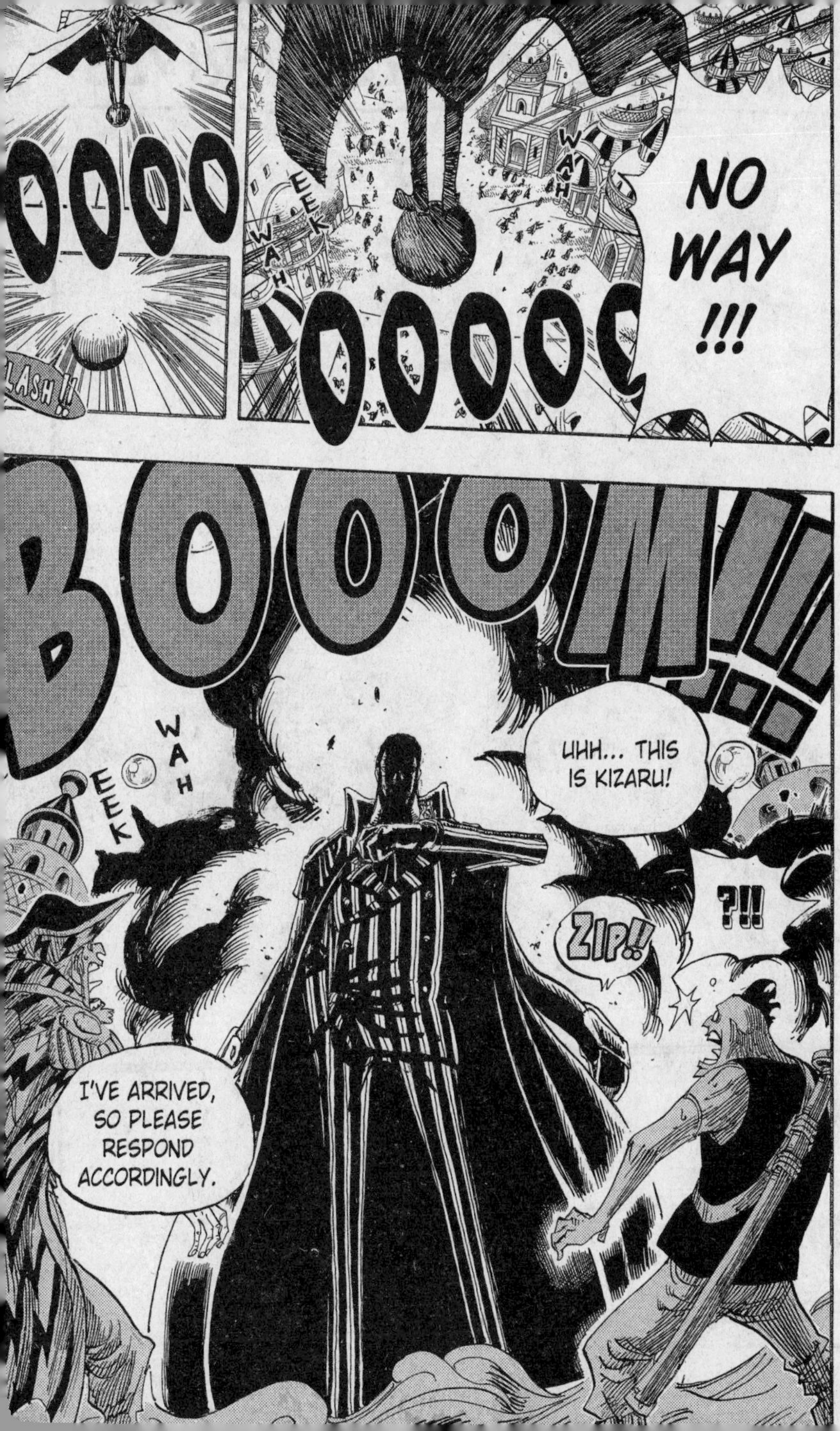
NO WAY !!!
WAH
EEK
WAH
OOOOO
OOOO
LASH!!
BOOOM!!!
UHH... THIS IS KIZARU!
?!!
ZIP!!
WAH
EEK
I'VE ARRIVED, SO PLEASE RESPOND ACCORDINGLY.

Chapter 507: KIZARU ARRIVES

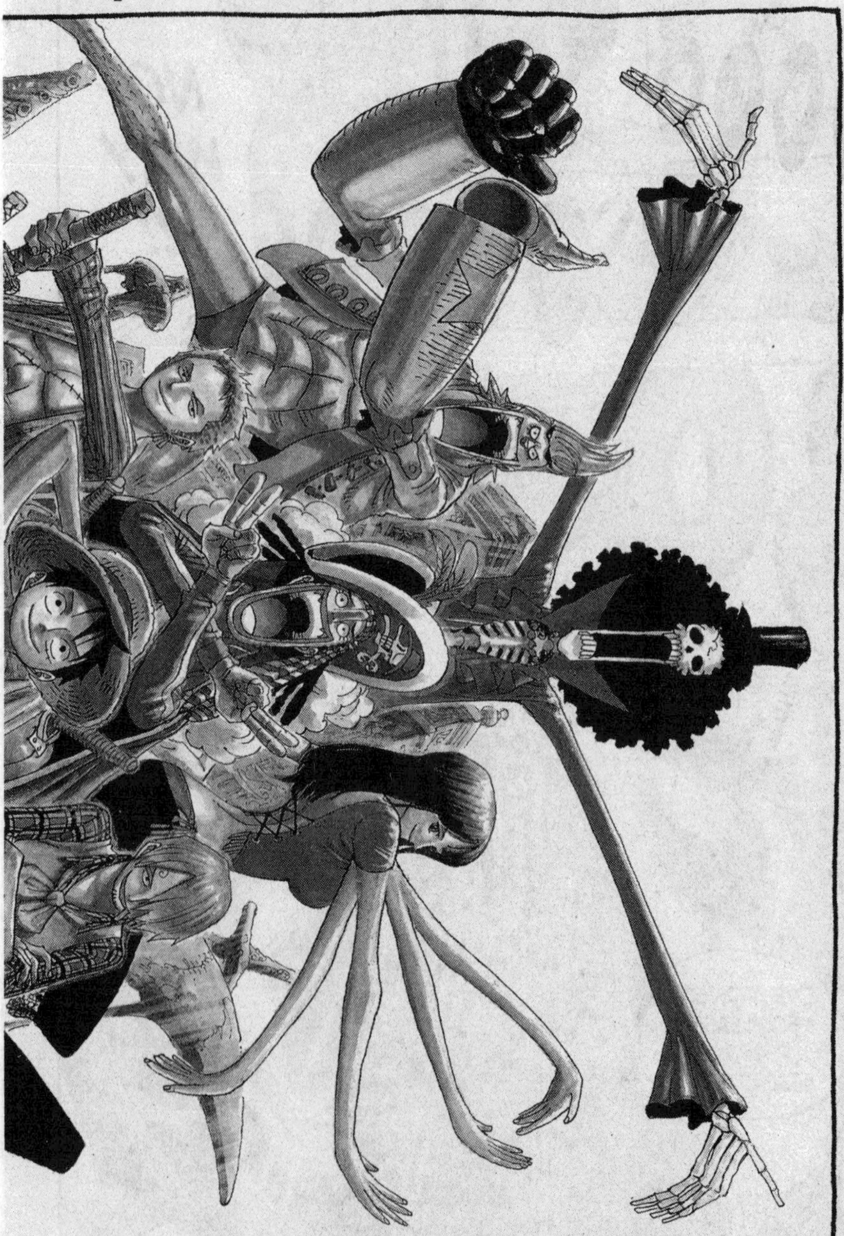

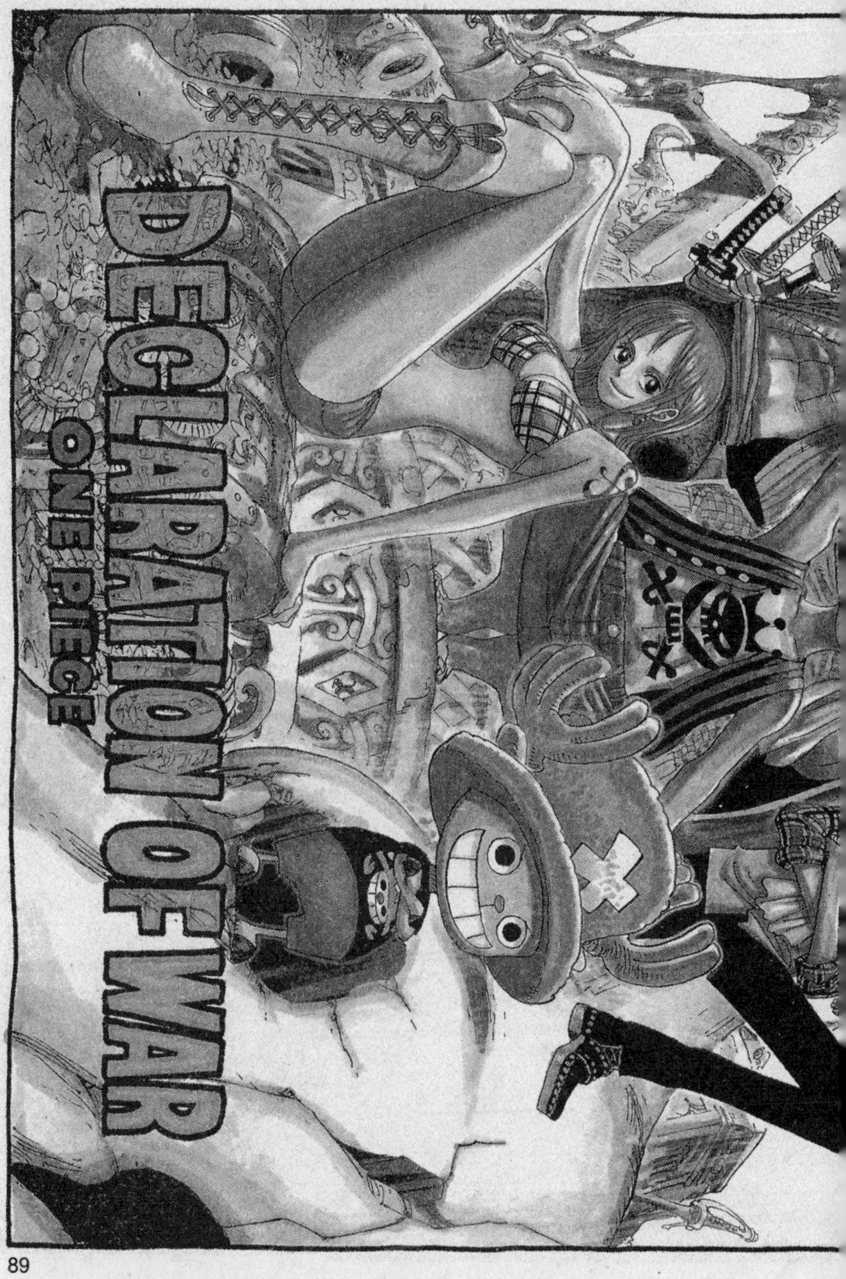
DECLARATION OF WAR
ONE PIECE

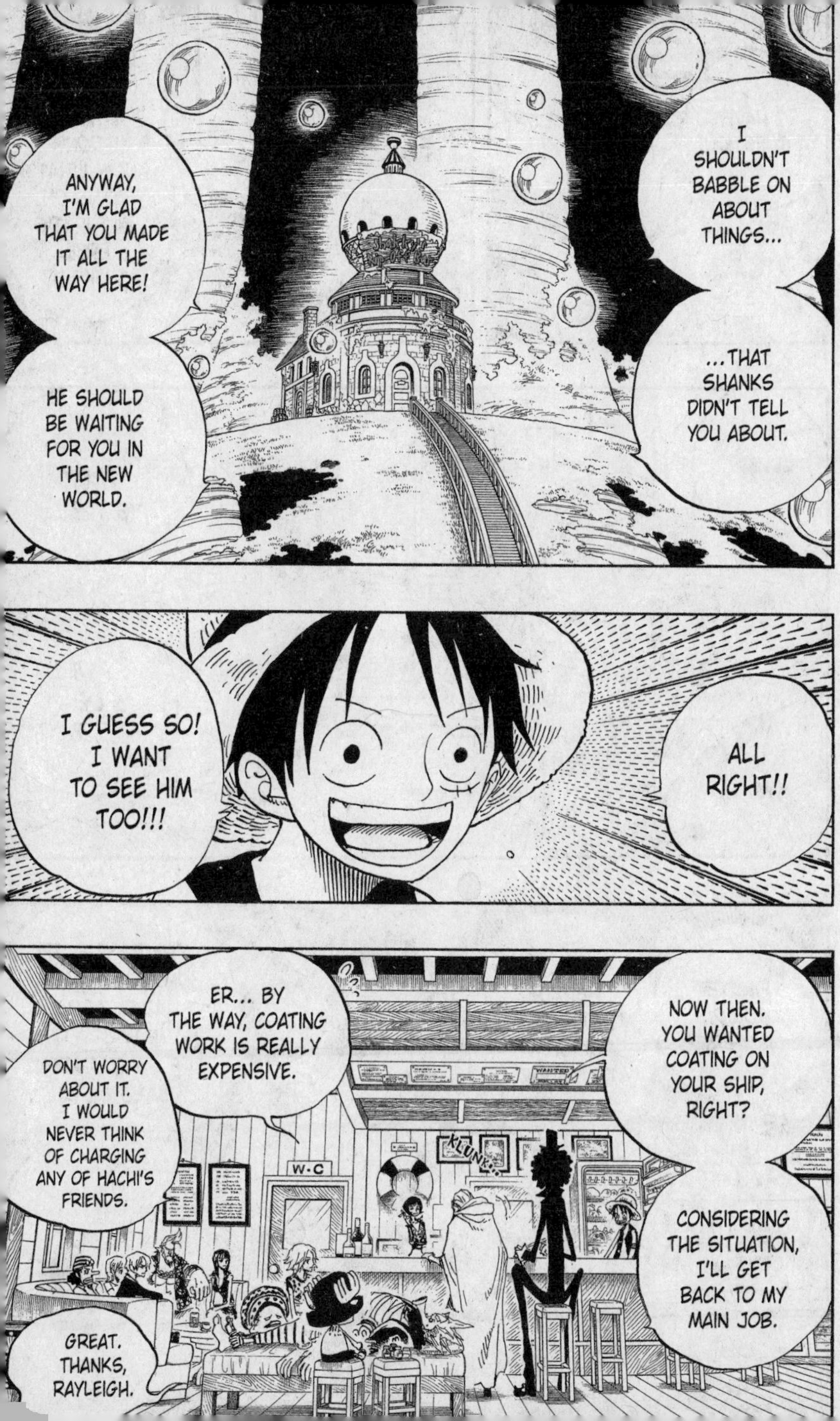
I SHOULDN'T BABBLE ON ABOUT THINGS...
...THAT SHANKS DIDN'T TELL YOU ABOUT.
ANYWAY, I'M GLAD THAT YOU MADE IT ALL THE WAY HERE!
HE SHOULD BE WAITING FOR YOU IN THE NEW WORLD.
ALL RIGHT!!
I GUESS SO! I WANT TO SEE HIM TOO!!!
NOW THEN. YOU WANTED COATING ON YOUR SHIP, RIGHT?
CONSIDERING THE SITUATION, I'LL GET BACK TO MY MAIN JOB.
KLUNK!!
WANTED
W-C
ER... BY THE WAY, COATING WORK IS REALLY EXPENSIVE.
DON'T WORRY ABOUT IT. I WOULD NEVER THINK OF CHARGING ANY OF HACHI'S FRIENDS.
GREAT. THANKS, RAYLEIGH.

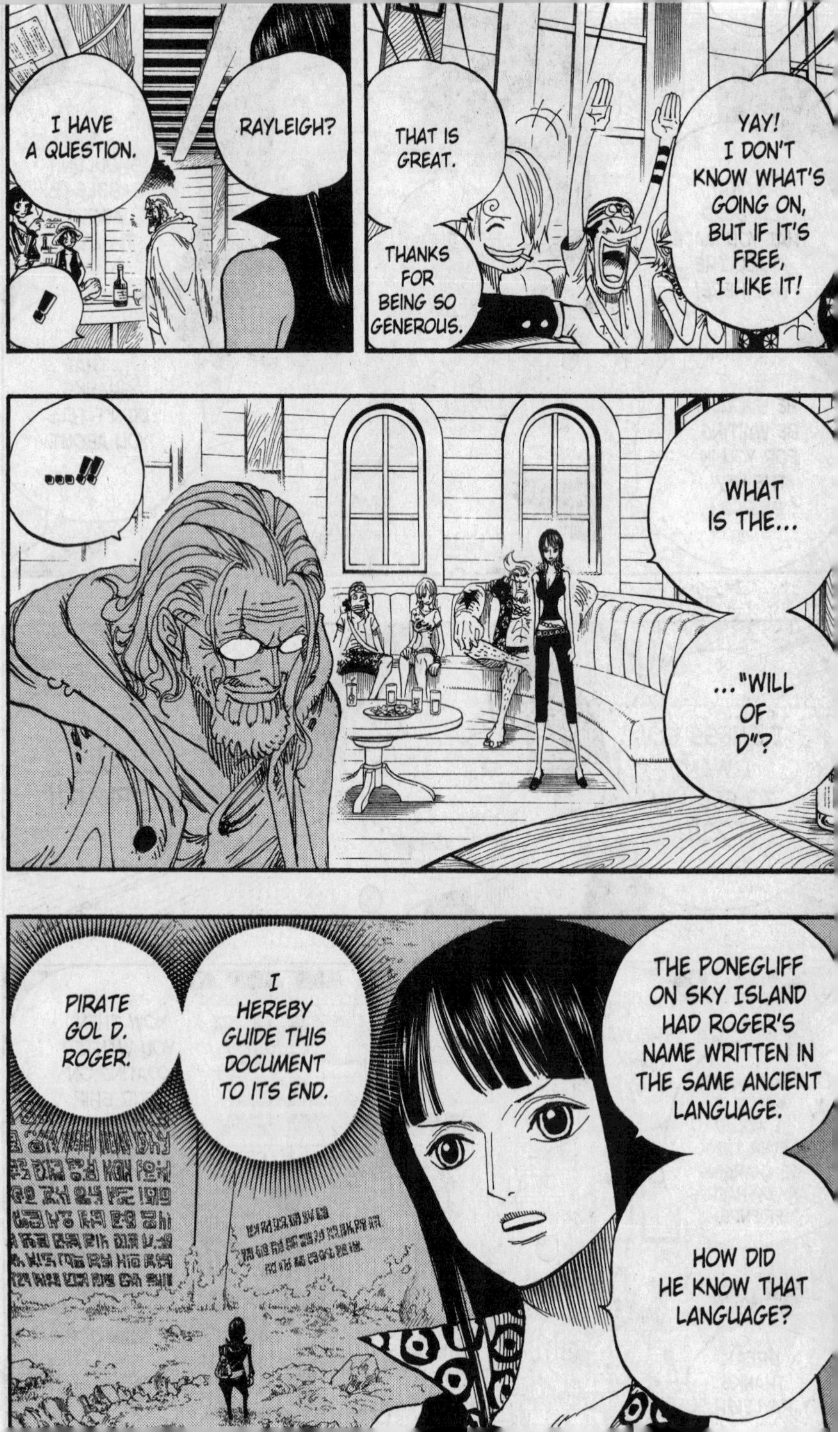
YAY! I DON'T KNOW WHAT'S GOING ON, BUT IF IT'S FREE, I LIKE IT!
THAT IS GREAT.
THANKS FOR BEING SO GENEROUS.
RAYLEIGH?
I HAVE A QUESTION.
!
WHAT IS THE...
..."WILL OF D"?
...!!
THE PONEGLIFF ON SKY ISLAND HAD ROGER'S NAME WRITTEN IN THE SAME ANCIENT LANGUAGE.
HOW DID HE KNOW THAT LANGUAGE?
I HEREBY GUIDE THIS DOCUMENT TO ITS END.
PIRATE GOL D. ROGER.

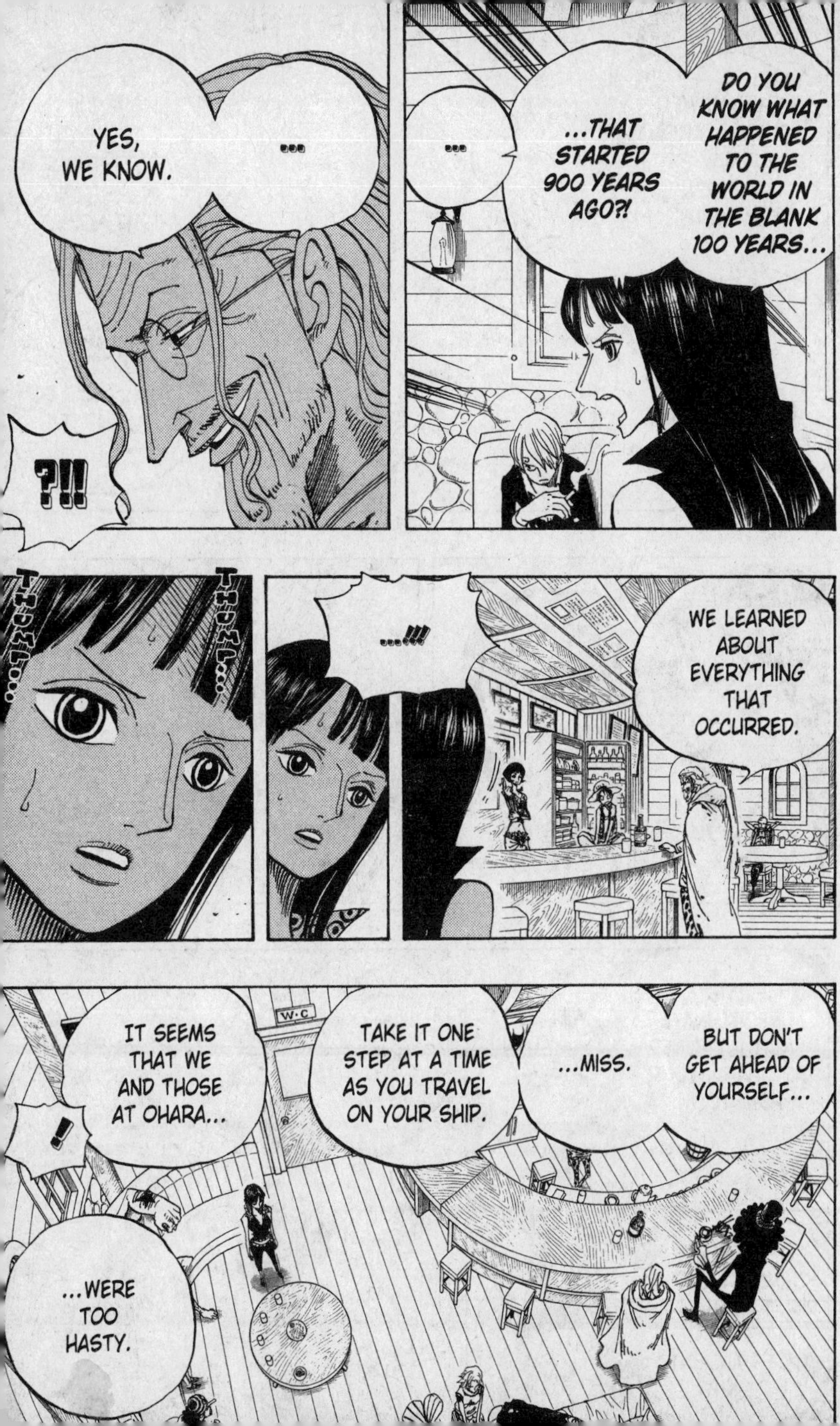
DO YOU KNOW WHAT HAPPENED TO THE WORLD IN THE BLANK 100 YEARS...
...THAT STARTED 900 YEARS AGO?!
...
...
YES, WE KNOW.
?!!
WE LEARNED ABOUT EVERYTHING THAT OCCURRED.
...!!!
THUMP...
THUMP...
BUT DON'T GET AHEAD OF YOURSELF...
...MISS.
TAKE IT ONE STEP AT A TIME AS YOU TRAVEL ON YOUR SHIP.
W.C
IT SEEMS THAT WE AND THOSE AT OHARA...
!
...WERE TOO HASTY.

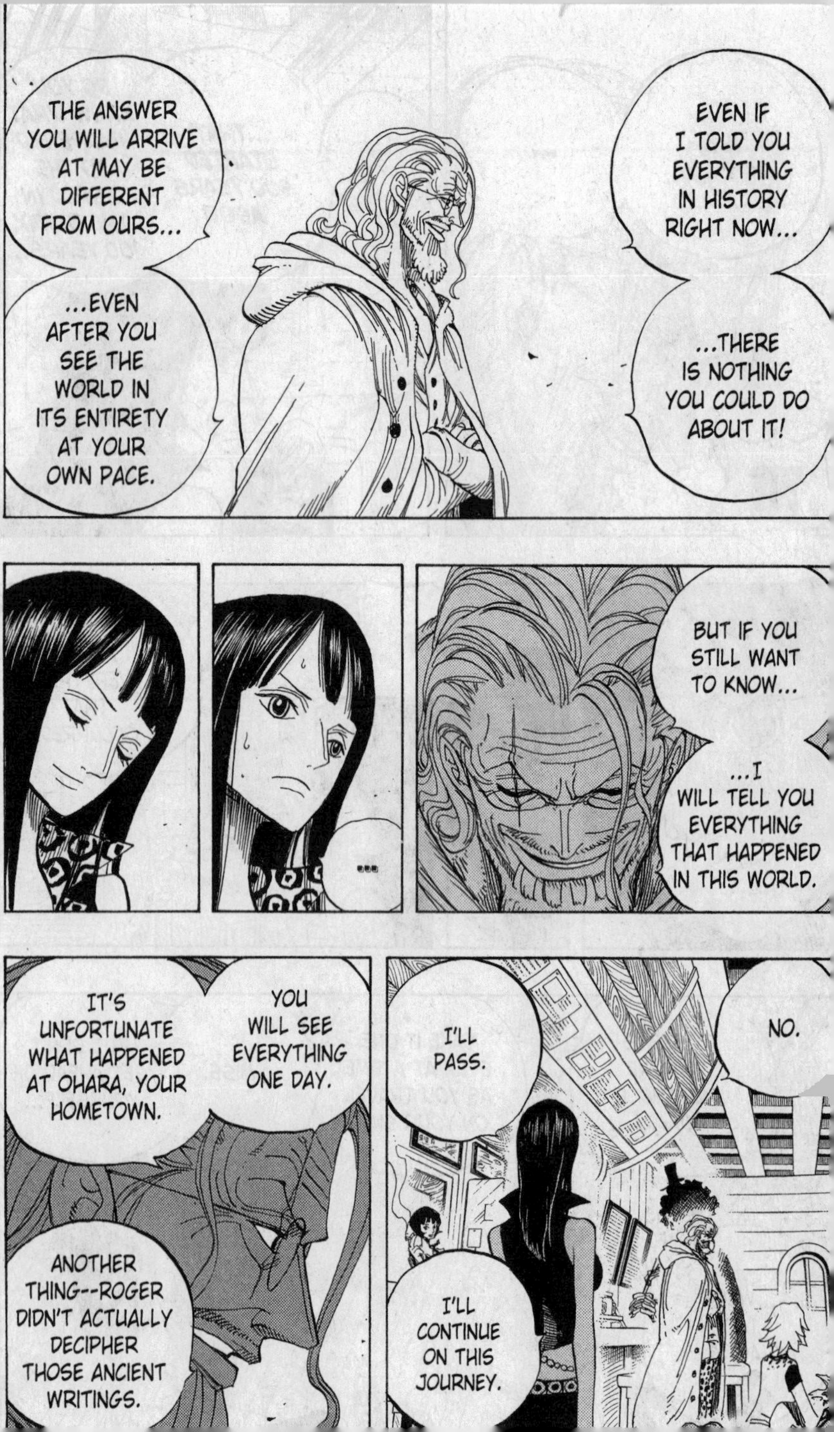
EVEN IF I TOLD YOU EVERYTHING IN HISTORY RIGHT NOW...
...THERE IS NOTHING YOU COULD DO ABOUT IT!
THE ANSWER YOU WILL ARRIVE AT MAY BE DIFFERENT FROM OURS...
...EVEN AFTER YOU SEE THE WORLD IN ITS ENTIRETY AT YOUR OWN PACE.
BUT IF YOU STILL WANT TO KNOW...
...I WILL TELL YOU EVERYTHING THAT HAPPENED IN THIS WORLD.
...
NO.
I'LL PASS.
I'LL CONTINUE ON THIS JOURNEY.
YOU WILL SEE EVERYTHING ONE DAY.
IT'S UNFORTUNATE WHAT HAPPENED AT OHARA, YOUR HOMETOWN.
ANOTHER THING--ROGER DIDN'T ACTUALLY DECIPHER THOSE ANCIENT WRITINGS.

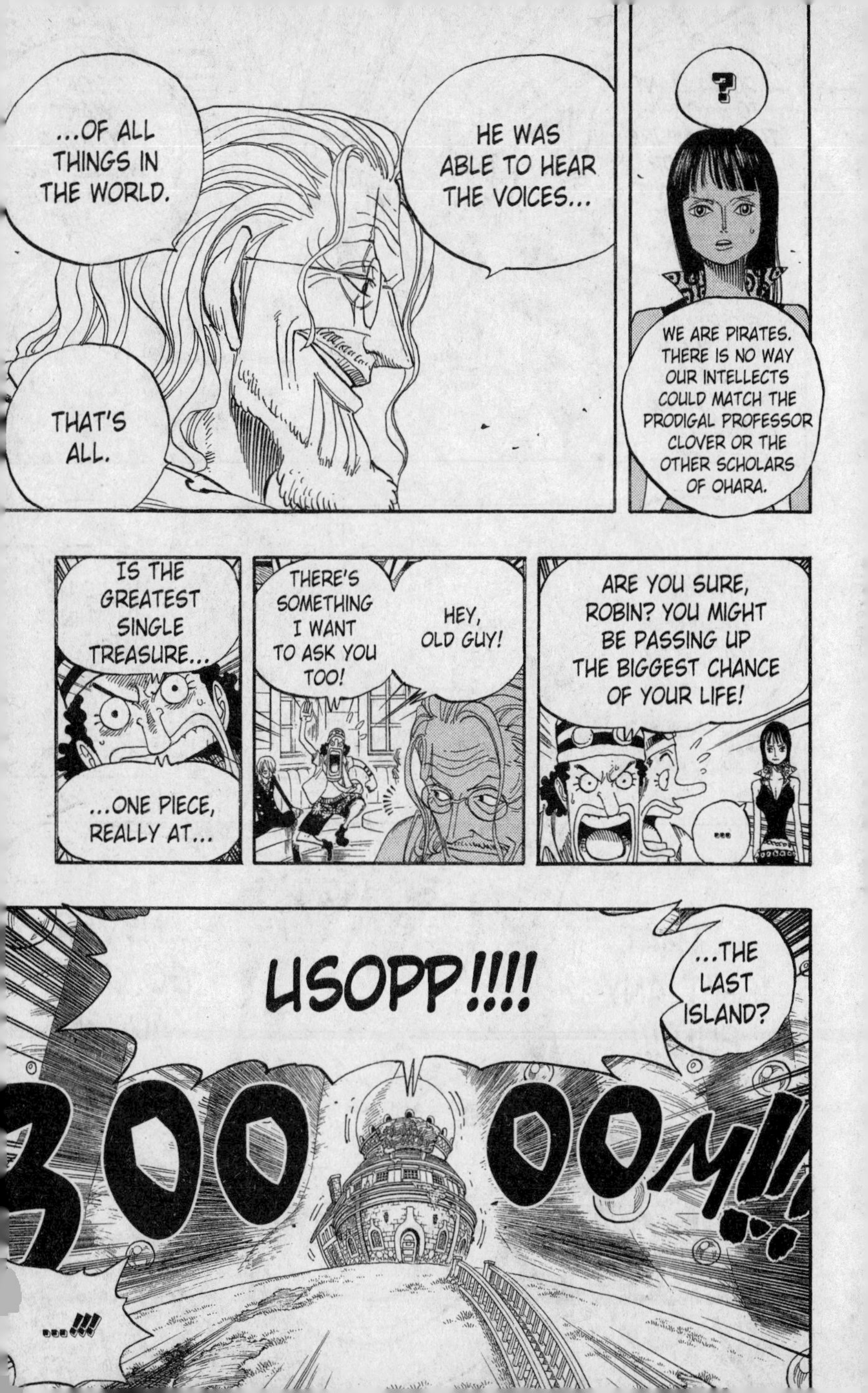
?
WE ARE PIRATES. THERE IS NO WAY OUR INTELLECTS COULD MATCH THE PRODIGAL PROFESSOR CLOVER OR THE OTHER SCHOLARS OF OHARA.
HE WAS ABLE TO HEAR THE VOICES...
...OF ALL THINGS IN THE WORLD.
THAT'S ALL.
ARE YOU SURE, ROBIN? YOU MIGHT BE PASSING UP THE BIGGEST CHANCE OF YOUR LIFE!
...
HEY, OLD GUY!
THERE'S SOMETHING I WANT TO ASK YOU TOO!
IS THE GREATEST SINGLE TREASURE...
...ONE PIECE, REALLY AT...
...THE LAST ISLAND?
USOPP!!!!
BOOOOM!!
...!!!

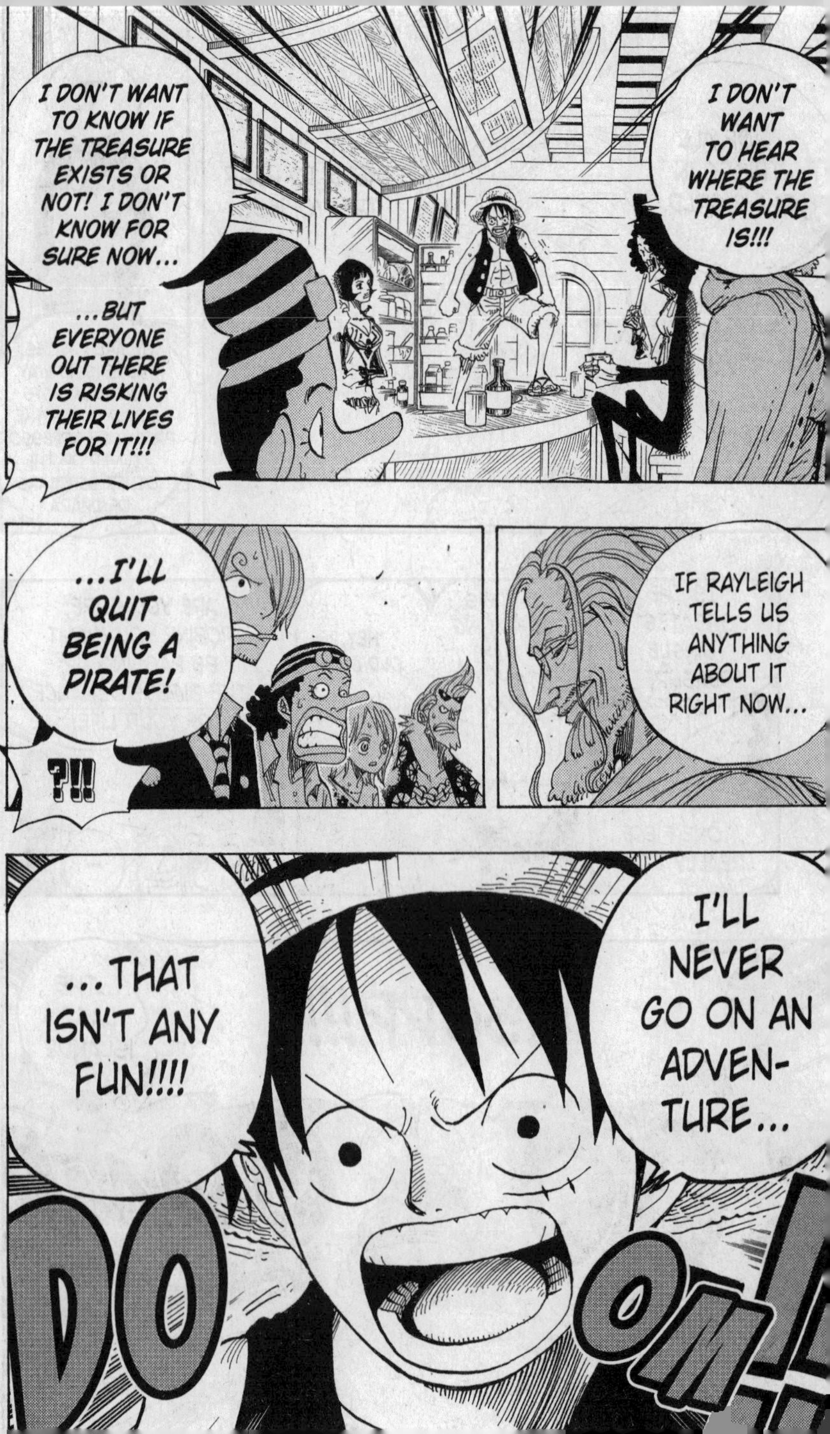
I DON'T WANT TO HEAR WHERE THE TREASURE IS!!!
I DON'T WANT TO KNOW IF THE TREASURE EXISTS OR NOT! I DON'T KNOW FOR SURE NOW...
...BUT EVERYONE OUT THERE IS RISKING THEIR LIVES FOR IT!!!
IF RAYLEIGH TELLS US ANYTHING ABOUT IT RIGHT NOW...
...I'LL QUIT BEING A PIRATE!
?!!
I'LL NEVER GO ON AN ADVEN-TURE...
...THAT ISN'T ANY FUN!!!!
DO

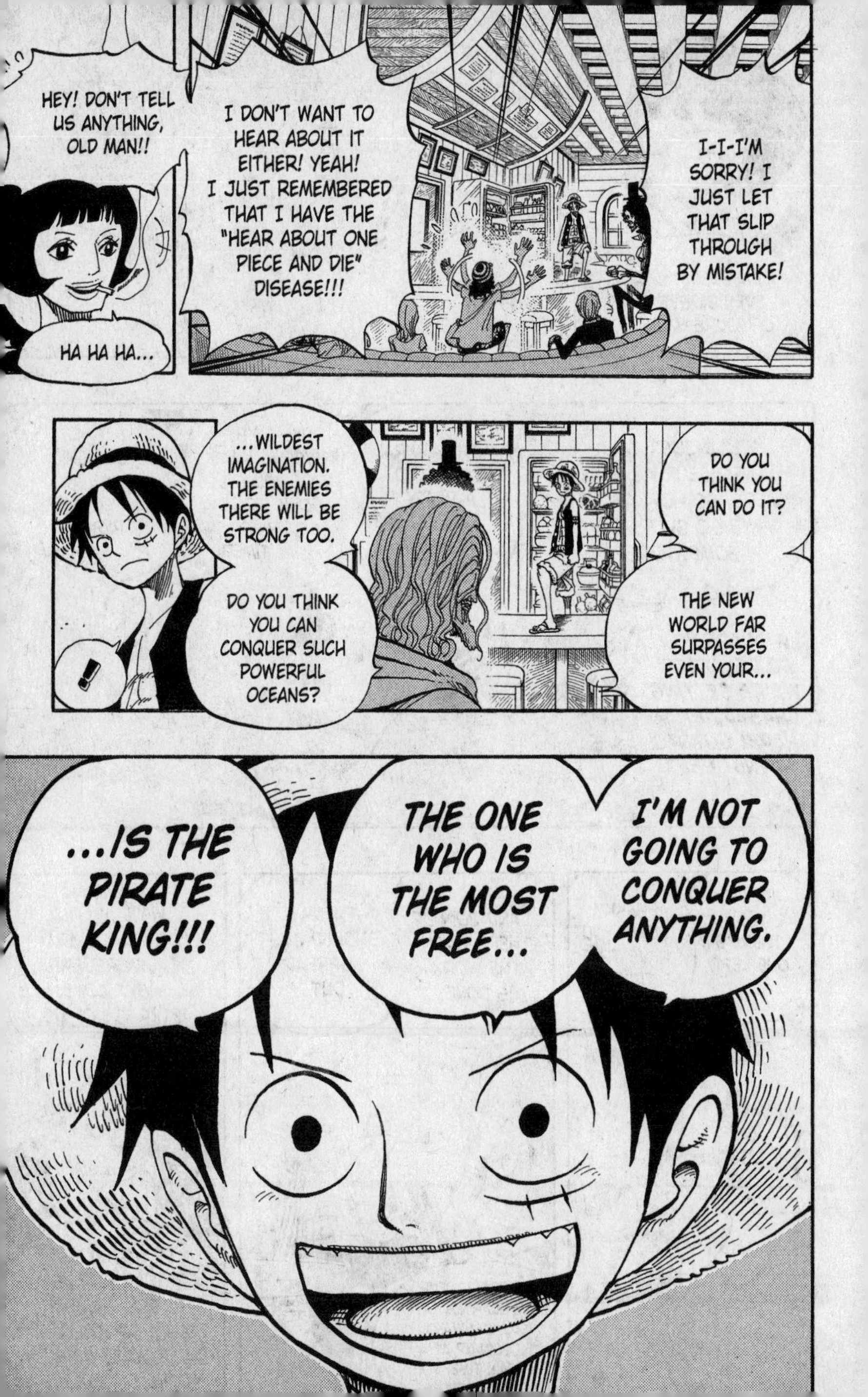
I-I-I'M SORRY! I JUST LET THAT SLIP THROUGH BY MISTAKE!
I DON'T WANT TO HEAR ABOUT IT EITHER! YEAH! I JUST REMEMBERED THAT I HAVE THE "HEAR ABOUT ONE PIECE AND DIE" DISEASE!!!
HEY! DON'T TELL US ANYTHING, OLD MAN!!
HA HA HA...
DO YOU THINK YOU CAN DO IT?
THE NEW WORLD FAR SURPASSES EVEN YOUR...
...WILDEST IMAGINATION. THE ENEMIES THERE WILL BE STRONG TOO.
DO YOU THINK YOU CAN CONQUER SUCH POWERFUL OCEANS?
!
I'M NOT GOING TO CONQUER ANYTHING.
THE ONE WHO IS THE MOST FREE...
...IS THE PIRATE KING!!!

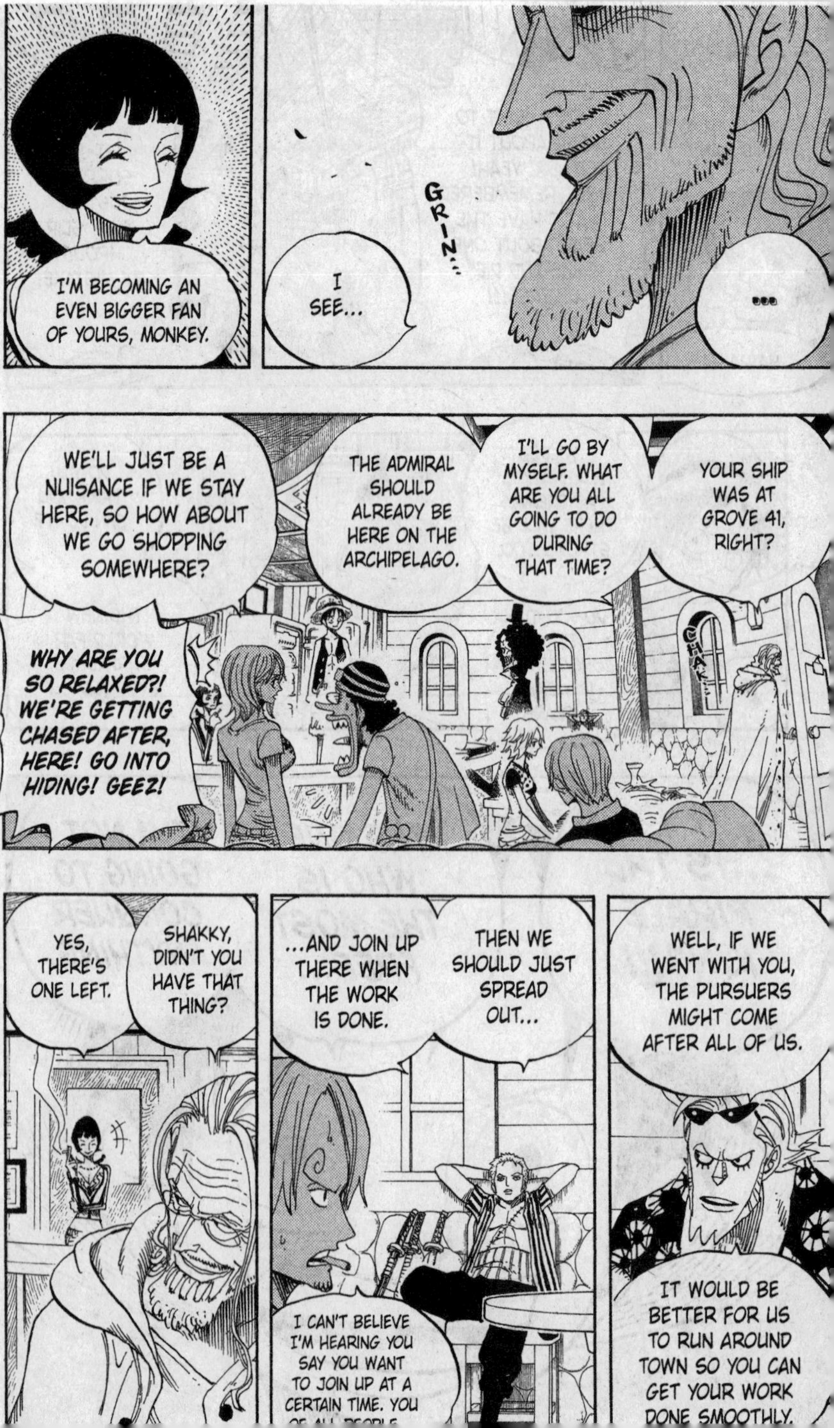
...
GRIN...
I SEE...
I'M BECOMING AN EVEN BIGGER FAN OF YOURS, MONKEY.
YOUR SHIP WAS AT GROVE 41, RIGHT?
I'LL GO BY MYSELF. WHAT ARE YOU ALL GOING TO DO DURING THAT TIME?
THE ADMIRAL SHOULD ALREADY BE HERE ON THE ARCHIPELAGO.
WE'LL JUST BE A NUISANCE IF WE STAY HERE, SO HOW ABOUT WE GO SHOPPING SOMEWHERE?
CHAK...
WHY ARE YOU SO RELAXED?! WE'RE GETTING CHASED AFTER, HERE! GO INTO HIDING! GEEZ!
WELL, IF WE WENT WITH YOU, THE PURSUERS MIGHT COME AFTER ALL OF US.
IT WOULD BE BETTER FOR US TO RUN AROUND TOWN SO YOU CAN GET YOUR WORK DONE SMOOTHLY.
THEN WE SHOULD JUST SPREAD OUT...
...AND JOIN UP THERE WHEN THE WORK IS DONE.
I CAN'T BELIEVE I'M HEARING YOU SAY YOU WANT TO JOIN UP AT A CERTAIN TIME. YOU
SHAKKY, DIDN'T YOU HAVE THAT THING?
YES, THERE'S ONE LEFT.

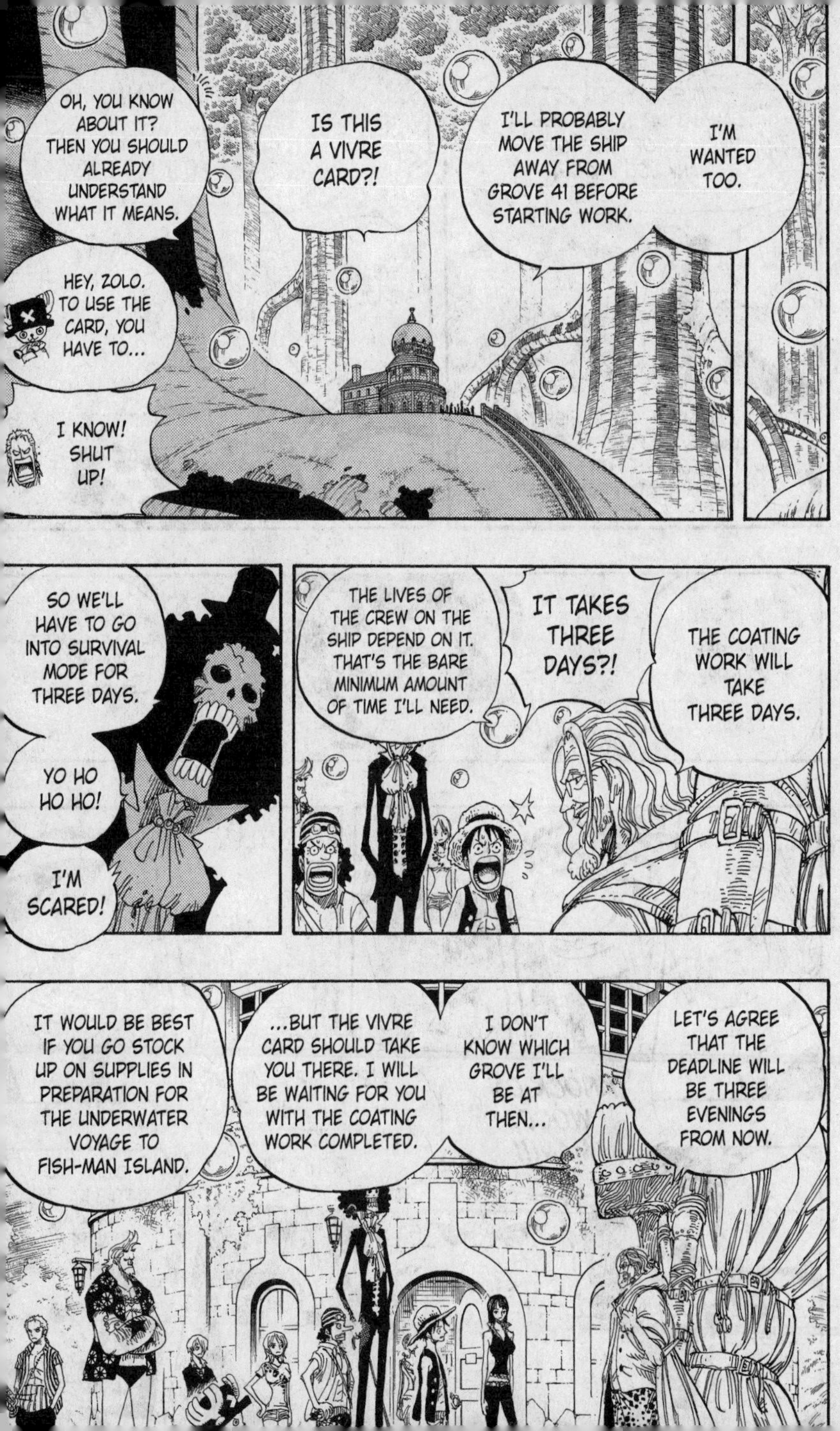
I'M WANTED TOO.
I'LL PROBABLY MOVE THE SHIP AWAY FROM GROVE 41 BEFORE STARTING WORK.
IS THIS A VIVRE CARD?!
OH, YOU KNOW ABOUT IT? THEN YOU SHOULD ALREADY UNDERSTAND WHAT IT MEANS.
HEY, ZOLO. TO USE THE CARD, YOU HAVE TO...
I KNOW! SHUT UP!
THE COATING WORK WILL TAKE THREE DAYS.
IT TAKES THREE DAYS?!
THE LIVES OF THE CREW ON THE SHIP DEPEND ON IT. THAT'S THE BARE MINIMUM AMOUNT OF TIME I'LL NEED.
SO WE'LL HAVE TO GO INTO SURVIVAL MODE FOR THREE DAYS.
YO HO HO HO!
I'M SCARED!
LET'S AGREE THAT THE DEADLINE WILL BE THREE EVENINGS FROM NOW.
I DON'T KNOW WHICH GROVE I'LL BE AT THEN...
...BUT THE VIVRE CARD SHOULD TAKE YOU THERE. I WILL BE WAITING FOR YOU WITH THE COATING WORK COMPLETED.
IT WOULD BE BEST IF YOU GO STOCK UP ON SUPPLIES IN PREPARATION FOR THE UNDERWATER VOYAGE TO FISH-MAN ISLAND.

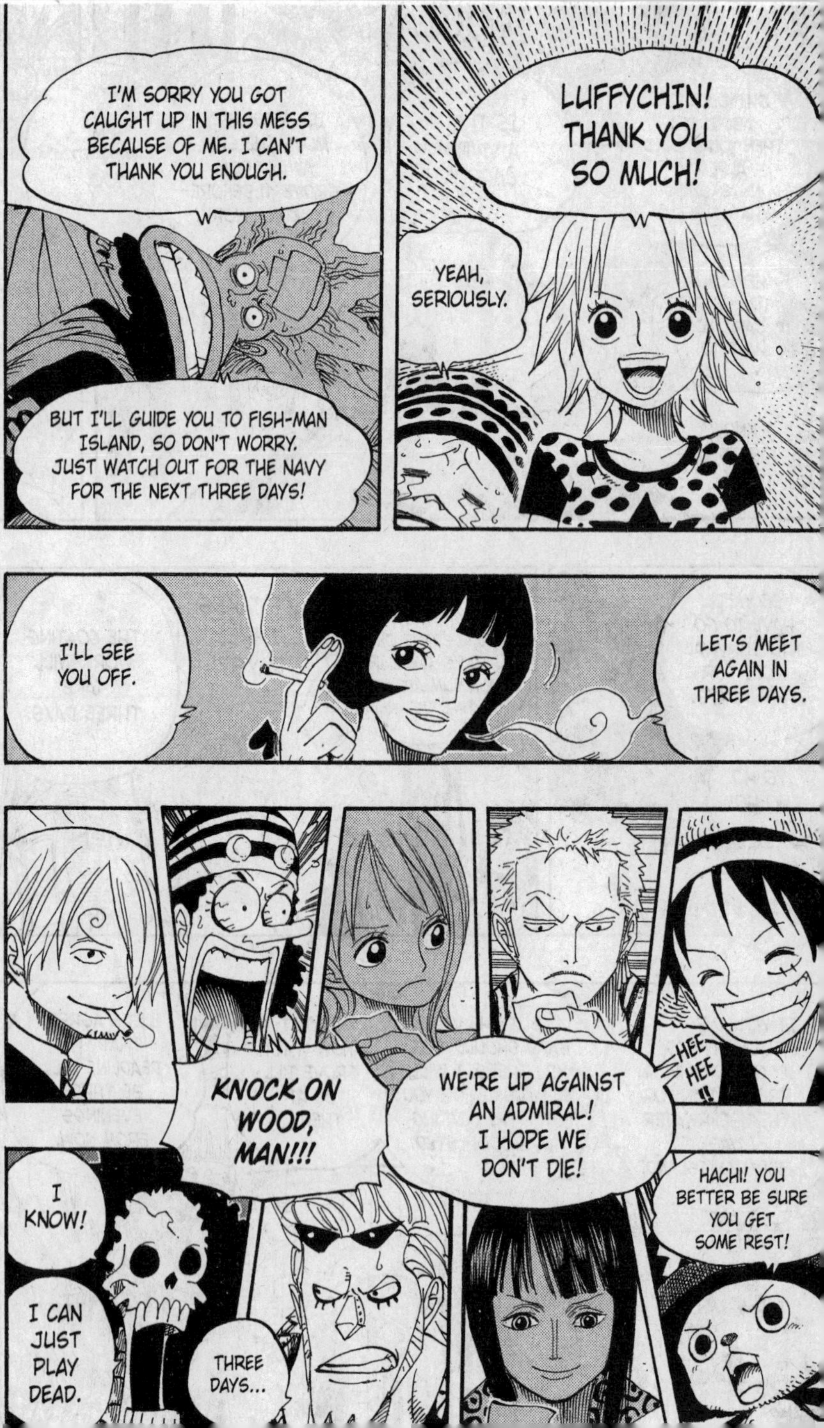
LUFFYCHIN! THANK YOU SO MUCH!
YEAH, SERIOUSLY.
I'M SORRY YOU GOT CAUGHT UP IN THIS MESS BECAUSE OF ME. I CAN'T THANK YOU ENOUGH.
BUT I'LL GUIDE YOU TO FISH-MAN ISLAND, SO DON'T WORRY. JUST WATCH OUT FOR THE NAVY FOR THE NEXT THREE DAYS!
LET'S MEET AGAIN IN THREE DAYS.
I'LL SEE YOU OFF.
HEE HEE!!
WE'RE UP AGAINST AN ADMIRAL! I HOPE WE DON'T DIE!
KNOCK ON WOOD, MAN!!!
HACHI! YOU BETTER BE SURE YOU GET SOME REST!
THREE DAYS...
I KNOW!
I CAN JUST PLAY DEAD.

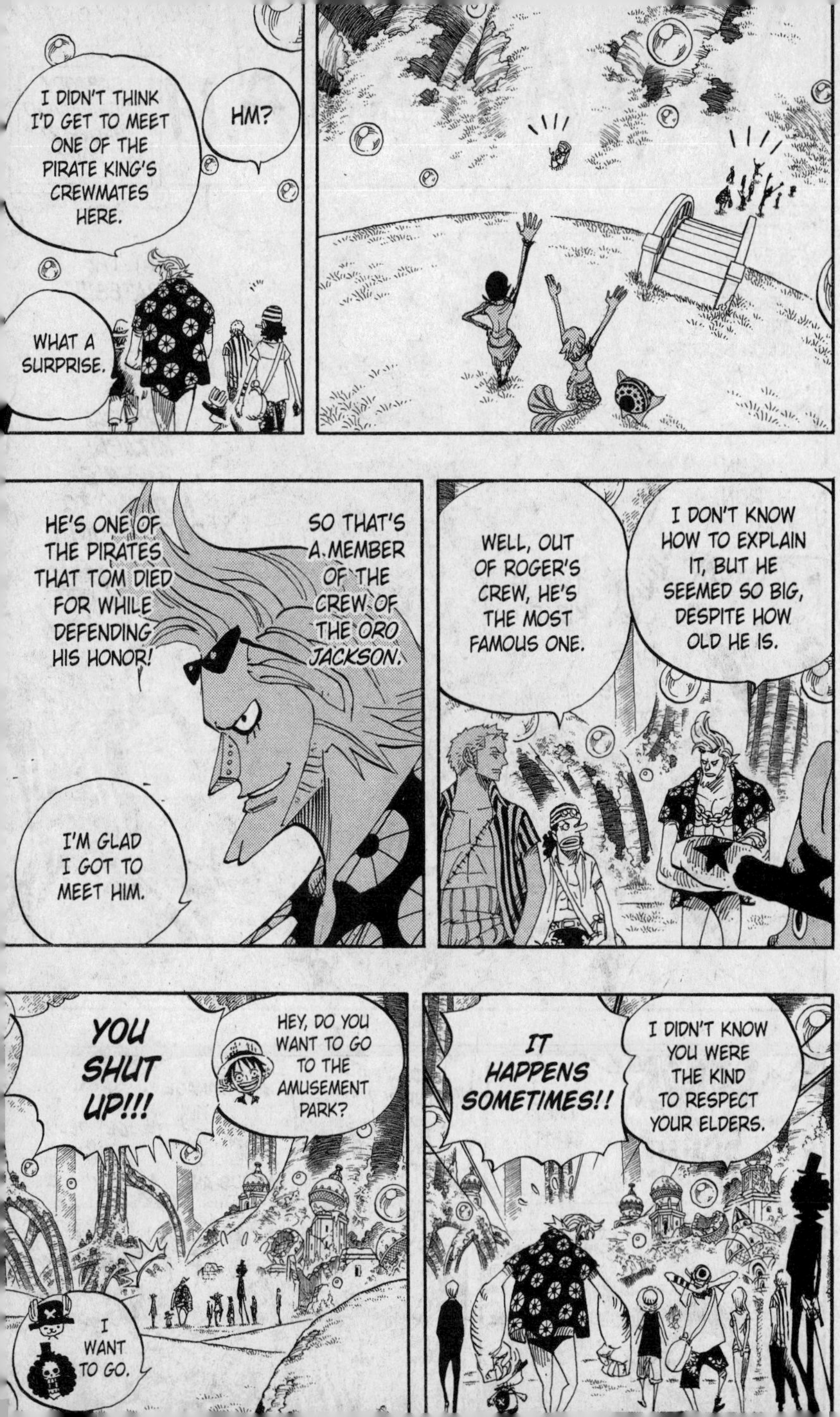
I DIDN'T THINK I'D GET TO MEET ONE OF THE PIRATE KING'S CREWMATES HERE.
HM?
WHAT A SURPRISE.
I DON'T KNOW HOW TO EXPLAIN IT, BUT HE SEEMED SO BIG, DESPITE HOW OLD HE IS.
WELL, OUT OF ROGER'S CREW, HE'S THE MOST FAMOUS ONE.
SO THAT'S A MEMBER OF THE CREW OF THE ORO JACKSON.
HE'S ONE OF THE PIRATES THAT TOM DIED FOR WHILE DEFENDING HIS HONOR!
I'M GLAD I GOT TO MEET HIM.
I DIDN'T KNOW YOU WERE THE KIND TO RESPECT YOUR ELDERS.
IT HAPPENS SOMETIMES!!
HEY, DO YOU WANT TO GO TO THE AMUSEMENT PARK?
YOU SHUT UP!!!
I WANT TO GO.

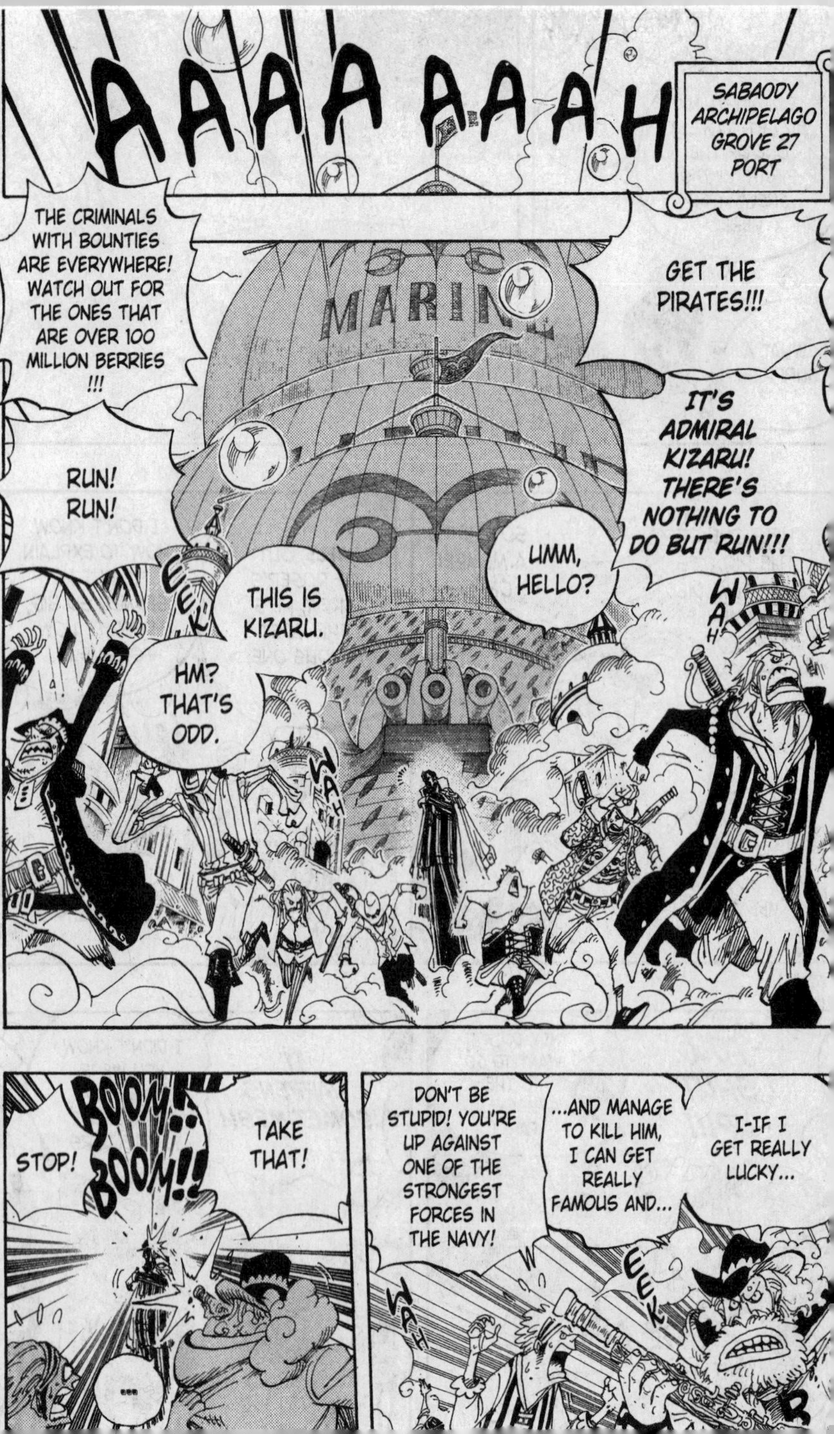
SABAODY ARCHIPELAGO GROVE 27 PORT
AAAAAAAH
GET THE PIRATES!!!
THE CRIMINALS WITH BOUNTIES ARE EVERYWHERE! WATCH OUT FOR THE ONES THAT ARE OVER 100 MILLION BERRIES !!!
IT'S ADMIRAL KIZARU! THERE'S NOTHING TO DO BUT RUN!!!
RUN! RUN!
WAH
UMM, HELLO?
EEK
THIS IS KIZARU.
HM? THAT'S ODD.
WAH
I-IF I GET REALLY LUCKY...
...AND MANAGE TO KILL HIM, I CAN GET REALLY FAMOUS AND...
DON'T BE STUPID! YOU'RE UP AGAINST ONE OF THE STRONGEST FORCES IN THE NAVY!
EEK
W
WAH
TAKE THAT!
BOOM!! BOOM!!
STOP!
...

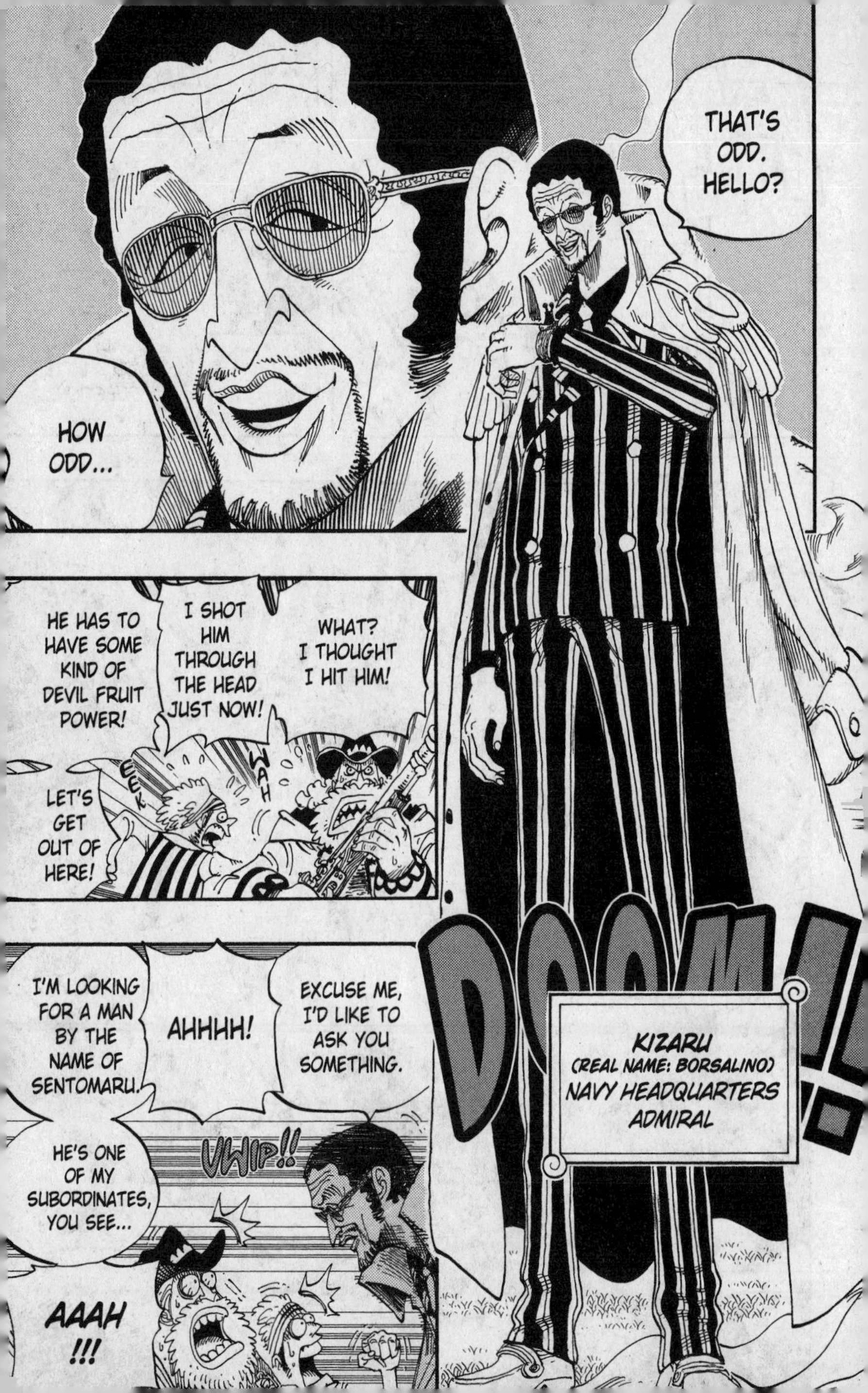
THAT'S ODD. HELLO?
HOW ODD...
WHAT? I THOUGHT I HIT HIM!
I SHOT HIM THROUGH THE HEAD JUST NOW!
HE HAS TO HAVE SOME KIND OF DEVIL FRUIT POWER!
WAAH
EEEK
LET'S GET OUT OF HERE!
EXCUSE ME, I'D LIKE TO ASK YOU SOMETHING.
AHHHH!
I'M LOOKING FOR A MAN BY THE NAME OF SENTOMARU.
HE'S ONE OF MY SUBORDINATES, YOU SEE...
WHIP!!
AAAH !!!
DOOM!!
KIZARU
(REAL NAME: BORSALINO)
NAVY HEADQUARTERS ADMIRAL

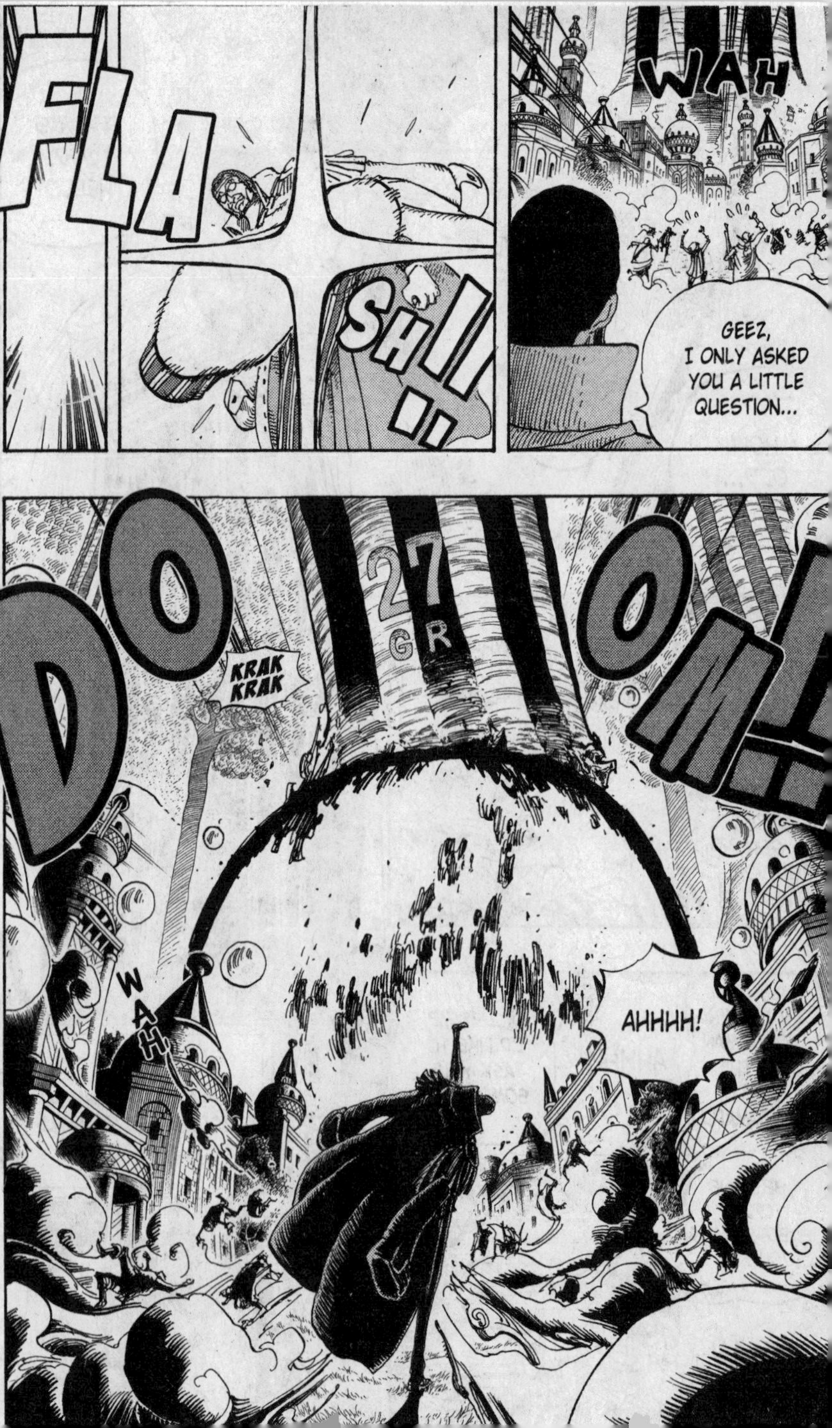
WAH
GEEZ, I ONLY ASKED YOU A LITTLE QUESTION...
FLA
SHI!!
DOOM!!
27 GR
KRAK KRAK
AHHHH!
WAH

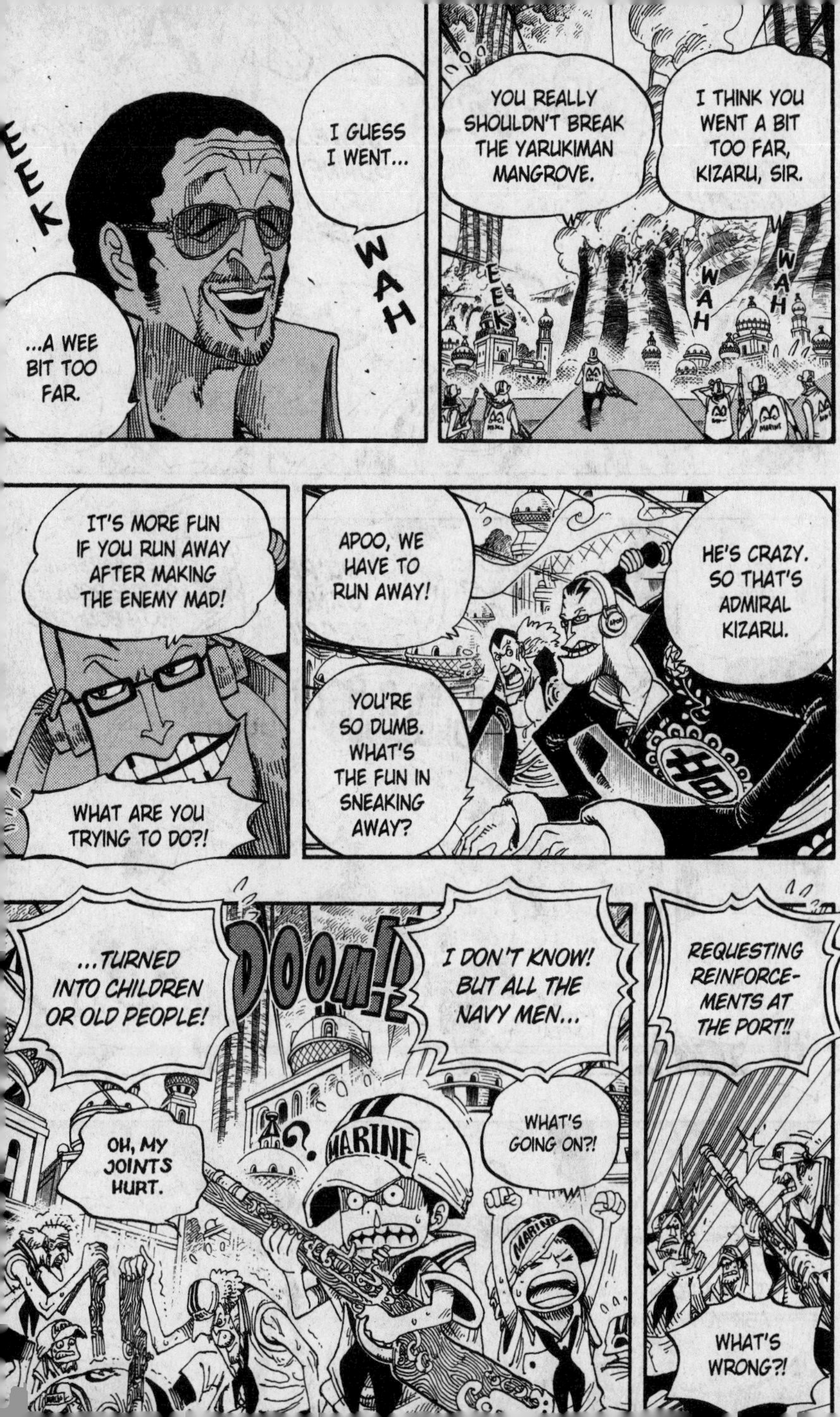
I THINK YOU WENT A BIT TOO FAR, KIZARU, SIR.
YOU REALLY SHOULDN'T BREAK THE YARUKIMAN MANGROVE.
WAH
WAH
EEK
I GUESS I WENT...
WAH
EEK
...A WEE BIT TOO FAR.
HE'S CRAZY. SO THAT'S ADMIRAL KIZARU.
APOO, WE HAVE TO RUN AWAY!
YOU'RE SO DUMB. WHAT'S THE FUN IN SNEAKING AWAY?
IT'S MORE FUN IF YOU RUN AWAY AFTER MAKING THE ENEMY MAD!
WHAT ARE YOU TRYING TO DO?!
REQUESTING REINFORCEMENTS AT THE PORT!!
WHAT'S WRONG?!
I DON'T KNOW! BUT ALL THE NAVY MEN...
WHAT'S GOING ON?!
DOOM
...TURNED INTO CHILDREN OR OLD PEOPLE!
OH, MY JOINTS HURT.

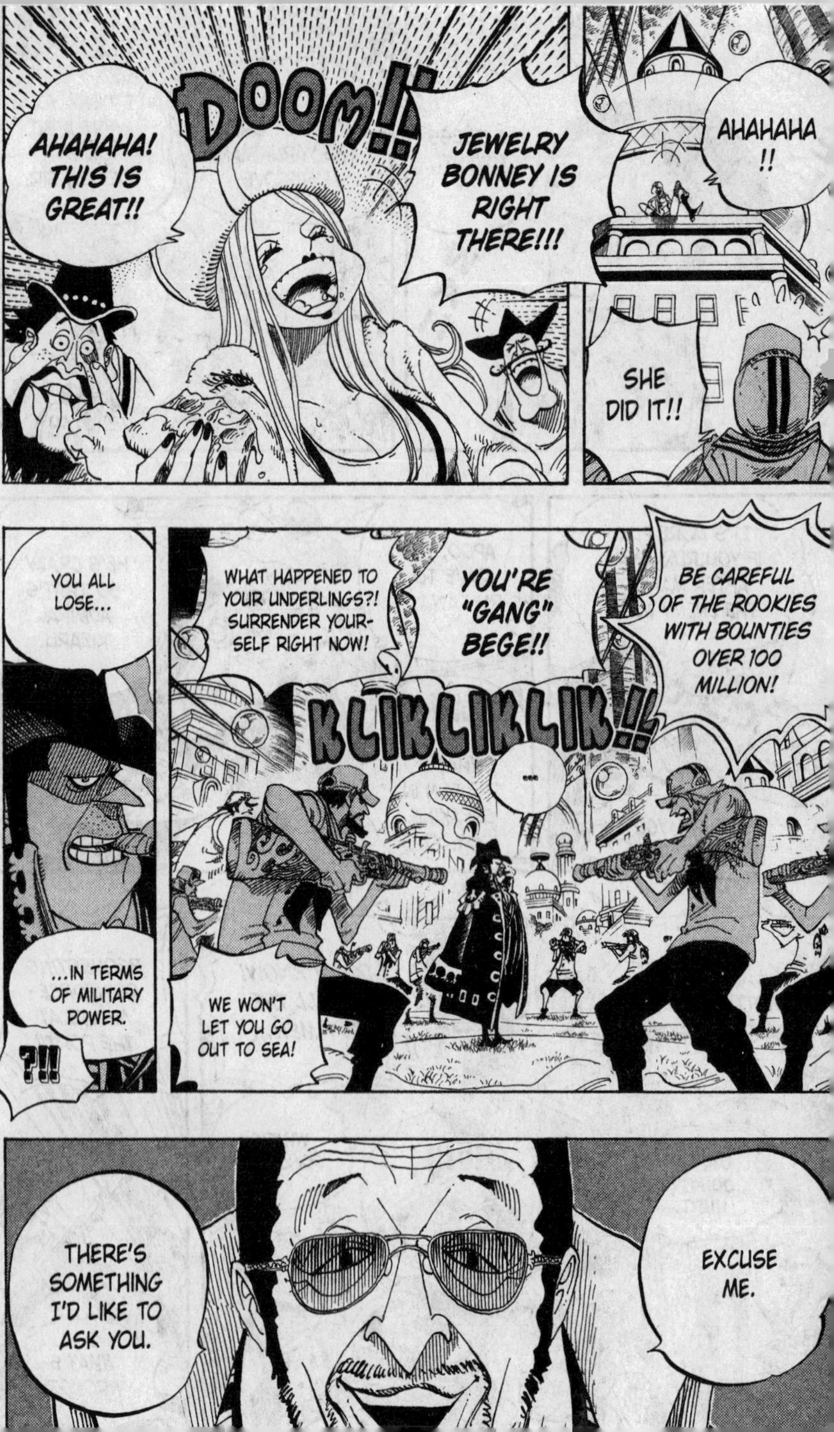
AHAHAHA !!
SHE DID IT!!
JEWELRY BONNEY IS RIGHT THERE!!!
DOOM!!
AHAHAHA! THIS IS GREAT!!
BE CAREFUL OF THE ROOKIES WITH BOUNTIES OVER 100 MILLION!
YOU'RE "GANG" BEGE!!
WHAT HAPPENED TO YOUR UNDERLINGS?! SURRENDER YOURSELF RIGHT NOW!
KLIKLIKLIK!!
...
WE WON'T LET YOU GO OUT TO SEA!
YOU ALL LOSE...
...IN TERMS OF MILITARY POWER.
?!!
EXCUSE ME.
THERE'S SOMETHING I'D LIKE TO ASK YOU.

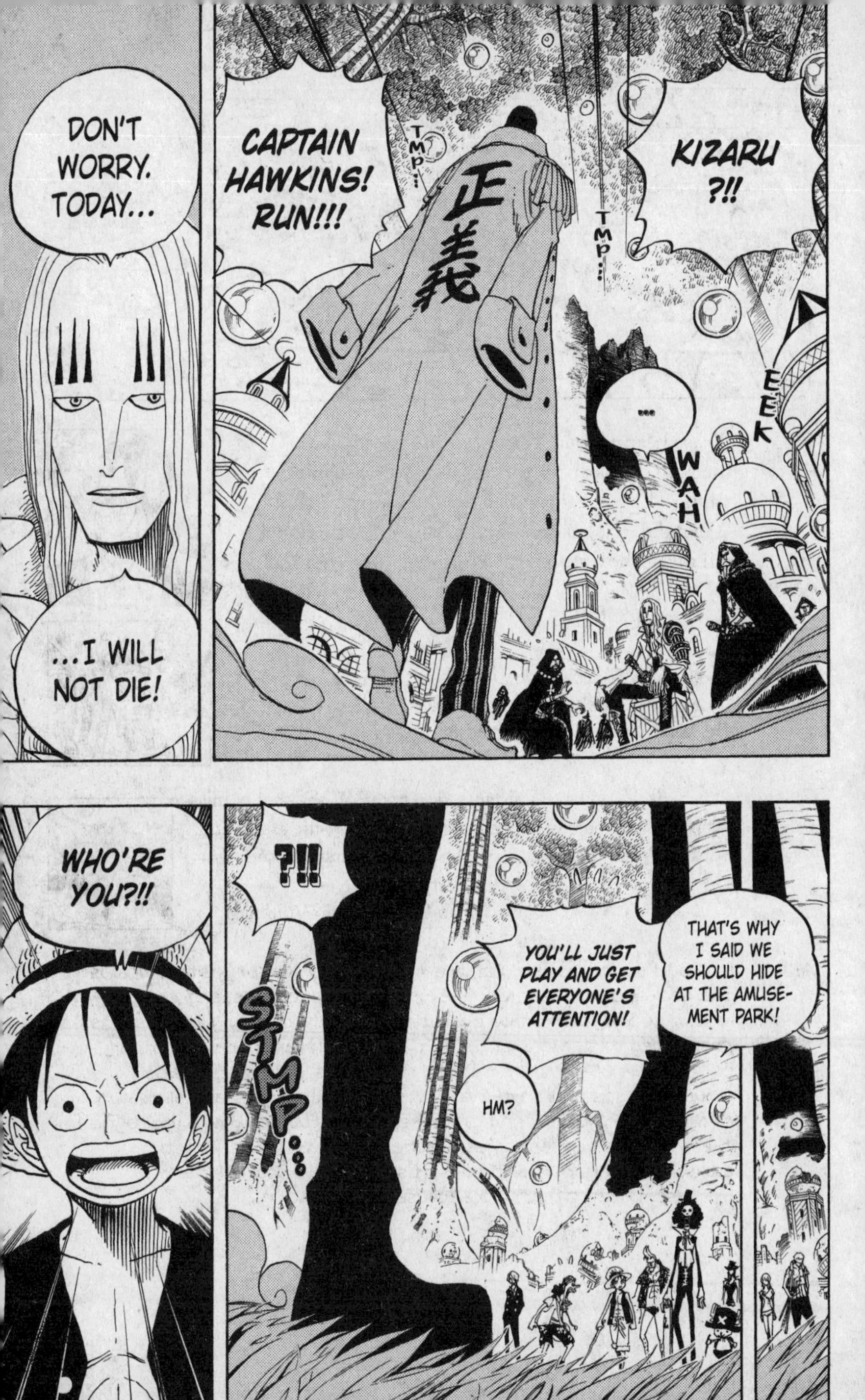
KIZARU ?!!
TMP...
EEK
CAPTAIN HAWKINS! RUN!!!
TMP...
...
WAH
DON'T WORRY. TODAY...
...I WILL NOT DIE!
THAT'S WHY I SAID WE SHOULD HIDE AT THE AMUSEMENT PARK!
YOU'LL JUST PLAY AND GET EVERYONE'S ATTENTION!
?!!
HM?
STMP...
WHO'RE YOU?!!

SBS Question Corner

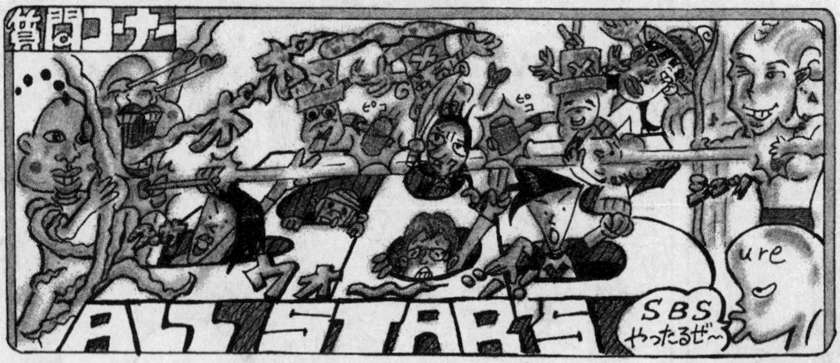
SBS
やったるぜ〜
ure

(T.M. Luffy, Aomori)

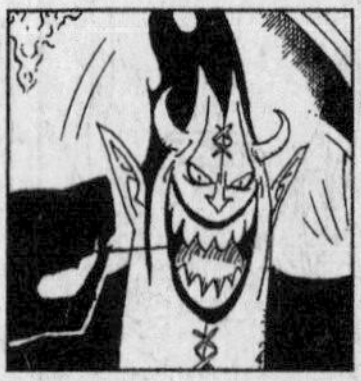

Q: Please hear me out! Yesterday, when I got out of the bath, I was about to wear my favorite tighty-whities. I then realized that my shadow was gone! When did that happen? And what kind of marionette did my shadow turn into? Please ask Moria for me!

-- Iwashi-chan

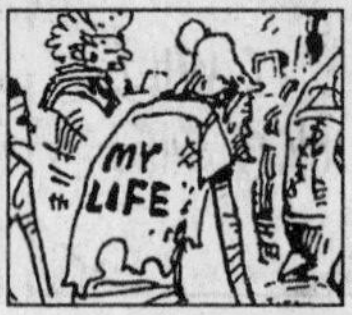
MY
LIFE

Oda: Well, Moria?
Moria: Ki shi shi! Shut up! You answer him!
Oda: Okay, I found him. It's this guy (→). He was getting lectured by Luffy.

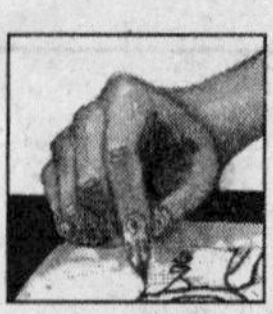

Q: Oda Sensei, you have assistants, don't you? With other comics, it's pretty obvious which drawings are done by the assistants, but I can't tell with *One Piece* even from the first volume! Do you draw the sketches for everything?

--Woman Who Re-read from Volume 1

A: It would be impossible for me to do everything. My staff draws the backgrounds for me. They look at my rough sketches and groundwork, then draw everything up very carefully. My staff is really filled with many great people. The difference with other comics is probably that things like crowds, animals, smoke, clouds, oceans and anything that "lives and moves" are all drawn by me. When you depend on other people to draw moving things, the presentation becomes a little off sometimes. A little awkward, even. But with this, it's more like something that I refuse to let others do because I'm stubborn.

Chapter 508:
ISLAND OF CARNAGE

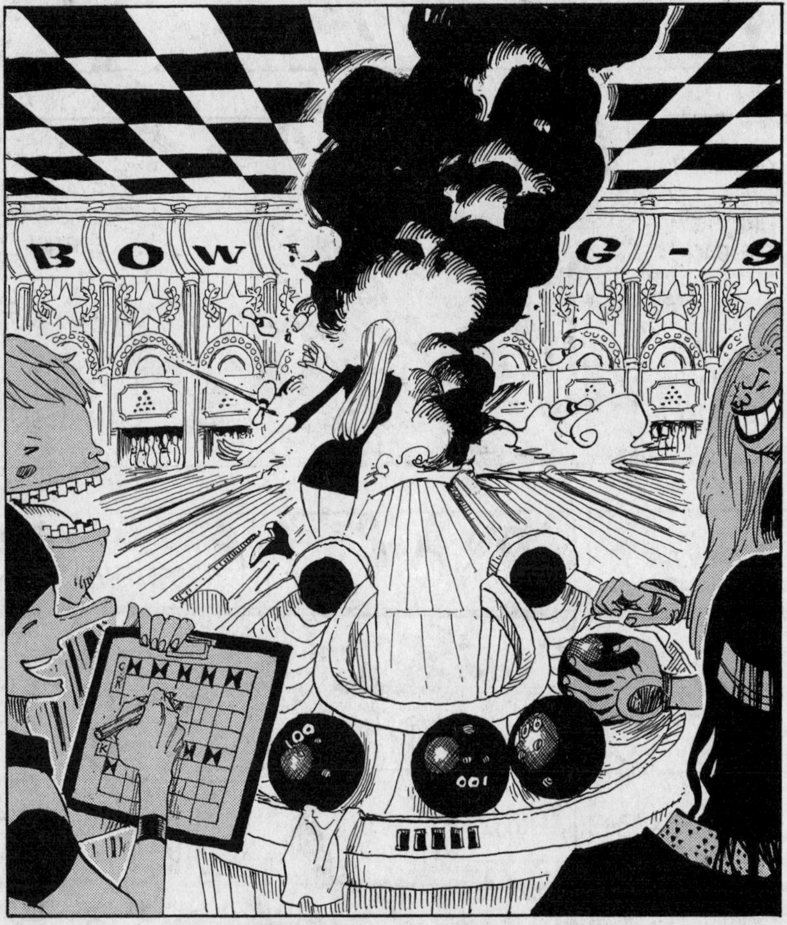
BOW G-9

CP9'S INDEPENDENT REPORT, VOL. 16:
"FUN BOWLING EXCURSION"

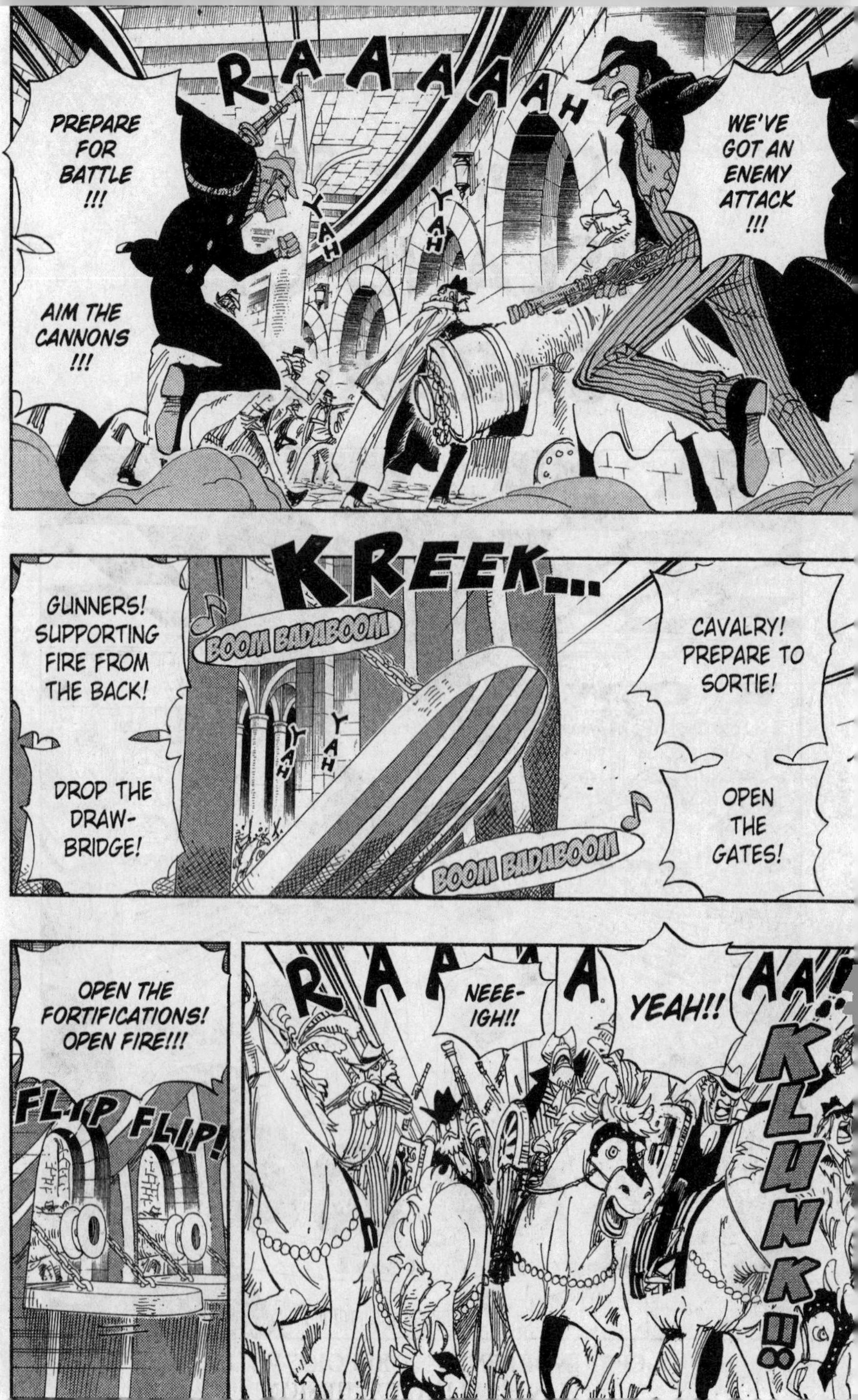
RAAAAAAH
WE'VE GOT AN ENEMY ATTACK!!!
YAH
YAH
PREPARE FOR BATTLE!!!
AIM THE CANNONS!!!
KREEK...
CAVALRY! PREPARE TO SORTIE!
OPEN THE GATES!
BOOM BADABOOM
YAH
YAH
BOOM BADABOOM
GUNNERS! SUPPORTING FIRE FROM THE BACK!
DROP THE DRAW-BRIDGE!
RAAAAAA!
YEAH!!
NEEE-IGH!!
KLUNK!!
OPEN THE FORTIFICATIONS! OPEN FIRE!!!
FLIP FLIP!

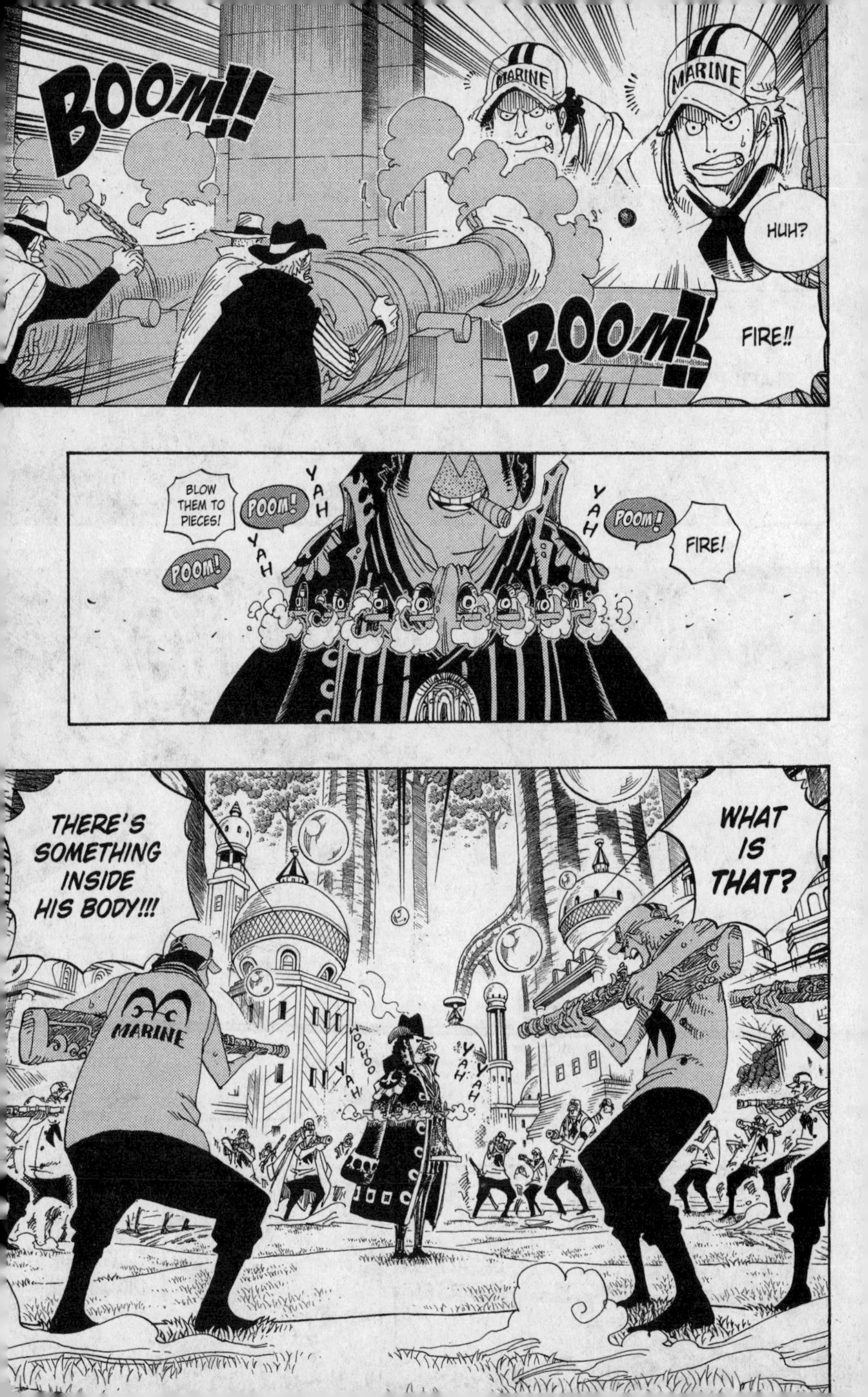
MARINE
MARINE
HUH?
FIRE!!
BOOM!!
BOOM!!
FIRE!
POOM!
YAH
POOM!
YAH
BLOW THEM TO PIECES!
POOM!
YAH
WHAT IS THAT?
YAH
YAH
WOOHOO
YAH
MARINE
THERE'S SOMETHING INSIDE HIS BODY!!!

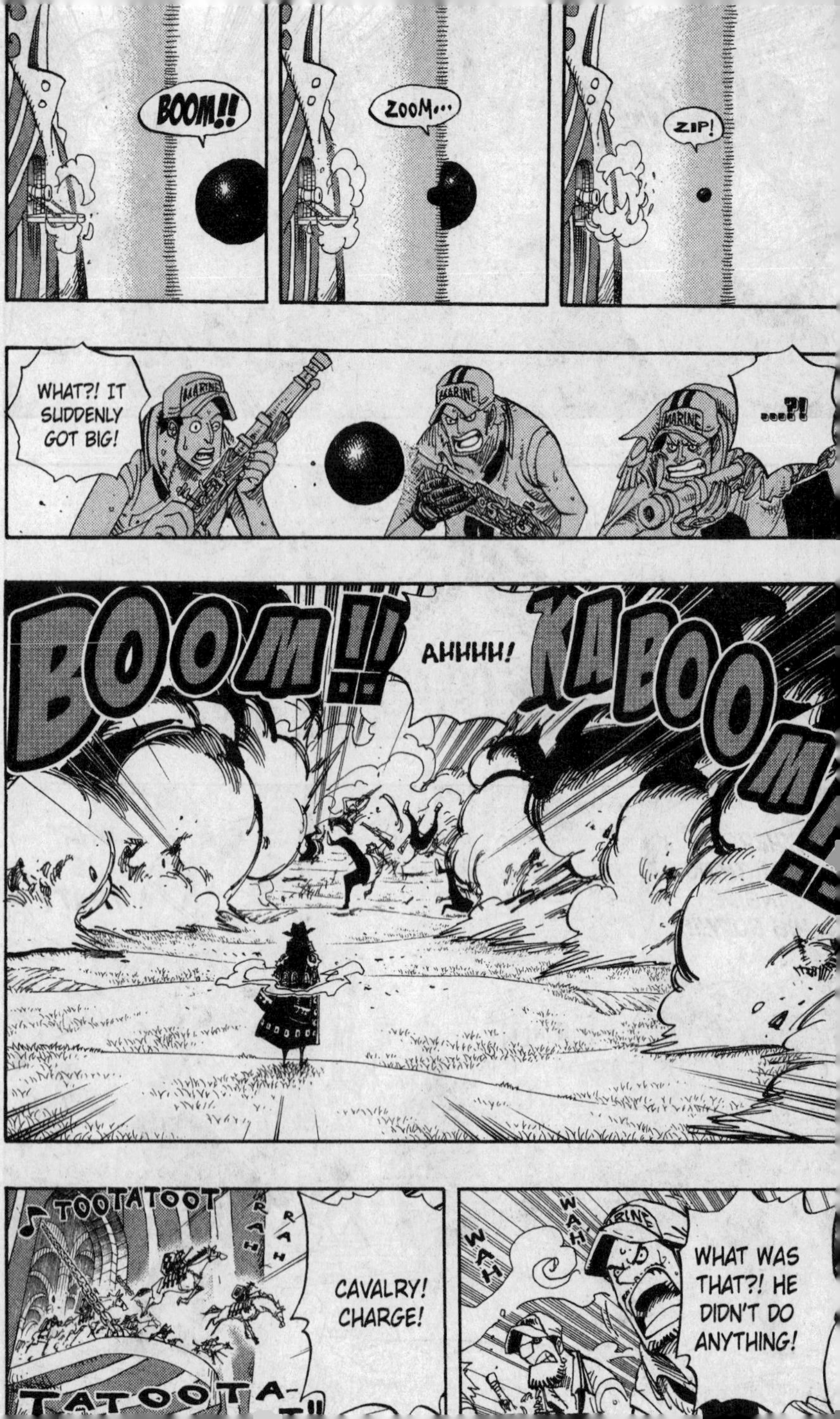
ZIP!
ZOOM...
BOOM!!
...?!
WHAT?! IT SUDDENLY GOT BIG!
KABOOM!!
AHHHH!
BOOM!!
WAH
WAH
WHAT WAS THAT?! HE DIDN'T DO ANYTHING!
RAH
RAH
TOOTATOOT
CAVALRY! CHARGE!
TATOOTA-!!

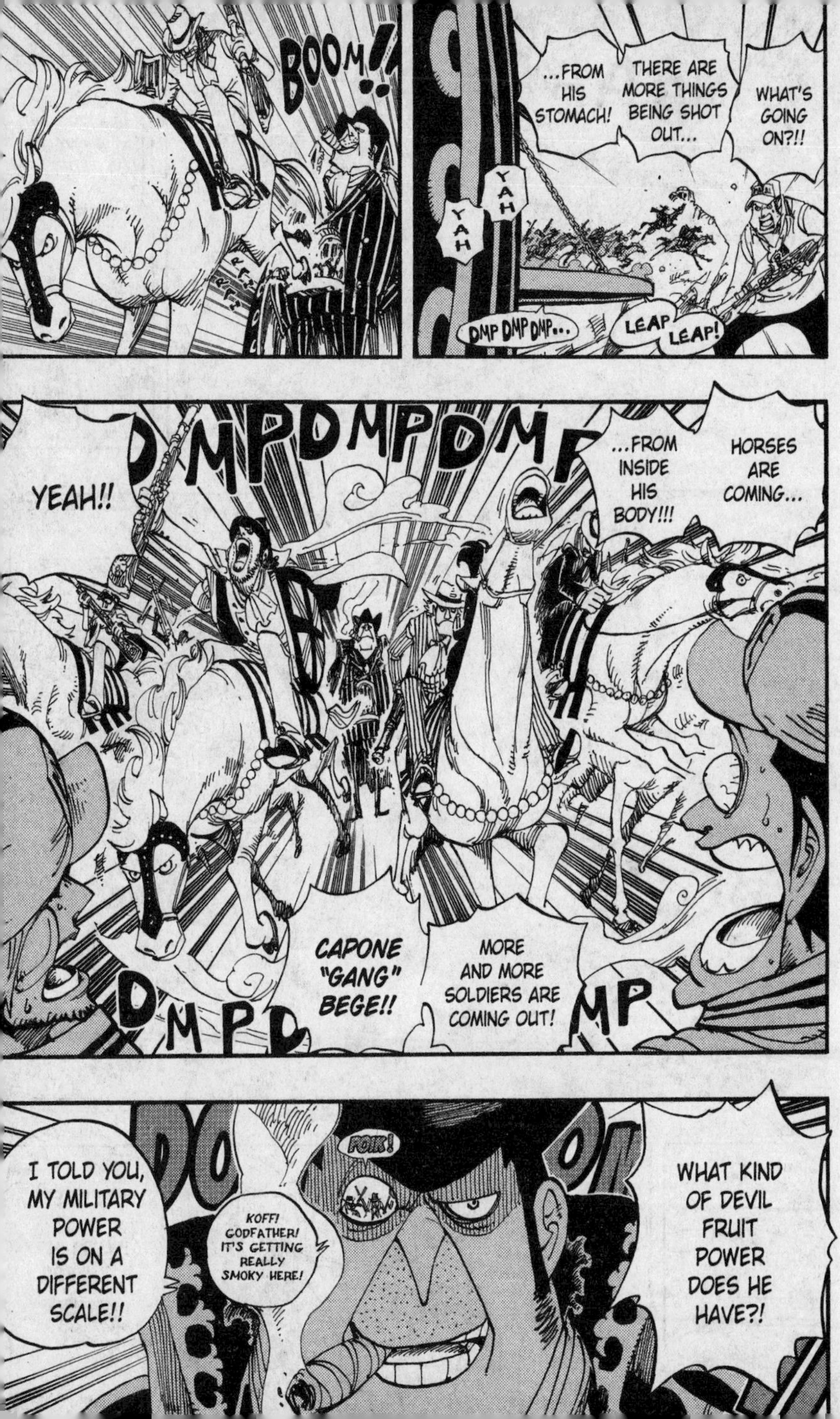
WHAT'S GOING ON?!!
THERE ARE MORE THINGS BEING SHOT OUT...
...FROM HIS STOMACH!
YAH
YAH
LEAP LEAP!
DMP DMP DMP...
BOOM!!
HORSES ARE COMING...
...FROM INSIDE HIS BODY!!!
DMPDMPDMP
YEAH!!
MP
MORE AND MORE SOLDIERS ARE COMING OUT!
CAPONE "GANG" BEGE!!
DMPD
WHAT KIND OF DEVIL FRUIT POWER DOES HE HAVE?!
POIK!
KOFF! GODFATHER! IT'S GETTING REALLY SMOKY HERE!
I TOLD YOU, MY MILITARY POWER IS ON A DIFFERENT SCALE!!

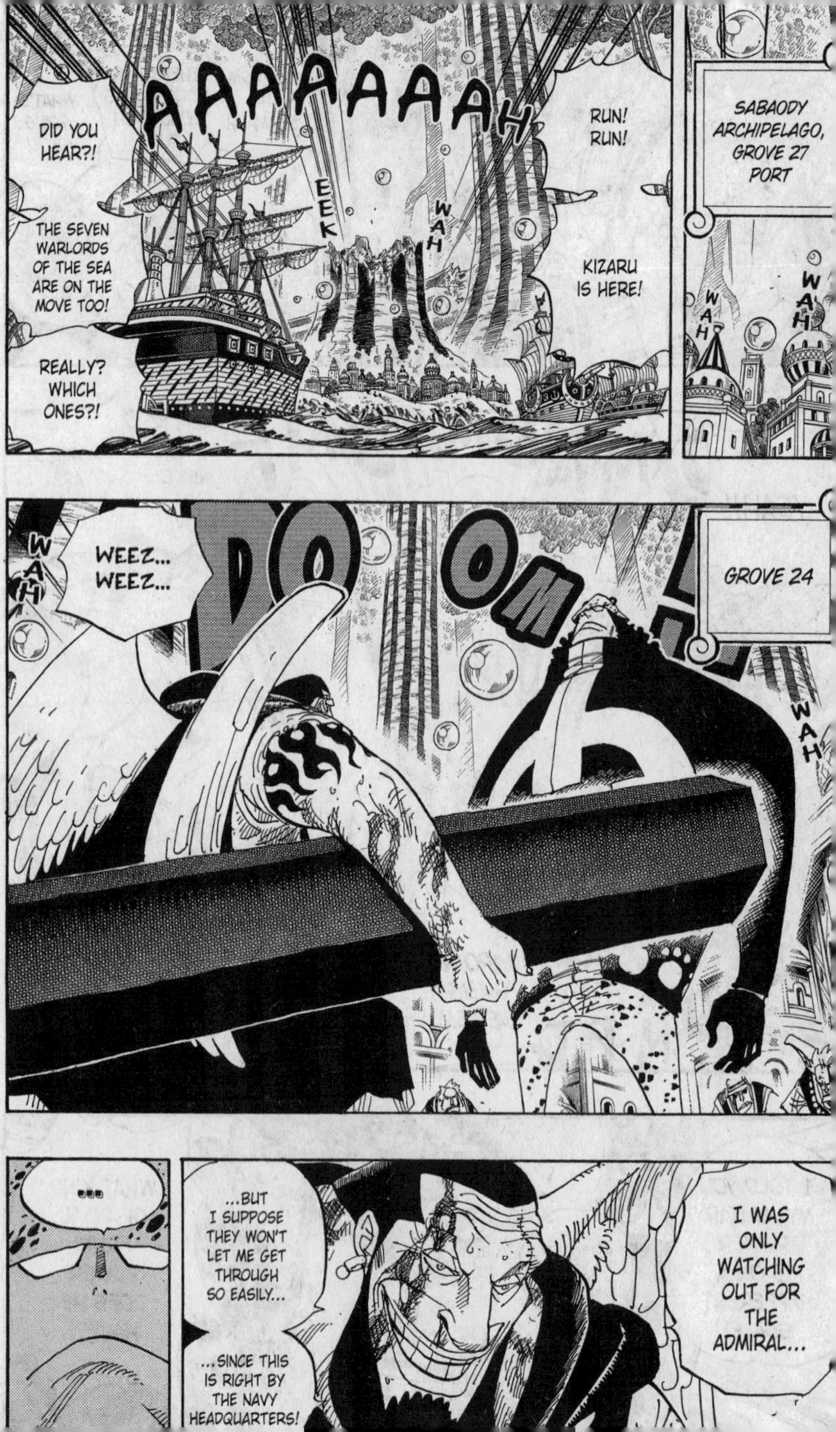
SABAODY ARCHIPELAGO, GROVE 27 PORT
WAH
WAH
AAAAAAAH
RUN! RUN!
EEK
WAH
KIZARU IS HERE!
DID YOU HEAR?!
THE SEVEN WARLORDS OF THE SEA ARE ON THE MOVE TOO!
REALLY? WHICH ONES?!
GROVE 24
WAH
DOOM
WEEZ... WEEZ...
WAH
I WAS ONLY WATCHING OUT FOR THE ADMIRAL...
...BUT I SUPPOSE THEY WON'T LET ME GET THROUGH SO EASILY...
...SINCE THIS IS RIGHT BY THE NAVY HEADQUARTERS!
...

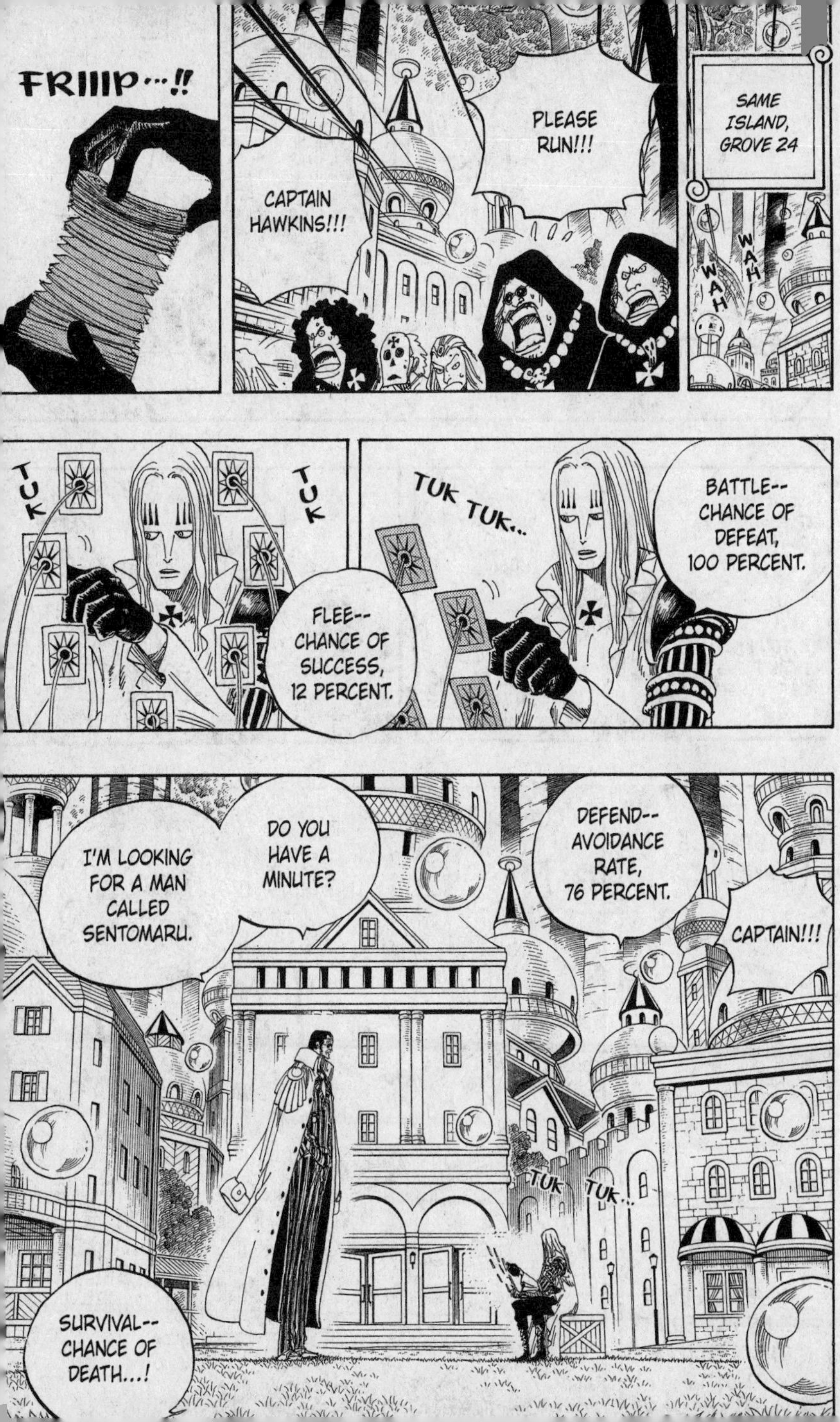
SAME ISLAND, GROVE 24
WAH WAH
PLEASE RUN!!!
CAPTAIN HAWKINS!!!
FRIIIP...!!
BATTLE--CHANCE OF DEFEAT, 100 PERCENT.
TUK TUK...
FLEE--CHANCE OF SUCCESS, 12 PERCENT.
TUK TUK
CAPTAIN!!!
DEFEND--AVOIDANCE RATE, 76 PERCENT.
DO YOU HAVE A MINUTE?
I'M LOOKING FOR A MAN CALLED SENTOMARU.
TUK TUK...
SURVIVAL--CHANCE OF DEATH...!

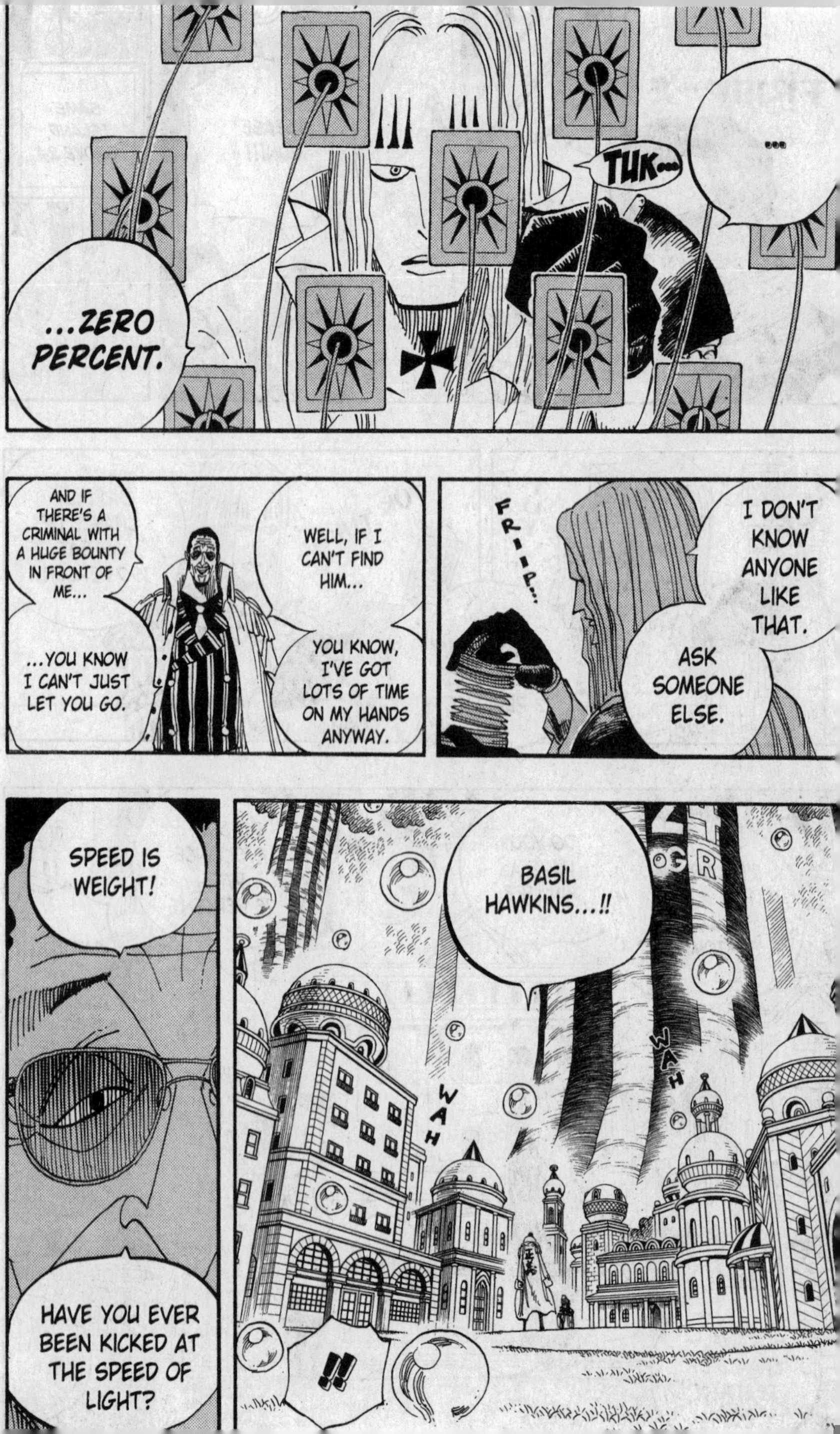
...
TUK...
...ZERO PERCENT.
FRIIIP...
I DON'T KNOW ANYONE LIKE THAT.
ASK SOMEONE ELSE.
WELL, IF I CAN'T FIND HIM...
YOU KNOW, I'VE GOT LOTS OF TIME ON MY HANDS ANYWAY.
AND IF THERE'S A CRIMINAL WITH A HUGE BOUNTY IN FRONT OF ME...
...YOU KNOW I CAN'T JUST LET YOU GO.
BASIL HAWKINS...!!
WAH
WAH
!!
SPEED IS WEIGHT!
HAVE YOU EVER BEEN KICKED AT THE SPEED OF LIGHT?

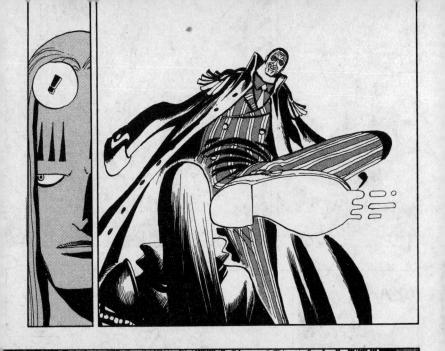

KRASH!!!

CAPTAIN!!!

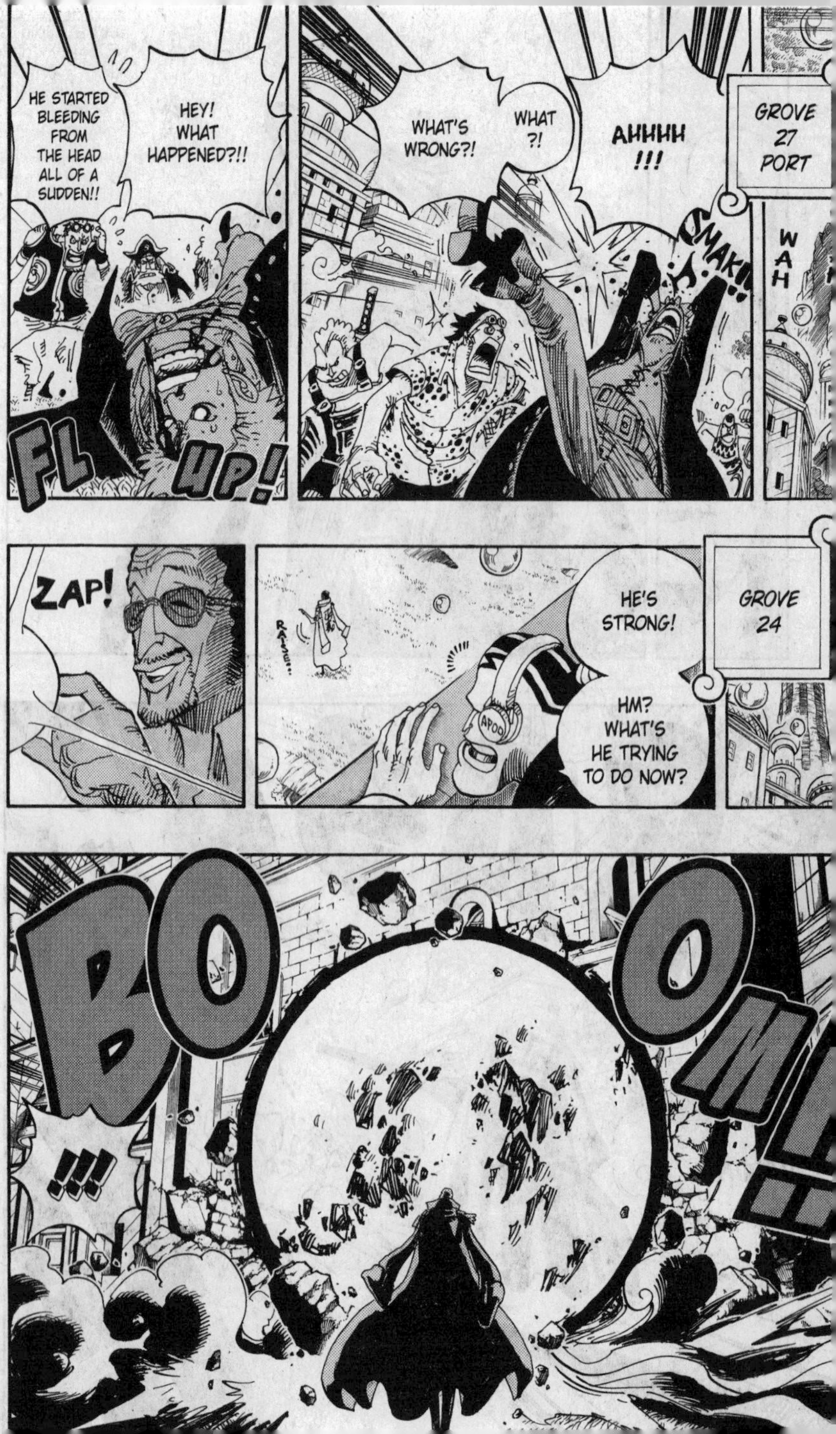
GROVE 27 PORT
WAH
AHHHH !!!
WHAT ?!
WHAT'S WRONG?!
SMAK!!
HEY! WHAT HAPPENED?!!
HE STARTED BLEEDING FROM THE HEAD ALL OF A SUDDEN!!
FLUP!
GROVE 24
HE'S STRONG!
HM? WHAT'S HE TRYING TO DO NOW?
APOO
ZAP!
BOOM!!
!!!

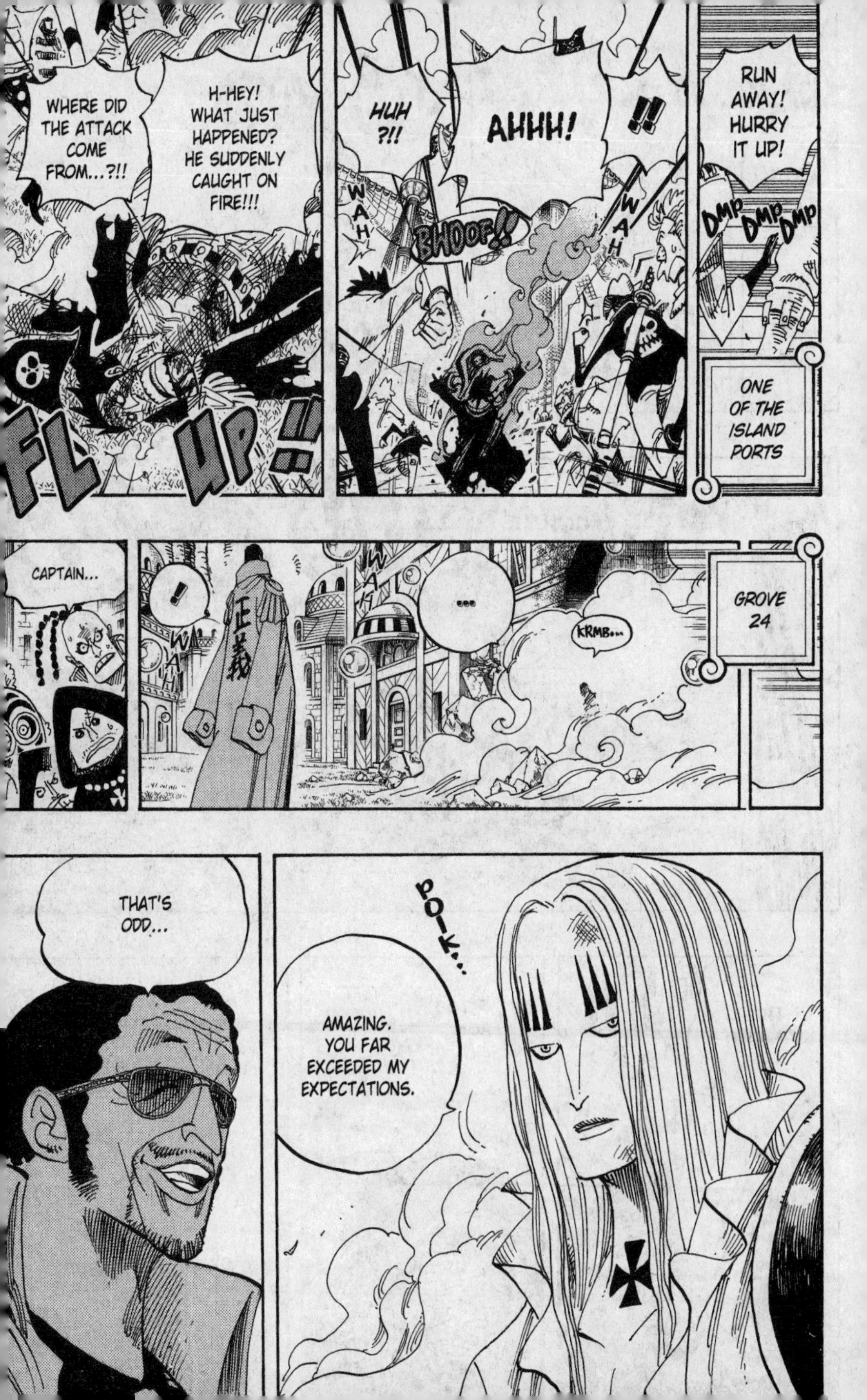
ONE OF THE ISLAND PORTS
RUN AWAY! HURRY IT UP!
DMP DMP DMP
!!
AHHH!
HUH ?!!
WAH
WAH
BWOOF!!
H-HEY! WHAT JUST HAPPENED? HE SUDDENLY CAUGHT ON FIRE!!!
WHERE DID THE ATTACK COME FROM...?!!
FLUP!!
GROVE 24
KRMB...
...
WAH
!
WAH
CAPTAIN...
POIK...
AMAZING. YOU FAR EXCEEDED MY EXPECTATIONS.
THAT'S ODD...

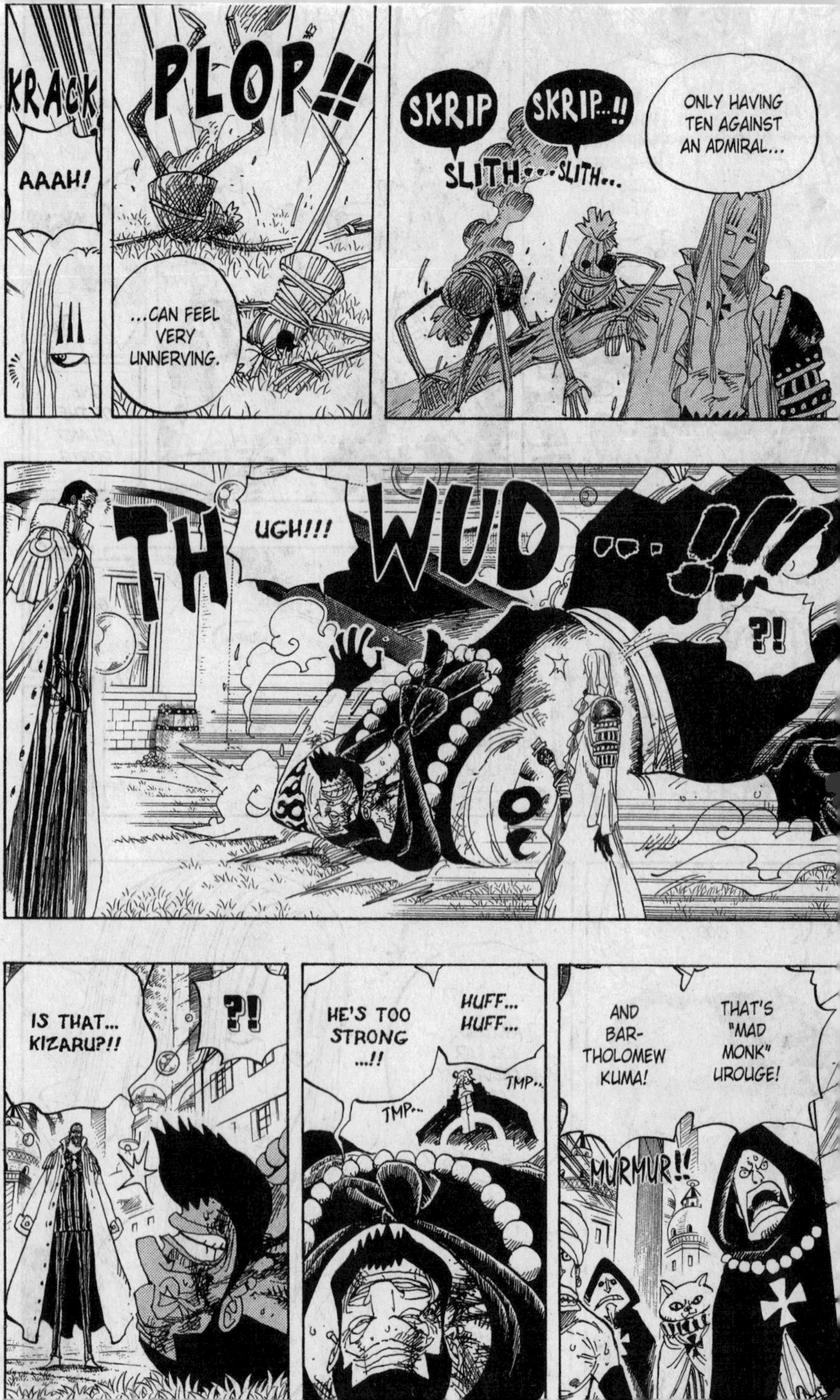
ONLY HAVING TEN AGAINST AN ADMIRAL...
SKRIP...!!
SKRIP
SLITH... SLITH...
PLOP!!
...CAN FEEL VERY UNNERVING.
KRACK
AAAH!
?!
WUD
UGH!!!
TH
THAT'S "MAD MONK" UROUGE!
AND BAR-THOLOMEW KUMA!
MURMUR!!
HUFF... HUFF...
HE'S TOO STRONG ...!!
TMP...
TMP...
?!
IS THAT... KIZARU?!!

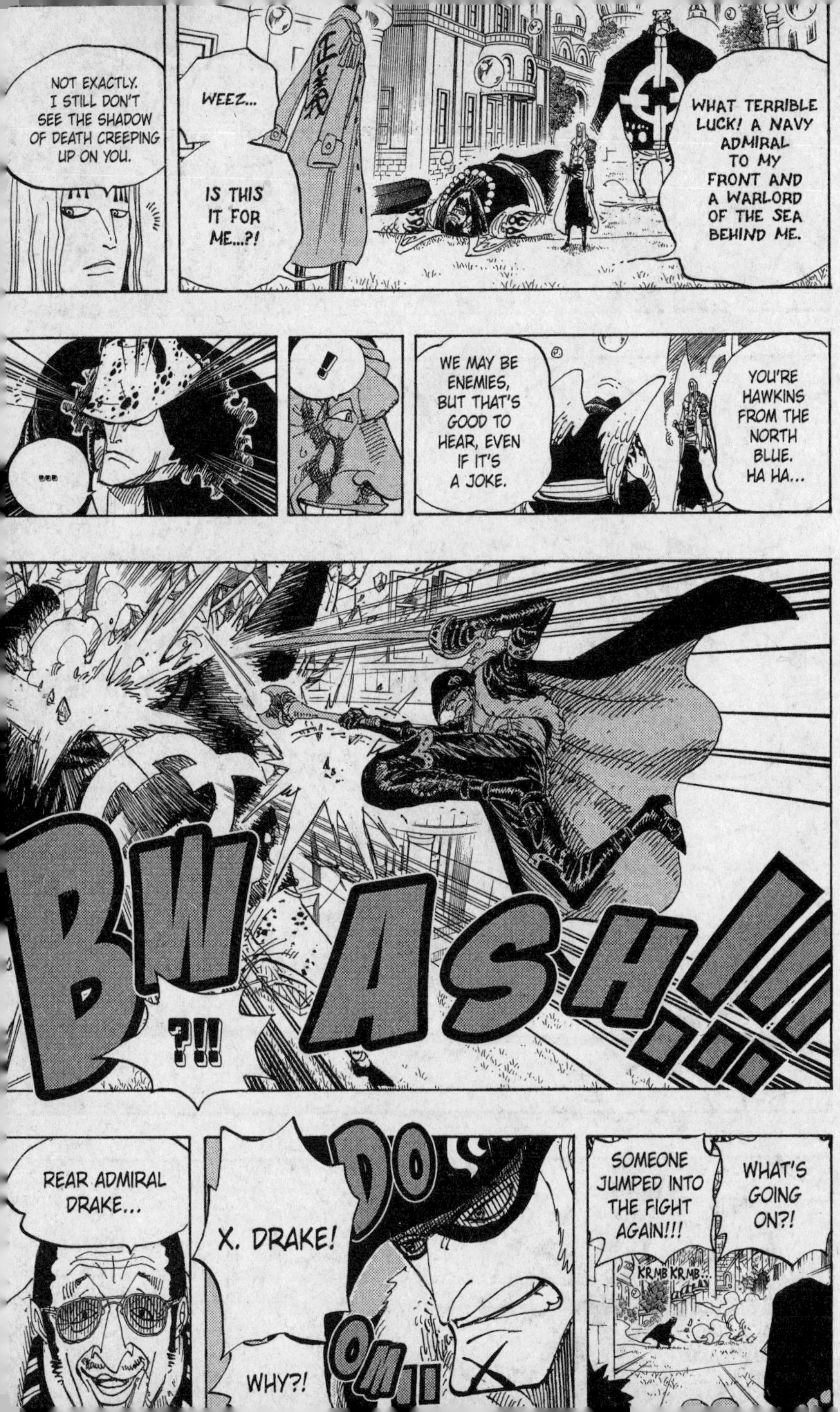
WHAT TERRIBLE LUCK! A NAVY ADMIRAL TO MY FRONT AND A WARLORD OF THE SEA BEHIND ME.
WEEZ...
IS THIS IT FOR ME...?!
NOT EXACTLY. I STILL DON'T SEE THE SHADOW OF DEATH CREEPING UP ON YOU.
YOU'RE HAWKINS FROM THE NORTH BLUE. HA HA...
WE MAY BE ENEMIES, BUT THAT'S GOOD TO HEAR, EVEN IF IT'S A JOKE.
!
...
BWASH!!!
?!!
WHAT'S GOING ON?!
SOMEONE JUMPED INTO THE FIGHT AGAIN!!!
KRMB KRMB...
DOOM!!
X. DRAKE!
WHY?!
REAR ADMIRAL DRAKE...

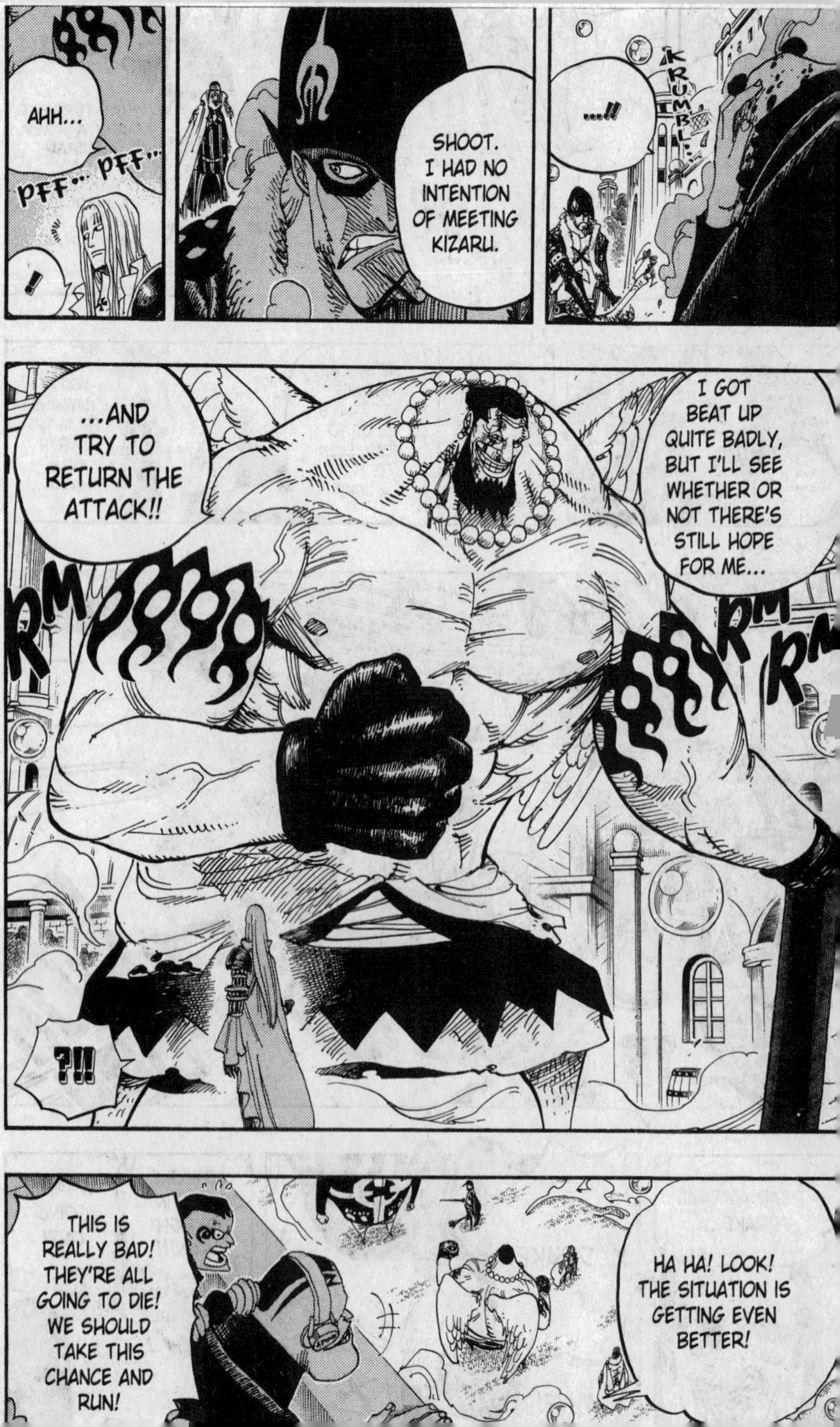
KRUMBL...
...!!
SHOOT. I HAD NO INTENTION OF MEETING KIZARU.
AHH...
PFF... PFF...
!
I GOT BEAT UP QUITE BADLY, BUT I'LL SEE WHETHER OR NOT THERE'S STILL HOPE FOR ME...
...AND TRY TO RETURN THE ATTACK!!
?!!
HA HA! LOOK! THE SITUATION IS GETTING EVEN BETTER!
THIS IS REALLY BAD! THEY'RE ALL GOING TO DIE! WE SHOULD TAKE THIS CHANCE AND RUN!

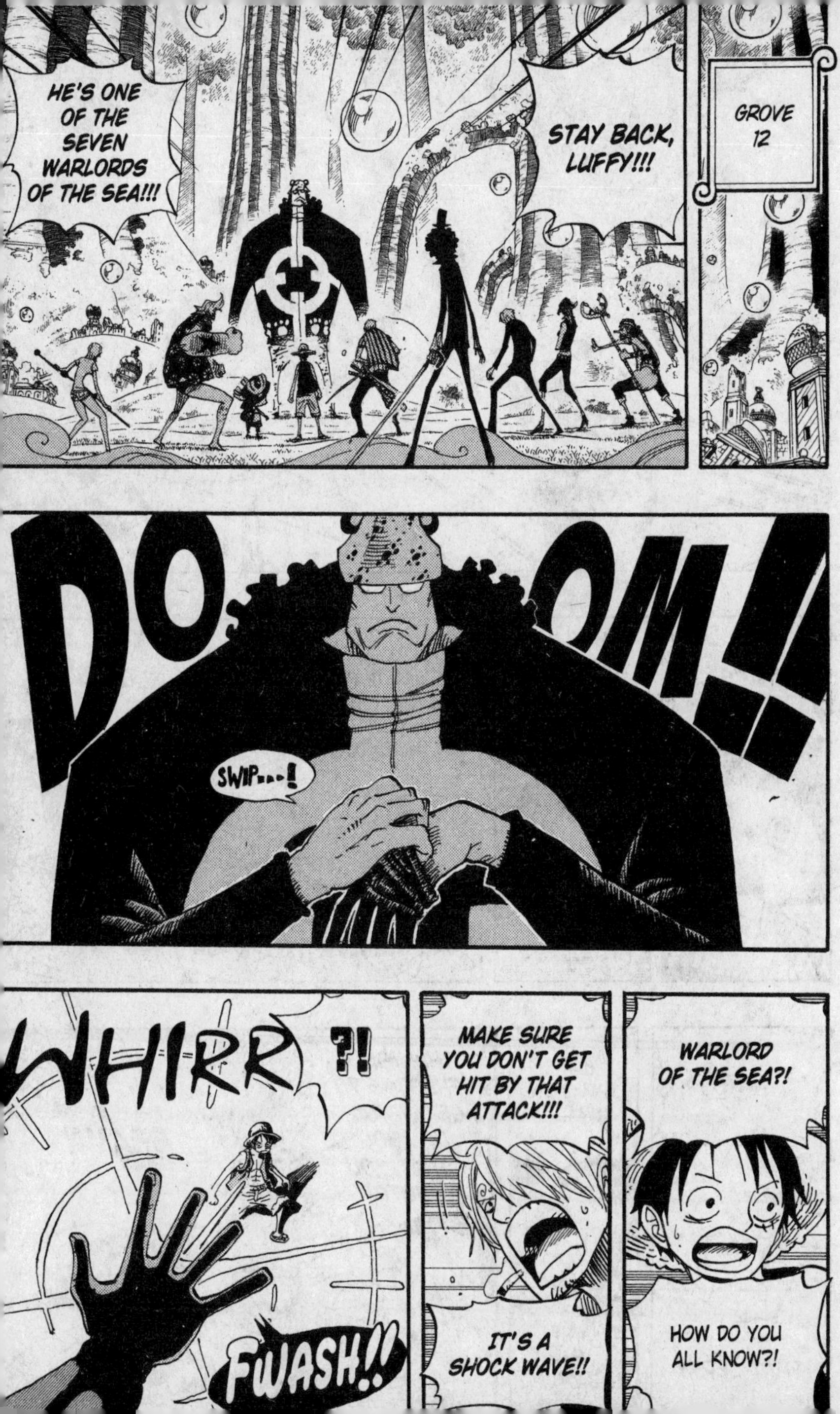
GROVE 12
STAY BACK, LUFFY!!!
HE'S ONE OF THE SEVEN WARLORDS OF THE SEA!!!
DOOM!!
SWIP...!
WARLORD OF THE SEA?!
HOW DO YOU ALL KNOW?!
MAKE SURE YOU DON'T GET HIT BY THAT ATTACK!!!
IT'S A SHOCK WAVE!!
?!
WHIRR
FWASH!!

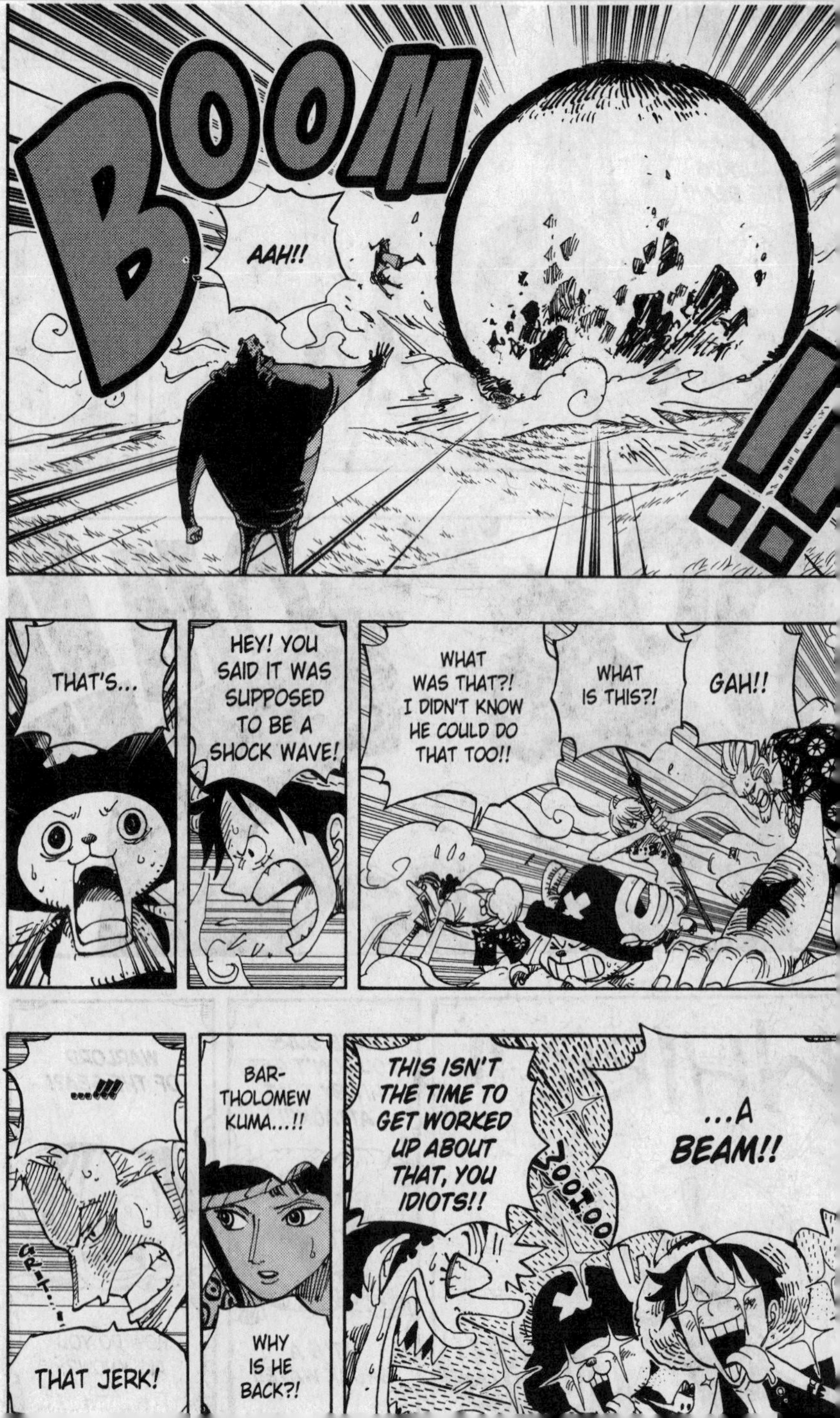
BOOM
AAH!!
!!!
GAH!!
WHAT IS THIS?!
WHAT WAS THAT?! I DIDN'T KNOW HE COULD DO THAT TOO!!
HEY! YOU SAID IT WAS SUPPOSED TO BE A SHOCK WAVE!
THAT'S...
...A BEAM!!
THIS ISN'T THE TIME TO GET WORKED UP ABOUT THAT, YOU IDIOTS!!
BAR-THOLOMEW KUMA...!!
WHY IS HE BACK?!
...!!!
THAT JERK!

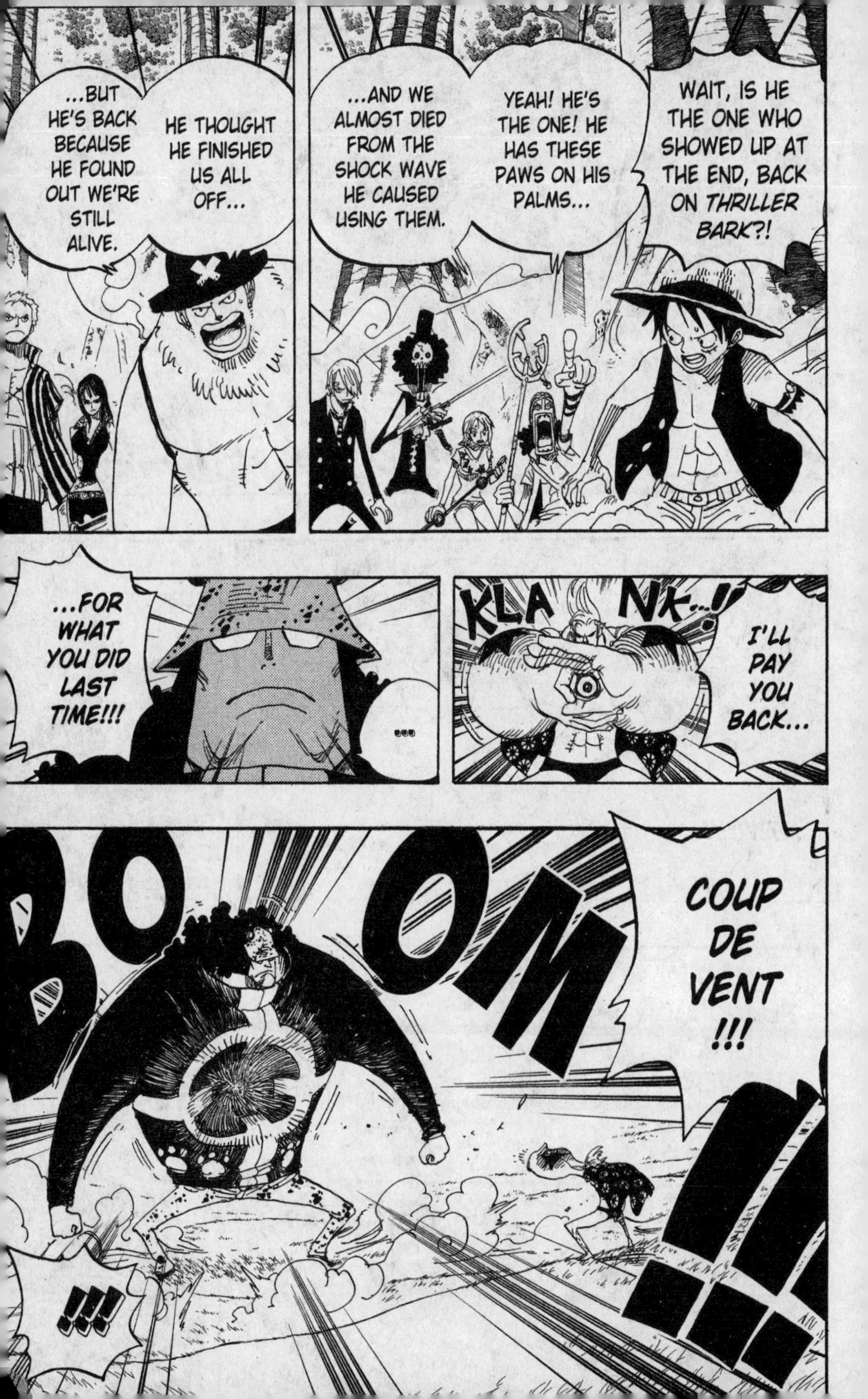
WAIT, IS HE THE ONE WHO SHOWED UP AT THE END, BACK ON *THRILLER BARK*?!
YEAH! HE'S THE ONE! HE HAS THESE PAWS ON HIS PALMS...
...AND WE ALMOST DIED FROM THE SHOCK WAVE HE CAUSED USING THEM.
HE THOUGHT HE FINISHED US ALL OFF...
...BUT HE'S BACK BECAUSE HE FOUND OUT WE'RE STILL ALIVE.
KLANK...!
I'LL PAY YOU BACK...
...FOR WHAT YOU DID LAST TIME!!!
...
COUP DE VENT !!!
BOOM
!!!
!!!

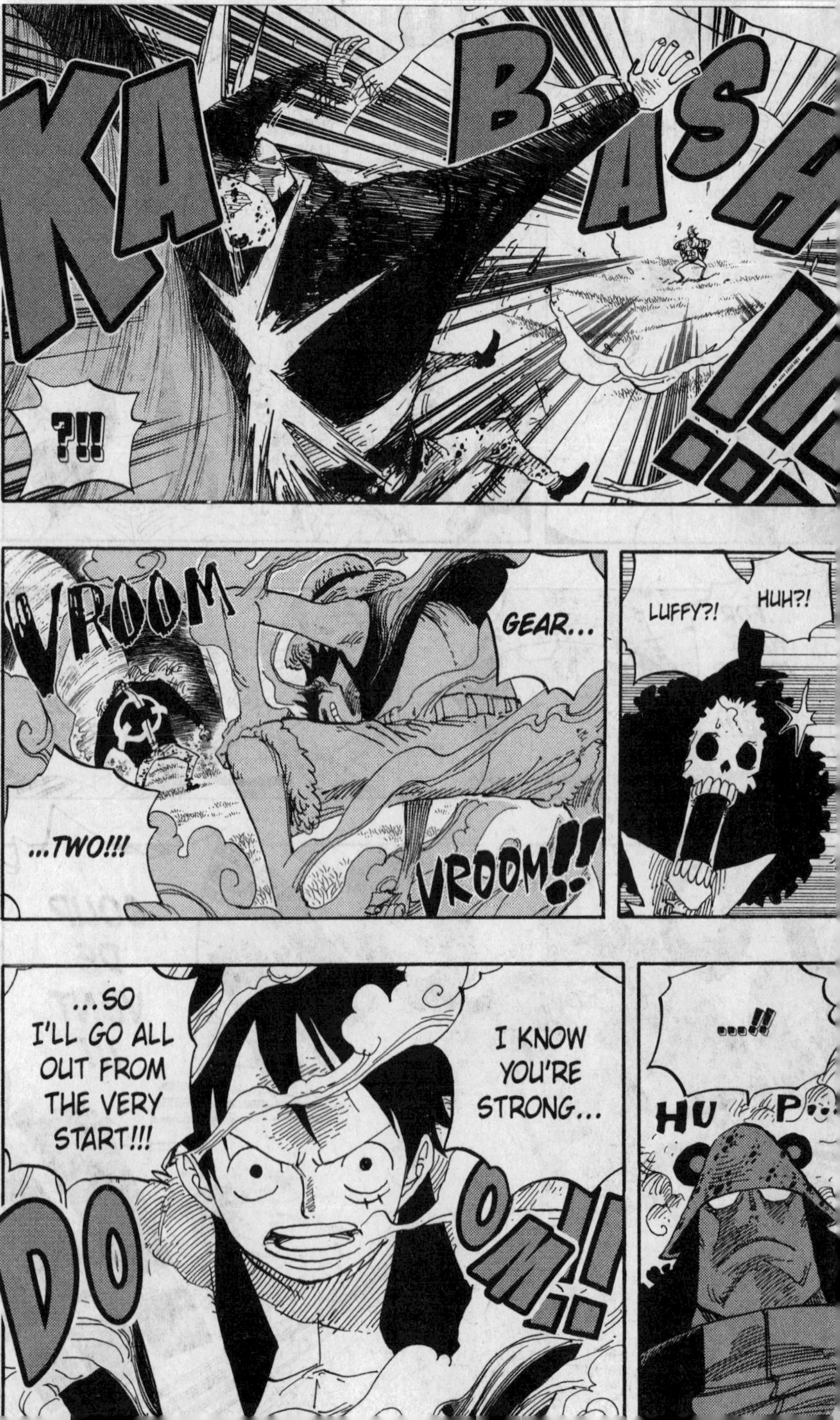
KABASH!!
?!!
HUH?!
LUFFY?!
GEAR...
VROOM
...TWO!!!
VROOM!!
...!!
HUP...
I KNOW YOU'RE STRONG...
...SO I'LL GO ALL OUT FROM THE VERY START!!!
DOOM!!

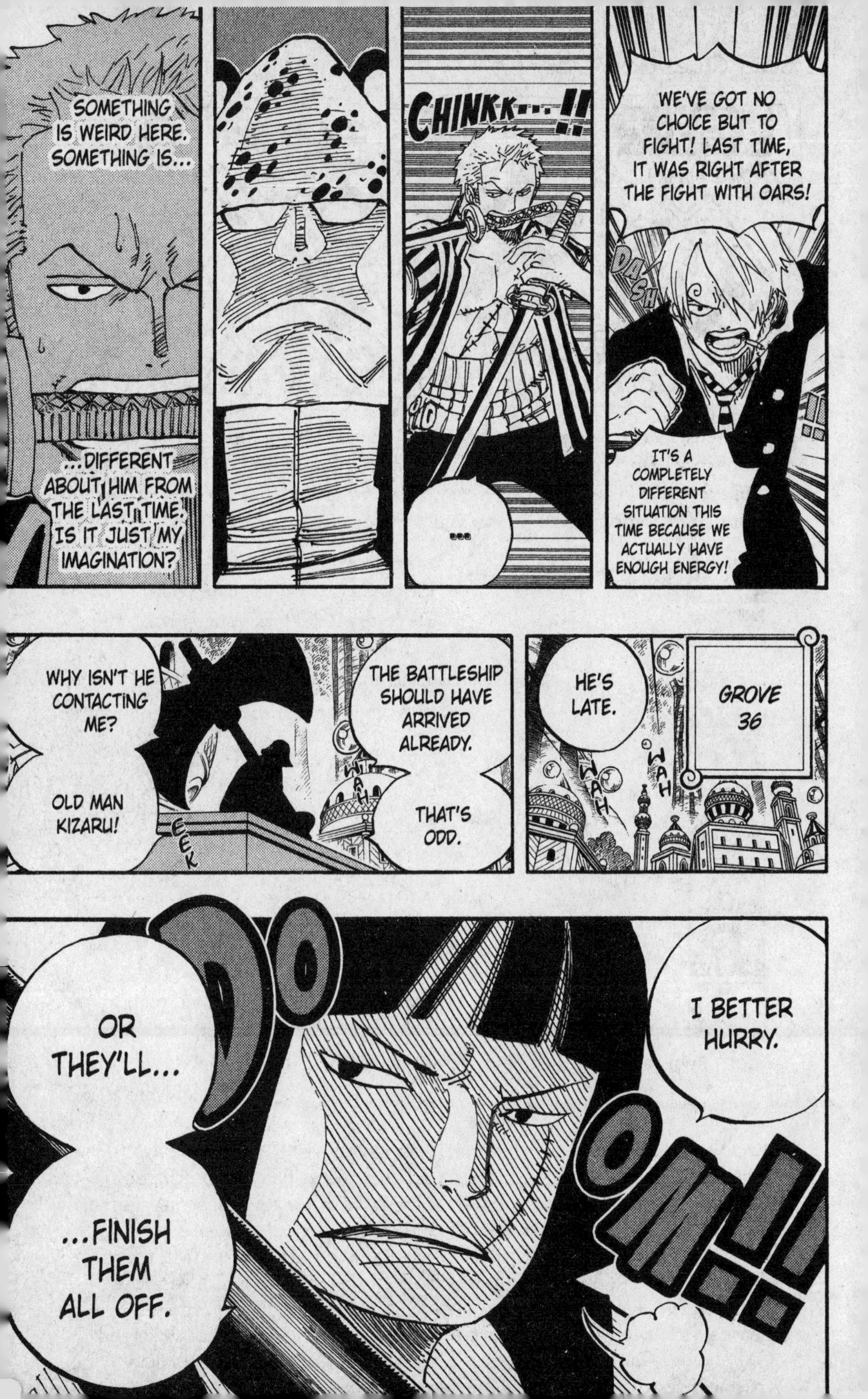
WE'VE GOT NO CHOICE BUT TO FIGHT! LAST TIME, IT WAS RIGHT AFTER THE FIGHT WITH OARS!
DASH
IT'S A COMPLETELY DIFFERENT SITUATION THIS TIME BECAUSE WE ACTUALLY HAVE ENOUGH ENERGY!
CHINKK...!!
...
SOMETHING IS WEIRD HERE. SOMETHING IS...
...DIFFERENT ABOUT HIM FROM THE LAST TIME. IS IT JUST MY IMAGINATION?
GROVE 36
HE'S LATE.
WAH
WAH
THE BATTLESHIP SHOULD HAVE ARRIVED ALREADY.
THAT'S ODD.
WAH
WHY ISN'T HE CONTACTING ME?
OLD MAN KIZARU!
EEK
I BETTER HURRY.
DOOM!!
OR THEY'LL...
...FINISH THEM ALL OFF.

SBS Question Corner

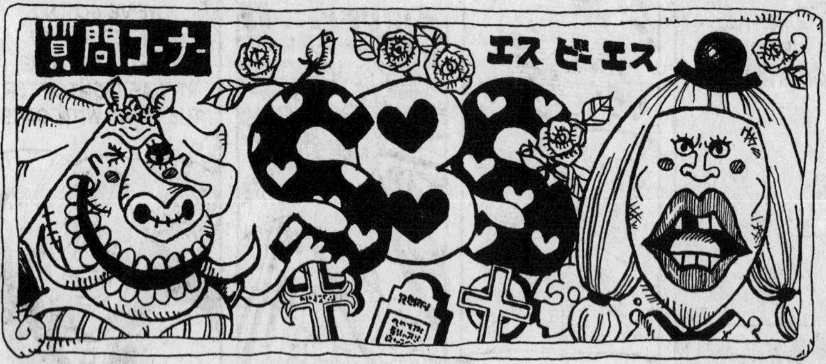
質問コーナー
エスビーエス
SBS

(Usopper, Gunma)

Q: Oda Sensei, hello. I have a question. I sometimes read up on the history of pirates, and I've been wondering about the "Supernova" rookies. I made a list below of where I think their names come from. What do you think of it?

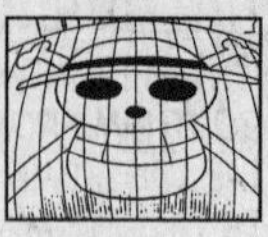

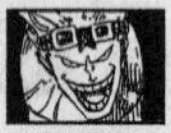	Eustass "Captain" Kid	=	13th century pirate monk Eustace + 17th century Scottish pirate William Kid
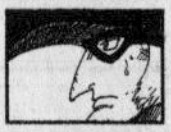	X. Drake	=	16th century English explorer, privateer and knight Francis Drake
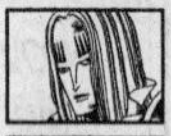	Basil Hawkins	=	Same as above, John Hawkins + 17th century pirate ship doctor Basil Ringrose
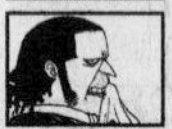	Capone "Gang" Bege	=	Same as above, Thomas Cavendish
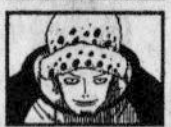	Trafalgar Law	=	18th century English pirate Edward Low
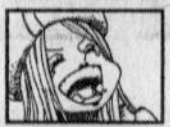	Jewelry Bonney	=	18th century female pirate Anne Bonny
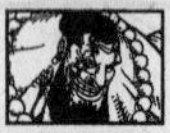	Urouge	=	16th century Turkish pirate Aruj Barbarossa
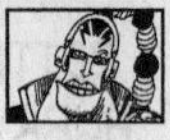	Scratchmen Apoo	=	19th century Chinese pirate Chui Apoo

I don't know about "Killer," but please correct me if I'm wrong!

--Chii-yan Mii-yan SP

A: Wonderful! Thank you so much! You saved me the trouble of explaining everything. But there is one thing I have to correct. Capone "Gang" Bege comes from the famous American gangster "Al Capone" and the English privateer William le Sauvage. You can think of privateers as pirates that are like the Seven Warlords of the Sea. Oh, and the name Killer is just made up. So yes, the rookies all have names taken from real pirates. But just the names. I think this should get a lot of pirate lovers really excited. Oh, and my Question Corner ends here! The special Question Corner section will start on page 148!

Chapter 509:
KIZARU VS. FOUR CAPTAINS

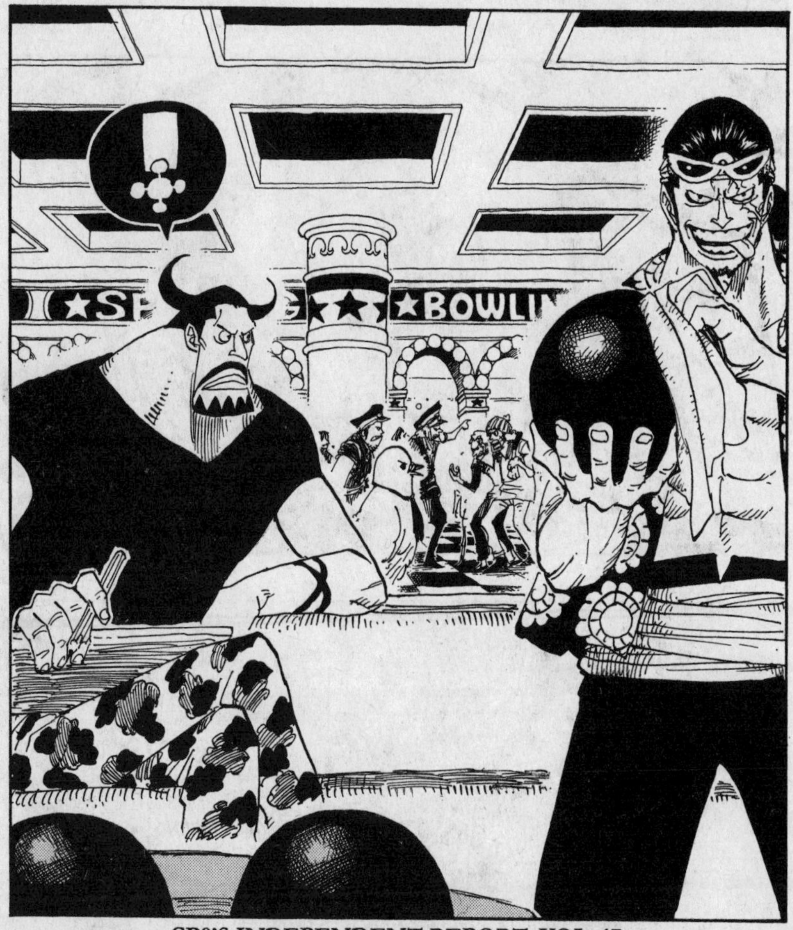
!
★SP
★BOWLI

CP9'S INDEPENDENT REPORT, VOL. 17:
"COMMOTION IN TOWN"

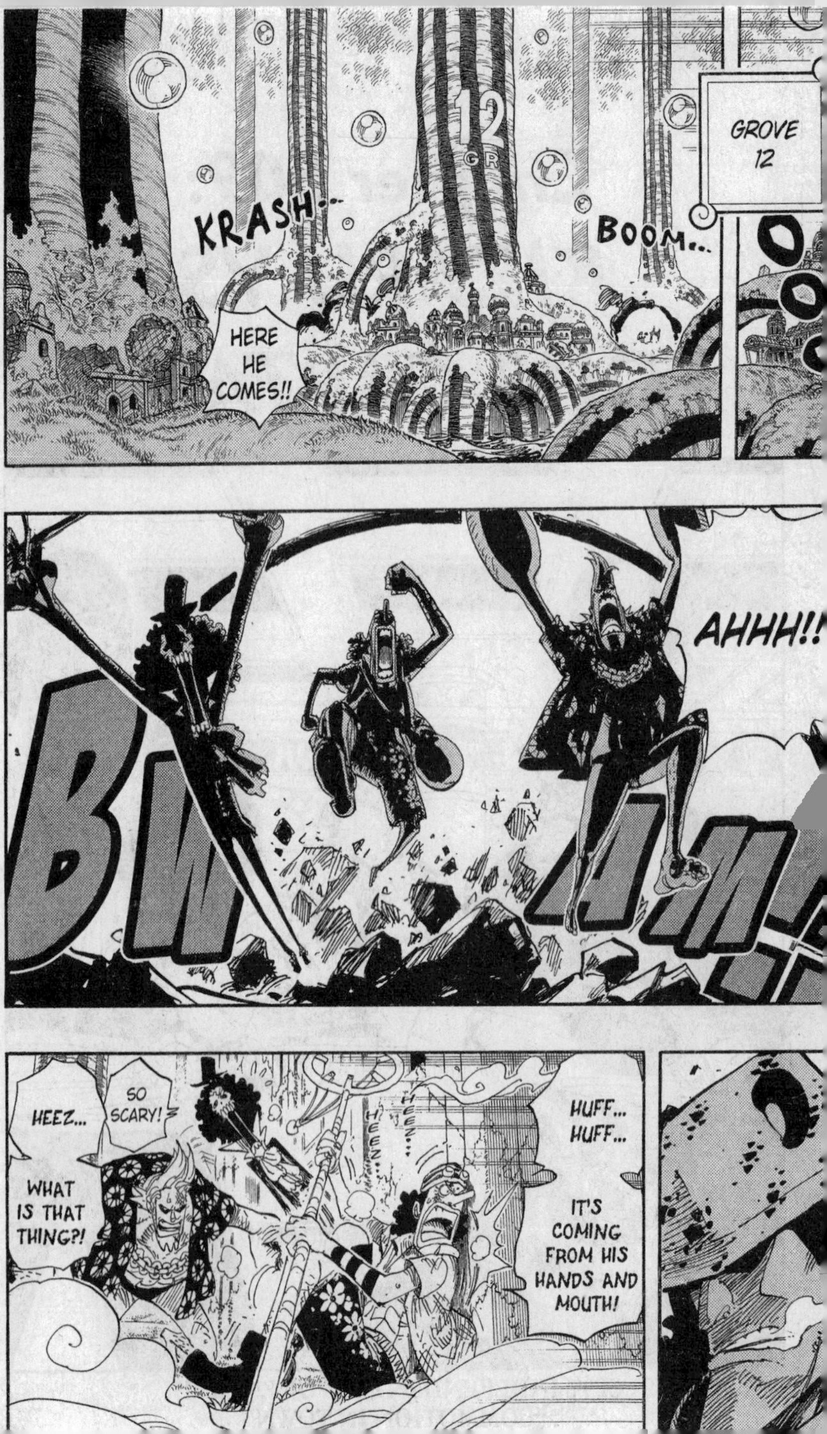
GROVE 12
BOOM...
KRASH...
HERE HE COMES!!
AHHH!!
HUFF... HUFF...
IT'S COMING FROM HIS HANDS AND MOUTH!
HEEZ...
SO SCARY!
HEEZ...
WHAT IS THAT THING?!

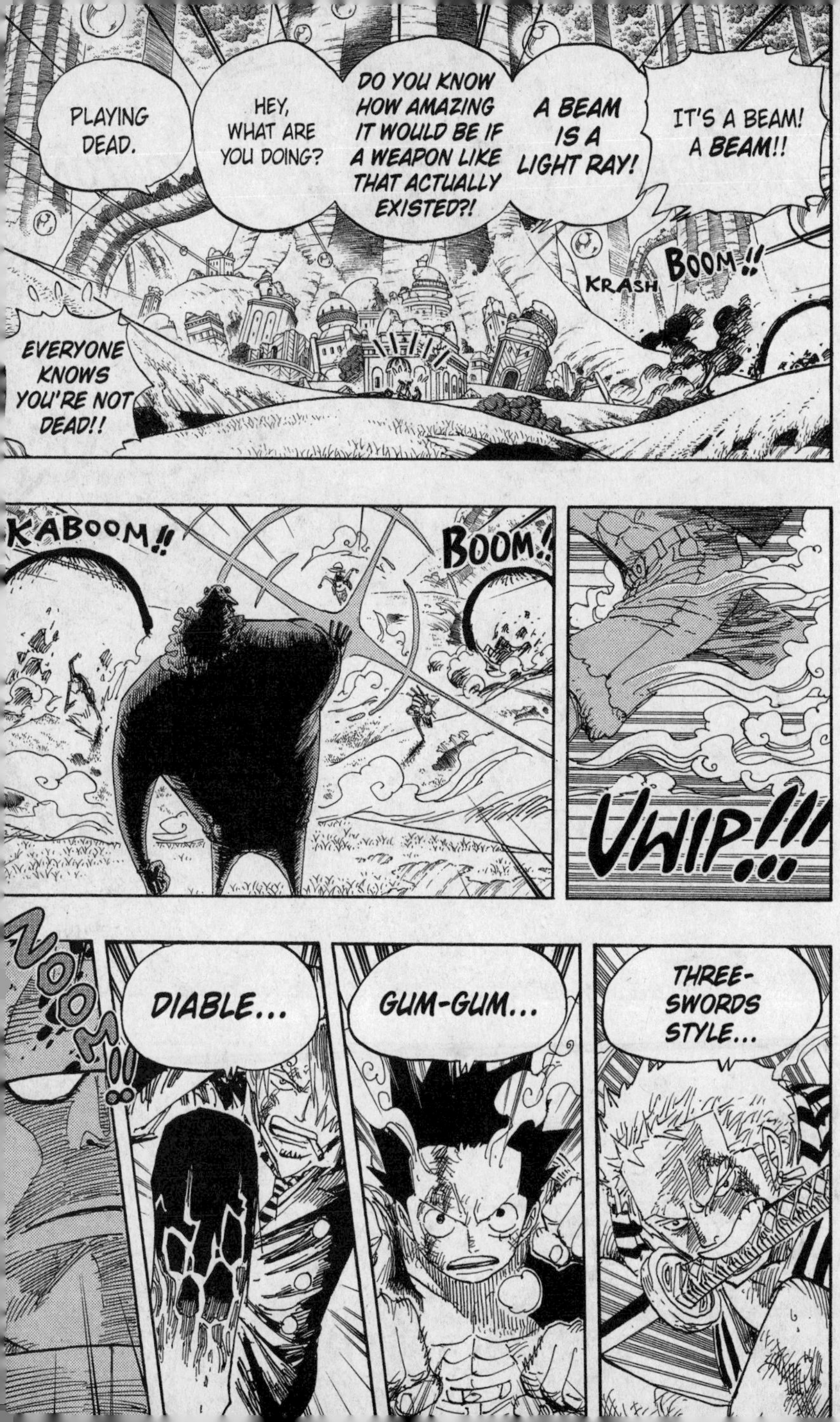
IT'S A BEAM! A BEAM!!
A BEAM IS A LIGHT RAY!
DO YOU KNOW HOW AMAZING IT WOULD BE IF A WEAPON LIKE THAT ACTUALLY EXISTED?!
HEY, WHAT ARE YOU DOING?
PLAYING DEAD.
BOOM!!
KRASH
EVERYONE KNOWS YOU'RE NOT DEAD!!
UWIP!!!
BOOM!!
KABOOM!!
THREE-SWORDS STYLE...
GUM-GUM...
DIABLE...
NOOOM!!

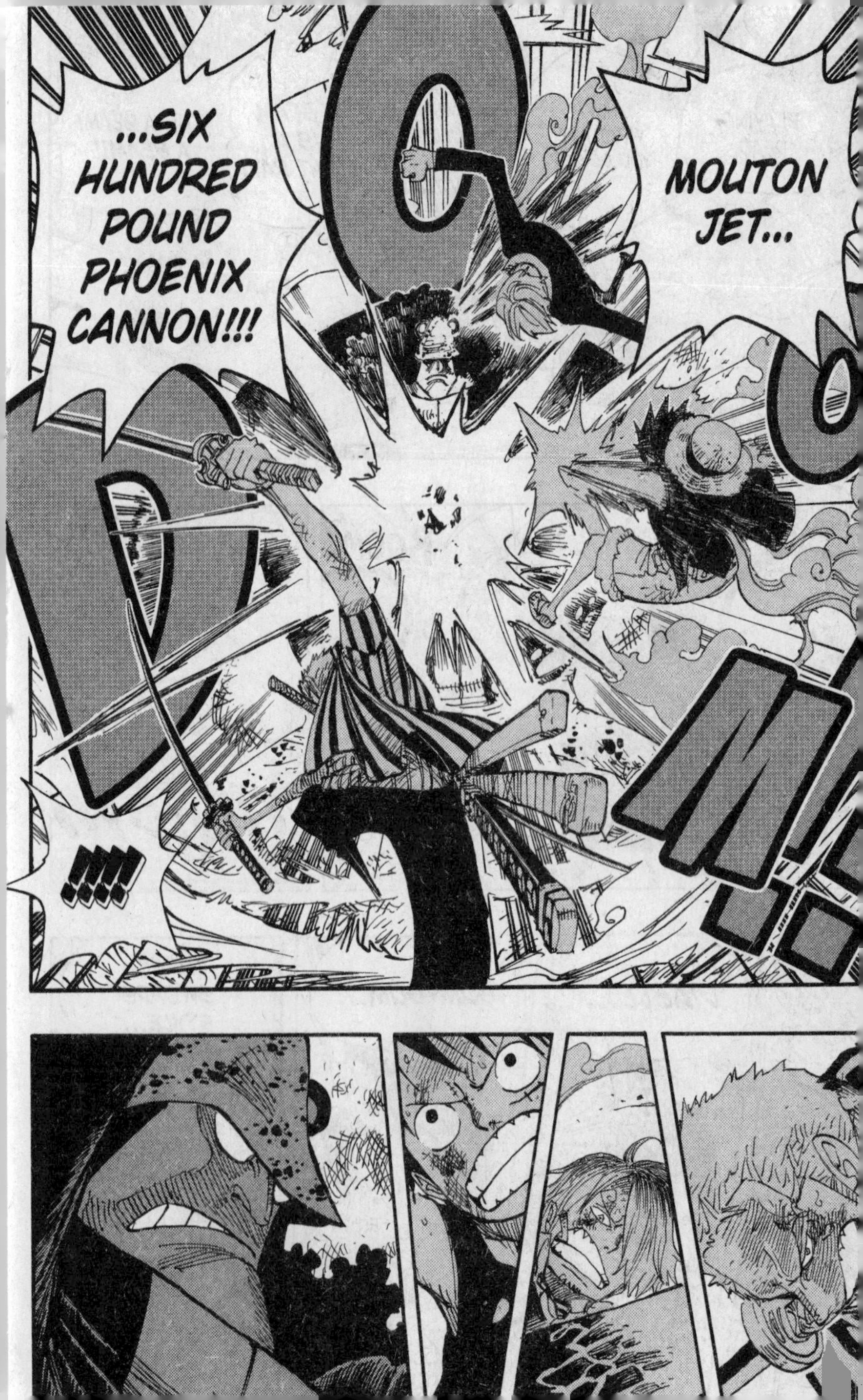
MOUTON JET...
...SIX HUNDRED POUND PHOENIX CANNON!!!
!!!!

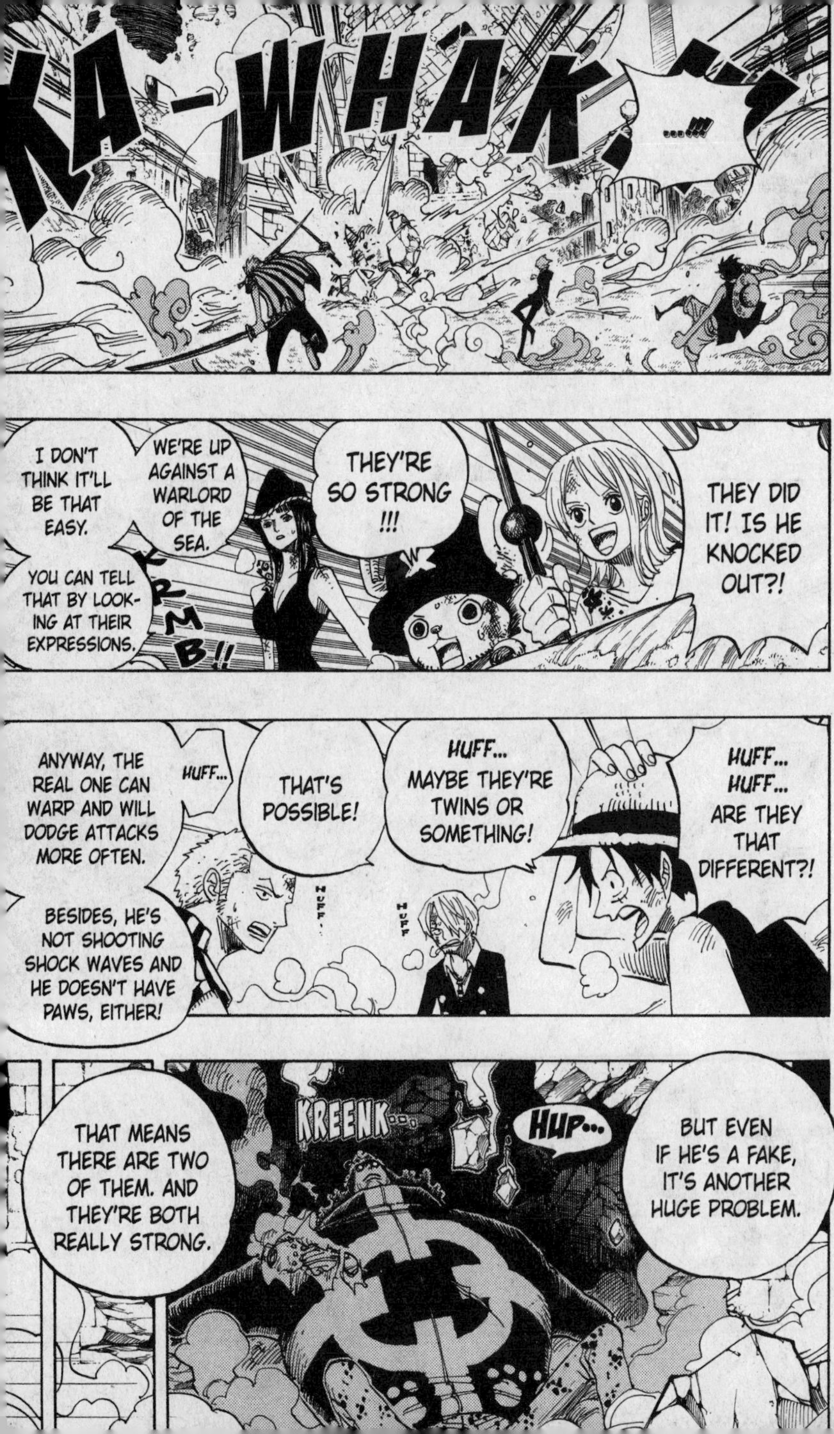
KA-WHAK...!!!
THEY DID IT! IS HE KNOCKED OUT?!
THEY'RE SO STRONG !!!
WE'RE UP AGAINST A WARLORD OF THE SEA.
I DON'T THINK IT'LL BE THAT EASY.
YOU CAN TELL THAT BY LOOKING AT THEIR EXPRESSIONS.
KRMB!!
HUFF... HUFF... ARE THEY THAT DIFFERENT?!
HUFF... MAYBE THEY'RE TWINS OR SOMETHING!
HUFF
THAT'S POSSIBLE!
HUFF...
HUFF...
ANYWAY, THE REAL ONE CAN WARP AND WILL DODGE ATTACKS MORE OFTEN.
BESIDES, HE'S NOT SHOOTING SHOCK WAVES AND HE DOESN'T HAVE PAWS, EITHER!
BUT EVEN IF HE'S A FAKE, IT'S ANOTHER HUGE PROBLEM.
HUP...
KREENK...
THAT MEANS THERE ARE TWO OF THEM. AND THEY'RE BOTH REALLY STRONG.

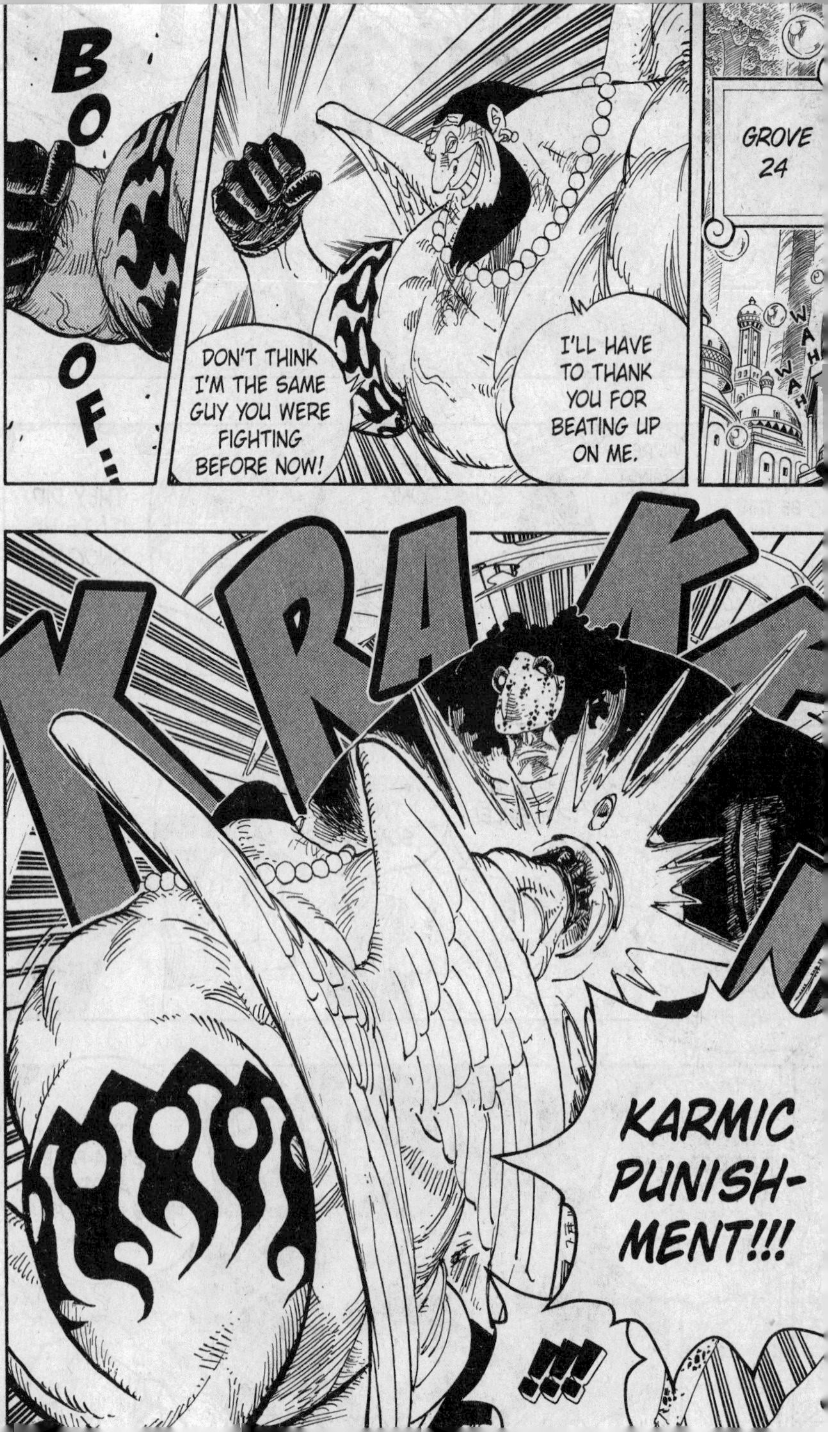
GROVE 24
WAH WAH
I'LL HAVE TO THANK YOU FOR BEATING UP ON ME.
DON'T THINK I'M THE SAME GUY YOU WERE FIGHTING BEFORE NOW!
BOOF...
KRAK
KARMIC PUNISH-MENT!!!
!!!

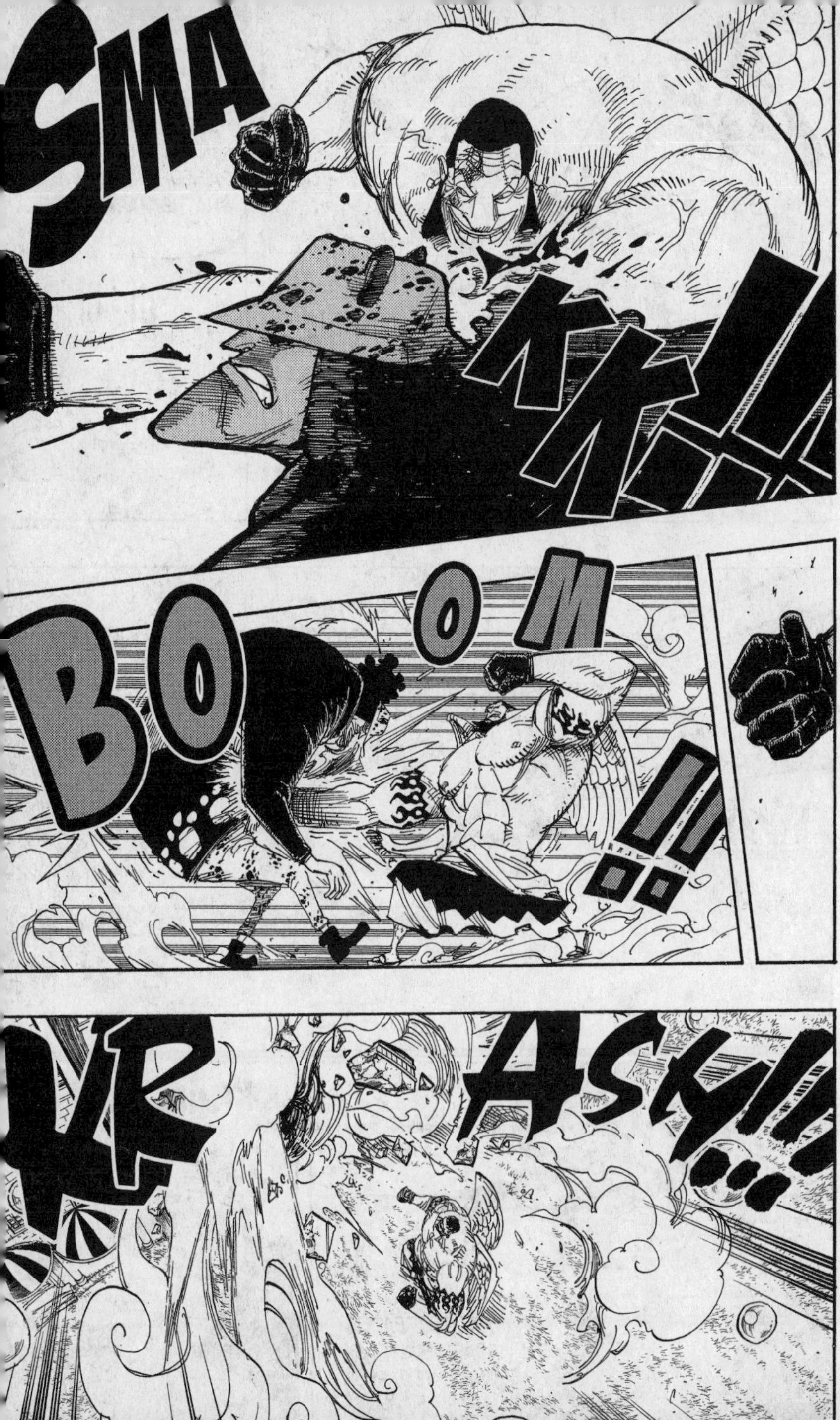
SMASH!!
BOOM!!
KRASH!!

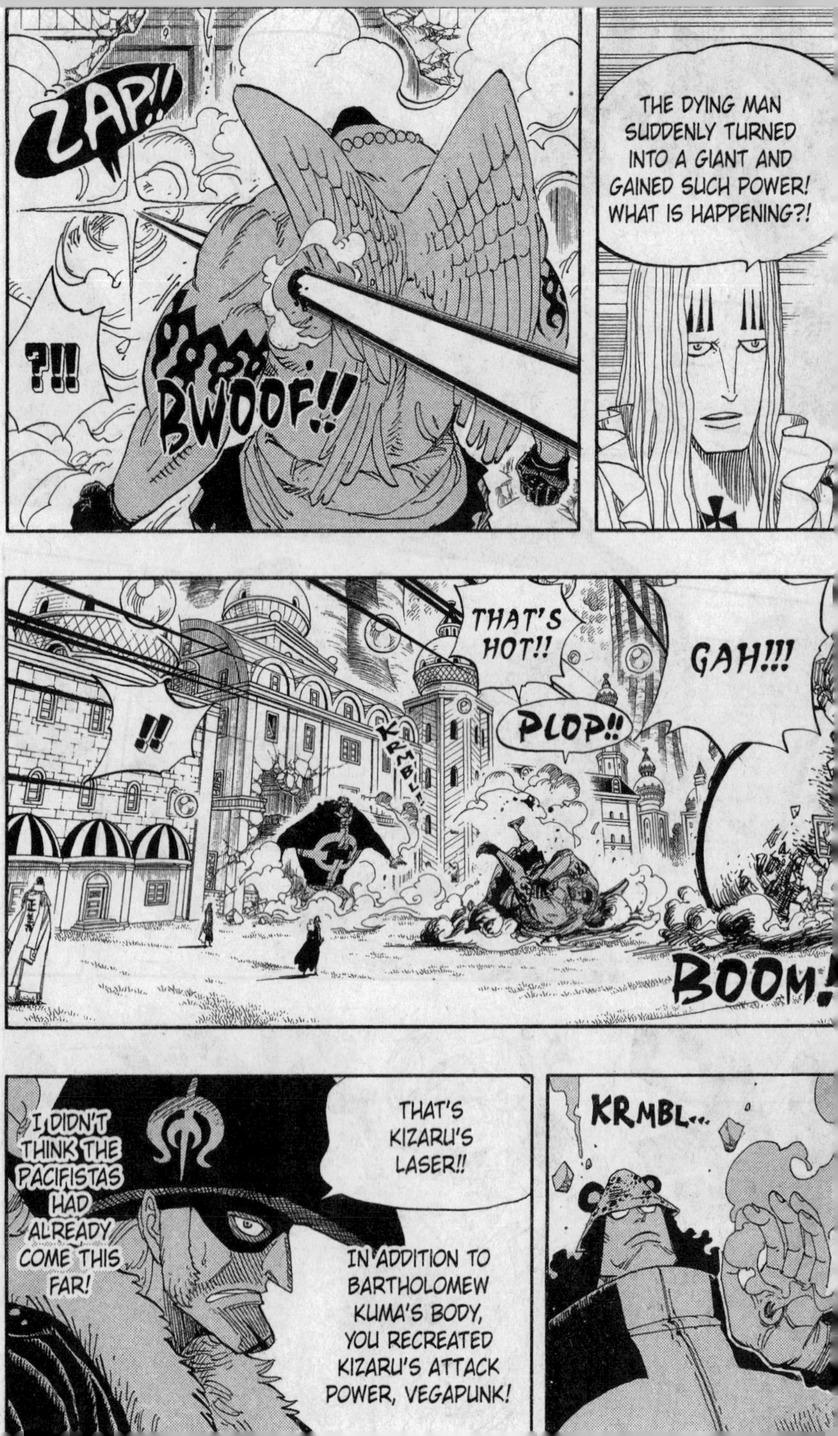
THE DYING MAN SUDDENLY TURNED INTO A GIANT AND GAINED SUCH POWER! WHAT IS HAPPENING?!
ZAP!!
?!!
BWOOF!!
GAH!!!
THAT'S HOT!!
PLOP!!
KRMBL!!
!!
BOOM!
KRMBL...
THAT'S KIZARU'S LASER!!
I DIDN'T THINK THE PACIFISTAS HAD ALREADY COME THIS FAR!
IN ADDITION TO BARTHOLOMEW KUMA'S BODY, YOU RECREATED KIZARU'S ATTACK POWER, VEGAPUNK!

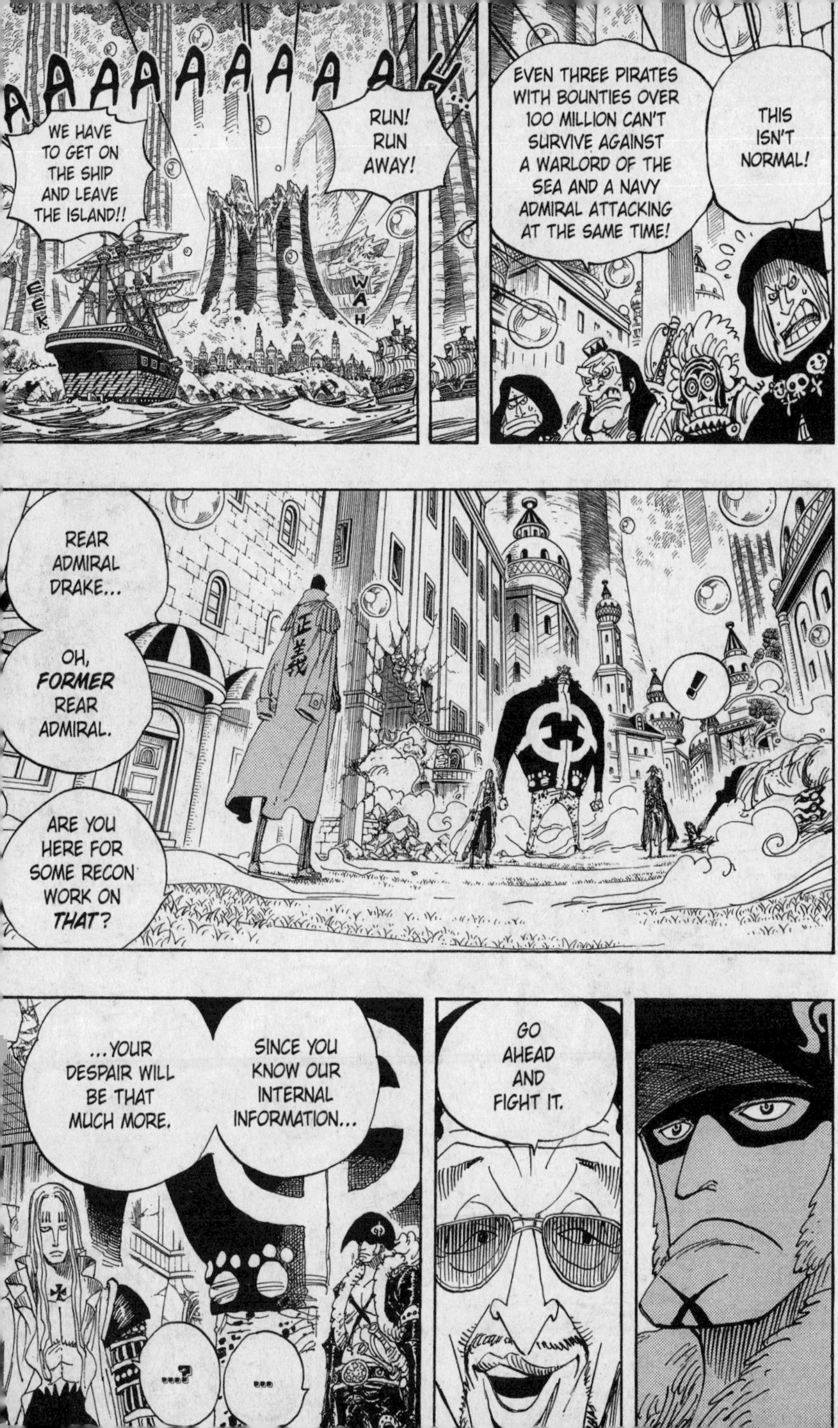
THIS ISN'T NORMAL!
EVEN THREE PIRATES WITH BOUNTIES OVER 100 MILLION CAN'T SURVIVE AGAINST A WARLORD OF THE SEA AND A NAVY ADMIRAL ATTACKING AT THE SAME TIME!
AAAAAAAAAH...
RUN! RUN AWAY!
WE HAVE TO GET ON THE SHIP AND LEAVE THE ISLAND!!
WAH
EEK
!
REAR ADMIRAL DRAKE...
OH, *FORMER* REAR ADMIRAL.
ARE YOU HERE FOR SOME RECON WORK ON *THAT*?
GO AHEAD AND FIGHT IT.
SINCE YOU KNOW OUR INTERNAL INFORMATION...
...YOUR DESPAIR WILL BE THAT MUCH MORE.
...
...?

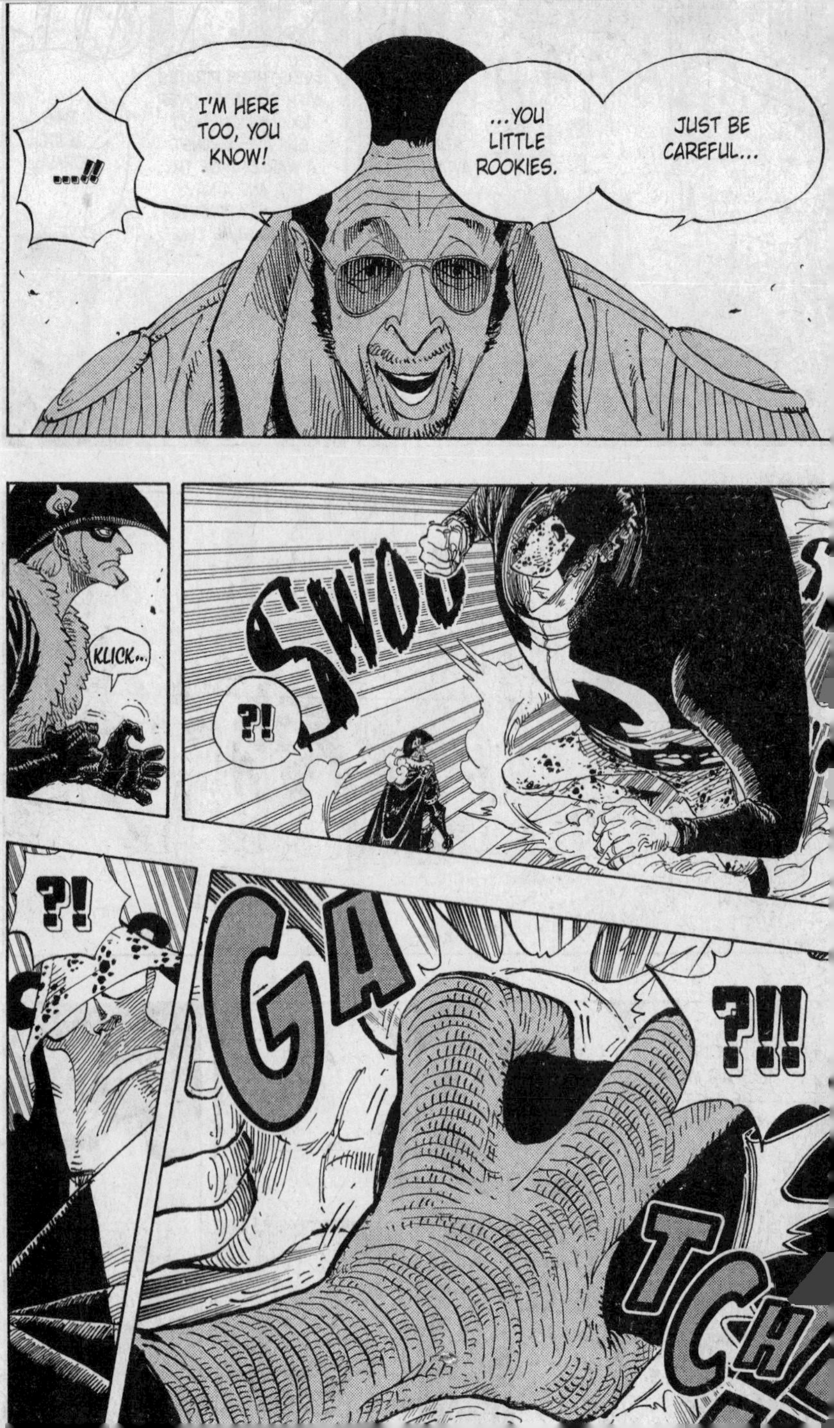
JUST BE CAREFUL...
...YOU LITTLE ROOKIES.
I'M HERE TOO, YOU KNOW!
...!!
SWO
?!
KLICK...
?!!
GA
TCH
?!

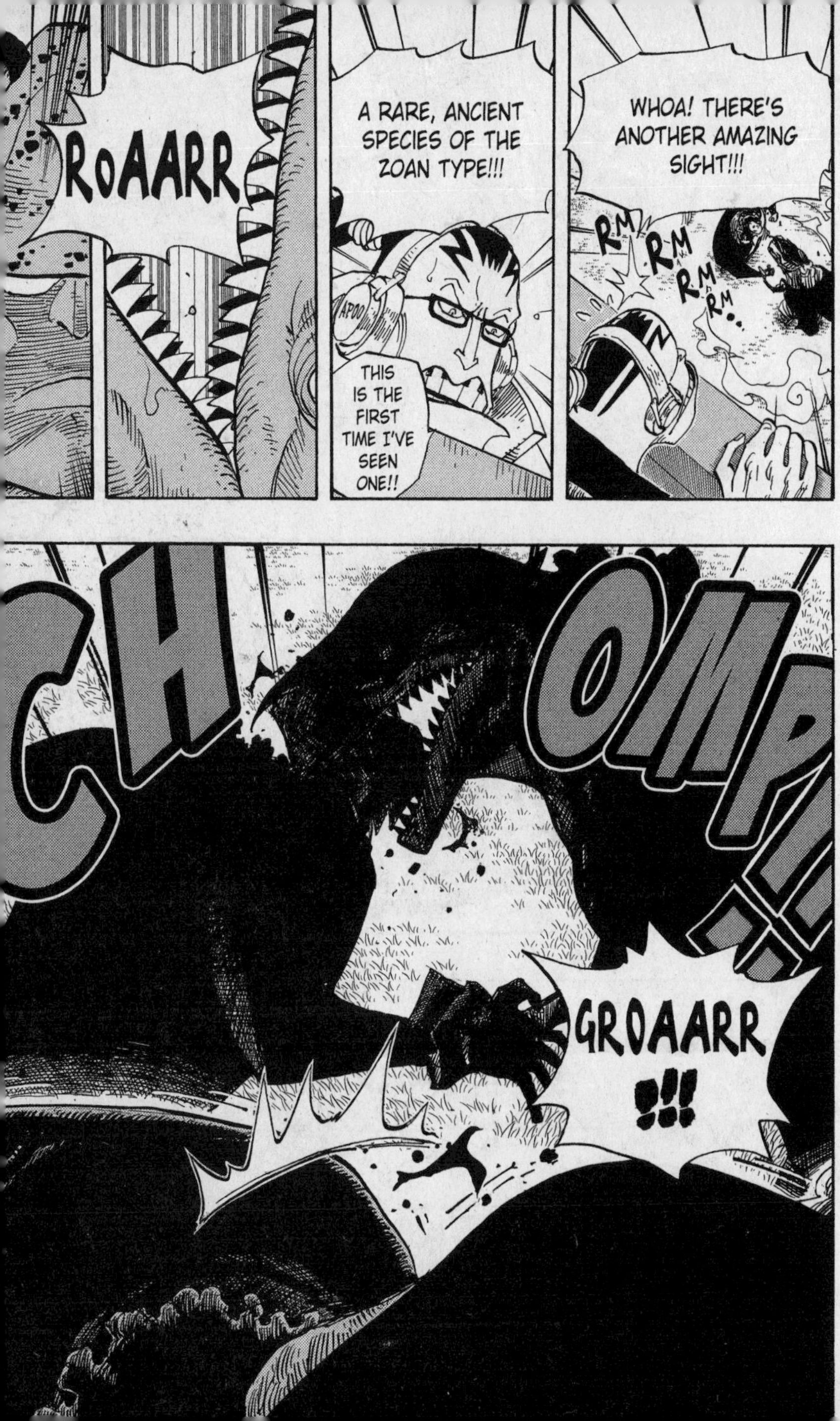
WHOA! THERE'S ANOTHER AMAZING SIGHT!!!
RM RM RM RM..
A RARE, ANCIENT SPECIES OF THE ZOAN TYPE!!!
APOO
THIS IS THE FIRST TIME I'VE SEEN ONE!!
ROAARR
CHOMP!!
GROAARR!!!

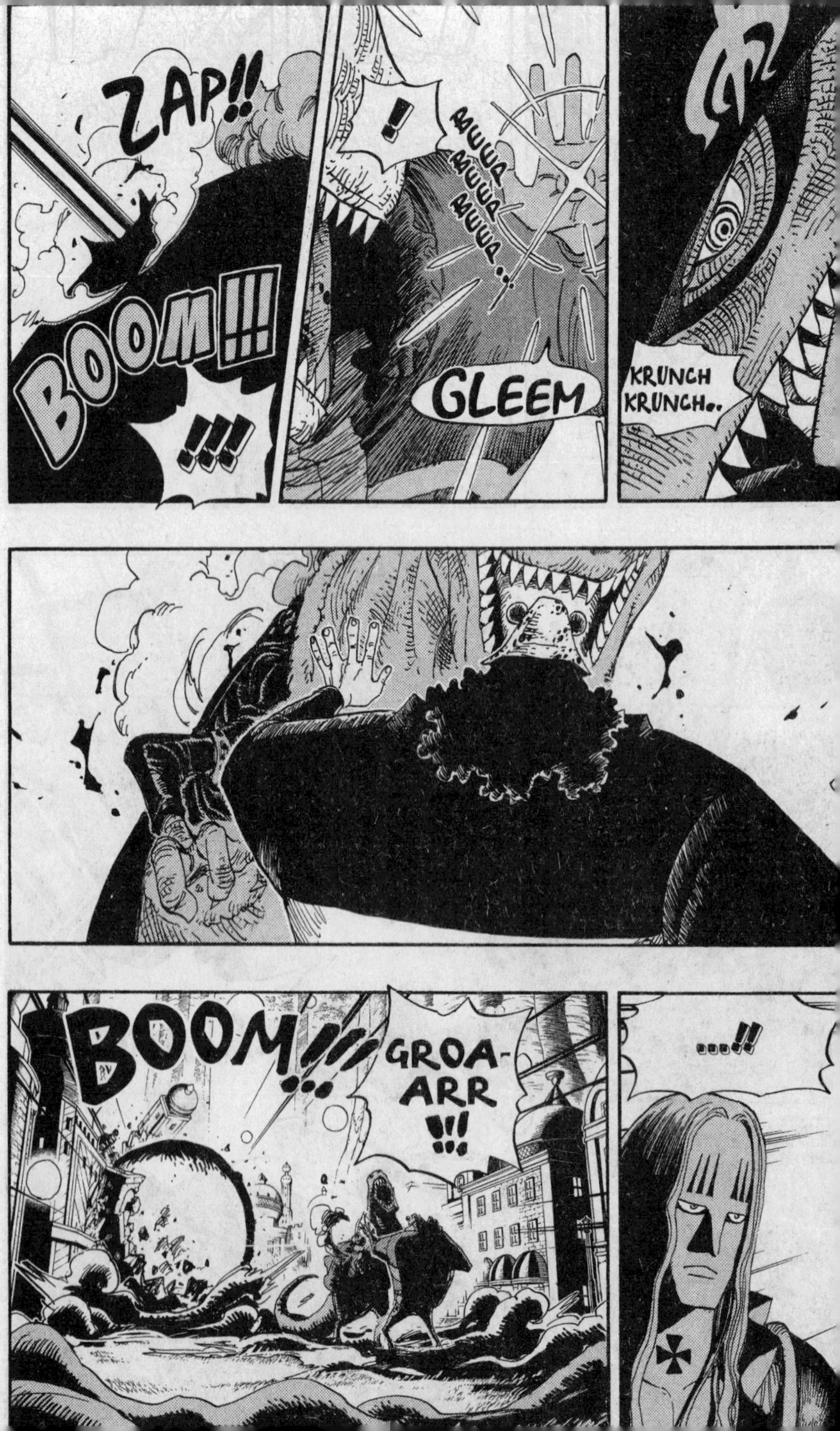
KRUNCH KRUNCH..
!
BWUA BWUA BWUA..
GLEEM
ZAP!!
BOOM!!!
!!!
...!!
GROA-ARR!!!
BOOM!!!...

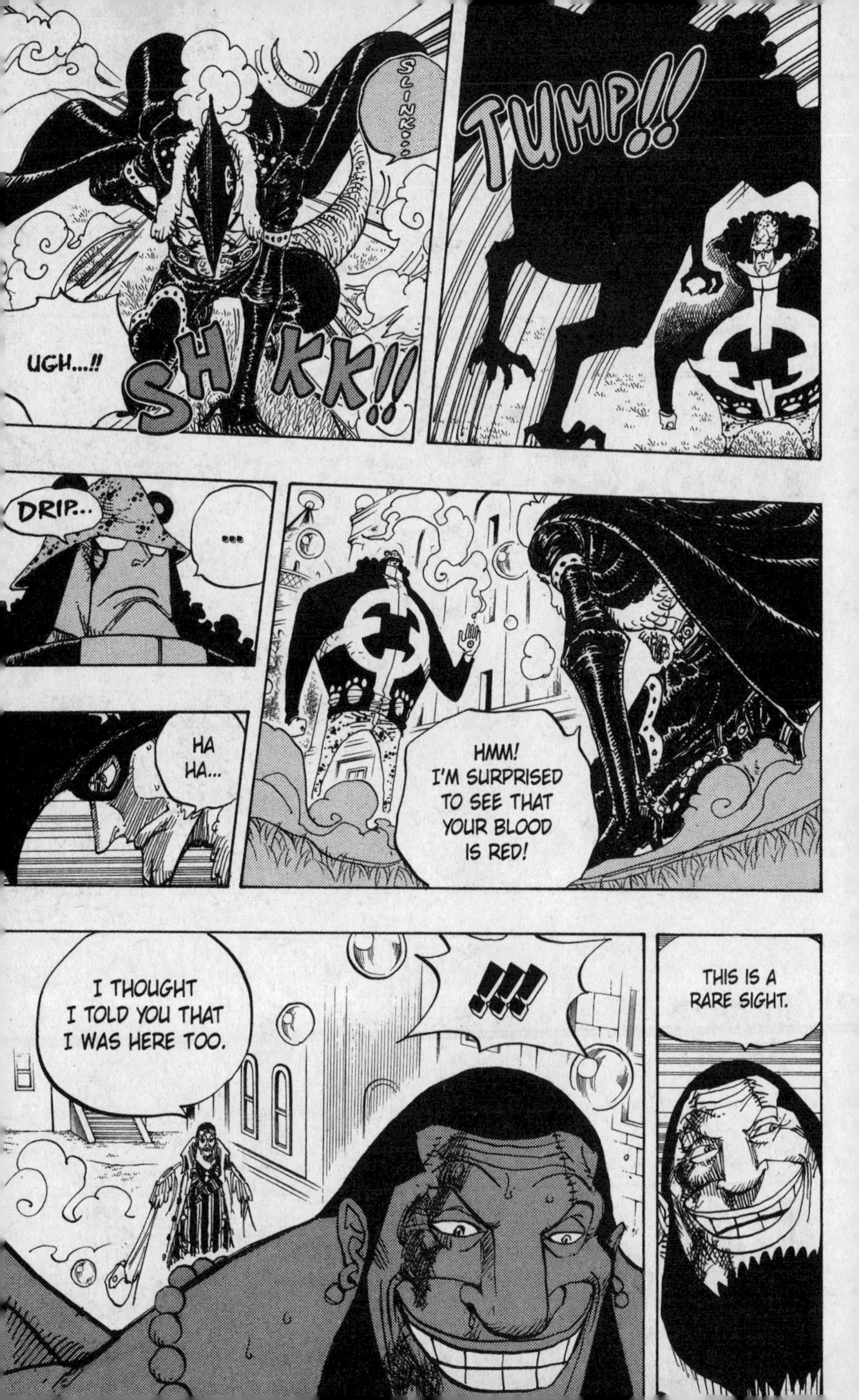
TUMP!!
SLINK...
SHKK!!
UGH...!!
HMM! I'M SURPRISED TO SEE THAT YOUR BLOOD IS RED!
DRIP...
...
HA HA...
THIS IS A RARE SIGHT.
!!!
I THOUGHT I TOLD YOU THAT I WAS HERE TOO.

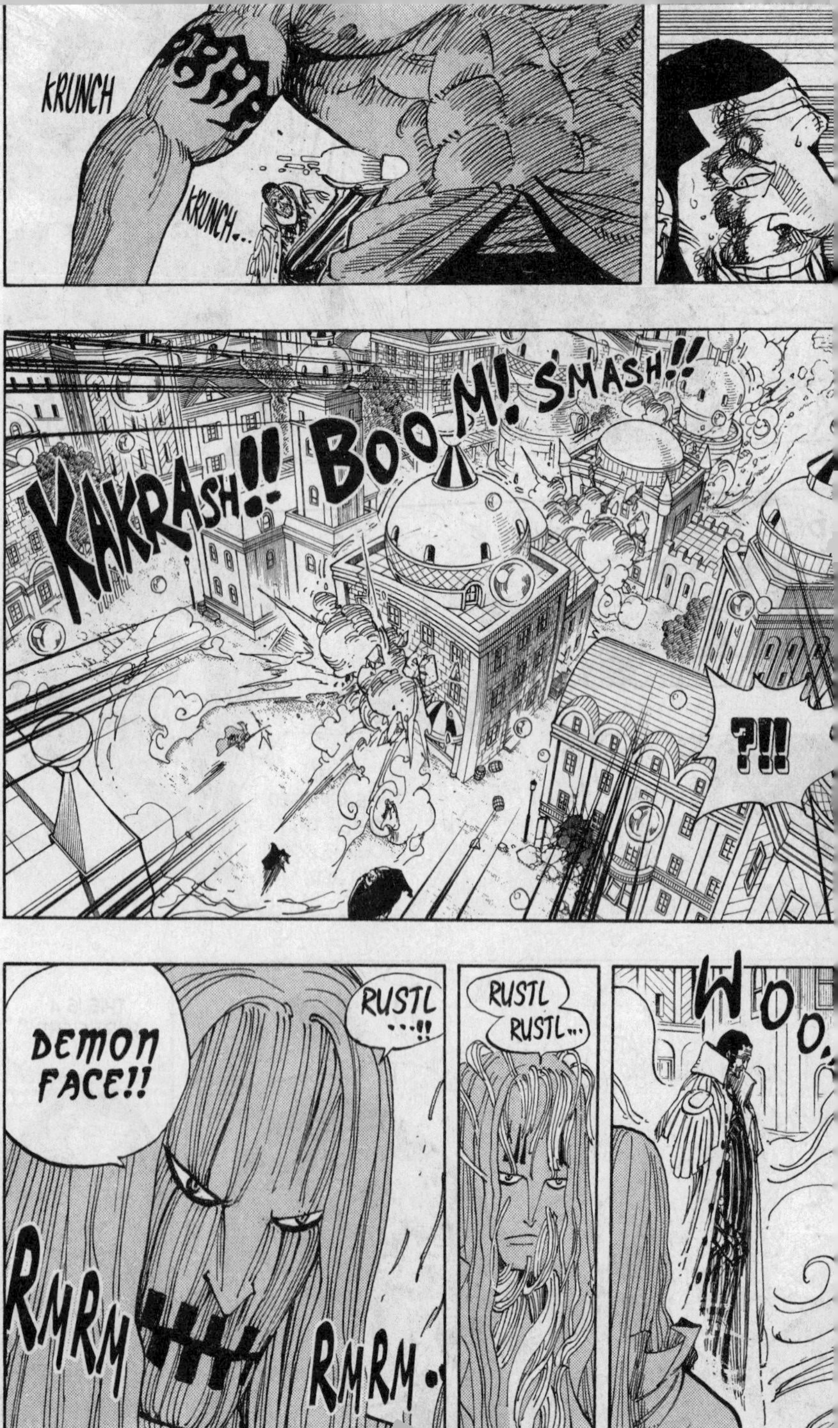
KRUNCH
KRUNCH...
SMASH!!
BOOM!
KAKRASH!!
?!!
WOO...
RUSTL RUSTL...
RUSTL...!!
DEMON FACE!!
RMRM
RMRM...

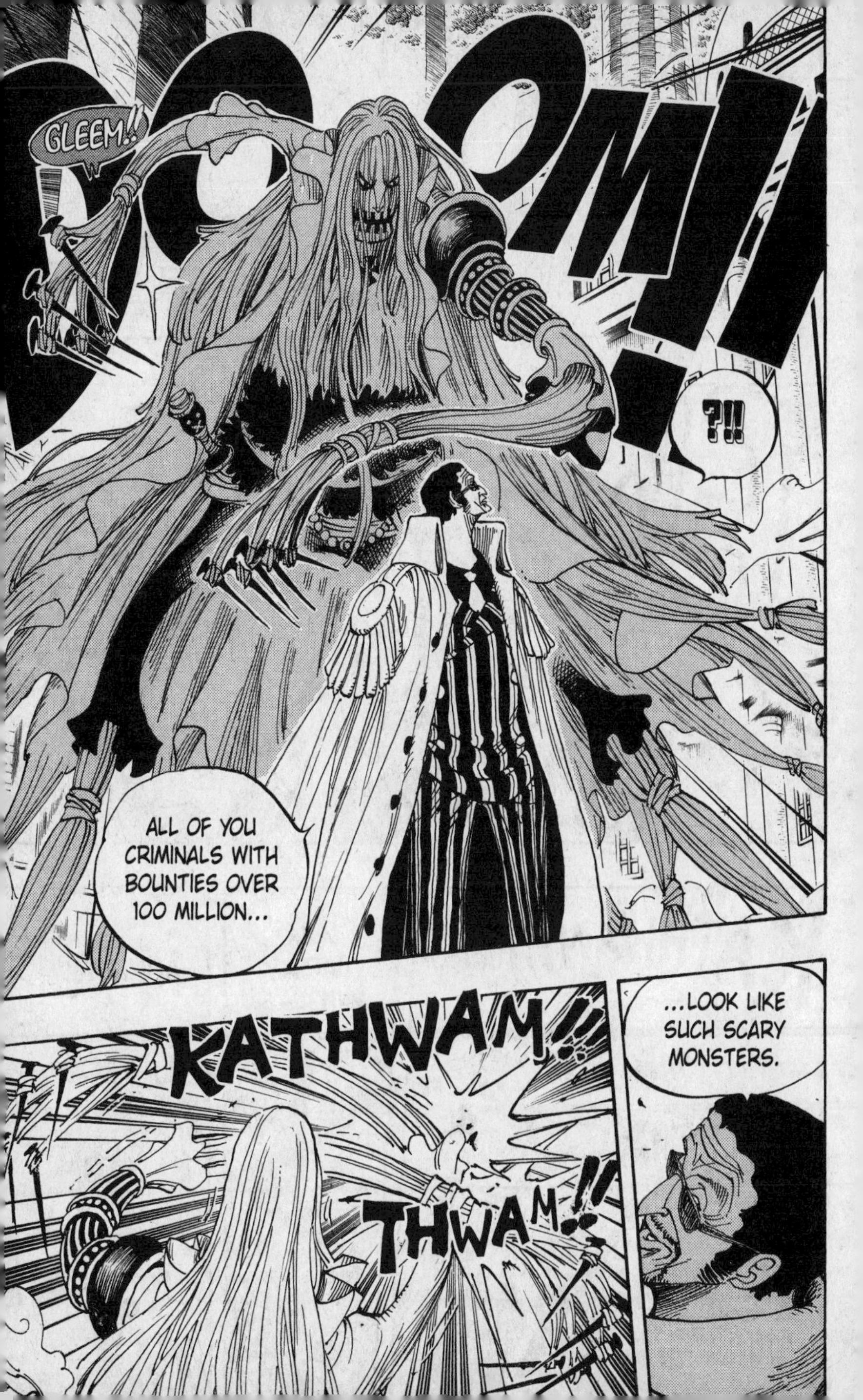
DOOM!!
?!!
GLEEM!!
ALL OF YOU CRIMINALS WITH BOUNTIES OVER 100 MILLION...
...LOOK LIKE SUCH SCARY MONSTERS.
KATHWAM!!
THWAM!!

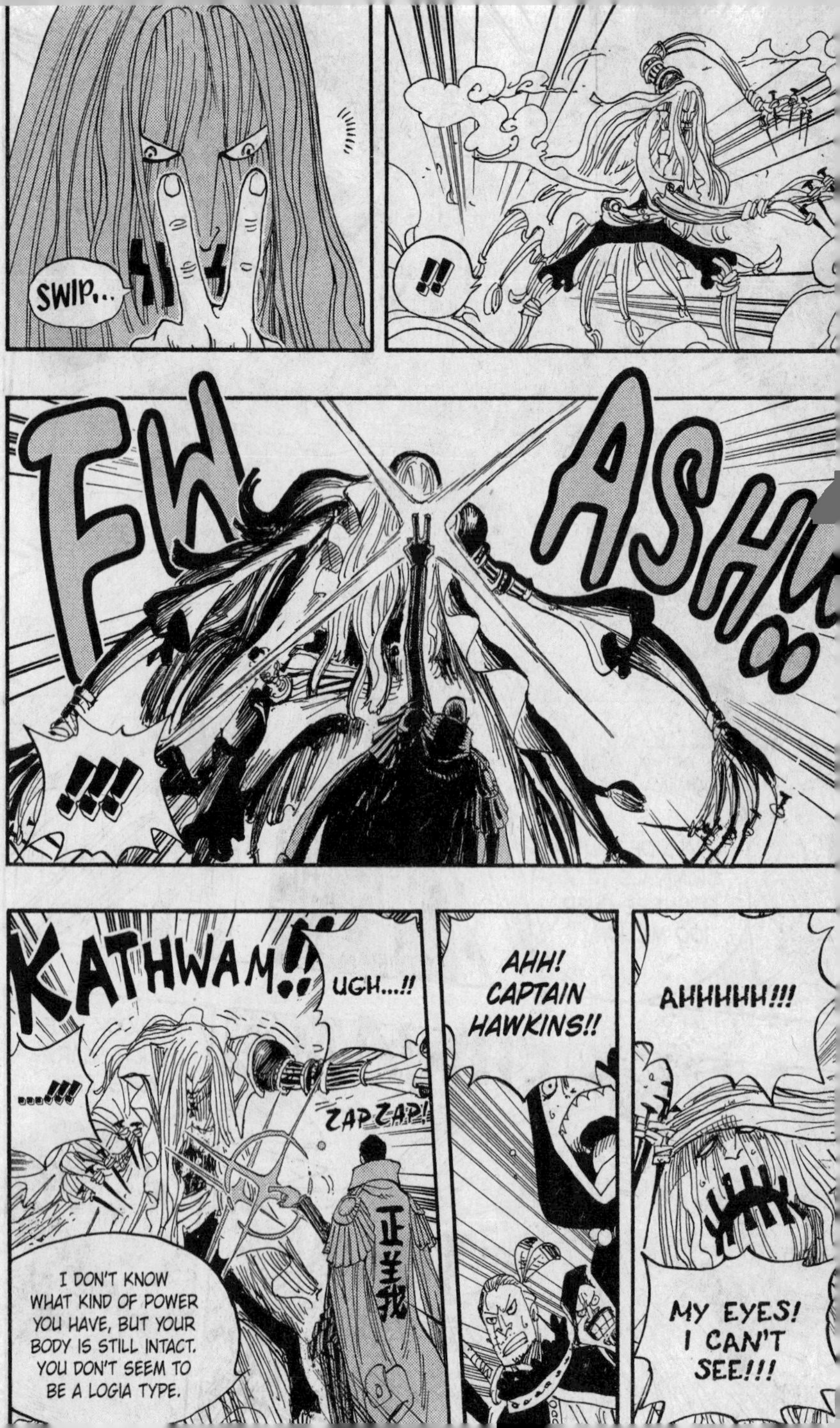
!!
SWIP...
FWASH!!
!!!
AHHHHH!!!
MY EYES! I CAN'T SEE!!!
AHH! CAPTAIN HAWKINS!!
KATHWAM!!
UGH...!!
...!!!
ZAP ZAP!
正義
I DON'T KNOW WHAT KIND OF POWER YOU HAVE, BUT YOUR BODY IS STILL INTACT. YOU DON'T SEEM TO BE A LOGIA TYPE.

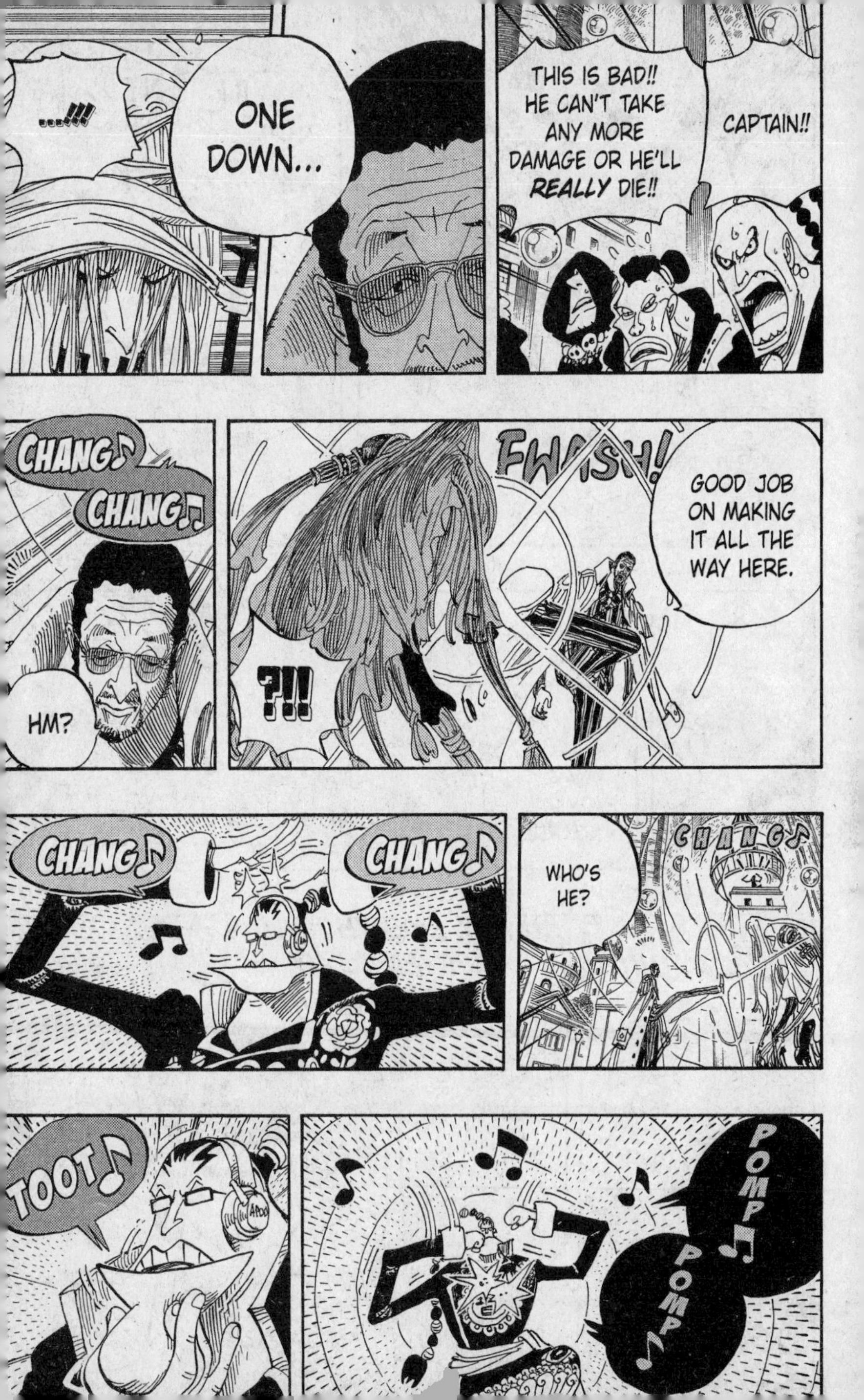
CAPTAIN!!
THIS IS BAD!! HE CAN'T TAKE ANY MORE DAMAGE OR HE'LL *REALLY* DIE!!
ONE DOWN...
...!!!
FWASH!
GOOD JOB ON MAKING IT ALL THE WAY HERE.
?!!
CHANG♪
CHANG♪
HM?
CHANG♪
WHO'S HE?
CHANG♪
CHANG♪
POMP♪
POMP♪
TOOT♪

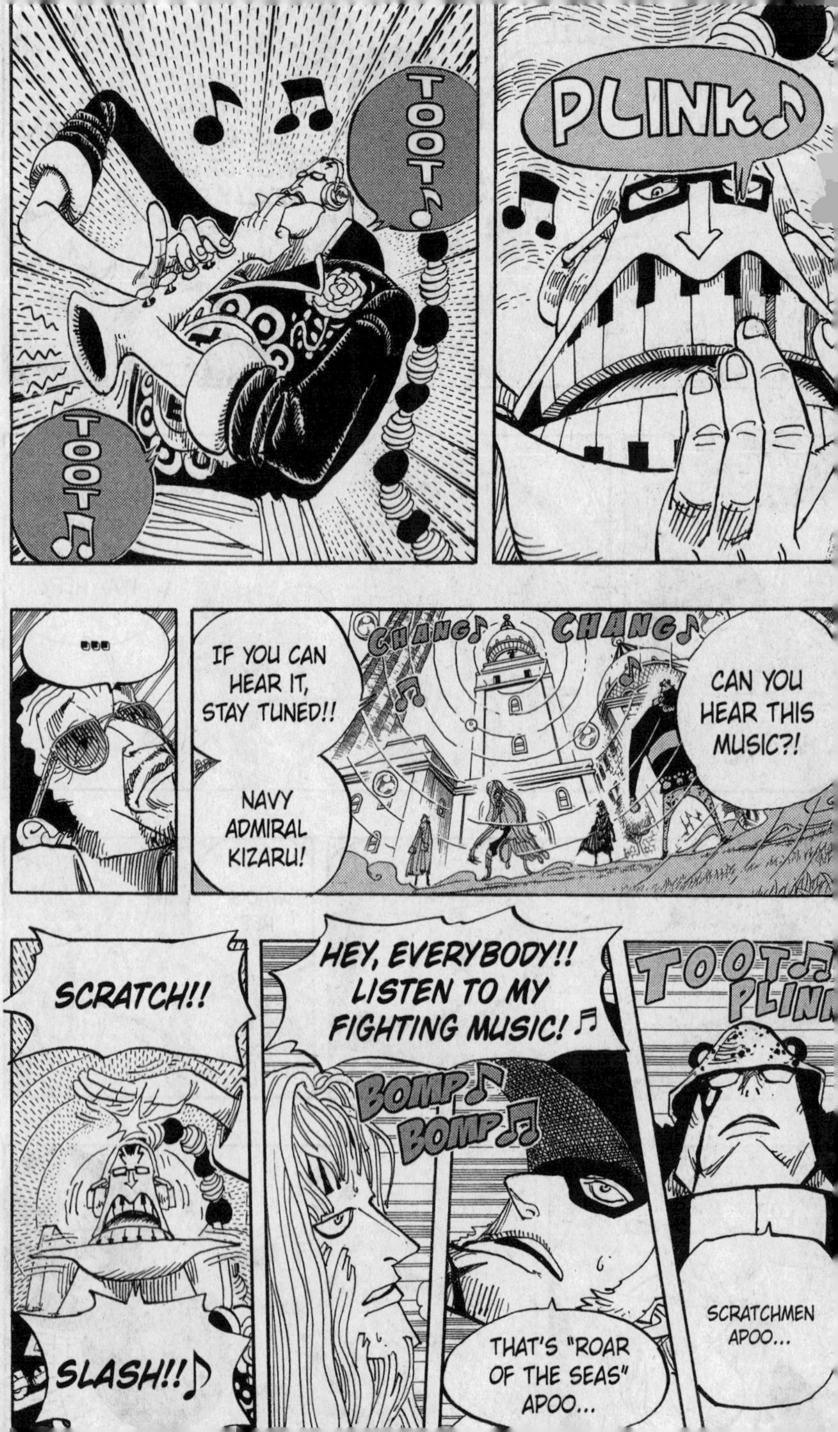
PLINK♪
TOOT♪
TOOT♪
CHANG♪ CHANG♪
CAN YOU HEAR THIS MUSIC?!
IF YOU CAN HEAR IT, STAY TUNED!!
NAVY ADMIRAL KIZARU!
...
TOOT♪♪
SCRATCHMEN APOO...
HEY, EVERYBODY!! LISTEN TO MY FIGHTING MUSIC! ♪
BOMP♪
BOMP♪
THAT'S "ROAR OF THE SEAS" APOO...
SCRATCH!!
SLASH!!♪

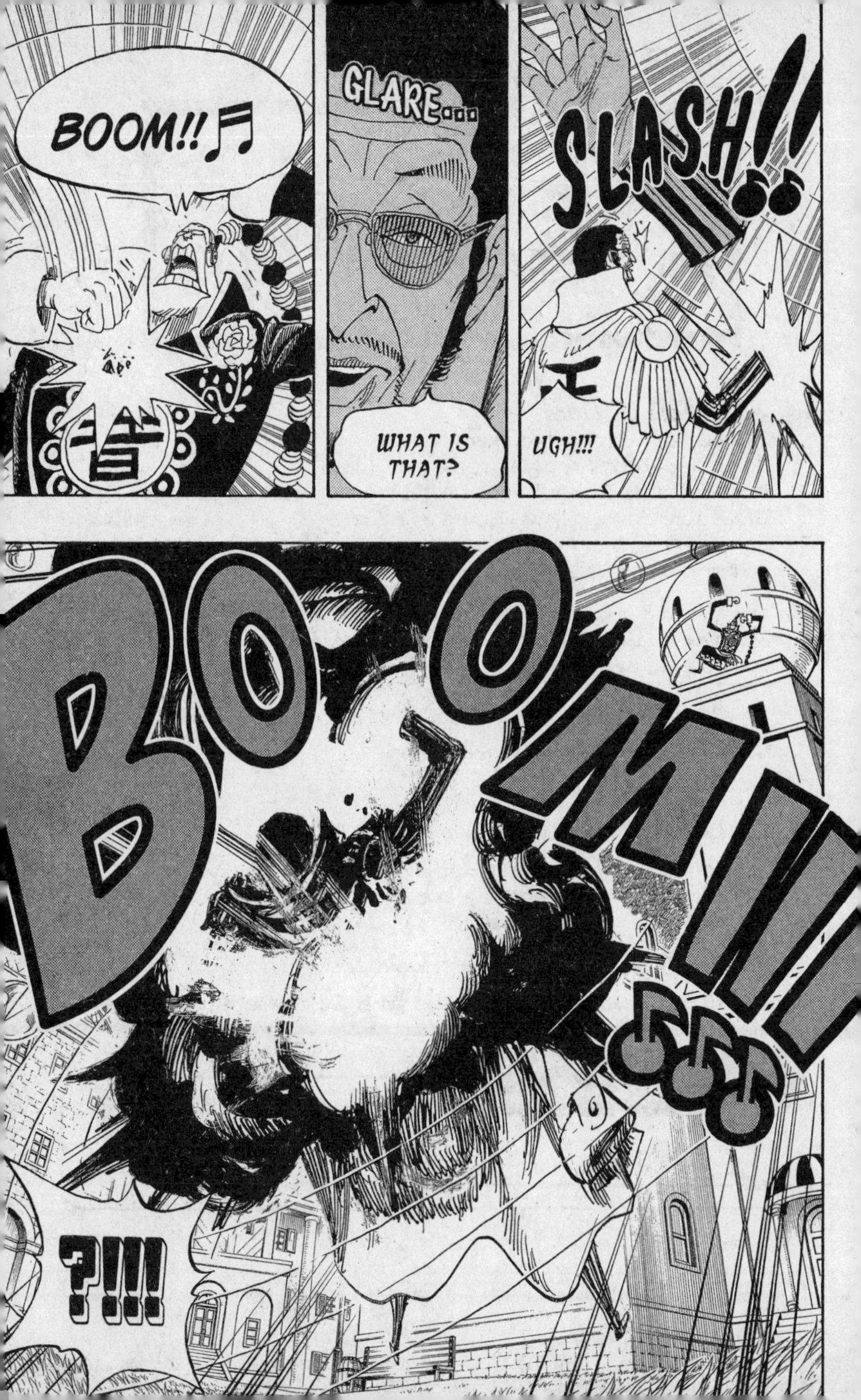
SLASH!!
UGH!!!
GLARE...
WHAT IS THAT?
BOOM!! ♫
BOOM!!
?!!!

SBS Question Corner

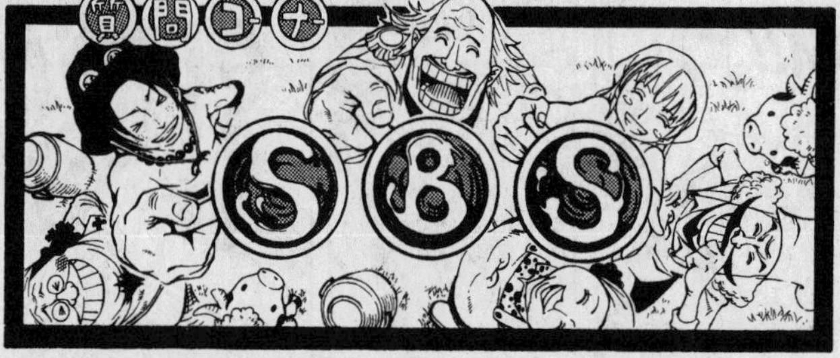
SBS

(Harry Milky, Tokyo)

D: ***HSK (Hello Silly Kids)***
Thanks for waiting. I've been receiving many letters asking for voice actors' profiles for a long time now. I wonder which volume it was where I first said, "then let's do a voice actor Question Corner"... I'm known as a grown-up who always fulfills his promises, even if it takes a little extra time. So here I am, fulfilling a promise! What's up, guys?!

D: Well, first things first, let's start with the voice of our hero, Monkey D. Luffy! The prodigal voice actress Mayumi Tanaka is in the house!

Oda: Hello, Mayumi.

Tanaka: Yes, hello. What's the matter?

O: We're doing an SBS today.

T: Oh, that. The (S)low (B)reaks done (S)lowly.

O: You're sort of right, but the right answer is... Well, just try it out yourself. Here are the postcards you have to answer (Drops a stack).

T: Oh? They sent in this many questions?

O: Yup. My readers do this all the time. So, please, answer them!

Preview for the next Voice Actor Question Corner

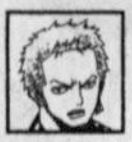

Zolo (Kazuya Nakai)

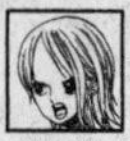

Nami (Akemi Okamura)

Chapter 510:
STRAW HAT PIRATES VS. WAR MACHINE

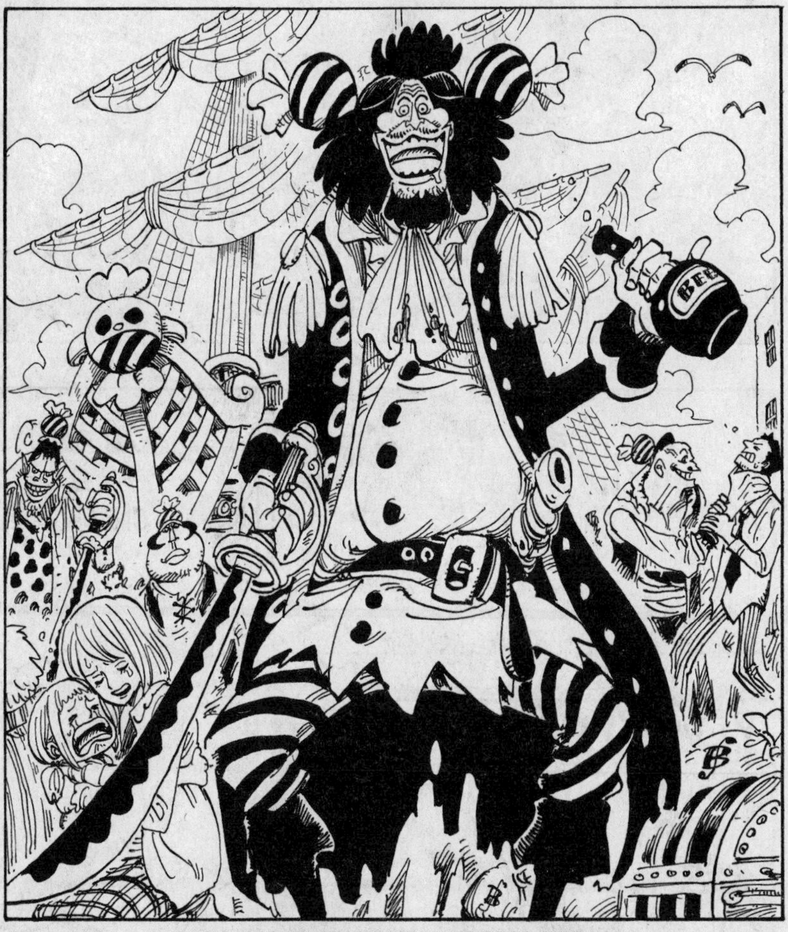

CP9'S INDEPENDENT REPORT, VOL. 18:
"CANDY PIRATES AT THE ST. POPLAR PORT!"

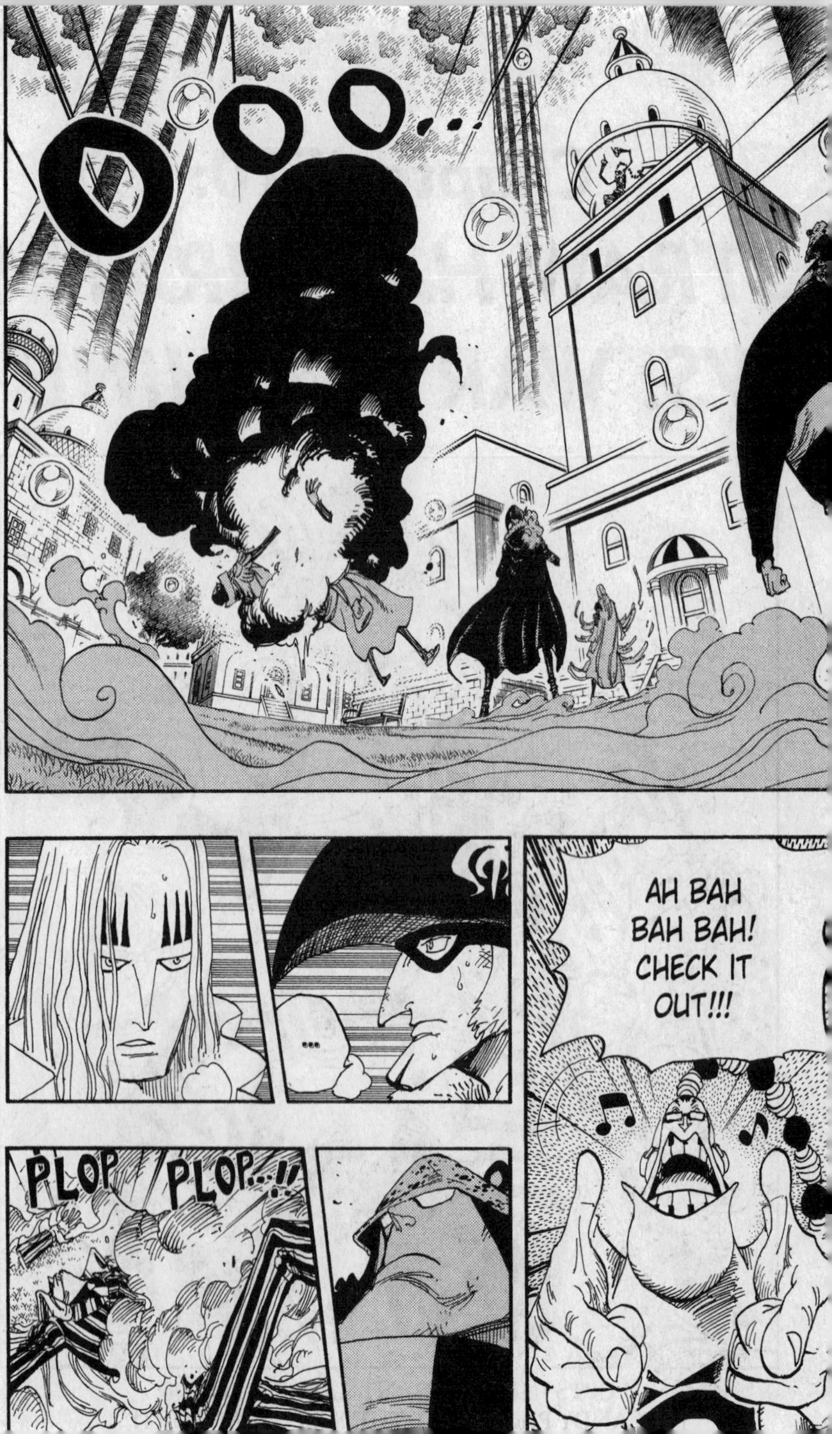
OOO...
AH BAH BAH BAH! CHECK IT OUT!!!
...
PLOP PLOP..!!

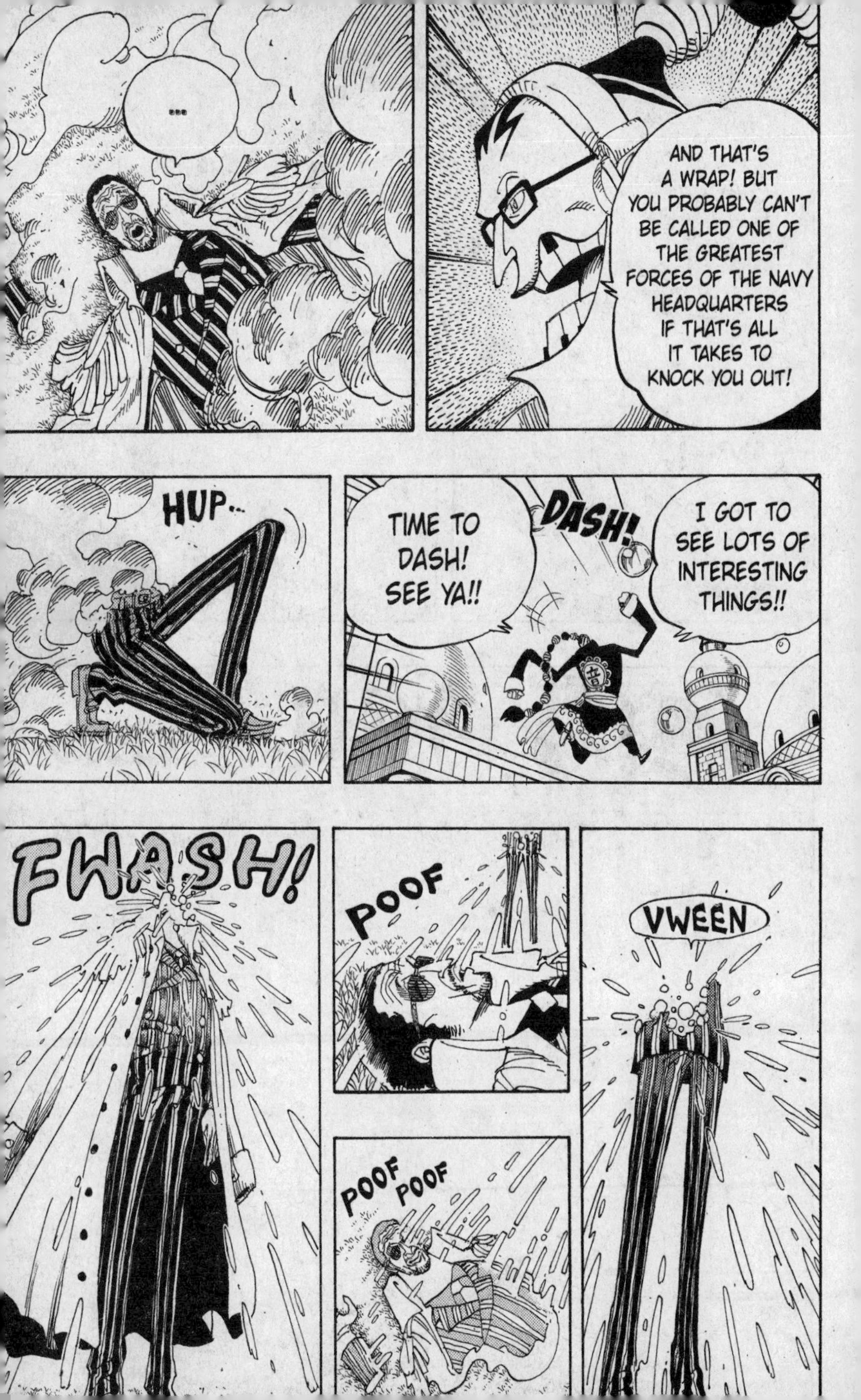
AND THAT'S A WRAP! BUT YOU PROBABLY CAN'T BE CALLED ONE OF THE GREATEST FORCES OF THE NAVY HEADQUARTERS IF THAT'S ALL IT TAKES TO KNOCK YOU OUT!
...
I GOT TO SEE LOTS OF INTERESTING THINGS!!
DASH!
TIME TO DASH! SEE YA!!
HUP...
VWEEN
POOF
POOF POOF
FWASH!

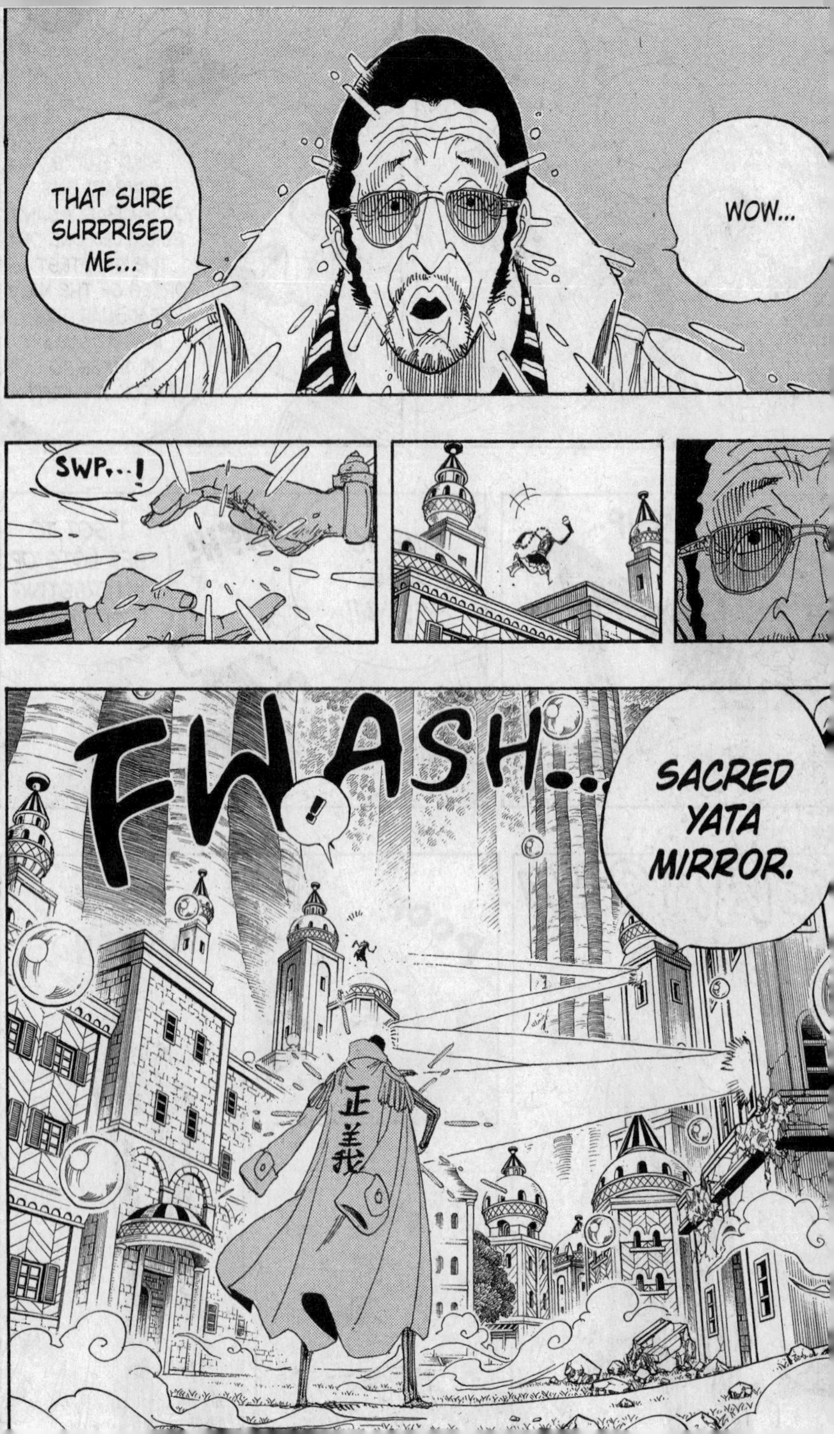
WOW...
THAT SURE SURPRISED ME...
SWP...!
SACRED YATA MIRROR.
FLASH...
!

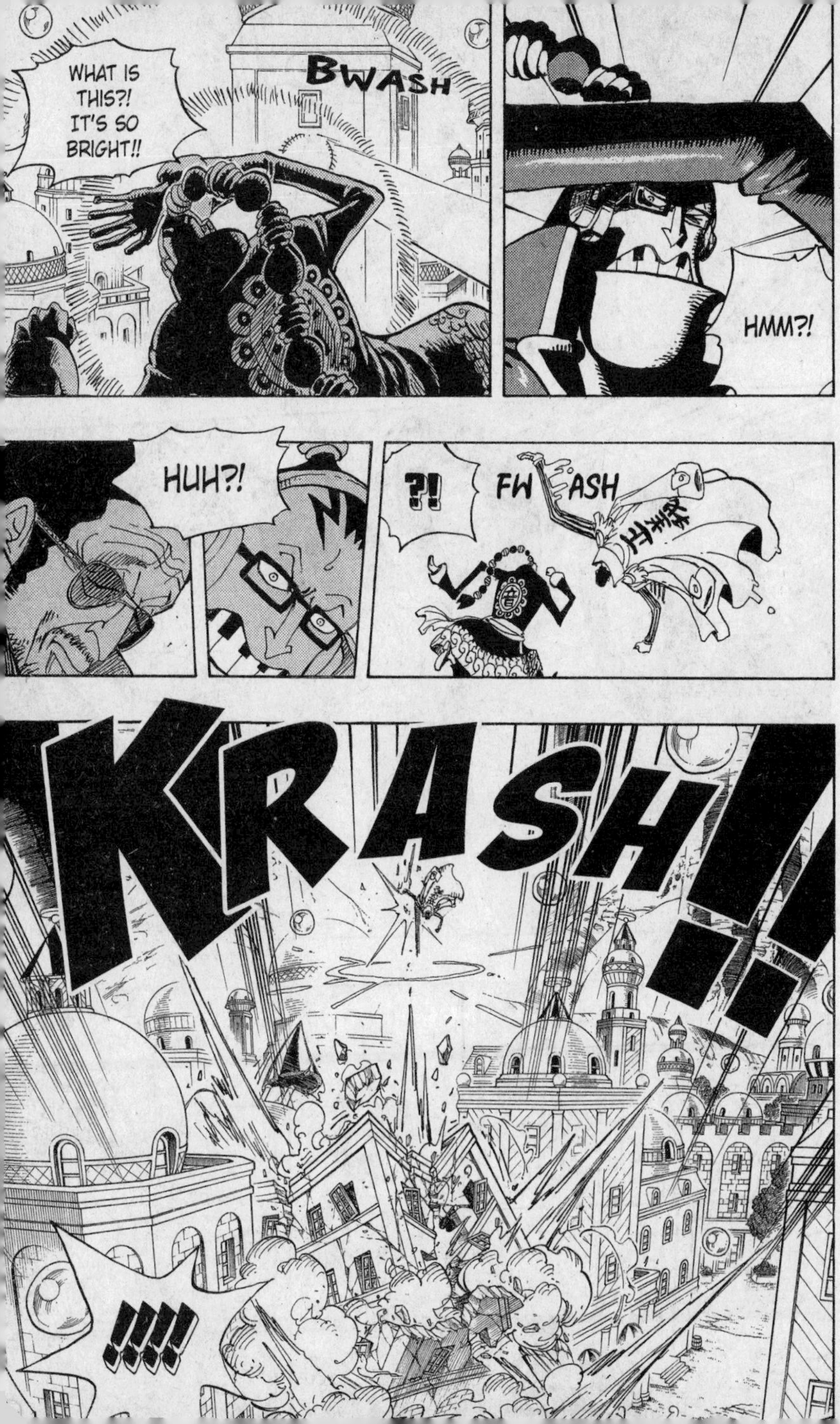
HMM?!
WHAT IS THIS?! IT'S SO BRIGHT!!
BWASH
?!
FW ASH
HUH?!
KRASH!!
!!!!

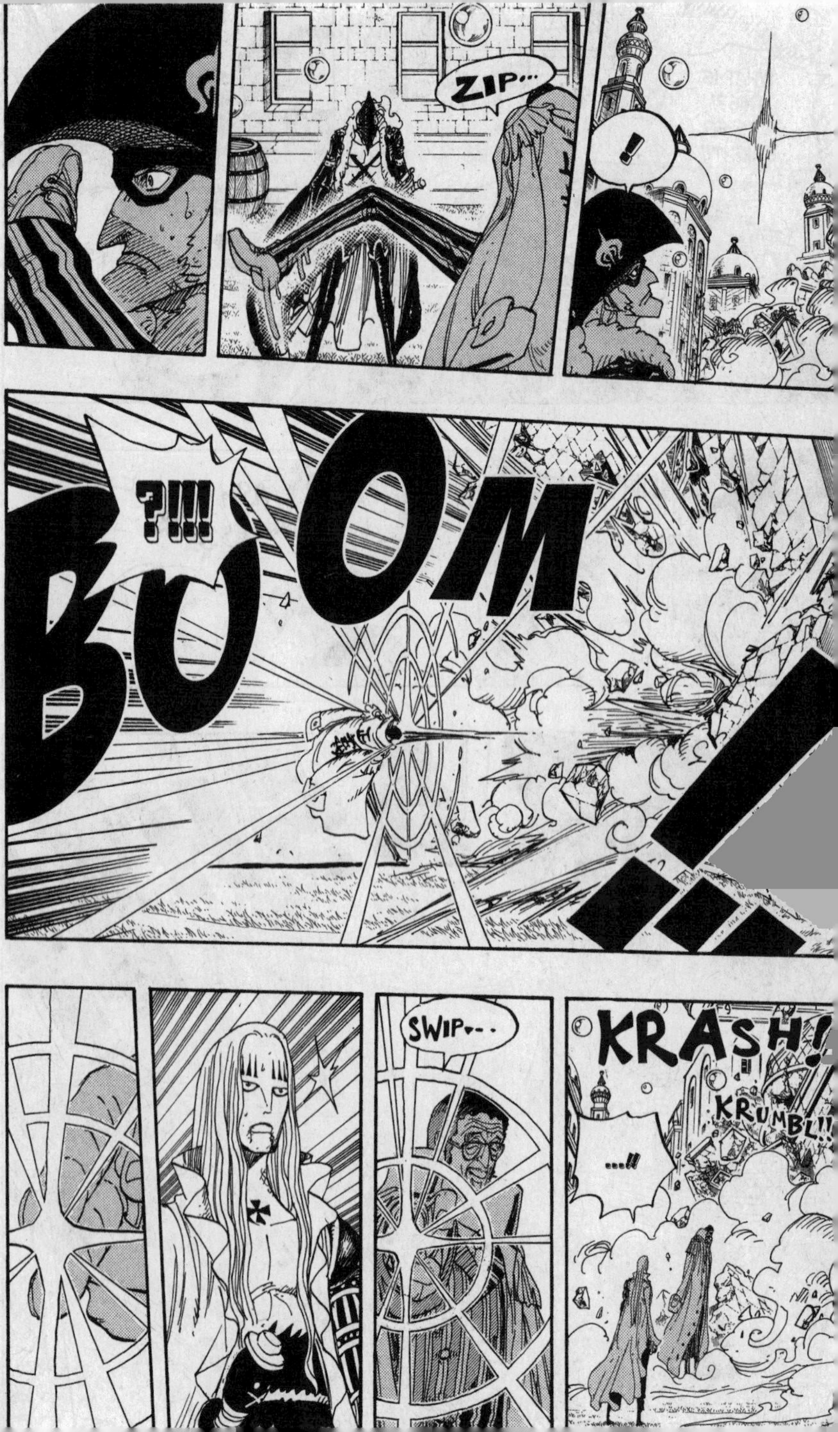
!
ZIP...
BOOM!!!
?!!!
KRASH!!
KRUMBL!!
...!!
SWIP...

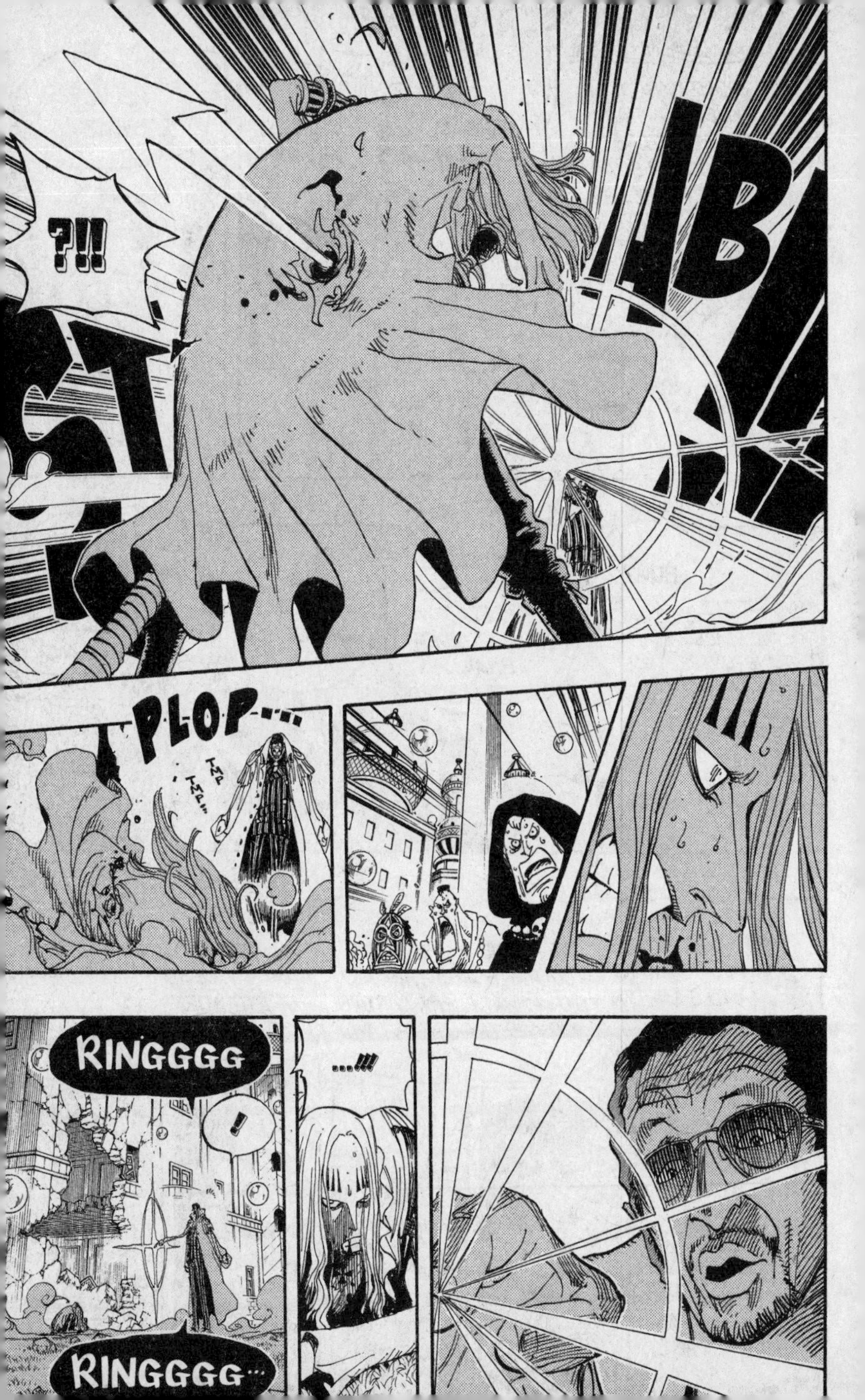
?!!
PLOP...
TMP TMP...
...!!!
RINGGGG
!
RINGGGG...

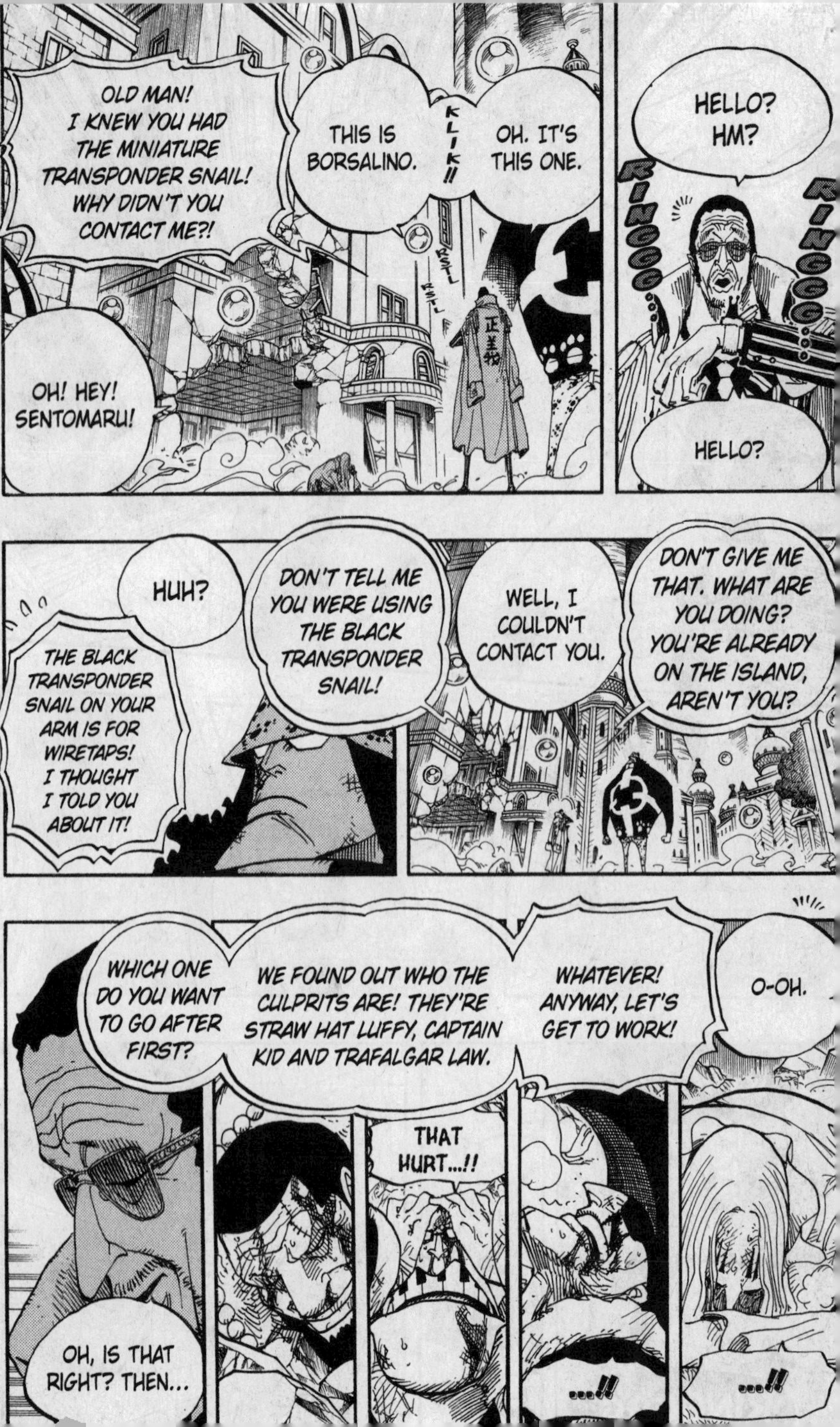
HELLO? HM?
RINGGG...
RINGGG...
HELLO?
OH. IT'S THIS ONE.
KLIK!!
THIS IS BORSALINO.
OLD MAN! I KNEW YOU HAD THE MINIATURE TRANSPONDER SNAIL! WHY DIDN'T YOU CONTACT ME?!
RSTL
RSTL
OH! HEY! SENTOMARU!
DON'T GIVE ME THAT. WHAT ARE YOU DOING? YOU'RE ALREADY ON THE ISLAND, AREN'T YOU?
WELL, I COULDN'T CONTACT YOU.
DON'T TELL ME YOU WERE USING THE BLACK TRANSPONDER SNAIL!
HUH?
THE BLACK TRANSPONDER SNAIL ON YOUR ARM IS FOR WIRETAPS! I THOUGHT I TOLD YOU ABOUT IT!
O-OH.
WHATEVER! ANYWAY, LET'S GET TO WORK!
WE FOUND OUT WHO THE CULPRITS ARE! THEY'RE STRAW HAT LUFFY, CAPTAIN KID AND TRAFALGAR LAW.
WHICH ONE DO YOU WANT TO GO AFTER FIRST?
...!!
...!!
THAT HURT...!!
OH, IS THAT RIGHT? THEN...

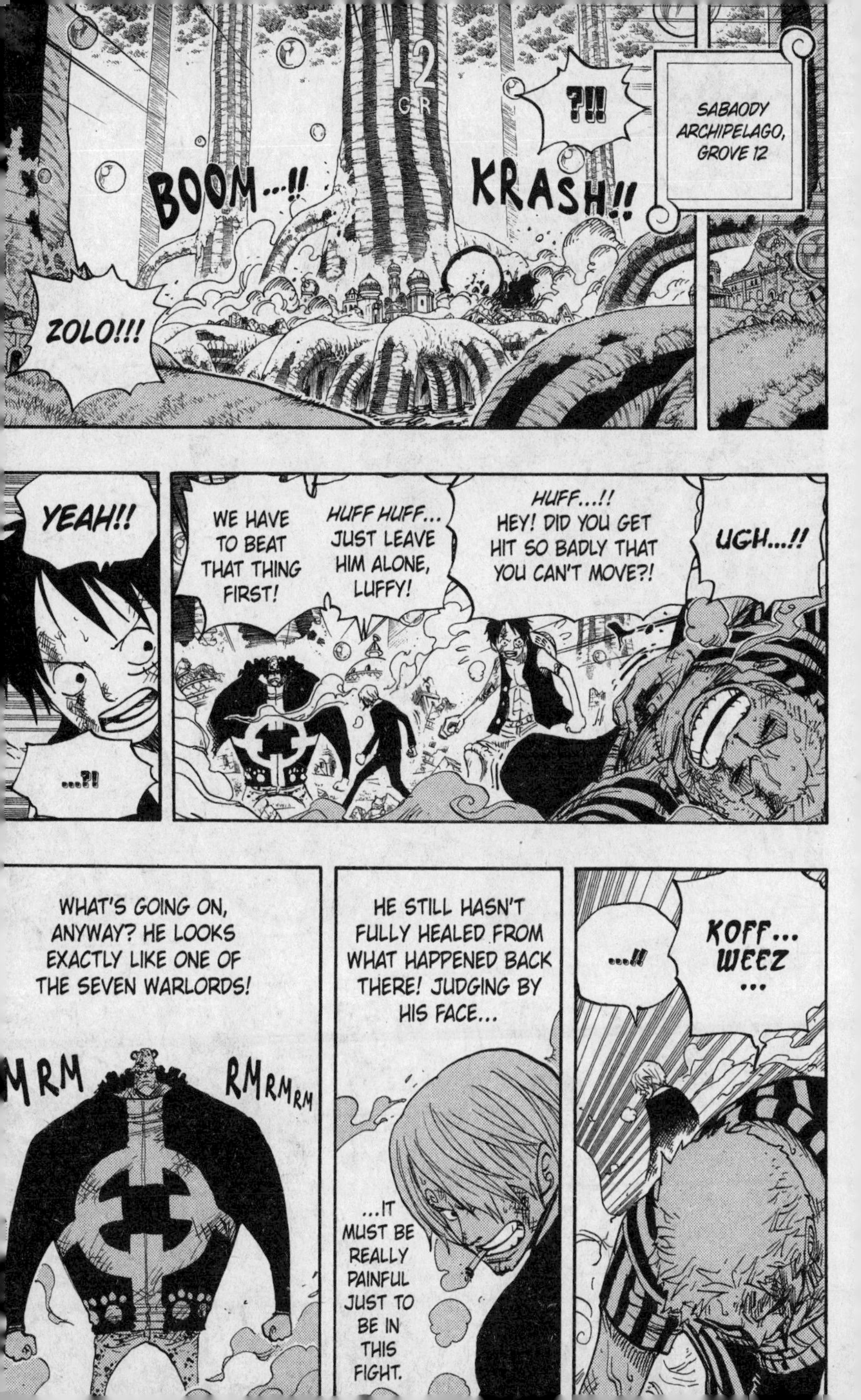
SABAODY ARCHIPELAGO, GROVE 12
12 GR
?!!
KRASH!!
BOOM...!!
ZOLO!!!
UGH...!!
HUFF...!! HEY! DID YOU GET HIT SO BADLY THAT YOU CAN'T MOVE?!
HUFF HUFF... JUST LEAVE HIM ALONE, LUFFY!
WE HAVE TO BEAT THAT THING FIRST!
YEAH!!
...?!
KOFF... WEEZ ...
...!!
HE STILL HASN'T FULLY HEALED FROM WHAT HAPPENED BACK THERE! JUDGING BY HIS FACE...
...IT MUST BE REALLY PAINFUL JUST TO BE IN THIS FIGHT.
WHAT'S GOING ON, ANYWAY? HE LOOKS EXACTLY LIKE ONE OF THE SEVEN WARLORDS!
RMRMRM
MRM

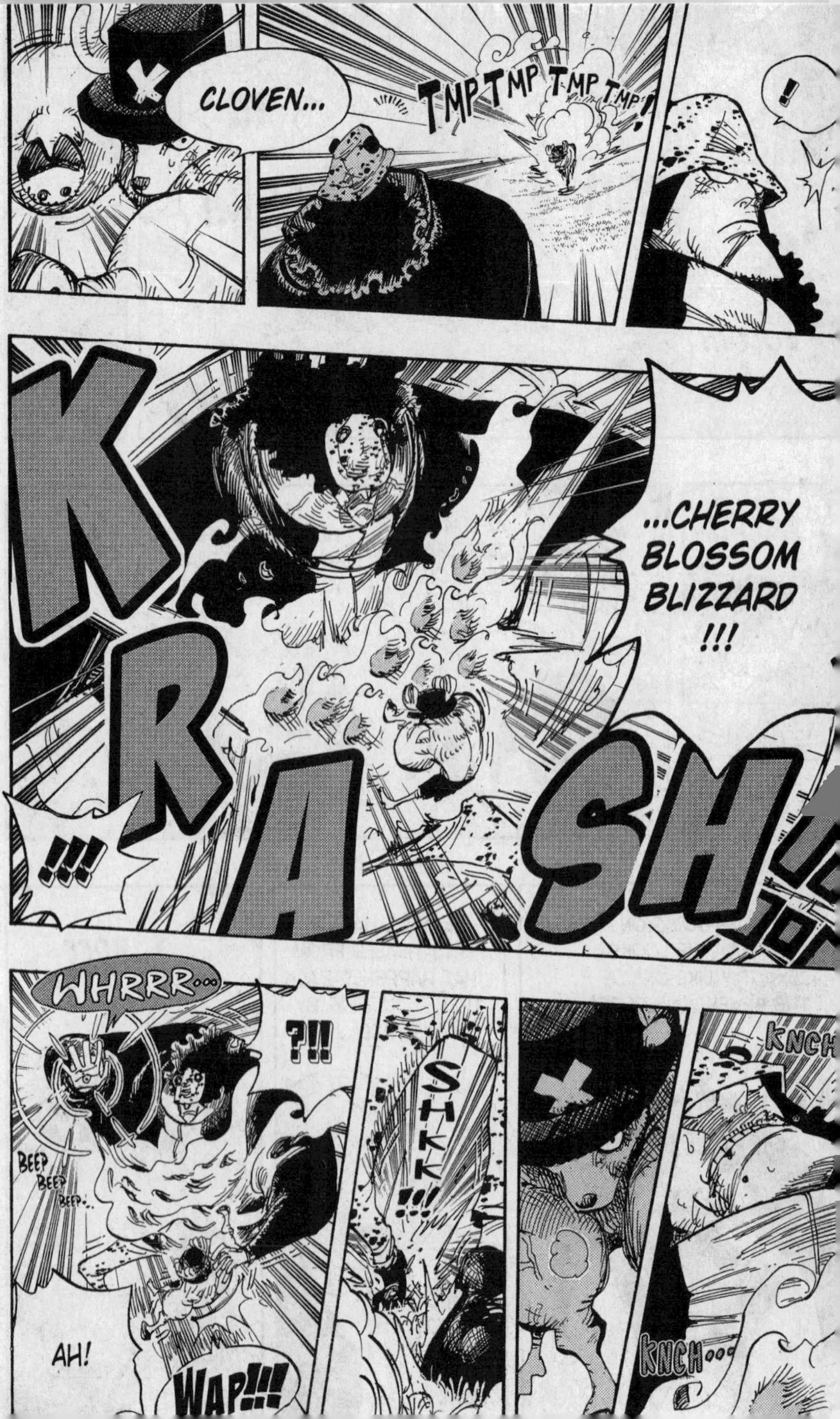
!
TMP TMP TMP TMP!
CLOVEN...
...CHERRY BLOSSOM BLIZZARD!!!
KRASH
!!!
KNCH
KNCH...
SHKK!!!
?!!
WHRRR...
BEEP BEEP BEEP...
AH!
WAP!!!

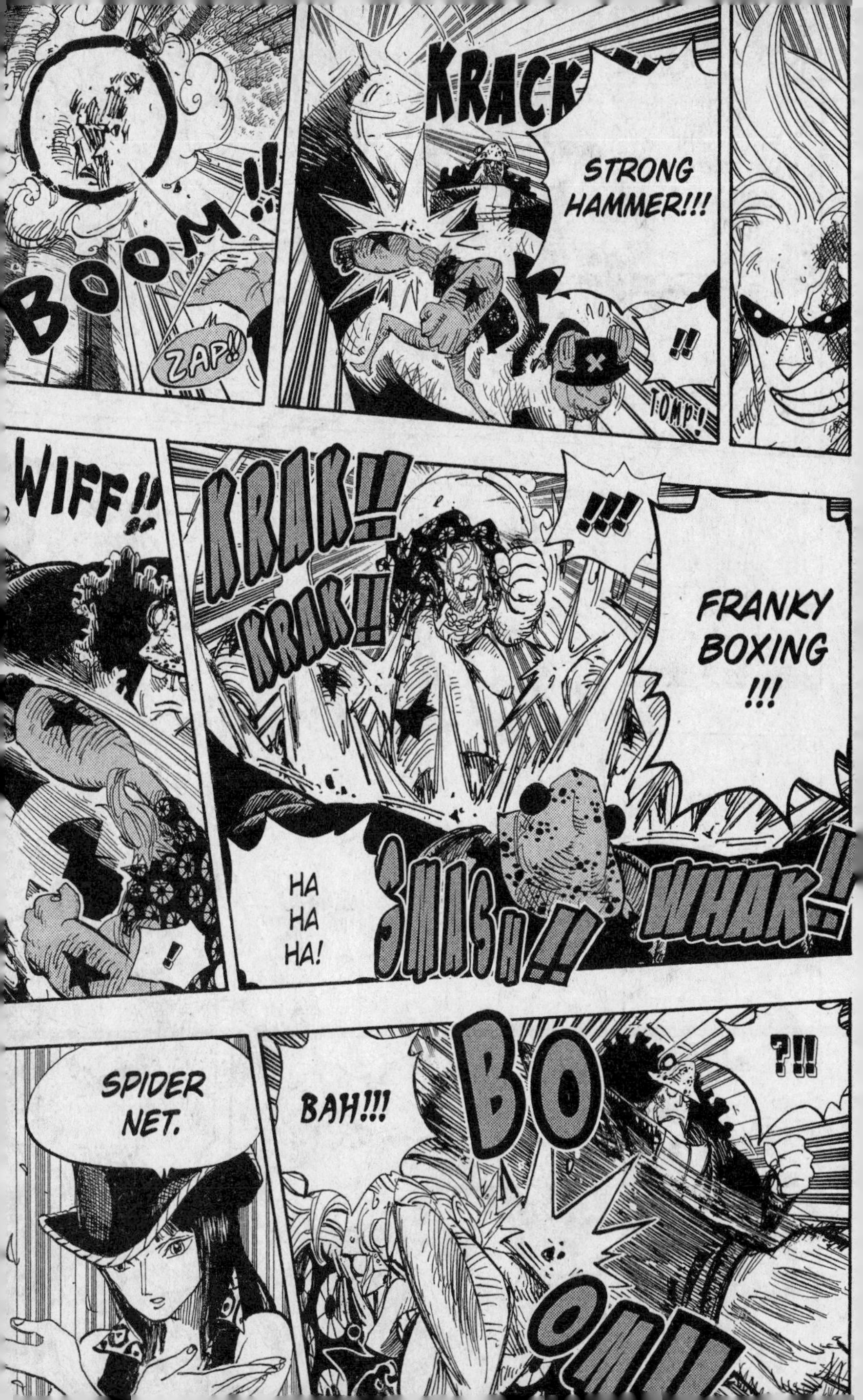
KRACK
STRONG HAMMER!!!
!!
TOMP!
BOOM!!
ZAP!!
!!!
FRANKY BOXING !!!
KRAK!!
KRAK!!
WHAK!!
SMASH!!
HA HA HA!
WIFF!!
!
?!!
BO
BAH!!!
OM!!
SPIDER NET.

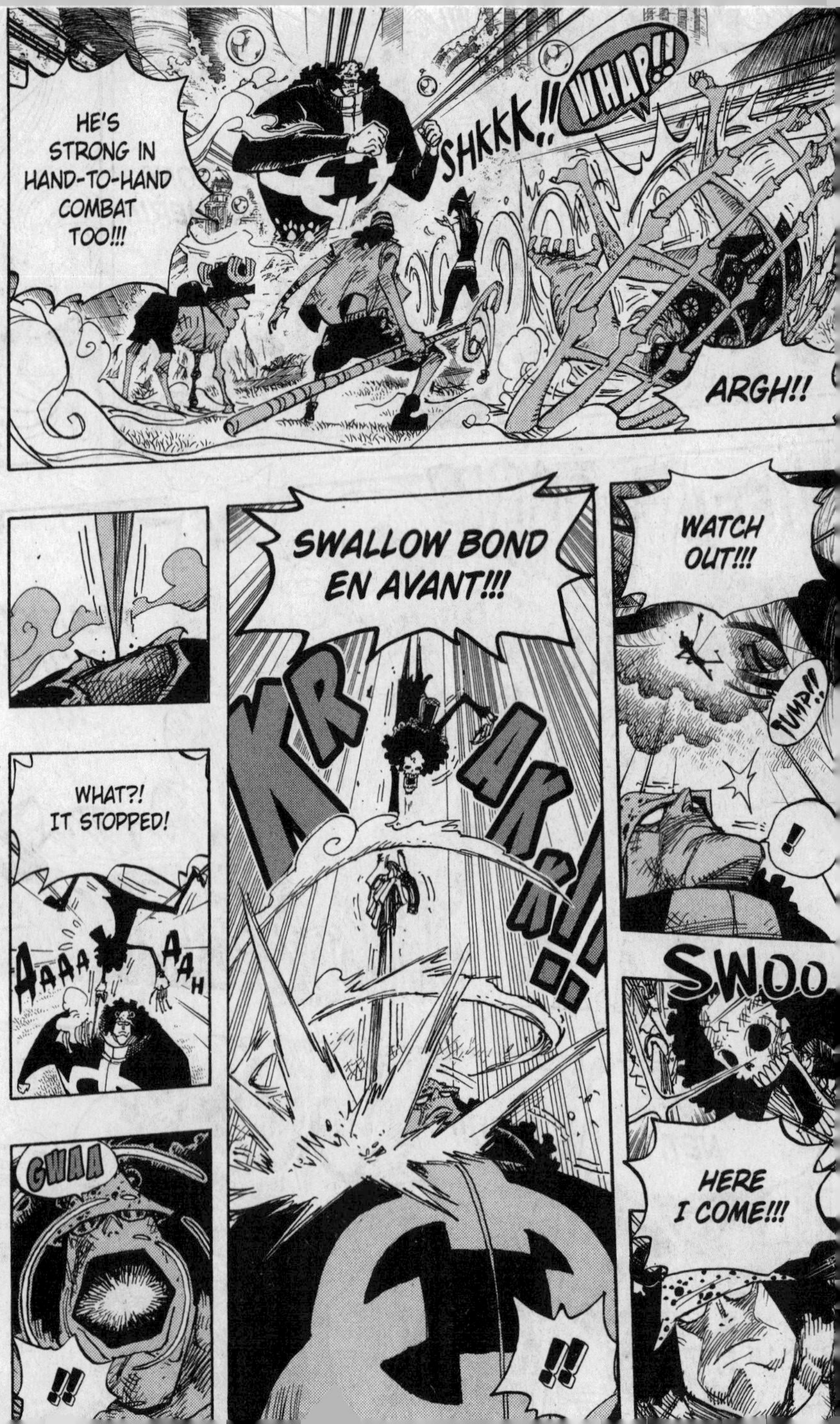

ARGH!!
WHAP!!
SHKKK!!
HE'S STRONG IN HAND-TO-HAND COMBAT TOO!!!
WATCH OUT!!!
TUMP!!
!
SWOO
HERE I COME!!!
SWALLOW BOND EN AVANT!!!
KRAKK!!
!!
WHAT?! IT STOPPED!
AAAA
AAH
GWAA
!!

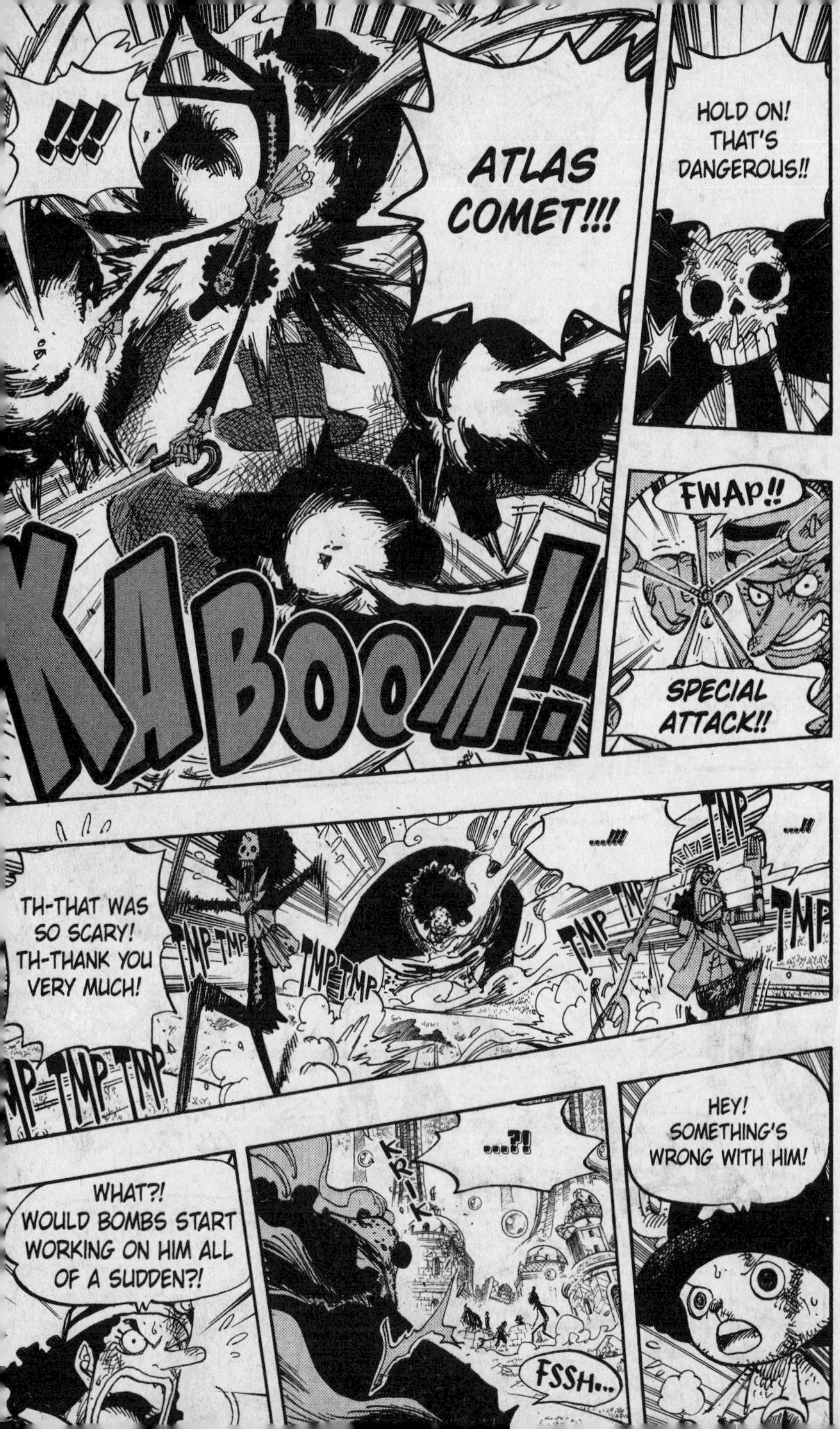

HOLD ON! THAT'S DANGEROUS!!
FWAP!!
SPECIAL ATTACK!!
ATLAS COMET!!!
!!!
KABOOM!!
...!!
TMP
TMP
...!!!
TMP TMP
TMP TMP
TMP TMP
TH-THAT WAS SO SCARY! TH-THANK YOU VERY MUCH!
TMP TMP TMP
HEY! SOMETHING'S WRONG WITH HIM!
...?!
KRIK
FSSH...
WHAT?! WOULD BOMBS START WORKING ON HIM ALL OF A SUDDEN?!

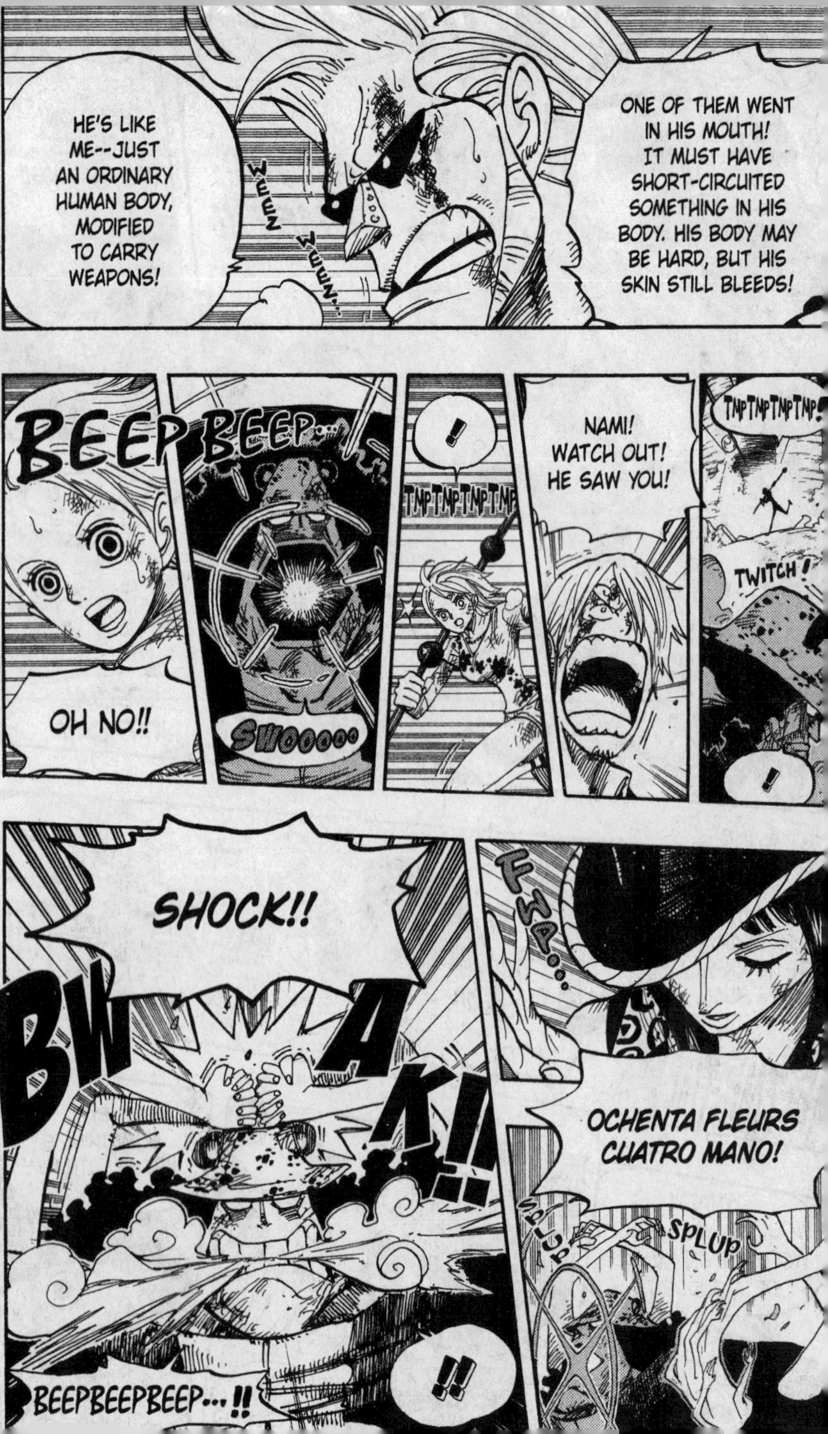
ONE OF THEM WENT IN HIS MOUTH! IT MUST HAVE SHORT-CIRCUITED SOMETHING IN HIS BODY. HIS BODY MAY BE HARD, BUT HIS SKIN STILL BLEEDS!
HE'S LIKE ME--JUST AN ORDINARY HUMAN BODY, MODIFIED TO CARRY WEAPONS!
WEEN
WEEN...
TMPTMPTMPTMP
TWITCH!
!
NAMI! WATCH OUT! HE SAW YOU!
!
TMPTMPTMPTMP
BEEP BEEP...
SWOOO...
OH NO!!
FWP...
OCHENTA FLEURS CUATRO MANO!
SPLUP
SPLUP
SHOCK!!
BWAK!!
!!
BEEPBEEPBEEP...!!

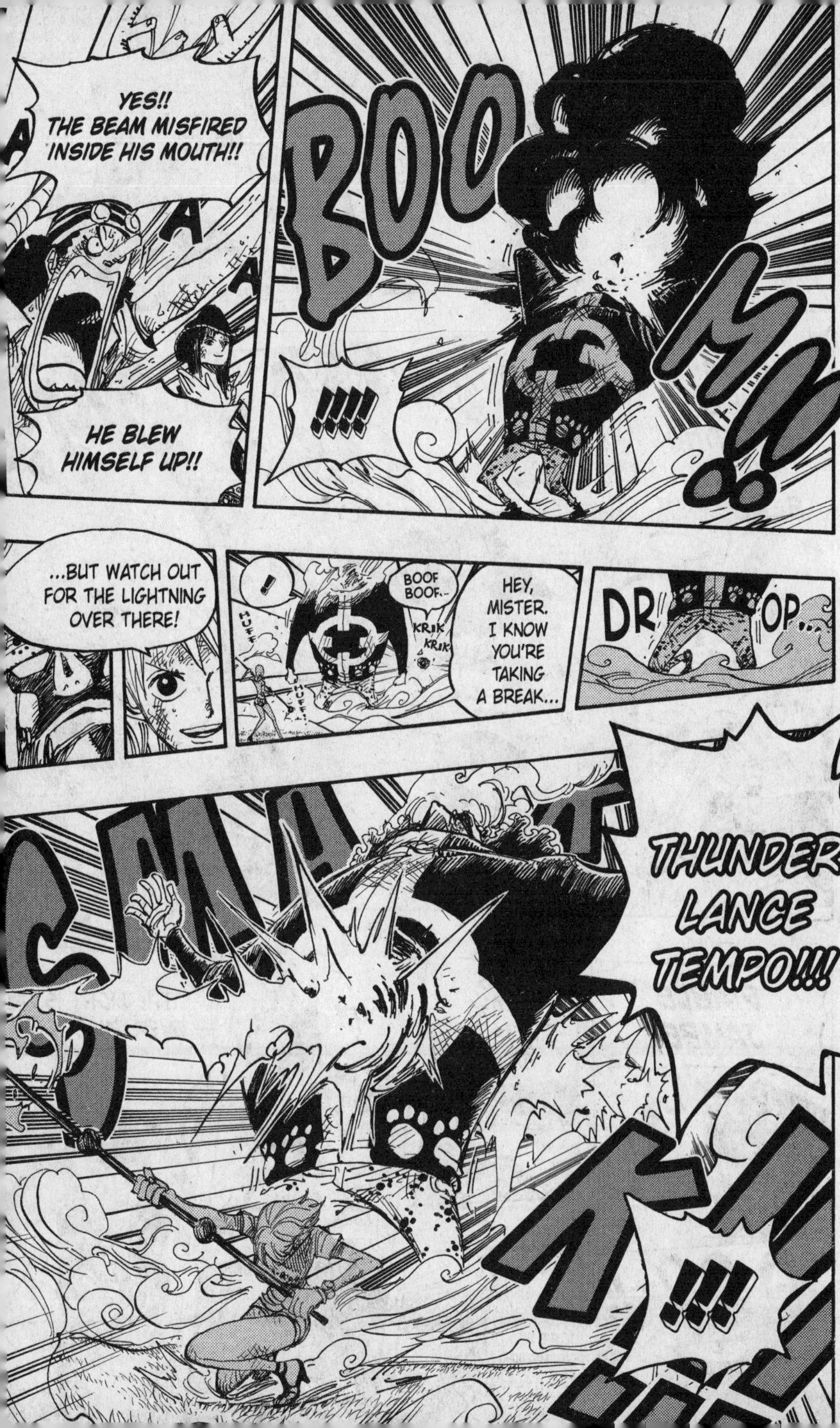
BOOOM!!
!!!!
YES!! THE BEAM MISFIRED INSIDE HIS MOUTH!!
HE BLEW HIMSELF UP!!
DROP...
HEY, MISTER. I KNOW YOU'RE TAKING A BREAK...
BOOF BOOF...
!
HUFF
HUFF
...BUT WATCH OUT FOR THE LIGHTNING OVER THERE!
THUNDER LANCE TEMPO!!!
!!!

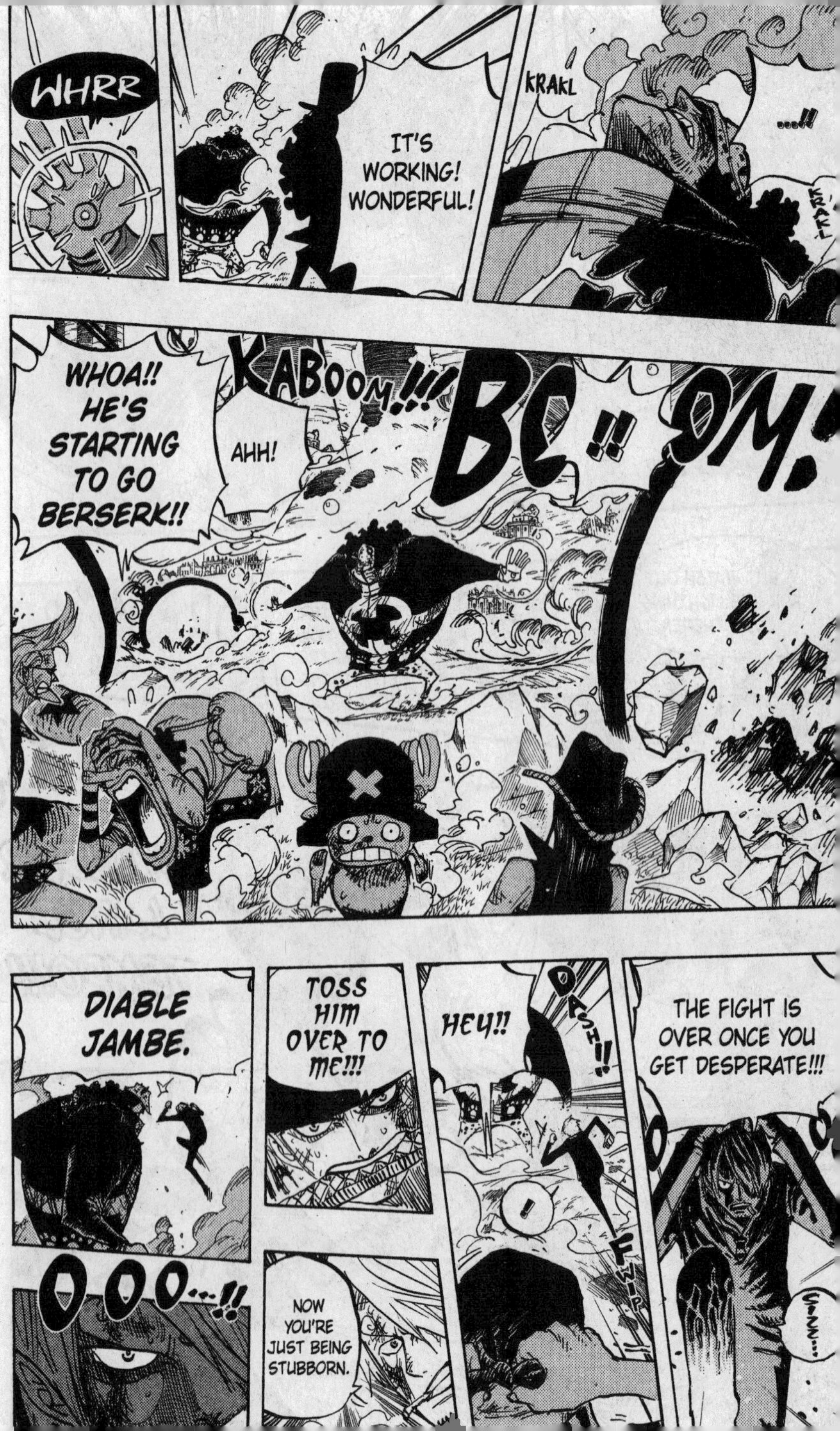
KRAKL
...!!
KRAKL
IT'S WORKING! WONDERFUL!
WHRR
KABOOM!!!
AHH!
WHOA!! HE'S STARTING TO GO BERSERK!!
THE FIGHT IS OVER ONCE YOU GET DESPERATE!!!
SIZZ...
HEY!!
DASH!!
!
FWIP
TOSS HIM OVER TO ME!!!
DIABLE JAMBE.
NOW YOU'RE JUST BEING STUBBORN.
O-O-O...!!

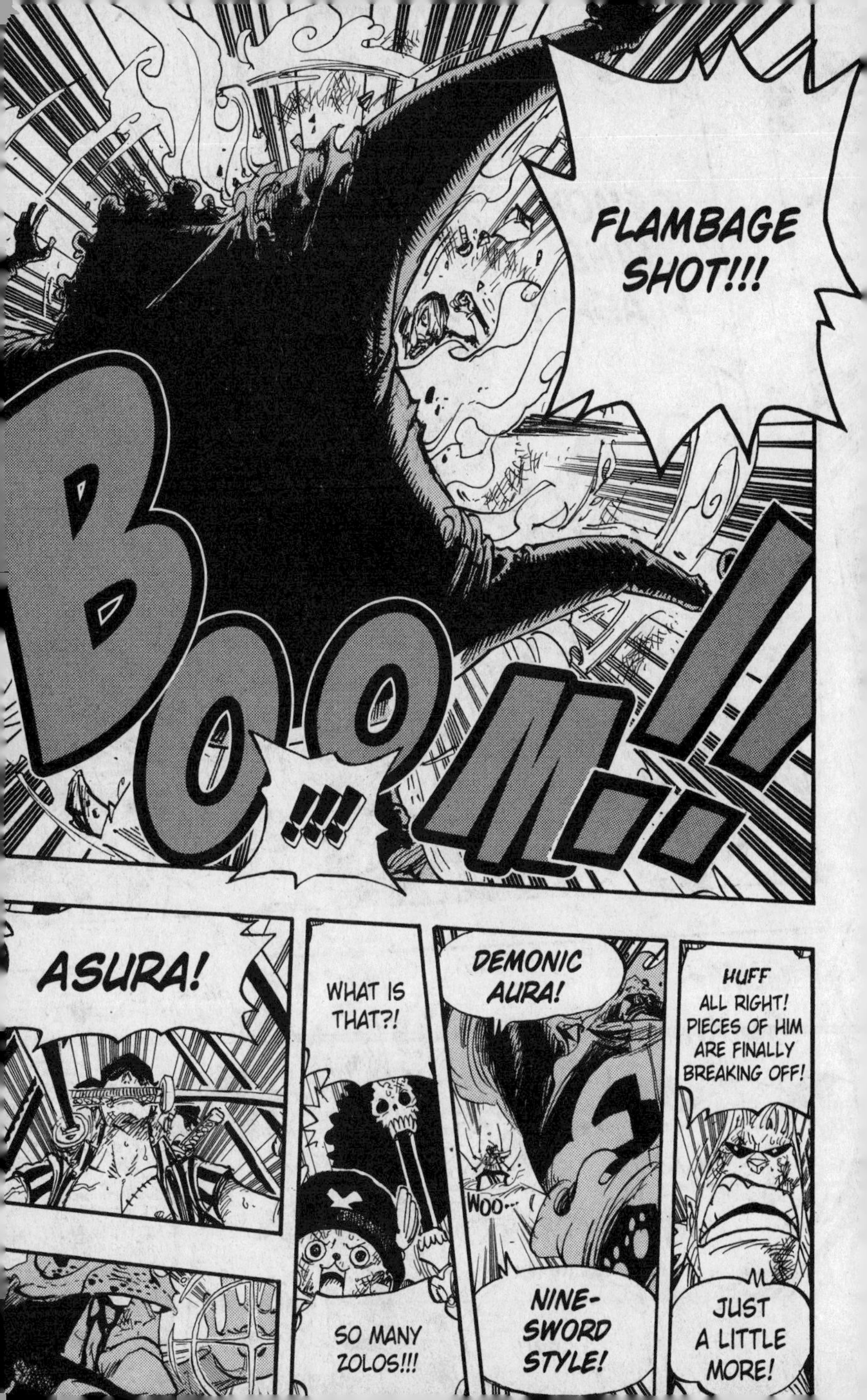
FLAMBAGE SHOT!!!
BOOM!!
!!!
HUFF
ALL RIGHT! PIECES OF HIM ARE FINALLY BREAKING OFF!
JUST A LITTLE MORE!
DEMONIC AURA!
WOO...
NINE-SWORD STYLE!
WHAT IS THAT?!
SO MANY ZOLOS!!!
ASURA!

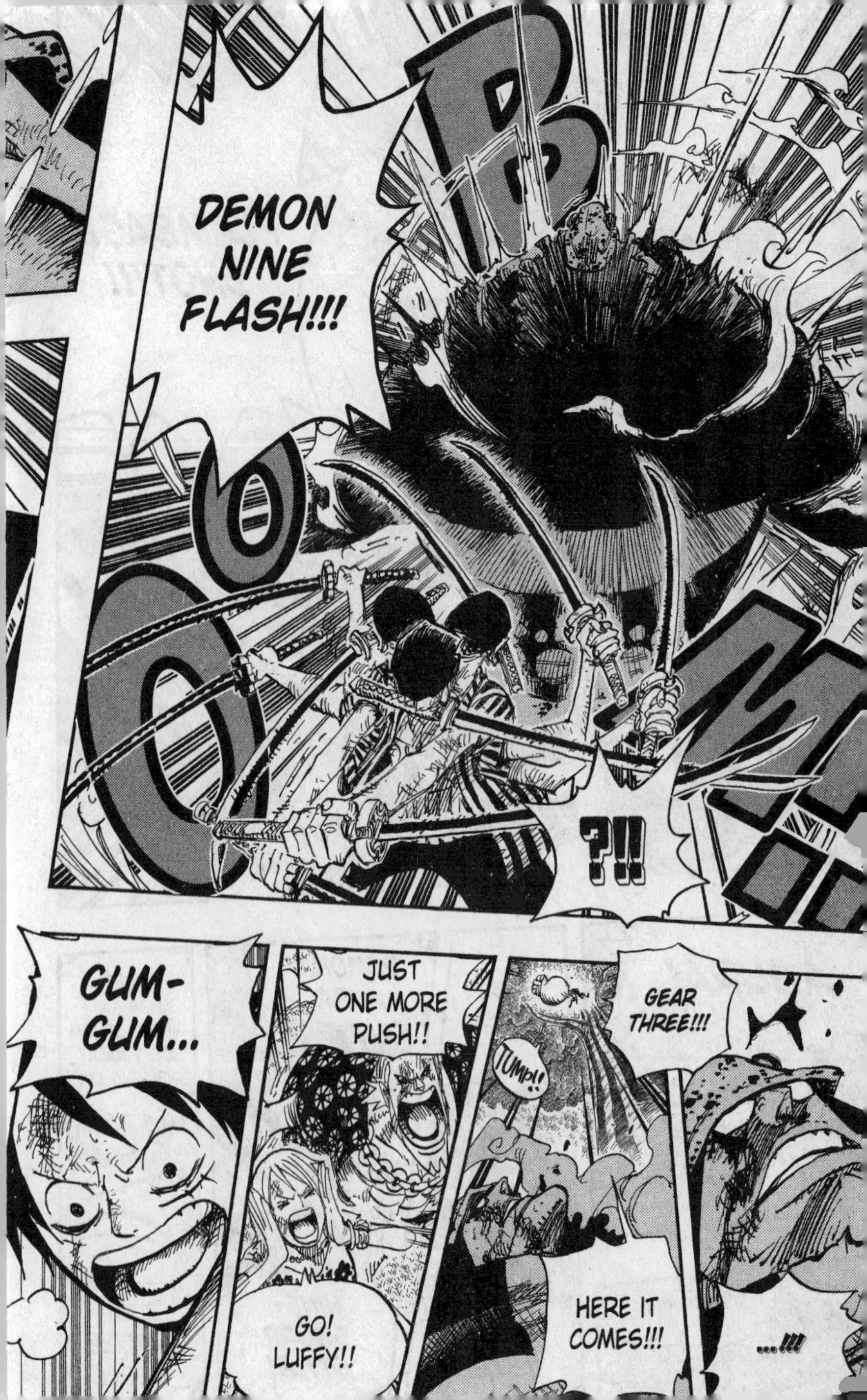
DEMON NINE FLASH!!!
?!!
...!!!
GEAR THREE!!!
TUMP!!
HERE IT COMES!!!
JUST ONE MORE PUSH!!
GO! LUFFY!!
GUM-GUM...

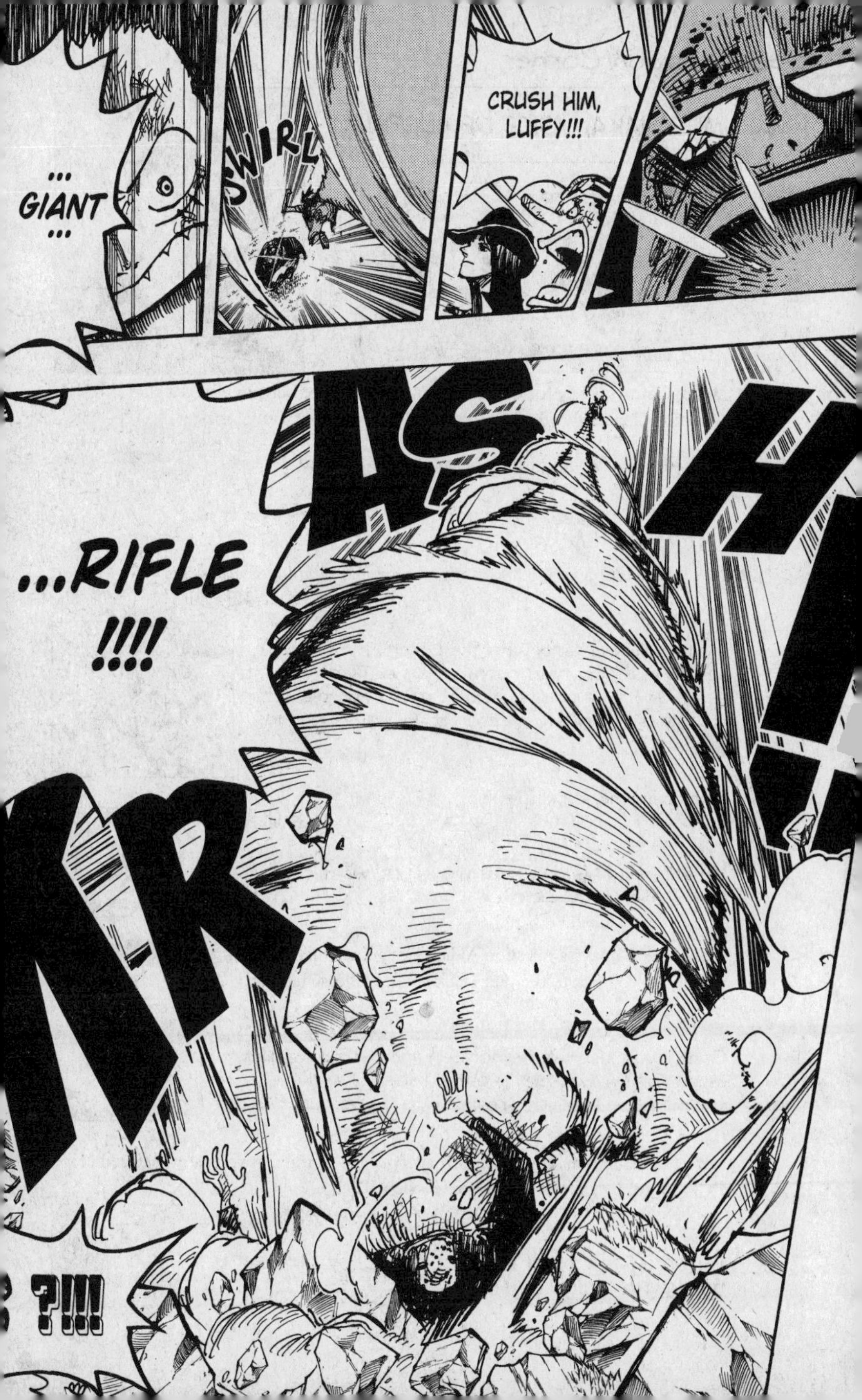
CRUSH HIM, LUFFY!!!
SWIRL
... GIANT ...
...RIFLE !!!!
?!!!

SBS Question Corner

MAYUMI TANAKA, VOICE OF LUFFY!

質問コーナー
それはね…
君の心の中さ。
そげきの島?

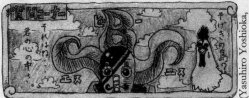

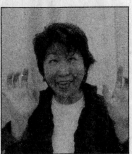

(Yasuhiro Yoshioka, Nagasaki)

Reader: Hello. Unfortunately for Odacchi, I'm going to have Mayumi Tanaka start the Question Corner this time (smooch!). Please start, Mayumi Tanaka.☆

--Rubosu

Tanaka: Let's start the (S)low (B)reaks done (S)lowly!

Oda: I said that's not what it stands for! Oh, wait. Maybe it is...

Reader: Have you ever partied with the other Straw Hat Pirates voice actors?

--Kanna Kawahito

CHEERS !!!
YOU GUYS ARE TOO KIND!!!

T: I had a takoyaki party with the other One Piece actors in my training room at home. There was some children's bedding in that room, and the actor who does Usopp fell asleep in it. He's a big pain in the butt.

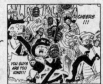

R: Don't mind me, just keep going.

--Usamickey

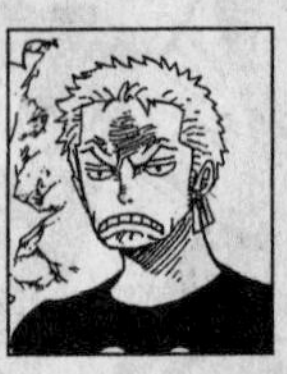

T: What? In Luffy's role? Usamickey, you want to play Luffy? Then I'll do Zolo.

R: Ms. Tanaka, I have a question. When you get telemarketers on the phone, do you talk to them in Luffy's voice? Please tell me.

--Windy

HEY, IS THAT YOU, SWAN?!
WHAT DO YOU WANT?

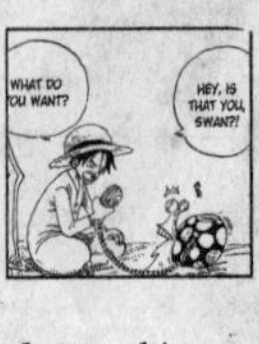

T: Once I was just talking normally and the telemarketer asked for my mother. I shouted back at him "I am the mom!" and he got freaked out. Serves him right!

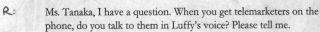

R: I'm a huge fan! I've seen practically every single anime that you were featured in. By the way… "Take this! Negative Hollow!"

--Maron

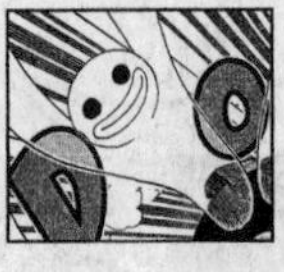

T: **I'M SO SORRY THAT A LITTLE OLD LADY LIKE ME IS DOING THE VOICE OF LUFFY...**

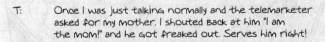

Chapter 511:
AXE-CARRYING SENTOMARU

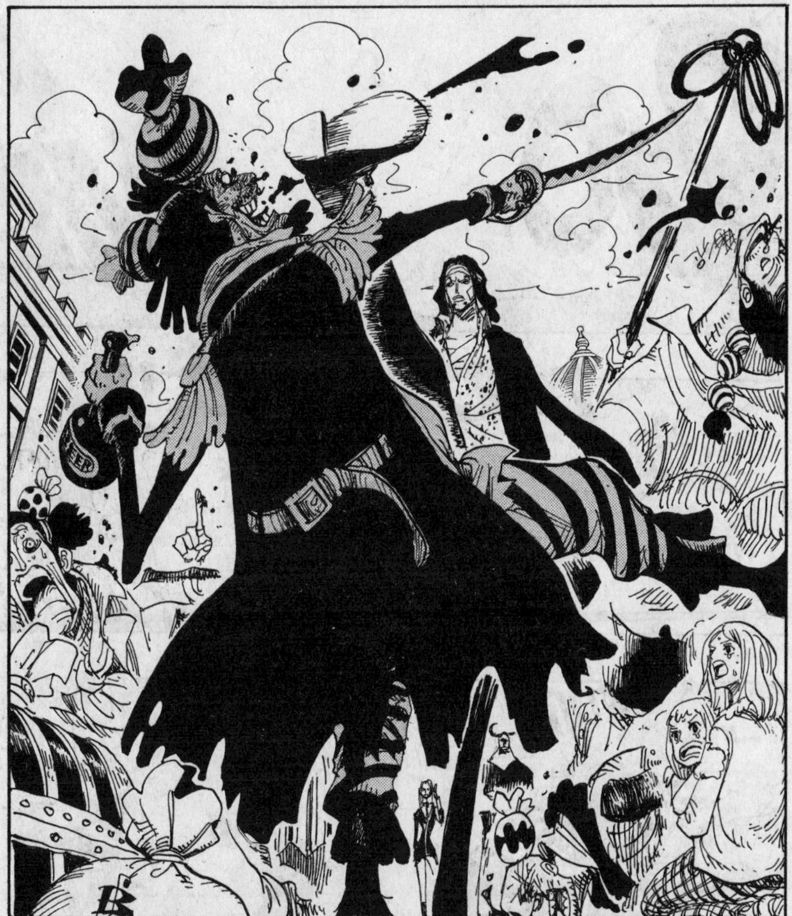

CP9'S INDEPENDENT REPORT, VOL. 19:
"MESSENGER OF JUSTICE"

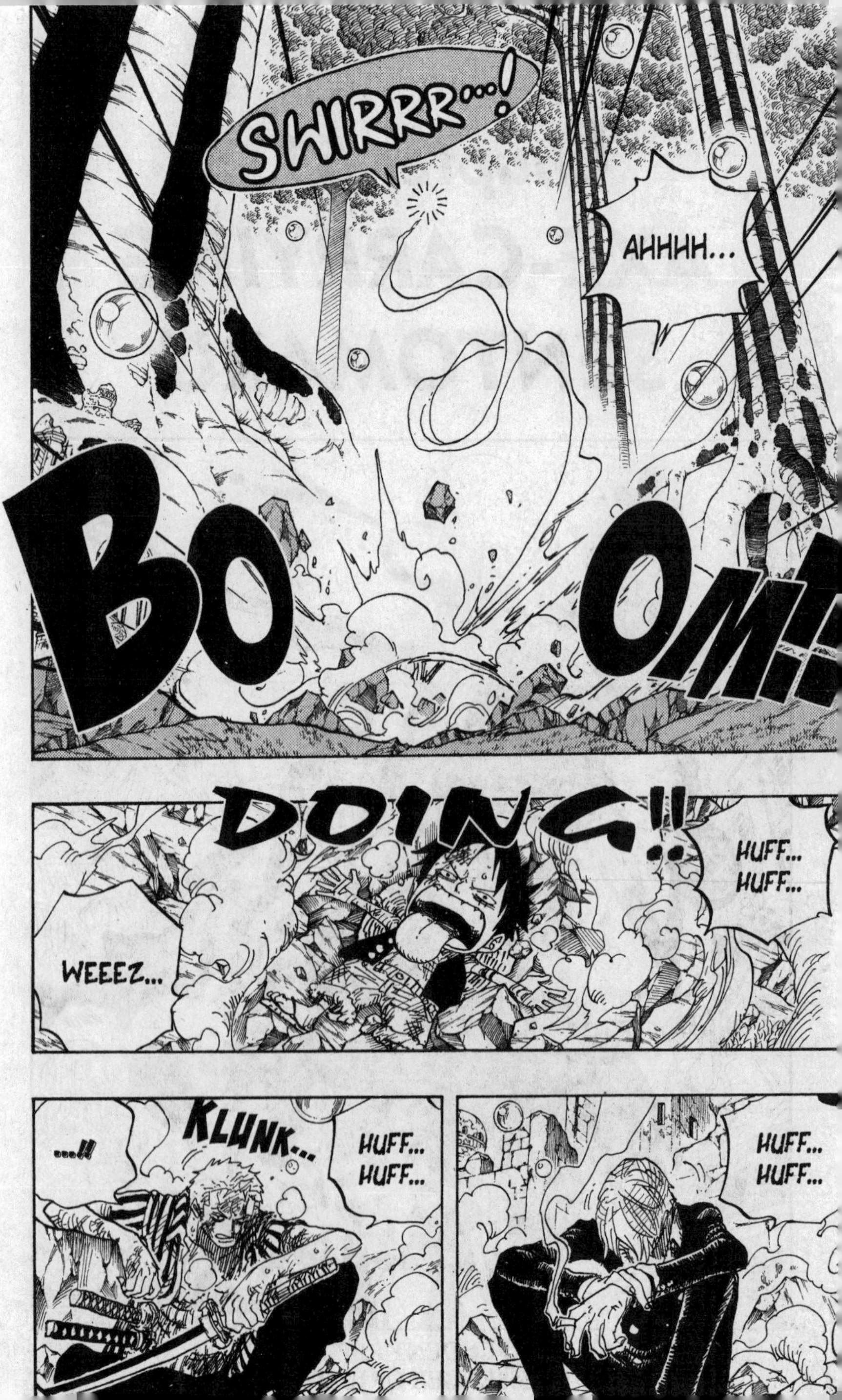

AHHHH...
SWIRRR...!
BOOM!!
DOING!!
HUFF... HUFF...
WEEEZ...
HUFF... HUFF...
HUFF... HUFF...
KLUNK...
...!!

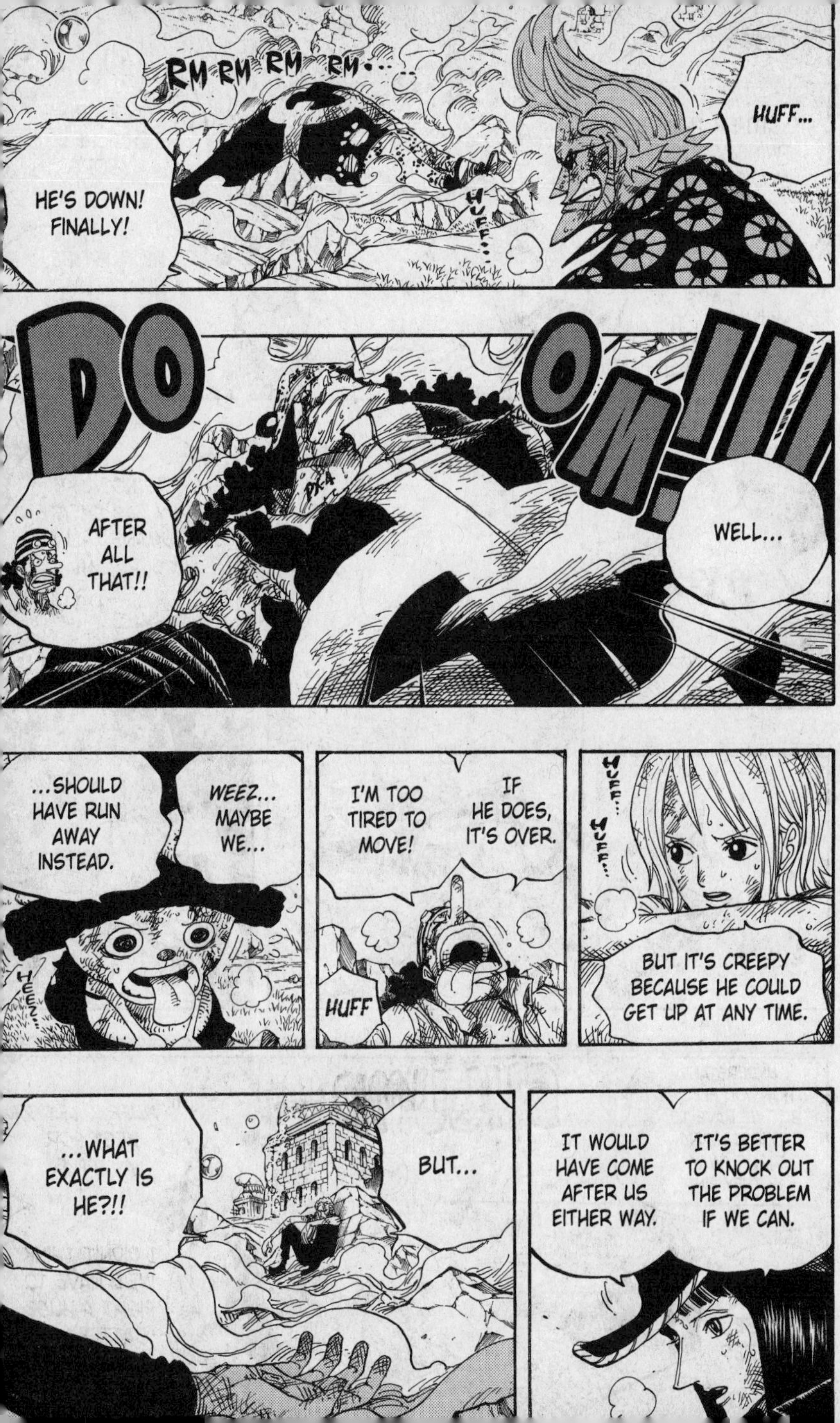
HUFF...
RM RM RM RM...
HE'S DOWN! FINALLY!
HUFF HUFF...
DOOOM!!
WELL...
AFTER ALL THAT!!
HUFF... HUFF...
BUT IT'S CREEPY BECAUSE HE COULD GET UP AT ANY TIME.
IF HE DOES, IT'S OVER.
I'M TOO TIRED TO MOVE!
HUFF
WEEZ... MAYBE WE...
...SHOULD HAVE RUN AWAY INSTEAD.
HEEZ...
IT'S BETTER TO KNOCK OUT THE PROBLEM IF WE CAN.
IT WOULD HAVE COME AFTER US EITHER WAY.
BUT...
...WHAT EXACTLY IS HE?!!

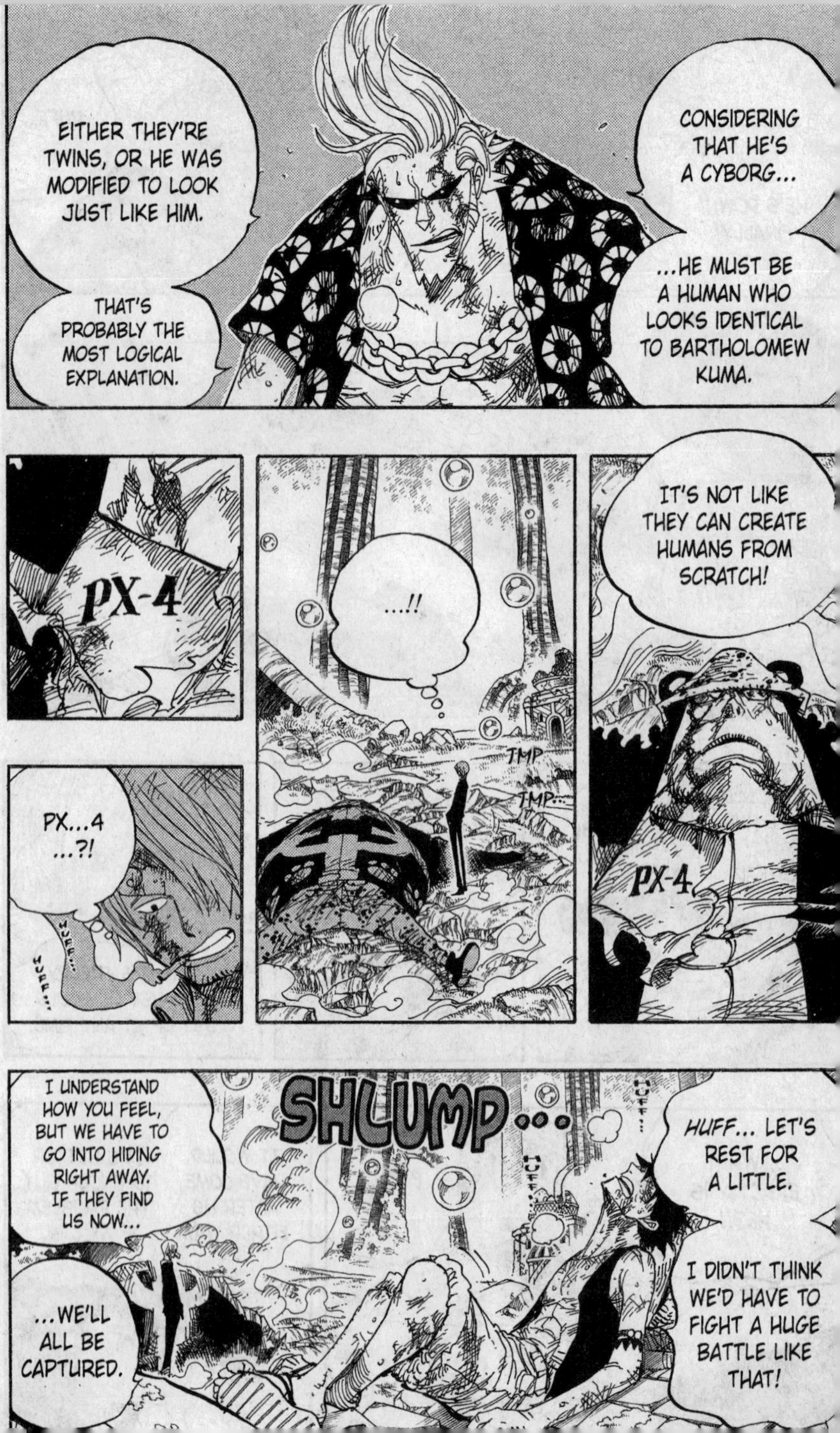
CONSIDERING THAT HE'S A CYBORG...
...HE MUST BE A HUMAN WHO LOOKS IDENTICAL TO BARTHOLOMEW KUMA.
EITHER THEY'RE TWINS, OR HE WAS MODIFIED TO LOOK JUST LIKE HIM.
THAT'S PROBABLY THE MOST LOGICAL EXPLANATION.
IT'S NOT LIKE THEY CAN CREATE HUMANS FROM SCRATCH!
PX-4
...!!
TMP
TMP...
PX-4
PX...4 ...?!
HUFF...
HUFF...
HUFF...
HUFF... LET'S REST FOR A LITTLE.
I DIDN'T THINK WE'D HAVE TO FIGHT A HUGE BATTLE LIKE THAT!
HUFF...
SHLUMP...
I UNDERSTAND HOW YOU FEEL, BUT WE HAVE TO GO INTO HIDING RIGHT AWAY. IF THEY FIND US NOW...
...WE'LL ALL BE CAPTURED.

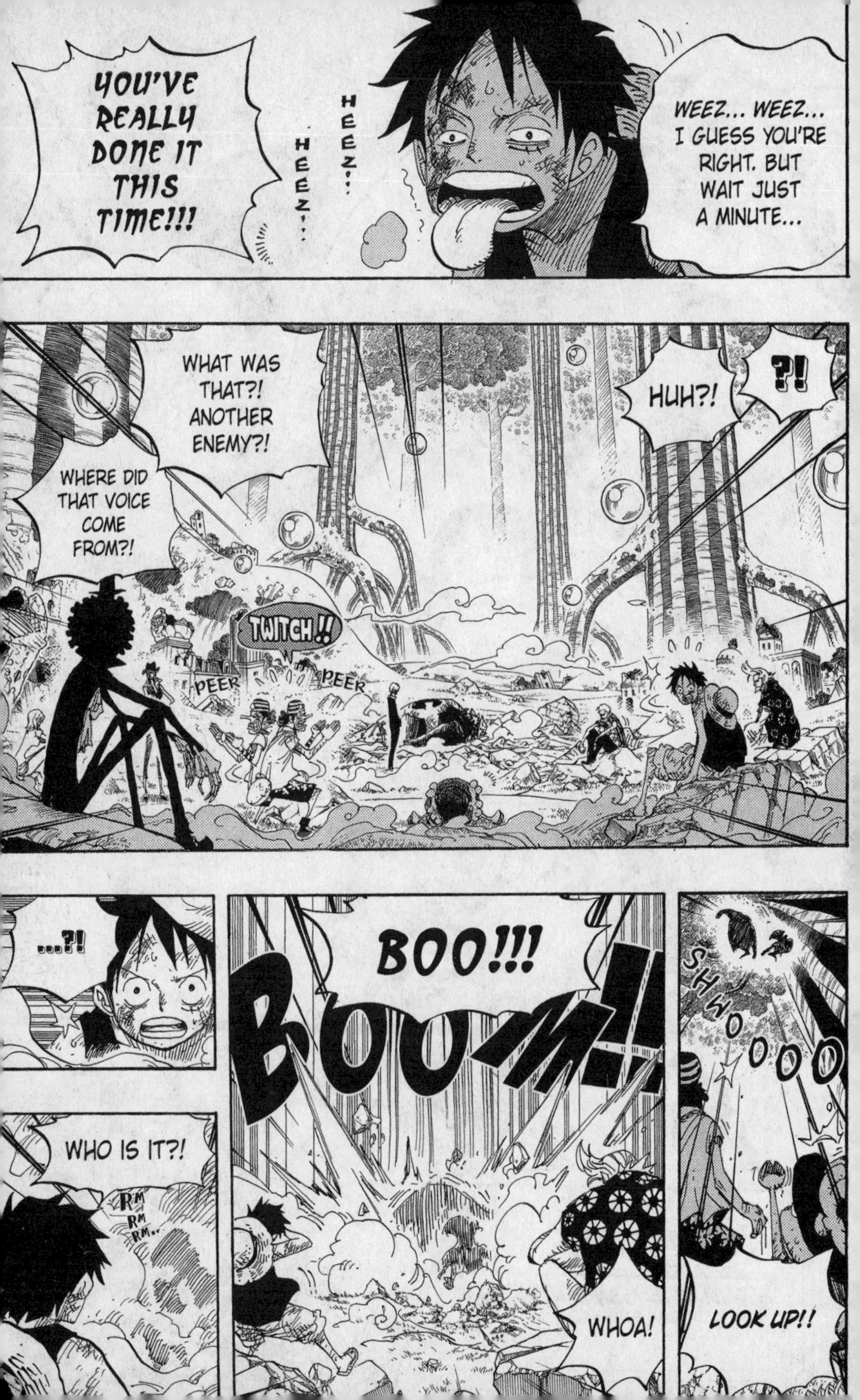
WEEZ... WEEZ... I GUESS YOU'RE RIGHT. BUT WAIT JUST A MINUTE...
HEEZ...
HEEZ...
YOU'VE REALLY DONE IT THIS TIME!!!
?!
HUH?!
WHAT WAS THAT?! ANOTHER ENEMY?!
WHERE DID THAT VOICE COME FROM?!
TWITCH!!
PEER
PEER
SHWOOOO
LOOK UP!!
BOO!!!
BOOM!!
WHOA!
...?!
WHO IS IT?!
RM RM RM...

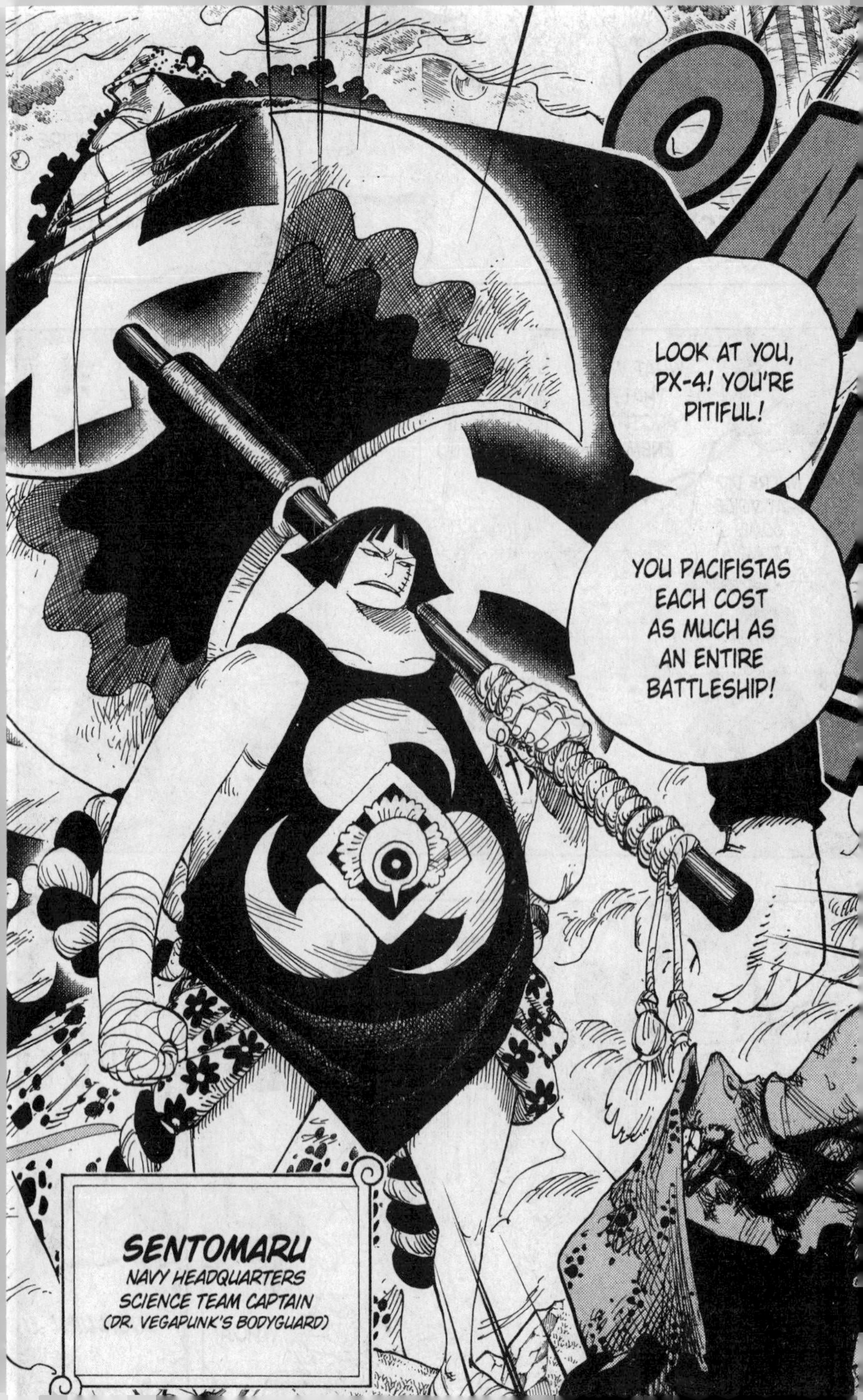
LOOK AT YOU, PX-4! YOU'RE PITIFUL!
YOU PACIFISTAS EACH COST AS MUCH AS AN ENTIRE BATTLESHIP!
SENTOMARU
NAVY HEADQUARTERS SCIENCE TEAM CAPTAIN (DR. VEGAPUNK'S BODYGUARD)

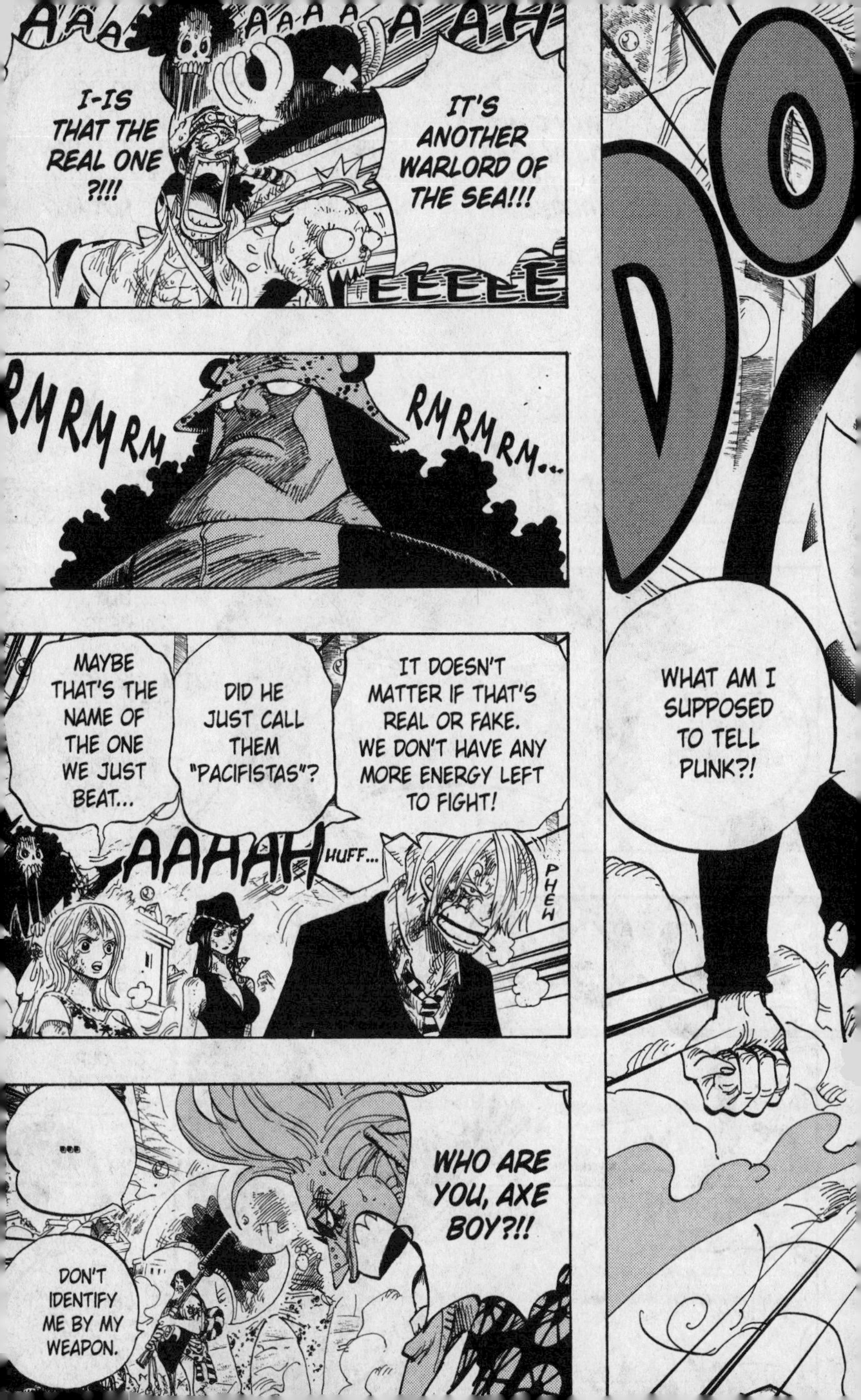
WHAT AM I SUPPOSED TO TELL PUNK?!
A A A A A AH
IT'S ANOTHER WARLORD OF THE SEA!!!
I-IS THAT THE REAL ONE ?!!!
EEEEEE
RMRMRM...
RMRMRM
IT DOESN'T MATTER IF THAT'S REAL OR FAKE. WE DON'T HAVE ANY MORE ENERGY LEFT TO FIGHT!
DID HE JUST CALL THEM "PACIFISTAS"?
MAYBE THAT'S THE NAME OF THE ONE WE JUST BEAT...
PHEW
HUFF...
AAAAH
WHO ARE YOU, AXE BOY?!!
...
DON'T IDENTIFY ME BY MY WEAPON.

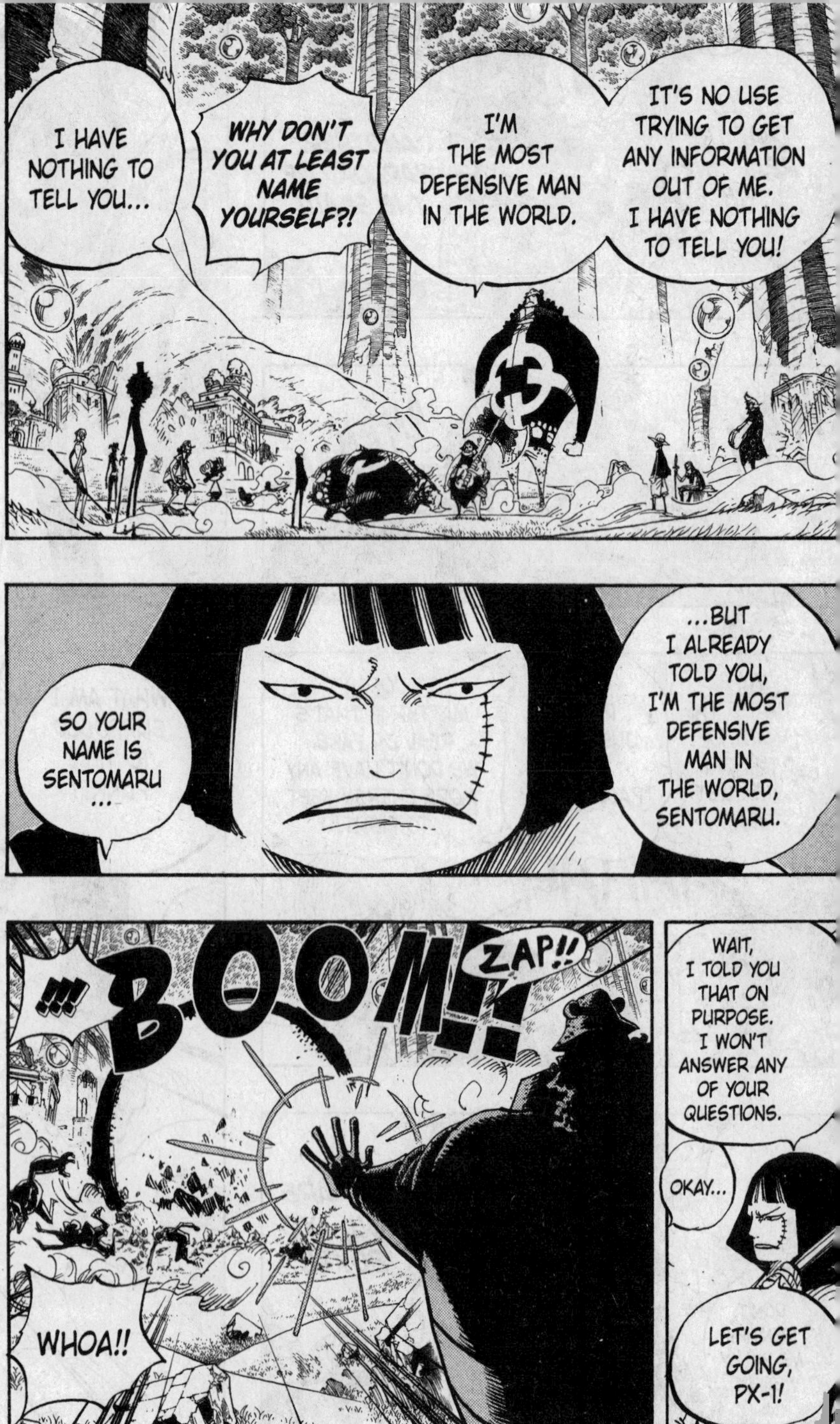
IT'S NO USE TRYING TO GET ANY INFORMATION OUT OF ME. I HAVE NOTHING TO TELL YOU!
I'M THE MOST DEFENSIVE MAN IN THE WORLD.
WHY DON'T YOU AT LEAST NAME YOURSELF?!
I HAVE NOTHING TO TELL YOU...
...BUT I ALREADY TOLD YOU, I'M THE MOST DEFENSIVE MAN IN THE WORLD, SENTOMARU.
SO YOUR NAME IS SENTOMARU ...
WAIT, I TOLD YOU THAT ON PURPOSE. I WON'T ANSWER ANY OF YOUR QUESTIONS.
OKAY...
LET'S GET GOING, PX-1!
ZAP!!
BOOM!!
!!!
WHOA!!

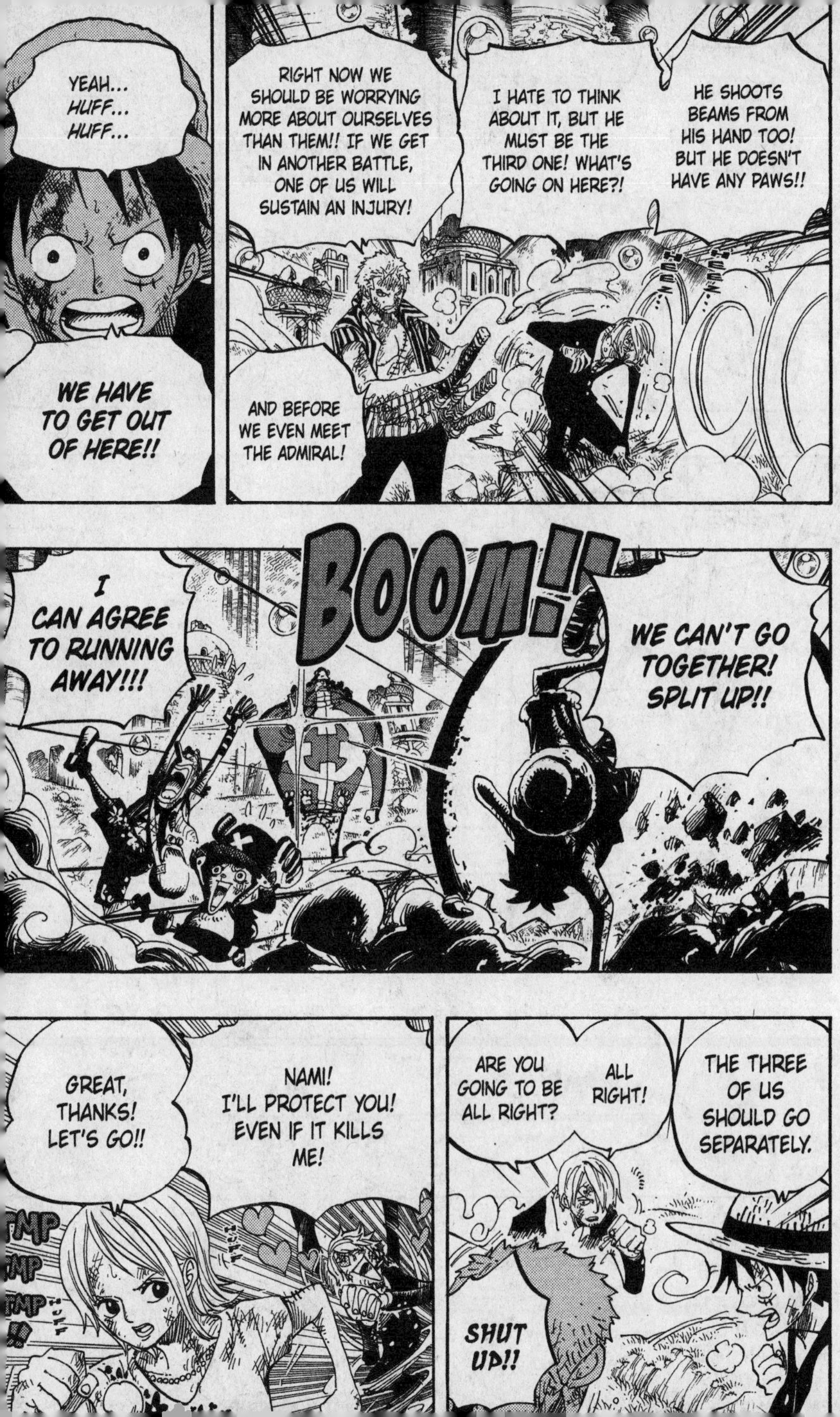
HE SHOOTS BEAMS FROM HIS HAND TOO! BUT HE DOESN'T HAVE ANY PAWS!!
I HATE TO THINK ABOUT IT, BUT HE MUST BE THE THIRD ONE! WHAT'S GOING ON HERE?!
RIGHT NOW WE SHOULD BE WORRYING MORE ABOUT OURSELVES THAN THEM!! IF WE GET IN ANOTHER BATTLE, ONE OF US WILL SUSTAIN AN INJURY!
AND BEFORE WE EVEN MEET THE ADMIRAL!
YEAH... HUFF... HUFF...
WE HAVE TO GET OUT OF HERE!!
BOOM!!
WE CAN'T GO TOGETHER! SPLIT UP!!
I CAN AGREE TO RUNNING AWAY!!!
THE THREE OF US SHOULD GO SEPARATELY.
ALL RIGHT!
ARE YOU GOING TO BE ALL RIGHT?
SHUT UP!!
NAMI! I'LL PROTECT YOU! EVEN IF IT KILLS ME!
GREAT, THANKS! LET'S GO!!
TMP
TMP
TMP
HUFF

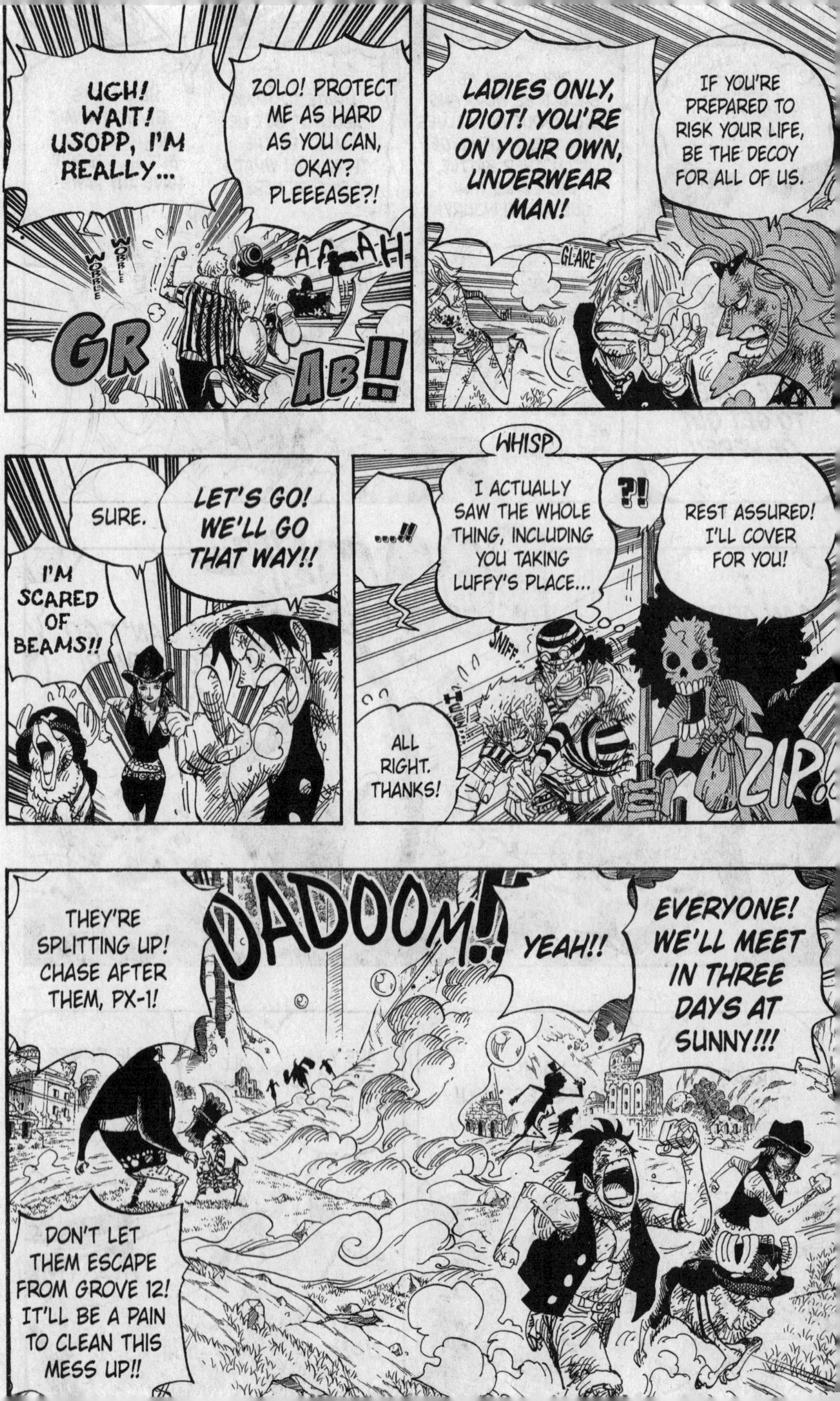
IF YOU'RE PREPARED TO RISK YOUR LIFE, BE THE DECOY FOR ALL OF US.
LADIES ONLY, IDIOT! YOU'RE ON YOUR OWN, UNDERWEAR MAN!
GLARE
ZOLO! PROTECT ME AS HARD AS YOU CAN, OKAY? PLEEEASE?!
UGH! WAIT! USOPP, I'M REALLY...
A-A-AH
GRAB!!
WOBBLE
WOBBLE
WHISP
REST ASSURED! I'LL COVER FOR YOU!
?!
I ACTUALLY SAW THE WHOLE THING, INCLUDING YOU TAKING LUFFY'S PLACE...
...!!
SNIFF...
ALL RIGHT. THANKS!
ZIP...
LET'S GO! WE'LL GO THAT WAY!!
SURE.
I'M SCARED OF BEAMS!!
EVERYONE! WE'LL MEET IN THREE DAYS AT SUNNY!!!
YEAH!!
DADOOM!!
THEY'RE SPLITTING UP! CHASE AFTER THEM, PX-1!
DON'T LET THEM ESCAPE FROM GROVE 12! IT'LL BE A PAIN TO CLEAN THIS MESS UP!!

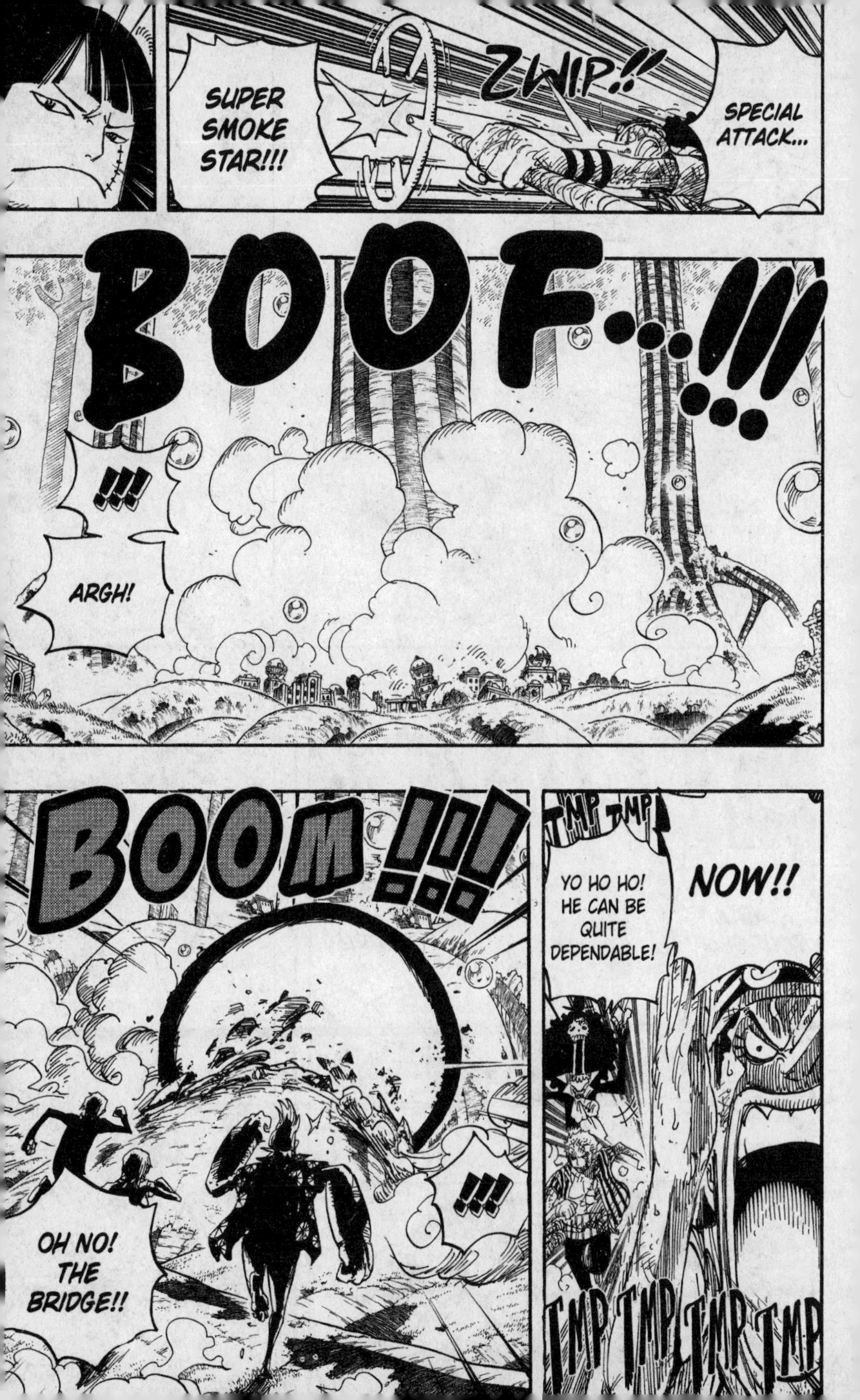
SPECIAL ATTACK...
ZWIP!!
SUPER SMOKE STAR!!!
BOOF...!!!
!!!
ARGH!
TMP TMP
NOW!!
YO HO HO! HE CAN BE QUITE DEPENDABLE!
TMP TMP TMP TMP
BOOM!!!
!!!
OH NO! THE BRIDGE!!

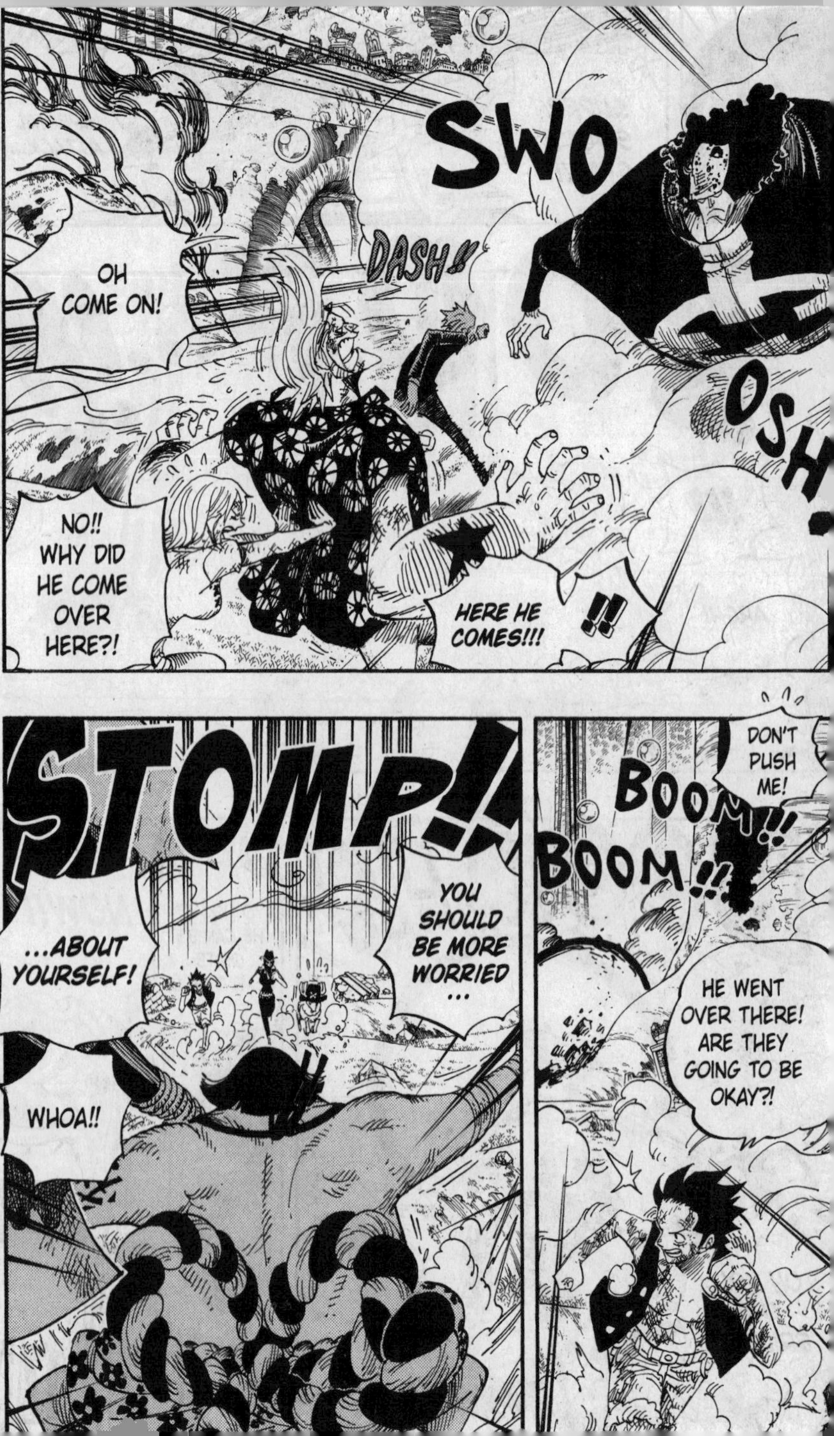
SWO
OSH
DASH!!
OH COME ON!
!!
HERE HE COMES!!!
NO!! WHY DID HE COME OVER HERE?!
DON'T PUSH ME!
BOOM!!
BOOM!!
HE WENT OVER THERE! ARE THEY GOING TO BE OKAY?!
STOMP!!
YOU SHOULD BE MORE WORRIED...
...ABOUT YOURSELF!
WHOA!!

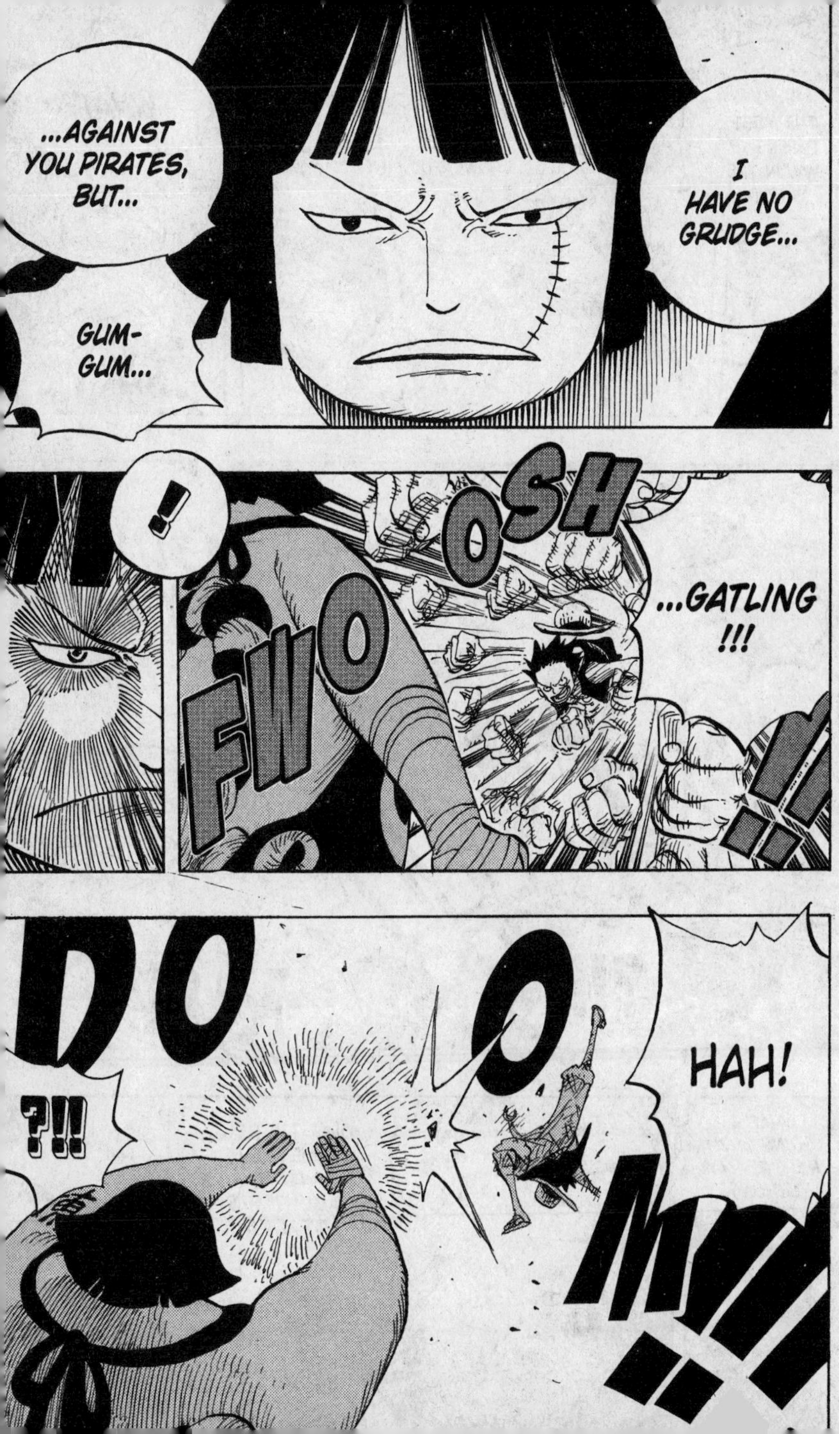
I HAVE NO GRUDGE...
...AGAINST YOU PIRATES, BUT...
GUM-GUM...
...GATLING!!!
FWOOSH
!
HAH!
DOOM!!
?!!

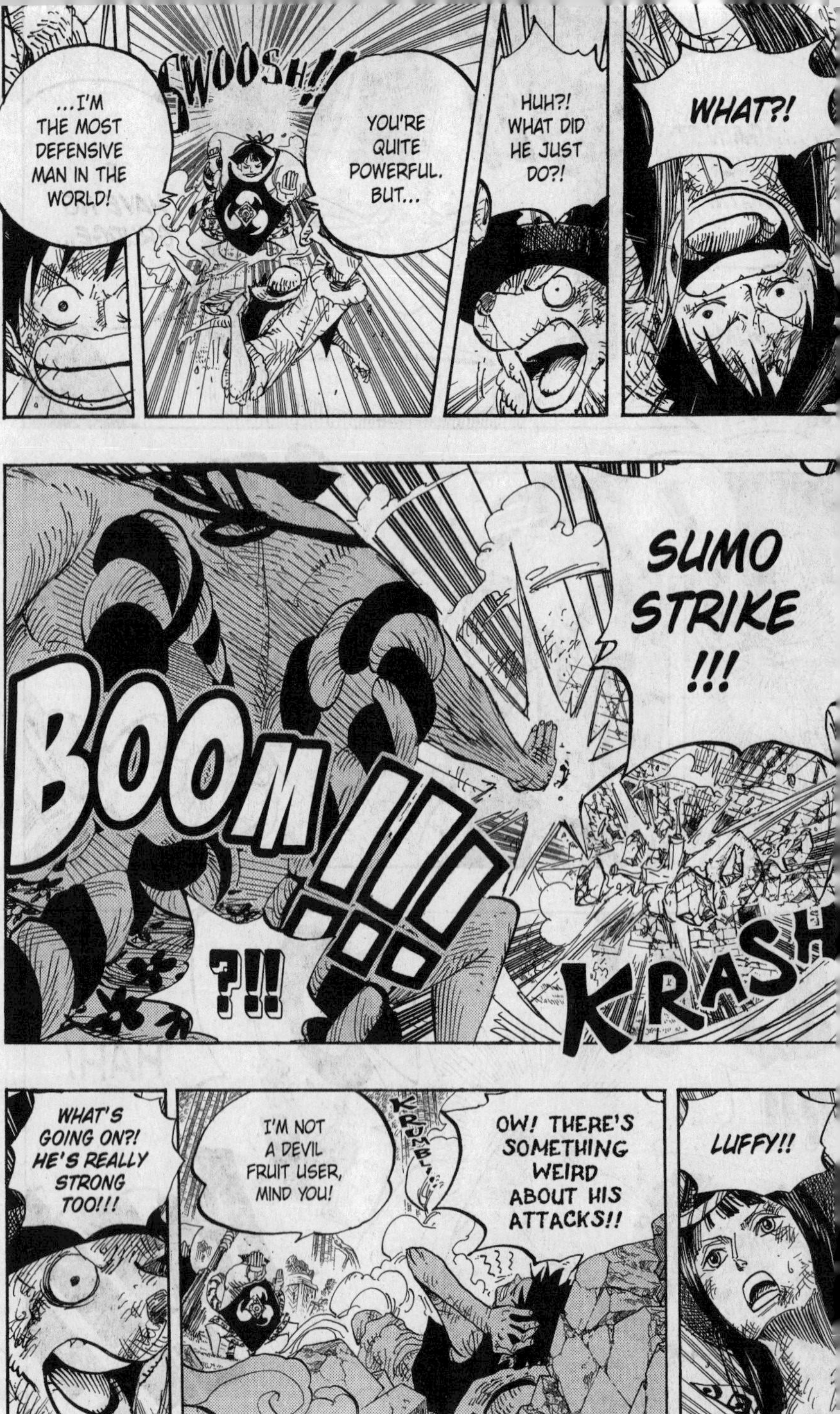
WHAT?!
HUH?! WHAT DID HE JUST DO?!
SWOOSH!!
YOU'RE QUITE POWERFUL. BUT...
...I'M THE MOST DEFENSIVE MAN IN THE WORLD!
SUMO STRIKE!!!
BOOM!!!
KRASH
?!!
LUFFY!!
OW! THERE'S SOMETHING WEIRD ABOUT HIS ATTACKS!!
KRUMBL
I'M NOT A DEVIL FRUIT USER, MIND YOU!
WHAT'S GOING ON?! HE'S REALLY STRONG TOO!!!

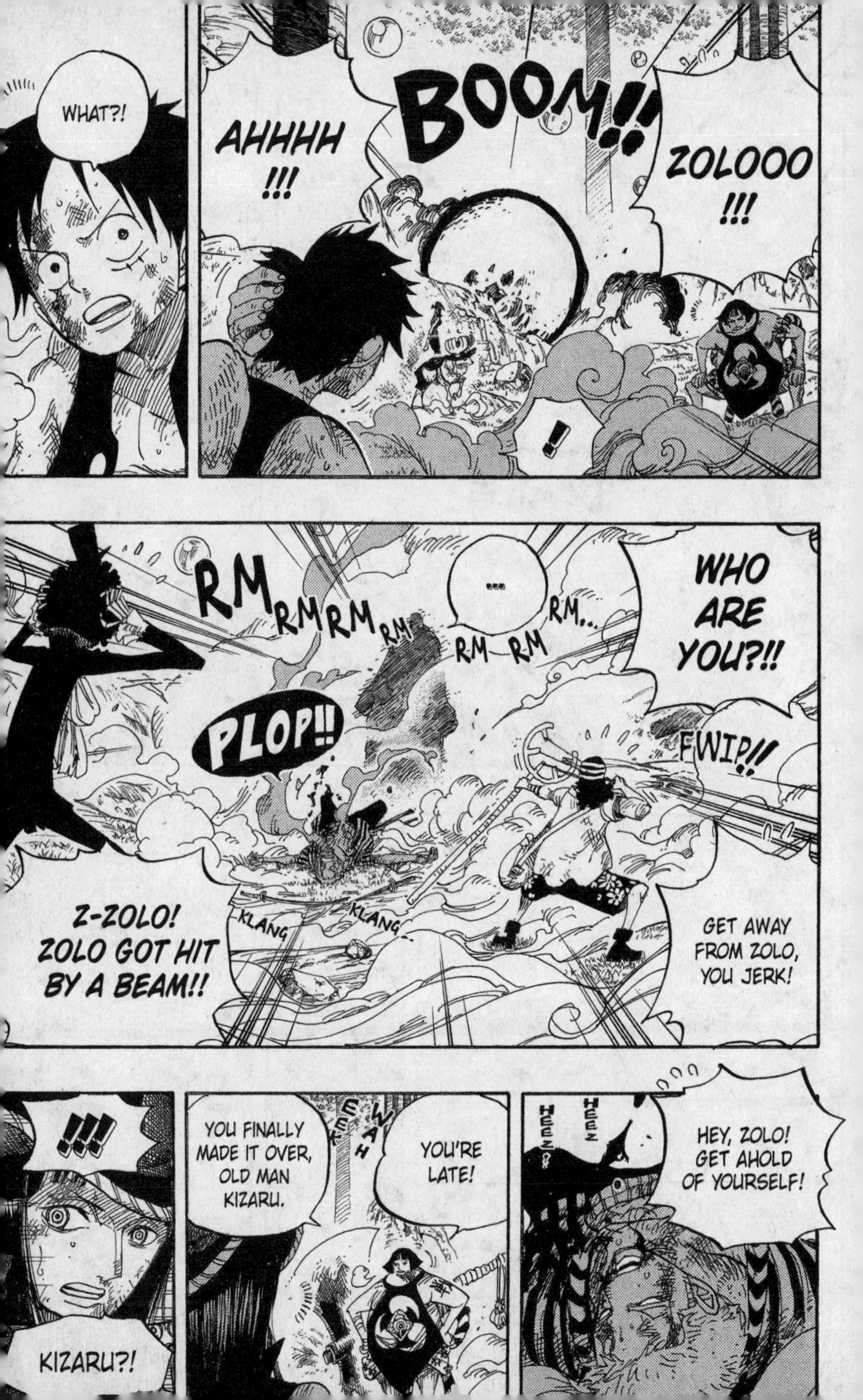
ZOLOOO !!!
BOOM!!
AHHHH !!!
!
WHAT?!
WHO ARE YOU?!!
...
RM RM RM RM RM RM RM...
FWIP!!
PLOP!!
GET AWAY FROM ZOLO, YOU JERK!
KLANG KLANG
Z-ZOLO! ZOLO GOT HIT BY A BEAM!!
HEEZ HEEZ
HEY, ZOLO! GET AHOLD OF YOURSELF!
WAH KEEK
YOU'RE LATE!
YOU FINALLY MADE IT OVER, OLD MAN KIZARU.
!!!
KIZARU?!

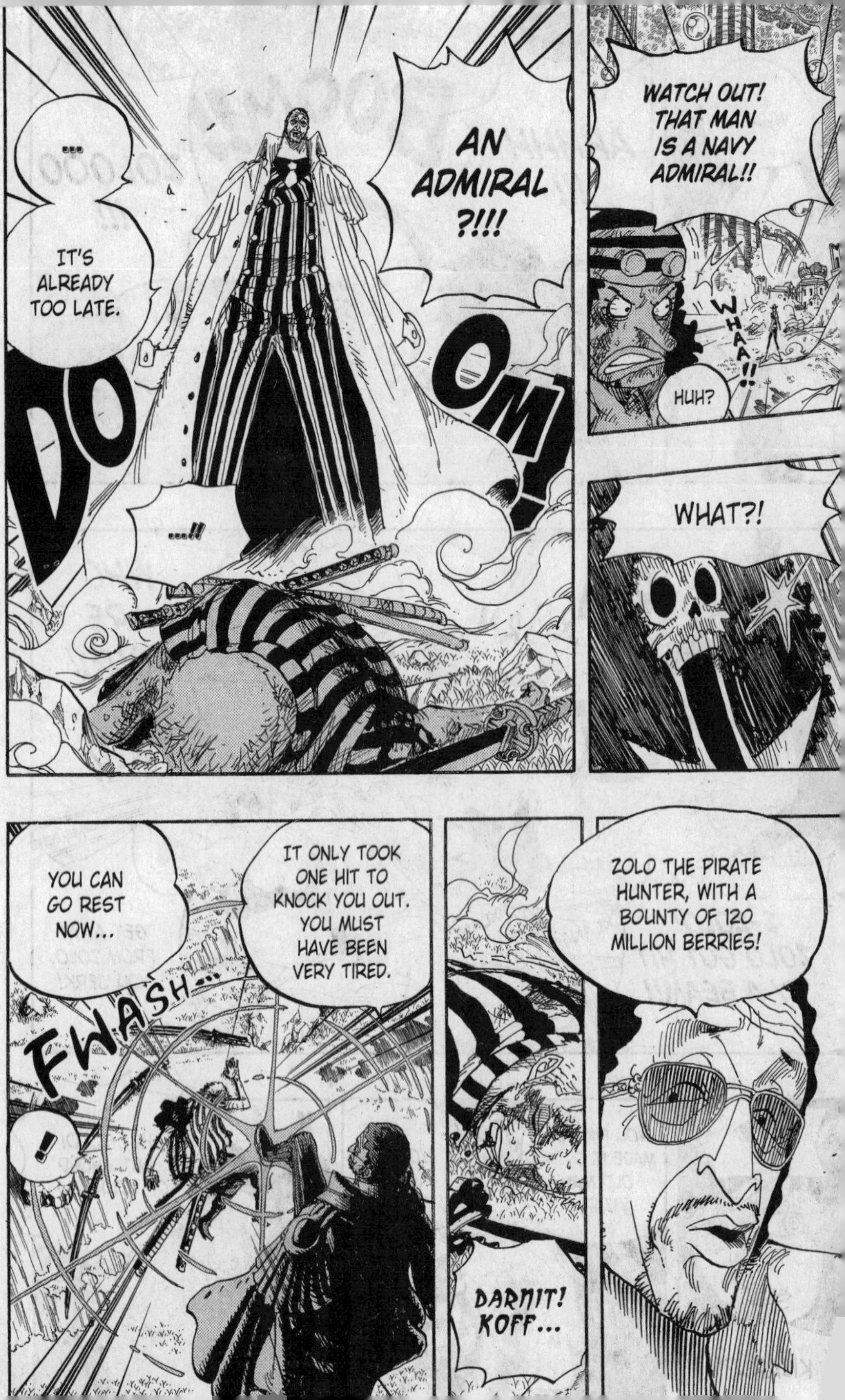
WATCH OUT! THAT MAN IS A NAVY ADMIRAL!!
WHAA!!
HUH?
WHAT?!
AN ADMIRAL ?!!!
...
IT'S ALREADY TOO LATE.
DOOM!
...!!
ZOLO THE PIRATE HUNTER, WITH A BOUNTY OF 120 MILLION BERRIES!
DARNIT! KOFF...
IT ONLY TOOK ONE HIT TO KNOCK YOU OUT. YOU MUST HAVE BEEN VERY TIRED.
YOU CAN GO REST NOW...
FWASH...
!

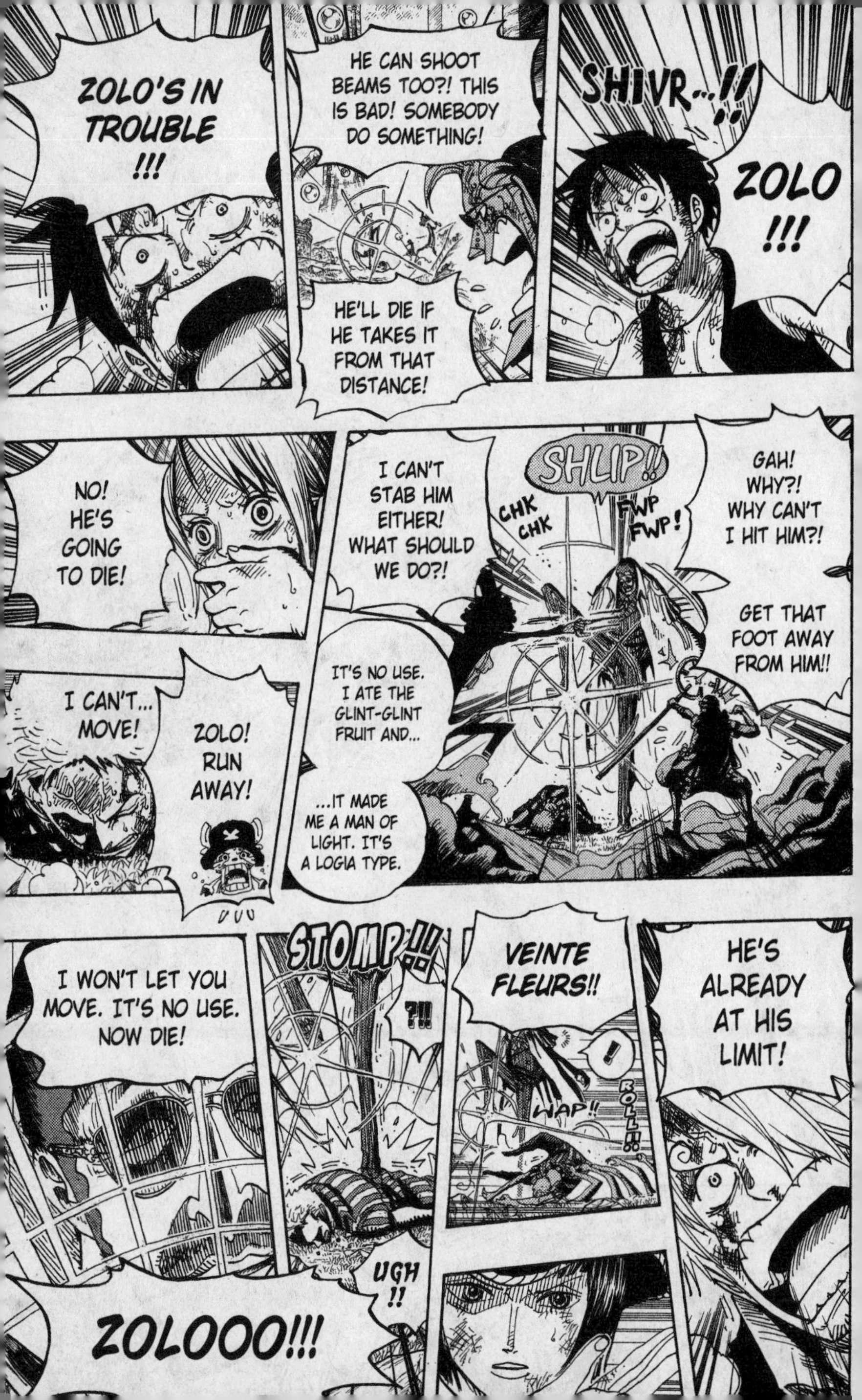

SHIVR...!!
ZOLO!!!
HE CAN SHOOT BEAMS TOO?! THIS IS BAD! SOMEBODY DO SOMETHING!
HE'LL DIE IF HE TAKES IT FROM THAT DISTANCE!
ZOLO'S IN TROUBLE!!!
GAH! WHY?! WHY CAN'T I HIT HIM?!
SHLIP!!
FWP FWP!
CHK CHK
I CAN'T STAB HIM EITHER! WHAT SHOULD WE DO?!
GET THAT FOOT AWAY FROM HIM!!
IT'S NO USE. I ATE THE GLINT-GLINT FRUIT AND...
...IT MADE ME A MAN OF LIGHT. IT'S A LOGIA TYPE.
NO! HE'S GOING TO DIE!
I CAN'T... MOVE!
ZOLO! RUN AWAY!
HE'S ALREADY AT HIS LIMIT!
VEINTE FLEURS!!
!
WAP!!
ROLL!!
STOMP!!
?!!
UGH!!
I WON'T LET YOU MOVE. IT'S NO USE. NOW DIE!
ZOLOOO!!!

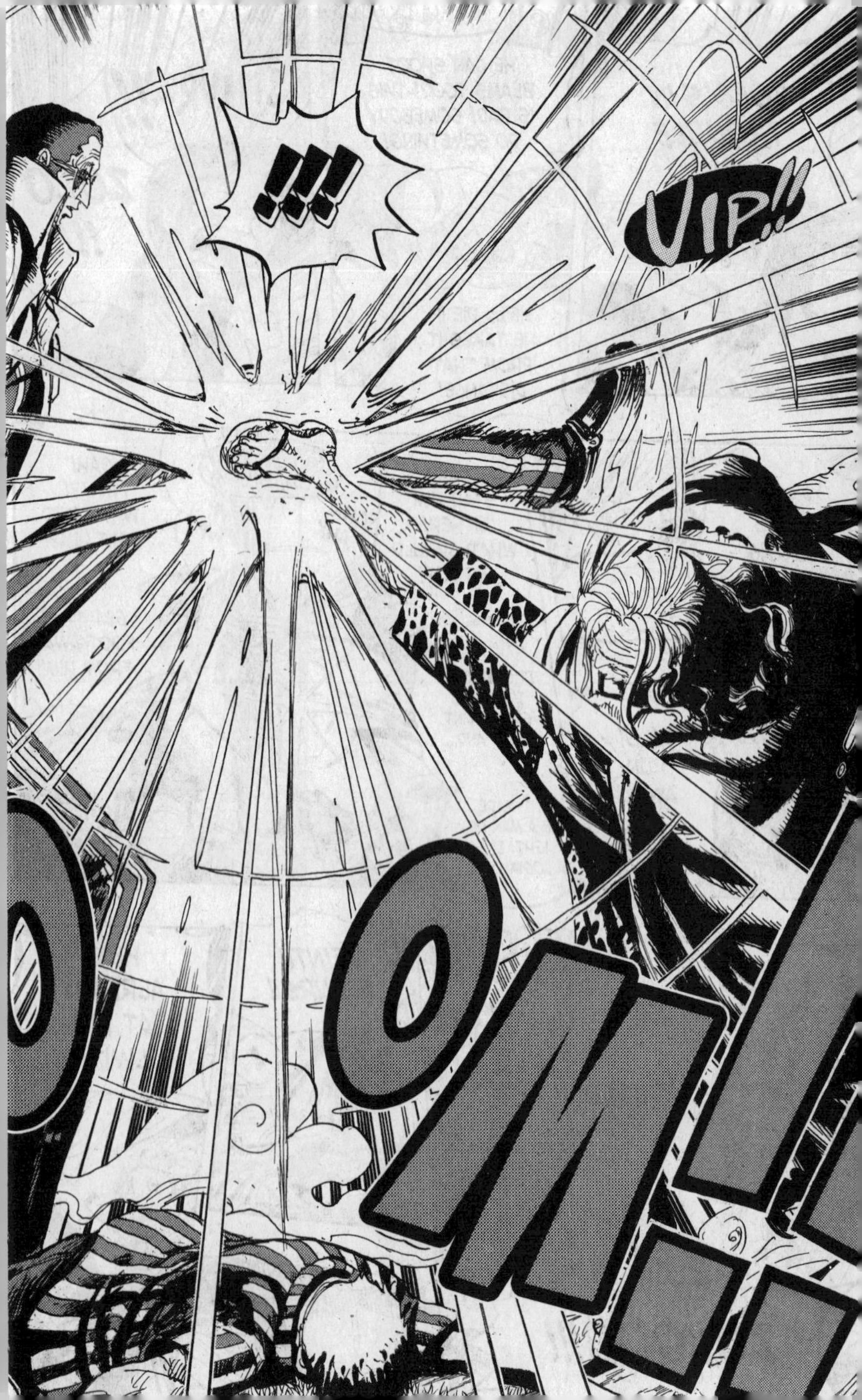
VIP!!
!!!
OOM!!

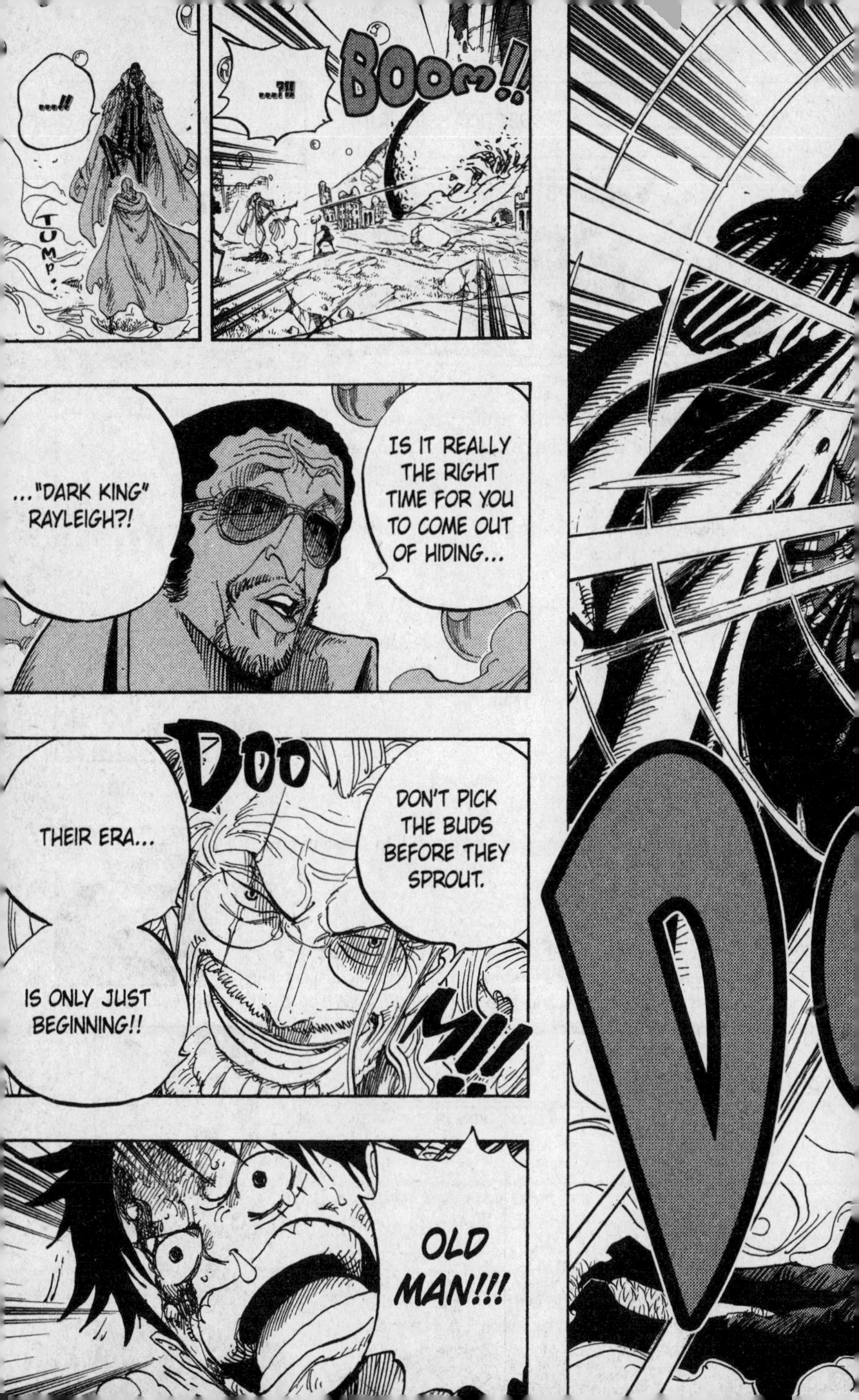
DO
...?!!
BOOM!!
...!!
TUMP
IS IT REALLY THE RIGHT TIME FOR YOU TO COME OUT OF HIDING...
..."DARK KING" RAYLEIGH?!
DOOM!!
DON'T PICK THE BUDS BEFORE THEY SPROUT.
THEIR ERA...
IS ONLY JUST BEGINNING!!
OLD MAN!!!

SBS Question Corner

CAPTAIN MAYUMI TANAKA'S QUESTION CORNER!!

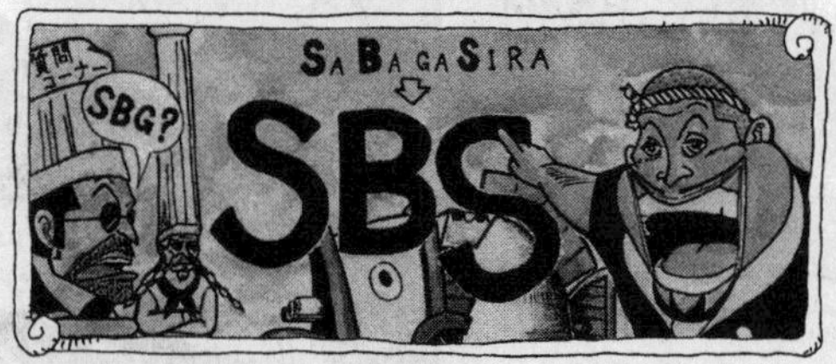

SBG?
SaBaGaSIRA
SBS

(Doromizu, Ibaraki)

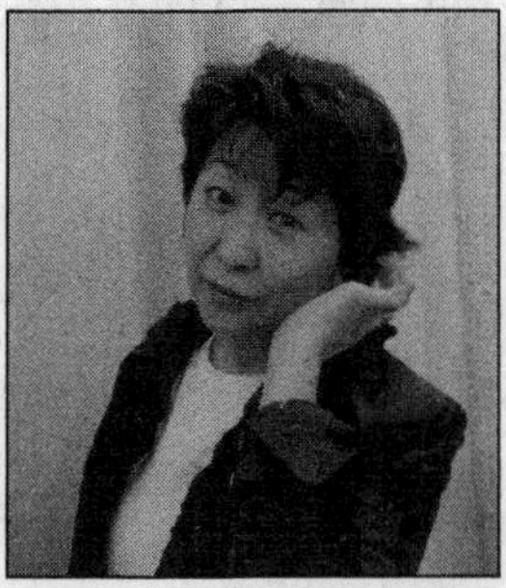

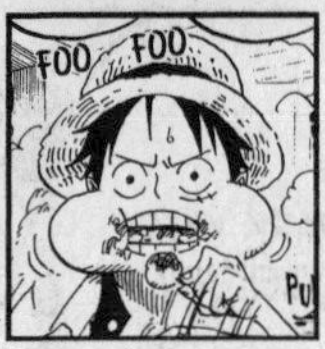

FOO FOO
PU

R: I see Luffy talk while he's eating very often... Do you eat while you're voice acting? I've always wondered about that!

--Ayako

T: I always go for realism! I'm always eating the stuff that Odacchi drew!

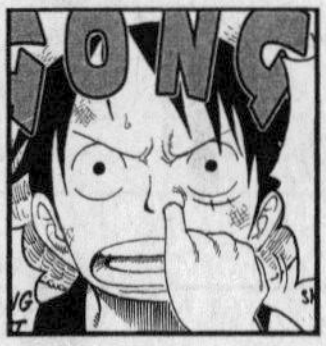

GONG

R: I enjoy watching the *One Piece* anime every week! When Luffy is talking while picking his nose, do you also imagine yourself picking your nose while saying it? Or do you actually pick your nose while you act?

--Hojirina III

T: I always go for realism! Always!

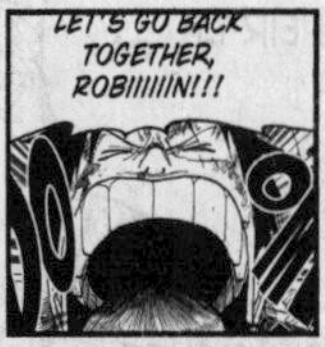

LET'S GO BACK TOGETHER, ROBIIIIIIN!!!

R: Luffy has a lot of lines that he shouts. Do those make you tired?!

--Calorie

T: I use up some strength every time I shout, and it makes me shorter. During the recording for the first episode of One Piece, I was 175 cm tall. But after ten years, I am now 147.5 cm.

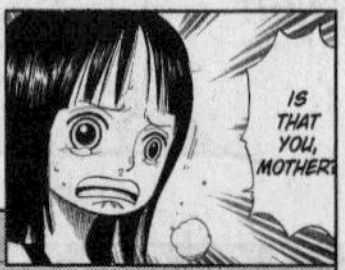

IS THAT YOU,

R: Please be my mom!

--High Socks in the Winter Last Me Three Days

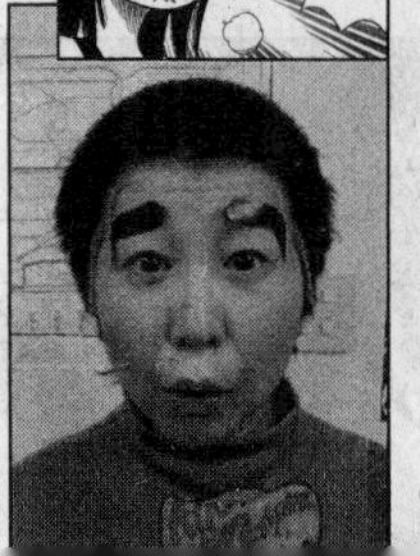

T: Sure. But I'll turn into your dad with a buzz cut sometimes. Are you sure you want that? (→)

O: What in the world are you doing?! Whatever! Look forward to the next Voice Actor Question Corner!

Chapter 512:
ZOLO, GONE

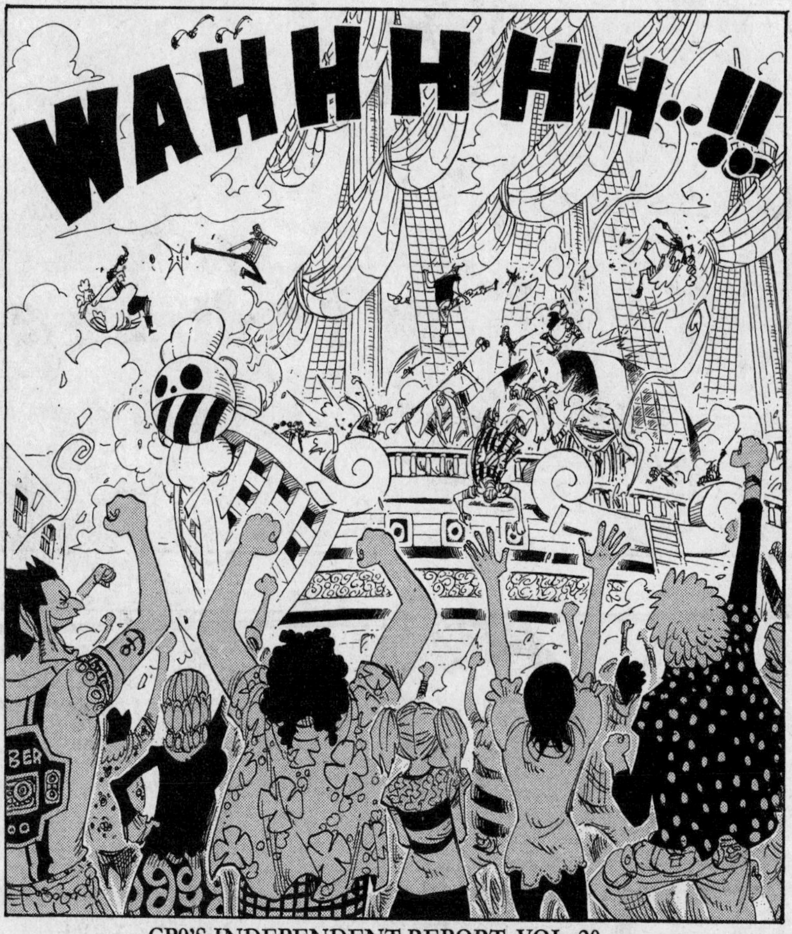
WAHHHHHH..!!

CP9'S INDEPENDENT REPORT, VOL. 20:
"THE HEROES NEVER SEEN BEFORE"

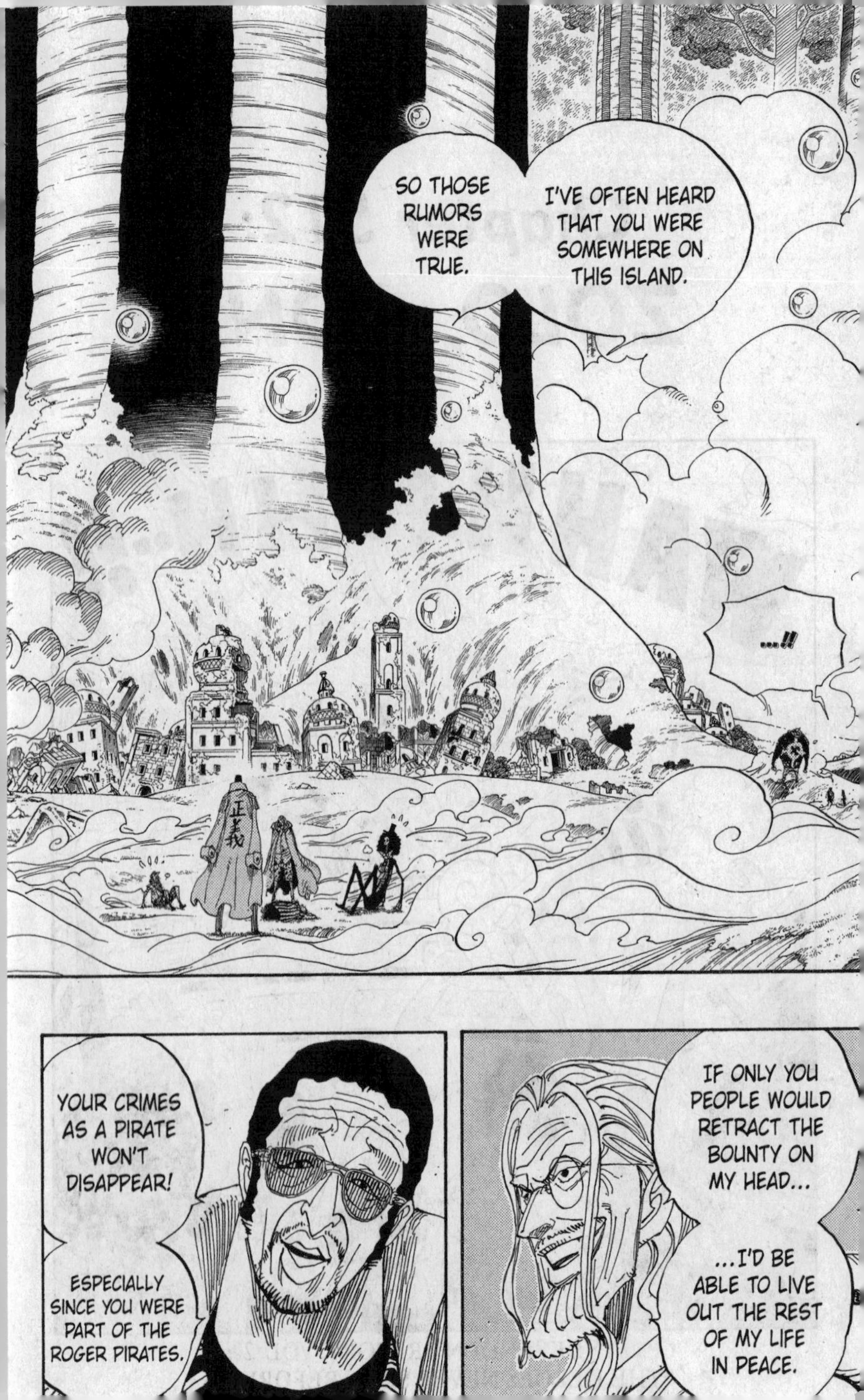
I'VE OFTEN HEARD THAT YOU WERE SOMEWHERE ON THIS ISLAND.
SO THOSE RUMORS WERE TRUE.
...!!
IF ONLY YOU PEOPLE WOULD RETRACT THE BOUNTY ON MY HEAD...
...I'D BE ABLE TO LIVE OUT THE REST OF MY LIFE IN PEACE.
YOUR CRIMES AS A PIRATE WON'T DISAPPEAR!
ESPECIALLY SINCE YOU WERE PART OF THE ROGER PIRATES.

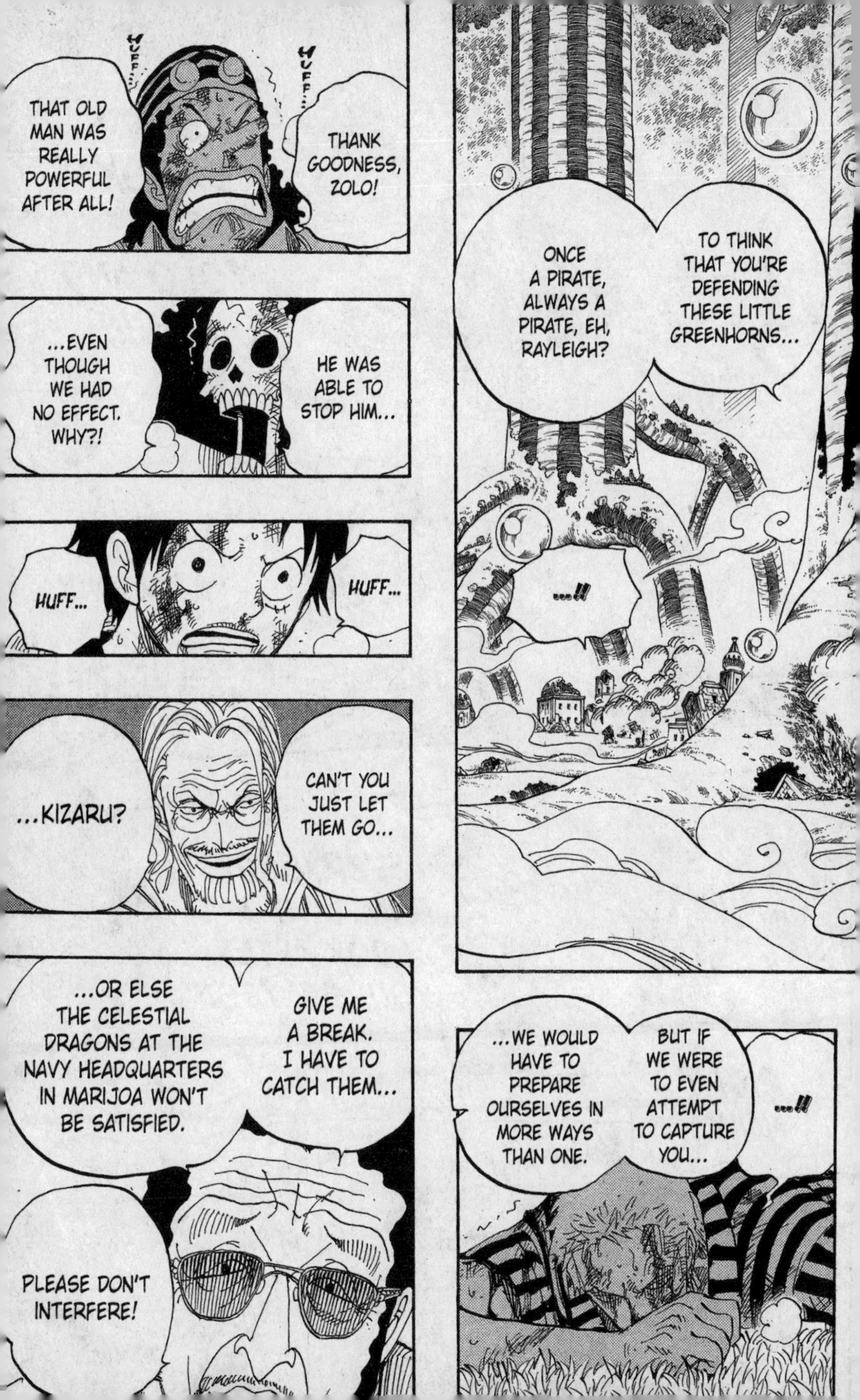
TO THINK THAT YOU'RE DEFENDING THESE LITTLE GREENHORNS...
ONCE A PIRATE, ALWAYS A PIRATE, EH, RAYLEIGH?
...!!
...!!
BUT IF WE WERE TO EVEN ATTEMPT TO CAPTURE YOU...
...WE WOULD HAVE TO PREPARE OURSELVES IN MORE WAYS THAN ONE.
HUFF...
HUFF...
THANK GOODNESS, ZOLO!
THAT OLD MAN WAS REALLY POWERFUL AFTER ALL!
HE WAS ABLE TO STOP HIM...
...EVEN THOUGH WE HAD NO EFFECT. WHY?!
HUFF...
HUFF...
CAN'T YOU JUST LET THEM GO...
...KIZARU?
GIVE ME A BREAK. I HAVE TO CATCH THEM...
...OR ELSE THE CELESTIAL DRAGONS AT THE NAVY HEADQUARTERS IN MARIJOA WON'T BE SATISFIED.
PLEASE DON'T INTERFERE!

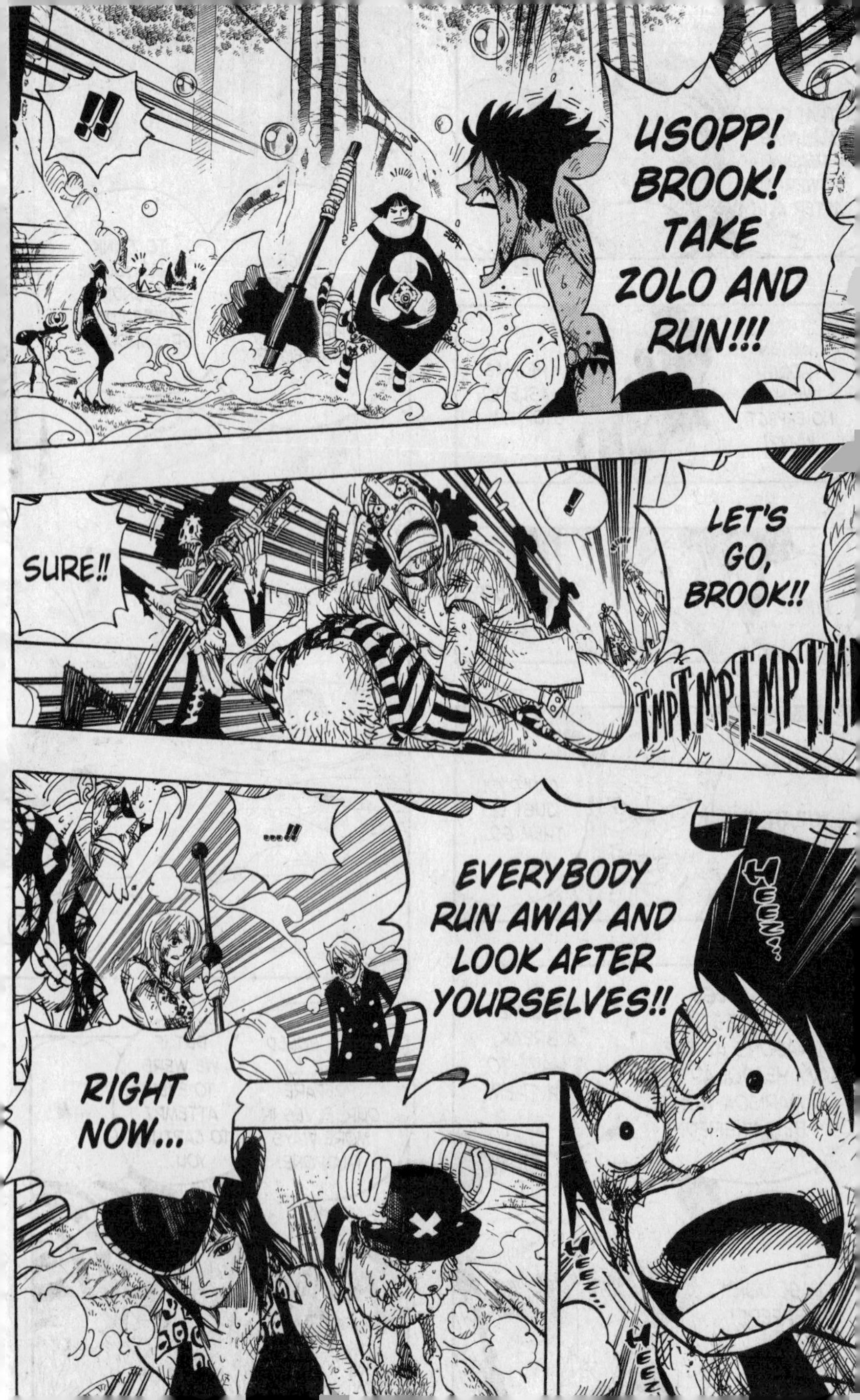

USOPP! BROOK! TAKE ZOLO AND RUN!!!
!!
LET'S GO, BROOK!!
!
SURE!!
TMP TMP TMP TMP
EVERYBODY RUN AWAY AND LOOK AFTER YOURSELVES!!
...!!
RIGHT NOW...

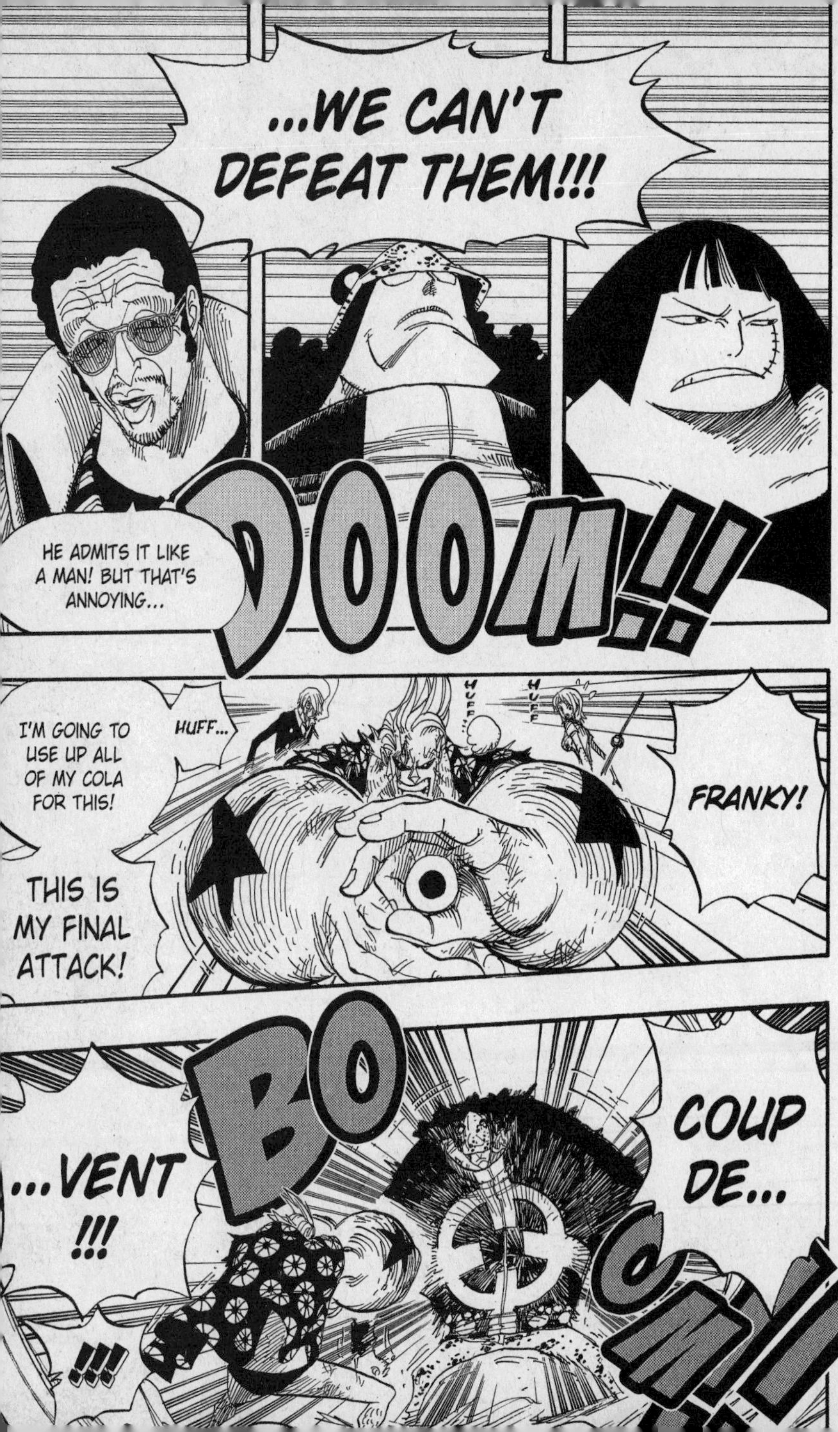
...WE CAN'T DEFEAT THEM!!!
HE ADMITS IT LIKE A MAN! BUT THAT'S ANNOYING...
DOOM!!
FRANKY!
HUFF
HUFF
HUFF...
I'M GOING TO USE UP ALL OF MY COLA FOR THIS!
THIS IS MY FINAL ATTACK!
COUP DE...
BOOM!!
...VENT !!!
!!!

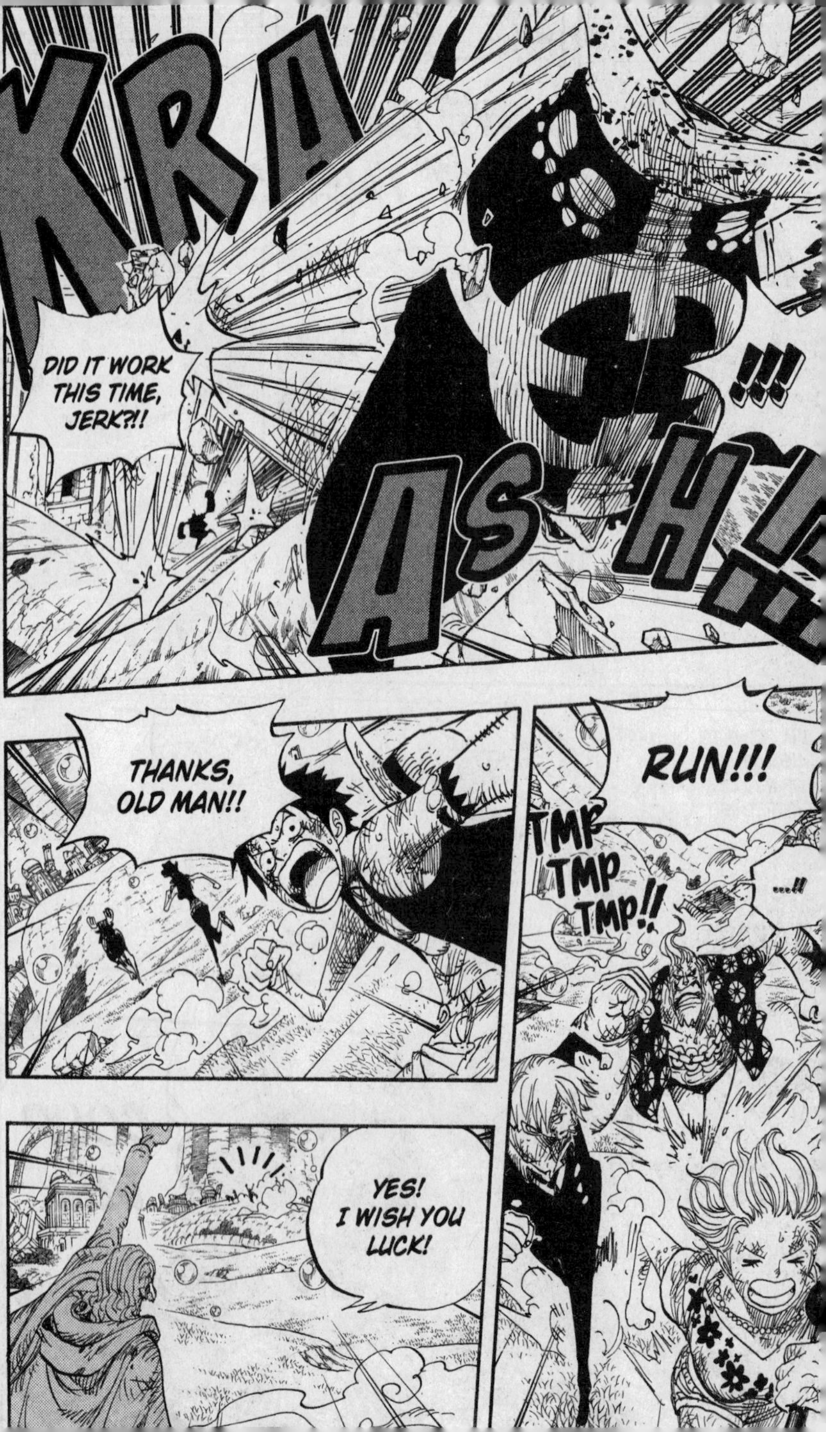
KRA
ASH!!!
DID IT WORK THIS TIME, JERK?!!
RUN!!!
TMP TMP TMP!!
...!!
THANKS, OLD MAN!!
YES! I WISH YOU LUCK!

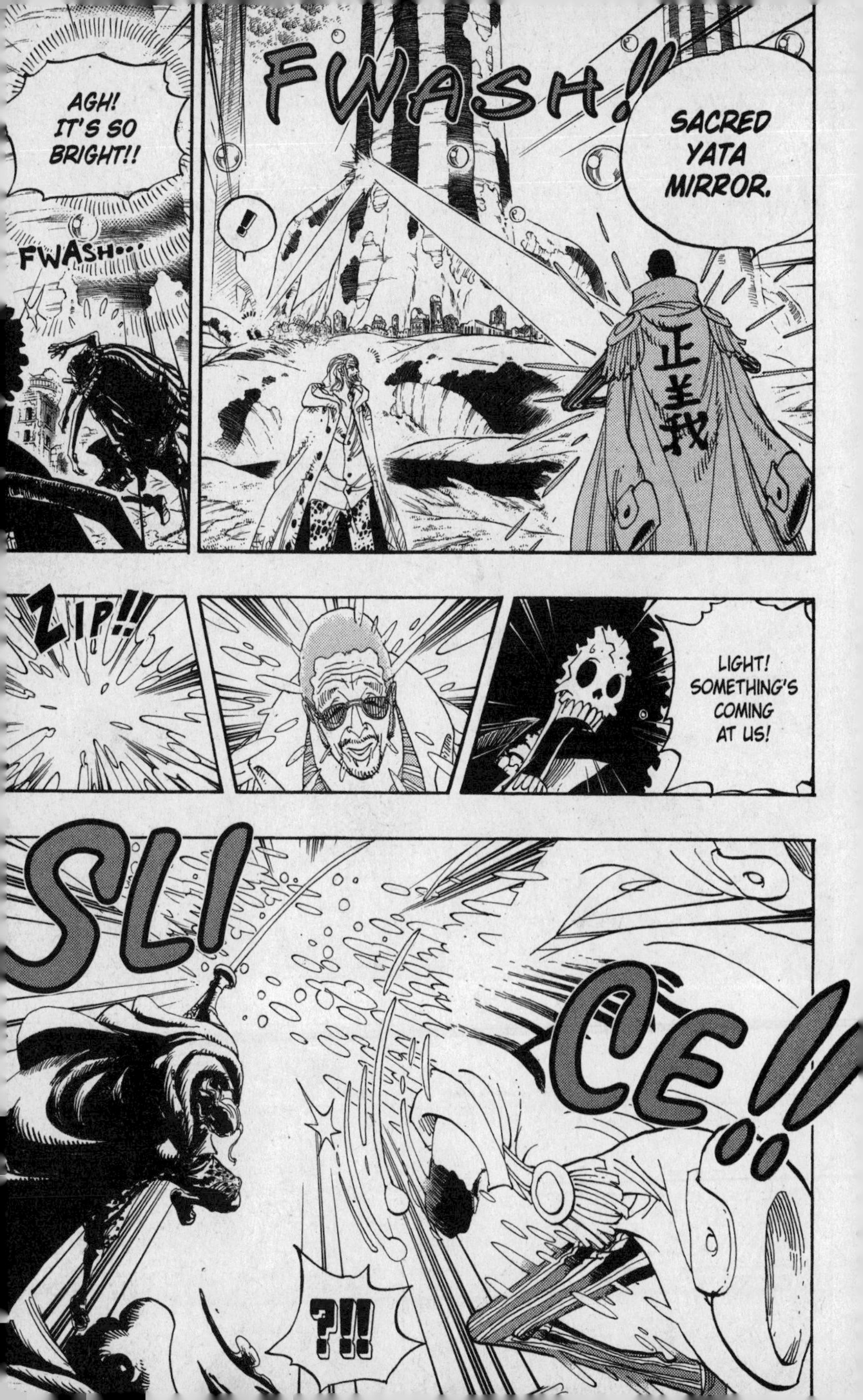
FWASH!!
SACRED YATA MIRROR.
!
AGH! IT'S SO BRIGHT!!
FWASH...
LIGHT! SOMETHING'S COMING AT US!
ZIP!!
SLICE!!
?!!

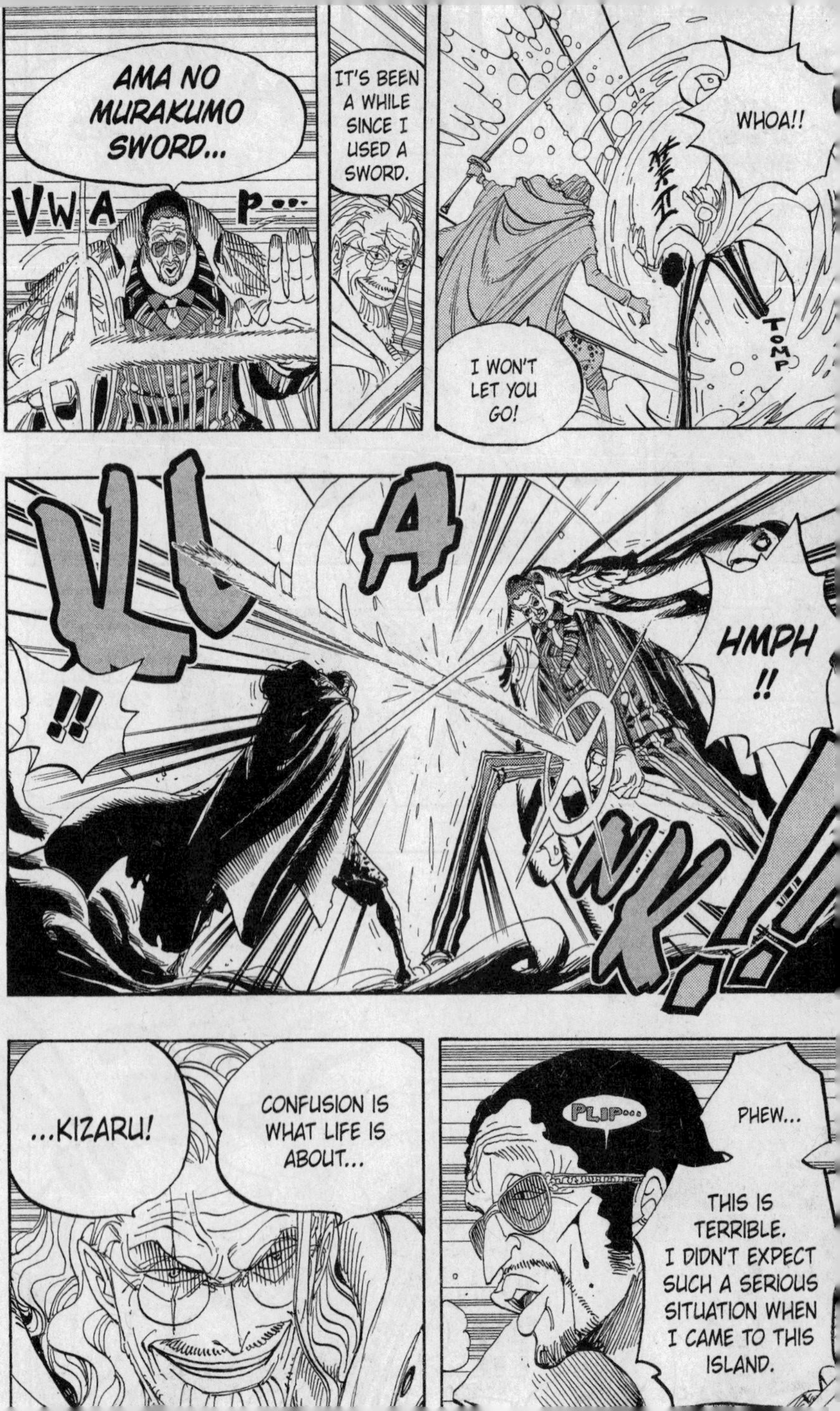
WHOA!!
TOMP
I WON'T LET YOU GO!
IT'S BEEN A WHILE SINCE I USED A SWORD.
AMA NO MURAKUMO SWORD...
VWAP...
HMPH!!
!!
PHEW...
PLIP...
THIS IS TERRIBLE. I DIDN'T EXPECT SUCH A SERIOUS SITUATION WHEN I CAME TO THIS ISLAND.
CONFUSION IS WHAT LIFE IS ABOUT...
...KIZARU!

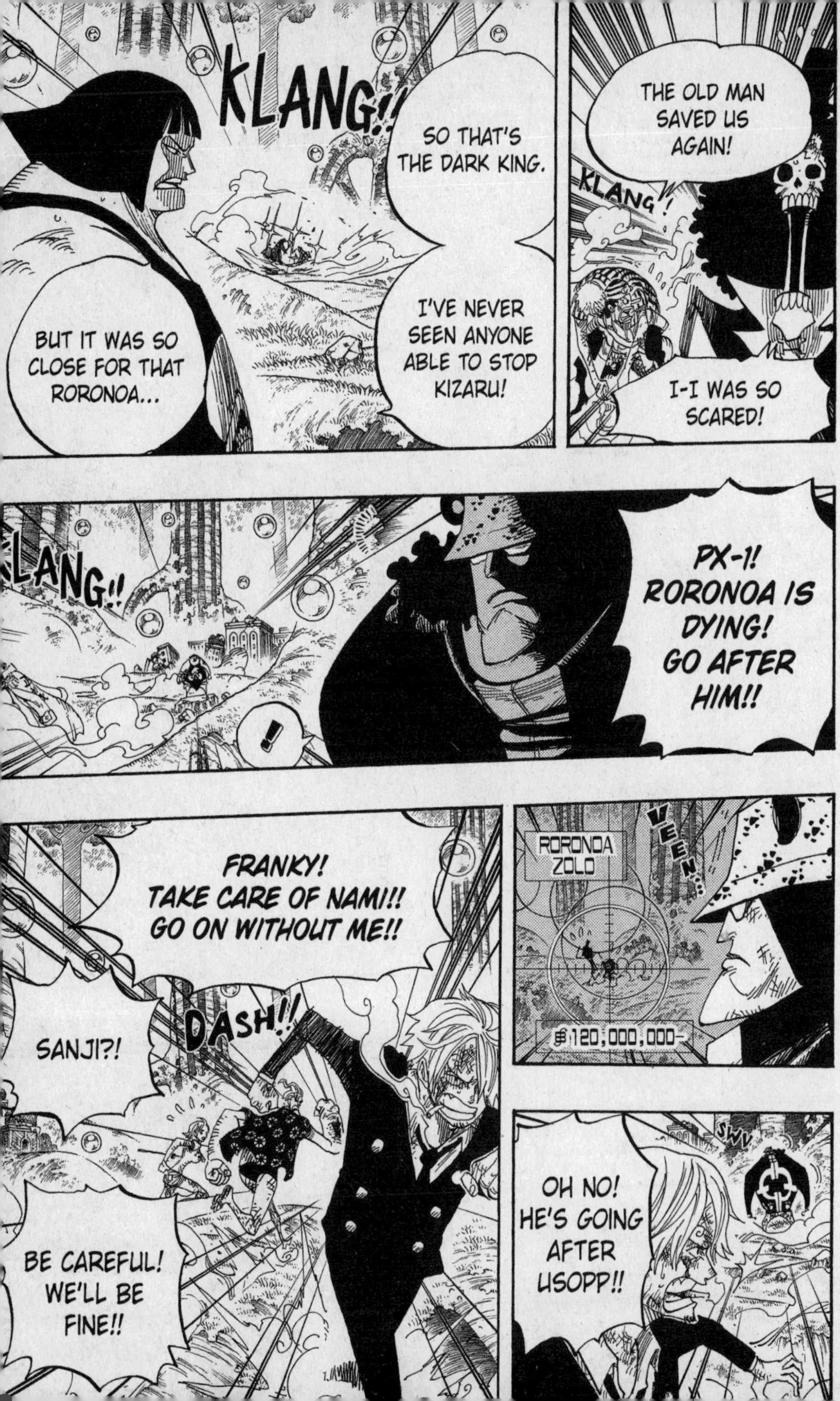
THE OLD MAN SAVED US AGAIN!
KLANG!
I-I WAS SO SCARED!
SO THAT'S THE DARK KING.
KLANG!!
I'VE NEVER SEEN ANYONE ABLE TO STOP KIZARU!
BUT IT WAS SO CLOSE FOR THAT RORONOA...
PX-1! RORONOA IS DYING! GO AFTER HIM!!
!
KLANG!!
VEEN...
RORONOA ZOLO
฿120,000,000-
SWV
OH NO! HE'S GOING AFTER USOPP!!
FRANKY! TAKE CARE OF NAMI!! GO ON WITHOUT ME!!
DASH!!
SANJI?!
BE CAREFUL! WE'LL BE FINE!!

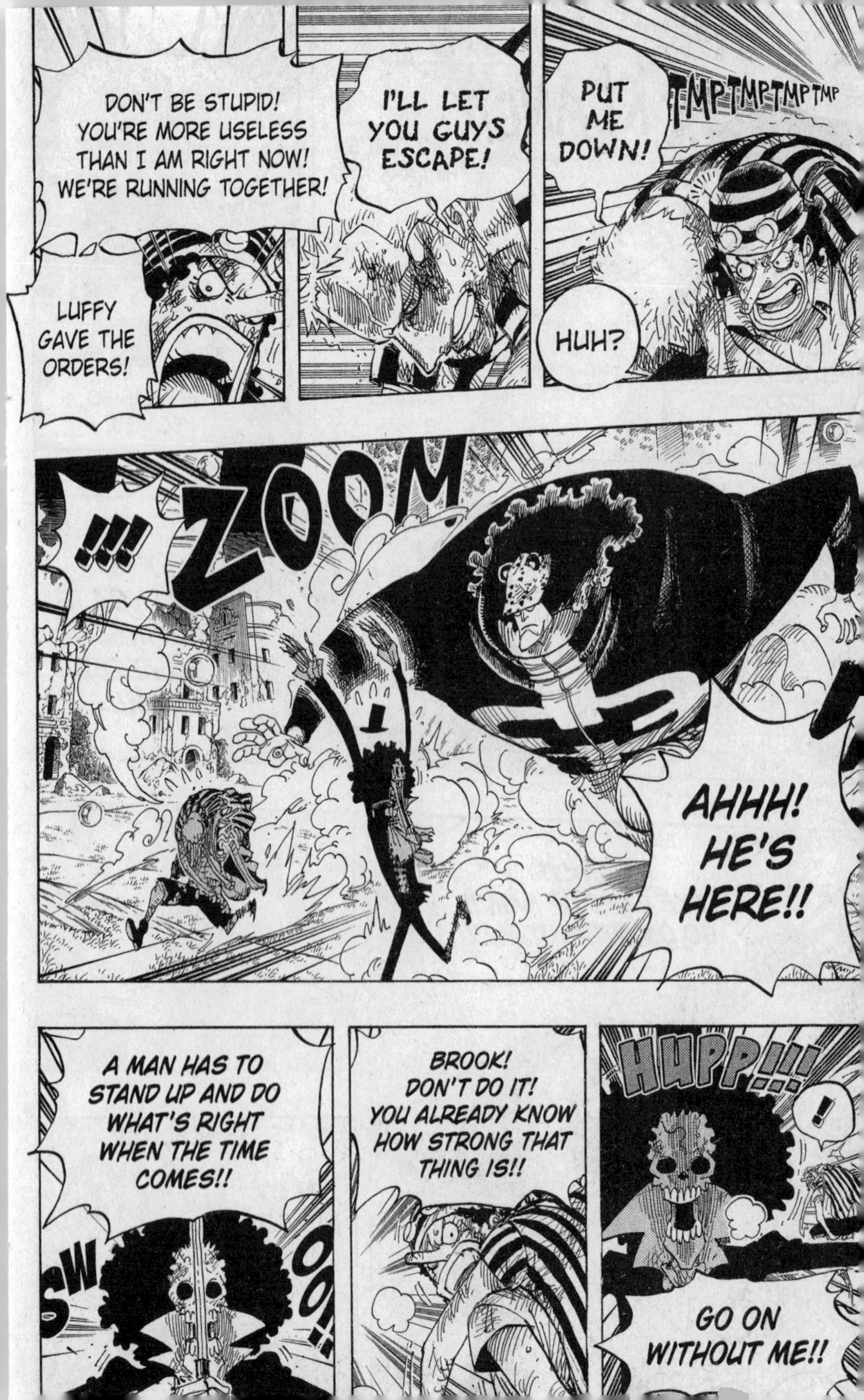
PUT ME DOWN!
TMPTMPTMPTMP
HUH?
I'LL LET YOU GUYS ESCAPE!
DON'T BE STUPID! YOU'RE MORE USELESS THAN I AM RIGHT NOW! WE'RE RUNNING TOGETHER!
LUFFY GAVE THE ORDERS!
ZOOM
!!!
AHHH! HE'S HERE!!
HUPP!!!
!
GO ON WITHOUT ME!!
BROOK! DON'T DO IT! YOU ALREADY KNOW HOW STRONG THAT THING IS!!
A MAN HAS TO STAND UP AND DO WHAT'S RIGHT WHEN THE TIME COMES!!
SW
OO!!

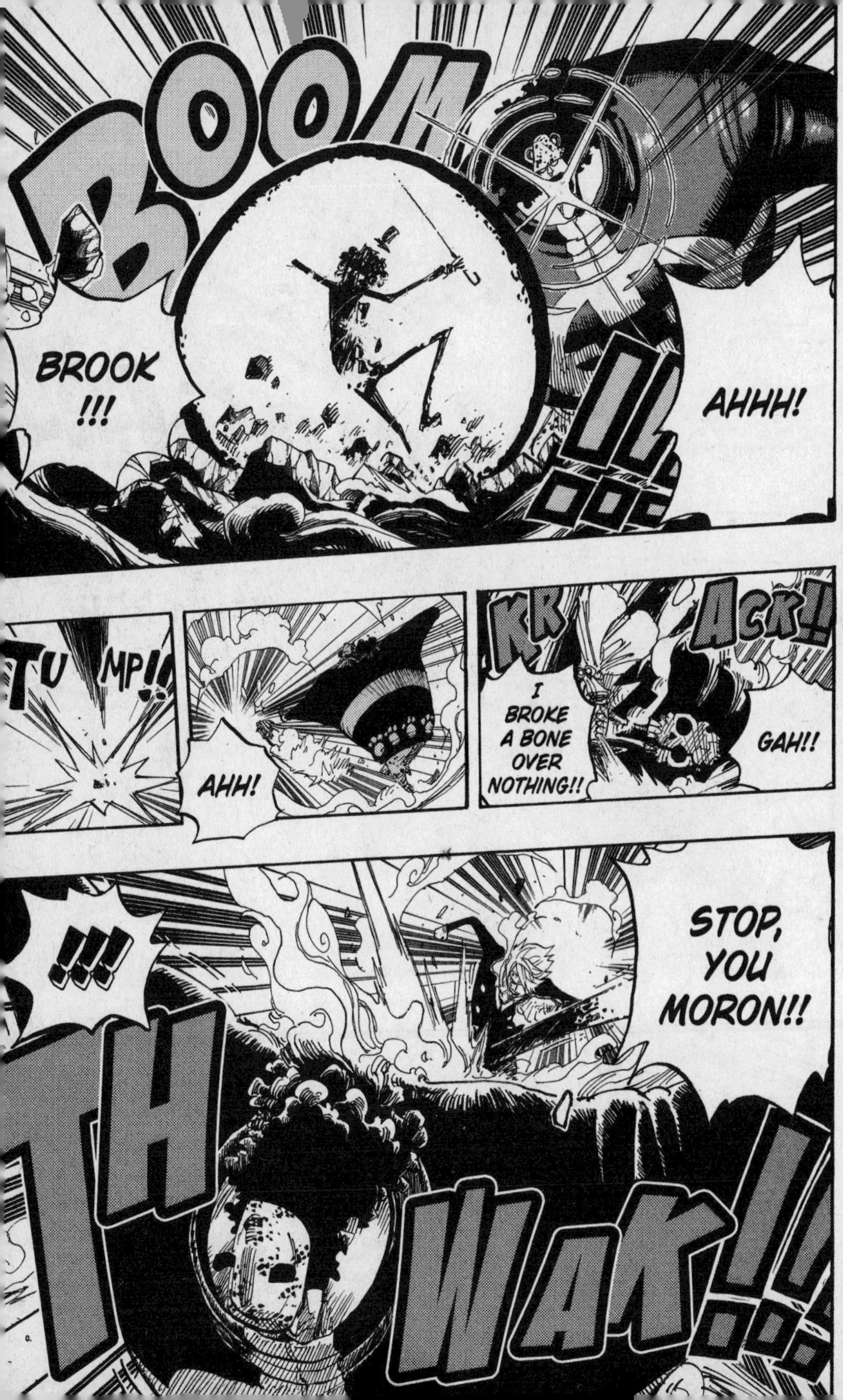
BOOM
AHHH!
BROOK !!!
KR ACK!!
GAH!!
I BROKE A BONE OVER NOTHING!!
AHH!
TU MP!!
STOP, YOU MORON!!
!!!
TH WAK!!

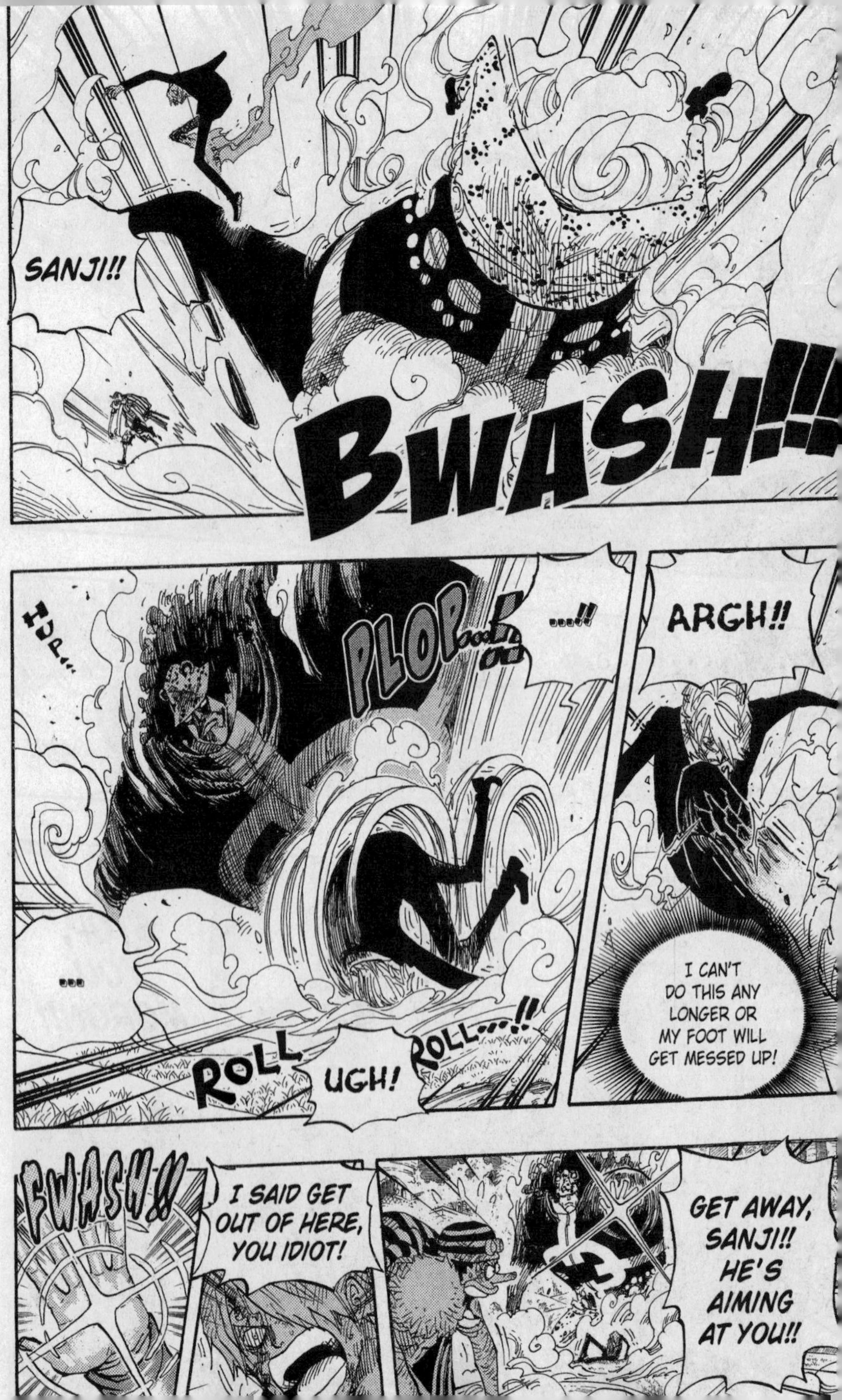
SANJI!!
BWASH!!!
ARGH!!
I CAN'T DO THIS ANY LONGER OR MY FOOT WILL GET MESSED UP!
...!!
PLOP...!
HUP...
...
ROLL...!!
UGH!
ROLL
GET AWAY, SANJI!! HE'S AIMING AT YOU!!
I SAID GET OUT OF HERE, YOU IDIOT!
FWASH!!

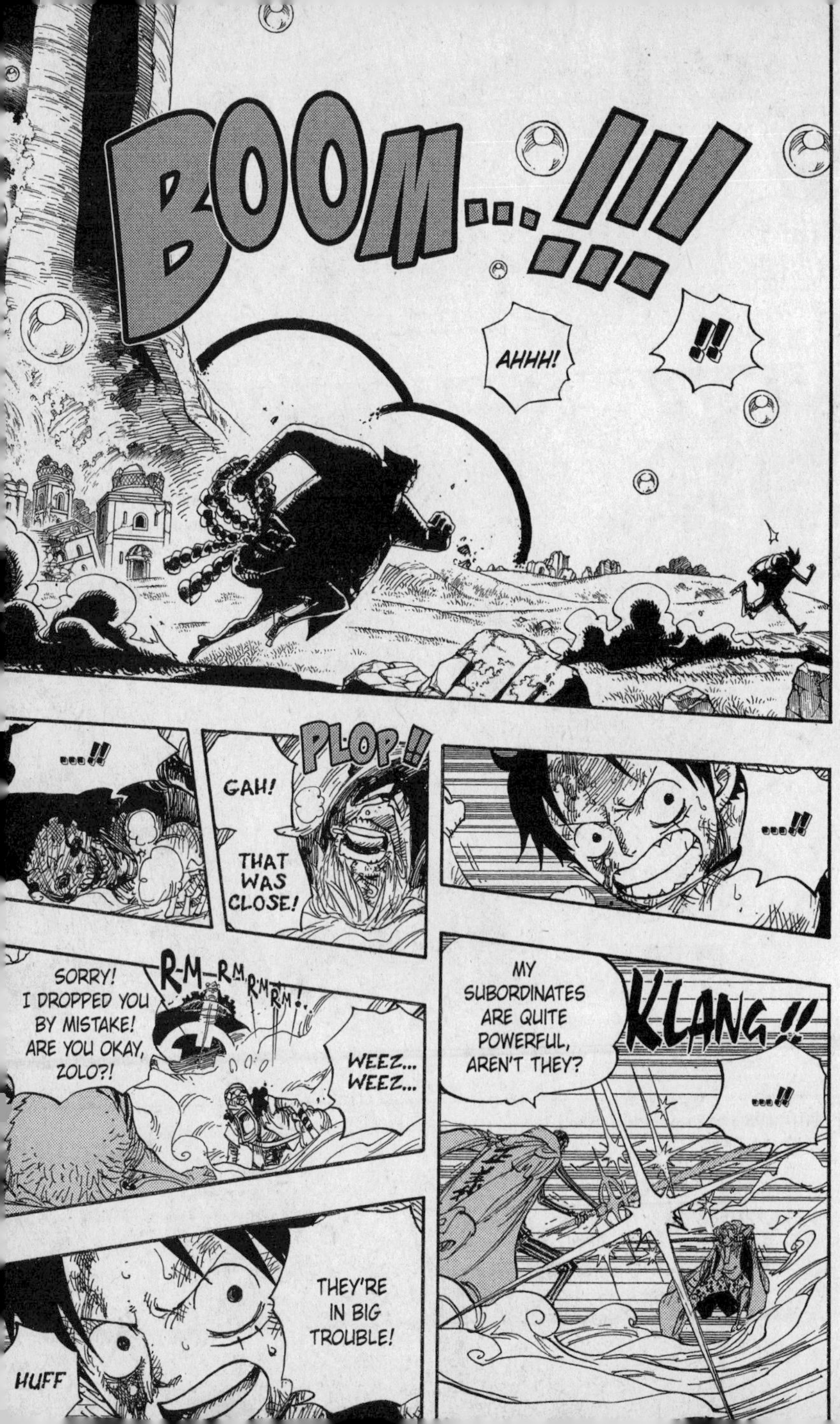
BOOM...!!!...
!!
AHHH!
...!!
PLOP!!
GAH!
THAT WAS CLOSE!
...!!
KLANG!!
MY SUBORDINATES ARE QUITE POWERFUL, AREN'T THEY?
...!!
R-M R-M R-M R-M
WEEZ... WEEZ...
SORRY! I DROPPED YOU BY MISTAKE! ARE YOU OKAY, ZOLO?!
THEY'RE IN BIG TROUBLE!
HUFF

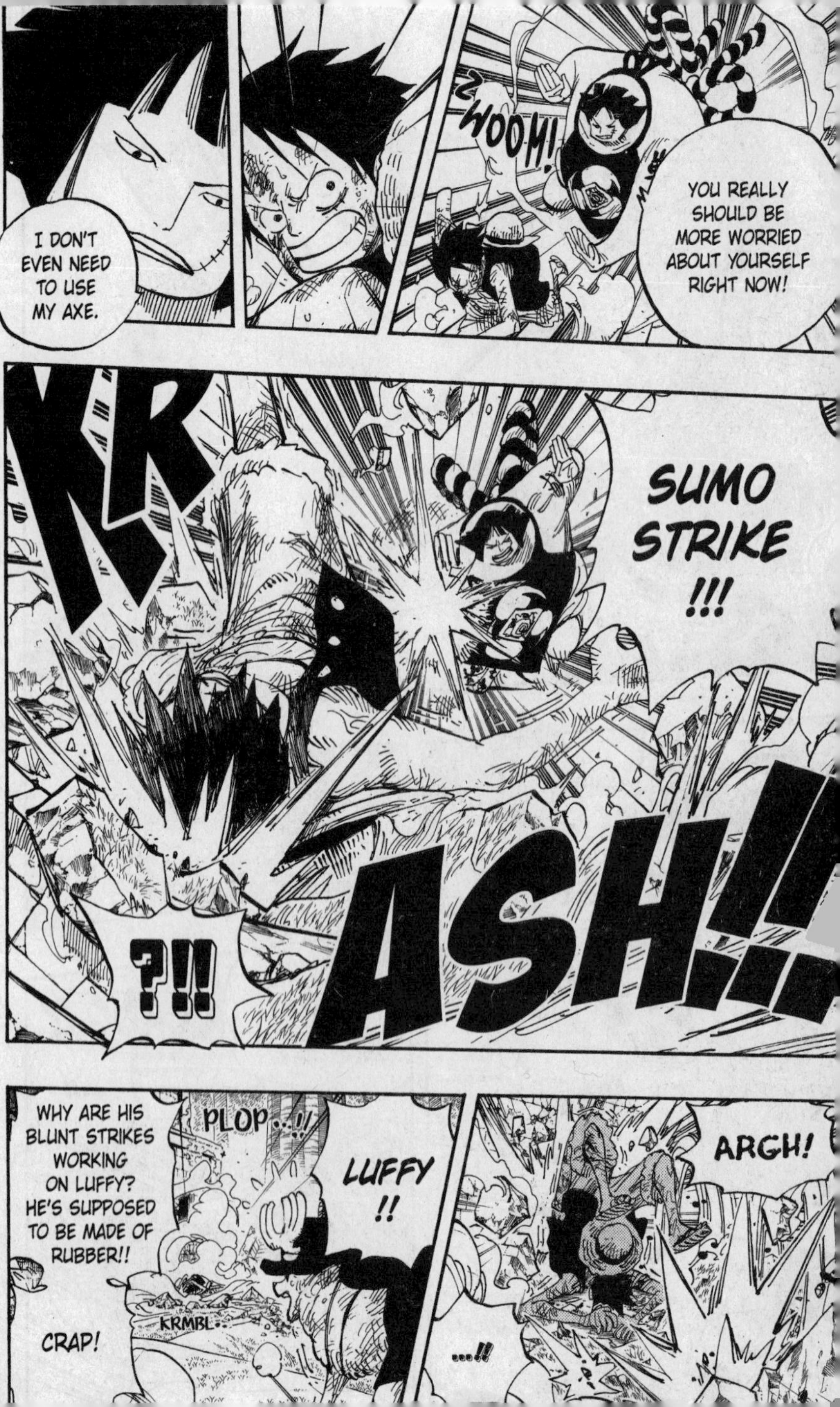
WOOM!
YOU REALLY SHOULD BE MORE WORRIED ABOUT YOURSELF RIGHT NOW!
I DON'T EVEN NEED TO USE MY AXE.
SUMO STRIKE !!!
KR
ASH!!
?!!
ARGH!
...!!
LUFFY !!
PLOP...!!
WHY ARE HIS BLUNT STRIKES WORKING ON LUFFY? HE'S SUPPOSED TO BE MADE OF RUBBER!!
KRMBL..
CRAP!

SANJI!!

?!

STOP IT!

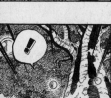

CHOPPER, WAIT!!

NO!! EVERYONE'S GOING TO DIE!!!

TMP. TMP. TMP.!!

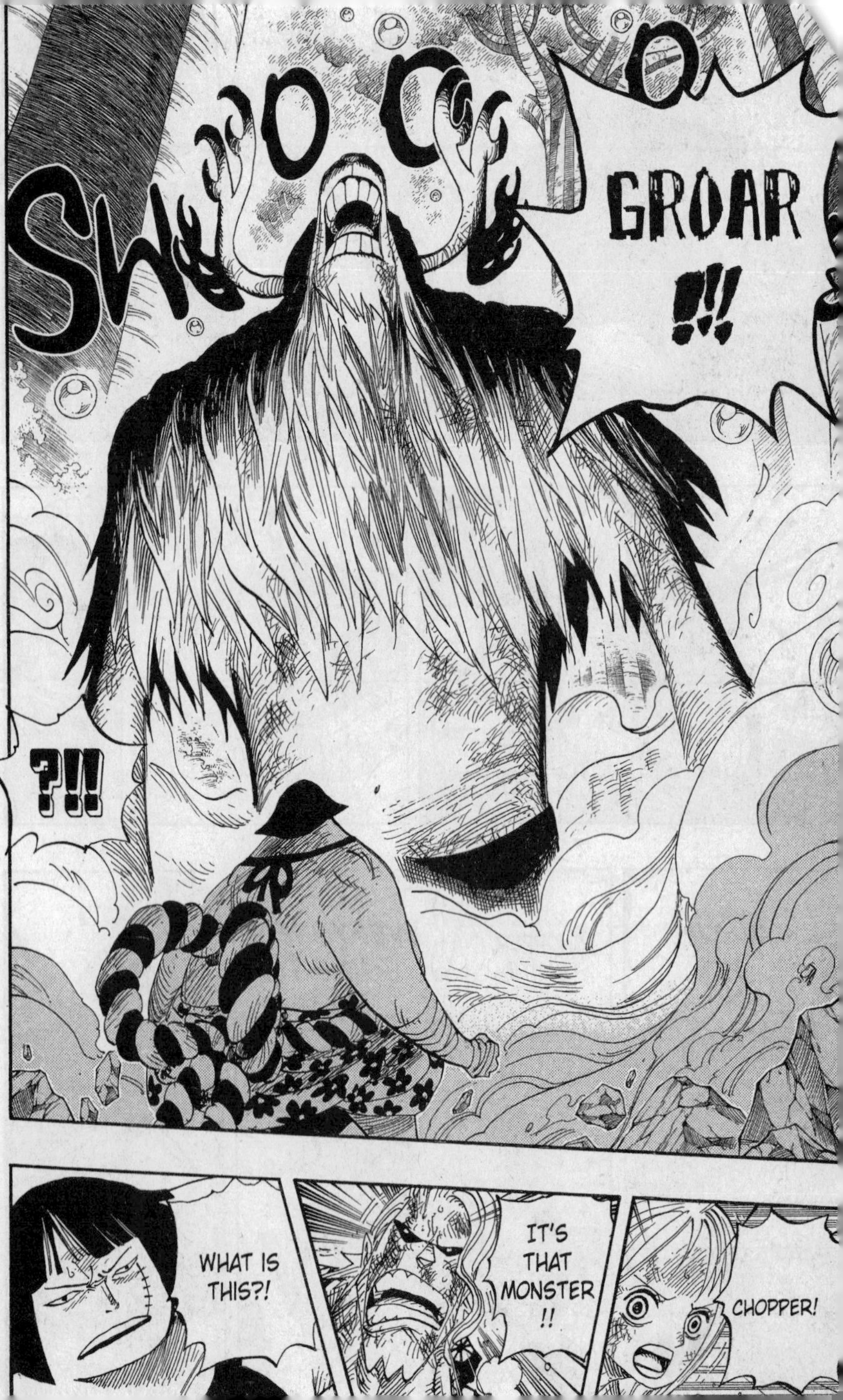
GROAR !!!
?!!
CHOPPER!
IT'S THAT MONSTER !!
WHAT IS THIS?!

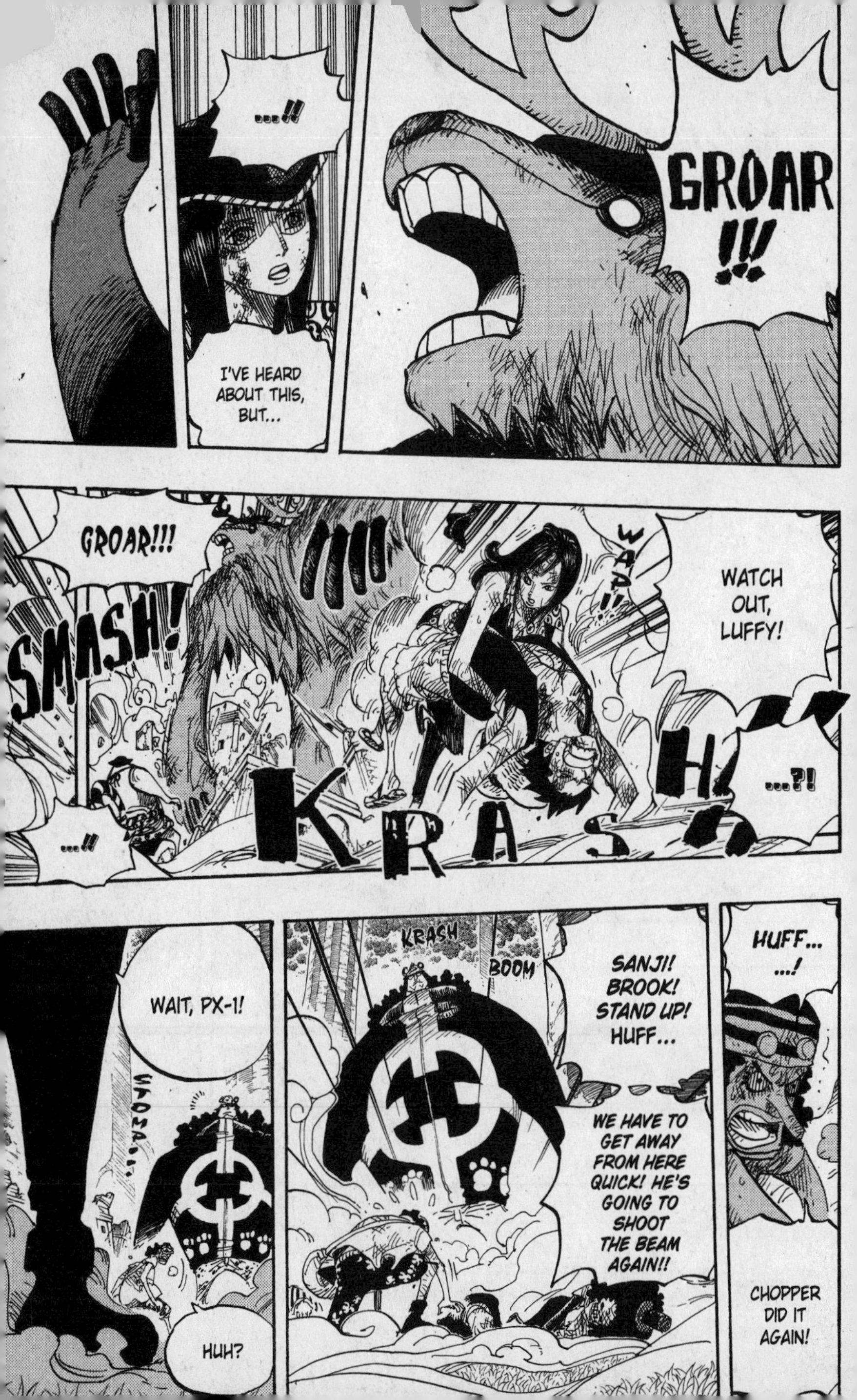
GROAR!!!
...!!
I'VE HEARD ABOUT THIS, BUT...
WATCH OUT, LUFFY!
WAP!!
...?!
KRASH
SMASH!
GROAR!!!
...!!
HUFF... ...!
CHOPPER DID IT AGAIN!
SANJI! BROOK! STAND UP! HUFF...
WE HAVE TO GET AWAY FROM HERE QUICK! HE'S GOING TO SHOOT THE BEAM AGAIN!!
BOOM
KRASH
WAIT, PX-1!
STOMP...
HUH?

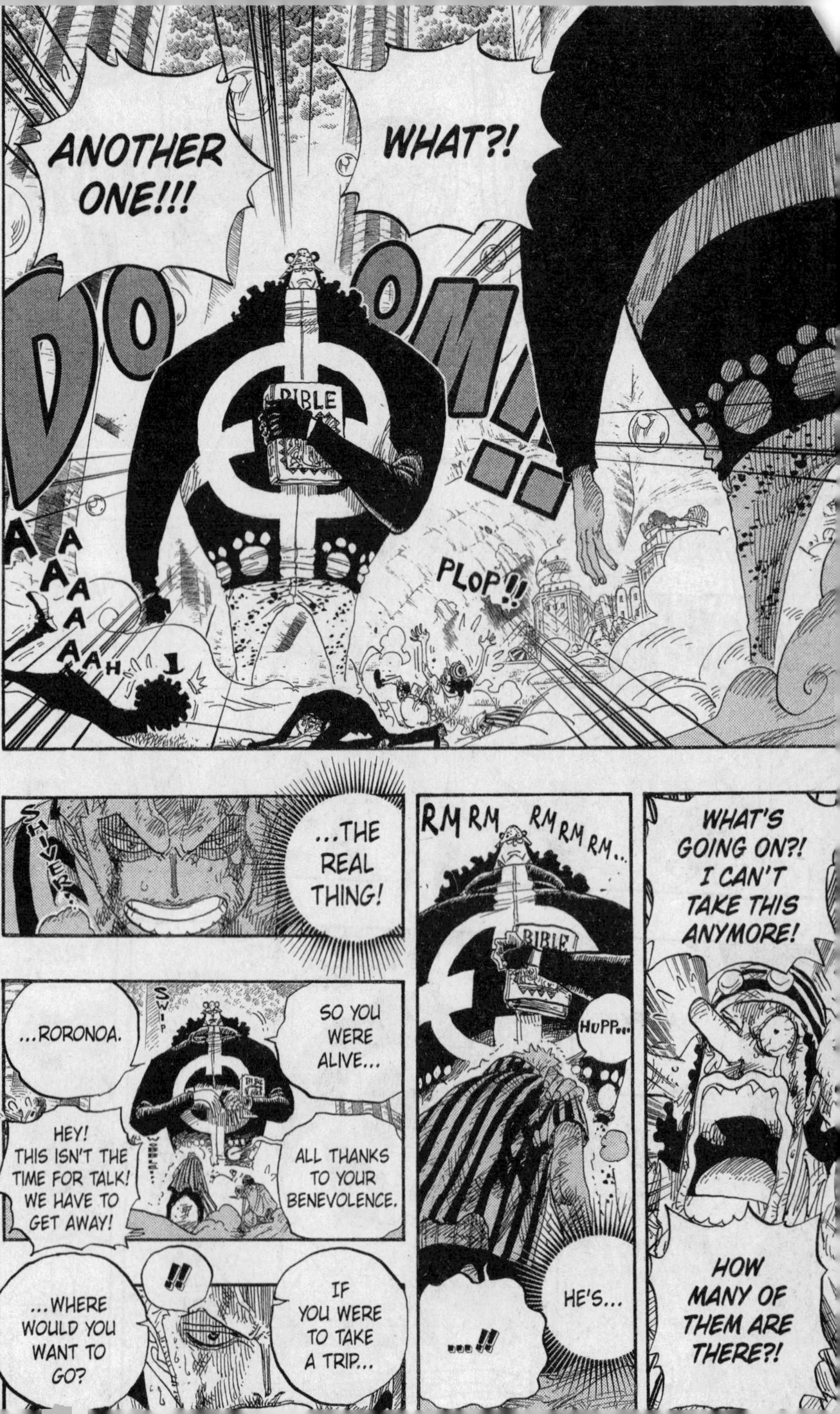
WHAT?!
ANOTHER ONE!!!
DOOM!!
PLOP!!
AAAAAAAAH
WHAT'S GOING ON?! I CAN'T TAKE THIS ANYMORE!
HOW MANY OF THEM ARE THERE?!
RM RM RM RM RM...
HUPP...
HE'S...
...!!
SHIVER
...THE REAL THING!
SWIP
...RORONOA.
SO YOU WERE ALIVE...
ALL THANKS TO YOUR BENEVOLENCE.
HEY! THIS ISN'T THE TIME FOR TALK! WE HAVE TO GET AWAY!
IF YOU WERE TO TAKE A TRIP...
!!
...WHERE WOULD YOU WANT TO GO?

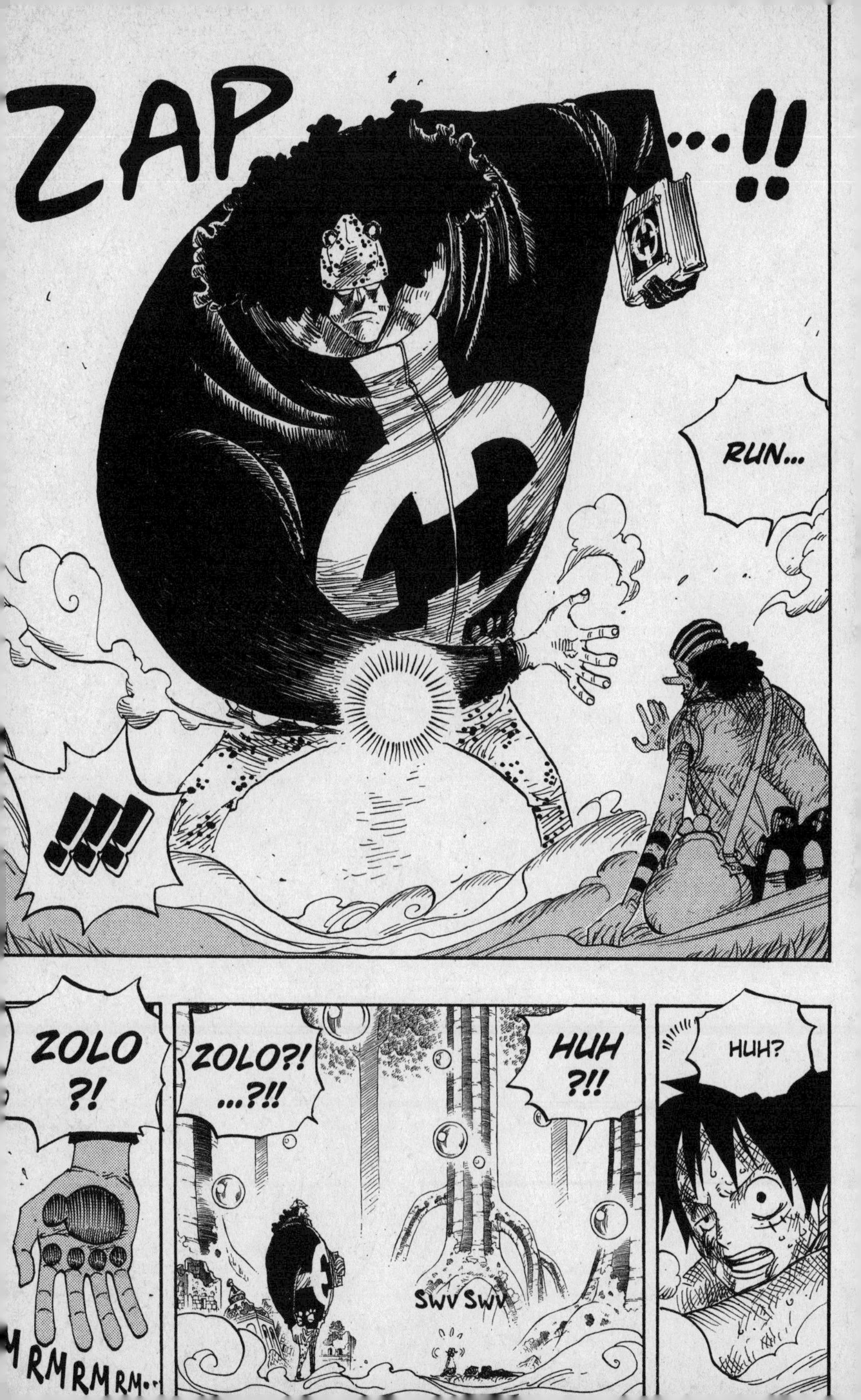

ZAP...!!
RUN...
!!!
HUH?
HUH ?!!
ZOLO?! ...?!!
SWV SWV
ZOLO ?!
RMRMRMRM...

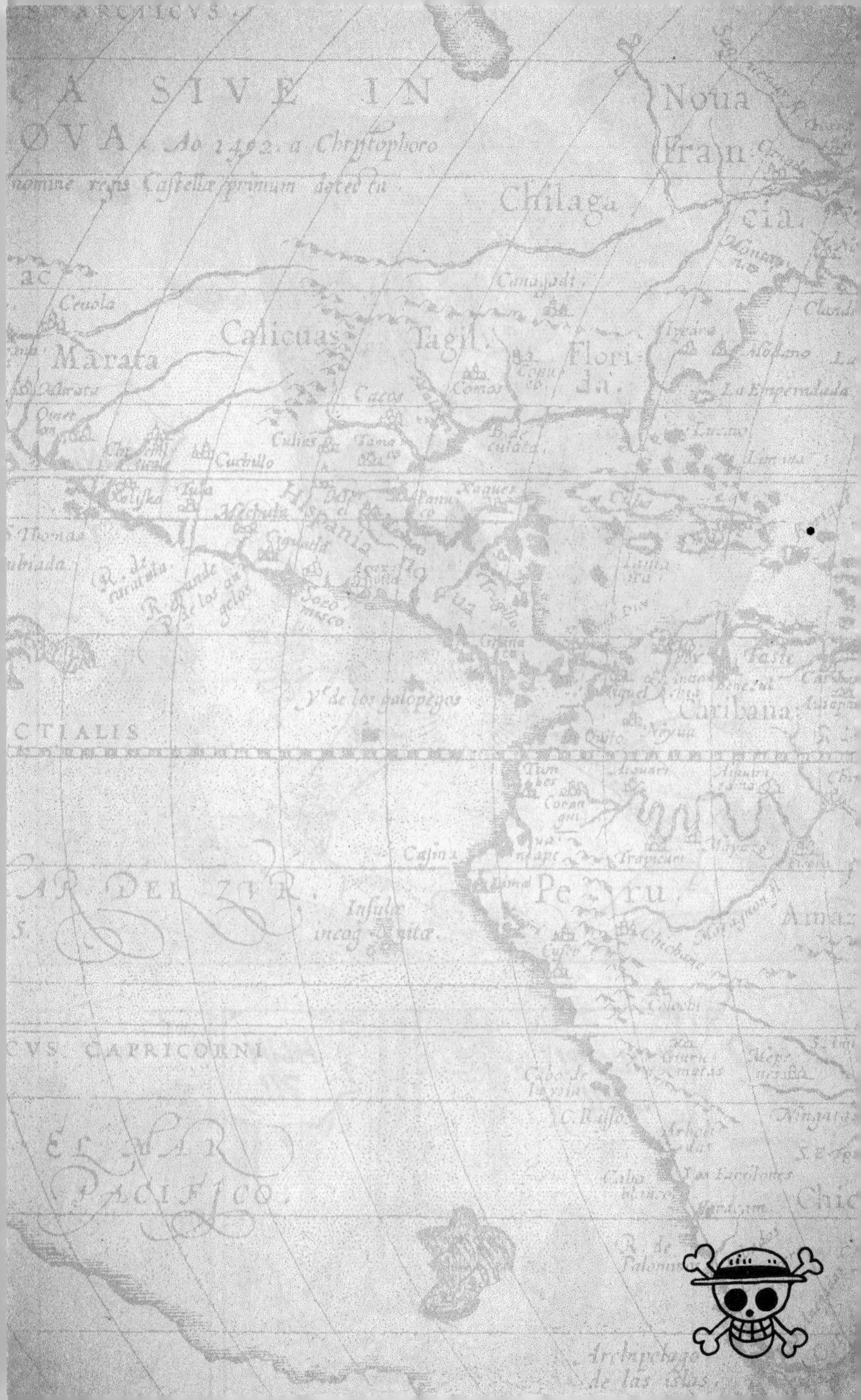

A SIVE IN
OVA, Ao 1492. a Chrystophoro
nomine regis Castellæ primum detec̄ tu

ac

Ceuola

Marata   Calicuas   Tagil.   Flori-

Odresta   da.
Onci   Culies   Tama   cudata.
on   Bu
Cuchillo

Rolisha   Tota   Michula   Bel-   Panu
Hispania

Thomas   Guibald   Cibola
ubiada   R. de   Mexo
              cannata.   mueo
              R. grande
              a los as
              Tolot

Y. de los galopegos

CTIALIS

AR DEL ZVR.   Insulæ
                    incoḡ nita.

CVS CAPRICORNI

EL MAR
PACIFICO.

Noua

Fran-
                                      cia.

Chilaga

Camapedi

La Emperluda

Lucius

Cuban

Nova

Taste
Caribana

Peru.   Amaz

Cabo de
Trystan

I.C. Basso

Cabo   Las Escobones
blanco   Chic

R. de
Paloma

Archipelago
de las islas

"Excuse me" or "Excuse me, I need to get off."
Whenever people say these things they take a
certain stance. I call it the "God Fist." It's a sort
of qigong pose that's been passed down from
ancient China. The qi that emits from the hand
causes the sea of people to part, like how Moses
did the waters, creating a bright, shining path...

Volume 53 starts now!

— Eiichiro Oda, 2009

ARCTICVS.

CA SIVE IN
QVA, Ao 1492 a Christophoro
nomine regis Castellæ primum detecta.

Noua
Fran
cia.

Chilaga

Canagua

Marata
Cewola
Marata
Quir

Calicuas
Cacos
Culias
Cuchillo
Tama

Tagil
Comos
Coru
culata

Flori
da.
La Emperadida
Lucuo

Hispania
Mechuacan
Guacit

Caques

T
uia
Tropic

Lama
Icuv

Thomas
nada

R. de
cacualia
R. grande
de los
pelos
Saco
mizco
Gina

Taste
Benecul
Caribo

Y de los galopegos

Quito
Neyua

Caribana
Aguar.

CTIALIS

Corangue

Casma
uia
nape
Fracuci

Mapa

Pe ru.
Cusco
Chichan

Amaz

Colochi

CVS. CAPRICORNI
AR DEL ZVR.
Insulæ
incog nitæ.

Cabo de
la Isla
C. Redso

Aruri
matas

Mepe
ni

Ningatas
S.E spi

EL
PACIFICO

Cabo
Blanco
Veragua

Chic

R. de
Palomin

Archipelago
de las Islas.

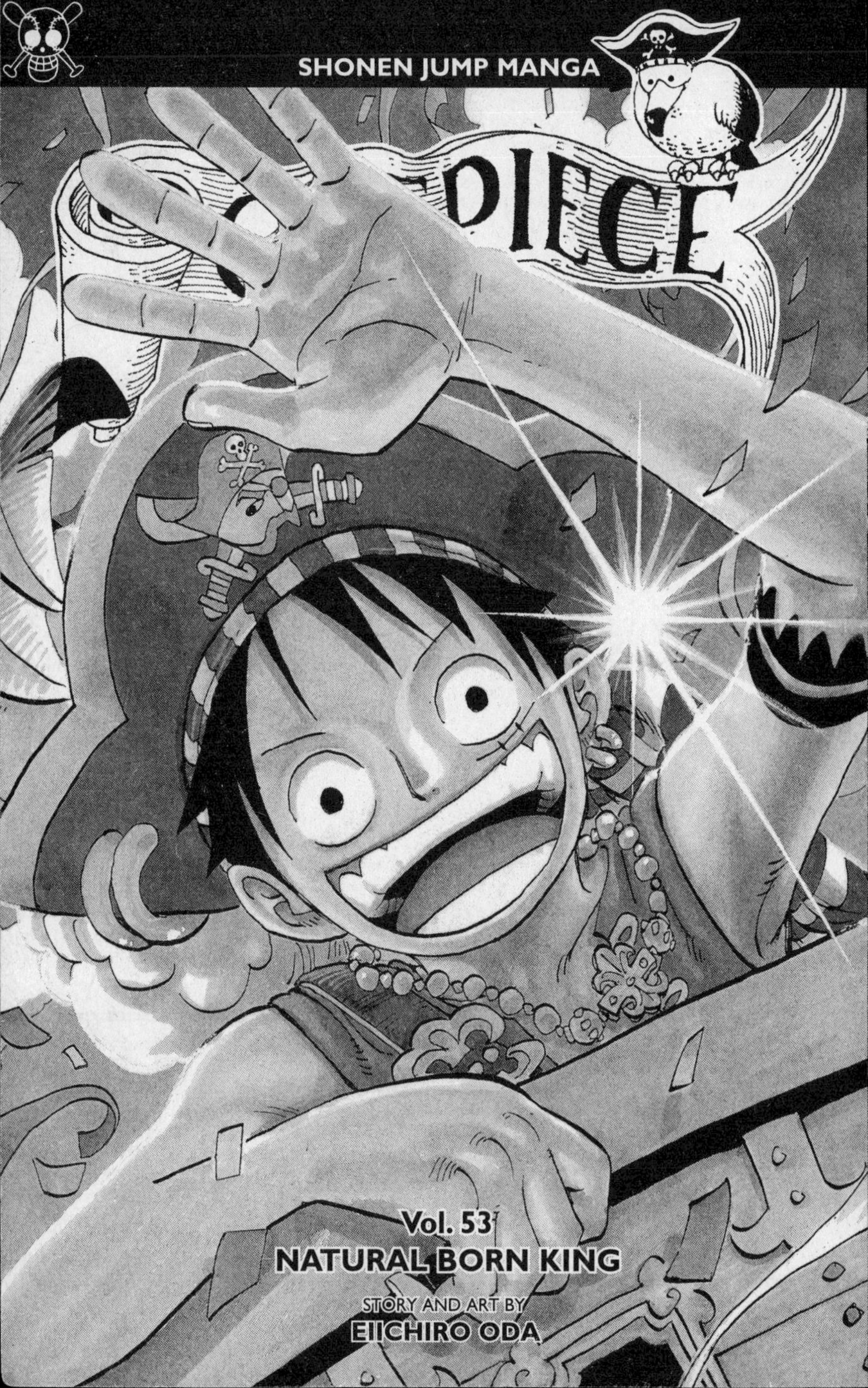
SHONEN JUMP MANGA
PIECE
Vol. 53
NATURAL BORN KING
STORY AND ART BY
EIICHIRO ODA

The Straw Hats

Total bounty: 700,000,050 berries

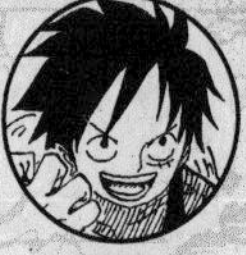

Boundlessly optimistic and able to stretch like rubber, he is determined to become King of the Pirates.
Bounty: 300 million berries

Monkey D. Luffy

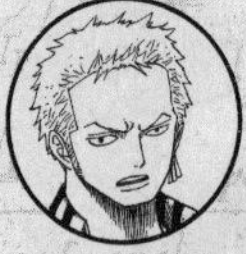

A former bounty hunter and master of the "three-sword"style. He aspires to be the world's greatest swordsman.
Bounty: 120 million berries

Roronoa Zolo

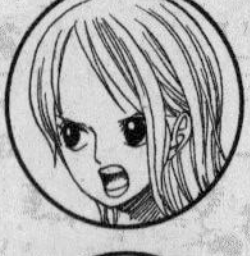

A thief who specializes in robbing pirates. Nami hates pirates, but Luffy convinced her to be his navigator.
Bounty: 16 million berries

Nami

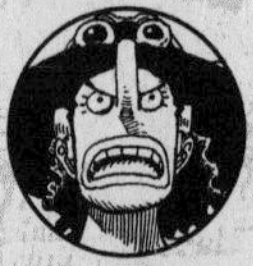

A village boy with a talent for telling tall tales. His father, Yasopp, is a member of Shanks's crew.
Bounty: 30 million berries

Usopp

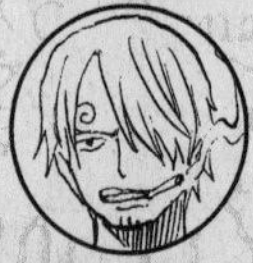

The kindhearted cook (and ladies' man) whose dream is to find the legendary sea, the "All Blue."
Bounty: 77 million berries

Sanji

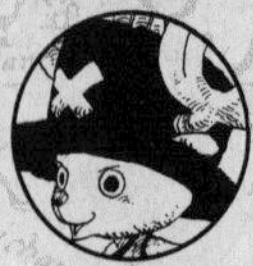

A blue-nosed man-reindeer and the ship's doctor.
Bounty: 50 berries

Tony Tony Chopper

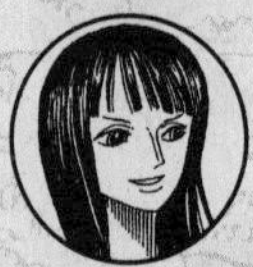

A mysterious woman in search of the Ponegliff on which true history is recorded.
Bounty: 80 million berries

Nico Robin

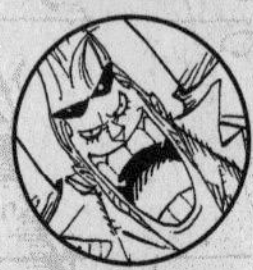

A softhearted cyborg and talented shipwright.
Bounty: 44 million berries

Franky

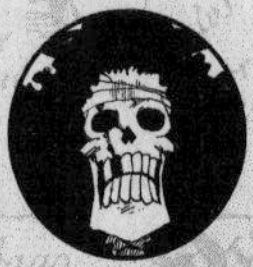

A skeleton warrior with an afro. He dreams of being reunited with Laboon, the tame whale he parted with fifty years ago.
Bounty: 33 million berries

Brook

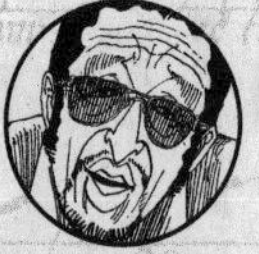

Navy Headquarters Admiral (real name: Borsalino)

Kizaru

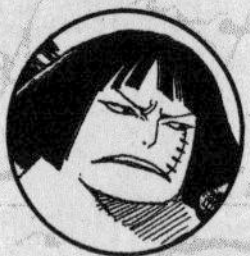

Navy Headquarters Science Team Leader and Dr. Vegapunk's bodyguard.

Sentomaru

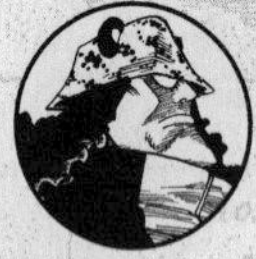

One of the Seven Warlords of the Sea; also known as "Tyrant" Kuma.

Bartholomew Kuma

THE STORY OF ONE PIECE • VOLUME 53 •

Monkey D. Luffy started out as just a kid with a dream—to become the greatest pirate in history! Stirred by the tales of pirate "Red-Haired" Shanks, Luffy vowed to become a pirate himself. That was before the enchanted Devil Fruit gave Luffy the power to stretch like rubber, at the cost of being unable to swim—a serious handicap for an aspiring sea dog. Undeterred, Luffy set out to sea and recruited some crewmates—master swordsman Zolo; treasure-hunting thief Nami; lying sharpshooter Usopp; the high-kicking chef Sanji; Chopper, the walkin' talkin' reindeer doctor; the mysterious archaeologist Robin; cyborg shipwright Franky; and Brook, a musical skeleton!

Now in the Grand Line, Luffy and the crew are headed for Fish-Man Island on their new vessel, *Thousand Sunny*. After defeating one of the Seven Warlords of the Sea, Gecko Moria, on the enormous ghost ship *Thriller Bark*, they meet up with a mermaid named Camie and the Fish-Man Hatchan. In order to reach the underwater Fish-Man Island and pass over the Red Line, *Thousand Sunny* will require a special coating, so the Straw Hats make their way to the renowned coating craftsman at Sabaody Archipelago, a gathering ground for high-bounty rookie pirates and Celestial Dragons! When his crew is threatened, Luffy strikes back, and a great battle with the rookie pirates ensues, staining Sabaody Archipelago with blood. Navy Admiral Kizaru arrives with Dr. Vegapunk's underling, Sentomaru. Shape-shifting Pacifistas in the form of Bartholomew Kuma also arrive, putting the crew at a serious disadvantage... And then the real Kuma shows up! Rayleigh jumps in to help, but not before Zolo is "erased" by Kuma's powers!!

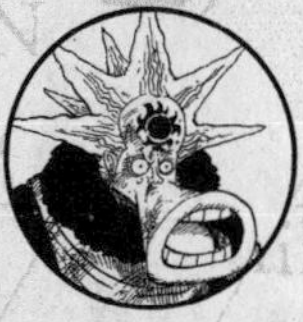

Octopus fritter store owner and former Arlong Pirate. Octopus Fish-Man.

HATCHAN (HACHI)

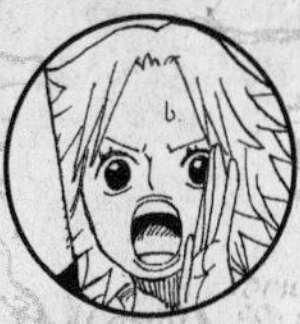

Designer in training and octopus fritter store clerk. Kissing Gourami Mermaid.

CAMIE

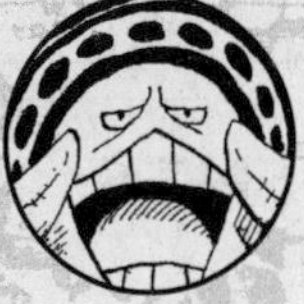

Starfish and designer of Criminal brand.

PAPPAGU

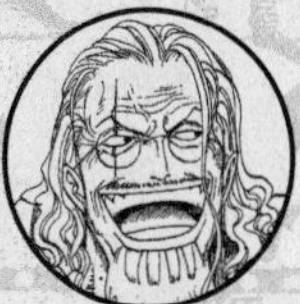

Former first mate with the Roger Pirates and the Pirate King's right-hand man.

SILVERS RAYLEIGH

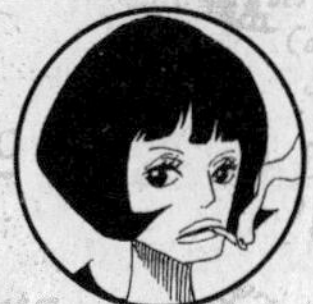

Bar owner and former pirate.

SHAKUYAKU (SHAKKY)

A pirate that Luffy idolizes. Shanks gave Luffy his trademark straw hat.

"RED-HAIRED" SHANKS

Vol. 53
Natural Born King

CONTENTS

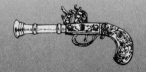

Chapter 513:
BEYOND RESCUE!!!

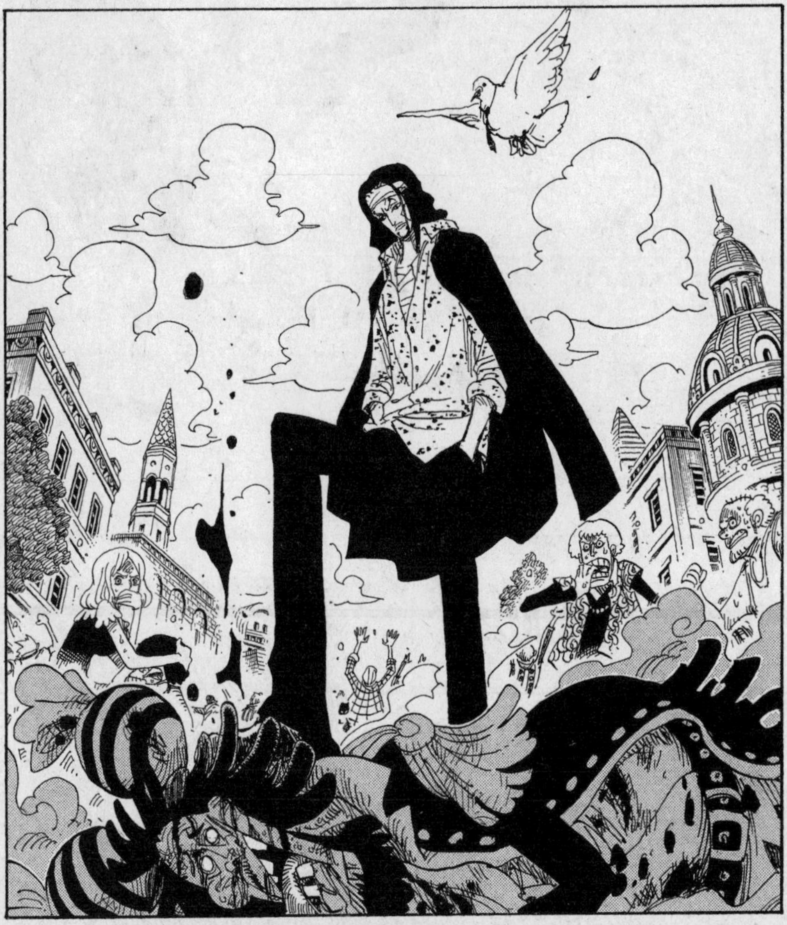

CP9'S INDEPENDENT REPORT, VOL. 21:
"EXCESSIVE JUSTICE"

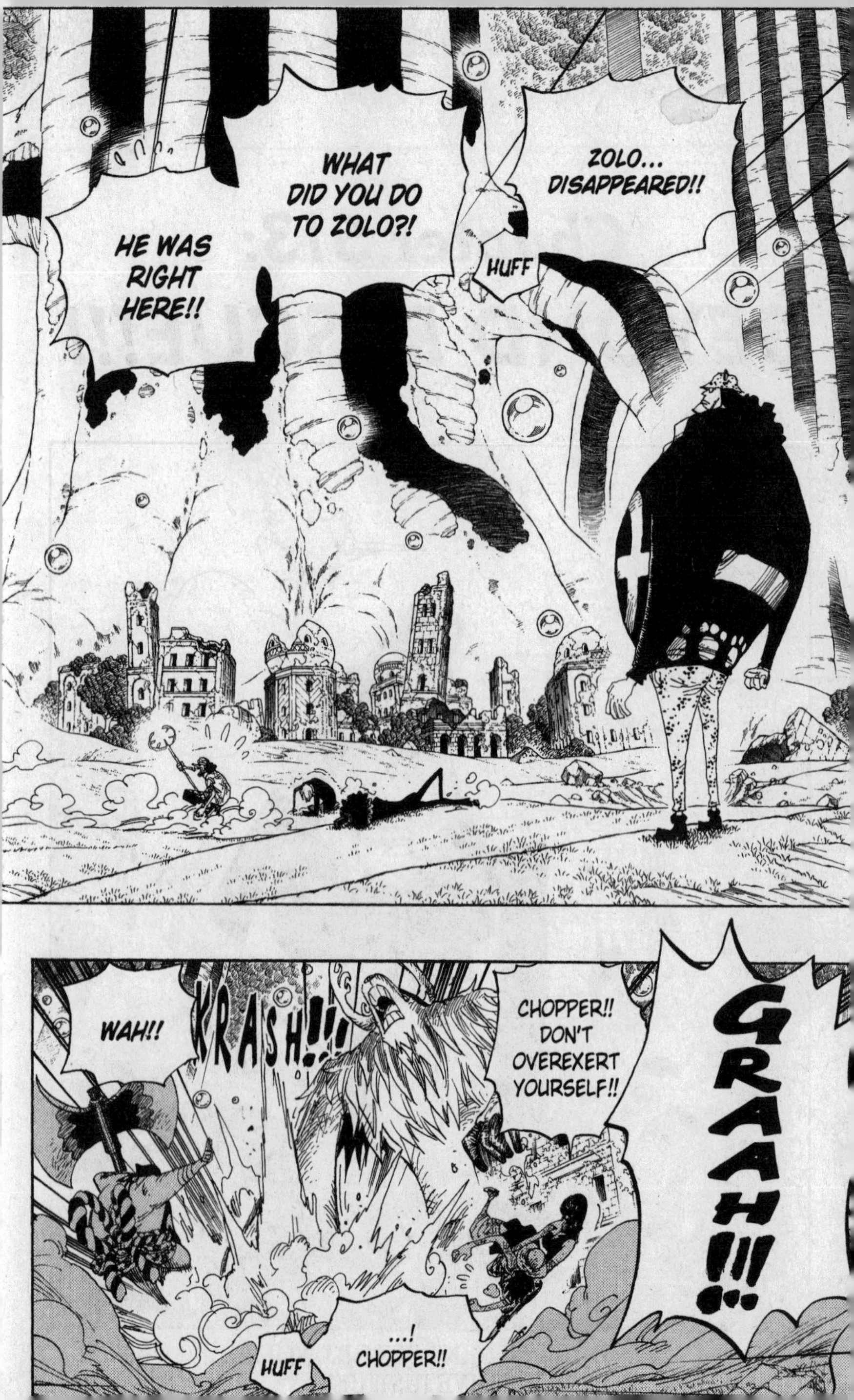
ZOLO... DISAPPEARED!!
HUFF
WHAT DID YOU DO TO ZOLO?!
HE WAS RIGHT HERE!!
GRAAH!!!
CHOPPER!! DON'T OVEREXERT YOURSELF!!
KRASH!!!
WAH!!
...! CHOPPER!!
HUFF

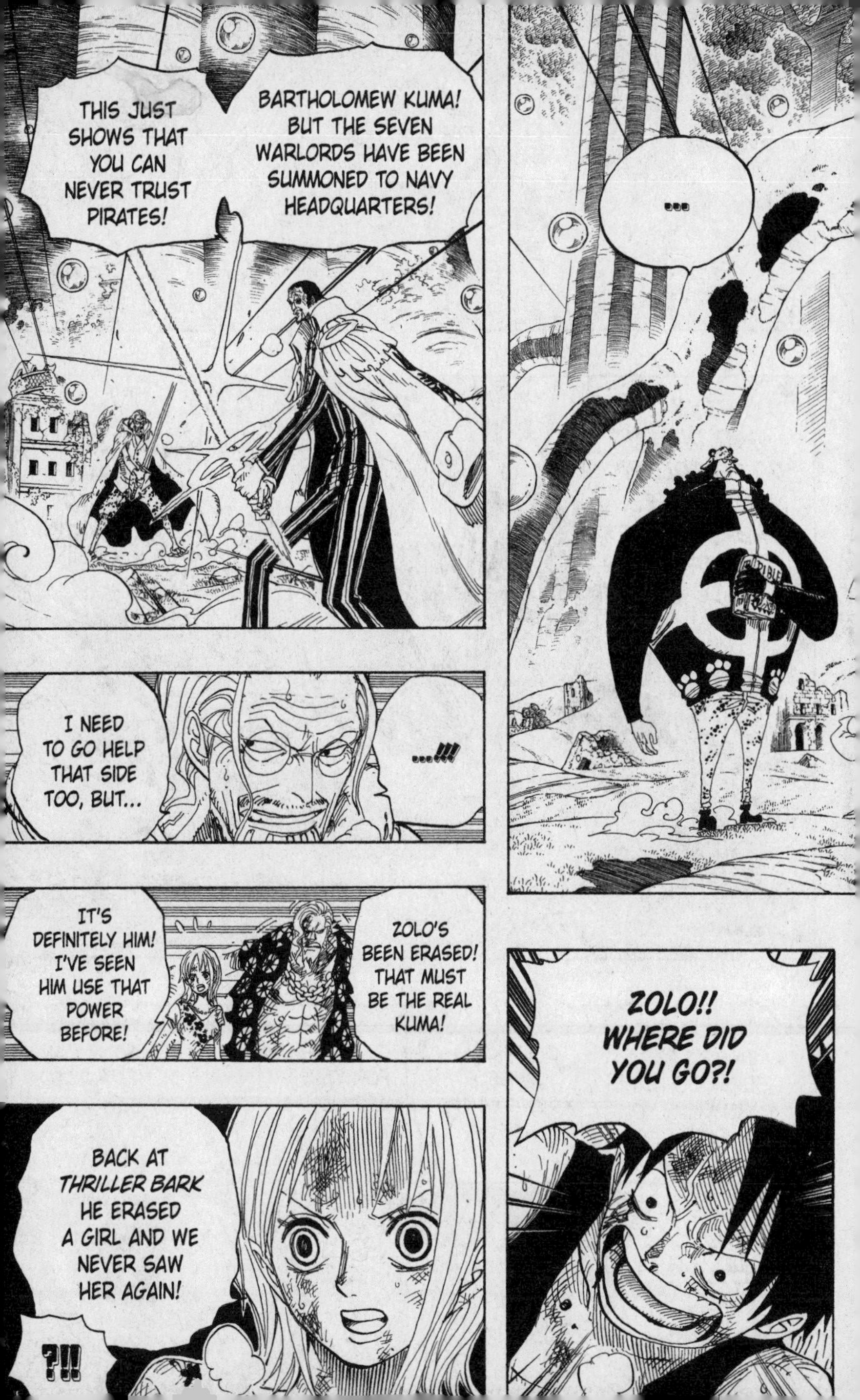
...
BARTHOLOMEW KUMA! BUT THE SEVEN WARLORDS HAVE BEEN SUMMONED TO NAVY HEADQUARTERS!
THIS JUST SHOWS THAT YOU CAN NEVER TRUST PIRATES!
...!!!
I NEED TO GO HELP THAT SIDE TOO, BUT...
ZOLO!! WHERE DID YOU GO?!
ZOLO'S BEEN ERASED! THAT MUST BE THE REAL KUMA!
IT'S DEFINITELY HIM! I'VE SEEN HIM USE THAT POWER BEFORE!
BACK AT *THRILLER BARK* HE ERASED A GIRL AND WE NEVER SAW HER AGAIN!
?!!

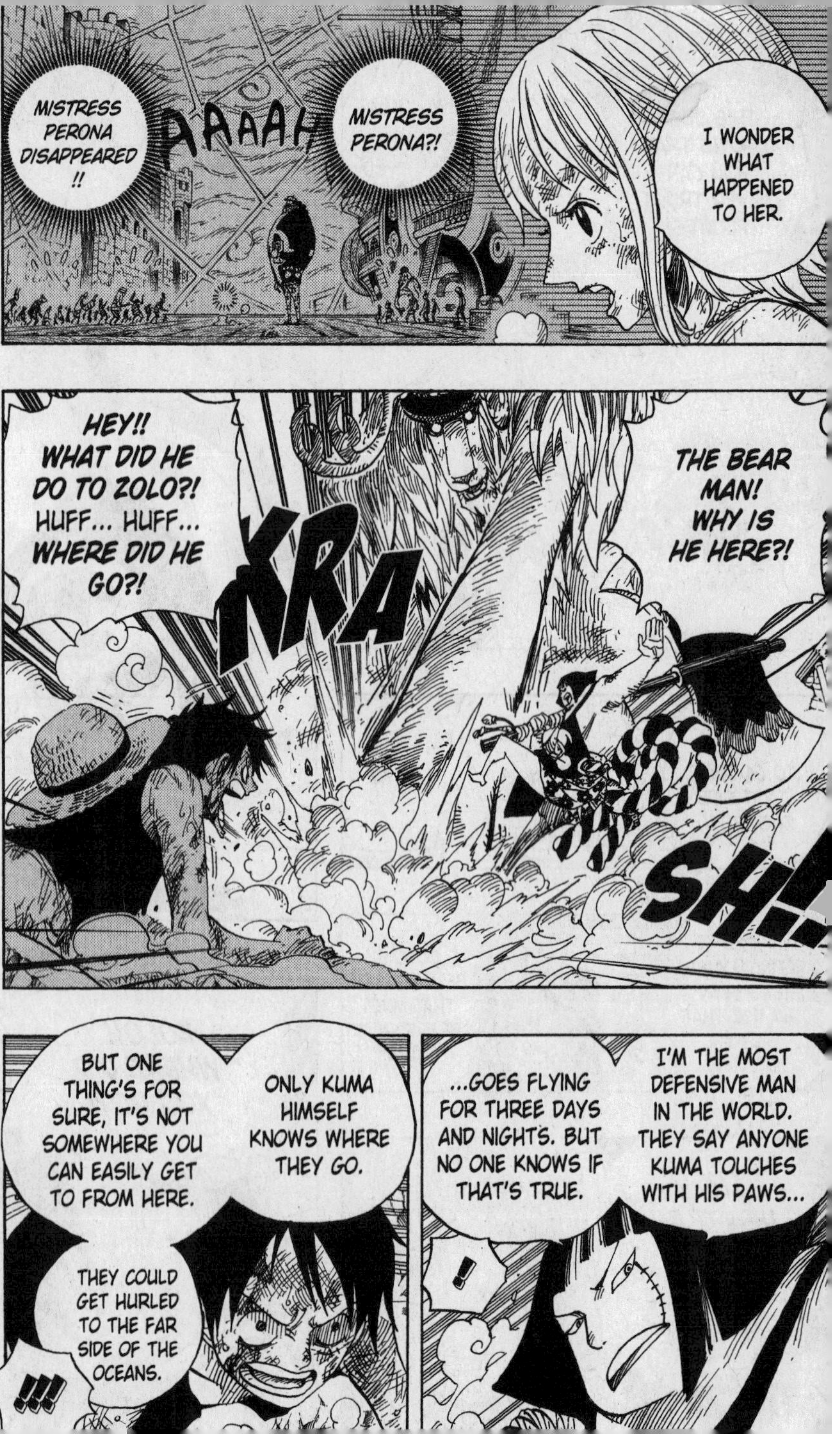

I WONDER WHAT HAPPENED TO HER.
MISTRESS PERONA?!
AAAAH
MISTRESS PERONA DISAPPEARED!!
THE BEAR MAN! WHY IS HE HERE?!
HEY!! WHAT DID HE DO TO ZOLO?! HUFF... HUFF... WHERE DID HE GO?!
KRA
SH
I'M THE MOST DEFENSIVE MAN IN THE WORLD. THEY SAY ANYONE KUMA TOUCHES WITH HIS PAWS...
...GOES FLYING FOR THREE DAYS AND NIGHTS. BUT NO ONE KNOWS IF THAT'S TRUE.
!
ONLY KUMA HIMSELF KNOWS WHERE THEY GO.
BUT ONE THING'S FOR SURE, IT'S NOT SOMEWHERE YOU CAN EASILY GET TO FROM HERE.
THEY COULD GET HURLED TO THE FAR SIDE OF THE OCEANS.
!!!

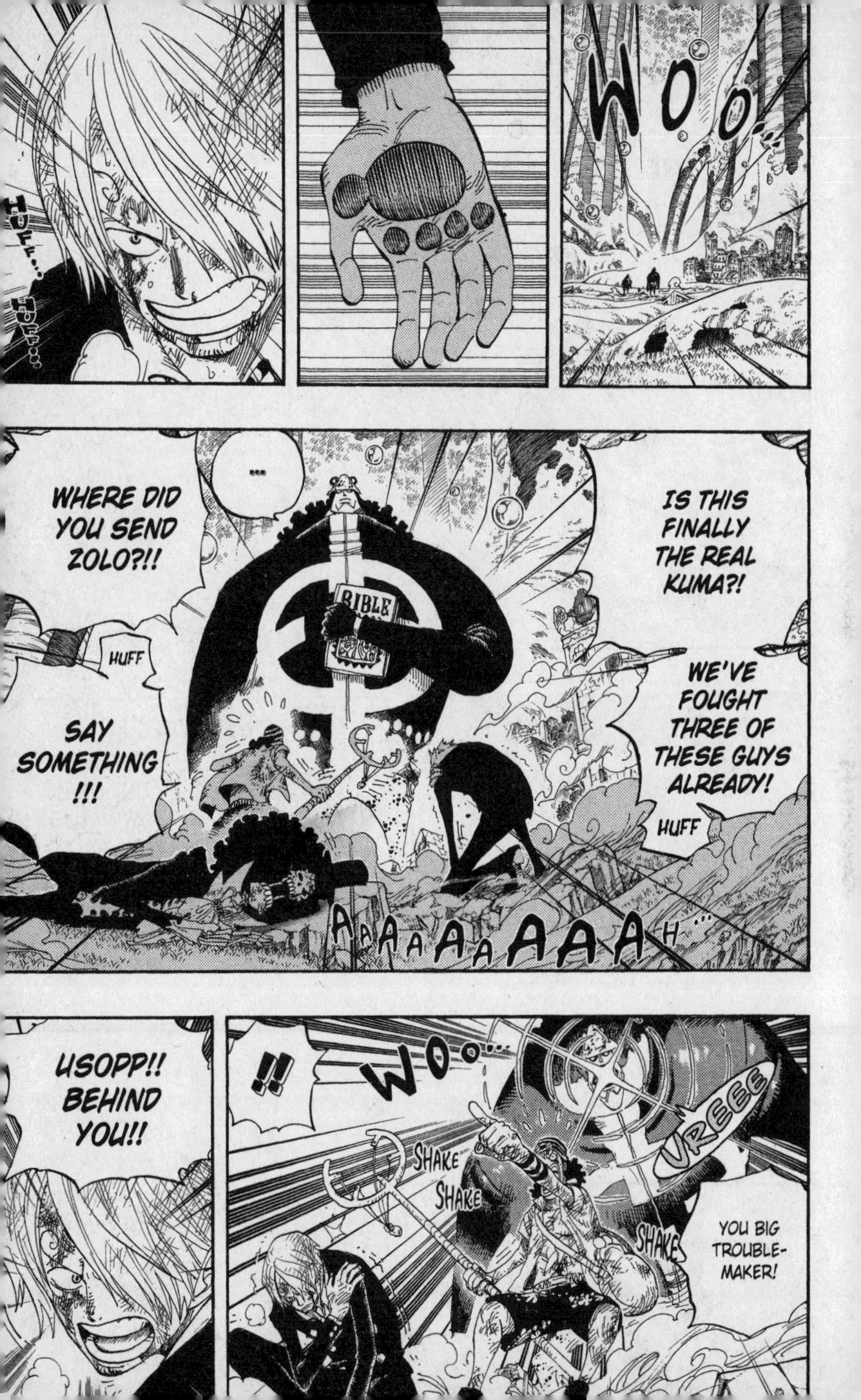
WOO
HUFF... HUFF...
IS THIS FINALLY THE REAL KUMA?!
WE'VE FOUGHT THREE OF THESE GUYS ALREADY!
HUFF
...
WHERE DID YOU SEND ZOLO?!!
HUFF
SAY SOMETHING!!!
AAAAAAAAAH...
VREEE
WOO...
!!
YOU BIG TROUBLE-MAKER!
SHAKE
SHAKE SHAKE
USOPP!! BEHIND YOU!!

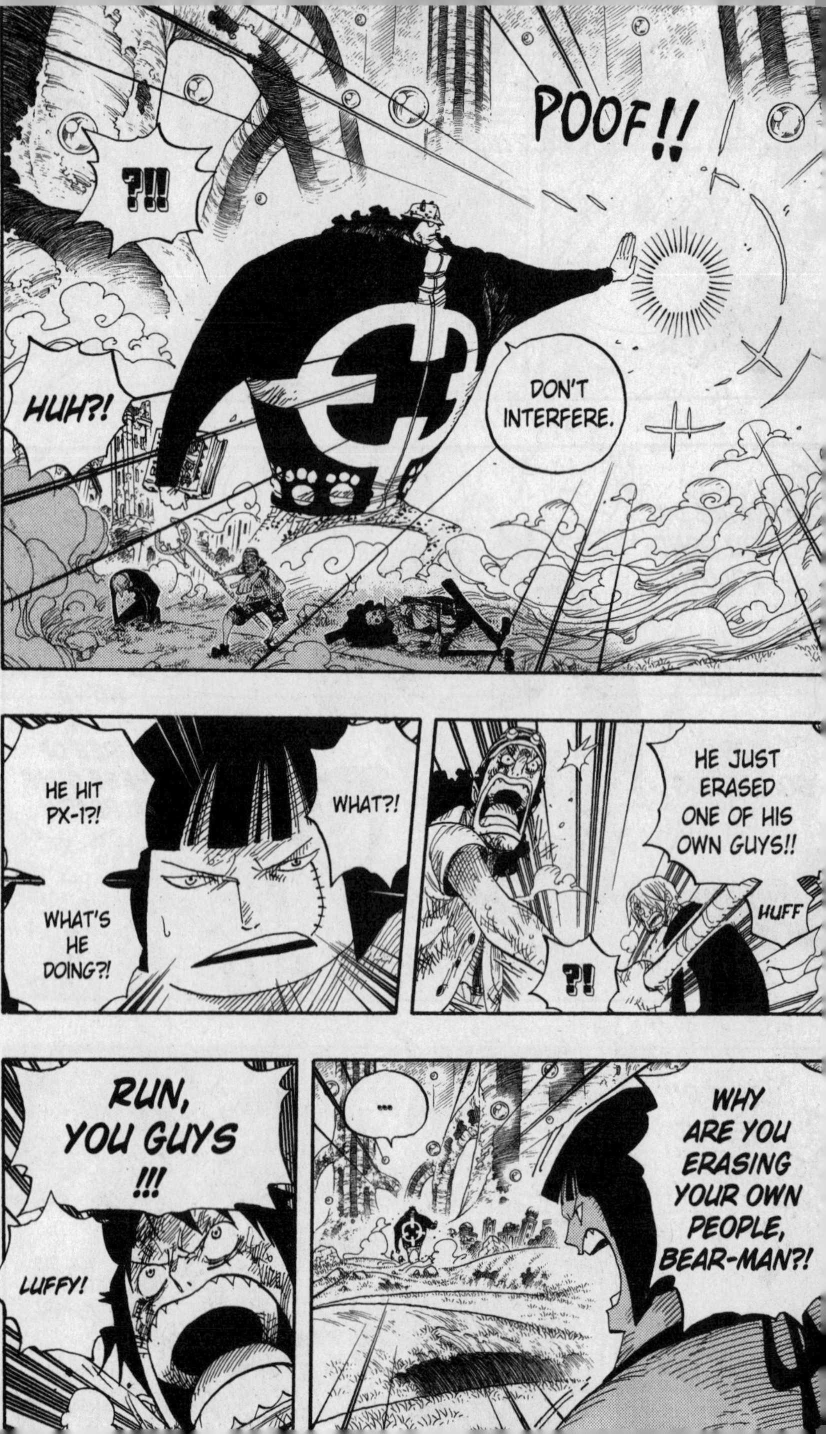
POOF!!
?!!
DON'T INTERFERE.
HUH?!
HE JUST ERASED ONE OF HIS OWN GUYS!!
HUFF
?!
WHAT?!
HE HIT PX-1?!
WHAT'S HE DOING?!
WHY ARE YOU ERASING YOUR OWN PEOPLE, BEAR-MAN?!
...
RUN, YOU GUYS!!!
LUFFY!

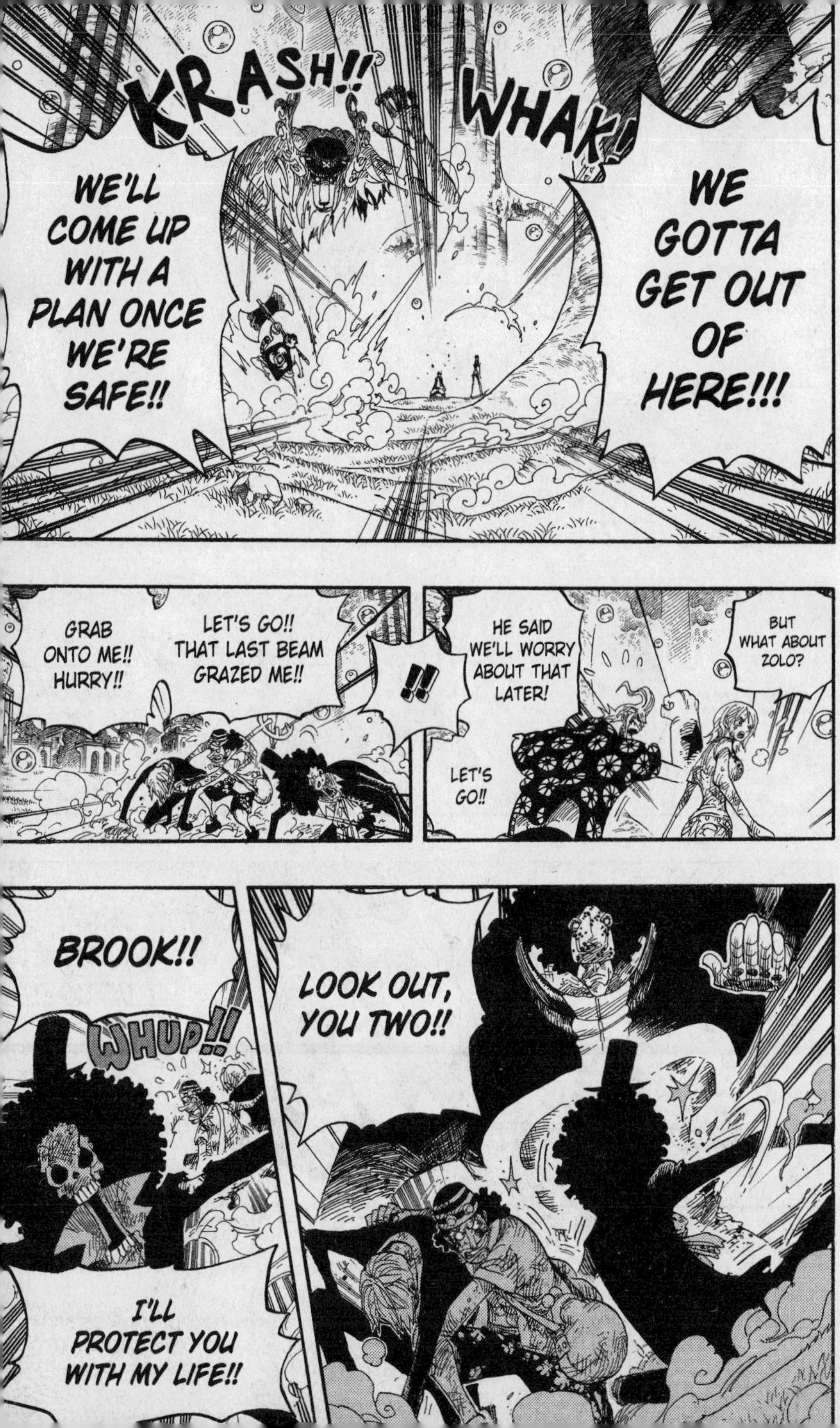
WHAK!
WE GOTTA GET OUT OF HERE!!!
KRASH!!
WE'LL COME UP WITH A PLAN ONCE WE'RE SAFE!!
BUT WHAT ABOUT ZOLO?
HE SAID WE'LL WORRY ABOUT THAT LATER!
LET'S GO!!
!!
LET'S GO!! THAT LAST BEAM GRAZED ME!!
GRAB ONTO ME!! HURRY!!
LOOK OUT, YOU TWO!!
BROOK!!
WHUP!!
I'LL PROTECT YOU WITH MY LIFE!!

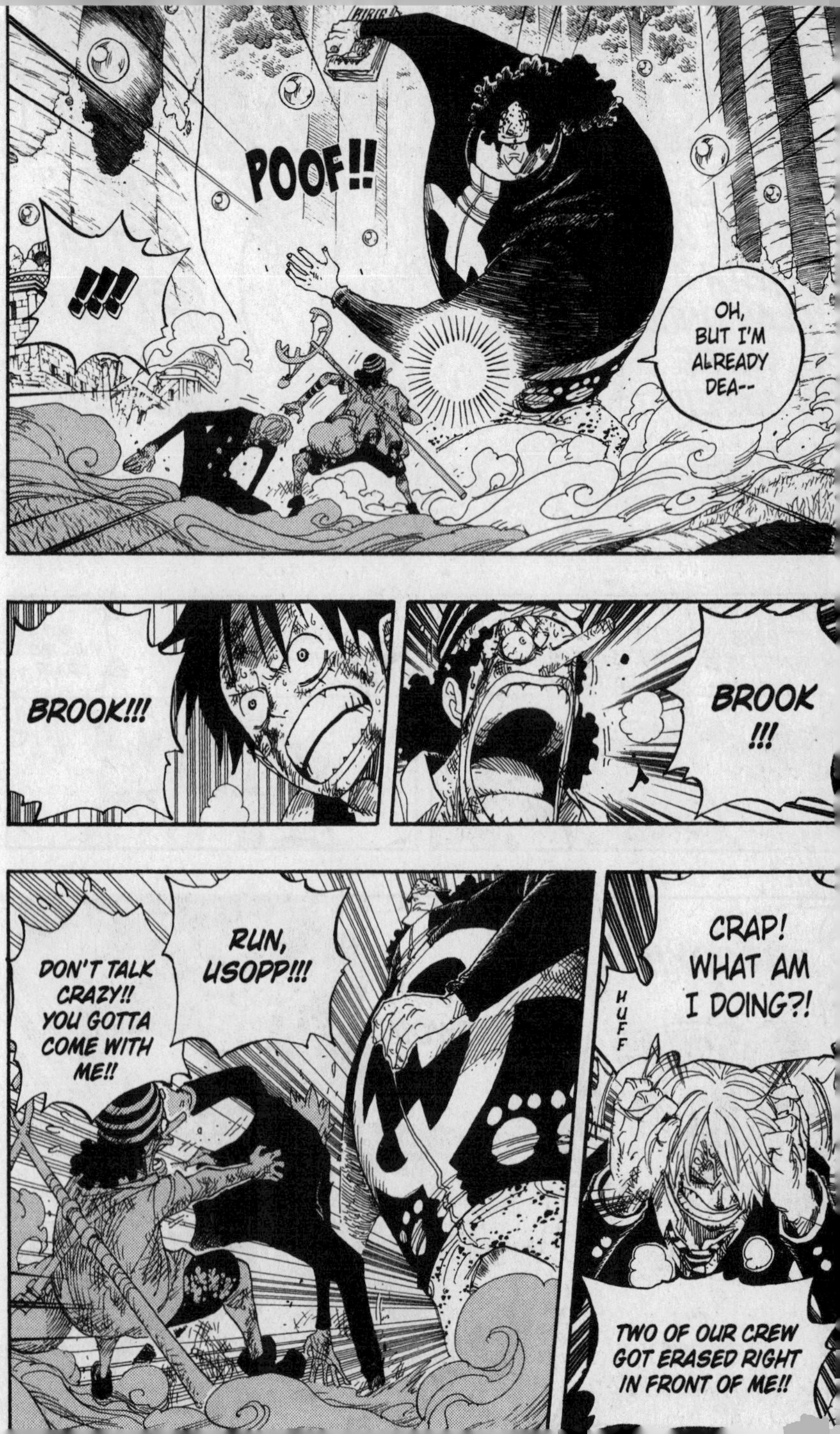
OH, BUT I'M ALREADY DEA--
POOF!!
!!!
BROOK !!!
BROOK!!!
CRAP! WHAT AM I DOING?!
HUFF
TWO OF OUR CREW GOT ERASED RIGHT IN FRONT OF ME!!
RUN, USOPP!!!
DON'T TALK CRAZY!! YOU GOTTA COME WITH ME!!

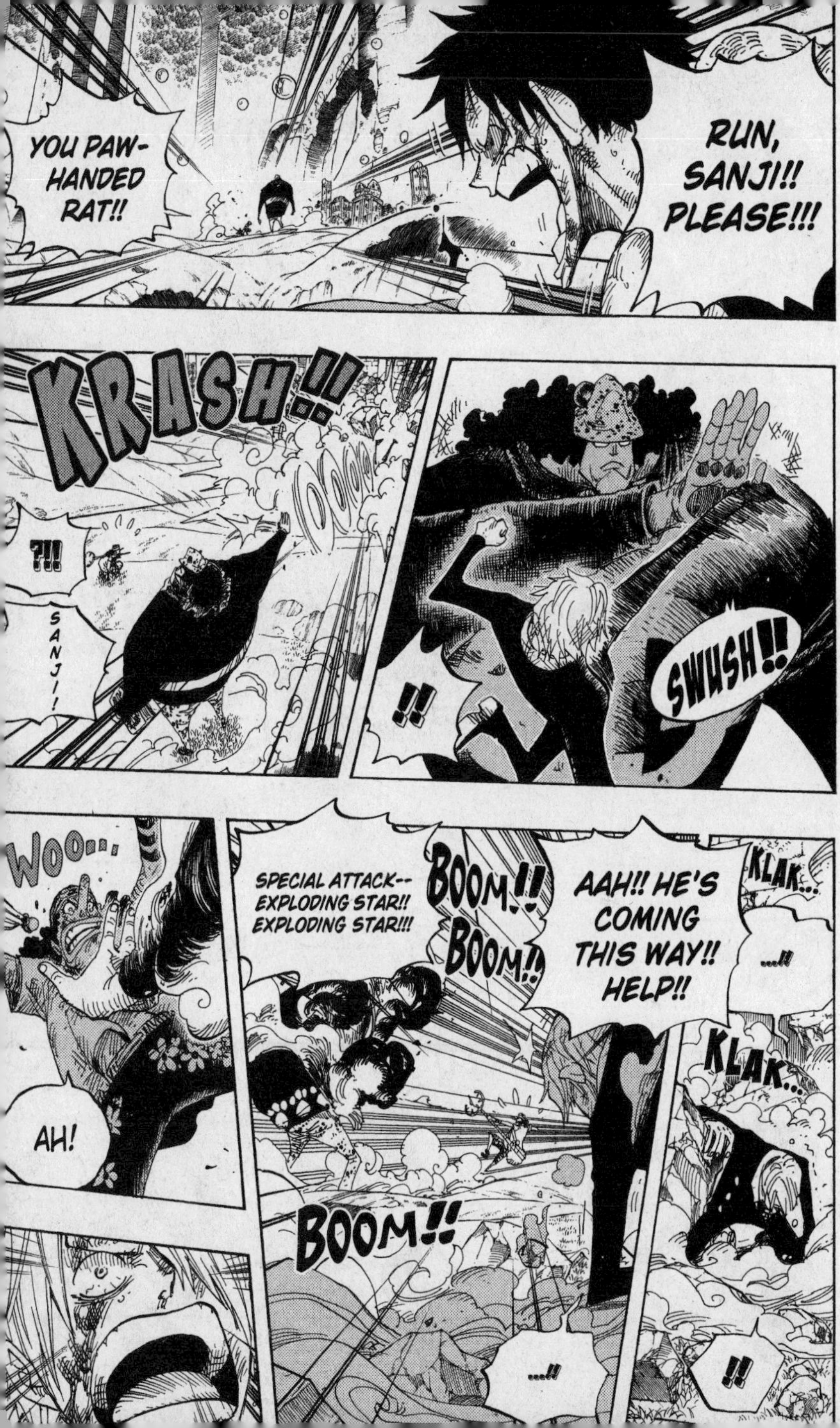
RUN, SANJI!! PLEASE!!!
YOU PAW-HANDED RAT!!
SWUSH!!
!!
KRASH!!!
?!!
SANJI!
KLAK...
...!!
KLAK...
!!
AAH!! HE'S COMING THIS WAY!! HELP!!
BOOM!!
BOOM!!
SPECIAL ATTACK--EXPLODING STAR!! EXPLODING STAR!!!
BOOM!!
...!!
WOO...
AH!

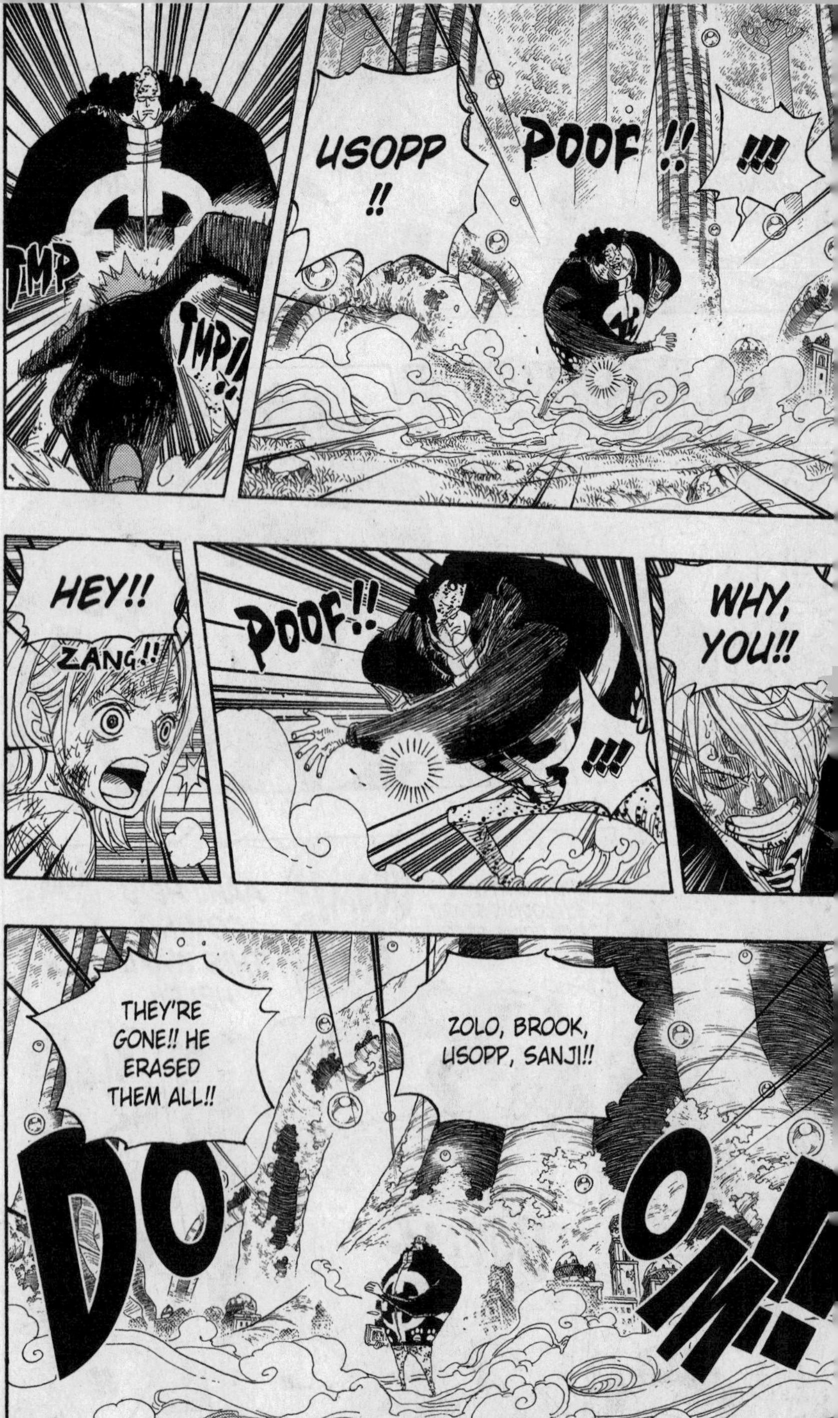
!!!
POOF!!
USOPP!!
TMP
TMP!!
WHY, YOU!!
!!!
POOF!!
HEY!!
ZANG!!
ZOLO, BROOK, USOPP, SANJI!!
THEY'RE GONE!! HE ERASED THEM ALL!!
DOOM!!

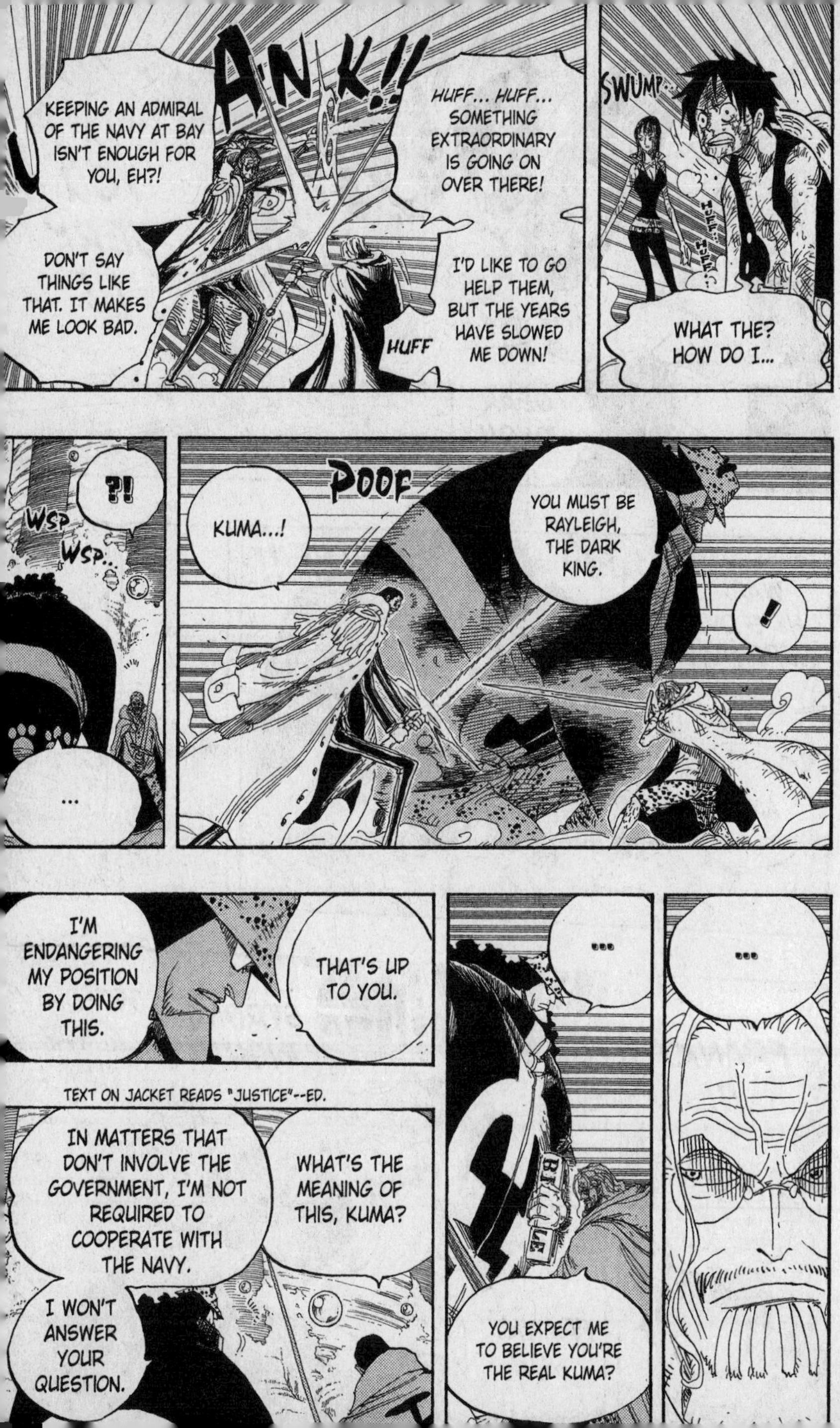
SWUMP...
HUFF... HUFF...
WHAT THE? HOW DO I...
ANK!!
HUFF... HUFF... SOMETHING EXTRAORDINARY IS GOING ON OVER THERE!
I'D LIKE TO GO HELP THEM, BUT THE YEARS HAVE SLOWED ME DOWN!
HUFF
KEEPING AN ADMIRAL OF THE NAVY AT BAY ISN'T ENOUGH FOR YOU, EH?!
DON'T SAY THINGS LIKE THAT. IT MAKES ME LOOK BAD.
POOF
YOU MUST BE RAYLEIGH, THE DARK KING.
KUMA...!
!
?!
WSP
WSP...
...
...
...
YOU EXPECT ME TO BELIEVE YOU'RE THE REAL KUMA?
THAT'S UP TO YOU.
I'M ENDANGERING MY POSITION BY DOING THIS.
TEXT ON JACKET READS "JUSTICE"--ED.
WHAT'S THE MEANING OF THIS, KUMA?
IN MATTERS THAT DON'T INVOLVE THE GOVERNMENT, I'M NOT REQUIRED TO COOPERATE WITH THE NAVY.
I WON'T ANSWER YOUR QUESTION.

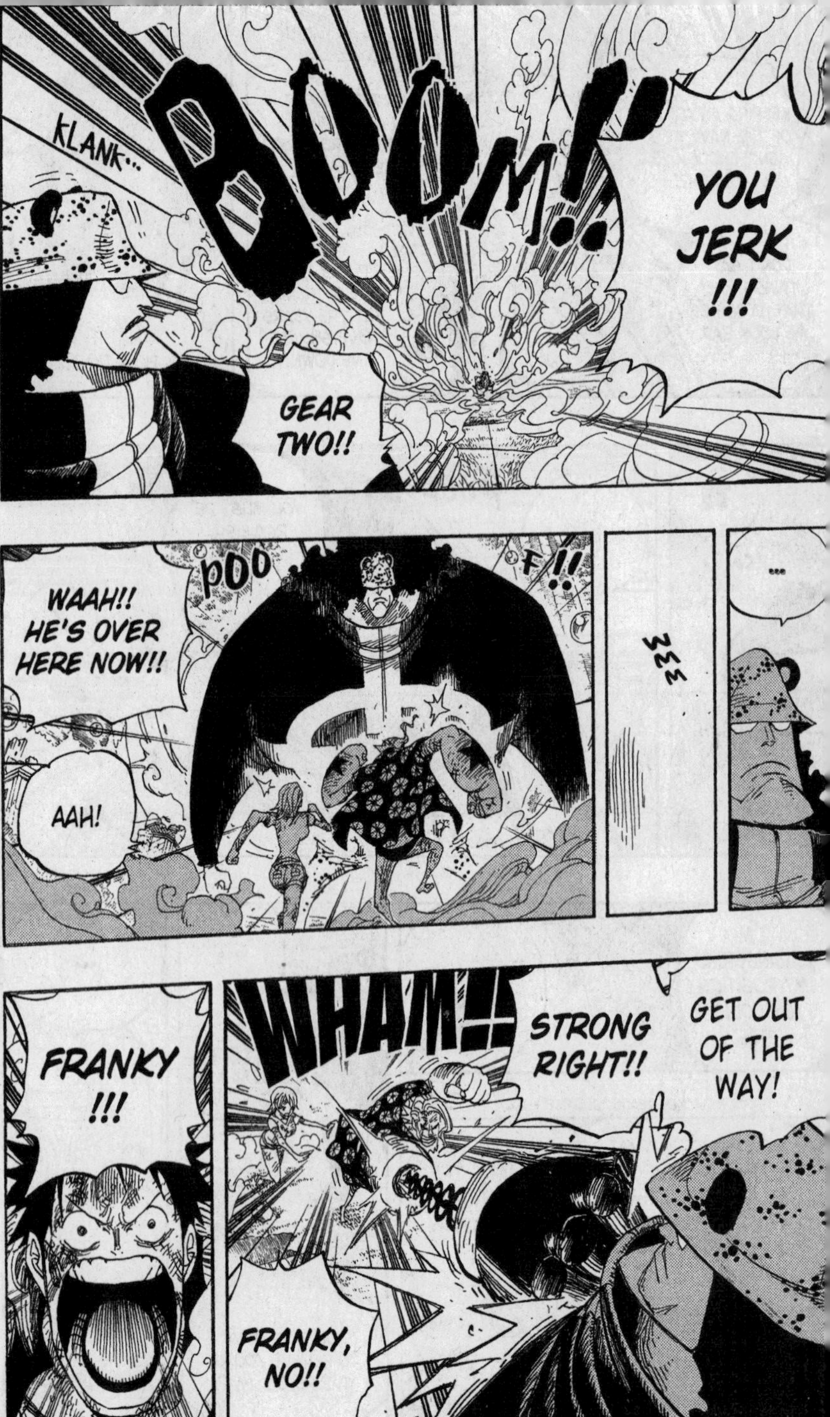
YOU JERK!!!
BOOM!!
KLANK...
GEAR TWO!!
...
POOF!!
WAAH!! HE'S OVER HERE NOW!!
AAH!
GET OUT OF THE WAY!
STRONG RIGHT!!
WHAM!!
FRANKY, NO!!
FRANKY!!!

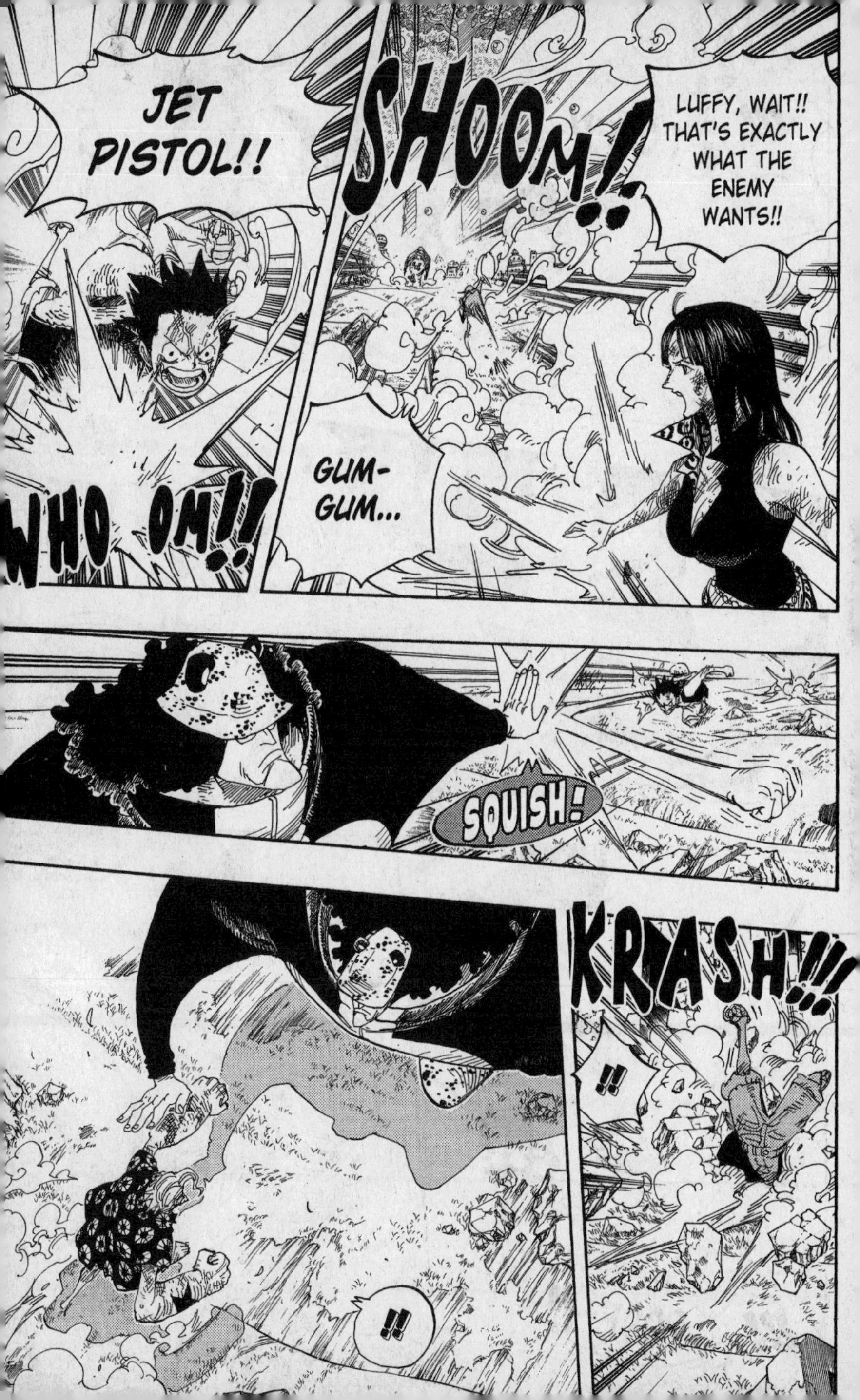
LUFFY, WAIT!! THAT'S EXACTLY WHAT THE ENEMY WANTS!!
SHOOM!
GUM-GUM...
JET PISTOL!!
WHOOM!!
SQUISH!
KRASH!!!
!!
!!

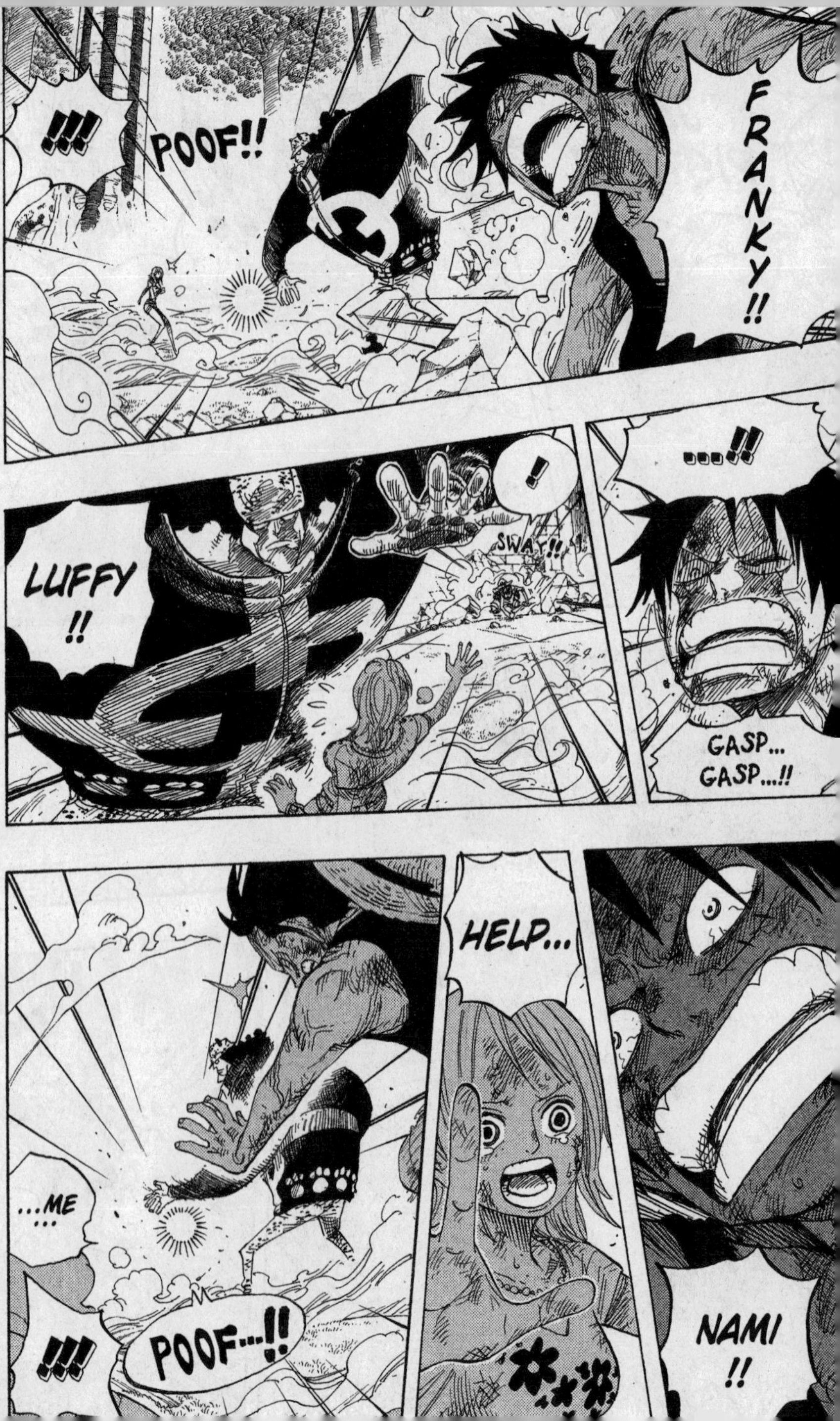
FRANKY!!
POOF!!
!!!
...!!
GASP... GASP...!!
!
SWAY!!
LUFFY !!
NAMI !!
HELP...
...ME ...
POOF...!!
!!!

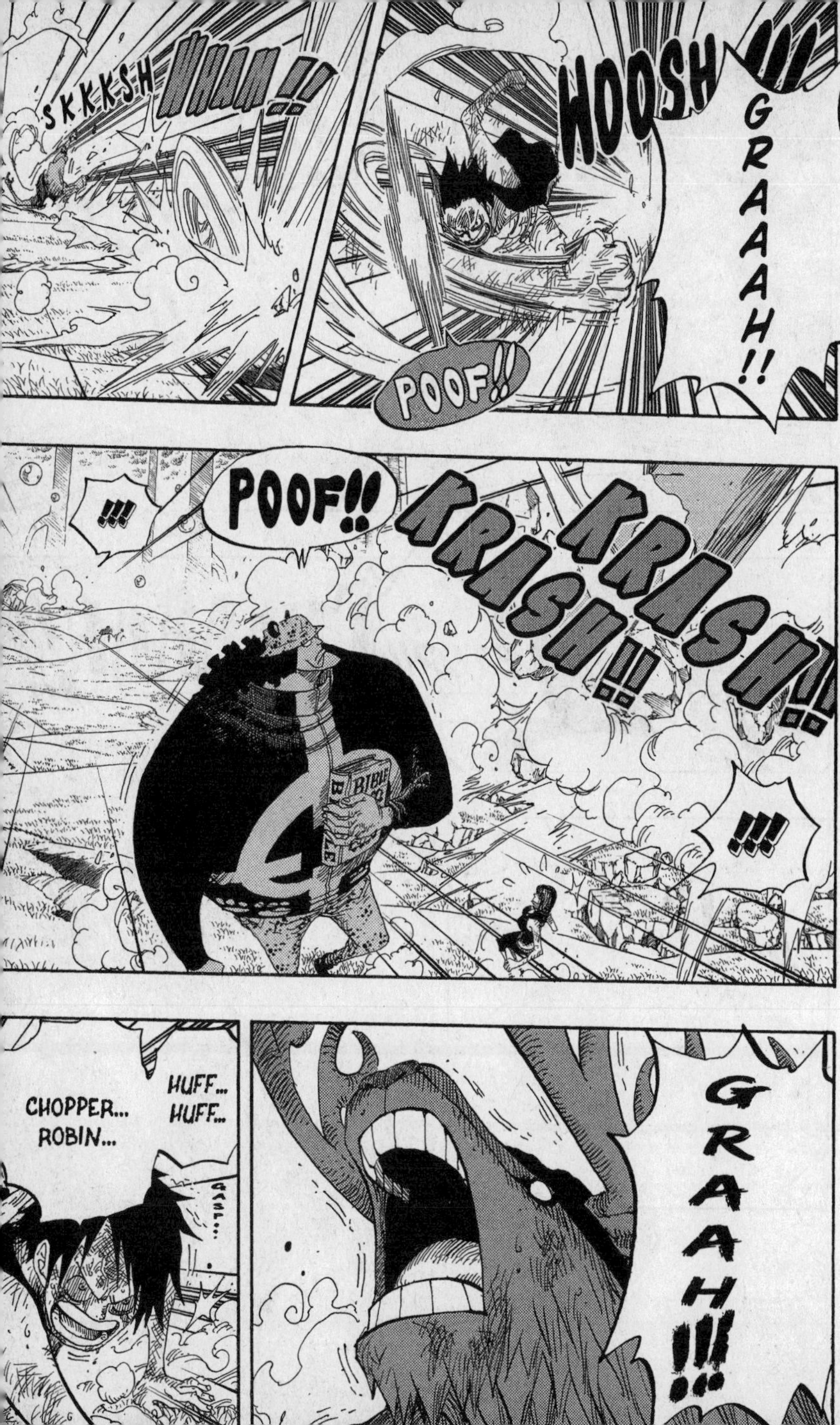
WHOOSH
GRAAAAH!!
POOF!!
WHAM!!
SKKKSH
KRISH
KRISH!!
!!!
POOF!!
!!!
GRAAH!!!
HUFF... HUFF...
CHOPPER... ROBIN...
GASP...

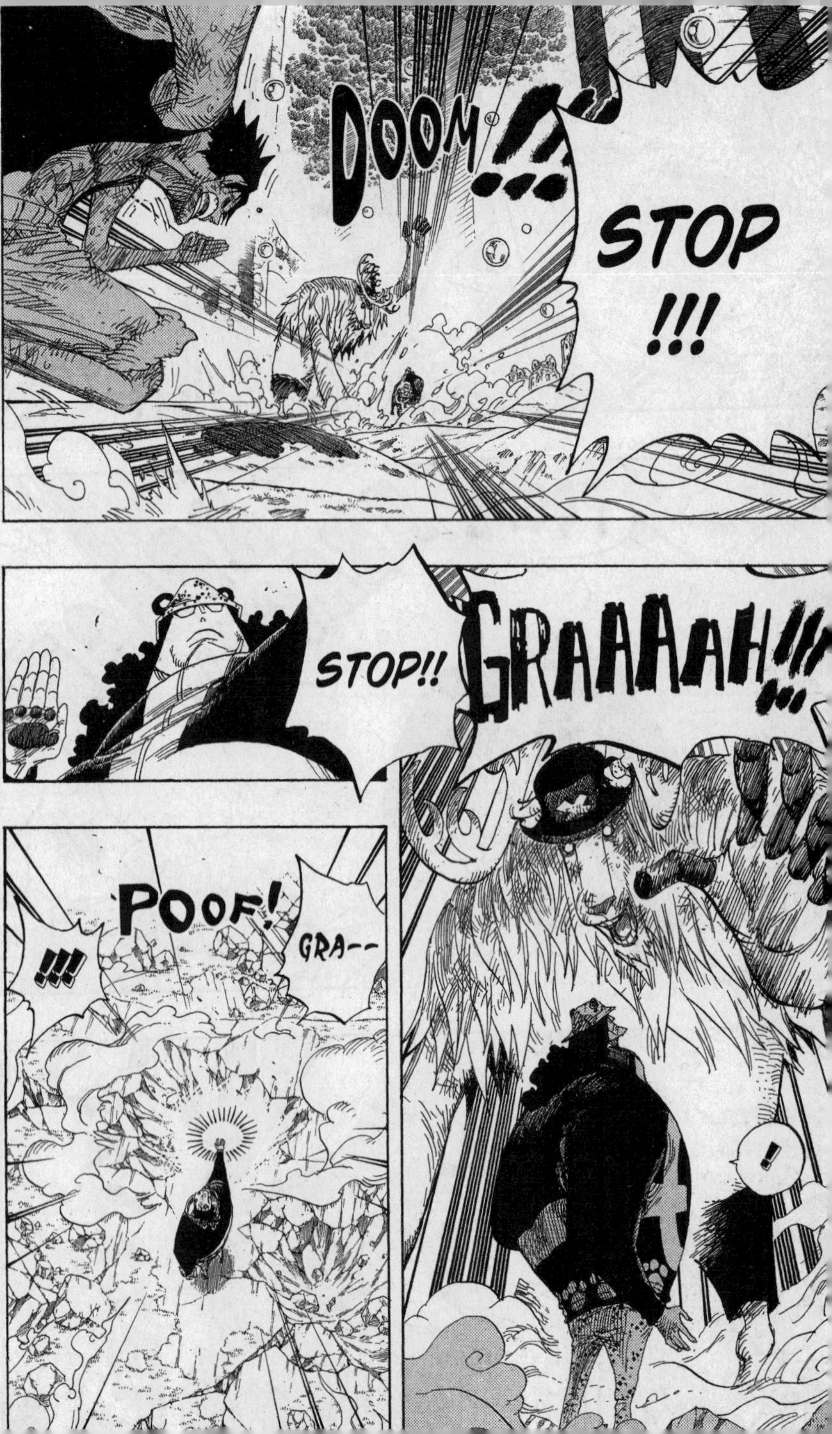
DOOM!!
STOP!!!
GRAAAAH!!!
!
STOP!!
POOF!
GRA--
!!!

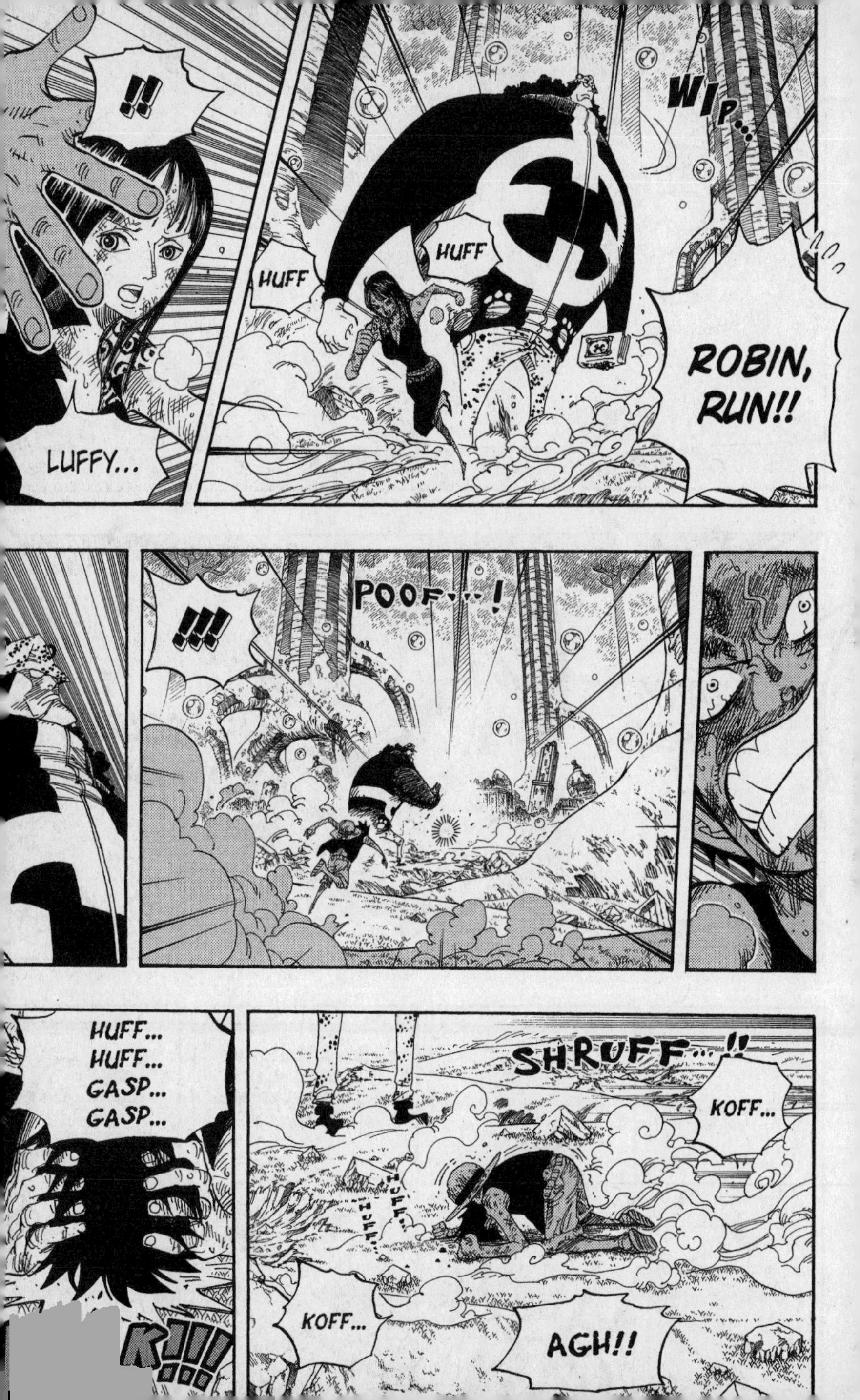
WIP...
ROBIN, RUN!!
HUFF
HUFF
!!
LUFFY...
POOF...!
!!!
SHRUFF...!!
KOFF...
HUFF... HUFF...
KOFF...
AGH!!
HUFF...
HUFF...
GASP...
GASP...
K!!!!

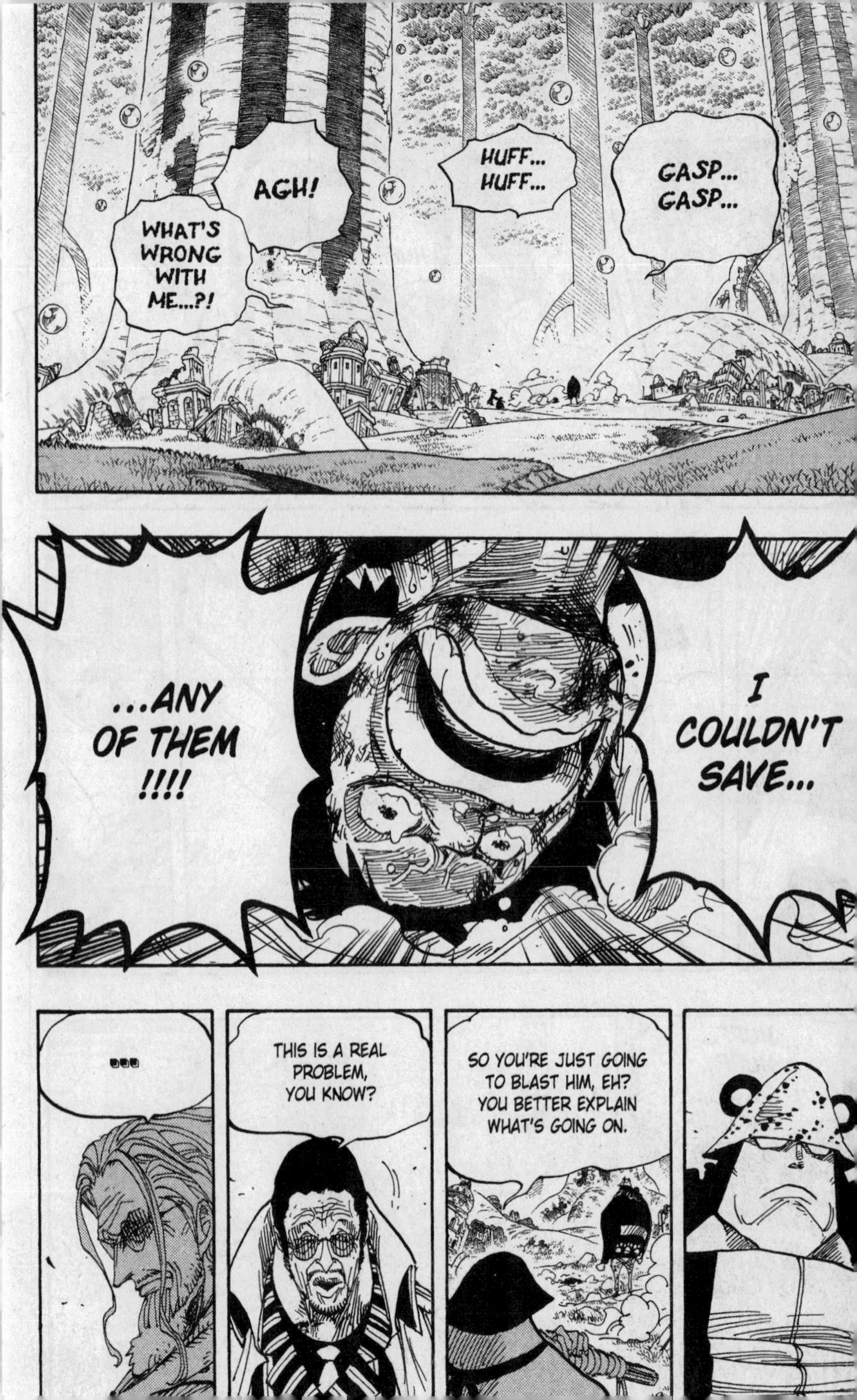
GASP... GASP...
HUFF... HUFF...
AGH!
WHAT'S WRONG WITH ME...?!
I COULDN'T SAVE...
...ANY OF THEM !!!!
SO YOU'RE JUST GOING TO BLAST HIM, EH? YOU BETTER EXPLAIN WHAT'S GOING ON.
THIS IS A REAL PROBLEM, YOU KNOW?
...

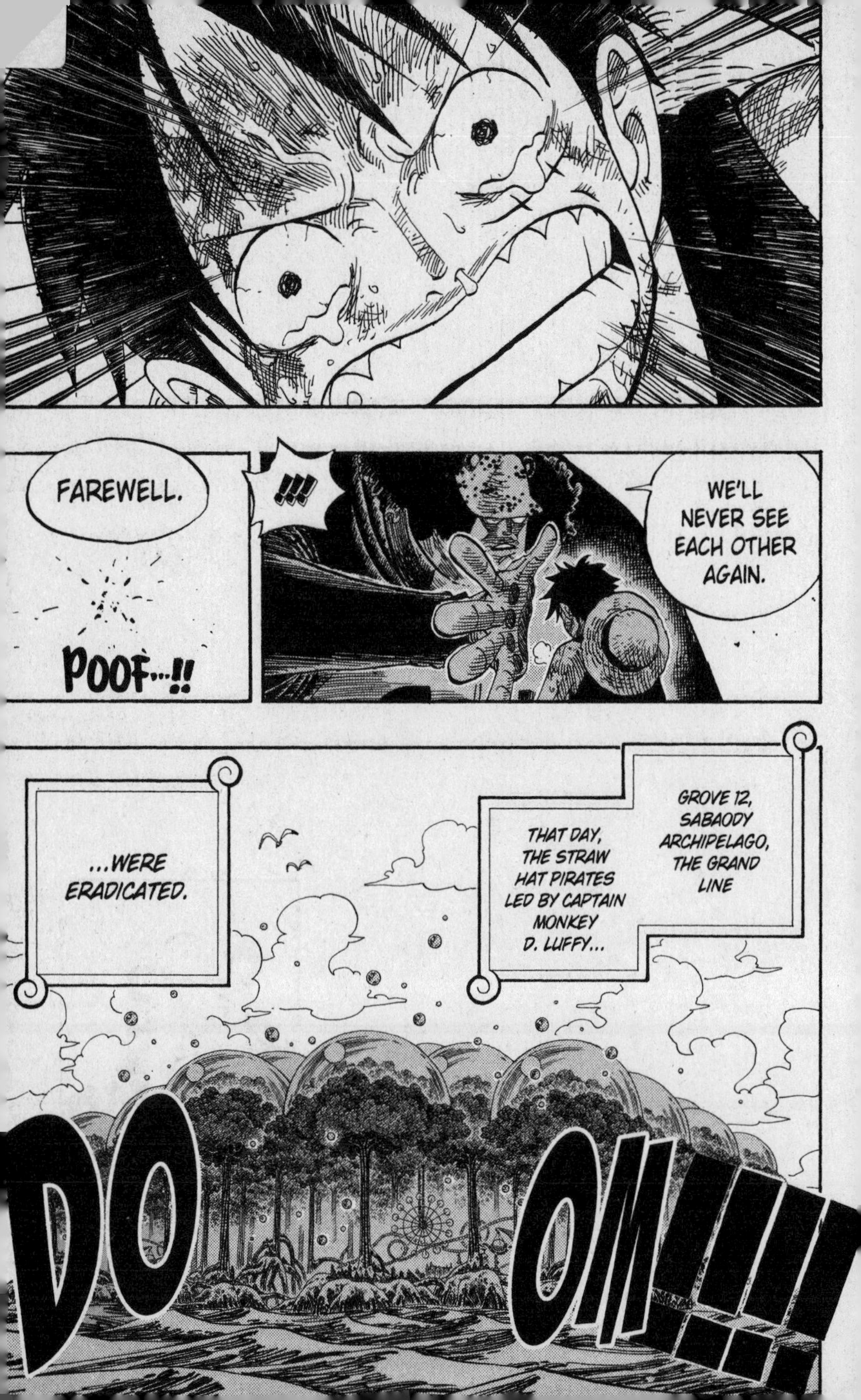

WE'LL NEVER SEE EACH OTHER AGAIN.
!!!
FAREWELL.
POOF...!!
GROVE 12, SABAODY ARCHIPELAGO, THE GRAND LINE
THAT DAY, THE STRAW HAT PIRATES LED BY CAPTAIN MONKEY D. LUFFY...
...WERE ERADICATED.
DO
ON!!!!

Chapter 514:
BODY PARASITE MUSHROOMS

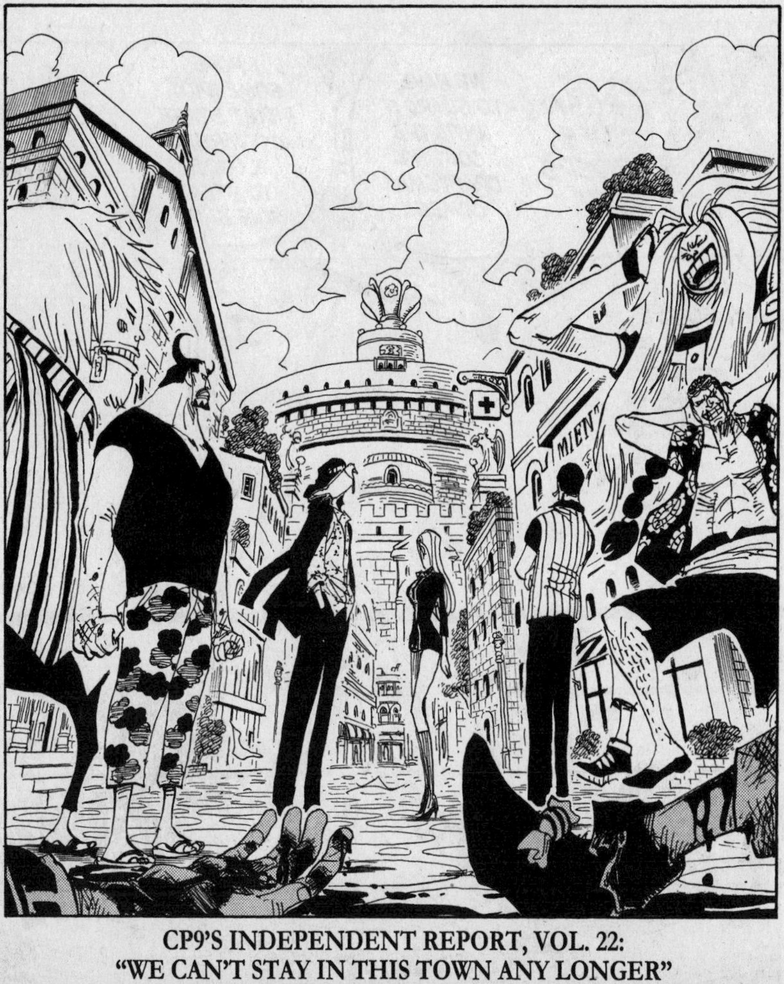

CP9'S INDEPENDENT REPORT, VOL. 22:
"WE CAN'T STAY IN THIS TOWN ANY LONGER"

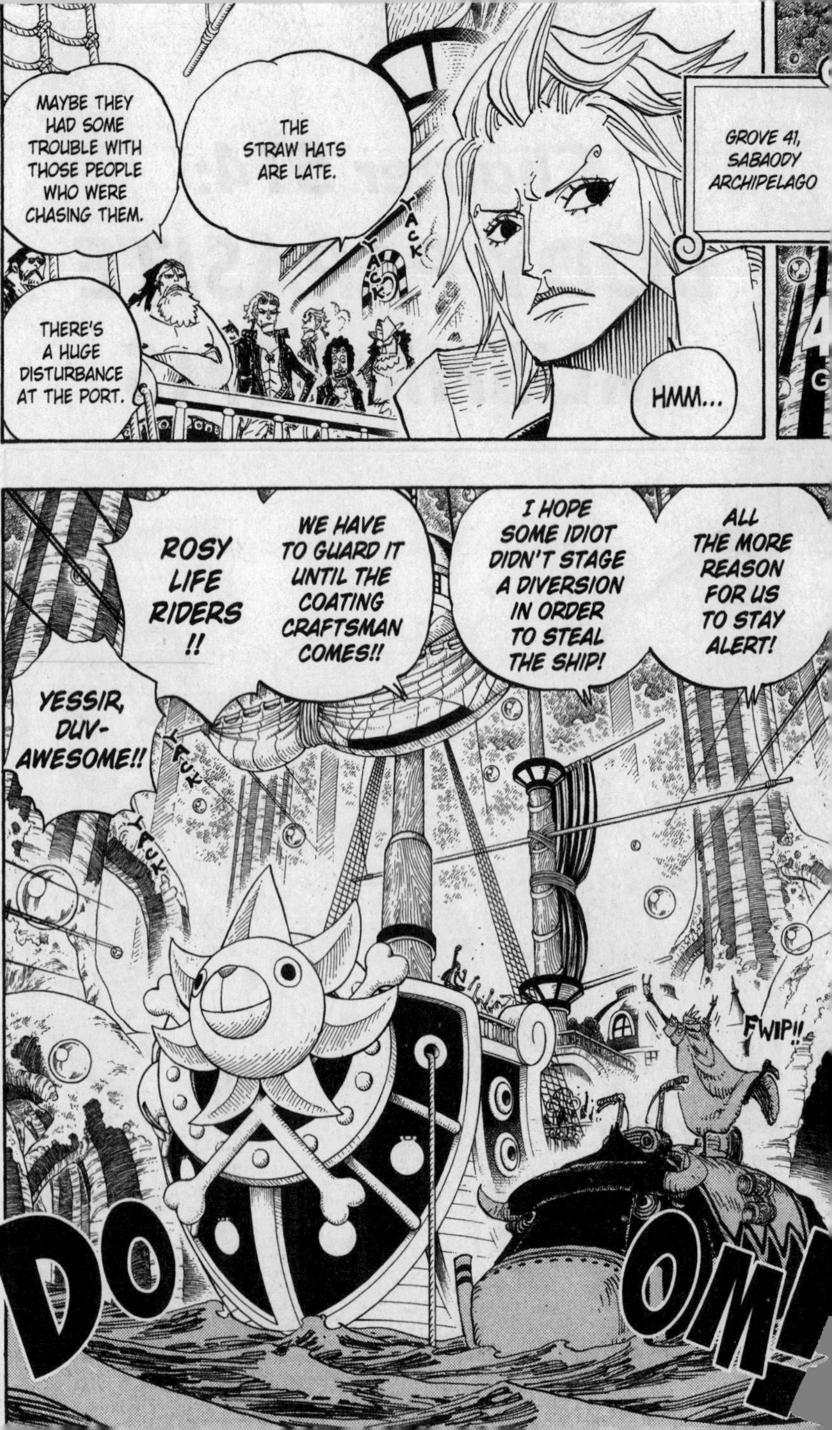
GROVE 41, SABAODY ARCHIPELAGO
THE STRAW HATS ARE LATE.
HMM...
YACK YACK
MAYBE THEY HAD SOME TROUBLE WITH THOSE PEOPLE WHO WERE CHASING THEM.
THERE'S A HUGE DISTURBANCE AT THE PORT.
ALL THE MORE REASON FOR US TO STAY ALERT!
I HOPE SOME IDIOT DIDN'T STAGE A DIVERSION IN ORDER TO STEAL THE SHIP!
WE HAVE TO GUARD IT UNTIL THE COATING CRAFTSMAN COMES!!
ROSY LIFE RIDERS !!
YESSIR, DUV-AWESOME!!
YAUK YAUK
FWIP!!
DOOM!!

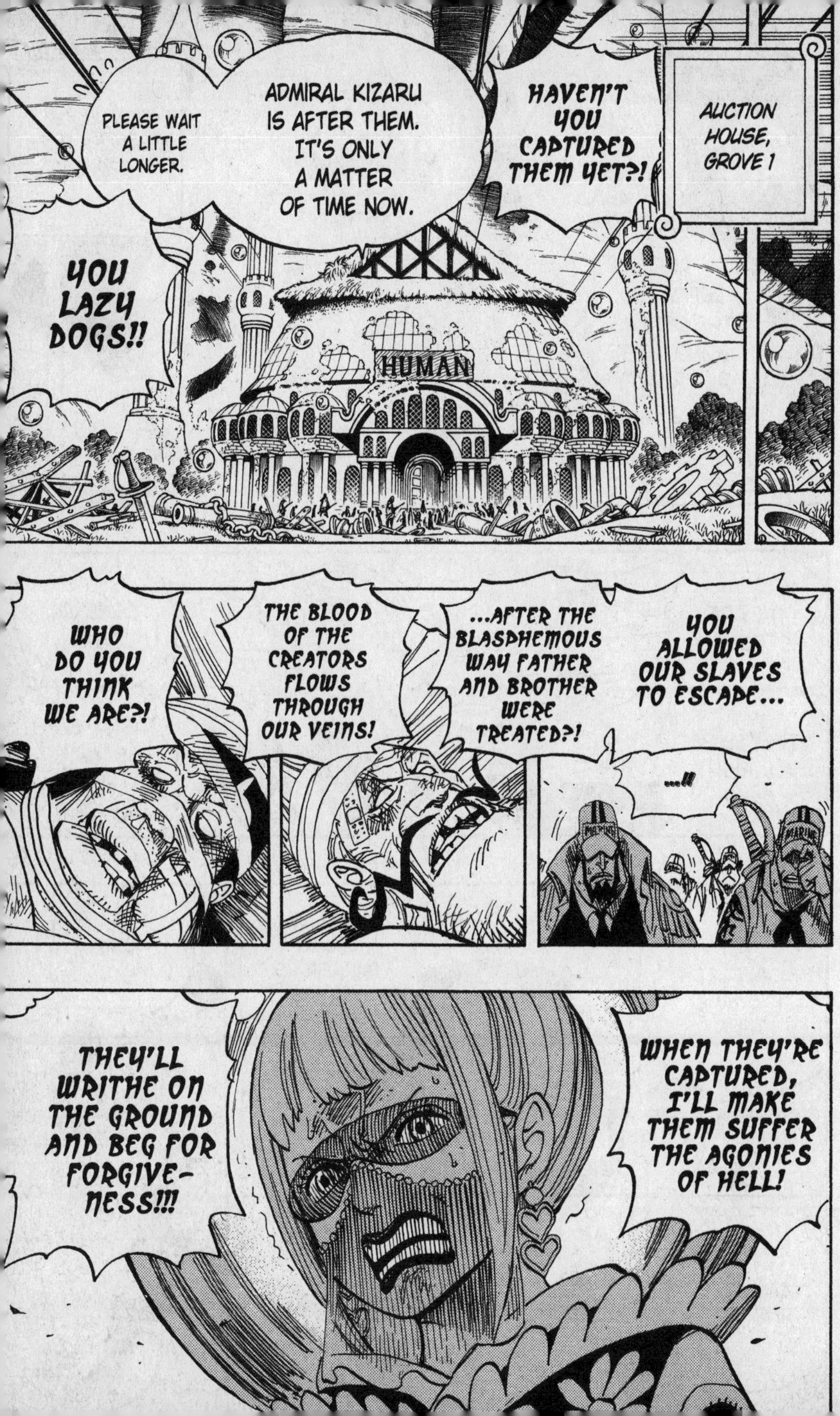
AUCTION HOUSE, GROVE 1
HAVEN'T YOU CAPTURED THEM YET?!
ADMIRAL KIZARU IS AFTER THEM. IT'S ONLY A MATTER OF TIME NOW.
PLEASE WAIT A LITTLE LONGER.
HUMAN
YOU LAZY DOGS!!
YOU ALLOWED OUR SLAVES TO ESCAPE...
...!!
...AFTER THE BLASPHEMOUS WAY FATHER AND BROTHER WERE TREATED?!
THE BLOOD OF THE CREATORS FLOWS THROUGH OUR VEINS!
WHO DO YOU THINK WE ARE?!
WHEN THEY'RE CAPTURED, I'LL MAKE THEM SUFFER THE AGONIES OF HELL!
THEY'LL WRITHE ON THE GROUND AND BEG FOR FORGIVE-NESS!!!

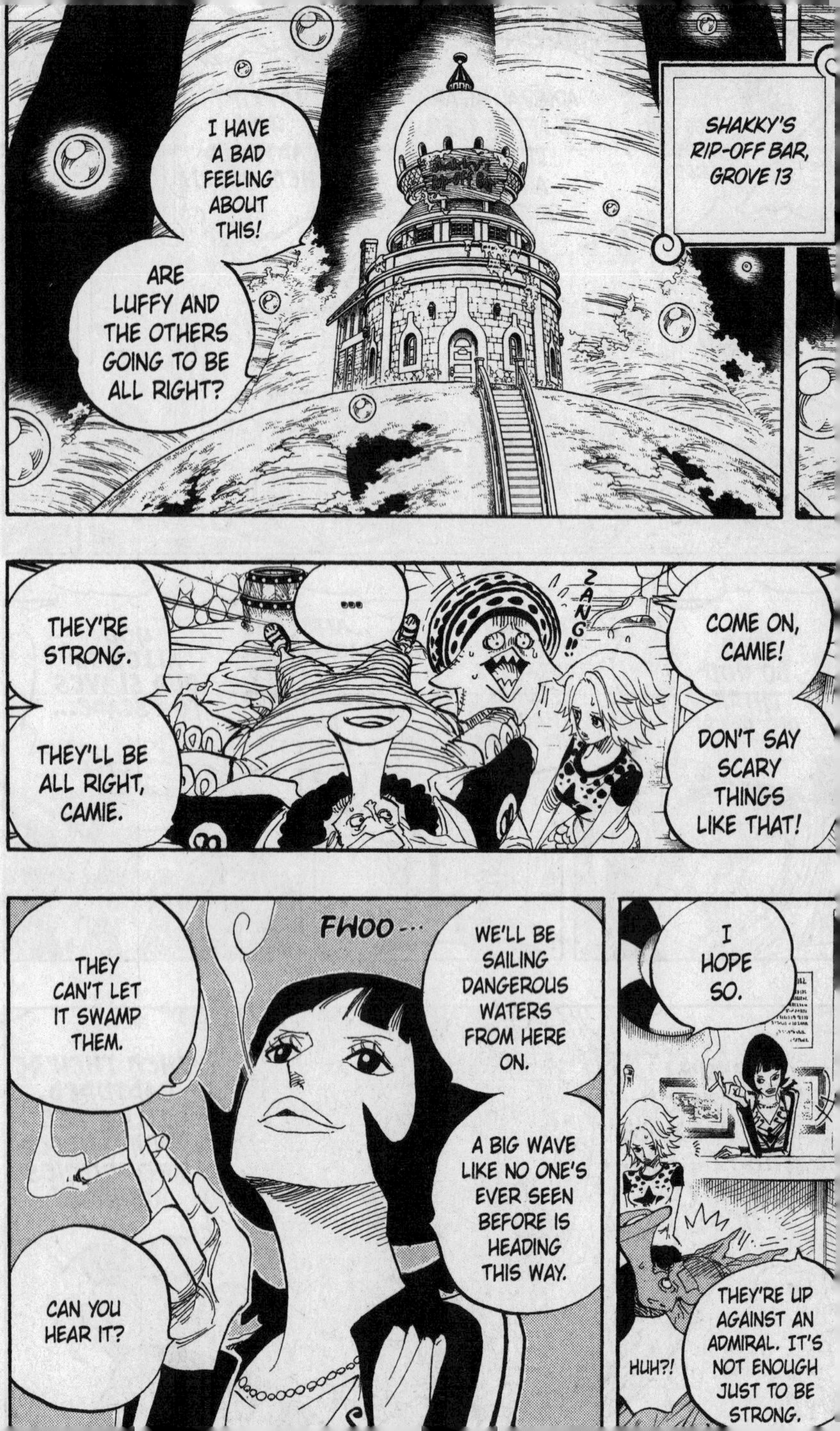
SHAKKY'S RIP-OFF BAR, GROVE 13
I HAVE A BAD FEELING ABOUT THIS!
ARE LUFFY AND THE OTHERS GOING TO BE ALL RIGHT?
COME ON, CAMIE!
DON'T SAY SCARY THINGS LIKE THAT!
ZANG!!
...
THEY'RE STRONG.
THEY'LL BE ALL RIGHT, CAMIE.
I HOPE SO.
THEY'RE UP AGAINST AN ADMIRAL. IT'S NOT ENOUGH JUST TO BE STRONG.
HUH?!
FWOO...
WE'LL BE SAILING DANGEROUS WATERS FROM HERE ON.
THEY CAN'T LET IT SWAMP THEM.
A BIG WAVE LIKE NO ONE'S EVER SEEN BEFORE IS HEADING THIS WAY.
CAN YOU HEAR IT?

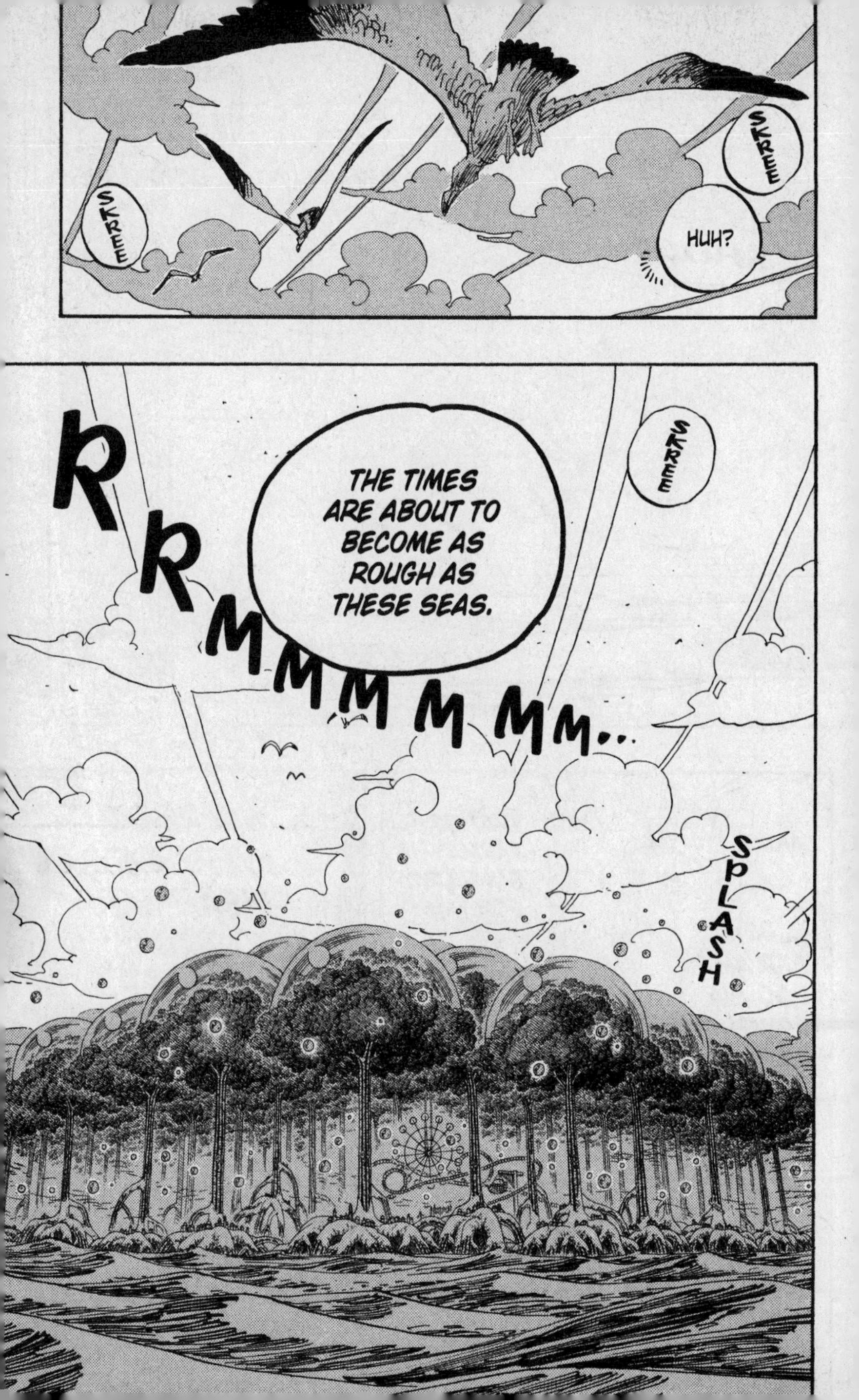
SKREE
HUH?
SKREE
SKREE
THE TIMES ARE ABOUT TO BECOME AS ROUGH AS THESE SEAS.
RRMMMMMM...
SPLASH

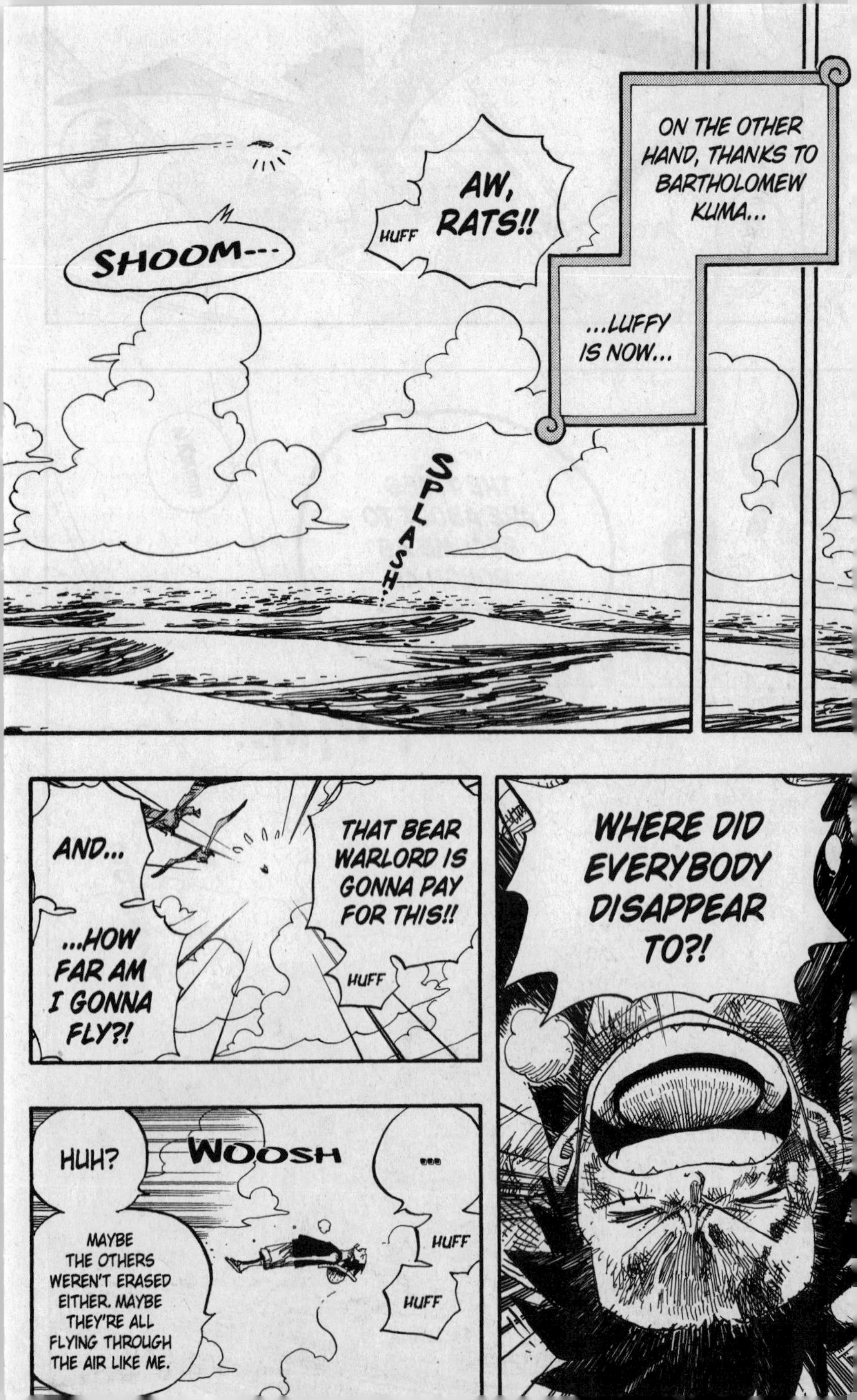
ON THE OTHER HAND, THANKS TO BARTHOLOMEW KUMA...
...LUFFY IS NOW...
AW, RATS!!
HUFF
SHOOM---
SPLASH!
WHERE DID EVERYBODY DISAPPEAR TO?!
THAT BEAR WARLORD IS GONNA PAY FOR THIS!!
HUFF
AND...
...HOW FAR AM I GONNA FLY?!
...
HUFF
HUFF
WOOSH
HUH?
MAYBE THE OTHERS WEREN'T ERASED EITHER. MAYBE THEY'RE ALL FLYING THROUGH THE AIR LIKE ME.

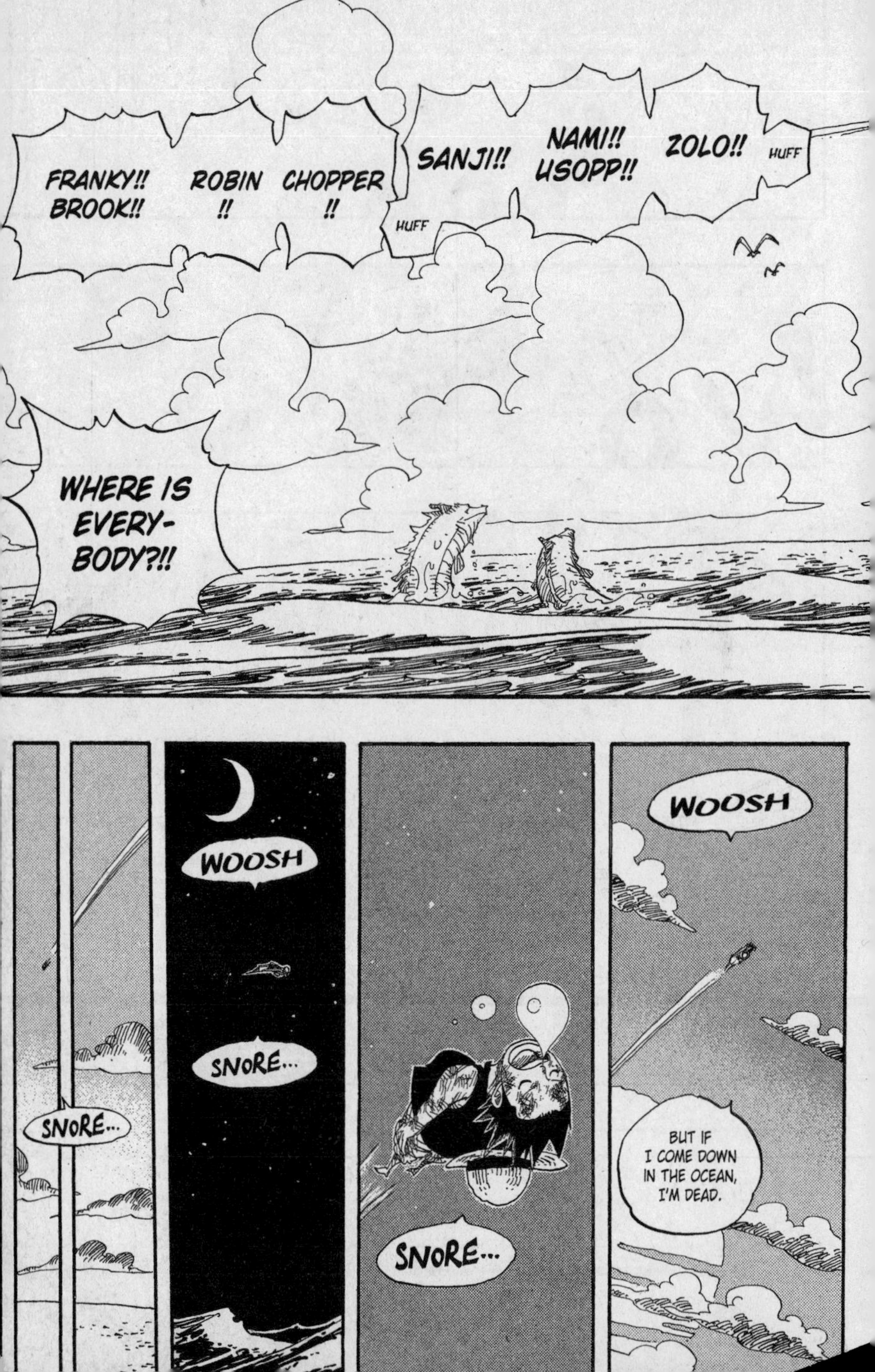
ZOLO!!
HUFF
NAMI!! USOPP!!
SANJI!!
HUFF
CHOPPER!!
ROBIN!!
FRANKY!! BROOK!!
WHERE IS EVERY-BODY?!!
WOOSH
BUT IF I COME DOWN IN THE OCEAN, I'M DEAD.
SNORE...
WOOSH
SNORE...
SNORE...

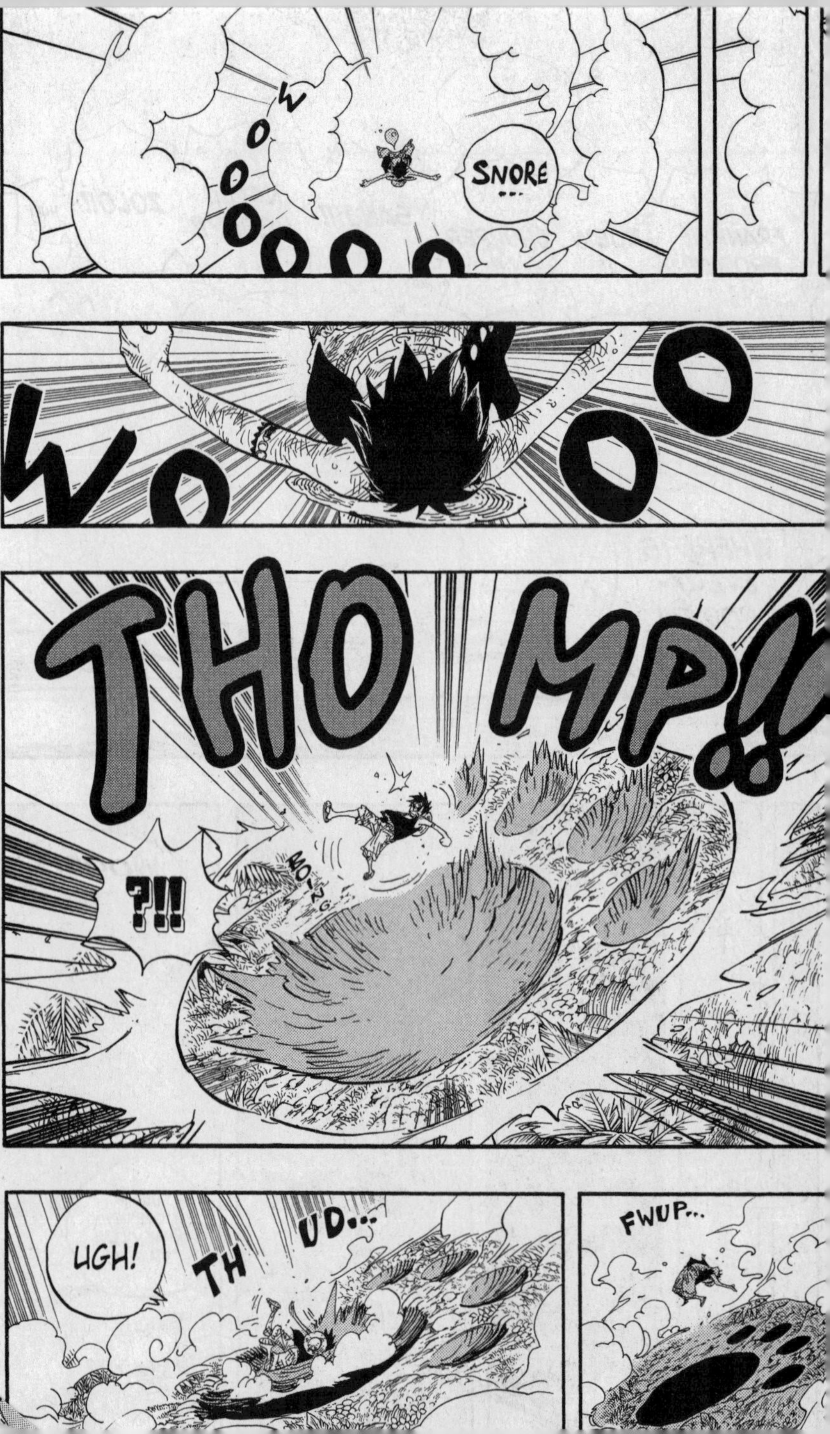

SNORE...
WOOOOOOO
WOOOO
THOMP!!
BOING
?!!
FWUP...
THUD...
UGH!

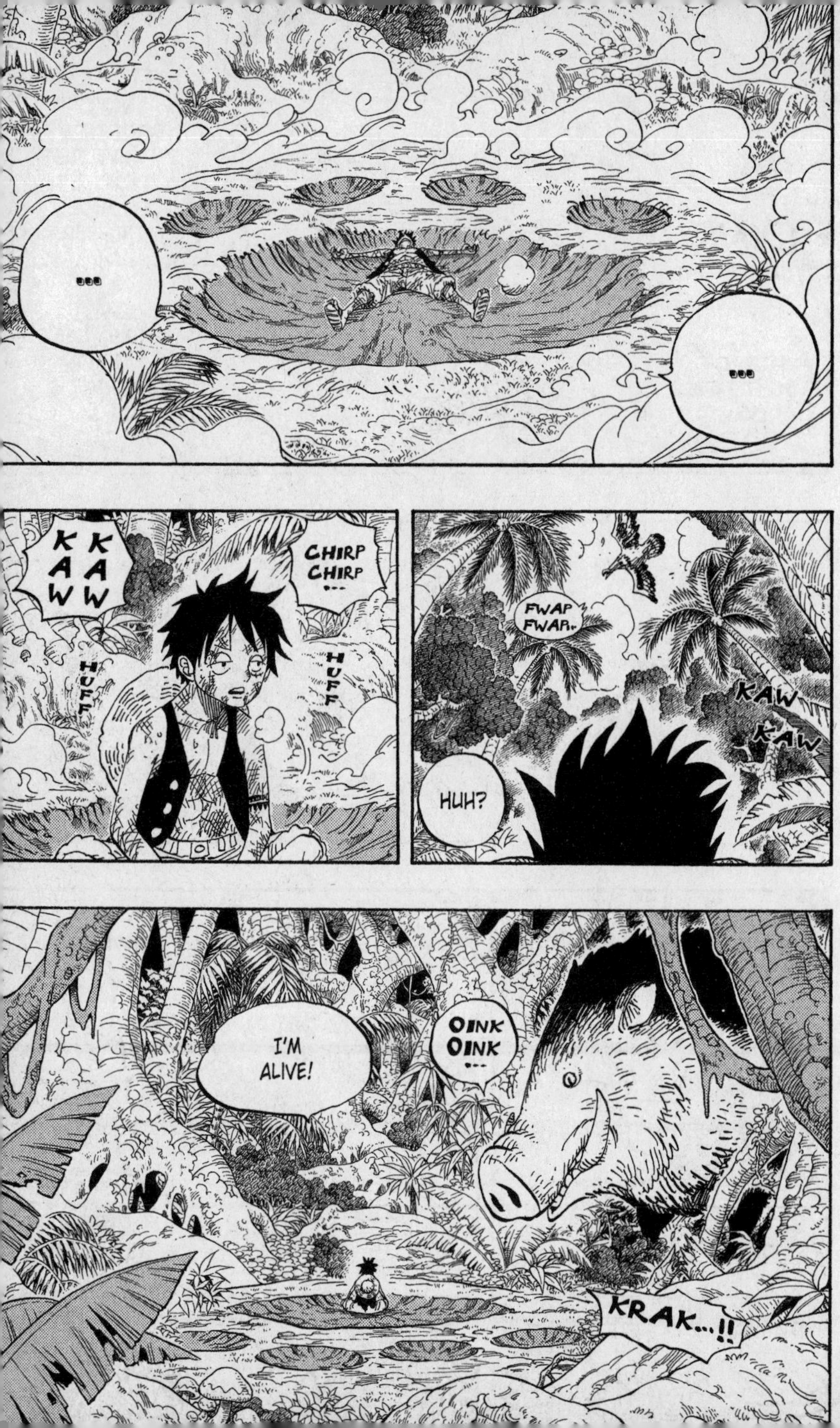
...
...
FWAP FWAP..
KAW KAW
HUH?
CHIRP CHIRP...
KAW KAW
HUFF
HUFF
OINK OINK...
I'M ALIVE!
KRAK...!!

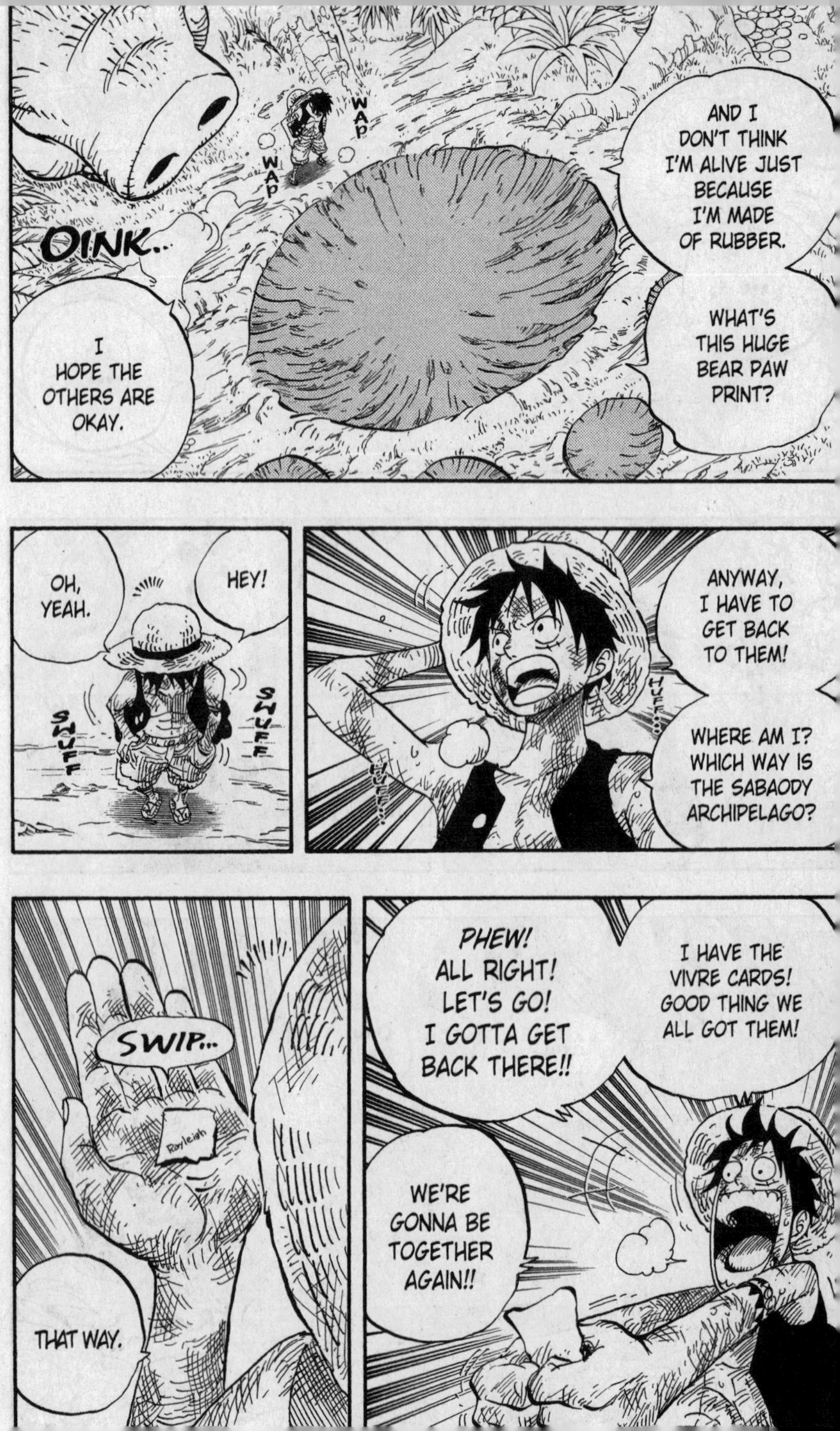
AND I DON'T THINK I'M ALIVE JUST BECAUSE I'M MADE OF RUBBER.
WHAT'S THIS HUGE BEAR PAW PRINT?
WAP
WAP
OINK...
I HOPE THE OTHERS ARE OKAY.
ANYWAY, I HAVE TO GET BACK TO THEM!
HUFF...
WHERE AM I? WHICH WAY IS THE SABAODY ARCHIPELAGO?
HUFF...
HEY!
OH, YEAH.
SHUFF
SHUFF
I HAVE THE VIVRE CARDS! GOOD THING WE ALL GOT THEM!
PHEW! ALL RIGHT! LET'S GO! I GOTTA GET BACK THERE!!
WE'RE GONNA BE TOGETHER AGAIN!!
SWIP...
Rayleigh
THAT WAY.

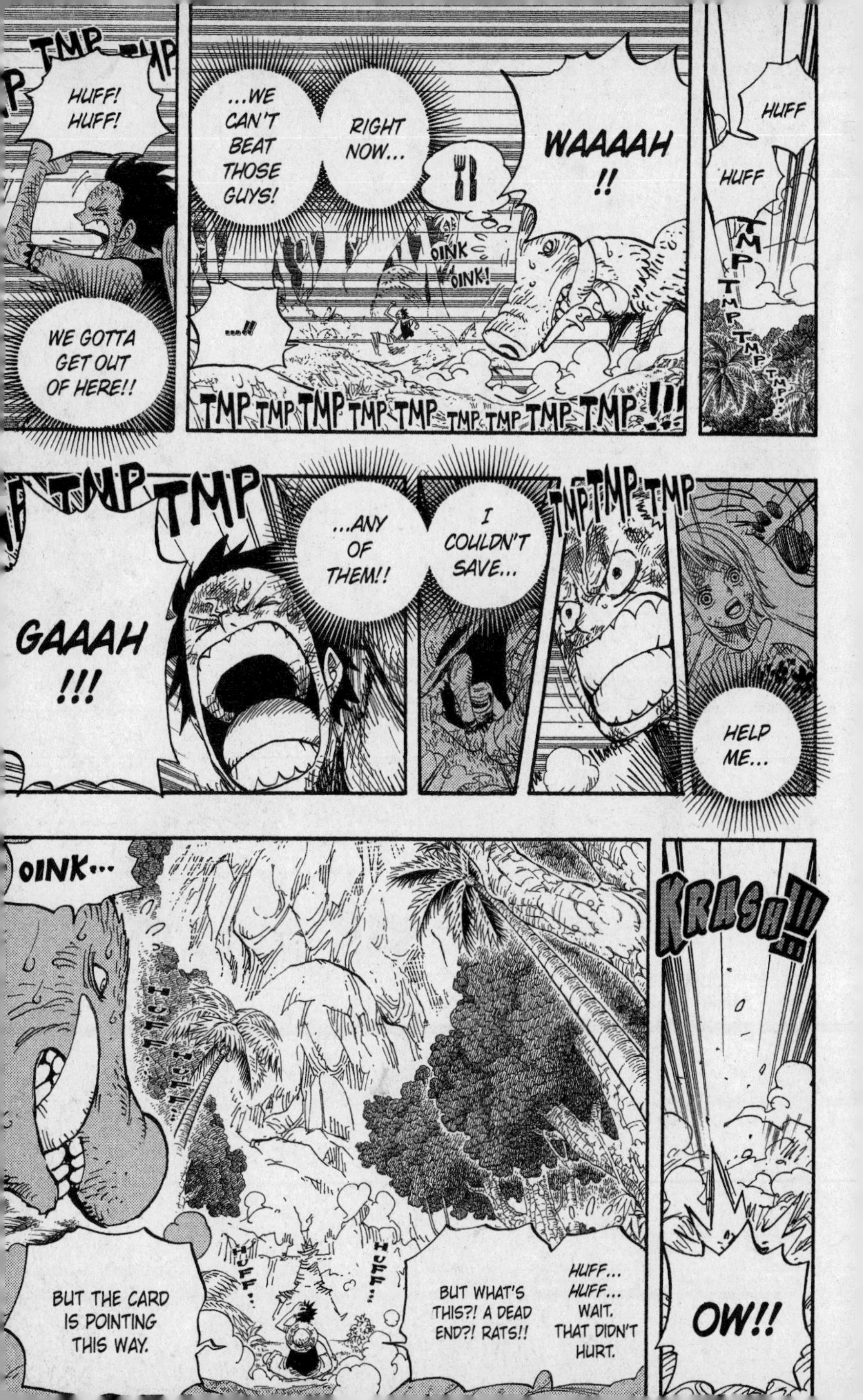
HUFF
HUFF
TMP TMP TMP TMP TMP TMP
WAAAAH!!
RIGHT NOW...
...WE CAN'T BEAT THOSE GUYS!
OINK OINK!
...!!
TMP TMP TMP TMP TMP TMP TMP TMP TMP!!!
TMP TMP
HUFF! HUFF!
WE GOTTA GET OUT OF HERE!!
TMP TMP TMP
HELP ME...
I COULDN'T SAVE...
...ANY OF THEM!!
TMP TMP
GAAAH!!!
KRASH!!!
OW!!
OINK...
HUFF... HUFF... WAIT. THAT DIDN'T HURT.
BUT WHAT'S THIS?! A DEAD END?! RATS!!
HUFF...
HUFF...
BUT THE CARD IS POINTING THIS WAY.

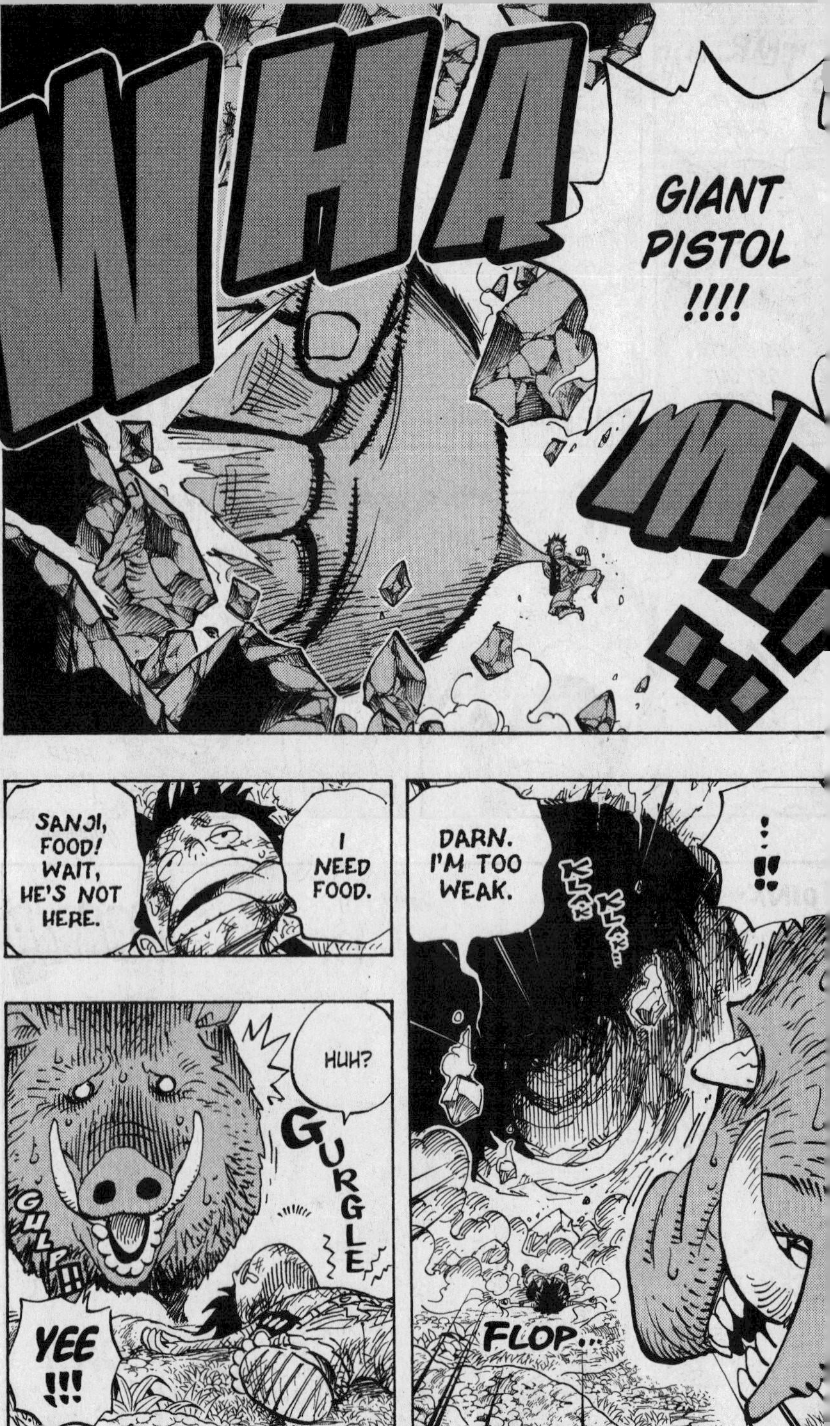
GIANT PISTOL!!!!
WHAM!!
...!!
DARN. I'M TOO WEAK.
KLAK KLAK...
FLOP...
I NEED FOOD.
SANJI, FOOD! WAIT, HE'S NOT HERE.
HUH?
GURGLE
GULP
YEE!!!

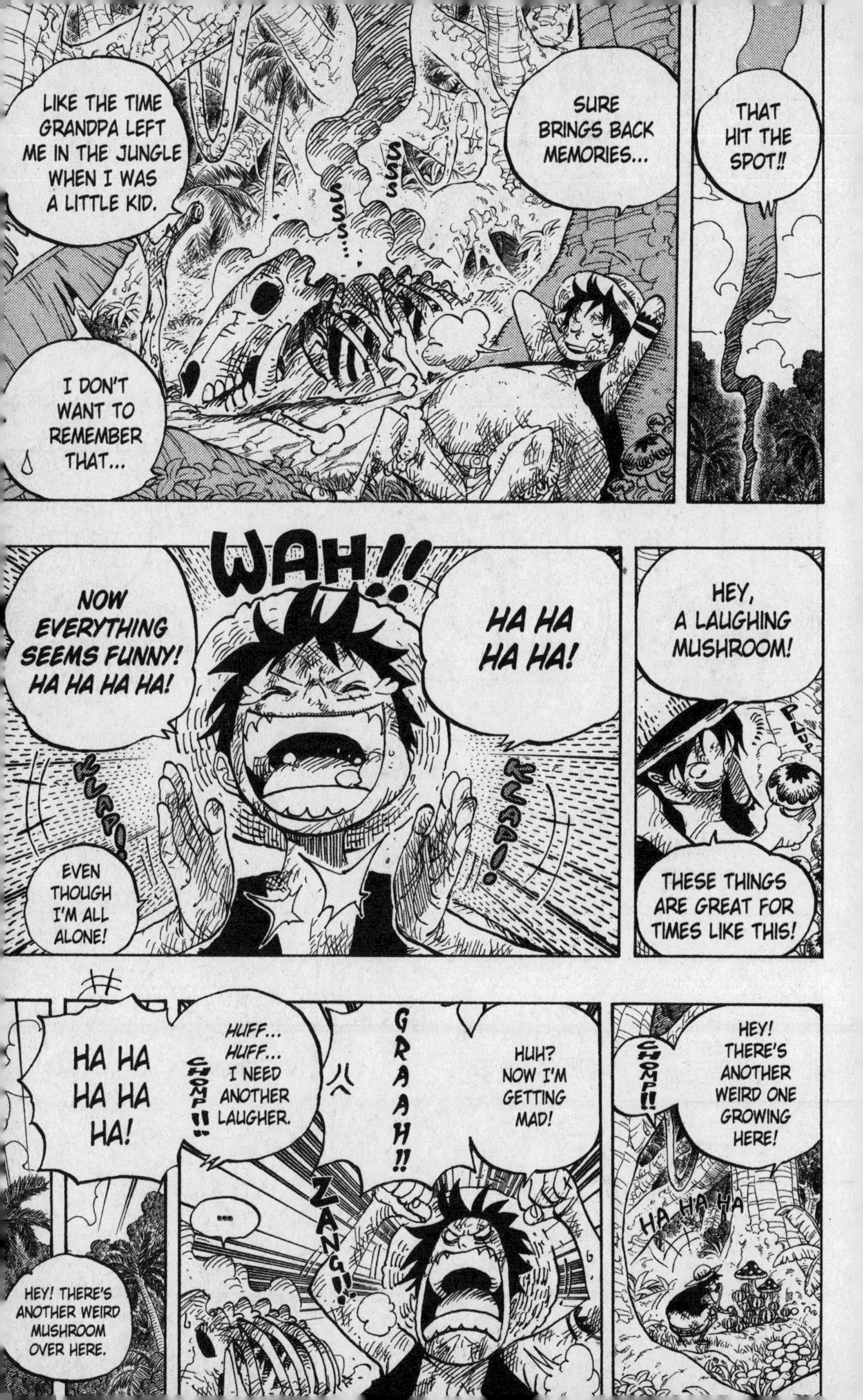
THAT HIT THE SPOT!!
SURE BRINGS BACK MEMORIES...
SSS
SSS...
LIKE THE TIME GRANDPA LEFT ME IN THE JUNGLE WHEN I WAS A LITTLE KID.
I DON'T WANT TO REMEMBER THAT...
HEY, A LAUGHING MUSHROOM!
PLUP
THESE THINGS ARE GREAT FOR TIMES LIKE THIS!
WAH!!
HA HA HA HA!
KLAP!!
NOW EVERYTHING SEEMS FUNNY! HA HA HA HA!
KLAP!!
EVEN THOUGH I'M ALL ALONE!
HEY! THERE'S ANOTHER WEIRD ONE GROWING HERE!
CHOMP!!
HA HA HA
HUH? NOW I'M GETTING MAD!
GRAAAH!!
ZANG!!
...
HA HA HA HA HA!
HUFF... HUFF... I NEED ANOTHER LAUGHER.
CHOMP!!
HEY! THERE'S ANOTHER WEIRD MUSHROOM OVER HERE.

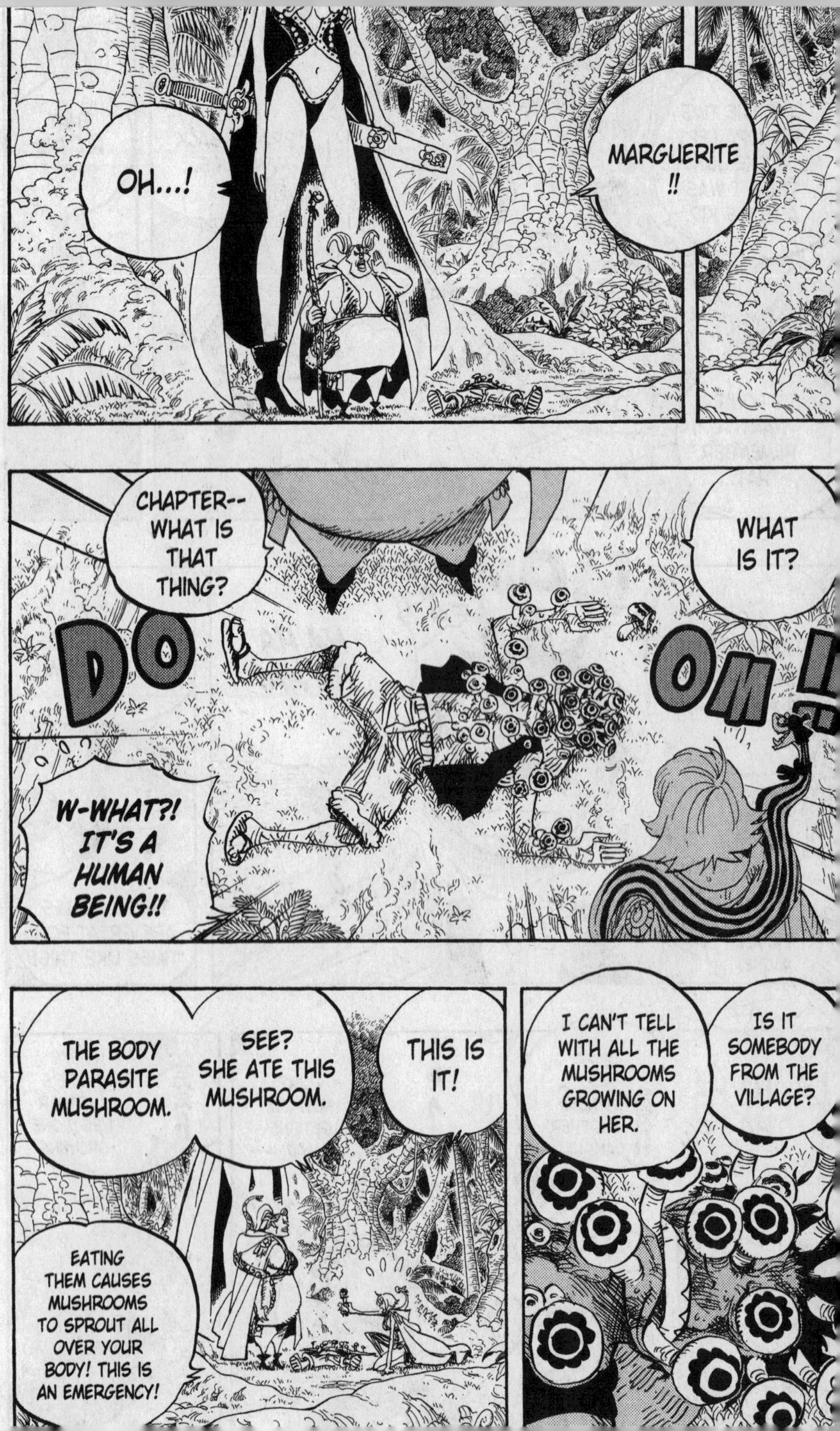
MARGUERITE!!
OH...!
WHAT IS IT?
CHAPTER-- WHAT IS THAT THING?
DOOM!!
W-WHAT?! IT'S A HUMAN BEING!!
IS IT SOMEBODY FROM THE VILLAGE?
I CAN'T TELL WITH ALL THE MUSHROOMS GROWING ON HER.
THIS IS IT!
SEE? SHE ATE THIS MUSHROOM.
THE BODY PARASITE MUSHROOM.
EATING THEM CAUSES MUSHROOMS TO SPROUT ALL OVER YOUR BODY! THIS IS AN EMERGENCY!

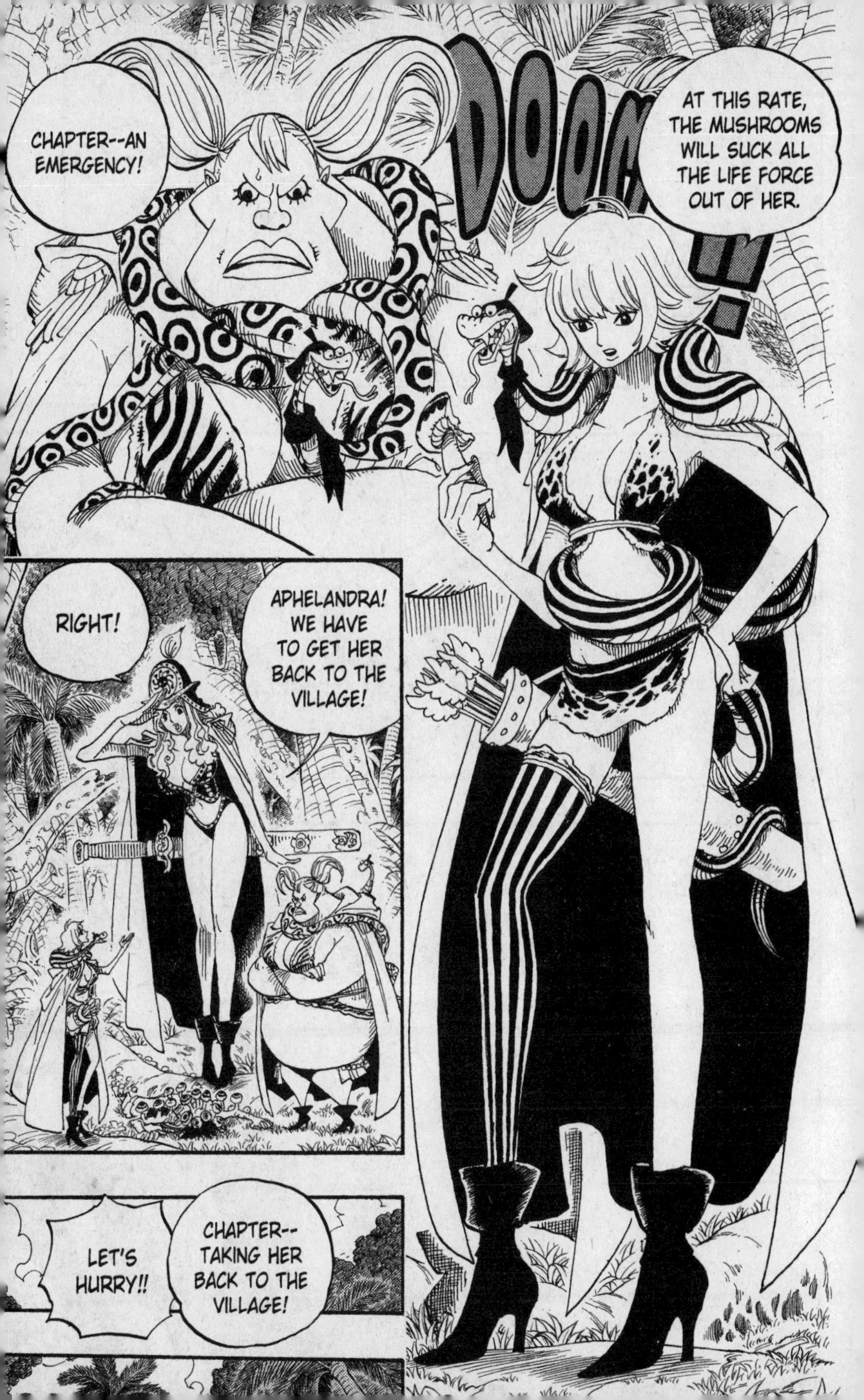
DOO
AT THIS RATE, THE MUSHROOMS WILL SUCK ALL THE LIFE FORCE OUT OF HER.
CHAPTER--AN EMERGENCY!
APHELANDRA! WE HAVE TO GET HER BACK TO THE VILLAGE!
RIGHT!
CHAPTER--TAKING HER BACK TO THE VILLAGE!
LET'S HURRY!!

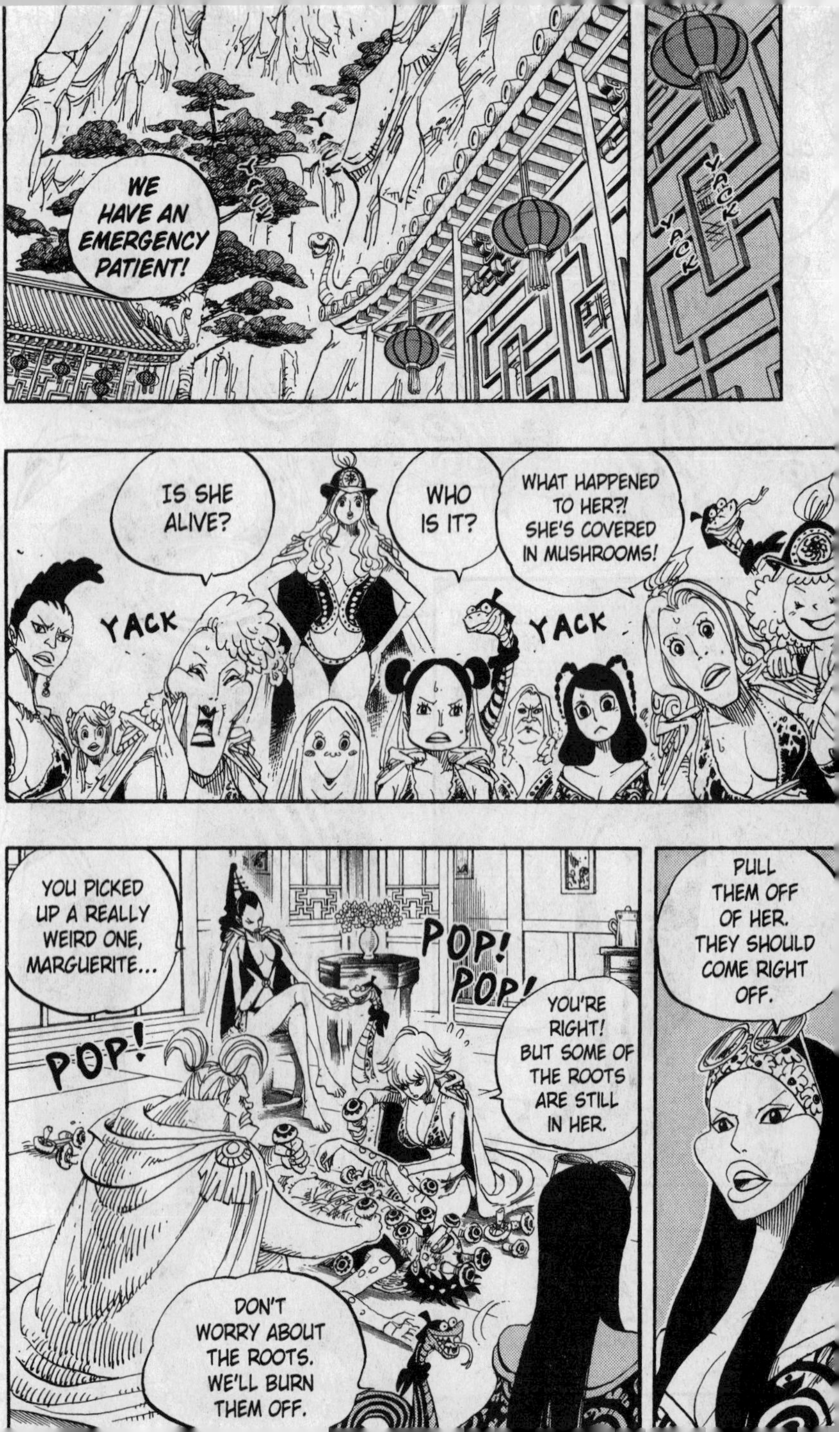
YACK
YACK
WE HAVE AN EMERGENCY PATIENT!
WHAT HAPPENED TO HER?! SHE'S COVERED IN MUSHROOMS!
YACK
WHO IS IT?
IS SHE ALIVE?
YACK
PULL THEM OFF OF HER. THEY SHOULD COME RIGHT OFF.
YOU'RE RIGHT! BUT SOME OF THE ROOTS ARE STILL IN HER.
POP! POP!
YOU PICKED UP A REALLY WEIRD ONE, MARGUERITE...
POP!
DON'T WORRY ABOUT THE ROOTS. WE'LL BURN THEM OFF.

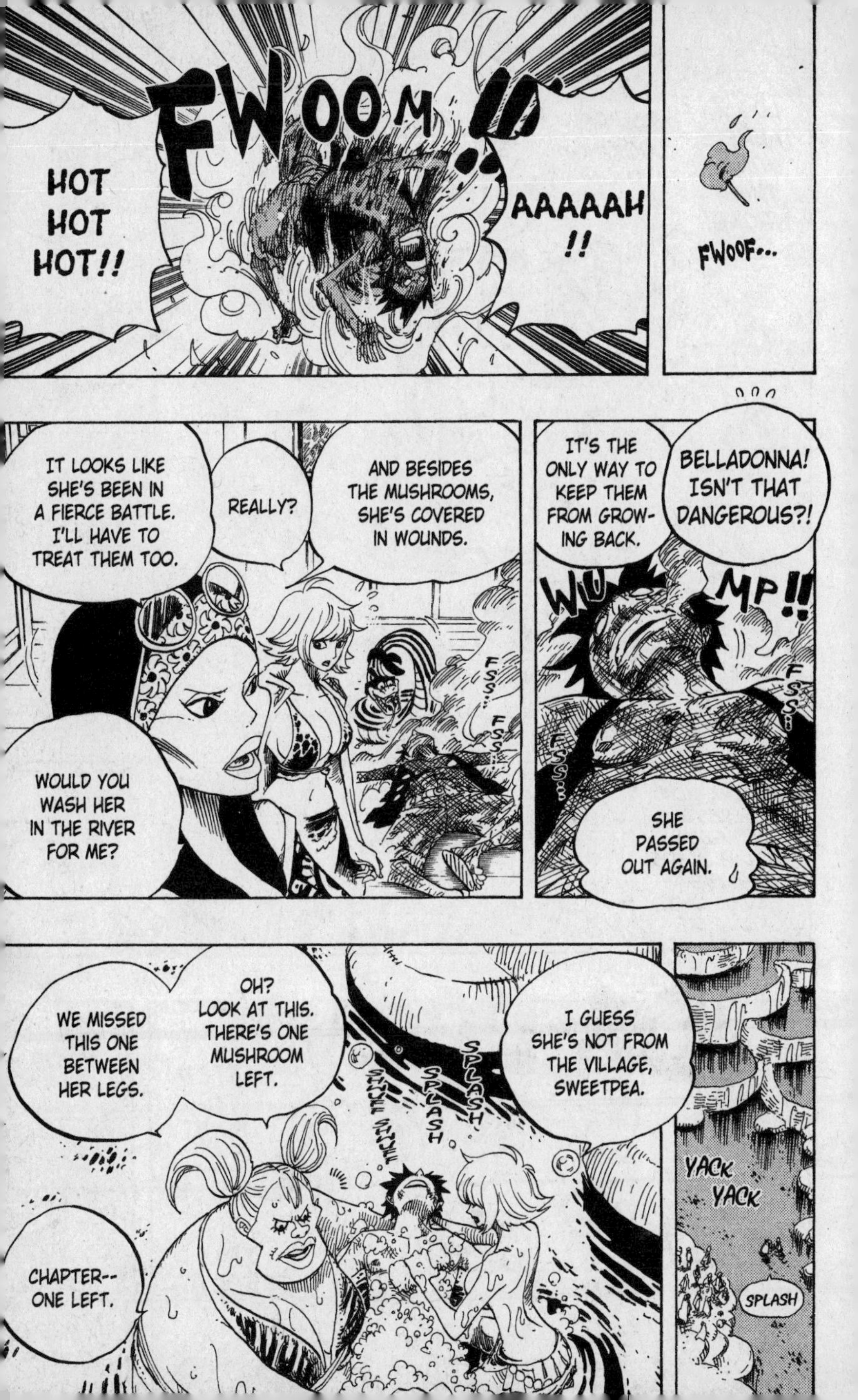
FWOOF...
FWOOM!!
AAAAAH!!
HOT HOT HOT!!
BELLADONNA! ISN'T THAT DANGEROUS?!
IT'S THE ONLY WAY TO KEEP THEM FROM GROW-ING BACK.
WUMP!!
FSS...
FSS...
SHE PASSED OUT AGAIN.
AND BESIDES THE MUSHROOMS, SHE'S COVERED IN WOUNDS.
REALLY?
IT LOOKS LIKE SHE'S BEEN IN A FIERCE BATTLE. I'LL HAVE TO TREAT THEM TOO.
FSS...
FSS...
WOULD YOU WASH HER IN THE RIVER FOR ME?
YACK YACK
SPLASH
I GUESS SHE'S NOT FROM THE VILLAGE, SWEETPEA.
SPLASH
SPLASH
OH? LOOK AT THIS. THERE'S ONE MUSHROOM LEFT.
WE MISSED THIS ONE BETWEEN HER LEGS.
CHAPTER-- ONE LEFT.

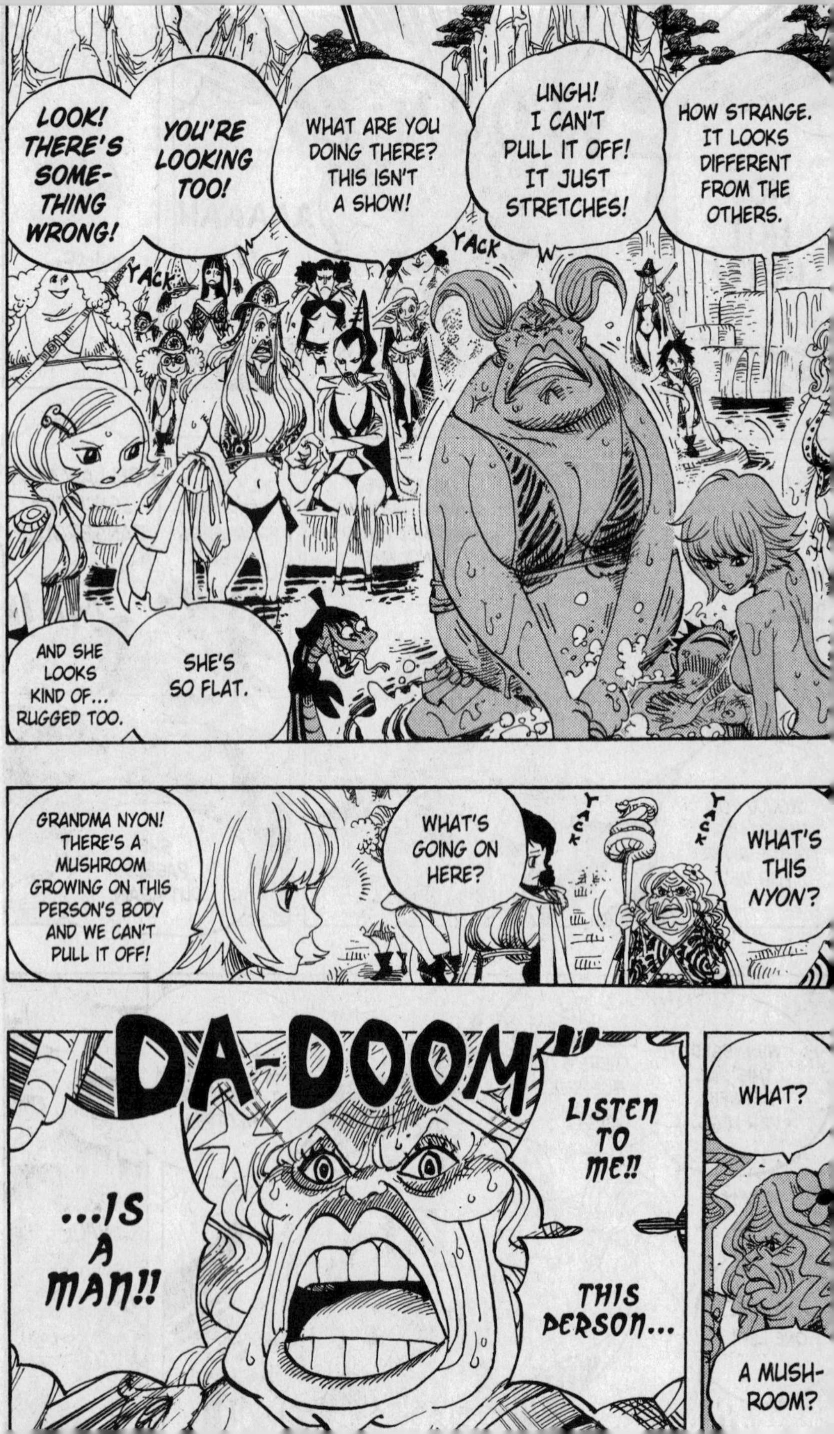
HOW STRANGE. IT LOOKS DIFFERENT FROM THE OTHERS.
UNGH! I CAN'T PULL IT OFF! IT JUST STRETCHES!
YACK
WHAT ARE YOU DOING THERE? THIS ISN'T A SHOW!
YOU'RE LOOKING TOO!
LOOK! THERE'S SOME-THING WRONG!
YACK
SHE'S SO FLAT.
AND SHE LOOKS KIND OF... RUGGED TOO.
WHAT'S THIS NYON?
YACK
YACK
WHAT'S GOING ON HERE?
GRANDMA NYON! THERE'S A MUSHROOM GROWING ON THIS PERSON'S BODY AND WE CAN'T PULL IT OFF!
WHAT?
A MUSH-ROOM?
DA-DOOM
LISTEN TO ME!!
THIS PERSON...
...IS A MAN!!

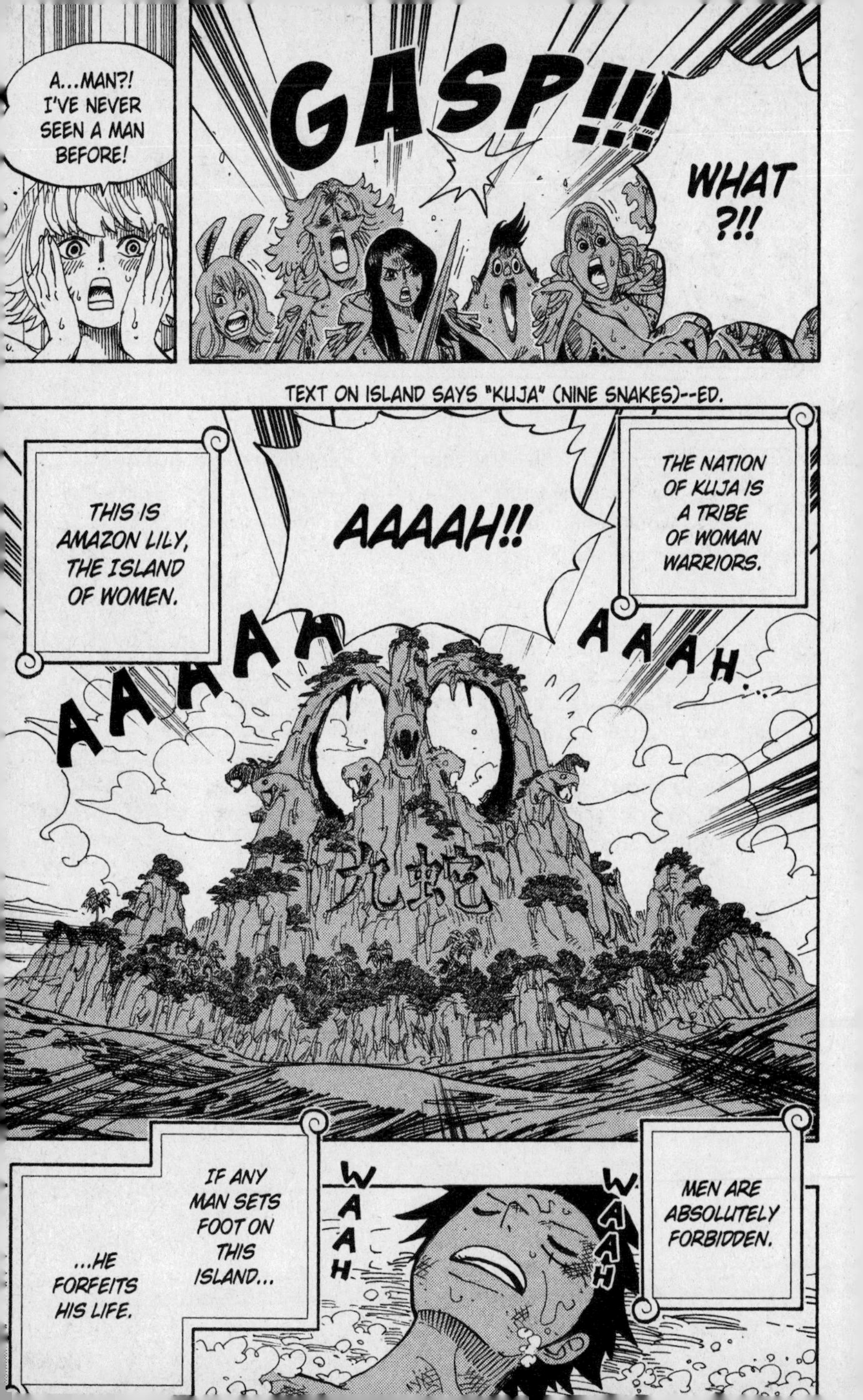
GASP!!!
WHAT ?!!
A...MAN?! I'VE NEVER SEEN A MAN BEFORE!
TEXT ON ISLAND SAYS "KUJA" (NINE SNAKES)--ED.
THE NATION OF KUJA IS A TRIBE OF WOMAN WARRIORS.
AAAAH!!
THIS IS AMAZON LILY, THE ISLAND OF WOMEN.
AAAAH.
AAAAAA
MEN ARE ABSOLUTELY FORBIDDEN.
WAAAH
WAAAH
IF ANY MAN SETS FOOT ON THIS ISLAND...
...HE FORFEITS HIS LIFE.

SBS Question Corner

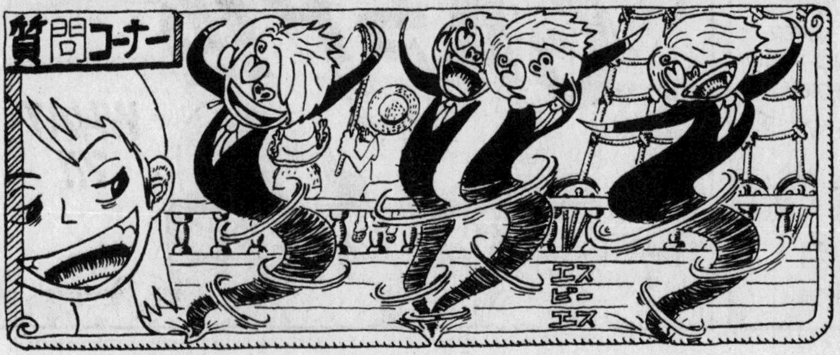
質問コーナー
エス
ピー
エス

(Yourikusai, Oita)

Leader(Q): In volume 51, chapter 502, the CP9's Independent Report shows Kalifa wearing the Criminal brand that's popular on Fish-Man Island! Why would a human be wearing that? And does Kalifa like brand-name stuff?

--MOTO

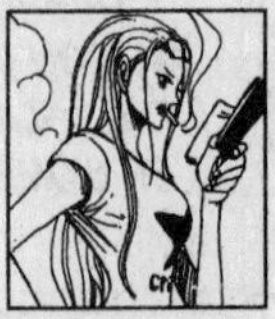

Oda(A): I'm glad you caught that. That is indeed a T-shirt of Pappagu's brand "Criminal." I get the feeling that Kalifa likes brand-name clothing. Criminal is very popular on Fish-Man Island, but it is sold on dry land too. Even Zolo was wearing it for a while. Now about the name "Criminal." The Japanese word for "criminal" can also mean "star." That's why it's star-shaped.

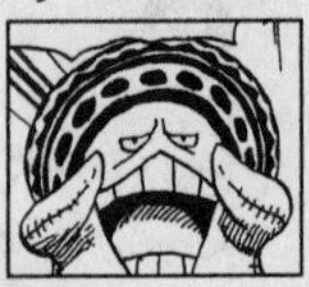

Q: Oda Sensei! Hello-Borsalino! This is about the super-cute mermaid Camie's birthday! The "Ca" in her name sounds like "K," the eleventh letter of the alphabet, so let's say it means eleven! Then "mie" rhymes with three (sort of)! So can her birthday be November 3?

--II TO ITTE!

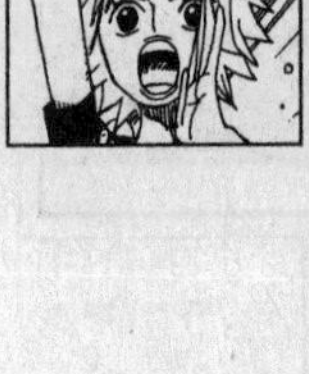

A: Hello-Borsalino! Sure. Sure-Borsalino!

Chapter 515: ADVENTURE ON THE ISLAND OF WOMEN

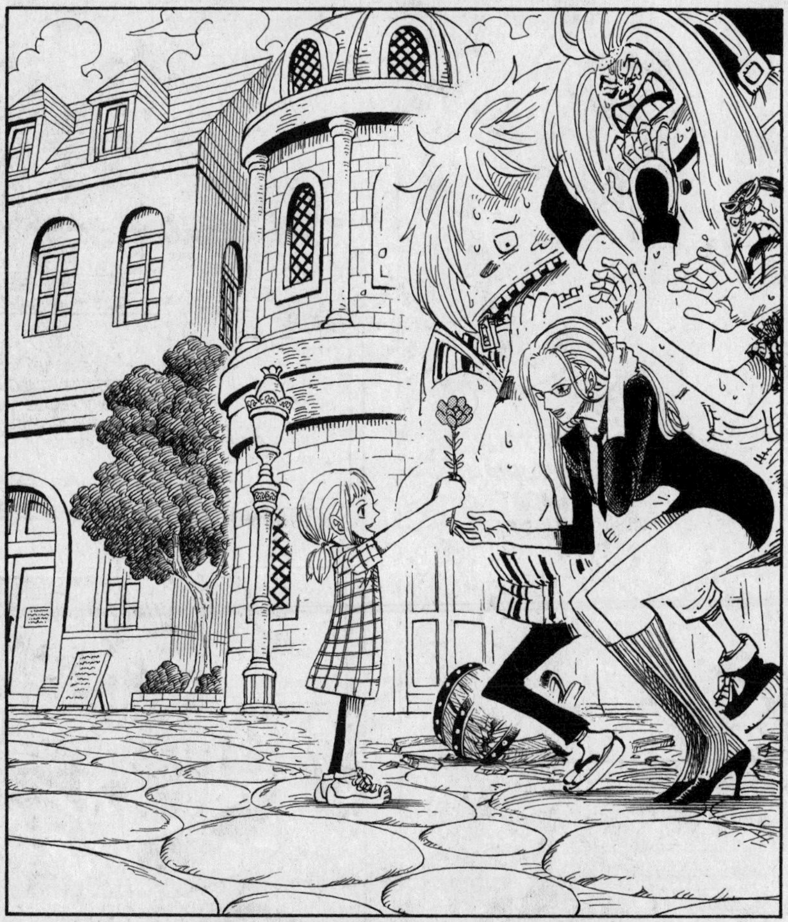

CP9'S INDEPENDENT REPORT, VOL. 23:
"A FLOWER IS A GIFT THAT SHINES BRIGHTLY"

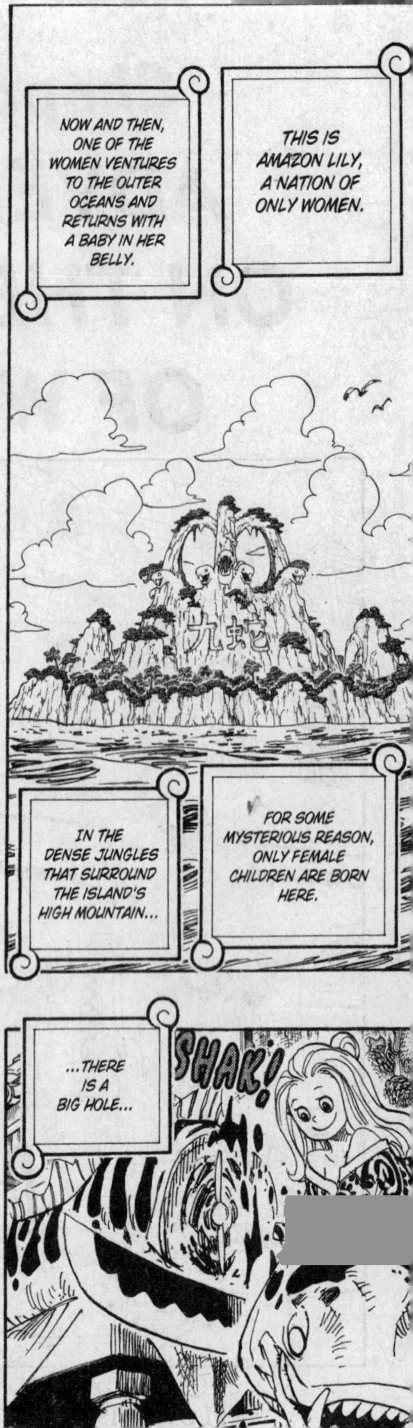
THIS IS AMAZON LILY, A NATION OF ONLY WOMEN.
NOW AND THEN, ONE OF THE WOMEN VENTURES TO THE OUTER OCEANS AND RETURNS WITH A BABY IN HER BELLY.
FOR SOME MYSTERIOUS REASON, ONLY FEMALE CHILDREN ARE BORN HERE.
IN THE DENSE JUNGLES THAT SURROUND THE ISLAND'S HIGH MOUNTAIN...
...THERE IS A BIG HOLE...
SHAK!
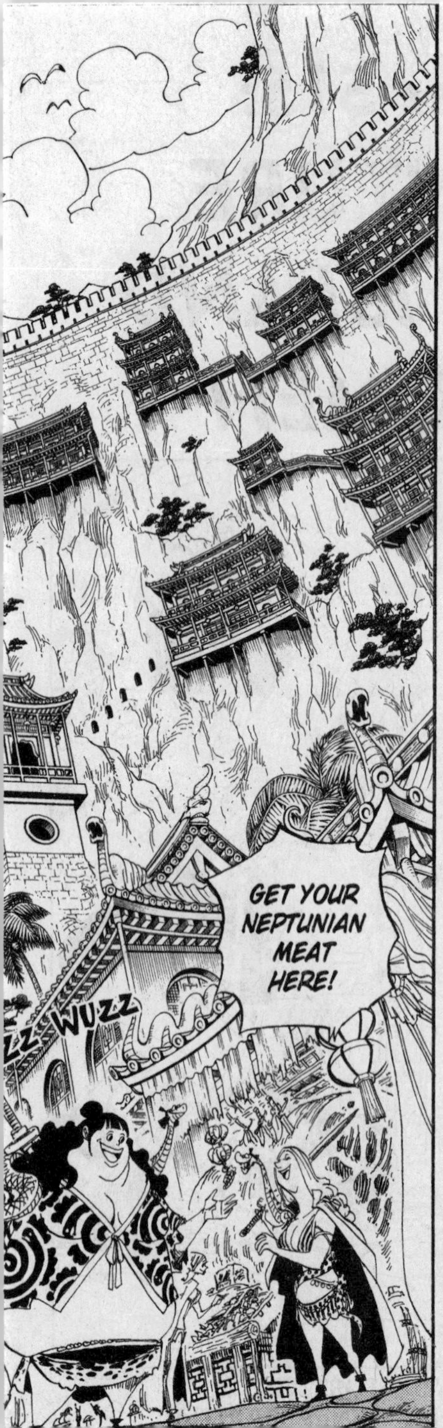
GET YOUR NEPTUNIAN MEAT HERE!
WUZZ
ZZ

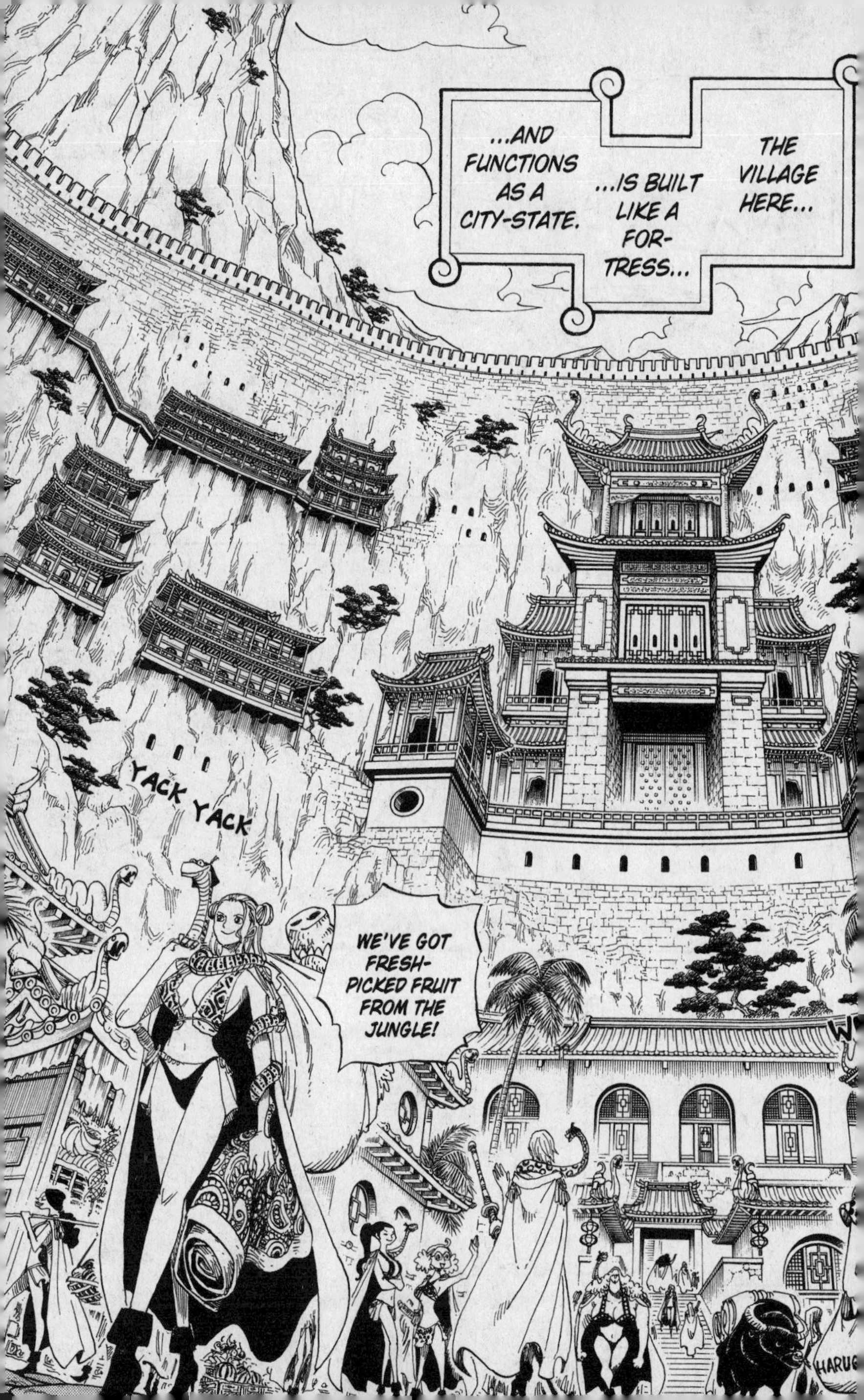
THE VILLAGE HERE...
...IS BUILT LIKE A FOR-TRESS...
...AND FUNCTIONS AS A CITY-STATE.
WE'VE GOT FRESH-PICKED FRUIT FROM THE JUNGLE!
YACK YACK

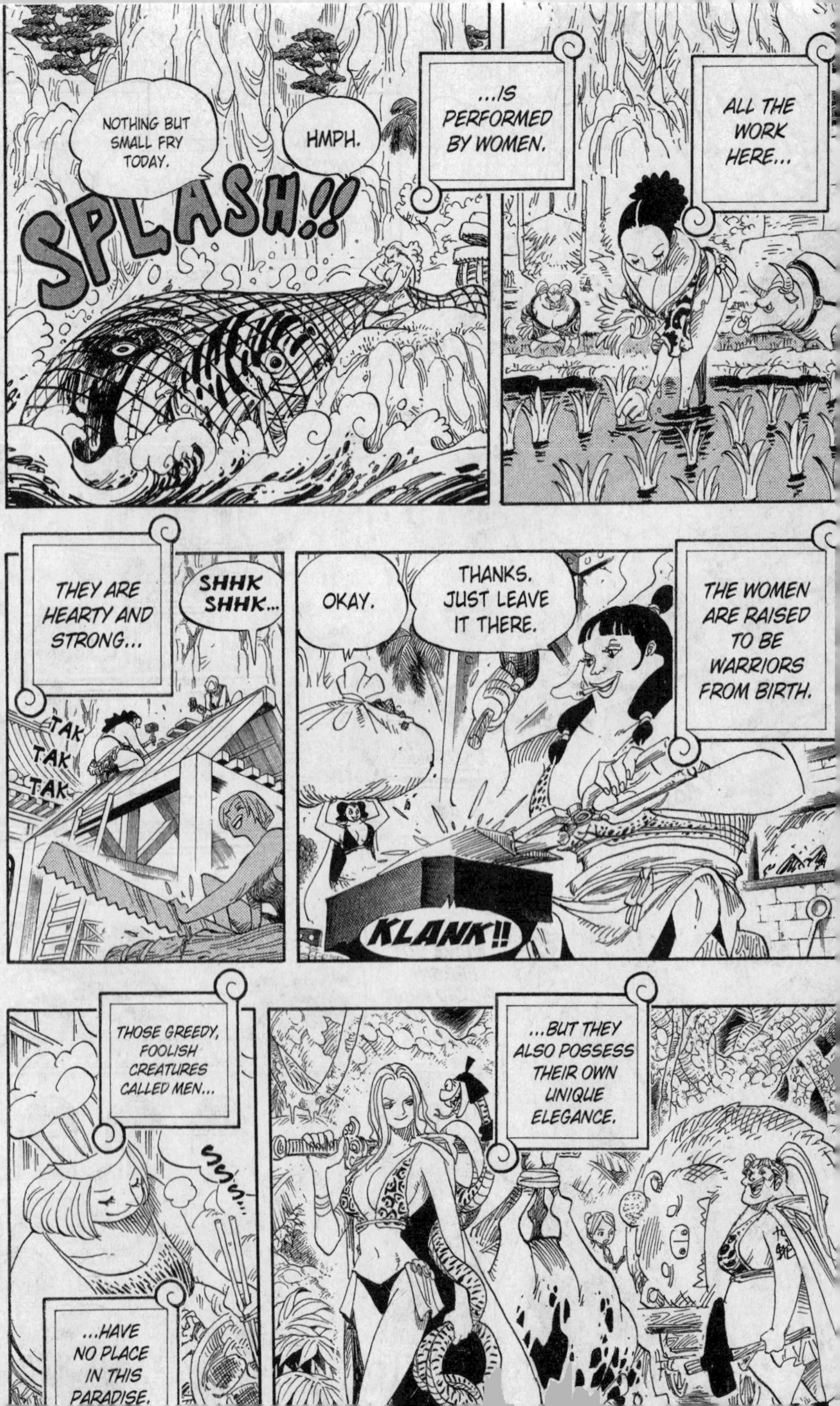
ALL THE WORK HERE...
...IS PERFORMED BY WOMEN.
HMPH.
NOTHING BUT SMALL FRY TODAY.
SPLASH!!
THE WOMEN ARE RAISED TO BE WARRIORS FROM BIRTH.
THANKS. JUST LEAVE IT THERE.
OKAY.
KLANK!!
THEY ARE HEARTY AND STRONG...
SHHK SHHK...
TAK TAK TAK
...BUT THEY ALSO POSSESS THEIR OWN UNIQUE ELEGANCE.
THOSE GREEDY, FOOLISH CREATURES CALLED MEN...
...HAVE NO PLACE IN THIS PARADISE.

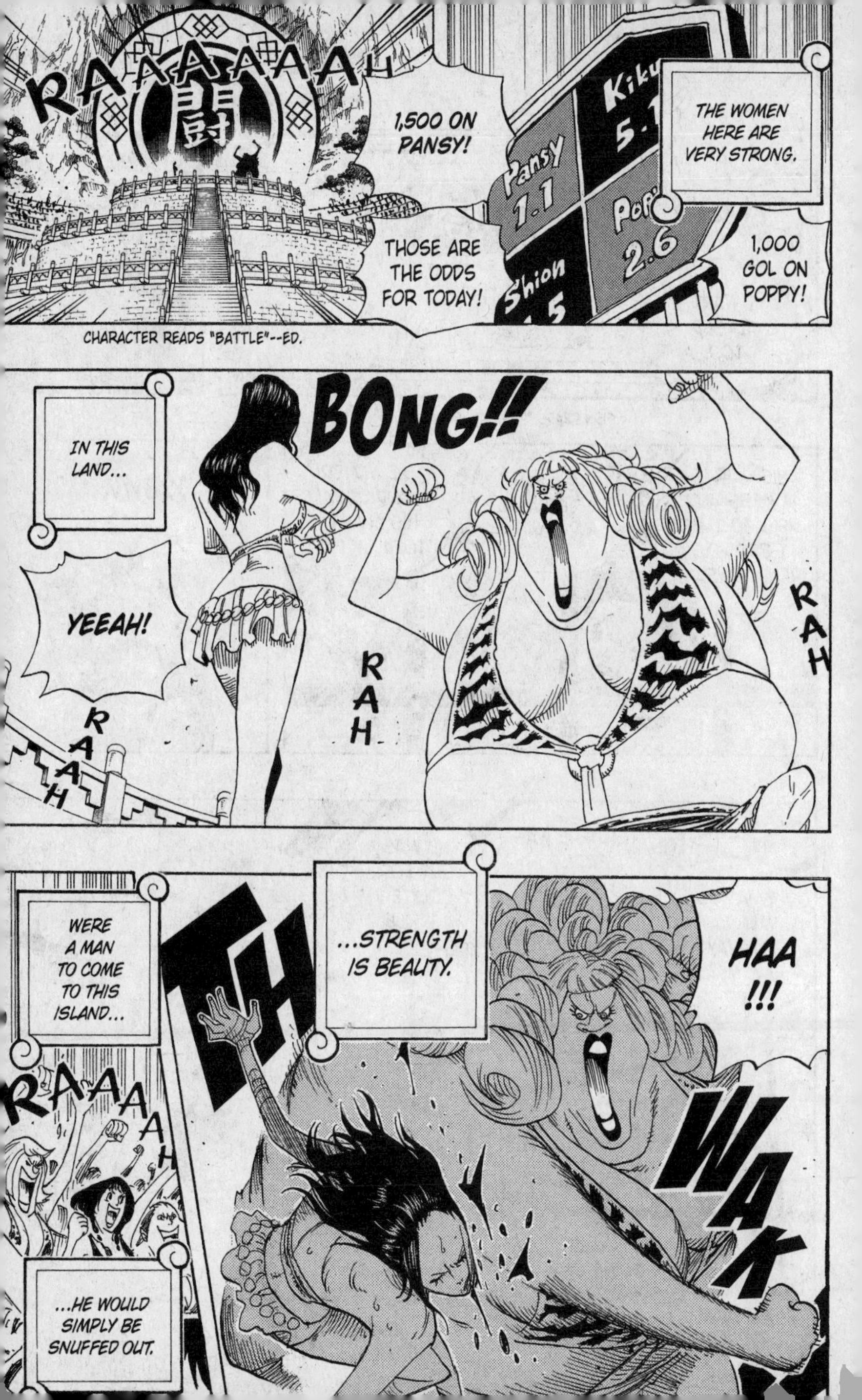
THE WOMEN HERE ARE VERY STRONG.
1,000 GOL ON POPPY!
Kiku 5.1
Pansy 7.1
Pop 2.6
Shion
1,500 ON PANSY!
THOSE ARE THE ODDS FOR TODAY!
RAAAAAAAH
闘
CHARACTER READS "BATTLE"--ED.
RAH
BONG!!
IN THIS LAND...
YEEAH!
RAH
RAAH
HAA!!!
WAK
...STRENGTH IS BEAUTY.
TH
WERE A MAN TO COME TO THIS ISLAND...
RAAAAH
...HE WOULD SIMPLY BE SNUFFED OUT.

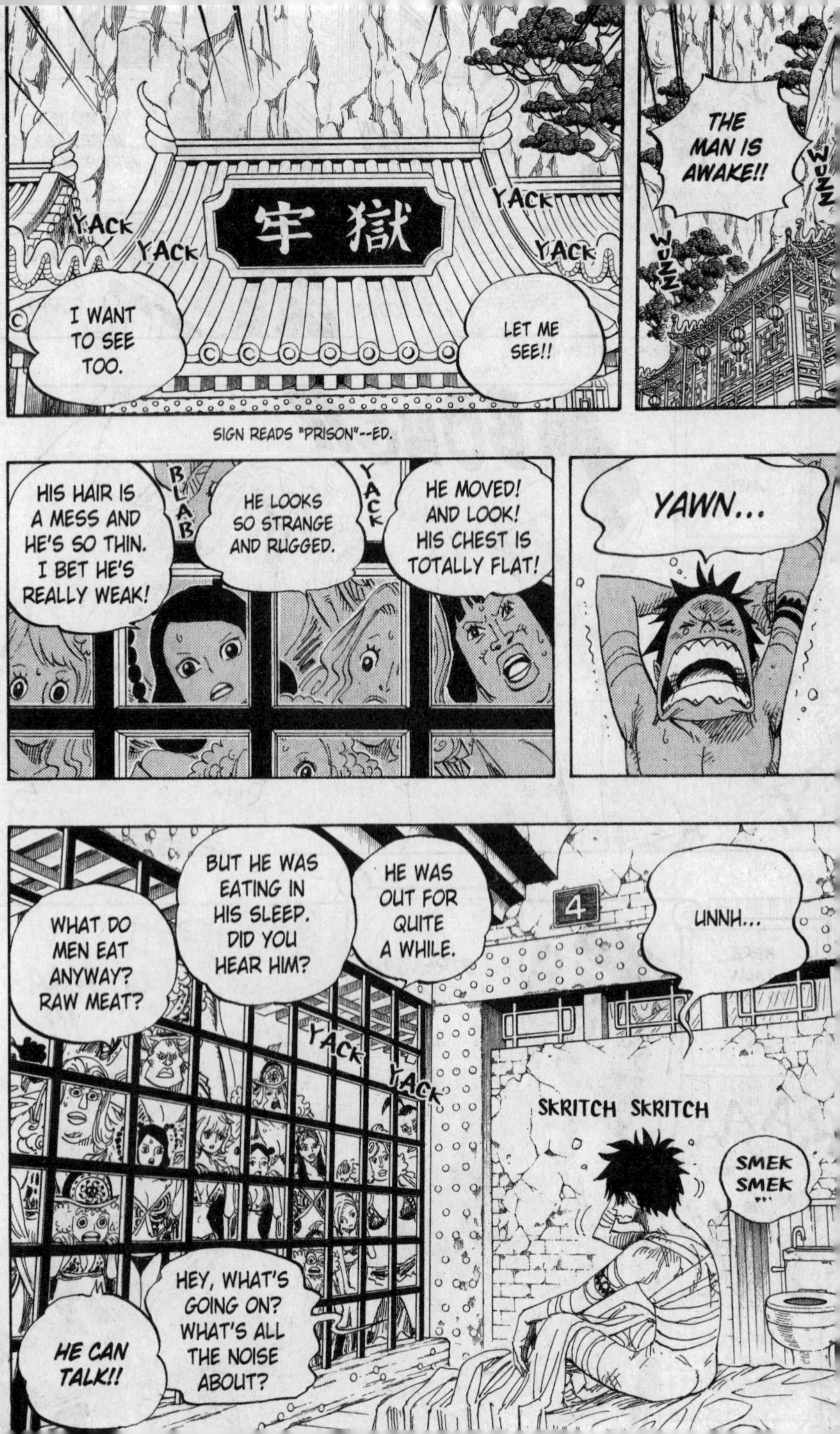
THE MAN IS AWAKE!!
WUZZ
WUZZ
YACK
YACK
牢獄
LET ME SEE!!
YACK
YACK
I WANT TO SEE TOO.
YAWN...
HE MOVED! AND LOOK! HIS CHEST IS TOTALLY FLAT!
YACK
HE LOOKS SO STRANGE AND RUGGED.
BLAB
HIS HAIR IS A MESS AND HE'S SO THIN. I BET HE'S REALLY WEAK!
UNNH...
4
HE WAS OUT FOR QUITE A WHILE.
BUT HE WAS EATING IN HIS SLEEP. DID YOU HEAR HIM?
WHAT DO MEN EAT ANYWAY? RAW MEAT?
YACK
YACK
SKRITCH SKRITCH
SMEK SMEK
HEY, WHAT'S GOING ON? WHAT'S ALL THE NOISE ABOUT?
HE CAN TALK!!
SIGN READS "PRISON"--ED.

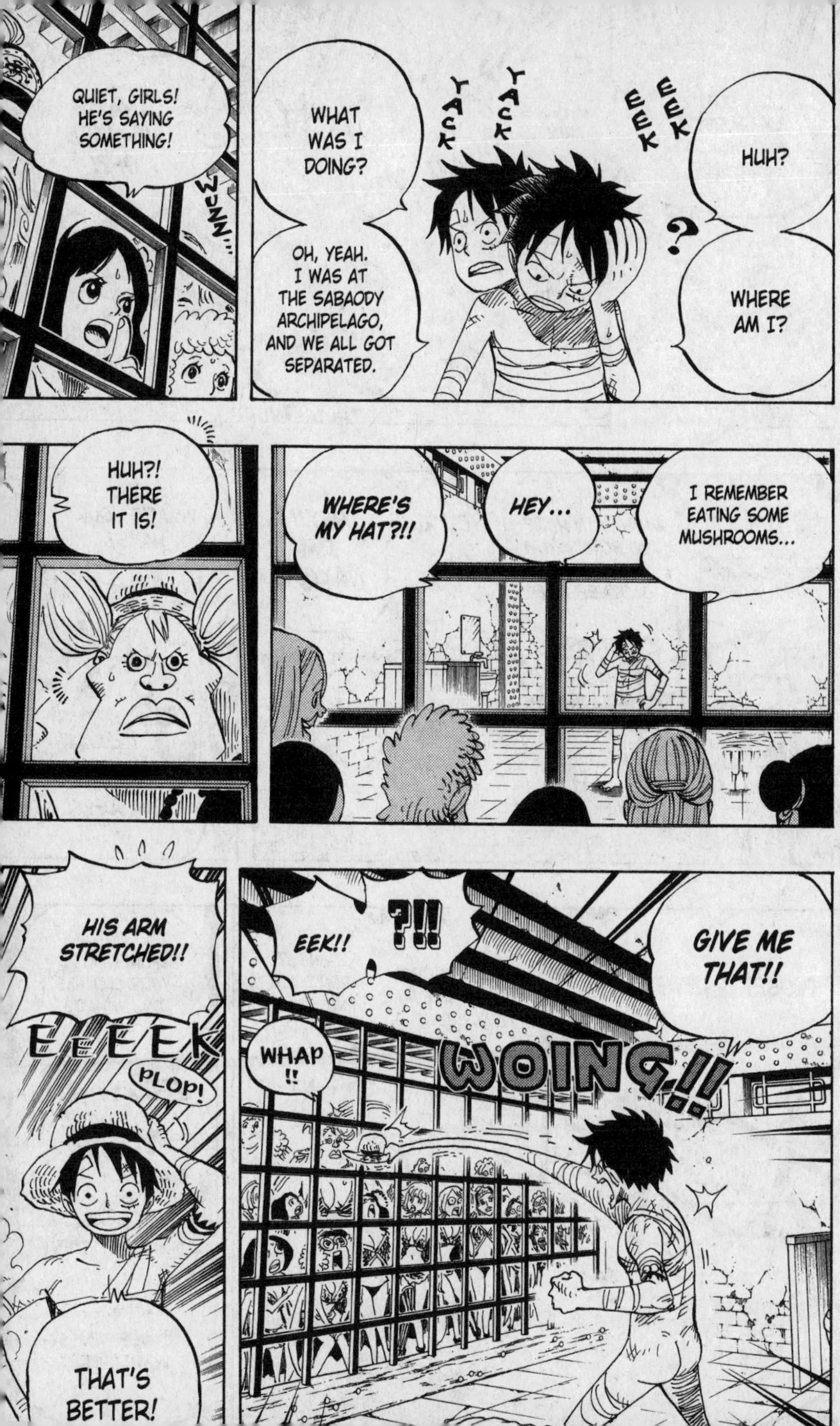
HUH?
WHERE AM I?
EEK EEK
YACK YACK
WHAT WAS I DOING?
OH, YEAH. I WAS AT THE SABAODY ARCHIPELAGO, AND WE ALL GOT SEPARATED.
QUIET, GIRLS! HE'S SAYING SOMETHING!
WUZZ...
I REMEMBER EATING SOME MUSHROOMS...
HEY...
WHERE'S MY HAT?!!
HUH?! THERE IT IS!
GIVE ME THAT!!
?!!
EEK!!
WOING!!
WHAP !!
HIS ARM STRETCHED!!
EEEEK
PLOP!
THAT'S BETTER!

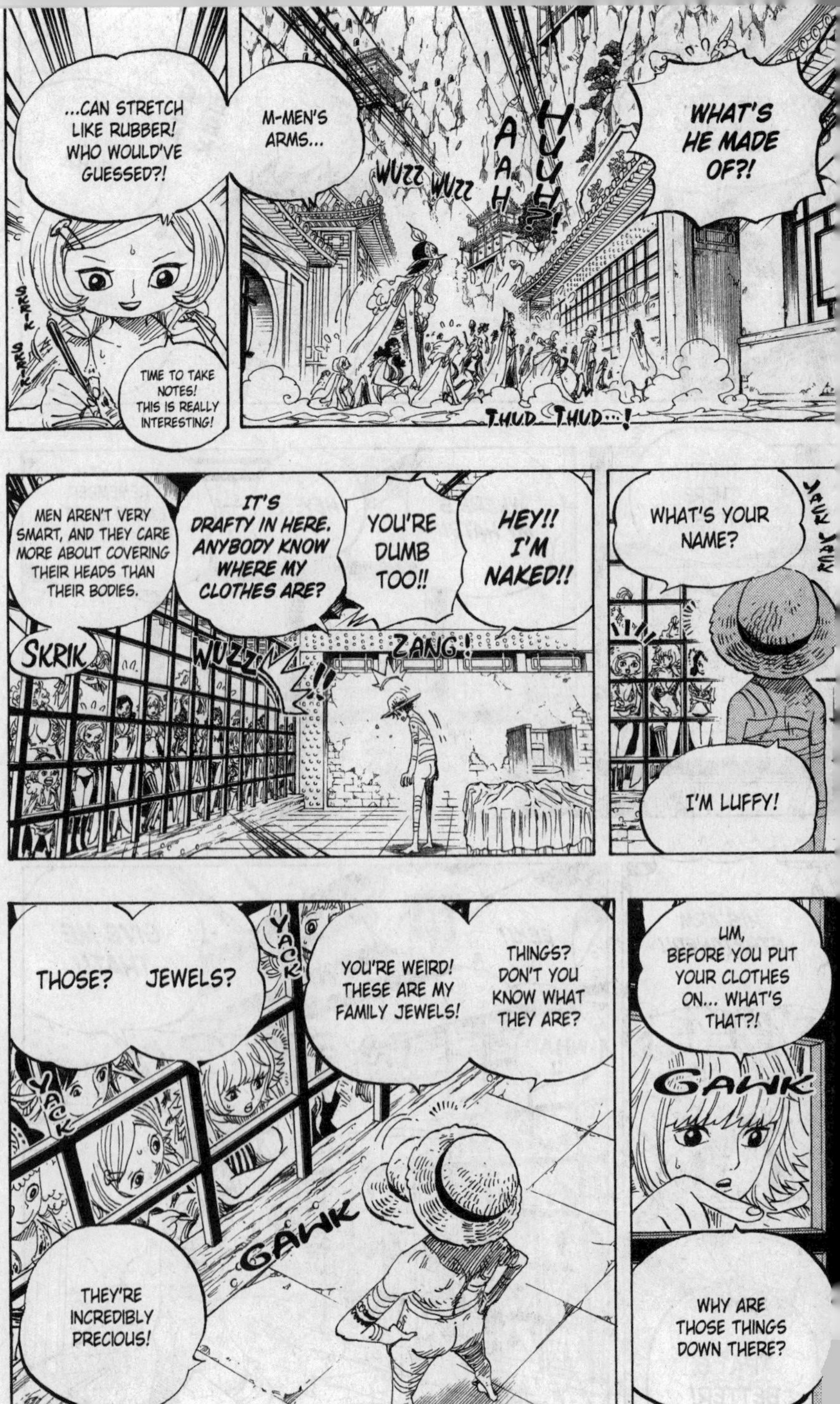
WHAT'S HE MADE OF?!
HUUH?!
AAAH
WUZZ WUZZ
THUD THUD...!
M-MEN'S ARMS...
...CAN STRETCH LIKE RUBBER! WHO WOULD'VE GUESSED?!
SKRIK SKRIK
TIME TO TAKE NOTES! THIS IS REALLY INTERESTING!
YACK YACK
WHAT'S YOUR NAME?
I'M LUFFY!
HEY!! I'M NAKED!!
YOU'RE DUMB TOO!!
IT'S DRAFTY IN HERE. ANYBODY KNOW WHERE MY CLOTHES ARE?
MEN AREN'T VERY SMART, AND THEY CARE MORE ABOUT COVERING THEIR HEADS THAN THEIR BODIES.
ZANG!
WUZZ
SKRIK
UM, BEFORE YOU PUT YOUR CLOTHES ON... WHAT'S THAT?!
GAWK
WHY ARE THOSE THINGS DOWN THERE?
THINGS? DON'T YOU KNOW WHAT THEY ARE?
YOU'RE WEIRD! THESE ARE MY FAMILY JEWELS!
YACK
JEWELS?
THOSE?
YACK
GAWK
THEY'RE INCREDIBLY PRECIOUS!

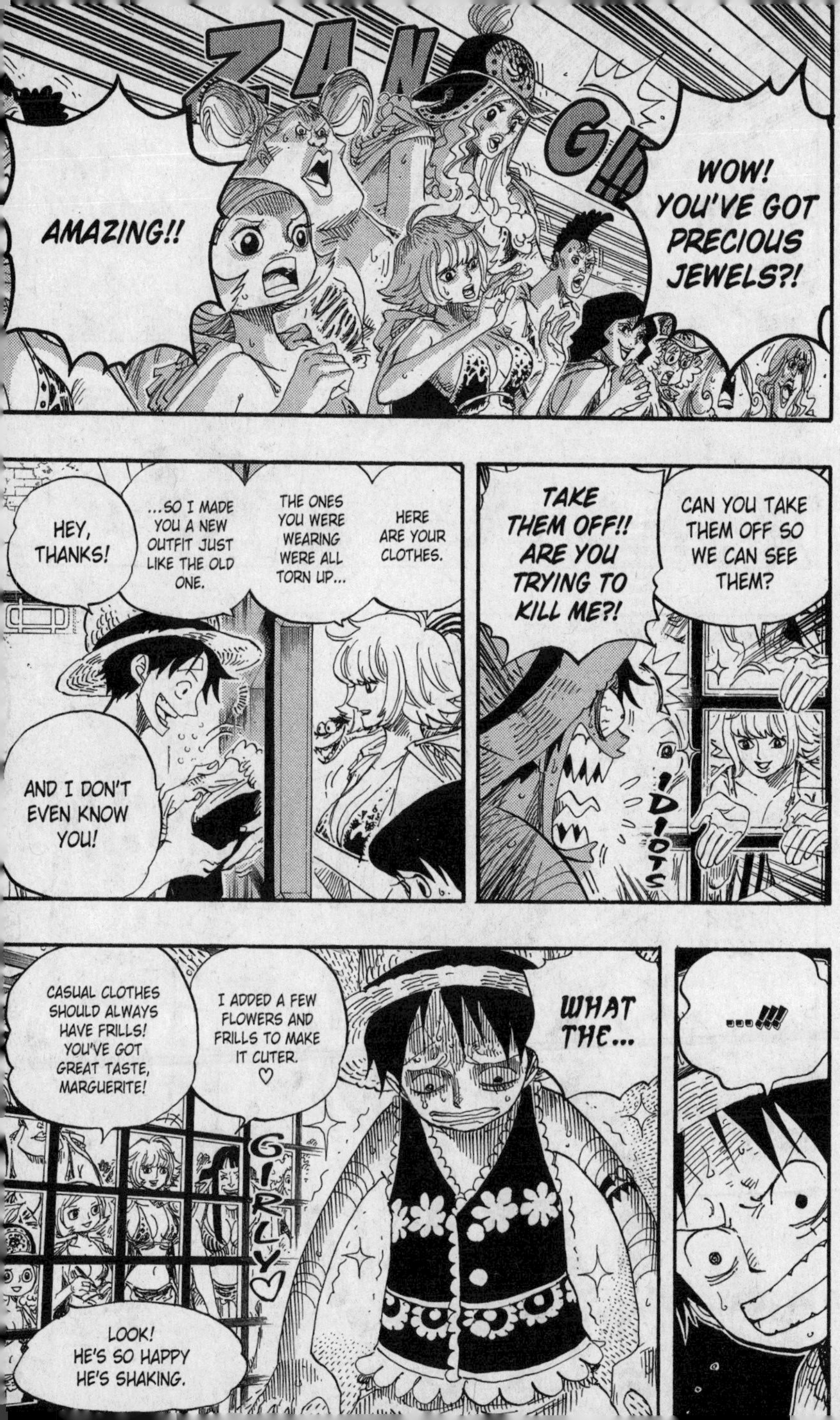
ZAN
GI!!
WOW! YOU'VE GOT PRECIOUS JEWELS?!
AMAZING!!
CAN YOU TAKE THEM OFF SO WE CAN SEE THEM?
TAKE THEM OFF!! ARE YOU TRYING TO KILL ME?!
IDIOTS
HERE ARE YOUR CLOTHES.
THE ONES YOU WERE WEARING WERE ALL TORN UP...
...SO I MADE YOU A NEW OUTFIT JUST LIKE THE OLD ONE.
HEY, THANKS!
AND I DON'T EVEN KNOW YOU!
...!!!
WHAT THE...
I ADDED A FEW FLOWERS AND FRILLS TO MAKE IT CUTER. ♡
CASUAL CLOTHES SHOULD ALWAYS HAVE FRILLS! YOU'VE GOT GREAT TASTE, MARGUERITE!
GIRLY♡
LOOK! HE'S SO HAPPY HE'S SHAKING.

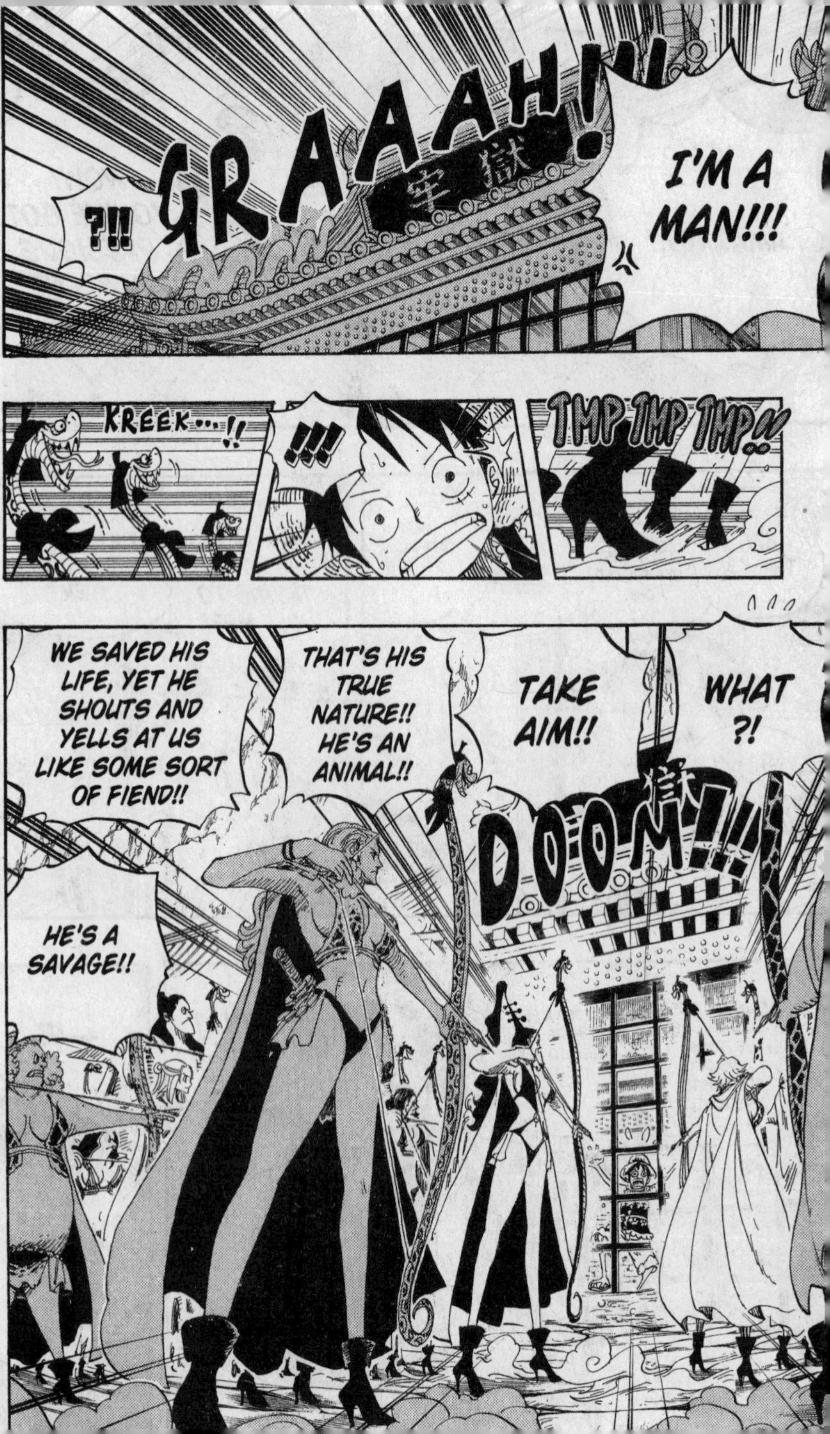
I'M A MAN!!!
GRAAAH!!!
牢獄
?!!
TMP TMP TMP!!
!!!
KREEK...!!
WHAT ?!
TAKE AIM!!
DOOM!!!
THAT'S HIS TRUE NATURE!! HE'S AN ANIMAL!!
WE SAVED HIS LIFE, YET HE SHOUTS AND YELLS AT US LIKE SOME SORT OF FIEND!!
HE'S A SAVAGE!!

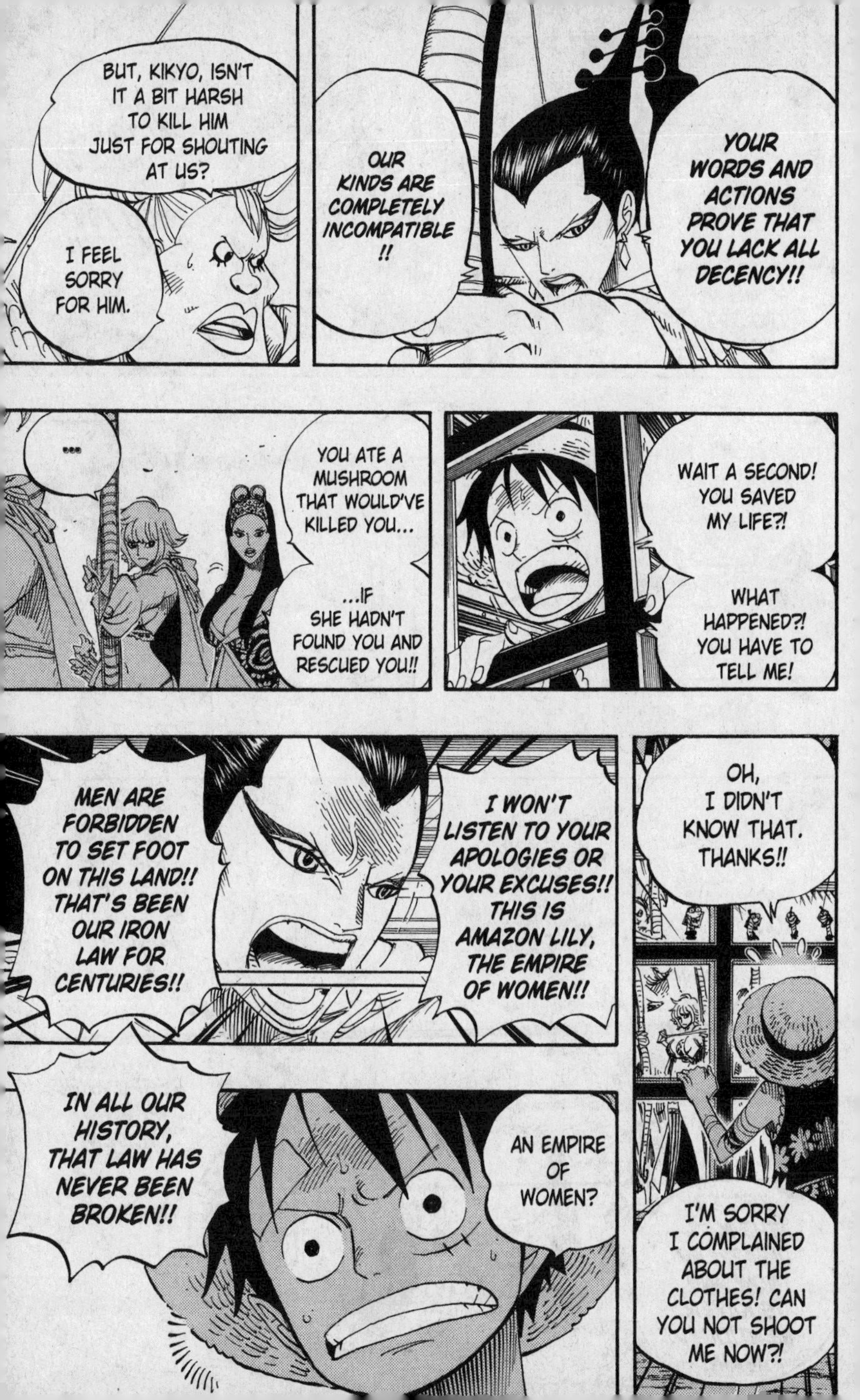
YOUR WORDS AND ACTIONS PROVE THAT YOU LACK ALL DECENCY!!
OUR KINDS ARE COMPLETELY INCOMPATIBLE !!
BUT, KIKYO, ISN'T IT A BIT HARSH TO KILL HIM JUST FOR SHOUTING AT US?
I FEEL SORRY FOR HIM.
WAIT A SECOND! YOU SAVED MY LIFE?!
WHAT HAPPENED?! YOU HAVE TO TELL ME!
YOU ATE A MUSHROOM THAT WOULD'VE KILLED YOU...
...IF SHE HADN'T FOUND YOU AND RESCUED YOU!!
...
OH, I DIDN'T KNOW THAT. THANKS!!
I'M SORRY I COMPLAINED ABOUT THE CLOTHES! CAN YOU NOT SHOOT ME NOW?!
I WON'T LISTEN TO YOUR APOLOGIES OR YOUR EXCUSES!! THIS IS AMAZON LILY, THE EMPIRE OF WOMEN!!
MEN ARE FORBIDDEN TO SET FOOT ON THIS LAND!! THAT'S BEEN OUR IRON LAW FOR CENTURIES!!
AN EMPIRE OF WOMEN?
IN ALL OUR HISTORY, THAT LAW HAS NEVER BEEN BROKEN!!

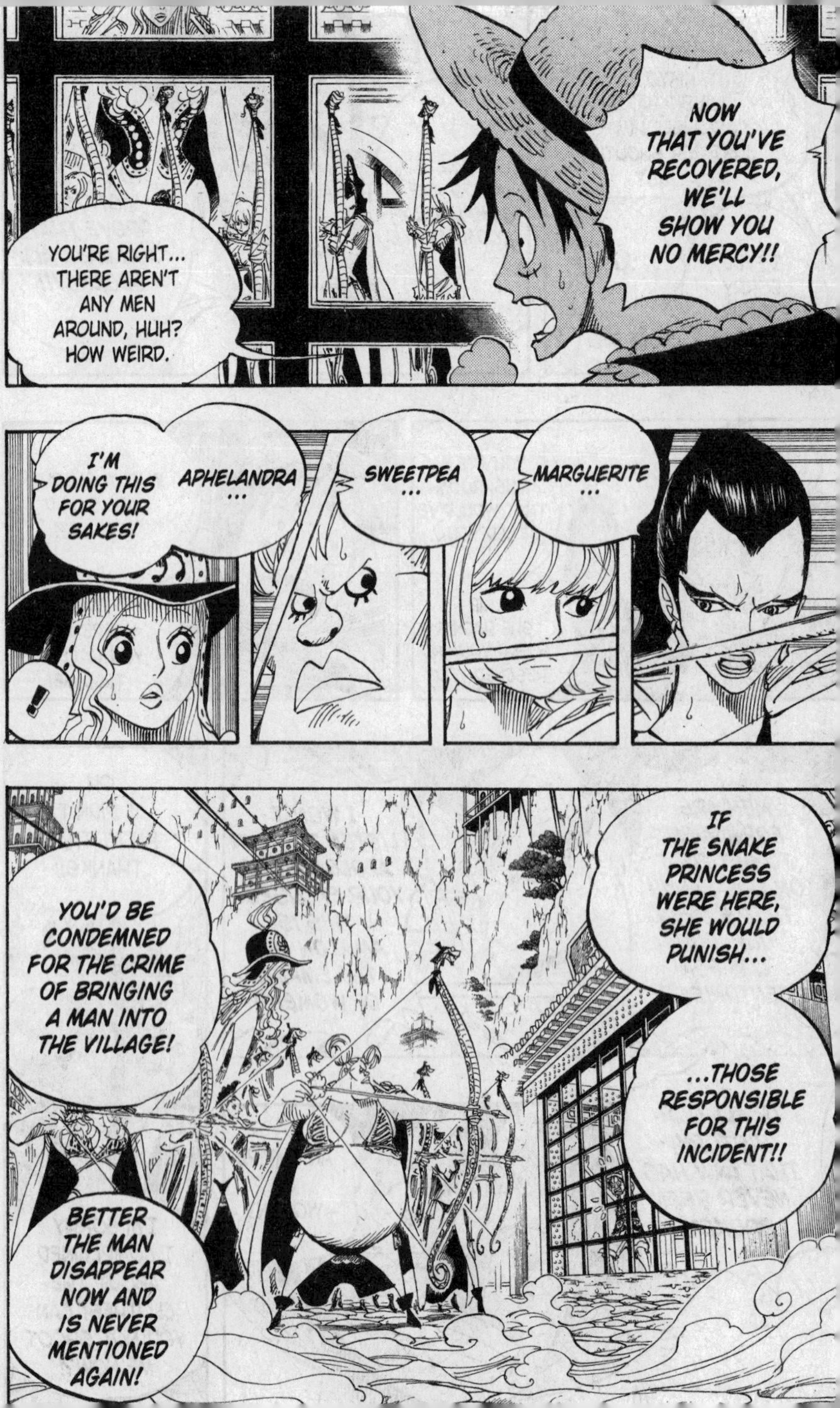
NOW THAT YOU'VE RECOVERED, WE'LL SHOW YOU NO MERCY!!
YOU'RE RIGHT... THERE AREN'T ANY MEN AROUND, HUH? HOW WEIRD.
MARGUERITE...
SWEETPEA...
APHELANDRA...
I'M DOING THIS FOR YOUR SAKES!
!
IF THE SNAKE PRINCESS WERE HERE, SHE WOULD PUNISH...
...THOSE RESPONSIBLE FOR THIS INCIDENT!!
YOU'D BE CONDEMNED FOR THE CRIME OF BRINGING A MAN INTO THE VILLAGE!
BETTER THE MAN DISAPPEAR NOW AND IS NEVER MENTIONED AGAIN!

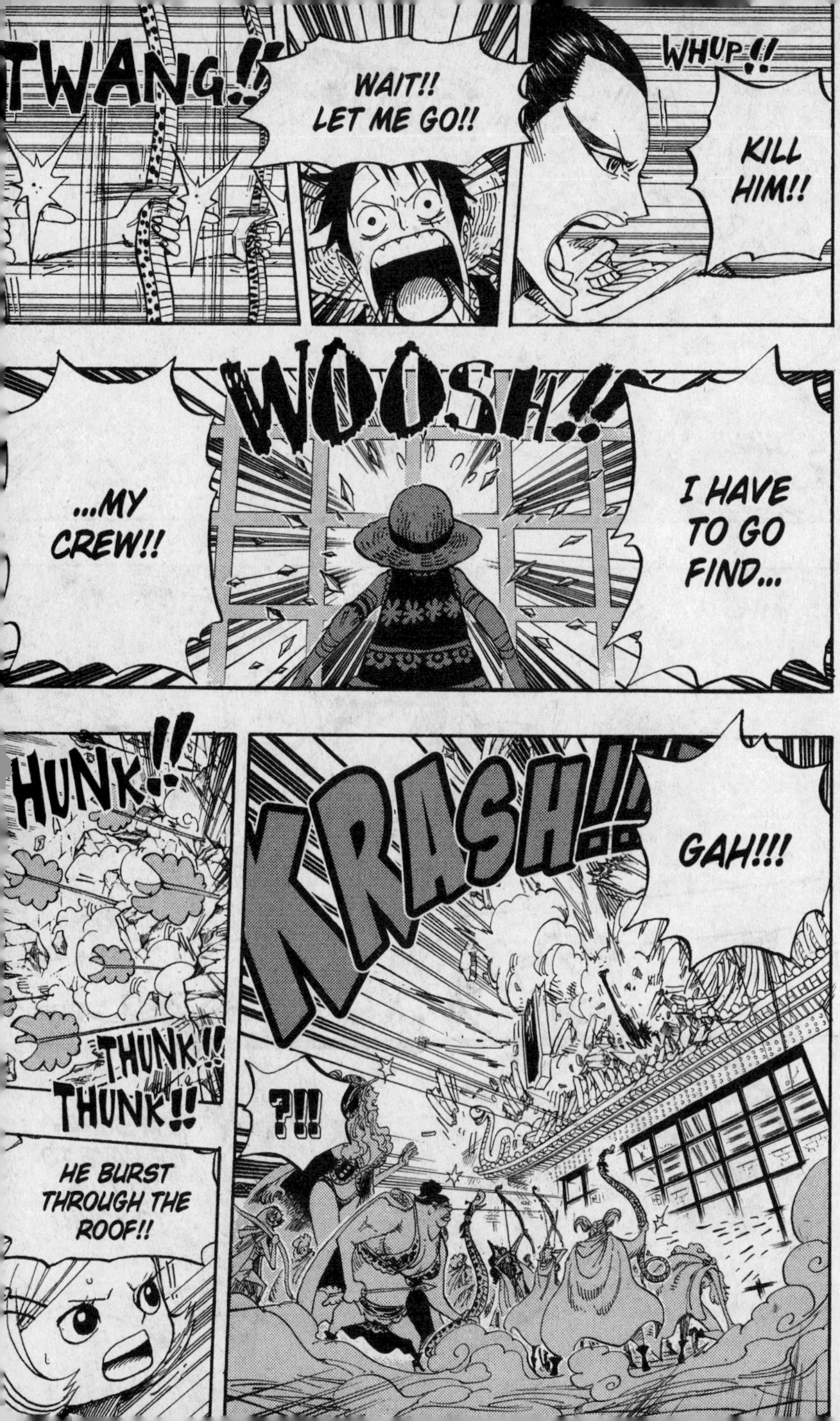
WHUP!!
KILL HIM!!
WAIT!! LET ME GO!!
TWANG!!
WOOSH!!
I HAVE TO GO FIND...
...MY CREW!!
KRASH!!
GAH!!!
?!!
HUNK!!
THUNK!!
THUNK!!
HE BURST THROUGH THE ROOF!!

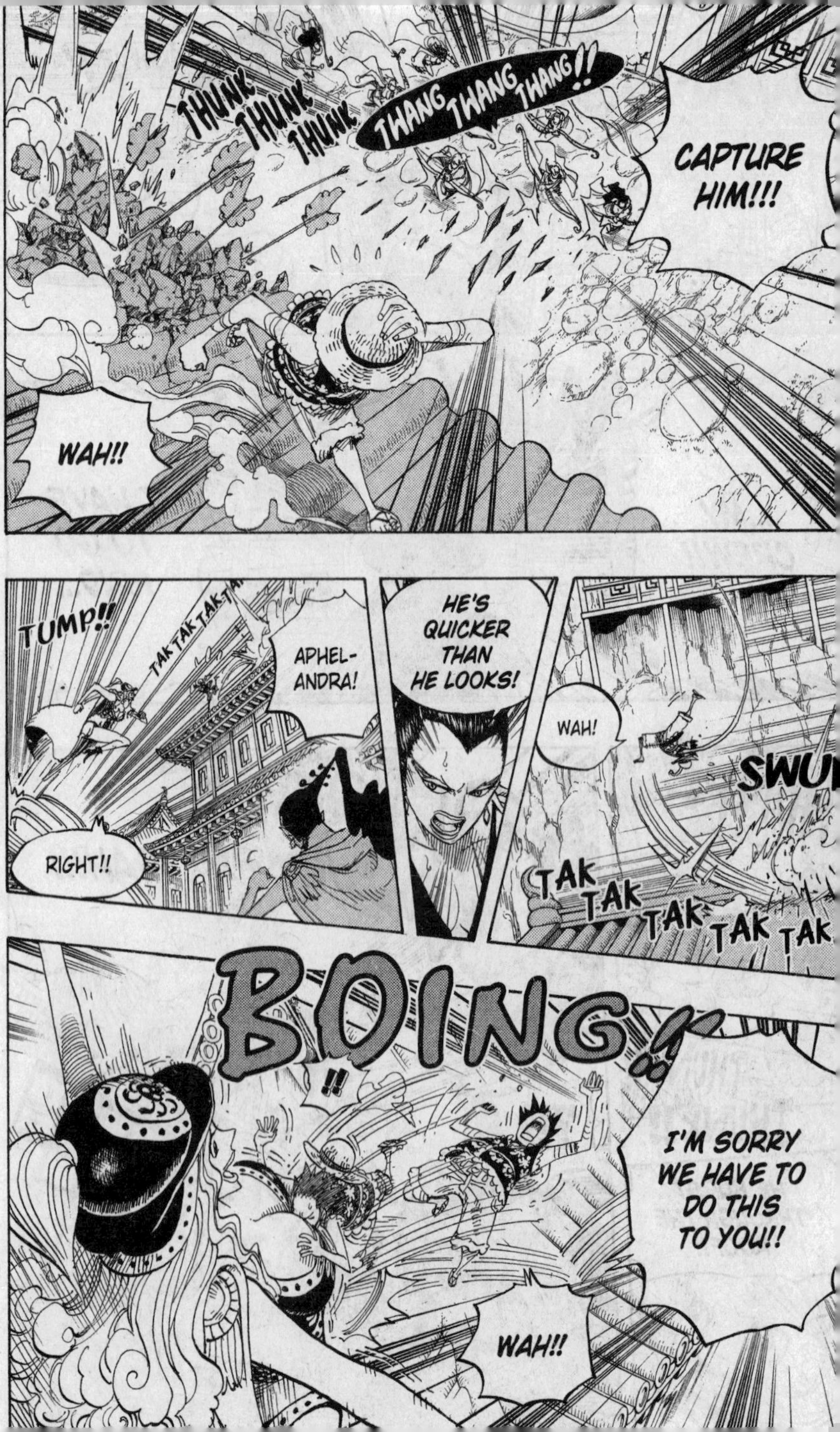
CAPTURE HIM!!!
THANG THANG THANG!!
THUNK THUNK THUNK
WAH!!
SWU
TAK TAK TAK TAK TAK
WAH!
HE'S QUICKER THAN HE LOOKS!
TUMP!!
TAKTAKTAKTAK
APHEL-ANDRA!
RIGHT!!
BOING!!
!!
I'M SORRY WE HAVE TO DO THIS TO YOU!!
WAH!!

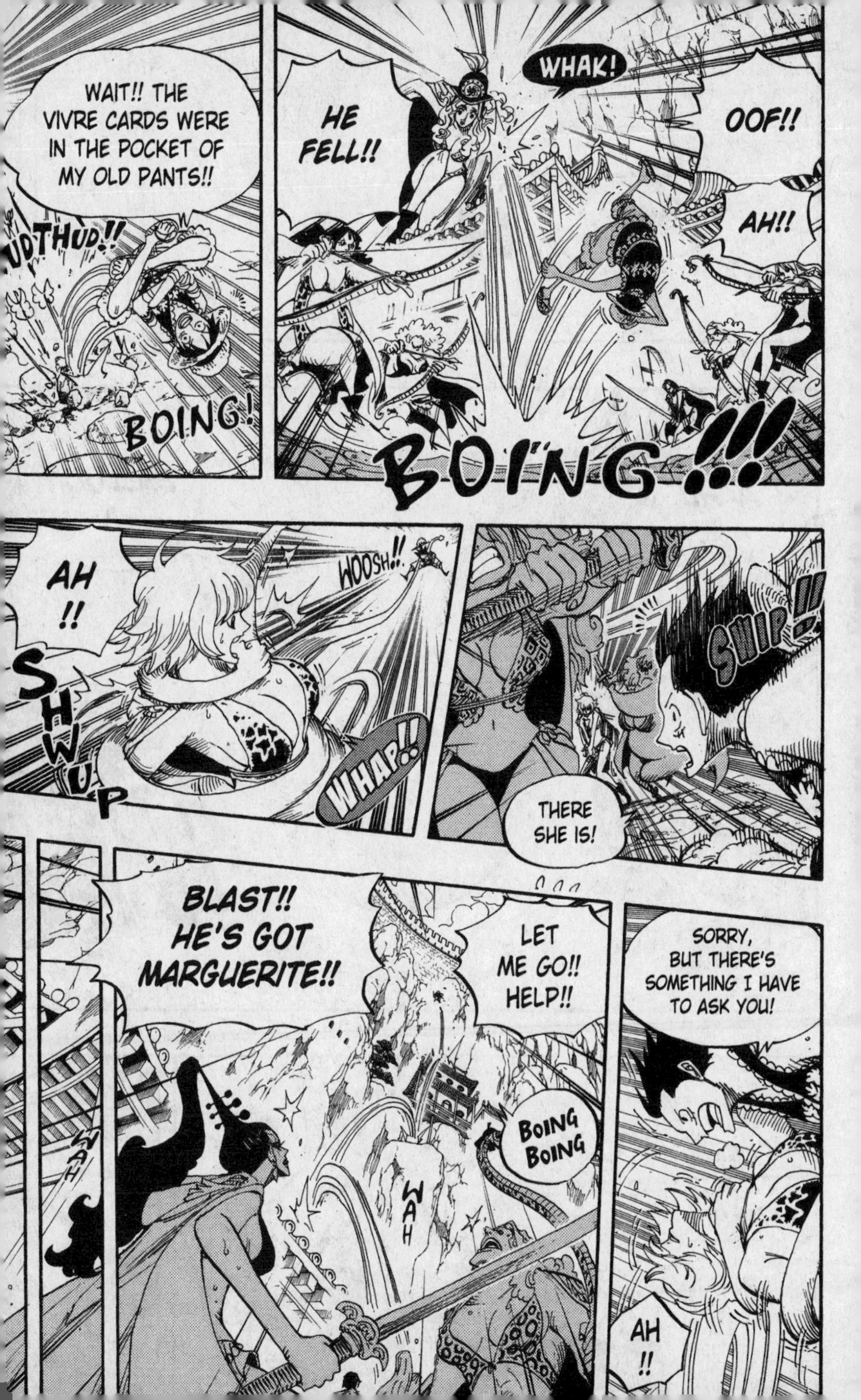
WHAK!
OOF!!
HE FELL!!
AH!!
BOING!!!
WAIT!! THE VIVRE CARDS WERE IN THE POCKET OF MY OLD PANTS!!
UDTHUD!!
BOING!
SWIP!!
THERE SHE IS!
WOOSH!!
AH !!
SHWUP
WHAP!!
SORRY, BUT THERE'S SOMETHING I HAVE TO ASK YOU!
AH !!
LET ME GO!! HELP!!
BOING BOING
WAH
BLAST!! HE'S GOT MARGUERITE!!
WAH

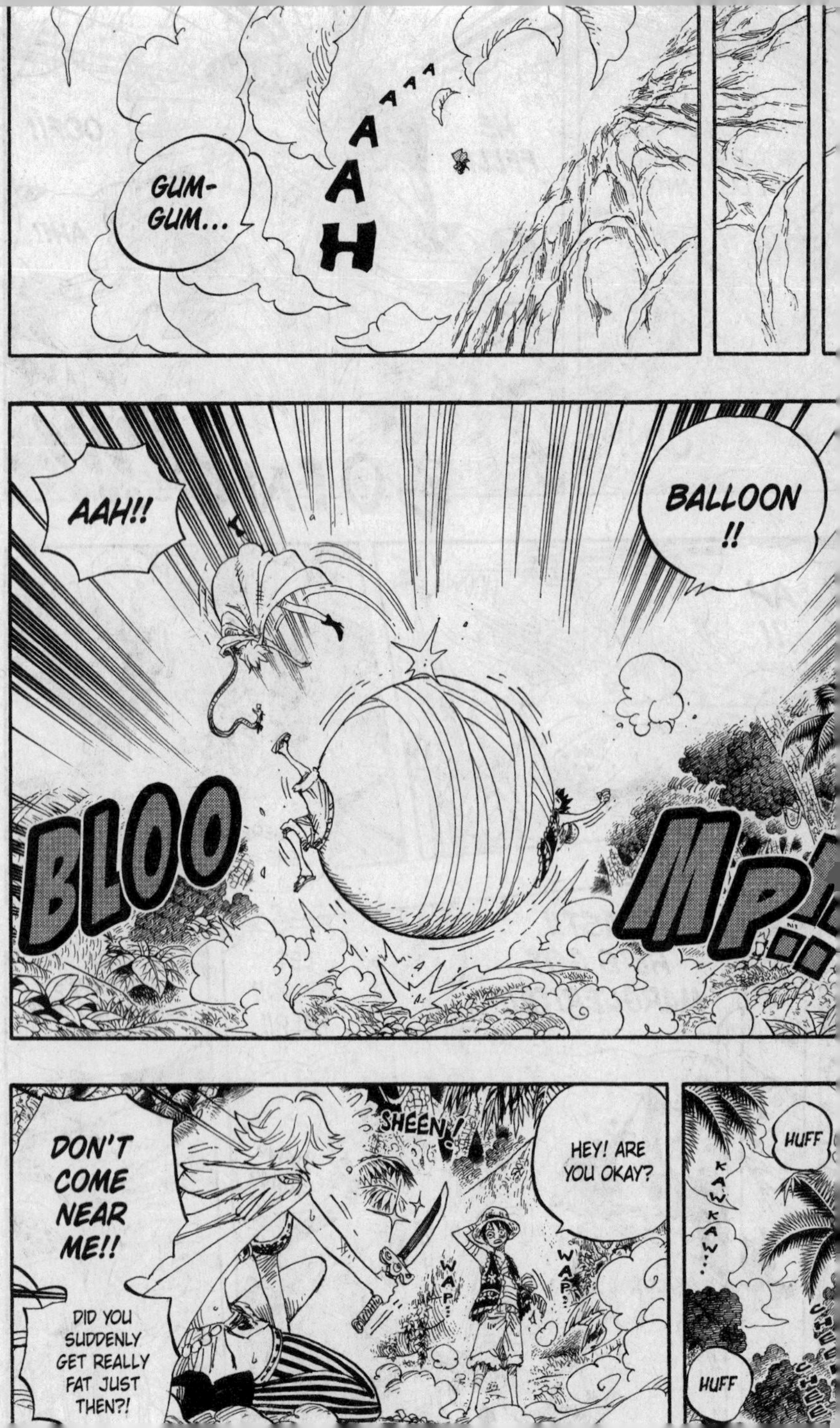
GUM-GUM...
AAAAAAH
BALLOON!!
AAH!!
BLOOMP!!
HUFF
KAW KAW...
HUFF
HEY! ARE YOU OKAY?
SHEEN!
WAP...
WAP...
DON'T COME NEAR ME!!
DID YOU SUDDENLY GET REALLY FAT JUST THEN?!

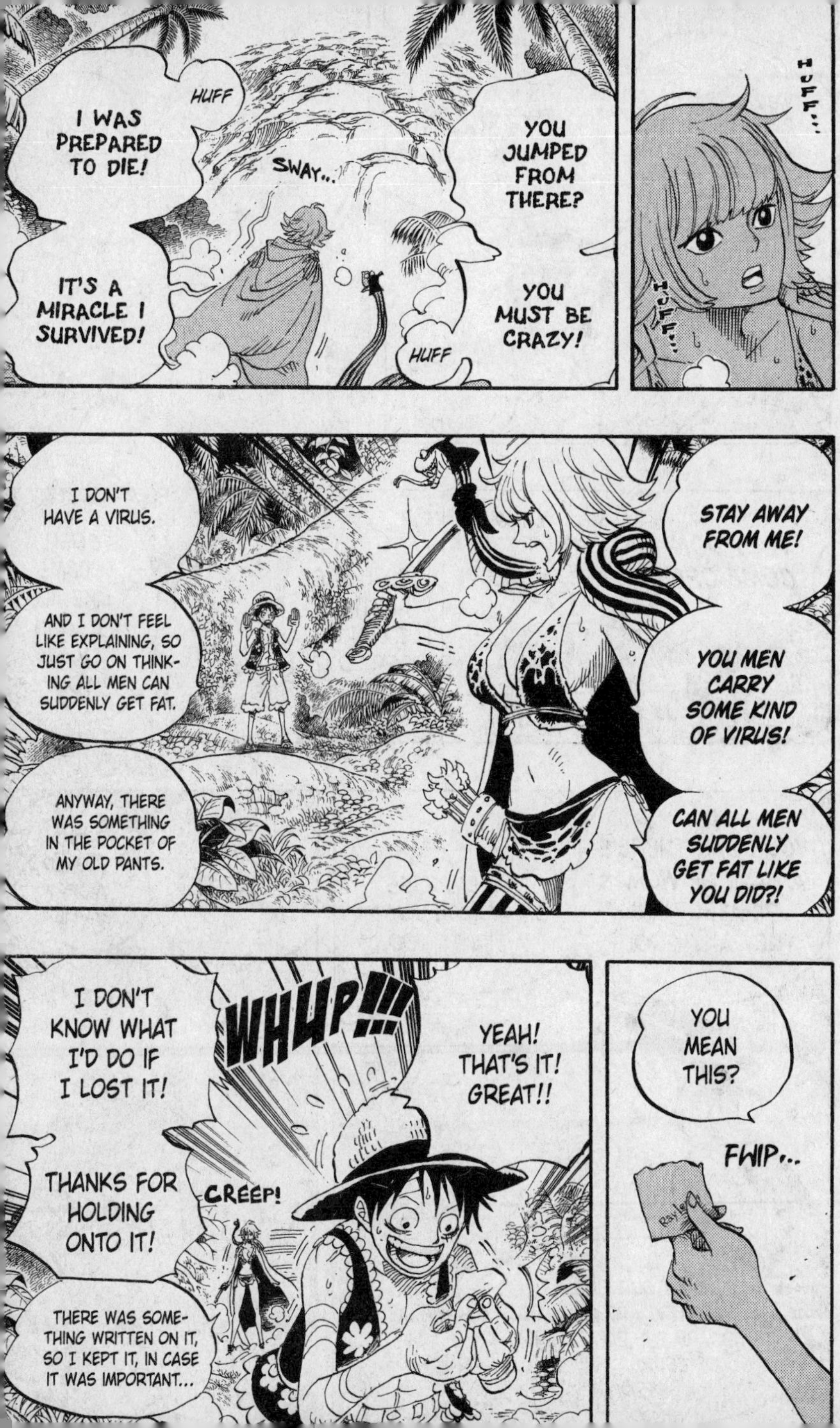
HUFF...
HUFF...
YOU JUMPED FROM THERE?
YOU MUST BE CRAZY!
HUFF
SWAY...
HUFF
I WAS PREPARED TO DIE!
IT'S A MIRACLE I SURVIVED!
STAY AWAY FROM ME!
YOU MEN CARRY SOME KIND OF VIRUS!
CAN ALL MEN SUDDENLY GET FAT LIKE YOU DID?!
I DON'T HAVE A VIRUS.
AND I DON'T FEEL LIKE EXPLAINING, SO JUST GO ON THINKING ALL MEN CAN SUDDENLY GET FAT.
ANYWAY, THERE WAS SOMETHING IN THE POCKET OF MY OLD PANTS.
YOU MEAN THIS?
FWIP...
YEAH! THAT'S IT! GREAT!!
WHUP!!!
I DON'T KNOW WHAT I'D DO IF I LOST IT!
THANKS FOR HOLDING ONTO IT!
CREEP!
THERE WAS SOMETHING WRITTEN ON IT, SO I KEPT IT, IN CASE IT WAS IMPORTANT...

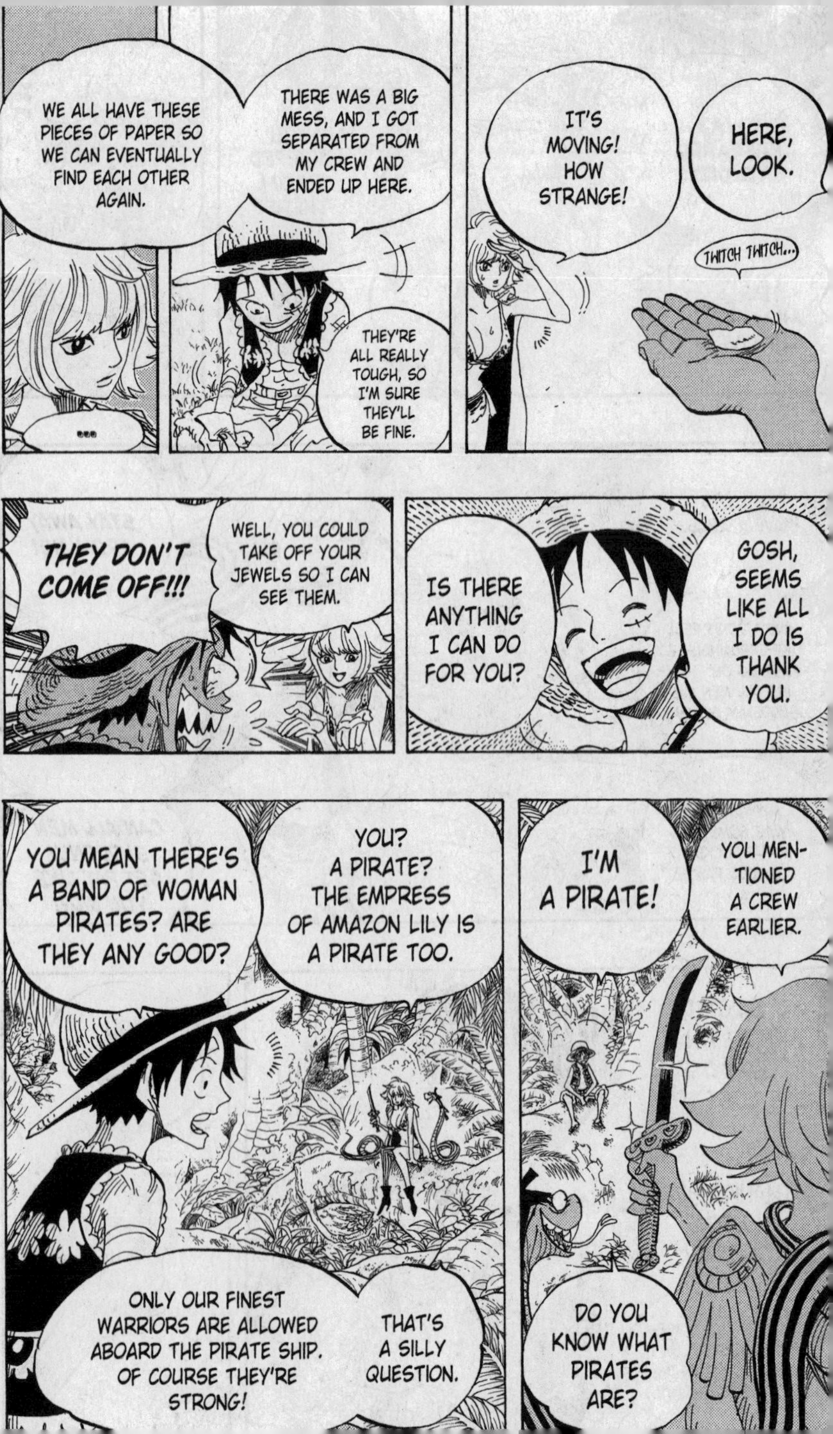
HERE, LOOK.
TWITCH TWITCH...
IT'S MOVING! HOW STRANGE!
THERE WAS A BIG MESS, AND I GOT SEPARATED FROM MY CREW AND ENDED UP HERE.
THEY'RE ALL REALLY TOUGH, SO I'M SURE THEY'LL BE FINE.
WE ALL HAVE THESE PIECES OF PAPER SO WE CAN EVENTUALLY FIND EACH OTHER AGAIN.
...
GOSH, SEEMS LIKE ALL I DO IS THANK YOU.
IS THERE ANYTHING I CAN DO FOR YOU?
WELL, YOU COULD TAKE OFF YOUR JEWELS SO I CAN SEE THEM.
THEY DON'T COME OFF!!!
YOU MENTIONED A CREW EARLIER.
I'M A PIRATE!
DO YOU KNOW WHAT PIRATES ARE?
YOU? A PIRATE? THE EMPRESS OF AMAZON LILY IS A PIRATE TOO.
YOU MEAN THERE'S A BAND OF WOMAN PIRATES? ARE THEY ANY GOOD?
THAT'S A SILLY QUESTION.
ONLY OUR FINEST WARRIORS ARE ALLOWED ABOARD THE PIRATE SHIP. OF COURSE THEY'RE STRONG!

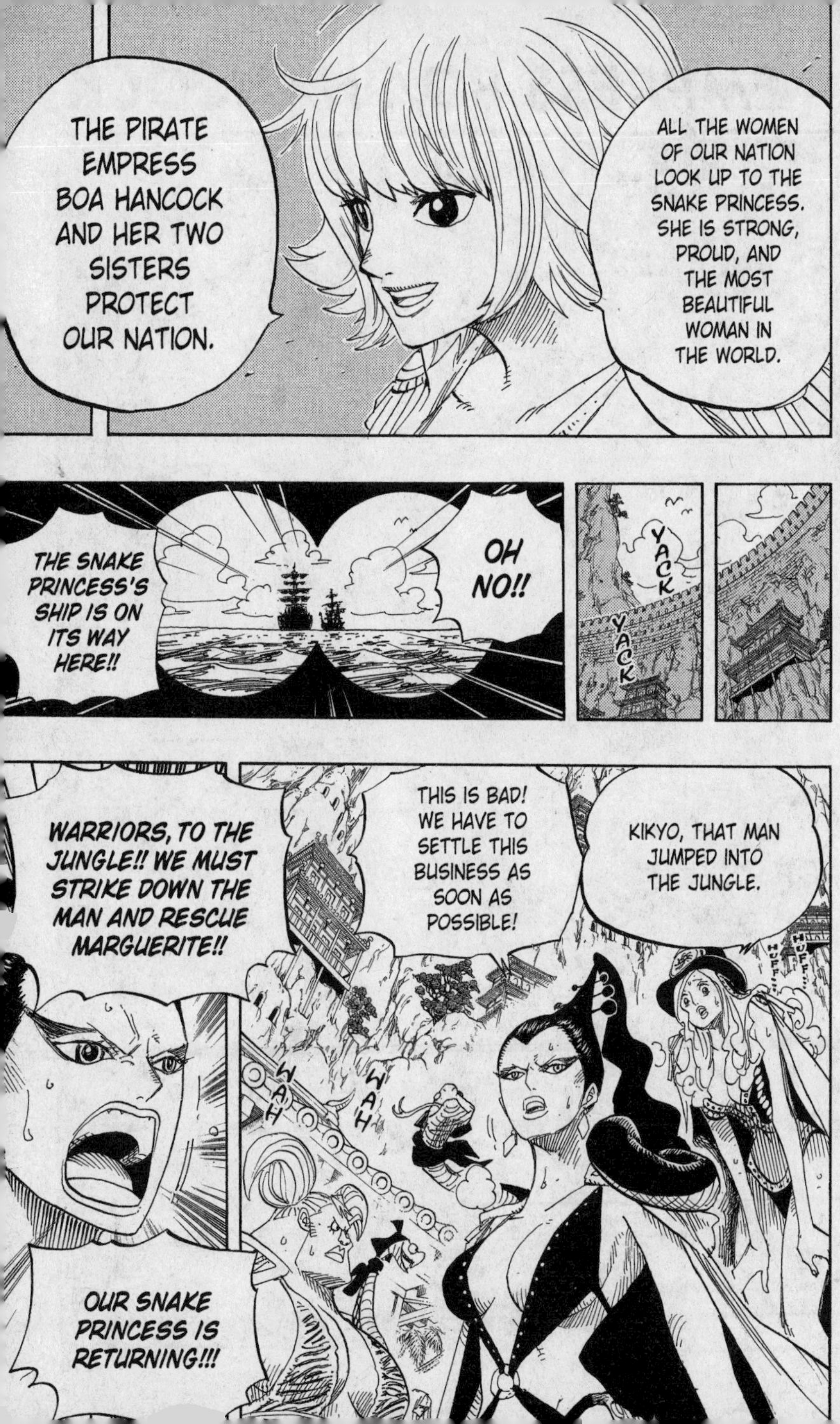
ALL THE WOMEN OF OUR NATION LOOK UP TO THE SNAKE PRINCESS. SHE IS STRONG, PROUD, AND THE MOST BEAUTIFUL WOMAN IN THE WORLD.
THE PIRATE EMPRESS BOA HANCOCK AND HER TWO SISTERS PROTECT OUR NATION.
YACK
YACK
OH NO!!
THE SNAKE PRINCESS'S SHIP IS ON ITS WAY HERE!!
KIKYO, THAT MAN JUMPED INTO THE JUNGLE.
HUFF...
HUFF...
THIS IS BAD! WE HAVE TO SETTLE THIS BUSINESS AS SOON AS POSSIBLE!
WAH
WAH
WARRIORS, TO THE JUNGLE!! WE MUST STRIKE DOWN THE MAN AND RESCUE MARGUERITE!!
OUR SNAKE PRINCESS IS RETURNING!!!

EMPRESS BOA HANCOCK

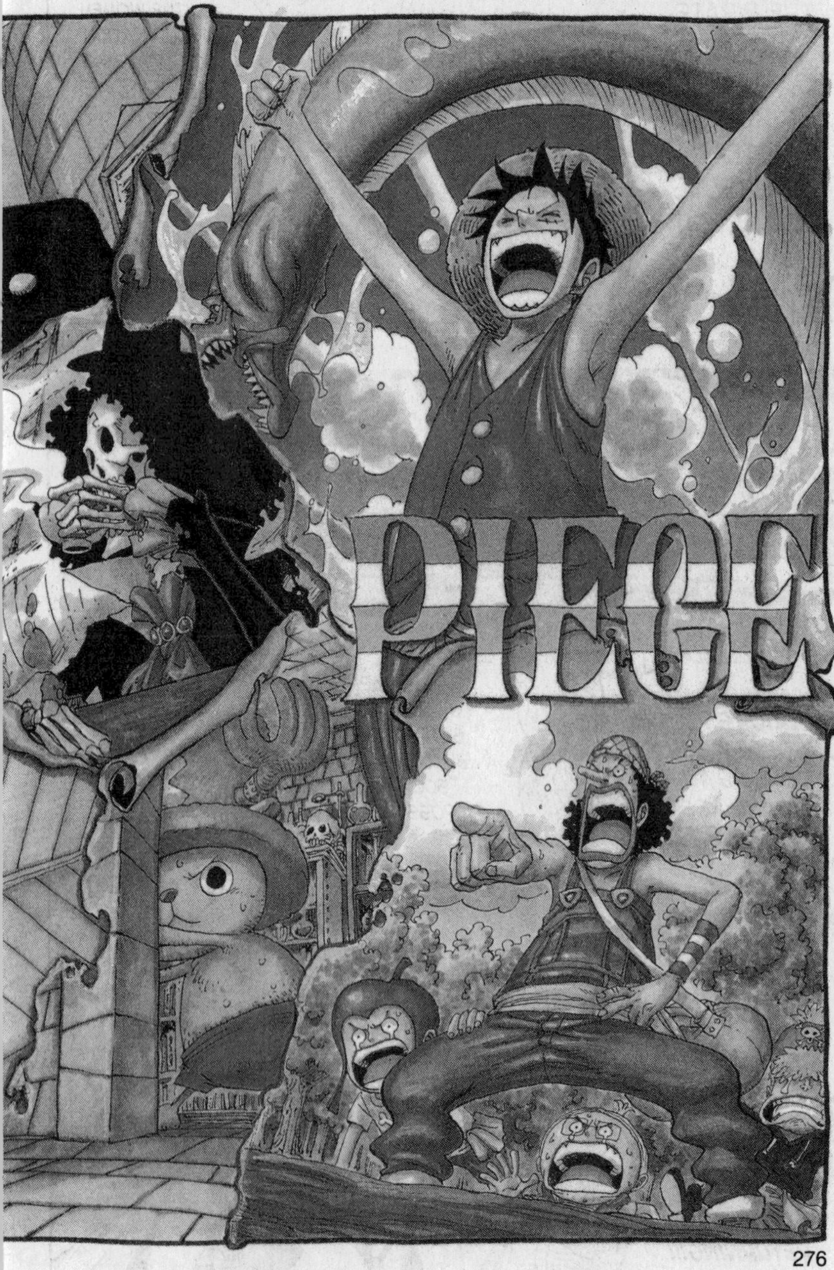
PIECE

Chapter 516: PIRATE

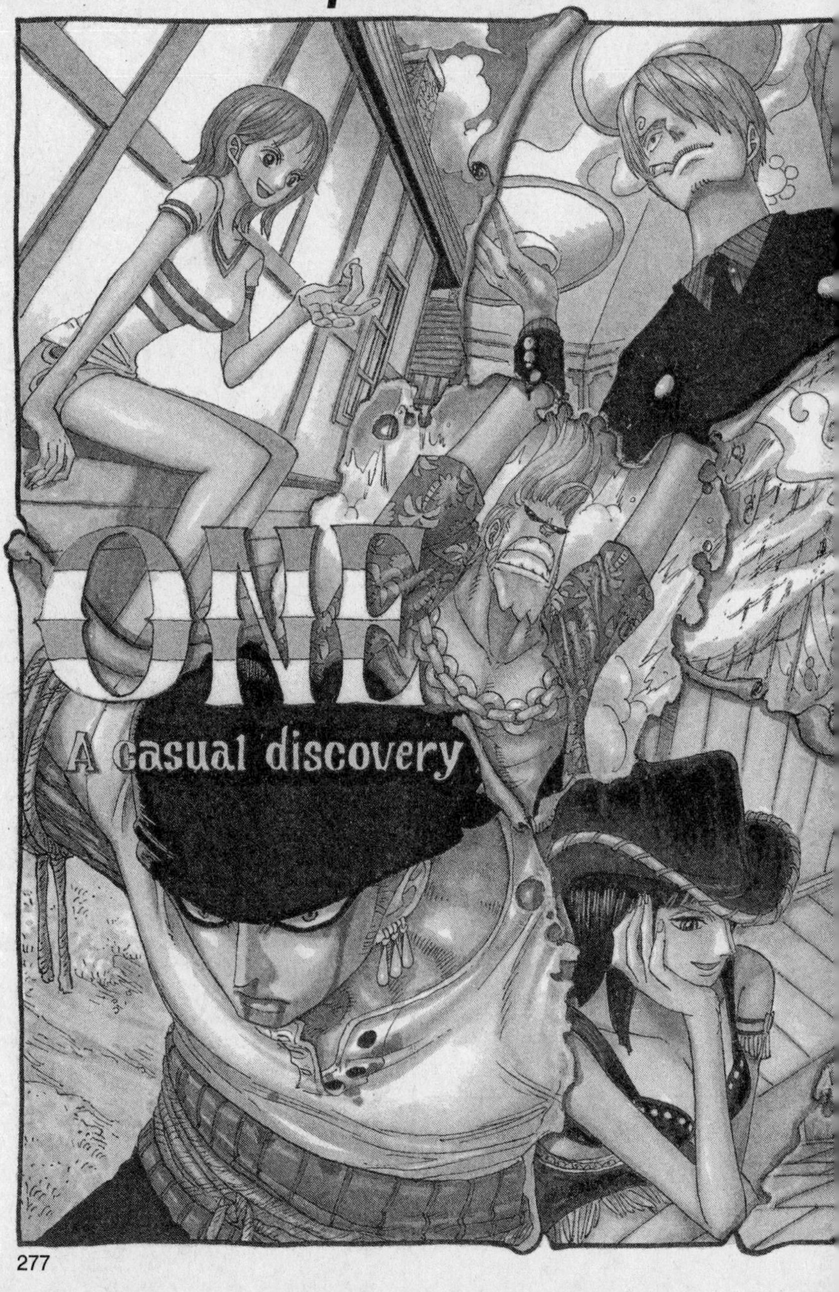
ONE
A casual discovery

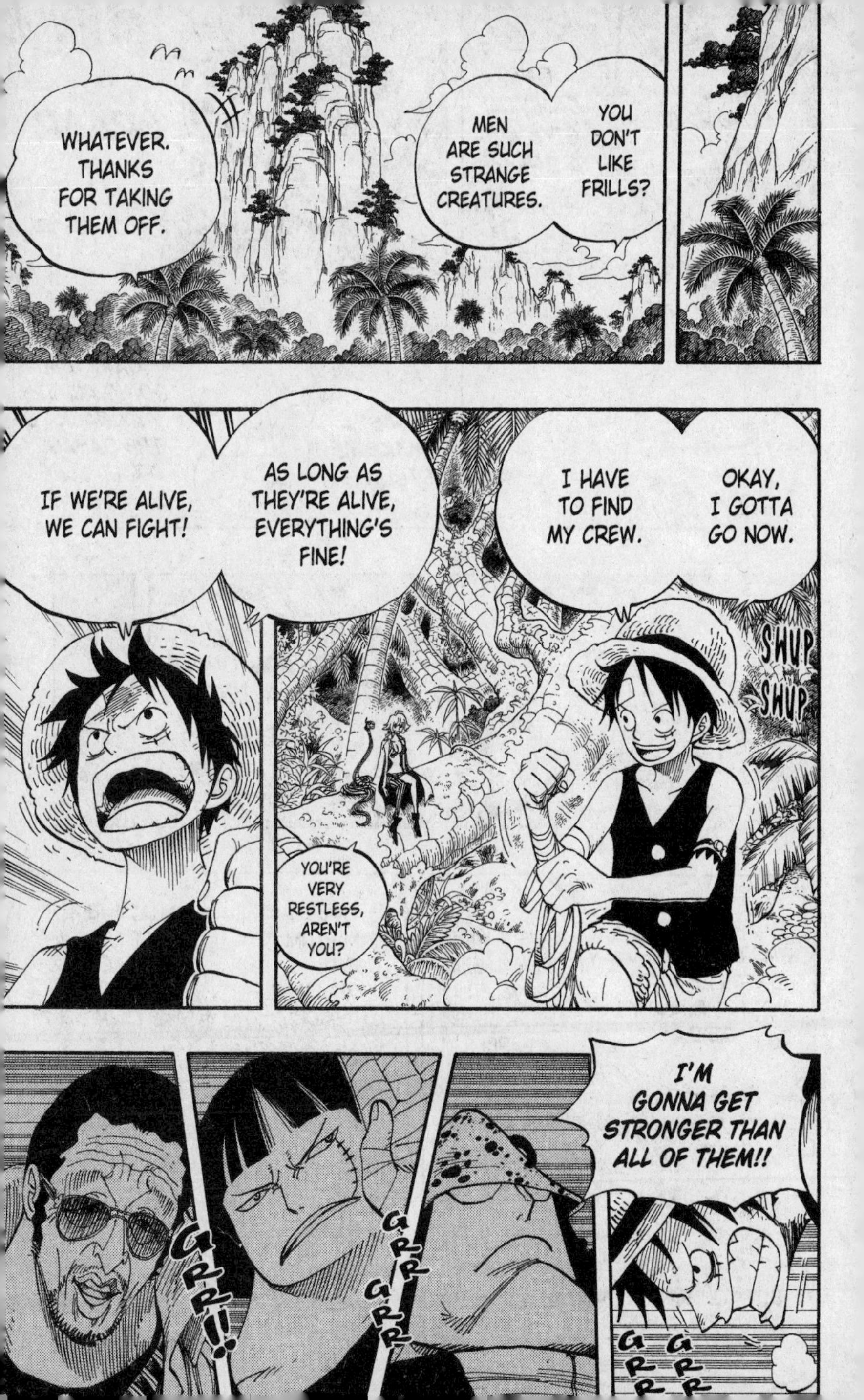
YOU DON'T LIKE FRILLS?
MEN ARE SUCH STRANGE CREATURES.
WHATEVER. THANKS FOR TAKING THEM OFF.
OKAY, I GOTTA GO NOW.
I HAVE TO FIND MY CREW.
SHUP SHUP
YOU'RE VERY RESTLESS, AREN'T YOU?
AS LONG AS THEY'RE ALIVE, EVERYTHING'S FINE!
IF WE'RE ALIVE, WE CAN FIGHT!
I'M GONNA GET STRONGER THAN ALL OF THEM!!
GRR GRR
GRR GRR
GRR!!

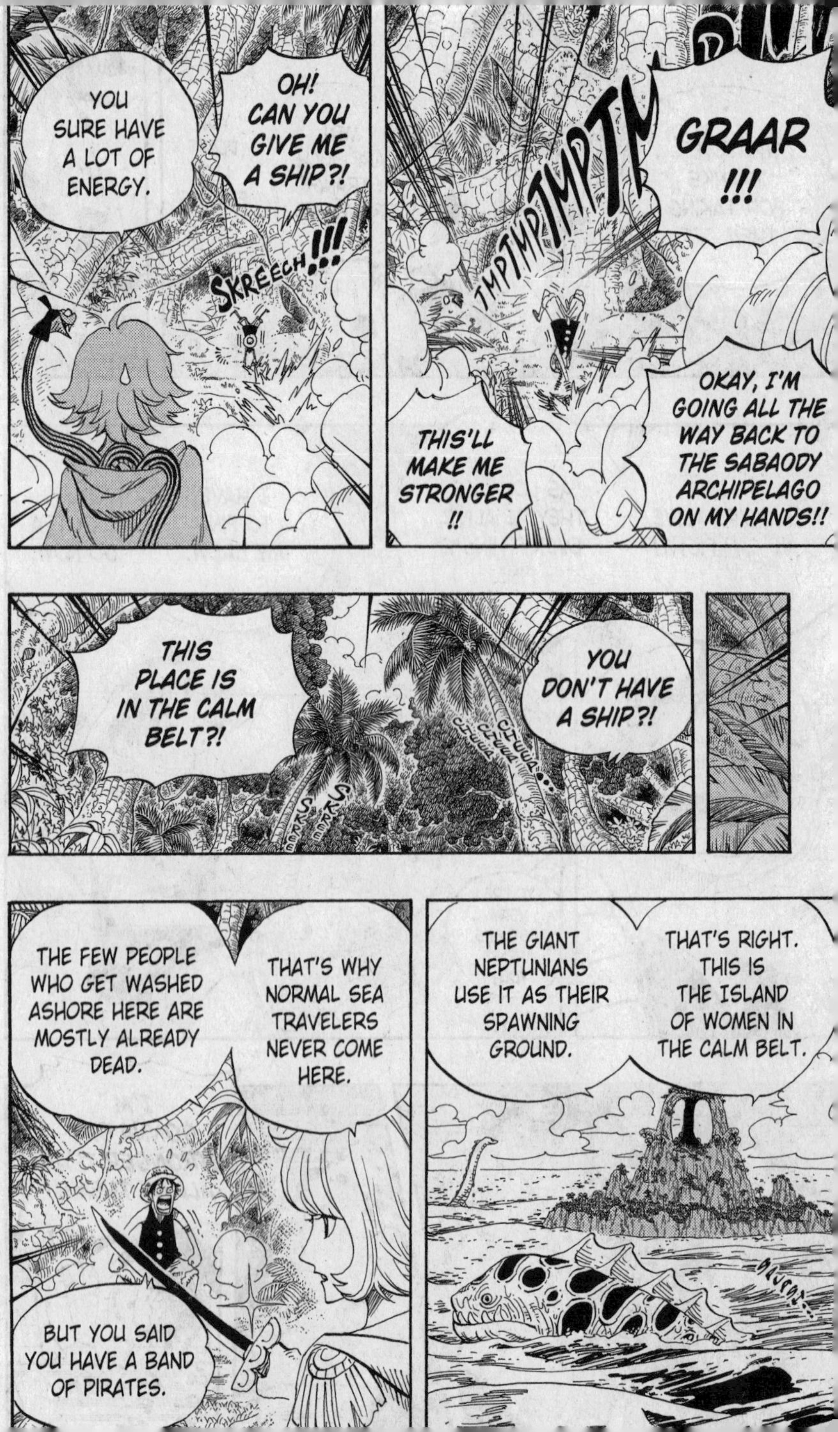
GRAAR!!!
TMPTMPTMPTM
OKAY, I'M GOING ALL THE WAY BACK TO THE SABAODY ARCHIPELAGO ON MY HANDS!!
THIS'LL MAKE ME STRONGER!!
OH! CAN YOU GIVE ME A SHIP?!
YOU SURE HAVE A LOT OF ENERGY.
SKREECH!!!
YOU DON'T HAVE A SHIP?!
THIS PLACE IS IN THE CALM BELT?!
THAT'S RIGHT. THIS IS THE ISLAND OF WOMEN IN THE CALM BELT.
THE GIANT NEPTUNIANS USE IT AS THEIR SPAWNING GROUND.
THAT'S WHY NORMAL SEA TRAVELERS NEVER COME HERE.
THE FEW PEOPLE WHO GET WASHED ASHORE HERE ARE MOSTLY ALREADY DEAD.
BUT YOU SAID YOU HAVE A BAND OF PIRATES.

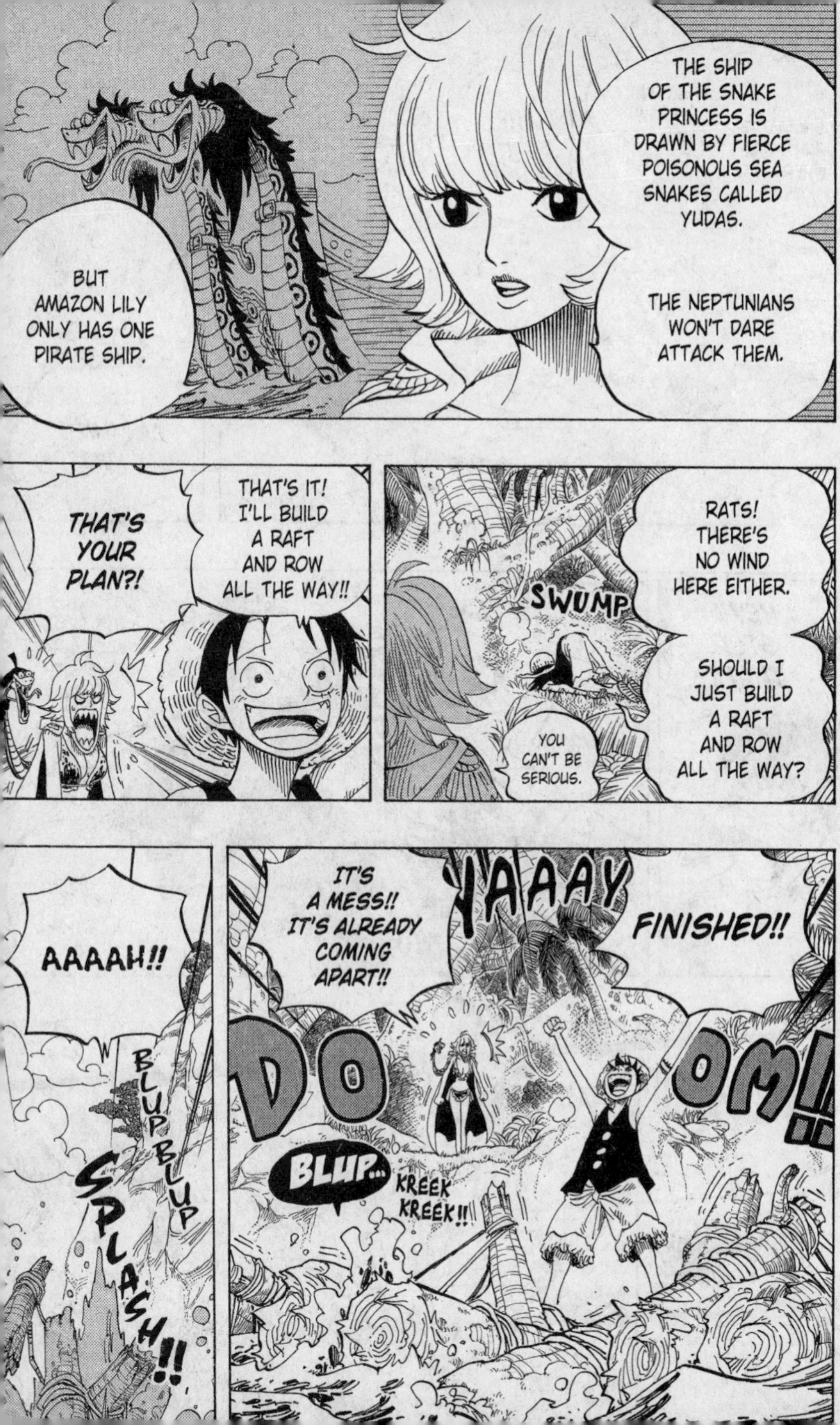
THE SHIP OF THE SNAKE PRINCESS IS DRAWN BY FIERCE POISONOUS SEA SNAKES CALLED YUDAS.
THE NEPTUNIANS WON'T DARE ATTACK THEM.
BUT AMAZON LILY ONLY HAS ONE PIRATE SHIP.
RATS! THERE'S NO WIND HERE EITHER.
SWUMP
SHOULD I JUST BUILD A RAFT AND ROW ALL THE WAY?
YOU CAN'T BE SERIOUS.
THAT'S IT! I'LL BUILD A RAFT AND ROW ALL THE WAY!!
THAT'S YOUR PLAN?!
YAAAY
FINISHED!!
IT'S A MESS!! IT'S ALREADY COMING APART!!
DOOM!!
BLUP...
KREEK KREEK!!
AAAAH!!
BLUP BLUP BLUP
SPLASH!!

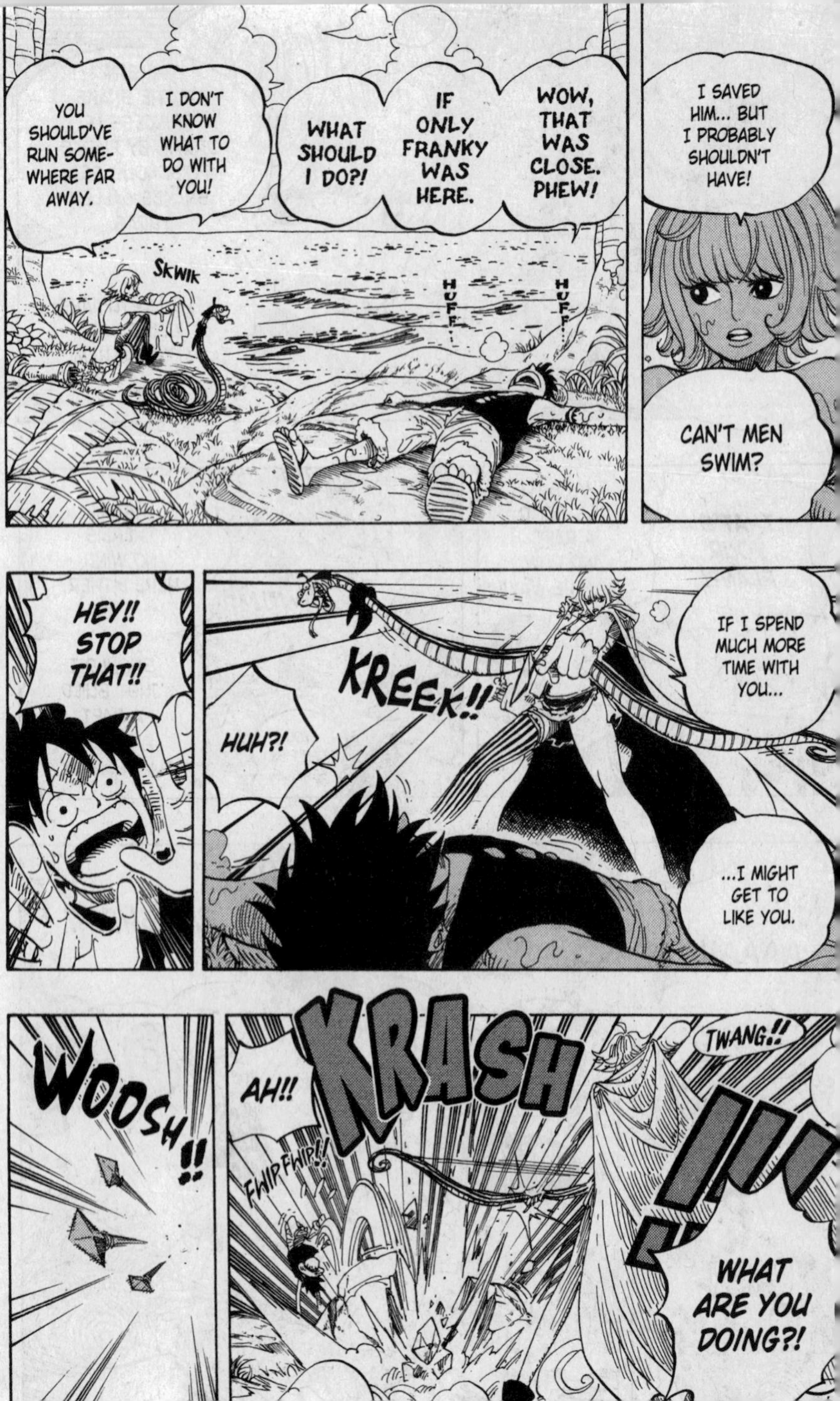
I SAVED HIM... BUT I PROBABLY SHOULDN'T HAVE!
CAN'T MEN SWIM?
WOW, THAT WAS CLOSE. PHEW!
IF ONLY FRANKY WAS HERE.
WHAT SHOULD I DO?!
I DON'T KNOW WHAT TO DO WITH YOU!
YOU SHOULD'VE RUN SOME-WHERE FAR AWAY.
HUFF...
HUFF...
SKWIK
IF I SPEND MUCH MORE TIME WITH YOU...
...I MIGHT GET TO LIKE YOU.
KREEK!!
HUH?!
HEY!! STOP THAT!!
TWANG!!
WHAT ARE YOU DOING?!
KRASH
AH!!
FWIP FWIP!!
WOOSH!!

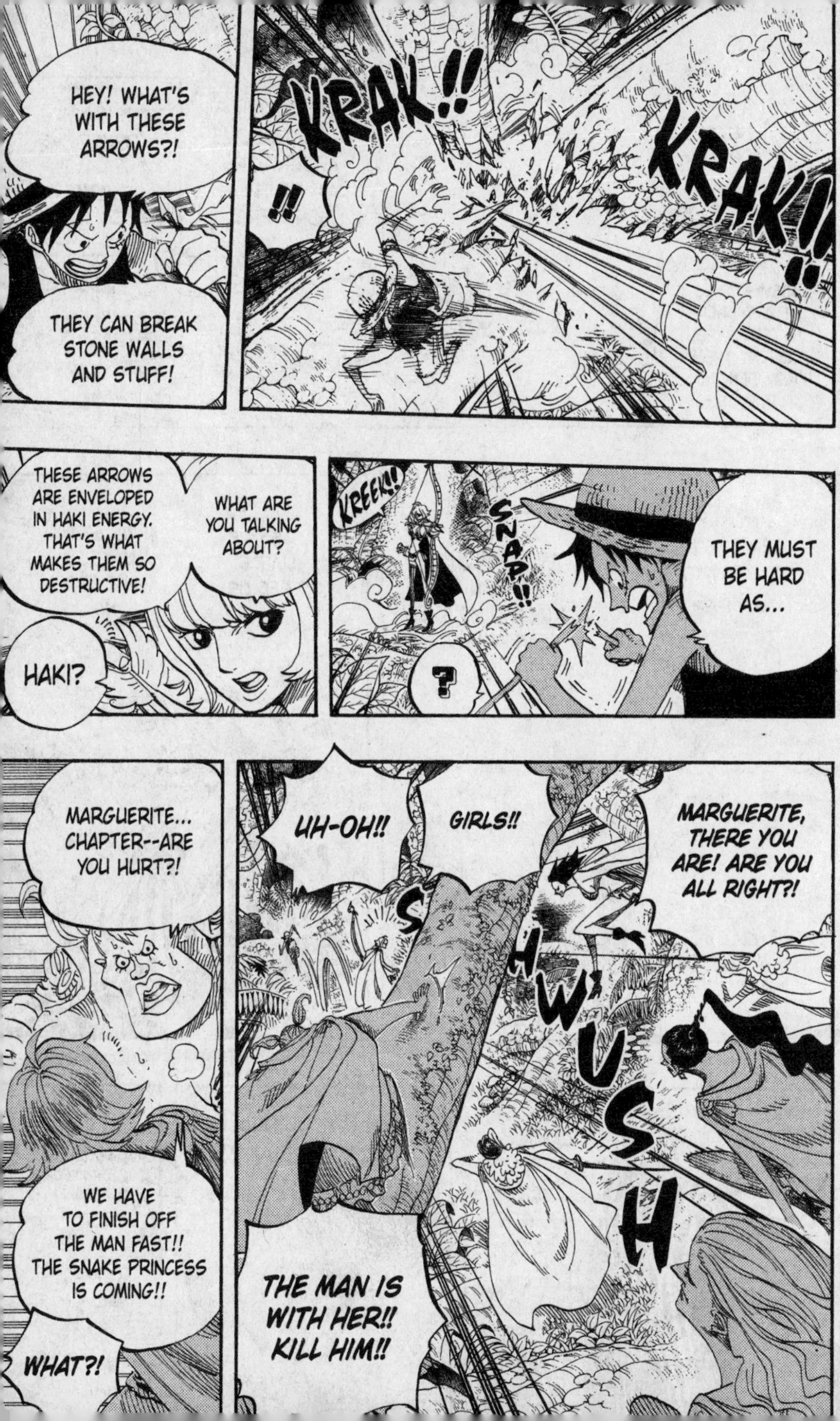
KRAK!!
KRAK!!
!!
HEY! WHAT'S WITH THESE ARROWS?!
THEY CAN BREAK STONE WALLS AND STUFF!
THEY MUST BE HARD AS...
SNAP!!
KREEK!!
?
WHAT ARE YOU TALKING ABOUT?
THESE ARROWS ARE ENVELOPED IN HAKI ENERGY. THAT'S WHAT MAKES THEM SO DESTRUCTIVE!
HAKI?
MARGUERITE, THERE YOU ARE! ARE YOU ALL RIGHT?!
GIRLS!!
UH-OH!!
SHWUSH
THE MAN IS WITH HER!! KILL HIM!!
MARGUERITE... CHAPTER--ARE YOU HURT?!
WE HAVE TO FINISH OFF THE MAN FAST!! THE SNAKE PRINCESS IS COMING!!
WHAT?!

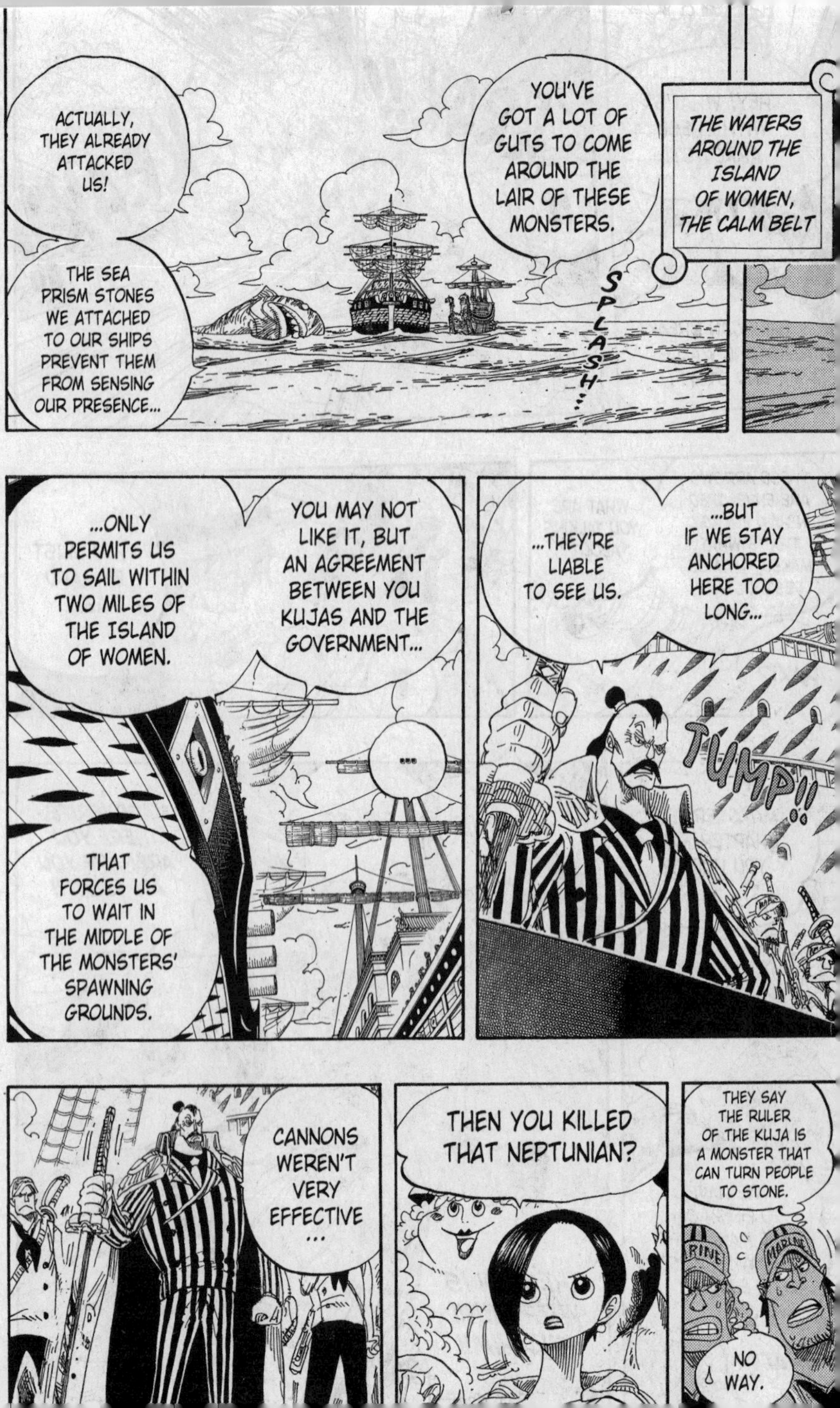
THE WATERS AROUND THE ISLAND OF WOMEN, THE CALM BELT
YOU'VE GOT A LOT OF GUTS TO COME AROUND THE LAIR OF THESE MONSTERS.
SPLASH...
ACTUALLY, THEY ALREADY ATTACKED US!
THE SEA PRISM STONES WE ATTACHED TO OUR SHIPS PREVENT THEM FROM SENSING OUR PRESENCE...
...BUT IF WE STAY ANCHORED HERE TOO LONG...
...THEY'RE LIABLE TO SEE US.
TUMP!!
YOU MAY NOT LIKE IT, BUT AN AGREEMENT BETWEEN YOU KUJAS AND THE GOVERNMENT...
...ONLY PERMITS US TO SAIL WITHIN TWO MILES OF THE ISLAND OF WOMEN.
THAT FORCES US TO WAIT IN THE MIDDLE OF THE MONSTERS' SPAWNING GROUNDS.
THEY SAY THE RULER OF THE KUJA IS A MONSTER THAT CAN TURN PEOPLE TO STONE.
NO WAY.
THEN YOU KILLED THAT NEPTUNIAN?
CANNONS WEREN'T VERY EFFECTIVE ...

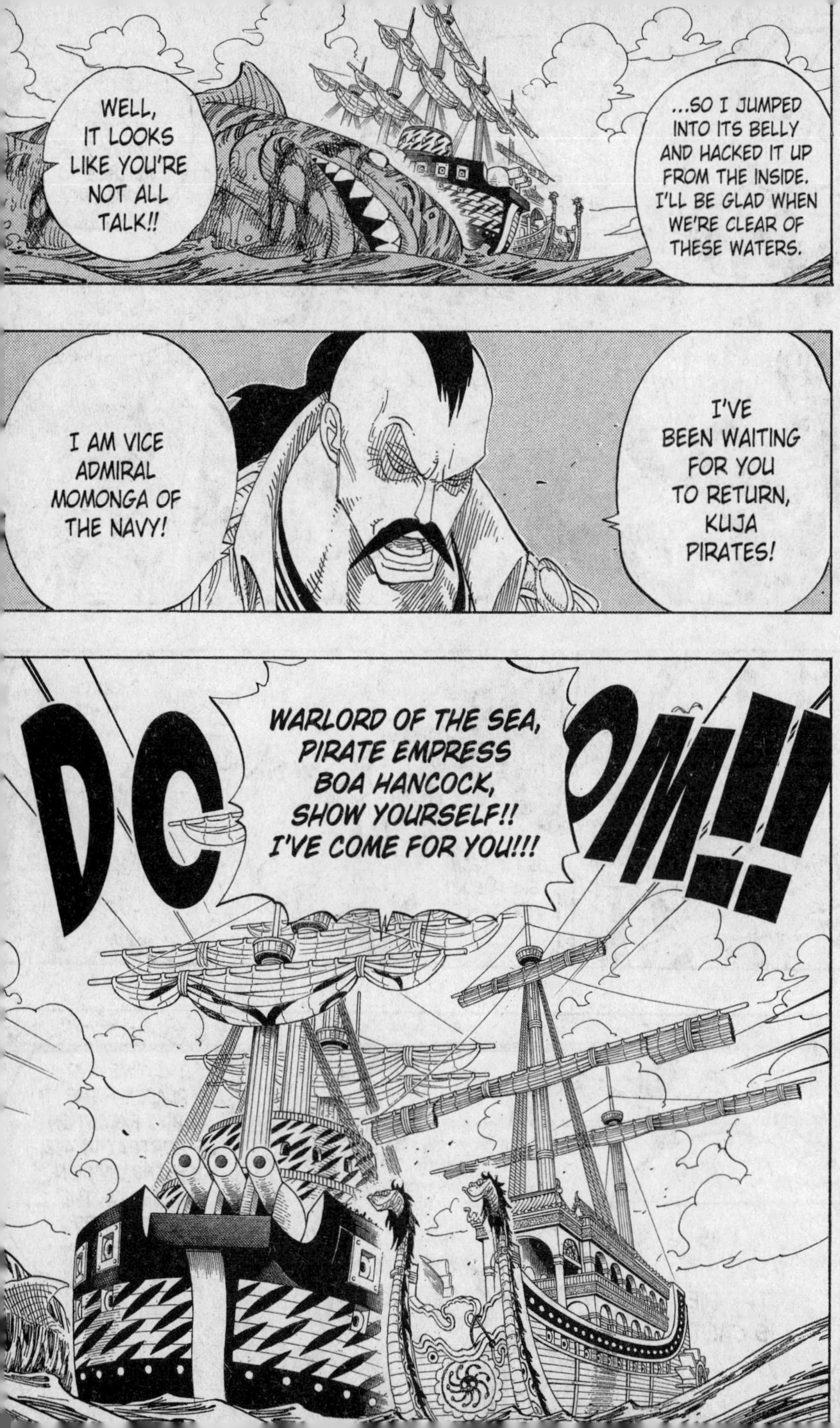
...SO I JUMPED INTO ITS BELLY AND HACKED IT UP FROM THE INSIDE. I'LL BE GLAD WHEN WE'RE CLEAR OF THESE WATERS.
WELL, IT LOOKS LIKE YOU'RE NOT ALL TALK!!
I'VE BEEN WAITING FOR YOU TO RETURN, KUJA PIRATES!
I AM VICE ADMIRAL MOMONGA OF THE NAVY!
DO
OM!!
WARLORD OF THE SEA, PIRATE EMPRESS BOA HANCOCK, SHOW YOURSELF!! I'VE COME FOR YOU!!!

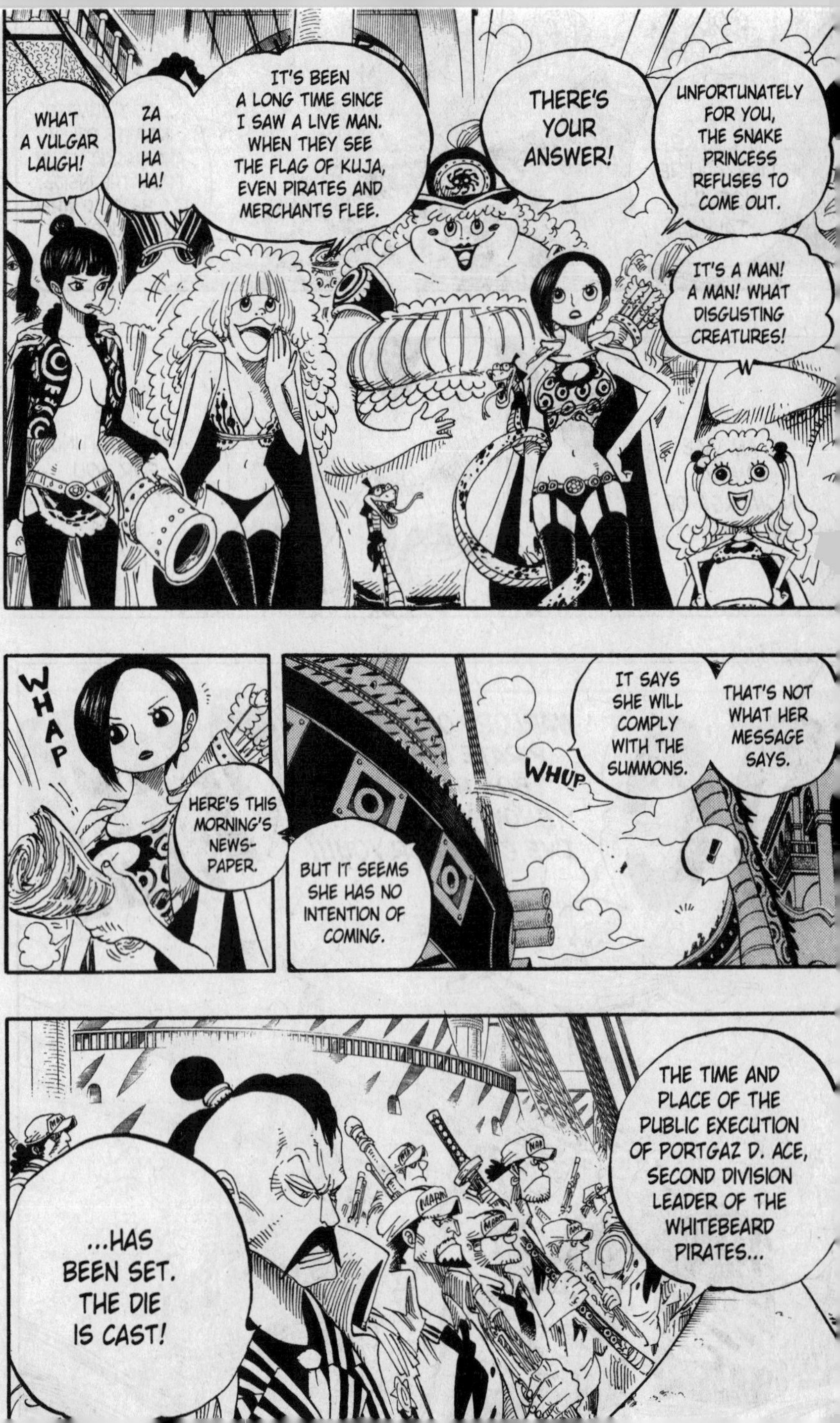
UNFORTUNATELY FOR YOU, THE SNAKE PRINCESS REFUSES TO COME OUT.
THERE'S YOUR ANSWER!
IT'S A MAN! A MAN! WHAT DISGUSTING CREATURES!
IT'S BEEN A LONG TIME SINCE I SAW A LIVE MAN. WHEN THEY SEE THE FLAG OF KUJA, EVEN PIRATES AND MERCHANTS FLEE.
ZA HA HA HA!
WHAT A VULGAR LAUGH!
THAT'S NOT WHAT HER MESSAGE SAYS.
IT SAYS SHE WILL COMPLY WITH THE SUMMONS.
WHUP
!
BUT IT SEEMS SHE HAS NO INTENTION OF COMING.
WHAP
HERE'S THIS MORNING'S NEWS-PAPER.
THE TIME AND PLACE OF THE PUBLIC EXECUTION OF PORTGAZ D. ACE, SECOND DIVISION LEADER OF THE WHITEBEARD PIRATES...
...HAS BEEN SET. THE DIE IS CAST!

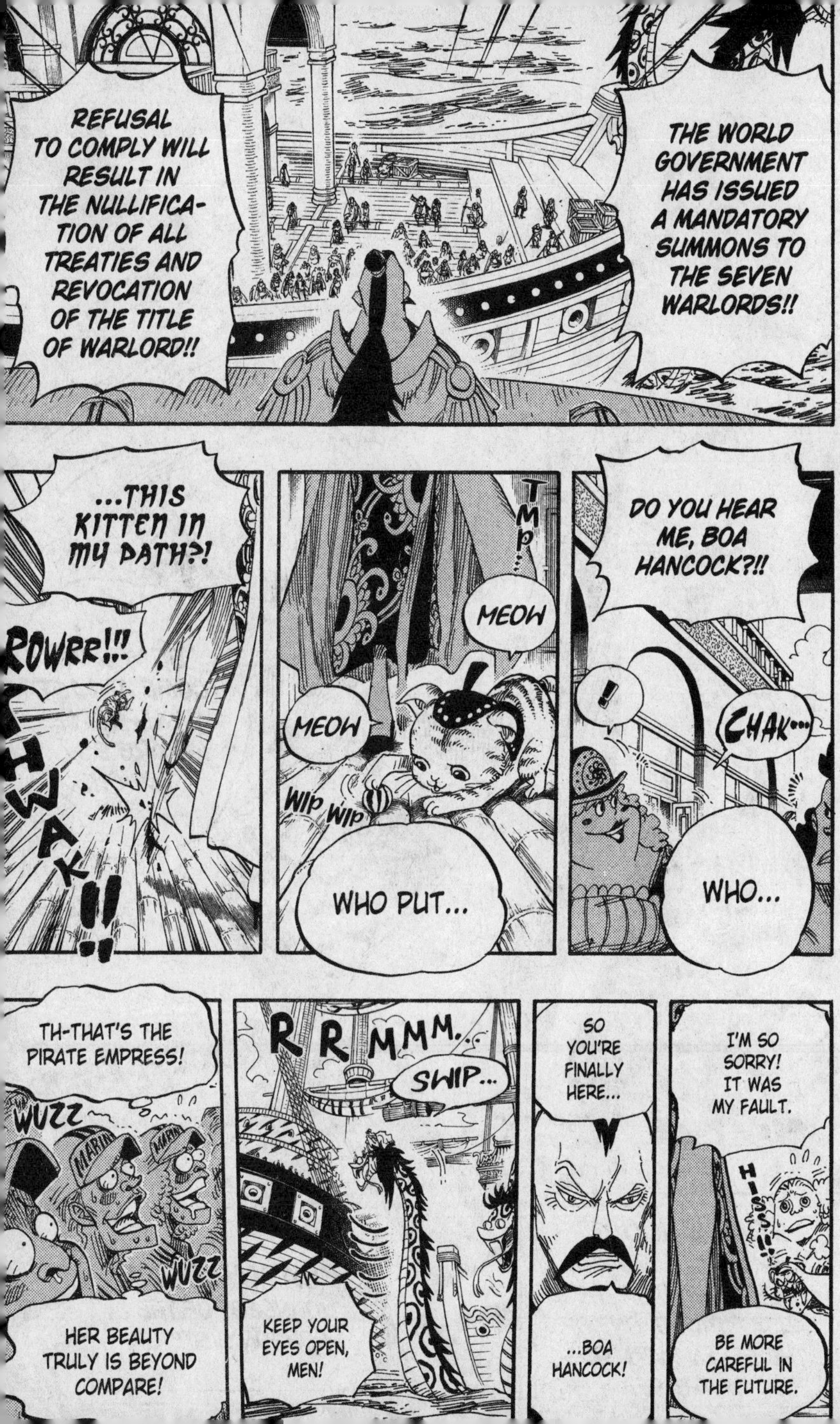

THE WORLD GOVERNMENT HAS ISSUED A MANDATORY SUMMONS TO THE SEVEN WARLORDS!!
REFUSAL TO COMPLY WILL RESULT IN THE NULLIFICATION OF ALL TREATIES AND REVOCATION OF THE TITLE OF WARLORD!!
DO YOU HEAR ME, BOA HANCOCK?!!
!
CHAK...
WHO...
TMP...
MEOW
MEOW
WIP WIP
WHO PUT...
...THIS KITTEN IN MY PATH?!
ROWRR!!!
THWAK!!!
I'M SO SORRY! IT WAS MY FAULT.
HISS!!
BE MORE CAREFUL IN THE FUTURE.
SO YOU'RE FINALLY HERE...
...BOA HANCOCK!
RRMMM.
SWIP...
KEEP YOUR EYES OPEN, MEN!
TH-THAT'S THE PIRATE EMPRESS!
WUZZ
WUZZ
HER BEAUTY TRULY IS BEYOND COMPARE!

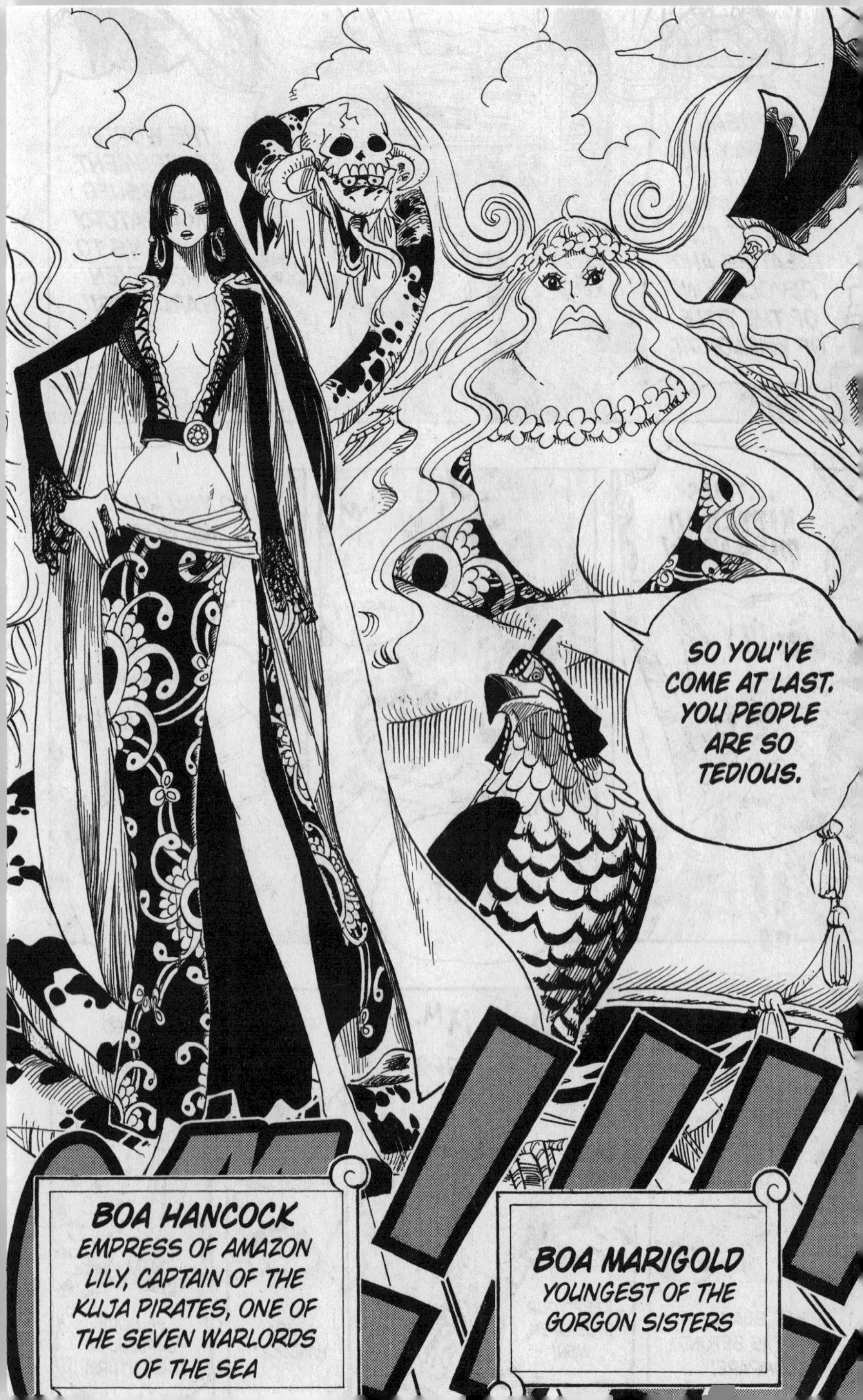
SO YOU'VE COME AT LAST. YOU PEOPLE ARE SO TEDIOUS.
BOA MARIGOLD
YOUNGEST OF THE GORGON SISTERS
BOA HANCOCK
EMPRESS OF AMAZON LILY, CAPTAIN OF THE KUJA PIRATES, ONE OF THE SEVEN WARLORDS OF THE SEA

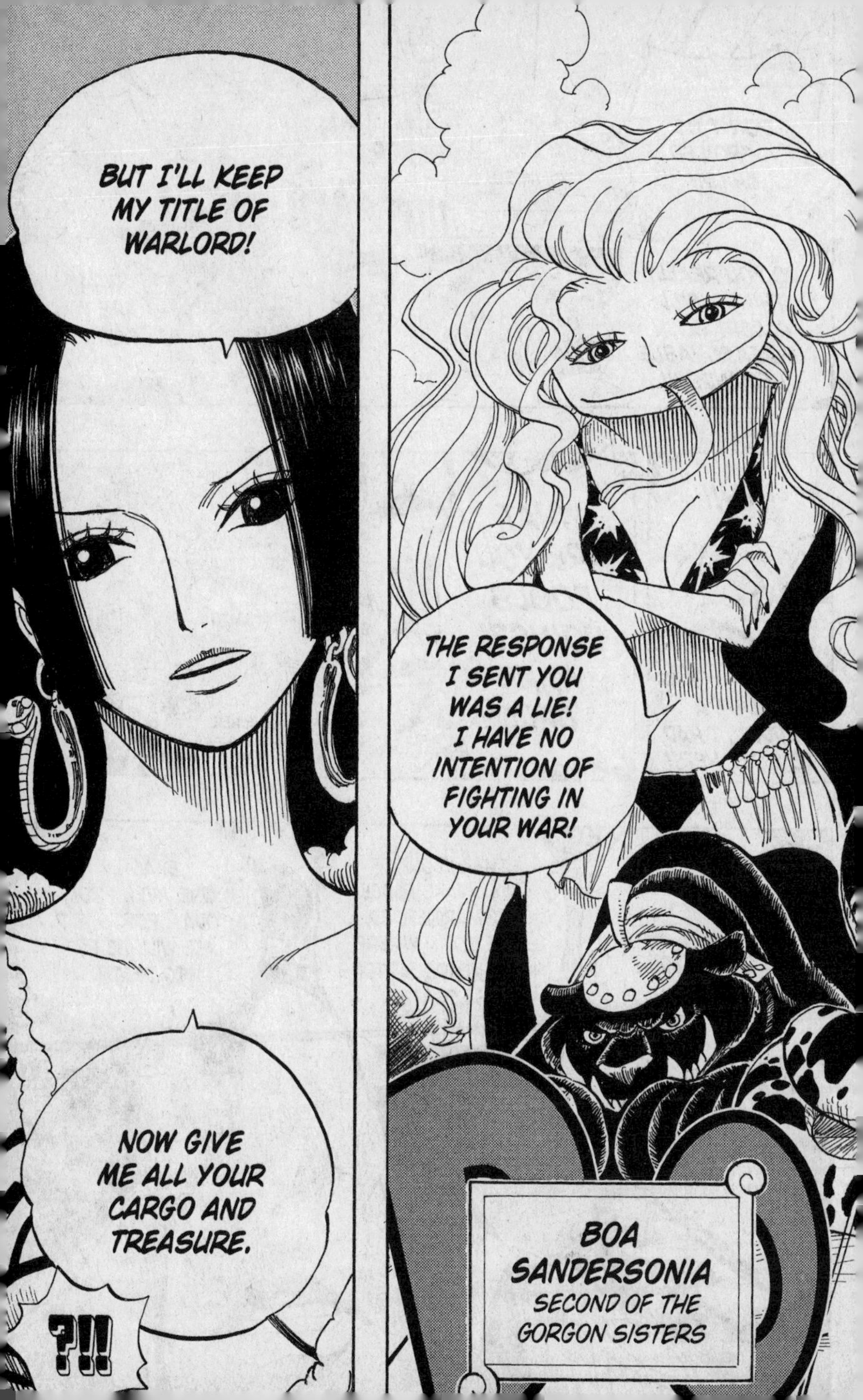
THE RESPONSE I SENT YOU WAS A LIE! I HAVE NO INTENTION OF FIGHTING IN YOUR WAR!
BOA SANDERSONIA
SECOND OF THE GORGON SISTERS
BUT I'LL KEEP MY TITLE OF WARLORD!
NOW GIVE ME ALL YOUR CARGO AND TREASURE.
?!!

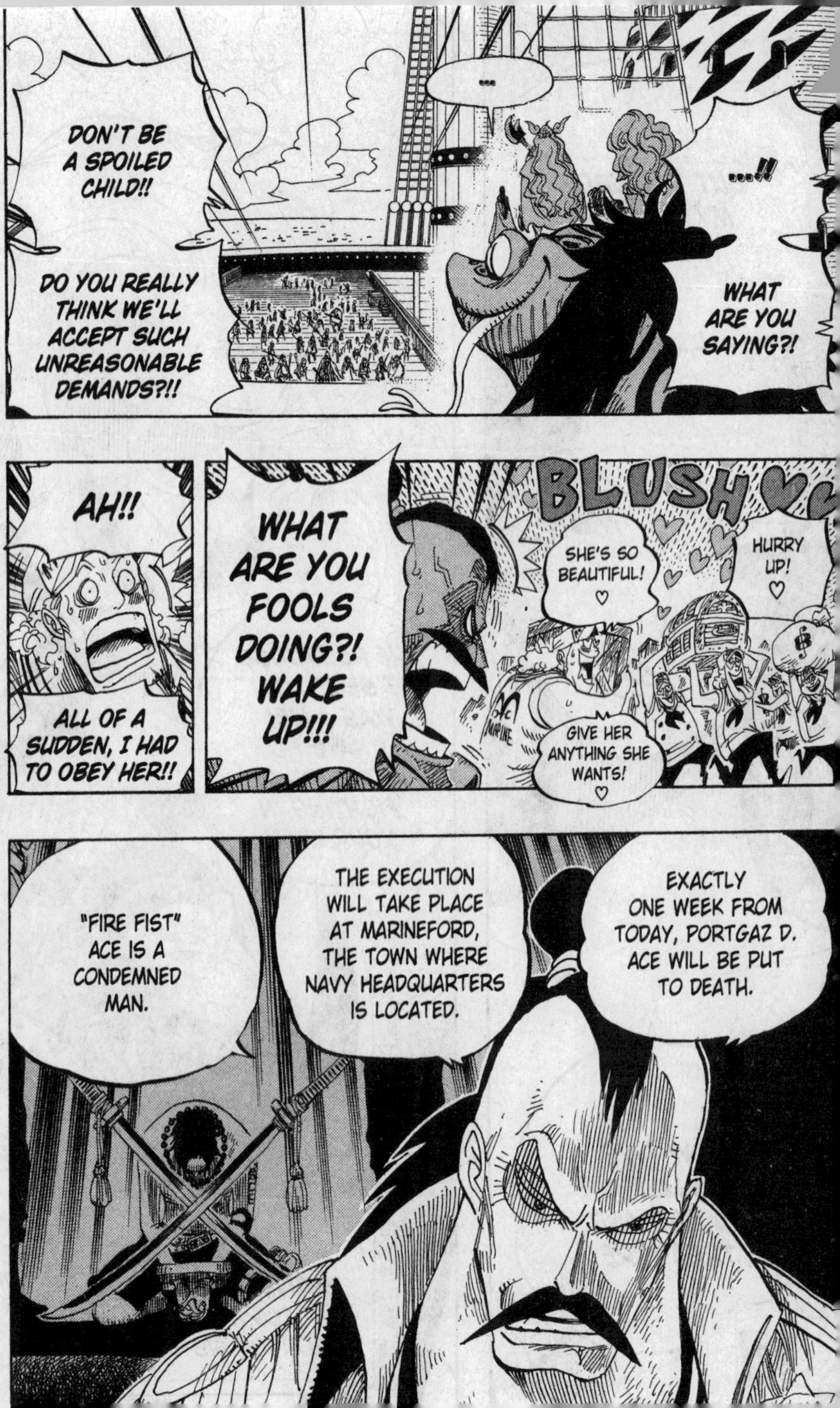
...!!
WHAT ARE YOU SAYING?!
...
DON'T BE A SPOILED CHILD!!
DO YOU REALLY THINK WE'LL ACCEPT SUCH UNREASONABLE DEMANDS?!!
BLUSH
HURRY UP! ♡
SHE'S SO BEAUTIFUL! ♡
GIVE HER ANYTHING SHE WANTS! ♡
MARINE
WHAT ARE YOU FOOLS DOING?! WAKE UP!!!
AH!!
ALL OF A SUDDEN, I HAD TO OBEY HER!!
EXACTLY ONE WEEK FROM TODAY, PORTGAZ D. ACE WILL BE PUT TO DEATH.
THE EXECUTION WILL TAKE PLACE AT MARINEFORD, THE TOWN WHERE NAVY HEADQUARTERS IS LOCATED.
"FIRE FIST" ACE IS A CONDEMNED MAN.

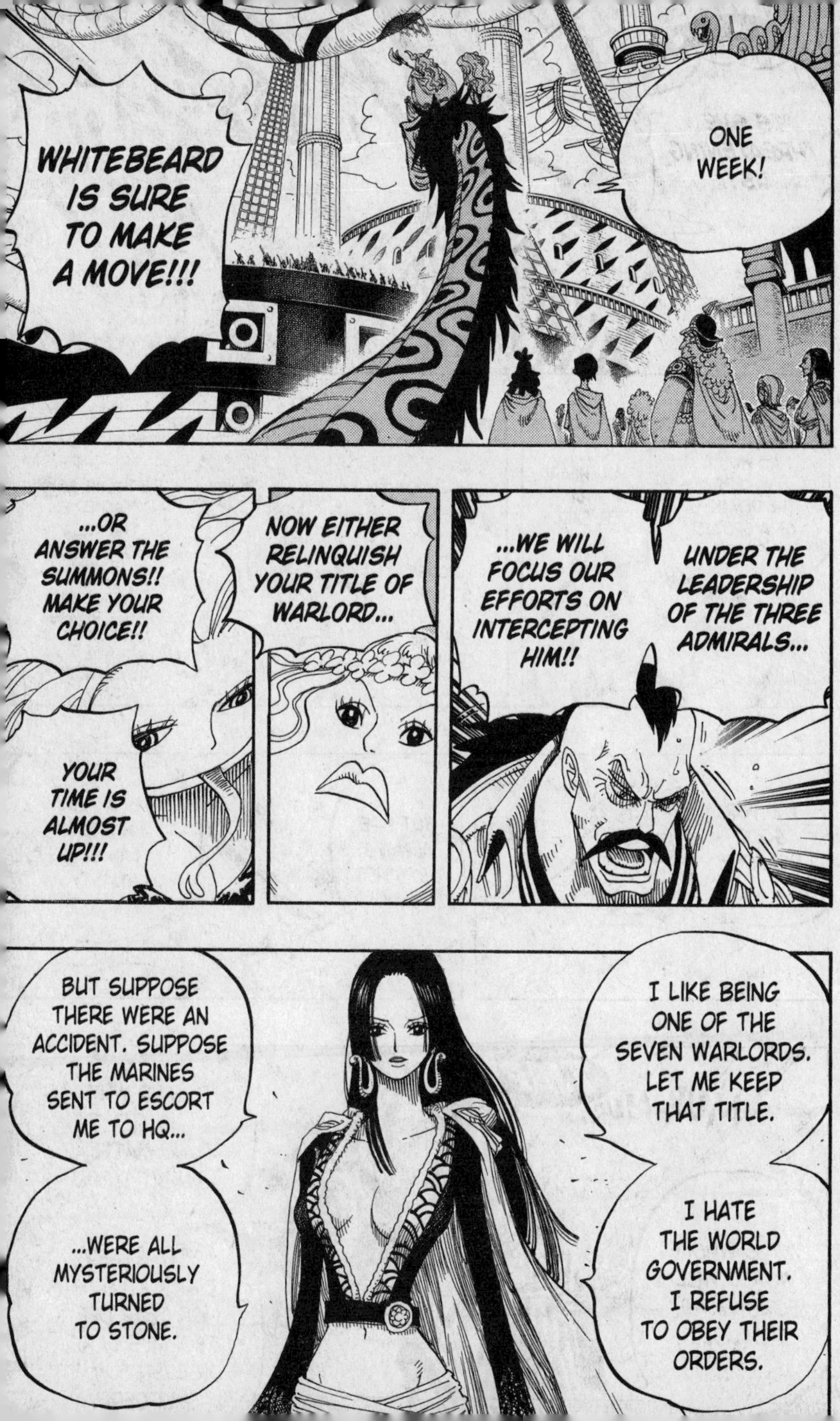
ONE WEEK!
WHITEBEARD IS SURE TO MAKE A MOVE!!!
UNDER THE LEADERSHIP OF THE THREE ADMIRALS...
...WE WILL FOCUS OUR EFFORTS ON INTERCEPTING HIM!!
NOW EITHER RELINQUISH YOUR TITLE OF WARLORD...
...OR ANSWER THE SUMMONS!! MAKE YOUR CHOICE!!
YOUR TIME IS ALMOST UP!!!
I LIKE BEING ONE OF THE SEVEN WARLORDS. LET ME KEEP THAT TITLE.
I HATE THE WORLD GOVERNMENT. I REFUSE TO OBEY THEIR ORDERS.
BUT SUPPOSE THERE WERE AN ACCIDENT. SUPPOSE THE MARINES SENT TO ESCORT ME TO HQ...
...WERE ALL MYSTERIOUSLY TURNED TO STONE.

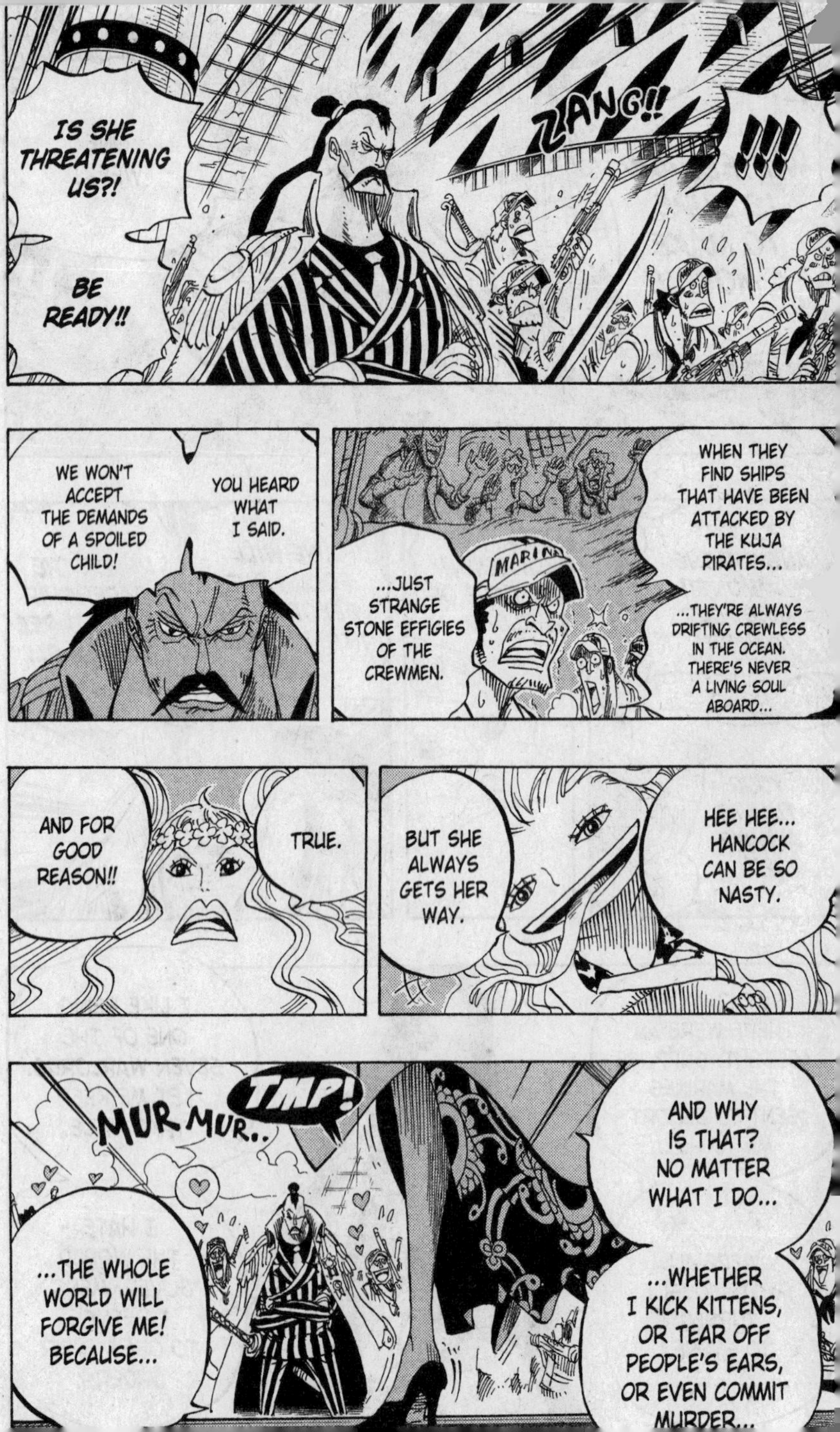
!!!
ZANG!!
IS SHE THREATENING US?!
BE READY!!
WHEN THEY FIND SHIPS THAT HAVE BEEN ATTACKED BY THE KUJA PIRATES...
...THEY'RE ALWAYS DRIFTING CREWLESS IN THE OCEAN. THERE'S NEVER A LIVING SOUL ABOARD...
...JUST STRANGE STONE EFFIGIES OF THE CREWMEN.
YOU HEARD WHAT I SAID.
WE WON'T ACCEPT THE DEMANDS OF A SPOILED CHILD!
HEE HEE... HANCOCK CAN BE SO NASTY.
BUT SHE ALWAYS GETS HER WAY.
TRUE.
AND FOR GOOD REASON!!
AND WHY IS THAT? NO MATTER WHAT I DO...
TMP!
MUR MUR..
...WHETHER I KICK KITTENS, OR TEAR OFF PEOPLE'S EARS, OR EVEN COMMIT MURDER...
...THE WHOLE WORLD WILL FORGIVE ME! BECAUSE...

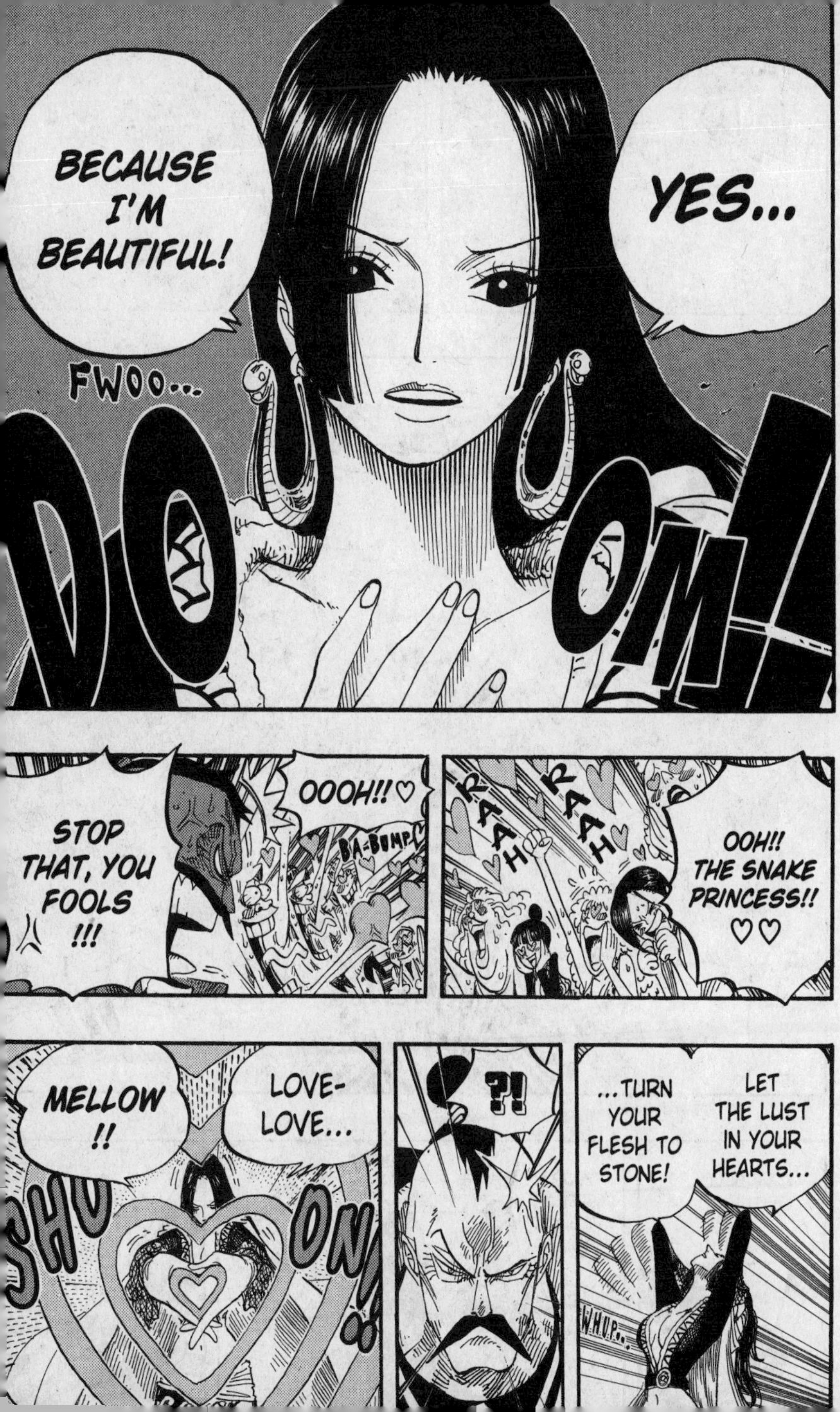
YES...
BECAUSE I'M BEAUTIFUL!
FWOO...
DOOM!!
RAAH
RAAH
OOH!! THE SNAKE PRINCESS!! ♡♡
OOOH!! ♡
BA-BUMP
STOP THAT, YOU FOOLS !!!
LET THE LUST IN YOUR HEARTS...
...TURN YOUR FLESH TO STONE!
WHUP..
?!
LOVE-LOVE...
MELLOW !!
SHOOM!!

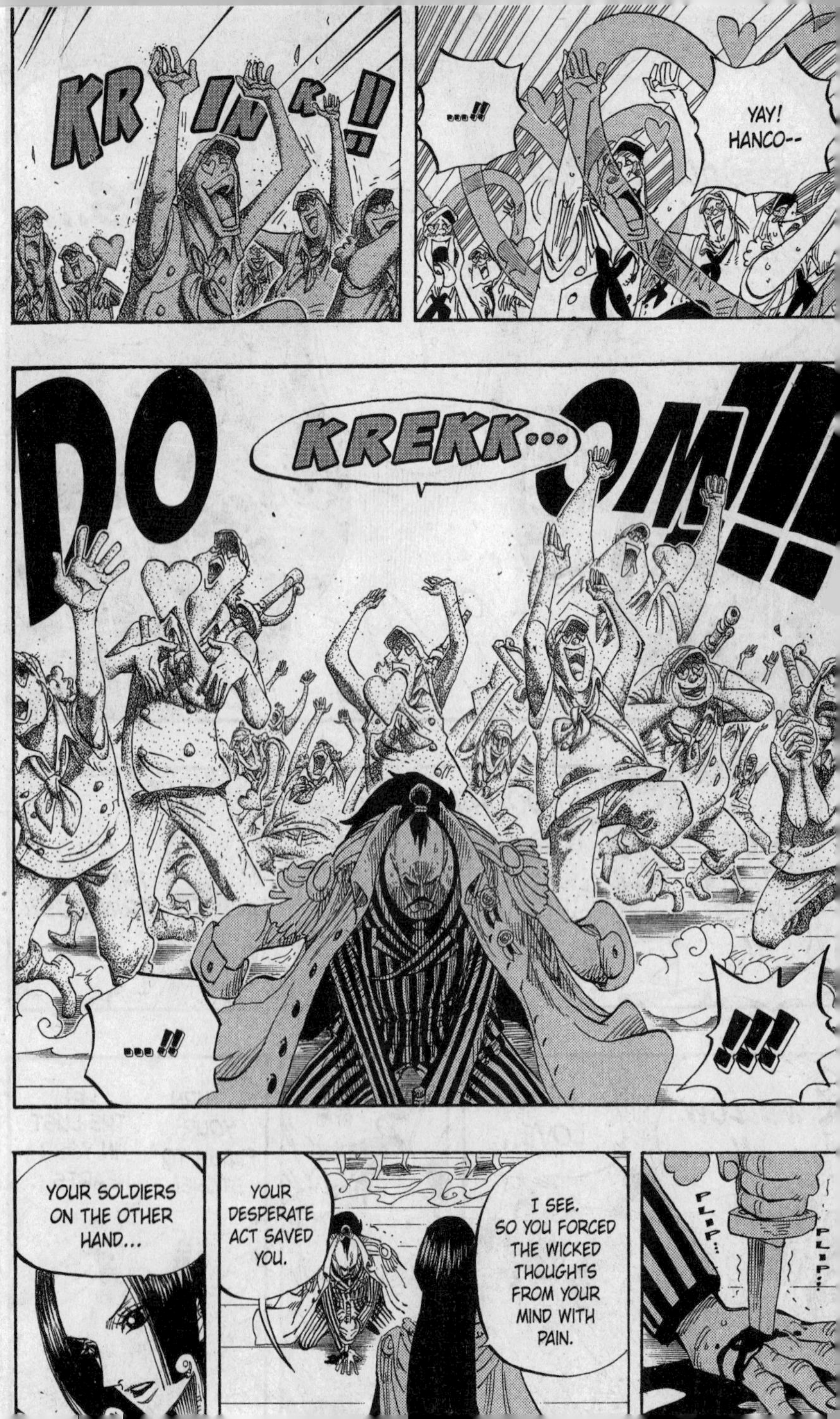
YAY! HANCO--
...!!
KRINK!!
DOOM!!
KREKK...
!!!
...!!
PLIP...
PLIP...
I SEE. SO YOU FORCED THE WICKED THOUGHTS FROM YOUR MIND WITH PAIN.
YOUR DESPERATE ACT SAVED YOU.
YOUR SOLDIERS ON THE OTHER HAND...

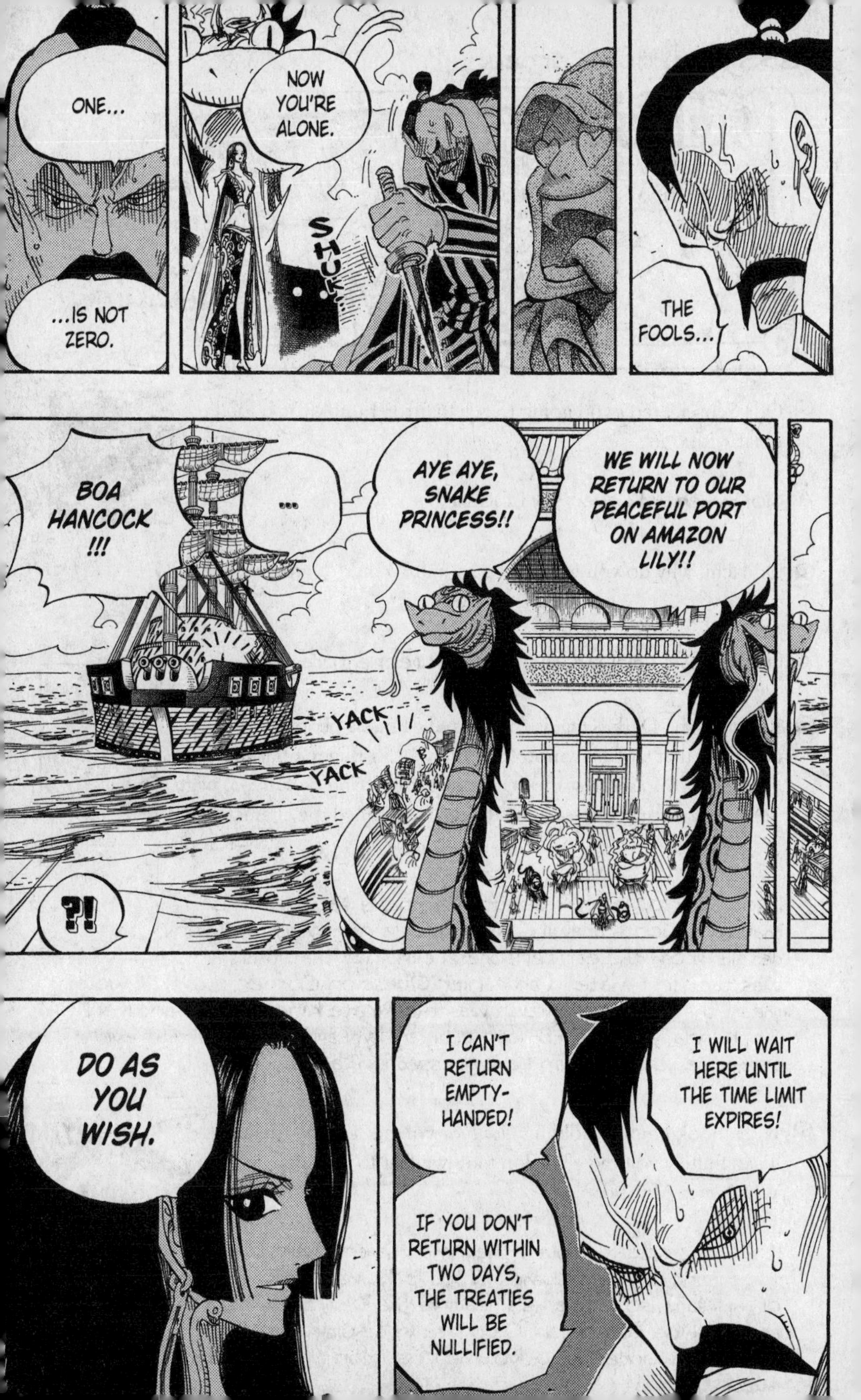
THE FOOLS...
NOW YOU'RE ALONE.
SHUK
ONE...
...IS NOT ZERO.
WE WILL NOW RETURN TO OUR PEACEFUL PORT ON AMAZON LILY!!
AYE AYE, SNAKE PRINCESS!!
...
BOA HANCOCK !!!
YACK
YACK
?!
I WILL WAIT HERE UNTIL THE TIME LIMIT EXPIRES!
I CAN'T RETURN EMPTY-HANDED!
IF YOU DON'T RETURN WITHIN TWO DAYS, THE TREATIES WILL BE NULLIFIED.
DO AS YOU WISH.

SBS Question Corner

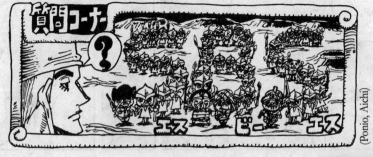

(Ponio, Aichi)

Q: Oda Sensei, aren't you going to get an afro? I think you'd look great with one. --Hiromu

A: No! When did I ever say I would?!

Q: Oddachi, why do you want to be a pirate? You're a grown-up now! ♡ --Ulmol

A: I never said I did! What's with you people today?

Q: Rayleigh, the Dark King, is too wicked. (I guess people don't use that word anymore.) By the way, in Buggy's flashback in chapter 19, I found a somewhat younger Rayleigh (volume 3, page 34). I was surprised to see you'd already designed the character that long ago. --Kanpla

A: I got a lot of letters about this. I really feel that this manga is worth drawing when people remember such tiny details from the early episodes. I explained that this person was the first mate in an earlier Question Corner, but that would mean that Silvers Rayleigh was the Pirate King's right-hand man! So, Kanpla, you're a 48-year-old man. I'm happy to know that even someone your age can be impressed by Rayleigh.

Q: Is the book Kuma's holding *One Piece* volume 12? My friend says it's definitely volume 13! I don't know what to tell him. Which is it, Mr. Oda? --YUMAx527

A: It would be right around the time the crew entered the Grand Line in volumes 12 and 13. Kuma always has that bored look on his face, so maybe he's reading the Davy Back Fight in volume 33 and laughing to himself. Or maybe he's holding volume 25, in which he debuted. I wonder which volume it is! I don't know. Let's all take a guess! Bye!

Chapter 517:
BATH TIME

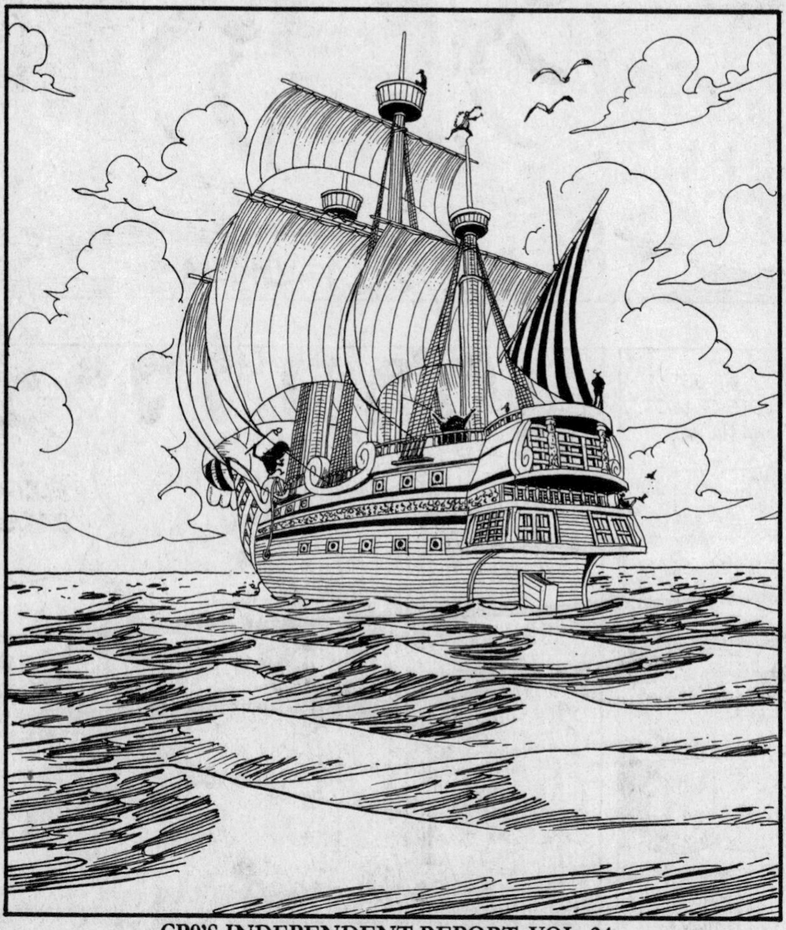

CP9'S INDEPENDENT REPORT, VOL. 24:
"CP9 SETS SAIL FROM ST. POPLAR"

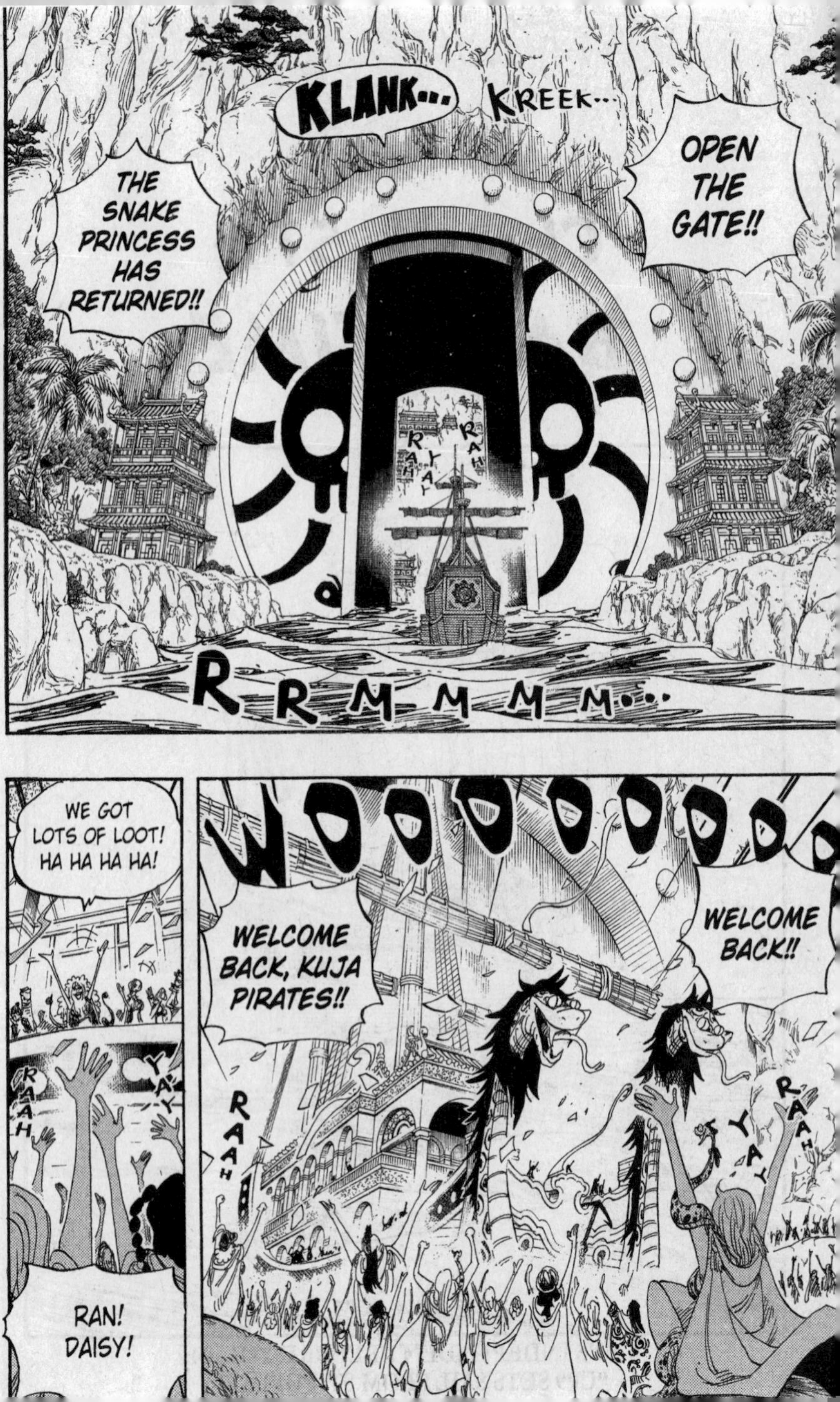

OPEN THE GATE!!
KREEK...
KLANK...
THE SNAKE PRINCESS HAS RETURNED!!
RAH
YAY
RAH
RRMMMMM...
WOOOOOOOOOO
WELCOME BACK!!
WELCOME BACK, KUJA PIRATES!!
RAAH
YAY
RAAH
WE GOT LOTS OF LOOT! HA HA HA HA!
YAY
RAAH
RAN! DAISY!

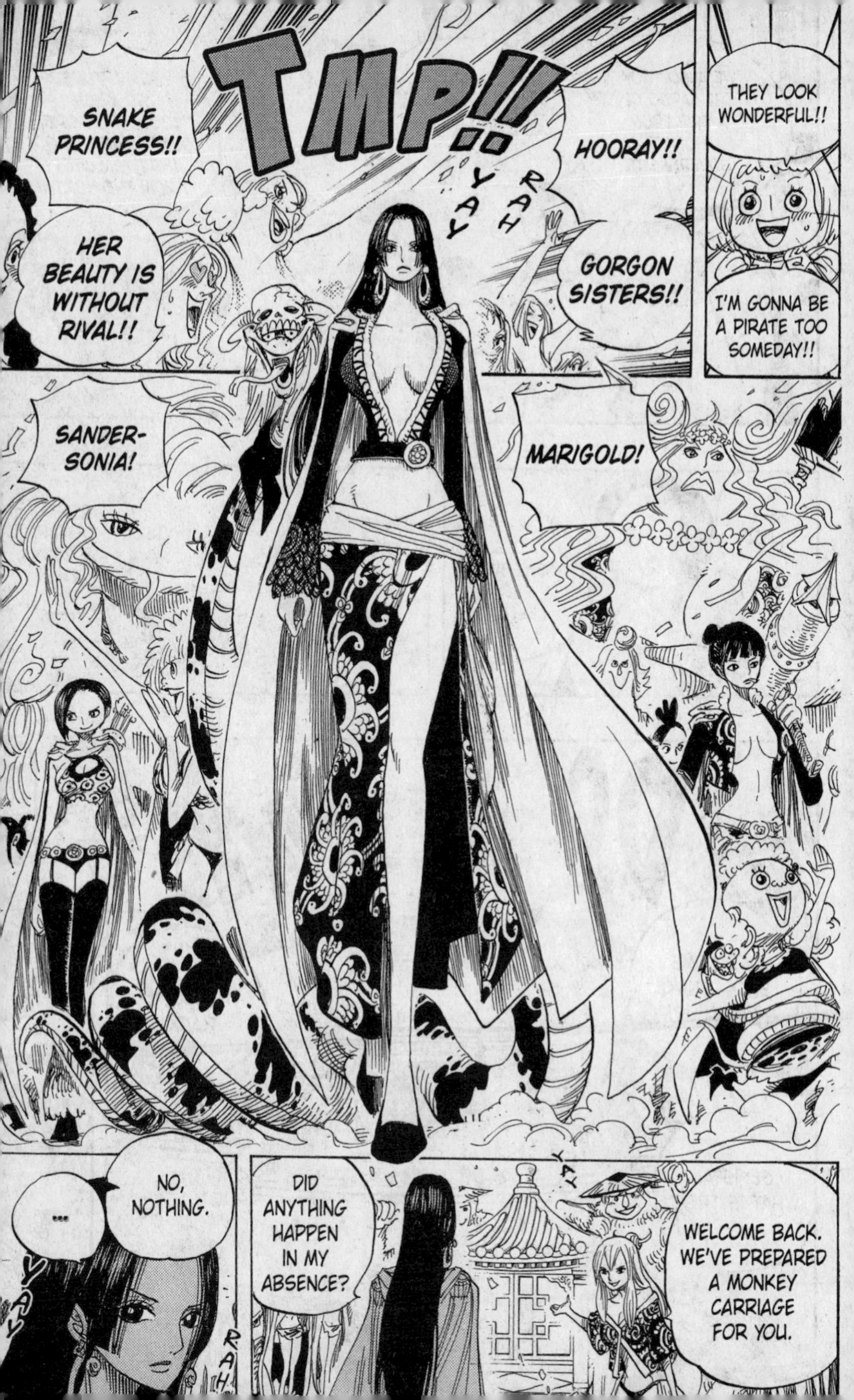
THEY LOOK WONDERFUL!!
I'M GONNA BE A PIRATE TOO SOMEDAY!!
HOORAY!!
RAH
YAY
TMP!!
SNAKE PRINCESS!!
GORGON SISTERS!!
HER BEAUTY IS WITHOUT RIVAL!!
MARIGOLD!
SANDER-SONIA!
YAY
WELCOME BACK. WE'VE PREPARED A MONKEY CARRIAGE FOR YOU.
DID ANYTHING HAPPEN IN MY ABSENCE?
NO, NOTHING.
...
YAY
RAH

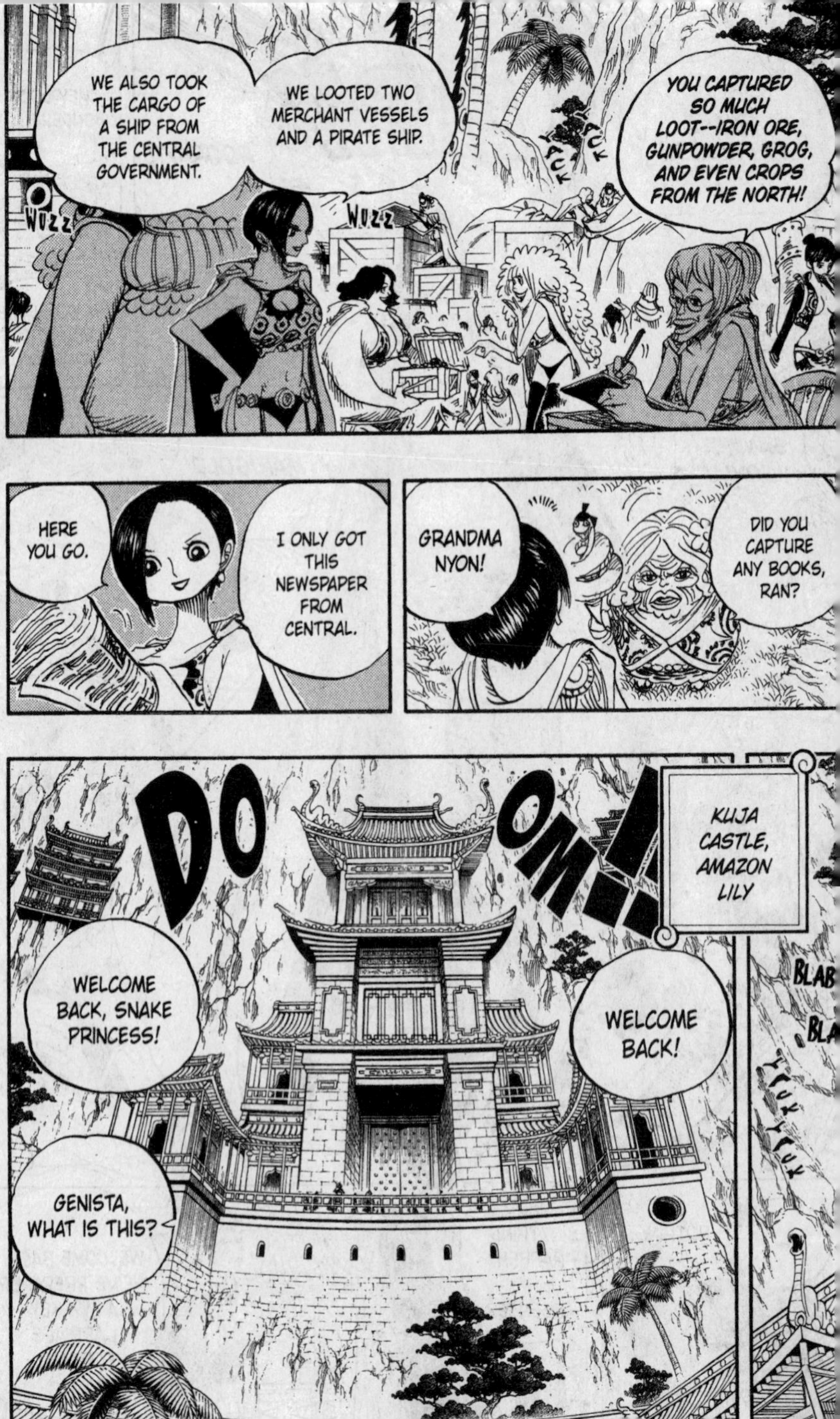
YOU CAPTURED SO MUCH LOOT--IRON ORE, GUNPOWDER, GROG, AND EVEN CROPS FROM THE NORTH!
YACK YACK
WE LOOTED TWO MERCHANT VESSELS AND A PIRATE SHIP.
WUZZ
WE ALSO TOOK THE CARGO OF A SHIP FROM THE CENTRAL GOVERNMENT.
WUZZ
DID YOU CAPTURE ANY BOOKS, RAN?
GRANDMA NYON!
I ONLY GOT THIS NEWSPAPER FROM CENTRAL.
HERE YOU GO.
BLAB
KUJA CASTLE, AMAZON LILY
DOOM!!
WELCOME BACK!
WELCOME BACK, SNAKE PRINCESS!
GENISTA, WHAT IS THIS?

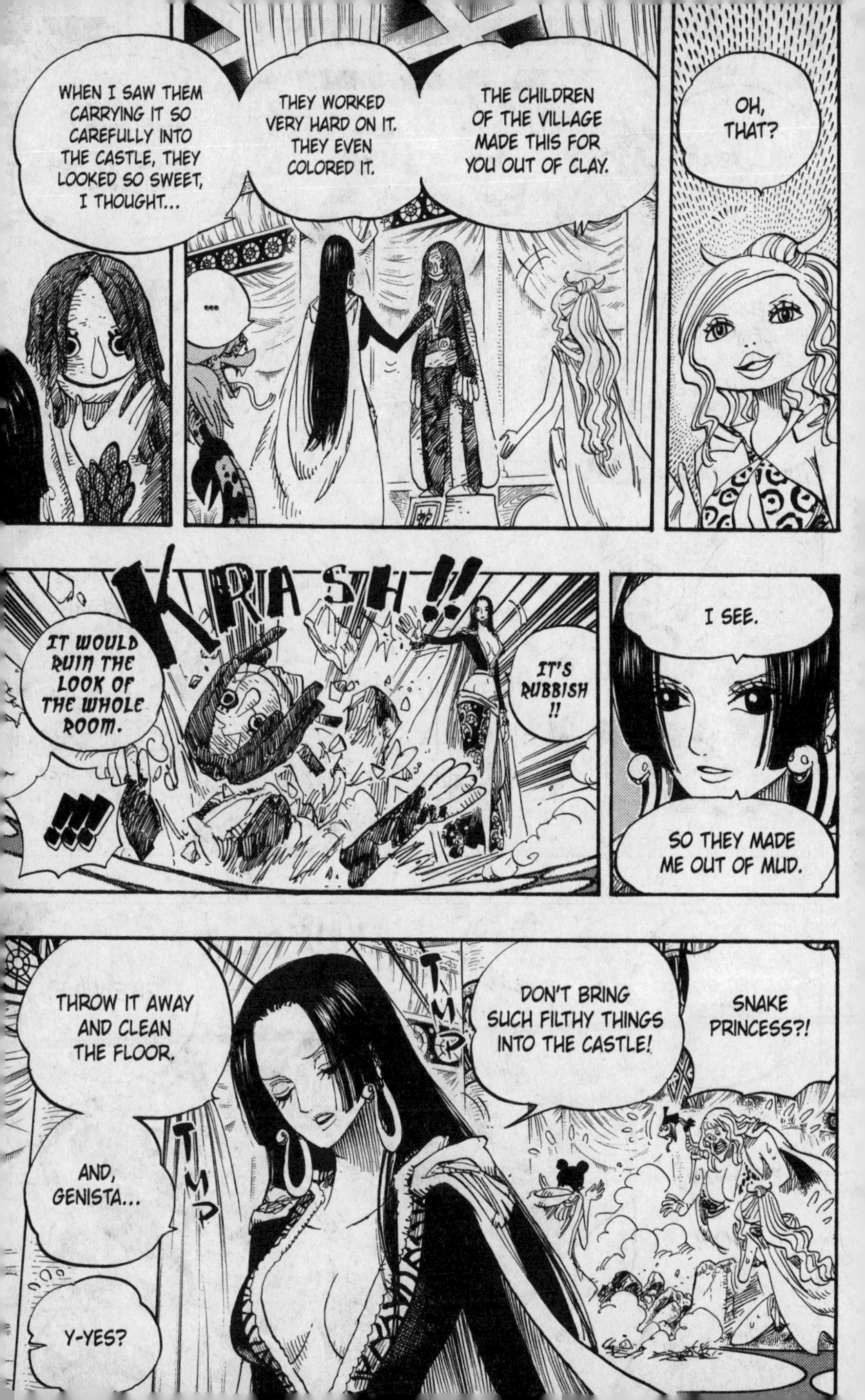
OH, THAT?
THE CHILDREN OF THE VILLAGE MADE THIS FOR YOU OUT OF CLAY.
THEY WORKED VERY HARD ON IT. THEY EVEN COLORED IT.
...
WHEN I SAW THEM CARRYING IT SO CAREFULLY INTO THE CASTLE, THEY LOOKED SO SWEET, I THOUGHT...
I SEE.
SO THEY MADE ME OUT OF MUD.
KRASH!!
IT'S RUBBISH!!
IT WOULD RUIN THE LOOK OF THE WHOLE ROOM.
!!!
SNAKE PRINCESS?!
DON'T BRING SUCH FILTHY THINGS INTO THE CASTLE!
TMP
THROW IT AWAY AND CLEAN THE FLOOR.
TMP
AND, GENISTA...
Y-YES?

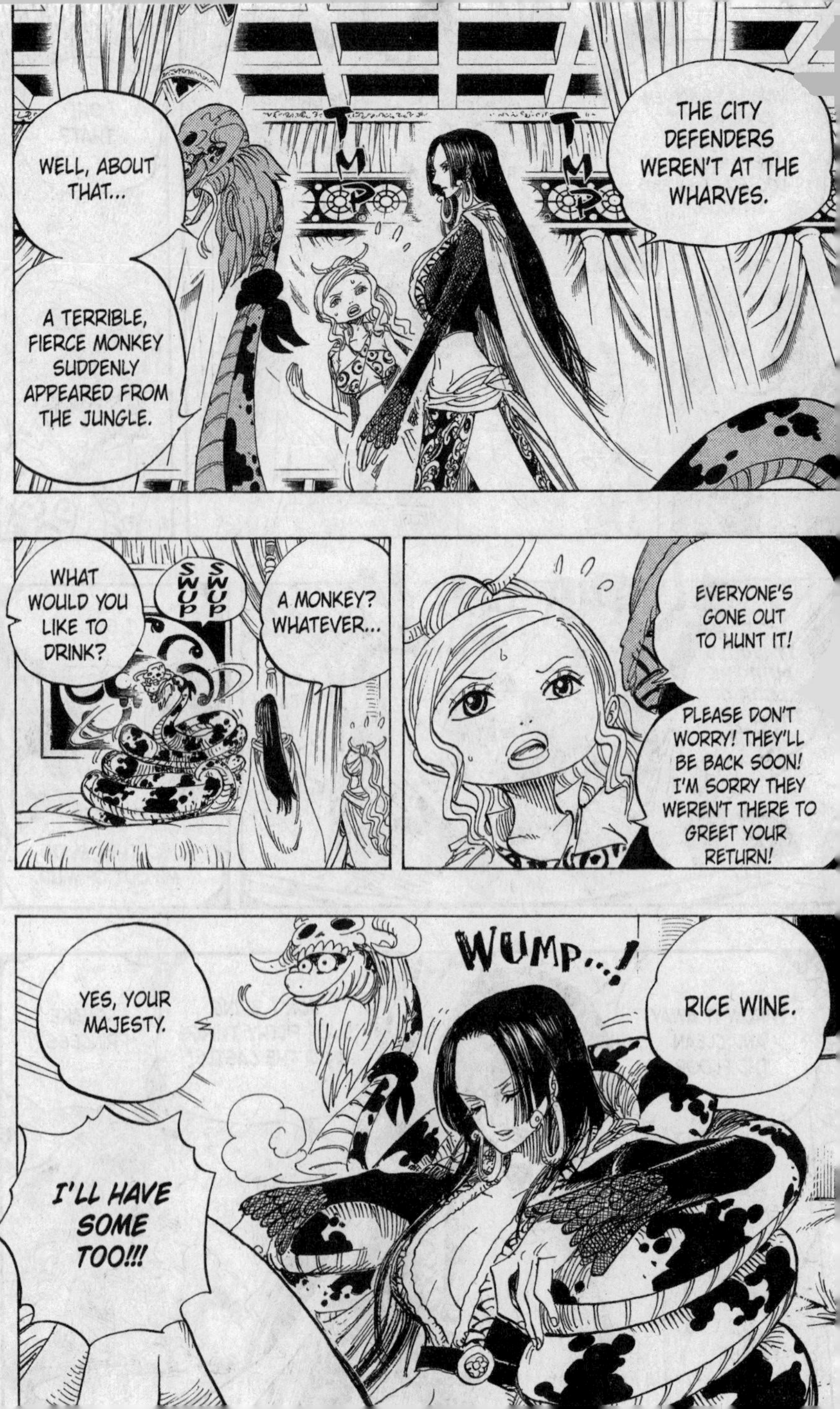
THE CITY DEFENDERS WEREN'T AT THE WHARVES.
TMP
TMP
WELL, ABOUT THAT...
A TERRIBLE, FIERCE MONKEY SUDDENLY APPEARED FROM THE JUNGLE.
EVERYONE'S GONE OUT TO HUNT IT!
PLEASE DON'T WORRY! THEY'LL BE BACK SOON! I'M SORRY THEY WEREN'T THERE TO GREET YOUR RETURN!
A MONKEY? WHATEVER...
SWUP SWUP
WHAT WOULD YOU LIKE TO DRINK?
RICE WINE.
WUMP...!
YES, YOUR MAJESTY.
I'LL HAVE SOME TOO!!!

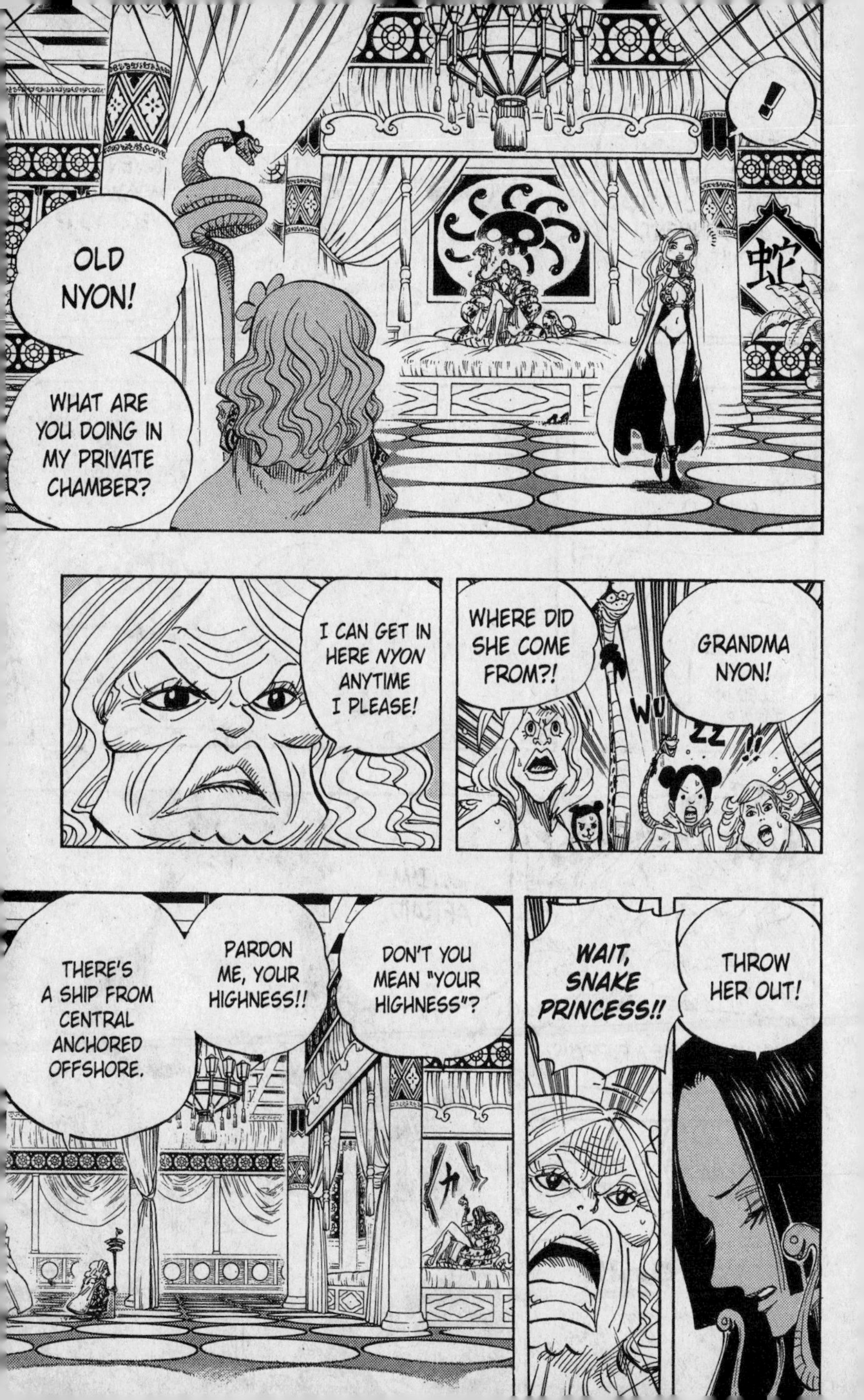
!
蛇
OLD NYON!
WHAT ARE YOU DOING IN MY PRIVATE CHAMBER?
GRANDMA NYON!
!!
WHERE DID SHE COME FROM?!
WUZZ
I CAN GET IN HERE *NYON* ANYTIME I PLEASE!
THROW HER OUT!
WAIT, SNAKE PRINCESS!!
DON'T YOU MEAN "YOUR HIGHNESS"?
PARDON ME, YOUR HIGHNESS!!
THERE'S A SHIP FROM CENTRAL ANCHORED OFFSHORE.

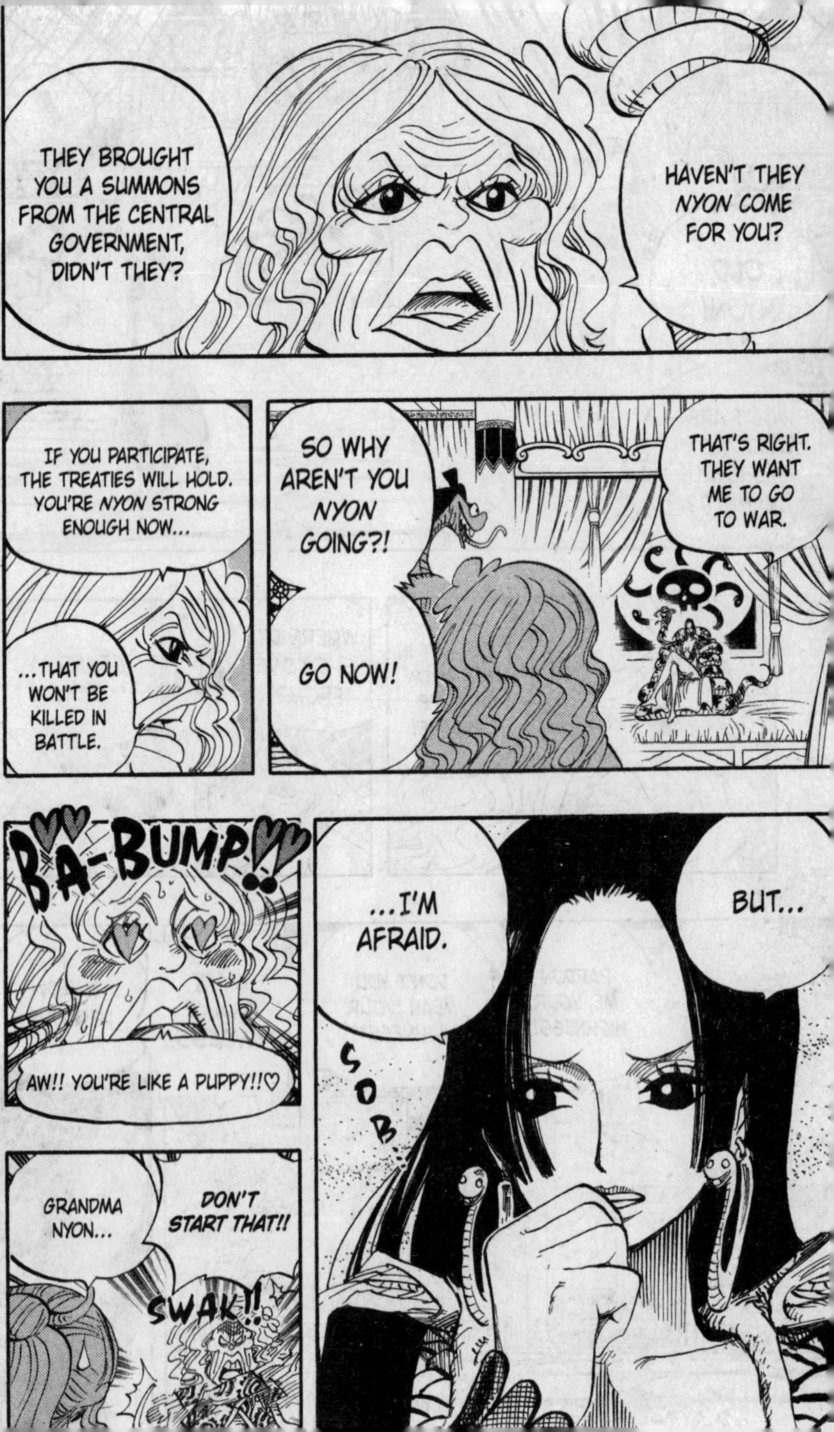

HAVEN'T THEY NYON COME FOR YOU?
THEY BROUGHT YOU A SUMMONS FROM THE CENTRAL GOVERNMENT, DIDN'T THEY?
THAT'S RIGHT. THEY WANT ME TO GO TO WAR.
SO WHY AREN'T YOU NYON GOING?!
GO NOW!
IF YOU PARTICIPATE, THE TREATIES WILL HOLD. YOU'RE NYON STRONG ENOUGH NOW...
...THAT YOU WON'T BE KILLED IN BATTLE.
BUT...
...I'M AFRAID.
SOB
BA-BUMP!!
AW!! YOU'RE LIKE A PUPPY!!♡
DON'T START THAT!!
GRANDMA NYON...
SWAK!!

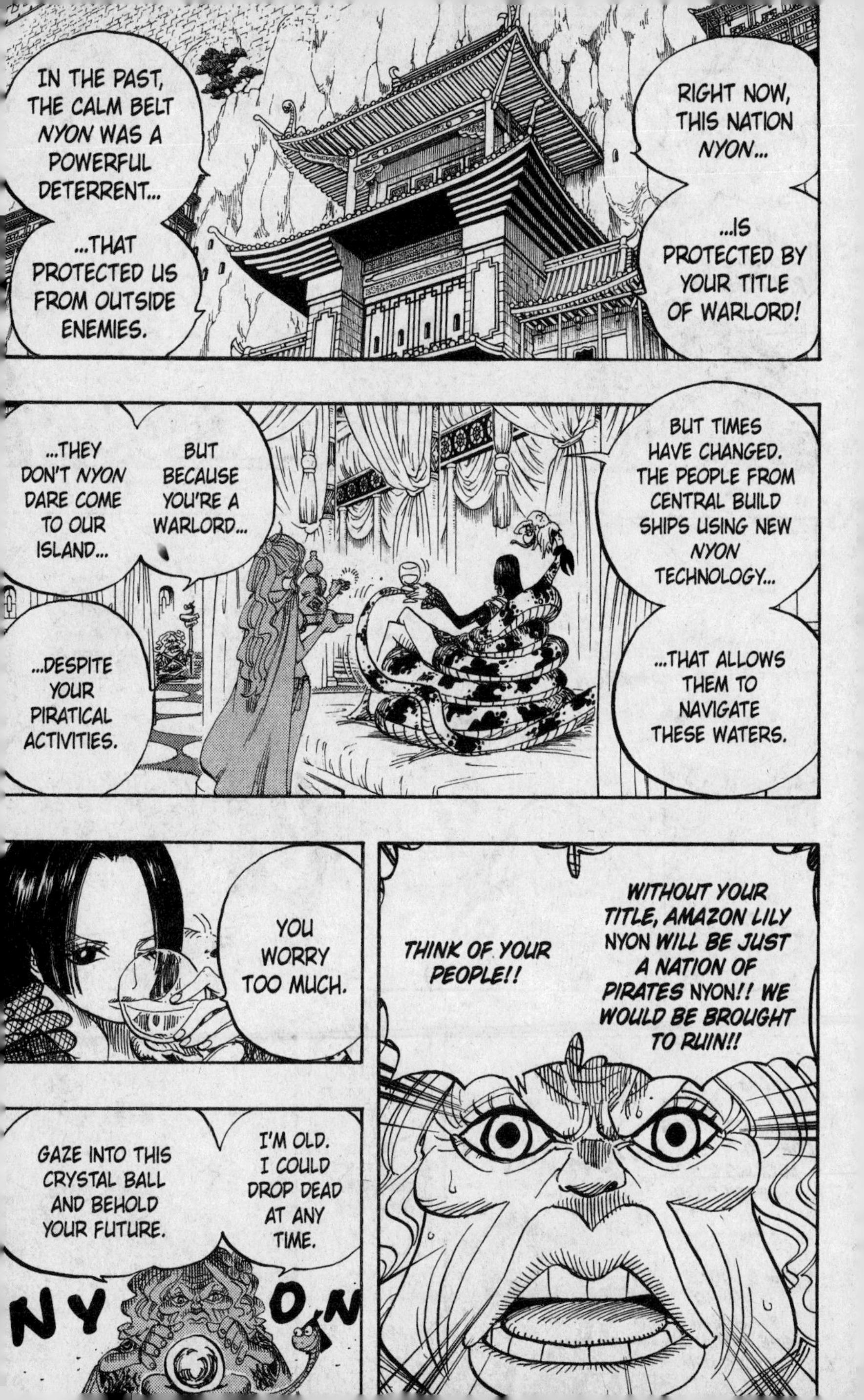
IN THE PAST, THE CALM BELT NYON WAS A POWERFUL DETERRENT...
...THAT PROTECTED US FROM OUTSIDE ENEMIES.
RIGHT NOW, THIS NATION NYON...
...IS PROTECTED BY YOUR TITLE OF WARLORD!
BUT TIMES HAVE CHANGED. THE PEOPLE FROM CENTRAL BUILD SHIPS USING NEW NYON TECHNOLOGY...
...THAT ALLOWS THEM TO NAVIGATE THESE WATERS.
BUT BECAUSE YOU'RE A WARLORD...
...THEY DON'T NYON DARE COME TO OUR ISLAND...
...DESPITE YOUR PIRATICAL ACTIVITIES.
WITHOUT YOUR TITLE, AMAZON LILY NYON WILL BE JUST A NATION OF PIRATES NYON!! WE WOULD BE BROUGHT TO RUIN!!
THINK OF YOUR PEOPLE!!
YOU WORRY TOO MUCH.
I'M OLD. I COULD DROP DEAD AT ANY TIME.
GAZE INTO THIS CRYSTAL BALL AND BEHOLD YOUR FUTURE.
NYON

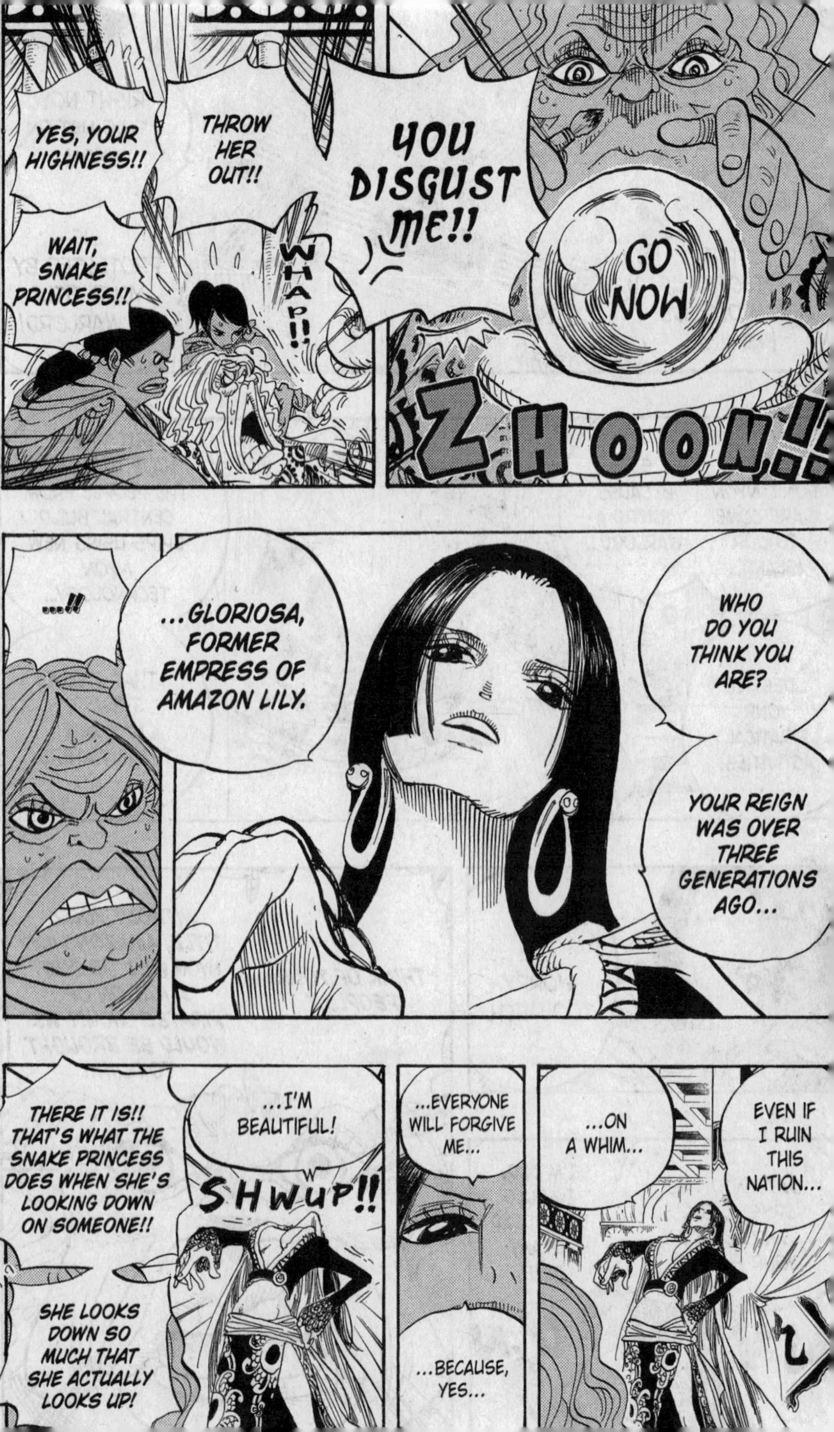
GO NOW
ZHOON!!
YOU DISGUST ME!!
THROW HER OUT!!
YES, YOUR HIGHNESS!!
WAIT, SNAKE PRINCESS!!
WHAP!!
WHO DO YOU THINK YOU ARE?
YOUR REIGN WAS OVER THREE GENERATIONS AGO...
...GLORIOSA, FORMER EMPRESS OF AMAZON LILY.
...!!
EVEN IF I RUIN THIS NATION...
...ON A WHIM...
...EVERYONE WILL FORGIVE ME...
...BECAUSE, YES...
...I'M BEAUTIFUL!
SHWUP!!
THERE IT IS!! THAT'S WHAT THE SNAKE PRINCESS DOES WHEN SHE'S LOOKING DOWN ON SOMEONE!!
SHE LOOKS DOWN SO MUCH THAT SHE ACTUALLY LOOKS UP!

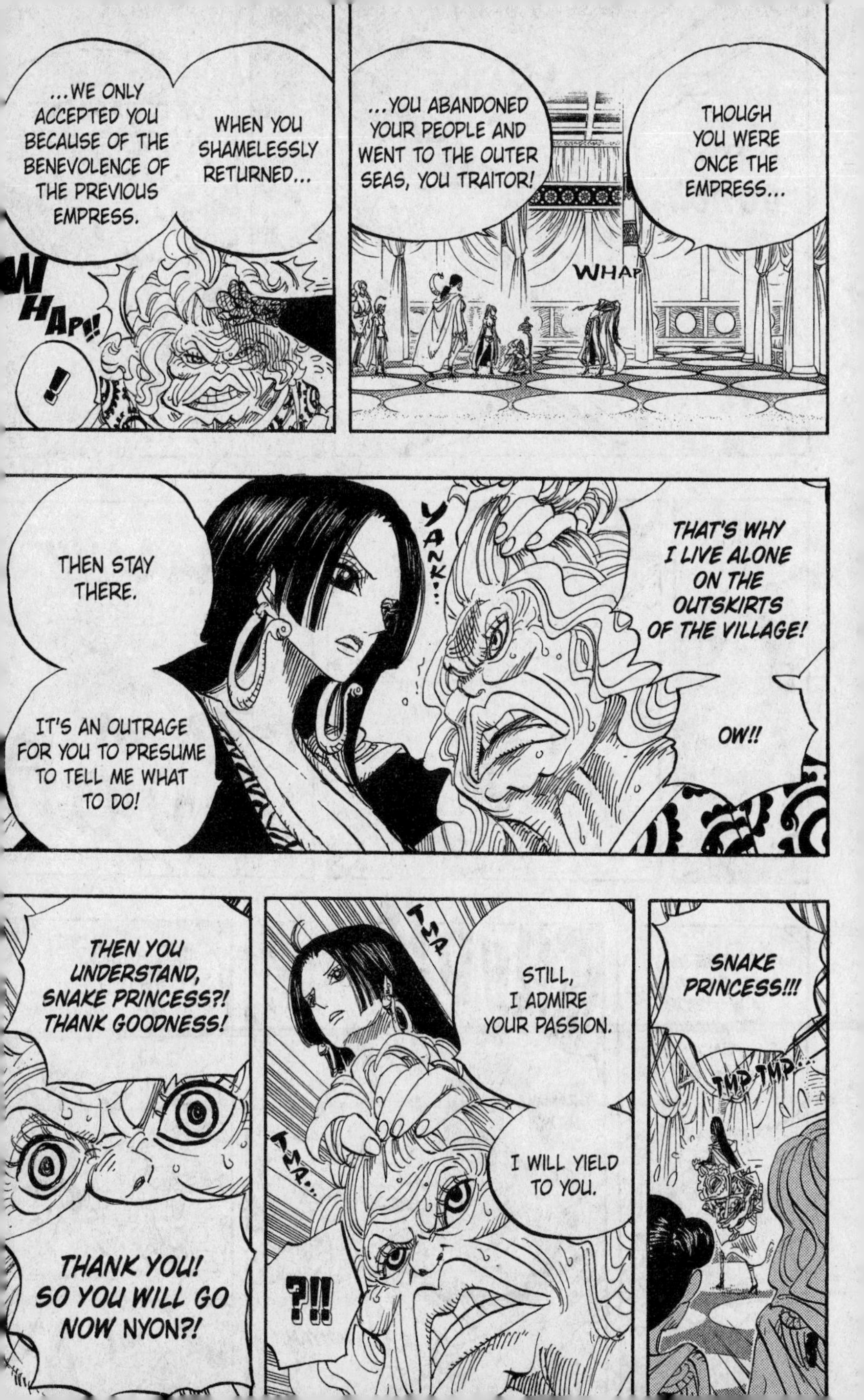

THOUGH YOU WERE ONCE THE EMPRESS...
...YOU ABANDONED YOUR PEOPLE AND WENT TO THE OUTER SEAS, YOU TRAITOR!
WHAP
WHEN YOU SHAMELESSLY RETURNED...
...WE ONLY ACCEPTED YOU BECAUSE OF THE BENEVOLENCE OF THE PREVIOUS EMPRESS.
WHAP!!
!
THAT'S WHY I LIVE ALONE ON THE OUTSKIRTS OF THE VILLAGE!
YANK...
OW!!
THEN STAY THERE.
IT'S AN OUTRAGE FOR YOU TO PRESUME TO TELL ME WHAT TO DO!
SNAKE PRINCESS!!!
TMP TMP...
TMA
STILL, I ADMIRE YOUR PASSION.
I WILL YIELD TO YOU.
TMA...
?!!
THEN YOU UNDERSTAND, SNAKE PRINCESS?! THANK GOODNESS!
THANK YOU! SO YOU WILL GO NOW NYON?!

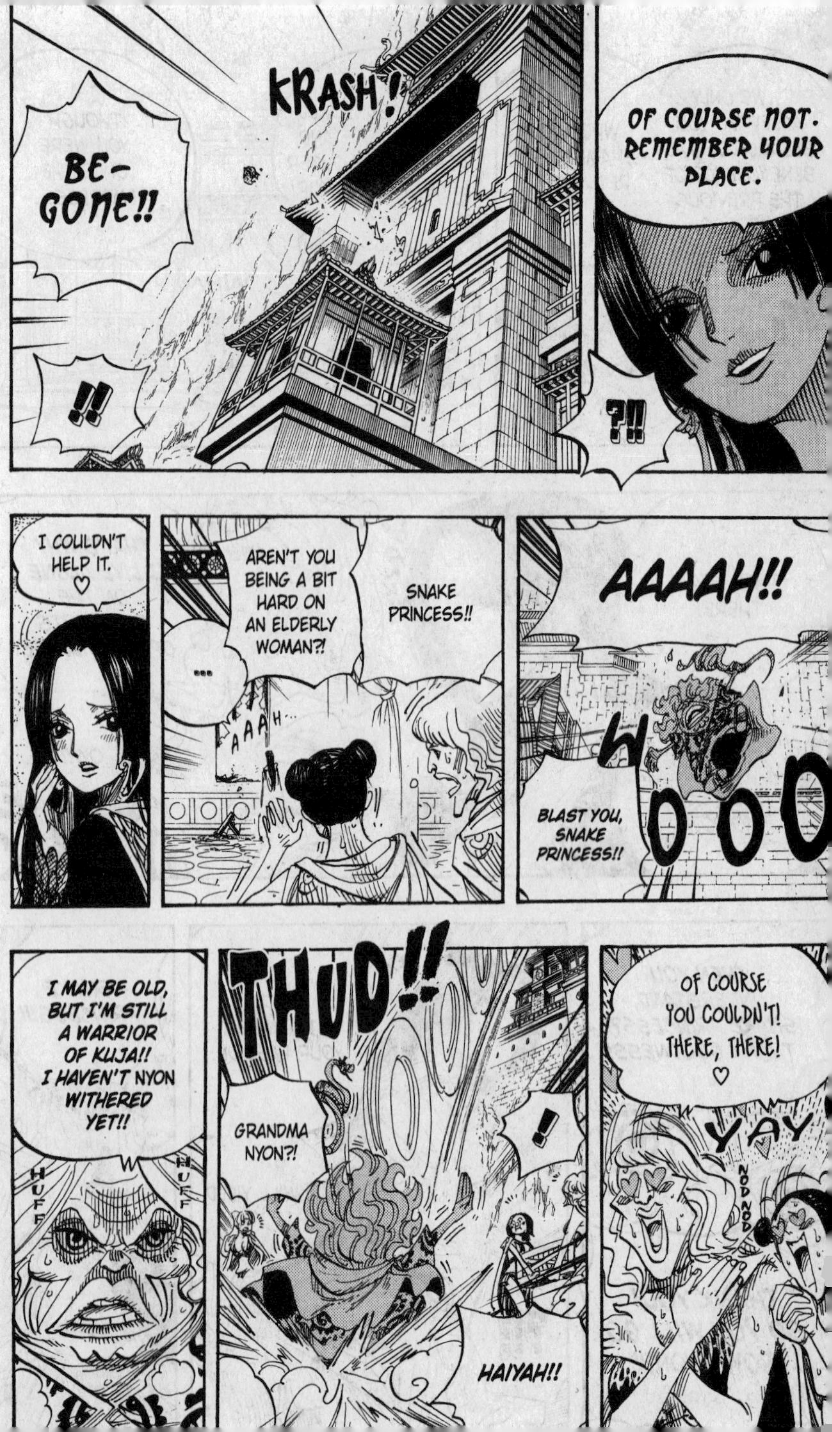
OF COURSE NOT. REMEMBER YOUR PLACE.
?!!
KRASH!
BE-GONE!!
!!
AAAAH!!
WOOOO
BLAST YOU, SNAKE PRINCESS!!
SNAKE PRINCESS!!
AREN'T YOU BEING A BIT HARD ON AN ELDERLY WOMAN?!
...
AAAH...
I COULDN'T HELP IT. ♡
OF COURSE YOU COULDN'T! THERE, THERE! ♡
YAY
NOD NOD
THUD!!
!
GRANDMA NYON?!
HAIYAH!!
I MAY BE OLD, BUT I'M STILL A WARRIOR OF KUJA!! I HAVEN'T NYON WITHERED YET!!
HUFF
HUFF

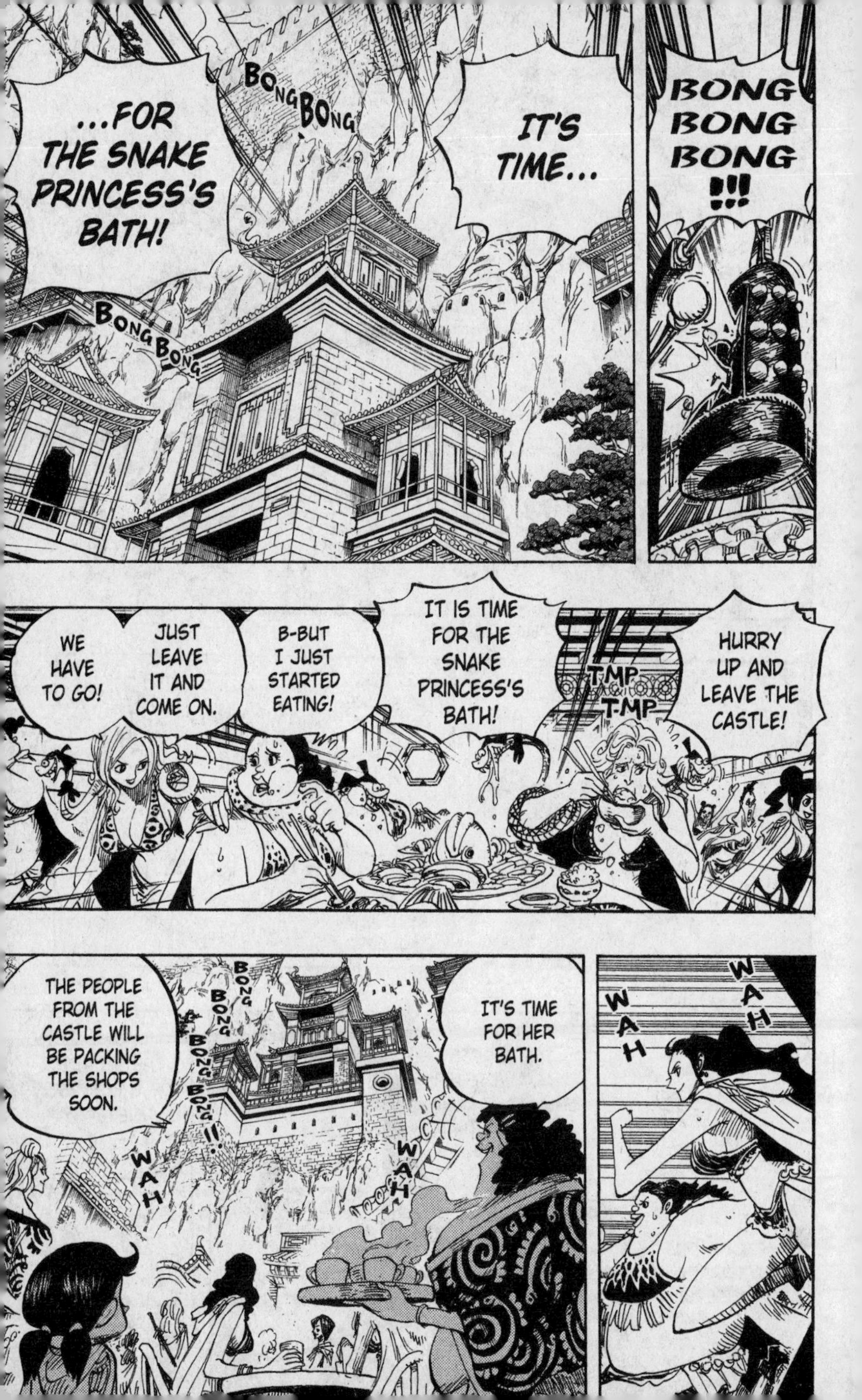
BONG BONG BONG!!!
IT'S TIME...
BONG BONG
...FOR THE SNAKE PRINCESS'S BATH!
BONG BONG
HURRY UP AND LEAVE THE CASTLE!
TMP TMP
IT IS TIME FOR THE SNAKE PRINCESS'S BATH!
B-BUT I JUST STARTED EATING!
JUST LEAVE IT AND COME ON.
WE HAVE TO GO!
WAH
WAH
IT'S TIME FOR HER BATH.
WAH
BONG BONG BONG BONG!!
THE PEOPLE FROM THE CASTLE WILL BE PACKING THE SHOPS SOON.
WAH

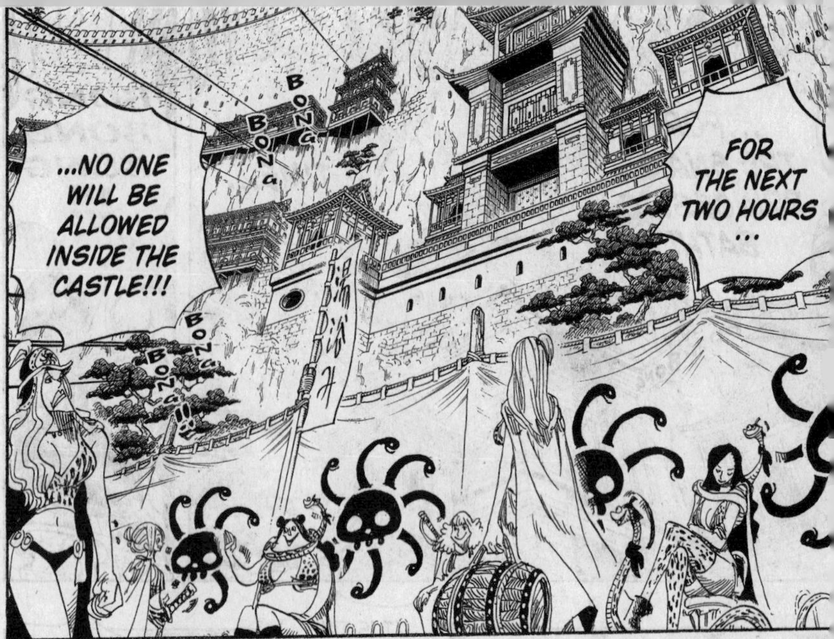
FOR THE NEXT TWO HOURS...
...NO ONE WILL BE ALLOWED INSIDE THE CASTLE!!!
BONG
BONG
BONG
BONG
BONG

BANNER READS "BATHING"--ED.

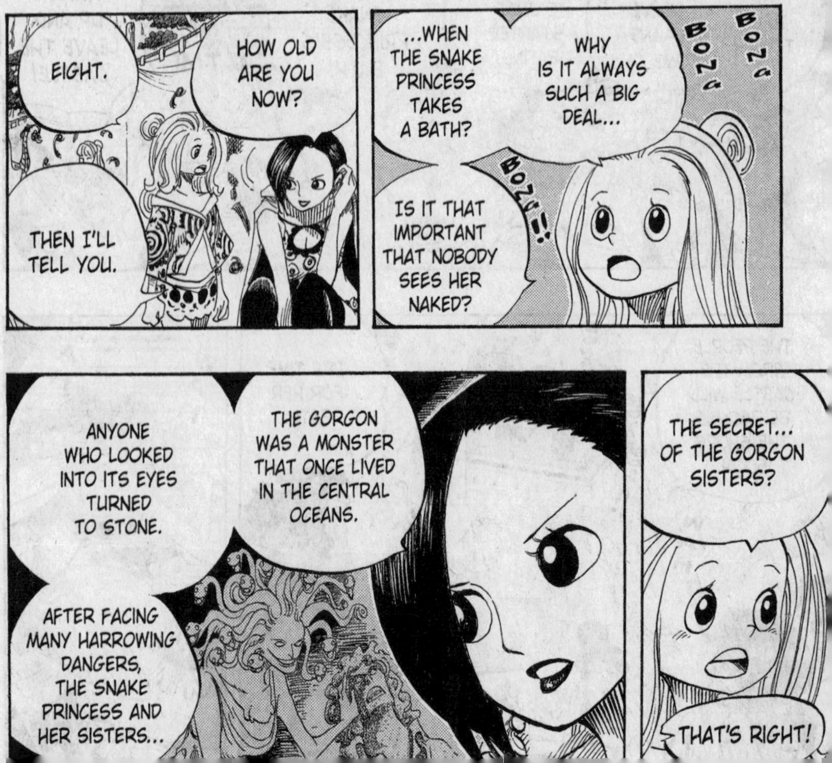
WHY IS IT ALWAYS SUCH A BIG DEAL...
...WHEN THE SNAKE PRINCESS TAKES A BATH?
BONG
BONG
BONG!!
IS IT THAT IMPORTANT THAT NOBODY SEES HER NAKED?
HOW OLD ARE YOU NOW?
EIGHT.
THEN I'LL TELL YOU.
THE SECRET... OF THE GORGON SISTERS?
THAT'S RIGHT!
THE GORGON WAS A MONSTER THAT ONCE LIVED IN THE CENTRAL OCEANS.
ANYONE WHO LOOKED INTO ITS EYES TURNED TO STONE.
AFTER FACING MANY HARROWING DANGERS, THE SNAKE PRINCESS AND HER SISTERS...

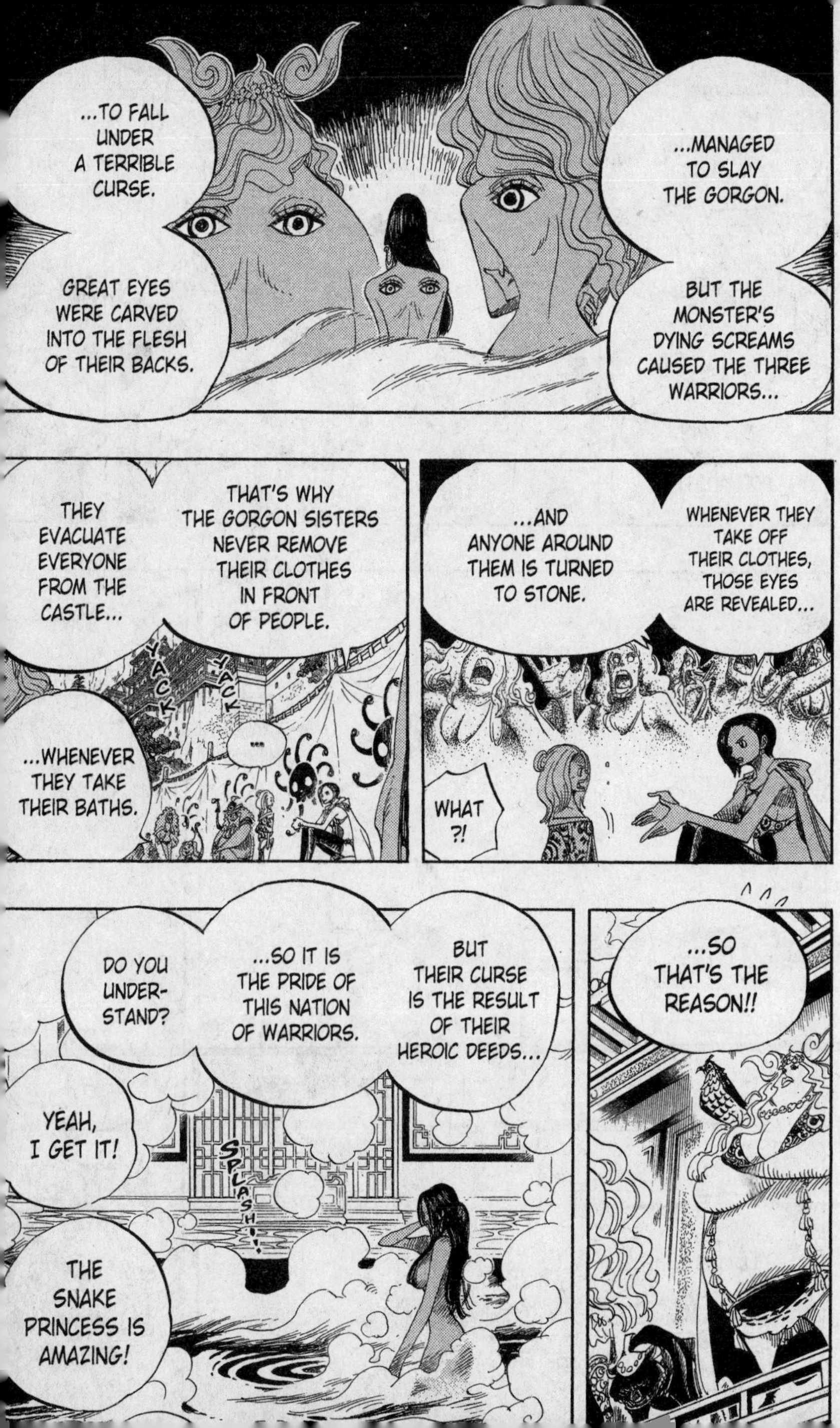
...MANAGED TO SLAY THE GORGON.
BUT THE MONSTER'S DYING SCREAMS CAUSED THE THREE WARRIORS...
...TO FALL UNDER A TERRIBLE CURSE.
GREAT EYES WERE CARVED INTO THE FLESH OF THEIR BACKS.
WHENEVER THEY TAKE OFF THEIR CLOTHES, THOSE EYES ARE REVEALED...
...AND ANYONE AROUND THEM IS TURNED TO STONE.
WHAT ?!
THAT'S WHY THE GORGON SISTERS NEVER REMOVE THEIR CLOTHES IN FRONT OF PEOPLE.
THEY EVACUATE EVERYONE FROM THE CASTLE...
YACK
YACK
...WHENEVER THEY TAKE THEIR BATHS.
...
...SO THAT'S THE REASON!!
BUT THEIR CURSE IS THE RESULT OF THEIR HEROIC DEEDS...
...SO IT IS THE PRIDE OF THIS NATION OF WARRIORS.
DO YOU UNDER-STAND?
SPLASH!!
YEAH, I GET IT!
THE SNAKE PRINCESS IS AMAZING!

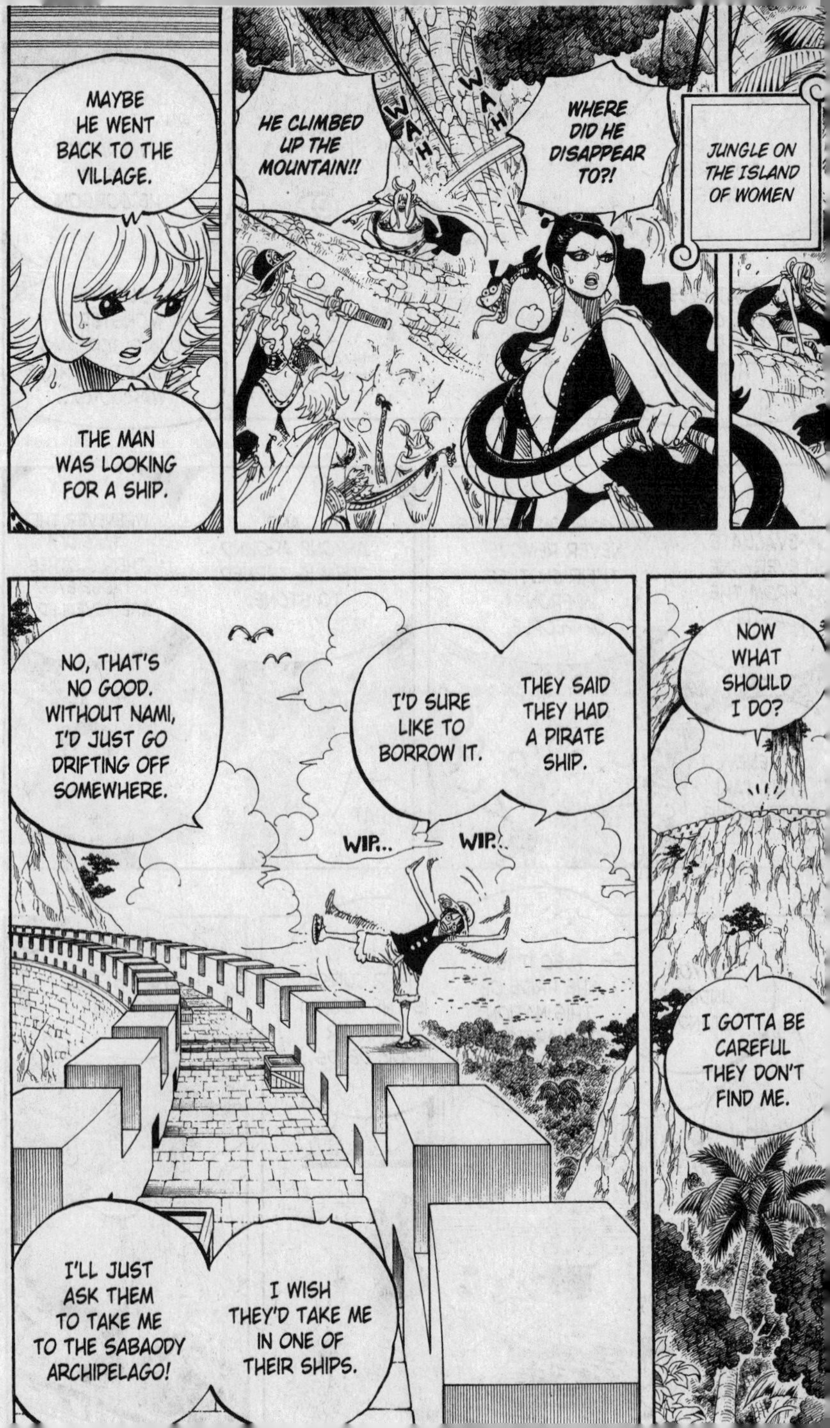
JUNGLE ON THE ISLAND OF WOMEN
WHERE DID HE DISAPPEAR TO?!
WAH WAH
HE CLIMBED UP THE MOUNTAIN!!
MAYBE HE WENT BACK TO THE VILLAGE.
THE MAN WAS LOOKING FOR A SHIP.
NOW WHAT SHOULD I DO?
I GOTTA BE CAREFUL THEY DON'T FIND ME.
THEY SAID THEY HAD A PIRATE SHIP.
I'D SURE LIKE TO BORROW IT.
NO, THAT'S NO GOOD. WITHOUT NAMI, I'D JUST GO DRIFTING OFF SOMEWHERE.
WIP..
WIP..
I WISH THEY'D TAKE ME IN ONE OF THEIR SHIPS.
I'LL JUST ASK THEM TO TAKE ME TO THE SABAODY ARCHIPELAGO!

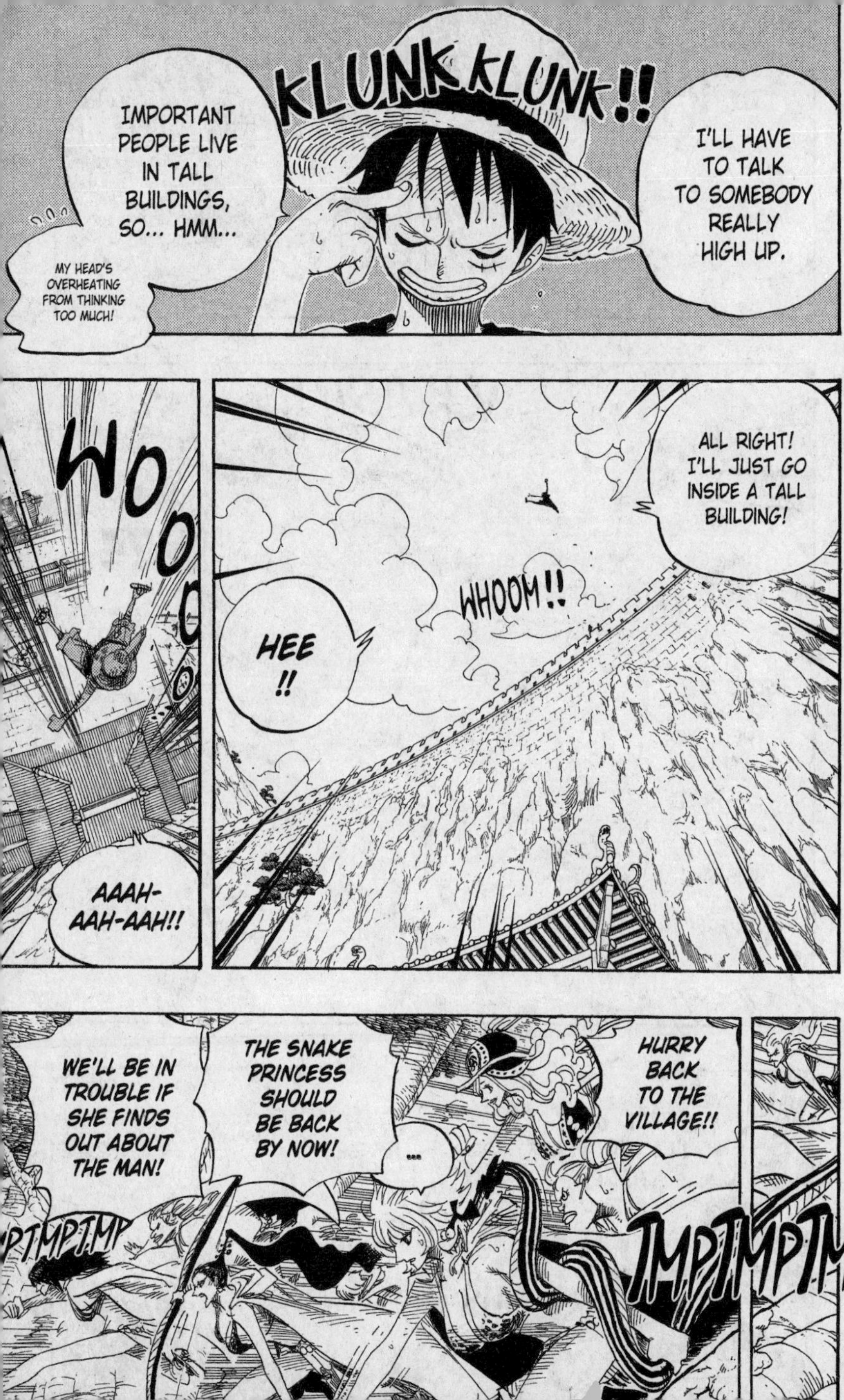
KLUNK KLUNK!!
I'LL HAVE TO TALK TO SOMEBODY REALLY HIGH UP.
IMPORTANT PEOPLE LIVE IN TALL BUILDINGS, SO... HMM...
MY HEAD'S OVERHEATING FROM THINKING TOO MUCH!
ALL RIGHT! I'LL JUST GO INSIDE A TALL BUILDING!
WHOOM!!
HEE!!
WOOO
AAAH-AAH-AAH!!
HURRY BACK TO THE VILLAGE!!
TMPTMPTM
...
THE SNAKE PRINCESS SHOULD BE BACK BY NOW!
WE'LL BE IN TROUBLE IF SHE FINDS OUT ABOUT THE MAN!
PTMPTMP

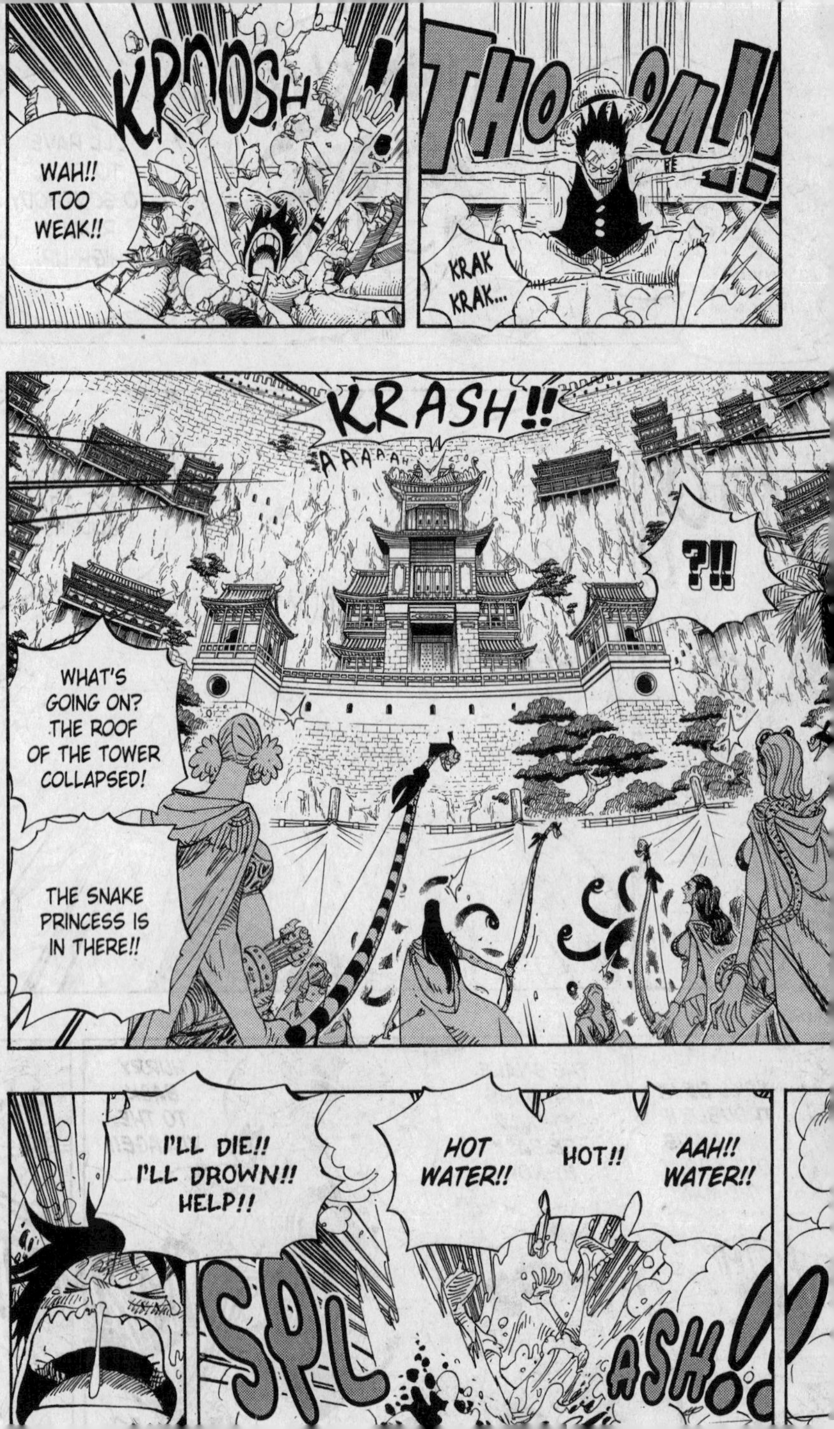
THO OM!!
KRAK KRAK...
KPOOSH!!
WAH!! TOO WEAK!!
KRASH!!
AAAAA
?!!
WHAT'S GOING ON? THE ROOF OF THE TOWER COLLAPSED!
THE SNAKE PRINCESS IS IN THERE!!
AAH!! WATER!!
HOT!!
HOT WATER!!
SPL ASH!!
I'LL DIE!! I'LL DROWN!! HELP!!

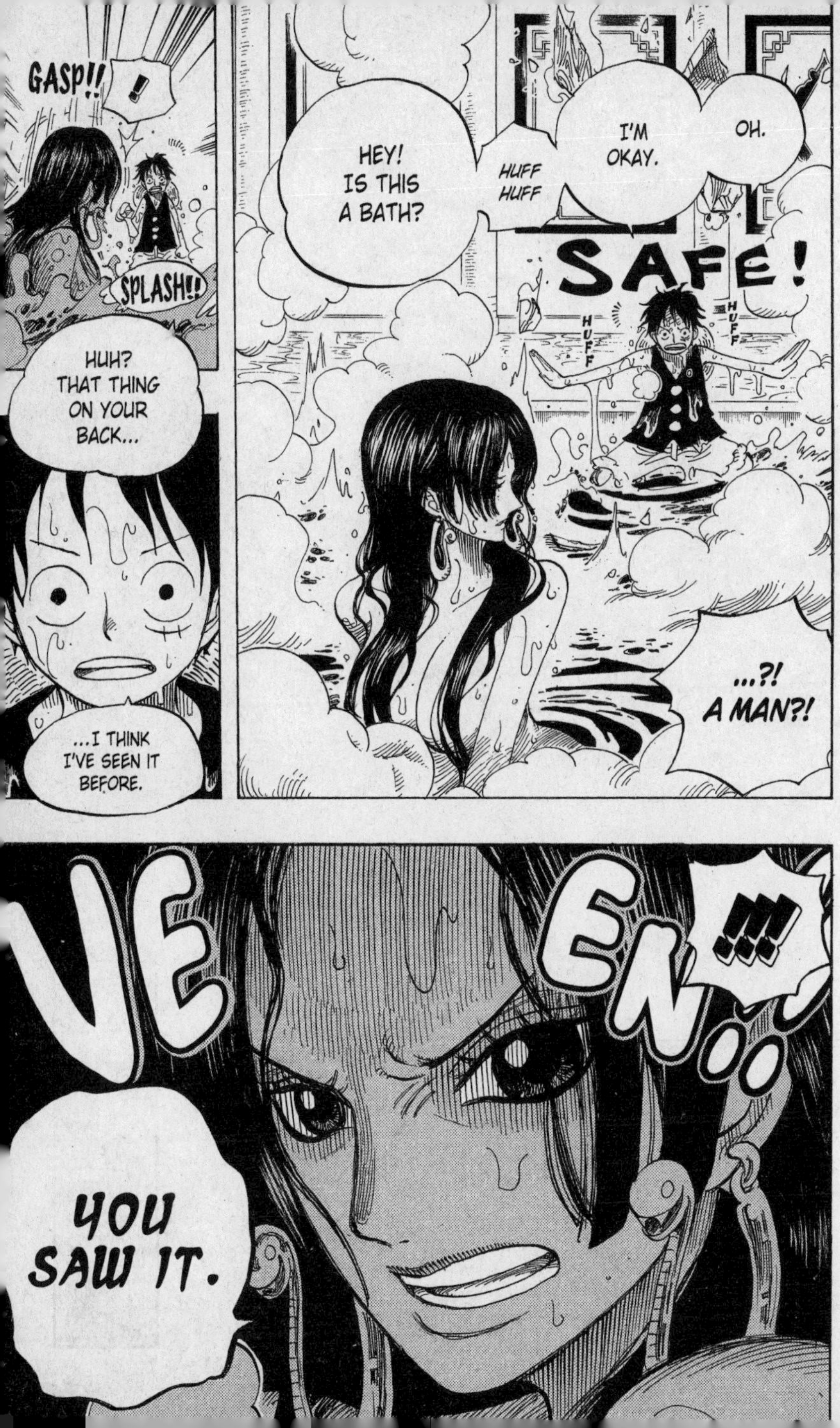
OH.
I'M OKAY.
HUFF HUFF
HEY! IS THIS A BATH?
SAFE!
HUFF HUFF
...?! A MAN?!
!
GASP!!
SPLASH!!
HUH? THAT THING ON YOUR BACK...
...I THINK I'VE SEEN IT BEFORE.
VE EN...!!!
YOU SAW IT.

Chapter 518:
COLISEUM

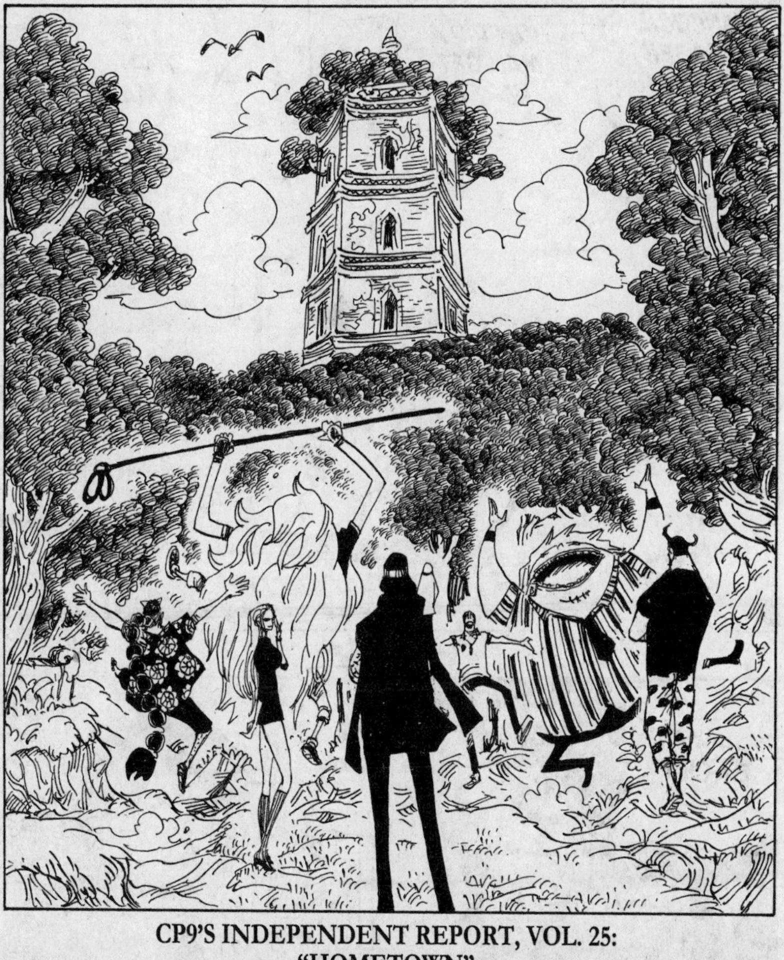

CP9'S INDEPENDENT REPORT, VOL. 25:
"HOMETOWN"

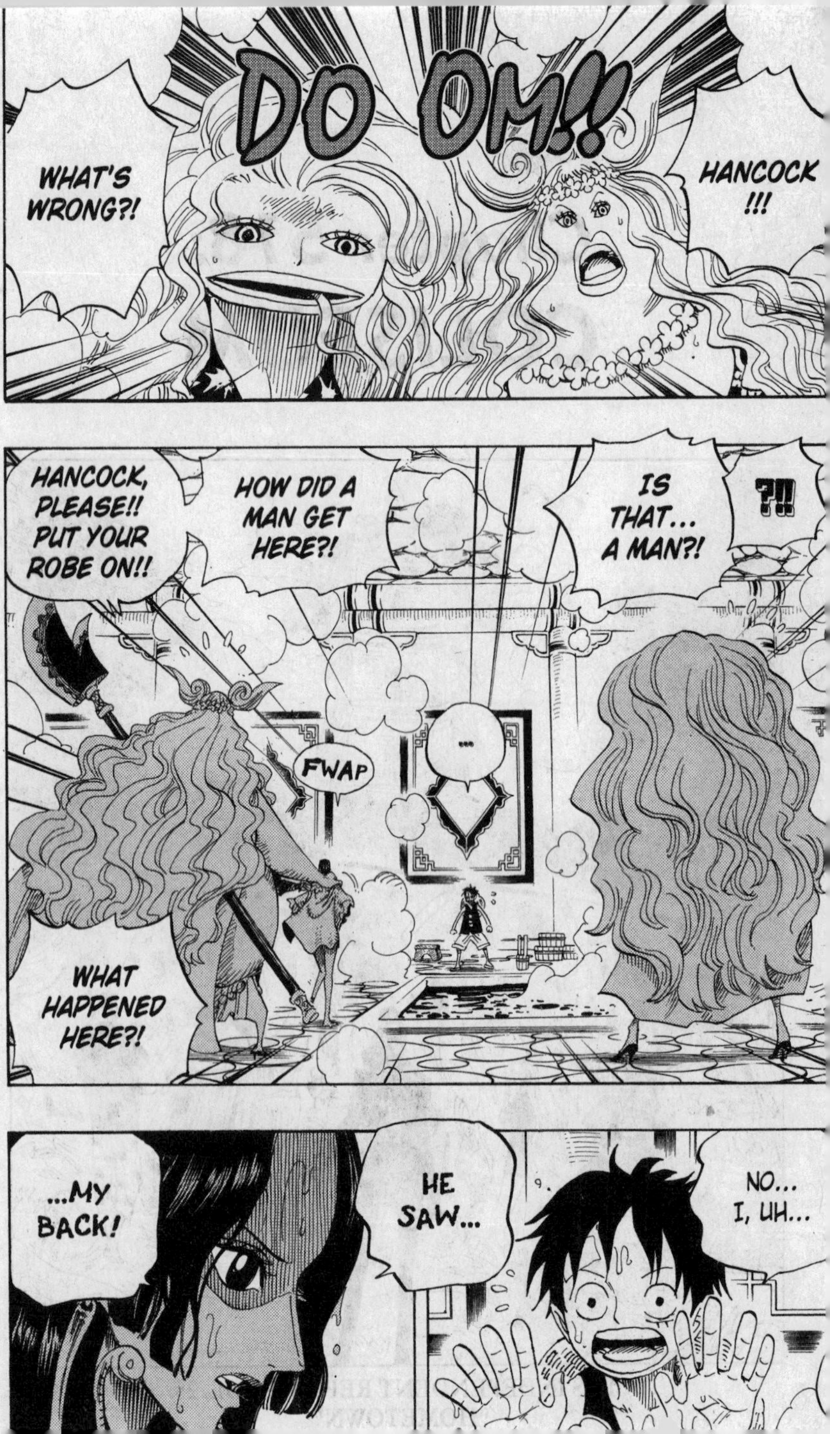
DO OM!!
HANCOCK !!!
WHAT'S WRONG?!
?!!
IS THAT... A MAN?!
HOW DID A MAN GET HERE?!
HANCOCK, PLEASE!! PUT YOUR ROBE ON!!
...
FWAP
WHAT HAPPENED HERE?!
NO... I, UH...
HE SAW...
...MY BACK!

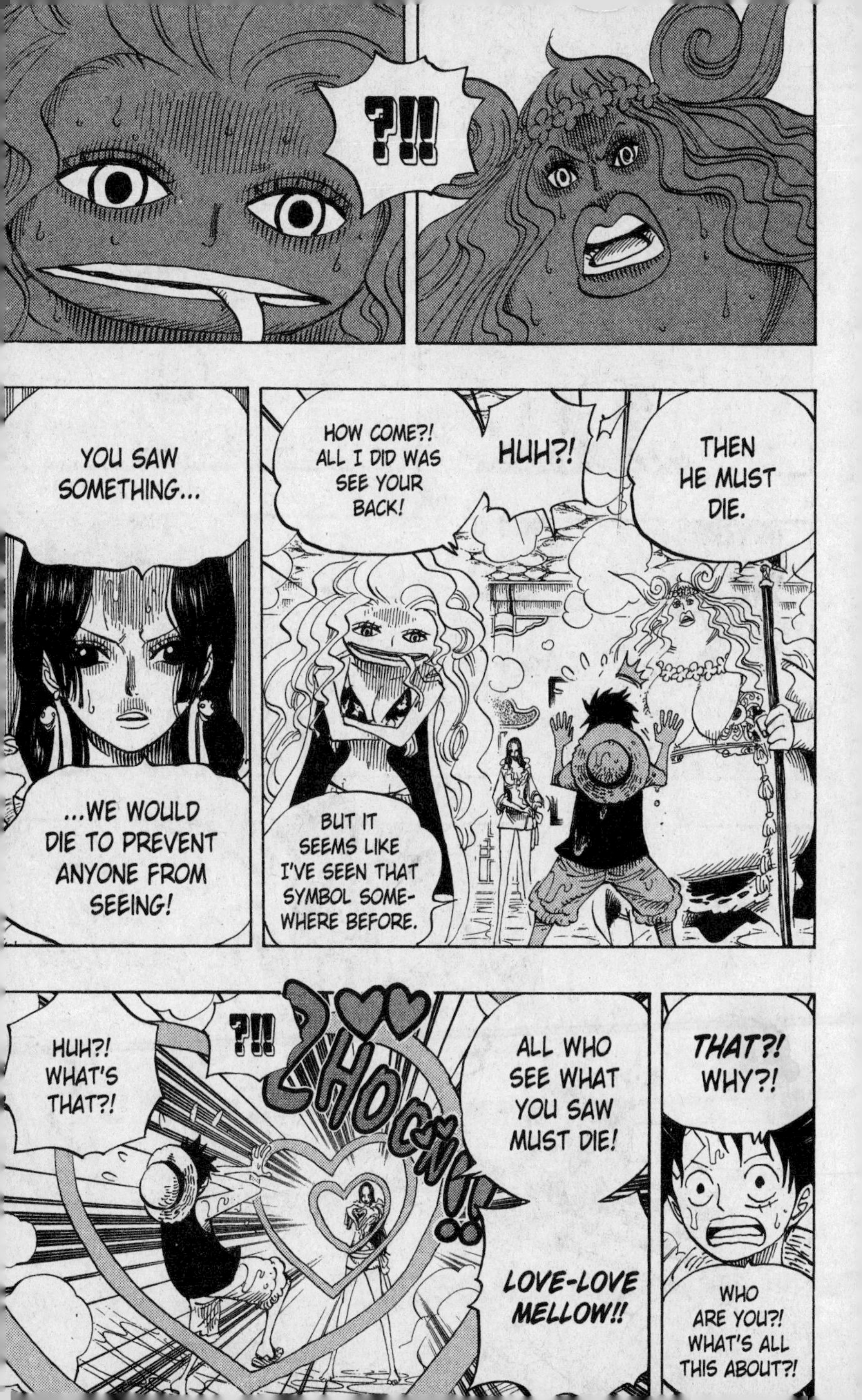
?!!
THEN HE MUST DIE.
HUH?!
HOW COME?! ALL I DID WAS SEE YOUR BACK!
BUT IT SEEMS LIKE I'VE SEEN THAT SYMBOL SOME-WHERE BEFORE.
YOU SAW SOMETHING...
...WE WOULD DIE TO PREVENT ANYONE FROM SEEING!
THAT?! WHY?!
WHO ARE YOU?! WHAT'S ALL THIS ABOUT?!
ALL WHO SEE WHAT YOU SAW MUST DIE!
?!!
HUH?! WHAT'S THAT?!
LOVE-LOVE MELLOW!!

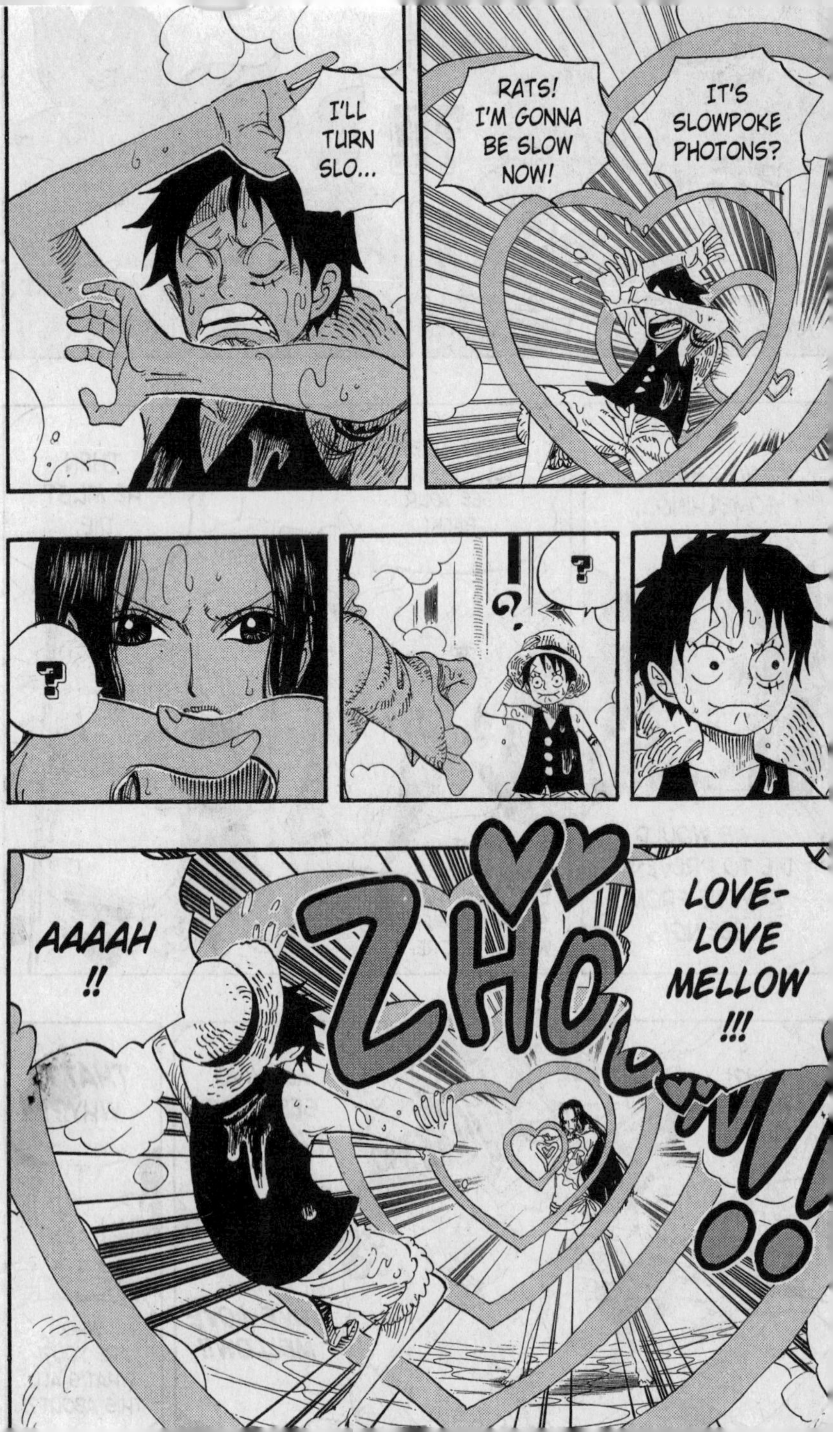
IT'S SLOWPOKE PHOTONS?
RATS! I'M GONNA BE SLOW NOW!
I'LL TURN SLO...
?
?
?
LOVE-LOVE MELLOW !!!
AAAAH !!

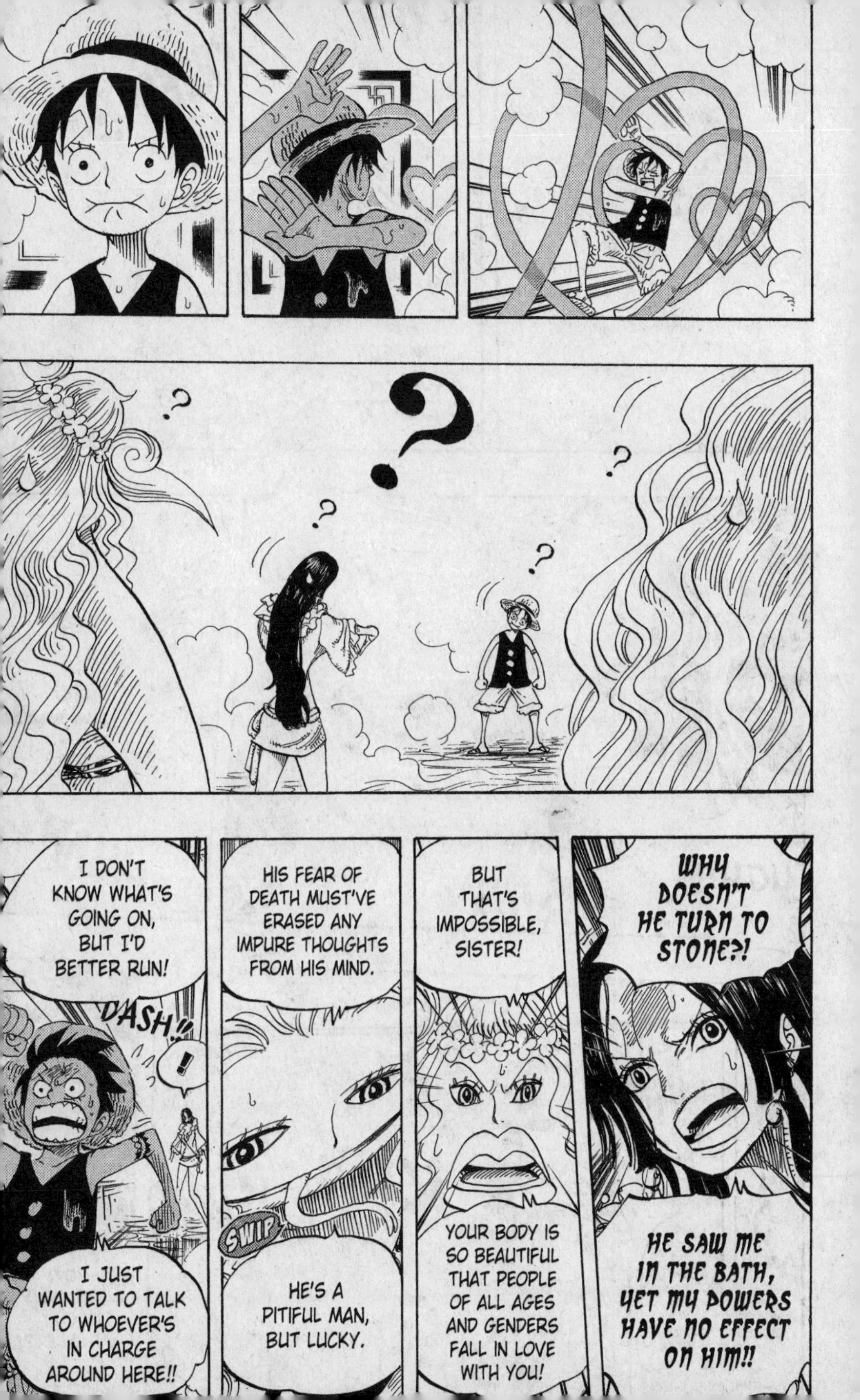
WHY DOESN'T HE TURN TO STONE?!
HE SAW ME IN THE BATH, YET MY POWERS HAVE NO EFFECT ON HIM!!
BUT THAT'S IMPOSSIBLE, SISTER!
YOUR BODY IS SO BEAUTIFUL THAT PEOPLE OF ALL AGES AND GENDERS FALL IN LOVE WITH YOU!
HIS FEAR OF DEATH MUST'VE ERASED ANY IMPURE THOUGHTS FROM HIS MIND.
SWIP
HE'S A PITIFUL MAN, BUT LUCKY.
I DON'T KNOW WHAT'S GOING ON, BUT I'D BETTER RUN!
DASH!!
!
I JUST WANTED TO TALK TO WHOEVER'S IN CHARGE AROUND HERE!!

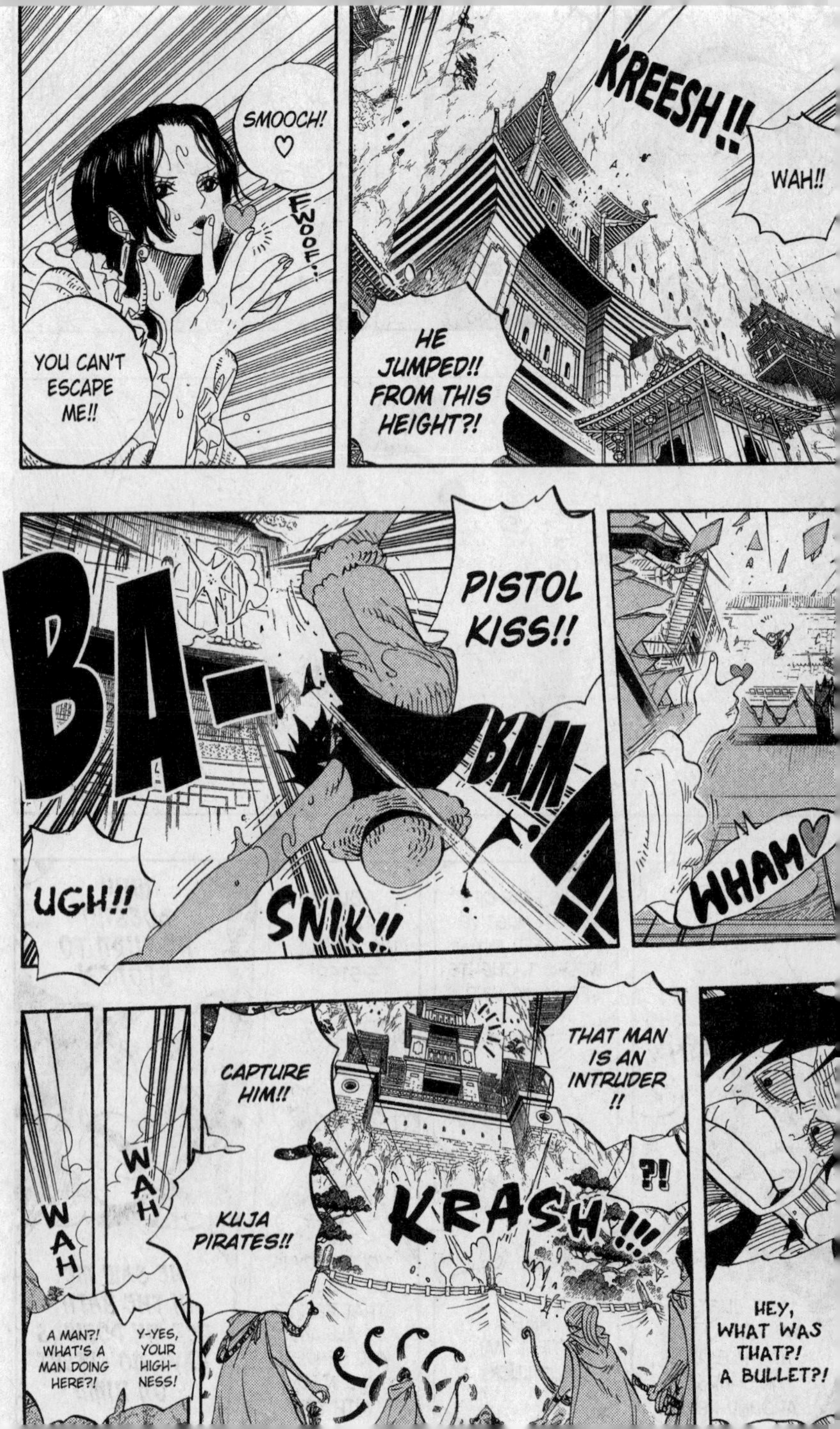
KREESH!!
WAH!!
HE JUMPED!! FROM THIS HEIGHT?!
SMOOCH! ♡
FWOOF!!
YOU CAN'T ESCAPE ME!!
WHAM♡
PISTOL KISS!!
BA-BAM!!
SNIK!!
UGH!!
HEY, WHAT WAS THAT?! A BULLET?!
THAT MAN IS AN INTRUDER!!
?!
CAPTURE HIM!!
KRASH!!!
KUJA PIRATES!!
WAH
Y-YES, YOUR HIGHNESS!
WAH
A MAN?! WHAT'S A MAN DOING HERE?!

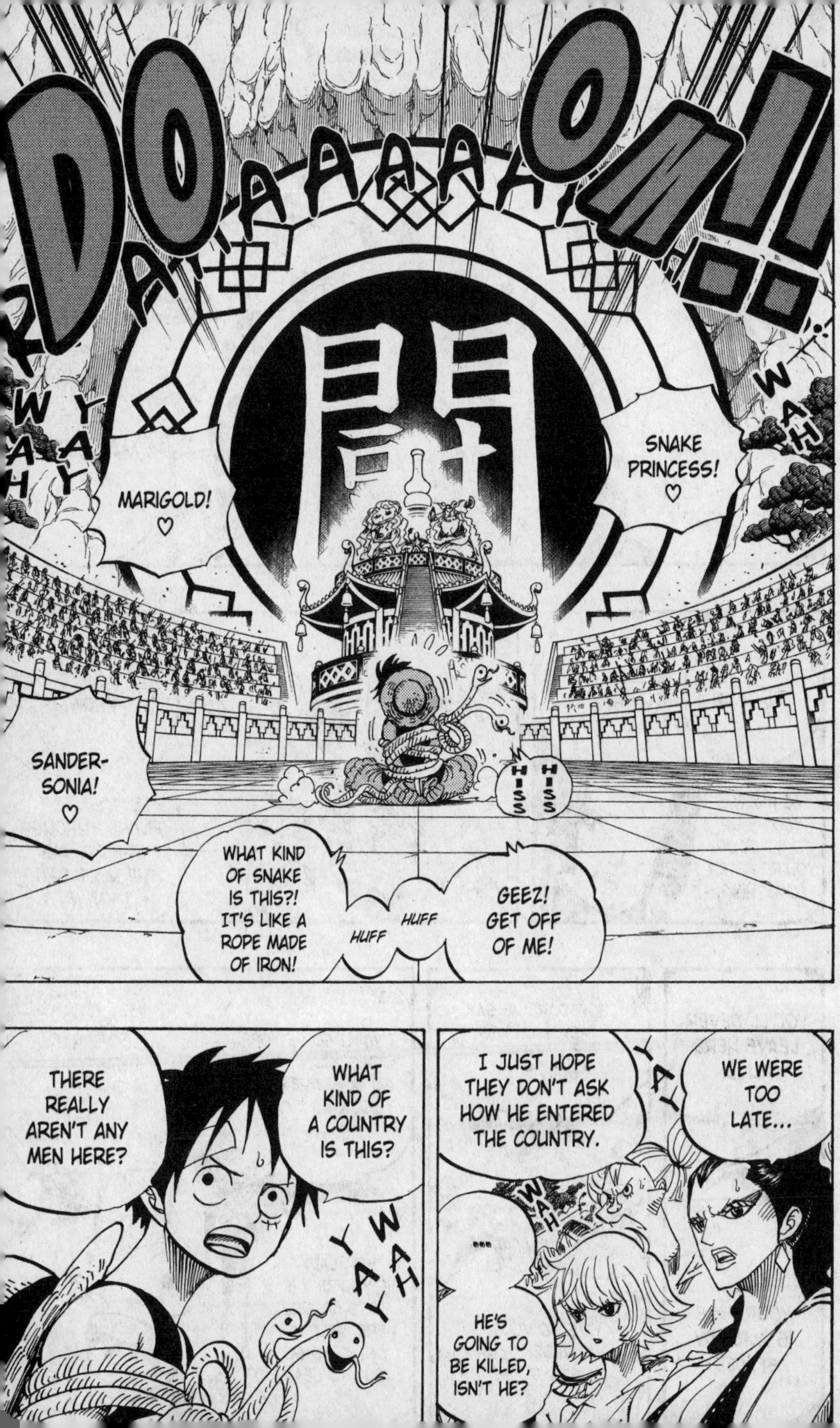
WAH
SNAKE PRINCESS! ♡
MARIGOLD! ♡
YAY
WAH
SANDER-SONIA! ♡
HISS HISS
GEEZ! GET OFF OF ME!
HUFF
HUFF
WHAT KIND OF SNAKE IS THIS?! IT'S LIKE A ROPE MADE OF IRON!
WE WERE TOO LATE...
YAY
I JUST HOPE THEY DON'T ASK HOW HE ENTERED THE COUNTRY.
WAH
...
HE'S GOING TO BE KILLED, ISN'T HE?
WHAT KIND OF A COUNTRY IS THIS?
THERE REALLY AREN'T ANY MEN HERE?
WAH
YAY

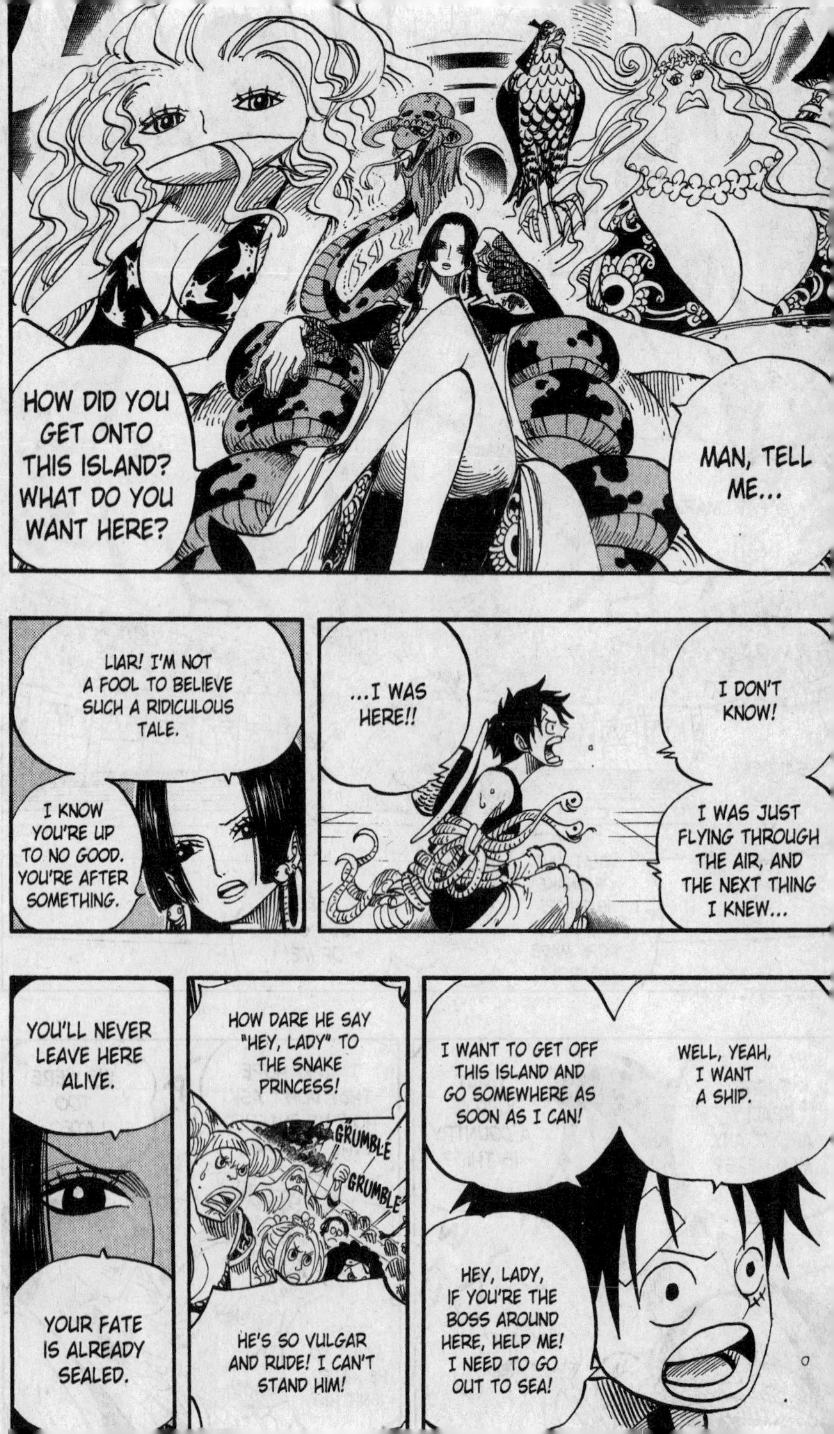
MAN, TELL ME...
HOW DID YOU GET ONTO THIS ISLAND? WHAT DO YOU WANT HERE?
I DON'T KNOW!
I WAS JUST FLYING THROUGH THE AIR, AND THE NEXT THING I KNEW...
...I WAS HERE!!
LIAR! I'M NOT A FOOL TO BELIEVE SUCH A RIDICULOUS TALE.
I KNOW YOU'RE UP TO NO GOOD. YOU'RE AFTER SOMETHING.
WELL, YEAH, I WANT A SHIP.
I WANT TO GET OFF THIS ISLAND AND GO SOMEWHERE AS SOON AS I CAN!
HEY, LADY, IF YOU'RE THE BOSS AROUND HERE, HELP ME! I NEED TO GO OUT TO SEA!
HOW DARE HE SAY "HEY, LADY" TO THE SNAKE PRINCESS!
GRUMBLE
GRUMBLE
HE'S SO VULGAR AND RUDE! I CAN'T STAND HIM!
YOU'LL NEVER LEAVE HERE ALIVE.
YOUR FATE IS ALREADY SEALED.

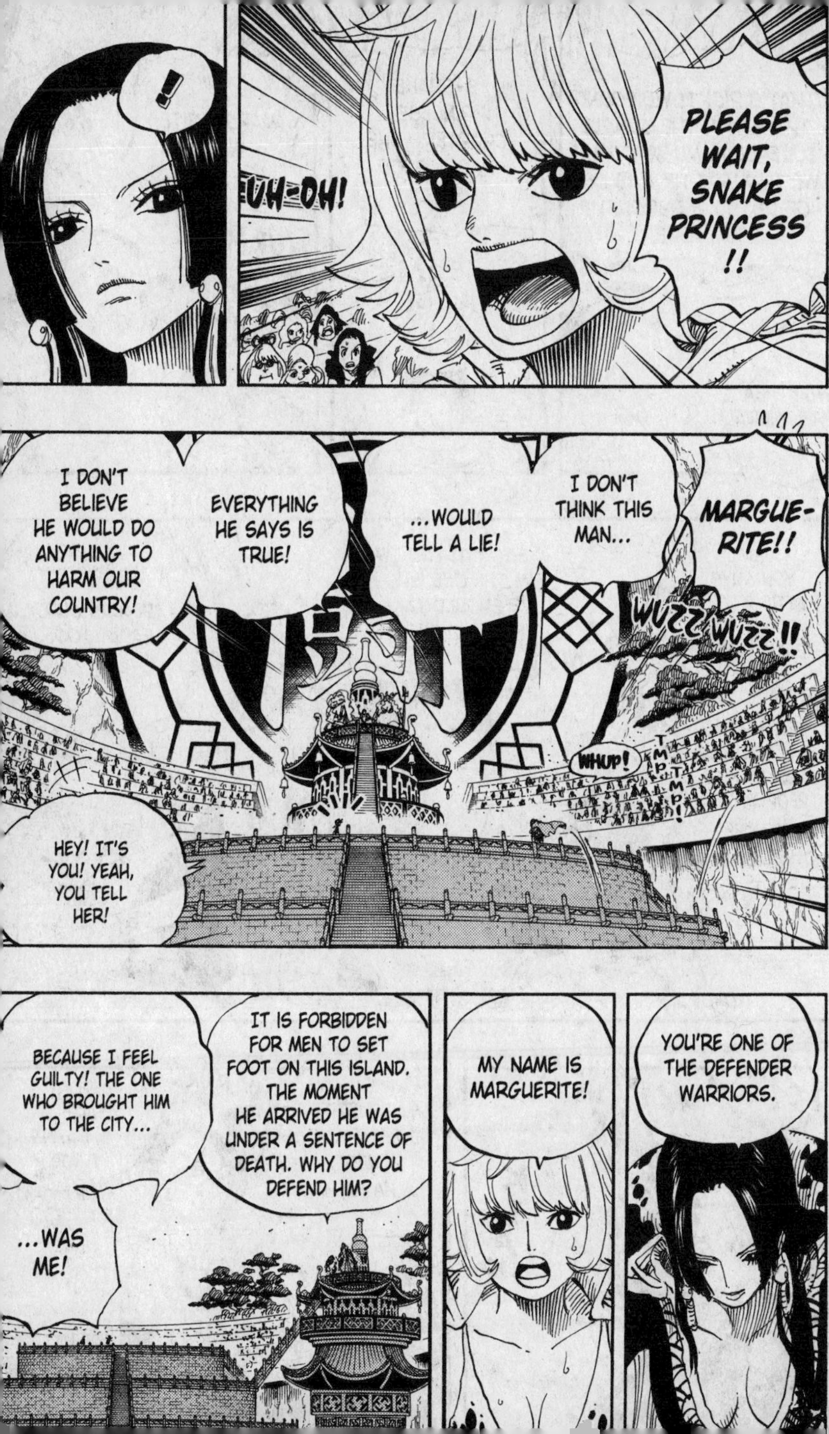
PLEASE WAIT, SNAKE PRINCESS!!
UH-OH!
!
MARGUE-RITE!!
WUZZ WUZZ!!
I DON'T THINK THIS MAN...
...WOULD TELL A LIE!
EVERYTHING HE SAYS IS TRUE!
I DON'T BELIEVE HE WOULD DO ANYTHING TO HARM OUR COUNTRY!
TMP TMP!
WHUP!
HEY! IT'S YOU! YEAH, YOU TELL HER!
YOU'RE ONE OF THE DEFENDER WARRIORS.
MY NAME IS MARGUERITE!
IT IS FORBIDDEN FOR MEN TO SET FOOT ON THIS ISLAND. THE MOMENT HE ARRIVED HE WAS UNDER A SENTENCE OF DEATH. WHY DO YOU DEFEND HIM?
BECAUSE I FEEL GUILTY! THE ONE WHO BROUGHT HIM TO THE CITY...
...WAS ME!

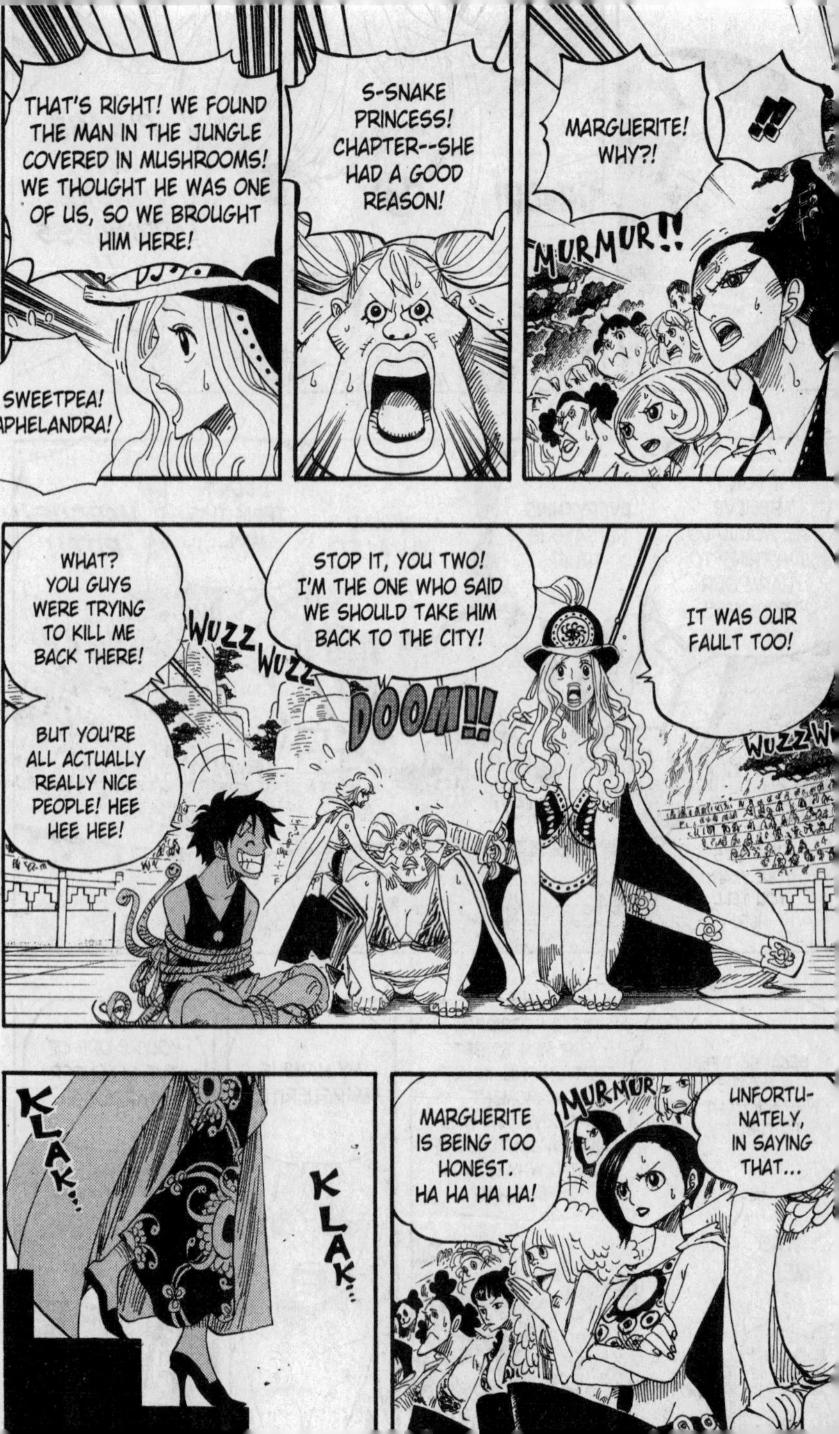
!!
MARGUERITE! WHY?!
MURMUR!!
S-SNAKE PRINCESS! CHAPTER--SHE HAD A GOOD REASON!
THAT'S RIGHT! WE FOUND THE MAN IN THE JUNGLE COVERED IN MUSHROOMS! WE THOUGHT HE WAS ONE OF US, SO WE BROUGHT HIM HERE!
SWEETPEA! APHELANDRA!
IT WAS OUR FAULT TOO!
WUZZW
STOP IT, YOU TWO! I'M THE ONE WHO SAID WE SHOULD TAKE HIM BACK TO THE CITY!
DOOM!!
WUZZ WUZZ
WHAT? YOU GUYS WERE TRYING TO KILL ME BACK THERE!
BUT YOU'RE ALL ACTUALLY REALLY NICE PEOPLE! HEE HEE HEE!
UNFORTU-NATELY, IN SAYING THAT...
MURMUR
MARGUERITE IS BEING TOO HONEST. HA HA HA HA!
KLAK...
KLAK...

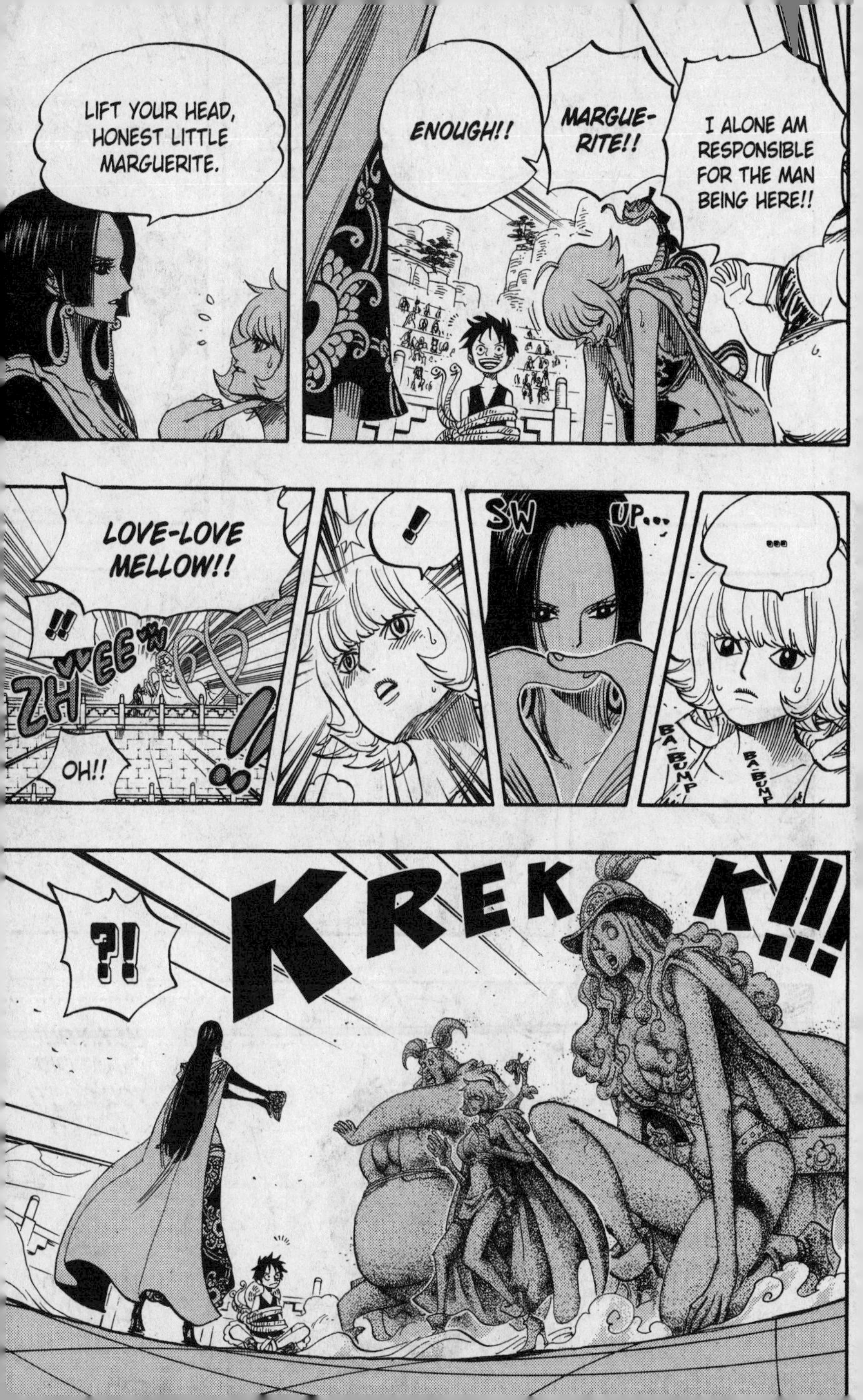
I ALONE AM RESPONSIBLE FOR THE MAN BEING HERE!!
MARGUE-RITE!!
ENOUGH!!
LIFT YOUR HEAD, HONEST LITTLE MARGUERITE.
...
BA-BUMP
BA-BUMP
SW UP...
!
LOVE-LOVE MELLOW!!
!!
ZHWEE'N
OH!!
KREKK!!!
?!

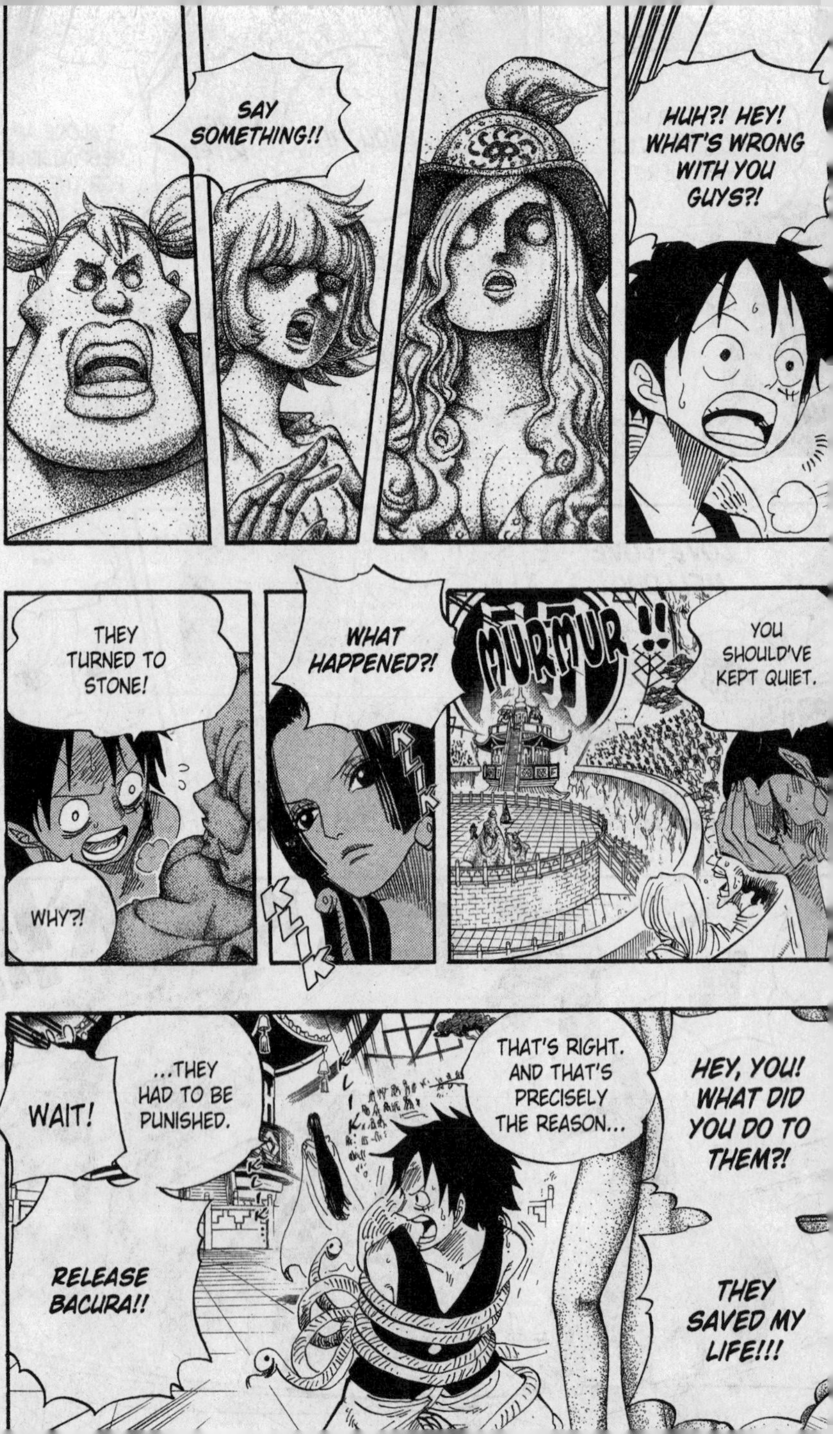
HUH?! HEY! WHAT'S WRONG WITH YOU GUYS?!
SAY SOMETHING!!
YOU SHOULD'VE KEPT QUIET.
MURMUR!!
WHAT HAPPENED?!
KLIK
KLIK
THEY TURNED TO STONE!
WHY?!
HEY, YOU! WHAT DID YOU DO TO THEM?!
THEY SAVED MY LIFE!!!
THAT'S RIGHT. AND THAT'S PRECISELY THE REASON...
...THEY HAD TO BE PUNISHED.
KLIK
KLIK
WAIT!
RELEASE BACURA!!

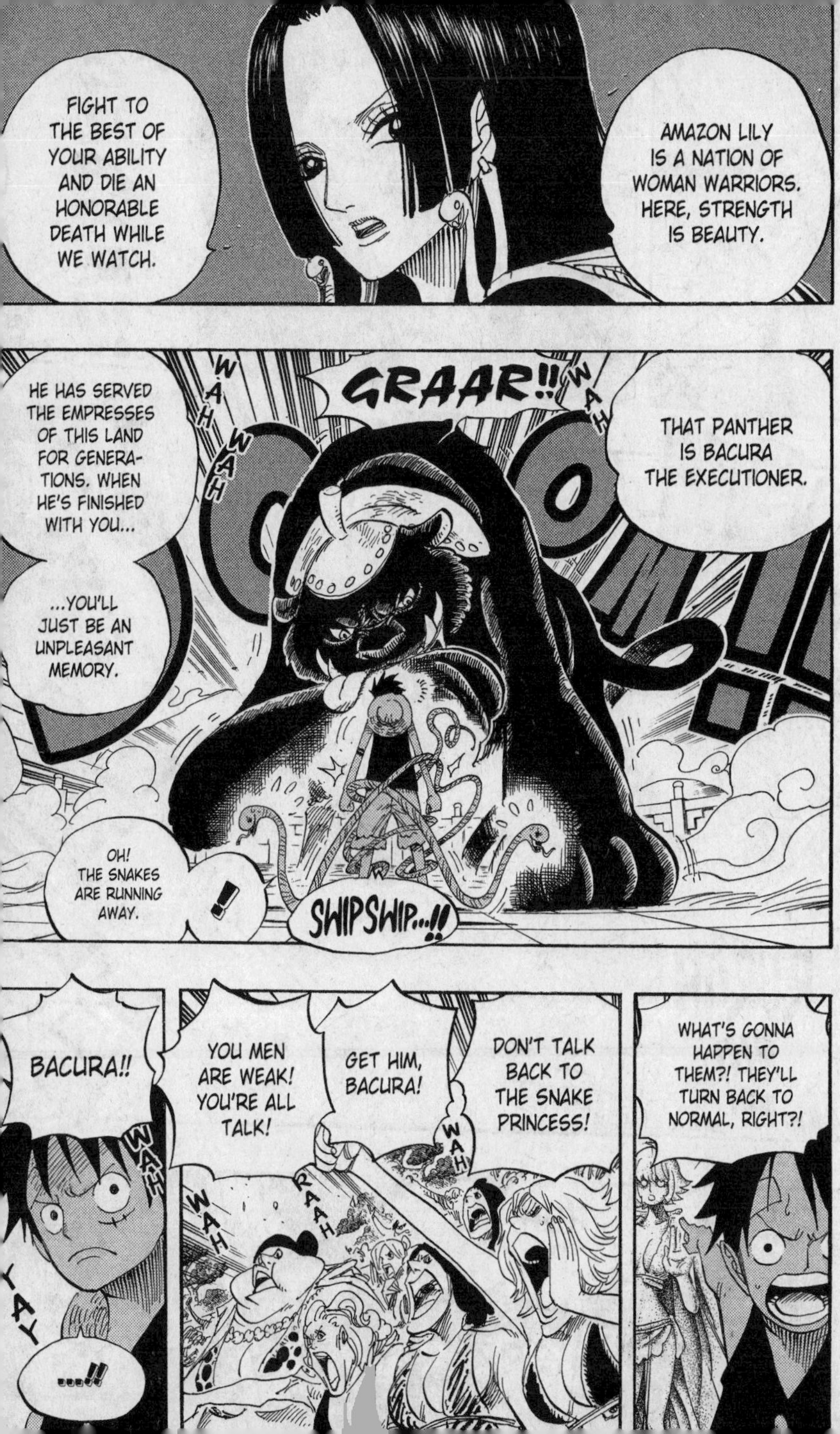
AMAZON LILY IS A NATION OF WOMAN WARRIORS. HERE, STRENGTH IS BEAUTY.
FIGHT TO THE BEST OF YOUR ABILITY AND DIE AN HONORABLE DEATH WHILE WE WATCH.
THAT PANTHER IS BACURA THE EXECUTIONER.
WAH
GRAAR!!
WAH WAH
HE HAS SERVED THE EMPRESSES OF THIS LAND FOR GENERATIONS. WHEN HE'S FINISHED WITH YOU...
...YOU'LL JUST BE AN UNPLEASANT MEMORY.
SWIPSWIP...!!
!
OH! THE SNAKES ARE RUNNING AWAY.
WHAT'S GONNA HAPPEN TO THEM?! THEY'LL TURN BACK TO NORMAL, RIGHT?!
DON'T TALK BACK TO THE SNAKE PRINCESS!
WAH
GET HIM, BACURA!
YOU MEN ARE WEAK! YOU'RE ALL TALK!
RAAH
WAH
BACURA!!
WAH
YAY
...!!

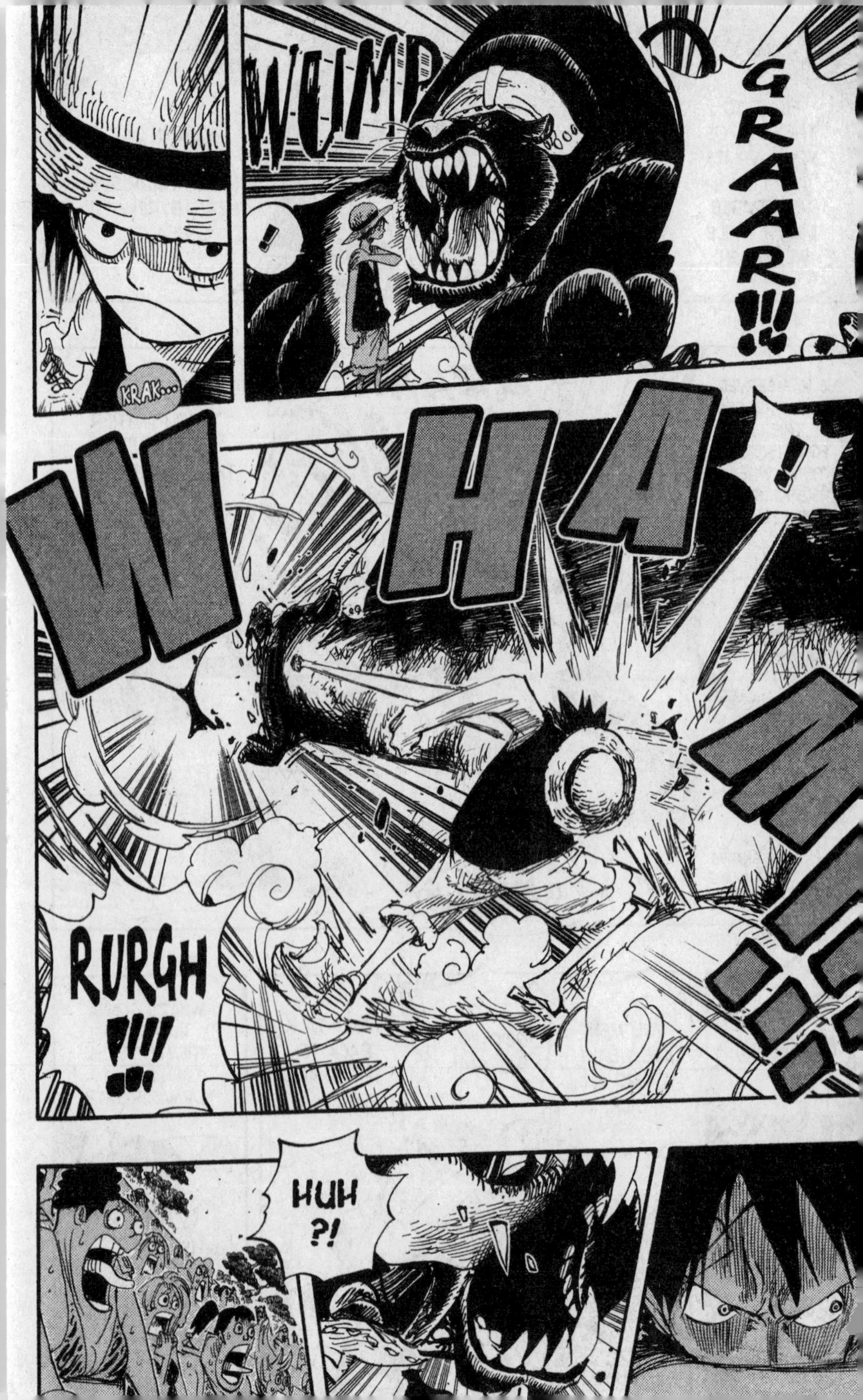
GRAAR!!!
WUMP
!
KRAK...
WHAM!!!
RURGH!!!!
HUH?!

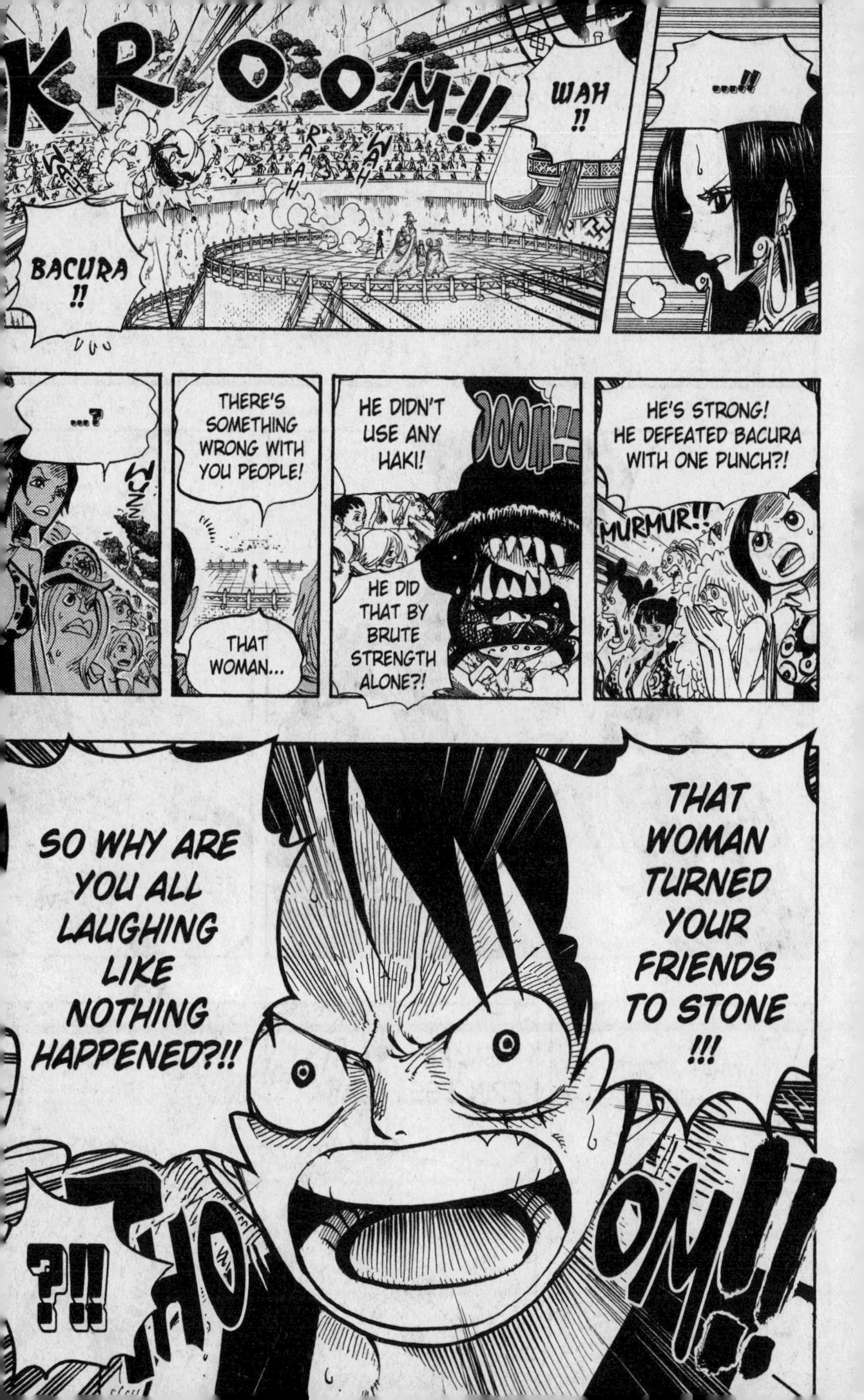
...!!
WAH !!
KROOM!!
WAH
RAAAH
WAH
BACURA !!
HE'S STRONG! HE DEFEATED BACURA WITH ONE PUNCH?!
MURMUR!!
DOOM!!
HE DIDN'T USE ANY HAKI!
HE DID THAT BY BRUTE STRENGTH ALONE?!
THERE'S SOMETHING WRONG WITH YOU PEOPLE!
THAT WOMAN...
...?
THAT WOMAN TURNED YOUR FRIENDS TO STONE !!!
SO WHY ARE YOU ALL LAUGHING LIKE NOTHING HAPPENED?!!
WHOOM!!
?!!

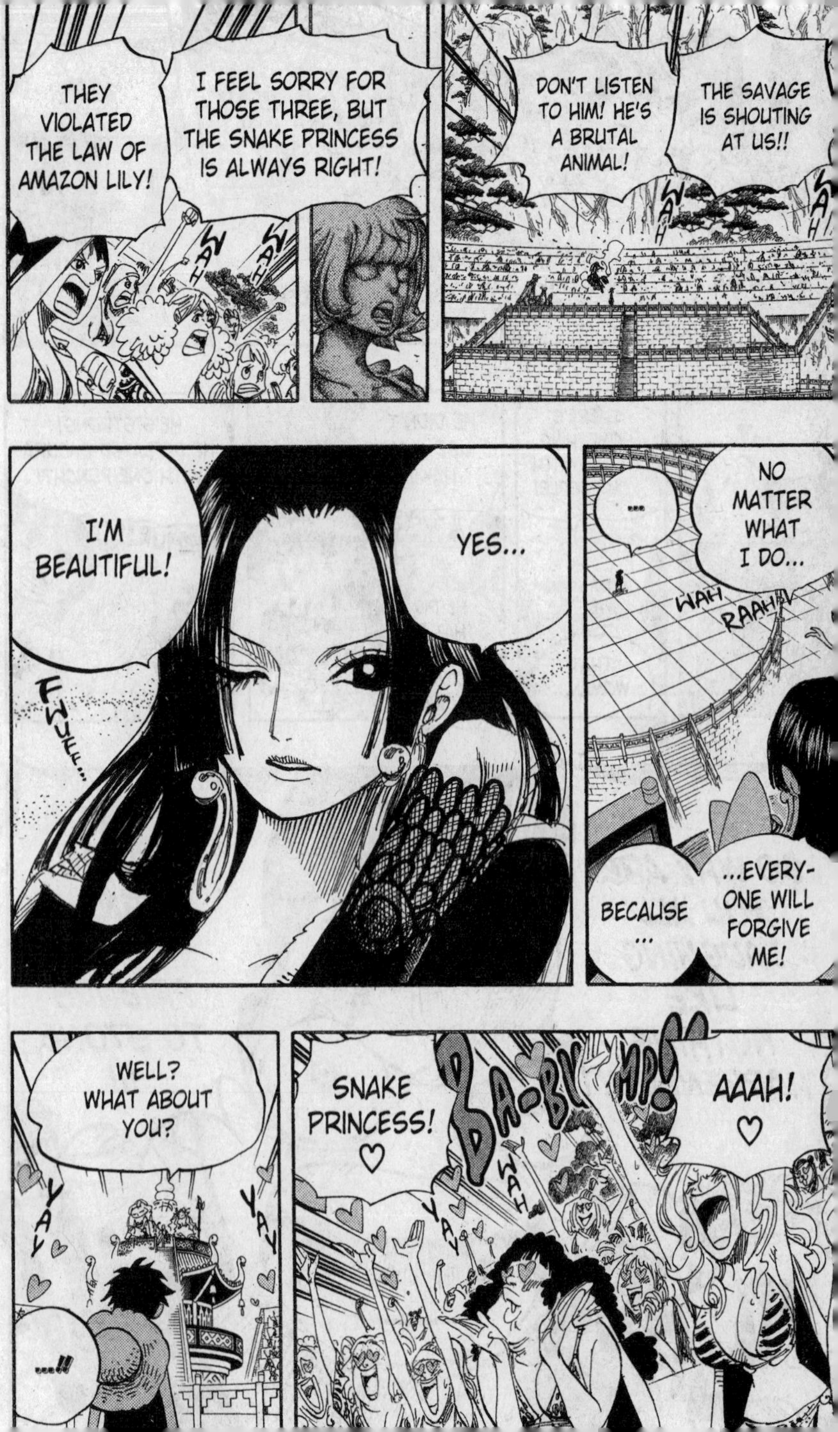
THE SAVAGE IS SHOUTING AT US!!
DON'T LISTEN TO HIM! HE'S A BRUTAL ANIMAL!
WAH
WAH
I FEEL SORRY FOR THOSE THREE, BUT THE SNAKE PRINCESS IS ALWAYS RIGHT!
THEY VIOLATED THE LAW OF AMAZON LILY!
WAH
WAH
NO MATTER WHAT I DO...
...
WAH
RAAH
...EVERY-ONE WILL FORGIVE ME!
BECAUSE ...
YES...
I'M BEAUTIFUL!
FWUFF...
AAAH! ♡
BA-BUMP!
SNAKE PRINCESS! ♡
WAH
YAY
WELL? WHAT ABOUT YOU?
YAY
YAY
...!!

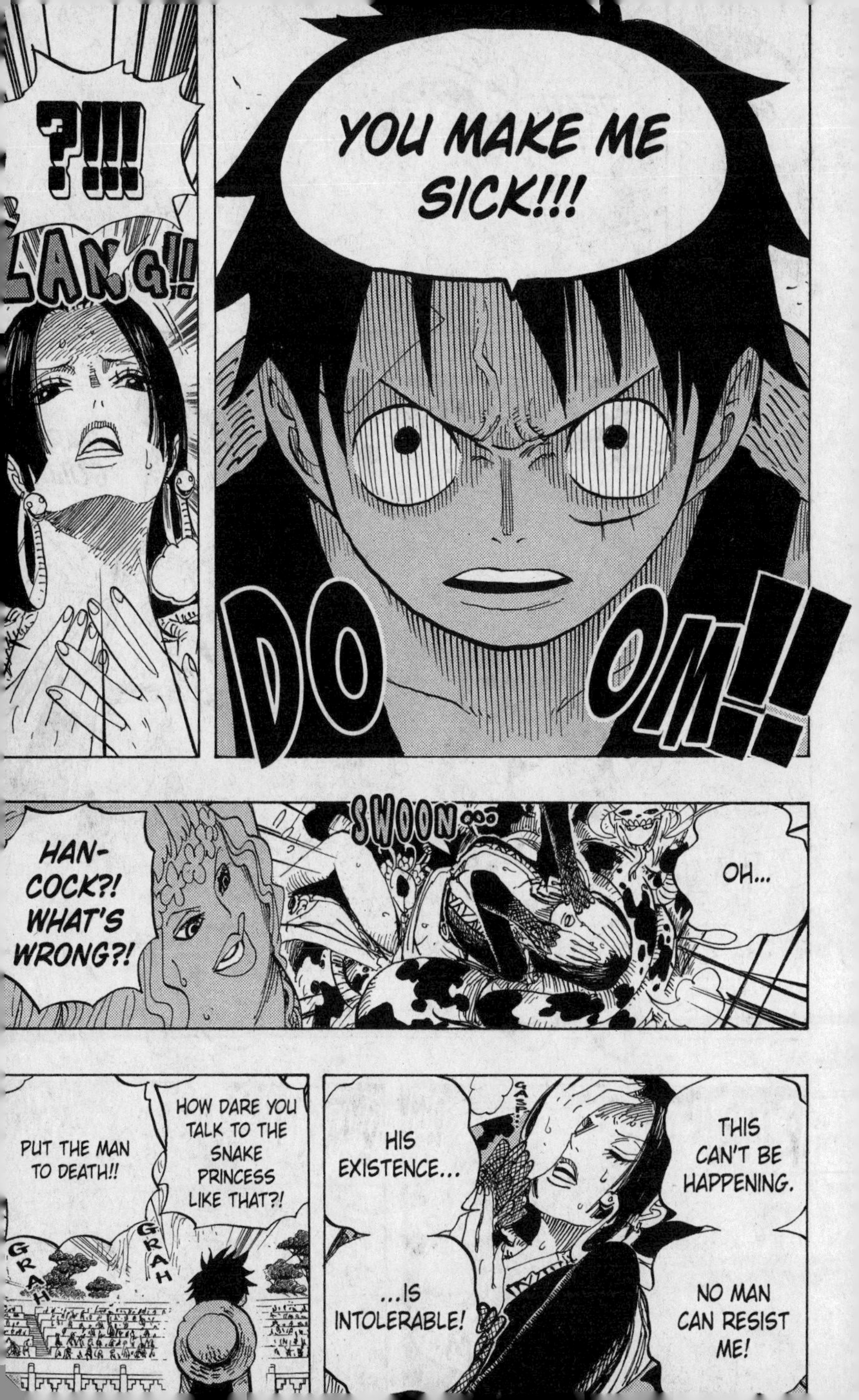
YOU MAKE ME SICK!!!
DO OM!!
?!!!
LANG!!
OH...
SWOON...
HAN-COCK?! WHAT'S WRONG?!
THIS CAN'T BE HAPPENING.
GASP...
HIS EXISTENCE...
NO MAN CAN RESIST ME!
...IS INTOLERABLE!
HOW DARE YOU TALK TO THE SNAKE PRINCESS LIKE THAT?!
GRAH
PUT THE MAN TO DEATH!!
GRAH

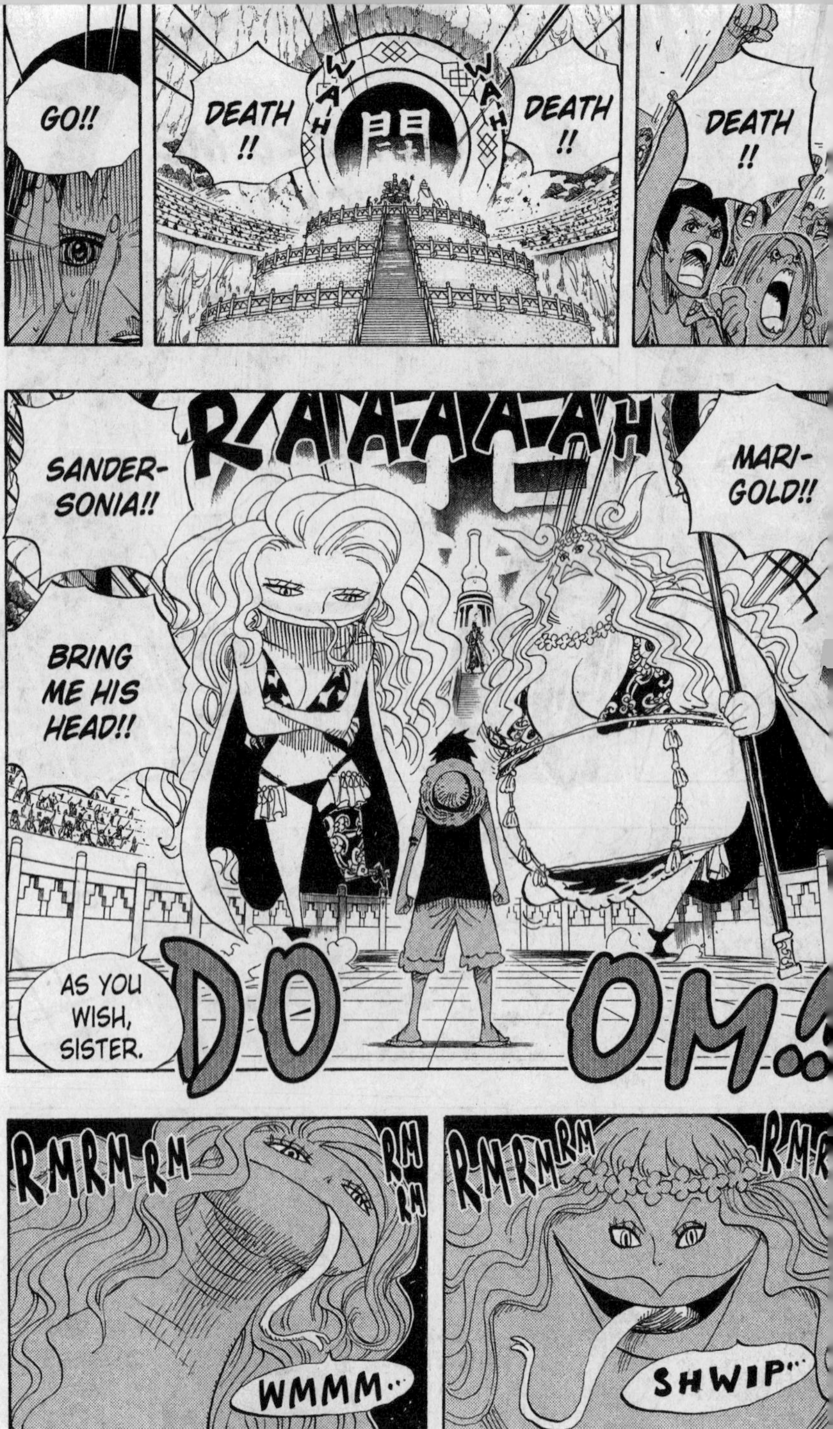
DEATH!!
DEATH!!
WAH
WAH
DEATH!!
GO!!
RAAAAAH
MARI-GOLD!!
SANDER-SONIA!!
BRING ME HIS HEAD!!
AS YOU WISH, SISTER.
DOOM!?
RMR
RMRMRMRM
SHWIP..
RMRMRMRM
RMRMRM
WMMM..

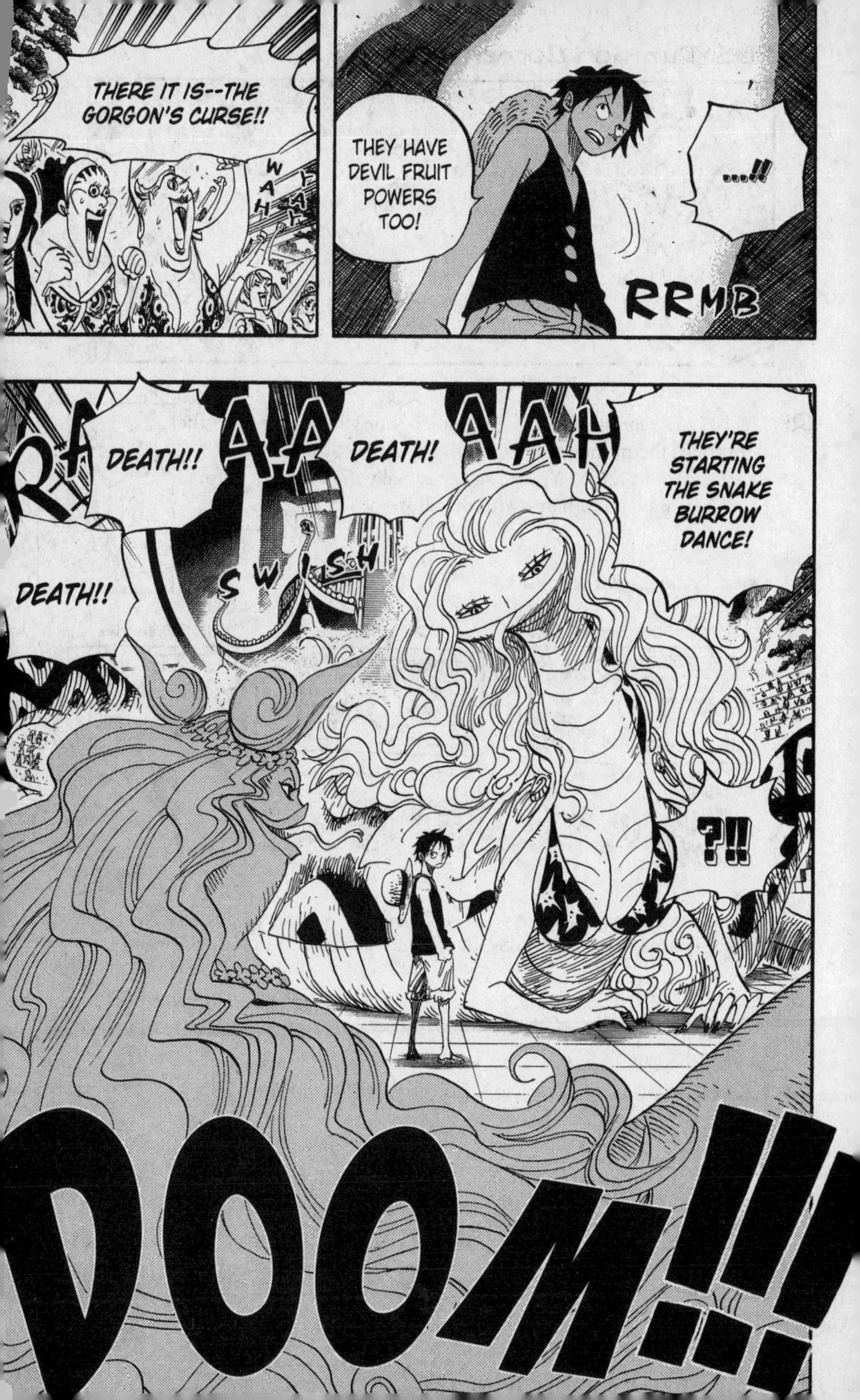
...!!
THEY HAVE DEVIL FRUIT POWERS TOO!
RRMB
THERE IT IS--THE GORGON'S CURSE!!
WAH HAH
THEY'RE STARTING THE SNAKE BURROW DANCE!
AAH
DEATH!
AA
DEATH!!
RA
DEATH!!
SWISH
?!!
DOOM!!!

SBS Question Corner

しつもんコーナー
エスビーエス

(Mall Osso, Tokyo)

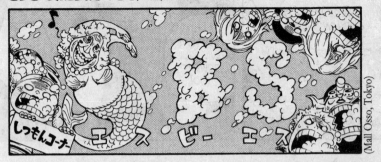

Q: Hello, Oda Sensei! This may be sudden, but whose face is on the berry bills, the money that's used in the world of *One Piece*? I really want to know! You've never actually drawn them before. So please draw them here--with details, mind you!

--Cat Burglar Aki

WELL THEN... IT'S NOT MUCH...
BUT HERE'S FIVE MILLION BERRIES...
IT'S JUST A TOKEN...

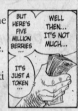

A: I see. I guess you're right.

10,000 Berries
Skeleton Yukichi
5,000 Berries
Bearmouth Ichiro
1,000 Berries
Rabbitmouth Hideyo
500 Berries
100 Berries
50 Berries
10 Berries
5 Berries
1 Berry

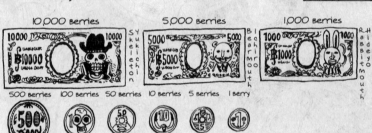

There, that's all of them. What? I'm just winging it? No, I'm not! Wait! I guess I am! Anyway, I'm making this official right now.

Q: In chapter 487, "That Song," there was a skeleton with a polka dot shirt that Brook picked up. And the guy who asked Brook how to fight with a sword has a sword stuck in his head. He's supposed to have died while singing, so how did the sword get in his head? When did it happen? And who did it?

--Copin

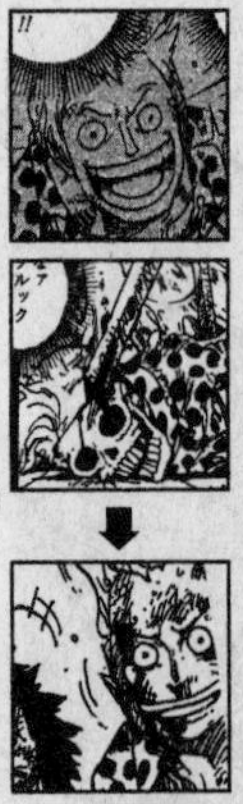

A: My readers have such keen eyes for these things! I'm really surprised. I received a couple of letters about this, so let me introduce them to you! Meet the Mizuuta twins!

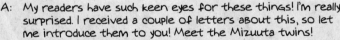

I died singing.
Elder Brother: Madaisky Mizuuta
Younger Brother: Mawaritosky
I got stabbed in the

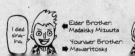

Chapter 519:
NATURAL BORN KING

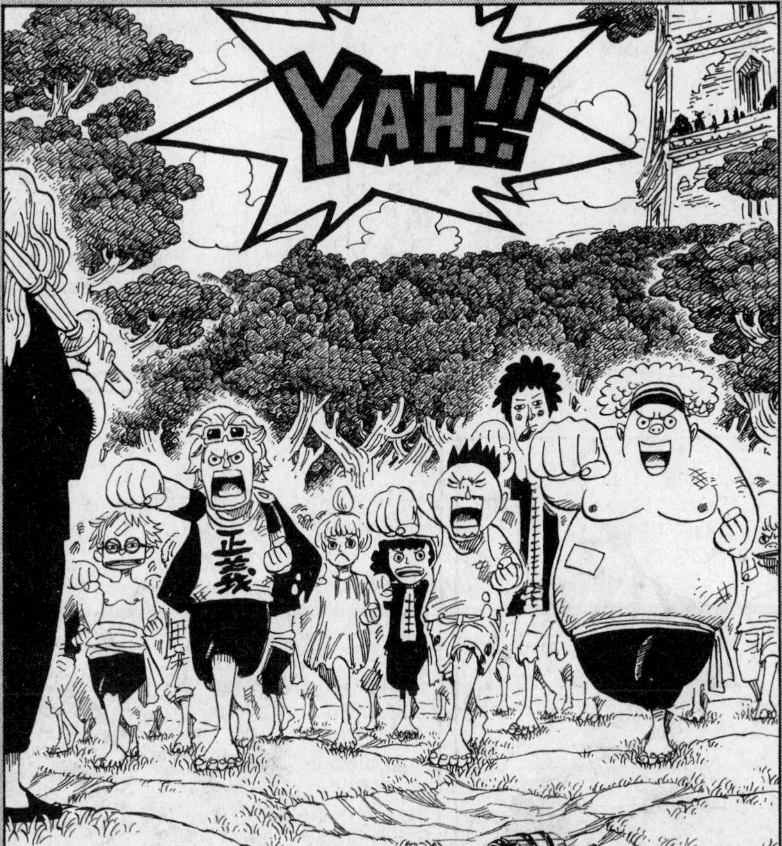
YAH!!

CP9'S INDEPENDENT REPORT, VOL. 26:
"NEXT GENERATION CP IN TRAINING"

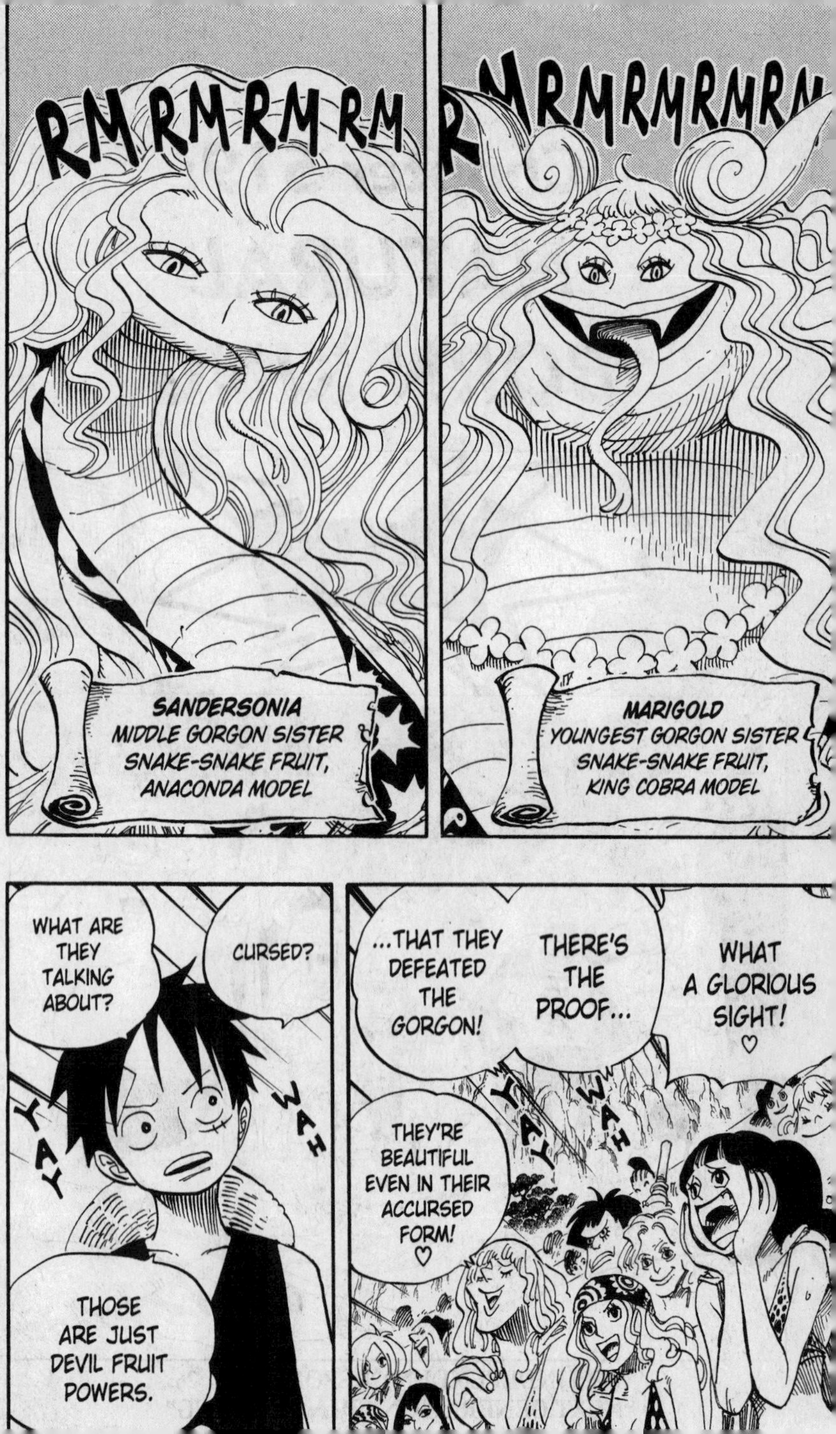

RMRMRMRMRN
MARIGOLD
YOUNGEST GORGON SISTER
SNAKE-SNAKE FRUIT,
KING COBRA MODEL
RMRMRMRMRM
SANDERSONIA
MIDDLE GORGON SISTER
SNAKE-SNAKE FRUIT,
ANACONDA MODEL
WHAT A GLORIOUS SIGHT! ♡
THERE'S THE PROOF...
...THAT THEY DEFEATED THE GORGON!
WAH
YAY
THEY'RE BEAUTIFUL EVEN IN THEIR ACCURSED FORM! ♡
CURSED?
WHAT ARE THEY TALKING ABOUT?
WAH
YAY
THOSE ARE JUST DEVIL FRUIT POWERS.

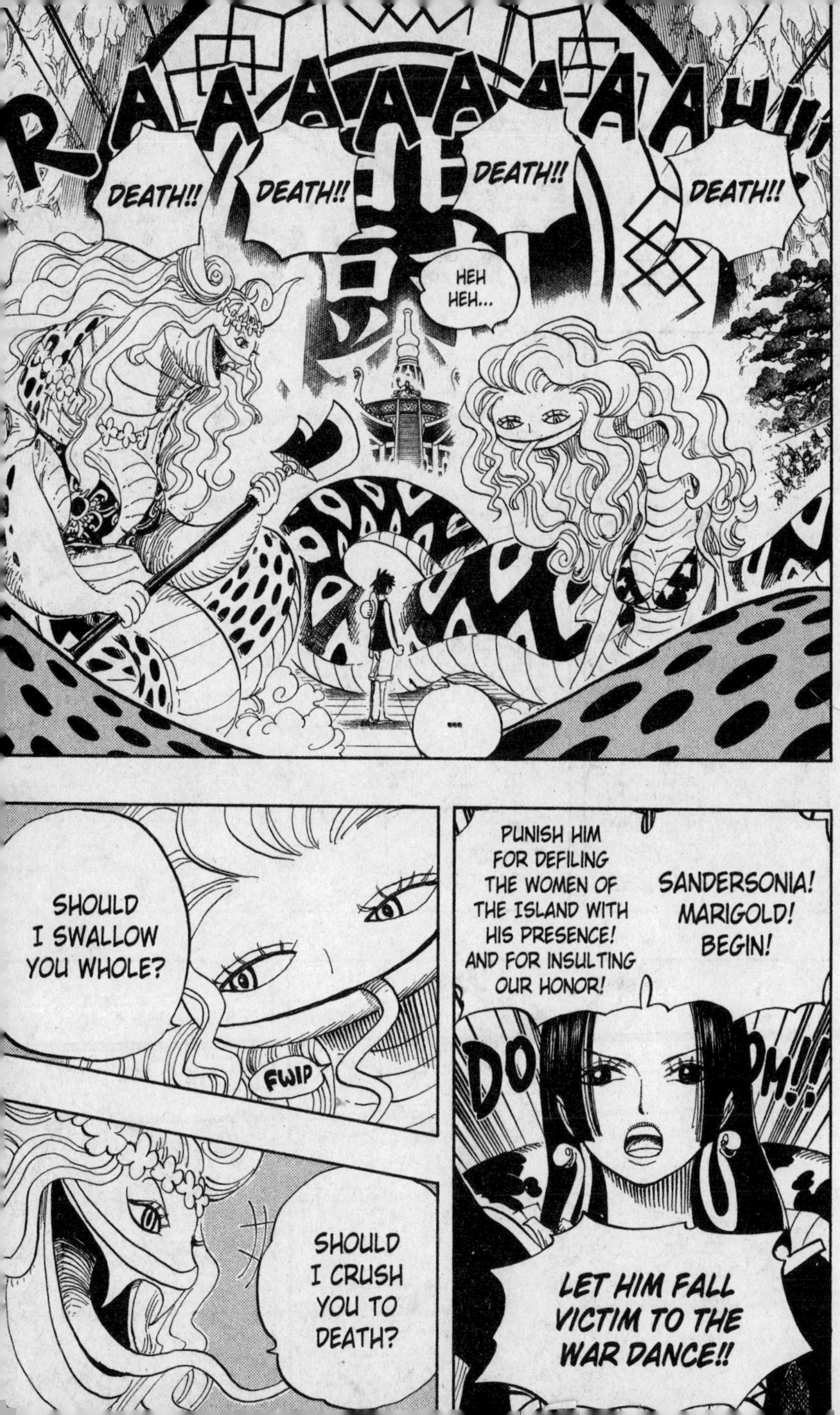
RAAAAAAAH!!!
DEATH!!
DEATH!!
DEATH!!
DEATH!!
HEH HEH...
...
SANDERSONIA! MARIGOLD! BEGIN!
PUNISH HIM FOR DEFILING THE WOMEN OF THE ISLAND WITH HIS PRESENCE! AND FOR INSULTING OUR HONOR!
DOOM!!!
LET HIM FALL VICTIM TO THE WAR DANCE!!
SHOULD I SWALLOW YOU WHOLE?
FWIP
SHOULD I CRUSH YOU TO DEATH?

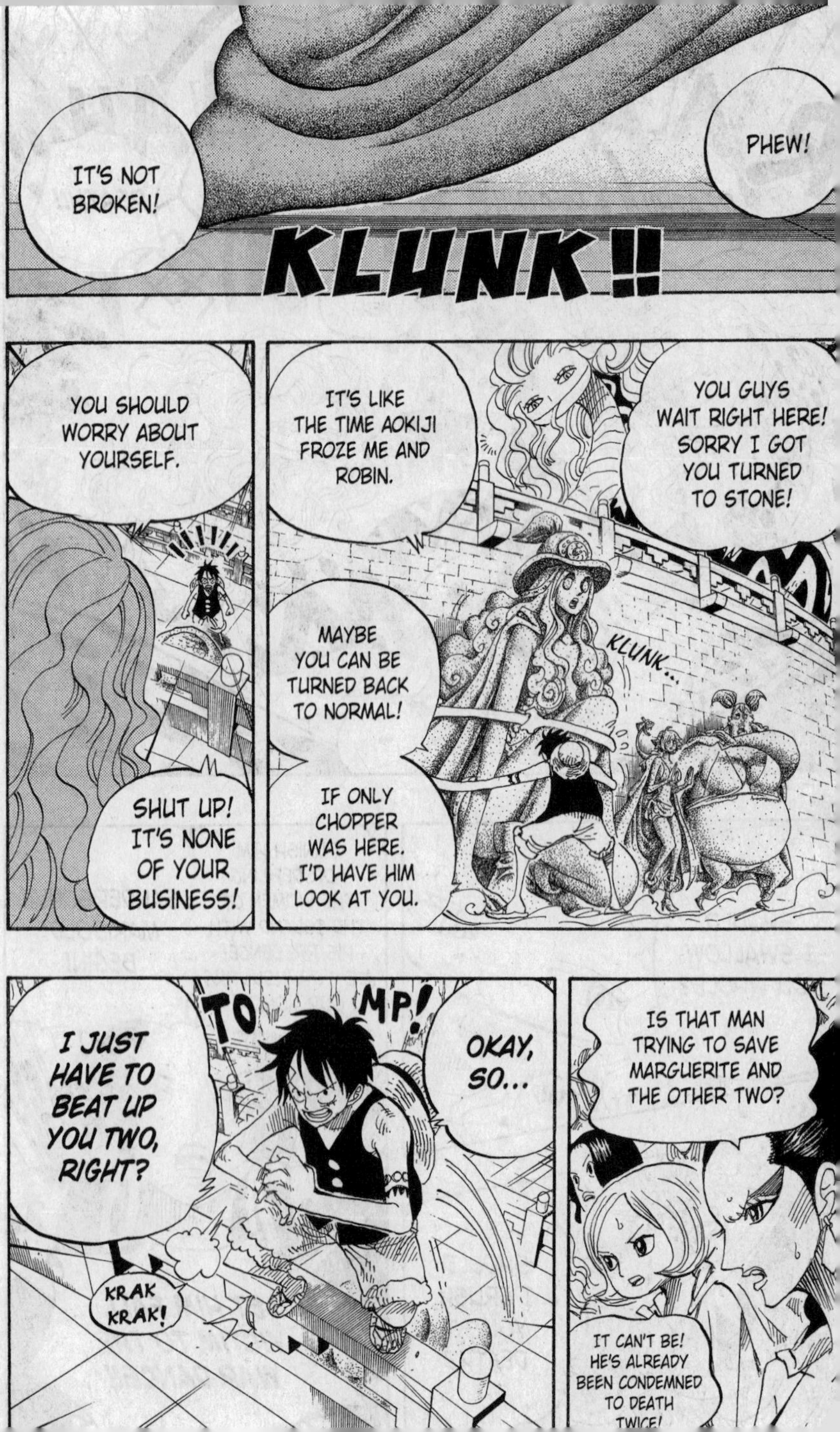
PHEW!
IT'S NOT BROKEN!
KLUNK!!
YOU GUYS WAIT RIGHT HERE! SORRY I GOT YOU TURNED TO STONE!
IT'S LIKE THE TIME AOKIJI FROZE ME AND ROBIN.
MAYBE YOU CAN BE TURNED BACK TO NORMAL!
KLUNK...
IF ONLY CHOPPER WAS HERE. I'D HAVE HIM LOOK AT YOU.
YOU SHOULD WORRY ABOUT YOURSELF.
SHUT UP! IT'S NONE OF YOUR BUSINESS!
IS THAT MAN TRYING TO SAVE MARGUERITE AND THE OTHER TWO?
IT CAN'T BE! HE'S ALREADY BEEN CONDEMNED TO DEATH TWICE!
OKAY, SO...
TOMP!
I JUST HAVE TO BEAT UP YOU TWO, RIGHT?
KRAK KRAK!

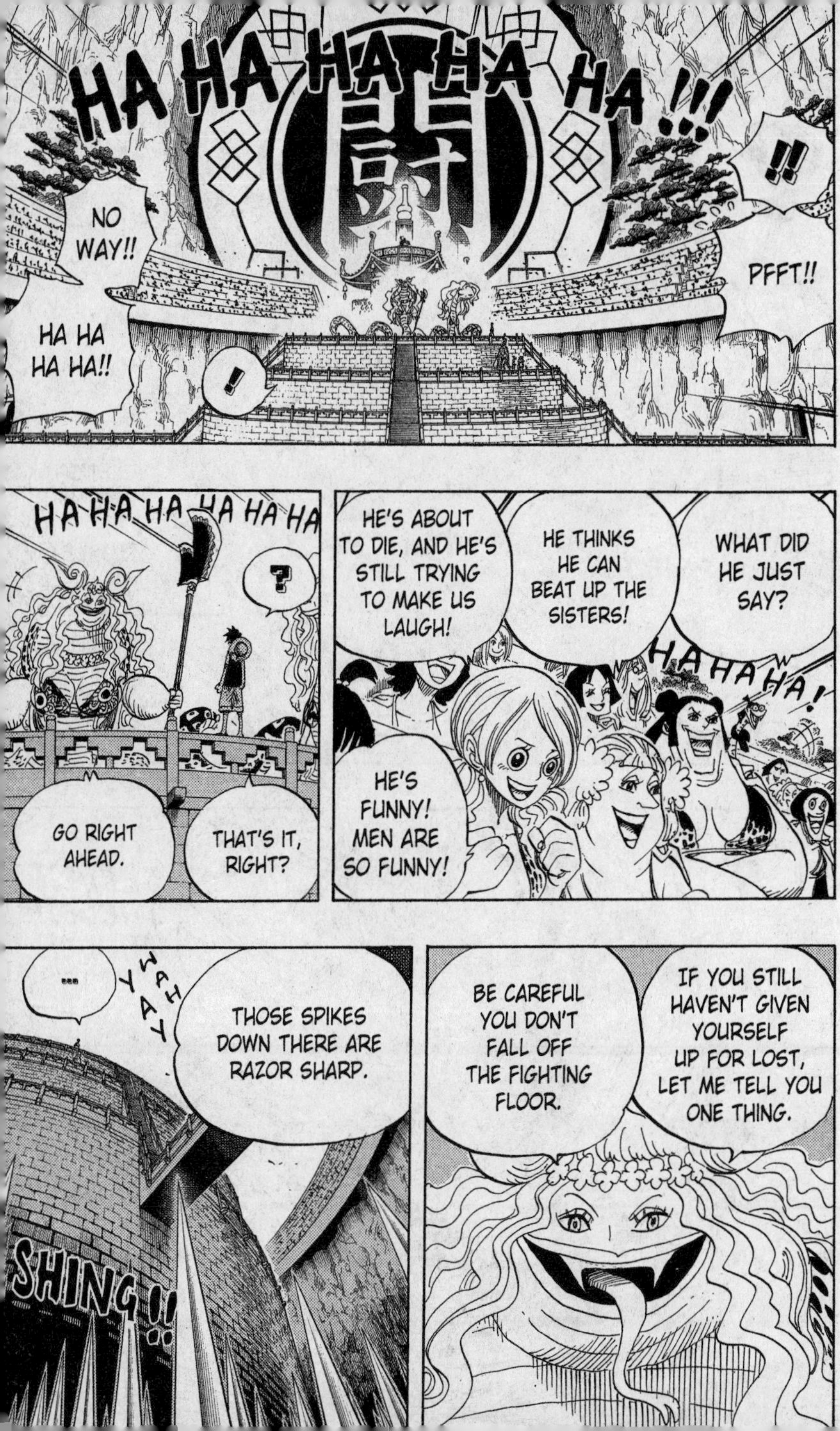
HA HA HA HA HA HA HA!!!
!!
PFFT!!
NO WAY!!
!
HA HA HA HA!!
WHAT DID HE JUST SAY?
HE THINKS HE CAN BEAT UP THE SISTERS!
HE'S ABOUT TO DIE, AND HE'S STILL TRYING TO MAKE US LAUGH!
HA HA HA HA!
HE'S FUNNY! MEN ARE SO FUNNY!
HA HA HA HA HA HA HA
?
THAT'S IT, RIGHT?
GO RIGHT AHEAD.
IF YOU STILL HAVEN'T GIVEN YOURSELF UP FOR LOST, LET ME TELL YOU ONE THING.
BE CAREFUL YOU DON'T FALL OFF THE FIGHTING FLOOR.
THOSE SPIKES DOWN THERE ARE RAZOR SHARP.
...
SHING!!

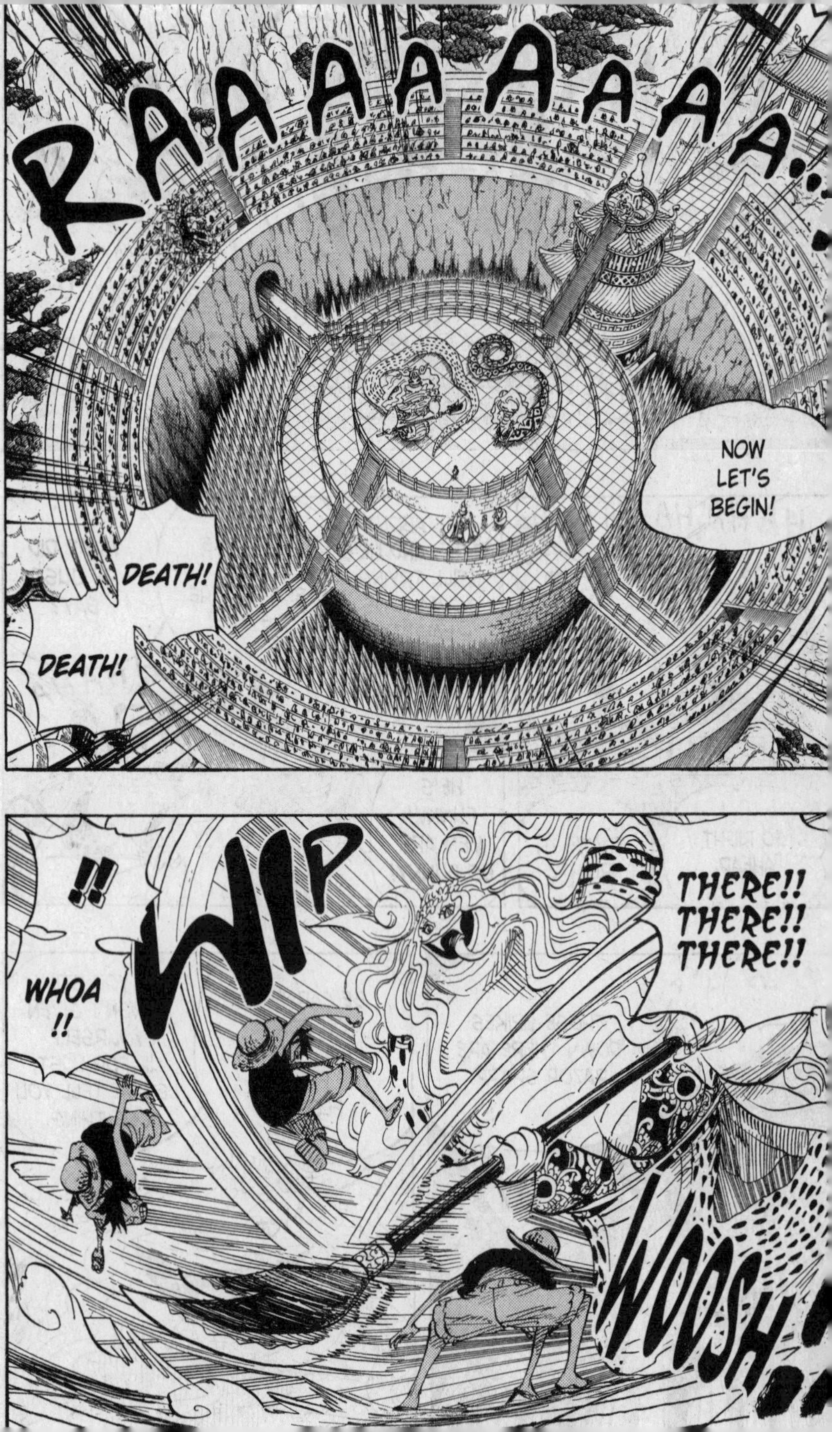
RAAAAAAAA...!!
NOW LET'S BEGIN!
DEATH!
DEATH!
THERE!! THERE!! THERE!!
WHOOSH...!!
WHIP
!!
WHOA !!

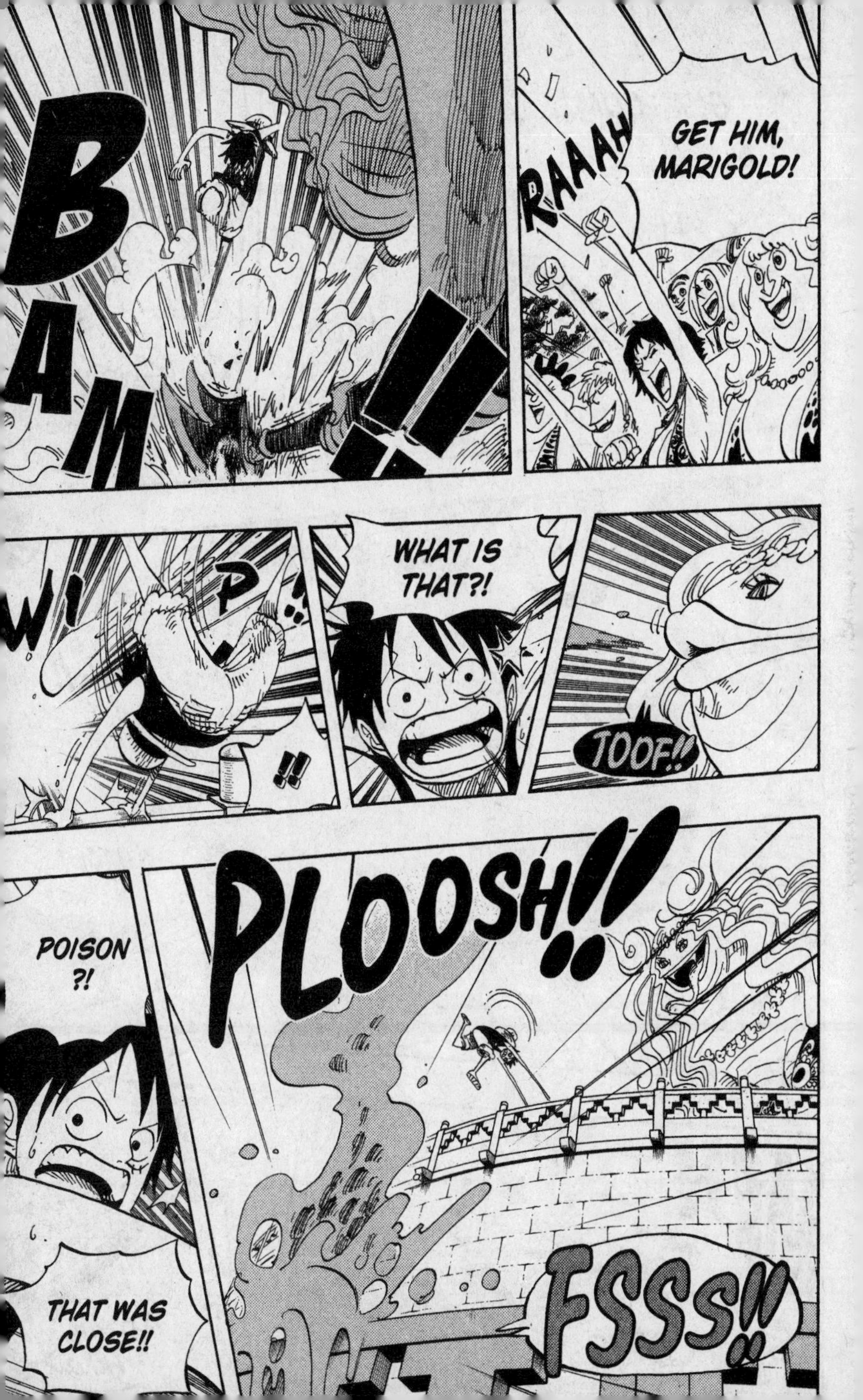
RAAAH
GET HIM, MARIGOLD!
BAM!!
TOOF!!
WHAT IS THAT?!
PLOOSH!!
FSSS!!
POISON ?!
THAT WAS CLOSE!!

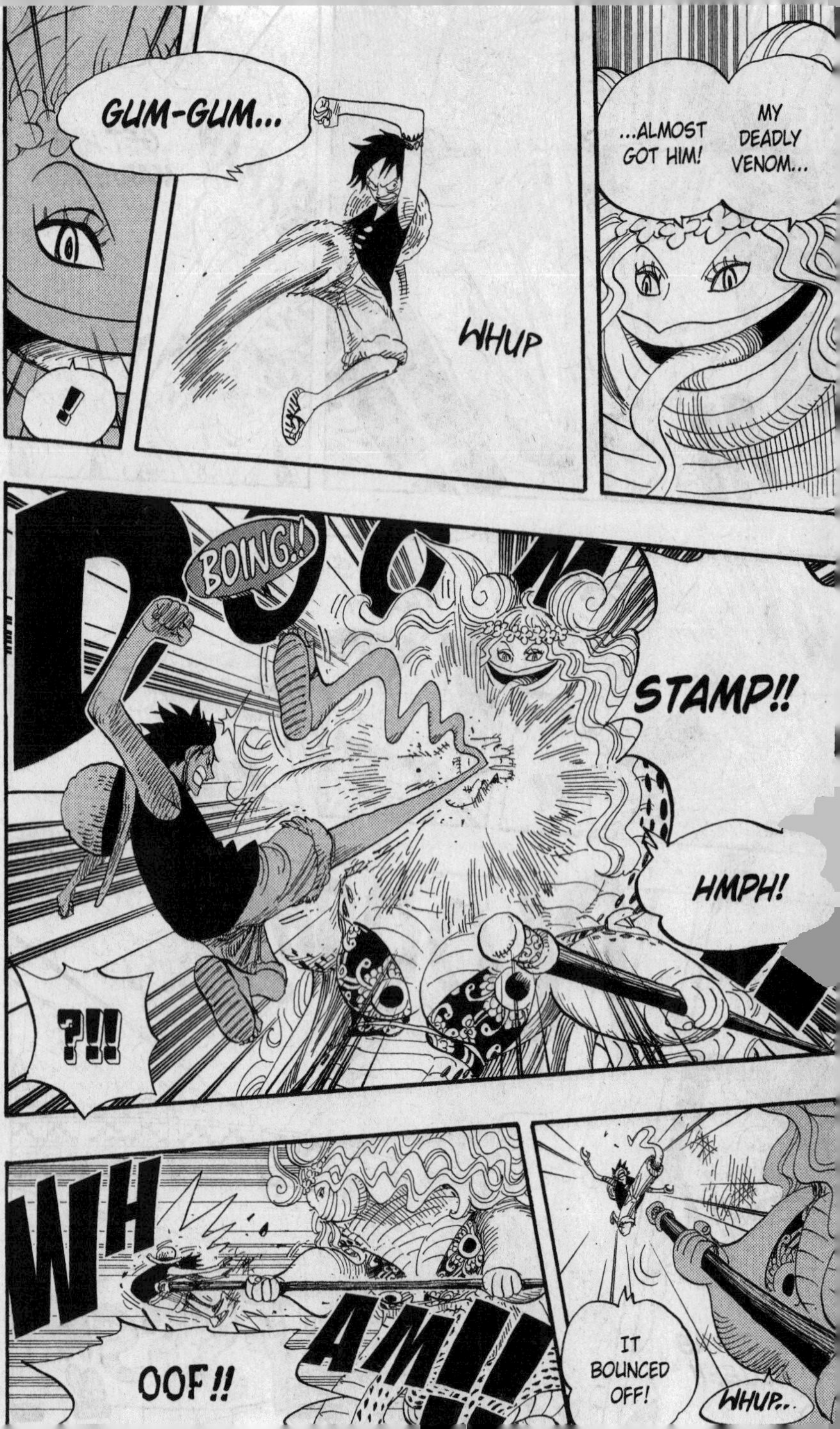
MY DEADLY VENOM...
...ALMOST GOT HIM!
GUM-GUM...
WHUP
!
BOING!!
STAMP!!
HMPH!
?!!
IT BOUNCED OFF!
WHUP...
WHAM!!
OOF!!

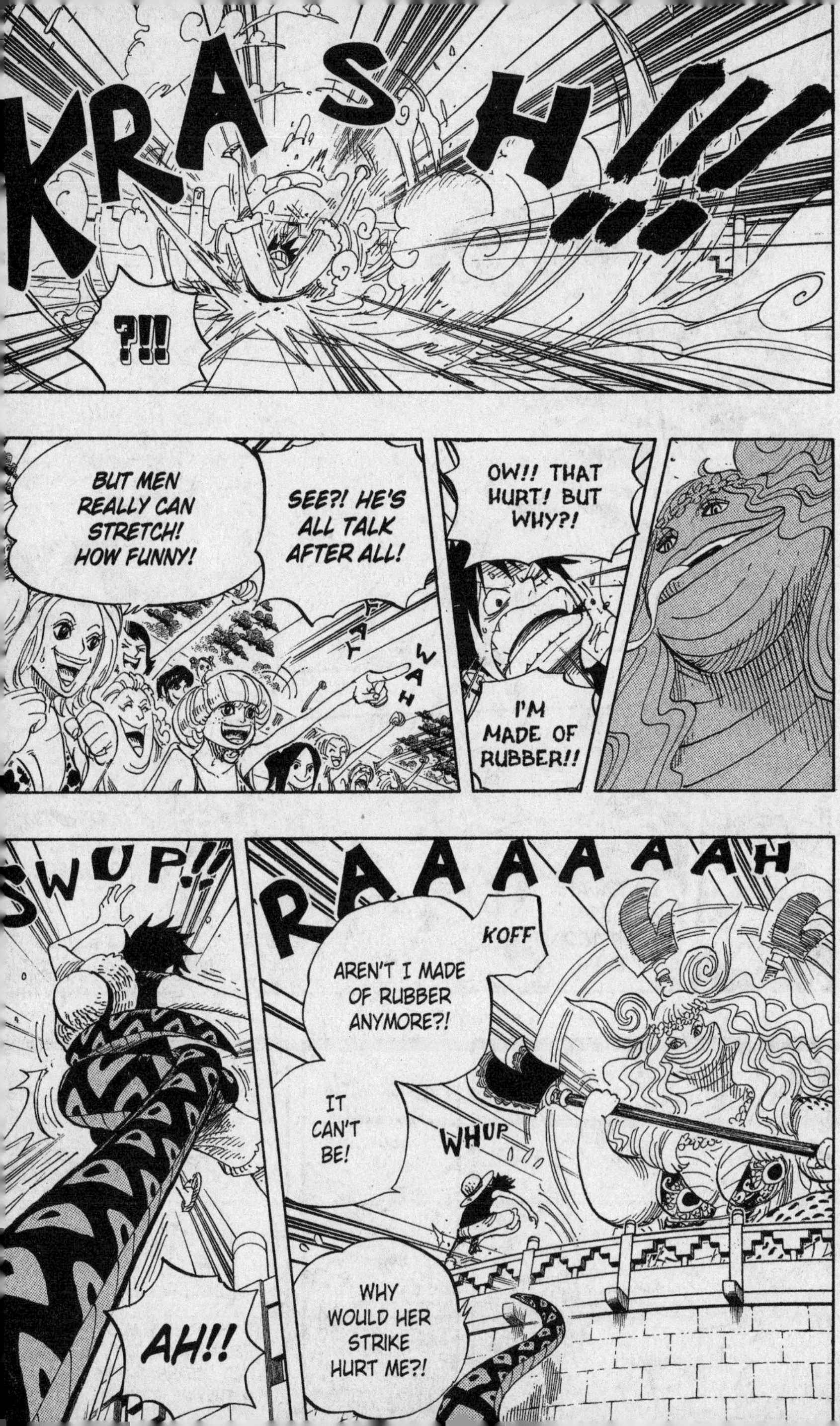
KRASH!!!
?!!
OW!! THAT HURT! BUT WHY?!
I'M MADE OF RUBBER!!
SEE?! HE'S ALL TALK AFTER ALL!
BUT MEN REALLY CAN STRETCH! HOW FUNNY!
RAAAAAAH
KOFF
AREN'T I MADE OF RUBBER ANYMORE?!
IT CAN'T BE!
WHUP
WHY WOULD HER STRIKE HURT ME?!
SWUP!!
AH!!

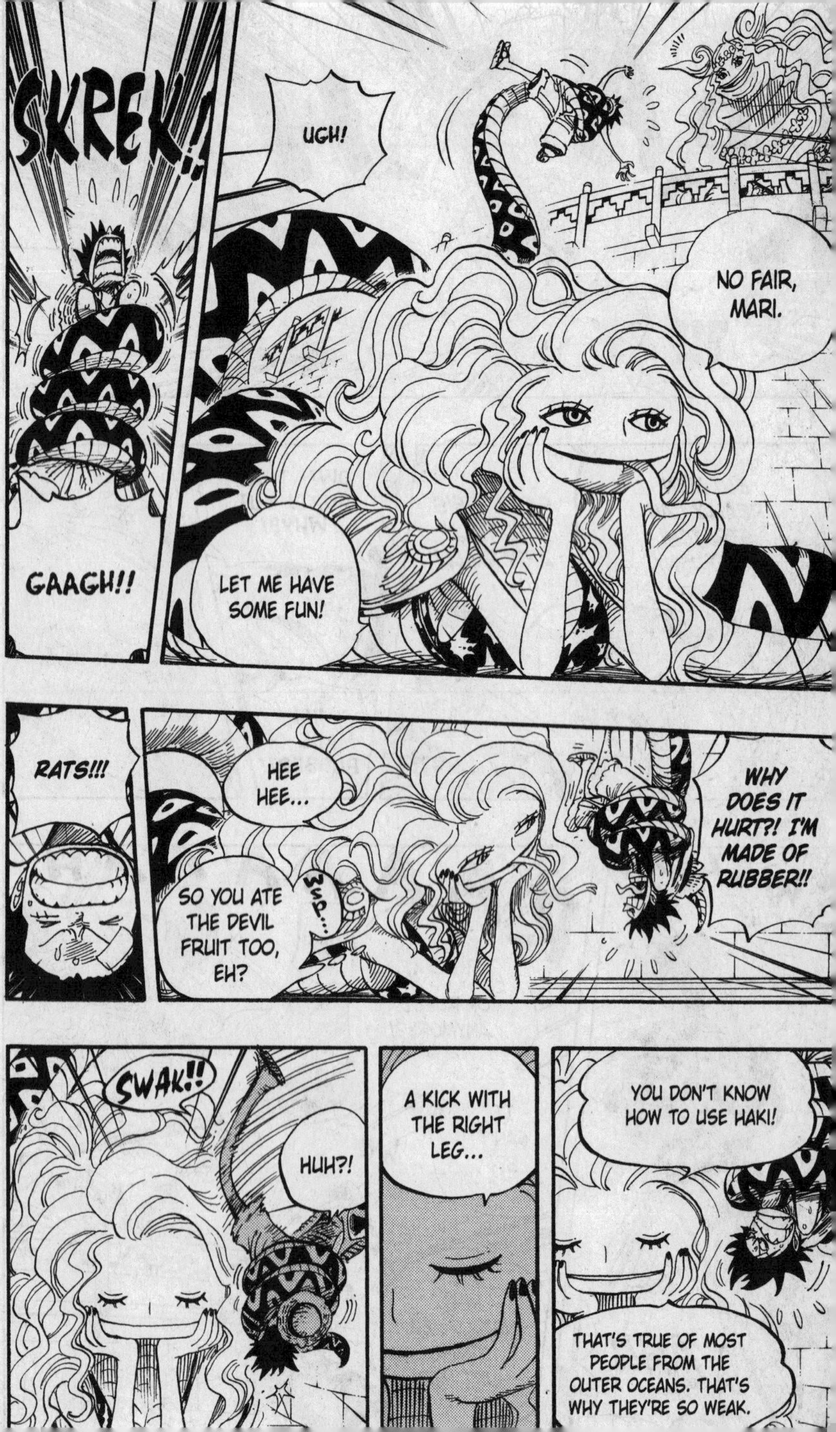
UGH!
NO FAIR, MARI.
LET ME HAVE SOME FUN!
SKREK!!
GAAGH!!
WHY DOES IT HURT?! I'M MADE OF RUBBER!!
HEE HEE...
WSP...
SO YOU ATE THE DEVIL FRUIT TOO, EH?
RATS!!!
YOU DON'T KNOW HOW TO USE HAKI!
THAT'S TRUE OF MOST PEOPLE FROM THE OUTER OCEANS. THAT'S WHY THEY'RE SO WEAK.
A KICK WITH THE RIGHT LEG...
SWAK!!
HUH?!

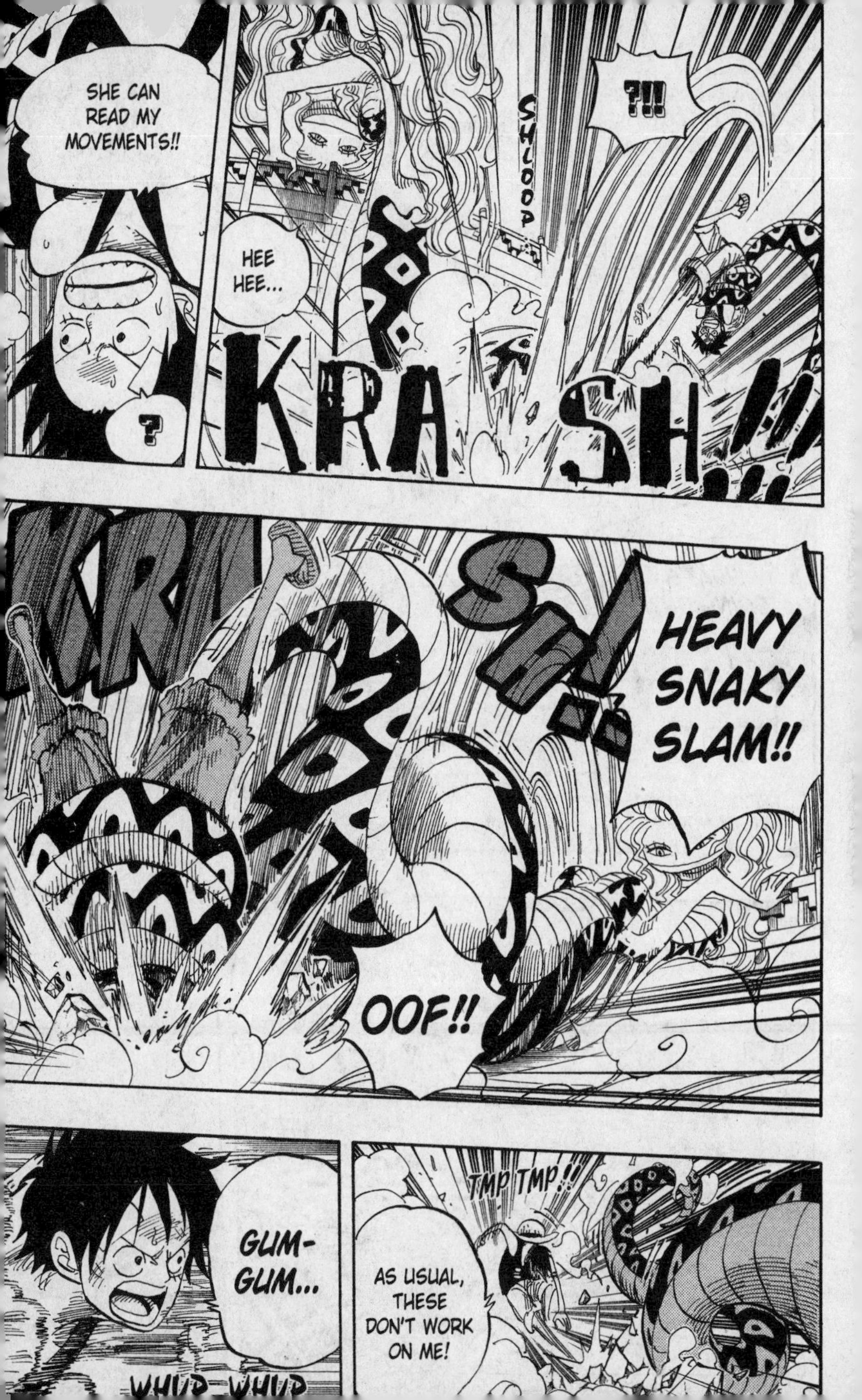
?!!
SHLOOP
HEE HEE...
KRASH!!
SHE CAN READ MY MOVEMENTS!!
?
HEAVY SNAKY SLAM!!
SH!!
OOF!!
TMP TMP!!
AS USUAL, THESE DON'T WORK ON ME!
GUM-GUM...
WHUD WHUD

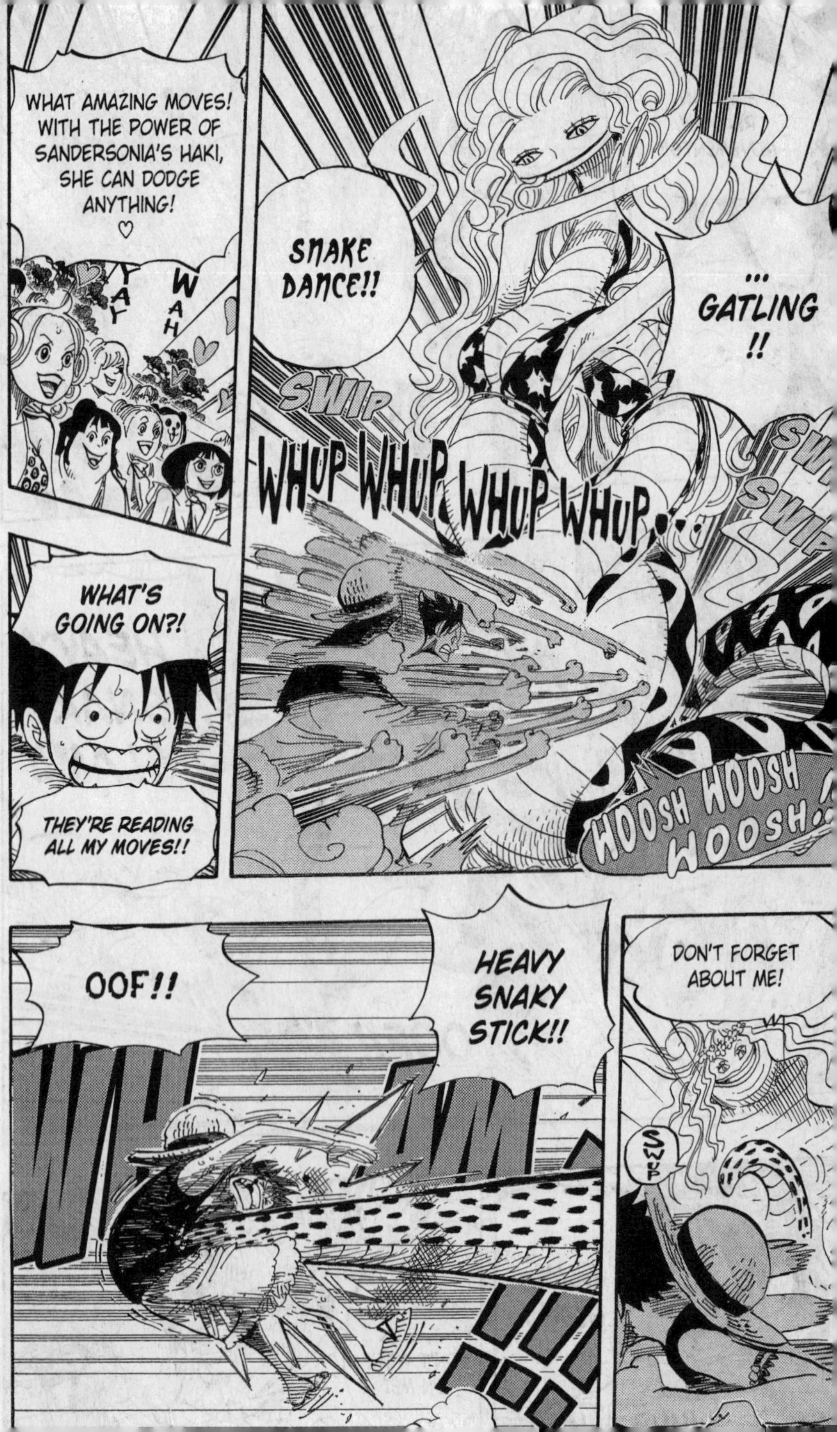
... GATLING !!
SNAKE DANCE!!
SWIP SWIP SWIP
SWIP
WHUP WHUP WHUP WHUP WHUP...
WOOSH WOOSH WOOSH...
WHAT AMAZING MOVES! WITH THE POWER OF SANDERSONIA'S HAKI, SHE CAN DODGE ANYTHING! ♡
WAH
YAY
WHAT'S GOING ON?!
THEY'RE READING ALL MY MOVES!!
DON'T FORGET ABOUT ME!
SWUP
HEAVY SNAKY STICK!!
OOF!!

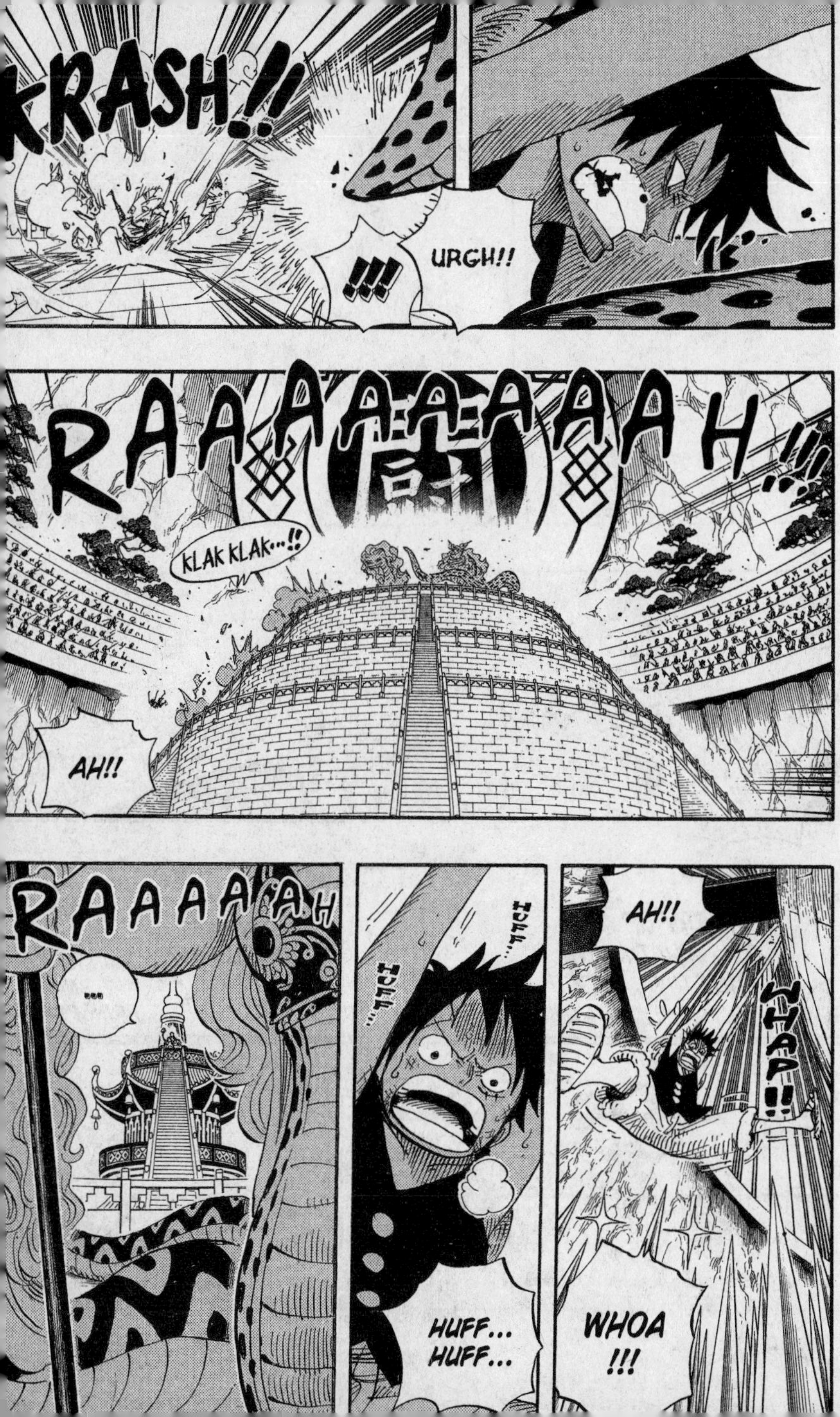
URGH!!
!!!
KRASH!!
RAAAAAAAAH!!!
KLAK KLAK...!!
AH!!
AH!!
WHAP!!
WHOA !!!
HUFF...
HUFF...
HUFF... HUFF...
RAAAAAAH
...

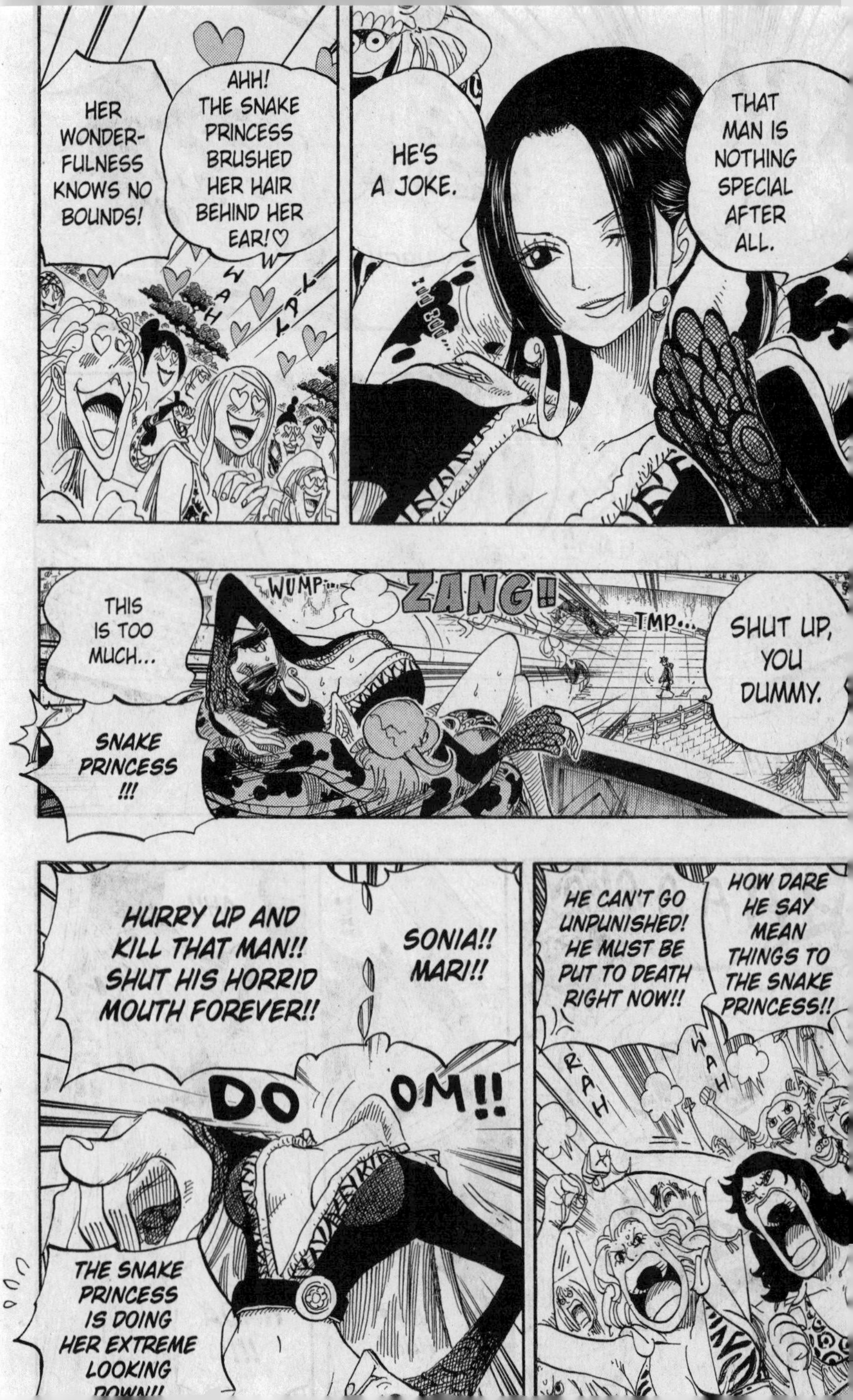
THAT MAN IS NOTHING SPECIAL AFTER ALL.
HE'S A JOKE.
AHH! THE SNAKE PRINCESS BRUSHED HER HAIR BEHIND HER EAR!♡
HER WONDER-FULNESS KNOWS NO BOUNDS!
WAH
SHUT UP, YOU DUMMY.
TMP...
ZANG!!
WUMP...
THIS IS TOO MUCH...
SNAKE PRINCESS!!!
HOW DARE HE SAY MEAN THINGS TO THE SNAKE PRINCESS!!
HE CAN'T GO UNPUNISHED! HE MUST BE PUT TO DEATH RIGHT NOW!!
WAH
RAH
SONIA!! MARI!!
HURRY UP AND KILL THAT MAN!! SHUT HIS HORRID MOUTH FOREVER!!
DO OM!!
THE SNAKE PRINCESS IS DOING HER EXTREME LOOKING DOWN!!

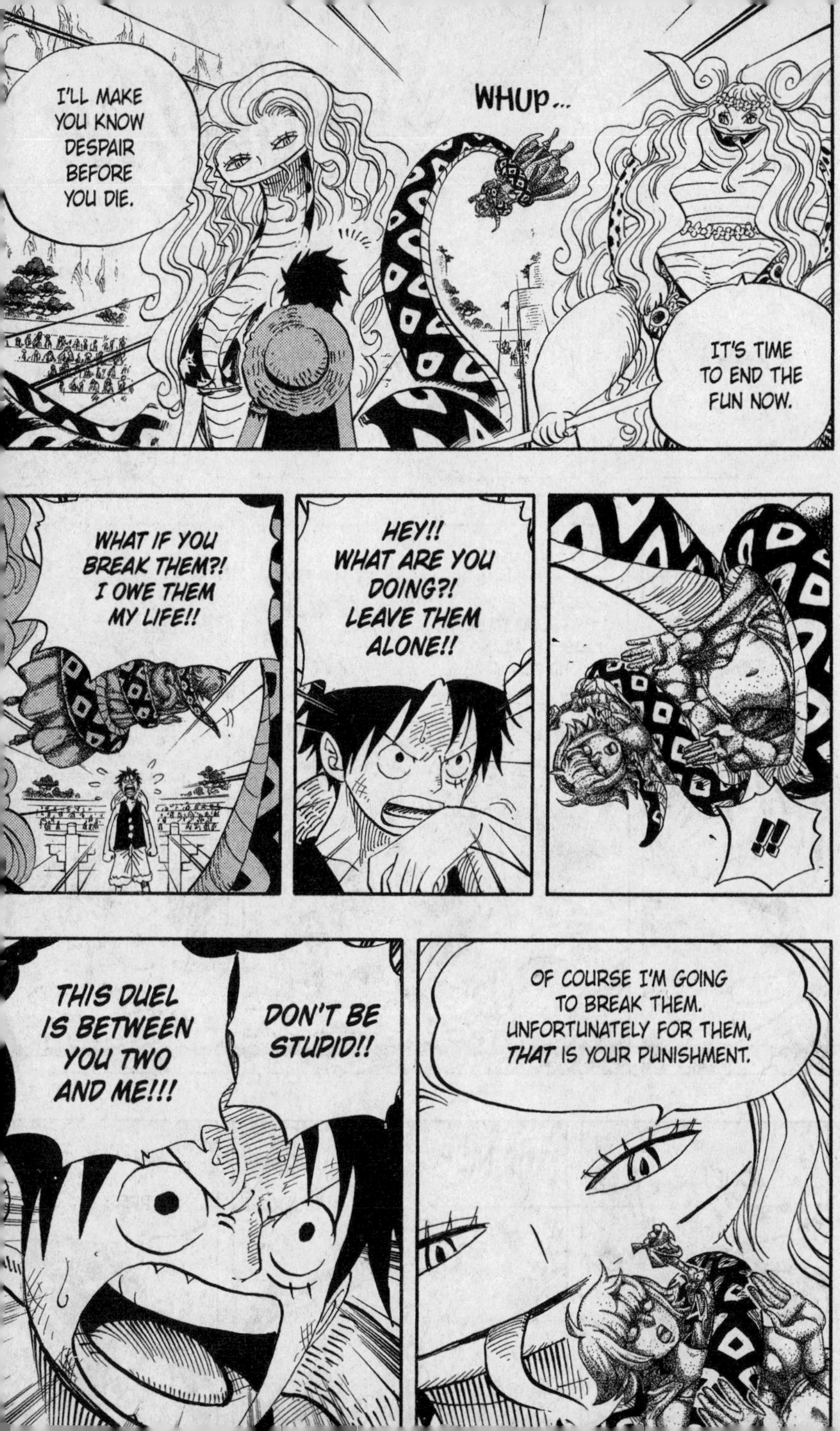
WHUP...
IT'S TIME TO END THE FUN NOW.
I'LL MAKE YOU KNOW DESPAIR BEFORE YOU DIE.
!!
HEY!! WHAT ARE YOU DOING?! LEAVE THEM ALONE!!
WHAT IF YOU BREAK THEM?! I OWE THEM MY LIFE!!
OF COURSE I'M GOING TO BREAK THEM. UNFORTUNATELY FOR THEM, THAT IS YOUR PUNISHMENT.
DON'T BE STUPID!!
THIS DUEL IS BETWEEN YOU TWO AND ME!!!

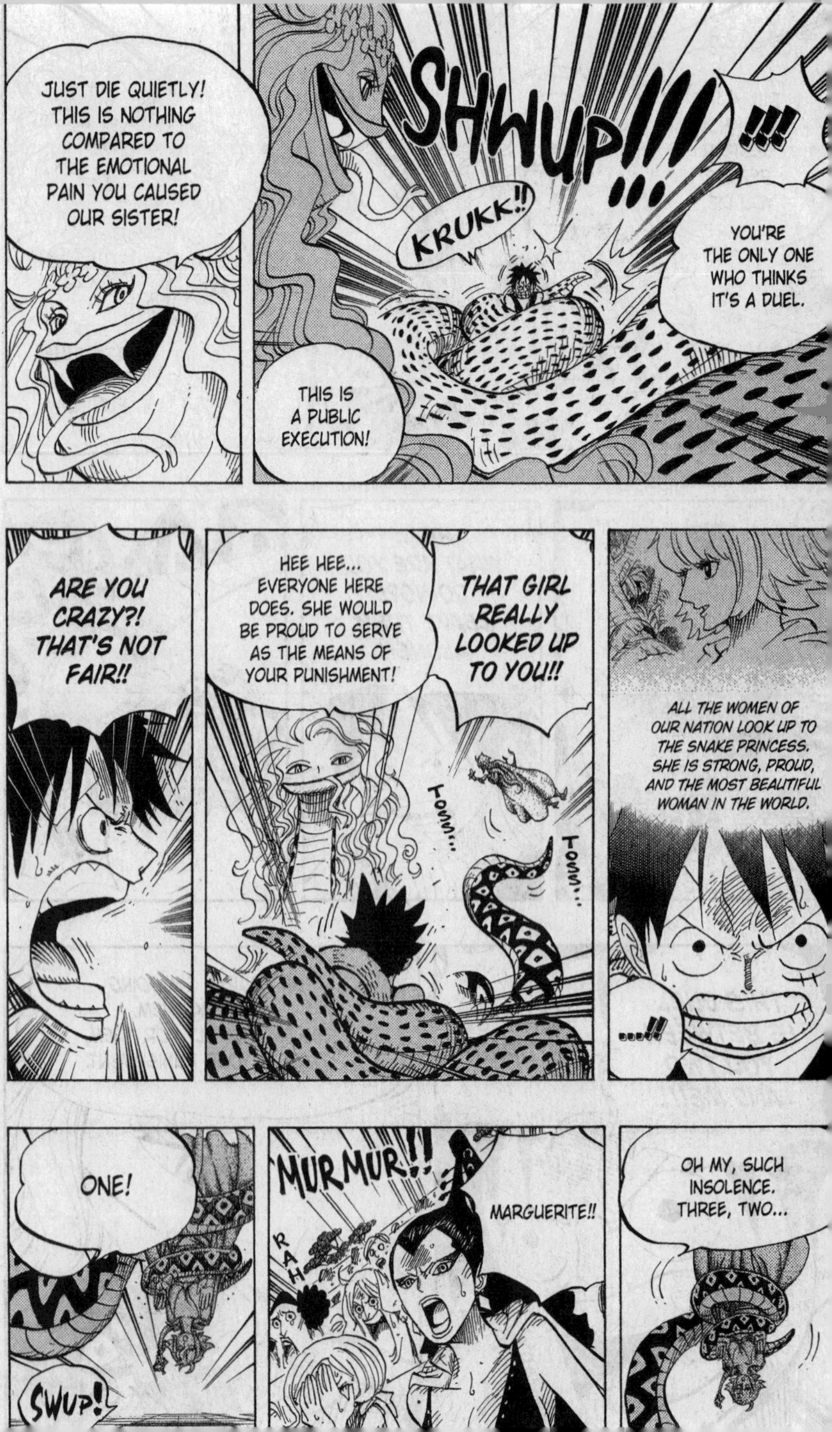
!!!
SHWUP!!!
YOU'RE THE ONLY ONE WHO THINKS IT'S A DUEL.
KRUKK!!
THIS IS A PUBLIC EXECUTION!
JUST DIE QUIETLY! THIS IS NOTHING COMPARED TO THE EMOTIONAL PAIN YOU CAUSED OUR SISTER!
ALL THE WOMEN OF OUR NATION LOOK UP TO THE SNAKE PRINCESS. SHE IS STRONG, PROUD, AND THE MOST BEAUTIFUL WOMAN IN THE WORLD.
...!!
THAT GIRL REALLY LOOKED UP TO YOU!!
HEE HEE... EVERYONE HERE DOES. SHE WOULD BE PROUD TO SERVE AS THE MEANS OF YOUR PUNISHMENT!
TOSS...
TOSS...
ARE YOU CRAZY?! THAT'S NOT FAIR!!
OH MY, SUCH INSOLENCE. THREE, TWO...
MARGUERITE!!
MURMUR!!
RAH
ONE!
SWUP!

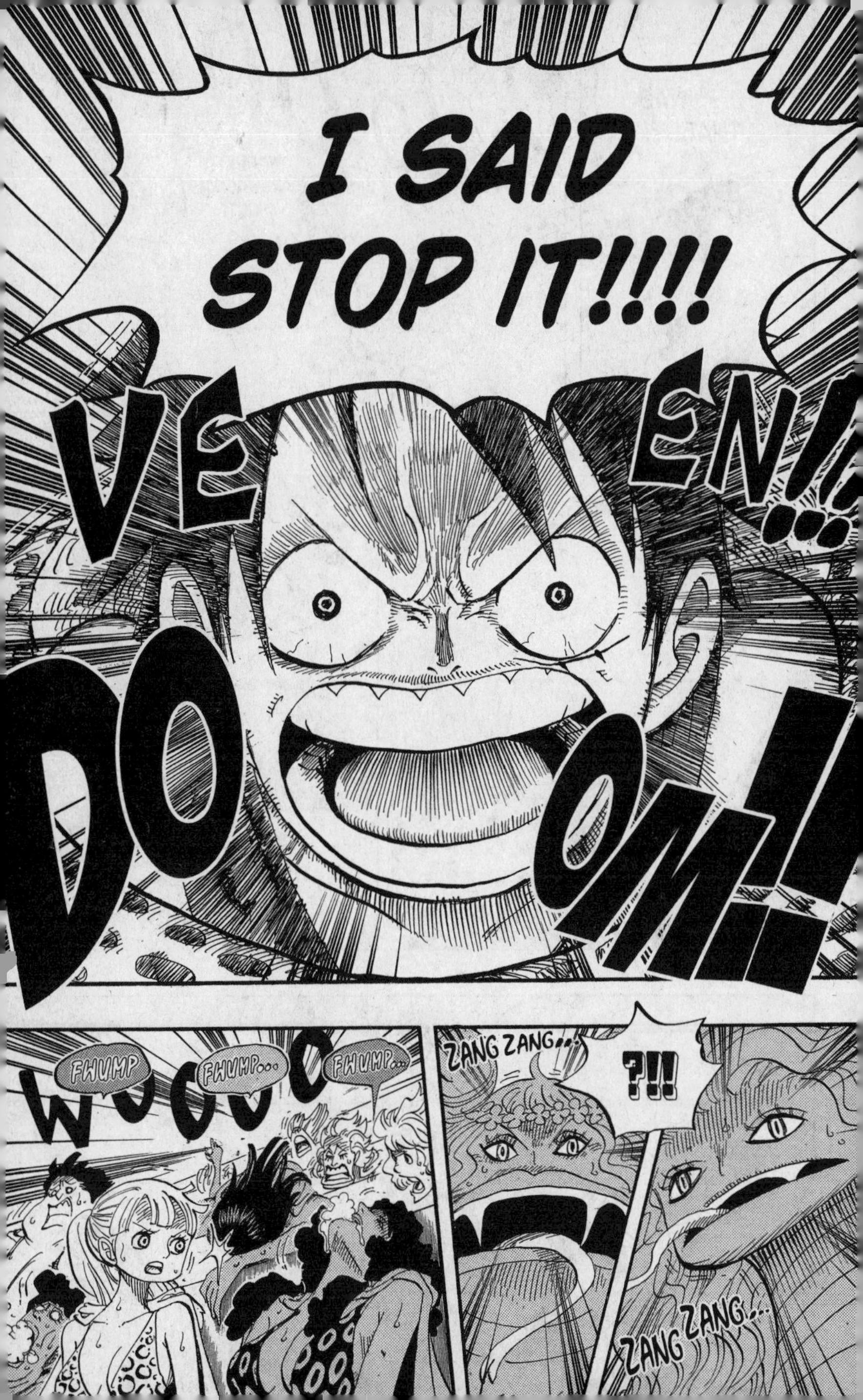
I SAID STOP IT!!!!
VE
EN!!...
DO
ON!!
ZANG ZANG...
?!!
ZANG ZANG...
FWUMP
FWUMP...
FWUMP...

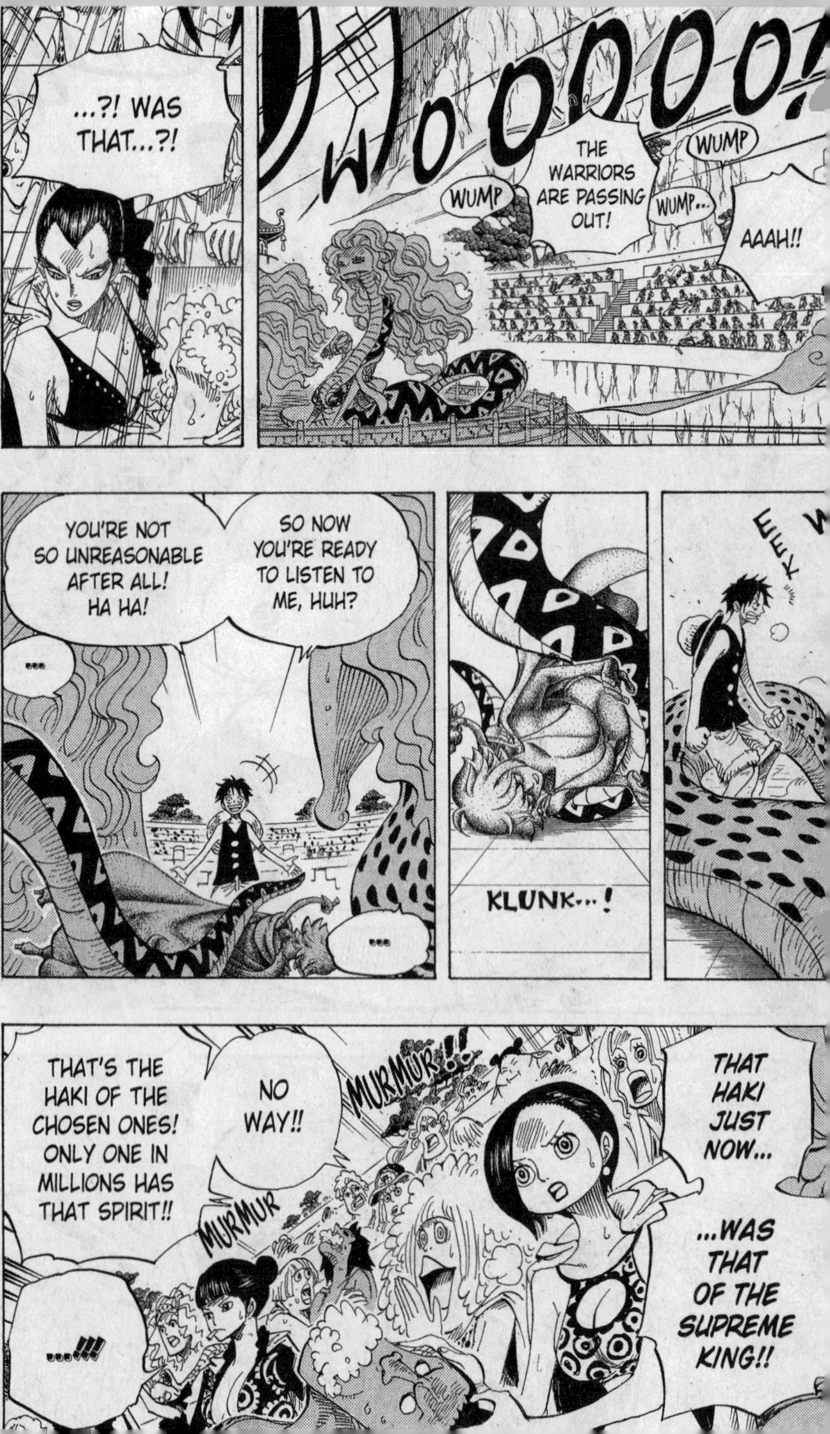
WHOOOOOO!
AAAH!!
WUMP
WUMP...
THE WARRIORS ARE PASSING OUT!
WUMP
...?! WAS THAT...?!
EEEK
KLUNK...!
SO NOW YOU'RE READY TO LISTEN TO ME, HUH?
YOU'RE NOT SO UNREASONABLE AFTER ALL! HA HA!
...
...
THAT HAKI JUST NOW...
...WAS THAT OF THE SUPREME KING!!
MURMUR
NO WAY!!
THAT'S THE HAKI OF THE CHOSEN ONES! ONLY ONE IN MILLIONS HAS THAT SPIRIT!!
MURMUR
...!!!

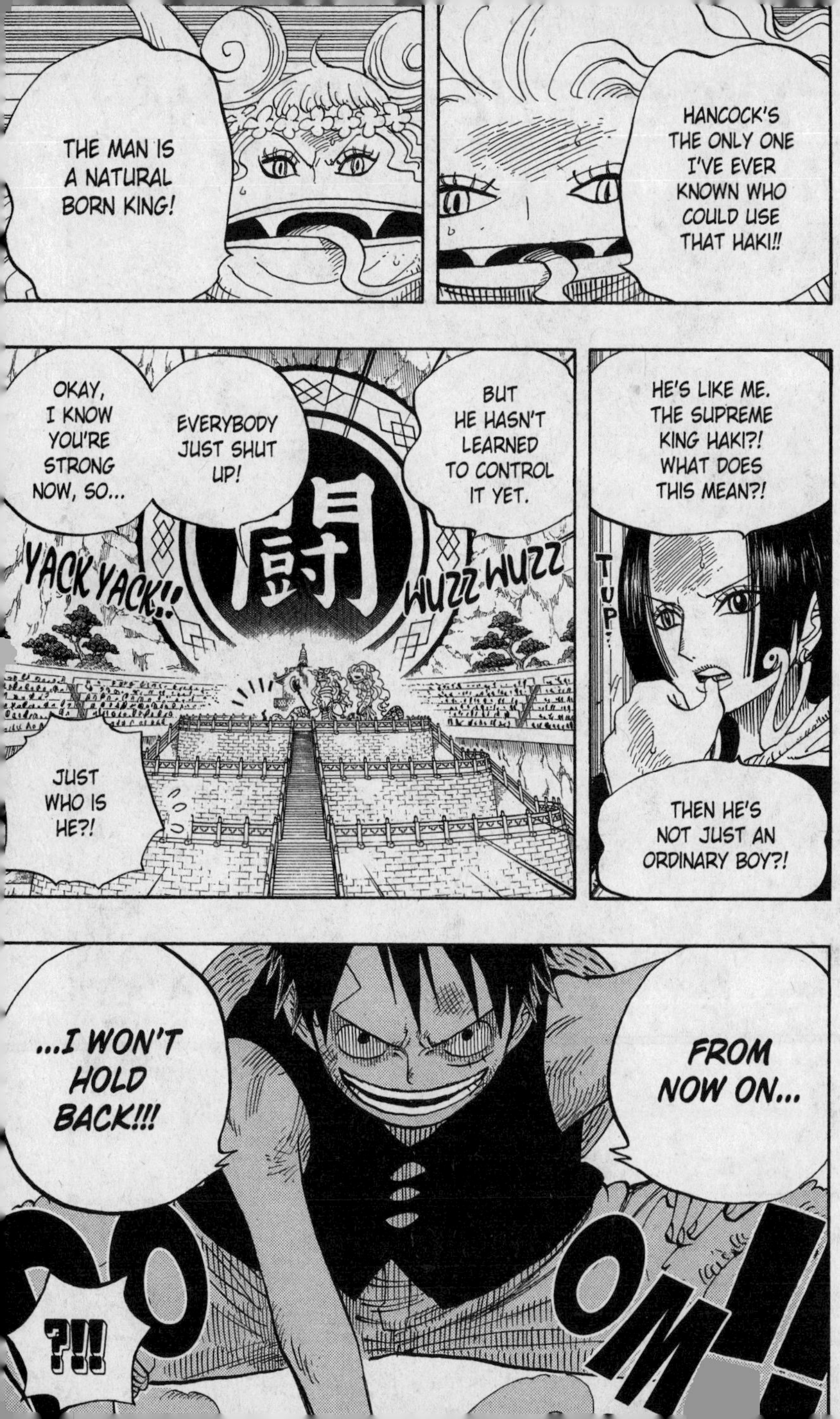
HANCOCK'S THE ONLY ONE I'VE EVER KNOWN WHO COULD USE THAT HAKI!!
THE MAN IS A NATURAL BORN KING!
HE'S LIKE ME. THE SUPREME KING HAKI?! WHAT DOES THIS MEAN?!
TUP
THEN HE'S NOT JUST AN ORDINARY BOY?!
BUT HE HASN'T LEARNED TO CONTROL IT YET.
WUZZ WUZZ
EVERYBODY JUST SHUT UP!
OKAY, I KNOW YOU'RE STRONG NOW, SO...
YACK YACK!!
JUST WHO IS HE?!
FROM NOW ON...
...I WON'T HOLD BACK!!!
OOM!
?!!

EYE OF THE GORGON

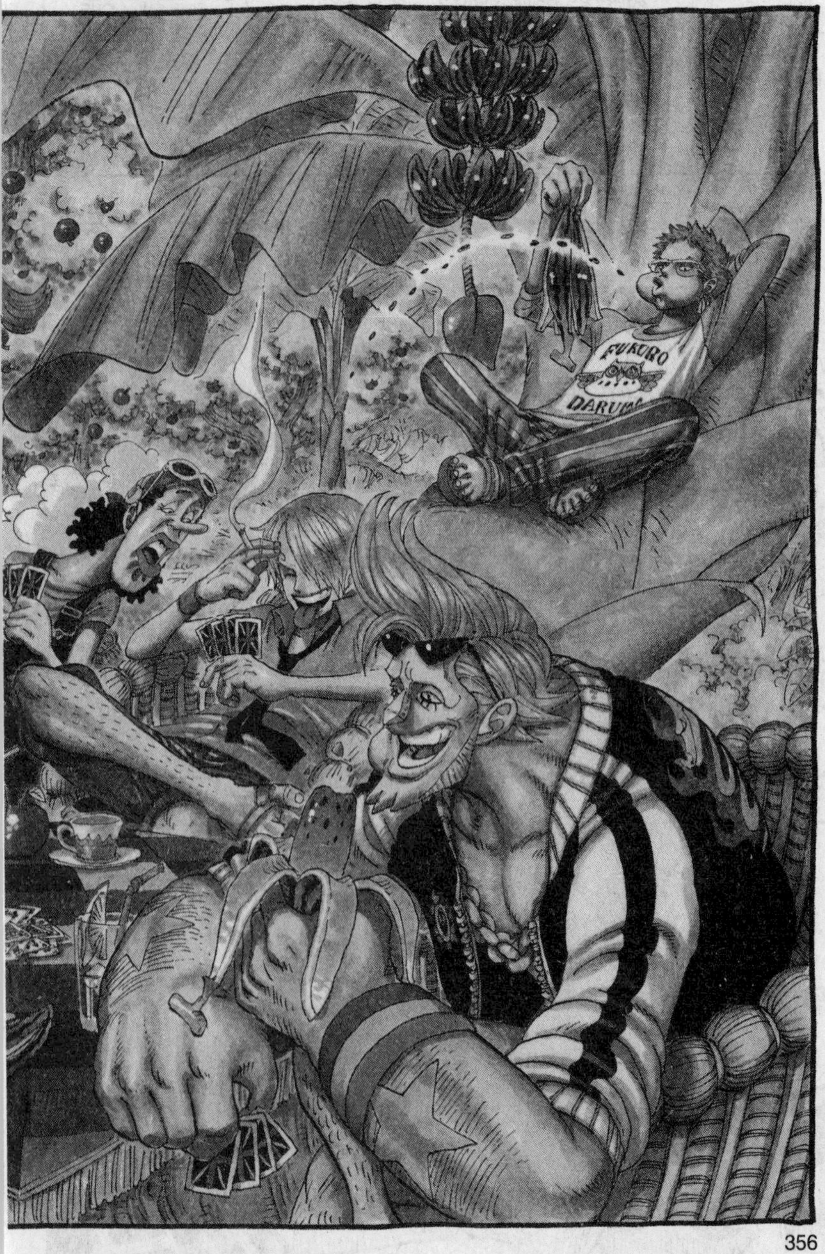
FUKURO
DARUMA

Chapter 520:

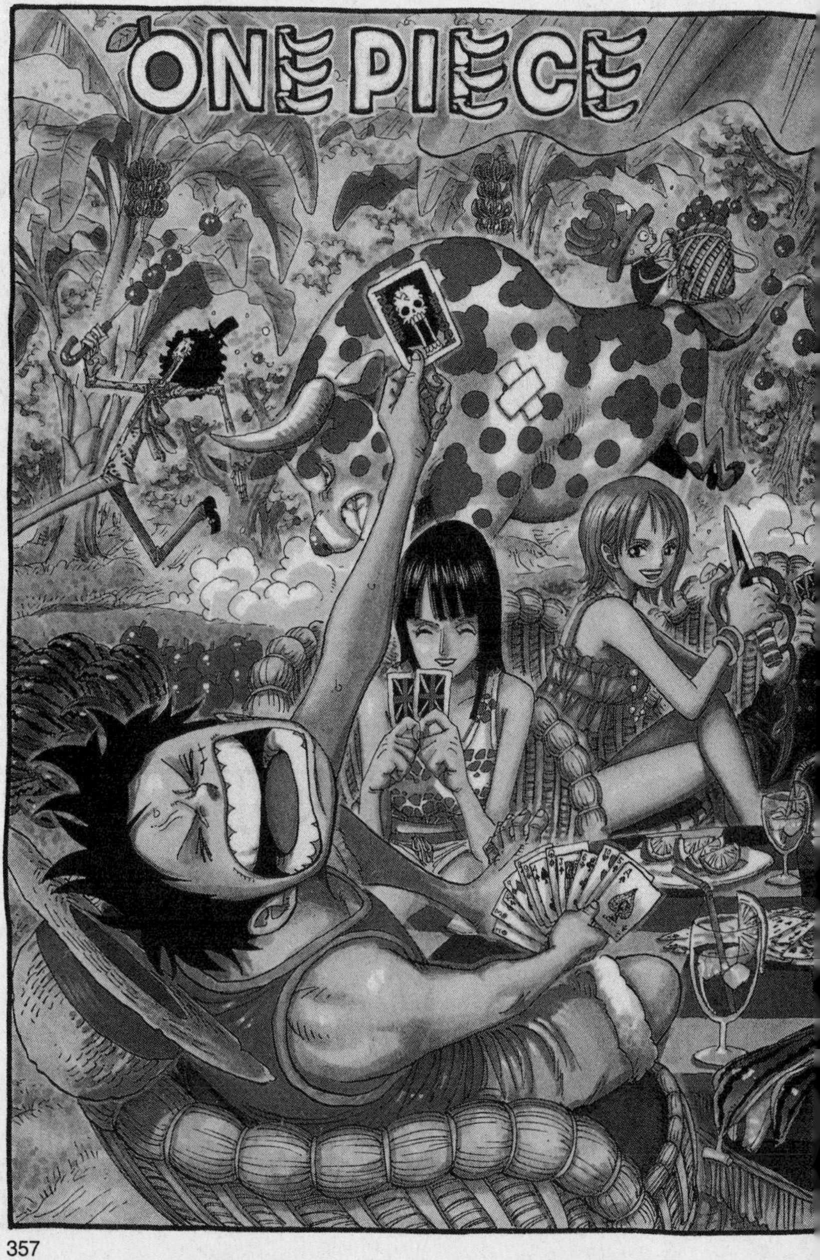
ONE PIECE

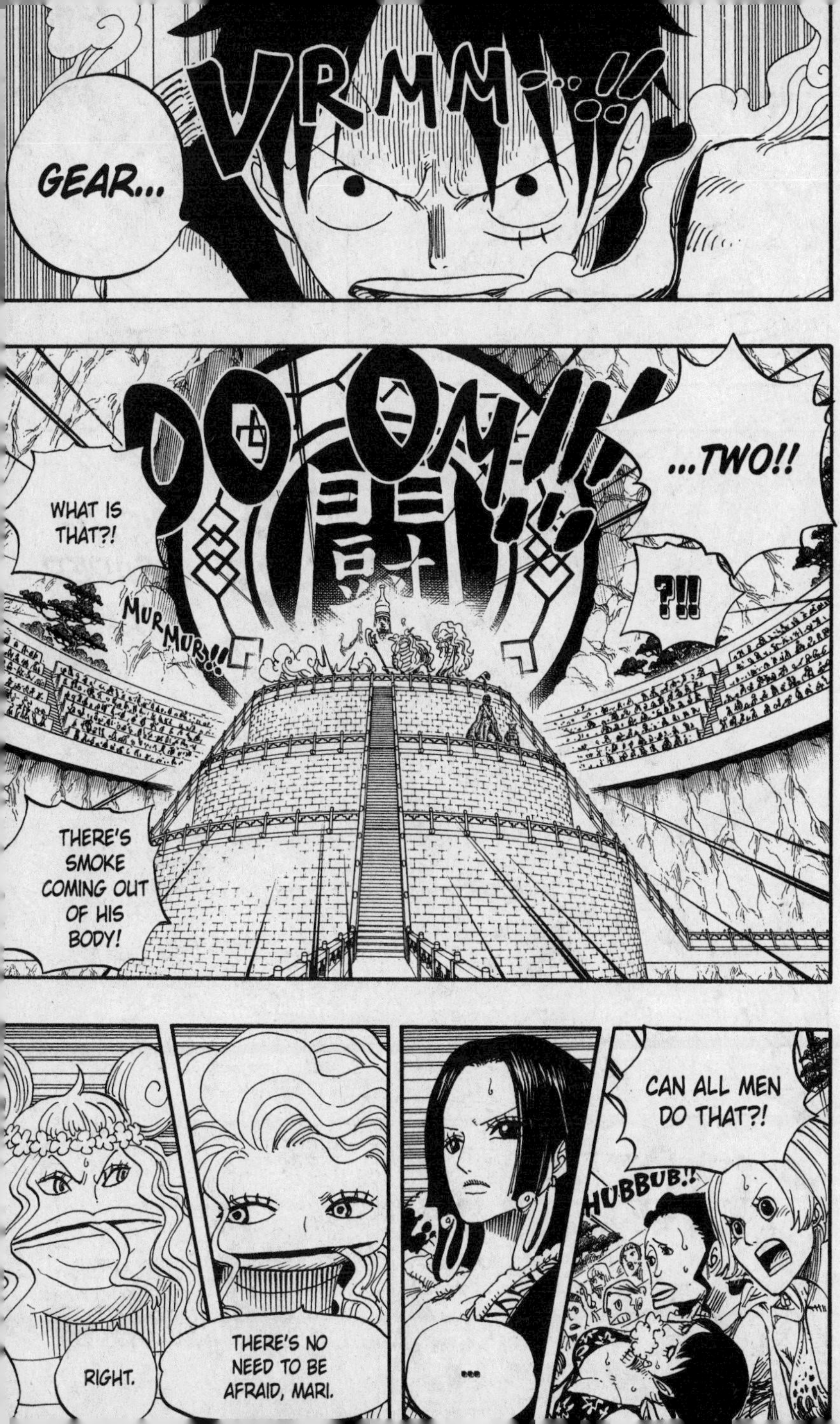
VRMM...!!
GEAR...
...TWO!!
?!!
DOOM!!
WHAT IS THAT?!
MURMUR!!
THERE'S SMOKE COMING OUT OF HIS BODY!
CAN ALL MEN DO THAT?!
HUBBUB!!
...
THERE'S NO NEED TO BE AFRAID, MARI.
RIGHT.

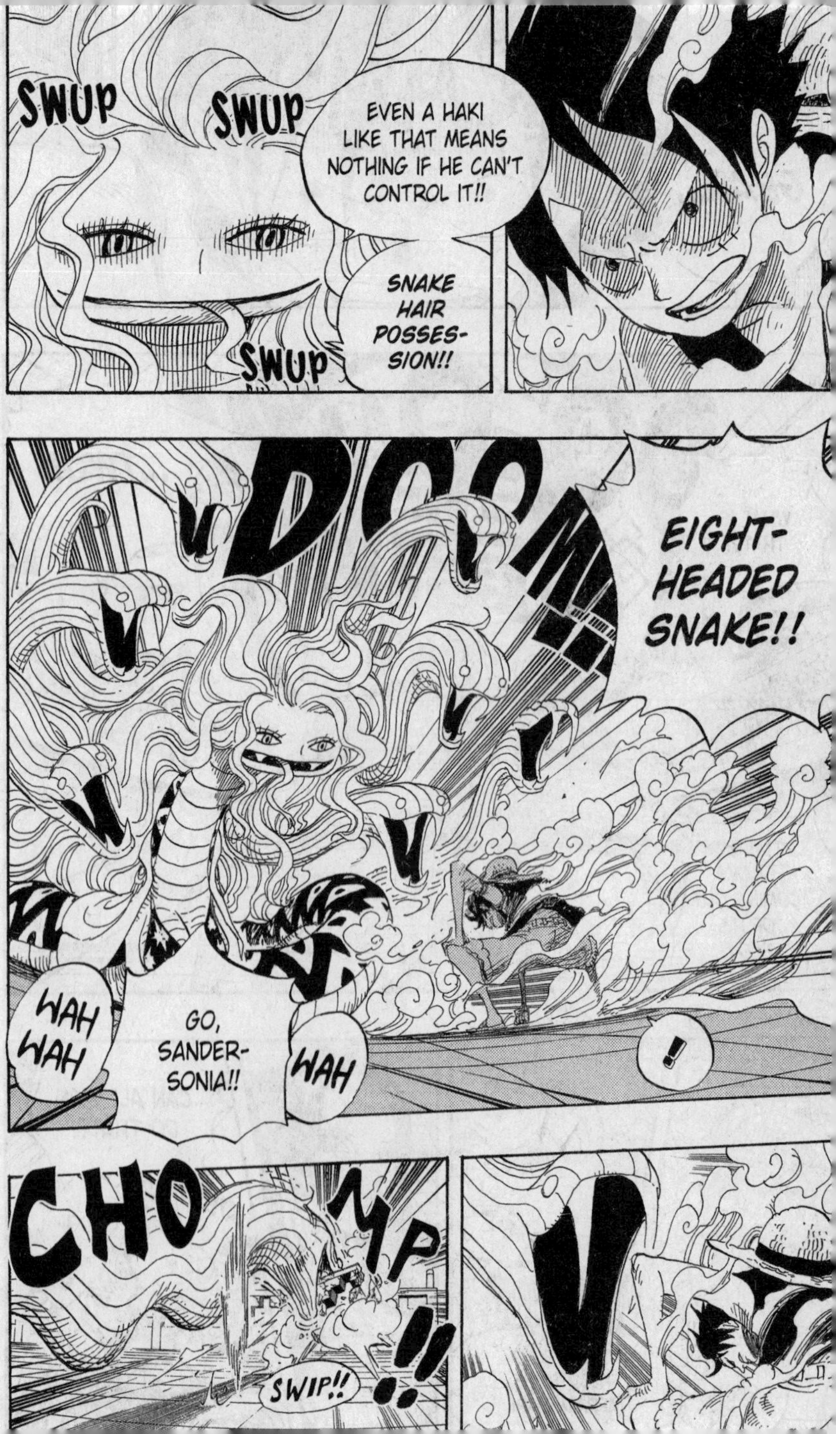
SWUP
SWUP
EVEN A HAKI LIKE THAT MEANS NOTHING IF HE CAN'T CONTROL IT!!
SNAKE HAIR POSSES-SION!!
SWUP
EIGHT-HEADED SNAKE!!
DOOM
!
WAH
GO, SANDER-SONIA!!
WAH WAH
CHOMP!!
SWIP!!

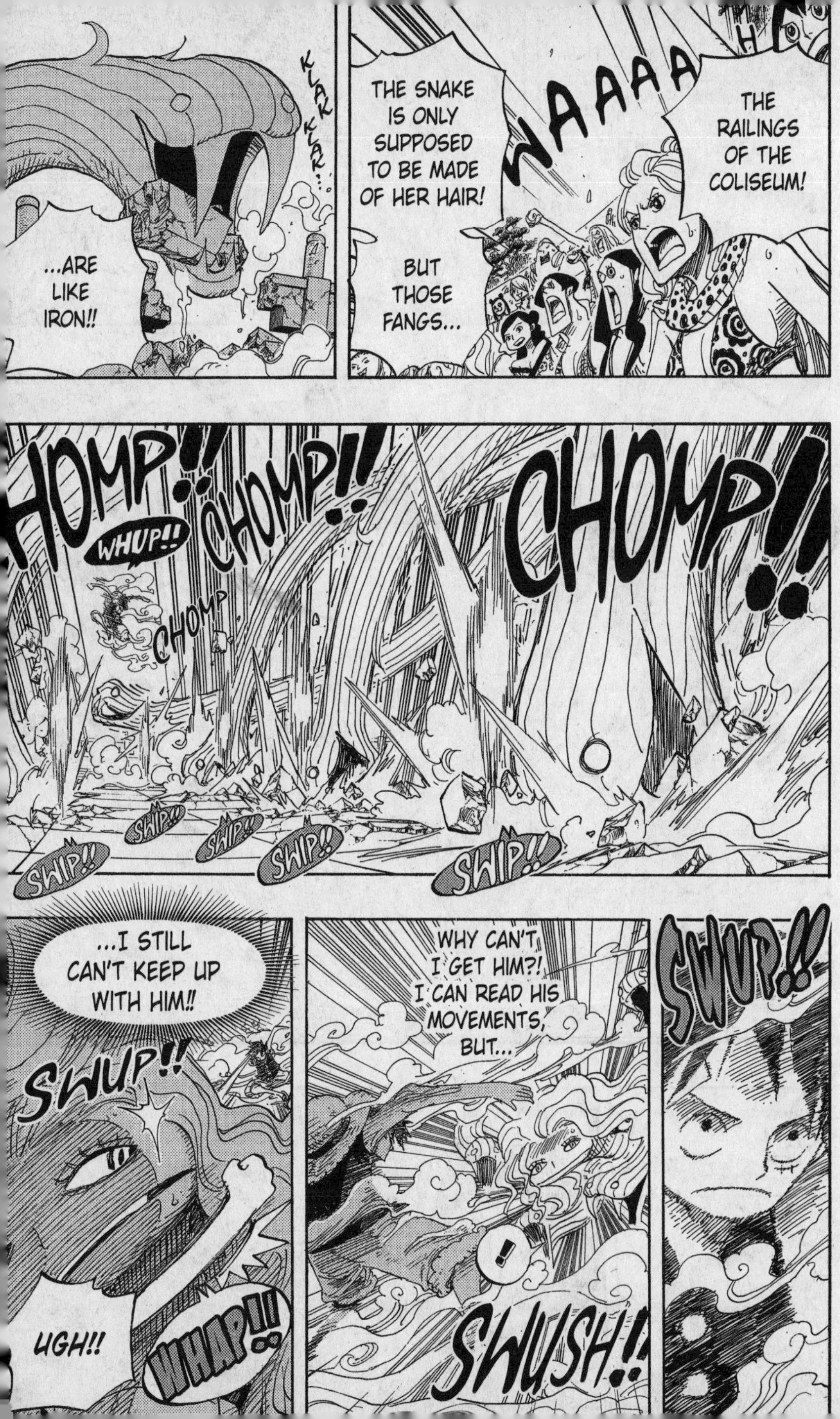
WAAAAA
THE RAILINGS OF THE COLISEUM!
THE SNAKE IS ONLY SUPPOSED TO BE MADE OF HER HAIR!
BUT THOSE FANGS...
KLAK KLAK...
...ARE LIKE IRON!!
CHOMP!!
CHOMP!!
CHOMP!!
WHUP!!
CHOMP
SWIP!!
SWIP!!
SWIP!!
SWIP!!
SWIP!!
SWUP!!
WHY CAN'T I GET HIM?! I CAN READ HIS MOVEMENTS, BUT...
!
SWUSH!!
...I STILL CAN'T KEEP UP WITH HIM!!
SWUP!!
UGH!!
WHAP!!

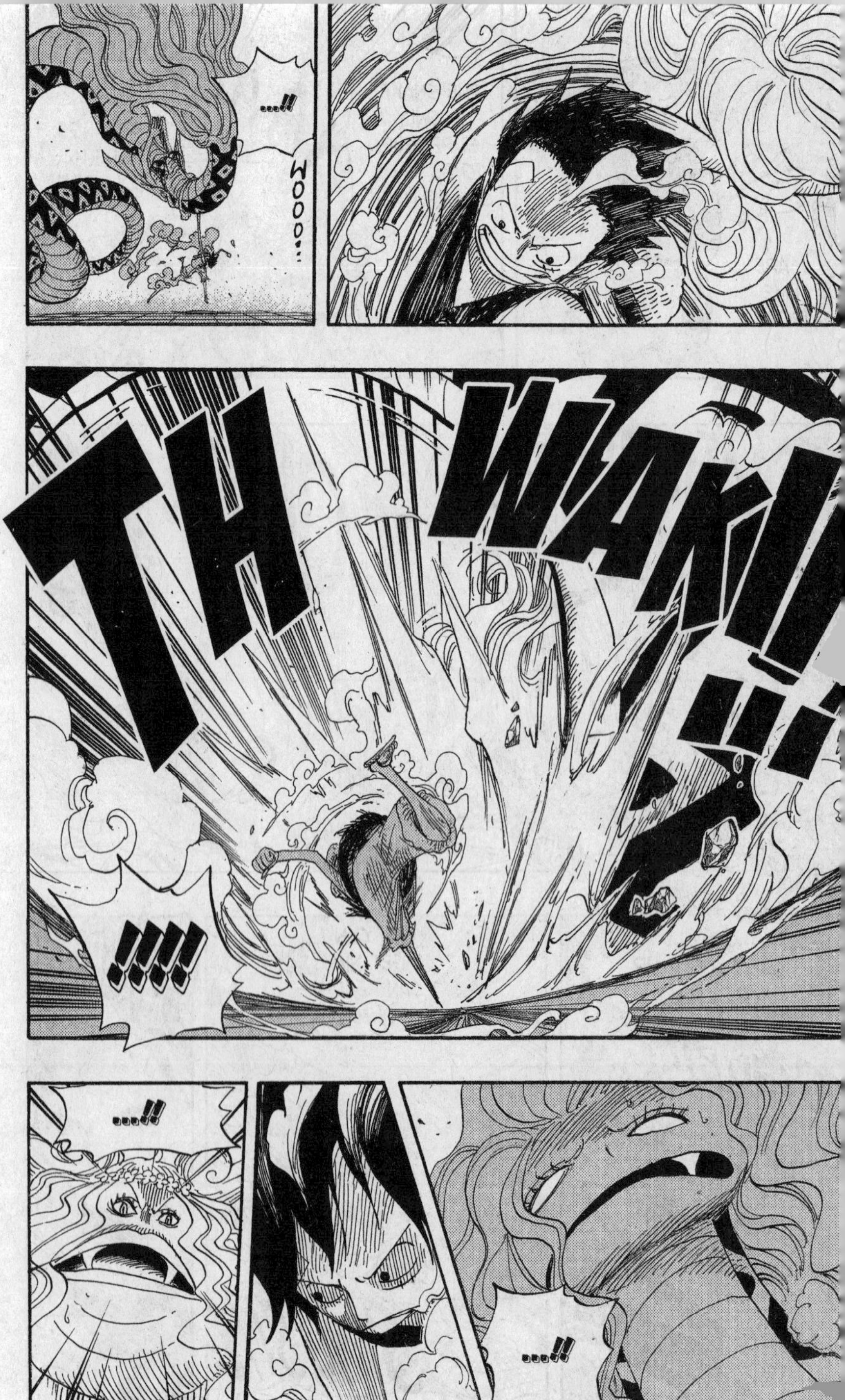

WOOOO...!!
...!!
THWAK!!!
!!!!
...!!
...!!

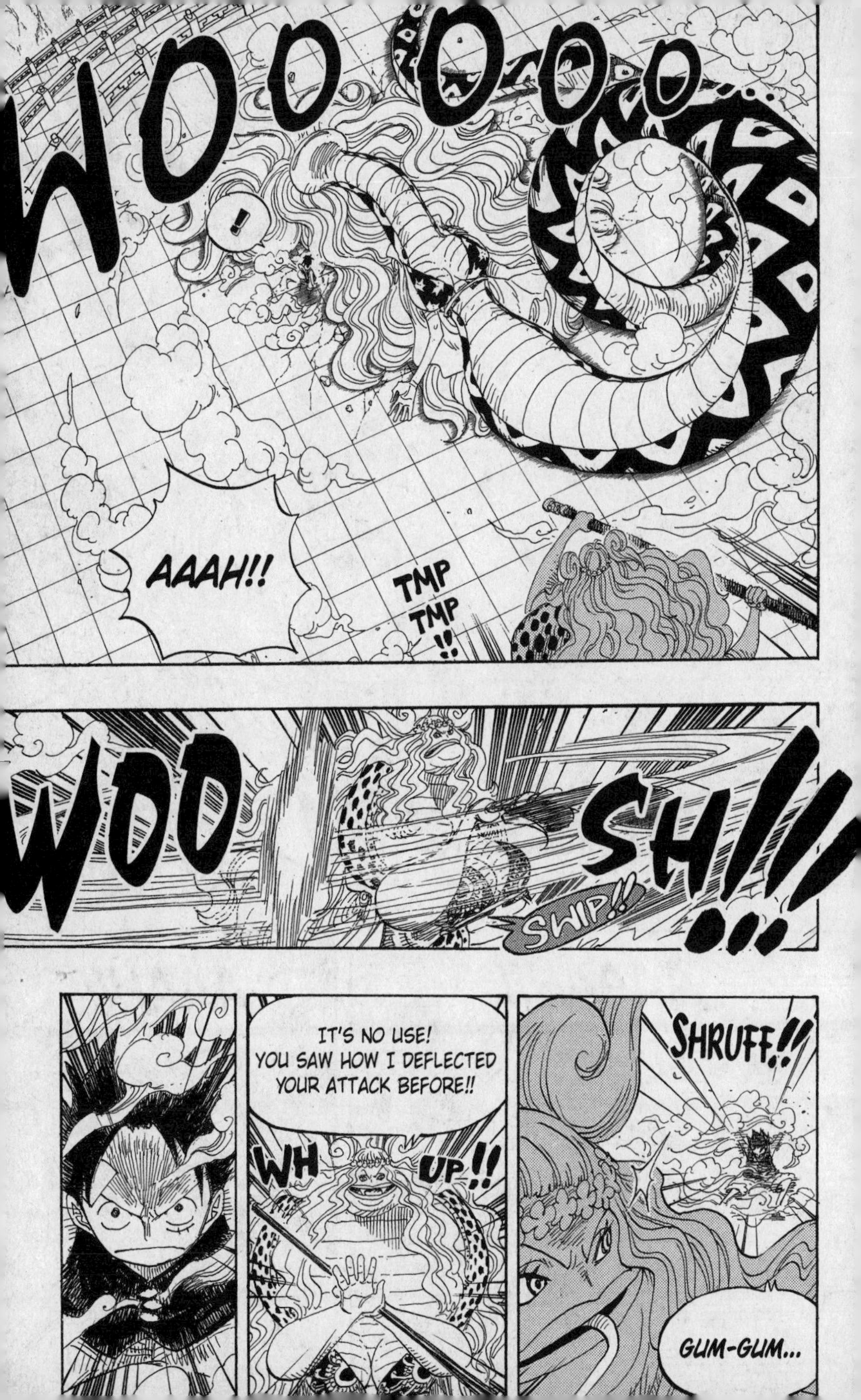
WOOOOOO...
!
TMP TMP!!
AAAH!!
WOOSH!!
SWIP!!
SHRUFF!!
GUM-GUM...
IT'S NO USE! YOU SAW HOW I DEFLECTED YOUR ATTACK BEFORE!!
WHUP!!

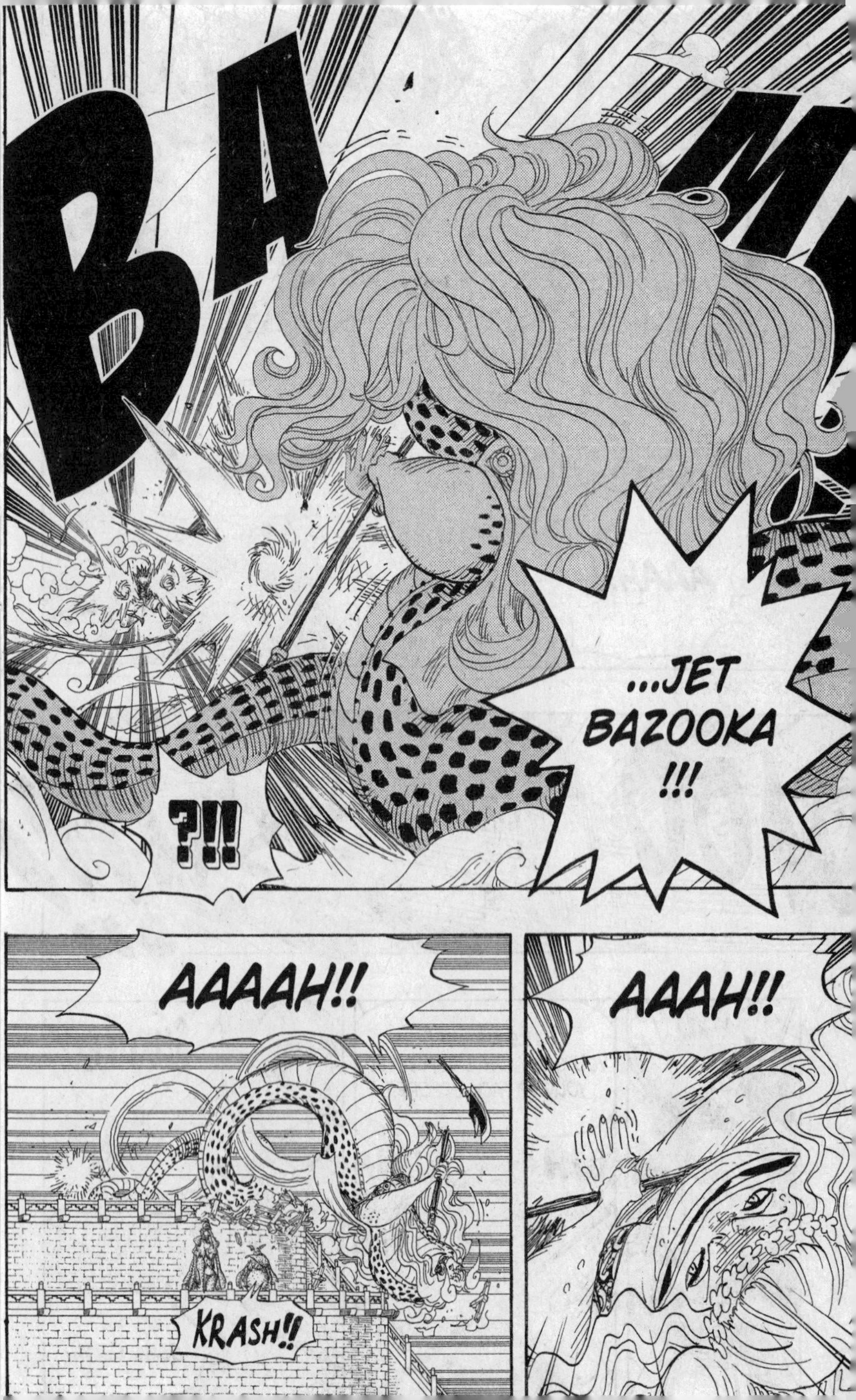
BAM
...JET BAZOOKA!!!
?!!
AAAH!!
AAAAH!!
KRASH!!

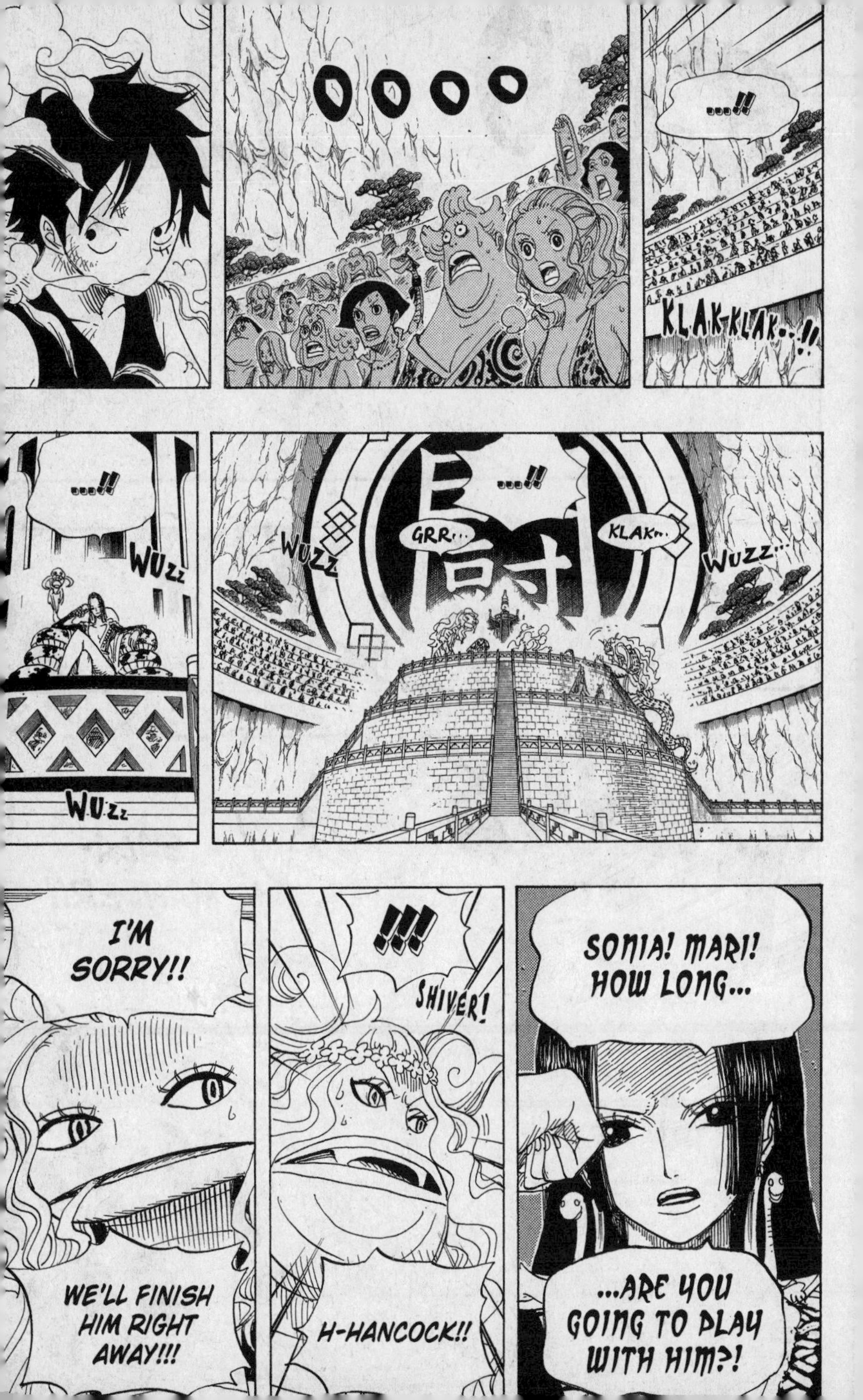
...!!
KLAK-KLAK..!!
...!!
WUZZ...
KLAK...
GRR...
WUZZ
...!!
WUZZ
WUZZ
SONIA! MARI! HOW LONG...
...ARE YOU GOING TO PLAY WITH HIM?!
!!!
SHIVER!
H-HANCOCK!!
I'M SORRY!!
WE'LL FINISH HIM RIGHT AWAY!!!

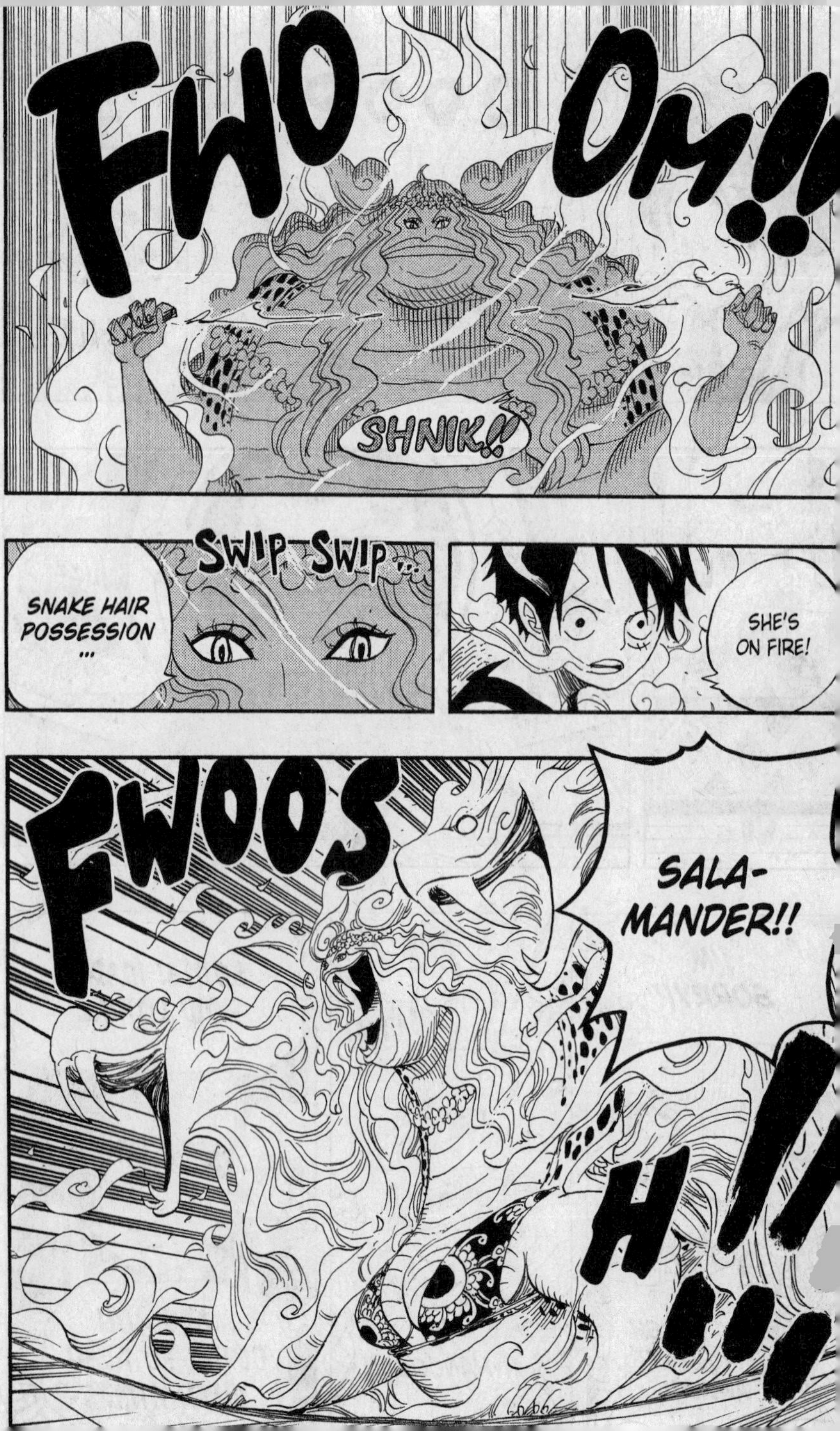
FWOOM!!
SHNIK!!
SHE'S ON FIRE!
SWIP SWIP...
SNAKE HAIR POSSESSION ...
SALA-MANDER!!
FWOOSH!!!

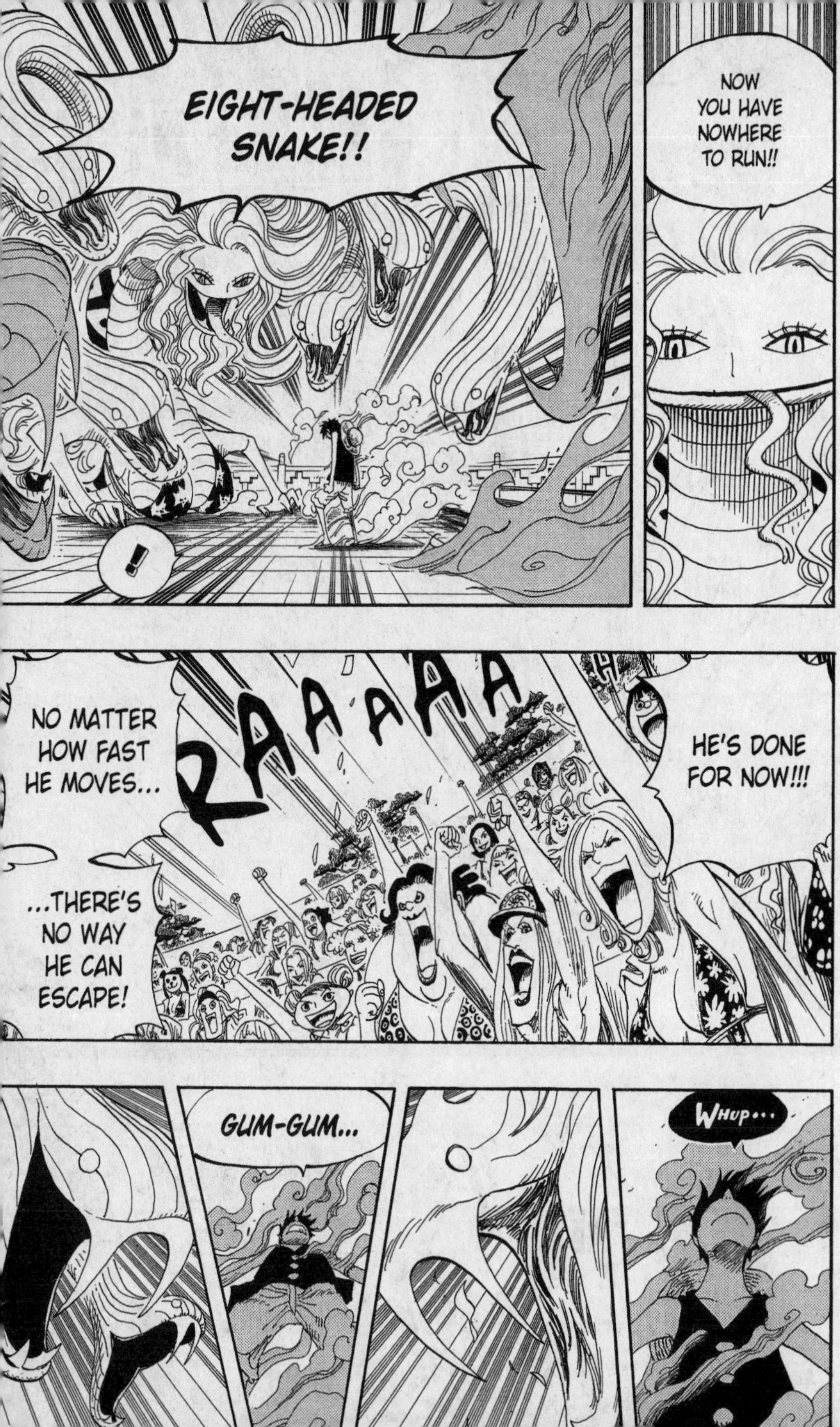
NOW YOU HAVE NOWHERE TO RUN!!
EIGHT-HEADED SNAKE!!
!
HE'S DONE FOR NOW!!!
RAAAAA
NO MATTER HOW FAST HE MOVES...
...THERE'S NO WAY HE CAN ESCAPE!
WHUP...
GUM-GUM...

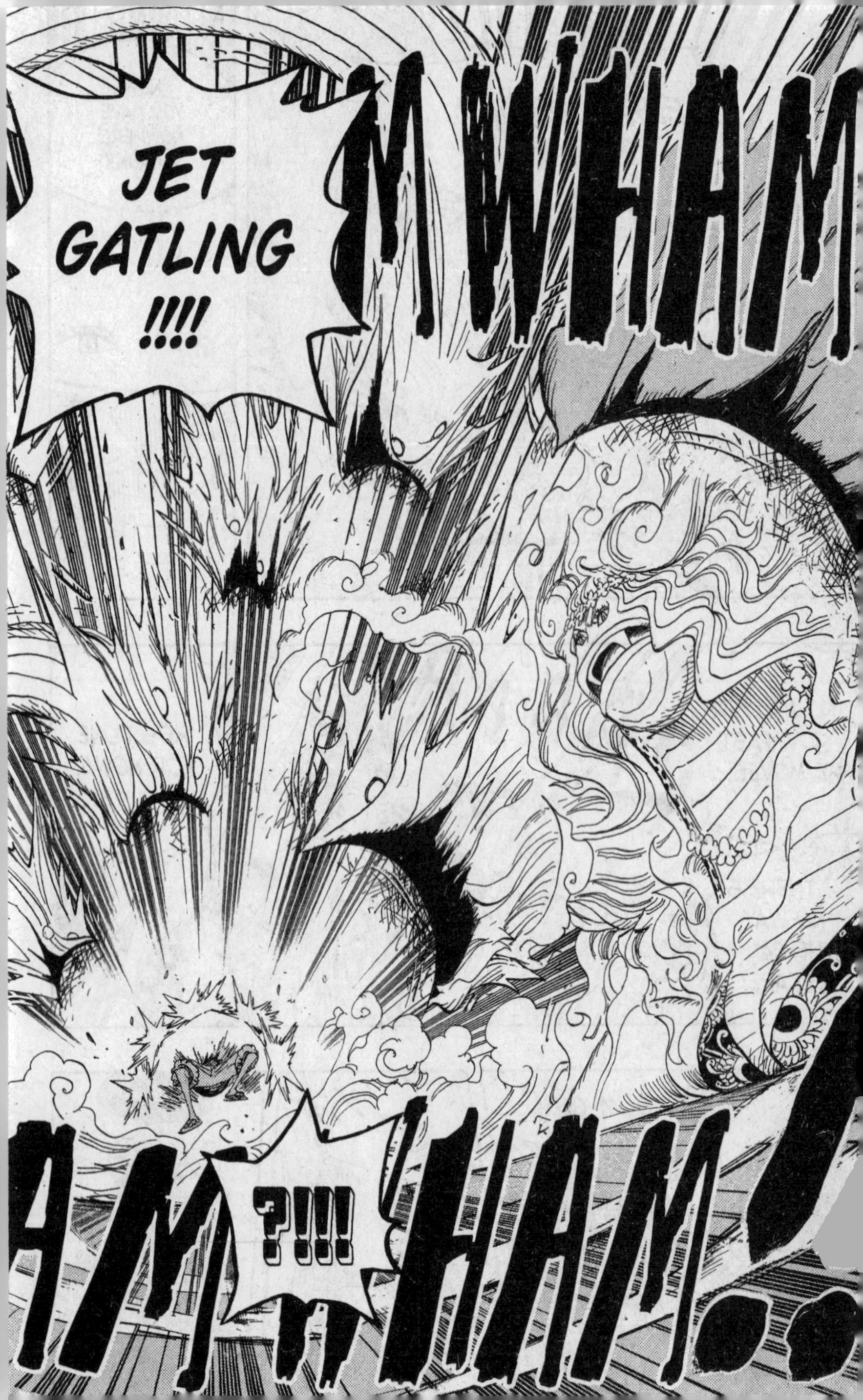
WHAM
JET GATLING !!!!
WHAM...
?!!!
AM...

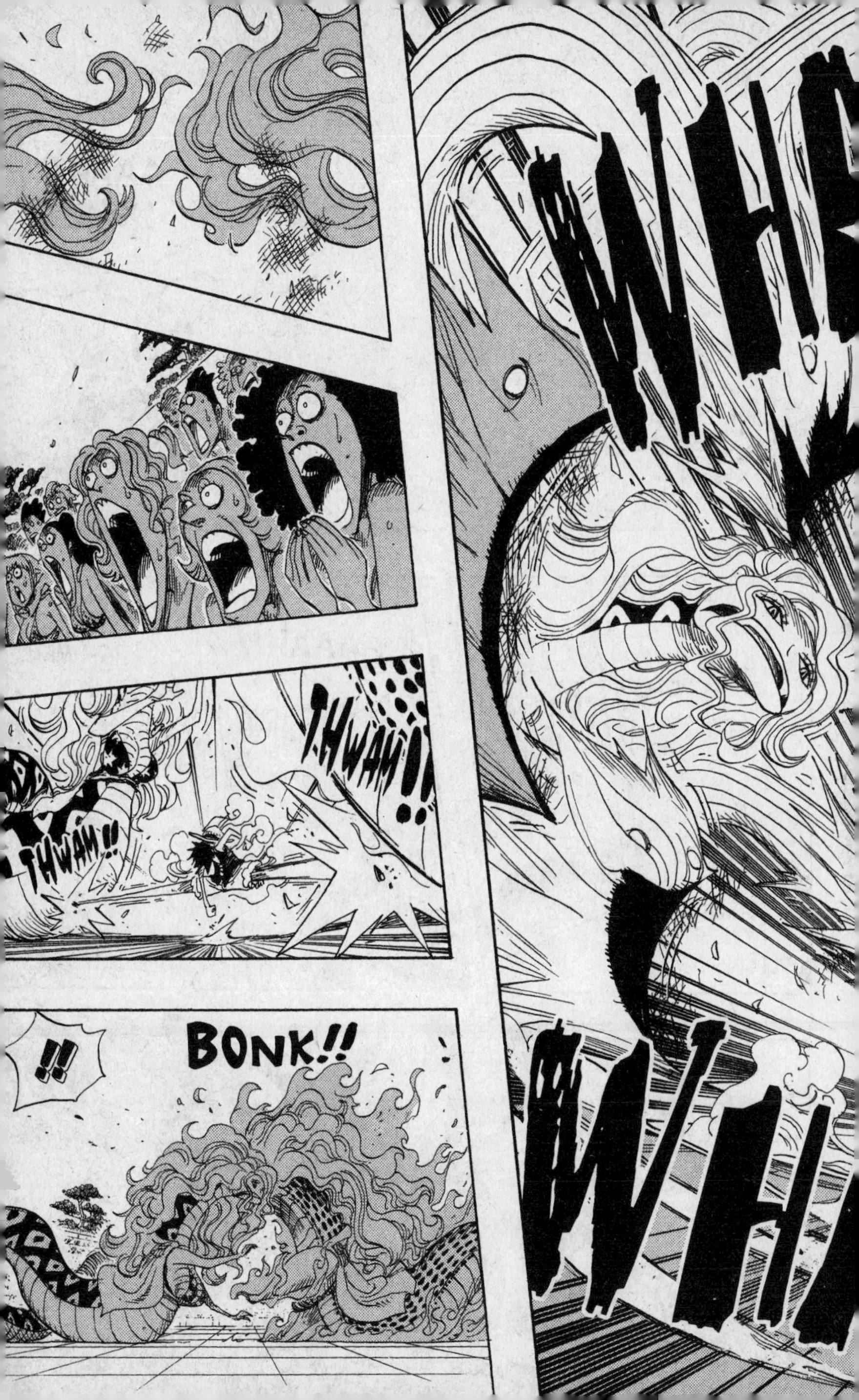
THWAM!!
THWAM!!
BONK!!
!!

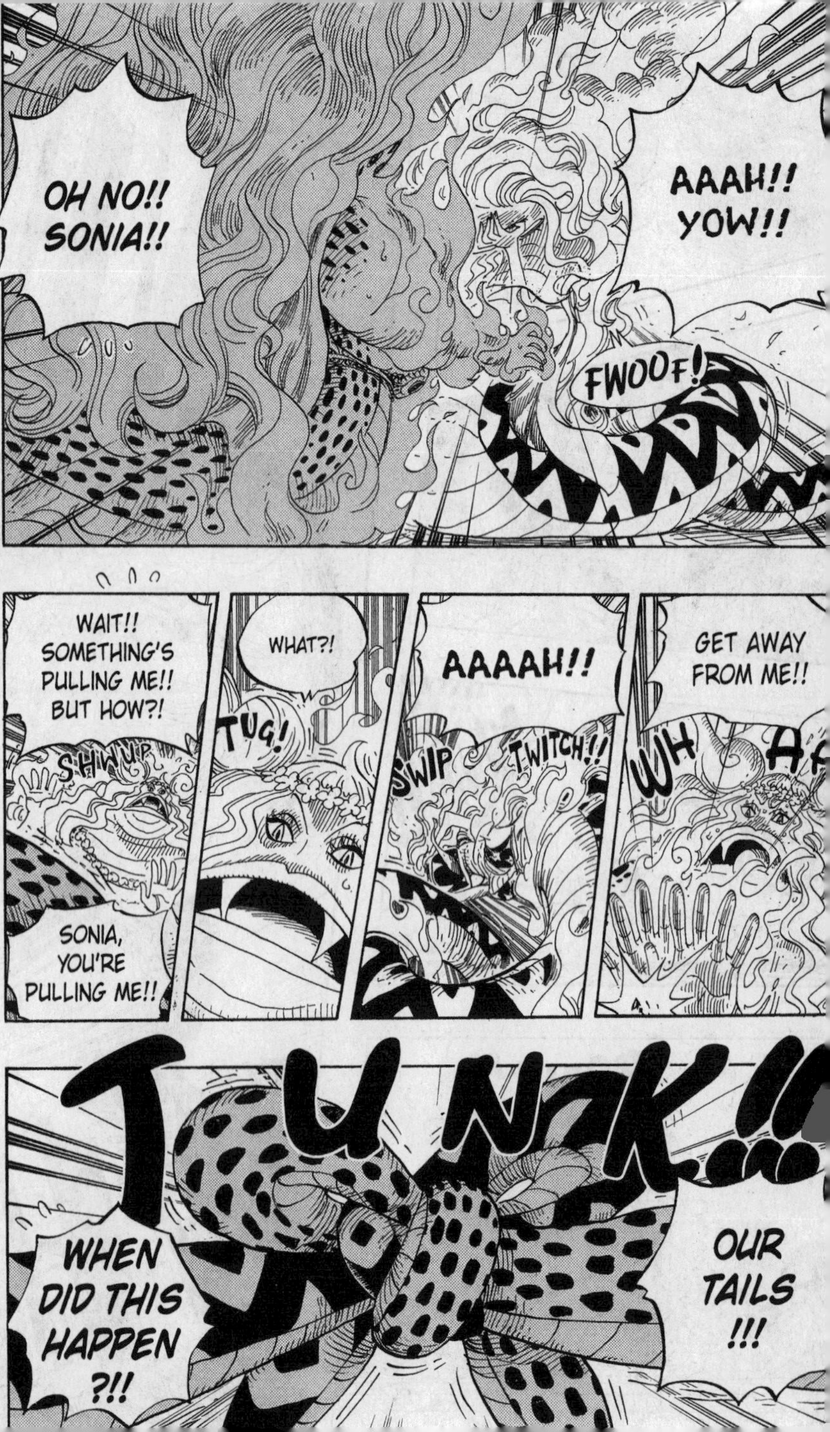
AAAH!! YOW!!
FWOOF!
OH NO!! SONIA!!
GET AWAY FROM ME!!
WH
AAAAH!!
TWITCH!!
SWIP
WHAT?!
TUG!
WAIT!! SOMETHING'S PULLING ME!! BUT HOW?!
SHWUP
SONIA, YOU'RE PULLING ME!!
TUNK!!
OUR TAILS!!!
WHEN DID THIS HAPPEN?!!

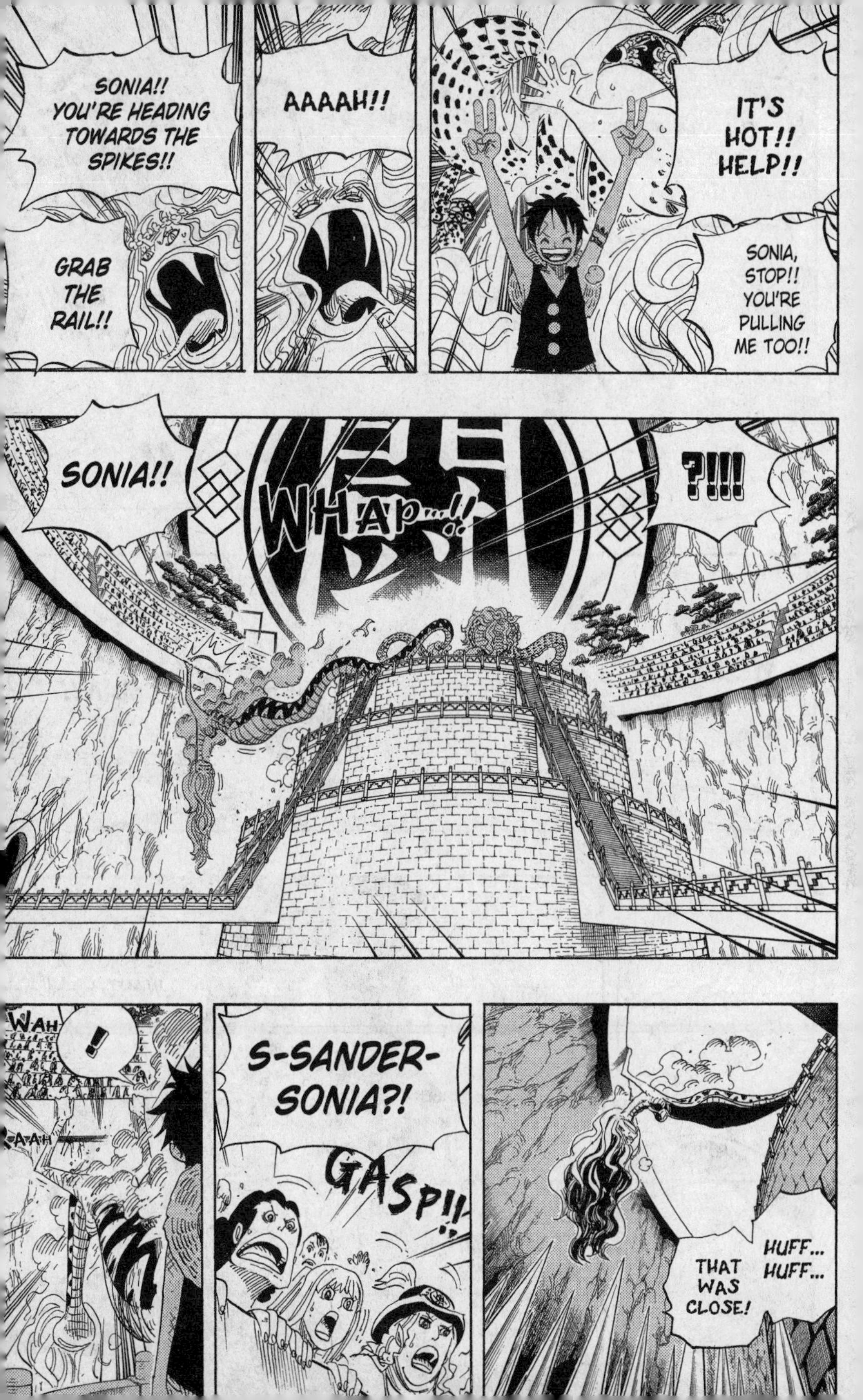
IT'S HOT!! HELP!!
SONIA, STOP!! YOU'RE PULLING ME TOO!!
AAAAH!!
SONIA!! YOU'RE HEADING TOWARDS THE SPIKES!!
GRAB THE RAIL!!
?!!!
SONIA!!
WHAP...!!
HUFF... HUFF...
THAT WAS CLOSE!
S-SANDER-SONIA?!
GASP!!
!
WAH
AAH

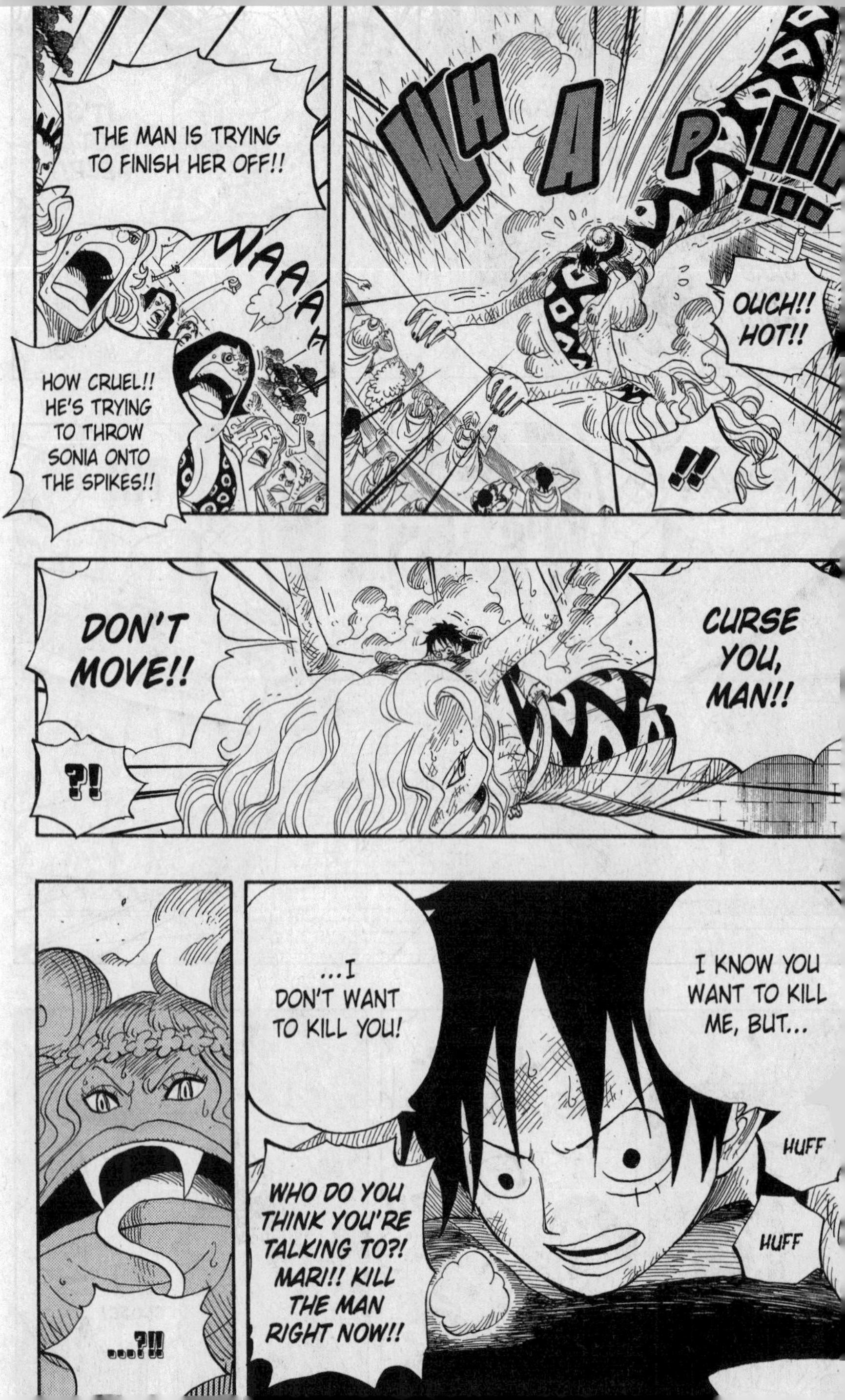
WHAP!!!
OUCH!! HOT!!
!!
THE MAN IS TRYING TO FINISH HER OFF!!
WAAAAH
HOW CRUEL!! HE'S TRYING TO THROW SONIA ONTO THE SPIKES!!
CURSE YOU, MAN!!
DON'T MOVE!!
?!
I KNOW YOU WANT TO KILL ME, BUT...
...I DON'T WANT TO KILL YOU!
HUFF
HUFF
WHO DO YOU THINK YOU'RE TALKING TO?! MARI!! KILL THE MAN RIGHT NOW!!
...?!!

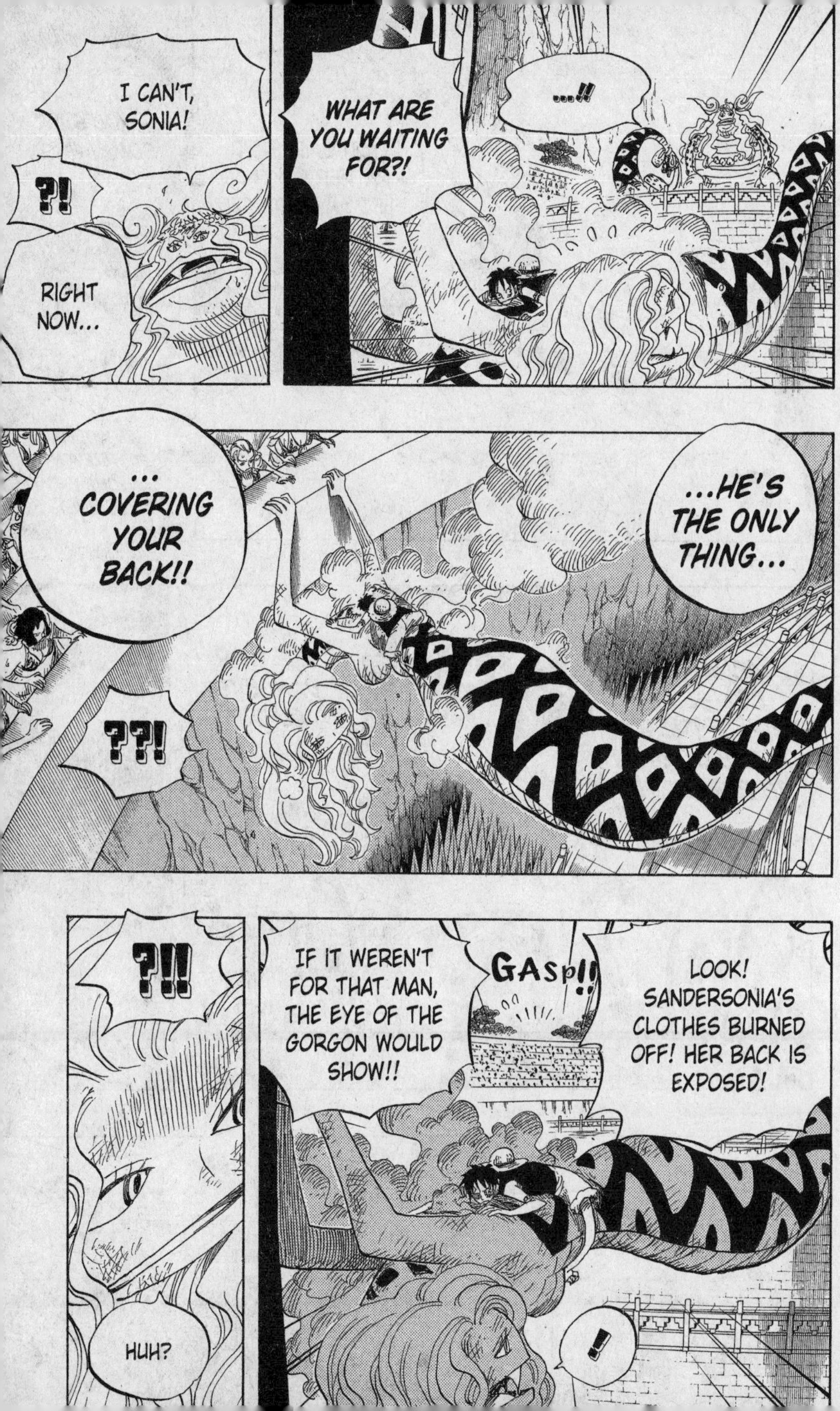
...!!
WHAT ARE YOU WAITING FOR?!
I CAN'T, SONIA!
?!
RIGHT NOW...
...HE'S THE ONLY THING...
...COVERING YOUR BACK!!
??!
LOOK! SANDERSONIA'S CLOTHES BURNED OFF! HER BACK IS EXPOSED!
GASp!!
IF IT WEREN'T FOR THAT MAN, THE EYE OF THE GORGON WOULD SHOW!!
!
?!!
HUH?

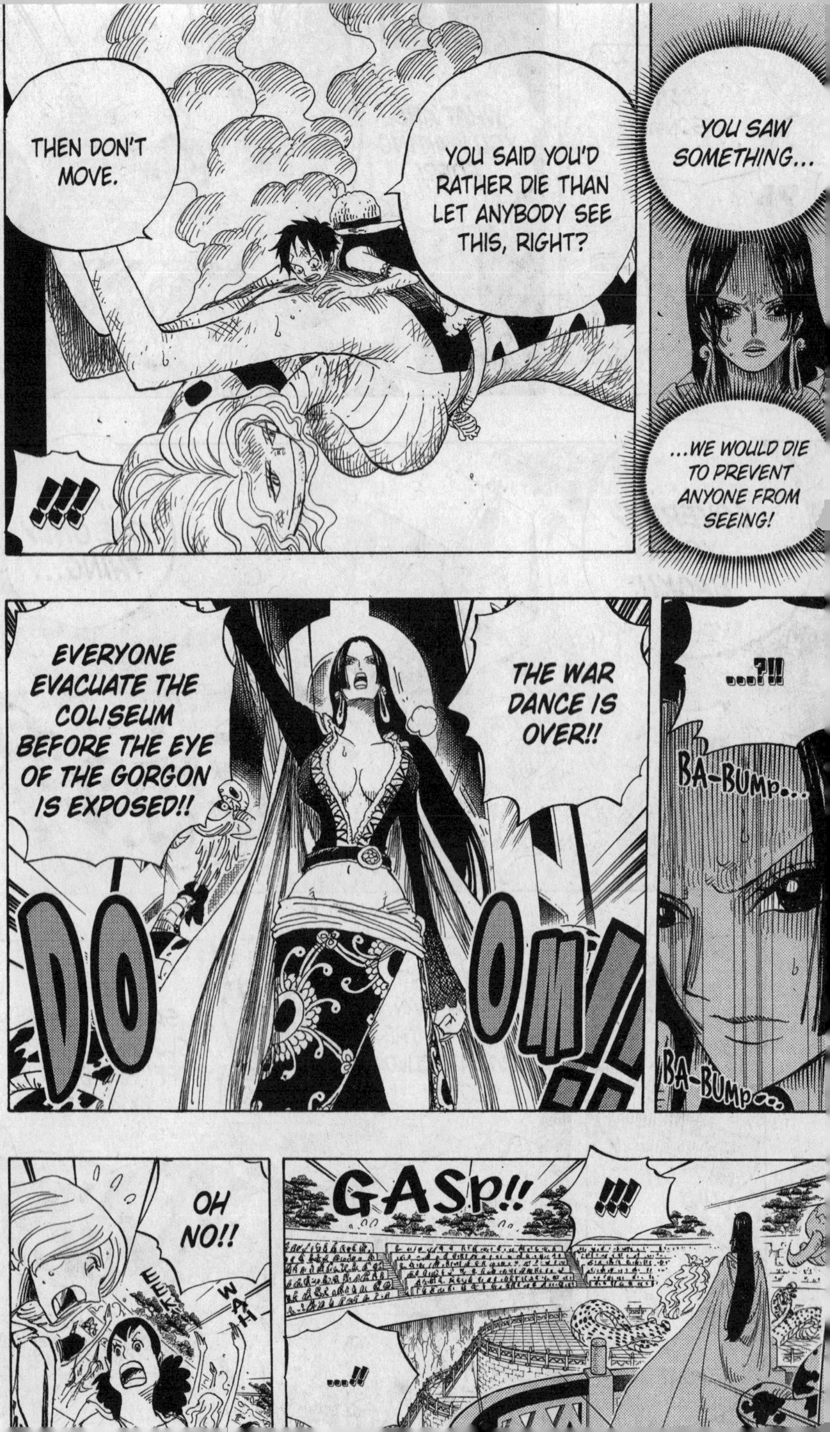
YOU SAW SOMETHING...
...WE WOULD DIE TO PREVENT ANYONE FROM SEEING!
YOU SAID YOU'D RATHER DIE THAN LET ANYBODY SEE THIS, RIGHT?
THEN DON'T MOVE.
!!!
...?!!
BA-BUMP...
BA-BUMP...
THE WAR DANCE IS OVER!!
EVERYONE EVACUATE THE COLISEUM BEFORE THE EYE OF THE GORGON IS EXPOSED!!
DO OM
GASP!!
!!!
...!!
OH NO!!
EEK
WAH

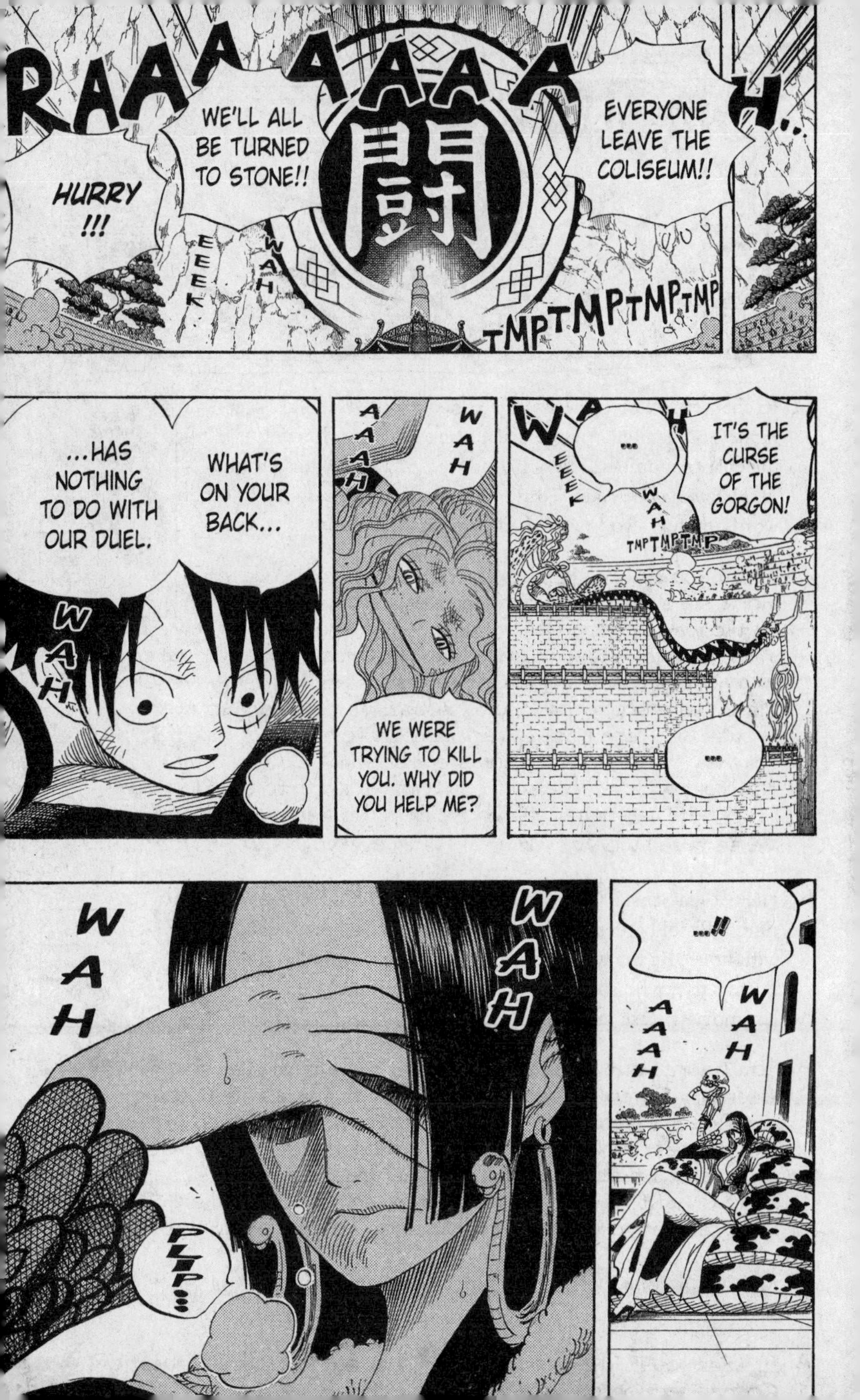
RAAAAAAAAH..
EVERYONE LEAVE THE COLISEUM!!
WE'LL ALL BE TURNED TO STONE!!
HURRY!!!
WAH
EEEEK
TMPTMPTMPTMP
WAH
IT'S THE CURSE OF THE GORGON!
...
EEEEK
WAH
TMPTMPTMP
...
WAH
AAAAH
WE WERE TRYING TO KILL YOU. WHY DID YOU HELP ME?
WHAT'S ON YOUR BACK...
...HAS NOTHING TO DO WITH OUR DUEL.
WAH
...!!
WAH
AAAAH
WAH
WAH
PLIP...

SBS Question Corner

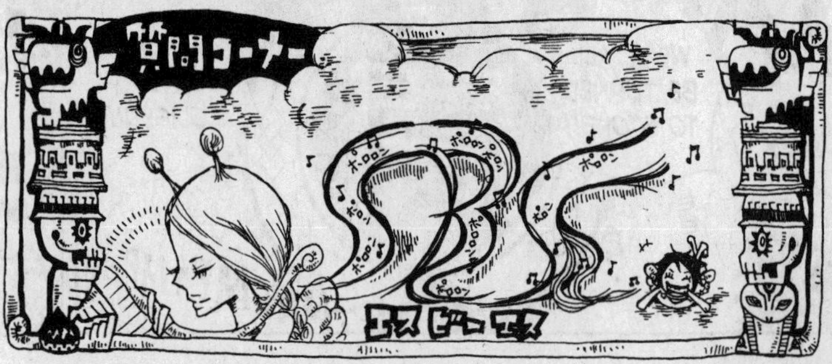
質問コーナー
エスビーエス

(Ena Taniguchi, Shimane)

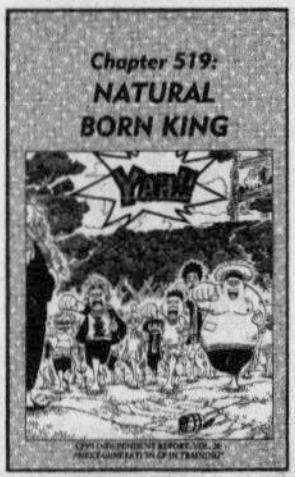
Chapter 519:
NATURAL BORN KING

Q: In chapter 519 of *One Piece*, you added tone to the title page, right? You painted one title page black too. After looking at the chapter number, I understood why. 519 is the final chapter of *Dragon Ball* by Akira Toriyama, an author you respect. In other words, that was your way of saying you'd caught up.

A: Wow, you figured it out. You're exactly right. Well, it's more like a milestone for me than a message.
By the way, *Dragon Ball* only has 42 volumes out, so some people already think I'm way beyond that. But *Dragon Ball* started off as a humorous comic and only had 15 pages per chapter, while One Piece was a story comic with 19 pages per chapter. So even though we were both in serialization for 12 years, I did 53 volumes. I'm sorry I made you spend so much extra money. I want to wrap up One Piece soon, but I don't want to abandon the story until I've tied up the loose ends. So please be patient with me because I won't stop until I wrap everything up.

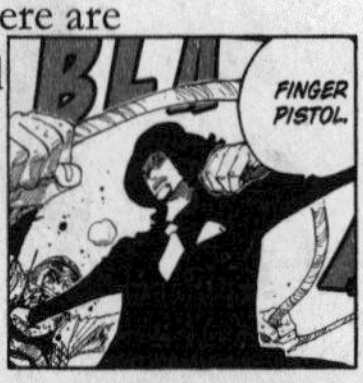
FINGER PISTOL.

Q: Hello, Oda Sensei. CP9 is extremely popular at my school. There are Finger Pistol battles every single day, so our bodies are riddled with holes. By the way, I heard you're the legendary Seven Powers user who surpasses even the Six Powers. What's the last move? Please tell me.

--CP608

A: You figured out my secret. Yes, that's right. I'm the legendary Seven Powers user. Six Powers means that you can use Finger Pistol, Moon Walk, Iron Body, Shave, Paper Art, and, uh... Tempest Kick! But there's one more special move that only I can use, and that's the Bother! When people are having a really serious fight, I get in between them and shout "Bother!" This gets really annoying really fast. So you got a problem with that?!

Q: Mr. Oda, if you were to take a trip, where would you go? ***Pop***!

--Junpei

A: !!... (See you in the next volume! Check out the special Question Corner section on page 188.)

Chapter 521:
HOOF OF THE CELESTIAL DRAGON

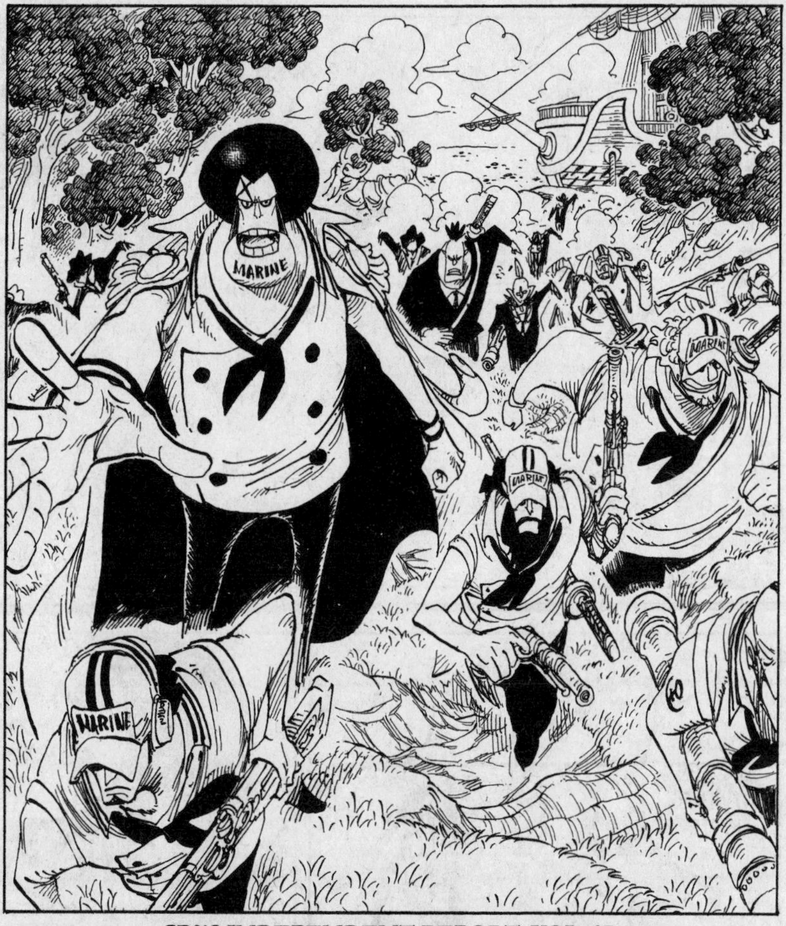
MARINE
MARINE
MARINE
MARINE

CP9'S INDEPENDENT REPORT, VOL. 27:
"PURSUERS ASHORE--CP9 CAPTURE MISSION"

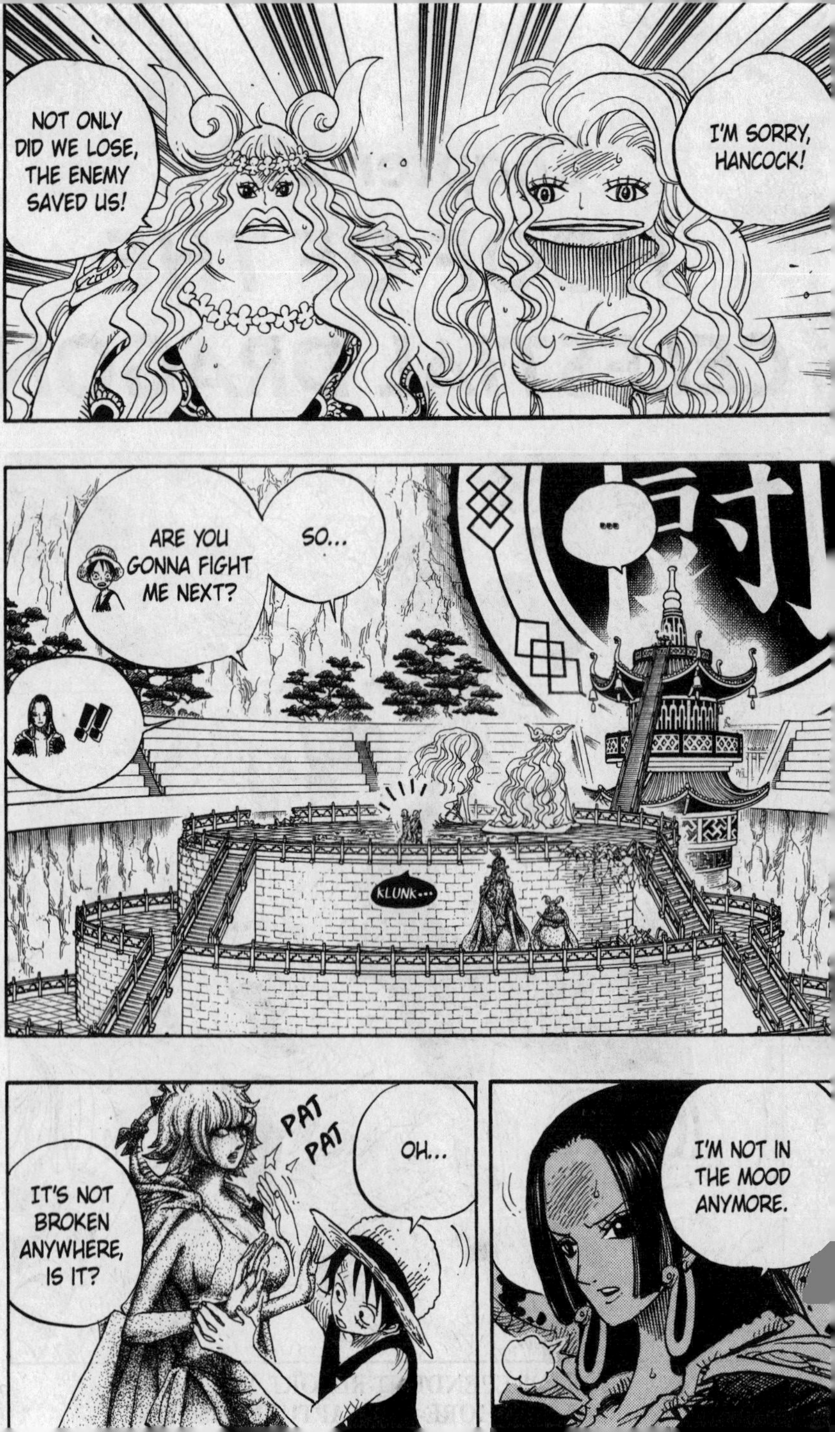
I'M SORRY, HANCOCK!
NOT ONLY DID WE LOSE, THE ENEMY SAVED US!
...
SO...
ARE YOU GONNA FIGHT ME NEXT?
!!
KLUNK...
I'M NOT IN THE MOOD ANYMORE.
OH...
PAT PAT
IT'S NOT BROKEN ANYWHERE, IS IT?

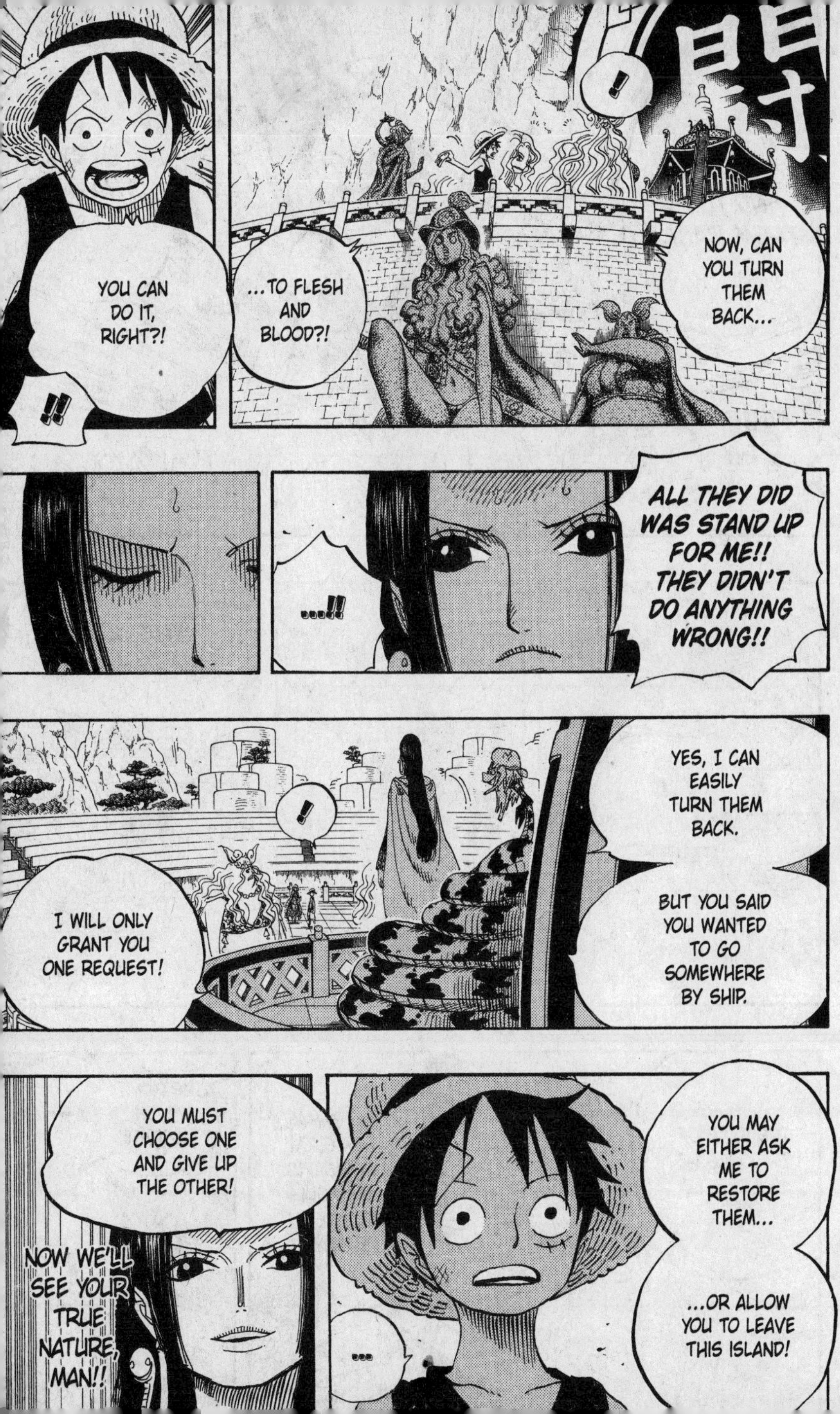

NOW, CAN YOU TURN THEM BACK...
...TO FLESH AND BLOOD?!
YOU CAN DO IT, RIGHT?!
!!
ALL THEY DID WAS STAND UP FOR ME!! THEY DIDN'T DO ANYTHING WRONG!!
...!!
YES, I CAN EASILY TURN THEM BACK.
BUT YOU SAID YOU WANTED TO GO SOMEWHERE BY SHIP.
I WILL ONLY GRANT YOU ONE REQUEST!
YOU MAY EITHER ASK ME TO RESTORE THEM...
...OR ALLOW YOU TO LEAVE THIS ISLAND!
...
YOU MUST CHOOSE ONE AND GIVE UP THE OTHER!
NOW WE'LL SEE YOUR TRUE NATURE, MAN!!

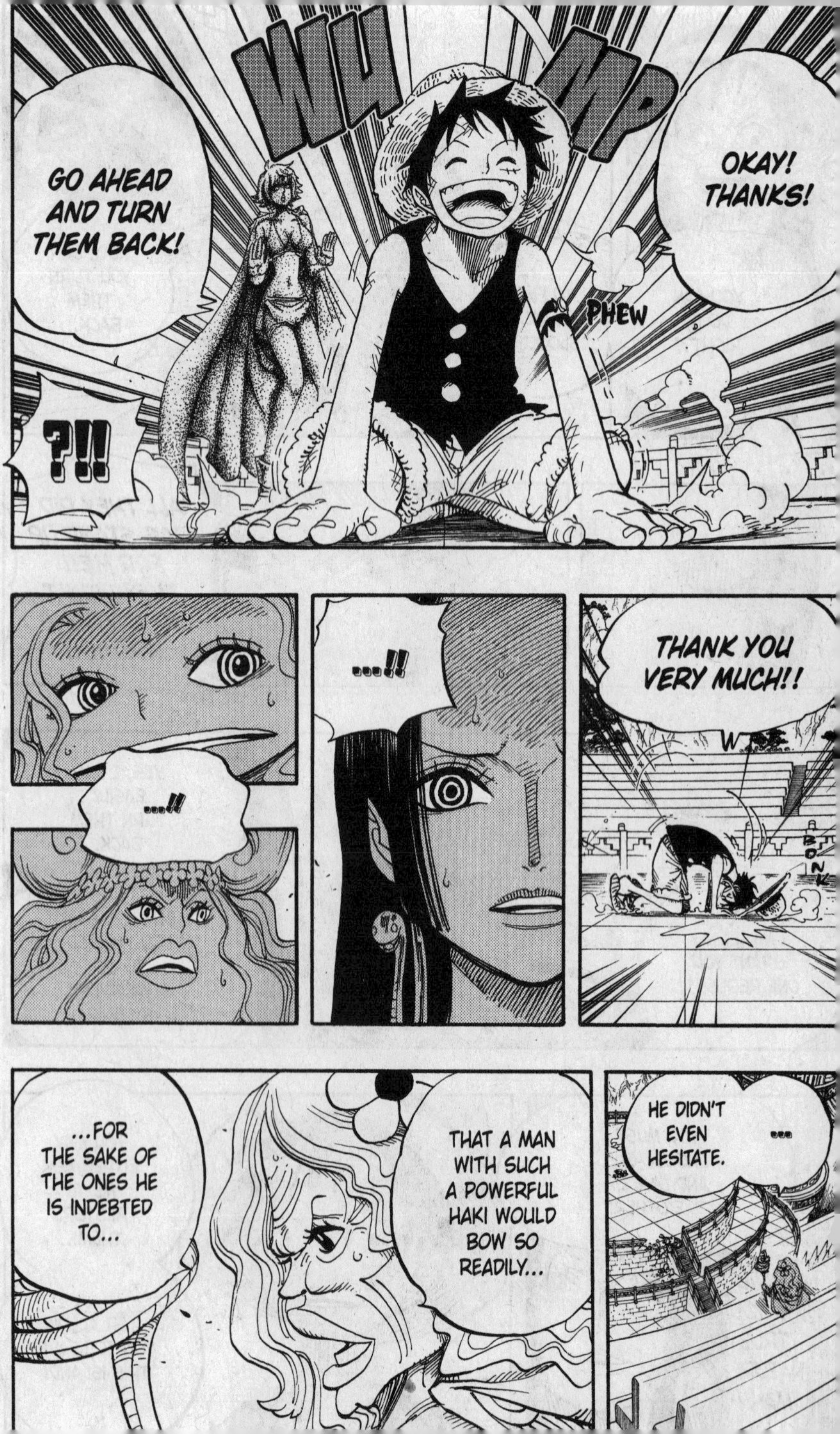
WHUMP
OKAY! THANKS!
PHEW
GO AHEAD AND TURN THEM BACK!
?!!
THANK YOU VERY MUCH!!
BONK
...!!
...!!
HE DIDN'T EVEN HESITATE.
...
THAT A MAN WITH SUCH A POWERFUL HAKI WOULD BOW SO READILY...
...FOR THE SAKE OF THE ONES HE IS INDEBTED TO...

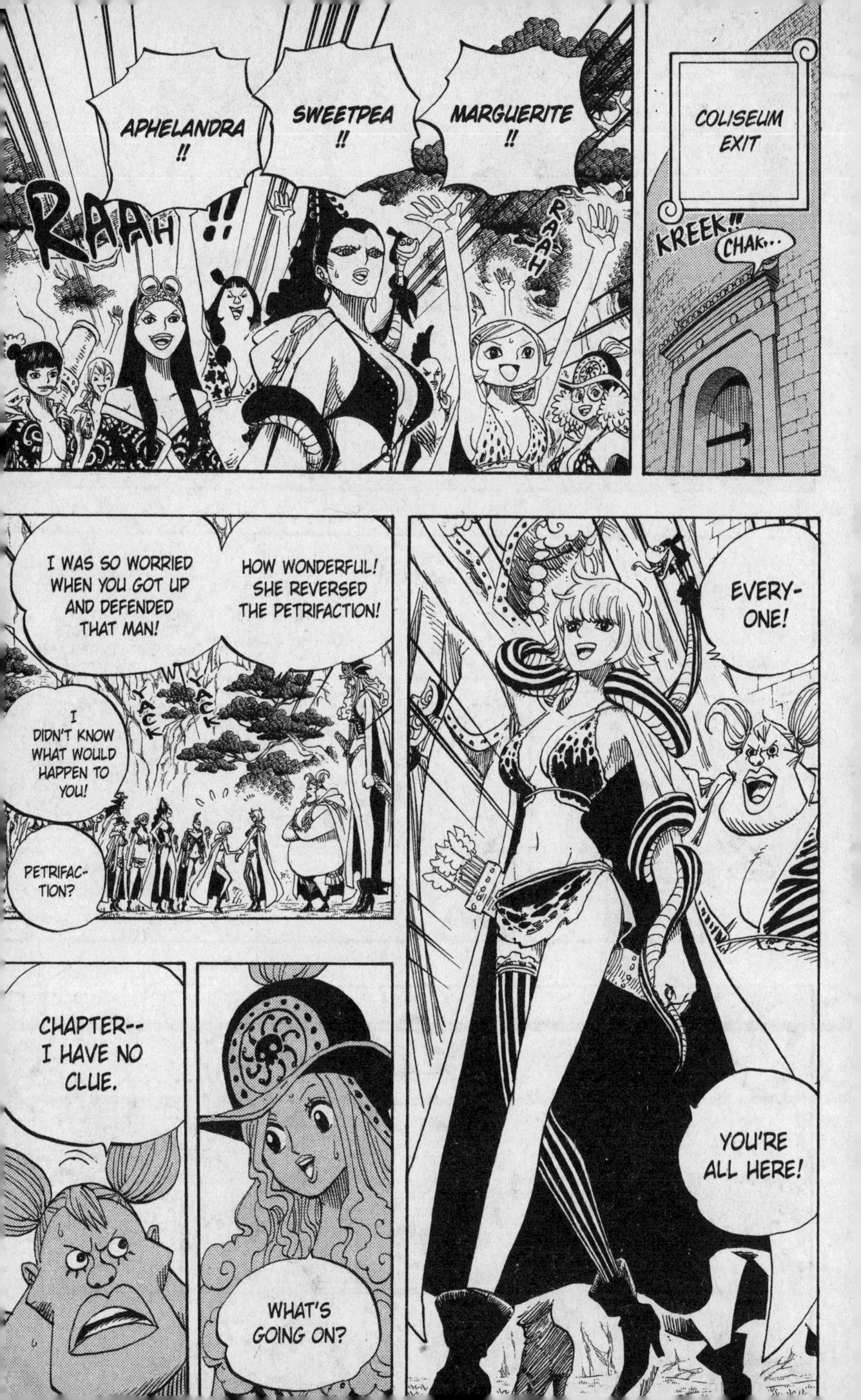
COLISEUM EXIT
KREEK!!
CHAK...
MARGUERITE !!
SWEETPEA !!
APHELANDRA !!
RAAH
RAAH !!
EVERY-ONE!
YOU'RE ALL HERE!
HOW WONDERFUL! SHE REVERSED THE PETRIFACTION!
I WAS SO WORRIED WHEN YOU GOT UP AND DEFENDED THAT MAN!
YACK
YACK
I DIDN'T KNOW WHAT WOULD HAPPEN TO YOU!
PETRIFAC-TION?
WHAT'S GOING ON?
CHAPTER-- I HAVE NO CLUE.

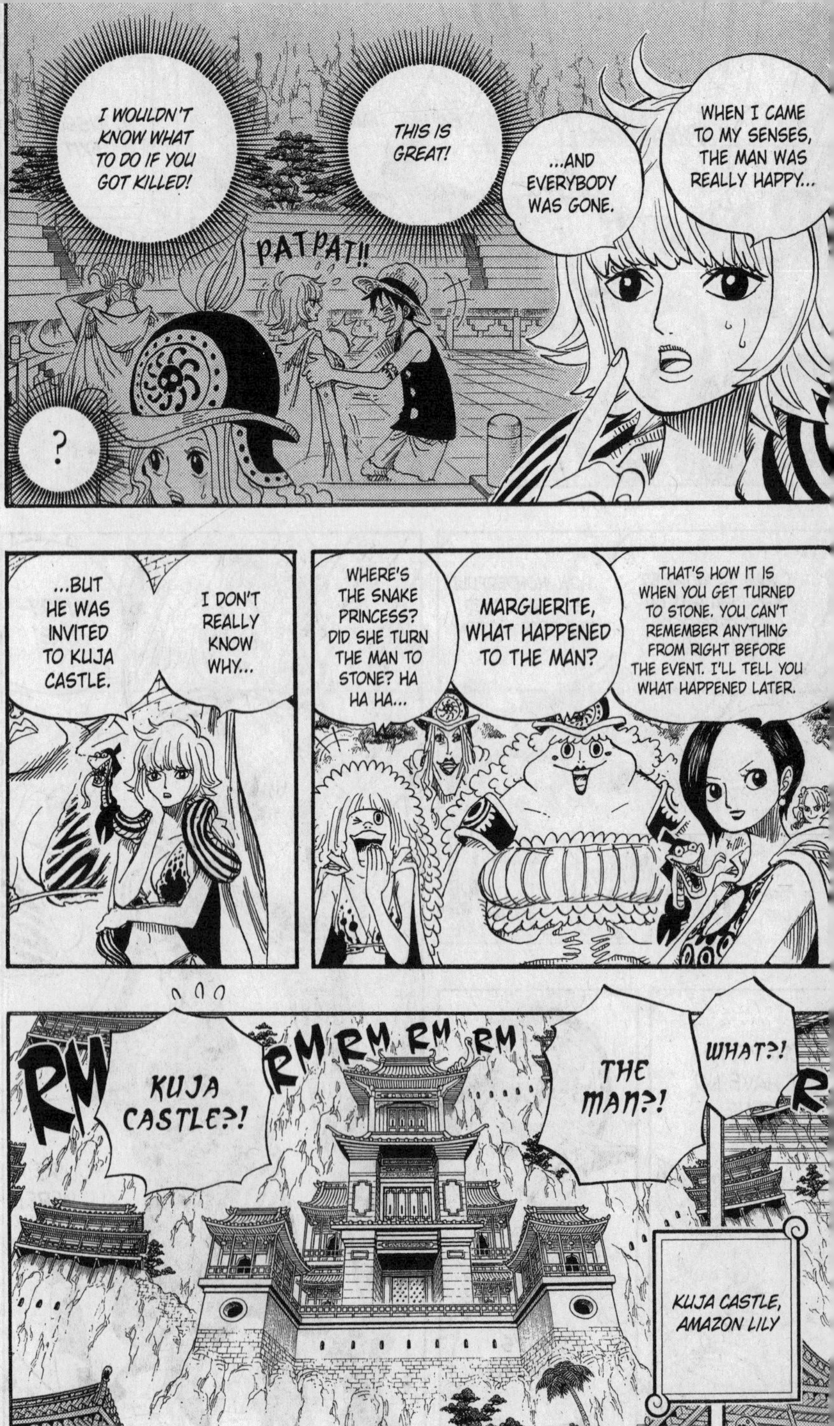
WHEN I CAME TO MY SENSES, THE MAN WAS REALLY HAPPY...
...AND EVERYBODY WAS GONE.
THIS IS GREAT!
I WOULDN'T KNOW WHAT TO DO IF YOU GOT KILLED!
PATPAT!!
?
THAT'S HOW IT IS WHEN YOU GET TURNED TO STONE. YOU CAN'T REMEMBER ANYTHING FROM RIGHT BEFORE THE EVENT. I'LL TELL YOU WHAT HAPPENED LATER.
MARGUERITE, WHAT HAPPENED TO THE MAN?
WHERE'S THE SNAKE PRINCESS? DID SHE TURN THE MAN TO STONE? HA HA HA...
I DON'T REALLY KNOW WHY...
...BUT HE WAS INVITED TO KUJA CASTLE.
WHAT?!
THE MAN?!
RM RM RM RM RM
KUJA CASTLE?!
KUJA CASTLE, AMAZON LILY

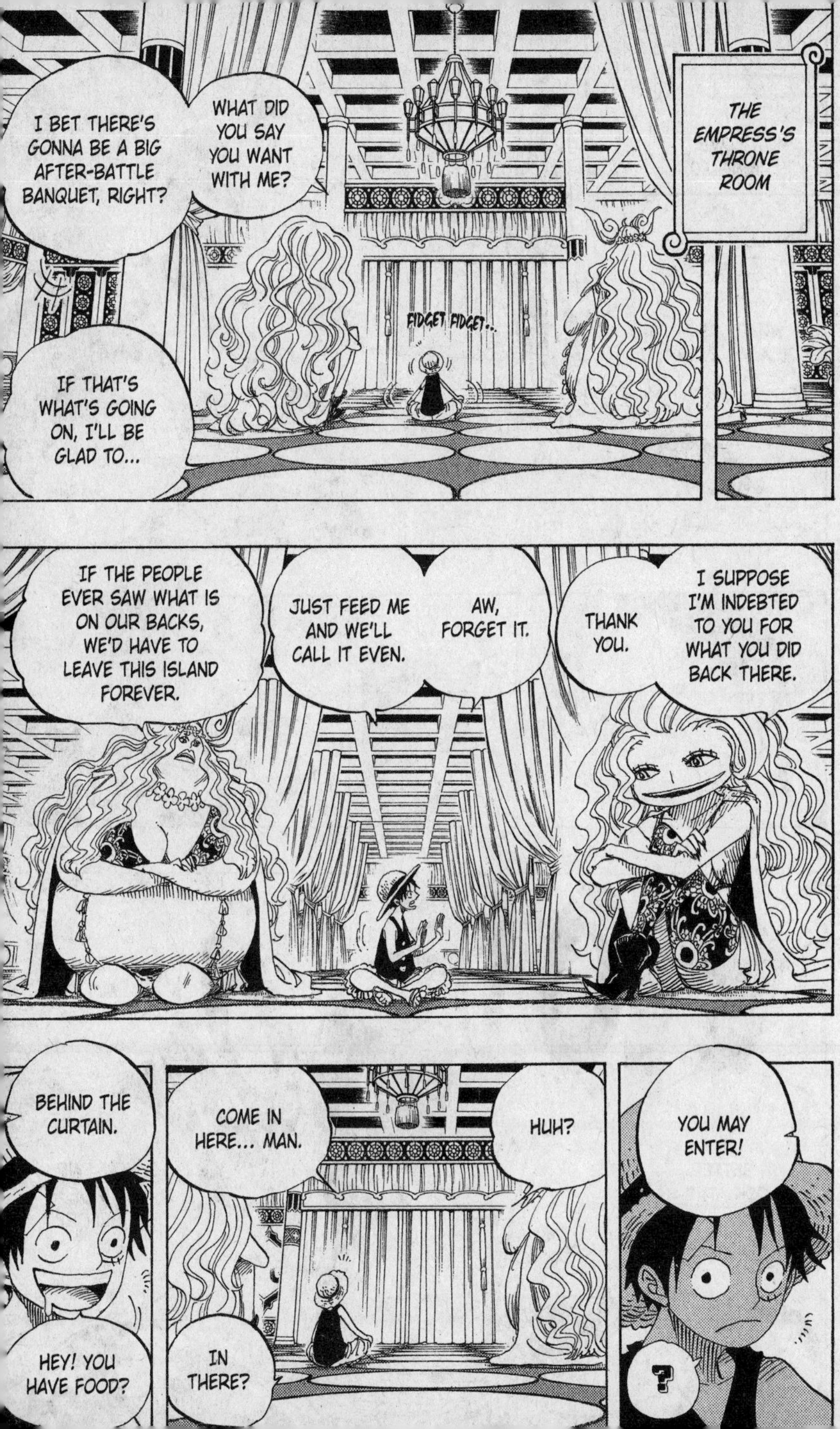
THE EMPRESS'S THRONE ROOM
WHAT DID YOU SAY YOU WANT WITH ME?
I BET THERE'S GONNA BE A BIG AFTER-BATTLE BANQUET, RIGHT?
FIDGET FIDGET...
IF THAT'S WHAT'S GOING ON, I'LL BE GLAD TO...
I SUPPOSE I'M INDEBTED TO YOU FOR WHAT YOU DID BACK THERE.
THANK YOU.
AW, FORGET IT.
JUST FEED ME AND WE'LL CALL IT EVEN.
IF THE PEOPLE EVER SAW WHAT IS ON OUR BACKS, WE'D HAVE TO LEAVE THIS ISLAND FOREVER.
YOU MAY ENTER!
?
HUH?
COME IN HERE... MAN.
IN THERE?
BEHIND THE CURTAIN.
HEY! YOU HAVE FOOD?

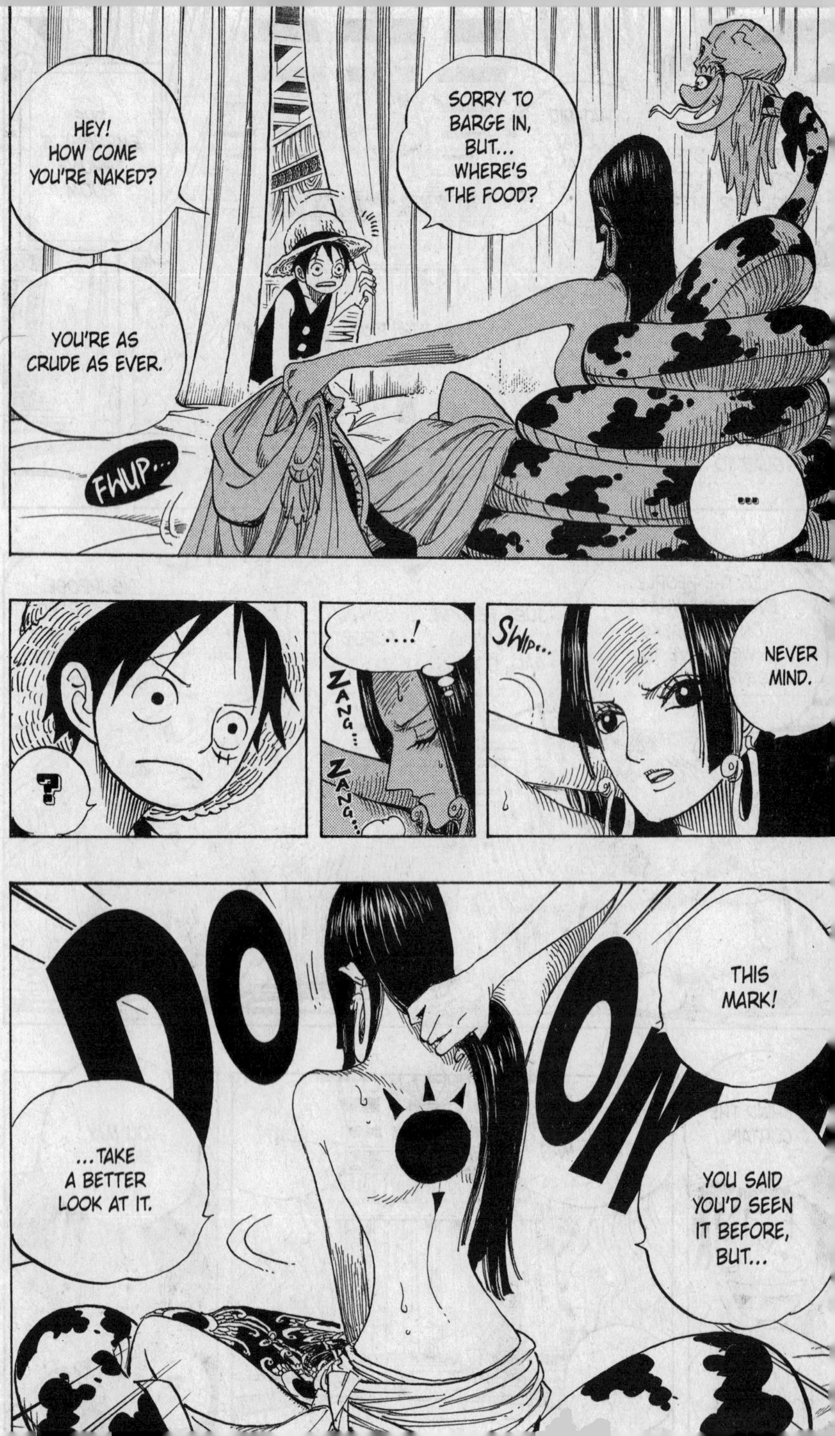
SORRY TO BARGE IN, BUT... WHERE'S THE FOOD?
HEY! HOW COME YOU'RE NAKED?
...
YOU'RE AS CRUDE AS EVER.
FWUP...
SWIP...
NEVER MIND.
...!
ZANG...
ZANG...
?
THIS MARK!
DOOM
YOU SAID YOU'D SEEN IT BEFORE, BUT...
...TAKE A BETTER LOOK AT IT.

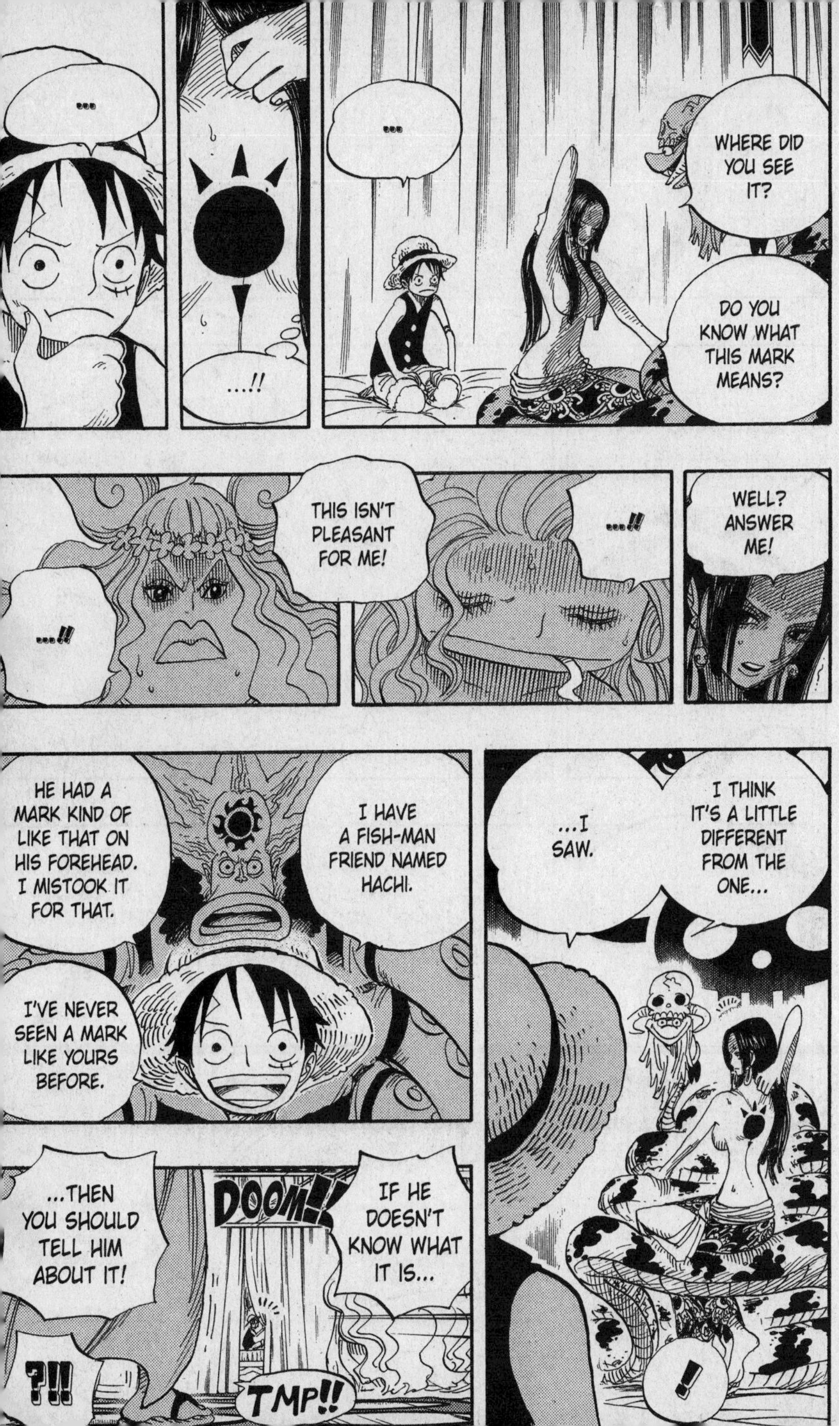
WHERE DID YOU SEE IT?
DO YOU KNOW WHAT THIS MARK MEANS?
...
...!!
...
WELL? ANSWER ME!
...!!
THIS ISN'T PLEASANT FOR ME!
...!!
I THINK IT'S A LITTLE DIFFERENT FROM THE ONE...
...I SAW.
!
I HAVE A FISH-MAN FRIEND NAMED HACHI.
HE HAD A MARK KIND OF LIKE THAT ON HIS FOREHEAD. I MISTOOK IT FOR THAT.
I'VE NEVER SEEN A MARK LIKE YOURS BEFORE.
IF HE DOESN'T KNOW WHAT IT IS...
DOOM!!
...THEN YOU SHOULD TELL HIM ABOUT IT!
TMP!!
?!!

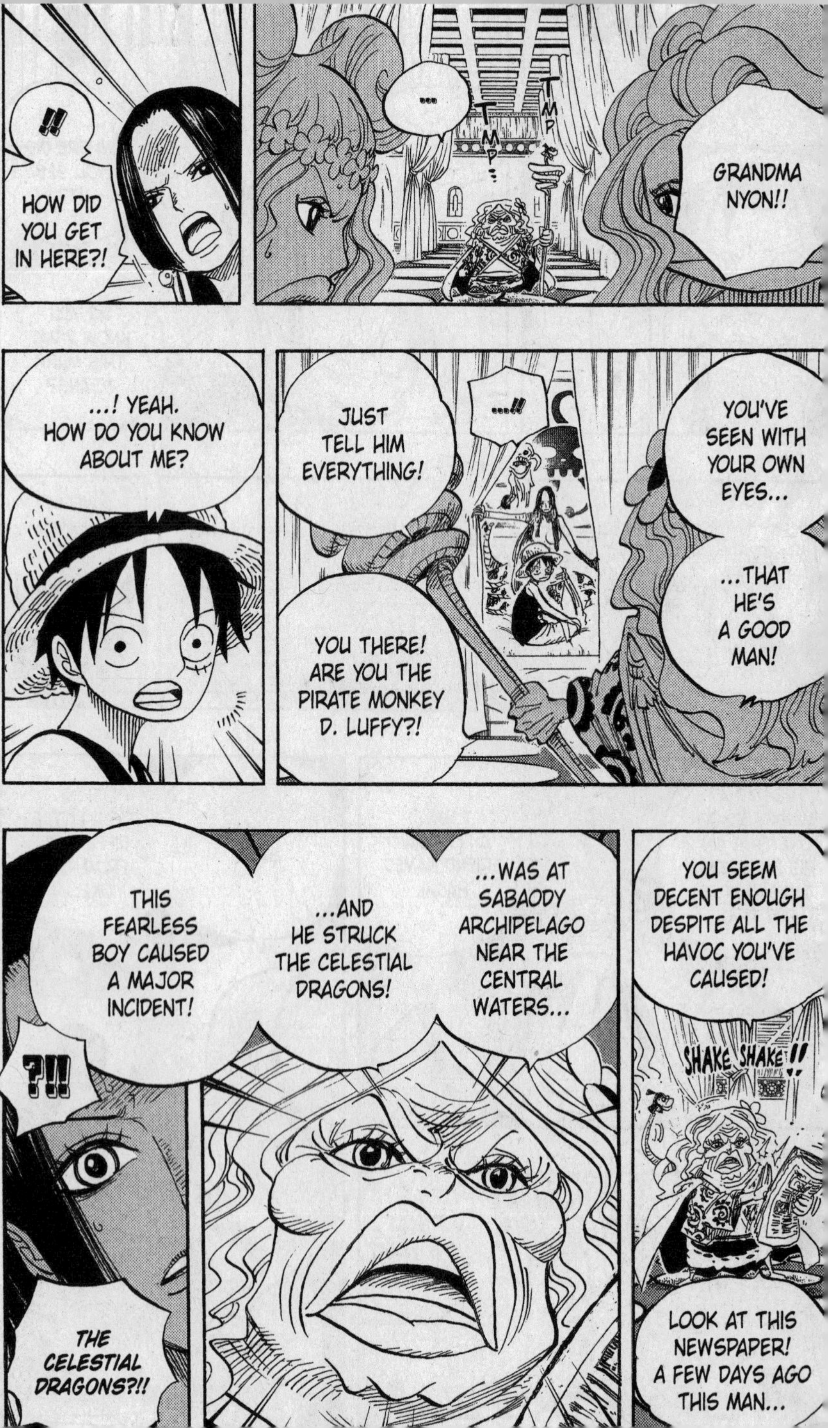
GRANDMA NYON!!
TMP TMP
...
!!
HOW DID YOU GET IN HERE?!
YOU'VE SEEN WITH YOUR OWN EYES...
...THAT HE'S A GOOD MAN!
...!!
JUST TELL HIM EVERYTHING!
YOU THERE! ARE YOU THE PIRATE MONKEY D. LUFFY?!
...! YEAH. HOW DO YOU KNOW ABOUT ME?
YOU SEEM DECENT ENOUGH DESPITE ALL THE HAVOC YOU'VE CAUSED!
SHAKE SHAKE!!
LOOK AT THIS NEWSPAPER! A FEW DAYS AGO THIS MAN...
...WAS AT SABAODY ARCHIPELAGO NEAR THE CENTRAL WATERS...
...AND HE STRUCK THE CELESTIAL DRAGONS!
THIS FEARLESS BOY CAUSED A MAJOR INCIDENT!
?!!
THE CELESTIAL DRAGONS?!!

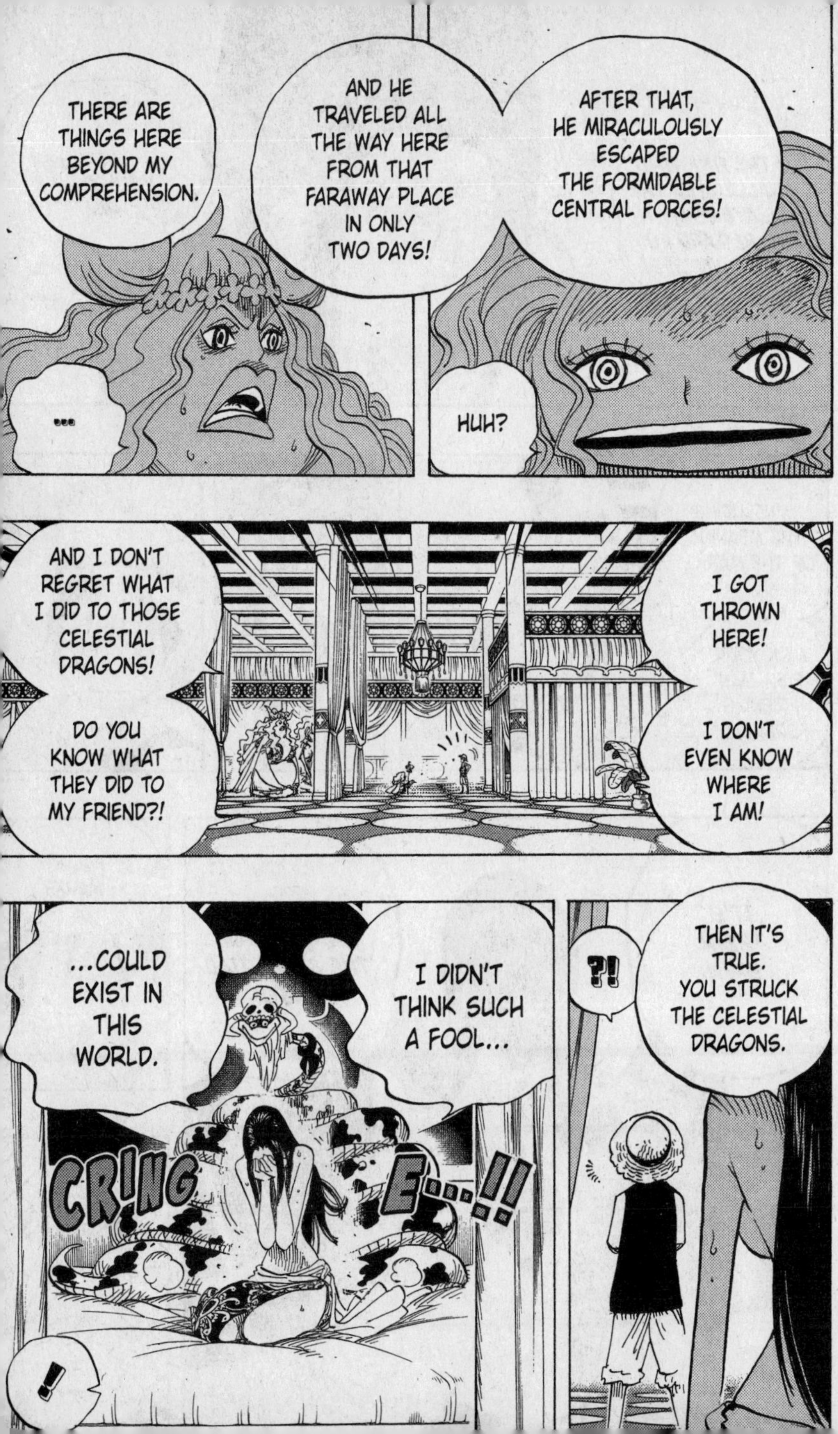
AFTER THAT, HE MIRACULOUSLY ESCAPED THE FORMIDABLE CENTRAL FORCES!
HUH?
AND HE TRAVELED ALL THE WAY HERE FROM THAT FARAWAY PLACE IN ONLY TWO DAYS!
THERE ARE THINGS HERE BEYOND MY COMPREHENSION.
...
I GOT THROWN HERE!
I DON'T EVEN KNOW WHERE I AM!
AND I DON'T REGRET WHAT I DID TO THOSE CELESTIAL DRAGONS!
DO YOU KNOW WHAT THEY DID TO MY FRIEND?!
THEN IT'S TRUE. YOU STRUCK THE CELESTIAL DRAGONS.
?!
I DIDN'T THINK SUCH A FOOL...
...COULD EXIST IN THIS WORLD.
CRINGE...!!
!

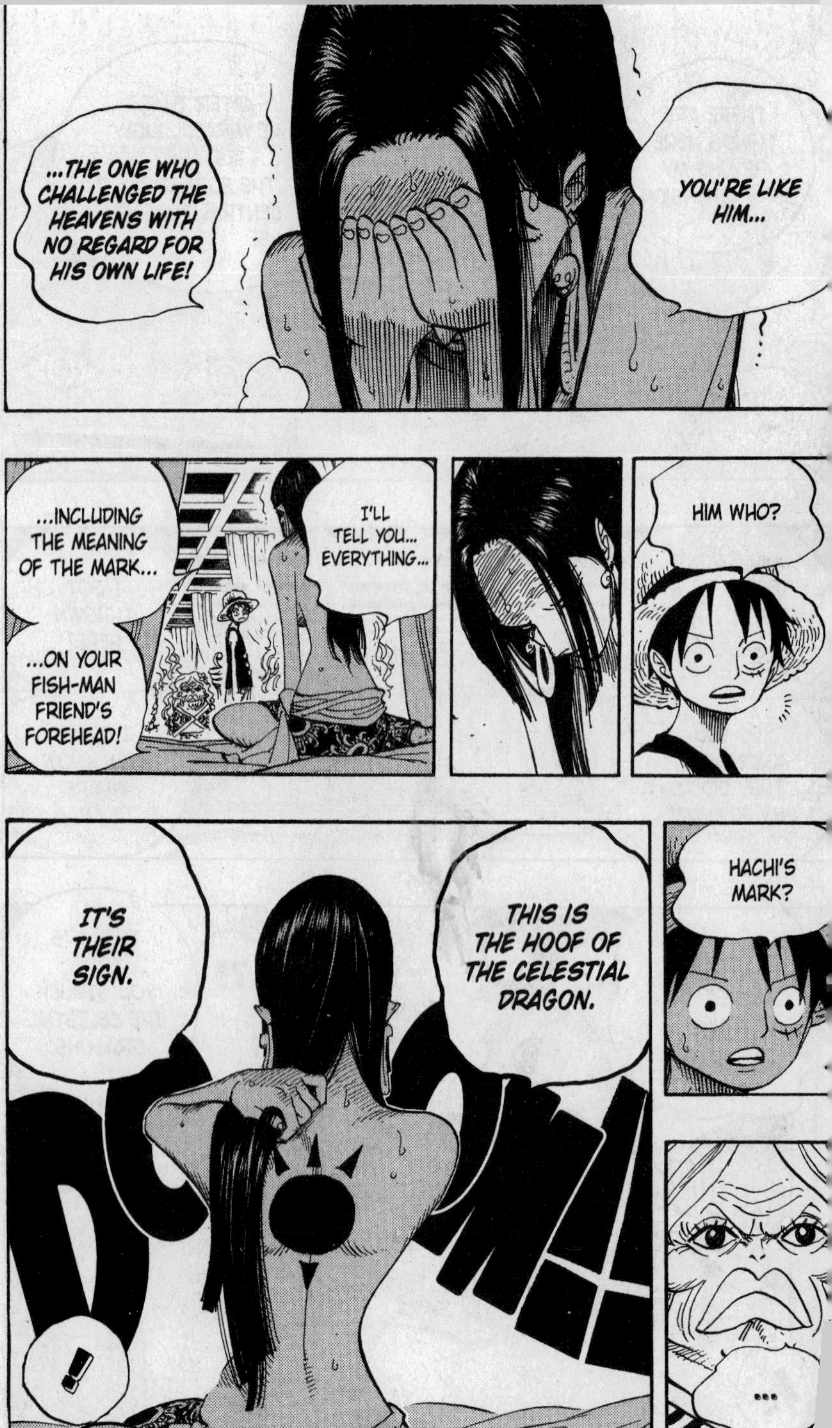
YOU'RE LIKE HIM...
...THE ONE WHO CHALLENGED THE HEAVENS WITH NO REGARD FOR HIS OWN LIFE!
HIM WHO?
I'LL TELL YOU... EVERYTHING...
...INCLUDING THE MEANING OF THE MARK...
...ON YOUR FISH-MAN FRIEND'S FOREHEAD!
HACHI'S MARK?
...
THIS IS THE HOOF OF THE CELESTIAL DRAGON.
IT'S THEIR SIGN.
!

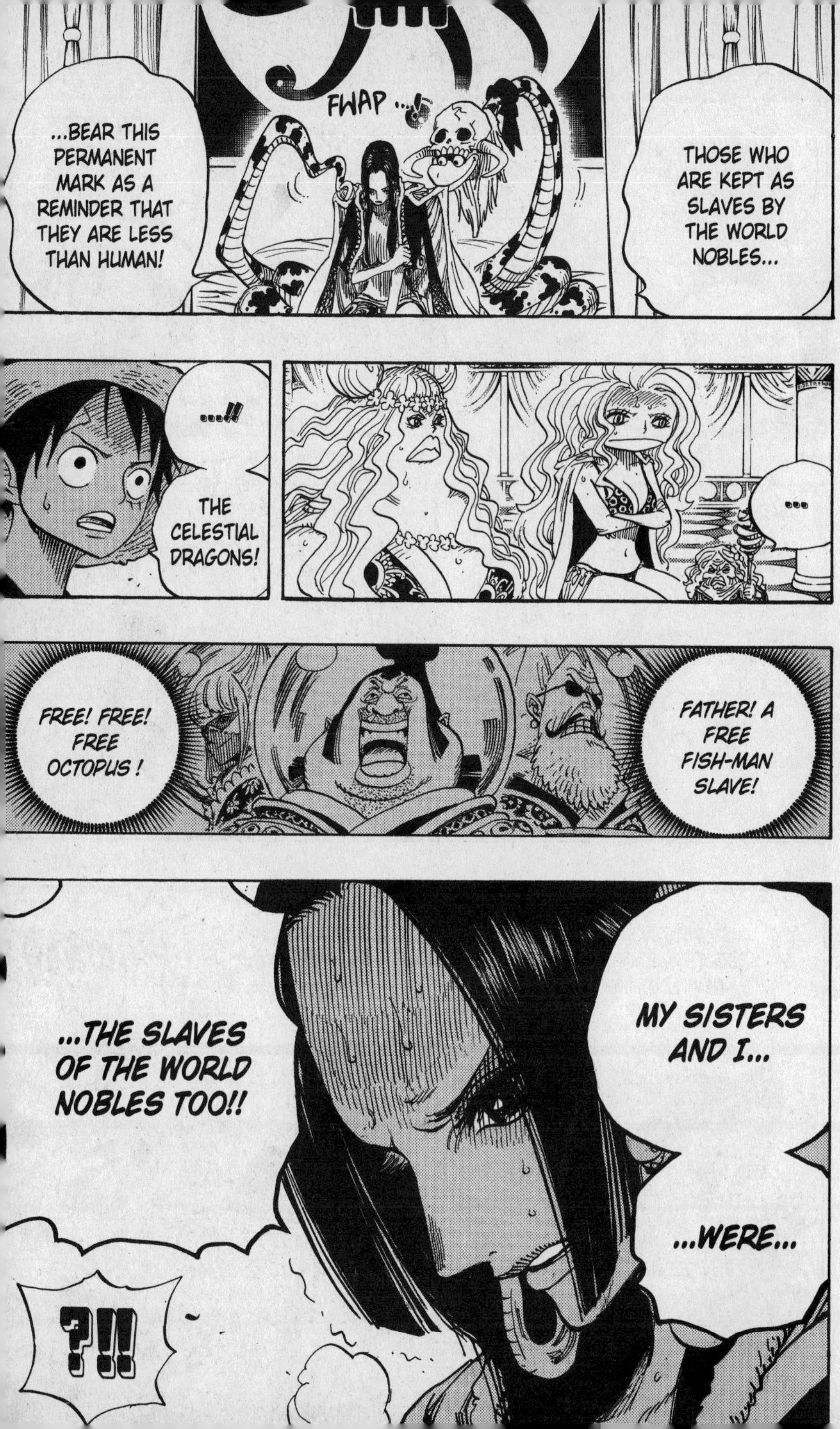
THOSE WHO ARE KEPT AS SLAVES BY THE WORLD NOBLES...
FWAP
...BEAR THIS PERMANENT MARK AS A REMINDER THAT THEY ARE LESS THAN HUMAN!
...
...!!
THE CELESTIAL DRAGONS!
FATHER! A FREE FISH-MAN SLAVE!
FREE! FREE! FREE OCTOPUS!
MY SISTERS AND I...
...WERE...
...THE SLAVES OF THE WORLD NOBLES TOO!!
?!!

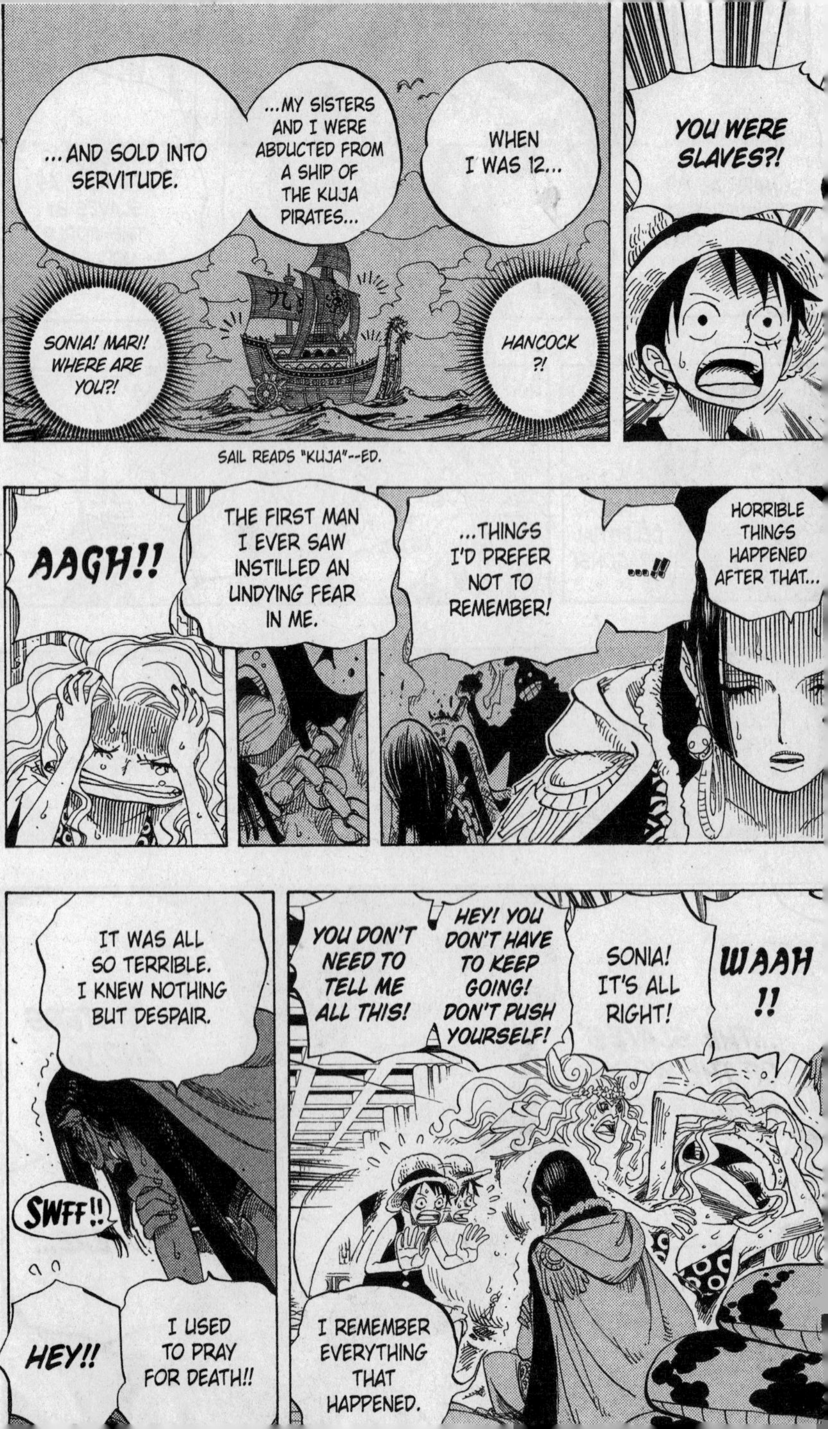
YOU WERE SLAVES?!
WHEN I WAS 12...
...MY SISTERS AND I WERE ABDUCTED FROM A SHIP OF THE KUJA PIRATES...
...AND SOLD INTO SERVITUDE.
HANCOCK ?!
SONIA! MARI! WHERE ARE YOU?!
SAIL READS "KUJA"--ED.
HORRIBLE THINGS HAPPENED AFTER THAT...
...!!
...THINGS I'D PREFER NOT TO REMEMBER!
THE FIRST MAN I EVER SAW INSTILLED AN UNDYING FEAR IN ME.
AAGH!!
WAAH !!
SONIA! IT'S ALL RIGHT!
HEY! YOU DON'T HAVE TO KEEP GOING! DON'T PUSH YOURSELF!
YOU DON'T NEED TO TELL ME ALL THIS!
I REMEMBER EVERYTHING THAT HAPPENED.
IT WAS ALL SO TERRIBLE. I KNEW NOTHING BUT DESPAIR.
SWFF!!
I USED TO PRAY FOR DEATH!!
HEY!!

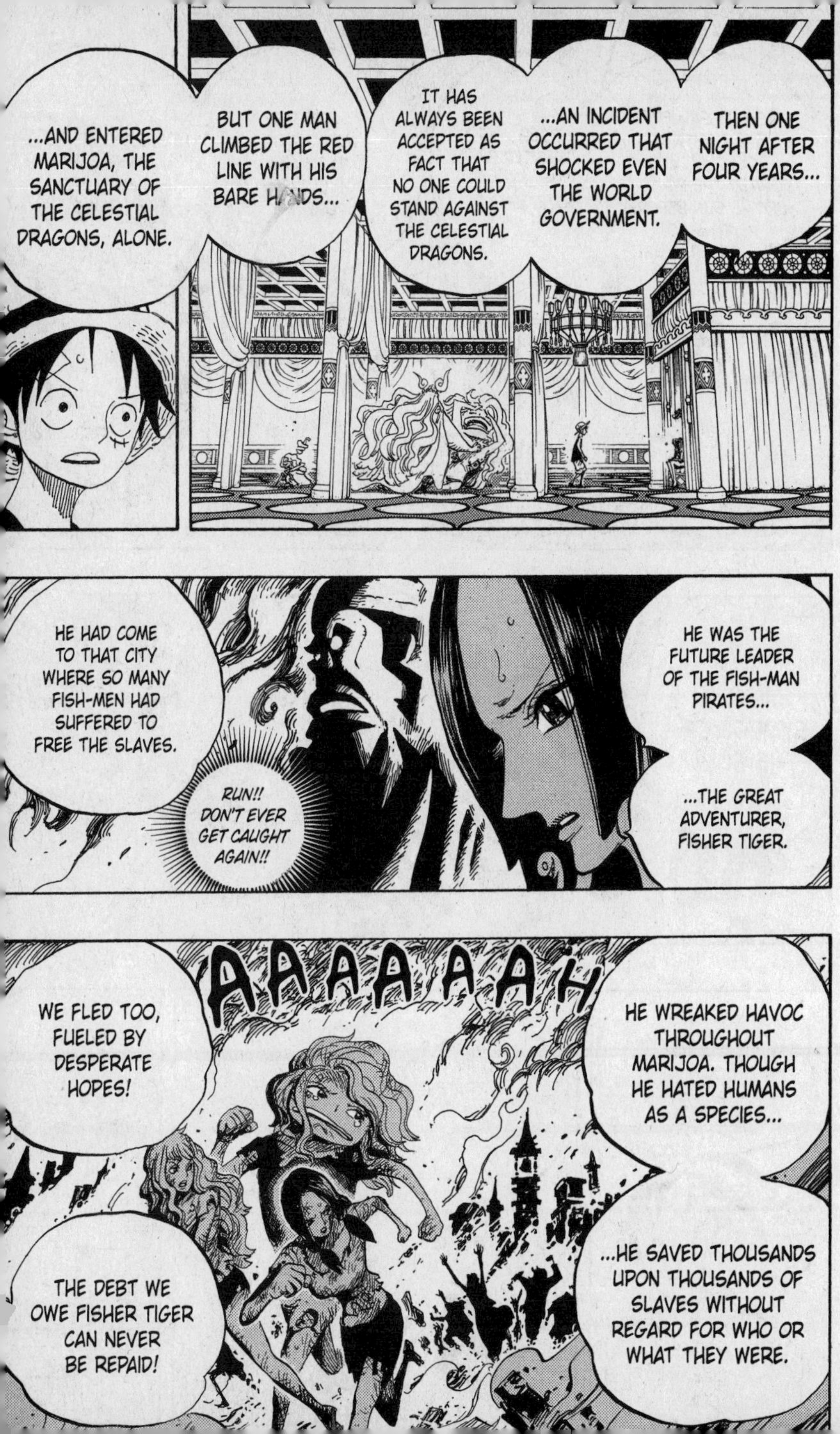
THEN ONE NIGHT AFTER FOUR YEARS...
...AN INCIDENT OCCURRED THAT SHOCKED EVEN THE WORLD GOVERNMENT.
IT HAS ALWAYS BEEN ACCEPTED AS FACT THAT NO ONE COULD STAND AGAINST THE CELESTIAL DRAGONS.
BUT ONE MAN CLIMBED THE RED LINE WITH HIS BARE HANDS...
...AND ENTERED MARIJOA, THE SANCTUARY OF THE CELESTIAL DRAGONS, ALONE.
HE WAS THE FUTURE LEADER OF THE FISH-MAN PIRATES...
...THE GREAT ADVENTURER, FISHER TIGER.
RUN!! DON'T EVER GET CAUGHT AGAIN!!
HE HAD COME TO THAT CITY WHERE SO MANY FISH-MEN HAD SUFFERED TO FREE THE SLAVES.
HE WREAKED HAVOC THROUGHOUT MARIJOA. THOUGH HE HATED HUMANS AS A SPECIES...
AAAAAAH
WE FLED TOO, FUELED BY DESPERATE HOPES!
...HE SAVED THOUSANDS UPON THOUSANDS OF SLAVES WITHOUT REGARD FOR WHO OR WHAT THEY WERE.
THE DEBT WE OWE FISHER TIGER CAN NEVER BE REPAID!

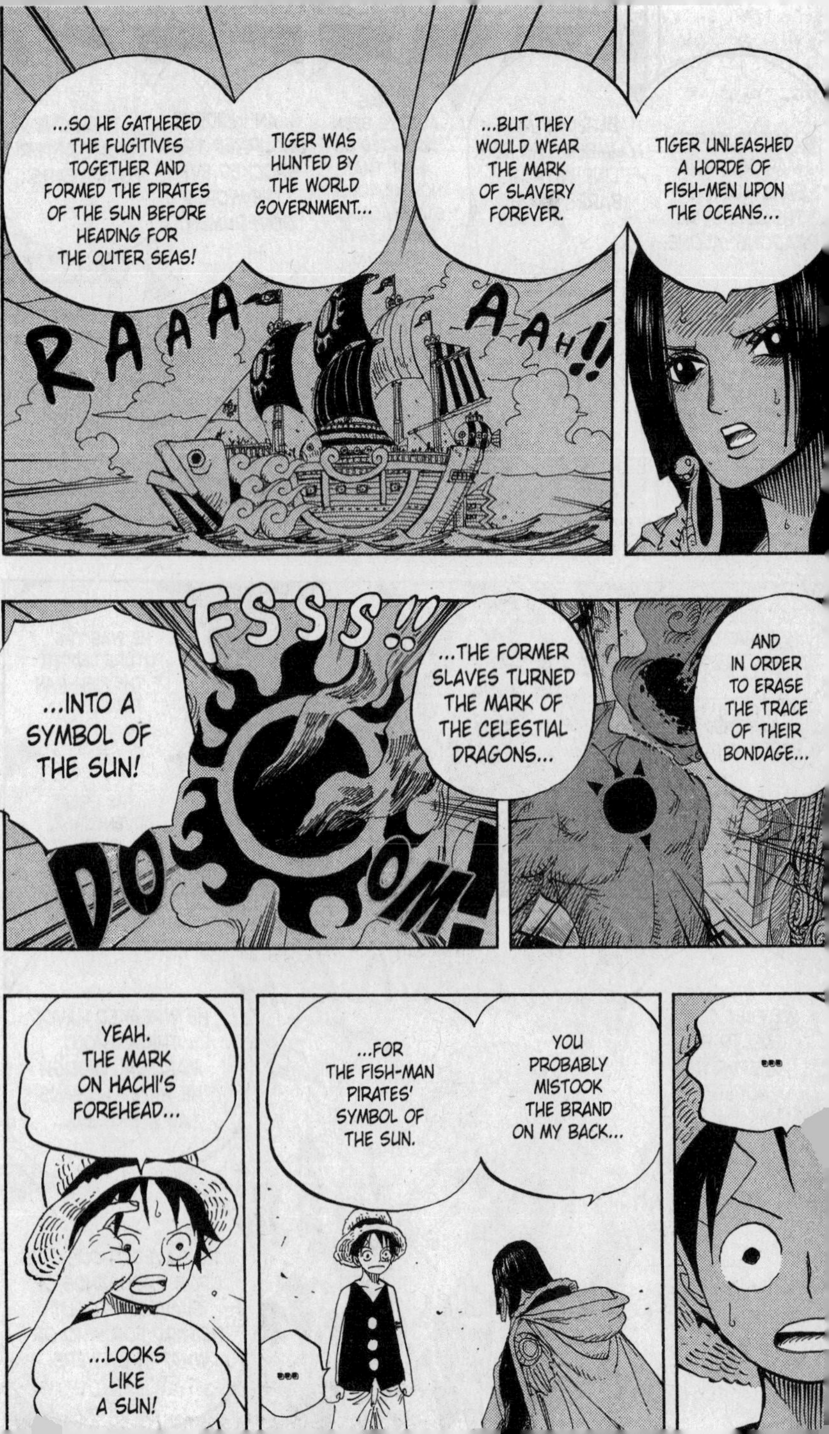
TIGER UNLEASHED A HORDE OF FISH-MEN UPON THE OCEANS...
...BUT THEY WOULD WEAR THE MARK OF SLAVERY FOREVER.
TIGER WAS HUNTED BY THE WORLD GOVERNMENT...
...SO HE GATHERED THE FUGITIVES TOGETHER AND FORMED THE PIRATES OF THE SUN BEFORE HEADING FOR THE OUTER SEAS!
RAAAAAH!!
AND IN ORDER TO ERASE THE TRACE OF THEIR BONDAGE...
...THE FORMER SLAVES TURNED THE MARK OF THE CELESTIAL DRAGONS...
FSSS!!
...INTO A SYMBOL OF THE SUN!
DOOOM!
...
YOU PROBABLY MISTOOK THE BRAND ON MY BACK...
...FOR THE FISH-MAN PIRATES' SYMBOL OF THE SUN.
...
YEAH. THE MARK ON HACHI'S FOREHEAD...
...LOOKS LIKE A SUN!

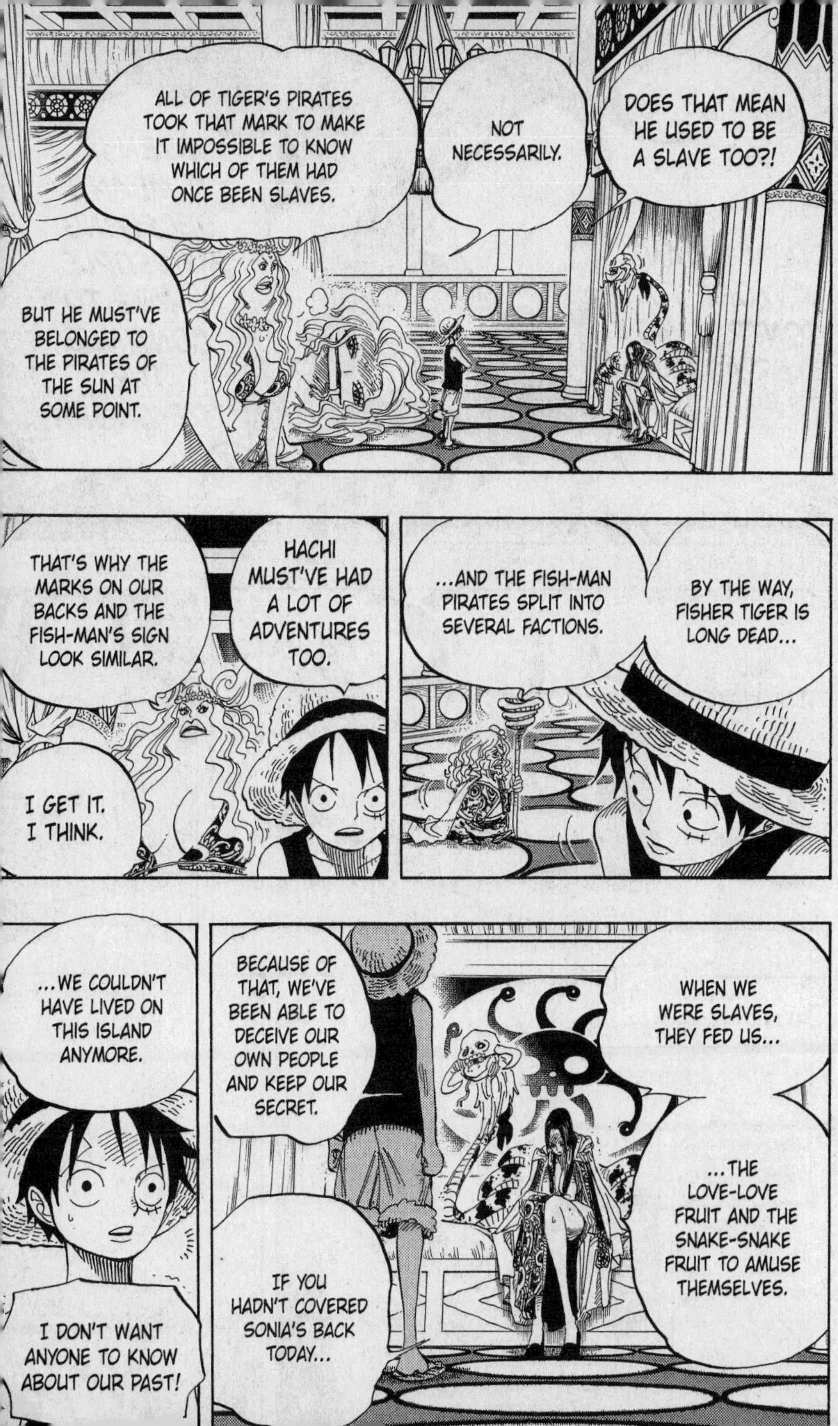
DOES THAT MEAN HE USED TO BE A SLAVE TOO?!
NOT NECESSARILY.
ALL OF TIGER'S PIRATES TOOK THAT MARK TO MAKE IT IMPOSSIBLE TO KNOW WHICH OF THEM HAD ONCE BEEN SLAVES.
BUT HE MUST'VE BELONGED TO THE PIRATES OF THE SUN AT SOME POINT.
BY THE WAY, FISHER TIGER IS LONG DEAD...
...AND THE FISH-MAN PIRATES SPLIT INTO SEVERAL FACTIONS.
HACHI MUST'VE HAD A LOT OF ADVENTURES TOO.
THAT'S WHY THE MARKS ON OUR BACKS AND THE FISH-MAN'S SIGN LOOK SIMILAR.
I GET IT. I THINK.
WHEN WE WERE SLAVES, THEY FED US...
...THE LOVE-LOVE FRUIT AND THE SNAKE-SNAKE FRUIT TO AMUSE THEMSELVES.
BECAUSE OF THAT, WE'VE BEEN ABLE TO DECEIVE OUR OWN PEOPLE AND KEEP OUR SECRET.
IF YOU HADN'T COVERED SONIA'S BACK TODAY...
...WE COULDN'T HAVE LIVED ON THIS ISLAND ANYMORE.
I DON'T WANT ANYONE TO KNOW ABOUT OUR PAST!

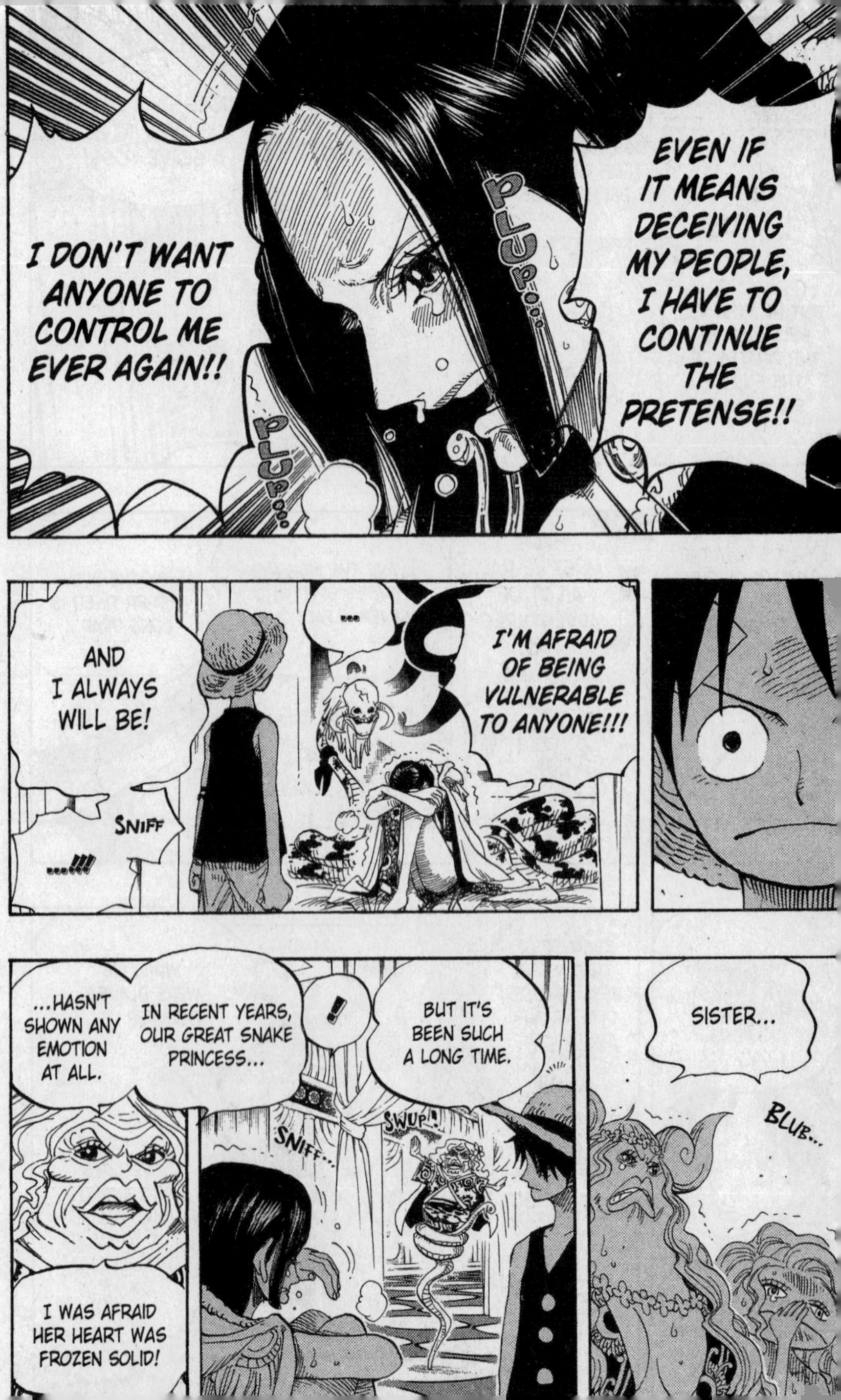
EVEN IF IT MEANS DECEIVING MY PEOPLE, I HAVE TO CONTINUE THE PRETENSE!!
PLUP...
I DON'T WANT ANYONE TO CONTROL ME EVER AGAIN!!
PLUP...
I'M AFRAID OF BEING VULNERABLE TO ANYONE!!!
...
AND I ALWAYS WILL BE!
SNIFF
...!!!
SISTER...
BLUB...
BUT IT'S BEEN SUCH A LONG TIME.
!
SWUP!
SNIFF...
IN RECENT YEARS, OUR GREAT SNAKE PRINCESS...
...HASN'T SHOWN ANY EMOTION AT ALL.
I WAS AFRAID HER HEART WAS FROZEN SOLID!

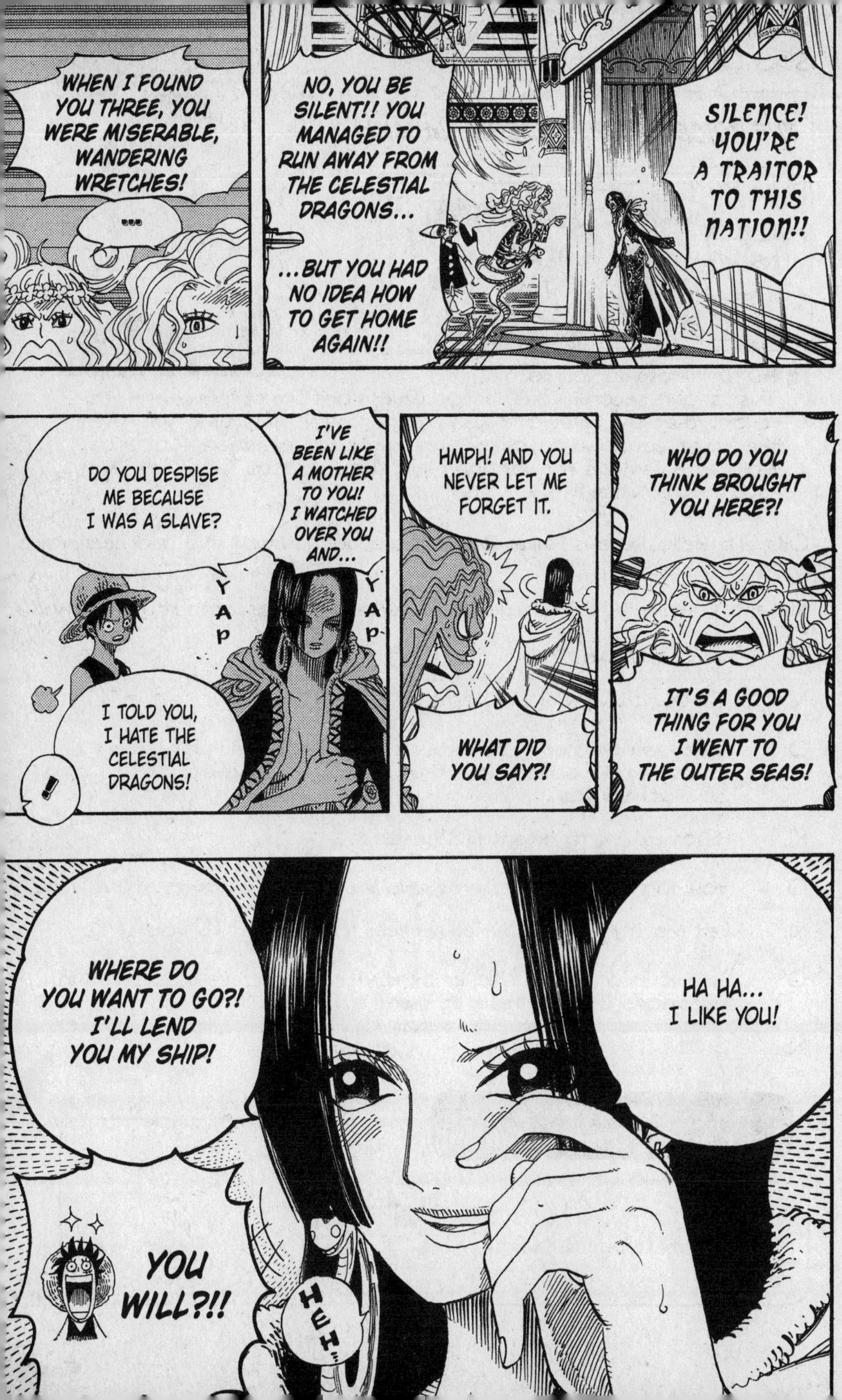
SILENCE! YOU'RE A TRAITOR TO THIS NATION!!
NO, YOU BE SILENT!! YOU MANAGED TO RUN AWAY FROM THE CELESTIAL DRAGONS...
...BUT YOU HAD NO IDEA HOW TO GET HOME AGAIN!!
WHEN I FOUND YOU THREE, YOU WERE MISERABLE, WANDERING WRETCHES!
...
WHO DO YOU THINK BROUGHT YOU HERE?!
IT'S A GOOD THING FOR YOU I WENT TO THE OUTER SEAS!
HMPH! AND YOU NEVER LET ME FORGET IT.
WHAT DID YOU SAY?!
I'VE BEEN LIKE A MOTHER TO YOU! I WATCHED OVER YOU AND...
YAP
DO YOU DESPISE ME BECAUSE I WAS A SLAVE?
YAP
I TOLD YOU, I HATE THE CELESTIAL DRAGONS!
!
HA HA... I LIKE YOU!
WHERE DO YOU WANT TO GO?! I'LL LEND YOU MY SHIP!
HEH...
YOU WILL?!!

SBS Question Corner

THE VOICE OF ZOLO, KAZUYA NAKAI!!

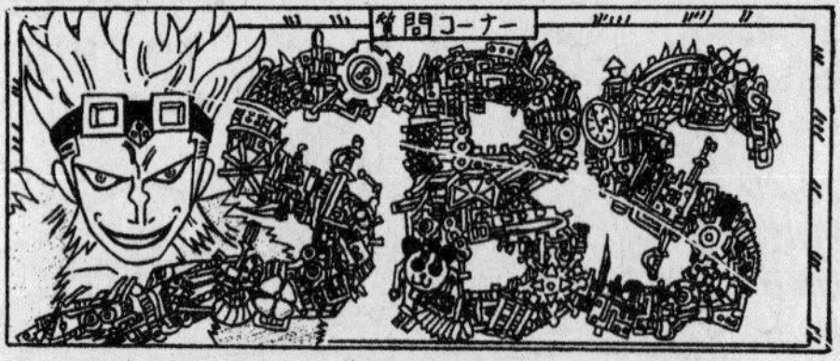
質問コーナー
SBS

(Kanta Yamamoto, Kyoto)

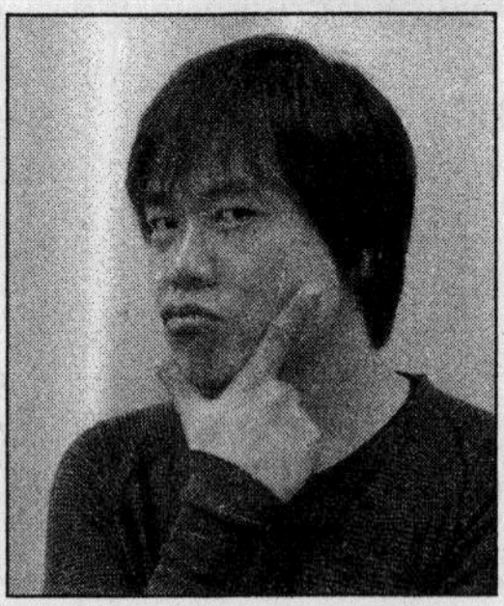

HDYD?! (How do you do?)
This is our second voice actor Question Corner. I'm happy to report that the first one was pretty popular. This time, we have the voice actor who voices our master swordsman, Roronoa Zolo. He's famous for farting while shouting out "Oni Giri!" We have Kazuya Nakai in the house!

Oda(O): Hello, here is Nakai. Please introduce yourself in a cool deep voice.

Nakai(N): Hello, this is Kazuya Nakai. My favorite dessert is Kashiwa-mochi.

O: Who asked you?

N: That's not very nice, Odachi.

O: Nice has nothing to do with it. We have limited space, so follow the script! Now then, do you know what SBS stands for?

N: (S)omething (B)latantly (S)enseless.

O: You don't know! Hey! Don't give me that "I was daydreaming" look!

N: Let me try again. (S)haved my head (B)ald but it (S)ucks.

O: Are you kidding me?! Never mind! Here. These are all letters with questions. (PLOP!) Have at them.

N: Sure.

More from Kazuya Nakai on page 208! ☞

In the next Voice Actor's Question Corner!

The next two voice actors will be...

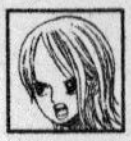

Akemi Okamura (Nami)

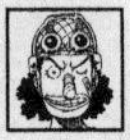

Kappei Yamaguchi (Usopp)

Chapter 522:

FATAL ILLNESS

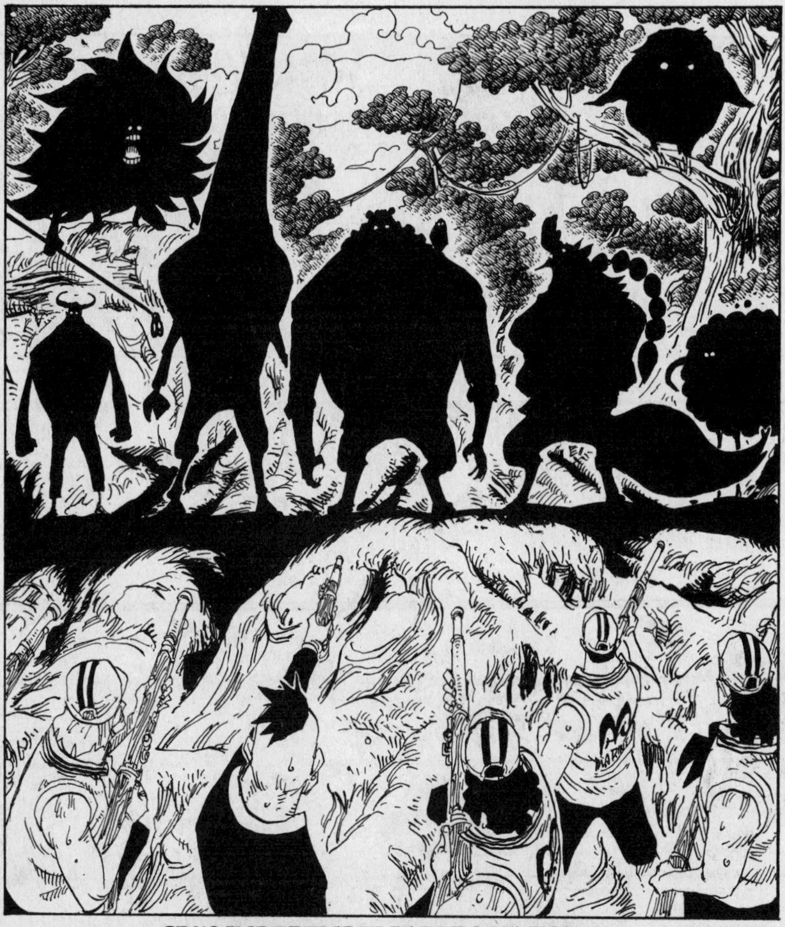

CP9'S INDEPENDENT REPORT, VOL. 28:
"DEFENDING OUR HOMETOWN"

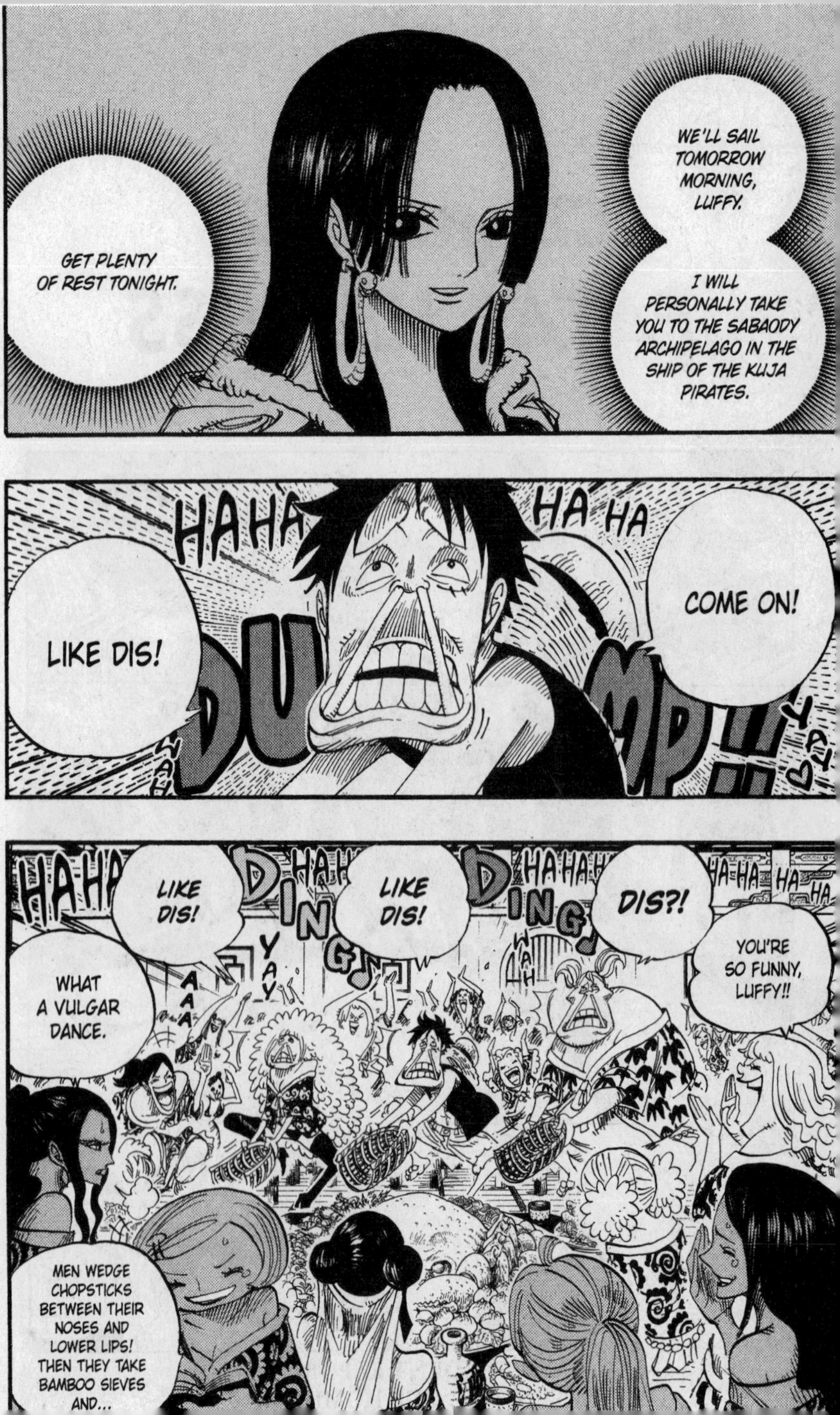
WE'LL SAIL TOMORROW MORNING, LUFFY.
I WILL PERSONALLY TAKE YOU TO THE SABAODY ARCHIPELAGO IN THE SHIP OF THE KUJA PIRATES.
GET PLENTY OF REST TONIGHT.
HA HA
COME ON!
DUMP!!
HAHA
LIKE DIS!
HA HA HA
YOU'RE SO FUNNY, LUFFY!!
DIS?!
DING
HA HA HA
LIKE DIS!
DING
HA HA
LIKE DIS!
YAY
HA HA
WHAT A VULGAR DANCE.
MEN WEDGE CHOPSTICKS BETWEEN THEIR NOSES AND LOWER LIPS! THEN THEY TAKE BAMBOO SIEVES AND...

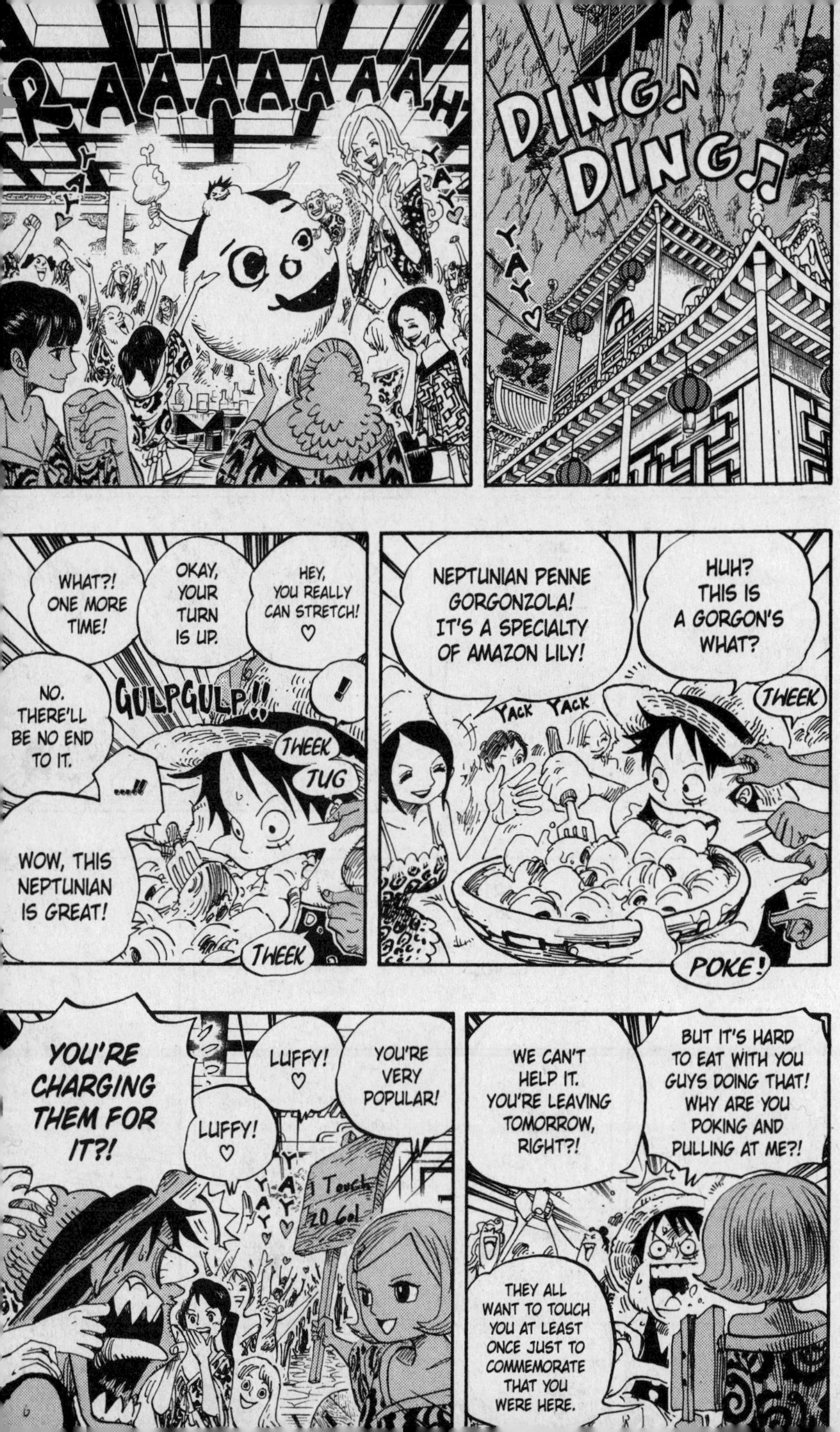
DING♪ DING♫
YAY♡
RAAAAAAAH
YAY♡
YAY♡
HUH? THIS IS A GORGON'S WHAT?
NEPTUNIAN PENNE GORGONZOLA! IT'S A SPECIALTY OF AMAZON LILY!
TWEEK
YACK YACK
POKE!
HEY, YOU REALLY CAN STRETCH! ♡
OKAY, YOUR TURN IS UP.
WHAT?! ONE MORE TIME!
!
GULPGULP!!
NO. THERE'LL BE NO END TO IT.
TWEEK
TUG
...!!
WOW, THIS NEPTUNIAN IS GREAT!
TWEEK
BUT IT'S HARD TO EAT WITH YOU GUYS DOING THAT! WHY ARE YOU POKING AND PULLING AT ME?!
WE CAN'T HELP IT. YOU'RE LEAVING TOMORROW, RIGHT?!
THEY ALL WANT TO TOUCH YOU AT LEAST ONCE JUST TO COMMEMORATE THAT YOU WERE HERE.
YOU'RE VERY POPULAR!
LUFFY! ♡
LUFFY! ♡
YAY♡
YAY♡
1 Touch 20 Gol
YOU'RE CHARGING THEM FOR IT?!

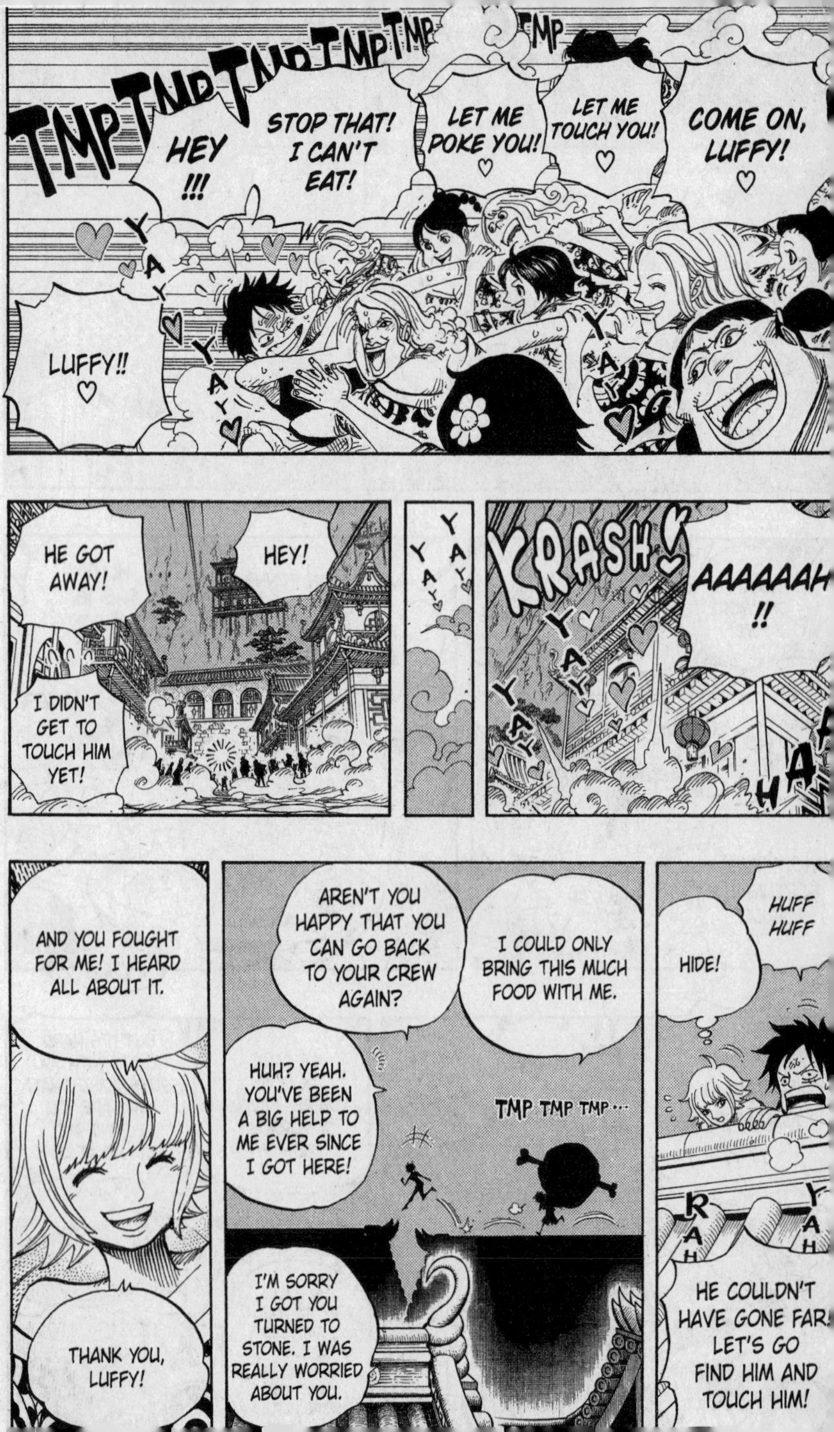
TMP TMP TMP TMP TMP TMP TMP
COME ON, LUFFY! ♡
LET ME TOUCH YOU! ♡
LET ME POKE YOU! ♡
STOP THAT! I CAN'T EAT!
HEY !!!
YAY
YAY
YAY
LUFFY!! ♡
KRASH!
AAAAAAH!!
YAY
HA
YAY
YAY
HEY!
HE GOT AWAY!
I DIDN'T GET TO TOUCH HIM YET!
HUFF HUFF
HIDE!
RAH
YAH
HE COULDN'T HAVE GONE FAR! LET'S GO FIND HIM AND TOUCH HIM!
I COULD ONLY BRING THIS MUCH FOOD WITH ME.
AREN'T YOU HAPPY THAT YOU CAN GO BACK TO YOUR CREW AGAIN?
HUH? YEAH. YOU'VE BEEN A BIG HELP TO ME EVER SINCE I GOT HERE!
TMP TMP TMP...
I'M SORRY I GOT YOU TURNED TO STONE. I WAS REALLY WORRIED ABOUT YOU.
AND YOU FOUGHT FOR ME! I HEARD ALL ABOUT IT.
THANK YOU, LUFFY!

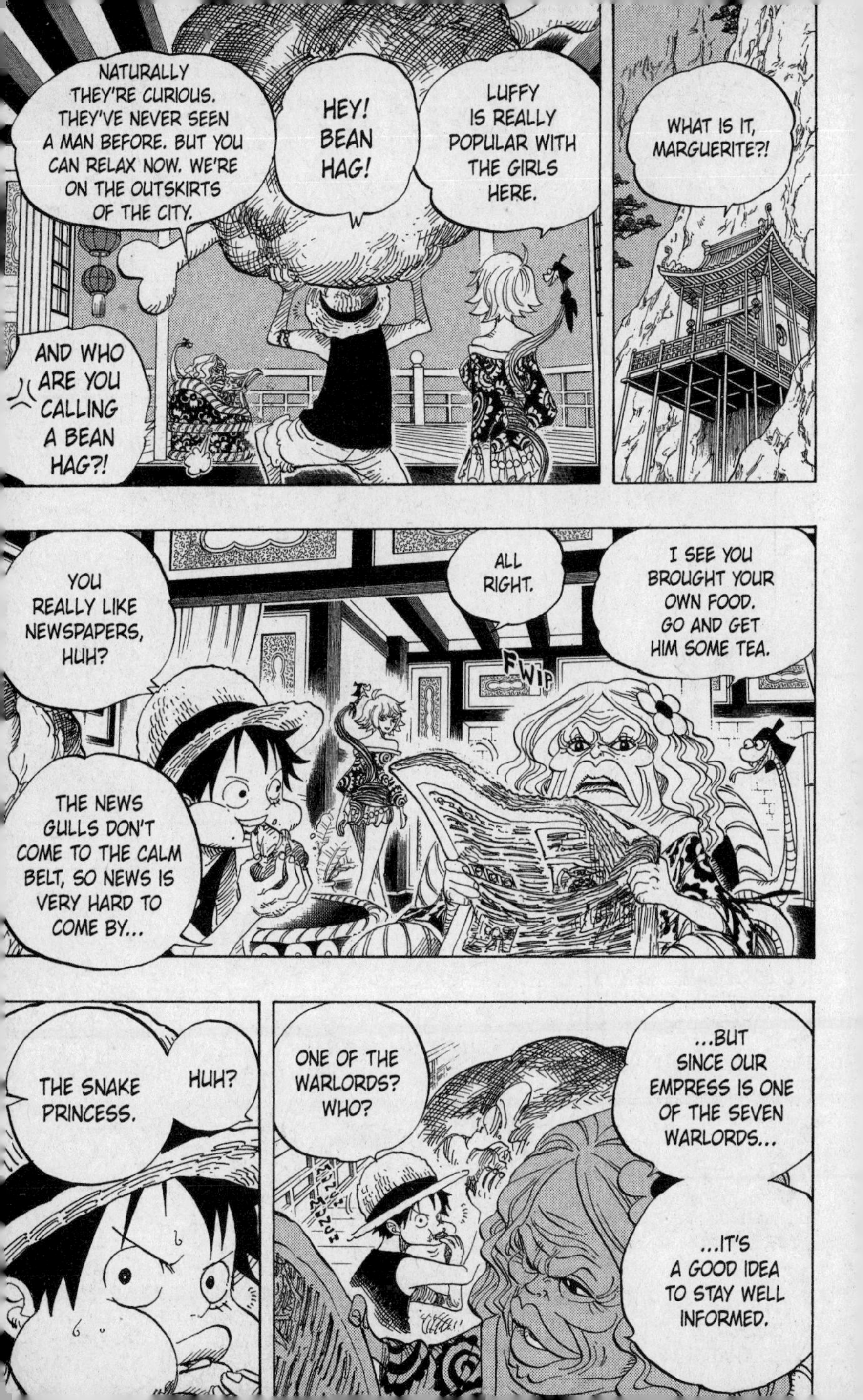
WHAT IS IT, MARGUERITE?!
LUFFY IS REALLY POPULAR WITH THE GIRLS HERE.
HEY! BEAN HAG!
NATURALLY THEY'RE CURIOUS. THEY'VE NEVER SEEN A MAN BEFORE. BUT YOU CAN RELAX NOW. WE'RE ON THE OUTSKIRTS OF THE CITY.
AND WHO ARE YOU CALLING A BEAN HAG?!
I SEE YOU BROUGHT YOUR OWN FOOD. GO AND GET HIM SOME TEA.
ALL RIGHT.
FWIP
YOU REALLY LIKE NEWSPAPERS, HUH?
THE NEWS GULLS DON'T COME TO THE CALM BELT, SO NEWS IS VERY HARD TO COME BY...
...BUT SINCE OUR EMPRESS IS ONE OF THE SEVEN WARLORDS...
...IT'S A GOOD IDEA TO STAY WELL INFORMED.
ONE OF THE WARLORDS? WHO?
HUH?
THE SNAKE PRINCESS.

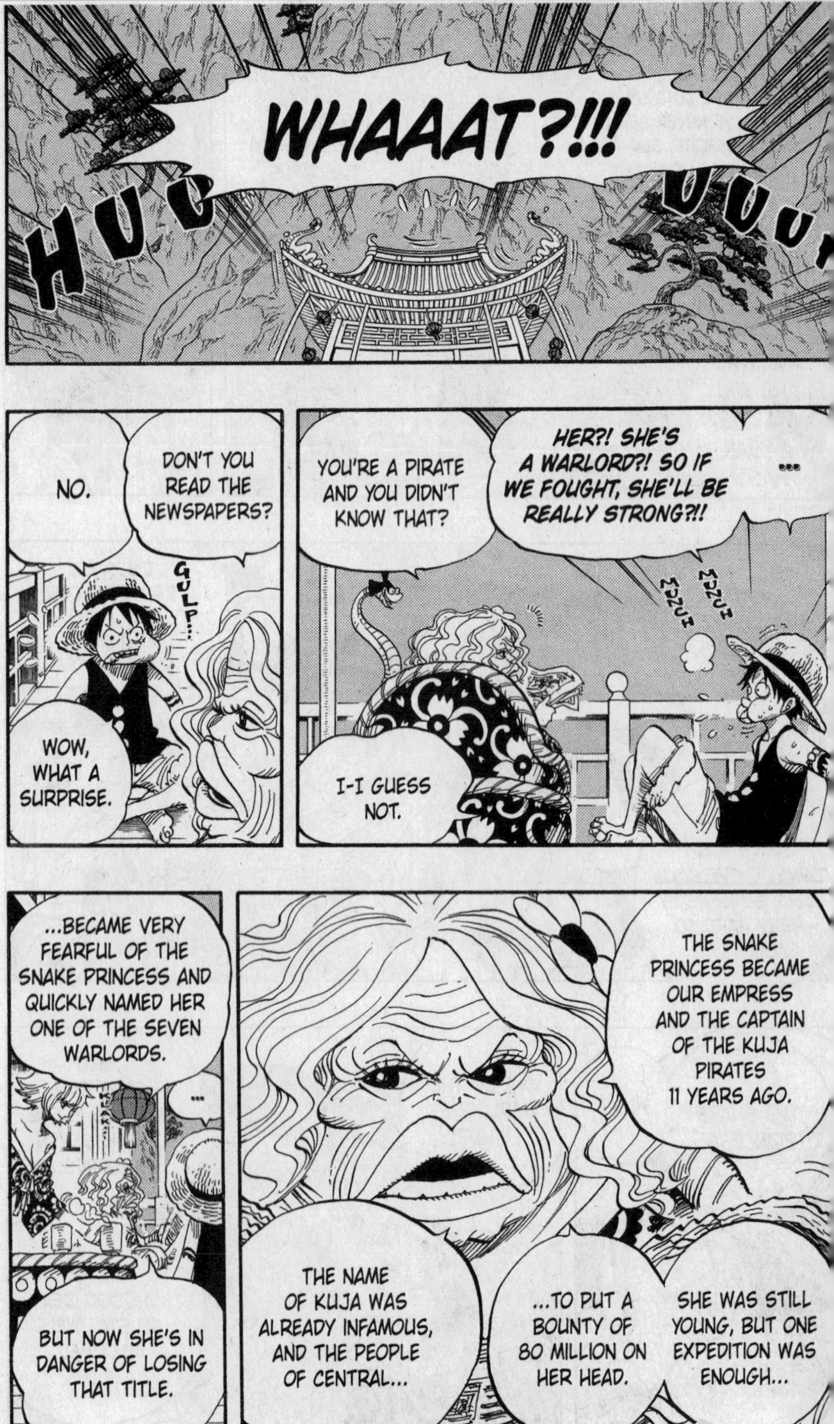
WHAAAT?!!!
HUU
UUU
...
HER?! SHE'S A WARLORD?! SO IF WE FOUGHT, SHE'LL BE REALLY STRONG?!!
YOU'RE A PIRATE AND YOU DIDN'T KNOW THAT?
ZUZUI
ZUZUI
I-I GUESS NOT.
DON'T YOU READ THE NEWSPAPERS?
NO.
GULP...
WOW, WHAT A SURPRISE.
THE SNAKE PRINCESS BECAME OUR EMPRESS AND THE CAPTAIN OF THE KUJA PIRATES 11 YEARS AGO.
SHE WAS STILL YOUNG, BUT ONE EXPEDITION WAS ENOUGH...
...TO PUT A BOUNTY OF 80 MILLION ON HER HEAD.
THE NAME OF KUJA WAS ALREADY INFAMOUS, AND THE PEOPLE OF CENTRAL...
...BECAME VERY FEARFUL OF THE SNAKE PRINCESS AND QUICKLY NAMED HER ONE OF THE SEVEN WARLORDS.
...
BUT NOW SHE'S IN DANGER OF LOSING THAT TITLE.

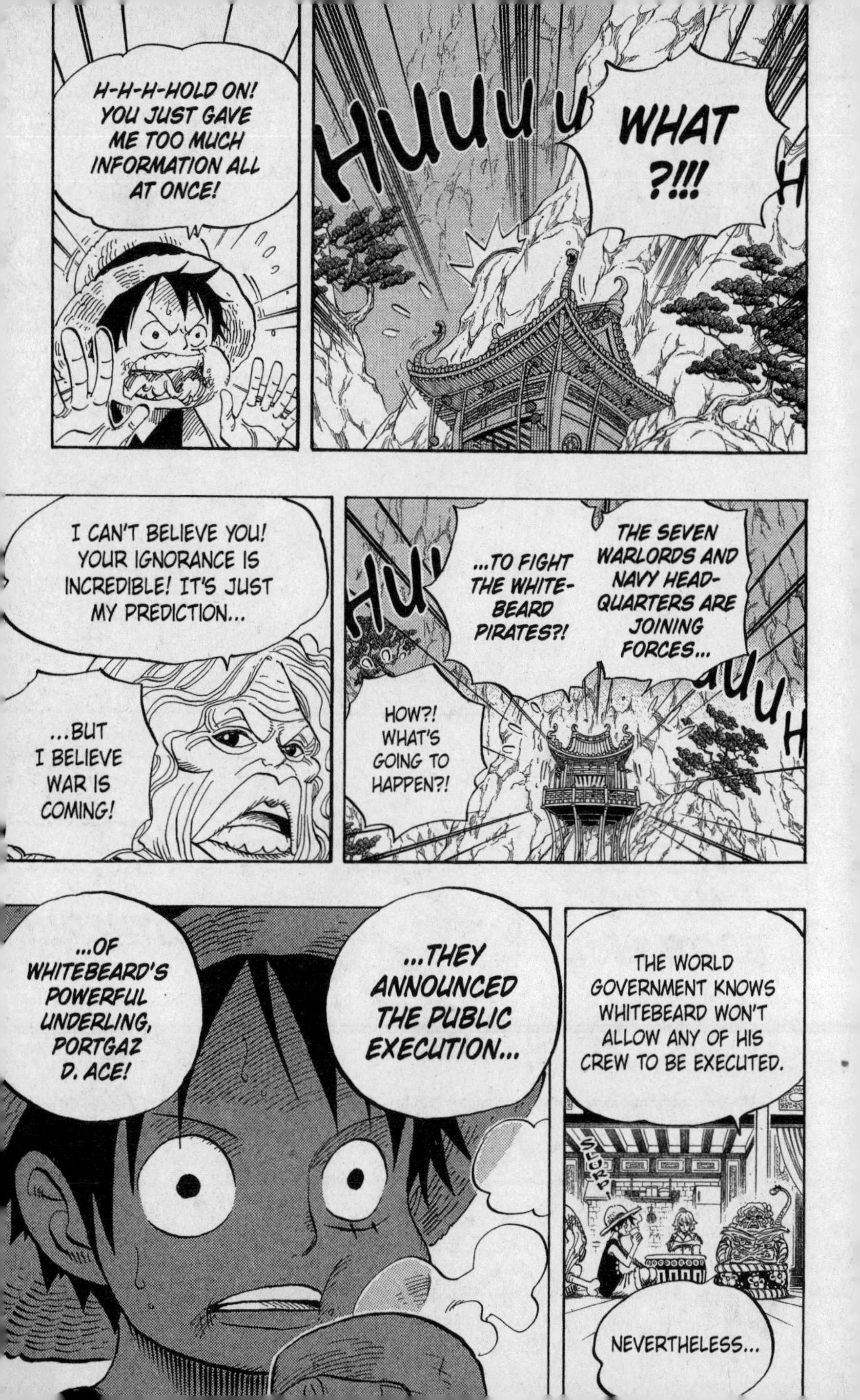
HUUUUU
WHAT ?!!!
H
H-H-H-HOLD ON! YOU JUST GAVE ME TOO MUCH INFORMATION ALL AT ONCE!
HU
THE SEVEN WARLORDS AND NAVY HEADQUARTERS ARE JOINING FORCES...
...TO FIGHT THE WHITEBEARD PIRATES?!
UUUH
HOW?! WHAT'S GOING TO HAPPEN?!
I CAN'T BELIEVE YOU! YOUR IGNORANCE IS INCREDIBLE! IT'S JUST MY PREDICTION...
...BUT I BELIEVE WAR IS COMING!
THE WORLD GOVERNMENT KNOWS WHITEBEARD WON'T ALLOW ANY OF HIS CREW TO BE EXECUTED.
SLURP
NEVERTHELESS...
...THEY ANNOUNCED THE PUBLIC EXECUTION...
...OF WHITEBEARD'S POWERFUL UNDERLING, PORTGAZ D. ACE!

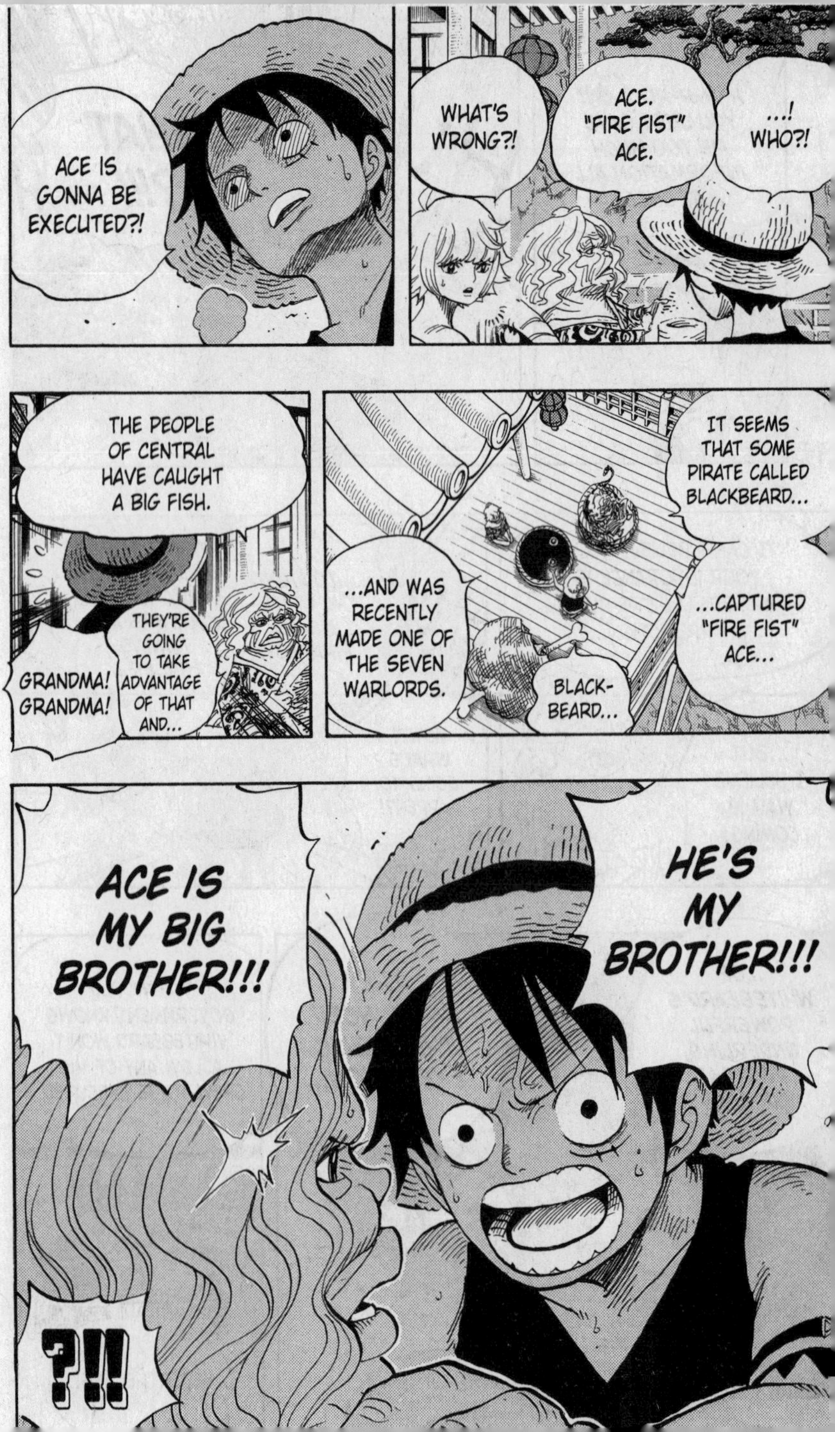
...! WHO?!
ACE. "FIRE FIST" ACE.
WHAT'S WRONG?!
ACE IS GONNA BE EXECUTED?!
IT SEEMS THAT SOME PIRATE CALLED BLACKBEARD...
...CAPTURED "FIRE FIST" ACE...
...AND WAS RECENTLY MADE ONE OF THE SEVEN WARLORDS.
BLACK-BEARD...
THE PEOPLE OF CENTRAL HAVE CAUGHT A BIG FISH.
THEY'RE GOING TO TAKE ADVANTAGE OF THAT AND...
GRANDMA! GRANDMA!
HE'S MY BROTHER!!!
ACE IS MY BIG BROTHER!!!
?!!

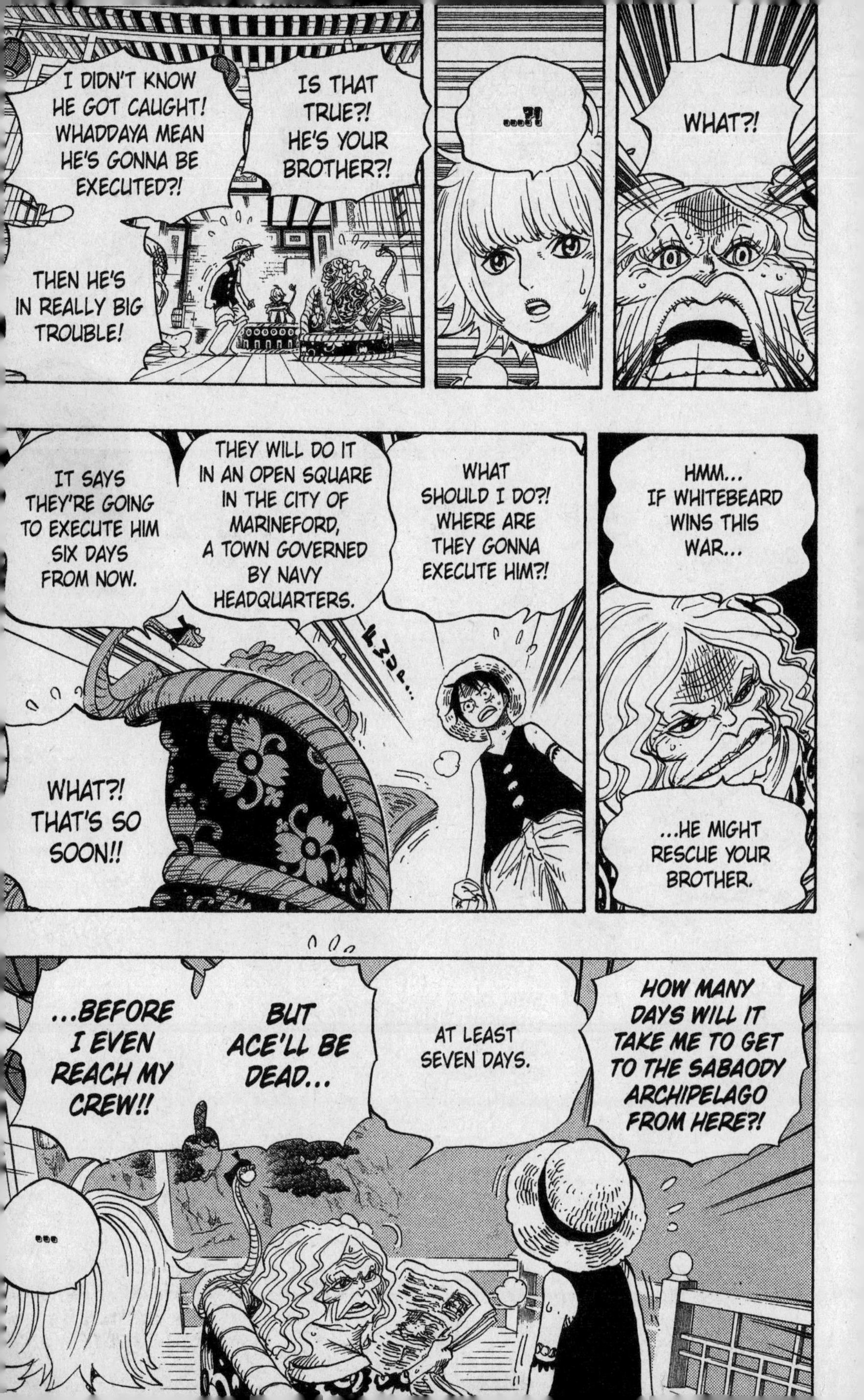
WHAT?!
...?!
IS THAT TRUE?! HE'S YOUR BROTHER?!
I DIDN'T KNOW HE GOT CAUGHT! WHADDAYA MEAN HE'S GONNA BE EXECUTED?!
THEN HE'S IN REALLY BIG TROUBLE!
HMM... IF WHITEBEARD WINS THIS WAR...
...HE MIGHT RESCUE YOUR BROTHER.
WHAT SHOULD I DO?! WHERE ARE THEY GONNA EXECUTE HIM?!
THEY WILL DO IT IN AN OPEN SQUARE IN THE CITY OF MARINEFORD, A TOWN GOVERNED BY NAVY HEADQUARTERS.
IT SAYS THEY'RE GOING TO EXECUTE HIM SIX DAYS FROM NOW.
WHAT?! THAT'S SO SOON!!
HOW MANY DAYS WILL IT TAKE ME TO GET TO THE SABAODY ARCHIPELAGO FROM HERE?!
AT LEAST SEVEN DAYS.
BUT ACE'LL BE DEAD...
...BEFORE I EVEN REACH MY CREW!!
...

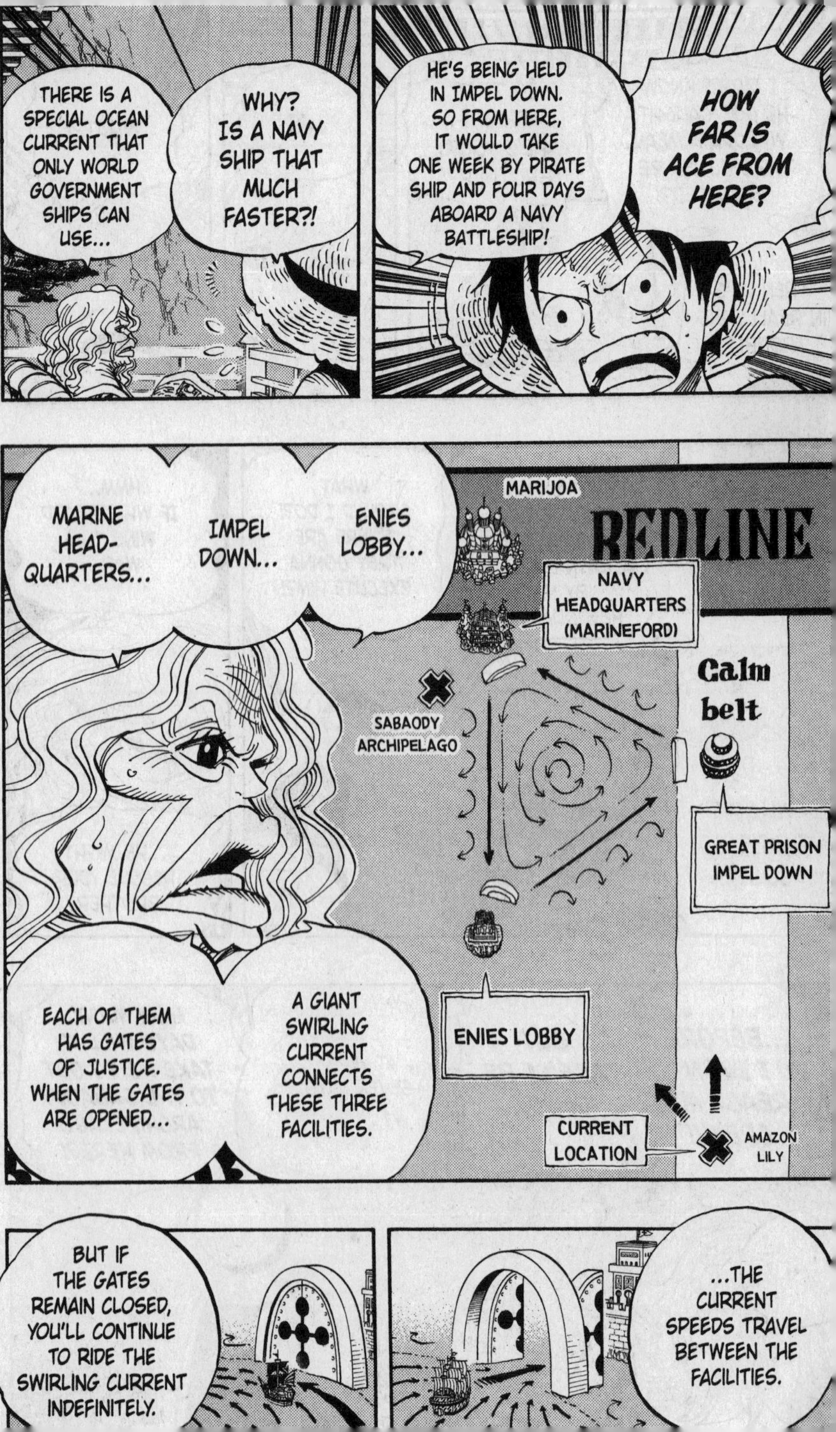
HOW FAR IS ACE FROM HERE?
HE'S BEING HELD IN IMPEL DOWN. SO FROM HERE, IT WOULD TAKE ONE WEEK BY PIRATE SHIP AND FOUR DAYS ABOARD A NAVY BATTLESHIP!
WHY? IS A NAVY SHIP THAT MUCH FASTER?!
THERE IS A SPECIAL OCEAN CURRENT THAT ONLY WORLD GOVERNMENT SHIPS CAN USE...
ENIES LOBBY...
IMPEL DOWN...
MARINE HEAD-QUARTERS...
MARIJOA
REDLINE
NAVY HEADQUARTERS (MARINEFORD)
Calm belt
SABAODY ARCHIPELAGO
GREAT PRISON IMPEL DOWN
ENIES LOBBY
CURRENT LOCATION
AMAZON LILY
A GIANT SWIRLING CURRENT CONNECTS THESE THREE FACILITIES.
EACH OF THEM HAS GATES OF JUSTICE. WHEN THE GATES ARE OPENED...
...THE CURRENT SPEEDS TRAVEL BETWEEN THE FACILITIES.
BUT IF THE GATES REMAIN CLOSED, YOU'LL CONTINUE TO RIDE THE SWIRLING CURRENT INDEFINITELY.

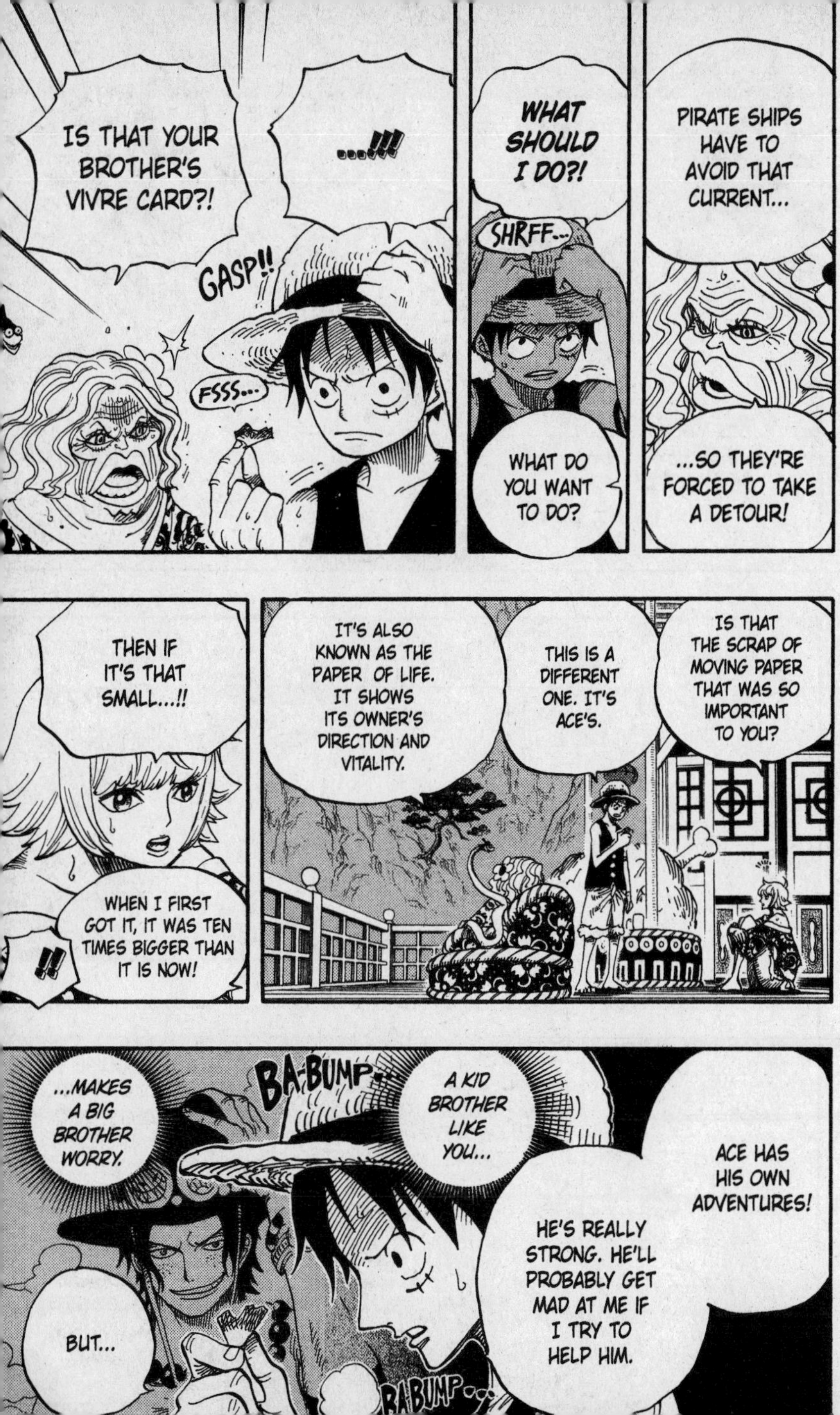
PIRATE SHIPS HAVE TO AVOID THAT CURRENT...
...SO THEY'RE FORCED TO TAKE A DETOUR!
WHAT SHOULD I DO?!
SHRFF...
WHAT DO YOU WANT TO DO?
...!!!
IS THAT YOUR BROTHER'S VIVRE CARD?!
GASP!!
FSSS...
IS THAT THE SCRAP OF MOVING PAPER THAT WAS SO IMPORTANT TO YOU?
THIS IS A DIFFERENT ONE. IT'S ACE'S.
IT'S ALSO KNOWN AS THE PAPER OF LIFE. IT SHOWS ITS OWNER'S DIRECTION AND VITALITY.
THEN IF IT'S THAT SMALL...!!
WHEN I FIRST GOT IT, IT WAS TEN TIMES BIGGER THAN IT IS NOW!
!!
ACE HAS HIS OWN ADVENTURES!
HE'S REALLY STRONG. HE'LL PROBABLY GET MAD AT ME IF I TRY TO HELP HIM.
A KID BROTHER LIKE YOU...
BA-BUMP...
...MAKES A BIG BROTHER WORRY.
BUT...
BA-BUMP...

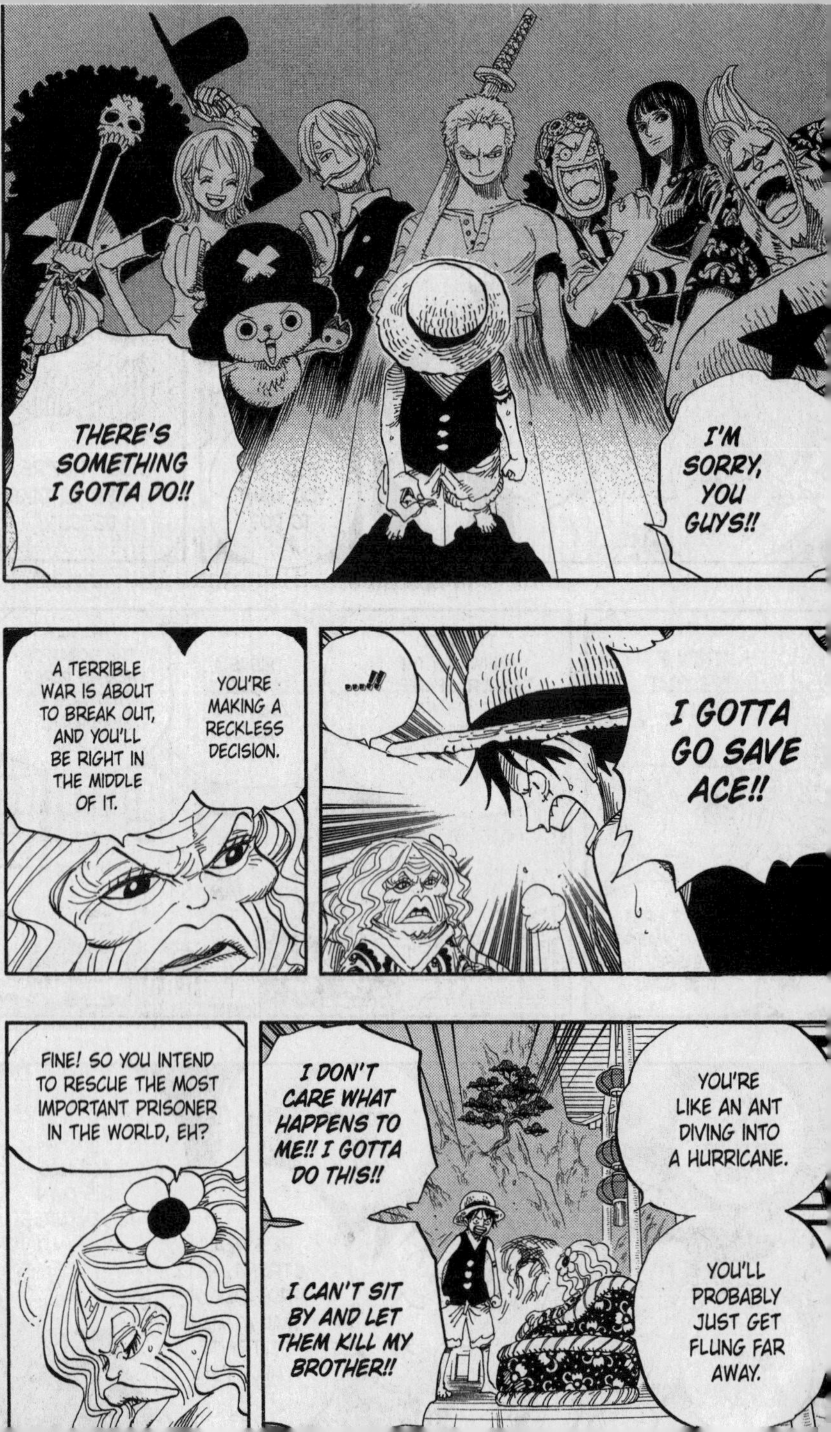
I'M SORRY, YOU GUYS!!
THERE'S SOMETHING I GOTTA DO!!
I GOTTA GO SAVE ACE!!
...!!
YOU'RE MAKING A RECKLESS DECISION.
A TERRIBLE WAR IS ABOUT TO BREAK OUT, AND YOU'LL BE RIGHT IN THE MIDDLE OF IT.
YOU'RE LIKE AN ANT DIVING INTO A HURRICANE.
YOU'LL PROBABLY JUST GET FLUNG FAR AWAY.
I DON'T CARE WHAT HAPPENS TO ME!! I GOTTA DO THIS!!
I CAN'T SIT BY AND LET THEM KILL MY BROTHER!!
FINE! SO YOU INTEND TO RESCUE THE MOST IMPORTANT PRISONER IN THE WORLD, EH?

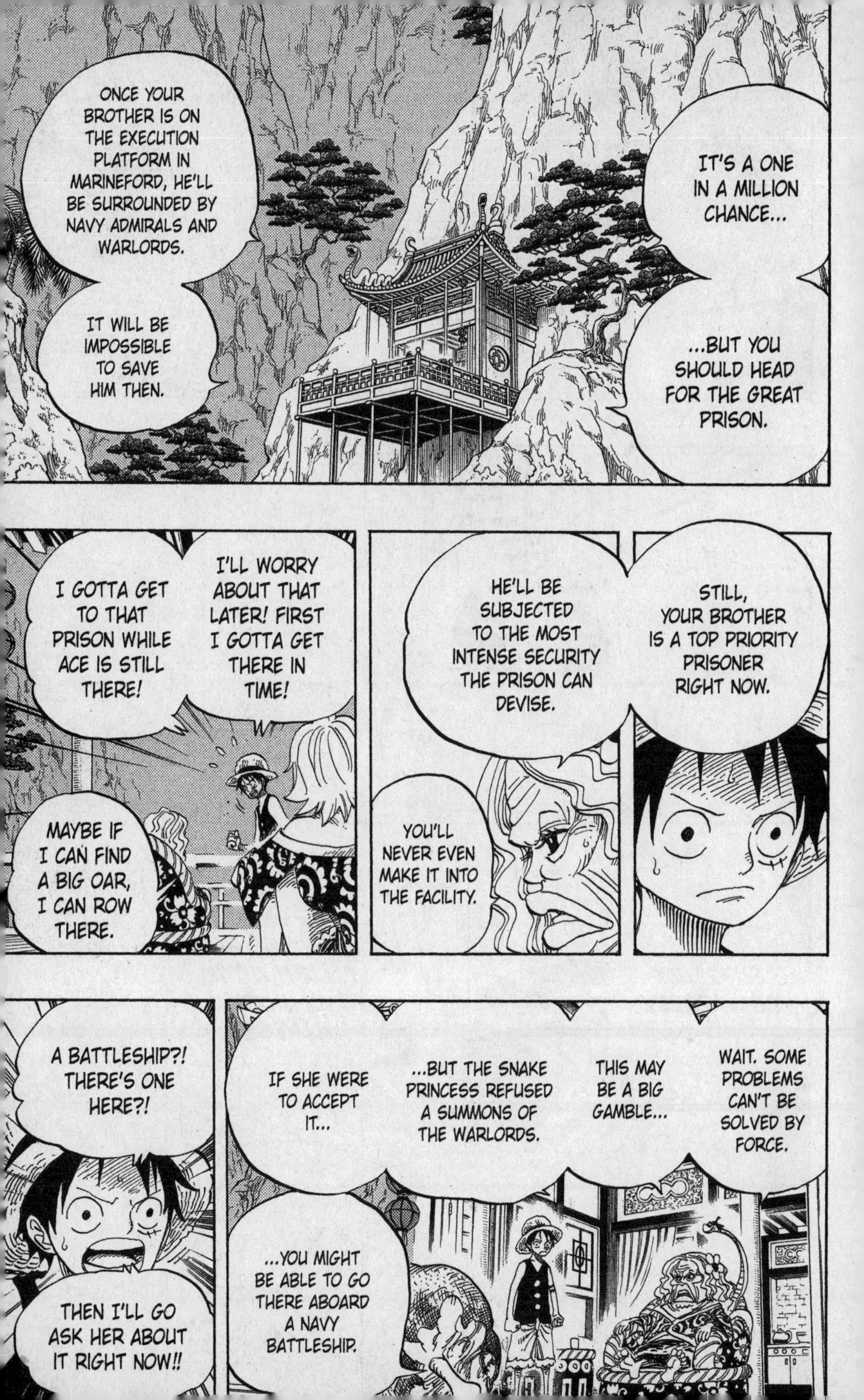
IT'S A ONE IN A MILLION CHANCE...
...BUT YOU SHOULD HEAD FOR THE GREAT PRISON.
ONCE YOUR BROTHER IS ON THE EXECUTION PLATFORM IN MARINEFORD, HE'LL BE SURROUNDED BY NAVY ADMIRALS AND WARLORDS.
IT WILL BE IMPOSSIBLE TO SAVE HIM THEN.
STILL, YOUR BROTHER IS A TOP PRIORITY PRISONER RIGHT NOW.
HE'LL BE SUBJECTED TO THE MOST INTENSE SECURITY THE PRISON CAN DEVISE.
YOU'LL NEVER EVEN MAKE IT INTO THE FACILITY.
I'LL WORRY ABOUT THAT LATER! FIRST I GOTTA GET THERE IN TIME!
I GOTTA GET TO THAT PRISON WHILE ACE IS STILL THERE!
MAYBE IF I CAN FIND A BIG OAR, I CAN ROW THERE.
WAIT. SOME PROBLEMS CAN'T BE SOLVED BY FORCE.
THIS MAY BE A BIG GAMBLE...
...BUT THE SNAKE PRINCESS REFUSED A SUMMONS OF THE WARLORDS.
IF SHE WERE TO ACCEPT IT...
...YOU MIGHT BE ABLE TO GO THERE ABOARD A NAVY BATTLESHIP.
A BATTLESHIP?! THERE'S ONE HERE?!
THEN I'LL GO ASK HER ABOUT IT RIGHT NOW!!

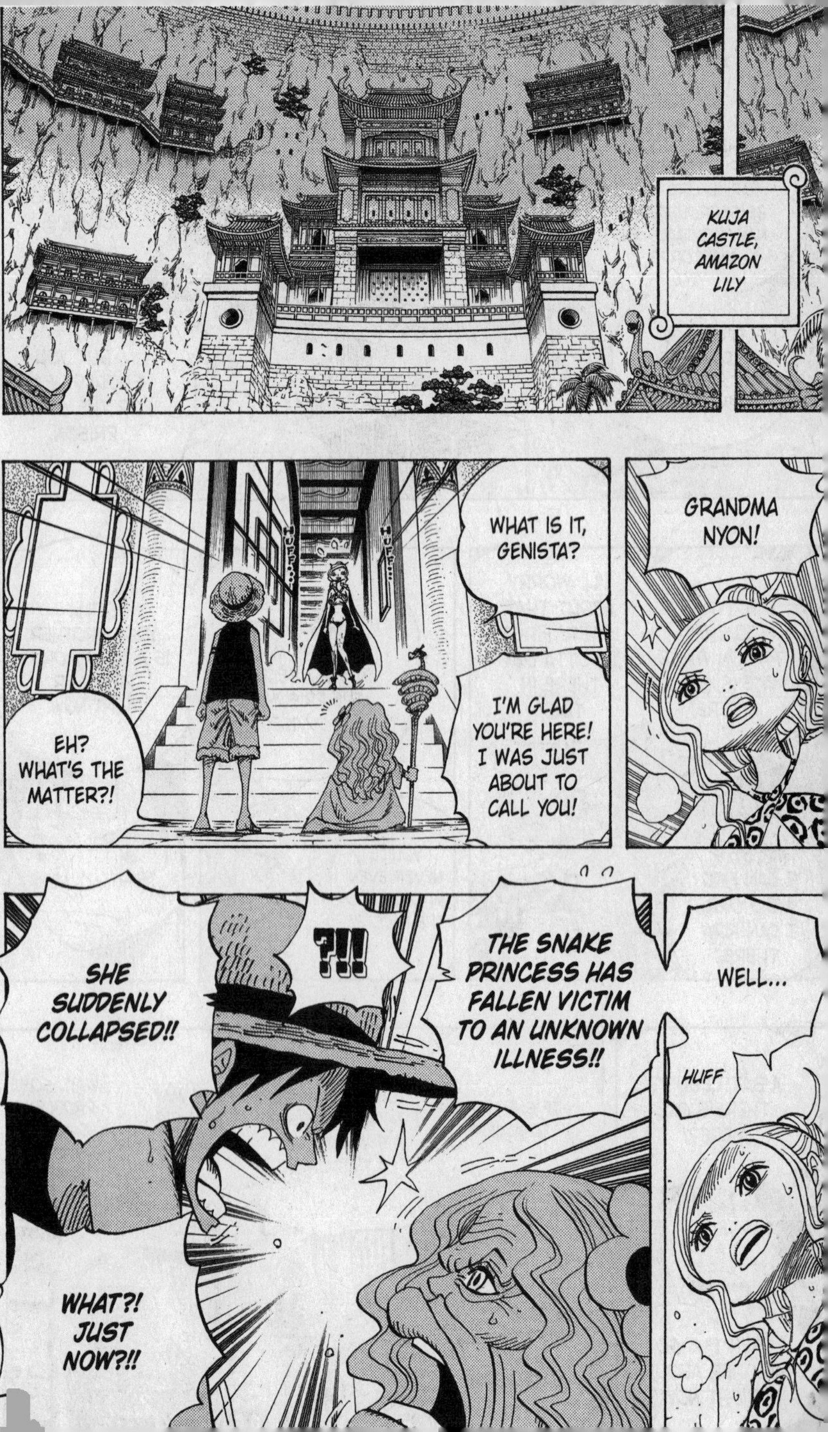
KUJA CASTLE, AMAZON LILY
GRANDMA NYON!
WHAT IS IT, GENISTA?
HUFF...
HUFF...
I'M GLAD YOU'RE HERE! I WAS JUST ABOUT TO CALL YOU!
EH? WHAT'S THE MATTER?!
WELL...
HUFF
THE SNAKE PRINCESS HAS FALLEN VICTIM TO AN UNKNOWN ILLNESS!!
?!!
SHE SUDDENLY COLLAPSED!!
WHAT?! JUST NOW?!!

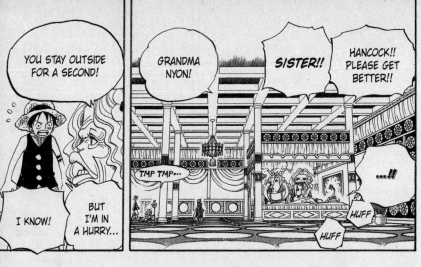

HANCOCK!! PLEASE GET BETTER!!
SISTER!!
GRANDMA NYON!
...!!
HUFF
HUFF
TMP TMP...
YOU STAY OUTSIDE FOR A SECOND!
BUT I'M IN A HURRY...
I KNOW!
HUFF HUFF
HUFF...
HUFF...
OH, THE PAIN!
DOOM!!
SHE KEEPS CLUTCHING HER CHEST! I WAS AFRAID THERE WAS SOMETHING WRONG WITH HER HEART!
BUT I DON'T THINK THERE IS. I'VE NEVER SEEN SYMPTOMS LIKE THESE BEFORE.
I DON'T EVEN KNOW WHAT MEDICINE TO PRESCRIBE HER!
BUT SHE'S IN TERRIBLE PAIN!
HUFF...
HUFF...
AND SHE REFUSES TO EAT ANYTHING.

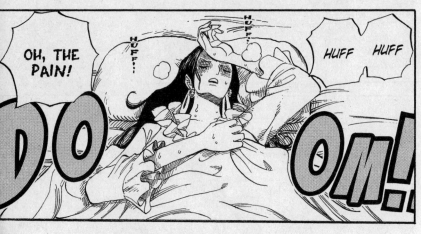

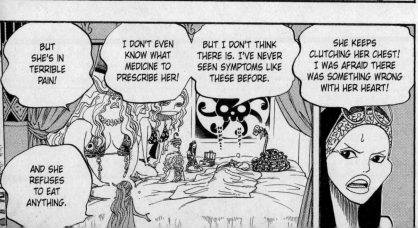

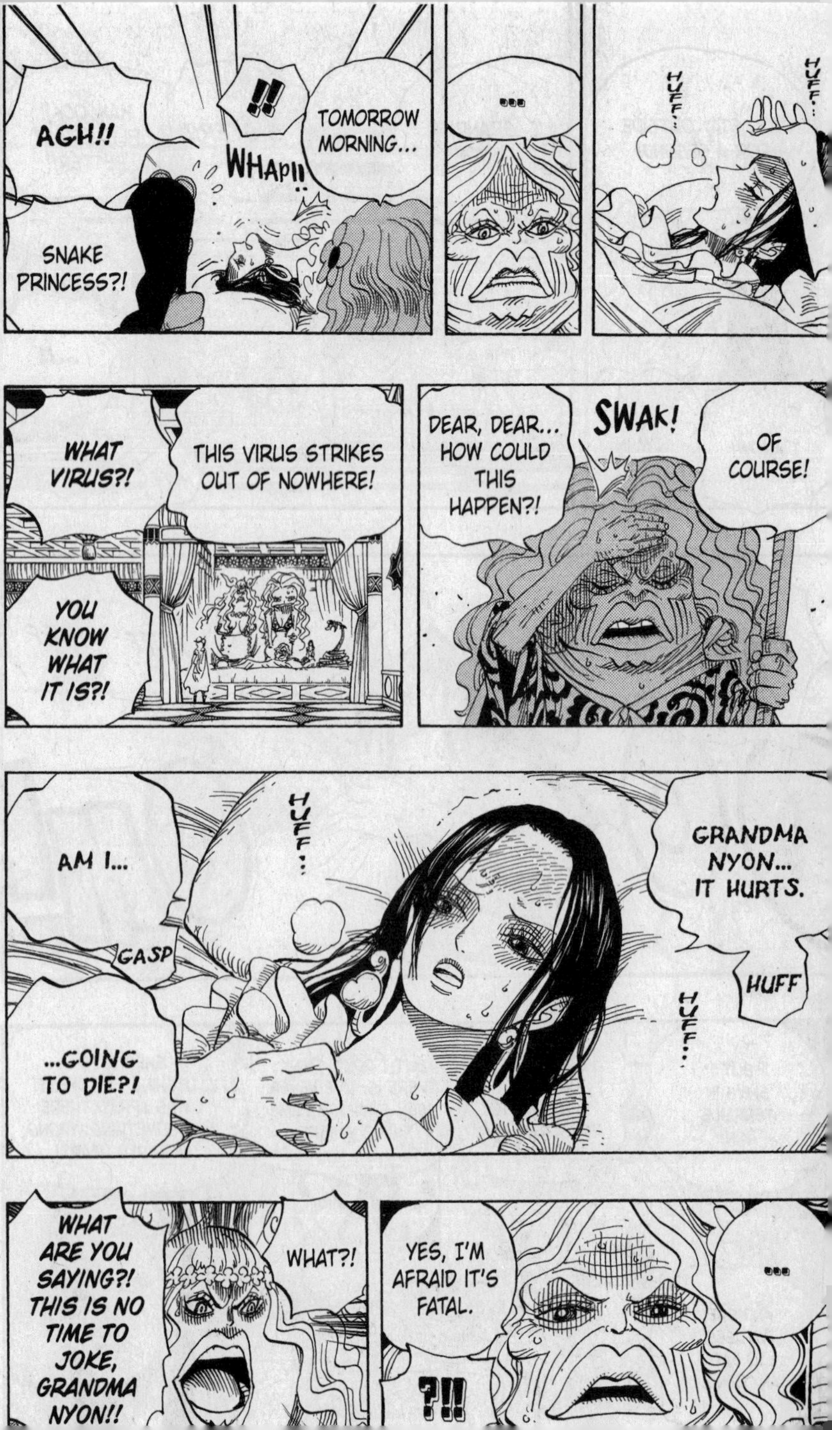
HUFF...
HUFF...
...
TOMORROW MORNING...
!!
WHAP!!
AGH!!
SNAKE PRINCESS?!
OF COURSE!
SWAK!
DEAR, DEAR... HOW COULD THIS HAPPEN?!
THIS VIRUS STRIKES OUT OF NOWHERE!
WHAT VIRUS?!
YOU KNOW WHAT IT IS?!
GRANDMA NYON... IT HURTS.
HUFF
HUFF...
HUFF...
AM I...
GASP
...GOING TO DIE?!
...
YES, I'M AFRAID IT'S FATAL.
?!!
WHAT?!
WHAT ARE YOU SAYING?! THIS IS NO TIME TO JOKE, GRANDMA NYON!!

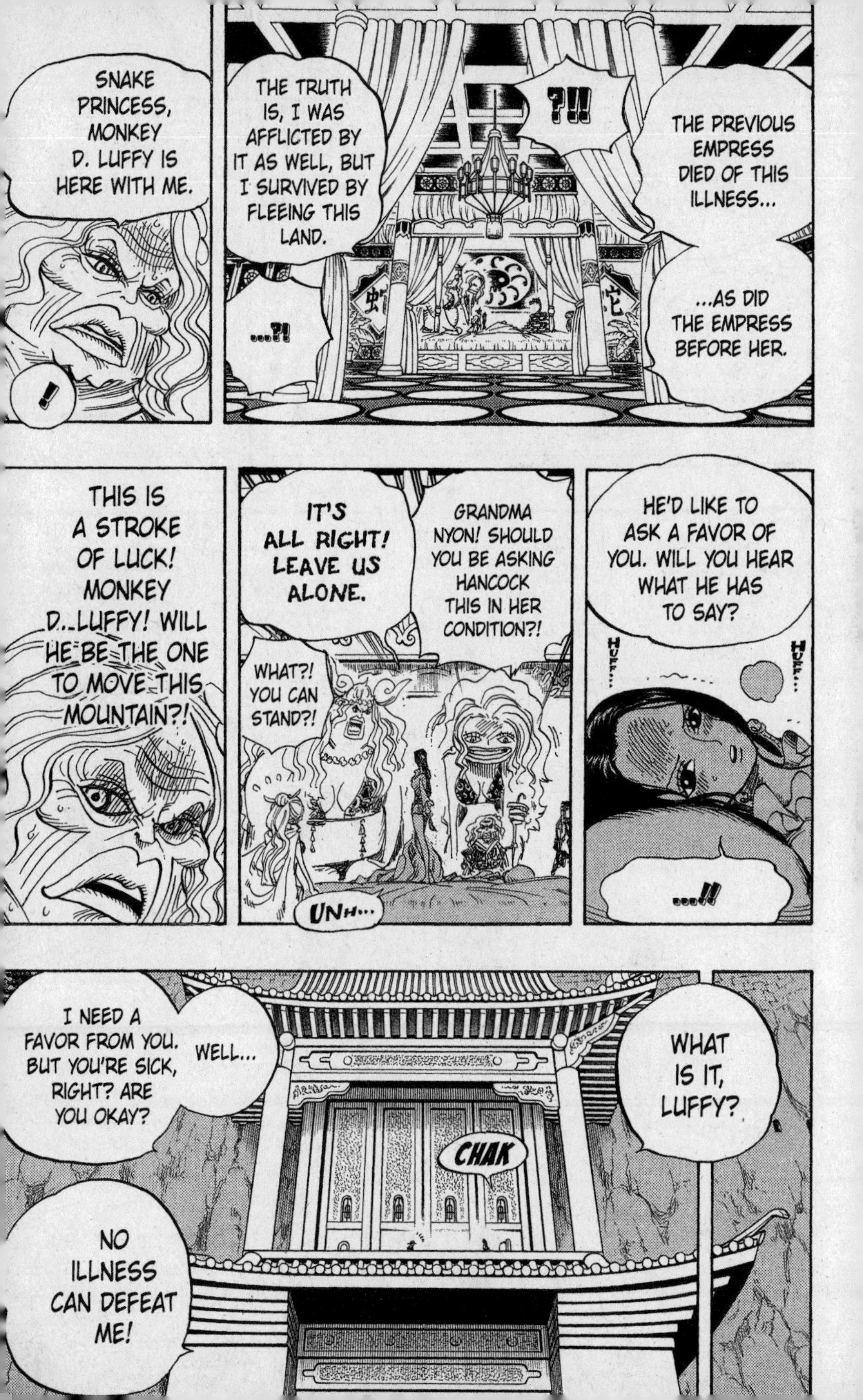
THE PREVIOUS EMPRESS DIED OF THIS ILLNESS...
?!!
...AS DID THE EMPRESS BEFORE HER.
THE TRUTH IS, I WAS AFFLICTED BY IT AS WELL, BUT I SURVIVED BY FLEEING THIS LAND.
...?!
SNAKE PRINCESS, MONKEY D. LUFFY IS HERE WITH ME.
!
HE'D LIKE TO ASK A FAVOR OF YOU. WILL YOU HEAR WHAT HE HAS TO SAY?
HUFF...
HUFF...
...!!
GRANDMA NYON! SHOULD YOU BE ASKING HANCOCK THIS IN HER CONDITION?!
IT'S ALL RIGHT! LEAVE US ALONE.
WHAT?! YOU CAN STAND?!
UNH...
THIS IS A STROKE OF LUCK! MONKEY D...LUFFY! WILL HE BE THE ONE TO MOVE THIS MOUNTAIN?!
WHAT IS IT, LUFFY?
CHAK
WELL...
I NEED A FAVOR FROM YOU. BUT YOU'RE SICK, RIGHT? ARE YOU OKAY?
NO ILLNESS CAN DEFEAT ME!

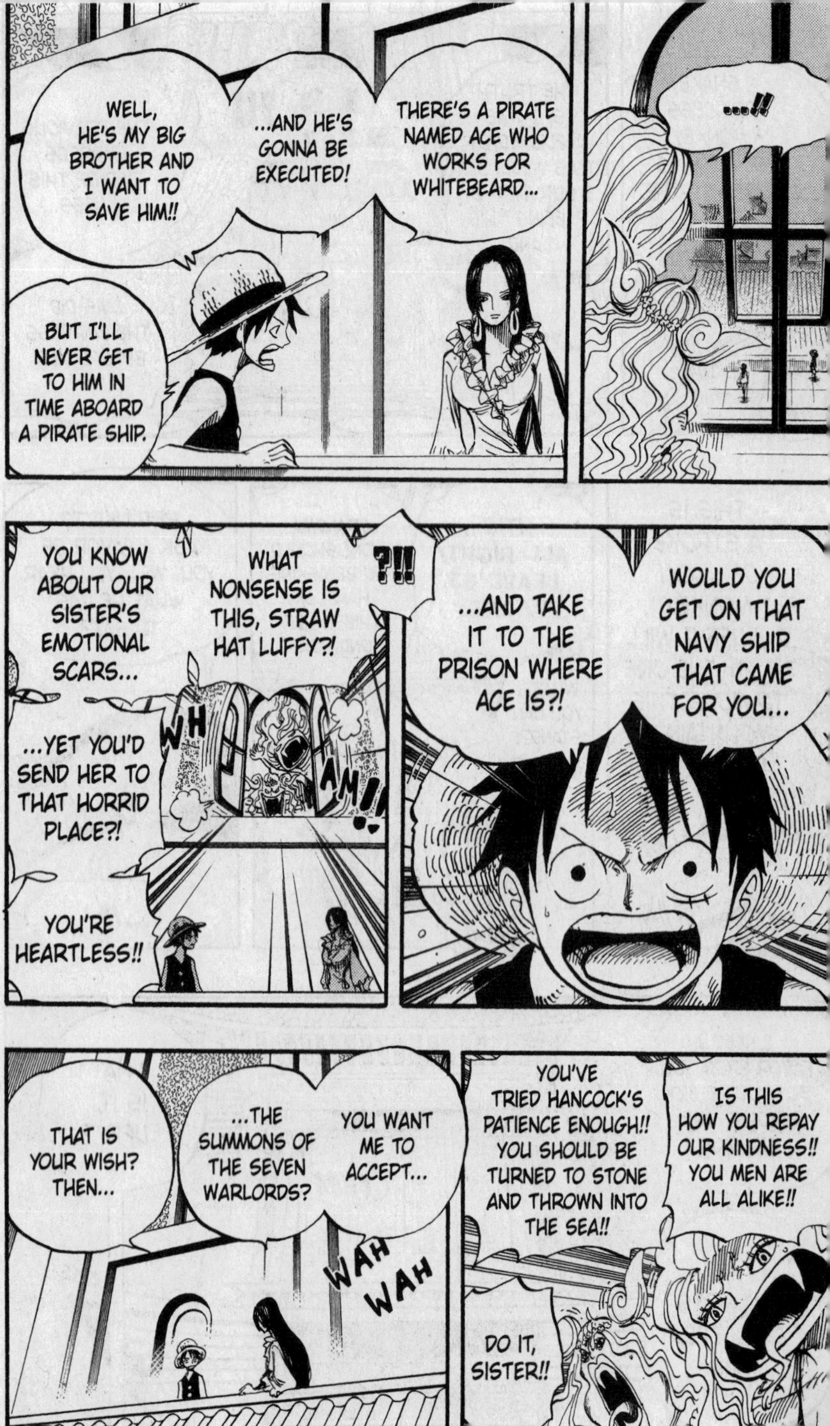
...!!
THERE'S A PIRATE NAMED ACE WHO WORKS FOR WHITEBEARD...
...AND HE'S GONNA BE EXECUTED!
WELL, HE'S MY BIG BROTHER AND I WANT TO SAVE HIM!!
BUT I'LL NEVER GET TO HIM IN TIME ABOARD A PIRATE SHIP.
WOULD YOU GET ON THAT NAVY SHIP THAT CAME FOR YOU...
...AND TAKE IT TO THE PRISON WHERE ACE IS?!
?!!
WHAT NONSENSE IS THIS, STRAW HAT LUFFY?!
WHAM!!
YOU KNOW ABOUT OUR SISTER'S EMOTIONAL SCARS...
...YET YOU'D SEND HER TO THAT HORRID PLACE?!
YOU'RE HEARTLESS!!
IS THIS HOW YOU REPAY OUR KINDNESS!! YOU MEN ARE ALL ALIKE!!
YOU'VE TRIED HANCOCK'S PATIENCE ENOUGH!! YOU SHOULD BE TURNED TO STONE AND THROWN INTO THE SEA!!
DO IT, SISTER!!
YOU WANT ME TO ACCEPT...
...THE SUMMONS OF THE SEVEN WARLORDS?
WAH WAH
THAT IS YOUR WISH? THEN...

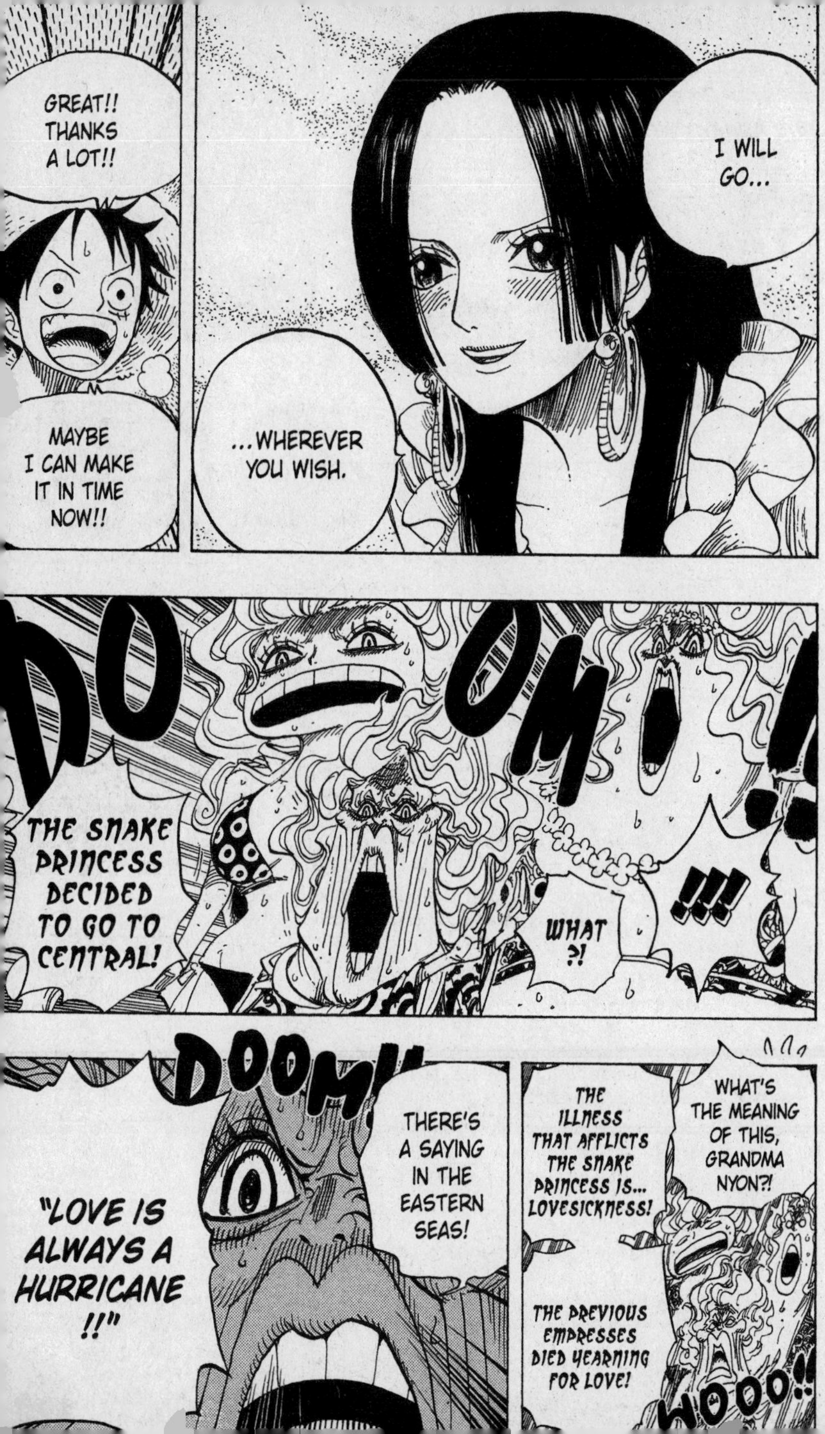
I WILL GO...
...WHEREVER YOU WISH.
GREAT!! THANKS A LOT!!
MAYBE I CAN MAKE IT IN TIME NOW!!
WHAT ?!
!!!
THE SNAKE PRINCESS DECIDED TO GO TO CENTRAL!
WHAT'S THE MEANING OF THIS, GRANDMA NYON?!
THE ILLNESS THAT AFFLICTS THE SNAKE PRINCESS IS... LOVESICKNESS!
THE PREVIOUS EMPRESSES DIED YEARNING FOR LOVE!
WOOO!!
DOOM!!
THERE'S A SAYING IN THE EASTERN SEAS!
"LOVE IS ALWAYS A HURRICANE !!"

SBS Question Corner

OUR GREAT SWORDSMAN, KAZUYA NAKAI!!

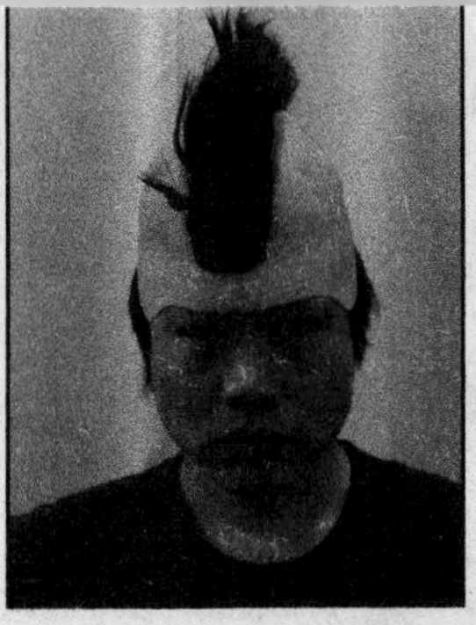

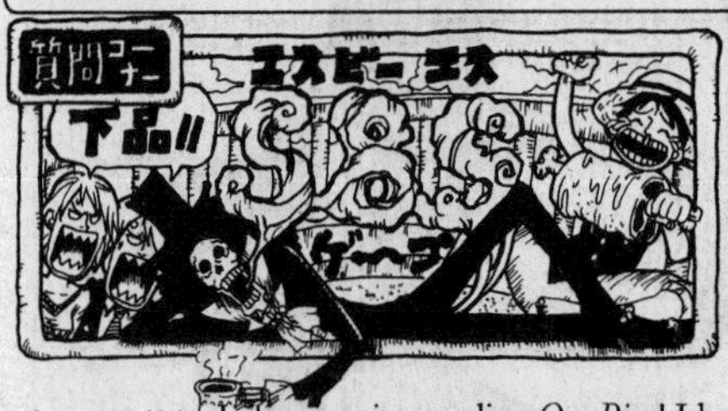
質問コーナー
下品!!

(Moto-Chan, Tokyo)

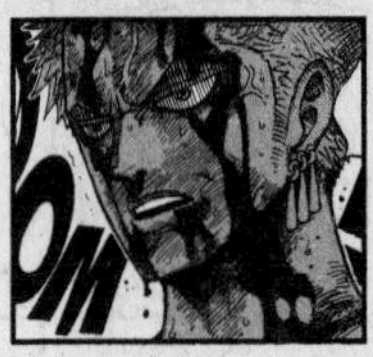

Reader(R): I always enjoy reading *One Piece*! I have a question for Mr. Nakai. Of all the characters in *One Piece*, Zolo seems to get injured the most. So do you suffer any kind of damage when he does? Please tell me!

--Spirit of Zero

Nakai(N): You remember how our captain said we aim for realism? Everybody beats on me in those scenes!

R: Nakai, please be my brother!

--Marimokorigori

N: Don't call me Brother! I have the heart of a girl! (Spoken on impulse)

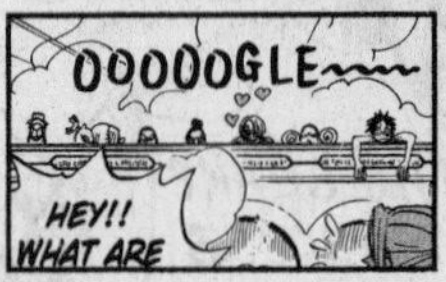
OOOOOGLE~~
HEY!! WHAT ARE

R: Hello, Mr. Nakai. In the Alabasta arc, all the guys except Zolo were peeping at the bathing women. Would you have peeped if you'd been there?

--Harason Beam

N: No. I'm a grown man. It's more fun to listen to the peepers talk about it and fantasize. Because I'm a grown-up.

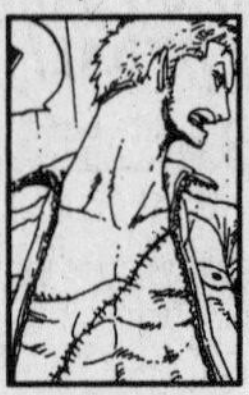

R: Mr. Nakai, I bet your abs are as cut as Zolo's! Tell me exactly how great they are!

--Yo

N: I don't know about my abs, but my butt has a deep cut down the center.

R: Mr. Nakai, have you ever cut your hair? I have. My hair used to be down to my waist, but I cut it to shoulder length.

--Snake

N: If you don't have anything to say, don't call me.

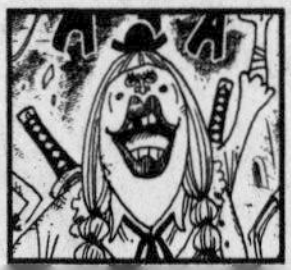

R: Nakai, I love you! Marry me! (voice of Lola the Proposer) Please answer me in a manly way, like Zolo. (Hee)

--Vague Suii

N: Streaming Wolf-Swords!!

R: Mr. Nakai, I have a question! Zolo is a weight-training freak, right? So do you lift weights to get into character? Oh! I know! I'll do the same thing I did with Mayumi Tanaka! Take this! Negative Hollow!

--Naocchi

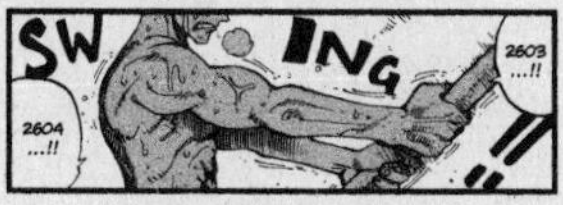
SWING
2603 ...!!
2604 ...!!

N: Ugh... Sorry, I may be Zolo, but I have 23 percent body fat.

R: Nakai! Take this! Oni Giri!! *Broot!!*
*Don't hold in your farts, just let them out! *Broot!!*

--Tony

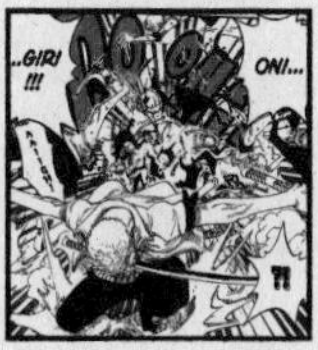
ONI...
..GIRI !!!

N: That was a devious special attack I used only once way back in the day! Use it with the greatest care: it can easily backfire.

R: I have a question for Kazuya Nakai. Do you and the voice actor for Sanji really get into fights? In the comic (and anime), you always seem to be at each other's throats.

--The South

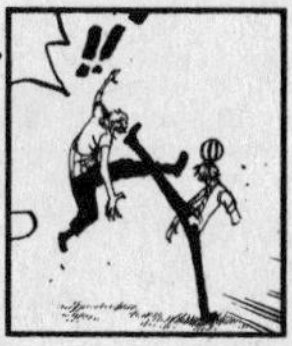
!!

N: Who's Sanji?

R: Please put a sword in your mouth and say, "Oni Giri!!"

--Kendo Club Spearhead

N: Mmrf! "Sword!" Oops! I mixed it up.

Oda: Thank you very much! Time's about up, Mr. Nakai. Hey! Why are you munching on rice balls?! Let's make the next postcard the last. Hey! Stop eating! And stop shouting "sword!" You're spraying rice everywhere!

R: Please think of a Zolo move that's also a pun. Thanks!

--By a thread

N: Leech! Loiter! Last!

Oda: That's useless! That ends this Voice Actor Question Corner! See you next time!

CA SIVE IN
OVA. *Ao 1492 a Chrytophoro*

nomine regis Castella primum detecta.

Noua
Fran cia

Chilaga

ac

Ceuola

Canagadi

Clandi

Marata   Calicuas   Tagil   Flori da

Morata
Cicre   Cacco   Como   Corn to   La Emperalula

Cuchillo   Cuias   Tara   Lucizo

Colisko   Tolla   Aschula   Hispania   Paniet   Aquer

S. Thomas   R. grande   de los   yelos   Coco   merco

V. de los galopeges

CTIALIS   Quito   Nagua   Caribana

Cajma   Pe ru

AR DEL ZVR.   Insulæ
                incognita.   Cuito

CVS CAPRICORNI   Cabo de
                    C. Rosso

EL MAR
PACIFICO.

R. de
Paomos

Ar. hipelago
de las Islas

I've heard it's possible for people to live 140 years, but most people's lives are shortened by the amount of work and stress they have to endure. I'm working day and night as a manga author, so I'll probably only live to be 135. (SULK) Life is too short. Time to start 54!

– *Eiichiro Oda, 2009*

CA SIVE IN
OVA. *Ao 1492. a Chrystophoro*
nomine regis Castella primum detecta.

Noua
Fran
cia

ARCTICVS

Chilaga

ac
Cunigaci
Cicuola
Clauda
Calicuas
Tagil
Flori
da.
Ispira
Moximo
La
Marata
Mirata
Coru
La Emperialada
Cacos
Comos
Quec
Lucaio
Cubas
Tania
cculata
Leri ma
Chsko
Cuchtla
Hispania
Cuba
Thomas
R. de cuchila
Michila
cguald
Socco meco
Gitana
Aose
Caribana
Carbar
Y de los galopego
Miguel
CTIALIS
Quito
Nepus
Turi
Araiar
Aurira
Conen gu
Casria
Iape
Graneari
Alaise
AR DEL ZVR
Pe ru.
Amaz
Insula incog nita.
Chchbi
Morropon
Colocli
VS. CAPRICORNI
Sciura matus
Cabo de layla
C. Rasso
EL MAR
PACIFICO
Arbori
Cabo blanco
los fordolores
Garagon
Chic
R. de Adorno
Archipelago de las Plas.

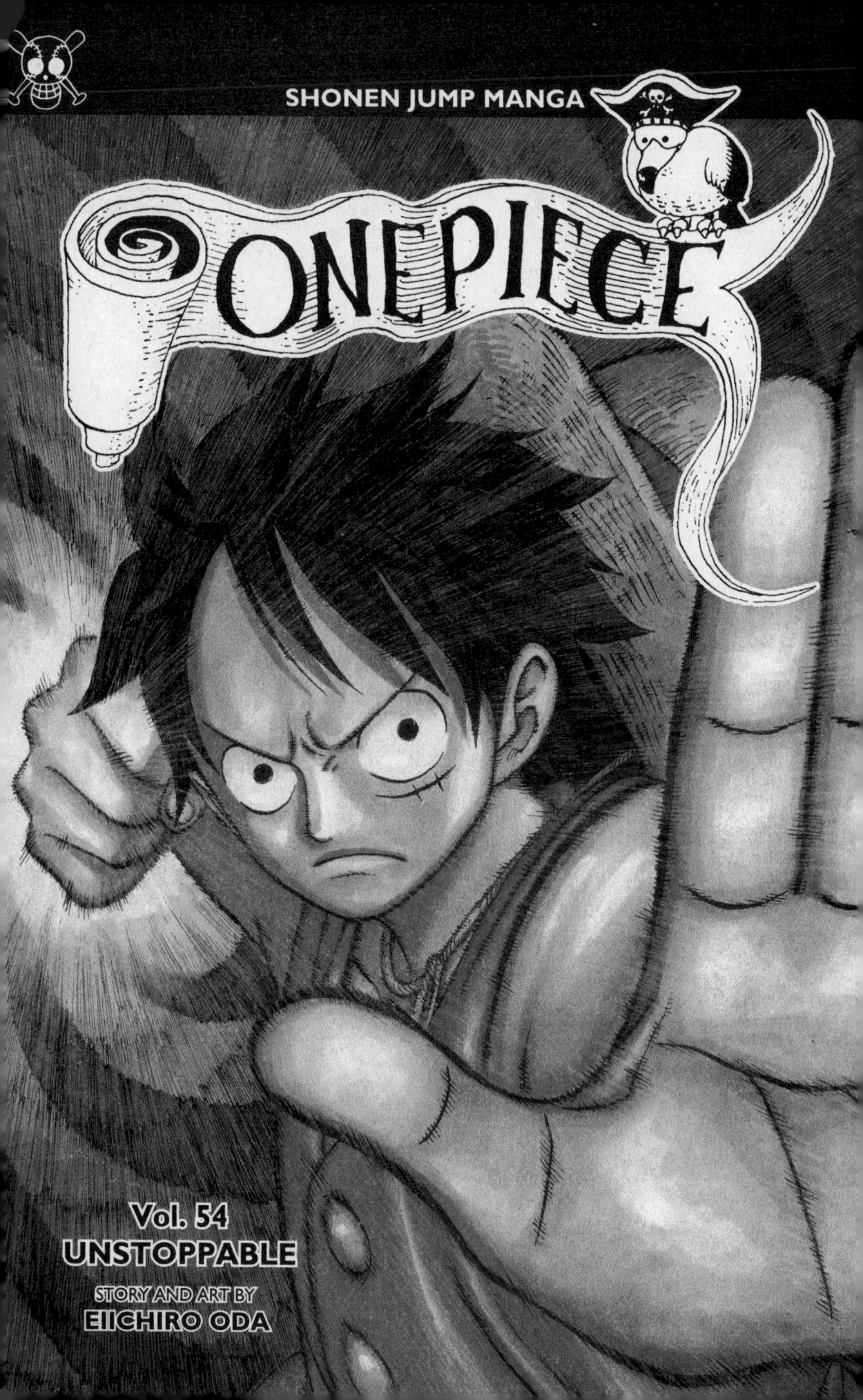
SHONEN JUMP MANGA
ONE PIECE
Vol. 54
UNSTOPPABLE
STORY AND ART BY
EIICHIRO ODA

Warriors of Kuja

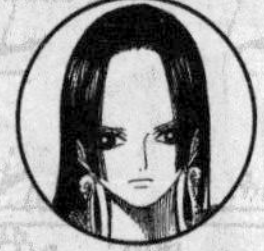

The empress of Amazon Lily, captain of the Kuja Pirates and one of the Seven Warlords of the Sea.

"Empress" Boa Hancock

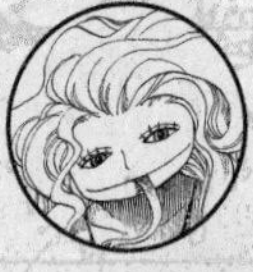

Second of the Gorgon Sisters.

Boa Sandersonia

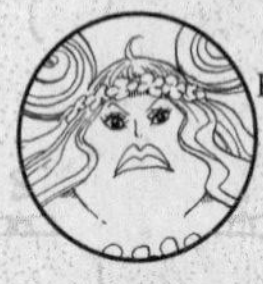

Youngest of the Gorgon Sisters.

Boa Marigold

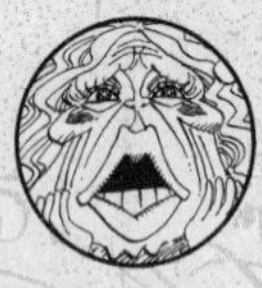

Former Empress of Amazon Lily.

Gloriosa (Grandma Nyon)

The Straw Hats

TOTAL BOUNTY: 700,000,050 BERRIES

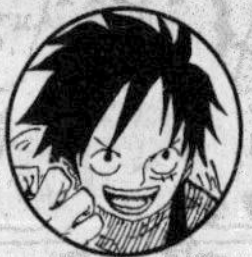

Boundlessly optimistic and able to stretch like rubber, he is determined to become King of the Pirates.

Bounty: 300 million berries

Monkey D. Luffy

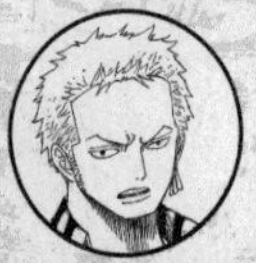

A former bounty hunter and master of the "three-sword"style. He aspires to be the world's greatest swordsman.

Bounty: 120 million berries

Roronoa Zolo

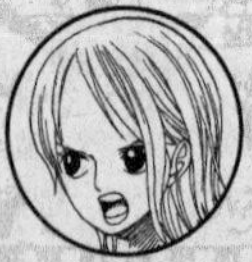

A thief who specializes in robbing pirates. Nami hates pirates, but Luffy convinced her to be his navigator.

Bounty: 16 million berries

Nami

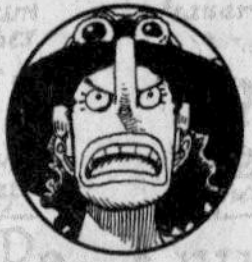

A village boy with a talent for telling tall tales. His father, Yasopp, is a member of Shanks's crew.

Bounty: 30 million berries

Usopp

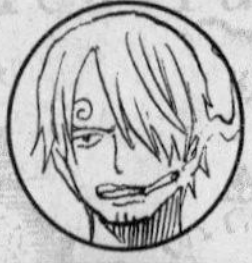

The kindhearted cook (and ladies' man) whose dream is to find the legendary sea, the "All Blue."

Bounty: 77 million berries

Sanji

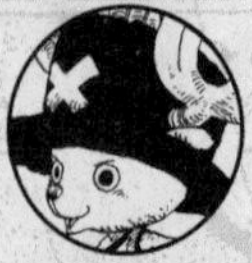

A blue-nosed man-reindeer and the ship's doctor.

Bounty: 50 berries

Tony Tony Chopper

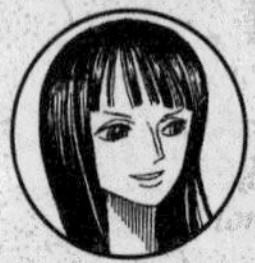

A mysterious woman in search of the Ponegliff on which true history is recorded.

Bounty: 80 million berries

Nico Robin

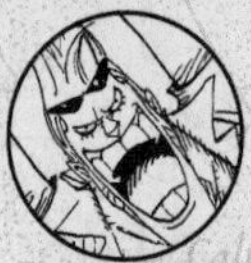

A softhearted cyborg and talented shipwright.

Bounty: 44 million berries

Franky

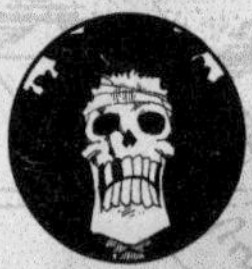

A skeleton warrior with an afro. He dreams of being reunited with Laboon, the tame whale he parted with fifty years ago.

Bounty: 33 million berries

Brook

THE STORY OF ONE PIECE • VOLUME 54 •

Monkey D. Luffy started out as just a kid with a dream—to become the greatest pirate in history! Stirred by the tales of pirate "Red-Haired" Shanks, Luffy vowed to become a pirate himself. That was before the enchanted Devil Fruit gave Luffy the power to stretch like rubber, at the cost of being unable to swim—a serious handicap for an aspiring sea dog. Undeterred, Luffy set out to sea and recruited some crewmates—master swordsman Zolo; treasure-hunting thief Nami; lying sharpshooter Usopp; the high-kicking chef Sanji; Chopper, the walkin' talkin' reindeer doctor; mysterious archaeologist Robin; cyborg shipwright Franky; and Brook, a musical skeleton!

Having entered the Grand Line, Luffy and crew get a new ship, the *Thousand Sunny*, to replace the *Merry Go*. They head for Fish-Man Island, but they soon find themselves encountering a number of strange and formidable characters on Saobody Archipelago, including the Celestial Dragons, Admiral Kizaru, and Kuma, who uses a mysterious power to scatter the crew far and wide.

Luffy ends up on Amazon Lily, an island of women forbidden to men, which is ruled by Boa Hancock, one of the Seven Warlords of the Sea. There he is nearly put to death when he discovers Hancock's secret. But Luffy wins her over, and empress and pirate decide to set forth together to rescue Luffy's brother Ace, who is to be executed in six days. But can they make it in time? And will the crew ever be reunited?

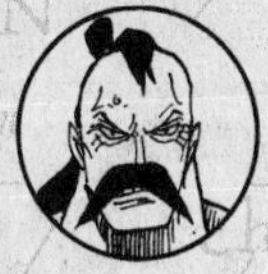

Navy Vice Admiral

MOMONGA

The Second Division Commander of the Whitebeard Pirates and Luffy's older brother. He was defeated by Blackbeard Teech and is currently imprisoned in Impel Down.

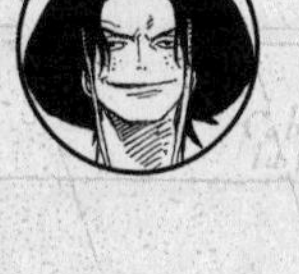

PORTGAZ D. ACE

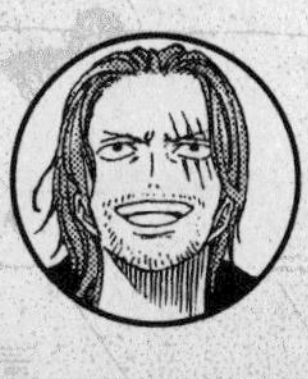

A pirate that Luffy idolizes. Shanks gave Luffy his trademark straw hat.

"RED-HAIRED" SHANKS

Vol. 54
Unstoppable

CONTENTS

Chapter 523:
HELL

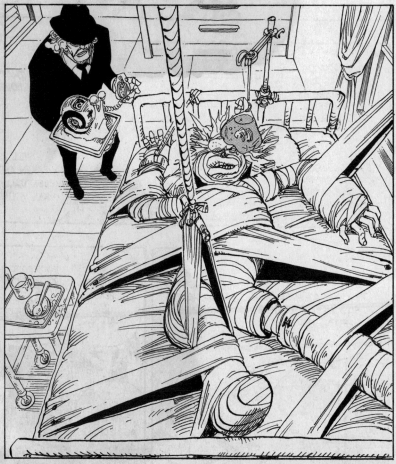

CP9'S INDEPENDENT REPORT, VOL. 29: "TRANSPONDER
SNAIL FOR SPANDAM IN THE INTENSIVE CARE UNIT"

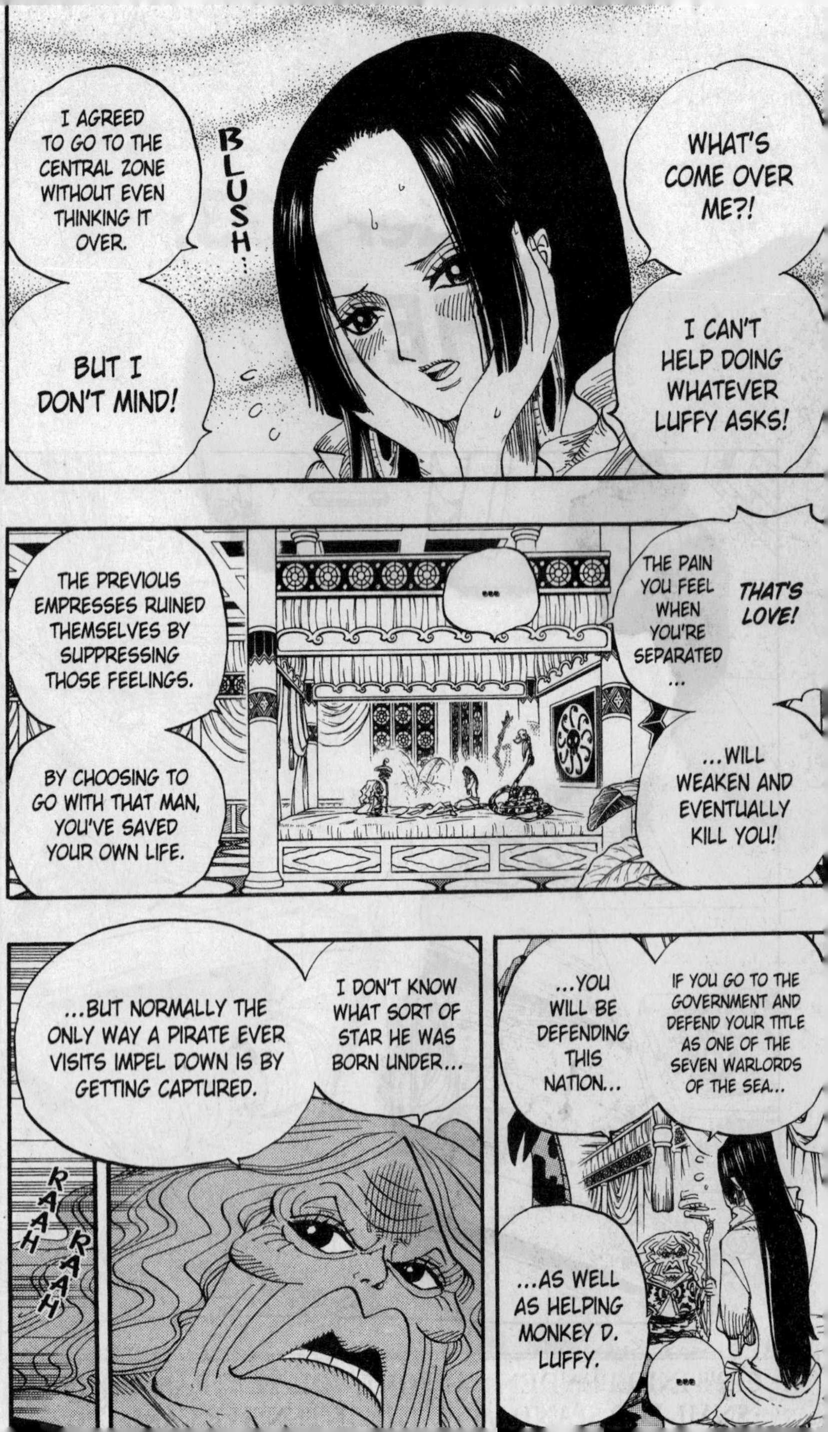
WHAT'S COME OVER ME?!
I CAN'T HELP DOING WHATEVER LUFFY ASKS!
BLUSH...
I AGREED TO GO TO THE CENTRAL ZONE WITHOUT EVEN THINKING IT OVER.
BUT I DON'T MIND!
THAT'S LOVE!
THE PAIN YOU FEEL WHEN YOU'RE SEPARATED...
...WILL WEAKEN AND EVENTUALLY KILL YOU!
...
THE PREVIOUS EMPRESSES RUINED THEMSELVES BY SUPPRESSING THOSE FEELINGS.
BY CHOOSING TO GO WITH THAT MAN, YOU'VE SAVED YOUR OWN LIFE.
IF YOU GO TO THE GOVERNMENT AND DEFEND YOUR TITLE AS ONE OF THE SEVEN WARLORDS OF THE SEA...
...YOU WILL BE DEFENDING THIS NATION...
...AS WELL AS HELPING MONKEY D. LUFFY.
...
I DON'T KNOW WHAT SORT OF STAR HE WAS BORN UNDER...
...BUT NORMALLY THE ONLY WAY A PIRATE EVER VISITS IMPEL DOWN IS BY GETTING CAPTURED.
RAAH RAAH RAAH

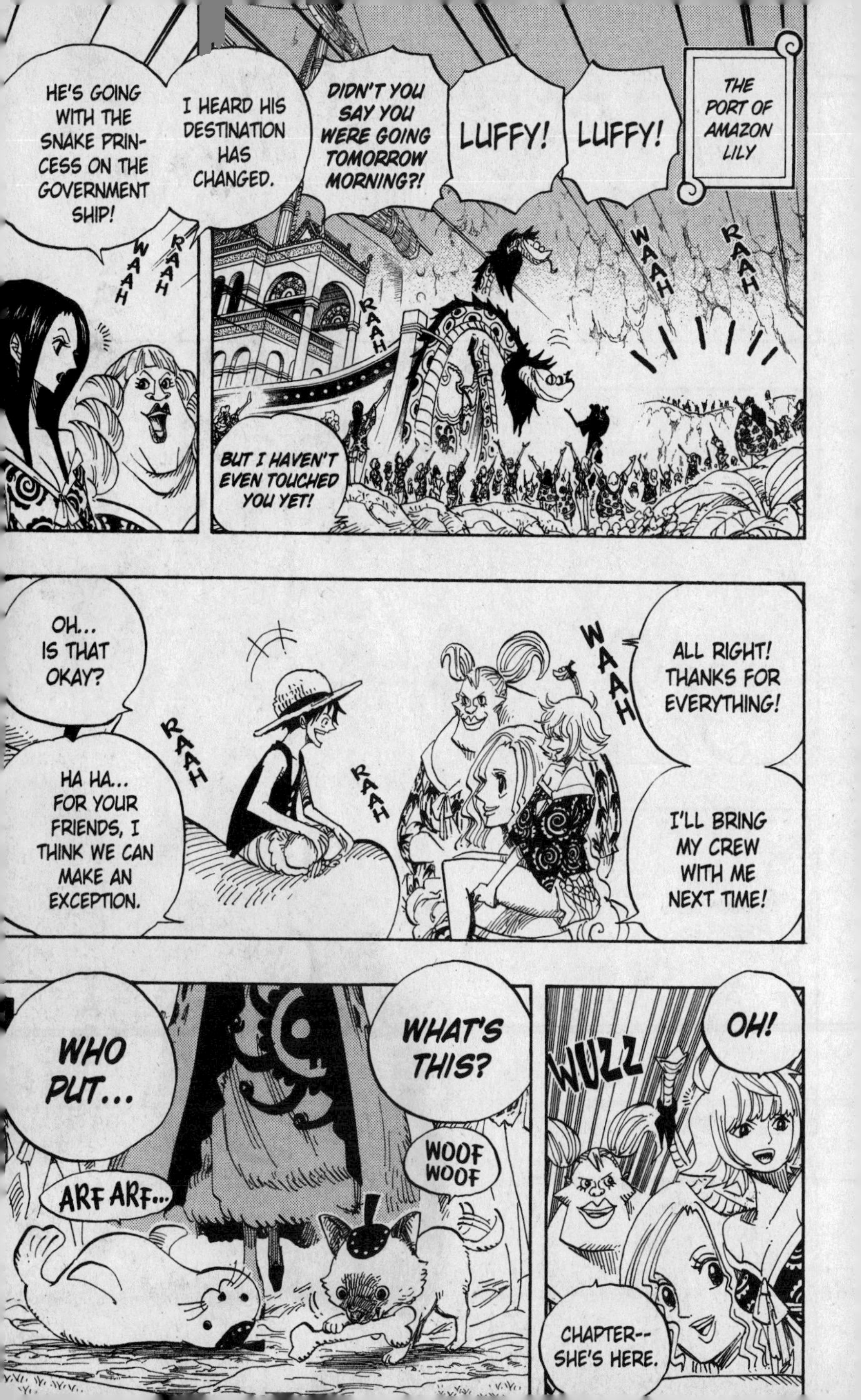
THE PORT OF AMAZON LILY
LUFFY!
LUFFY!
DIDN'T YOU SAY YOU WERE GOING TOMORROW MORNING?!
WAAH
RAAH
RAAH
BUT I HAVEN'T EVEN TOUCHED YOU YET!
I HEARD HIS DESTINATION HAS CHANGED.
HE'S GOING WITH THE SNAKE PRIN-CESS ON THE GOVERNMENT SHIP!
RAAH
WAAH
ALL RIGHT! THANKS FOR EVERYTHING!
I'LL BRING MY CREW WITH ME NEXT TIME!
WAAH
RAAH
RAAH
OH... IS THAT OKAY?
HA HA... FOR YOUR FRIENDS, I THINK WE CAN MAKE AN EXCEPTION.
OH!
WUZZ
CHAPTER-- SHE'S HERE.
WHAT'S THIS?
WOOF WOOF
WHO PUT...
ARF ARF...

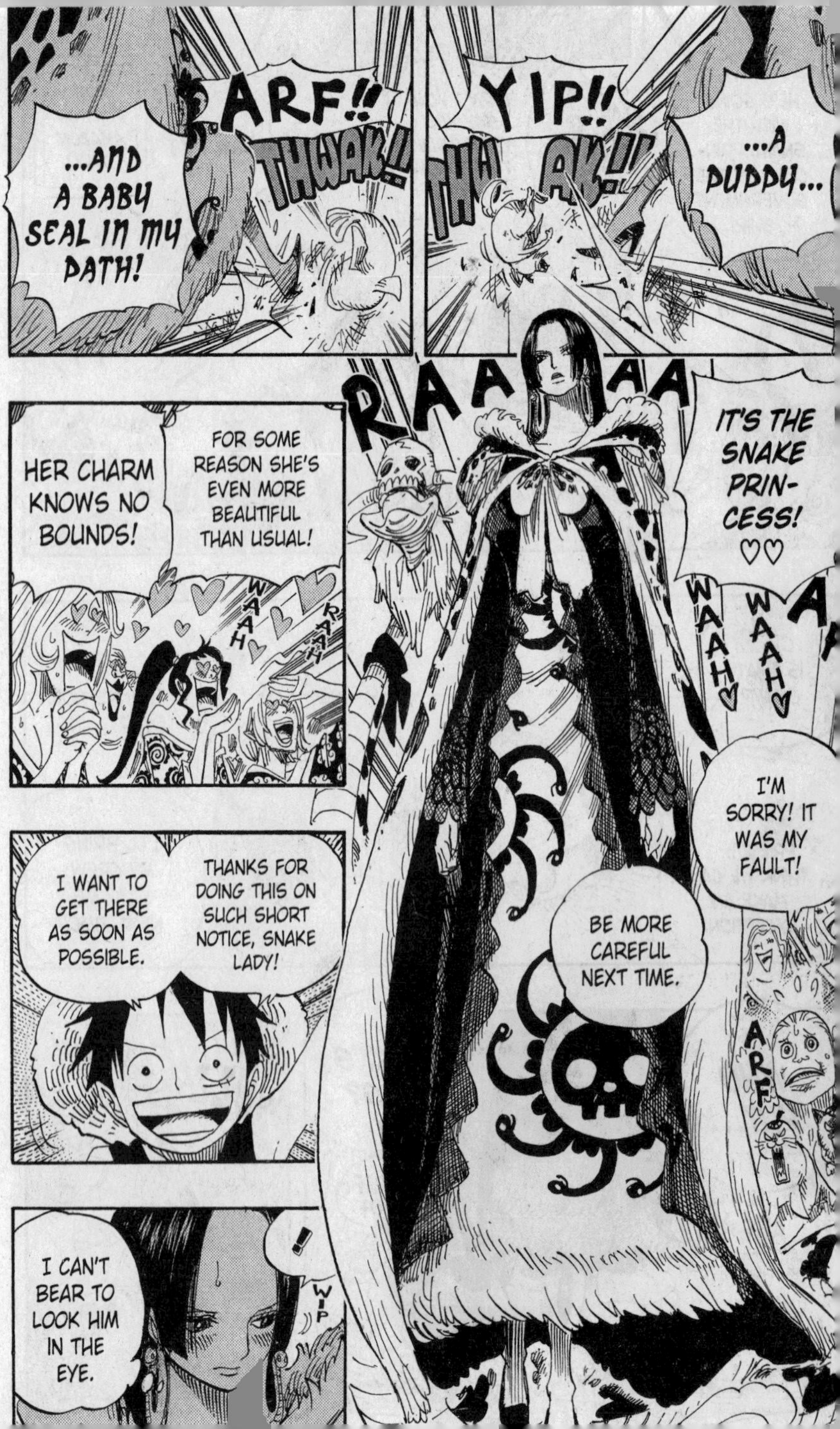
YIP!!
THW AK!!
...A PUPPY...
ARF!!
THWAK!!
...AND A BABY SEAL IN MY PATH!
RAAAAA
IT'S THE SNAKE PRINCESS! ♡♡
WAAH♡
WAAAH♡
I'M SORRY! IT WAS MY FAULT!
BE MORE CAREFUL NEXT TIME.
ARF
FOR SOME REASON SHE'S EVEN MORE BEAUTIFUL THAN USUAL!
HER CHARM KNOWS NO BOUNDS!
WAAH
RAAH
THANKS FOR DOING THIS ON SUCH SHORT NOTICE, SNAKE LADY!
I WANT TO GET THERE AS SOON AS POSSIBLE.
!
WIP
I CAN'T BEAR TO LOOK HIM IN THE EYE.

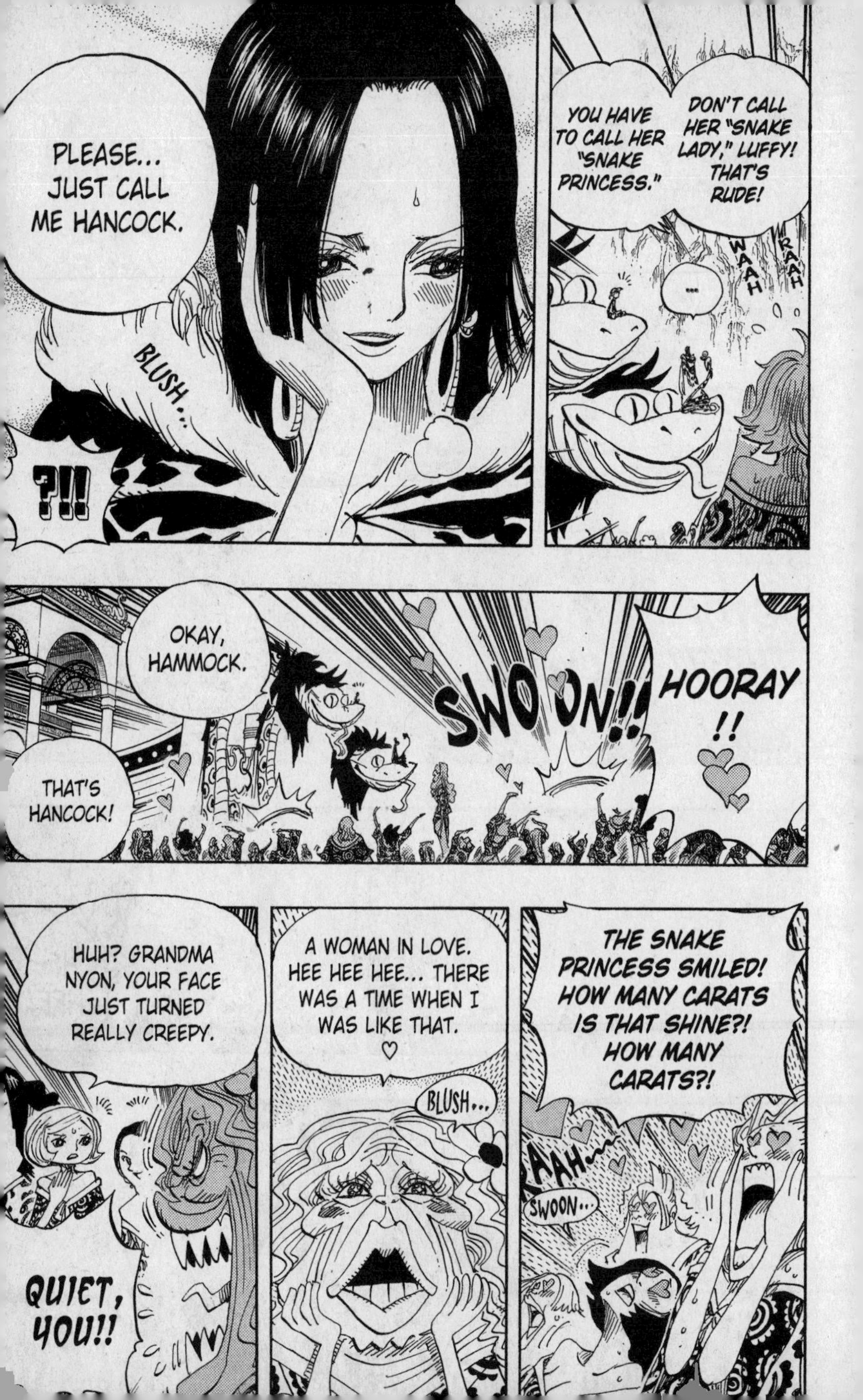
DON'T CALL HER "SNAKE LADY," LUFFY! THAT'S RUDE!
YOU HAVE TO CALL HER "SNAKE PRINCESS."
RAAH
WAAH
...
PLEASE... JUST CALL ME HANCOCK.
BLUSH...
?!!
HOORAY!!
SWOON!!
OKAY, HAMMOCK.
THAT'S HANCOCK!
THE SNAKE PRINCESS SMILED! HOW MANY CARATS IS THAT SHINE?! HOW MANY CARATS?!
RAAH...
SWOON...
A WOMAN IN LOVE. HEE HEE HEE... THERE WAS A TIME WHEN I WAS LIKE THAT. ♡
BLUSH...
HUH? GRANDMA NYON, YOUR FACE JUST TURNED REALLY CREEPY.
QUIET, YOU!!

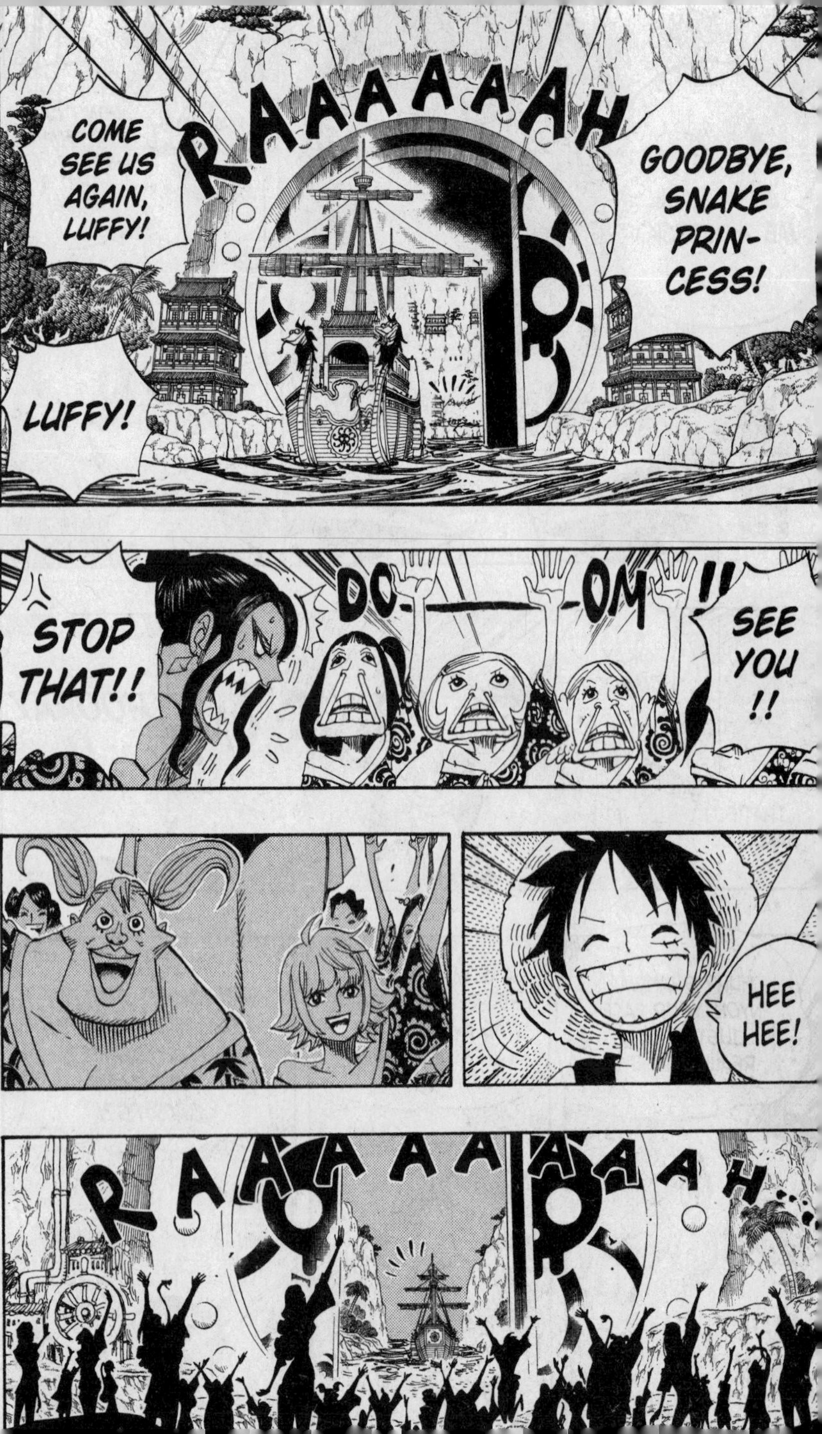
GOODBYE, SNAKE PRINCESS!
RAAAAAAH
COME SEE US AGAIN, LUFFY!
LUFFY!
SEE YOU!!
DO----OM!!
STOP THAT!!
HEE HEE!
RAAAAAAAAH

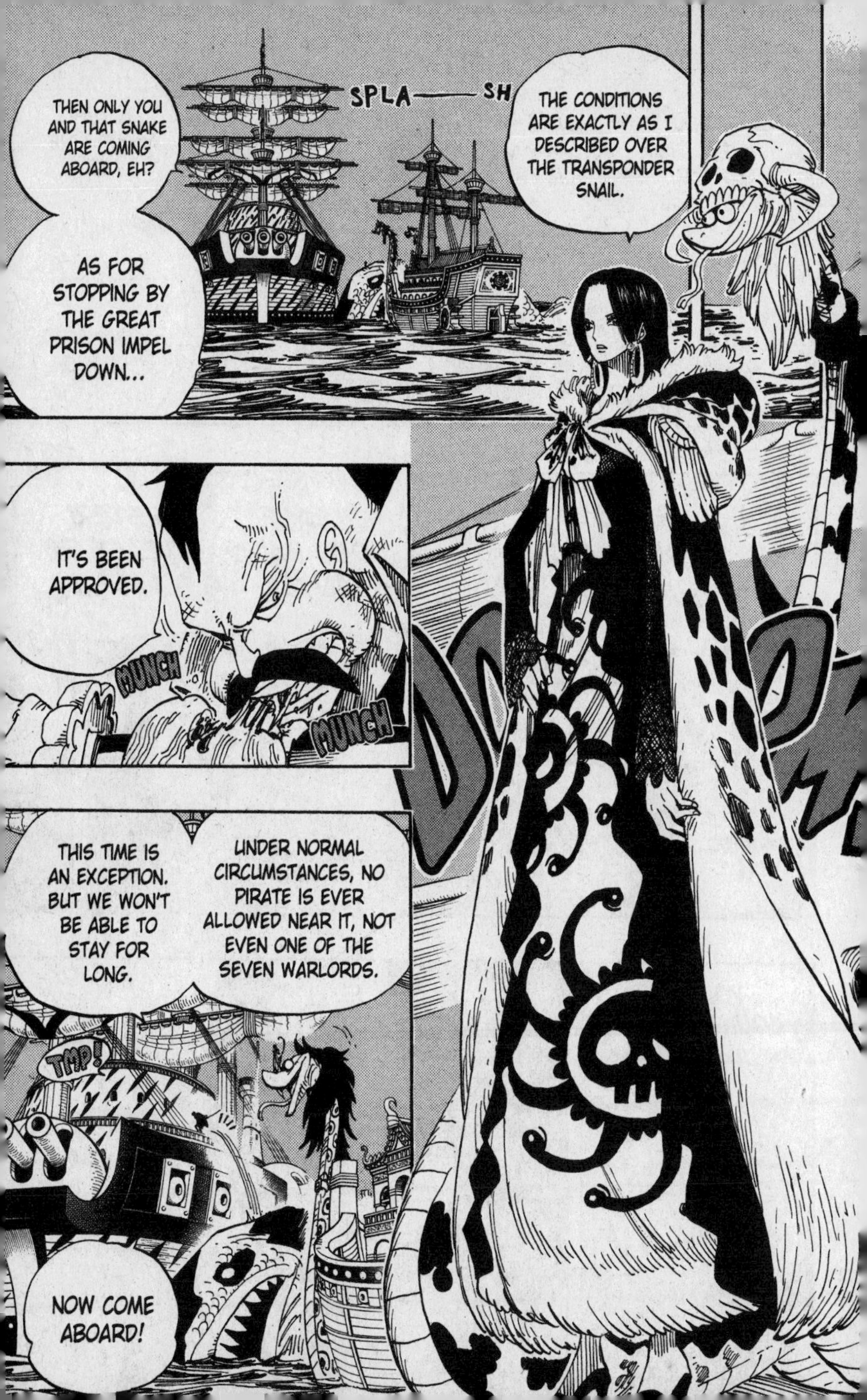
THE CONDITIONS ARE EXACTLY AS I DESCRIBED OVER THE TRANSPONDER SNAIL.
SPLA—SH
THEN ONLY YOU AND THAT SNAKE ARE COMING ABOARD, EH?
AS FOR STOPPING BY THE GREAT PRISON IMPEL DOWN...
IT'S BEEN APPROVED.
MUNCH
MUNCH
UNDER NORMAL CIRCUMSTANCES, NO PIRATE IS EVER ALLOWED NEAR IT, NOT EVEN ONE OF THE SEVEN WARLORDS.
THIS TIME IS AN EXCEPTION. BUT WE WON'T BE ABLE TO STAY FOR LONG.
TMP!
NOW COME ABOARD!

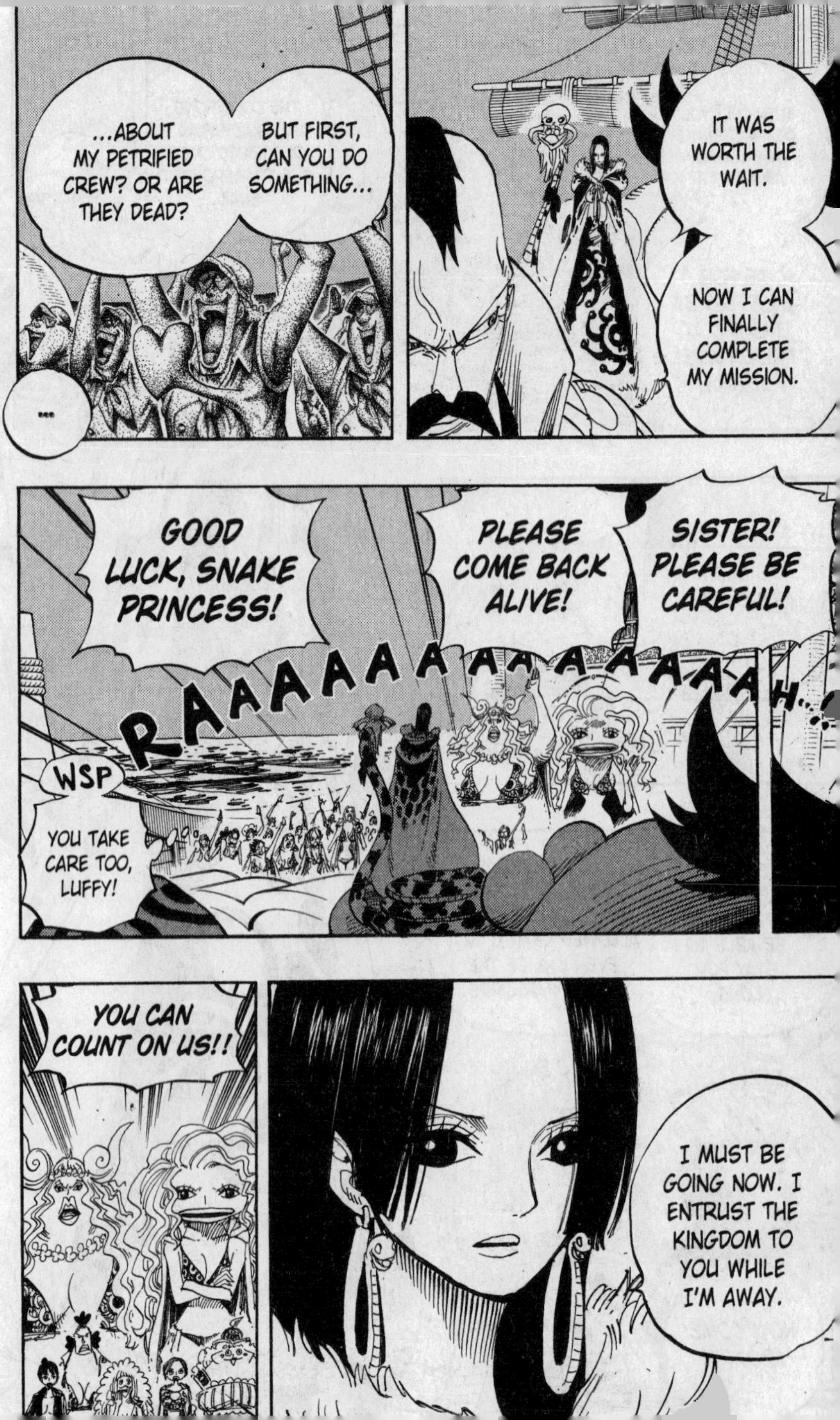
IT WAS WORTH THE WAIT.
NOW I CAN FINALLY COMPLETE MY MISSION.
BUT FIRST, CAN YOU DO SOMETHING...
...ABOUT MY PETRIFIED CREW? OR ARE THEY DEAD?
...
SISTER! PLEASE BE CAREFUL!
PLEASE COME BACK ALIVE!
GOOD LUCK, SNAKE PRINCESS!
RAAAAAAAAAAAAAAAH
WSP
YOU TAKE CARE TOO, LUFFY!
I MUST BE GOING NOW. I ENTRUST THE KINGDOM TO YOU WHILE I'M AWAY.
YOU CAN COUNT ON US!!

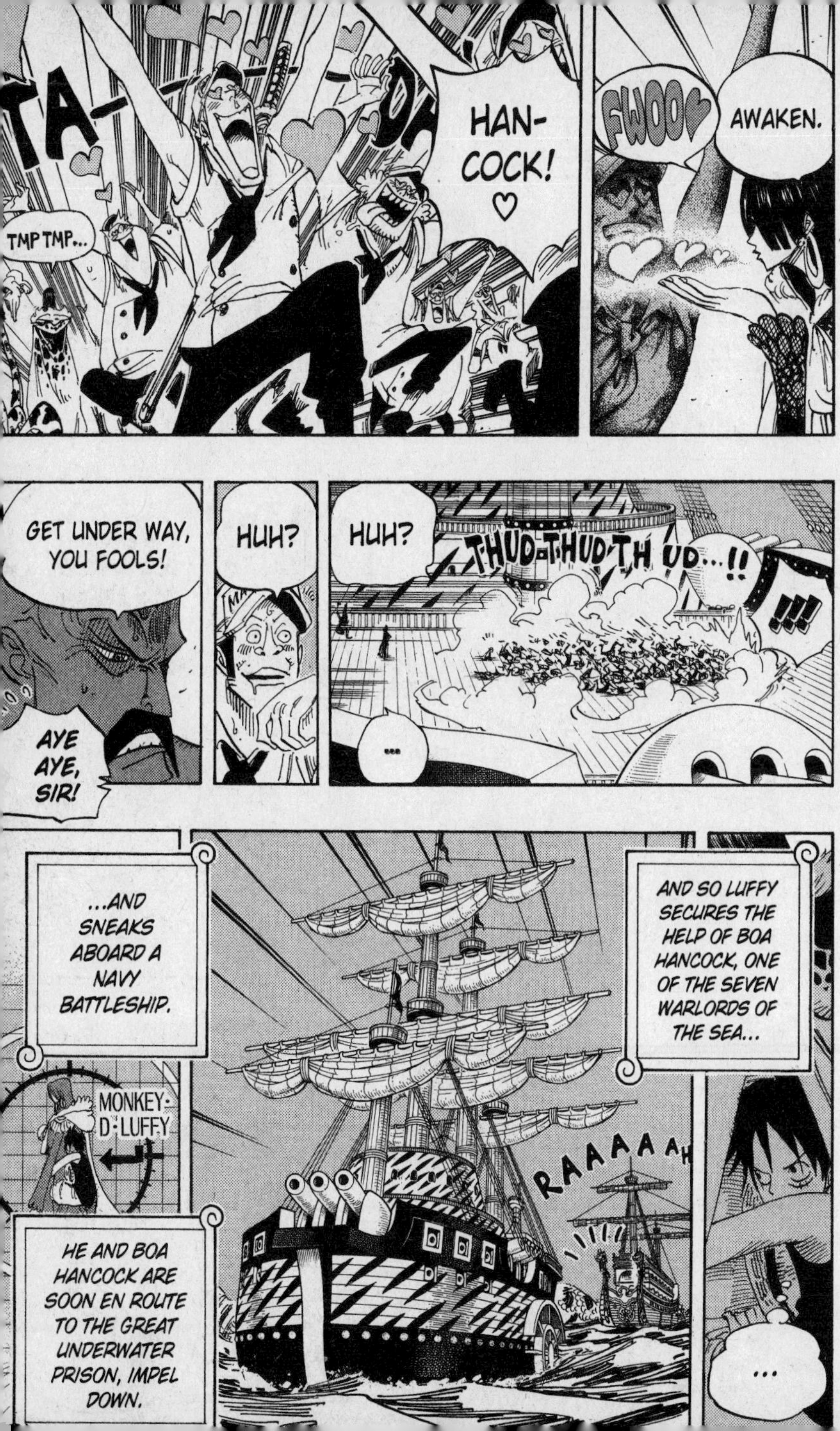
FWOO♥
AWAKEN.
HAN-COCK! ♥
TA-
TMP TMP...
THUD THUD THUD...!!
!!!
HUH?
...
HUH?
GET UNDER WAY, YOU FOOLS!
AYE AYE, SIR!
AND SO LUFFY SECURES THE HELP OF BOA HANCOCK, ONE OF THE SEVEN WARLORDS OF THE SEA...
...
RAAAAAH
...AND SNEAKS ABOARD A NAVY BATTLESHIP.
MONKEY D LUFFY
HE AND BOA HANCOCK ARE SOON EN ROUTE TO THE GREAT UNDERWATER PRISON, IMPEL DOWN.

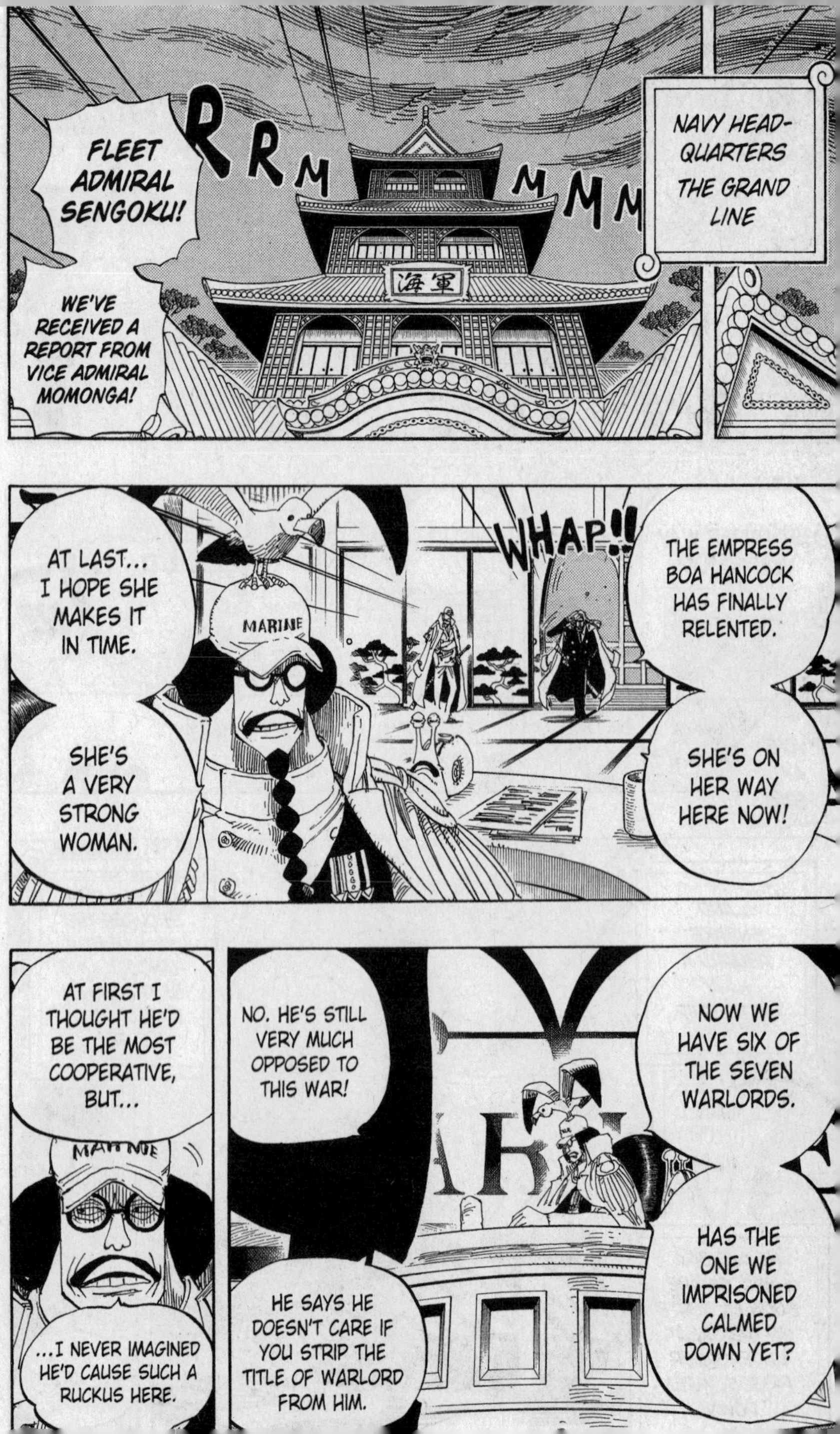
NAVY HEAD-QUARTERS THE GRAND LINE
RRMMMM
FLEET ADMIRAL SENGOKU!
WE'VE RECEIVED A REPORT FROM VICE ADMIRAL MOMONGA!
WHAP!!
THE EMPRESS BOA HANCOCK HAS FINALLY RELENTED.
SHE'S ON HER WAY HERE NOW!
AT LAST... I HOPE SHE MAKES IT IN TIME.
SHE'S A VERY STRONG WOMAN.
MARINE
NOW WE HAVE SIX OF THE SEVEN WARLORDS.
HAS THE ONE WE IMPRISONED CALMED DOWN YET?
NO. HE'S STILL VERY MUCH OPPOSED TO THIS WAR!
HE SAYS HE DOESN'T CARE IF YOU STRIP THE TITLE OF WARLORD FROM HIM.
AT FIRST I THOUGHT HE'D BE THE MOST COOPERATIVE, BUT...
...I NEVER IMAGINED HE'D CAUSE SUCH A RUCKUS HERE.

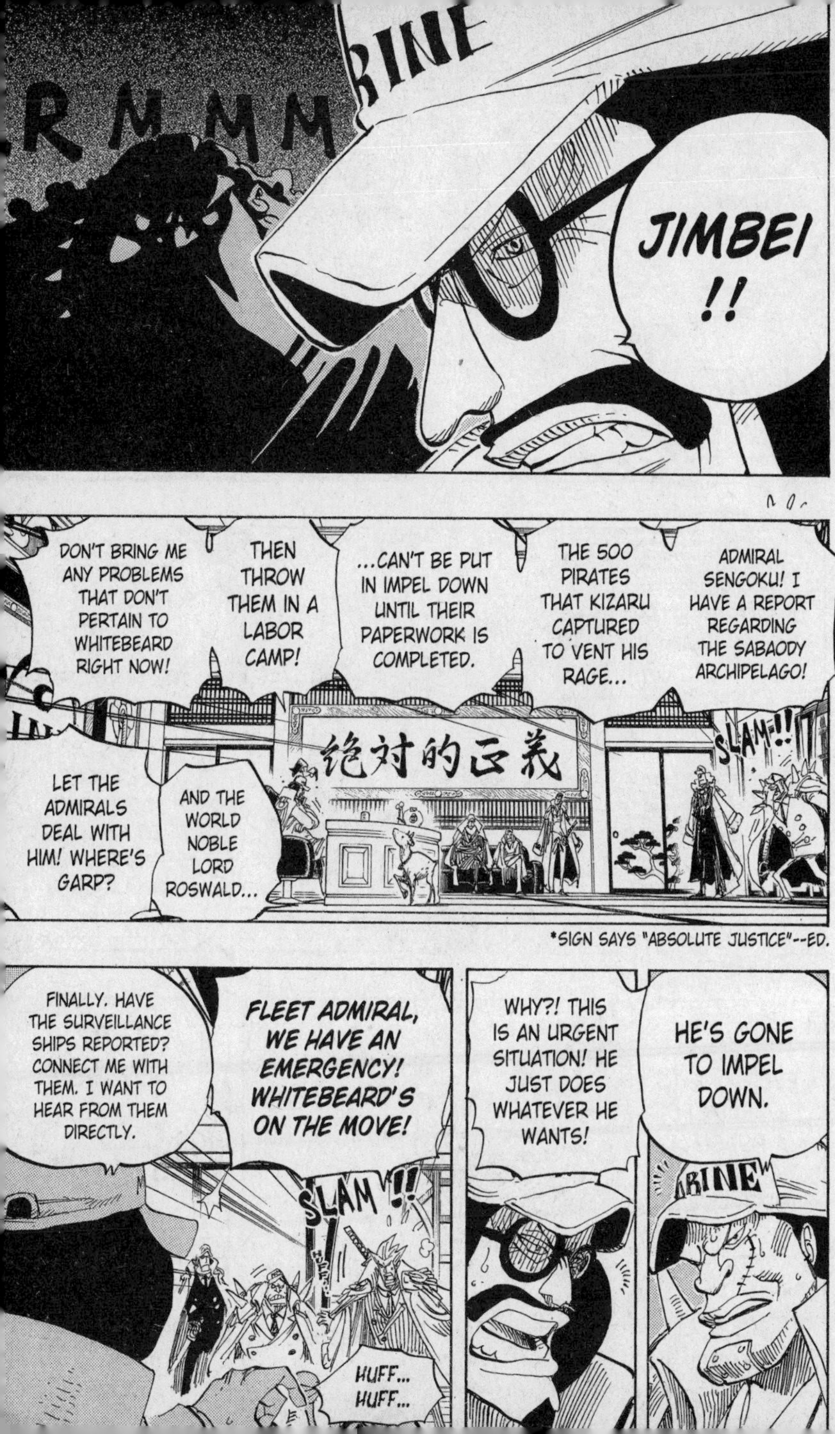
JIMBEI !!
RMMMM
ADMIRAL SENGOKU! I HAVE A REPORT REGARDING THE SABAODY ARCHIPELAGO!
THE 500 PIRATES THAT KIZARU CAPTURED TO VENT HIS RAGE...
...CAN'T BE PUT IN IMPEL DOWN UNTIL THEIR PAPERWORK IS COMPLETED.
THEN THROW THEM IN A LABOR CAMP!
DON'T BRING ME ANY PROBLEMS THAT DON'T PERTAIN TO WHITEBEARD RIGHT NOW!
SLAM!!
绝对的正義
AND THE WORLD NOBLE LORD ROSWALD...
LET THE ADMIRALS DEAL WITH HIM! WHERE'S GARP?
*SIGN SAYS "ABSOLUTE JUSTICE"--ED.
HE'S GONE TO IMPEL DOWN.
WHY?! THIS IS AN URGENT SITUATION! HE JUST DOES WHATEVER HE WANTS!
FLEET ADMIRAL, WE HAVE AN EMERGENCY! WHITEBEARD'S ON THE MOVE!
SLAM!!
HUFF... HUFF...
FINALLY. HAVE THE SURVEILLANCE SHIPS REPORTED? CONNECT ME WITH THEM. I WANT TO HEAR FROM THEM DIRECTLY.

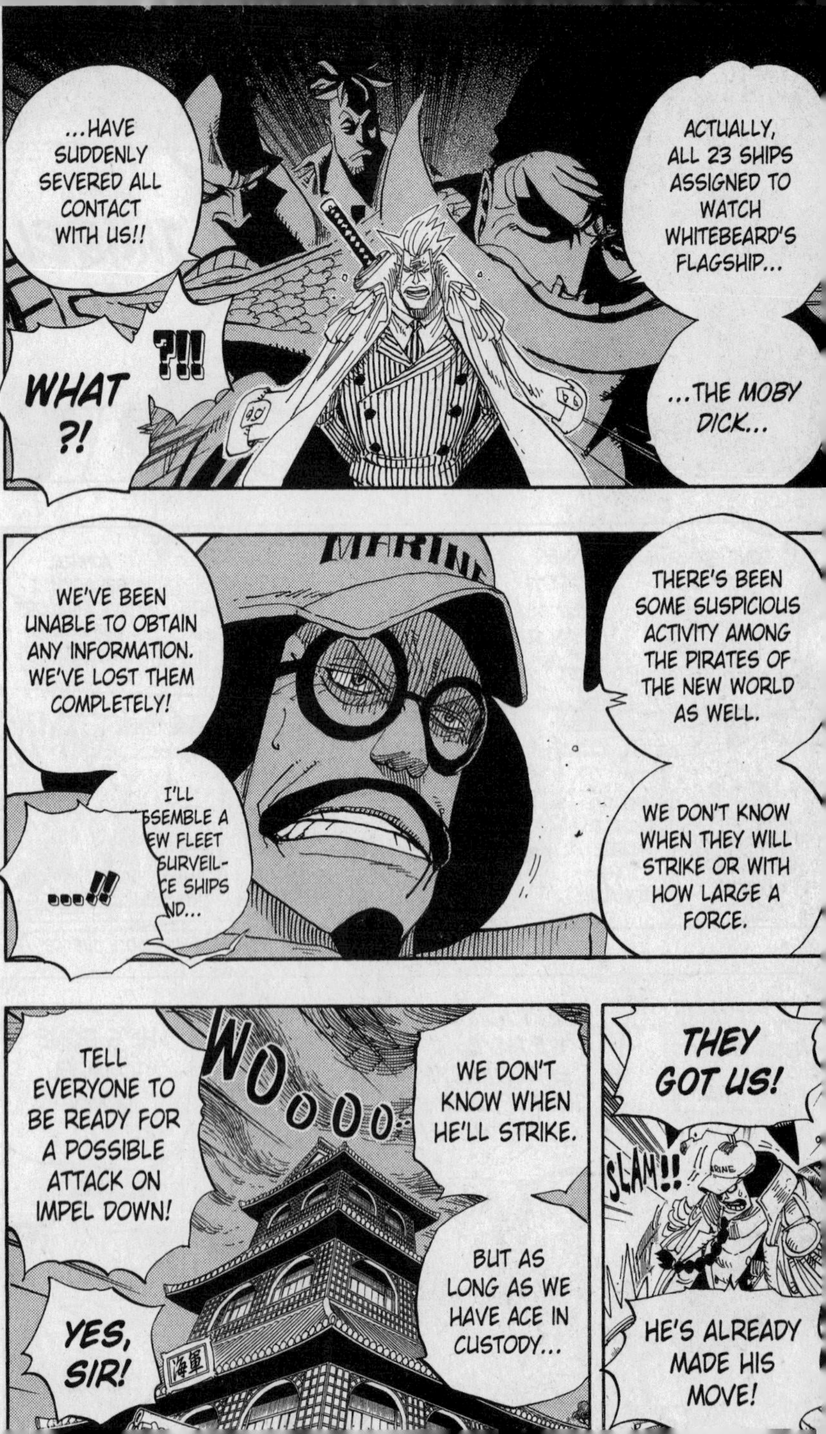
ACTUALLY, ALL 23 SHIPS ASSIGNED TO WATCH WHITEBEARD'S FLAGSHIP...
...THE MOBY DICK...
...HAVE SUDDENLY SEVERED ALL CONTACT WITH US!!
?!!
WHAT ?!
THERE'S BEEN SOME SUSPICIOUS ACTIVITY AMONG THE PIRATES OF THE NEW WORLD AS WELL.
WE DON'T KNOW WHEN THEY WILL STRIKE OR WITH HOW LARGE A FORCE.
WE'VE BEEN UNABLE TO OBTAIN ANY INFORMATION. WE'VE LOST THEM COMPLETELY!
I'LL SSEMBLE A EW FLEET SURVEIL- CE SHIPS ND...
...!!
THEY GOT US!
SLAM!!
HE'S ALREADY MADE HIS MOVE!
WE DON'T KNOW WHEN HE'LL STRIKE.
BUT AS LONG AS WE HAVE ACE IN CUSTODY...
WOOOO...
TELL EVERYONE TO BE READY FOR A POSSIBLE ATTACK ON IMPEL DOWN!
YES, SIR!

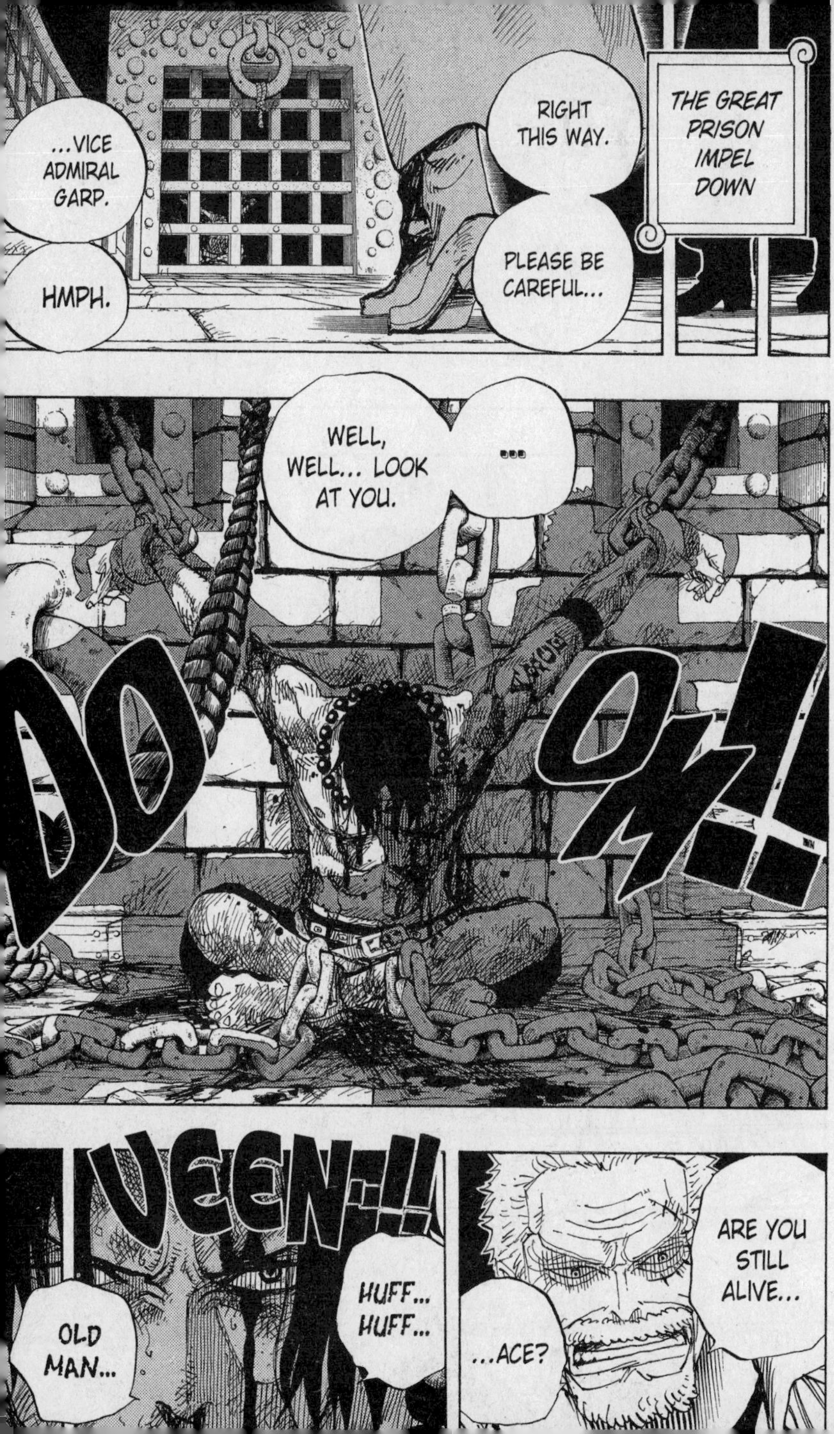
THE GREAT PRISON IMPEL DOWN
RIGHT THIS WAY.
PLEASE BE CAREFUL...
...VICE ADMIRAL GARP.
HMPH.
...
WELL, WELL... LOOK AT YOU.
DOON!!
UEEN!!!
ARE YOU STILL ALIVE...
...ACE?
HUFF... HUFF...
OLD MAN...

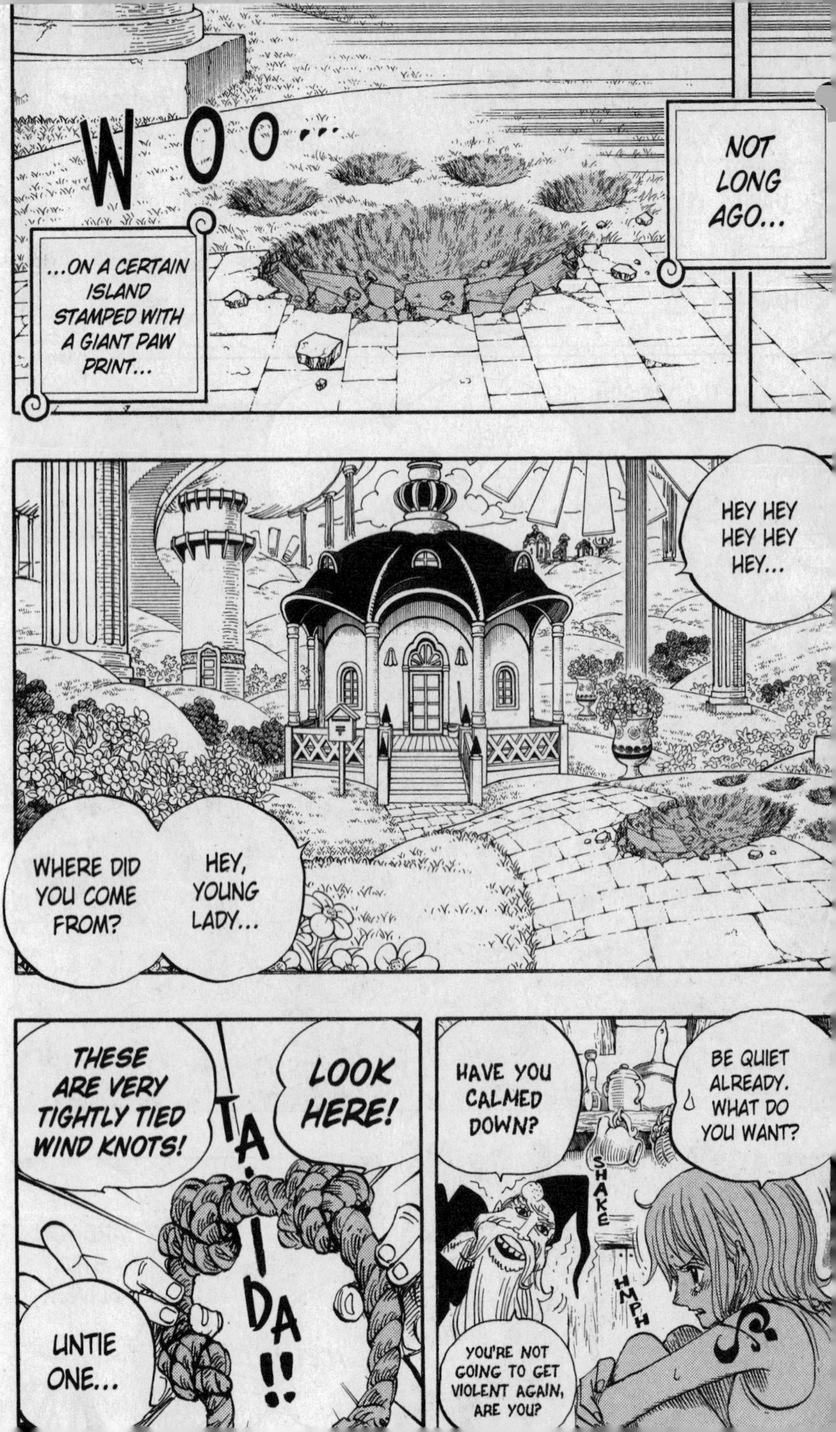
NOT LONG AGO...
...ON A CERTAIN ISLAND STAMPED WITH A GIANT PAW PRINT...
WOO...
HEY HEY HEY HEY HEY...
HEY, YOUNG LADY...
WHERE DID YOU COME FROM?
BE QUIET ALREADY. WHAT DO YOU WANT?
HAVE YOU CALMED DOWN?
SHAKE
HMPH
YOU'RE NOT GOING TO GET VIOLENT AGAIN, ARE YOU?
LOOK HERE!
THESE ARE VERY TIGHTLY TIED WIND KNOTS!
TA-DA!!
UNTIE ONE...

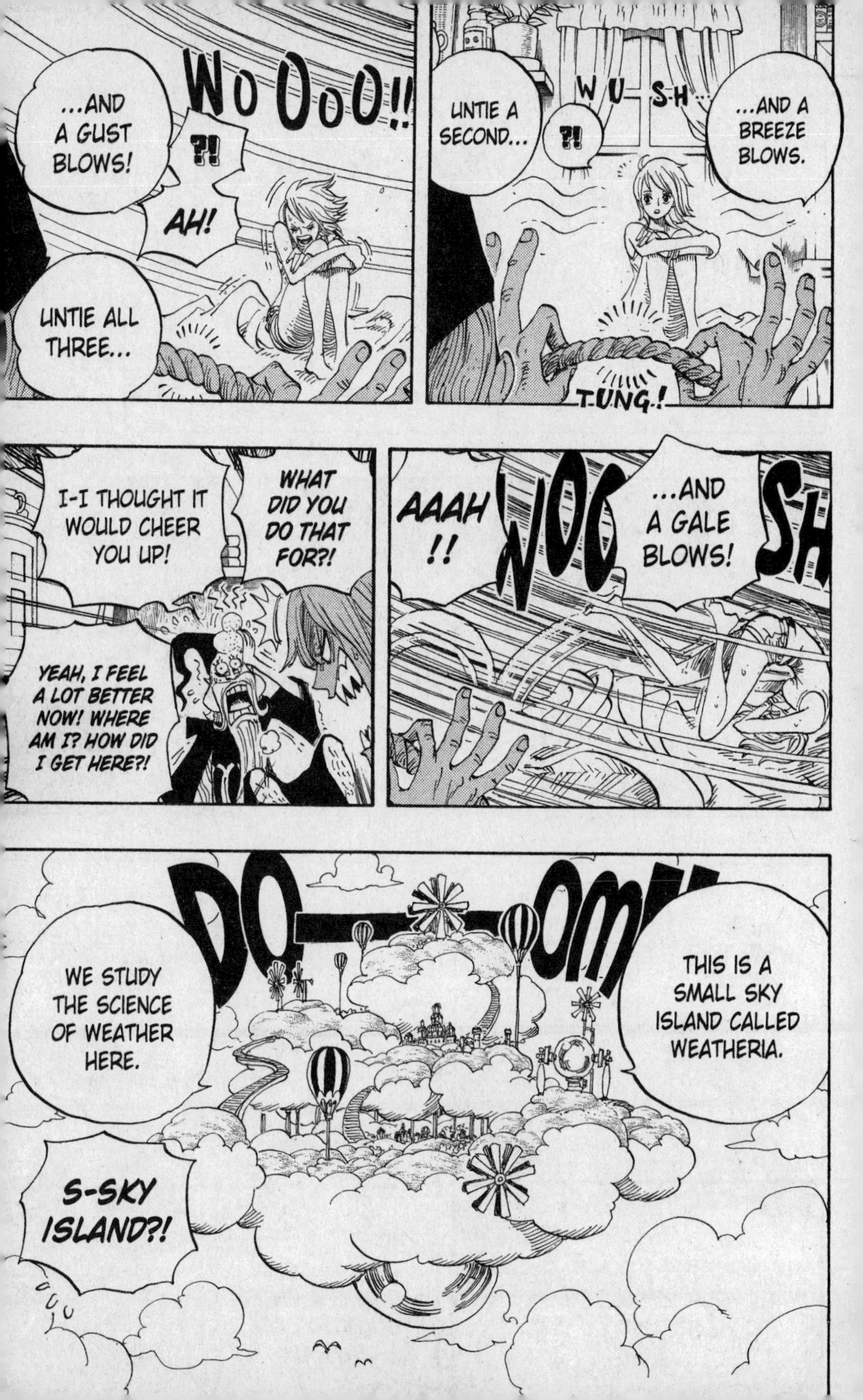
...AND A BREEZE BLOWS.
W U S H...
?!
UNTIE A SECOND...
TUNG.!
WOOOOO!!
...AND A GUST BLOWS!
?!
AH!
UNTIE ALL THREE...
...AND A GALE BLOWS!
AAAH!!
WHAT DID YOU DO THAT FOR?!
I-I THOUGHT IT WOULD CHEER YOU UP!
YEAH, I FEEL A LOT BETTER NOW! WHERE AM I? HOW DID I GET HERE?!
THIS IS A SMALL SKY ISLAND CALLED WEATHERIA.
WE STUDY THE SCIENCE OF WEATHER HERE.
S-SKY ISLAND?!

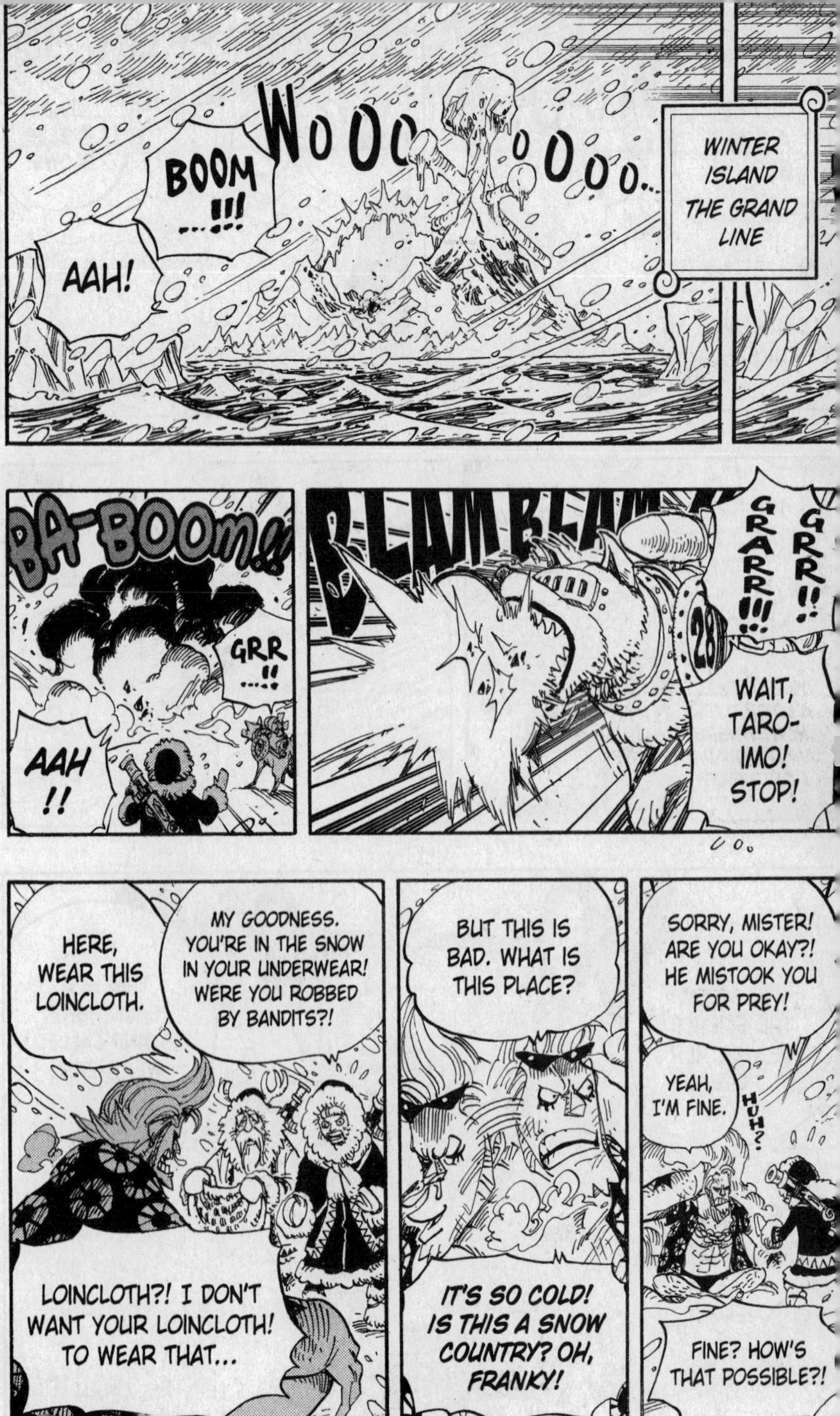
WINTER ISLAND THE GRAND LINE
WOOOOOOOO...
BOOM!!!...!!!
AAH!
BLAM BLAM
GRR!!
GRARR!!!...
WAIT, TARO-IMO! STOP!
BA-BOOM!!
GRR...!!
AAH!!
SORRY, MISTER! ARE YOU OKAY?! HE MISTOOK YOU FOR PREY!
YEAH, I'M FINE.
HUH?
FINE? HOW'S THAT POSSIBLE?!
BUT THIS IS BAD. WHAT IS THIS PLACE?
IT'S SO COLD! IS THIS A SNOW COUNTRY? OH, FRANKY!
MY GOODNESS. YOU'RE IN THE SNOW IN YOUR UNDERWEAR! WERE YOU ROBBED BY BANDITS?!
HERE, WEAR THIS LOINCLOTH.
LOINCLOTH?! I DON'T WANT YOUR LOINCLOTH! TO WEAR THAT...

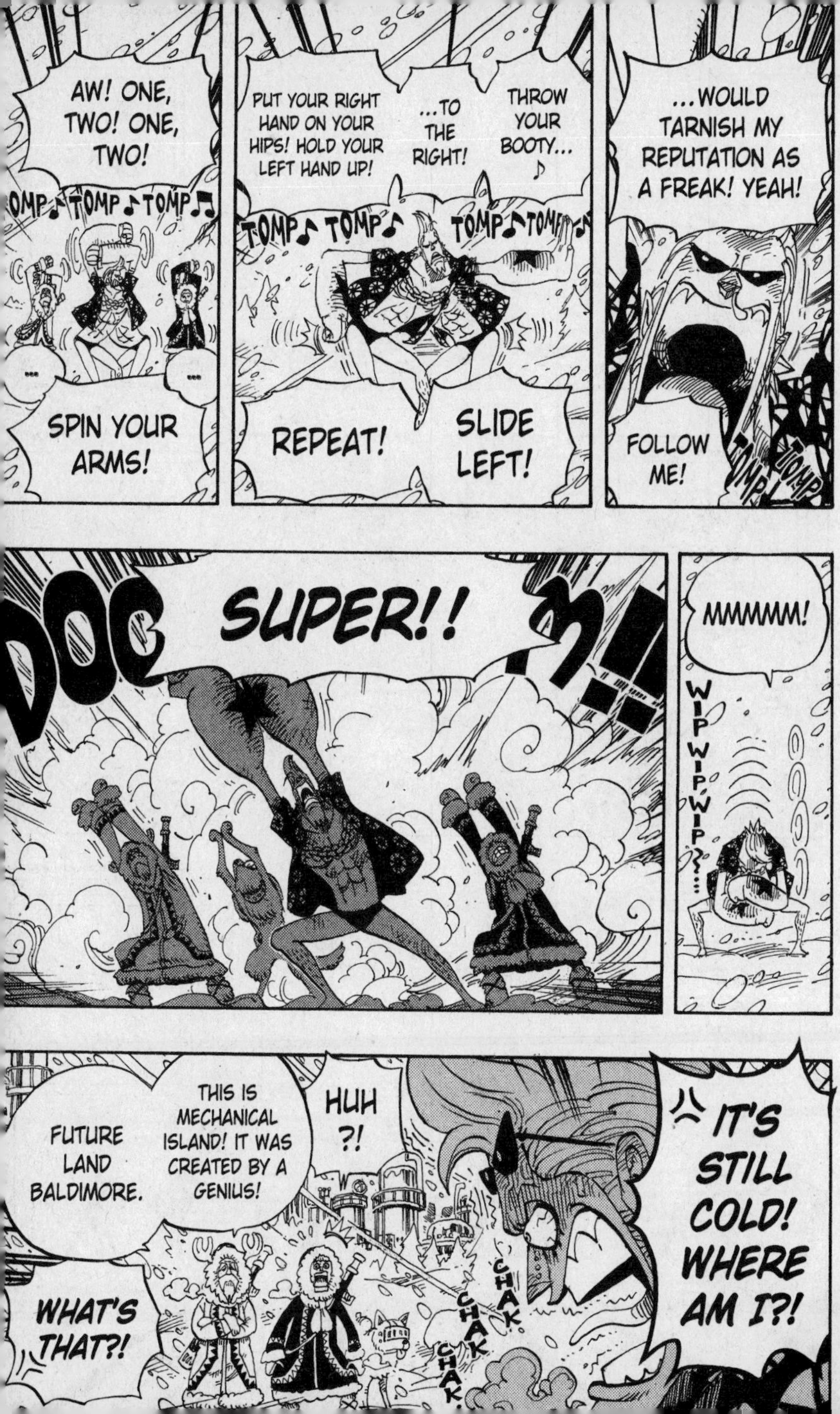
...WOULD TARNISH MY REPUTATION AS A FREAK! YEAH!
FOLLOW ME!
TOMP TOMP
THROW YOUR BOOTY... ♪
...TO THE RIGHT!
PUT YOUR RIGHT HAND ON YOUR HIPS! HOLD YOUR LEFT HAND UP!
TOMP♪ TOMP♪ TOMP♪ TOMP♪
SLIDE LEFT!
REPEAT!
AW! ONE, TWO! ONE, TWO!
TOMP♪ TOMP♪ TOMP♫
...
...
SPIN YOUR ARMS!
MMMMM!
WIP WIP WIP WIP ?...
DOO
SUPER!!
M!!
IT'S STILL COLD! WHERE AM I?!
CHAK CHAK CHAK CHAK
HUH ?!
THIS IS MECHANICAL ISLAND! IT WAS CREATED BY A GENIUS!
FUTURE LAND BALDIMORE.
WHAT'S THAT?!

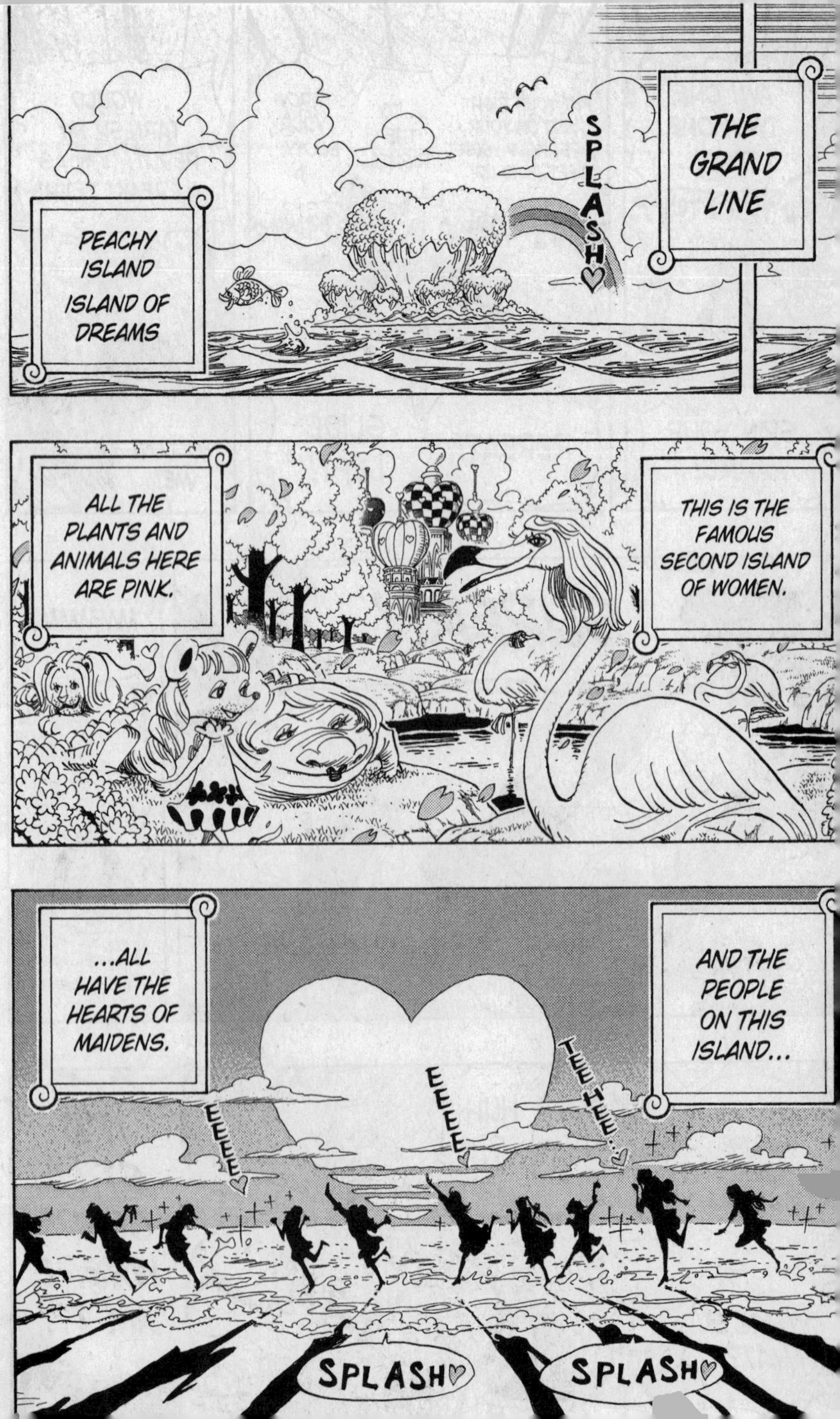
THE GRAND LINE
SPLASH♡
PEACHY ISLAND
ISLAND OF DREAMS
THIS IS THE FAMOUS SECOND ISLAND OF WOMEN.
ALL THE PLANTS AND ANIMALS HERE ARE PINK.
AND THE PEOPLE ON THIS ISLAND...
...ALL HAVE THE HEARTS OF MAIDENS.
TEE HEE...♡
EEEE♡
EEEE♡
SPLASH♡
SPLASH♡

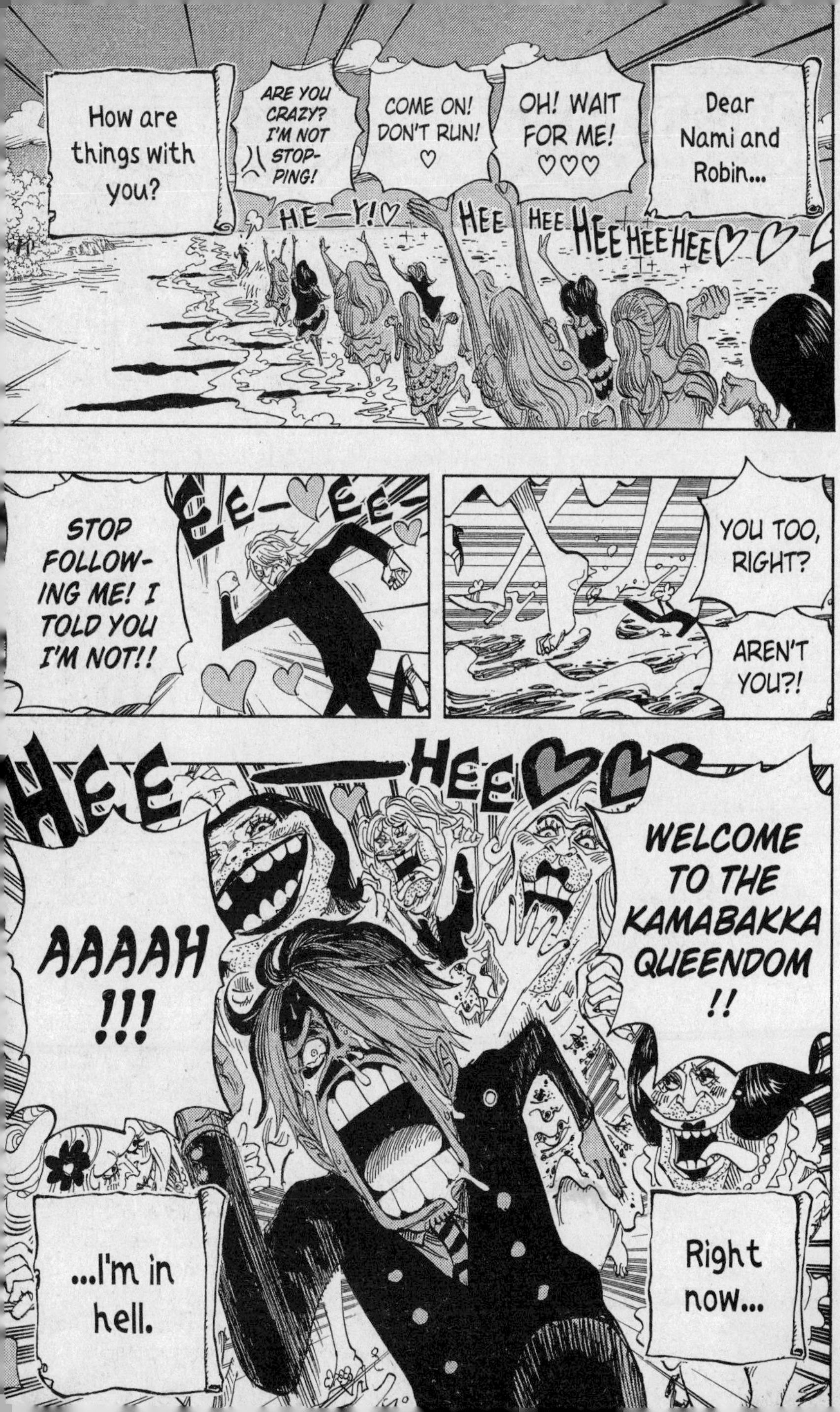
Dear Nami and Robin...
OH! WAIT FOR ME! ♡♡♡
COME ON! DON'T RUN! ♡
ARE YOU CRAZY? I'M NOT STOP-PING!
How are things with you?
HEE HEE HEE HEE HEE ♡♡
HE—Y! ♡
YOU TOO, RIGHT?
AREN'T YOU?!
EE—EE—
STOP FOLLOW-ING ME! I TOLD YOU I'M NOT!!
Right now...
WELCOME TO THE KAMABAKKA QUEENDOM!!
HEE—HEE
AAAAH!!!
...I'm in hell.

SBS Question Corner

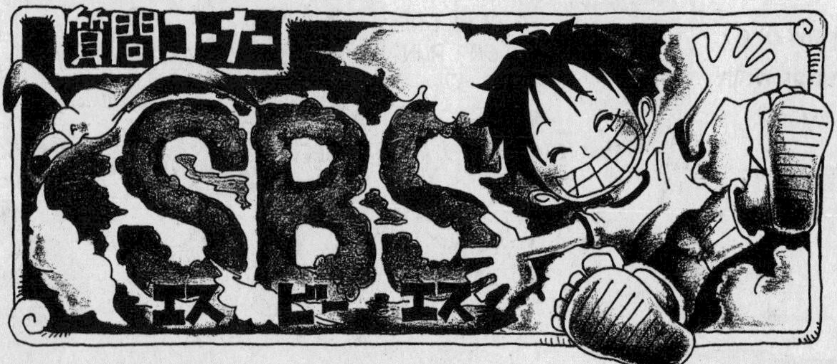

質問コーナー
SBS
エス ビー エス

(Tomomi Surimachi, Saitama)

Reader(Q): I don't know who you are, but there's something I have to tell you. Gack! The Question Corner is starting! (Drops dead.)

--Horsemeat Man

Oda(A): Hey, Horsemeat Man! Horsemeat Man! Get ahold of yourself! You told me you'd give this engagement ring to her! Horsemeat Man! Shut up! Okay, the Question Corner is starting now.

Q: I want to see Killer unmasked.

--Choco

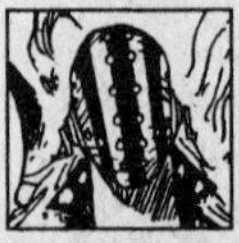

A: Yeah, me too.

Q: Hello, Mr. Oda. In volume 53, chapter 518, Luffy was unaffected by Boa Hancock's Love-Love Mellow, but he did react to Nami's "Happiness Punch" in chapter 213 of volume 23. Why was Nami's body effective against him but not the Snake Princess's? Is Nami that much better?

--Kazu

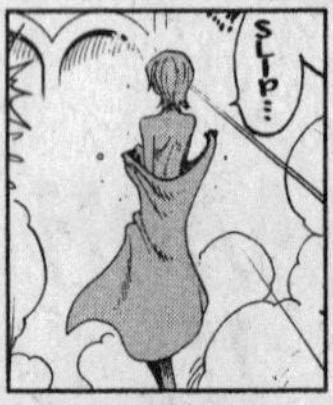

SLIP...

A: I get this question a lot. I'm surprised how many of you guys noticed it! Maybe you should stop reading manga and study harder for school! But then I'm the one drawing this stuff. Anyway, I noticed this when I was drawing it, but I thought everybody would be confused if Luffy got a nosebleed when he saw Hancock's form. As for Luffy reacting to Nami, I think it happened twice: once in volume 18 and again in volume 23. And Usopp was present both times! So he's the culprit here! In other words, Luffy reacted to Hancock as he normally would when he's alone. But Usopp's the same age as Luffy, so when he's around, Luffy behaves like a schoolboy on a field trip! So you see there's no contradiction here! The problem is Usopp!

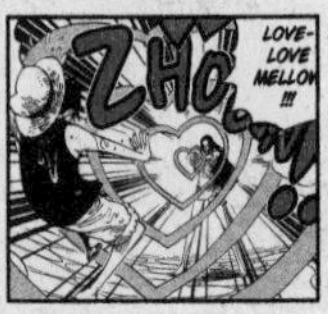

LOVE-LOVE MELLOW!!!

Chapter 524:
UNSTOPPABLE

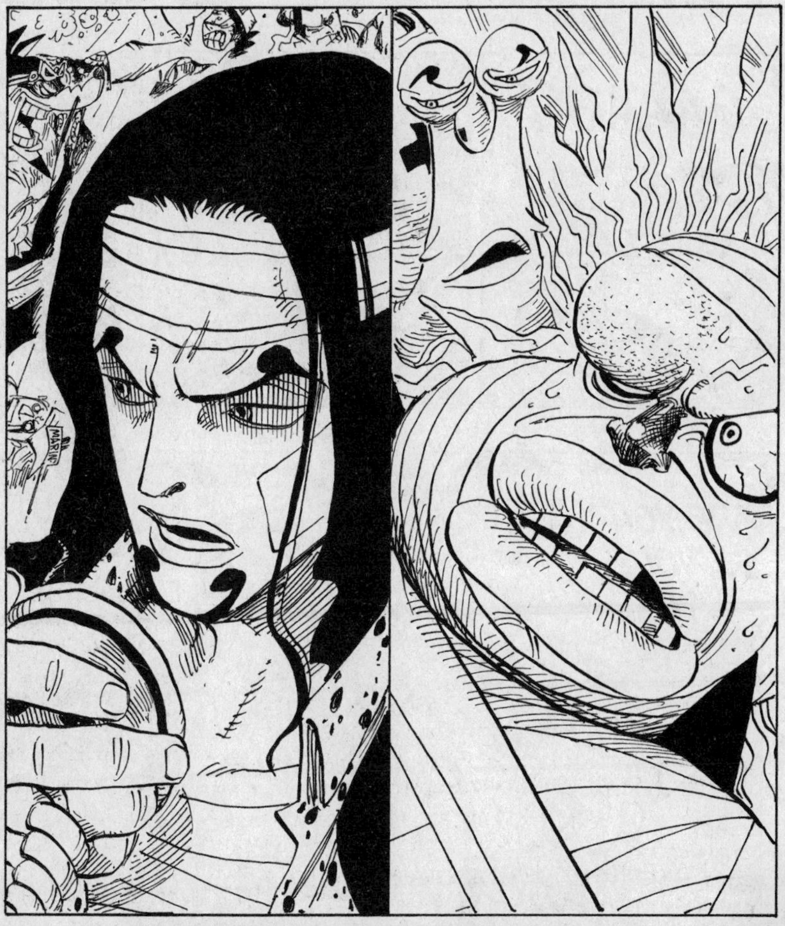
MARINE

CP9 INDEPENDENT REPORT, VOL. 30:
"THIS IS YOUR FORMER SUBORDINATE. ROB LUCCI."

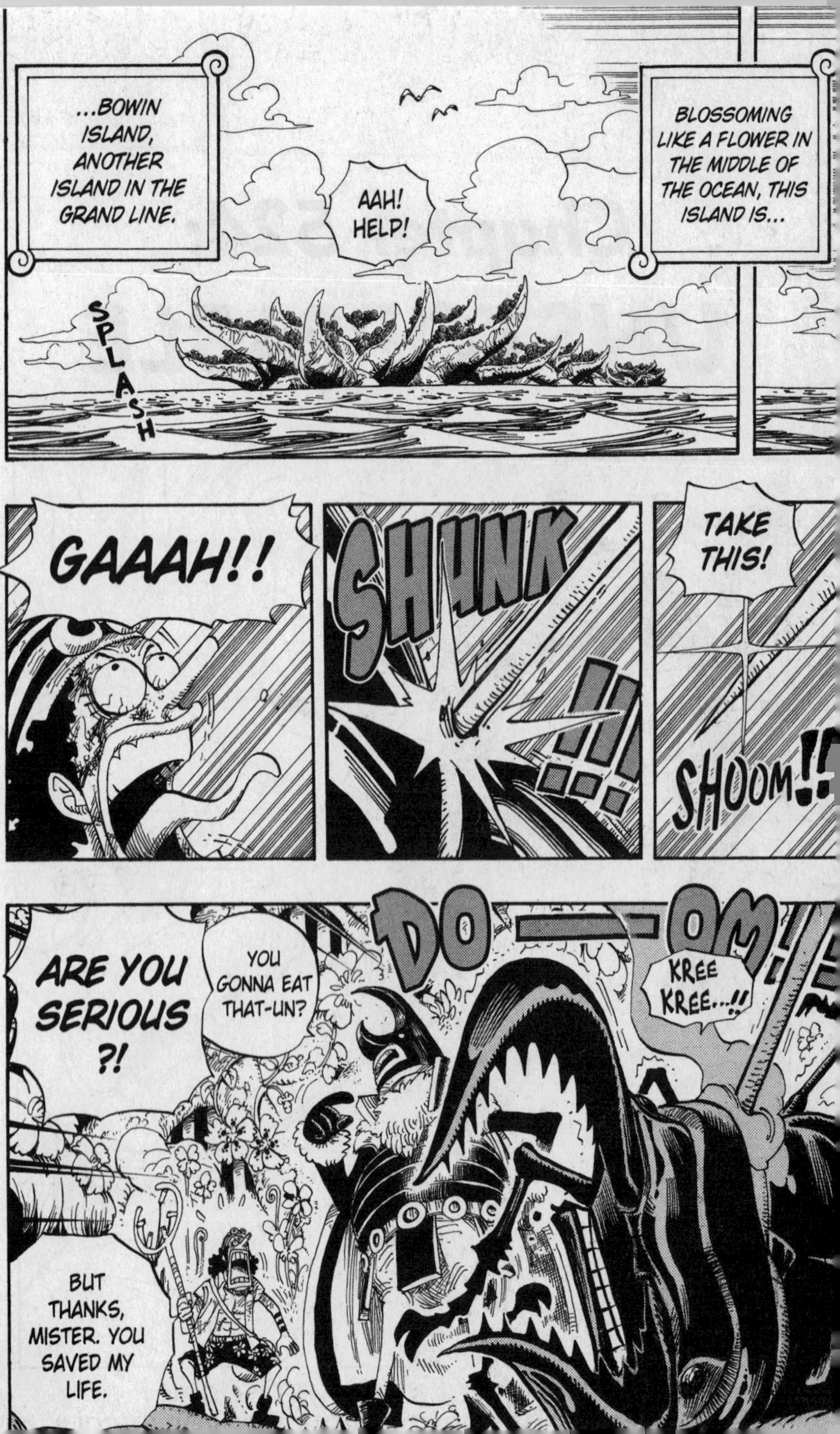

BLOSSOMING LIKE A FLOWER IN THE MIDDLE OF THE OCEAN, THIS ISLAND IS...
...BOWIN ISLAND, ANOTHER ISLAND IN THE GRAND LINE.
AAH! HELP!
SPLASH
TAKE THIS!
SHOOM!!
SHUNK
!!...!!
GAAAH!!
DO—OM!!
KREE KREE...!!
YOU GONNA EAT THAT-UN?
ARE YOU SERIOUS?!
BUT THANKS, MISTER. YOU SAVED MY LIFE.

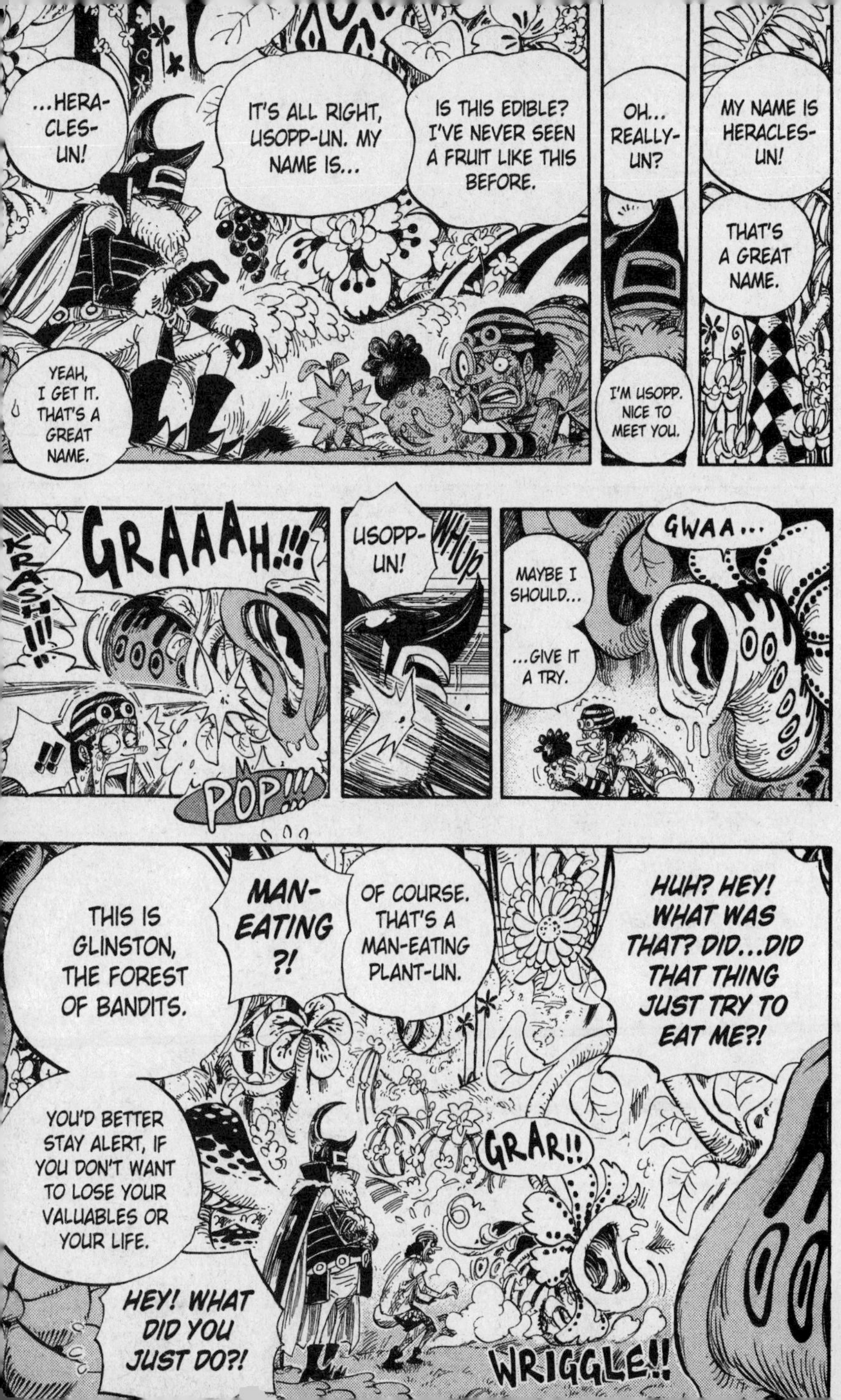
MY NAME IS HERACLES-UN!
THAT'S A GREAT NAME.
OH... REALLY-UN?
I'M USOPP. NICE TO MEET YOU.
IS THIS EDIBLE? I'VE NEVER SEEN A FRUIT LIKE THIS BEFORE.
IT'S ALL RIGHT, USOPP-UN. MY NAME IS...
...HERACLES-UN!
YEAH, I GET IT. THAT'S A GREAT NAME.
GWAA...
MAYBE I SHOULD...
...GIVE IT A TRY.
USOPP-UN!
WHUP
GRAAAH!!!
KRASH!!!
!!
POP!!!
HUH? HEY! WHAT WAS THAT? DID...DID THAT THING JUST TRY TO EAT ME?!
OF COURSE. THAT'S A MAN-EATING PLANT-UN.
MAN-EATING?!
THIS IS GLINSTON, THE FOREST OF BANDITS.
GRAR!!
YOU'D BETTER STAY ALERT, IF YOU DON'T WANT TO LOSE YOUR VALUABLES OR YOUR LIFE.
WRIGGLE!!
HEY! WHAT DID YOU JUST DO?!

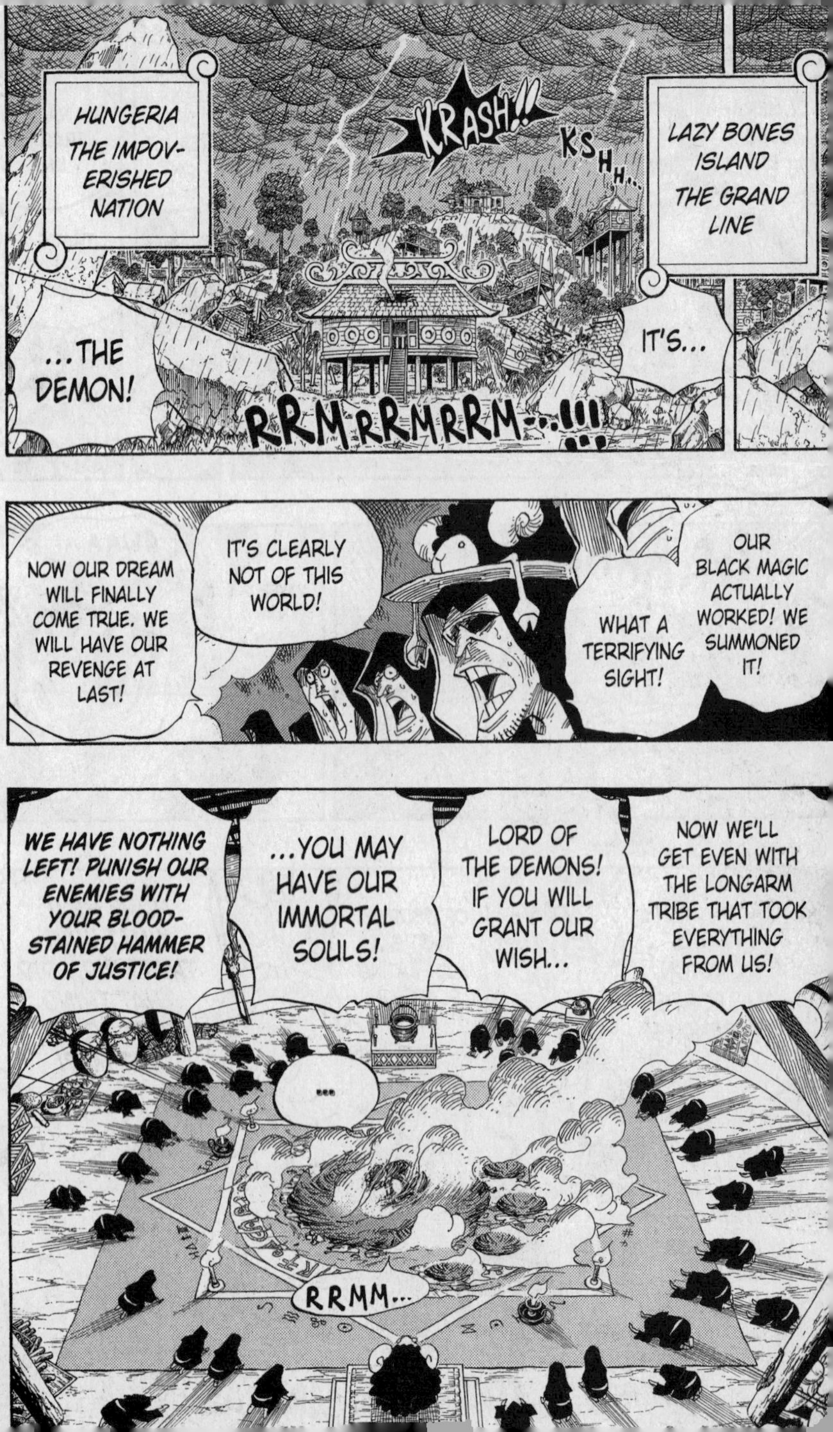
LAZY BONES ISLAND THE GRAND LINE
HUNGERIA THE IMPOVERISHED NATION
KRASH!!
KSHH...
IT'S...
...THE DEMON!
RRMRRMRRM...!!!
OUR BLACK MAGIC ACTUALLY WORKED! WE SUMMONED IT!
WHAT A TERRIFYING SIGHT!
IT'S CLEARLY NOT OF THIS WORLD!
NOW OUR DREAM WILL FINALLY COME TRUE. WE WILL HAVE OUR REVENGE AT LAST!
NOW WE'LL GET EVEN WITH THE LONGARM TRIBE THAT TOOK EVERYTHING FROM US!
LORD OF THE DEMONS! IF YOU WILL GRANT OUR WISH...
...YOU MAY HAVE OUR IMMORTAL SOULS!
WE HAVE NOTHING LEFT! PUNISH OUR ENEMIES WITH YOUR BLOOD-STAINED HAMMER OF JUSTICE!
...
RRMM...

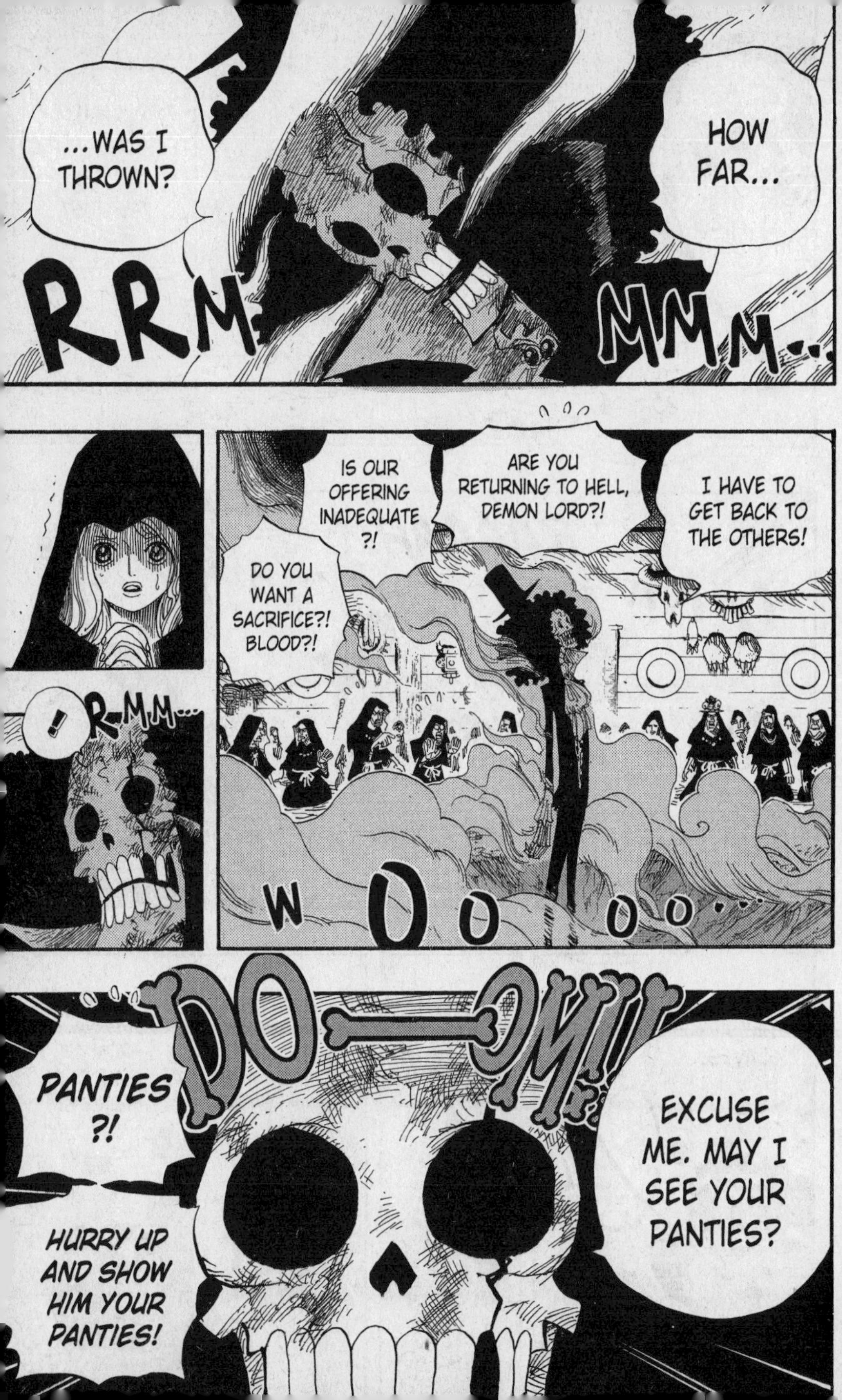
HOW FAR...
...WAS I THROWN?
RRM MMM...
I HAVE TO GET BACK TO THE OTHERS!
ARE YOU RETURNING TO HELL, DEMON LORD?!
IS OUR OFFERING INADEQUATE?!
DO YOU WANT A SACRIFICE?! BLOOD?!
W O O O O...
!
RMM...
EXCUSE ME. MAY I SEE YOUR PANTIES?
DO—OM!!
PANTIES?!
HURRY UP AND SHOW HIM YOUR PANTIES!

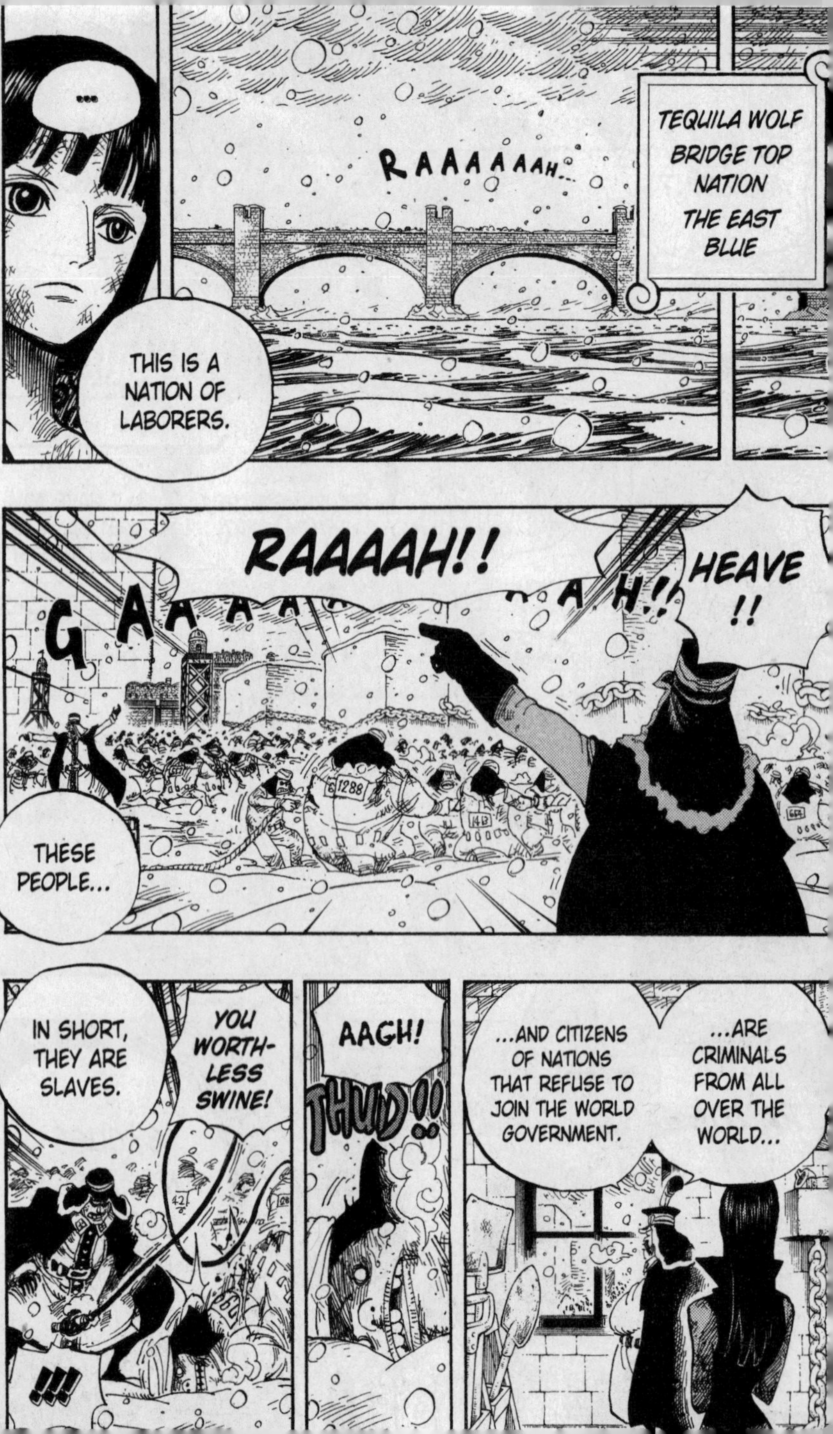
TEQUILA WOLF BRIDGE TOP NATION THE EAST BLUE
RAAAAAAH...
...
THIS IS A NATION OF LABORERS.
HEAVE!!
RAAAAH!!
THESE PEOPLE...
...ARE CRIMINALS FROM ALL OVER THE WORLD...
...AND CITIZENS OF NATIONS THAT REFUSE TO JOIN THE WORLD GOVERNMENT.
AAGH!
THUD!!
YOU WORTHLESS SWINE!
IN SHORT, THEY ARE SLAVES.

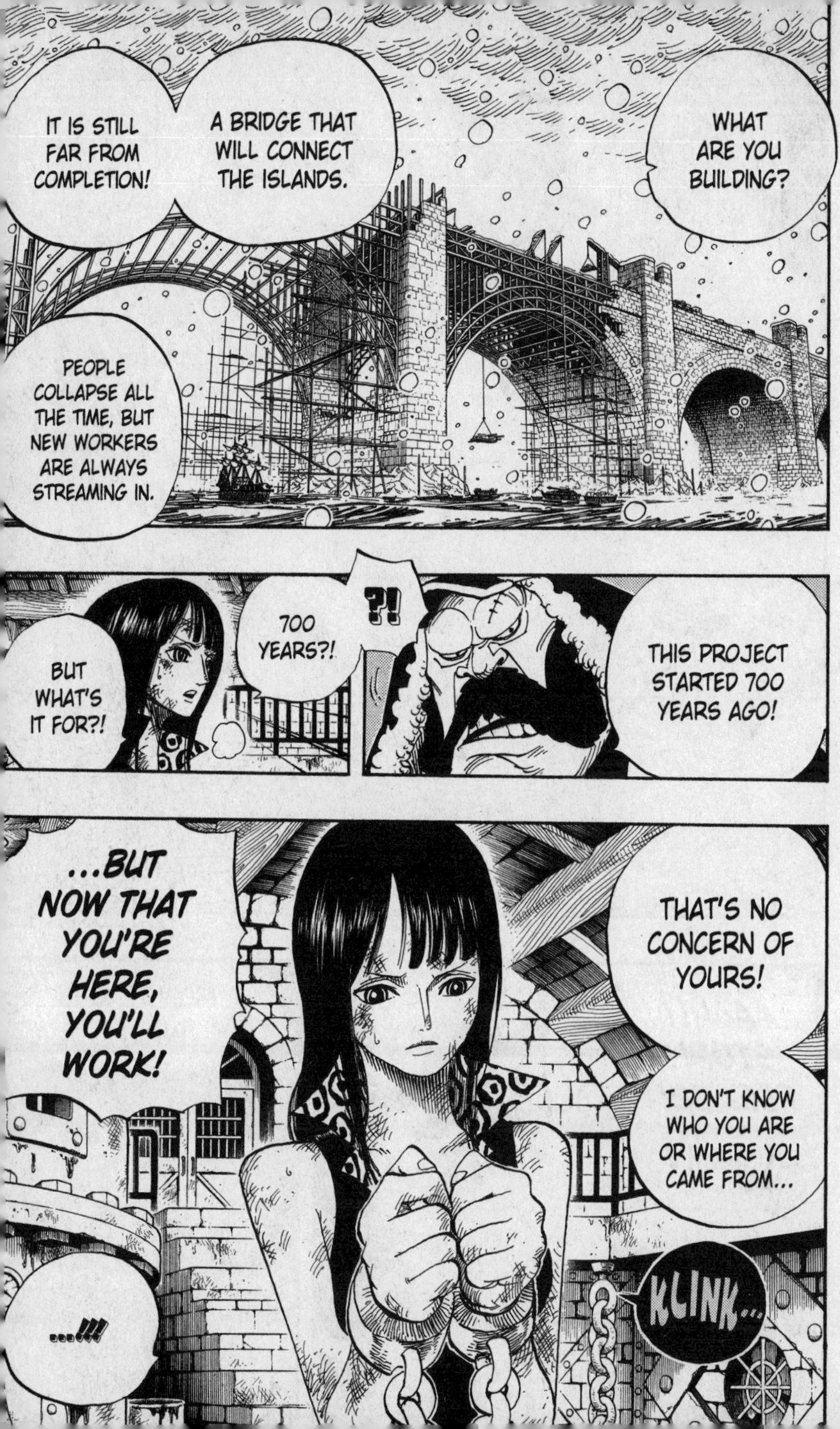
WHAT ARE YOU BUILDING?
A BRIDGE THAT WILL CONNECT THE ISLANDS.
IT IS STILL FAR FROM COMPLETION!
PEOPLE COLLAPSE ALL THE TIME, BUT NEW WORKERS ARE ALWAYS STREAMING IN.
THIS PROJECT STARTED 700 YEARS AGO!
?!
700 YEARS?!
BUT WHAT'S IT FOR?!
THAT'S NO CONCERN OF YOURS!
I DON'T KNOW WHO YOU ARE OR WHERE YOU CAME FROM...
...BUT NOW THAT YOU'RE HERE, YOU'LL WORK!
KLINK...
...!!!

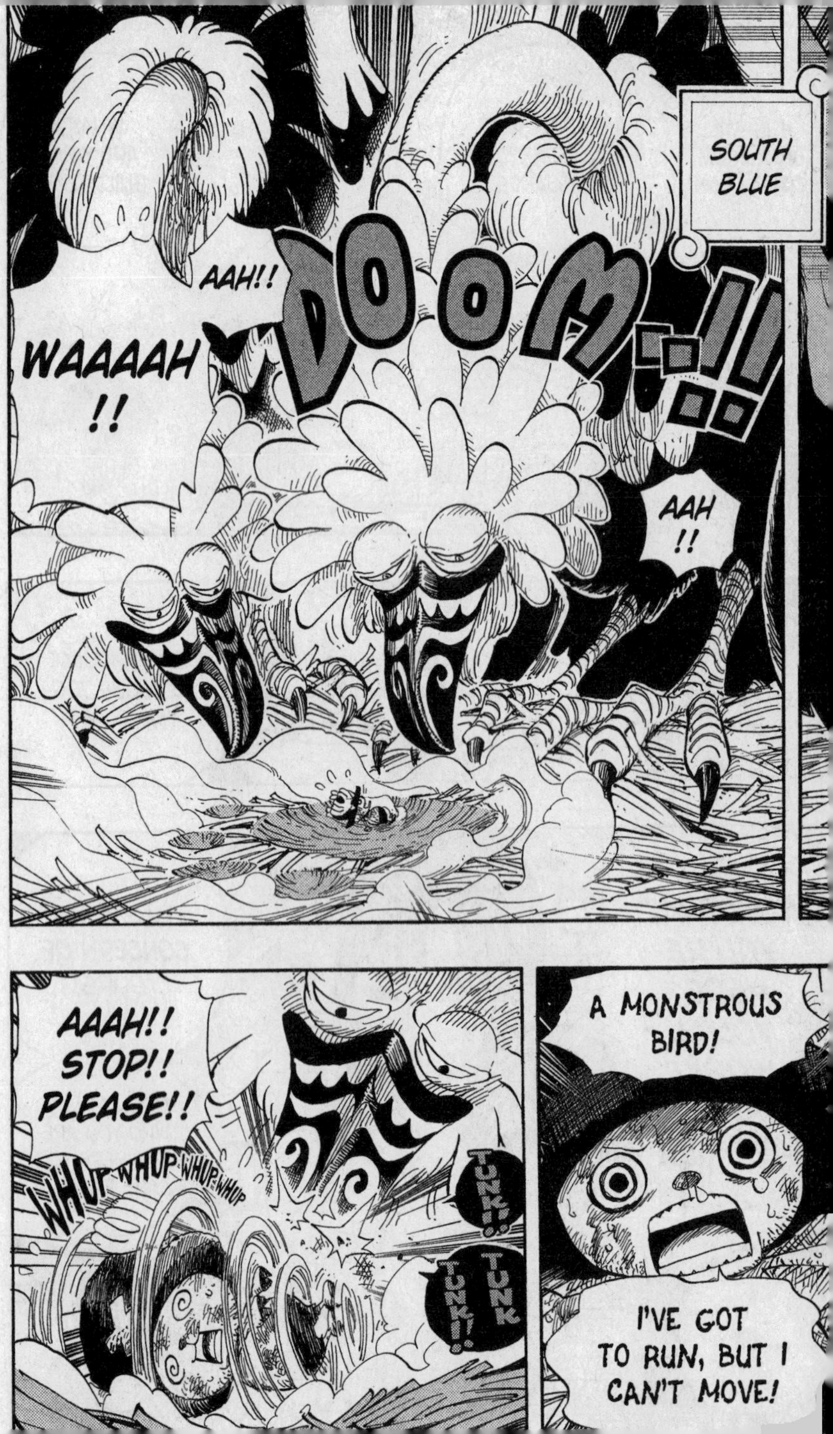
SOUTH BLUE
DOOM..!!
AAH!!
WAAAAH!!
AAH!!
A MONSTROUS BIRD!
I'VE GOT TO RUN, BUT I CAN'T MOVE!
TUNK!!
TUNK TUNK!!
AAAH!! STOP!! PLEASE!!
WHUP WHUP WHUP WHUP

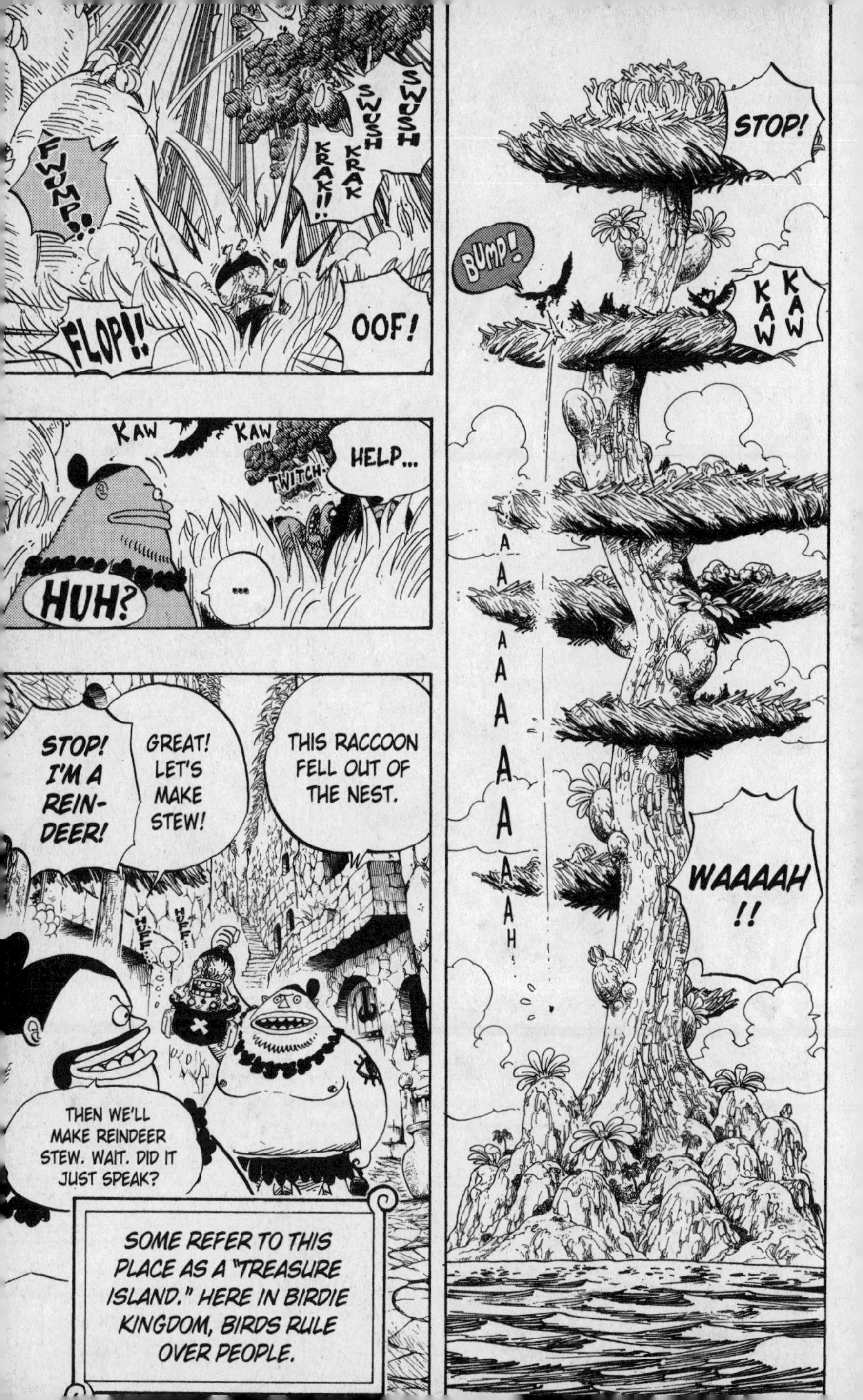
STOP!
BUMP!
KAW KAW
AAAAAAAAAAAH
WAAAAH!!
SWUSH SWUSH
KRAK KRAK!!
FWUMP!!
OOF!
FLOP!!
HELP...
TWITCH
KAW KAW
HUH?
...
THIS RACCOON FELL OUT OF THE NEST.
GREAT! LET'S MAKE STEW!
STOP! I'M A REIN-DEER!
HUFF HUFF
THEN WE'LL MAKE REINDEER STEW. WAIT. DID IT JUST SPEAK?
SOME REFER TO THIS PLACE AS A "TREASURE ISLAND." HERE IN BIRDIE KINGDOM, BIRDS RULE OVER PEOPLE.

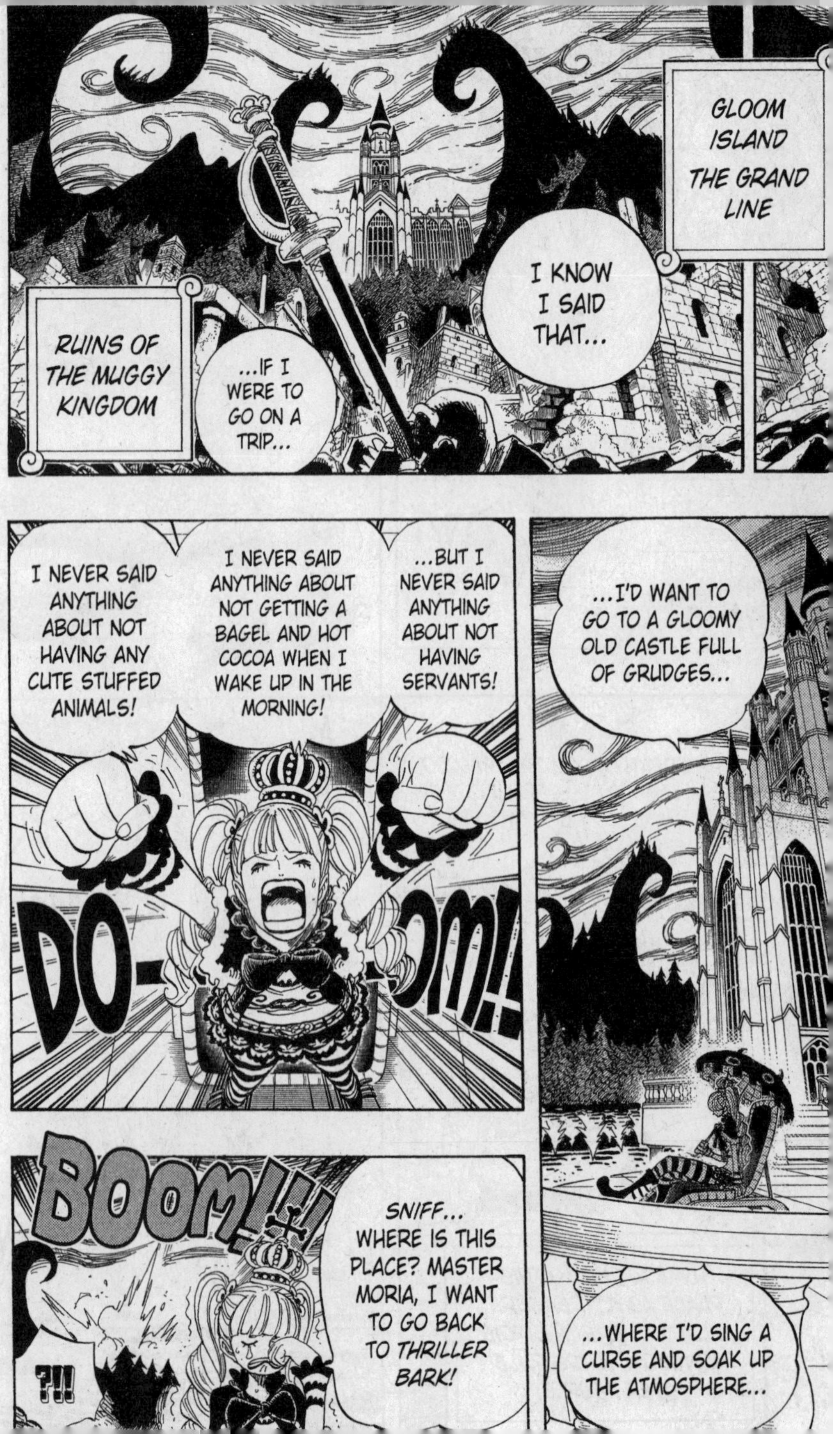
GLOOM ISLAND THE GRAND LINE
I KNOW I SAID THAT...
RUINS OF THE MUGGY KINGDOM
...IF I WERE TO GO ON A TRIP...
...I'D WANT TO GO TO A GLOOMY OLD CASTLE FULL OF GRUDGES...
...WHERE I'D SING A CURSE AND SOAK UP THE ATMOSPHERE...
...BUT I NEVER SAID ANYTHING ABOUT NOT HAVING SERVANTS!
I NEVER SAID ANYTHING ABOUT NOT GETTING A BAGEL AND HOT COCOA WHEN I WAKE UP IN THE MORNING!
I NEVER SAID ANYTHING ABOUT NOT HAVING ANY CUTE STUFFED ANIMALS!
DO-OM!!
BOOM!!!
SNIFF... WHERE IS THIS PLACE? MASTER MORIA, I WANT TO GO BACK TO *THRILLER BARK*!
?!!

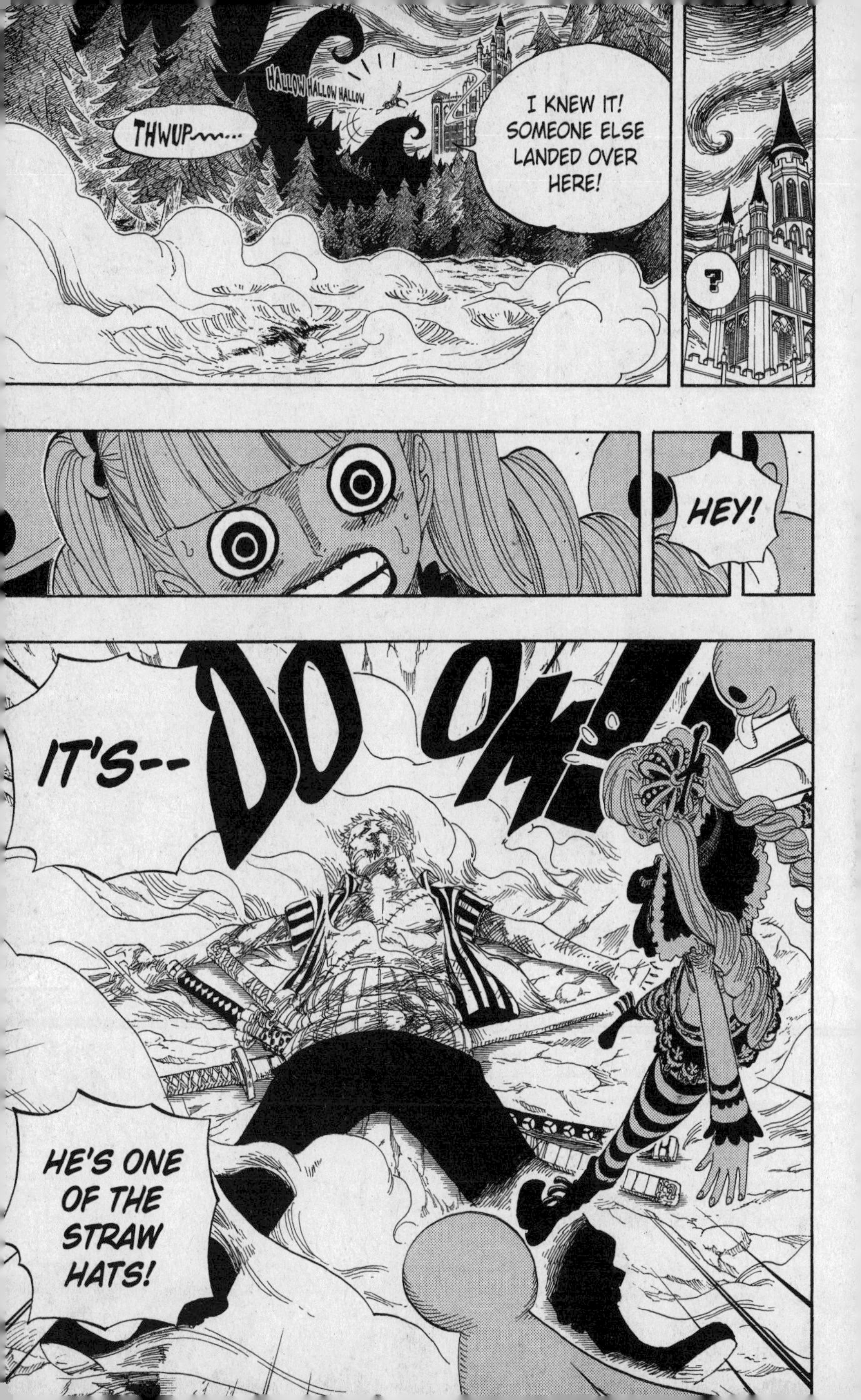
?
I KNEW IT! SOMEONE ELSE LANDED OVER HERE!
HALLOW HALLOW HALLOW
THWUP~~...
HEY!
DOOM!!
IT'S--
HE'S ONE OF THE STRAW HATS!

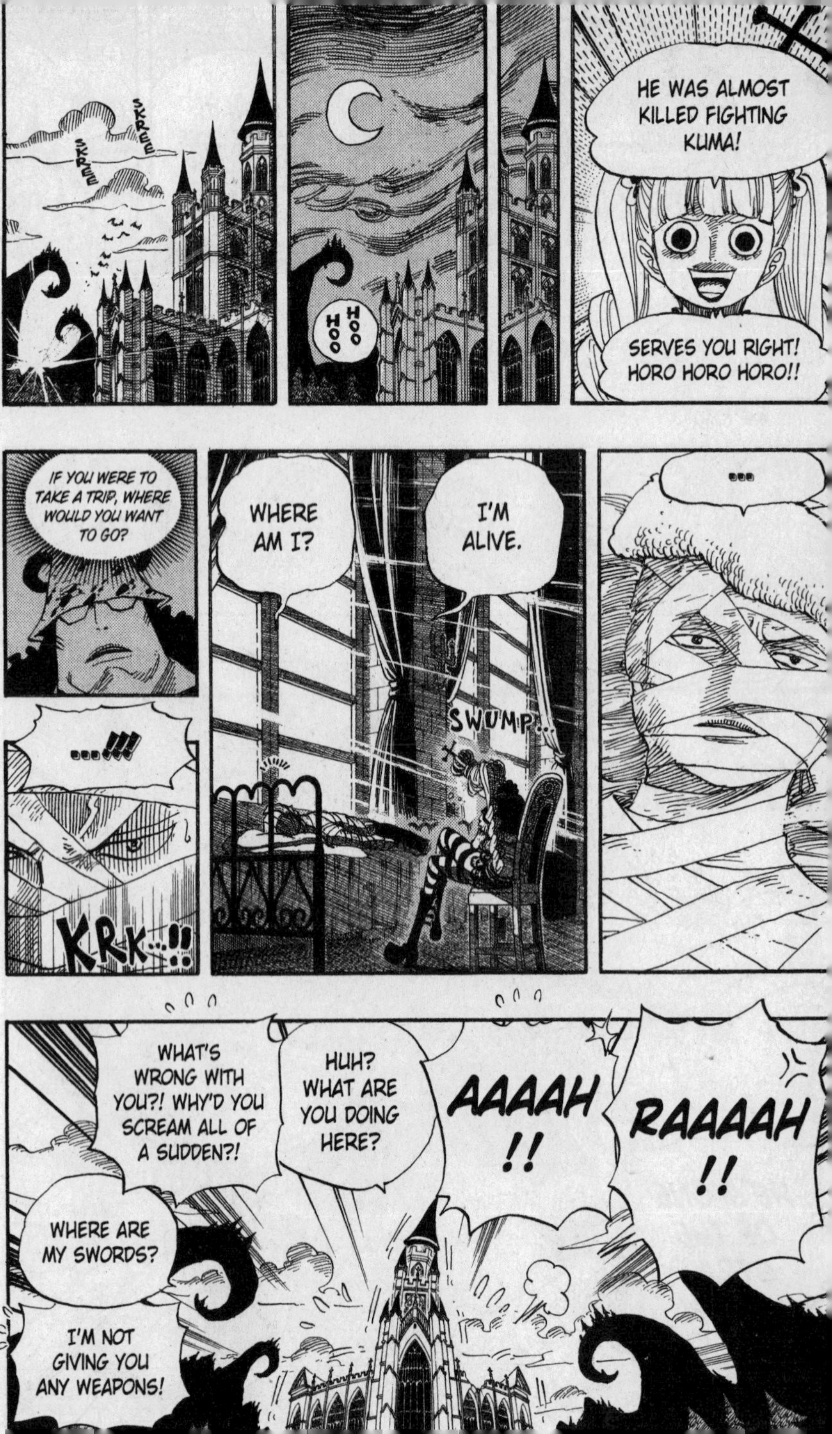
HE WAS ALMOST KILLED FIGHTING KUMA!
SERVES YOU RIGHT! HORO HORO HORO!!
HOO HOO
SKREE
SKREE
...
I'M ALIVE.
WHERE AM I?
SWUMP...
IF YOU WERE TO TAKE A TRIP, WHERE WOULD YOU WANT TO GO?
...!!!
KRK...!!
RAAAAH!!
AAAAH!!
HUH? WHAT ARE YOU DOING HERE?
WHAT'S WRONG WITH YOU?! WHY'D YOU SCREAM ALL OF A SUDDEN?!
WHERE ARE MY SWORDS?
I'M NOT GIVING YOU ANY WEAPONS!

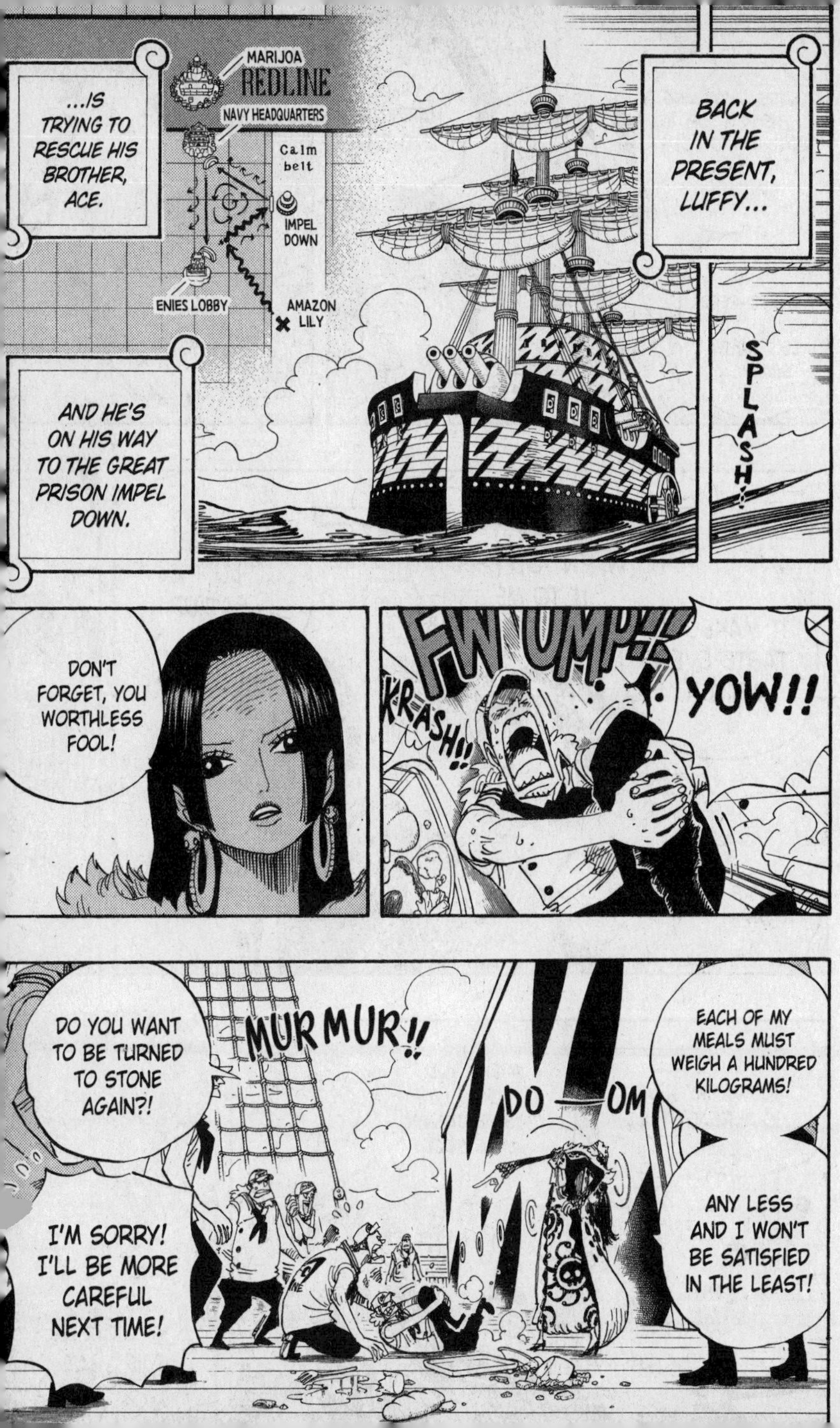

BACK IN THE PRESENT, LUFFY...
SPLASH!!
MARIJOA
REDLINE
NAVY HEADQUARTERS
Calm belt
IMPEL DOWN
ENIES LOBBY
AMAZON LILY
...IS TRYING TO RESCUE HIS BROTHER, ACE.
AND HE'S ON HIS WAY TO THE GREAT PRISON IMPEL DOWN.
FWUMP!!
KRASH!!
YOW!!
DON'T FORGET, YOU WORTHLESS FOOL!
EACH OF MY MEALS MUST WEIGH A HUNDRED KILOGRAMS!
ANY LESS AND I WON'T BE SATISFIED IN THE LEAST!
DO—OM
MURMUR!!
DO YOU WANT TO BE TURNED TO STONE AGAIN?!
I'M SORRY! I'LL BE MORE CAREFUL NEXT TIME!

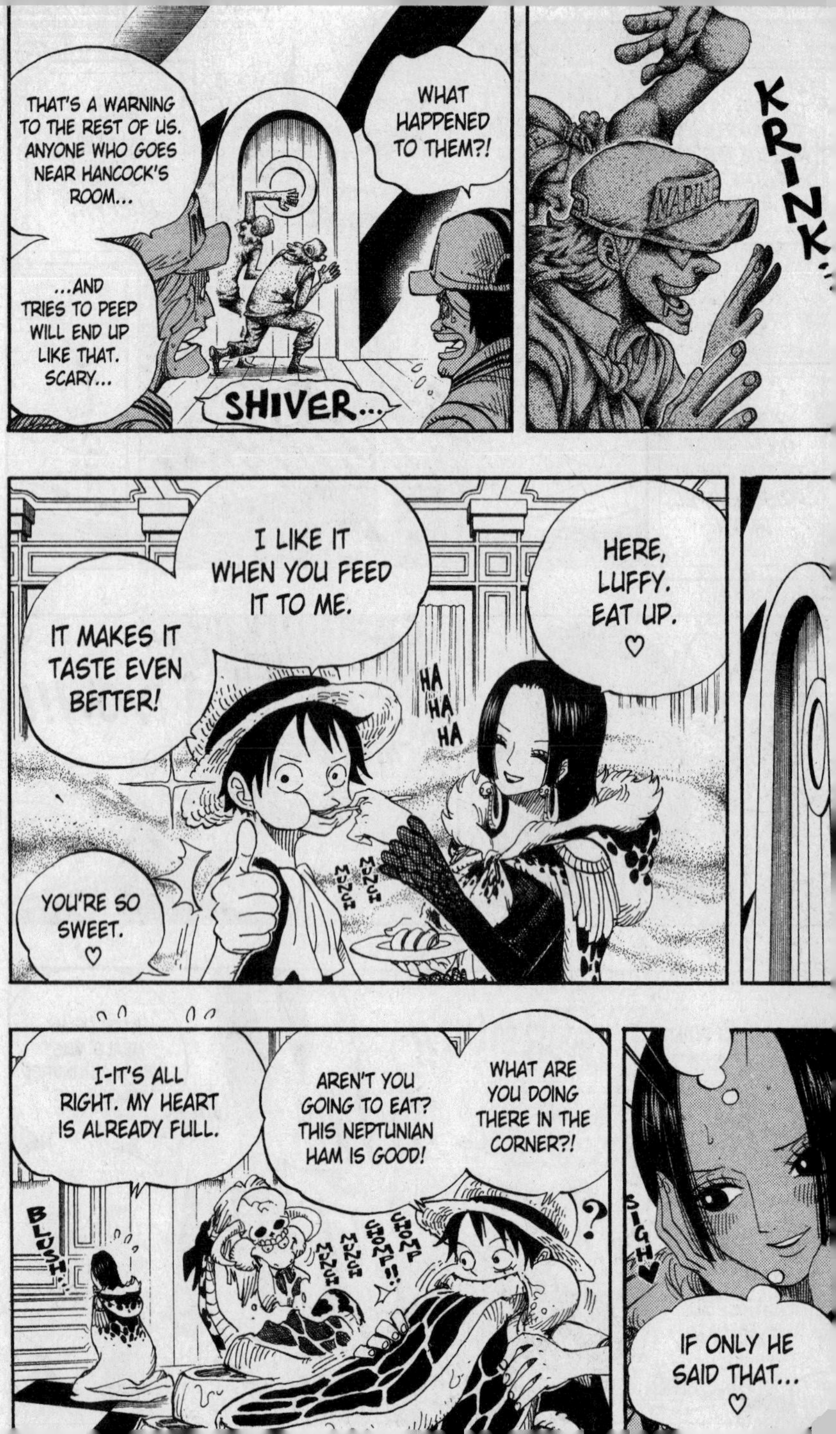
KRINK...
WHAT HAPPENED TO THEM?!
THAT'S A WARNING TO THE REST OF US. ANYONE WHO GOES NEAR HANCOCK'S ROOM...
...AND TRIES TO PEEP WILL END UP LIKE THAT. SCARY...
SHIVER...
HERE, LUFFY. EAT UP. ♡
HA HA HA
I LIKE IT WHEN YOU FEED IT TO ME.
IT MAKES IT TASTE EVEN BETTER!
MUNCH MUNCH
YOU'RE SO SWEET. ♡
SIGH♥
IF ONLY HE SAID THAT... ♡
WHAT ARE YOU DOING THERE IN THE CORNER?!
?
AREN'T YOU GOING TO EAT? THIS NEPTUNIAN HAM IS GOOD!
CHOMP CHOMP!!
MUNCH MUNCH
I-IT'S ALL RIGHT. MY HEART IS ALREADY FULL.
BLUSH...

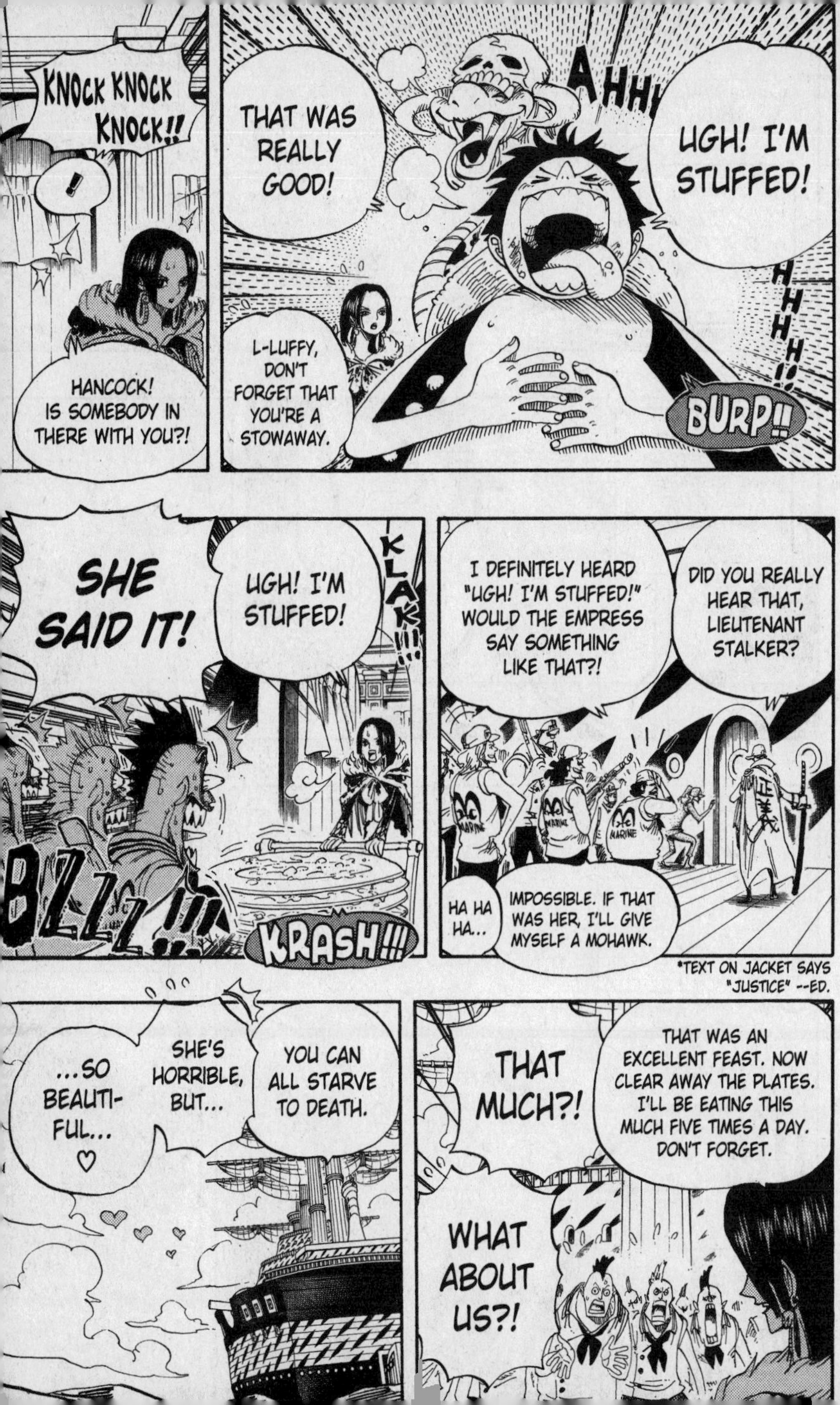
UGH! I'M STUFFED!
AHHHHHHH!!
THAT WAS REALLY GOOD!
BURP!!
L-LUFFY, DON'T FORGET THAT YOU'RE A STOWAWAY.
KNOCK KNOCK KNOCK!!
!
HANCOCK! IS SOMEBODY IN THERE WITH YOU?!
DID YOU REALLY HEAR THAT, LIEUTENANT STALKER?
I DEFINITELY HEARD "UGH! I'M STUFFED!" WOULD THE EMPRESS SAY SOMETHING LIKE THAT?!
IMPOSSIBLE. IF THAT WAS HER, I'LL GIVE MYSELF A MOHAWK.
HA HA HA...
KLAK!!!
UGH! I'M STUFFED!
SHE SAID IT!
KRASH!!!
BZZZZ!!!
THAT WAS AN EXCELLENT FEAST. NOW CLEAR AWAY THE PLATES. I'LL BE EATING THIS MUCH FIVE TIMES A DAY. DON'T FORGET.
THAT MUCH?!
WHAT ABOUT US?!
YOU CAN ALL STARVE TO DEATH.
SHE'S HORRIBLE, BUT...
...SO BEAUTIFUL... ♡
*TEXT ON JACKET SAYS "JUSTICE" --ED.

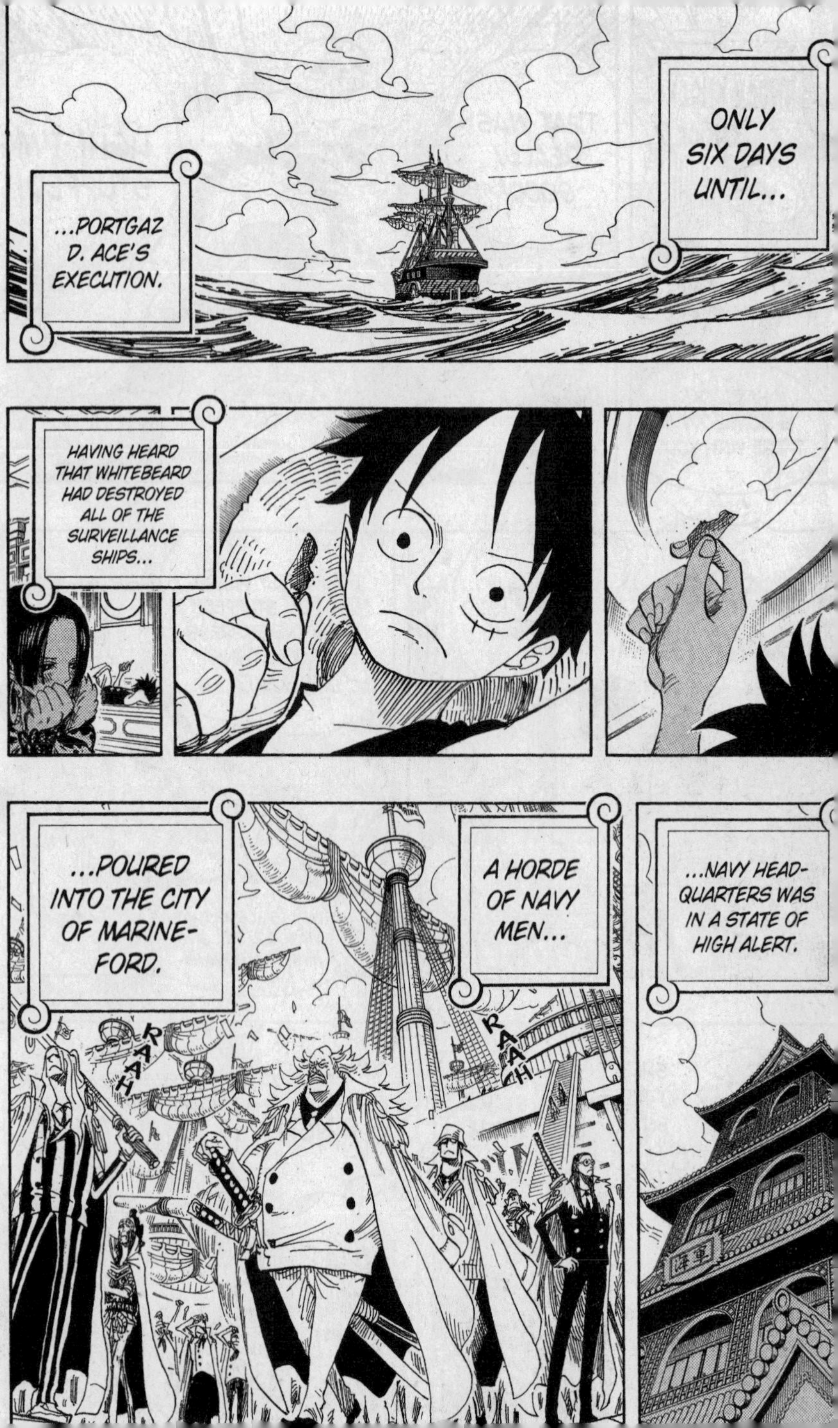
ONLY SIX DAYS UNTIL...
...PORTGAZ D. ACE'S EXECUTION.
HAVING HEARD THAT WHITEBEARD HAD DESTROYED ALL OF THE SURVEILLANCE SHIPS...
...NAVY HEAD-QUARTERS WAS IN A STATE OF HIGH ALERT.
A HORDE OF NAVY MEN...
RAAAH
...POURED INTO THE CITY OF MARINE-FORD.
RAAAH

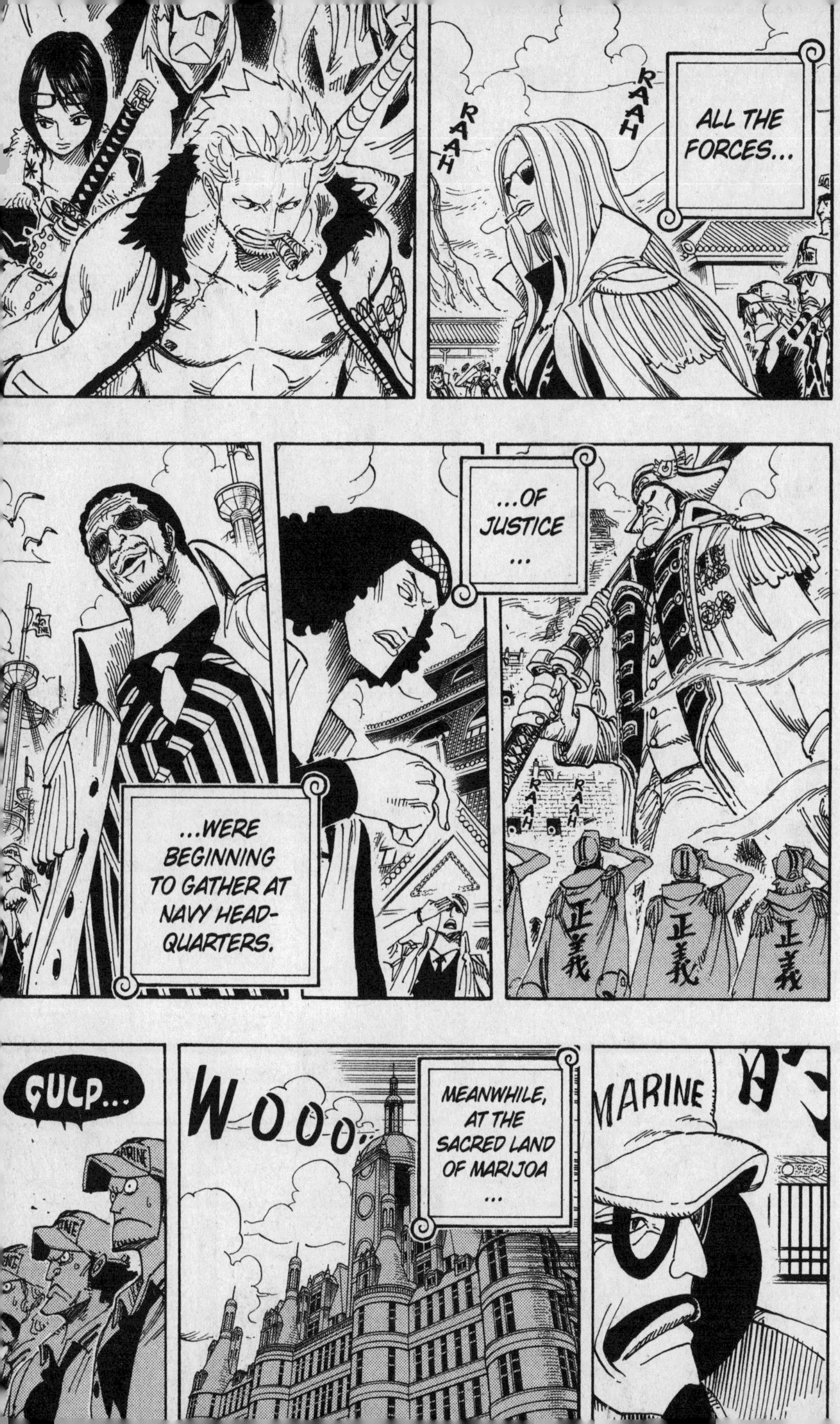
ALL THE FORCES...
RAAH
RAAH
...OF JUSTICE ...
RAAH
RAAH
...WERE BEGINNING TO GATHER AT NAVY HEAD-QUARTERS.
MARINE
MEANWHILE, AT THE SACRED LAND OF MARIJOA ...
WOOO
GULP...

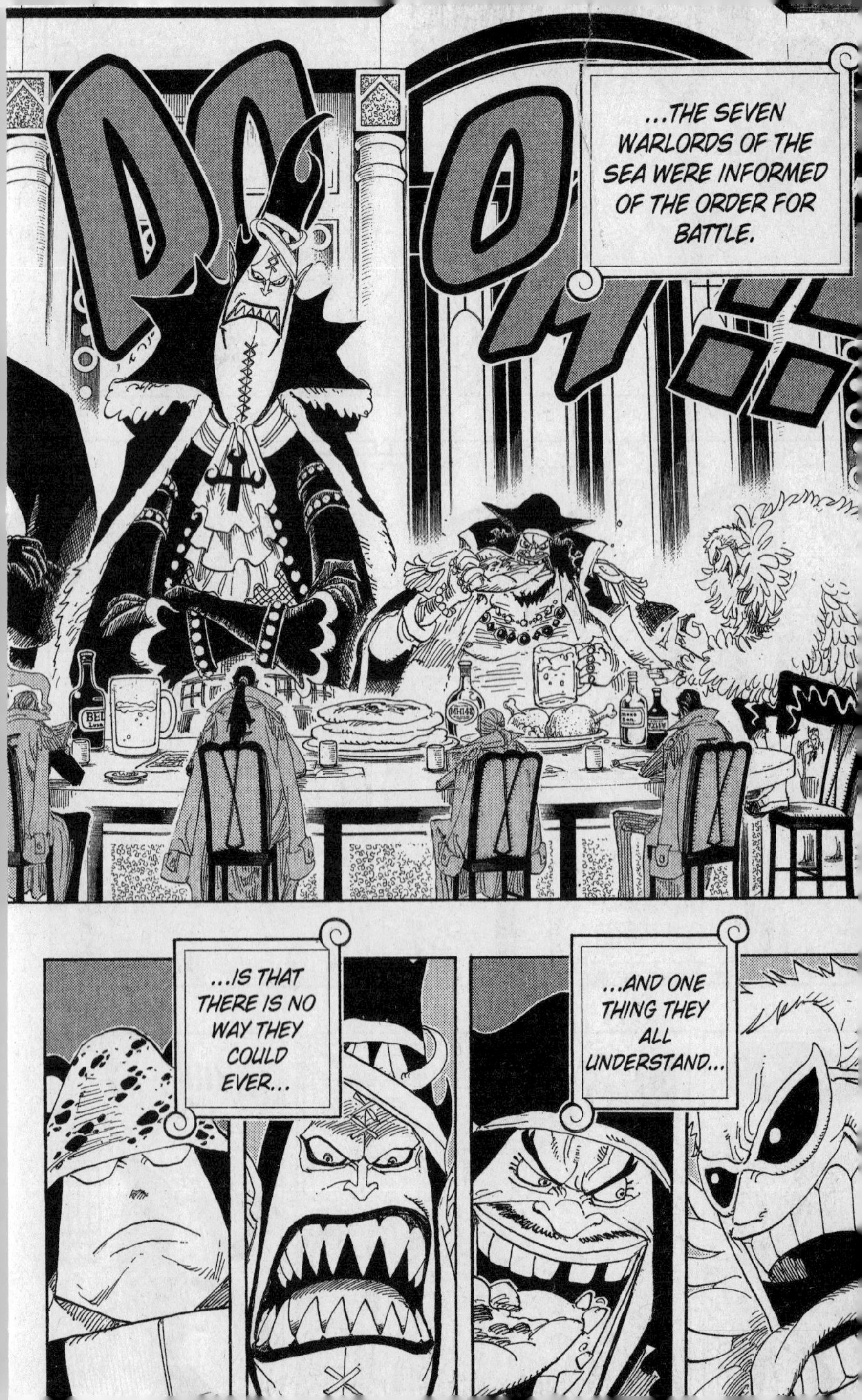
...THE SEVEN WARLORDS OF THE SEA WERE INFORMED OF THE ORDER FOR BATTLE.
...AND ONE THING THEY ALL UNDERSTAND...
...IS THAT THERE IS NO WAY THEY COULD EVER...

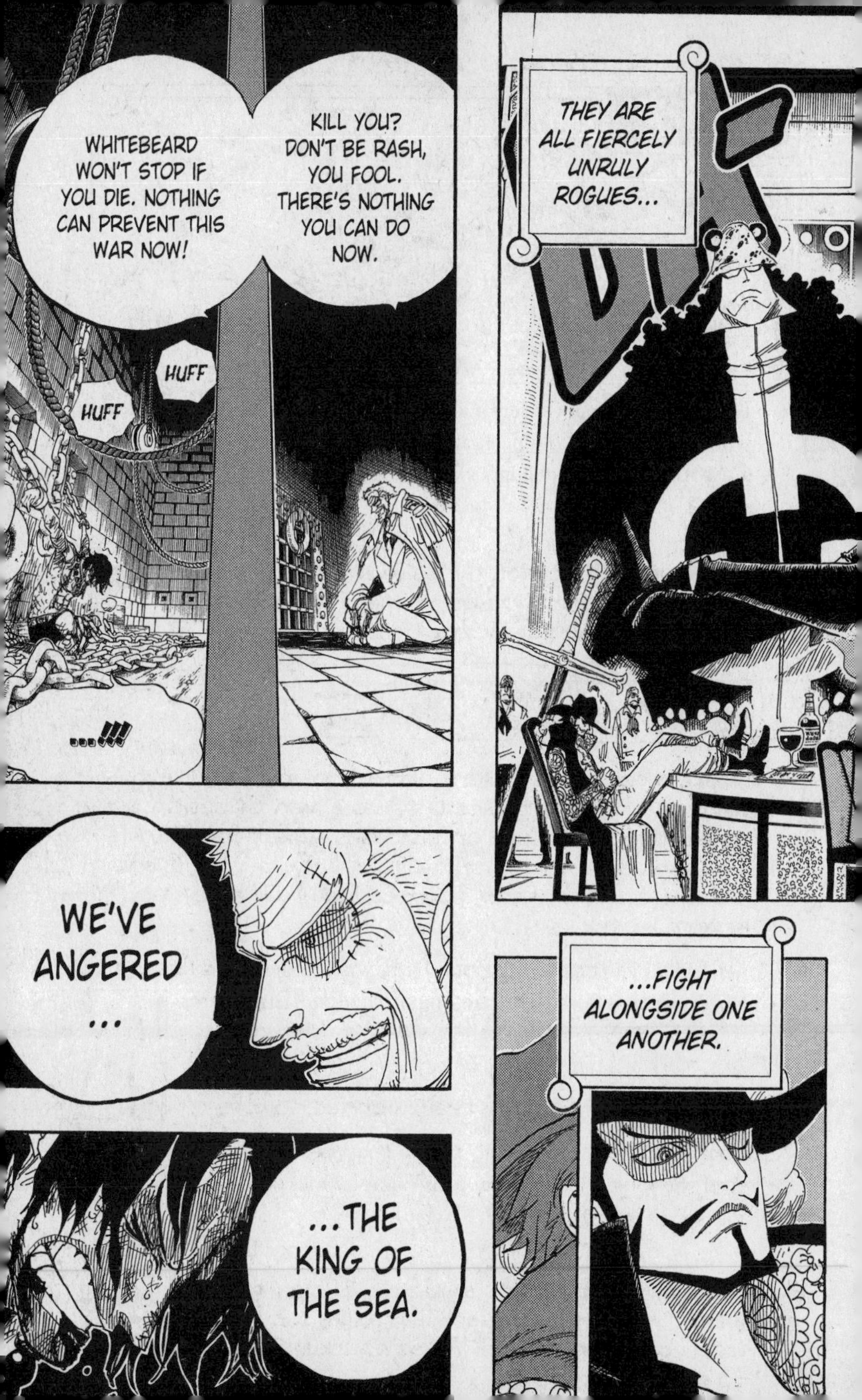

THEY ARE ALL FIERCELY UNRULY ROGUES...
...FIGHT ALONGSIDE ONE ANOTHER.
KILL YOU? DON'T BE RASH, YOU FOOL. THERE'S NOTHING YOU CAN DO NOW.
WHITEBEARD WON'T STOP IF YOU DIE. NOTHING CAN PREVENT THIS WAR NOW!
HUFF
HUFF
...!!!
WE'VE ANGERED ...
...THE KING OF THE SEA.

SBS Question Corner

質問コーナー
エスビーエス

(Mari Chiba, Iwate)

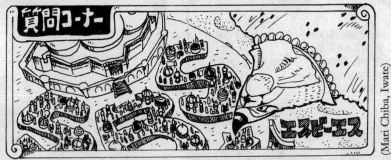

Q: Hello, I am an avid reader of *One Piece*. Here's my question. I reread the whole series from volume 1, and I noticed that Luffy almost never has any sort of internal dialogue. Why is that?

--Aqua Ribbon

A: And you didn't see this until volume 54? It's my policy to depict things in a certain way. It's just one of those things I decided to do from the beginning. In Luffy's case:

This should work.
But what if... What's that?
Let me see...
That's...
For this...

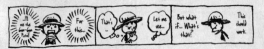

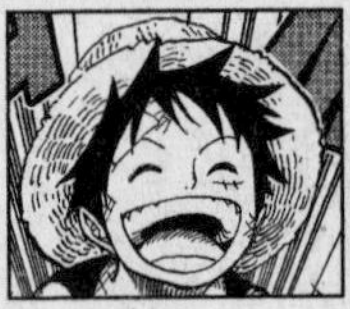

I make a conscious effort not to do anything like this. I want the readers to see Luffy as a man of action, so he always thinks out loud or just does something. During the Sky Island arc, I used internal dialogue with Montblanc Cricket, but that hardly counted. Luffy will always act before he thinks.

Q: Mr. Oda, I can't close my zipper! Oh, wait, forget I said that. Anyway, here's my question. Is Wanze one of the Four Emperors? All my friends think that's the case.

--Slacking Pirates

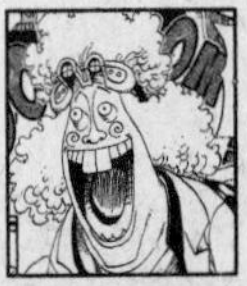

A: How's your zipper?! I'm really worried now.

Q: I have a question. On page 183, in chapter 521, Marigold is so thin! And she looks really pretty too! What happened to her?! Please tell me! ♡

--Chopper Lover ♡

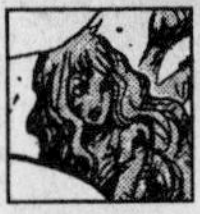

A: She didn't get fat! It's all muscle! She gained weight to get stronger! That's why she worked out and got all those muscles! She had to eat a lot too!

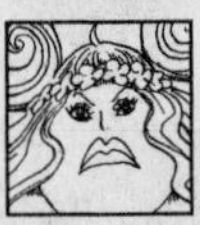

Chapter 525: THE UNDERWATER PRISON IMPEL DOWN

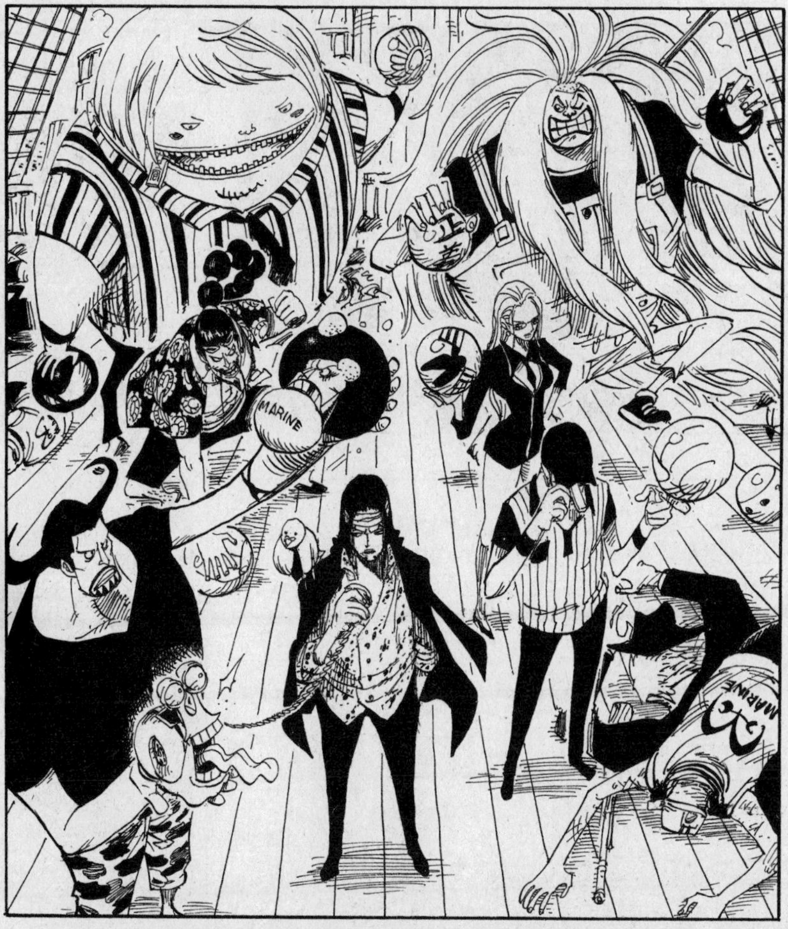
MARINE
MARINE

CP9 INDEPENDENT REPORT, VOL. 31:
"WE WILL RETURN ONE DAY"

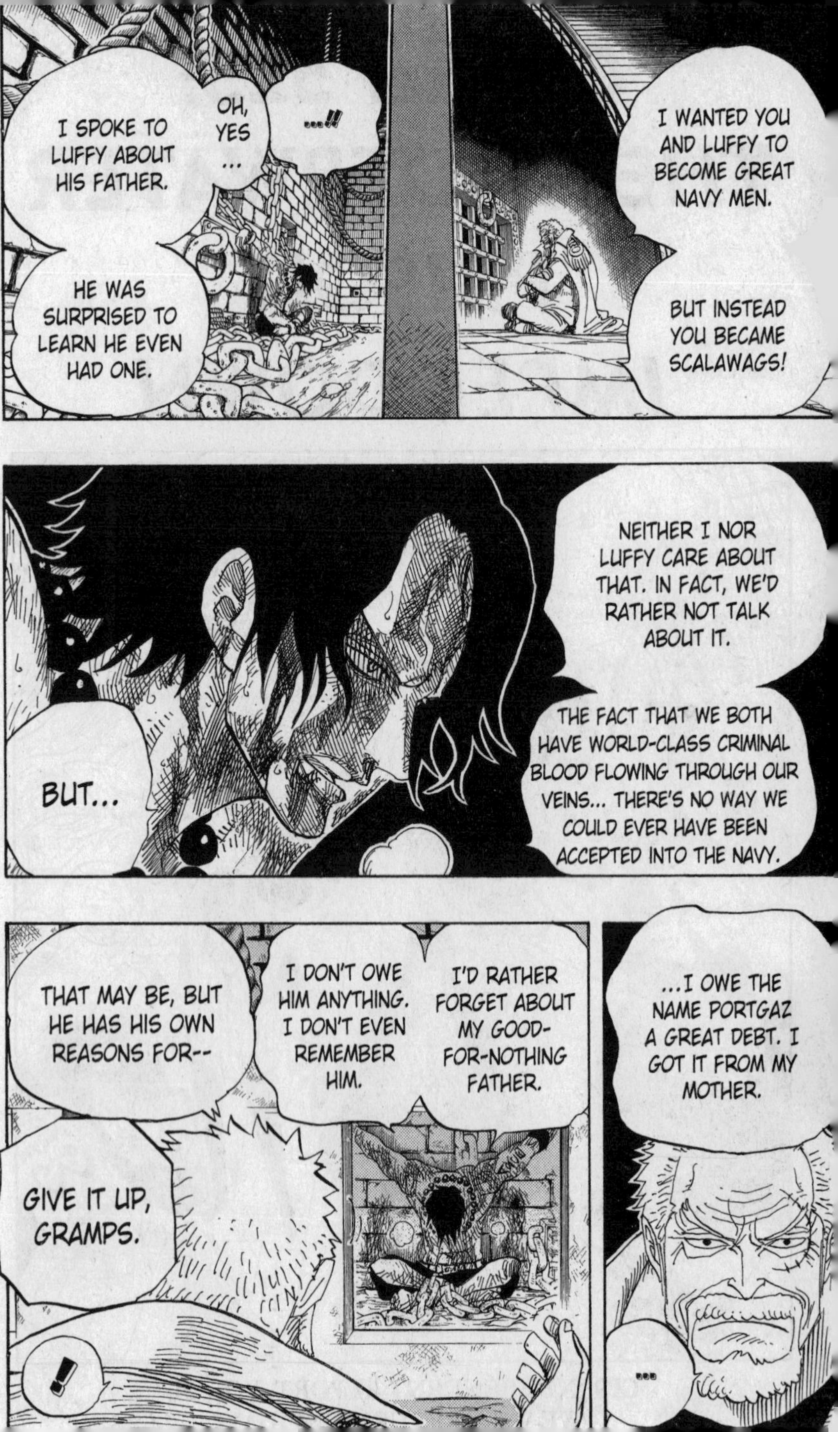
I WANTED YOU AND LUFFY TO BECOME GREAT NAVY MEN.
BUT INSTEAD YOU BECAME SCALAWAGS!
...!!
OH, YES ...
I SPOKE TO LUFFY ABOUT HIS FATHER.
HE WAS SURPRISED TO LEARN HE EVEN HAD ONE.
NEITHER I NOR LUFFY CARE ABOUT THAT. IN FACT, WE'D RATHER NOT TALK ABOUT IT.
THE FACT THAT WE BOTH HAVE WORLD-CLASS CRIMINAL BLOOD FLOWING THROUGH OUR VEINS... THERE'S NO WAY WE COULD EVER HAVE BEEN ACCEPTED INTO THE NAVY.
BUT...
...I OWE THE NAME PORTGAZ A GREAT DEBT. I GOT IT FROM MY MOTHER.
...
I'D RATHER FORGET ABOUT MY GOOD-FOR-NOTHING FATHER.
I DON'T OWE HIM ANYTHING. I DON'T EVEN REMEMBER HIM.
THAT MAY BE, BUT HE HAS HIS OWN REASONS FOR--
GIVE IT UP, GRAMPS.
!

...?!

IT WOULD BE A WASTE IF YOU DIED NOW, SONNY.

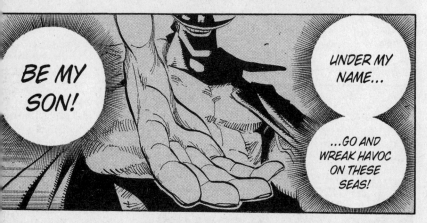

BE MY SON!

UNDER MY NAME...

...GO AND WREAK HAVOC ON THESE SEAS!

...IS MY ONLY FATHER!!

WHITE-BEARD...

...

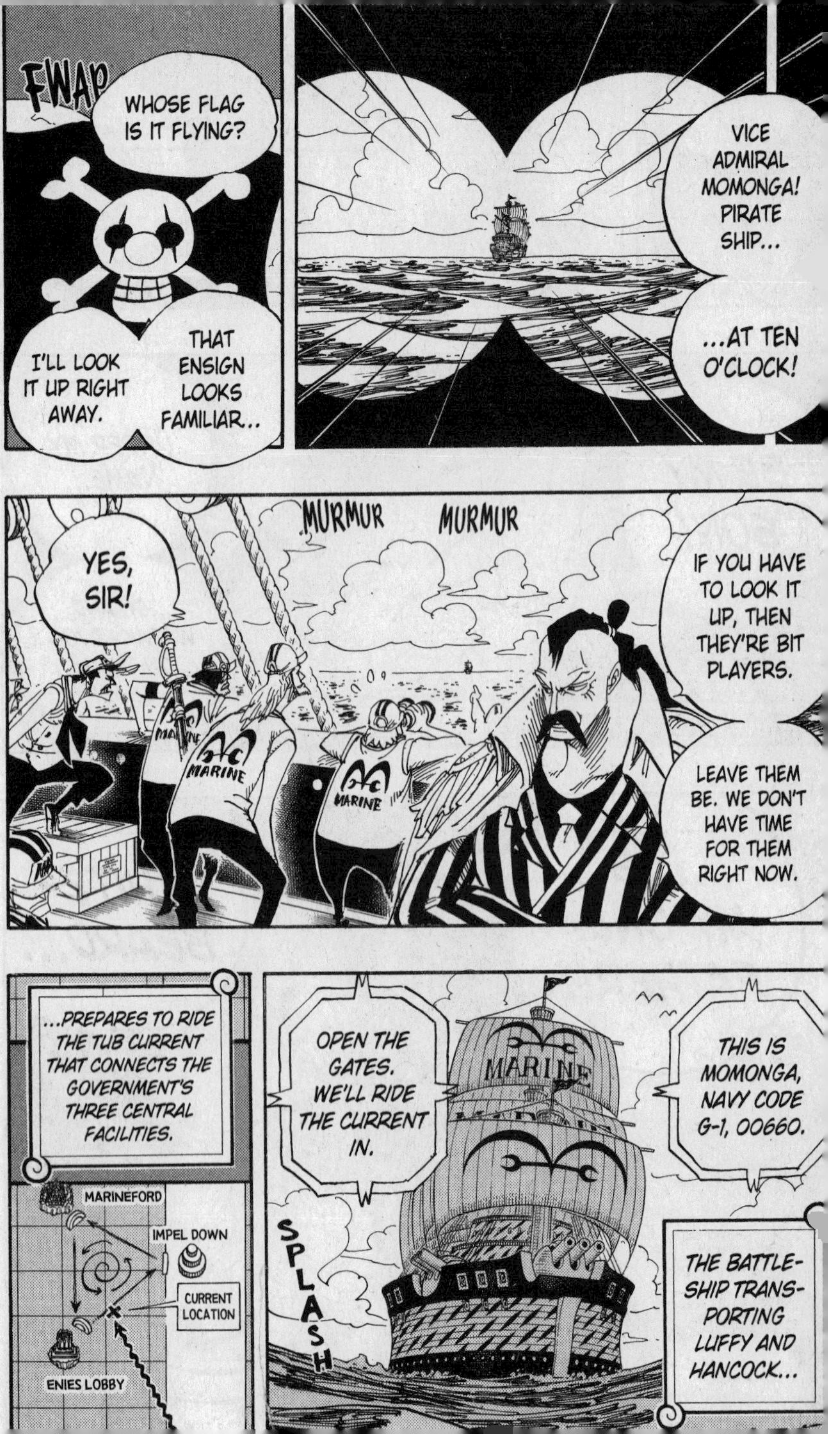
VICE ADMIRAL MOMONGA! PIRATE SHIP...
...AT TEN O'CLOCK!
WHOSE FLAG IS IT FLYING?
FWAP
THAT ENSIGN LOOKS FAMILIAR...
I'LL LOOK IT UP RIGHT AWAY.
MURMUR
MURMUR
IF YOU HAVE TO LOOK IT UP, THEN THEY'RE BIT PLAYERS.
LEAVE THEM BE. WE DON'T HAVE TIME FOR THEM RIGHT NOW.
YES, SIR!
MARINE
MARINE
MARINE
THIS IS MOMONGA, NAVY CODE G-1, 00660.
OPEN THE GATES. WE'LL RIDE THE CURRENT IN.
MARINE
SPLASH
THE BATTLESHIP TRANSPORTING LUFFY AND HANCOCK...
...PREPARES TO RIDE THE TUB CURRENT THAT CONNECTS THE GOVERNMENT'S THREE CENTRAL FACILITIES.
MARINEFORD
IMPEL DOWN
CURRENT LOCATION
ENIES LOBBY

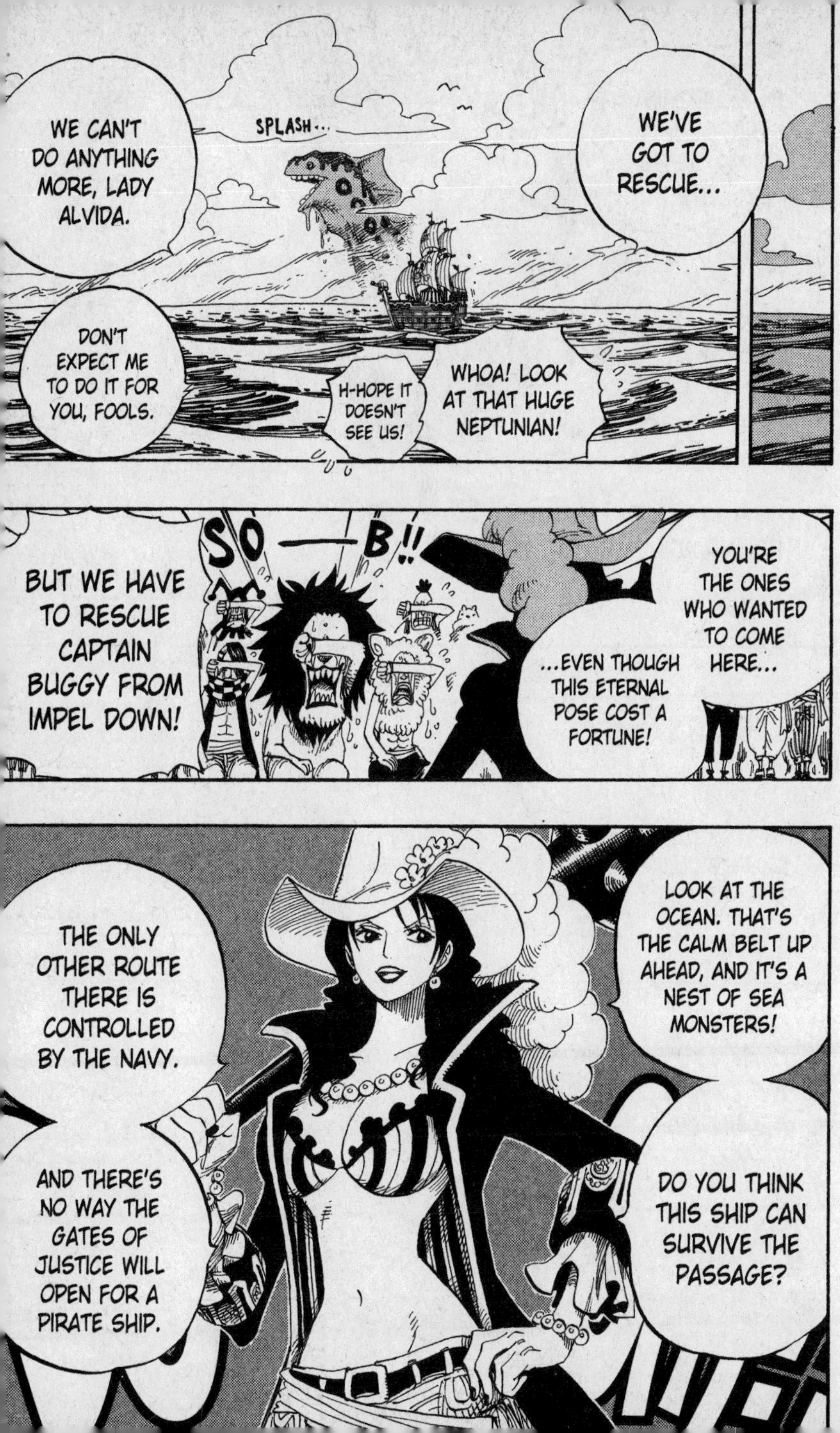
WE'VE GOT TO RESCUE...
WE CAN'T DO ANYTHING MORE, LADY ALVIDA.
SPLASH...
WHOA! LOOK AT THAT HUGE NEPTUNIAN!
H-HOPE IT DOESN'T SEE US!
DON'T EXPECT ME TO DO IT FOR YOU, FOOLS.
YOU'RE THE ONES WHO WANTED TO COME HERE...
...EVEN THOUGH THIS ETERNAL POSE COST A FORTUNE!
SO——B!!
BUT WE HAVE TO RESCUE CAPTAIN BUGGY FROM IMPEL DOWN!
LOOK AT THE OCEAN. THAT'S THE CALM BELT UP AHEAD, AND IT'S A NEST OF SEA MONSTERS!
THE ONLY OTHER ROUTE THERE IS CONTROLLED BY THE NAVY.
DO YOU THINK THIS SHIP CAN SURVIVE THE PASSAGE?
AND THERE'S NO WAY THE GATES OF JUSTICE WILL OPEN FOR A PIRATE SHIP.

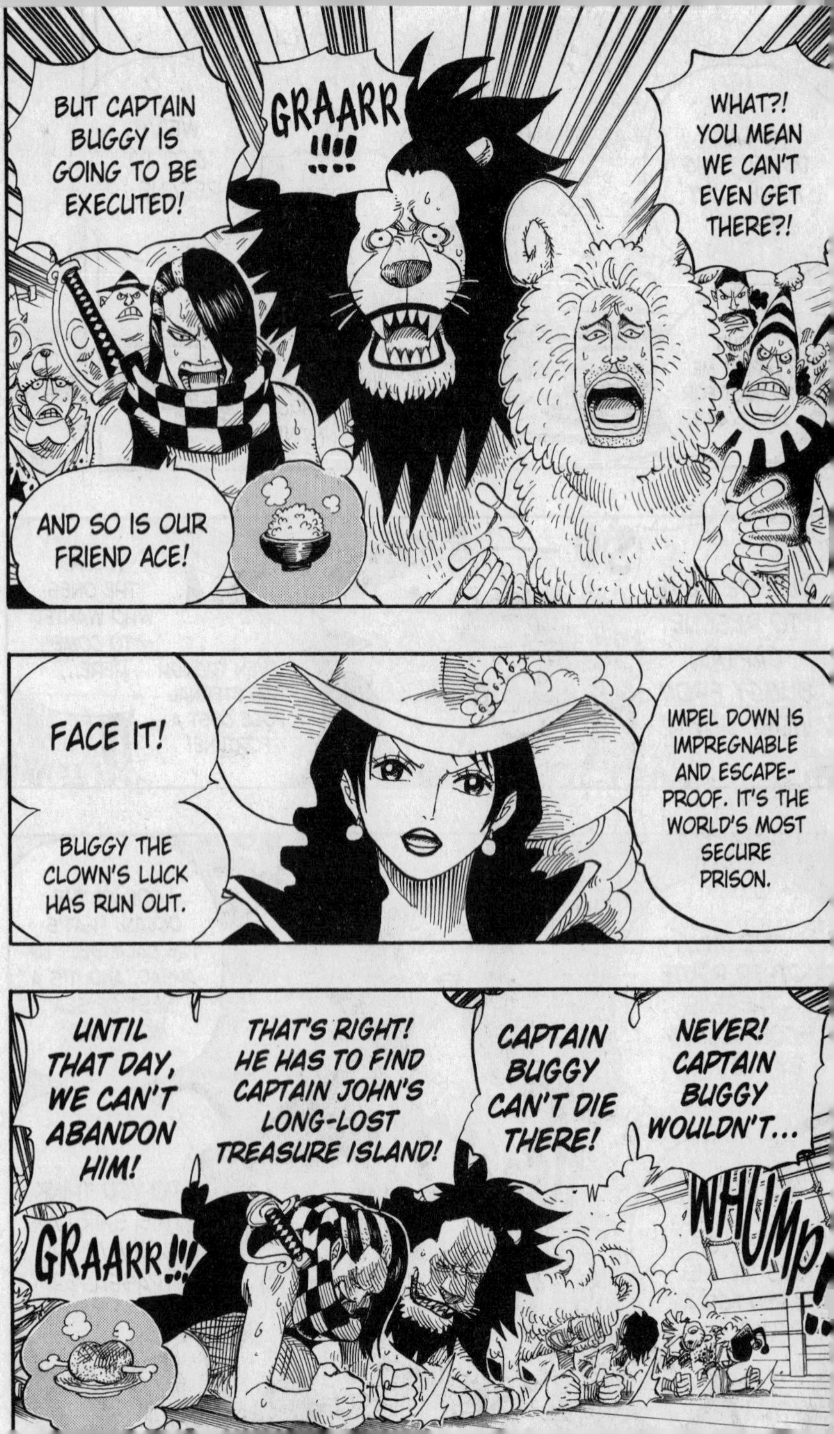
WHAT?! YOU MEAN WE CAN'T EVEN GET THERE?!
GRAARR !!!!
BUT CAPTAIN BUGGY IS GOING TO BE EXECUTED!
AND SO IS OUR FRIEND ACE!
IMPEL DOWN IS IMPREGNABLE AND ESCAPE-PROOF. IT'S THE WORLD'S MOST SECURE PRISON.
FACE IT!
BUGGY THE CLOWN'S LUCK HAS RUN OUT.
NEVER! CAPTAIN BUGGY WOULDN'T...
CAPTAIN BUGGY CAN'T DIE THERE!
THAT'S RIGHT! HE HAS TO FIND CAPTAIN JOHN'S LONG-LOST TREASURE ISLAND!
UNTIL THAT DAY, WE CAN'T ABANDON HIM!
WHUMP
GRAARR!!!

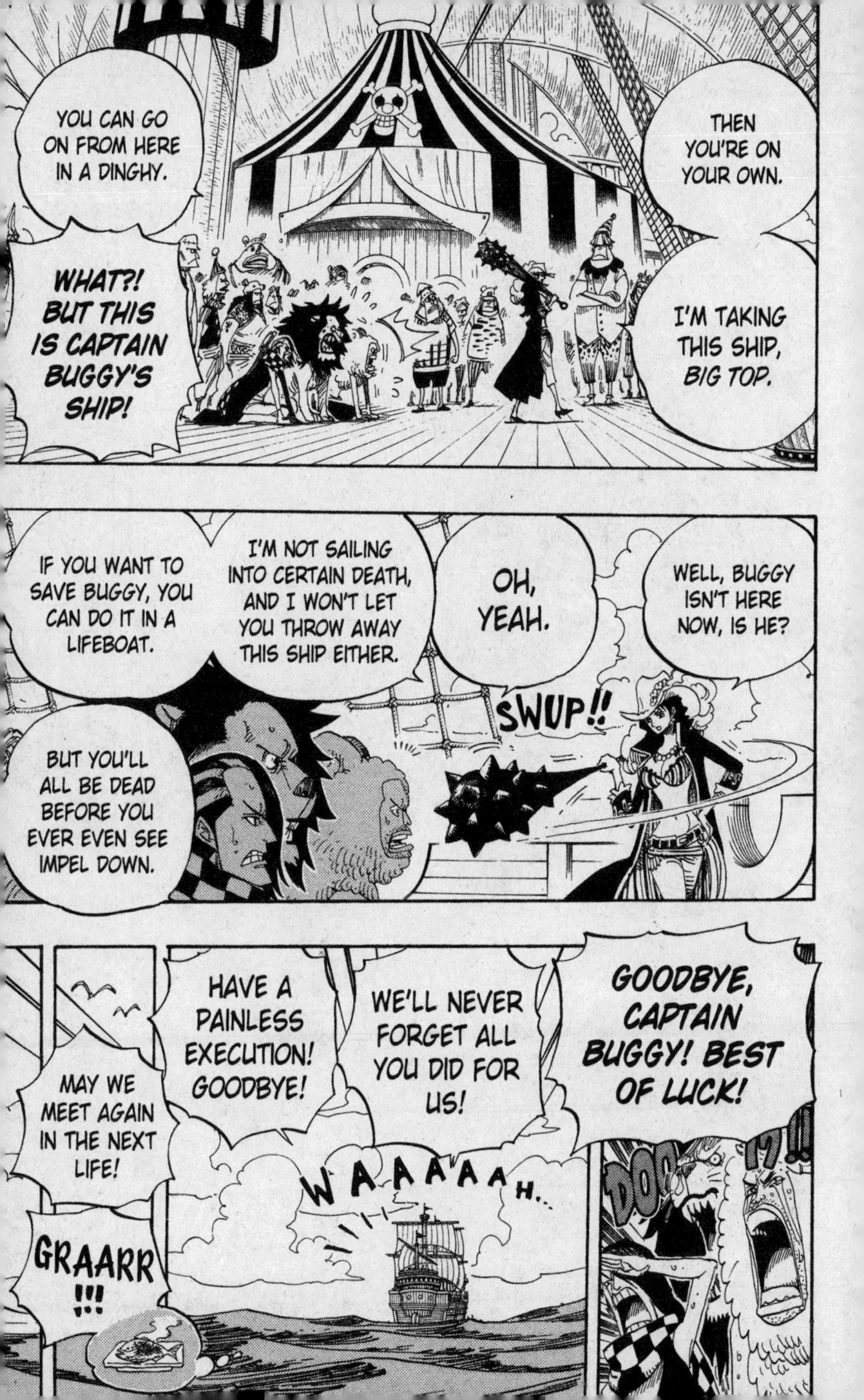
THEN YOU'RE ON YOUR OWN.
I'M TAKING THIS SHIP, BIG TOP.
YOU CAN GO ON FROM HERE IN A DINGHY.
WHAT?! BUT THIS IS CAPTAIN BUGGY'S SHIP!
WELL, BUGGY ISN'T HERE NOW, IS HE?
OH, YEAH.
I'M NOT SAILING INTO CERTAIN DEATH, AND I WON'T LET YOU THROW AWAY THIS SHIP EITHER.
IF YOU WANT TO SAVE BUGGY, YOU CAN DO IT IN A LIFEBOAT.
SWUP!!
BUT YOU'LL ALL BE DEAD BEFORE YOU EVER EVEN SEE IMPEL DOWN.
GOODBYE, CAPTAIN BUGGY! BEST OF LUCK!
DOO
!?!!
WE'LL NEVER FORGET ALL YOU DID FOR US!
HAVE A PAINLESS EXECUTION! GOODBYE!
MAY WE MEET AGAIN IN THE NEXT LIFE!
WAAAAAH..
GRAARR!!!

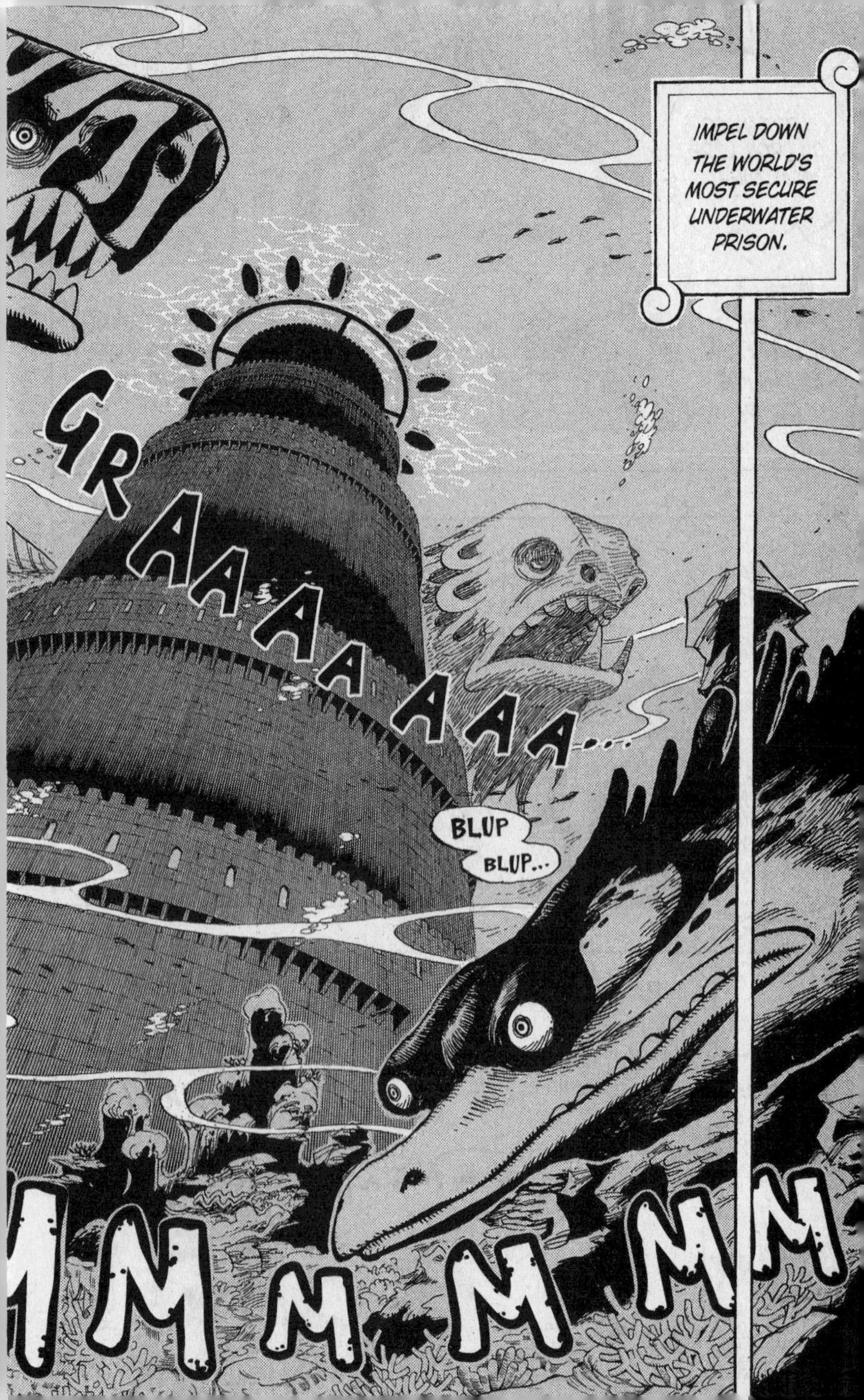
IMPEL DOWN
THE WORLD'S MOST SECURE UNDERWATER PRISON.
GRAAAAAAAA...
BLUP BLUP...
MMMMMM

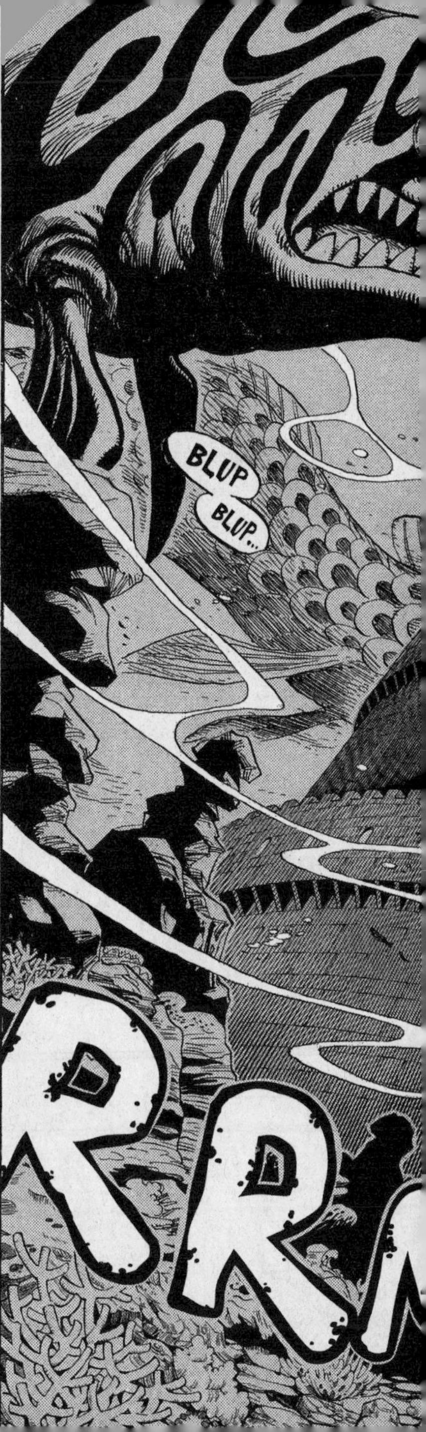
BLUP
BLUP...
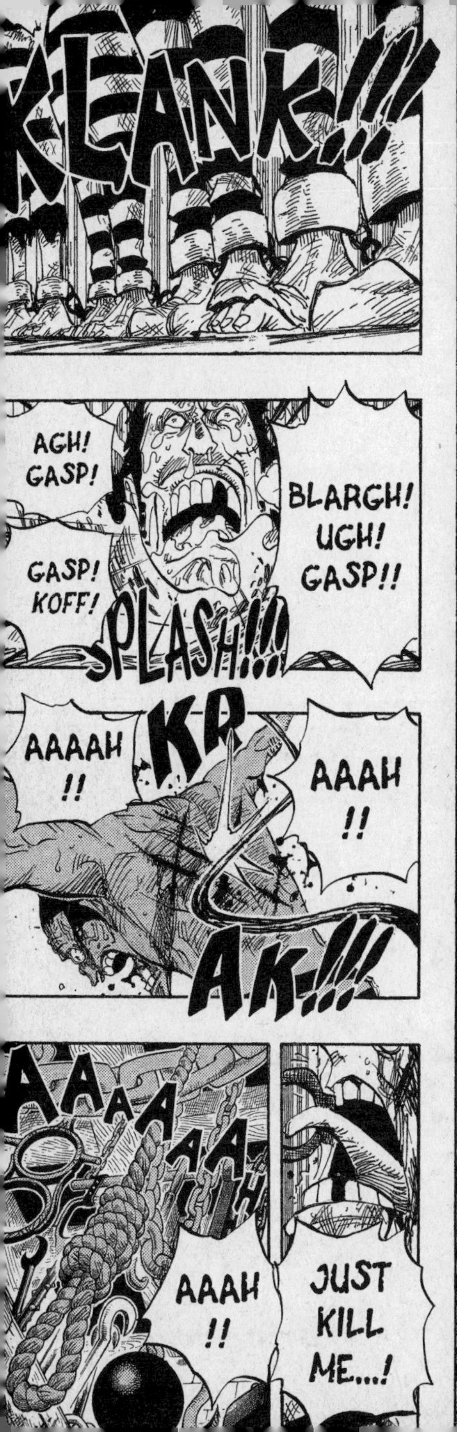
KLANK!!!
BLARGH! UGH! GASP!!
AGH! GASP!
GASP! KOFF!
SPLASH!!!
AAAH!!
AAAAH!!
KRAK!!!
JUST KILL ME...!
AAAAAAAAH
AAAH!!

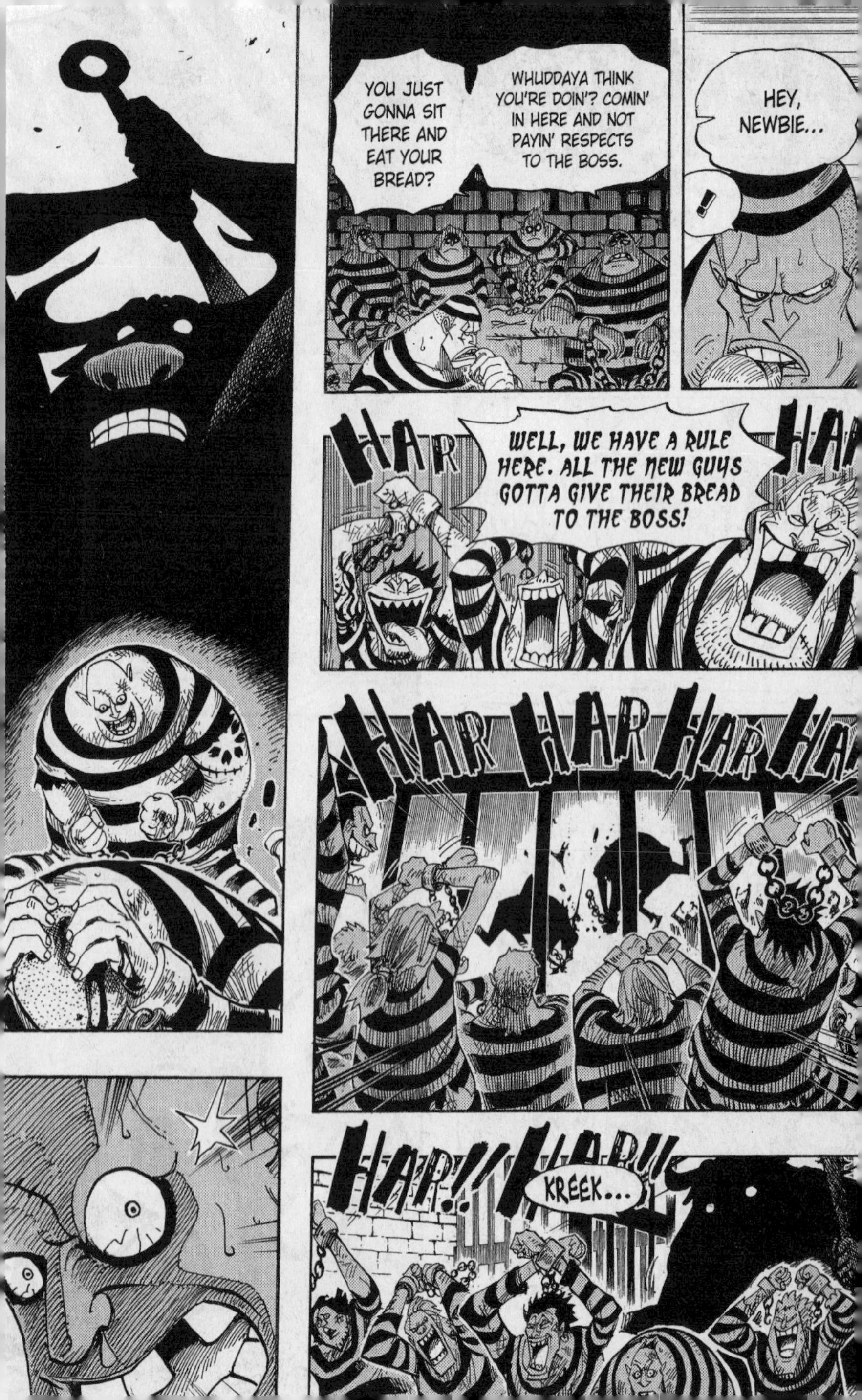
HEY, NEWBIE...
!
WHUDDAYA THINK YOU'RE DOIN'? COMIN' IN HERE AND NOT PAYIN' RESPECTS TO THE BOSS.
YOU JUST GONNA SIT THERE AND EAT YOUR BREAD?
HAR
WELL, WE HAVE A RULE HERE. ALL THE NEW GUYS GOTTA GIVE THEIR BREAD TO THE BOSS!
HAR
HAR HAR HAR HAR
HAR!! HAR!!
KREEK...

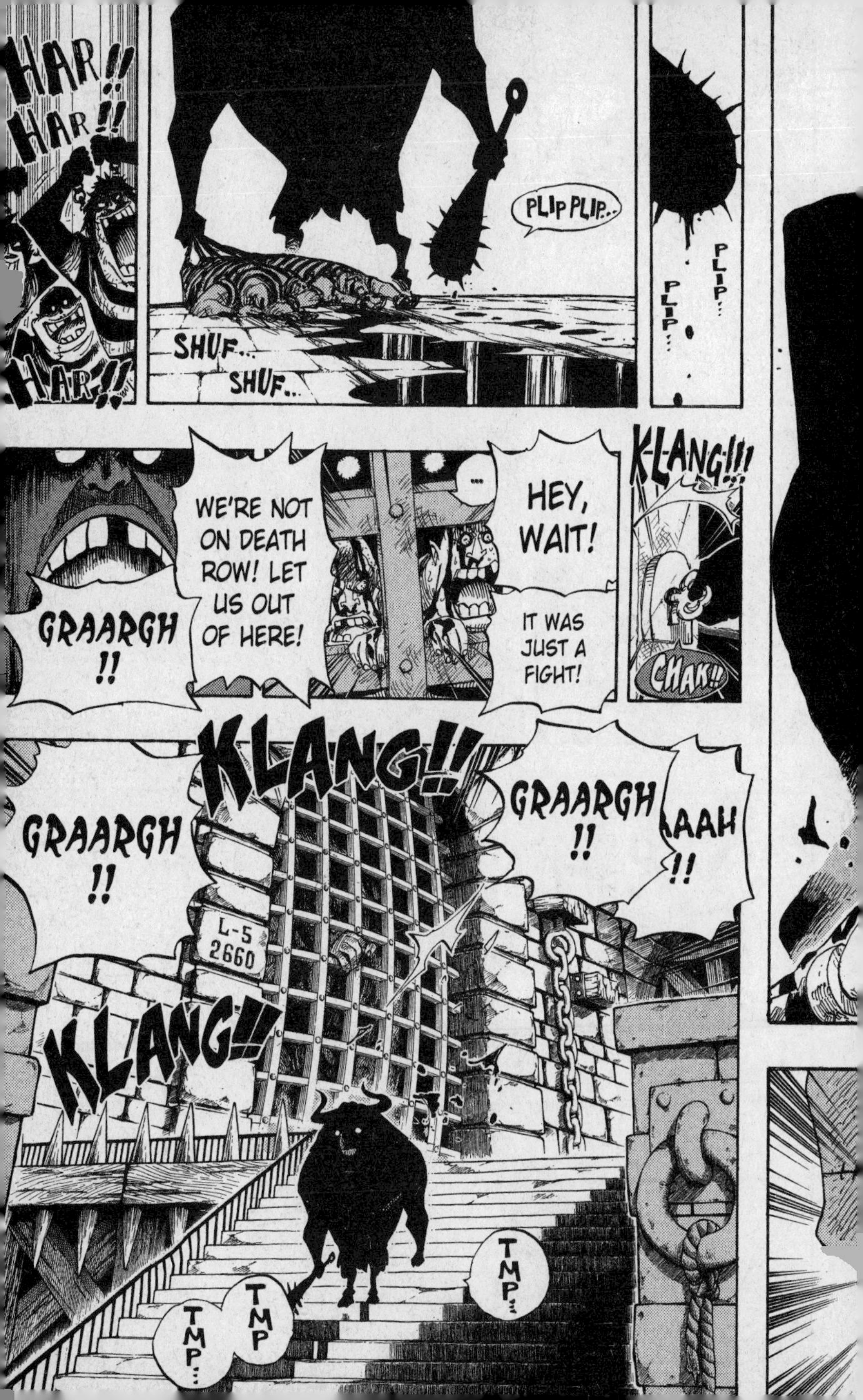
PLIP...
PLIP...
PLIP PLIP...
SHUF...
SHUF...
HAR!!
HAR!!
HAR!!
KLANG!!!
CHAK!!
...
HEY, WAIT!
IT WAS JUST A FIGHT!
WE'RE NOT ON DEATH ROW! LET US OUT OF HERE!
GRAARGH!!
KLANG!!
AAH!!
GRAARGH!!
GRAARGH!!
L-5 2660
KLANG!!
TMP...
TMP
TMP...

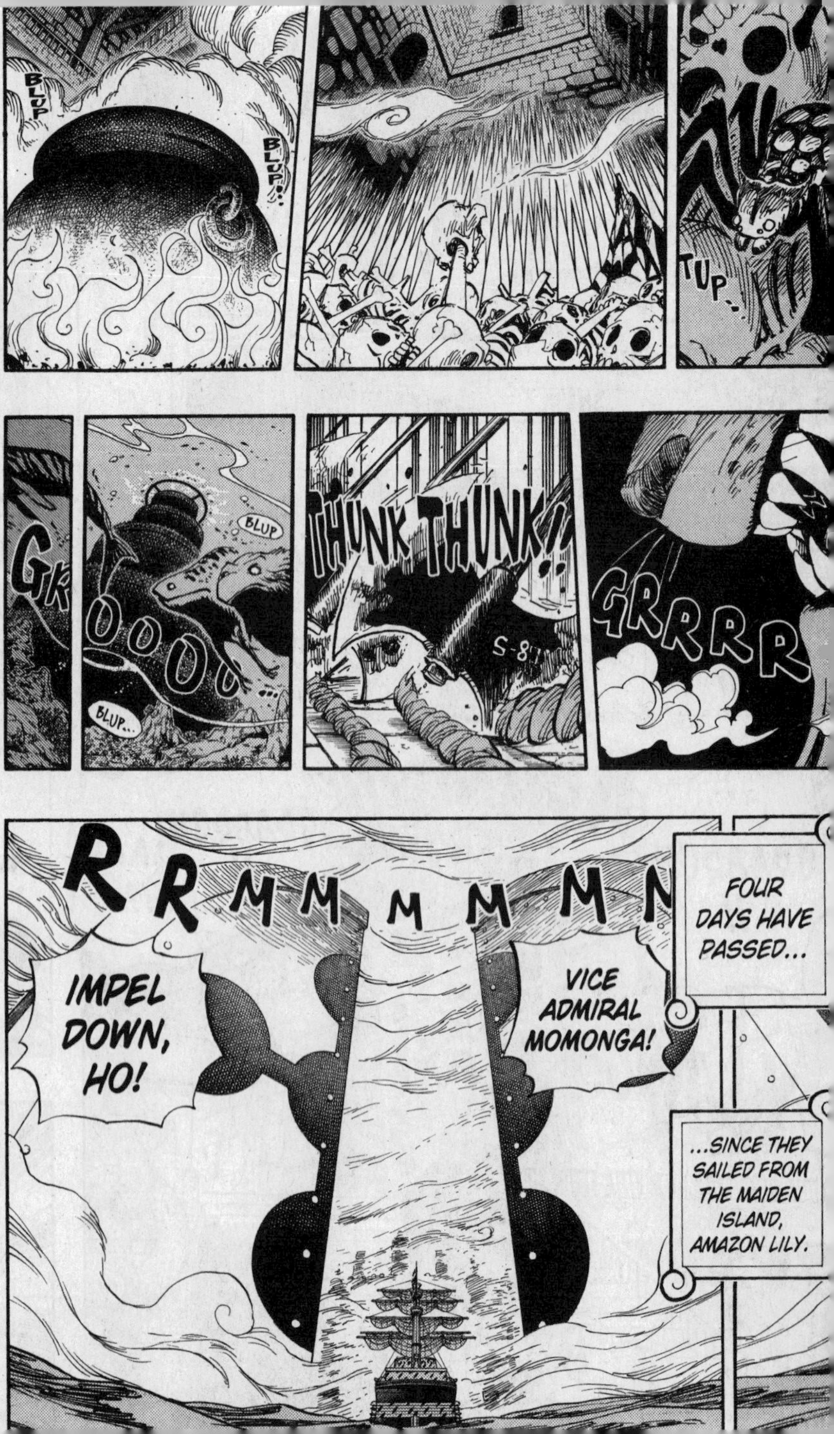
TUP...
BLUP
BLUP...
GRRRRR
THUNK THUNK!!
S-81
BLUP
GROOOOO
BLUP...
FOUR DAYS HAVE PASSED...
...SINCE THEY SAILED FROM THE MAIDEN ISLAND, AMAZON LILY.
RRMMMMMM
VICE ADMIRAL MOMONGA!
IMPEL DOWN, HO!

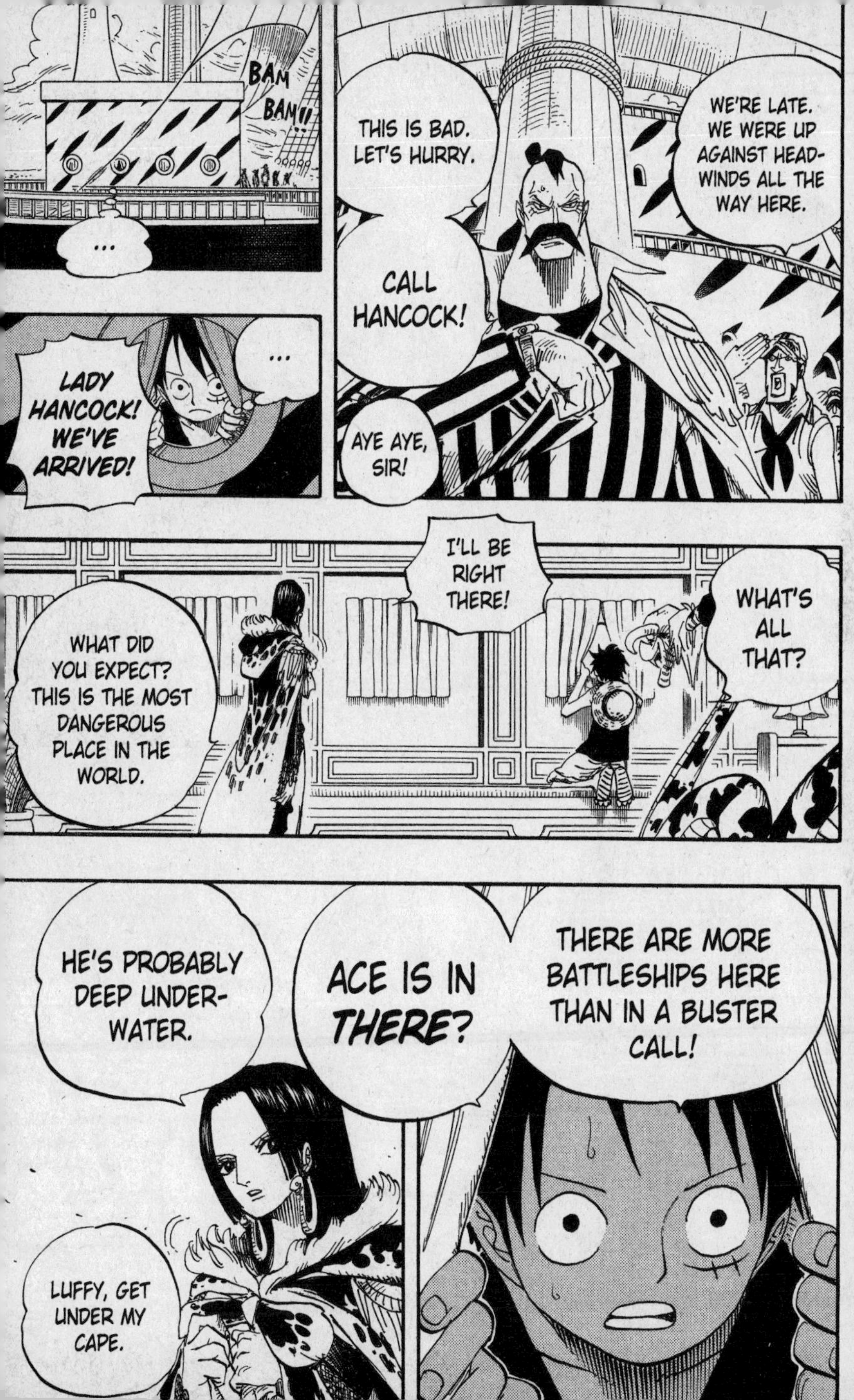
WE'RE LATE. WE WERE UP AGAINST HEAD-WINDS ALL THE WAY HERE.
THIS IS BAD. LET'S HURRY.
CALL HANCOCK!
AYE AYE, SIR!
BAM BAM!!
...
...
LADY HANCOCK! WE'VE ARRIVED!
I'LL BE RIGHT THERE!
WHAT'S ALL THAT?
WHAT DID YOU EXPECT? THIS IS THE MOST DANGEROUS PLACE IN THE WORLD.
THERE ARE MORE BATTLESHIPS HERE THAN IN A BUSTER CALL!
ACE IS IN THERE?
HE'S PROBABLY DEEP UNDER-WATER.
LUFFY, GET UNDER MY CAPE.

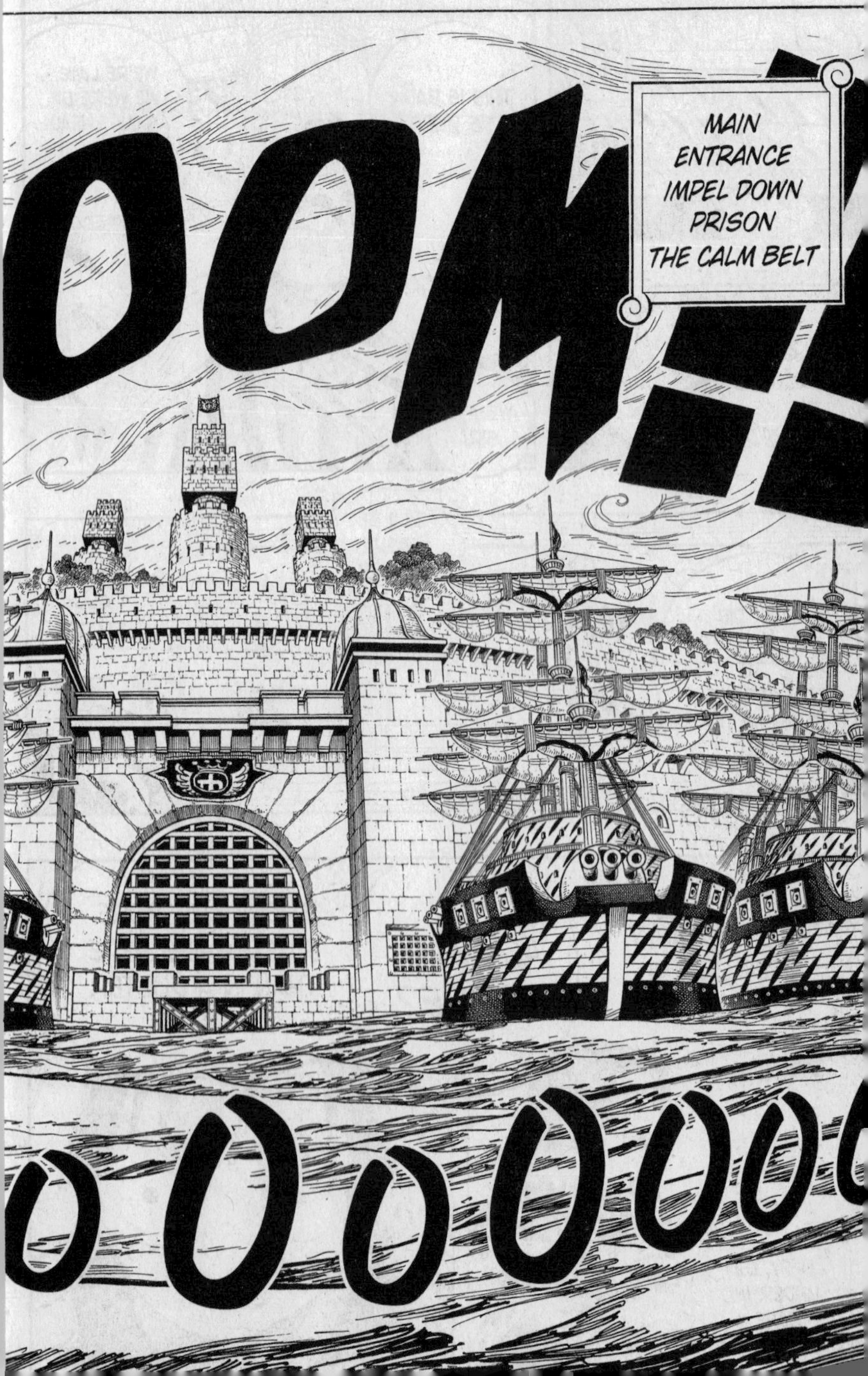
OOM!!
MAIN ENTRANCE
IMPEL DOWN PRISON
THE CALM BELT
OOOOOOO

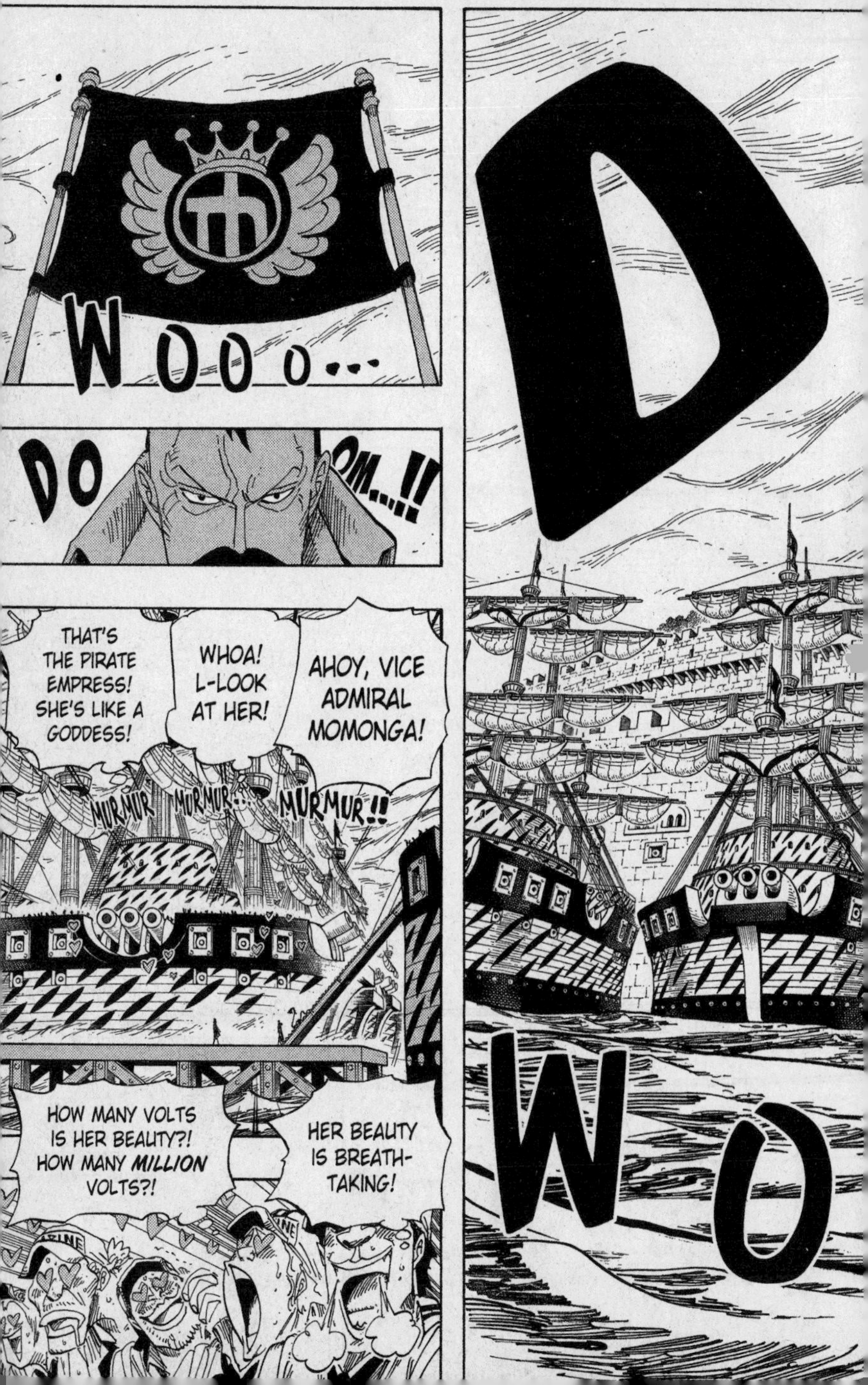
D
WO
WOOO...
DO
OM...!!
AHOY, VICE ADMIRAL MOMONGA!
WHOA! L-LOOK AT HER!
THAT'S THE PIRATE EMPRESS! SHE'S LIKE A GODDESS!
MURMUR!!
MURMUR...
MURMUR
HER BEAUTY IS BREATH-TAKING!
HOW MANY VOLTS IS HER BEAUTY?! HOW MANY *MILLION* VOLTS?!

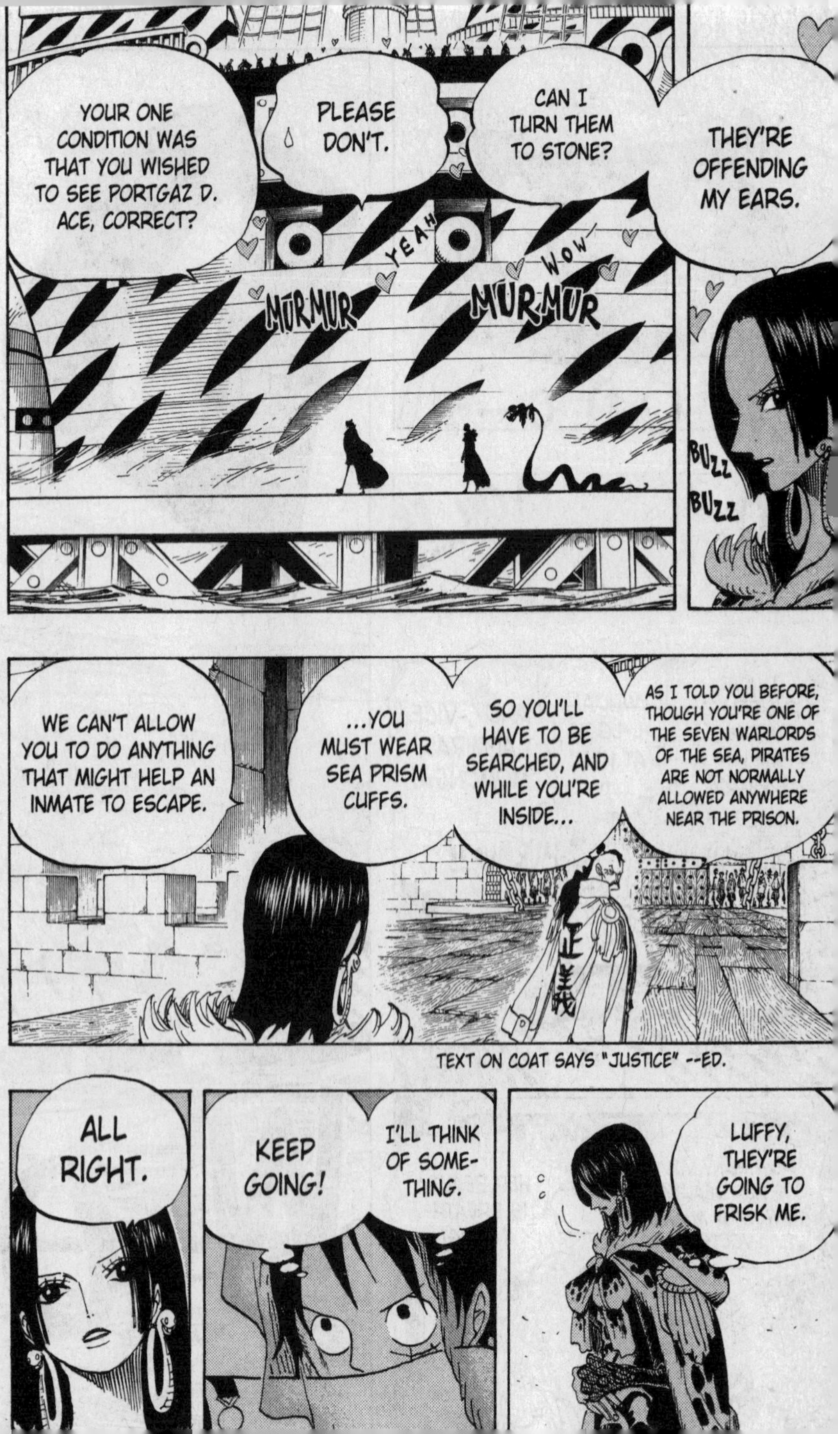
THEY'RE OFFENDING MY EARS.
BUZZ
BUZZ
CAN I TURN THEM TO STONE?
PLEASE DON'T.
YOUR ONE CONDITION WAS THAT YOU WISHED TO SEE PORTGAZ D. ACE, CORRECT?
WOW
MURMUR
YEAH
MURMUR
AS I TOLD YOU BEFORE, THOUGH YOU'RE ONE OF THE SEVEN WARLORDS OF THE SEA, PIRATES ARE NOT NORMALLY ALLOWED ANYWHERE NEAR THE PRISON.
SO YOU'LL HAVE TO BE SEARCHED, AND WHILE YOU'RE INSIDE...
...YOU MUST WEAR SEA PRISM CUFFS.
WE CAN'T ALLOW YOU TO DO ANYTHING THAT MIGHT HELP AN INMATE TO ESCAPE.
TEXT ON COAT SAYS "JUSTICE" --ED.
LUFFY, THEY'RE GOING TO FRISK ME.
I'LL THINK OF SOME-THING.
KEEP GOING!
ALL RIGHT.

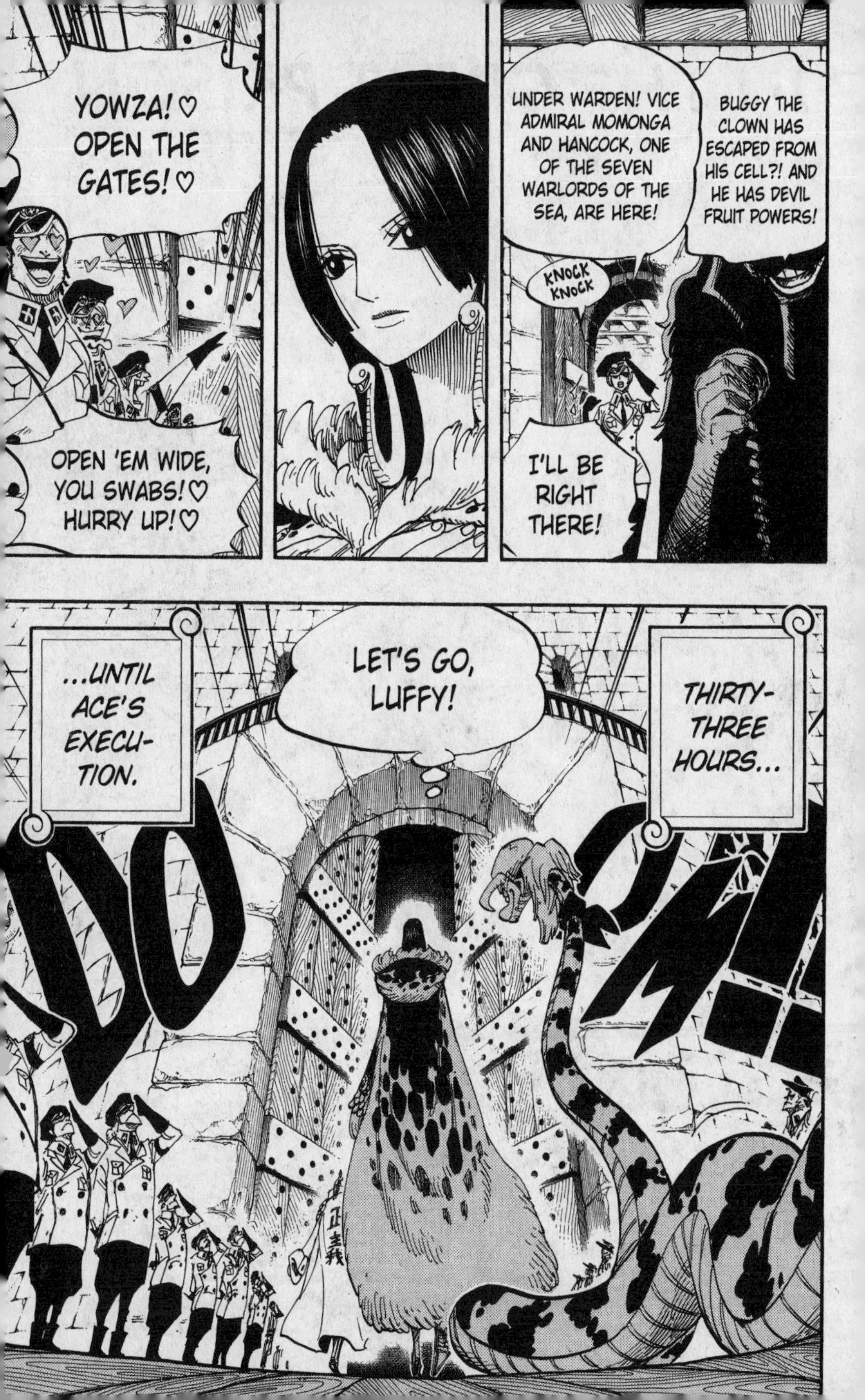
BUGGY THE CLOWN HAS ESCAPED FROM HIS CELL?! AND HE HAS DEVIL FRUIT POWERS!
UNDER WARDEN! VICE ADMIRAL MOMONGA AND HANCOCK, ONE OF THE SEVEN WARLORDS OF THE SEA, ARE HERE!
KNOCK KNOCK
I'LL BE RIGHT THERE!
YOWZA! ♡ OPEN THE GATES! ♡
OPEN 'EM WIDE, YOU SWABS! ♡ HURRY UP! ♡
THIRTY-THREE HOURS...
LET'S GO, LUFFY!
...UNTIL ACE'S EXECUTION.
DOOM

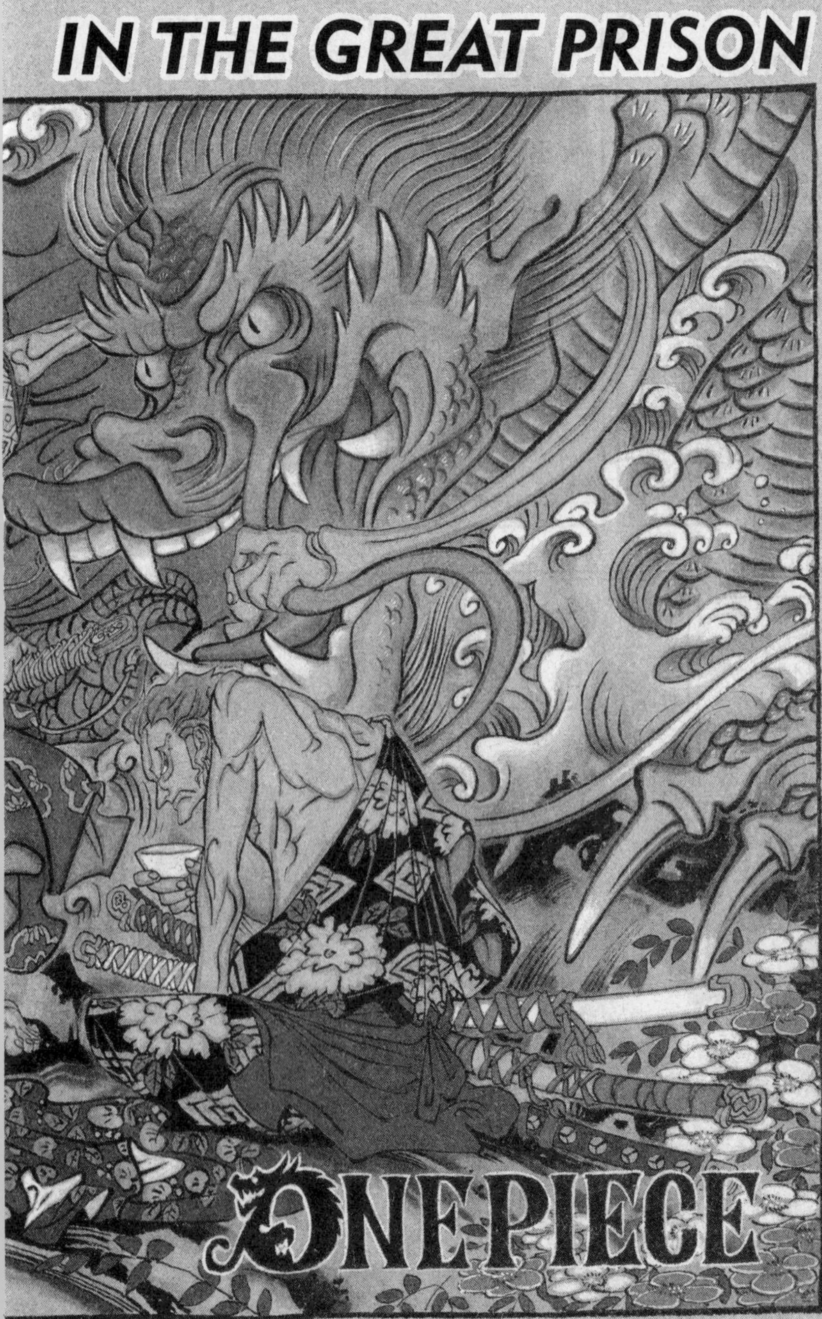
IN THE GREAT PRISON
ONE PIECE

Chapter 526: ADVENTURE

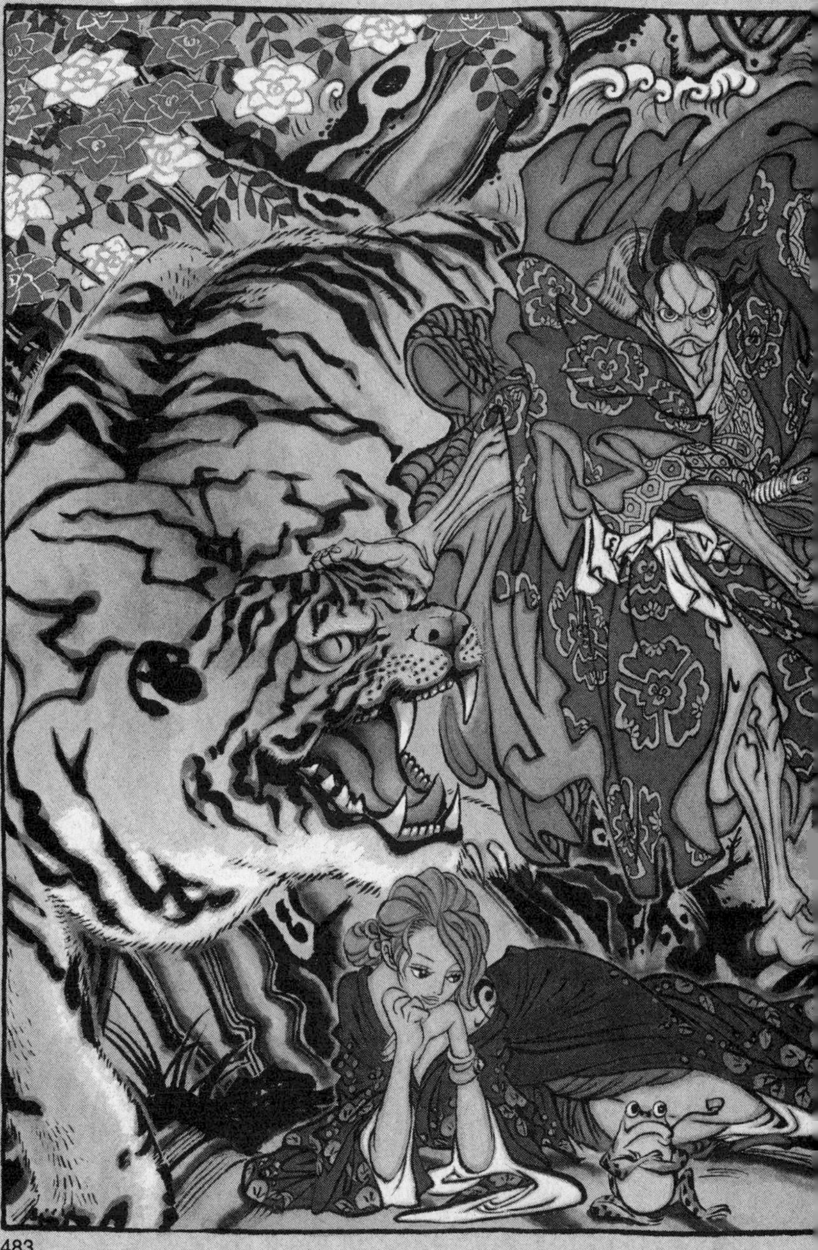

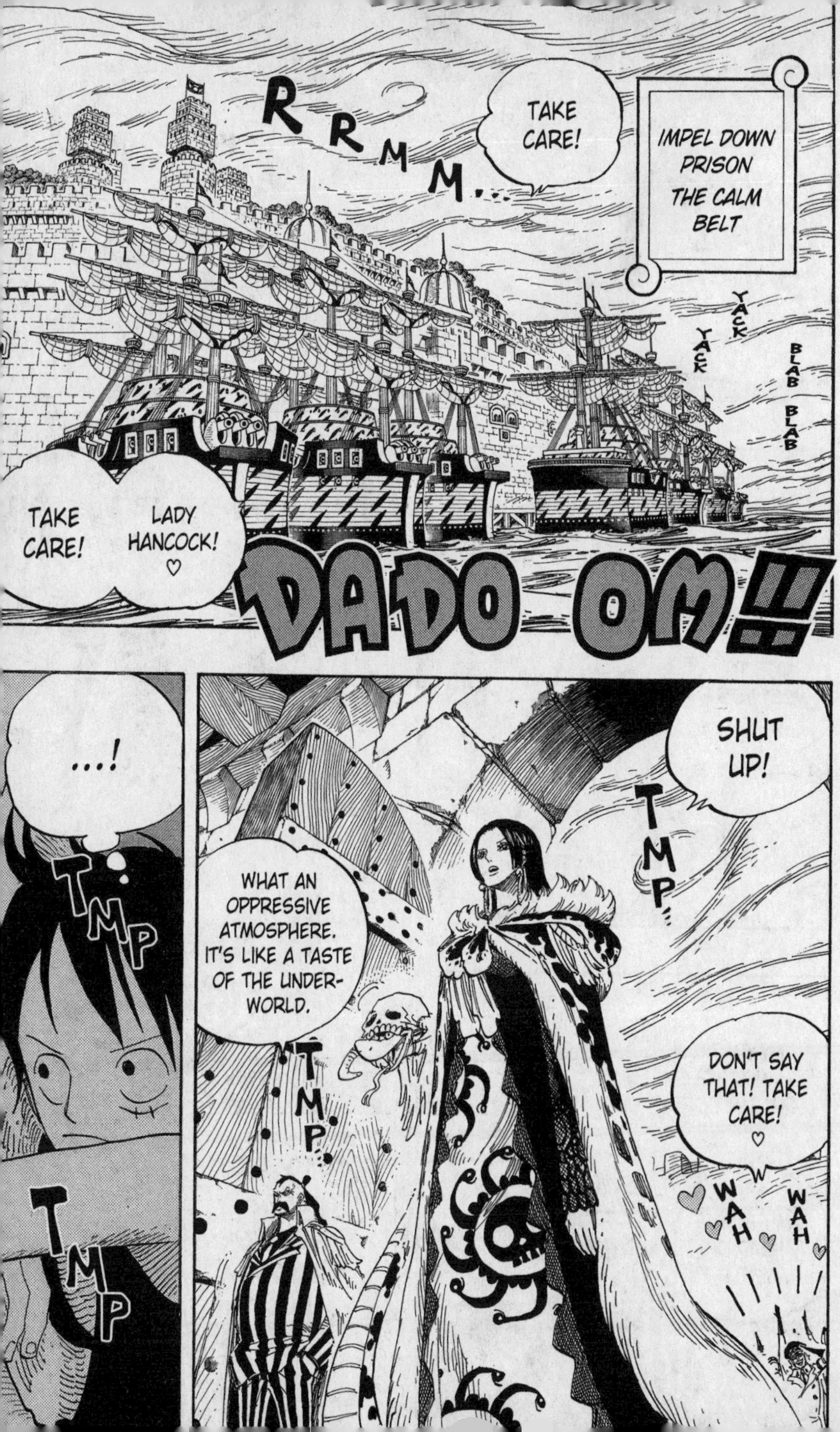
IMPEL DOWN PRISON THE CALM BELT
YACK YACK
BLAB BLAB
TAKE CARE!
RRMM...
LADY HANCOCK! ♡
TAKE CARE!
DADO OM!!
SHUT UP!
TMP
WHAT AN OPPRESSIVE ATMOSPHERE. IT'S LIKE A TASTE OF THE UNDER-WORLD.
DON'T SAY THAT! TAKE CARE! ♡
WAH WAH
TMP
...!
TMP
TMP

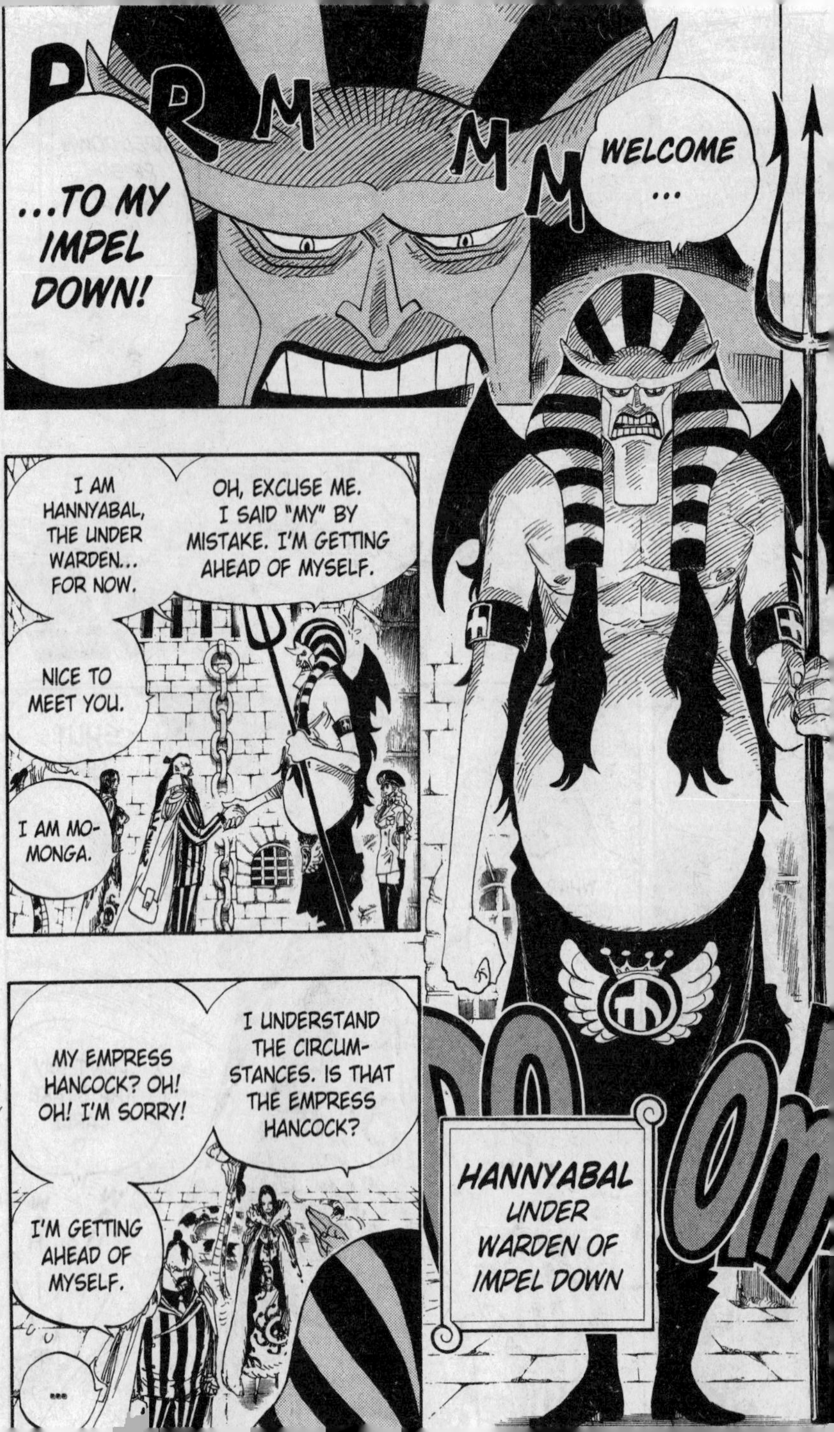
DRMMM
WELCOME…
…TO MY IMPEL DOWN!
DOOM
HANNYABAL UNDER WARDEN OF IMPEL DOWN
OH, EXCUSE ME. I SAID "MY" BY MISTAKE. I'M GETTING AHEAD OF MYSELF.
I AM HANNYABAL, THE UNDER WARDEN… FOR NOW.
NICE TO MEET YOU.
I AM MO-MONGA.
I UNDERSTAND THE CIRCUM-STANCES. IS THAT THE EMPRESS HANCOCK?
MY EMPRESS HANCOCK? OH! OH! I'M SORRY!
I'M GETTING AHEAD OF MYSELF.
…

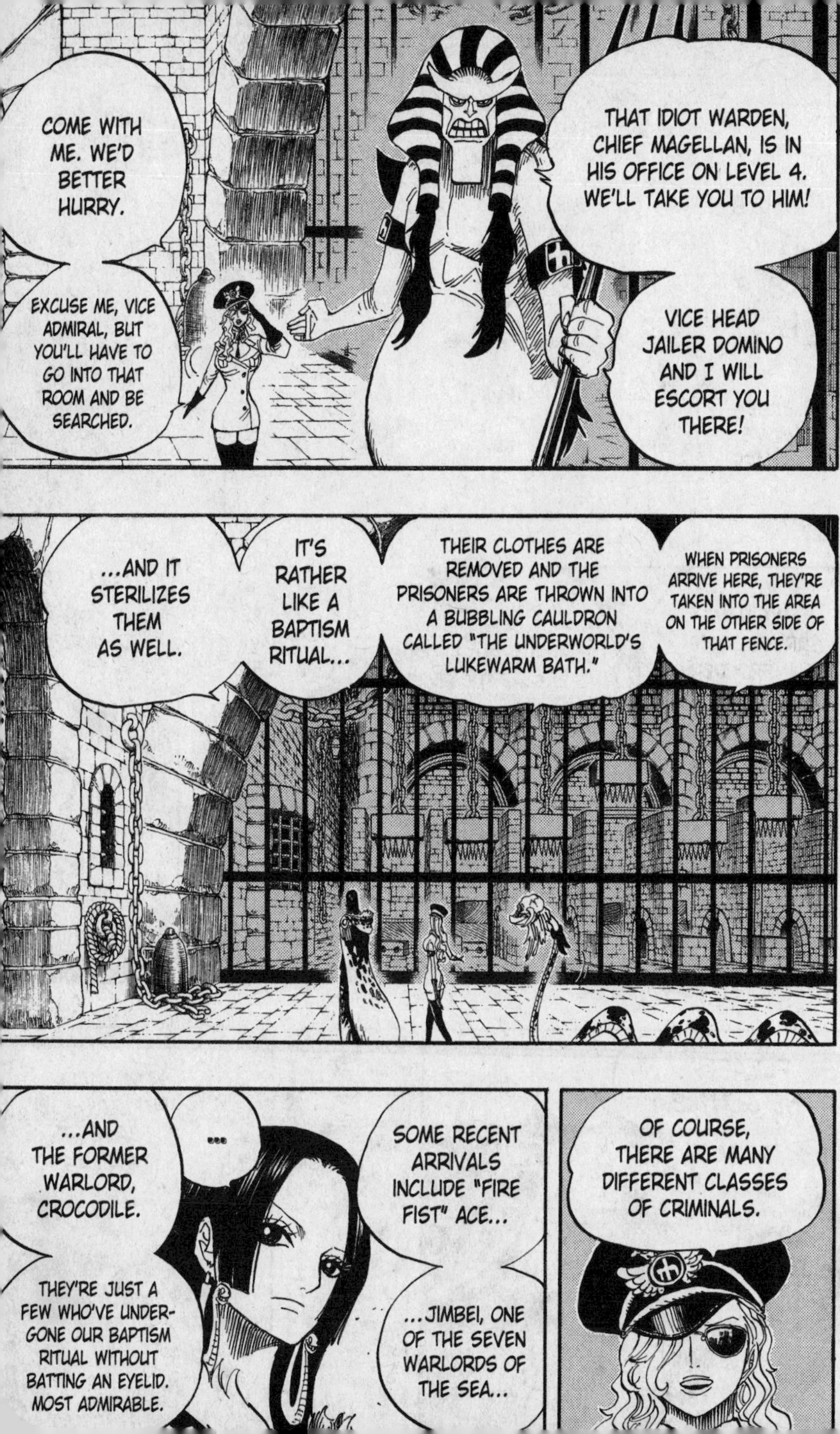
THAT IDIOT WARDEN, CHIEF MAGELLAN, IS IN HIS OFFICE ON LEVEL 4. WE'LL TAKE YOU TO HIM!
VICE HEAD JAILER DOMINO AND I WILL ESCORT YOU THERE!
COME WITH ME. WE'D BETTER HURRY.
EXCUSE ME, VICE ADMIRAL, BUT YOU'LL HAVE TO GO INTO THAT ROOM AND BE SEARCHED.
WHEN PRISONERS ARRIVE HERE, THEY'RE TAKEN INTO THE AREA ON THE OTHER SIDE OF THAT FENCE.
THEIR CLOTHES ARE REMOVED AND THE PRISONERS ARE THROWN INTO A BUBBLING CAULDRON CALLED "THE UNDERWORLD'S LUKEWARM BATH."
IT'S RATHER LIKE A BAPTISM RITUAL...
...AND IT STERILIZES THEM AS WELL.
OF COURSE, THERE ARE MANY DIFFERENT CLASSES OF CRIMINALS.
SOME RECENT ARRIVALS INCLUDE "FIRE FIST" ACE...
...JIMBEI, ONE OF THE SEVEN WARLORDS OF THE SEA...
...AND THE FORMER WARLORD, CROCODILE.
...
THEY'RE JUST A FEW WHO'VE UNDERGONE OUR BAPTISM RITUAL WITHOUT BATTING AN EYELID. MOST ADMIRABLE.

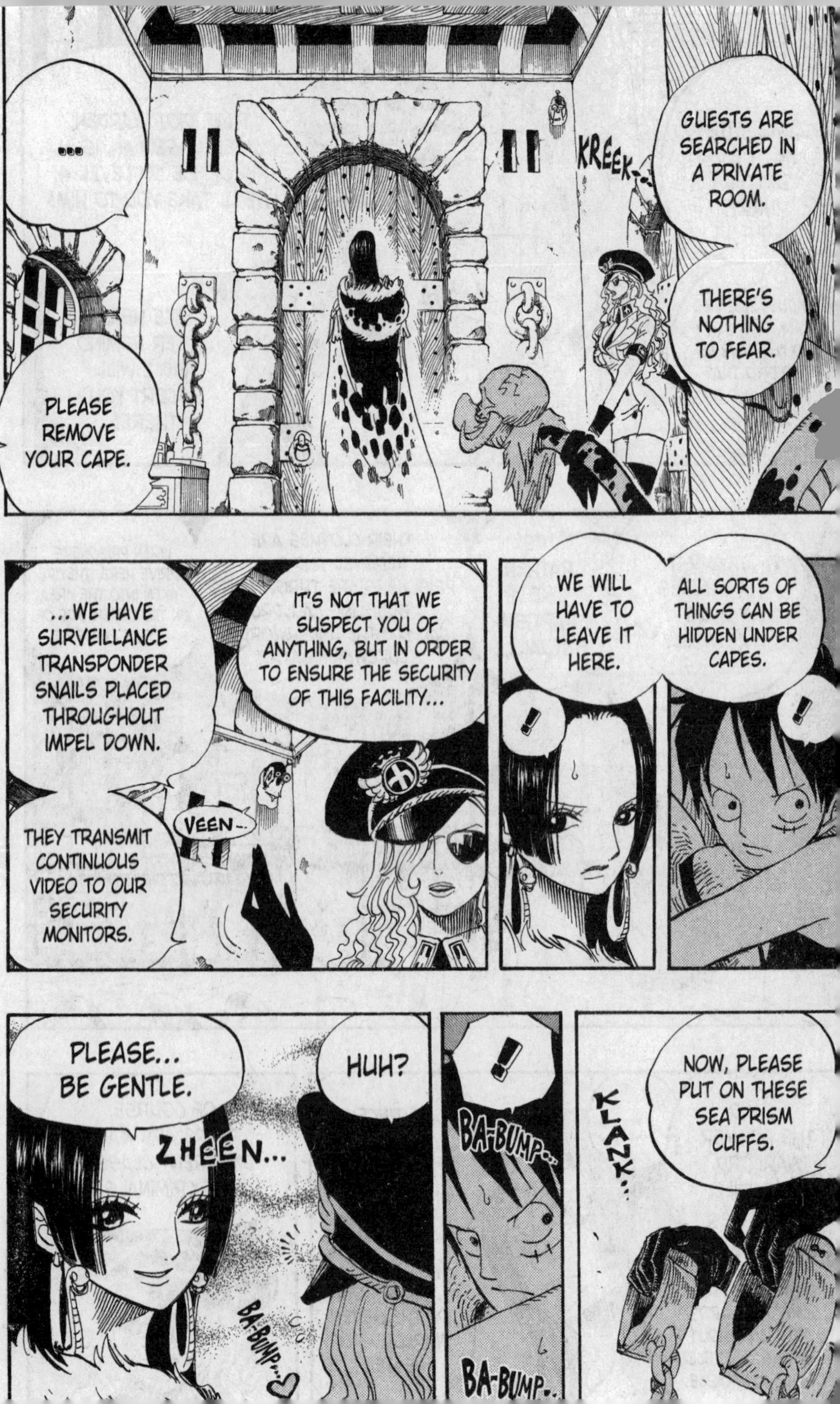
GUESTS ARE SEARCHED IN A PRIVATE ROOM.
THERE'S NOTHING TO FEAR.
KREEK...
...
PLEASE REMOVE YOUR CAPE.
ALL SORTS OF THINGS CAN BE HIDDEN UNDER CAPES.
!
WE WILL HAVE TO LEAVE IT HERE.
!
IT'S NOT THAT WE SUSPECT YOU OF ANYTHING, BUT IN ORDER TO ENSURE THE SECURITY OF THIS FACILITY...
...WE HAVE SURVEILLANCE TRANSPONDER SNAILS PLACED THROUGHOUT IMPEL DOWN.
VEEN..
THEY TRANSMIT CONTINUOUS VIDEO TO OUR SECURITY MONITORS.
NOW, PLEASE PUT ON THESE SEA PRISM CUFFS.
KLANK..
!
BA-BUMP...
BA-BUMP...
HUH?
PLEASE... BE GENTLE.
ZHEEN...
BA-BUMP...

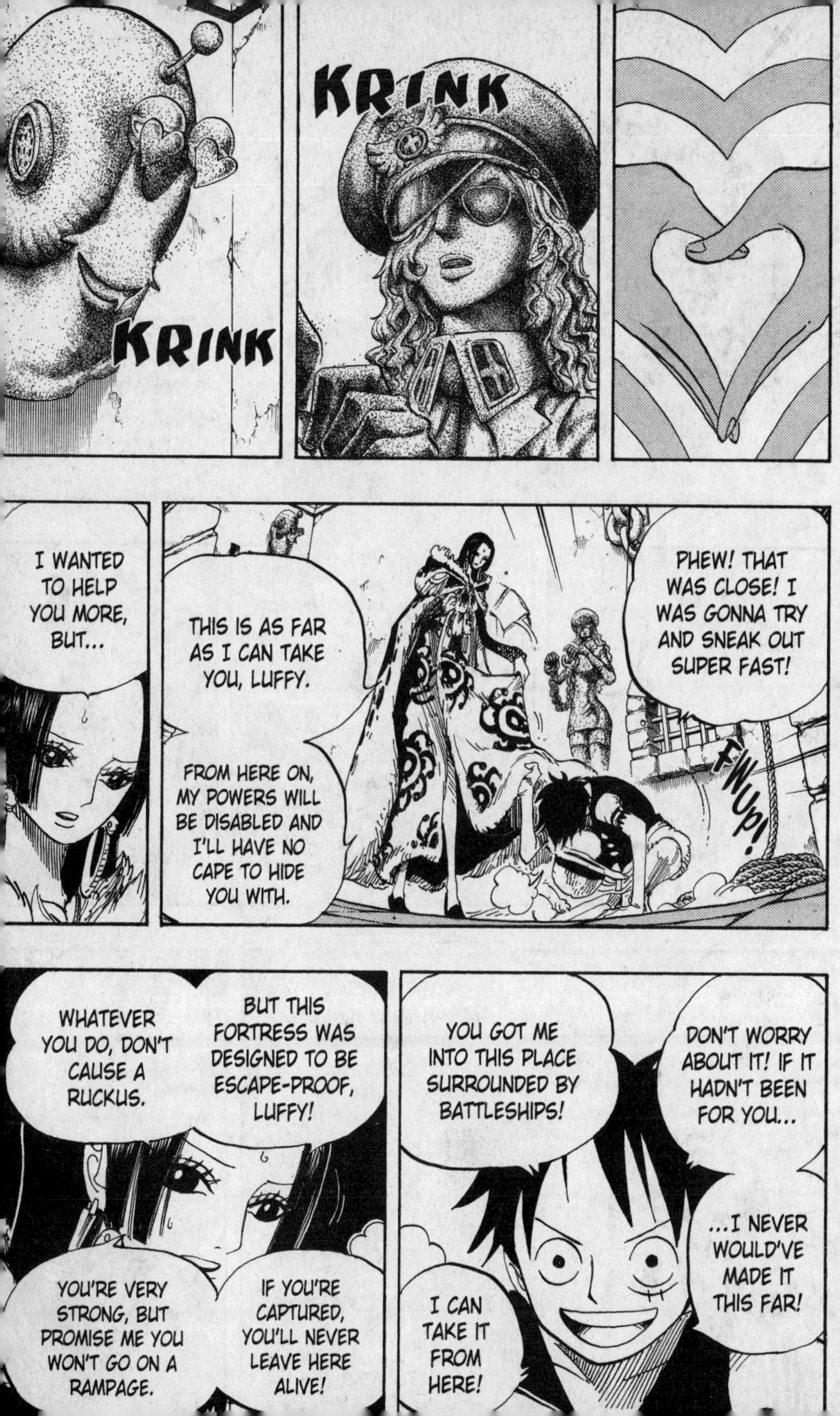
KRINK
KRINK
PHEW! THAT WAS CLOSE! I WAS GONNA TRY AND SNEAK OUT SUPER FAST!
FWUP!
THIS IS AS FAR AS I CAN TAKE YOU, LUFFY.
FROM HERE ON, MY POWERS WILL BE DISABLED AND I'LL HAVE NO CAPE TO HIDE YOU WITH.
I WANTED TO HELP YOU MORE, BUT...
DON'T WORRY ABOUT IT! IF IT HADN'T BEEN FOR YOU...
YOU GOT ME INTO THIS PLACE SURROUNDED BY BATTLESHIPS!
...I NEVER WOULD'VE MADE IT THIS FAR!
I CAN TAKE IT FROM HERE!
BUT THIS FORTRESS WAS DESIGNED TO BE ESCAPE-PROOF, LUFFY!
WHATEVER YOU DO, DON'T CAUSE A RUCKUS.
IF YOU'RE CAPTURED, YOU'LL NEVER LEAVE HERE ALIVE!
YOU'RE VERY STRONG, BUT PROMISE ME YOU WON'T GO ON A RAMPAGE.

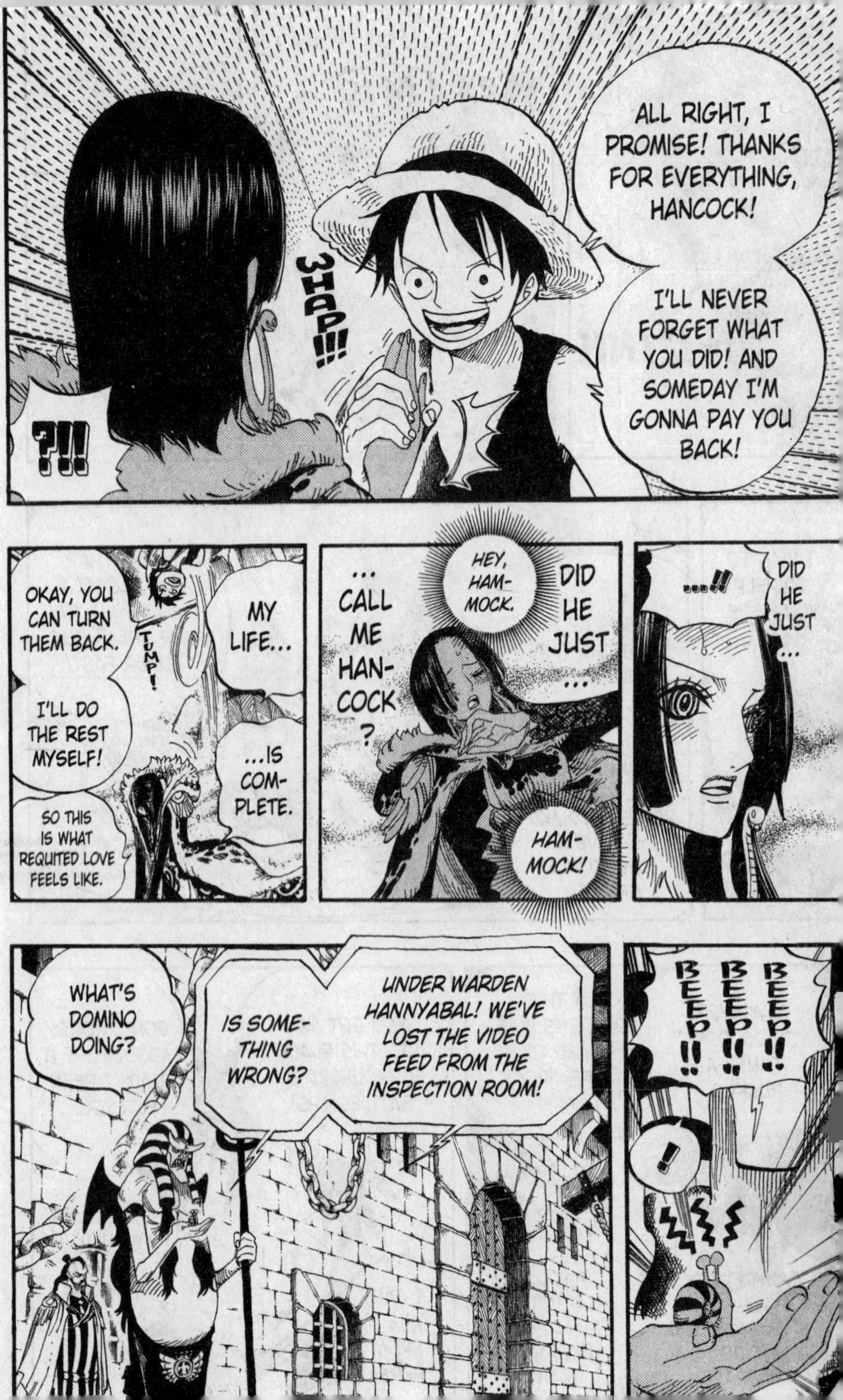
ALL RIGHT, I PROMISE! THANKS FOR EVERYTHING, HANCOCK!
I'LL NEVER FORGET WHAT YOU DID! AND SOMEDAY I'M GONNA PAY YOU BACK!
WHAP!!!
?!!
DID HE JUST ...
...!!
HEY, HAM-MOCK.
DID HE JUST ...
... CALL ME HAN-COCK?
HAM-MOCK!
MY LIFE...
OKAY, YOU CAN TURN THEM BACK.
TUMP!
I'LL DO THE REST MYSELF!
...IS COM-PLETE.
SO THIS IS WHAT REQUITED LOVE FEELS LIKE.
BEEP!!
BEEP!!
BEEP!!
!
UNDER WARDEN HANNYABAL! WE'VE LOST THE VIDEO FEED FROM THE INSPECTION ROOM!
IS SOME-THING WRONG?
WHAT'S DOMINO DOING?

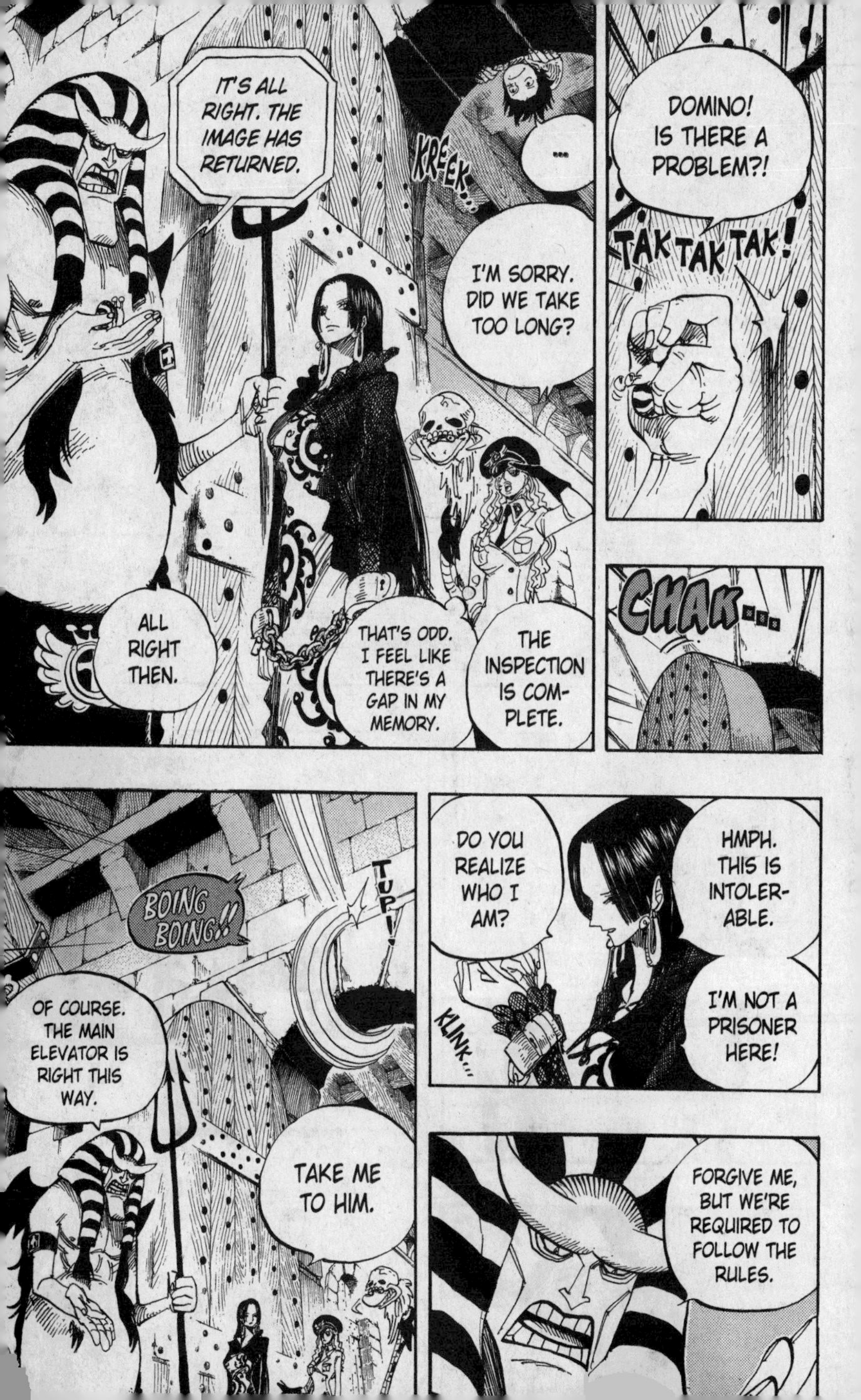
DOMINO! IS THERE A PROBLEM?!
TAK TAK TAK!
CHAK...
KREEK...
...
I'M SORRY. DID WE TAKE TOO LONG?
IT'S ALL RIGHT. THE IMAGE HAS RETURNED.
THE INSPECTION IS COMPLETE.
THAT'S ODD. I FEEL LIKE THERE'S A GAP IN MY MEMORY.
ALL RIGHT THEN.
HMPH. THIS IS INTOLERABLE.
DO YOU REALIZE WHO I AM?
KLINK...
I'M NOT A PRISONER HERE!
FORGIVE ME, BUT WE'RE REQUIRED TO FOLLOW THE RULES.
TUP!
BOING BOING!!
TAKE ME TO HIM.
OF COURSE. THE MAIN ELEVATOR IS RIGHT THIS WAY.

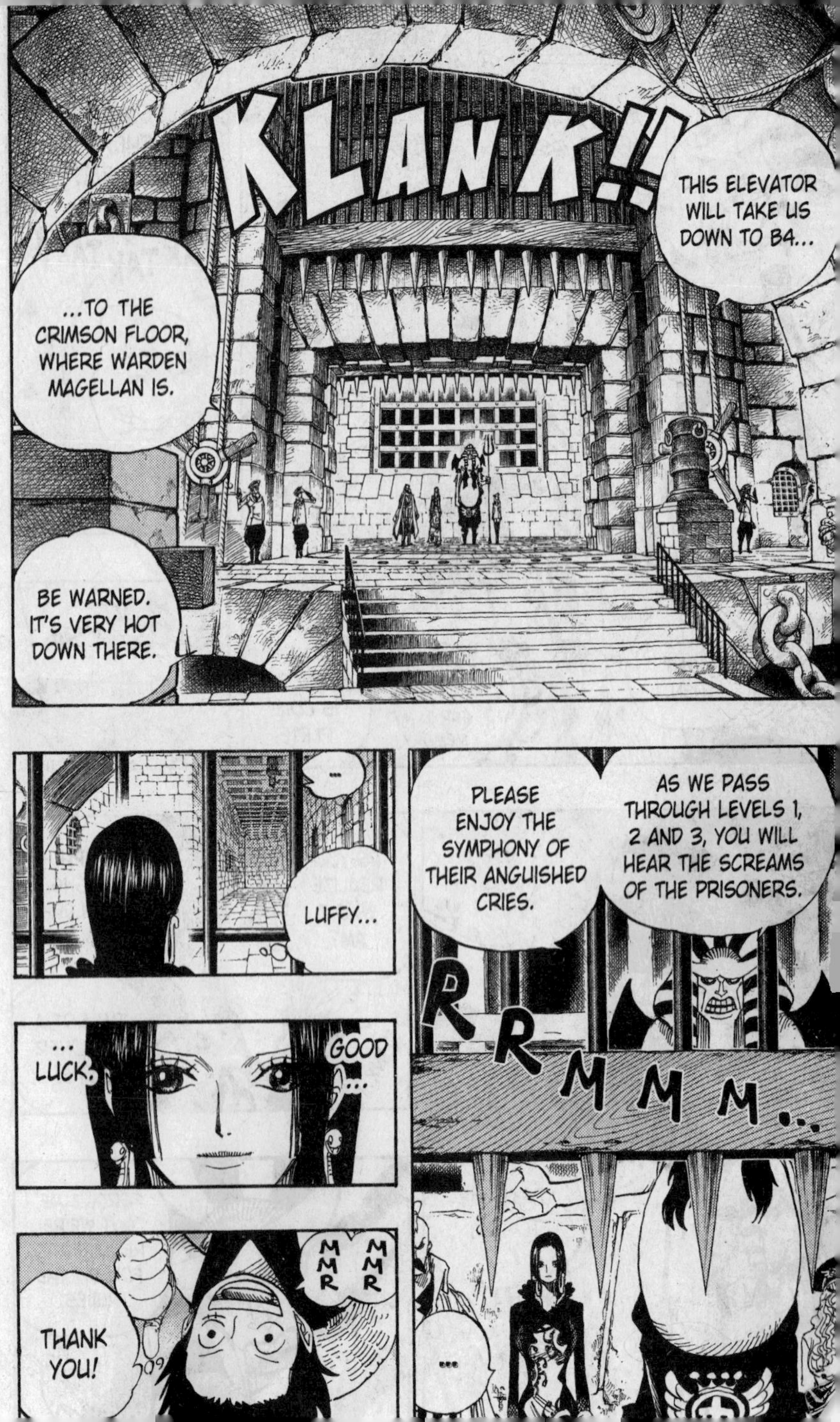
KLANK!!
THIS ELEVATOR WILL TAKE US DOWN TO B4...
...TO THE CRIMSON FLOOR, WHERE WARDEN MAGELLAN IS.
BE WARNED. IT'S VERY HOT DOWN THERE.
AS WE PASS THROUGH LEVELS 1, 2 AND 3, YOU WILL HEAR THE SCREAMS OF THE PRISONERS.
PLEASE ENJOY THE SYMPHONY OF THEIR ANGUISHED CRIES.
RRMMM..
...
...
LUFFY...
GOOD...
...LUCK.
MMR
MMR
THANK YOU!

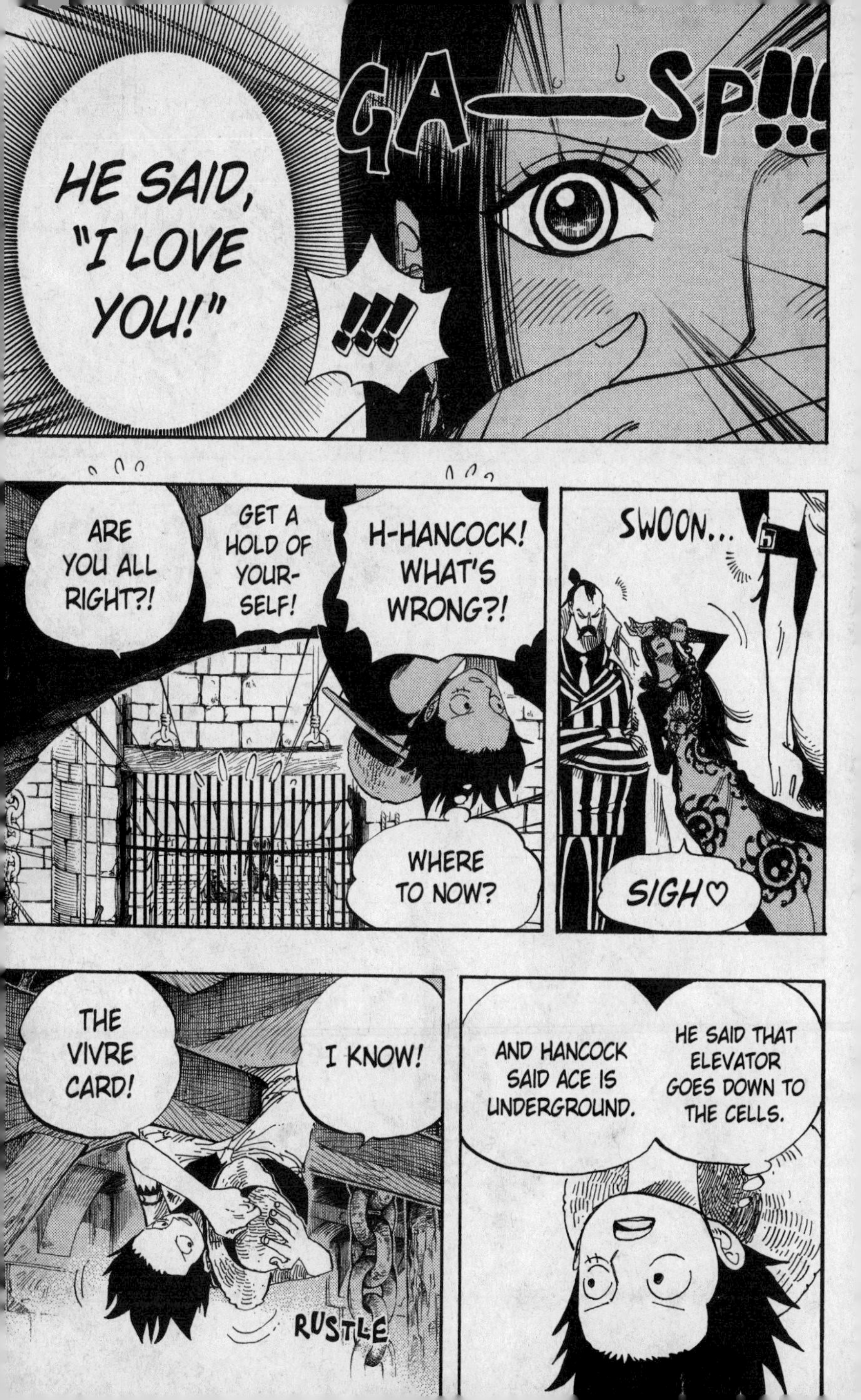
GA—SP!!!
HE SAID, "I LOVE YOU!"
!!!
SWOON...
SIGH♡
H-HANCOCK! WHAT'S WRONG?!
GET A HOLD OF YOUR-SELF!
ARE YOU ALL RIGHT?!
WHERE TO NOW?
HE SAID THAT ELEVATOR GOES DOWN TO THE CELLS.
AND HANCOCK SAID ACE IS UNDERGROUND.
I KNOW!
THE VIVRE CARD!
RUSTLE

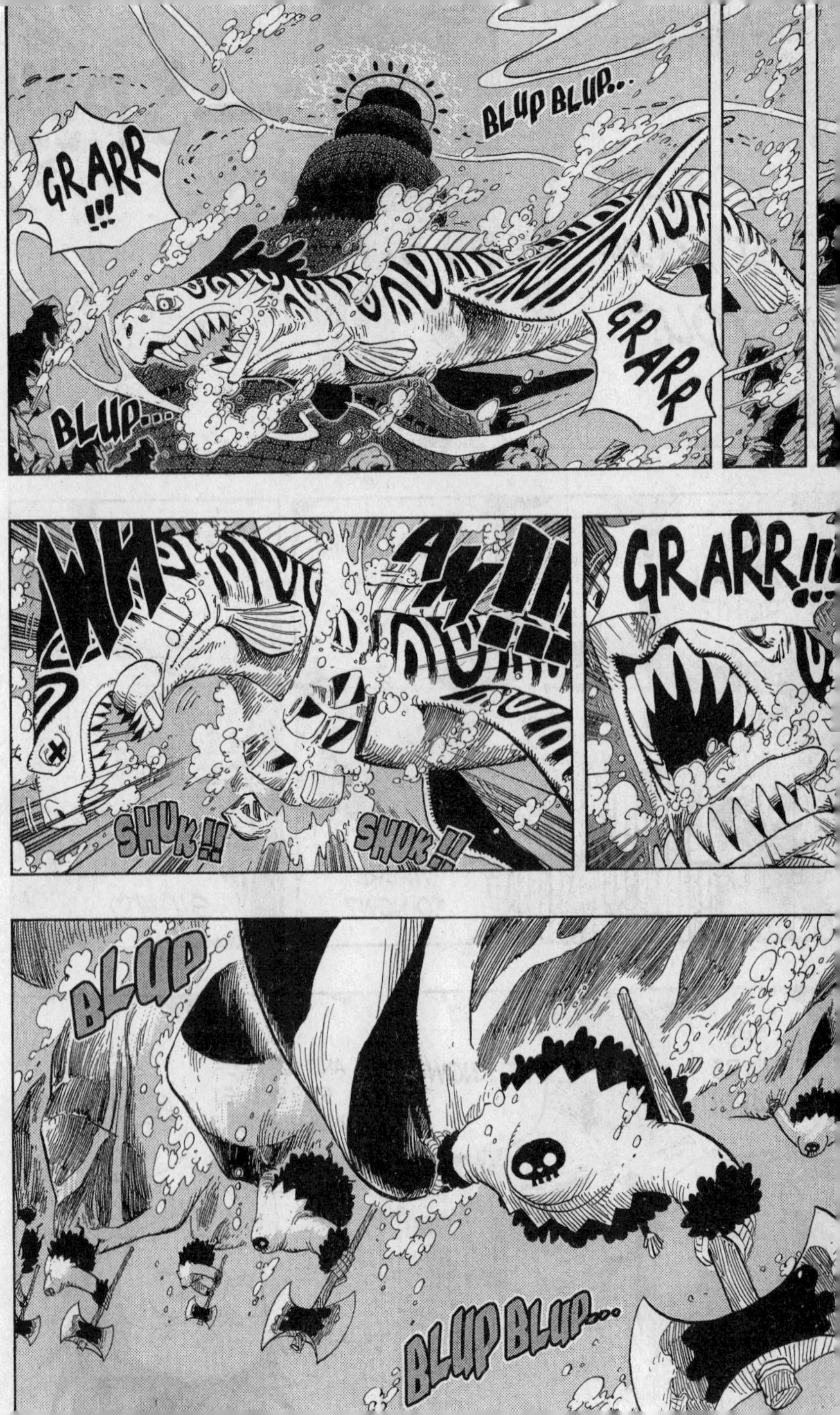
BLUP BLUP...
GRARR
GRARR !!!
BLUP...
GRARR!!!
WHAM!!
SHUK!!
SHUK!!
BLUP
BLUP BLUP...

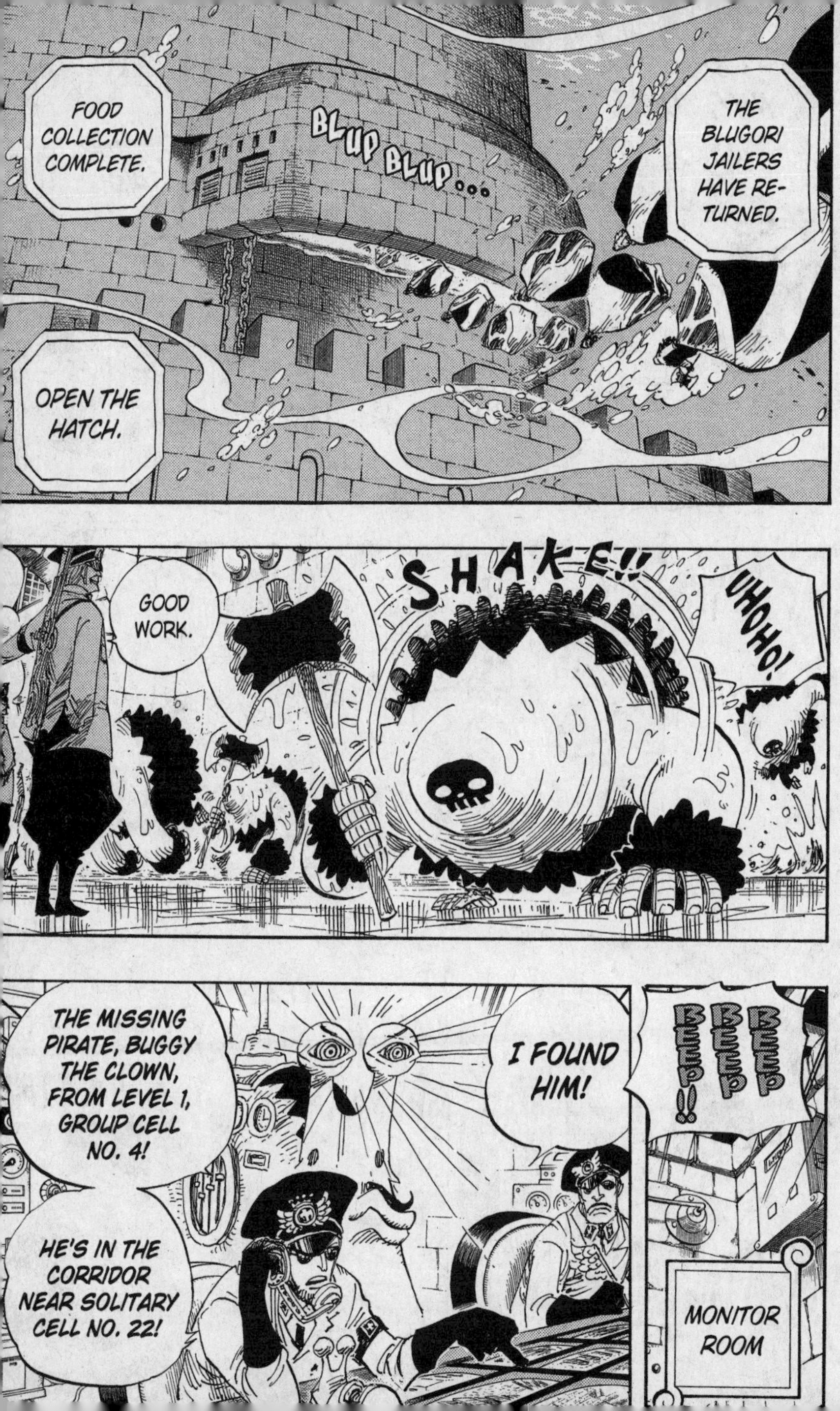
THE BLUGORI JAILERS HAVE RE-TURNED.
BLUP BLUP...
FOOD COLLECTION COMPLETE.
OPEN THE HATCH.
UHOHO!
SHAKE!!
GOOD WORK.
BEEP BEEP BEEP!!
MONITOR ROOM
I FOUND HIM!
THE MISSING PIRATE, BUGGY THE CLOWN, FROM LEVEL 1, GROUP CELL NO. 4!
HE'S IN THE CORRIDOR NEAR SOLITARY CELL NO. 22!

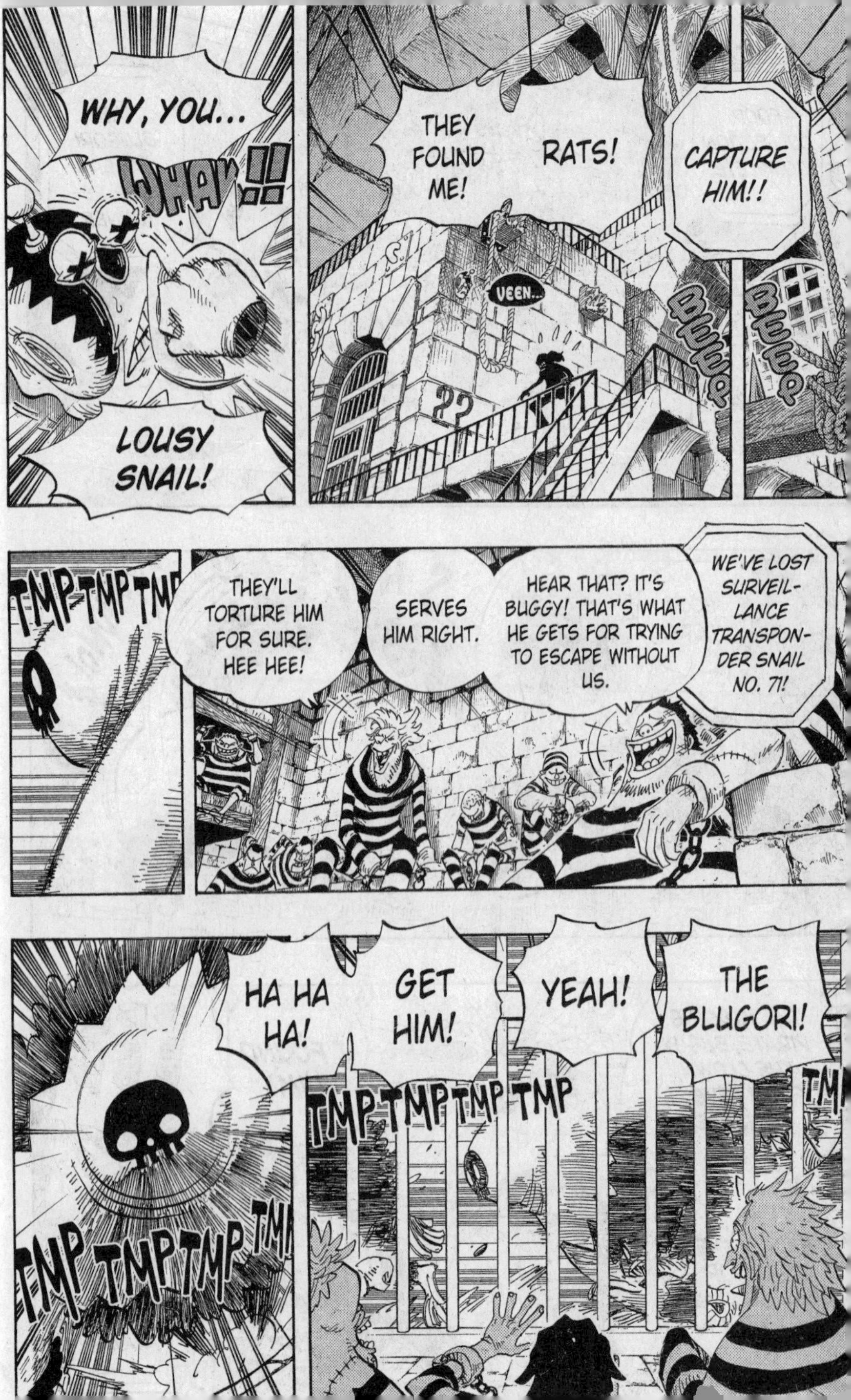
CAPTURE HIM!!
RATS!
THEY FOUND ME!
VEEN...
??
WHY, YOU...
WHAK!!
LOUSY SNAIL!
WE'VE LOST SURVEIL-LANCE TRANSPON-DER SNAIL NO. 71!
HEAR THAT? IT'S BUGGY! THAT'S WHAT HE GETS FOR TRYING TO ESCAPE WITHOUT US.
SERVES HIM RIGHT.
THEY'LL TORTURE HIM FOR SURE. HEE HEE!
TMP TMP TMP
THE BLUGORI!
YEAH!
GET HIM!
HA HA HA!
TMP TMP TMP TMP
TMP TMP TMP

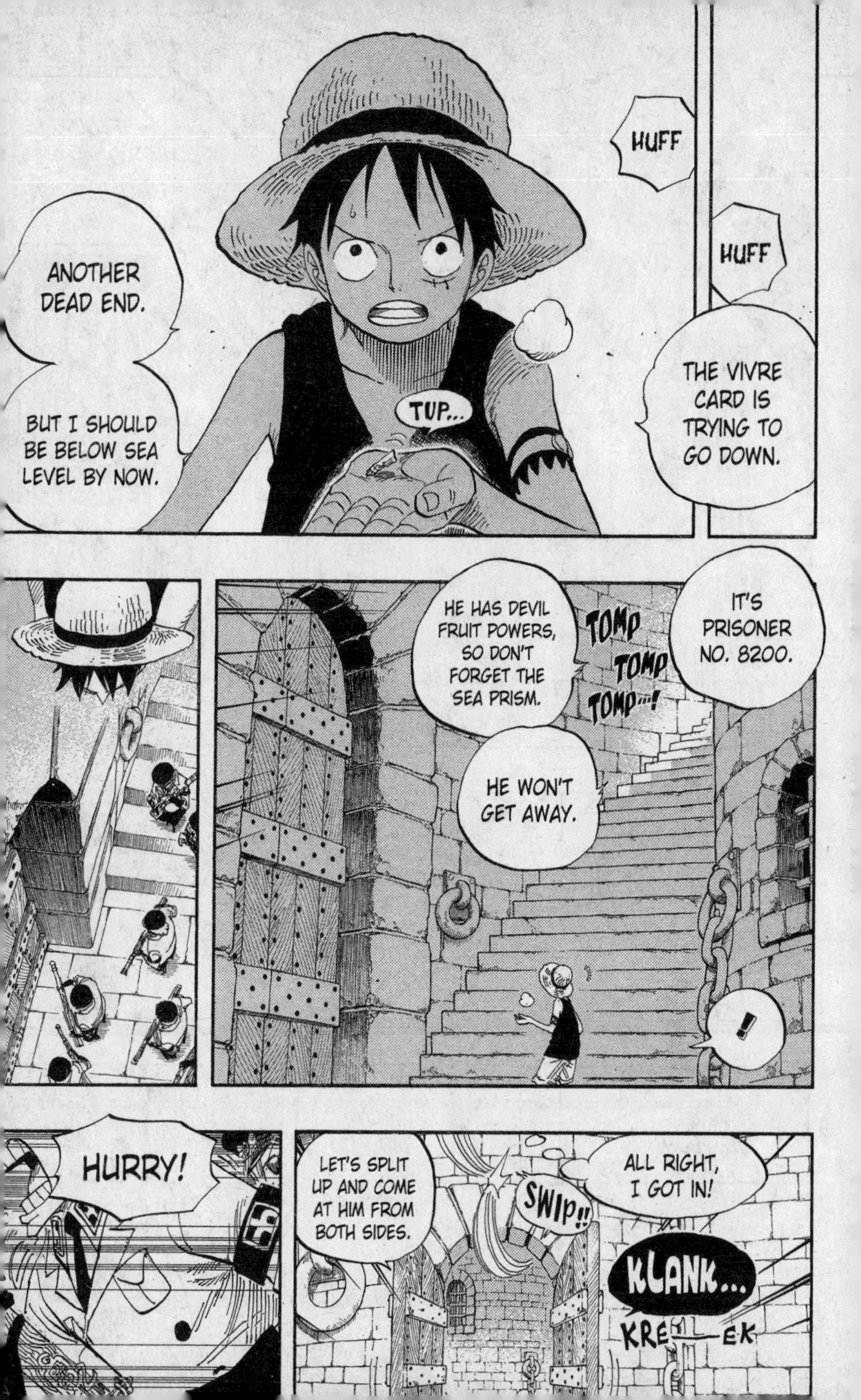
HUFF
HUFF
THE VIVRE CARD IS TRYING TO GO DOWN.
ANOTHER DEAD END.
TUP...
BUT I SHOULD BE BELOW SEA LEVEL BY NOW.
IT'S PRISONER NO. 8200.
HE HAS DEVIL FRUIT POWERS, SO DON'T FORGET THE SEA PRISM.
TOMP TOMP TOMP...!
HE WON'T GET AWAY.
!
ALL RIGHT, I GOT IN!
SWIP!!
LET'S SPLIT UP AND COME AT HIM FROM BOTH SIDES.
KLANK...
KRE-EK
HURRY!

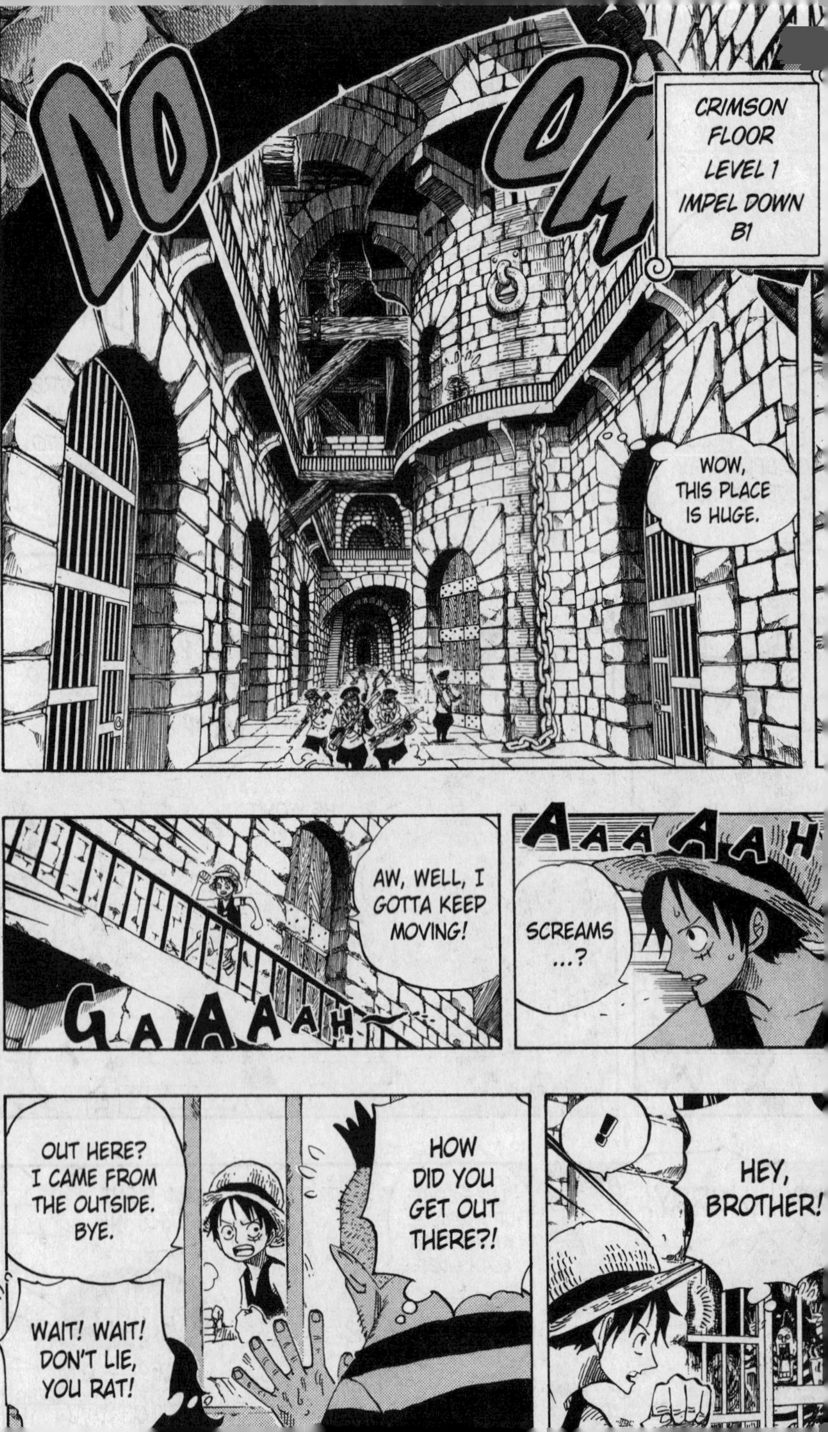
CRIMSON FLOOR LEVEL 1 IMPEL DOWN B1
DO
WOW, THIS PLACE IS HUGE.
AAAAAH
SCREAMS ...?
AW, WELL, I GOTTA KEEP MOVING!
GAAAAH
!
HEY, BROTHER!
HOW DID YOU GET OUT THERE?!
OUT HERE? I CAME FROM THE OUTSIDE. BYE.
WAIT! WAIT! DON'T LIE, YOU RAT!

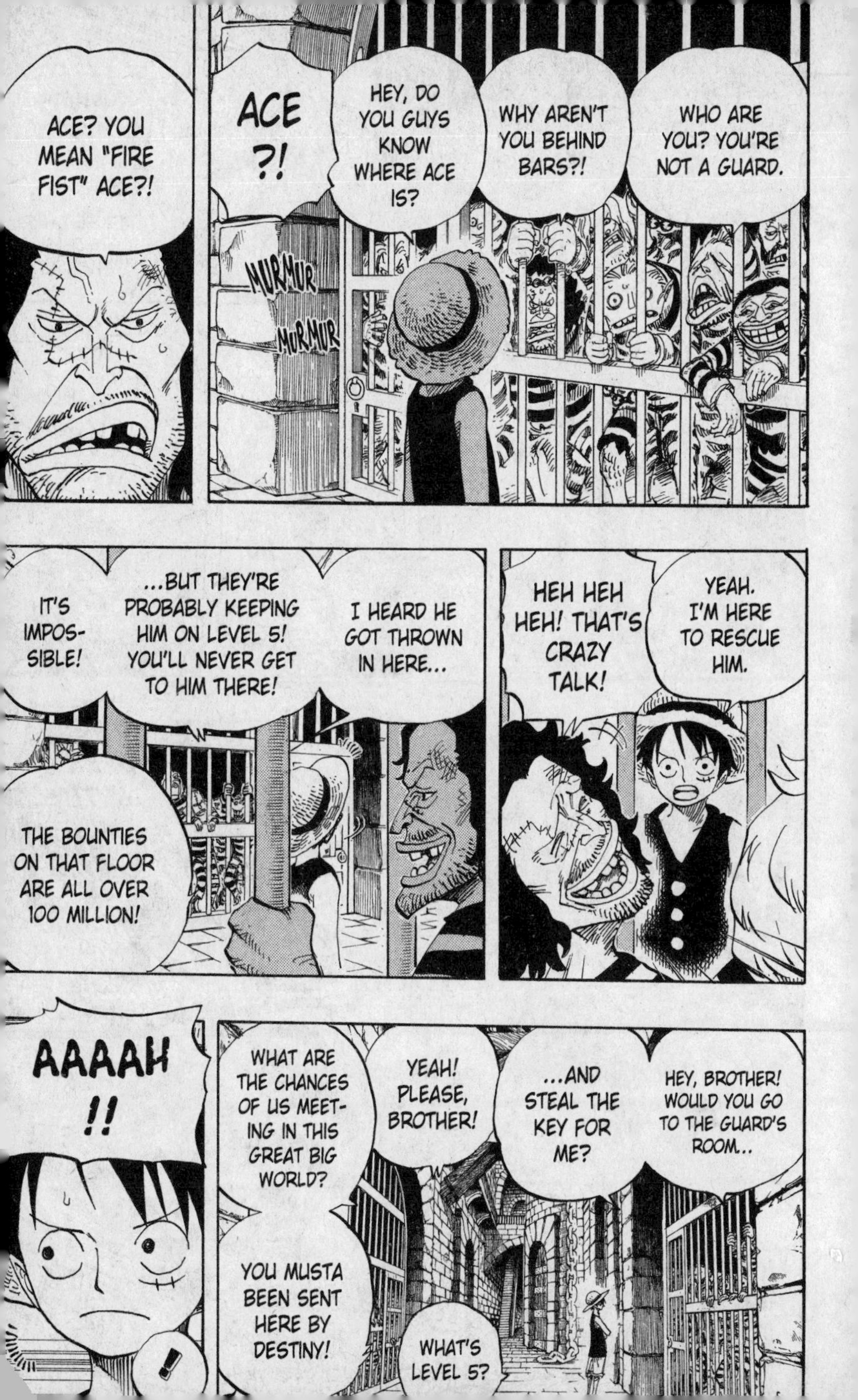
WHO ARE YOU? YOU'RE NOT A GUARD.
WHY AREN'T YOU BEHIND BARS?!
HEY, DO YOU GUYS KNOW WHERE ACE IS?
ACE ?!
MURMUR
MURMUR
ACE? YOU MEAN "FIRE FIST" ACE?!
YEAH. I'M HERE TO RESCUE HIM.
HEH HEH HEH! THAT'S CRAZY TALK!
I HEARD HE GOT THROWN IN HERE...
...BUT THEY'RE PROBABLY KEEPING HIM ON LEVEL 5! YOU'LL NEVER GET TO HIM THERE!
IT'S IMPOS-SIBLE!
THE BOUNTIES ON THAT FLOOR ARE ALL OVER 100 MILLION!
HEY, BROTHER! WOULD YOU GO TO THE GUARD'S ROOM...
...AND STEAL THE KEY FOR ME?
YEAH! PLEASE, BROTHER!
WHAT ARE THE CHANCES OF US MEET-ING IN THIS GREAT BIG WORLD?
YOU MUSTA BEEN SENT HERE BY DESTINY!
WHAT'S LEVEL 5?
AAAAH !!
!

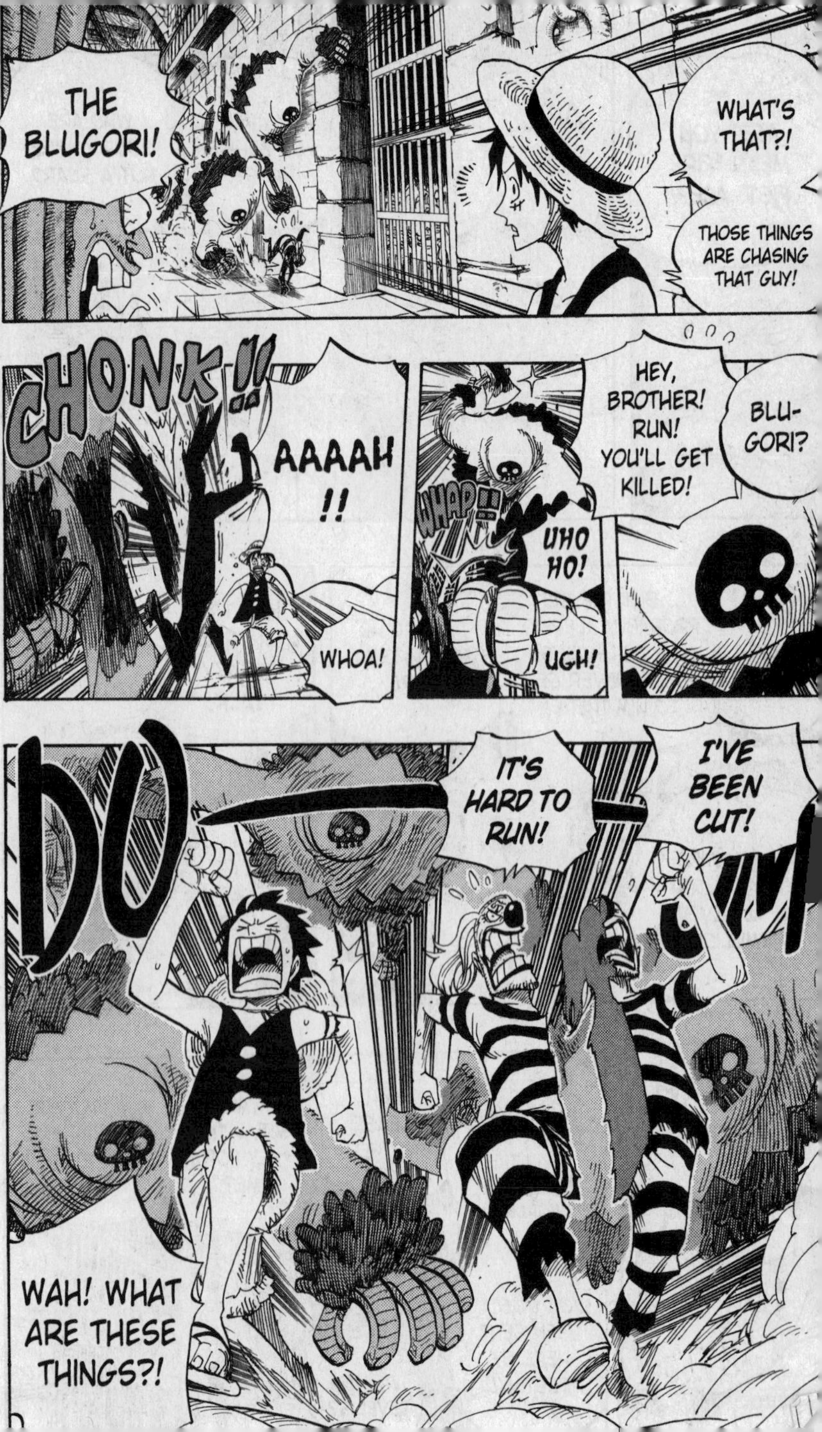
WHAT'S THAT?!
THOSE THINGS ARE CHASING THAT GUY!
THE BLUGORI!
BLU-GORI?
HEY, BROTHER! RUN! YOU'LL GET KILLED!
WHAP!!
UHO HO!
UGH!
CHONK!!
AAAAH!!
WHOA!
I'VE BEEN CUT!
IT'S HARD TO RUN!
DO
WAH! WHAT ARE THESE THINGS?!

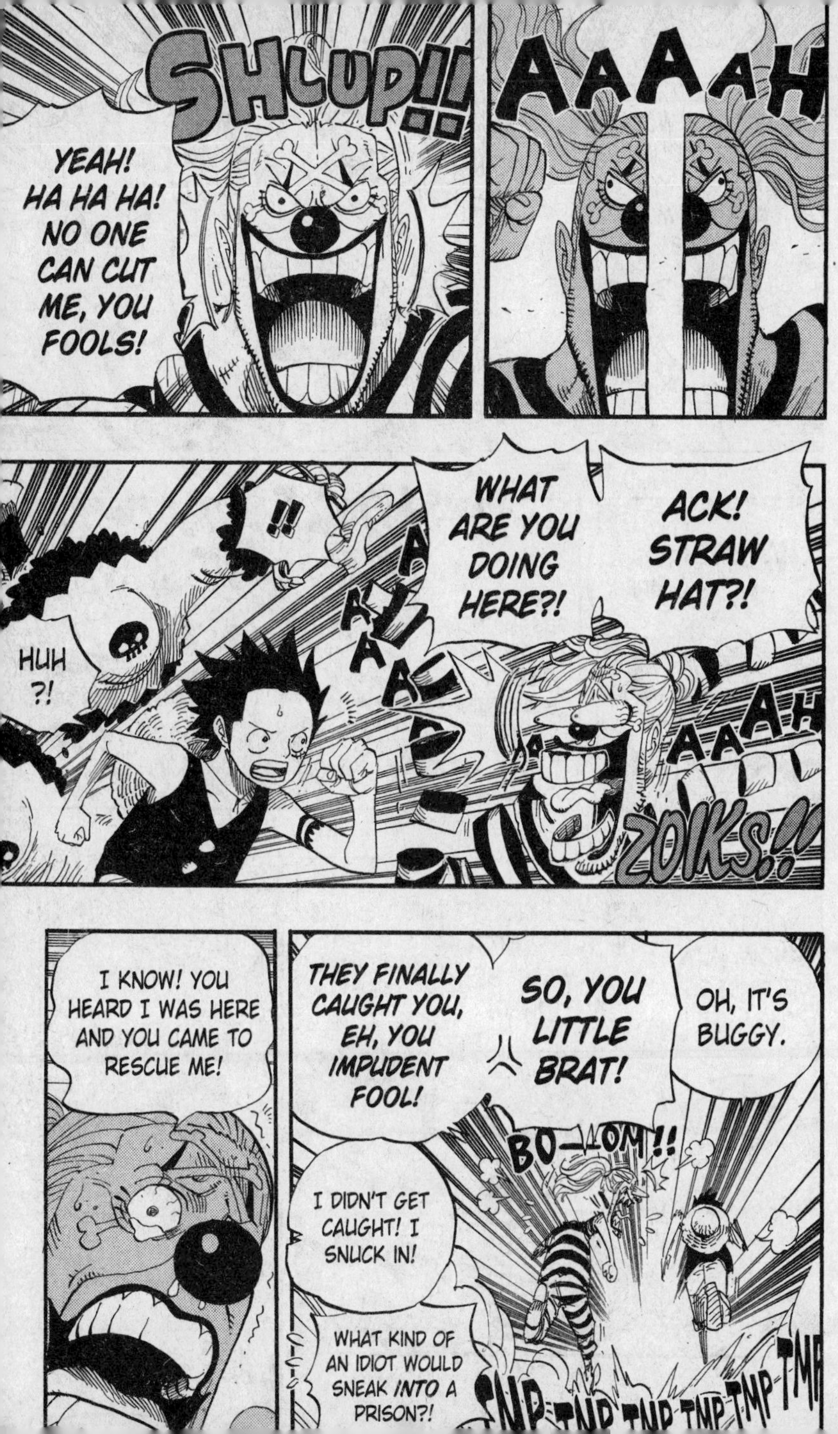
AAAAH
SHLUP!!
YEAH! HA HA HA! NO ONE CAN CUT ME, YOU FOOLS!
ACK! STRAW HAT?!
WHAT ARE YOU DOING HERE?!
AAAH
ZOIKS!!
!!
HUH ?!
OH, IT'S BUGGY.
SO, YOU LITTLE BRAT!
THEY FINALLY CAUGHT YOU, EH, YOU IMPUDENT FOOL!
BO—OM!!
I DIDN'T GET CAUGHT! I SNUCK IN!
WHAT KIND OF AN IDIOT WOULD SNEAK INTO A PRISON?!
TMP TMP TMP TMP TMP TMP
I KNOW! YOU HEARD I WAS HERE AND YOU CAME TO RESCUE ME!

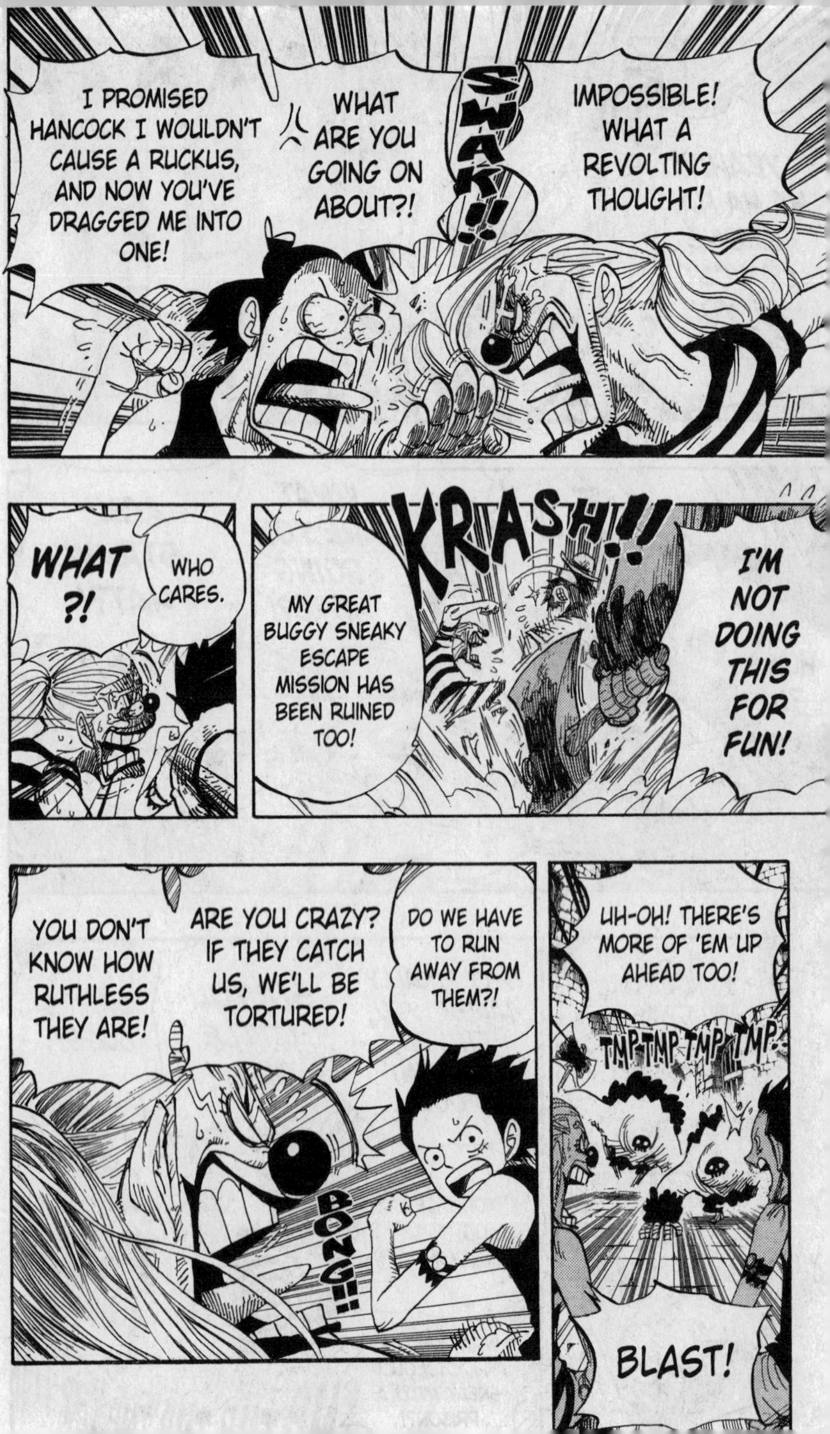
IMPOSSIBLE! WHAT A REVOLTING THOUGHT!
SWAK!!
WHAT ARE YOU GOING ON ABOUT?!
I PROMISED HANCOCK I WOULDN'T CAUSE A RUCKUS, AND NOW YOU'VE DRAGGED ME INTO ONE!
KRASH!!
I'M NOT DOING THIS FOR FUN!
MY GREAT BUGGY SNEAKY ESCAPE MISSION HAS BEEN RUINED TOO!
WHO CARES.
WHAT?!
UH-OH! THERE'S MORE OF 'EM UP AHEAD TOO!
TMP TMP TMP TMP
BLAST!
DO WE HAVE TO RUN AWAY FROM THEM?!
ARE YOU CRAZY? IF THEY CATCH US, WE'LL BE TORTURED!
YOU DON'T KNOW HOW RUTHLESS THEY ARE!
BONG!!

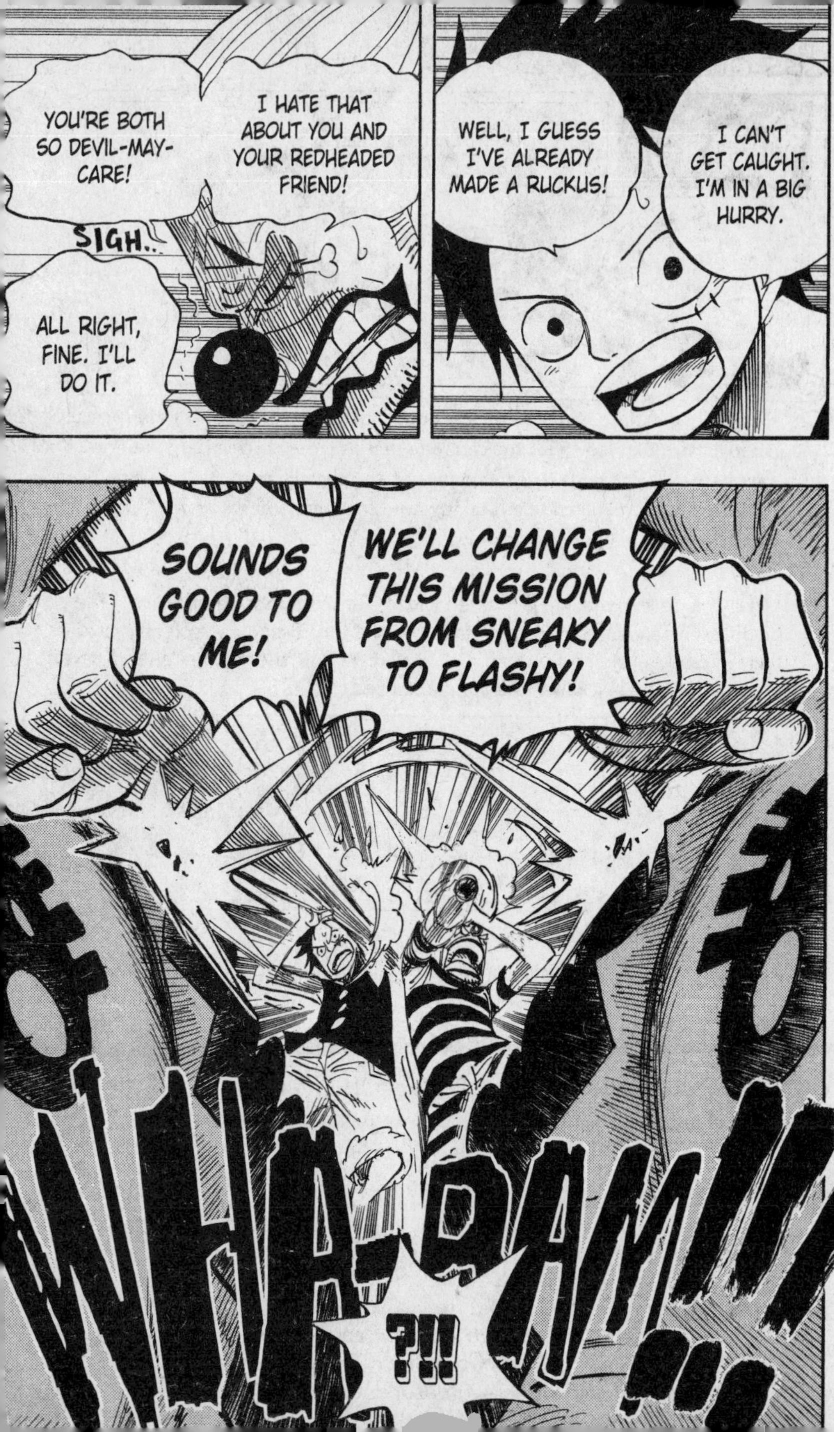
I CAN'T GET CAUGHT. I'M IN A BIG HURRY.
WELL, I GUESS I'VE ALREADY MADE A RUCKUS!
I HATE THAT ABOUT YOU AND YOUR REDHEADED FRIEND!
YOU'RE BOTH SO DEVIL-MAY-CARE!
SIGH...
ALL RIGHT, FINE. I'LL DO IT.
WE'LL CHANGE THIS MISSION FROM SNEAKY TO FLASHY!
SOUNDS GOOD TO ME!
WHA-BAM!!!
?!!

SBS Question Corner

(Yuki, Iwate)

Q: I'm in love with the Snake Princess and all of the Kuja Girls!♡ I'm especially in love with that lady with the cigarette that's wearing only a jacket on top of her bare skin! It seems that the names of the characters of Kuja haven't been shown anywhere. (like the girl taking notes or the members of the Kuja pirates) Please tell me their names!

--Ice Fish

A: They're called the Kuja Girls now? That sounds really nice. They do have names, but I just haven't shown them. I went through my sketchbook and picked them out from there. Go ahead and take a look if you're that interested.

Ran	Rindo	Daisy	Cosmos	Bluefan	Nerine	Belladonna	Genista
Kuja Pirates					Compulsive Note Taker	Doctor	Maid

Q: Oda... If you ate the Clear-Clear Fruit, what would you do?

--Lumberjack

A: Heh!♡ Heh heh...♡ Whoops! Moving on.

Good morning afternoon evening night! Hey, Odacchi!

Q: In volume 53, page 193, third panel, I saw Buggy on the newspaper that Grandma Nyon was reading. Did he finally get captured? What happened here?

--Okoge Riceball

A: Man, nothing gets past these readers... You're right. I did, in fact, draw Buggy. You'll find out why he's on the newspaper when you read this volume! Buggy got caught! He got caught by entering a navy garrison that he thought was a cave with Captain John's treasure. That's what the article says.

Chapter 527:
LEVEL 1: CRIMSON HELL

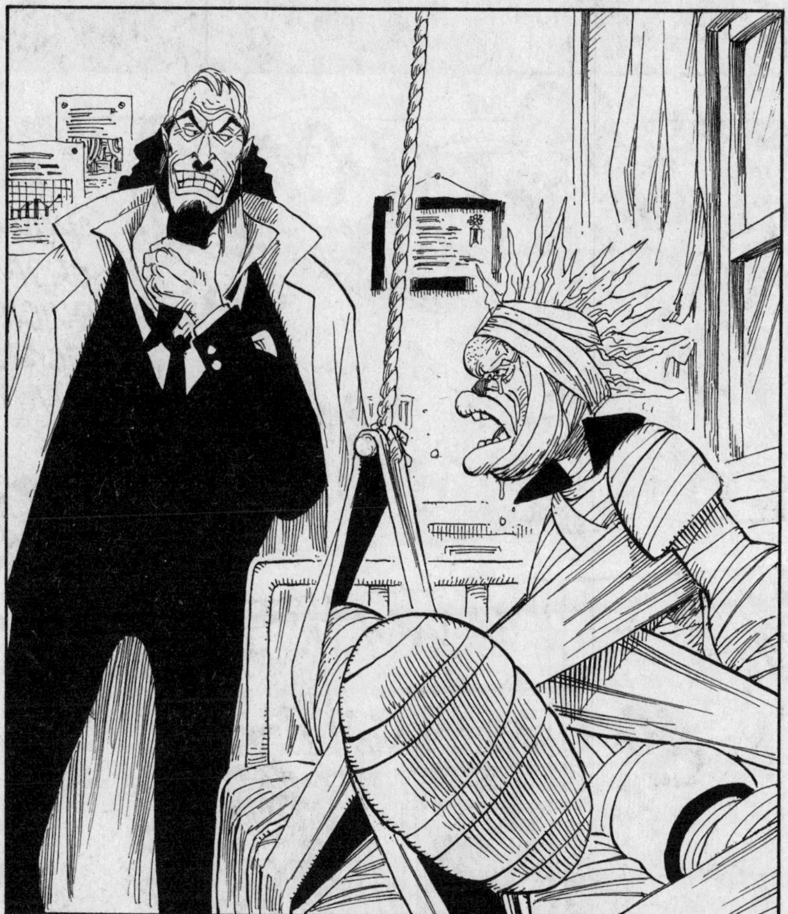

CP9 INDEPENDENT REPORT, VOL. 32:
"FATHER AND SON PLOTTING TO KILL CP9 AGENTS"

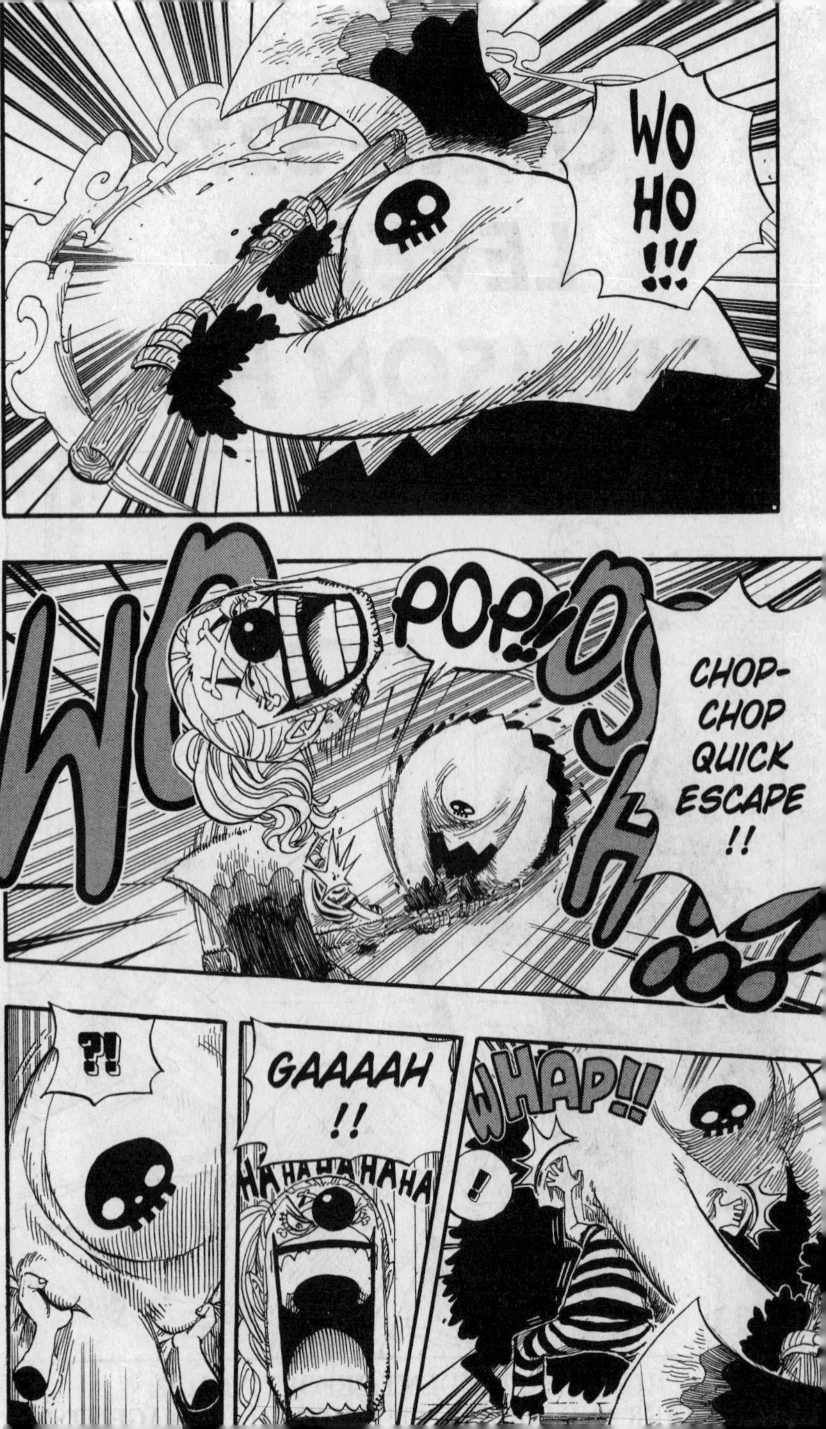
WO HO!!!
CHOP-CHOP QUICK ESCAPE !!
POP!!
WHAP!!
!
GAAAAH !!
HAHAHAHAHAHA
?!

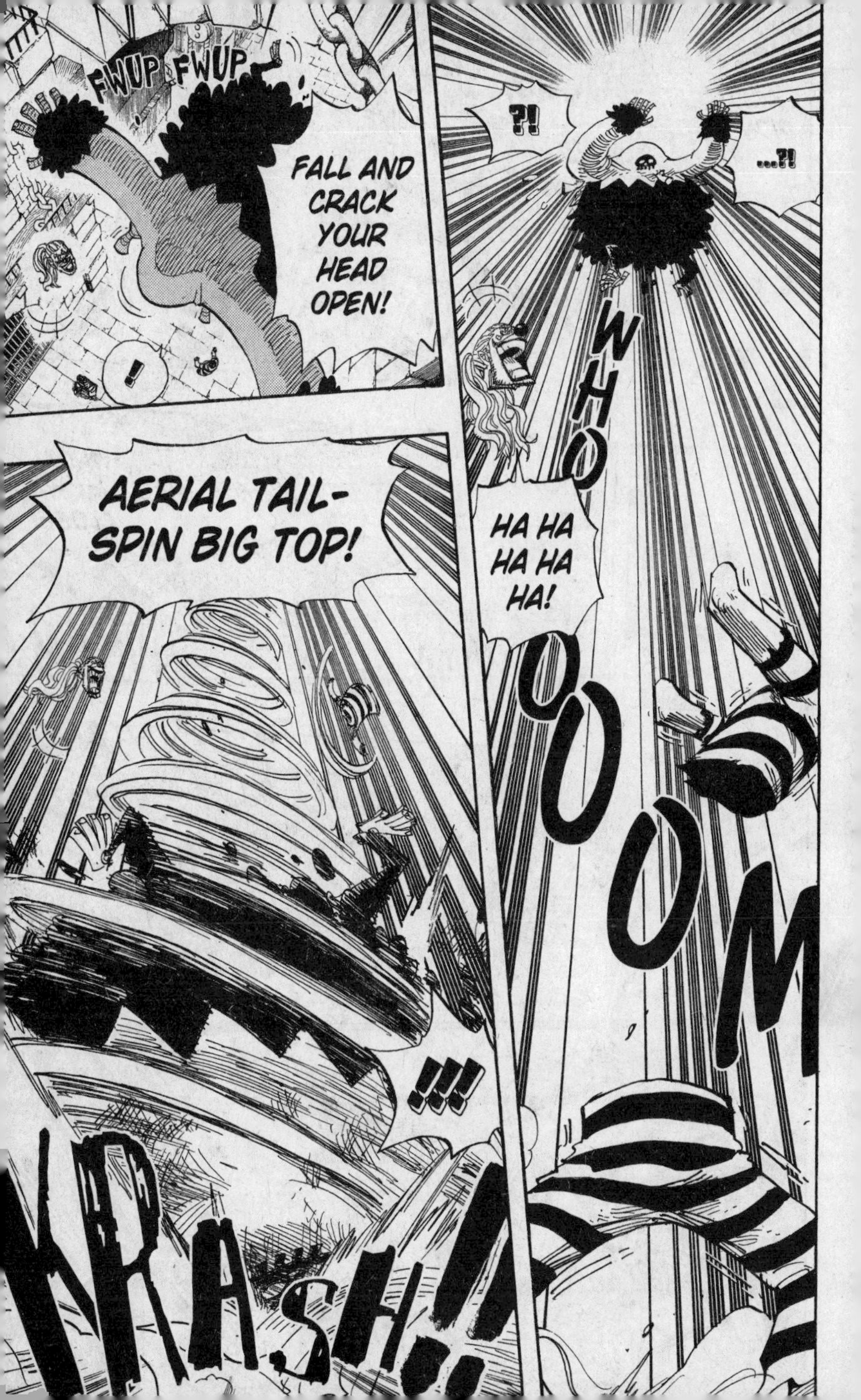
?!
...?!
WHOOOOM
HA HA HA HA HA!
FWUP FWUP
!
FALL AND CRACK YOUR HEAD OPEN!
AERIAL TAIL-SPIN BIG TOP!
!!!
KRASH!!

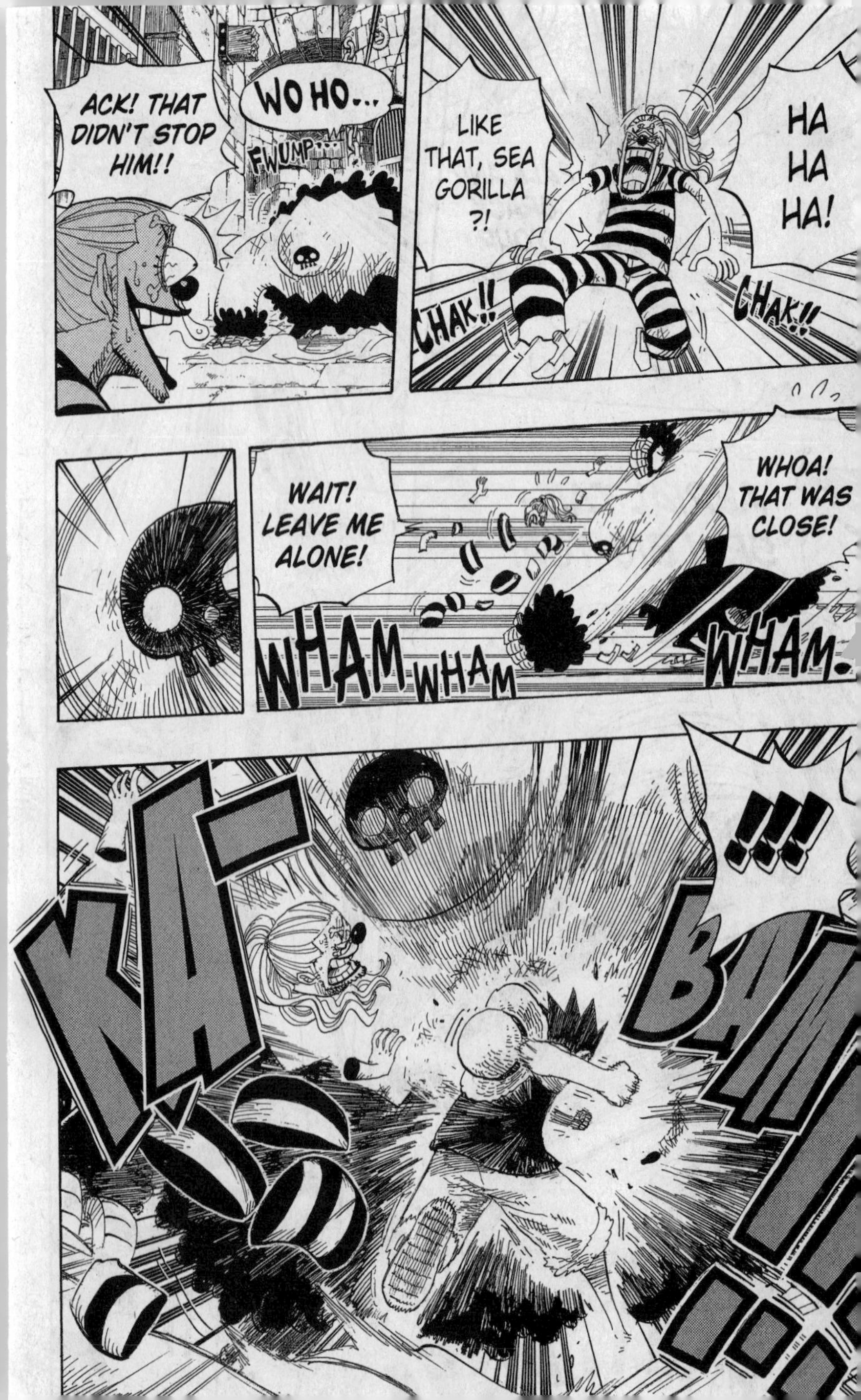
HA HA HA!
LIKE THAT, SEA GORILLA ?!
CHAK!!
CHAK!!
WO HO...
FWUMP...
ACK! THAT DIDN'T STOP HIM!!
WHOA! THAT WAS CLOSE!
WHAM.
WAIT! LEAVE ME ALONE!
WHAM
WHAM
!!!

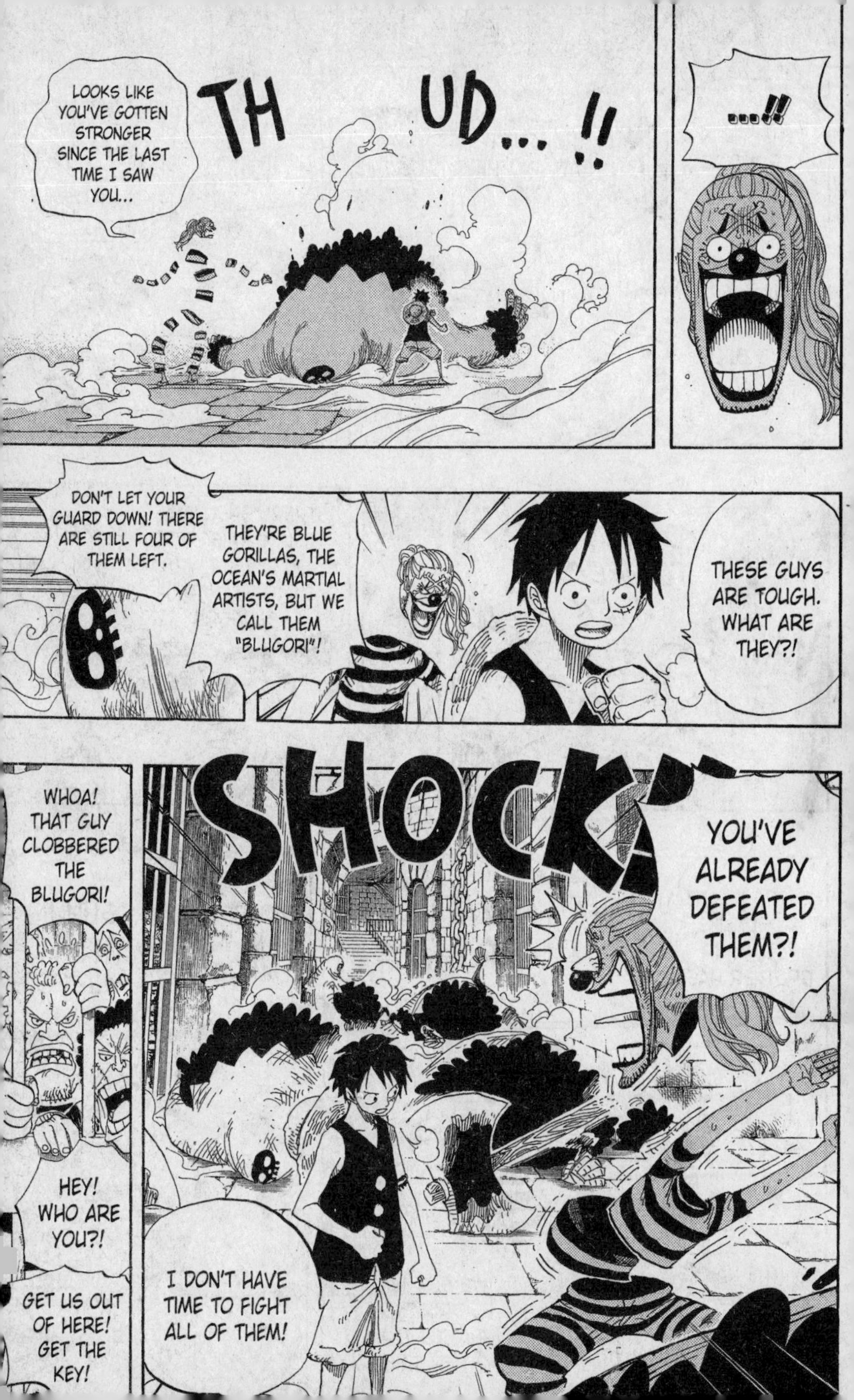
...!!
THUD...!!
LOOKS LIKE YOU'VE GOTTEN STRONGER SINCE THE LAST TIME I SAW YOU...
THESE GUYS ARE TOUGH. WHAT ARE THEY?!
THEY'RE BLUE GORILLAS, THE OCEAN'S MARTIAL ARTISTS, BUT WE CALL THEM "BLUGORI"!
DON'T LET YOUR GUARD DOWN! THERE ARE STILL FOUR OF THEM LEFT.
SHOCK
YOU'VE ALREADY DEFEATED THEM?!
I DON'T HAVE TIME TO FIGHT ALL OF THEM!
WHOA! THAT GUY CLOBBERED THE BLUGORI!
HEY! WHO ARE YOU?!
GET US OUT OF HERE! GET THE KEY!

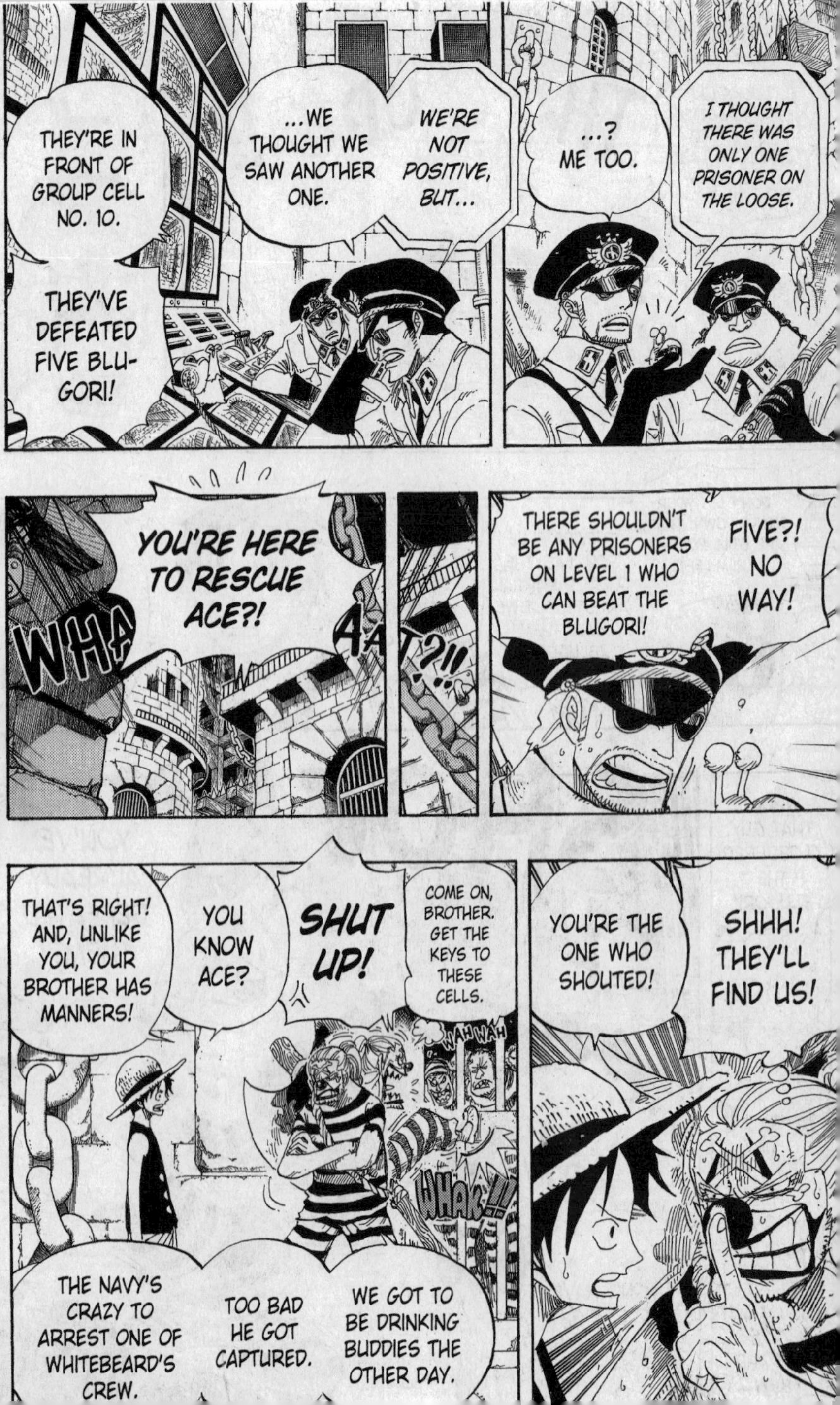
I THOUGHT THERE WAS ONLY ONE PRISONER ON THE LOOSE.
...? ME TOO.
WE'RE NOT POSITIVE, BUT...
...WE THOUGHT WE SAW ANOTHER ONE.
THEY'RE IN FRONT OF GROUP CELL NO. 10.
THEY'VE DEFEATED FIVE BLU-GORI!
FIVE?! NO WAY!
THERE SHOULDN'T BE ANY PRISONERS ON LEVEL 1 WHO CAN BEAT THE BLUGORI!
YOU'RE HERE TO RESCUE ACE?!
WHAAAT?!!
SHHH! THEY'LL FIND US!
YOU'RE THE ONE WHO SHOUTED!
COME ON, BROTHER. GET THE KEYS TO THESE CELLS.
SHUT UP!
YOU KNOW ACE?
THAT'S RIGHT! AND, UNLIKE YOU, YOUR BROTHER HAS MANNERS!
WAH WAH
WHAK!!
WE GOT TO BE DRINKING BUDDIES THE OTHER DAY.
TOO BAD HE GOT CAPTURED.
THE NAVY'S CRAZY TO ARREST ONE OF WHITEBEARD'S CREW.

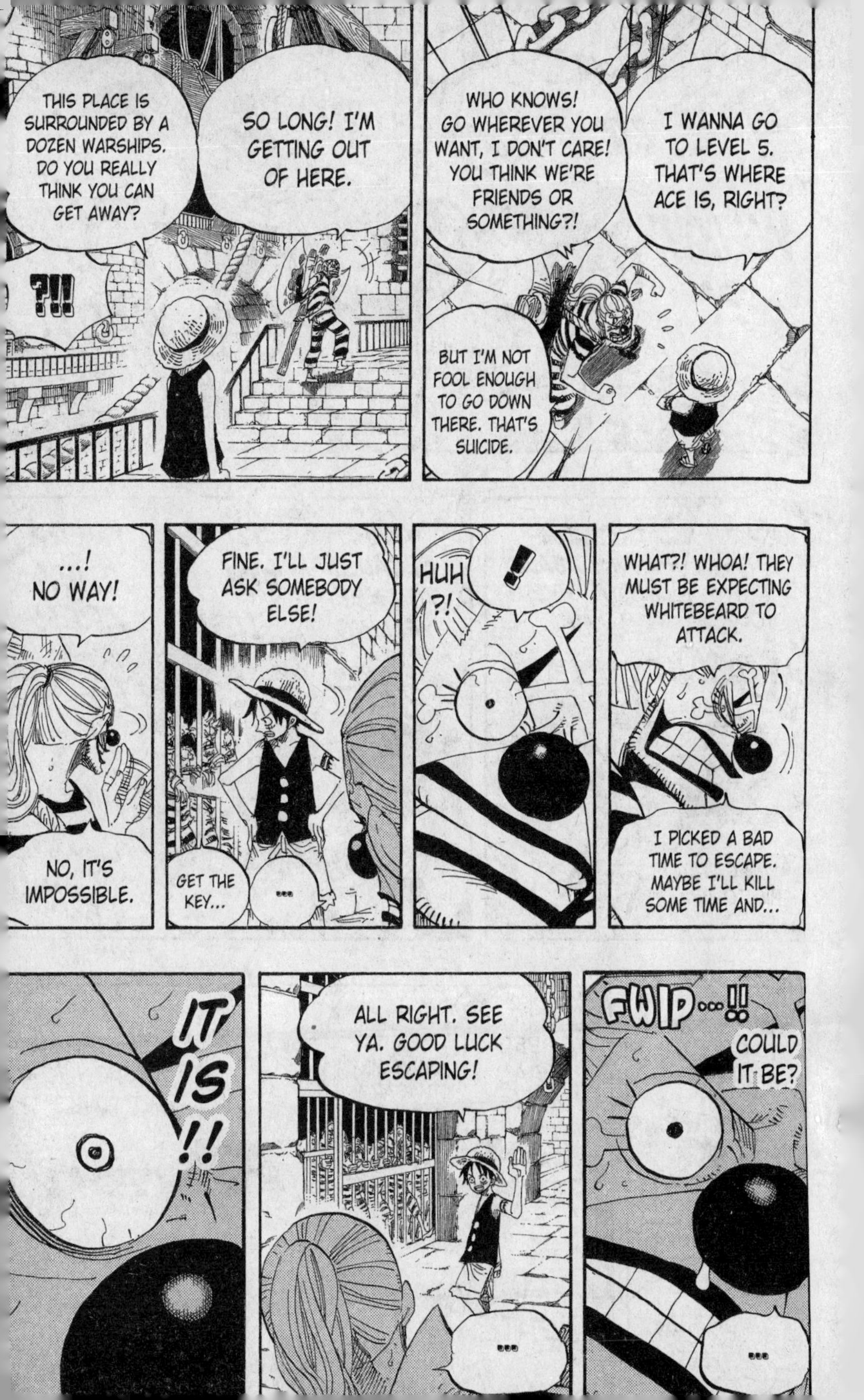
I WANNA GO TO LEVEL 5. THAT'S WHERE ACE IS, RIGHT?
WHO KNOWS! GO WHEREVER YOU WANT, I DON'T CARE! YOU THINK WE'RE FRIENDS OR SOMETHING?!
BUT I'M NOT FOOL ENOUGH TO GO DOWN THERE. THAT'S SUICIDE.
SO LONG! I'M GETTING OUT OF HERE.
THIS PLACE IS SURROUNDED BY A DOZEN WARSHIPS. DO YOU REALLY THINK YOU CAN GET AWAY?
?!!
WHAT?! WHOA! THEY MUST BE EXPECTING WHITEBEARD TO ATTACK.
I PICKED A BAD TIME TO ESCAPE. MAYBE I'LL KILL SOME TIME AND...
!
HUH ?!
FINE. I'LL JUST ASK SOMEBODY ELSE!
...
GET THE KEY...
...! NO WAY!
NO, IT'S IMPOSSIBLE.
FWIP...!!
COULD IT BE?
...
ALL RIGHT. SEE YA. GOOD LUCK ESCAPING!
...
IT IS!!

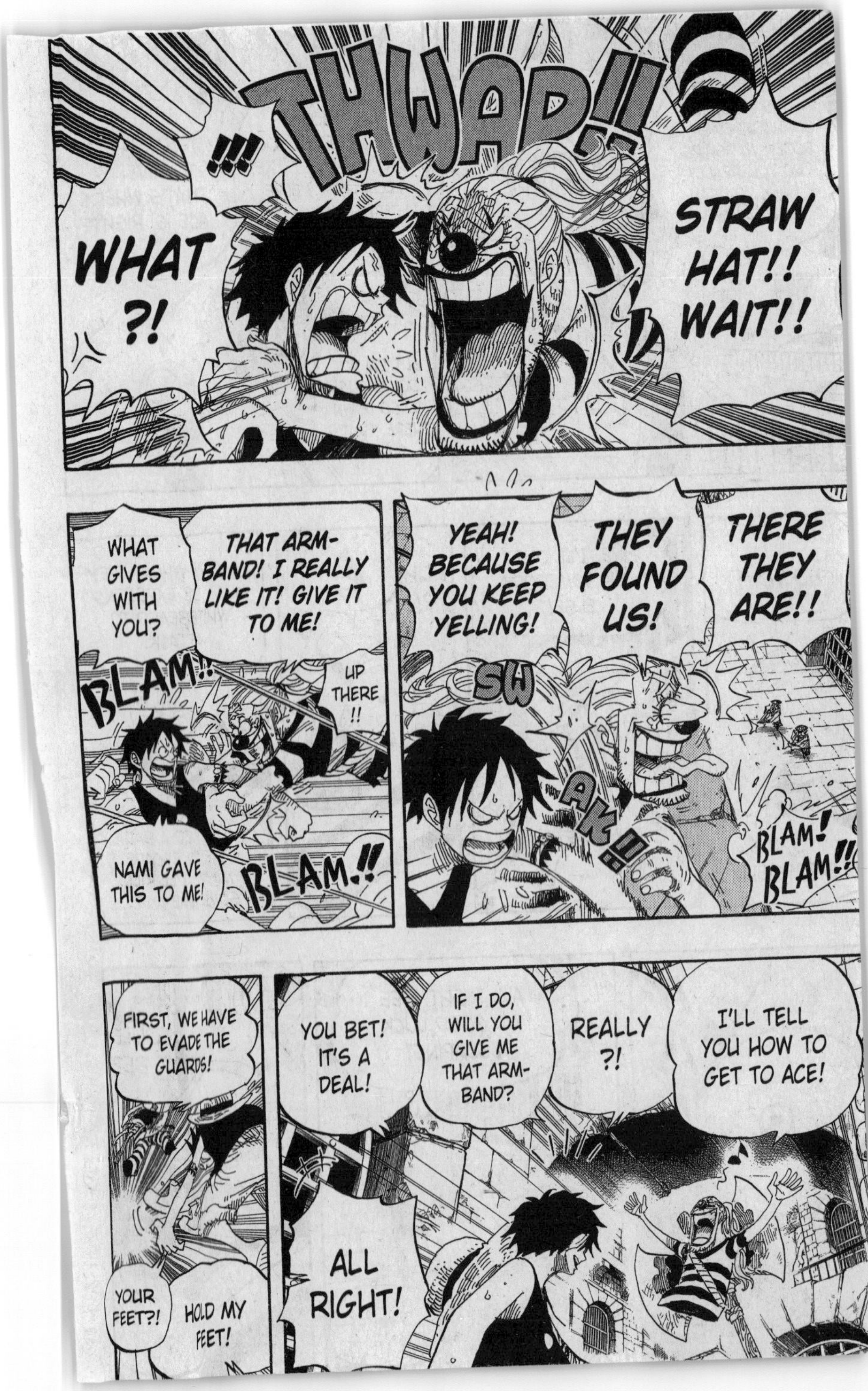
THWAP!!
STRAW HAT!! WAIT!!
!!!
WHAT ?!
THERE THEY ARE!!
THEY FOUND US!
YEAH! BECAUSE YOU KEEP YELLING!
SW
AK!!
BLAM! BLAM!!
THAT ARM-BAND! I REALLY LIKE IT! GIVE IT TO ME!
WHAT GIVES WITH YOU?
UP THERE!!
BLAM!!
NAMI GAVE THIS TO ME!
BLAM!!
I'LL TELL YOU HOW TO GET TO ACE!
REALLY ?!
IF I DO, WILL YOU GIVE ME THAT ARM-BAND?
YOU BET! IT'S A DEAL!
ALL RIGHT!
FIRST, WE HAVE TO EVADE THE GUARDS!
HOLD MY FEET!
YOUR FEET?!

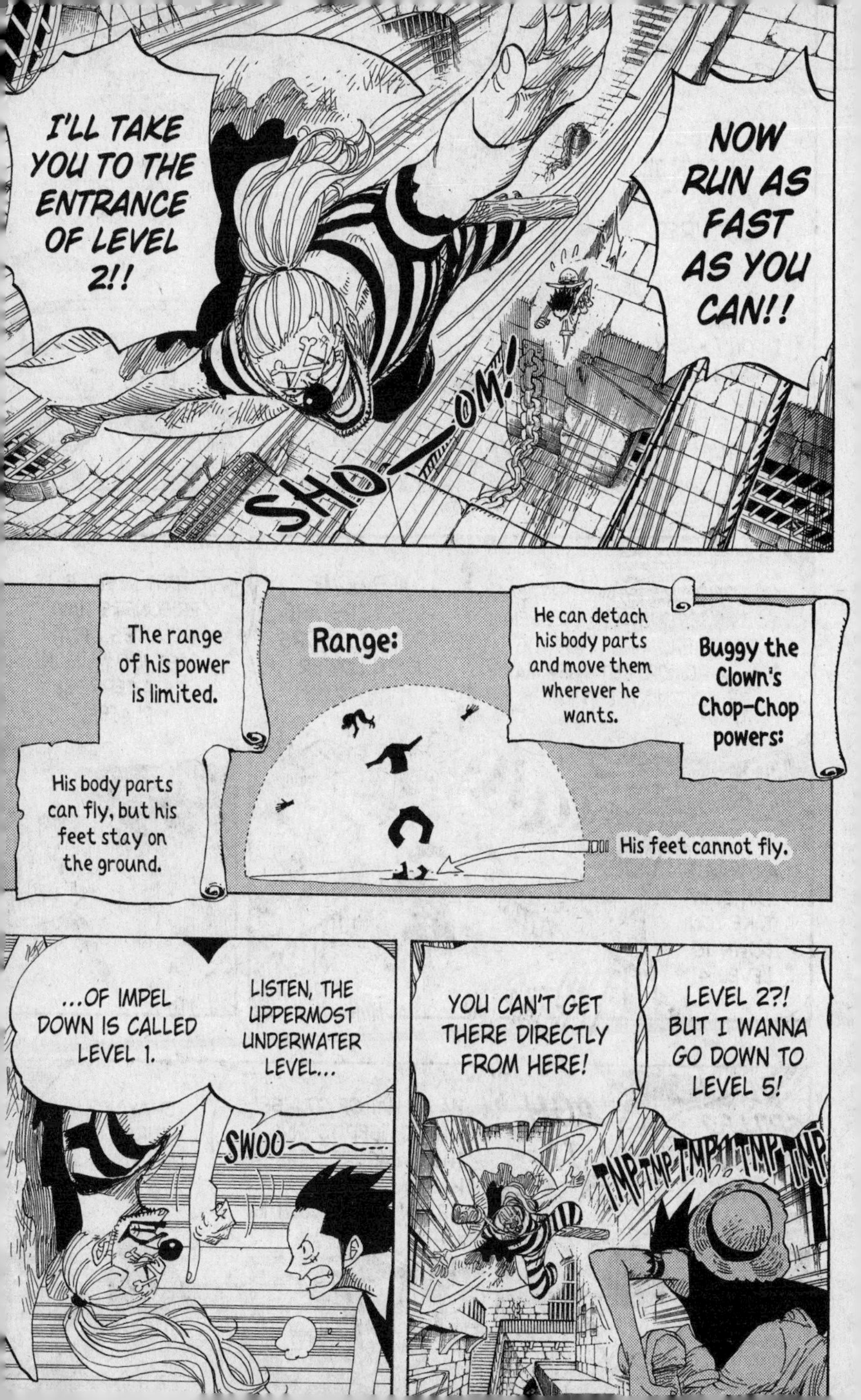
NOW RUN AS FAST AS YOU CAN!!
I'LL TAKE YOU TO THE ENTRANCE OF LEVEL 2!!
SHO—OM!
Buggy the Clown's Chop-Chop powers:
He can detach his body parts and move them wherever he wants.
Range:
The range of his power is limited.
His feet cannot fly.
His body parts can fly, but his feet stay on the ground.
LEVEL 2?! BUT I WANNA GO DOWN TO LEVEL 5!
YOU CAN'T GET THERE DIRECTLY FROM HERE!
TMP TMP TMP TMP TMP TMP
LISTEN, THE UPPERMOST UNDERWATER LEVEL...
...OF IMPEL DOWN IS CALLED LEVEL 1.
SWOO—

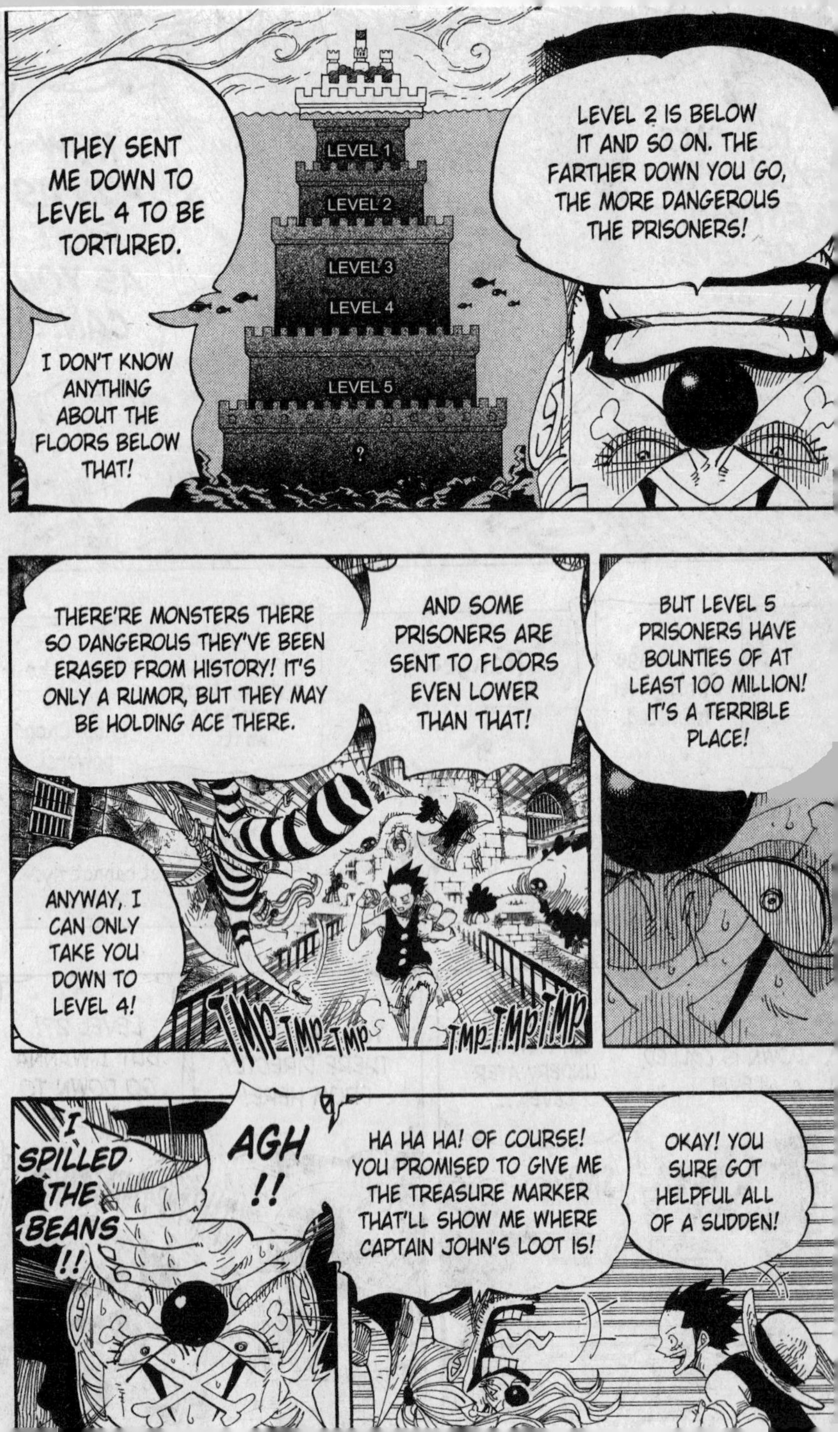
LEVEL 2 IS BELOW IT AND SO ON. THE FARTHER DOWN YOU GO, THE MORE DANGEROUS THE PRISONERS!
LEVEL 1
LEVEL 2
LEVEL 3
LEVEL 4
LEVEL 5
?
THEY SENT ME DOWN TO LEVEL 4 TO BE TORTURED.
I DON'T KNOW ANYTHING ABOUT THE FLOORS BELOW THAT!
BUT LEVEL 5 PRISONERS HAVE BOUNTIES OF AT LEAST 100 MILLION! IT'S A TERRIBLE PLACE!
AND SOME PRISONERS ARE SENT TO FLOORS EVEN LOWER THAN THAT!
THERE'RE MONSTERS THERE SO DANGEROUS THEY'VE BEEN ERASED FROM HISTORY! IT'S ONLY A RUMOR, BUT THEY MAY BE HOLDING ACE THERE.
ANYWAY, I CAN ONLY TAKE YOU DOWN TO LEVEL 4!
TMP TMP TMP
TMP TMP TMP
OKAY! YOU SURE GOT HELPFUL ALL OF A SUDDEN!
HA HA HA! OF COURSE! YOU PROMISED TO GIVE ME THE TREASURE MARKER THAT'LL SHOW ME WHERE CAPTAIN JOHN'S LOOT IS!
AGH !!
I SPILLED THE BEANS !!

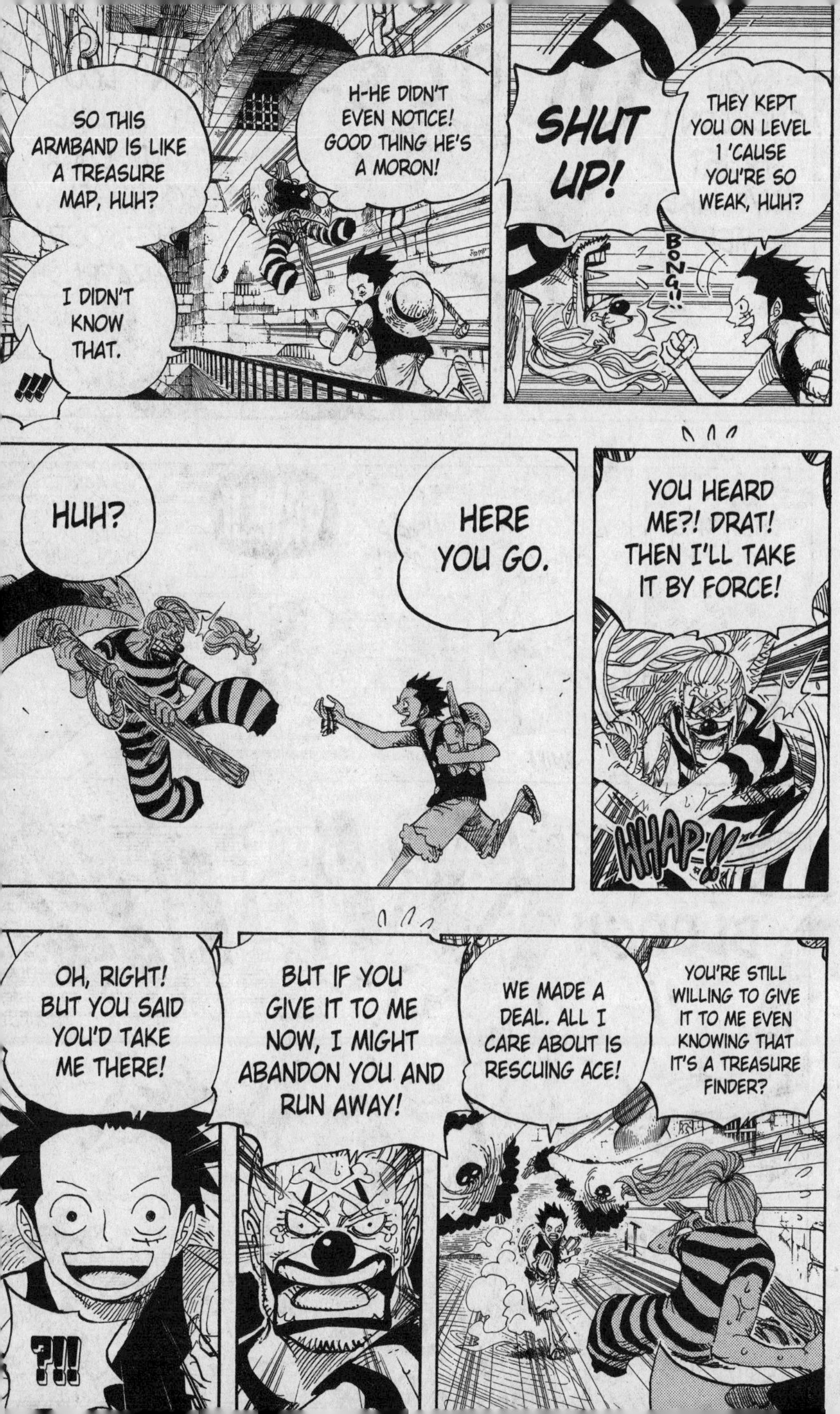
THEY KEPT YOU ON LEVEL 1 'CAUSE YOU'RE SO WEAK, HUH?
SHUT UP!
BONG!!
H-HE DIDN'T EVEN NOTICE! GOOD THING HE'S A MORON!
SO THIS ARMBAND IS LIKE A TREASURE MAP, HUH?
I DIDN'T KNOW THAT.
!!!
YOU HEARD ME?! DRAT! THEN I'LL TAKE IT BY FORCE!
WHAP!!
HERE YOU GO.
HUH?
YOU'RE STILL WILLING TO GIVE IT TO ME EVEN KNOWING THAT IT'S A TREASURE FINDER?
WE MADE A DEAL. ALL I CARE ABOUT IS RESCUING ACE!
BUT IF YOU GIVE IT TO ME NOW, I MIGHT ABANDON YOU AND RUN AWAY!
OH, RIGHT! BUT YOU SAID YOU'D TAKE ME THERE!
?!!

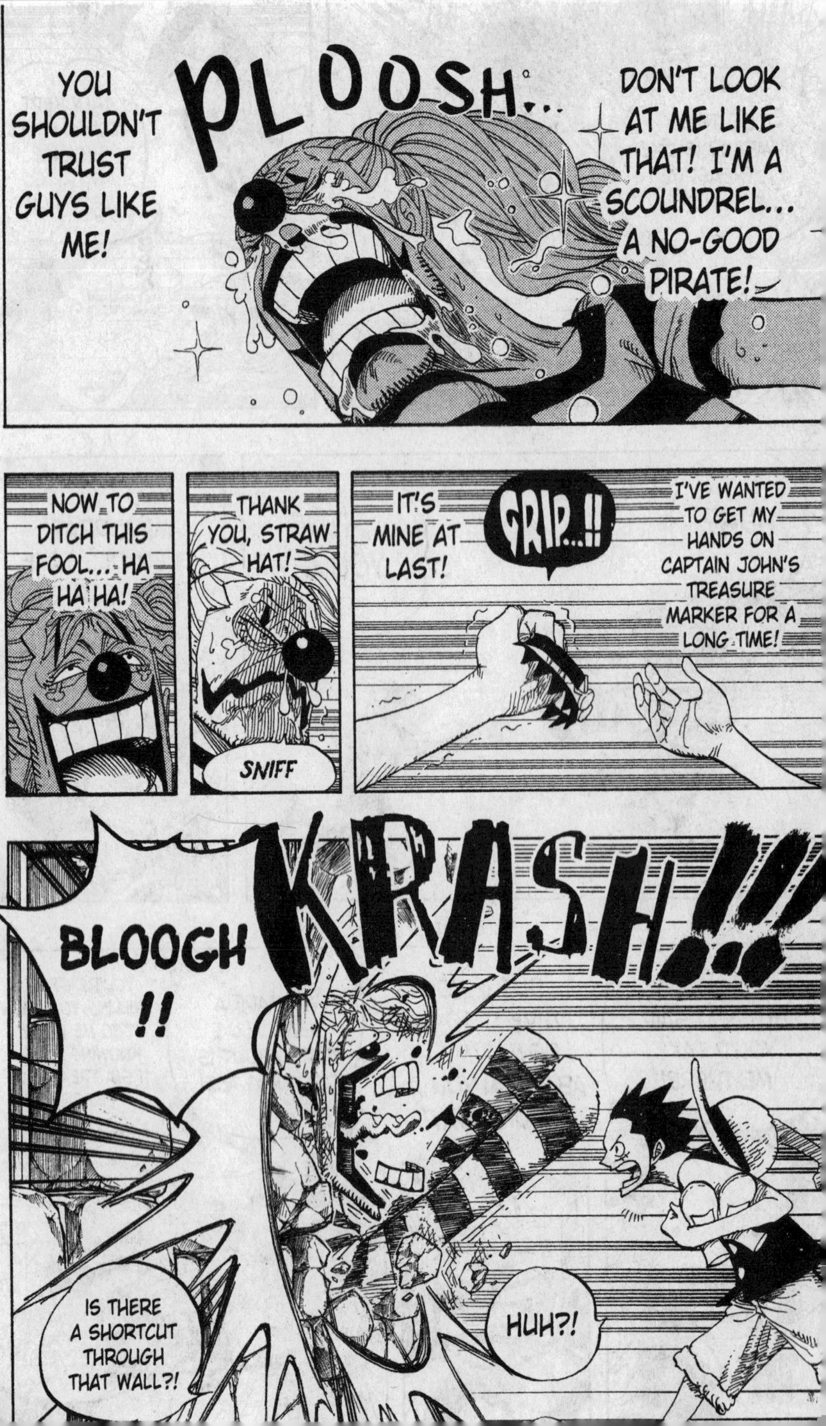
DON'T LOOK AT ME LIKE THAT! I'M A SCOUNDREL... A NO-GOOD PIRATE!
PLOOSH...
YOU SHOULDN'T TRUST GUYS LIKE ME!
I'VE WANTED TO GET MY HANDS ON CAPTAIN JOHN'S TREASURE MARKER FOR A LONG TIME!
GRIP...!!
IT'S MINE AT LAST!
THANK YOU, STRAW HAT!
SNIFF
NOW TO DITCH THIS FOOL... HA HA HA!
KRASH!!
BLOOGH !!
HUH?!
IS THERE A SHORTCUT THROUGH THAT WALL?!

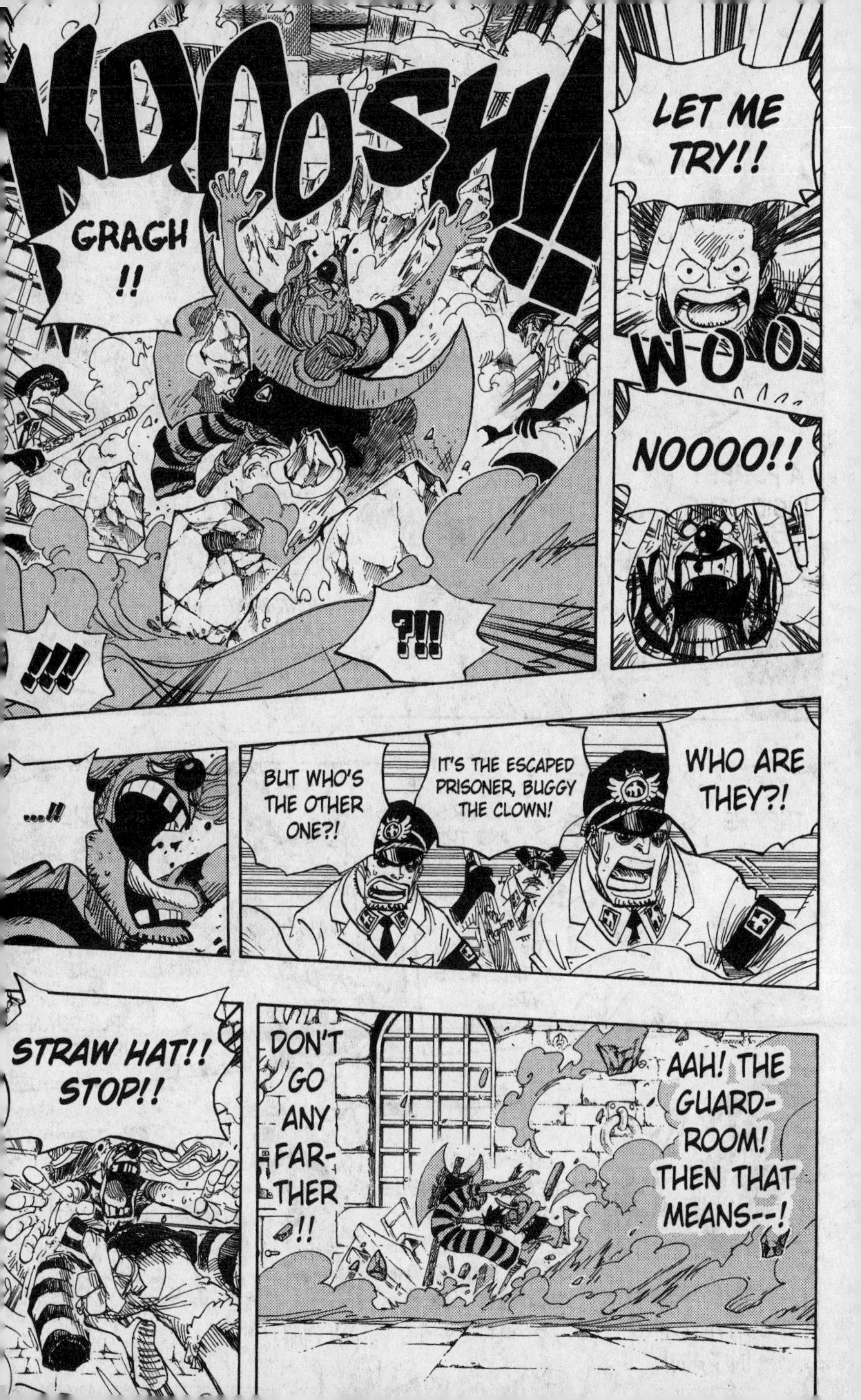
LET ME TRY!!
WOO
NOOOO!!
KDOOSH!!
GRAGH !!
?!!
!!!!
WHO ARE THEY?!
IT'S THE ESCAPED PRISONER, BUGGY THE CLOWN!
BUT WHO'S THE OTHER ONE?!
...!!
AAH! THE GUARD-ROOM! THEN THAT MEANS--!
DON'T GO ANY FAR-THER!!
STRAW HAT!! STOP!!

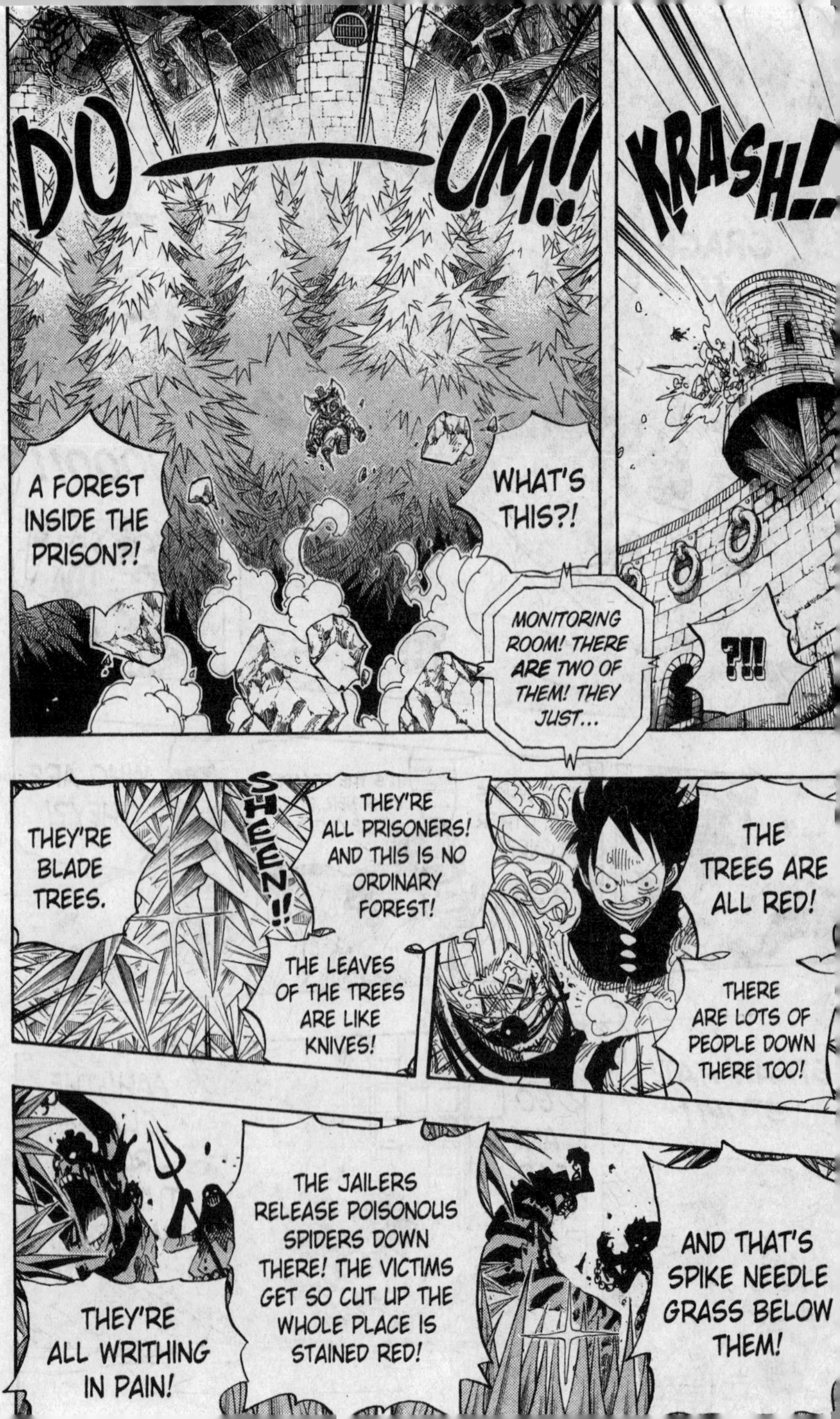
KRASH!!
?!!
MONITORING ROOM! THERE ARE TWO OF THEM! THEY JUST...
DO—OM!!
WHAT'S THIS?!
A FOREST INSIDE THE PRISON?!
THE TREES ARE ALL RED!
THERE ARE LOTS OF PEOPLE DOWN THERE TOO!
THEY'RE ALL PRISONERS! AND THIS IS NO ORDINARY FOREST!
SHEEN!!
THEY'RE BLADE TREES.
THE LEAVES OF THE TREES ARE LIKE KNIVES!
AND THAT'S SPIKE NEEDLE GRASS BELOW THEM!
THE JAILERS RELEASE POISONOUS SPIDERS DOWN THERE! THE VICTIMS GET SO CUT UP THE WHOLE PLACE IS STAINED RED!
THEY'RE ALL WRITHING IN PAIN!

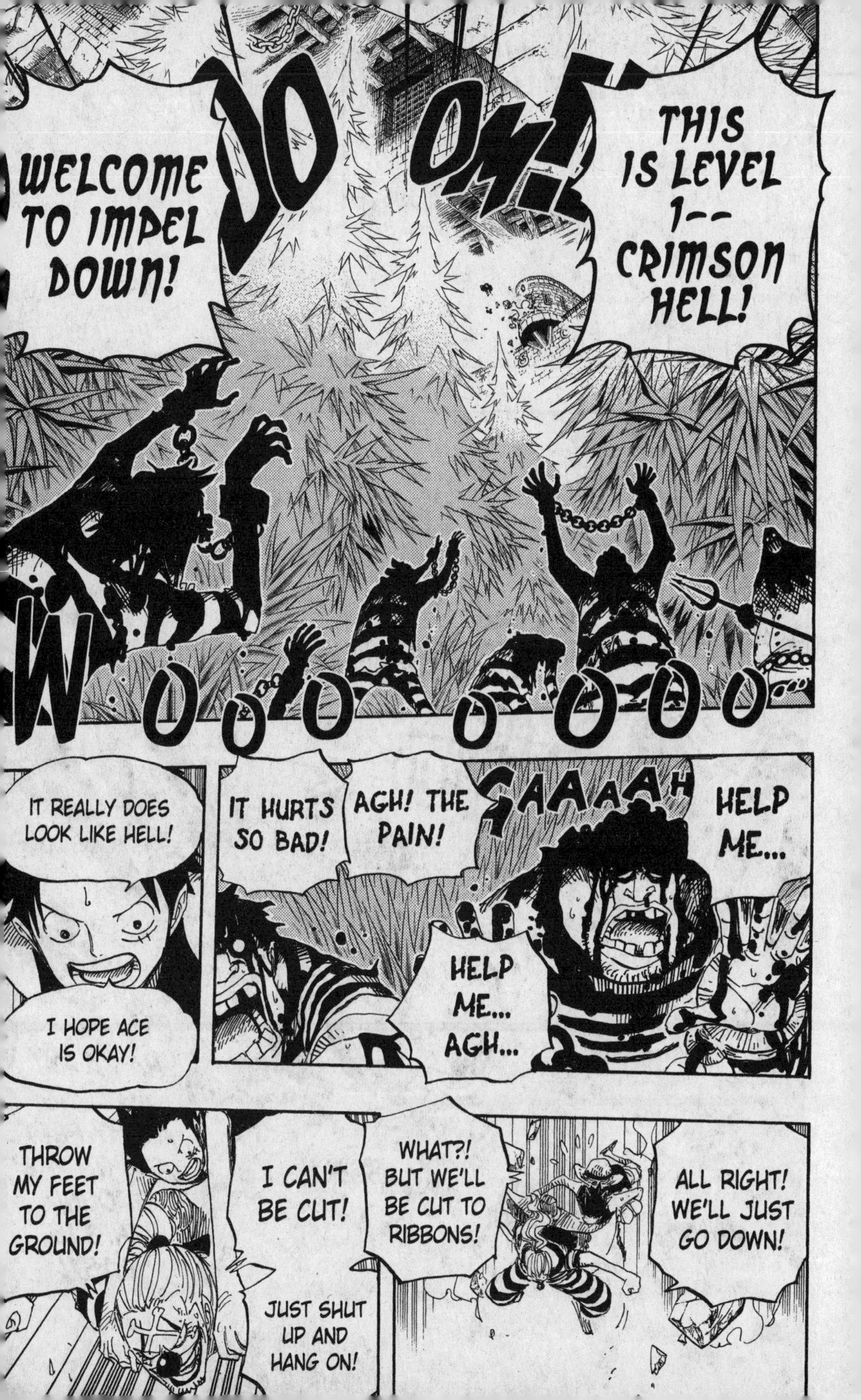
THIS IS LEVEL 1-- CRIMSON HELL!
DO ON!!
WELCOME TO IMPEL DOWN!
WOOOOOOO
HELP ME...
GAAAAAH
AGH! THE PAIN!
IT HURTS SO BAD!
HELP ME... AGH...
IT REALLY DOES LOOK LIKE HELL!
I HOPE ACE IS OKAY!
ALL RIGHT! WE'LL JUST GO DOWN!
WHAT?! BUT WE'LL BE CUT TO RIBBONS!
I CAN'T BE CUT!
JUST SHUT UP AND HANG ON!
THROW MY FEET TO THE GROUND!

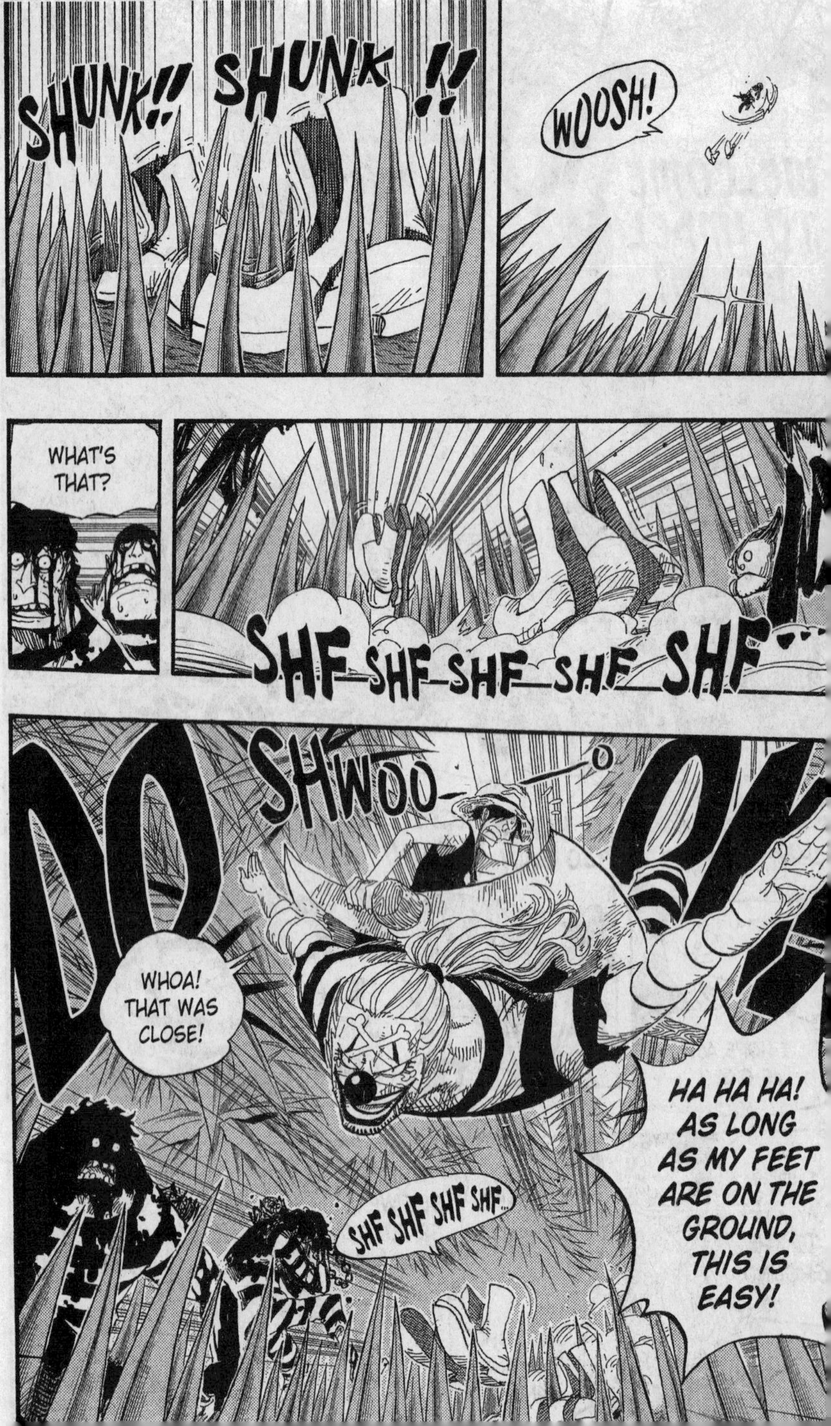
WOOSH!
SHUNK!! SHUNK!!
SHF SHF SHF SHF SHF...
WHAT'S THAT?
SHWOO
HA HA HA! AS LONG AS MY FEET ARE ON THE GROUND, THIS IS EASY!
WHOA! THAT WAS CLOSE!
SHF SHF SHF SHF...

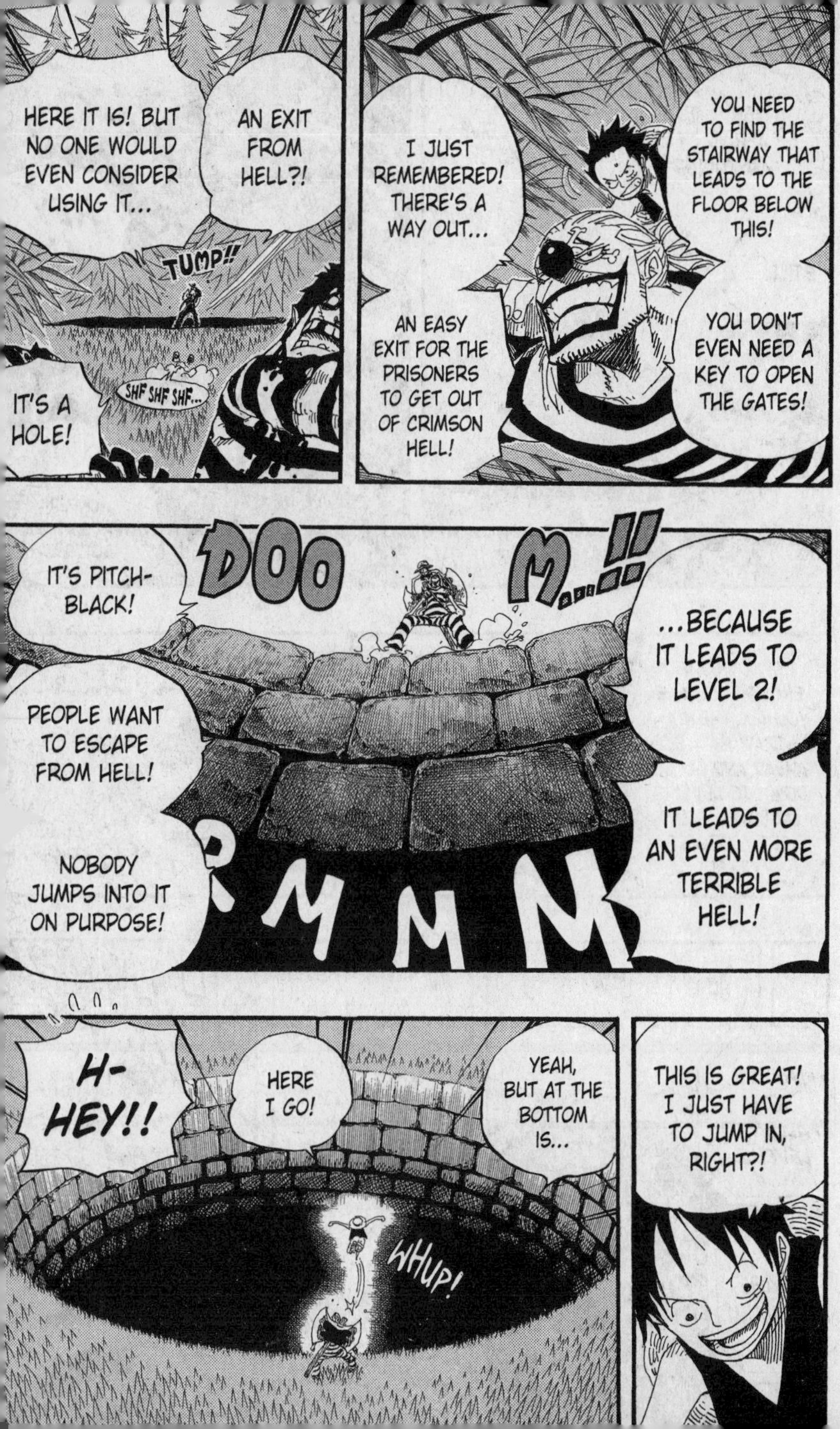

YOU NEED TO FIND THE STAIRWAY THAT LEADS TO THE FLOOR BELOW THIS!
I JUST REMEMBERED! THERE'S A WAY OUT...
YOU DON'T EVEN NEED A KEY TO OPEN THE GATES!
AN EASY EXIT FOR THE PRISONERS TO GET OUT OF CRIMSON HELL!
AN EXIT FROM HELL?!
HERE IT IS! BUT NO ONE WOULD EVEN CONSIDER USING IT...
TUMP!!
SHF SHF SHF...
IT'S A HOLE!
...BECAUSE IT LEADS TO LEVEL 2!
DOOM...!!
IT'S PITCH-BLACK!
IT LEADS TO AN EVEN MORE TERRIBLE HELL!
PEOPLE WANT TO ESCAPE FROM HELL!
MMM
NOBODY JUMPS INTO IT ON PURPOSE!
THIS IS GREAT! I JUST HAVE TO JUMP IN, RIGHT?!
YEAH, BUT AT THE BOTTOM IS...
HERE I GO!
H-HEY!!
WHUP!

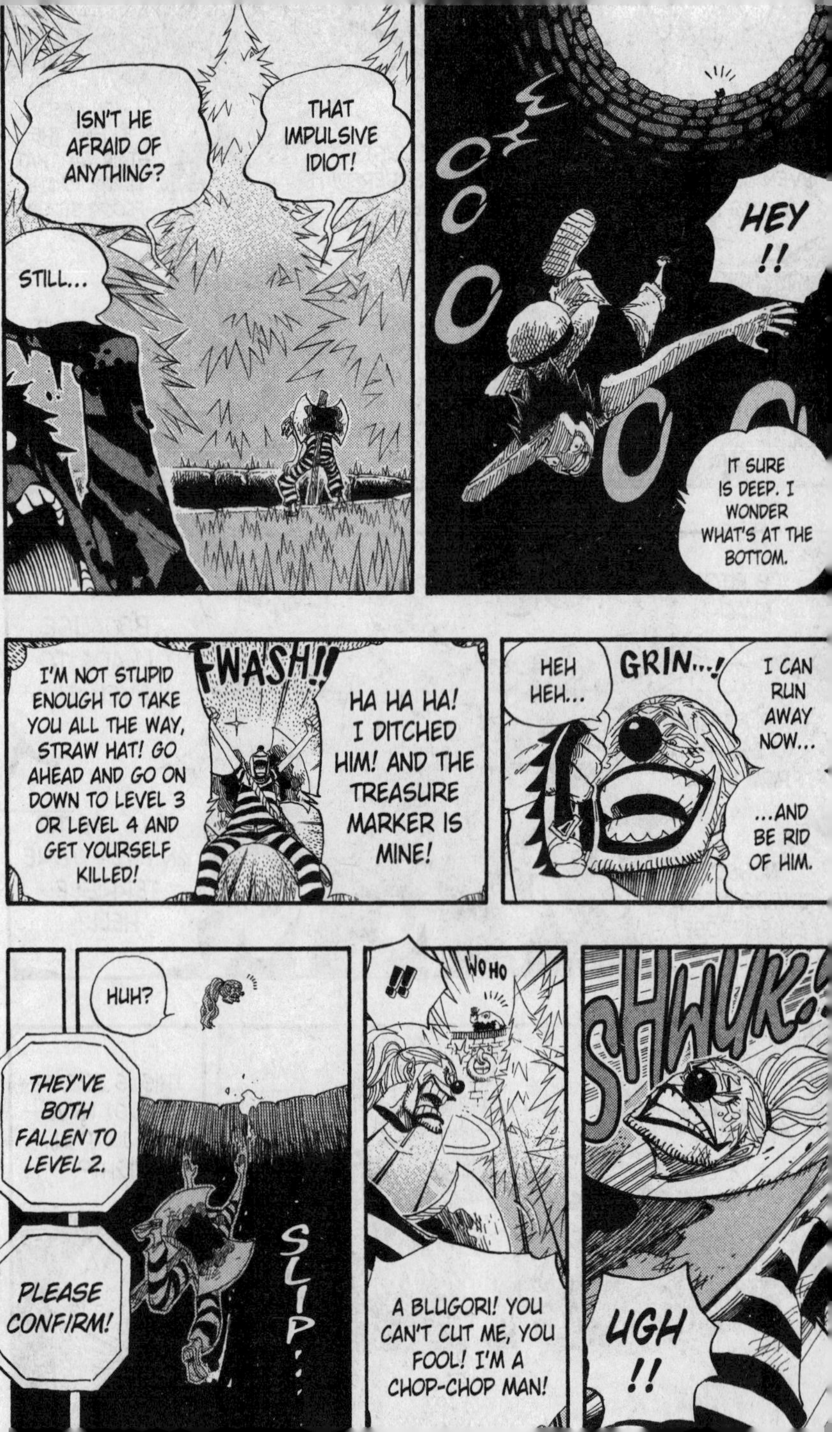
HEY!!
IT SURE IS DEEP. I WONDER WHAT'S AT THE BOTTOM.
THAT IMPULSIVE IDIOT!
ISN'T HE AFRAID OF ANYTHING?
STILL...
I CAN RUN AWAY NOW...
GRIN...!
HEH HEH...
...AND BE RID OF HIM.
FWASH!!
HA HA HA! I DITCHED HIM! AND THE TREASURE MARKER IS MINE!
I'M NOT STUPID ENOUGH TO TAKE YOU ALL THE WAY, STRAW HAT! GO AHEAD AND GO ON DOWN TO LEVEL 3 OR LEVEL 4 AND GET YOURSELF KILLED!
SHWUK!
UGH!!
!!
WOHO
A BLUGORI! YOU CAN'T CUT ME, YOU FOOL! I'M A CHOP-CHOP MAN!
HUH?
THEY'VE BOTH FALLEN TO LEVEL 2.
PLEASE CONFIRM!
SLIP...

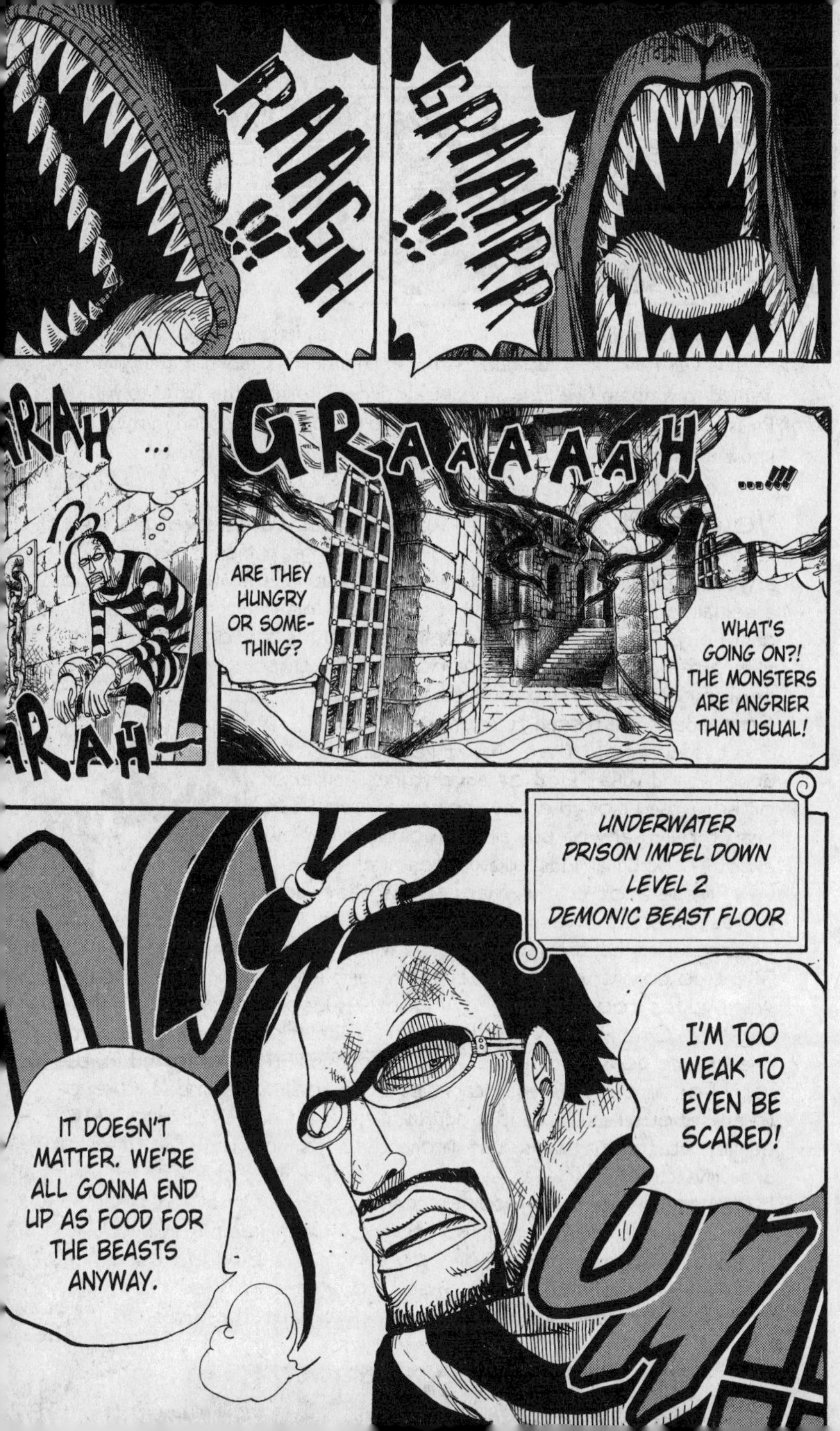
GRAAARRR!!!
RAAAGH!!!
GRAAAAAH...!!!
WHAT'S GOING ON?! THE MONSTERS ARE ANGRIER THAN USUAL!
ARE THEY HUNGRY OR SOME-THING?
RAH
...
RAH-
UNDERWATER PRISON IMPEL DOWN LEVEL 2 DEMONIC BEAST FLOOR
I'M TOO WEAK TO EVEN BE SCARED!
IT DOESN'T MATTER. WE'RE ALL GONNA END UP AS FOOD FOR THE BEASTS ANYWAY.

SBS Question Corner

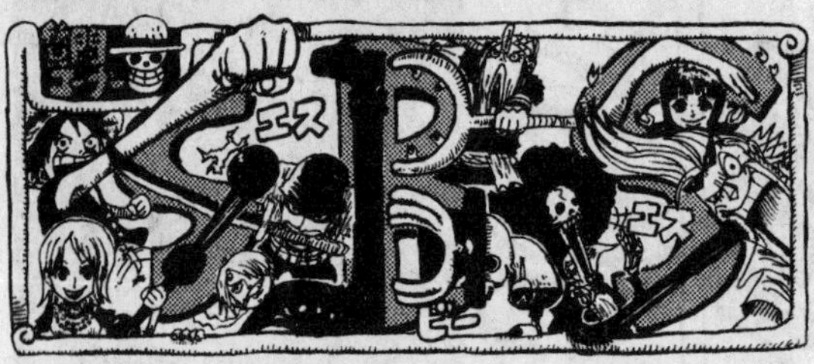

(Ponio, Aichi)

Introducing "One Piece Web"!

Q: Hello, Mr. Oda. This is the first time I've written a letter to you. I always enjoy reading *One Piece*. In a Question Corner in volume 53, you wrote that you wanted to wrap up *One Piece*, so I quickly decided to send this letter to you. Please don't say that. Please don't apologize for making us spend money! I know this is part of the Question Corner, but I don't have a question.

--Smoke

A: You don't?!? Anyway, I was surprised to receive lots of letters about what I said in volume 53. I really didn't mean anything significant when I said that! There is an "ideal length of a serialization" I believe, and it's "something that all readers can easily buy." This might be me being selfish as a storywriter, but the "Straw Hat Pirates" are now nine members strong. In the beginning, Luffy went out to sea alone!

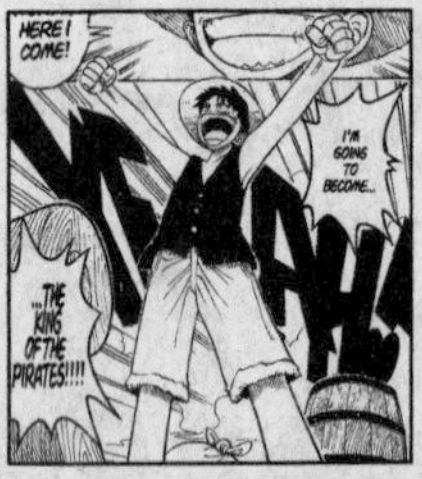
HERE I COME!
I'M GOING TO BECOME...
...THE KING OF THE PIRATES!!!!

So readers that read it from the middle don't even know that. I want people to understand what kind of adventures happened or how they got the new crewmembers! But I can't tell them to buy all 50 volumes! I know exactly how small kids' allowances are! That's why I made a lot of summary books that wrap up past stories. Every single time one is released, I asked the publishers to make it as cheap as possible. The two companies, Caramel Mama and Partyware, both did it for me! It's too cheap! Free, in fact! Awesome job! The Japanese website "One Piece Web" has been made! It's a story guide for the entire comic and it'll explain everything that happened in the past! For all the kids that can't buy the books, just read it here! Check it out now! (To the adults, please go buy the books) My earlier statement was just from that. It's not that I'm tired of drawing or anything. What I want to do hasn't changed at all. It's where all sorts of stories come together and "the final chapter is the most fun." The story of One Piece is still in the middle. If you have time, I hope you can read the whole thing through. I'm still challenging myself to create stories that no one has ever read before! Now go check out the website!

One Piece Web http://www.j-onepiece.com

Chapter 528:
JIMBEI, FIRST SON OF THE SEA

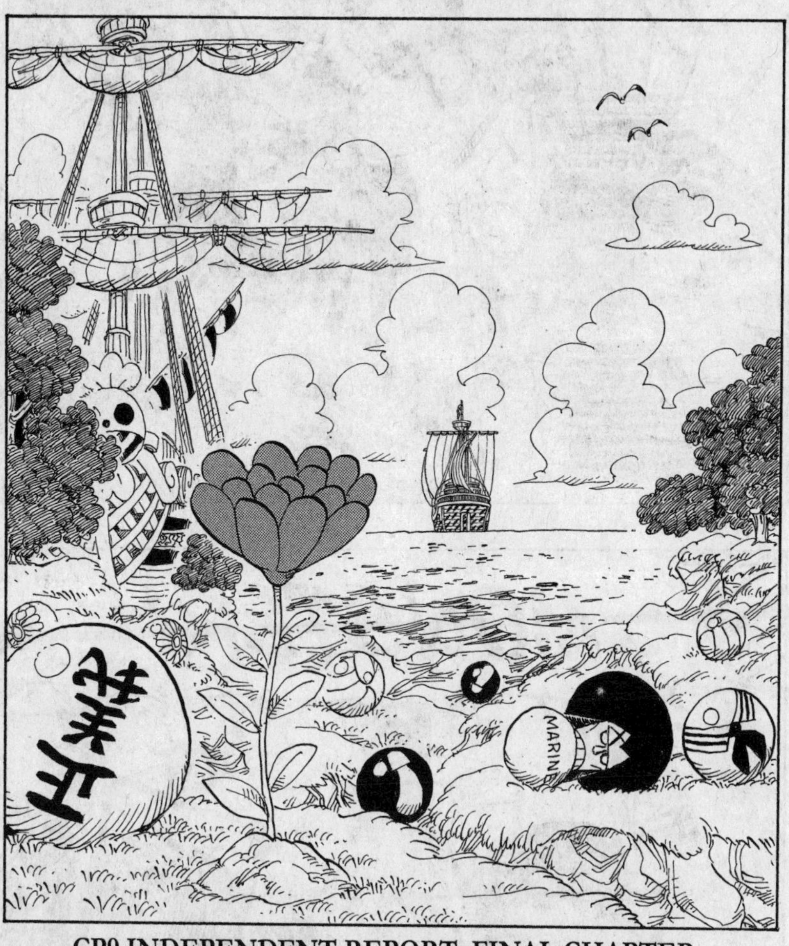

MARINE

TEXT ON BALL SAYS "JUSTICE" --ED.

CP9 INDEPENDENT REPORT, FINAL CHAPTER:
"THE SHIP DISAPPEARS INTO OBLIVION"

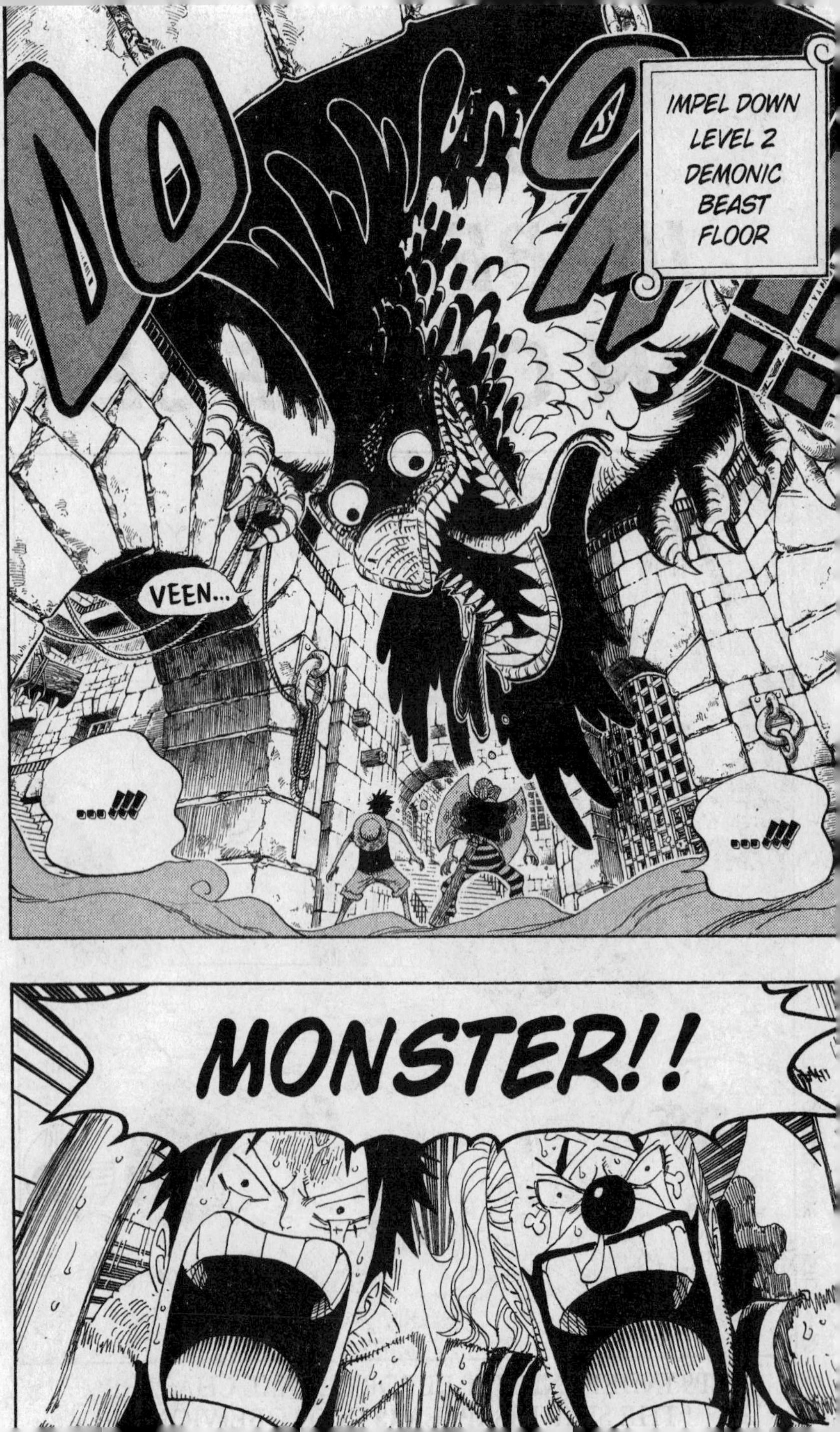

IMPEL DOWN LEVEL 2 DEMONIC BEAST FLOOR
DO
...!!!
VEEN...
...!!!
MONSTER!!

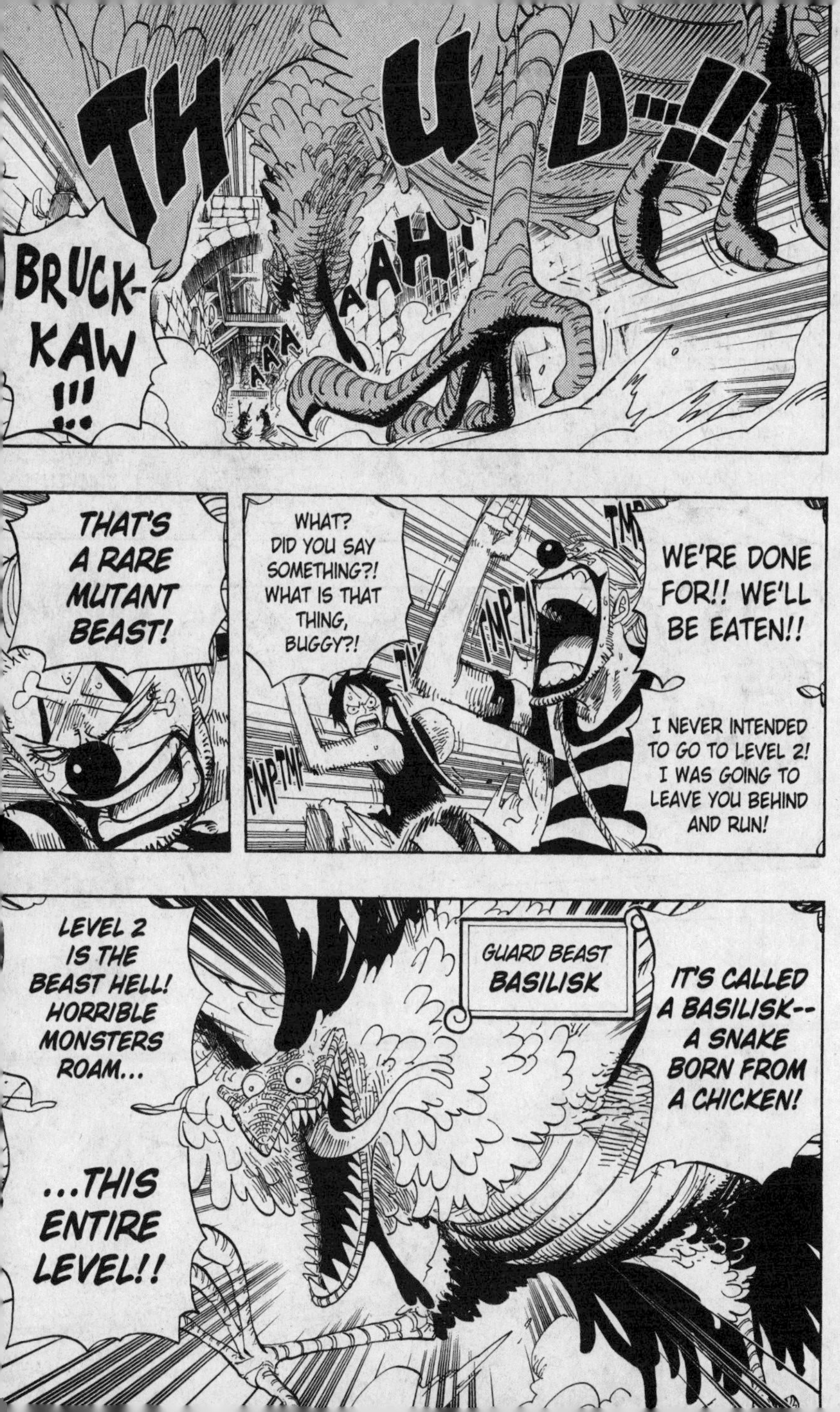
THUD--!!
AAAAH!
BRUCK-KAW!!!...
WE'RE DONE FOR!! WE'LL BE EATEN!!
TMP
TMPT
I NEVER INTENDED TO GO TO LEVEL 2! I WAS GOING TO LEAVE YOU BEHIND AND RUN!
WHAT? DID YOU SAY SOMETHING?! WHAT IS THAT THING, BUGGY?!
TMPTMP
THAT'S A RARE MUTANT BEAST!
IT'S CALLED A BASILISK-- A SNAKE BORN FROM A CHICKEN!
GUARD BEAST BASILISK
LEVEL 2 IS THE BEAST HELL! HORRIBLE MONSTERS ROAM...
...THIS ENTIRE LEVEL!!

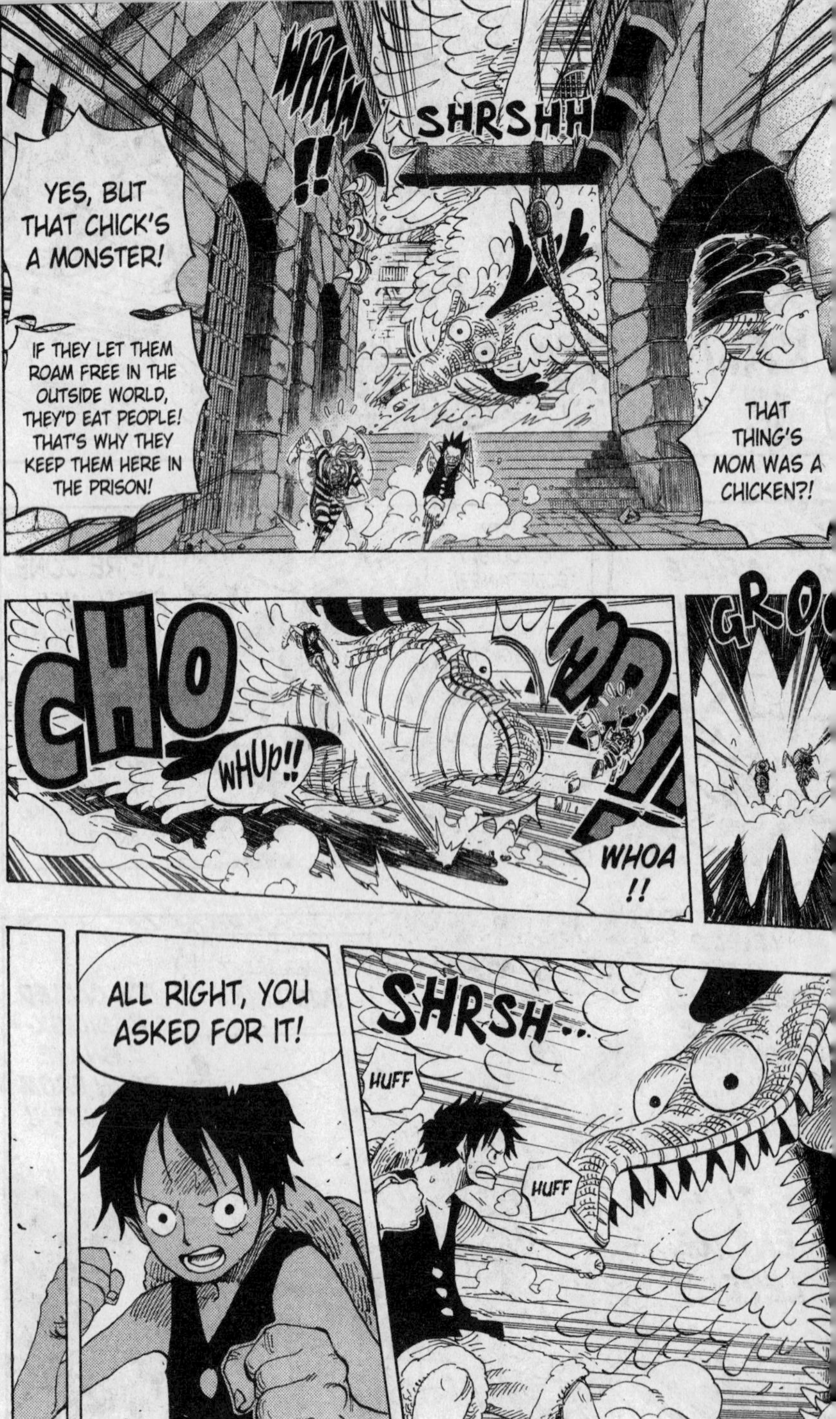
SHRSHH
WHAM!!
THAT THING'S MOM WAS A CHICKEN?!
YES, BUT THAT CHICK'S A MONSTER!
IF THEY LET THEM ROAM FREE IN THE OUTSIDE WORLD, THEY'D EAT PEOPLE! THAT'S WHY THEY KEEP THEM HERE IN THE PRISON!
GRO
WHOA !!
CHO
WHUP!!
SHRSH..
HUFF
HUFF
ALL RIGHT, YOU ASKED FOR IT!

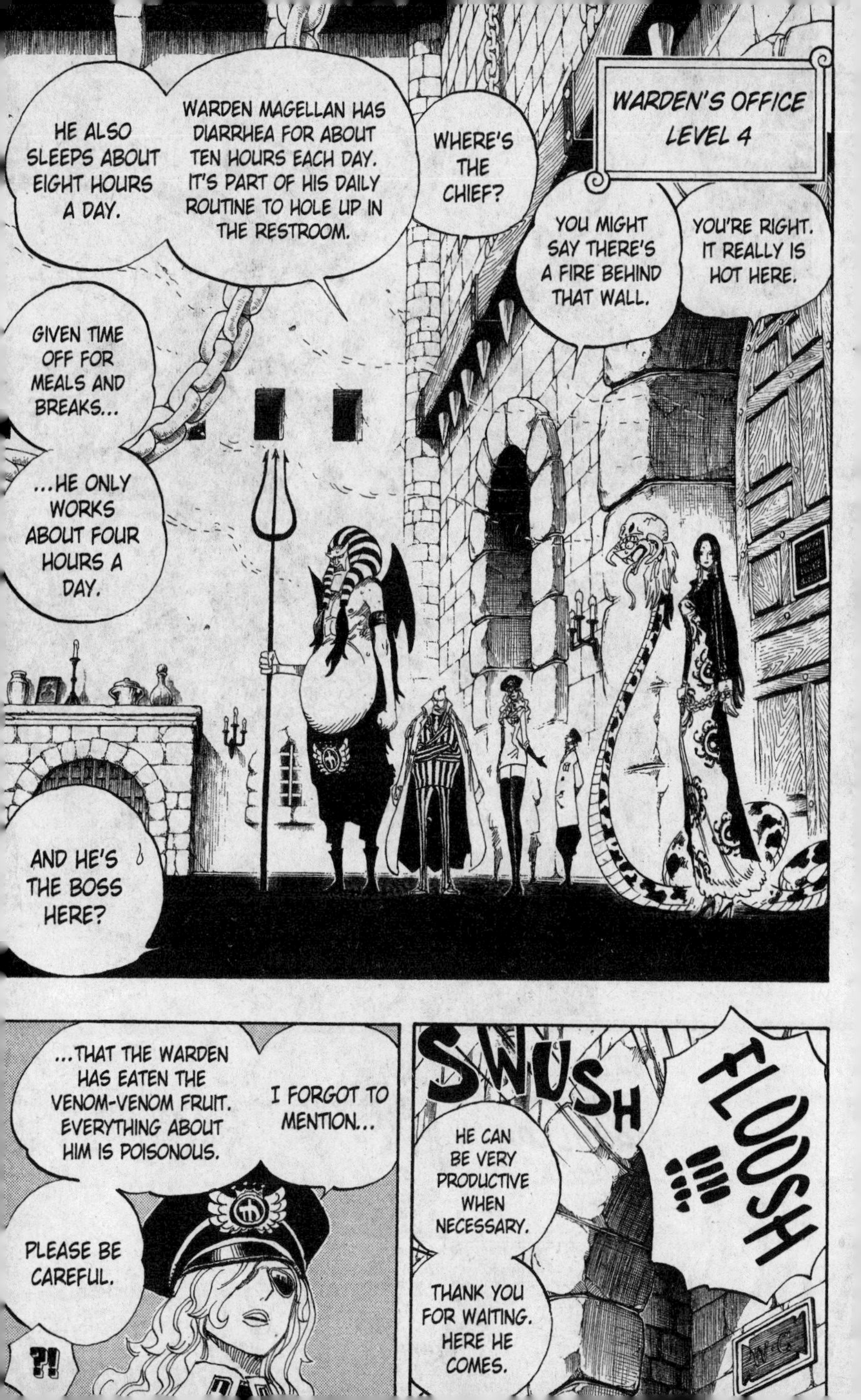
WARDEN'S OFFICE LEVEL 4
YOU'RE RIGHT. IT REALLY IS HOT HERE.
YOU MIGHT SAY THERE'S A FIRE BEHIND THAT WALL.
WHERE'S THE CHIEF?
WARDEN MAGELLAN HAS DIARRHEA FOR ABOUT TEN HOURS EACH DAY. IT'S PART OF HIS DAILY ROUTINE TO HOLE UP IN THE RESTROOM.
HE ALSO SLEEPS ABOUT EIGHT HOURS A DAY.
GIVEN TIME OFF FOR MEALS AND BREAKS...
...HE ONLY WORKS ABOUT FOUR HOURS A DAY.
AND HE'S THE BOSS HERE?
SWUSH
FLOOSH
HE CAN BE VERY PRODUCTIVE WHEN NECESSARY.
THANK YOU FOR WAITING. HERE HE COMES.
I FORGOT TO MENTION...
...THAT THE WARDEN HAS EATEN THE VENOM-VENOM FRUIT. EVERYTHING ABOUT HIM IS POISONOUS.
PLEASE BE CAREFUL.
?!

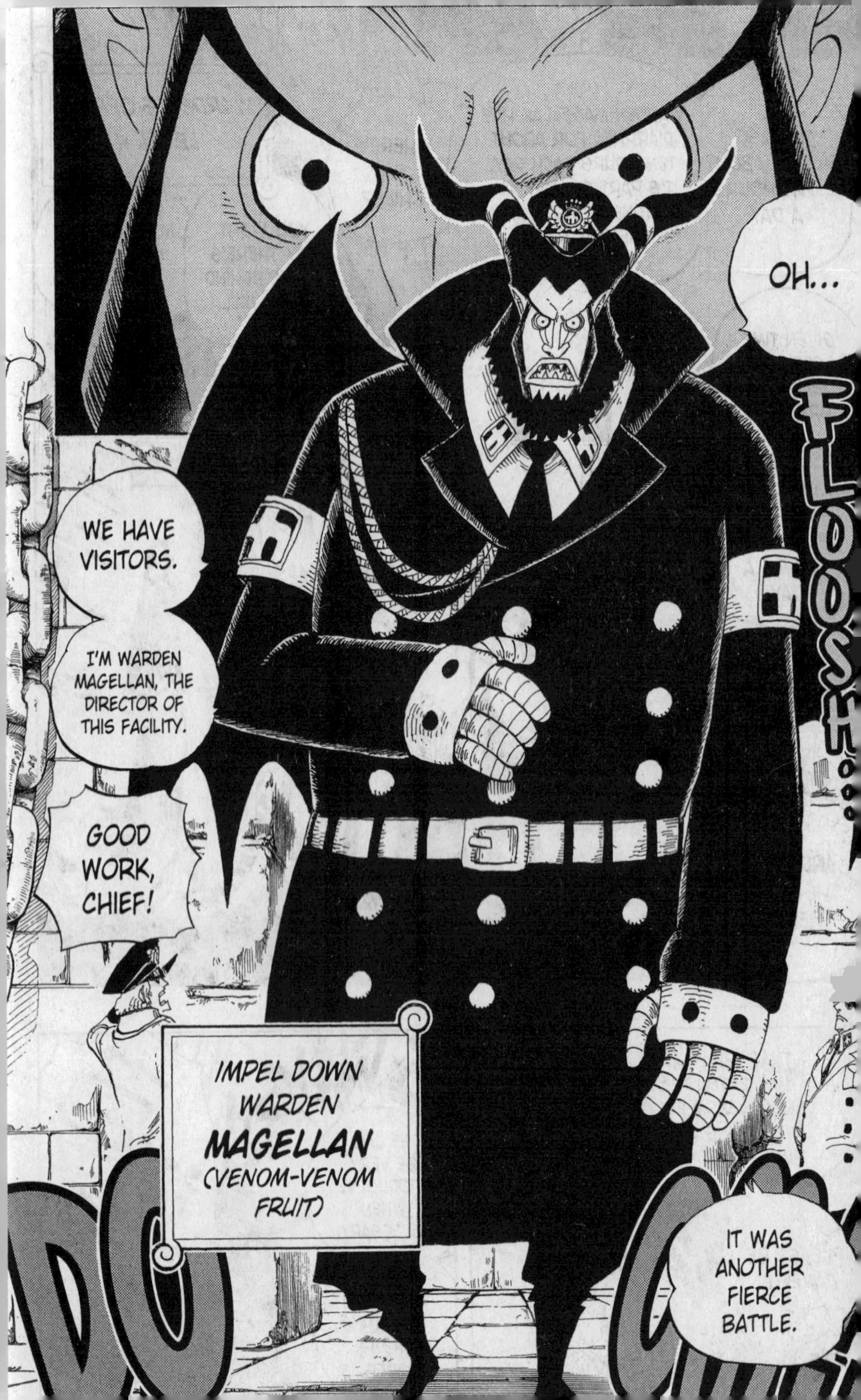
OH...
FLOOSH...
WE HAVE VISITORS.
I'M WARDEN MAGELLAN, THE DIRECTOR OF THIS FACILITY.
GOOD WORK, CHIEF!
IT WAS ANOTHER FIERCE BATTLE.
IMPEL DOWN WARDEN MAGELLAN (VENOM-VENOM FRUIT)

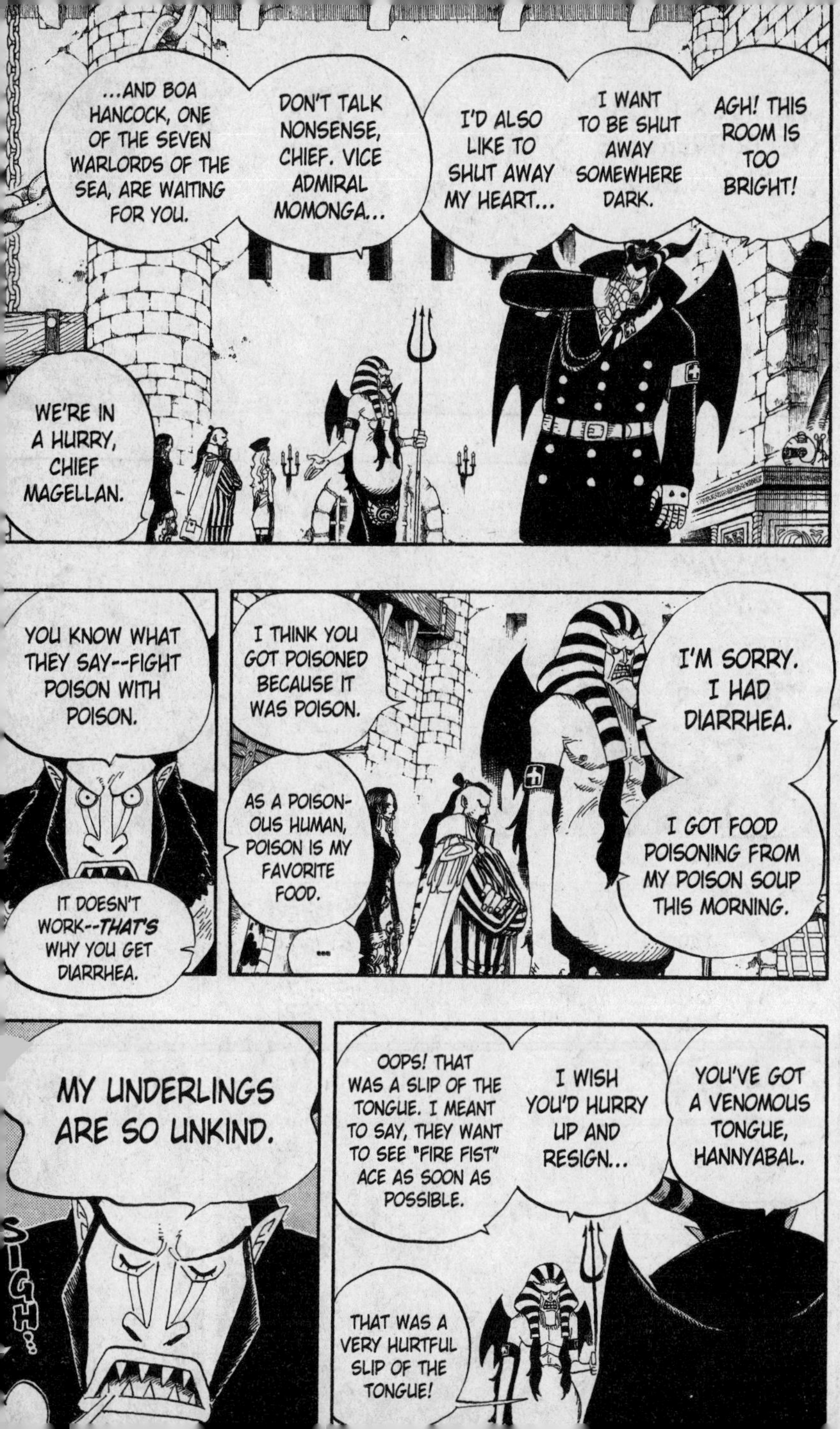
AGH! THIS ROOM IS TOO BRIGHT!
I WANT TO BE SHUT AWAY SOMEWHERE DARK.
I'D ALSO LIKE TO SHUT AWAY MY HEART...
DON'T TALK NONSENSE, CHIEF. VICE ADMIRAL MOMONGA...
...AND BOA HANCOCK, ONE OF THE SEVEN WARLORDS OF THE SEA, ARE WAITING FOR YOU.
WE'RE IN A HURRY, CHIEF MAGELLAN.
I'M SORRY. I HAD DIARRHEA.
I GOT FOOD POISONING FROM MY POISON SOUP THIS MORNING.
I THINK YOU GOT POISONED BECAUSE IT WAS POISON.
AS A POISONOUS HUMAN, POISON IS MY FAVORITE FOOD.
...
YOU KNOW WHAT THEY SAY--FIGHT POISON WITH POISON.
IT DOESN'T WORK--*THAT'S* WHY YOU GET DIARRHEA.
YOU'VE GOT A VENOMOUS TONGUE, HANNYABAL.
I WISH YOU'D HURRY UP AND RESIGN...
OOPS! THAT WAS A SLIP OF THE TONGUE. I MEANT TO SAY, THEY WANT TO SEE "FIRE FIST" ACE AS SOON AS POSSIBLE.
THAT WAS A VERY HURTFUL SLIP OF THE TONGUE!
MY UNDERLINGS ARE SO UNKIND.
SIGH...

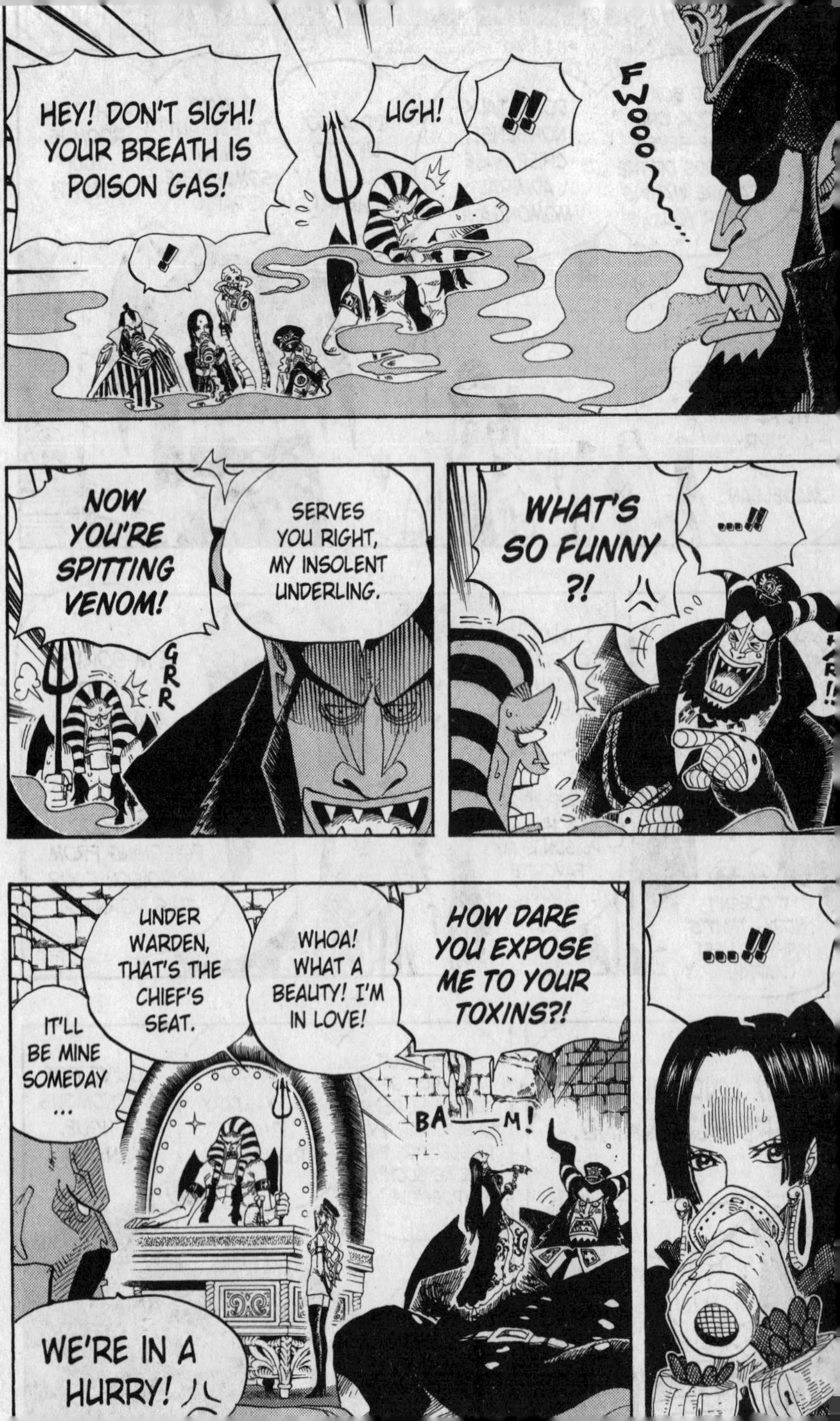
FWOOO~...
!!
UGH!
HEY! DON'T SIGH! YOUR BREATH IS POISON GAS!
!
...!!
WHAT'S SO FUNNY?!
SERVES YOU RIGHT, MY INSOLENT UNDERLING.
NOW YOU'RE SPITTING VENOM!
GRR
...!!
HOW DARE YOU EXPOSE ME TO YOUR TOXINS?!
BA—M!
WHOA! WHAT A BEAUTY! I'M IN LOVE!
UNDER WARDEN, THAT'S THE CHIEF'S SEAT.
IT'LL BE MINE SOMEDAY...
WE'RE IN A HURRY!

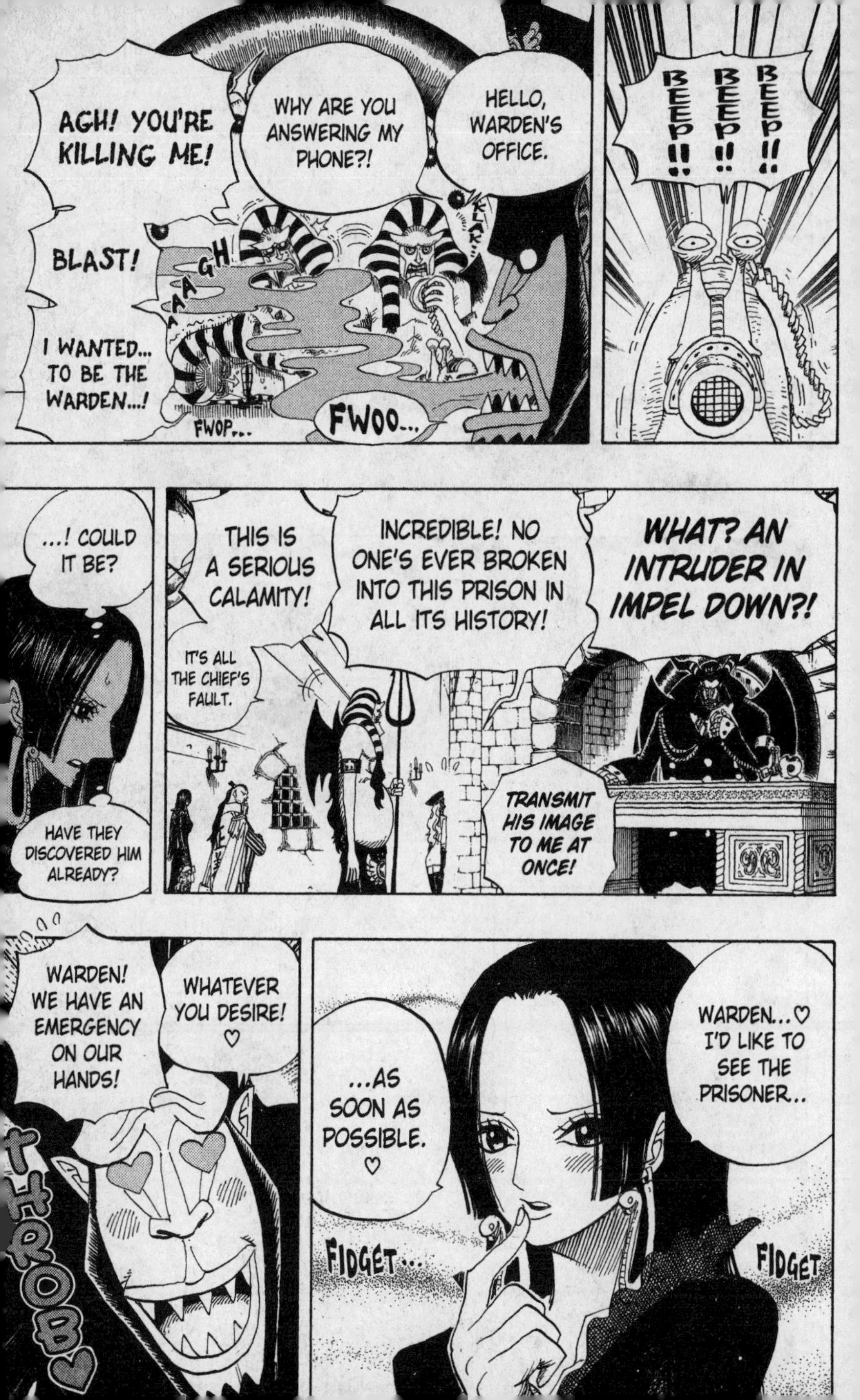
BEEP!! BEEP!! BEEP!!
HELLO, WARDEN'S OFFICE.
KLAK...
WHY ARE YOU ANSWERING MY PHONE?!
AGH! YOU'RE KILLING ME!
AAAGH
BLAST!
I WANTED... TO BE THE WARDEN...!
FWOO...
FWOP...
WHAT? AN INTRUDER IN IMPEL DOWN?!
INCREDIBLE! NO ONE'S EVER BROKEN INTO THIS PRISON IN ALL ITS HISTORY!
THIS IS A SERIOUS CALAMITY!
IT'S ALL THE CHIEF'S FAULT.
TRANSMIT HIS IMAGE TO ME AT ONCE!
...! COULD IT BE?
HAVE THEY DISCOVERED HIM ALREADY?
WARDEN...♡ I'D LIKE TO SEE THE PRISONER...
...AS SOON AS POSSIBLE. ♡
FIDGET
FIDGET...
WHATEVER YOU DESIRE! ♡
WARDEN! WE HAVE AN EMERGENCY ON OUR HANDS!
THROB♡

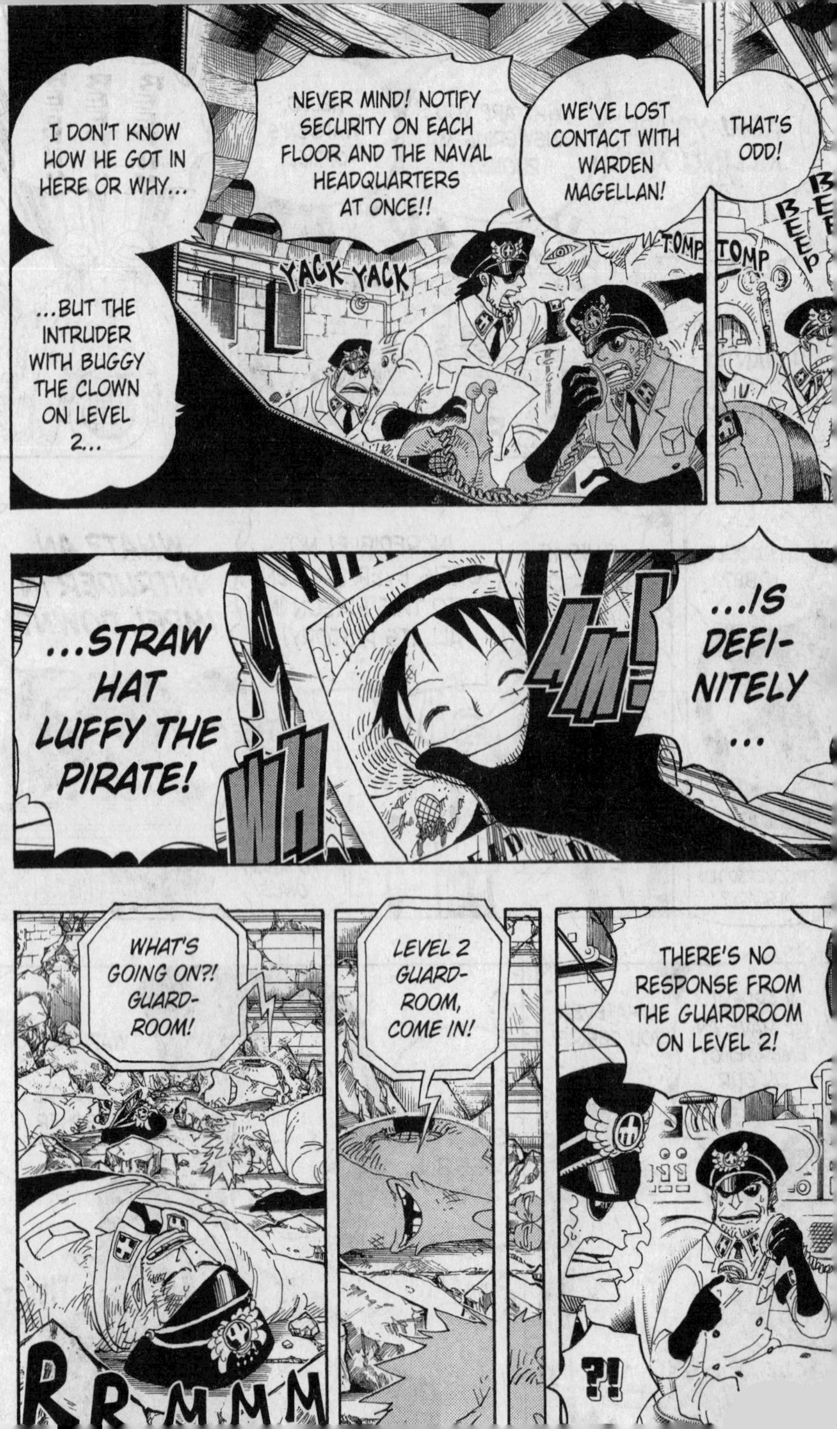
THAT'S ODD!
WE'VE LOST CONTACT WITH WARDEN MAGELLAN!
BEEP BEEP
TOMP TOMP
NEVER MIND! NOTIFY SECURITY ON EACH FLOOR AND THE NAVAL HEADQUARTERS AT ONCE!!
YACK YACK
I DON'T KNOW HOW HE GOT IN HERE OR WHY...
...BUT THE INTRUDER WITH BUGGY THE CLOWN ON LEVEL 2...
...IS DEFINITELY...
WHAM!
...STRAW HAT LUFFY THE PIRATE!
THERE'S NO RESPONSE FROM THE GUARDROOM ON LEVEL 2!
?!
LEVEL 2 GUARD-ROOM, COME IN!
WHAT'S GOING ON?! GUARD-ROOM!
RRMMM

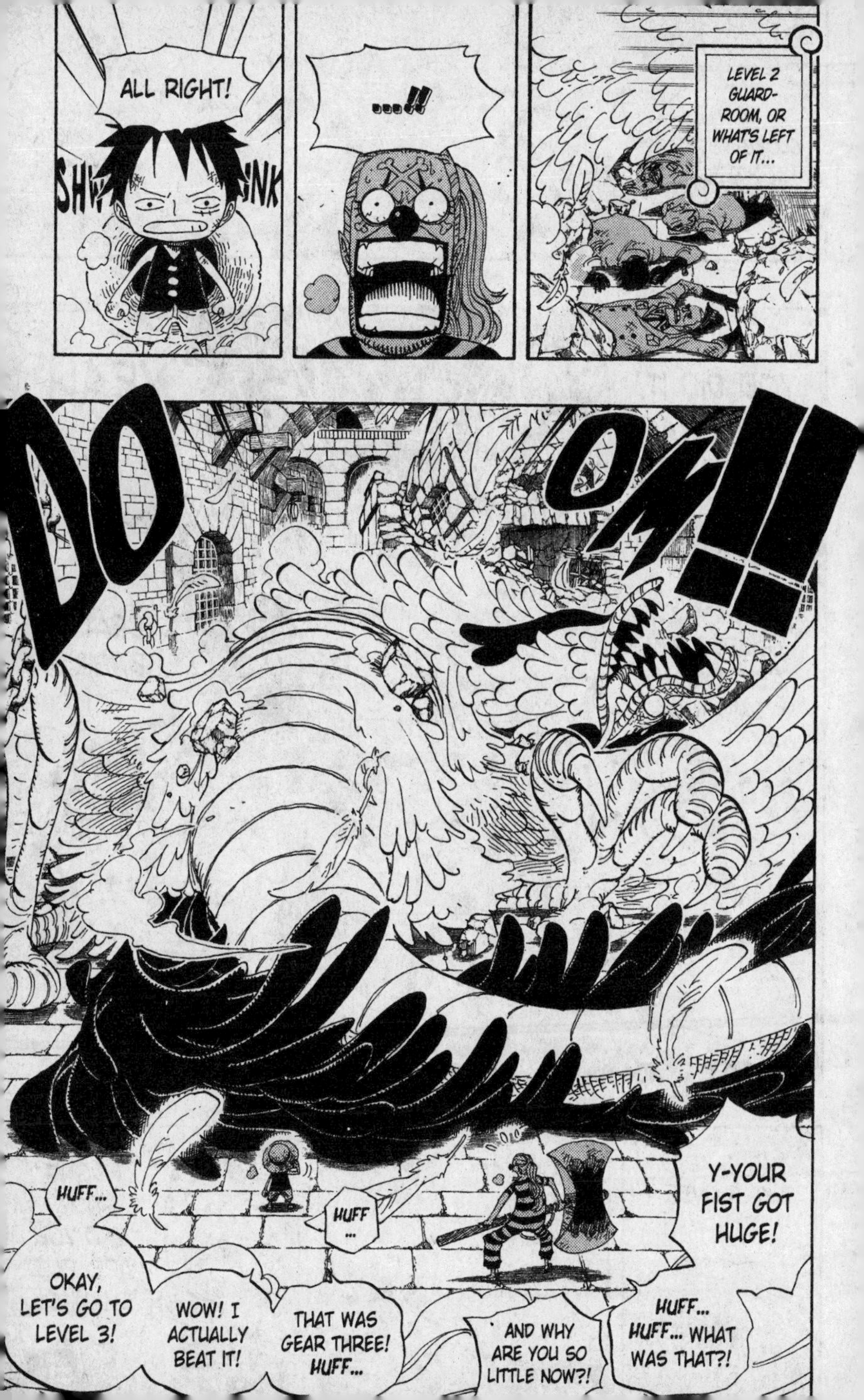
LEVEL 2 GUARD-ROOM, OR WHAT'S LEFT OF IT...
...!!
ALL RIGHT!
SHW
INK
DO
OM!!
Y-YOUR FIST GOT HUGE!
HUFF... HUFF... WHAT WAS THAT?!
AND WHY ARE YOU SO LITTLE NOW?!
HUFF ...
THAT WAS GEAR THREE! HUFF...
HUFF...
WOW! I ACTUALLY BEAT IT!
OKAY, LET'S GO TO LEVEL 3!

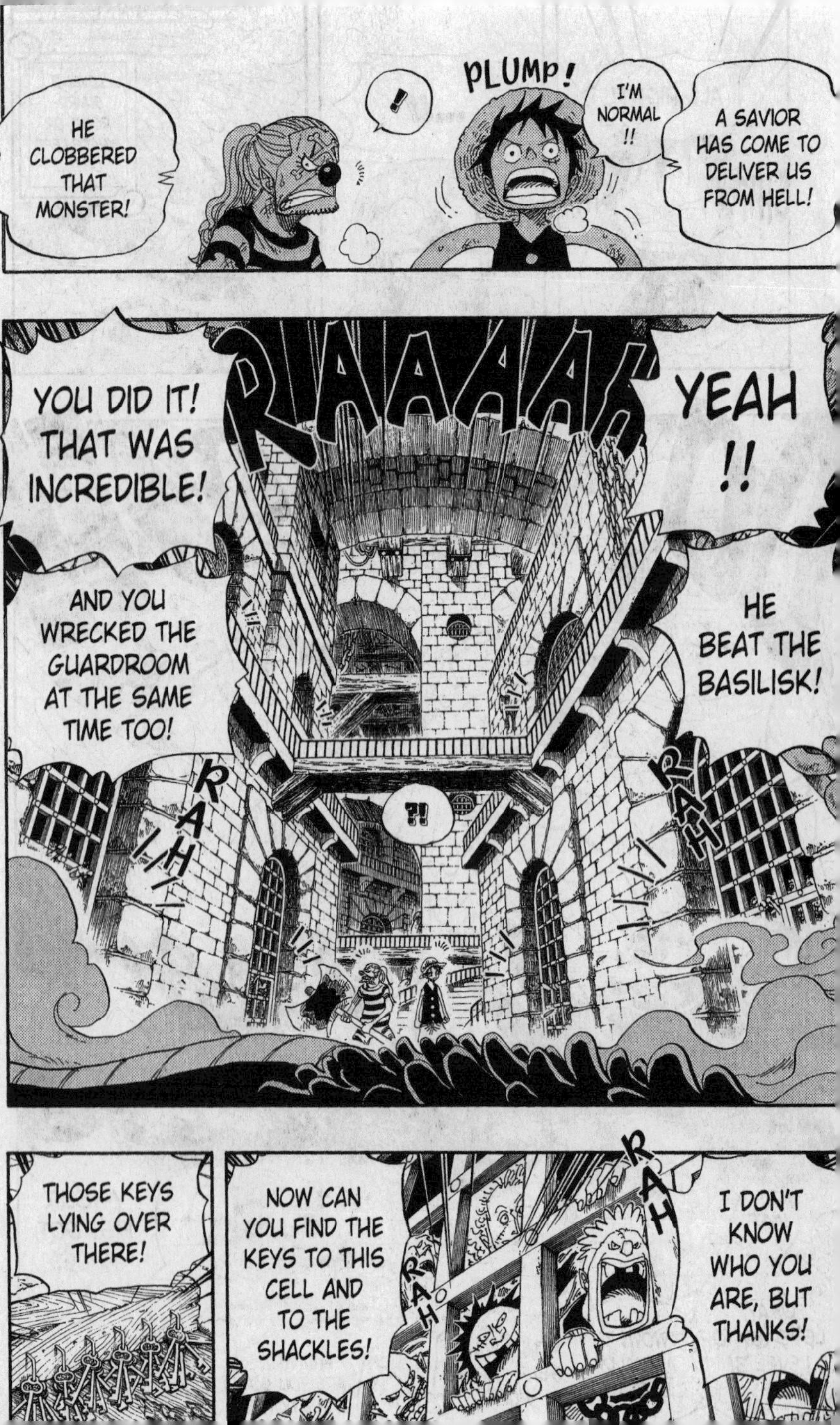
A SAVIOR HAS COME TO DELIVER US FROM HELL!
I'M NORMAL !!
PLUMP!
!
HE CLOBBERED THAT MONSTER!
YEAH !!
RAAAAAH
YOU DID IT! THAT WAS INCREDIBLE!
HE BEAT THE BASILISK!
AND YOU WRECKED THE GUARDROOM AT THE SAME TIME TOO!
RAH
RAH
?!
RAH
I DON'T KNOW WHO YOU ARE, BUT THANKS!
NOW CAN YOU FIND THE KEYS TO THIS CELL AND TO THE SHACKLES!
RAH
THOSE KEYS LYING OVER THERE!

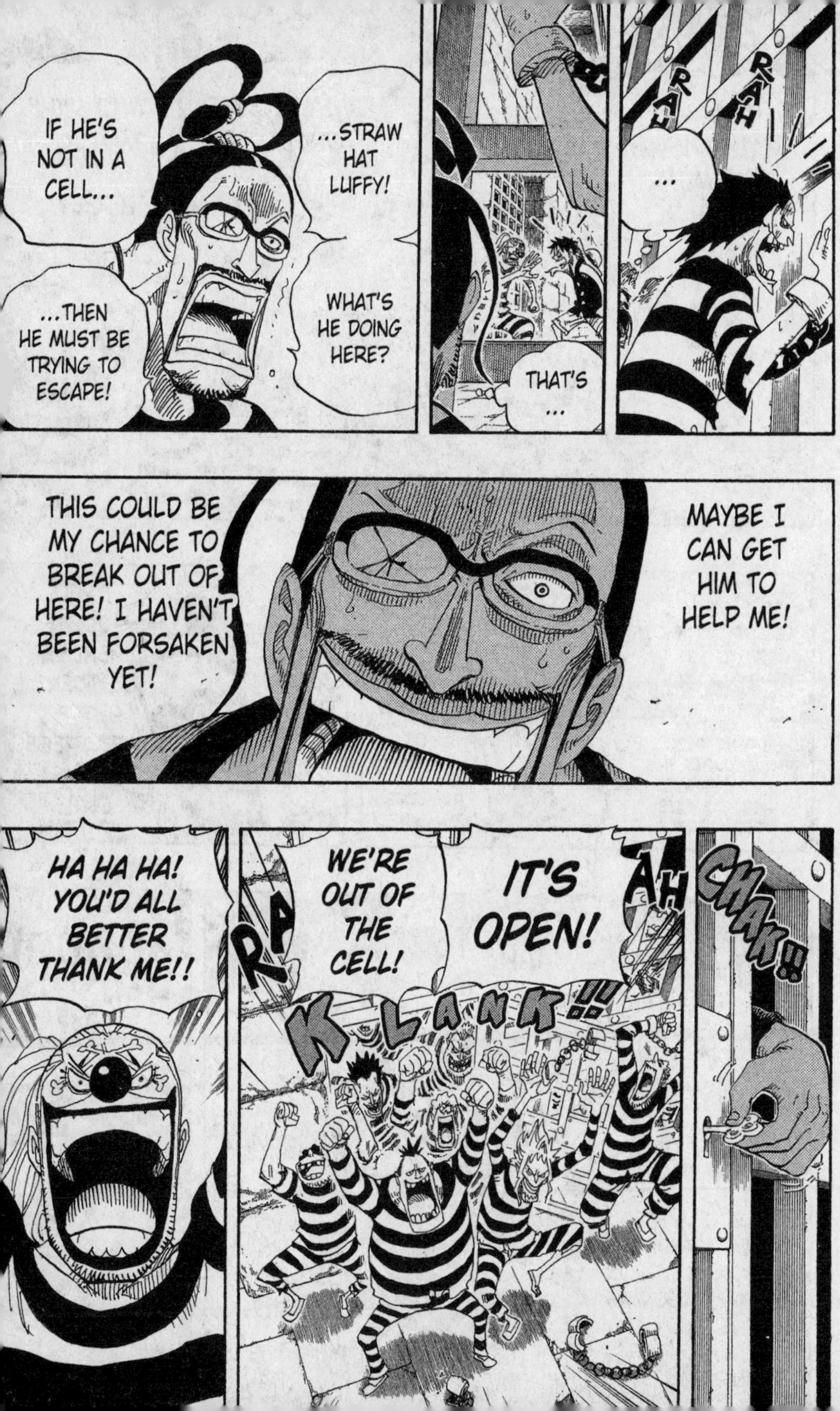
RAH
RAH
...
THAT'S ...
...STRAW HAT LUFFY!
WHAT'S HE DOING HERE?
IF HE'S NOT IN A CELL...
...THEN HE MUST BE TRYING TO ESCAPE!
THIS COULD BE MY CHANCE TO BREAK OUT OF HERE! I HAVEN'T BEEN FORSAKEN YET!
MAYBE I CAN GET HIM TO HELP ME!
CHAK!!
AH
IT'S OPEN!
WE'RE OUT OF THE CELL!
RA
KLANK!!
HA HA HA! YOU'D ALL BETTER THANK ME!!

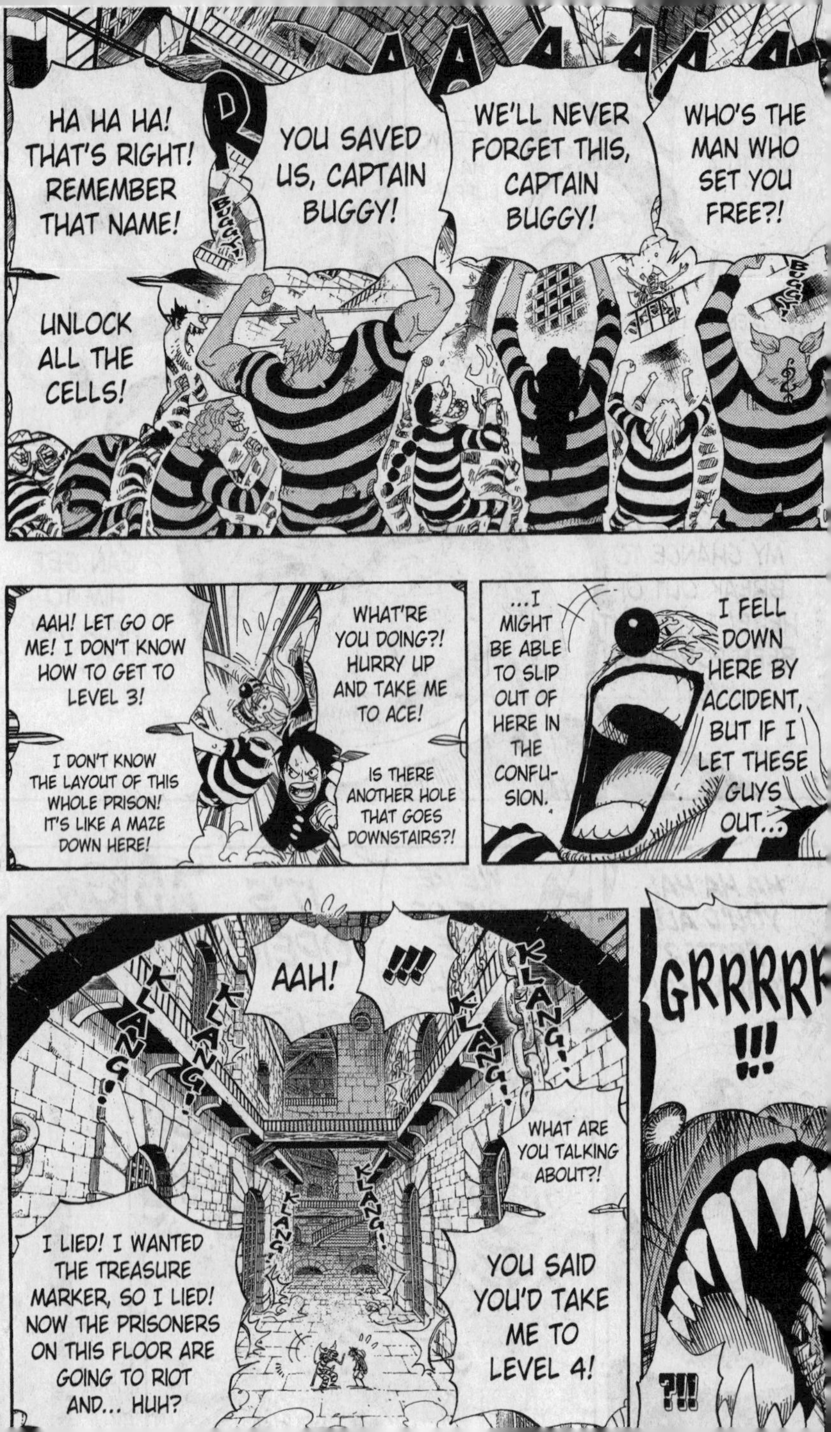
WHO'S THE MAN WHO SET YOU FREE?!
WE'LL NEVER FORGET THIS, CAPTAIN BUGGY!
YOU SAVED US, CAPTAIN BUGGY!
HA HA HA! THAT'S RIGHT! REMEMBER THAT NAME!
UNLOCK ALL THE CELLS!
I FELL DOWN HERE BY ACCIDENT, BUT IF I LET THESE GUYS OUT...
...I MIGHT BE ABLE TO SLIP OUT OF HERE IN THE CONFU-SION.
WHAT'RE YOU DOING?! HURRY UP AND TAKE ME TO ACE!
AAH! LET GO OF ME! I DON'T KNOW HOW TO GET TO LEVEL 3!
IS THERE ANOTHER HOLE THAT GOES DOWNSTAIRS?!
I DON'T KNOW THE LAYOUT OF THIS WHOLE PRISON! IT'S LIKE A MAZE DOWN HERE!
GRRRRR
!!!
?!!
!!!
AAH!
KLANG!
KLANG!
KLANG!
KLANG!
KLANG!
KLANG!
YOU SAID YOU'D TAKE ME TO LEVEL 4!
WHAT ARE YOU TALKING ABOUT?!
I LIED! I WANTED THE TREASURE MARKER, SO I LIED! NOW THE PRISONERS ON THIS FLOOR ARE GOING TO RIOT AND... HUH?

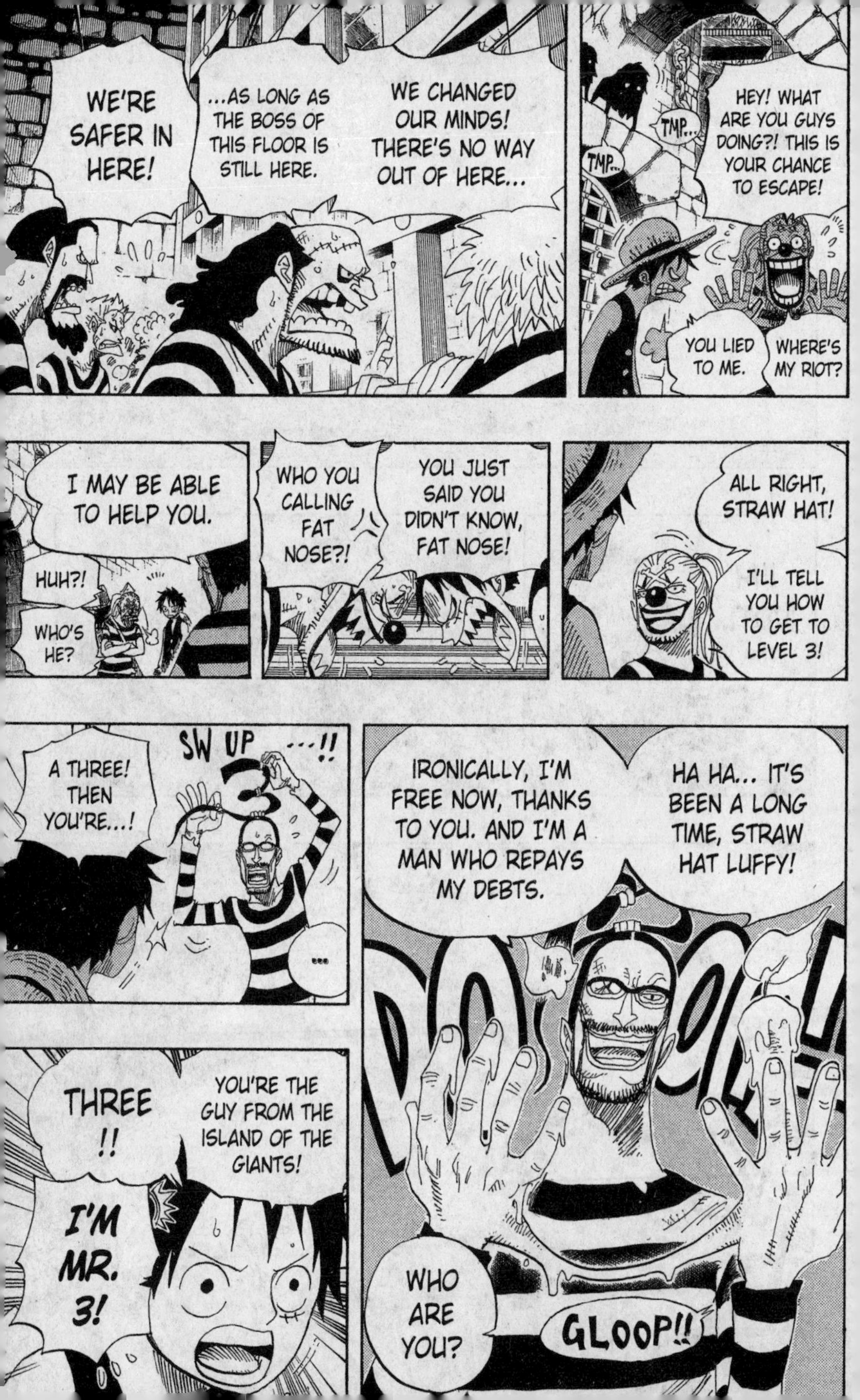
TMP...
TMP...
HEY! WHAT ARE YOU GUYS DOING?! THIS IS YOUR CHANCE TO ESCAPE!
WHERE'S MY RIOT?
YOU LIED TO ME.
WE CHANGED OUR MINDS! THERE'S NO WAY OUT OF HERE...
...AS LONG AS THE BOSS OF THIS FLOOR IS STILL HERE.
WE'RE SAFER IN HERE!
ALL RIGHT, STRAW HAT!
I'LL TELL YOU HOW TO GET TO LEVEL 3!
YOU JUST SAID YOU DIDN'T KNOW, FAT NOSE!
WHO YOU CALLING FAT NOSE?!
I MAY BE ABLE TO HELP YOU.
HUH?!
WHO'S HE?
HA HA... IT'S BEEN A LONG TIME, STRAW HAT LUFFY!
IRONICALLY, I'M FREE NOW, THANKS TO YOU. AND I'M A MAN WHO REPAYS MY DEBTS.
GLOOP!!
WHO ARE YOU?
SW UP
...!!
A THREE! THEN YOU'RE...!
...
YOU'RE THE GUY FROM THE ISLAND OF THE GIANTS!
THREE !!
I'M MR. 3!

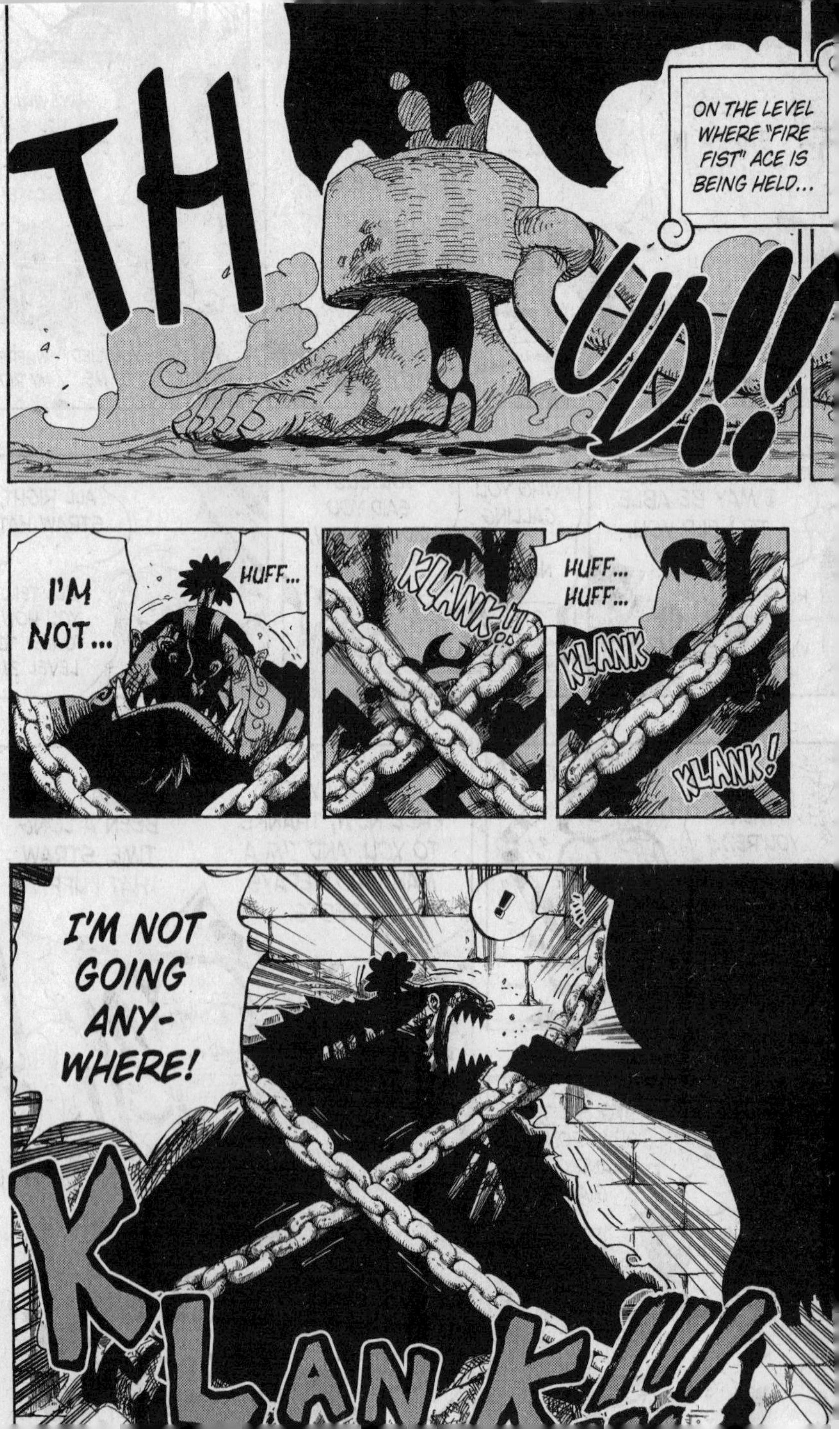
ON THE LEVEL WHERE "FIRE FIST" ACE IS BEING HELD...
THUD!!
HUFF...
I'M NOT...
KLANK!!
HUFF... HUFF...
KLANK
KLANK!
!
I'M NOT GOING ANY-WHERE!
KLANK!!!

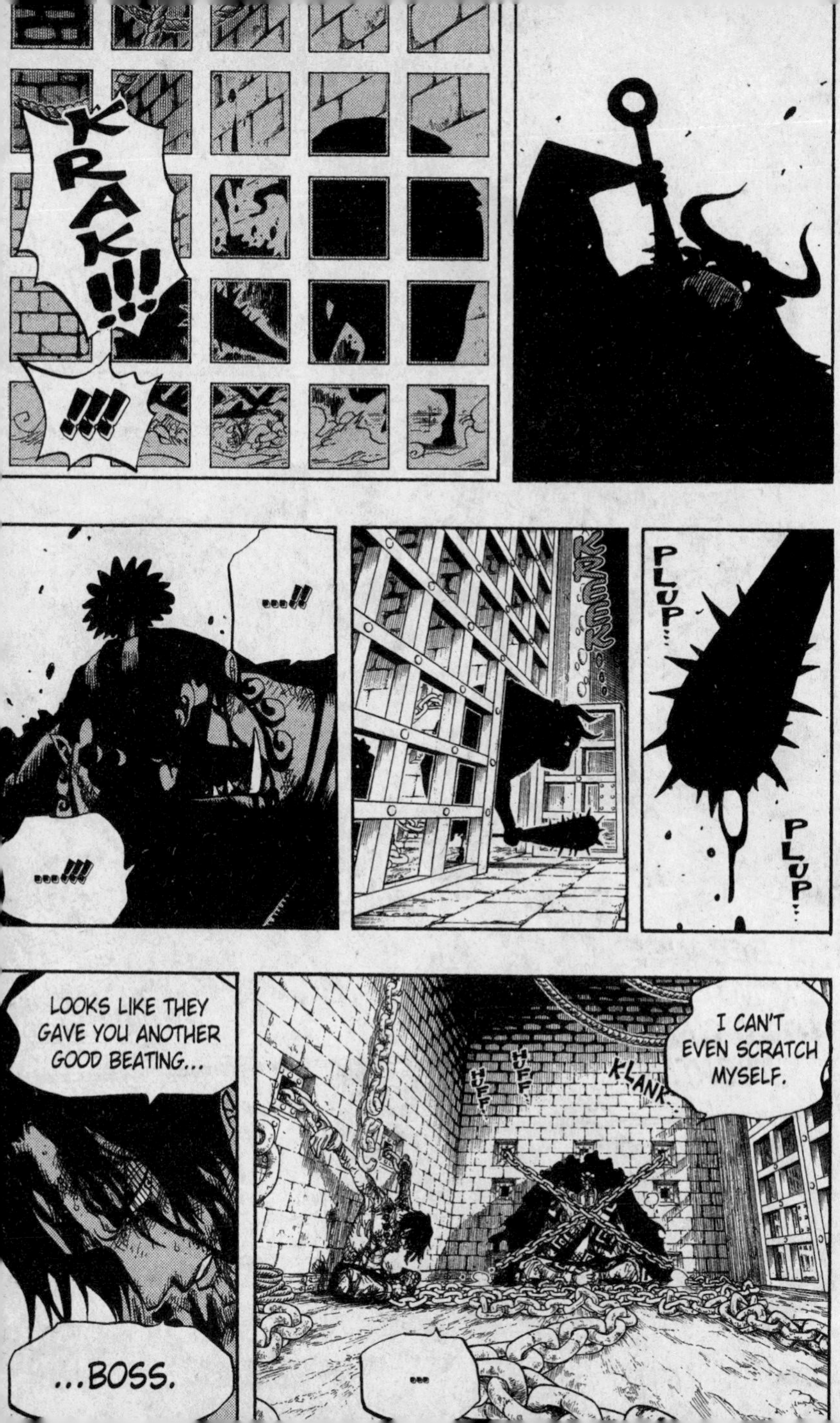
KRAK!!!
!!!
PLUP...
PLUP...
KREEK
...!!
...!!!
I CAN'T EVEN SCRATCH MYSELF.
KLANK
HUFF
HUFF
...
LOOKS LIKE THEY GAVE YOU ANOTHER GOOD BEATING...
...BOSS.

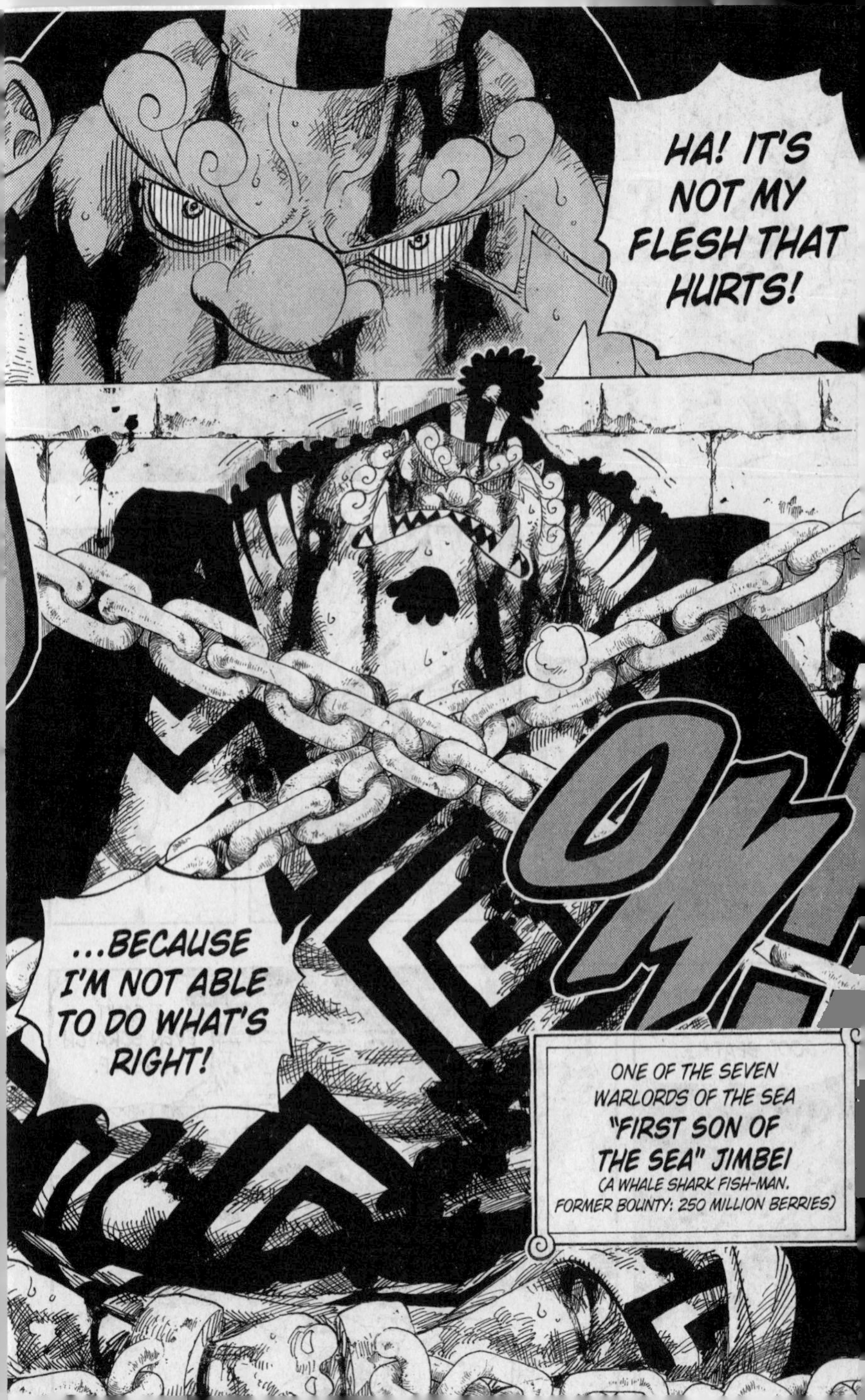
HA! IT'S NOT MY FLESH THAT HURTS!
...BECAUSE I'M NOT ABLE TO DO WHAT'S RIGHT!
ONE OF THE SEVEN WARLORDS OF THE SEA "FIRST SON OF THE SEA" JIMBEI (A WHALE SHARK FISH-MAN. FORMER BOUNTY: 250 MILLION BERRIES)

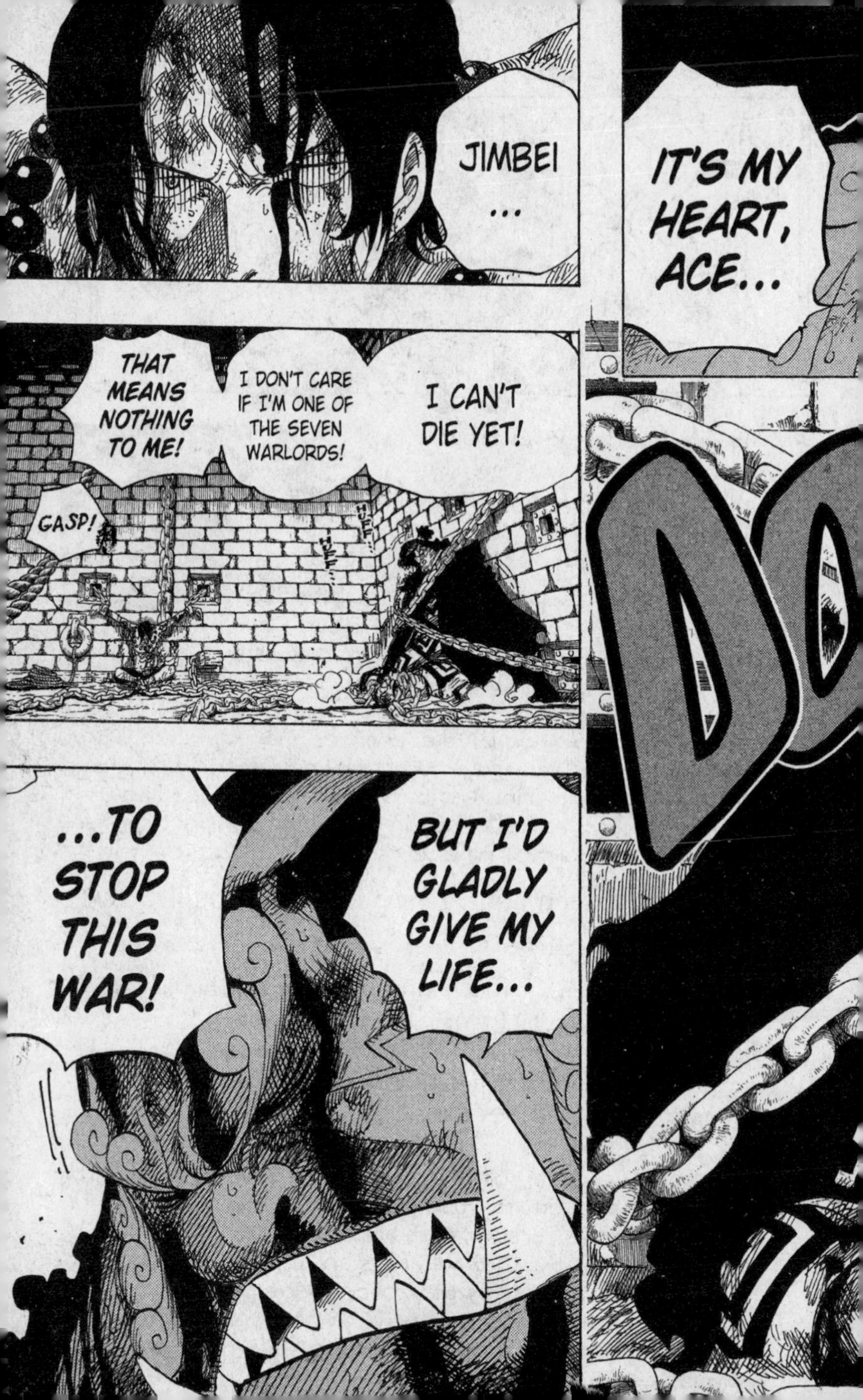
IT'S MY HEART, ACE...
JIMBEI ...
I CAN'T DIE YET!
I DON'T CARE IF I'M ONE OF THE SEVEN WARLORDS!
THAT MEANS NOTHING TO ME!
GASP!
HUFF
HUFF
BUT I'D GLADLY GIVE MY LIFE...
...TO STOP THIS WAR!

SBS Question Corner

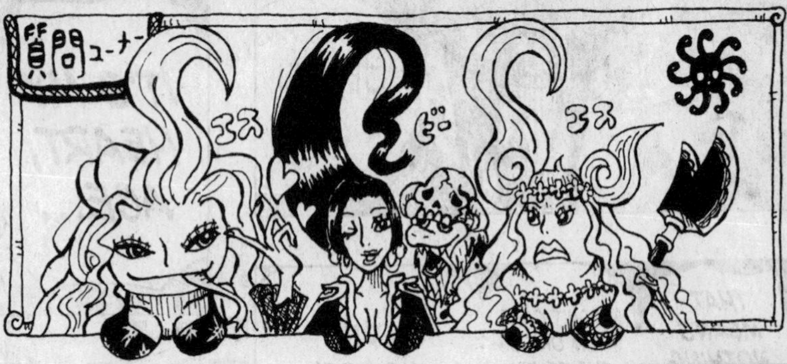

(Park won-Yong, Korea)

Q: Mr. Oda, Boa Hancock came out on the cover of *Jump* nine years ago! That really surprised me. Is this really her? Please tell me.

--PX-10000

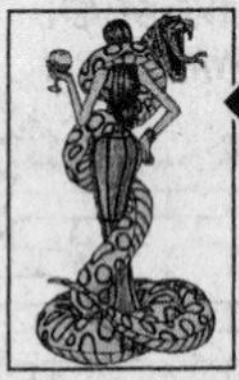

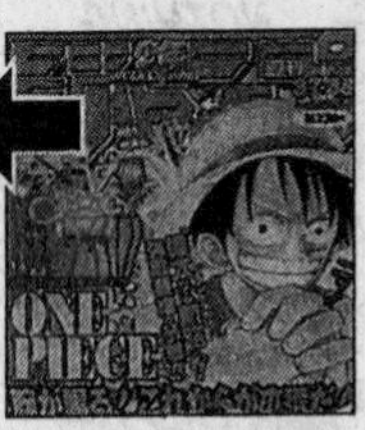
ONE PIECE

A: I'm the one who's surprised! People on the internet noticed this but I completely forgot about it. This picture was in the illustration collection, *Color Walk 2*, but during that time, the crew had just entered the Grand Line. The editors told me to draw the back view of the "enemies that will come." I drew about four, and I remember that Hancock was one of them. When I actually did bring her out in the comic, a lot about her is different, but that design is indeed Warlord Boa Hancock that I thought of nine years ago.

Q: Red light. Green light! I got you! Moss Ball! --Nashi

A: Haha! Zolo got caught! Neener neener neener! Okay.

Q: Hello, Odacchi. I am writing this letter from Liguria. (Liguria is a region of Italy, not Water Seven) I want to know the connections the two agents that went to Ohara with Spandine have with the current CP9 agents. I get the feeling that the guy with the glasses is Kalifa's father. Thank you for making Robin!

--Dario

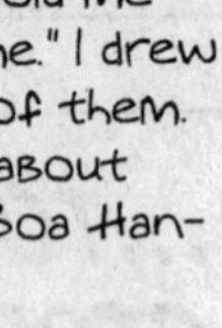

A: Kalifa's dad! You're absolutely right. I didn't give out any hints at all about it. I told my editor at the time about it, but this person (➡) is actually Kalifa's father. Most of the CP9 members are orphans that have been trained by the government, but we thought it might be interesting if among those children are some who belong to a long bloodline of agents. Kumadori's mom isn't one of them, by the way.

Chapter 529:
LEVEL 2: BEAST HELL

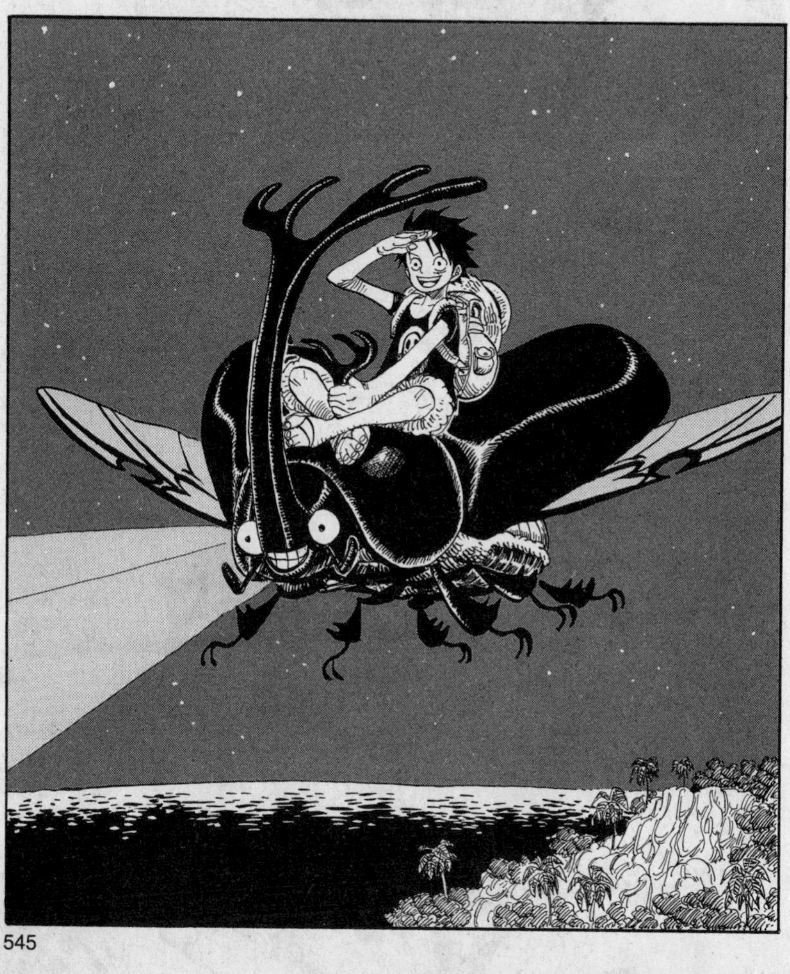

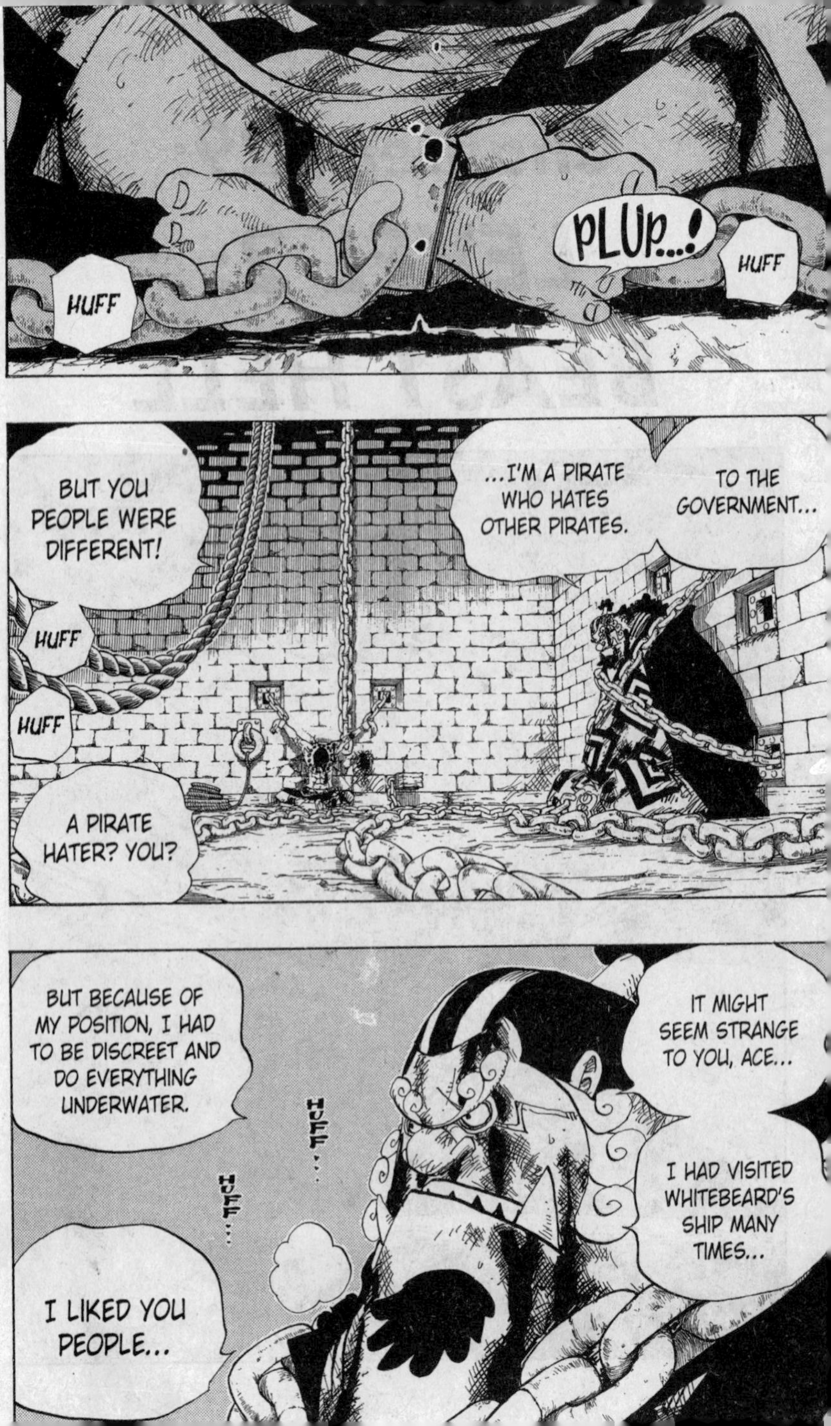
PLUP...!
HUFF
HUFF
TO THE GOVERNMENT...
...I'M A PIRATE WHO HATES OTHER PIRATES.
BUT YOU PEOPLE WERE DIFFERENT!
HUFF
HUFF
A PIRATE HATER? YOU?
IT MIGHT SEEM STRANGE TO YOU, ACE...
I HAD VISITED WHITEBEARD'S SHIP MANY TIMES...
BUT BECAUSE OF MY POSITION, I HAD TO BE DISCREET AND DO EVERYTHING UNDERWATER.
HUFF...
HUFF...
I LIKED YOU PEOPLE...

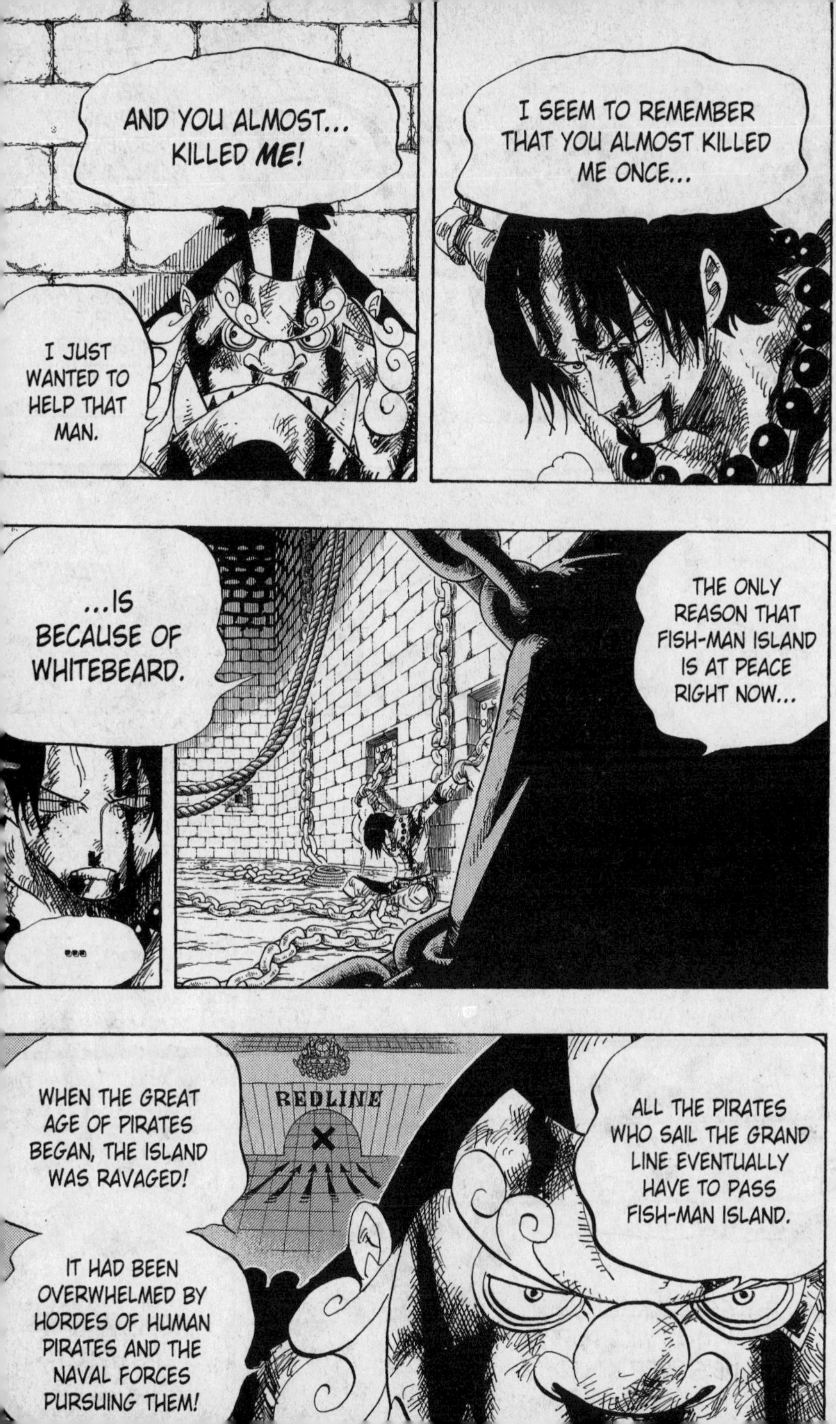
I SEEM TO REMEMBER THAT YOU ALMOST KILLED ME ONCE...
AND YOU ALMOST... KILLED *ME*!
I JUST WANTED TO HELP THAT MAN.
THE ONLY REASON THAT FISH-MAN ISLAND IS AT PEACE RIGHT NOW...
...IS BECAUSE OF WHITEBEARD.
...
ALL THE PIRATES WHO SAIL THE GRAND LINE EVENTUALLY HAVE TO PASS FISH-MAN ISLAND.
REDLINE
WHEN THE GREAT AGE OF PIRATES BEGAN, THE ISLAND WAS RAVAGED!
IT HAD BEEN OVERWHELMED BY HORDES OF HUMAN PIRATES AND THE NAVAL FORCES PURSUING THEM!

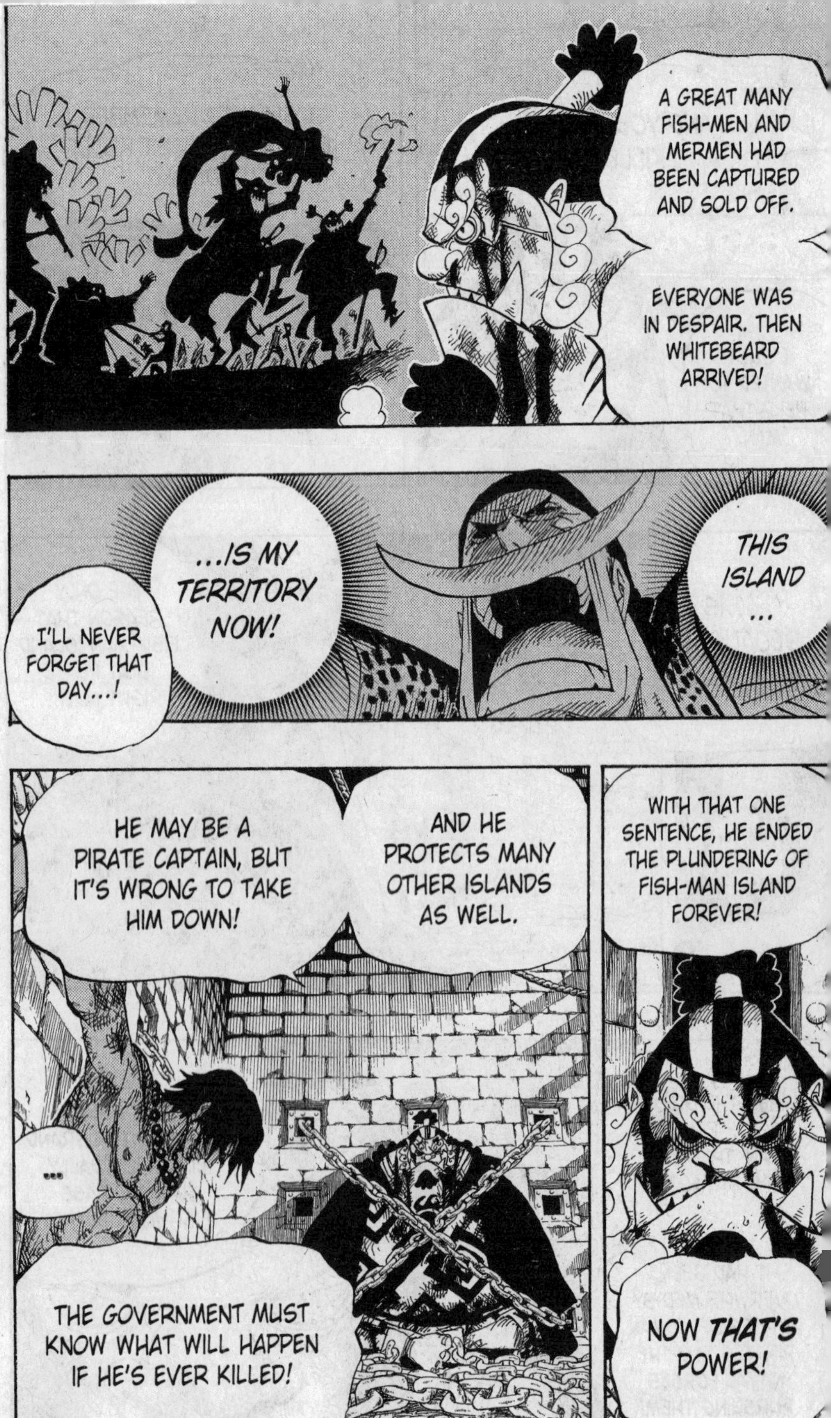
A GREAT MANY FISH-MEN AND MERMEN HAD BEEN CAPTURED AND SOLD OFF.
EVERYONE WAS IN DESPAIR. THEN WHITEBEARD ARRIVED!
THIS ISLAND ...
...IS MY TERRITORY NOW!
I'LL NEVER FORGET THAT DAY...!
WITH THAT ONE SENTENCE, HE ENDED THE PLUNDERING OF FISH-MAN ISLAND FOREVER!
NOW *THAT'S* POWER!
AND HE PROTECTS MANY OTHER ISLANDS AS WELL.
HE MAY BE A PIRATE CAPTAIN, BUT IT'S WRONG TO TAKE HIM DOWN!
...
THE GOVERNMENT MUST KNOW WHAT WILL HAPPEN IF HE'S EVER KILLED!

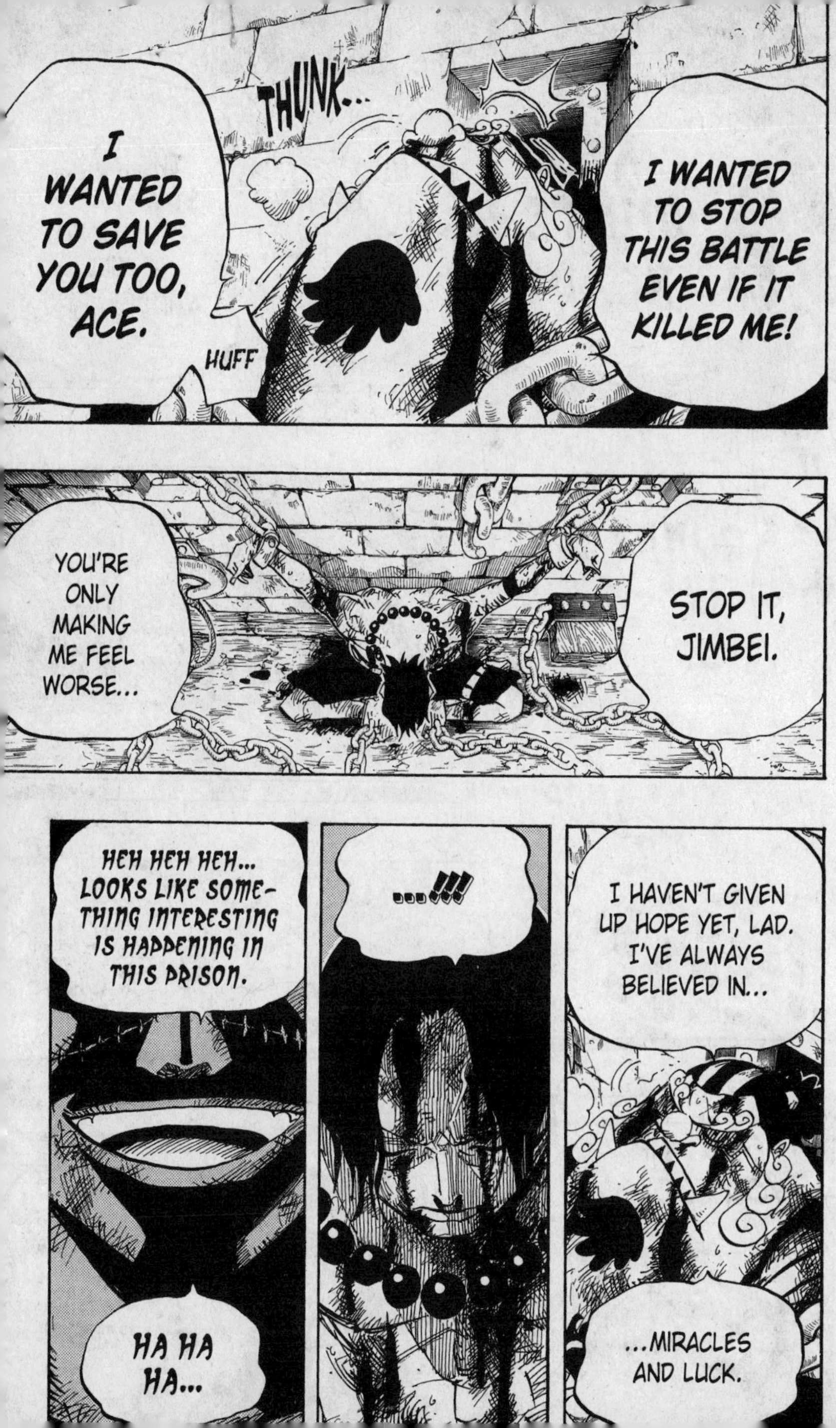
I WANTED TO STOP THIS BATTLE EVEN IF IT KILLED ME!
THUNK...
I WANTED TO SAVE YOU TOO, ACE.
HUFF
STOP IT, JIMBEI.
YOU'RE ONLY MAKING ME FEEL WORSE...
I HAVEN'T GIVEN UP HOPE YET, LAD. I'VE ALWAYS BELIEVED IN...
...MIRACLES AND LUCK.
...!!!
HEH HEH HEH... LOOKS LIKE SOME-THING INTERESTING IS HAPPENING IN THIS PRISON.
HA HA HA...

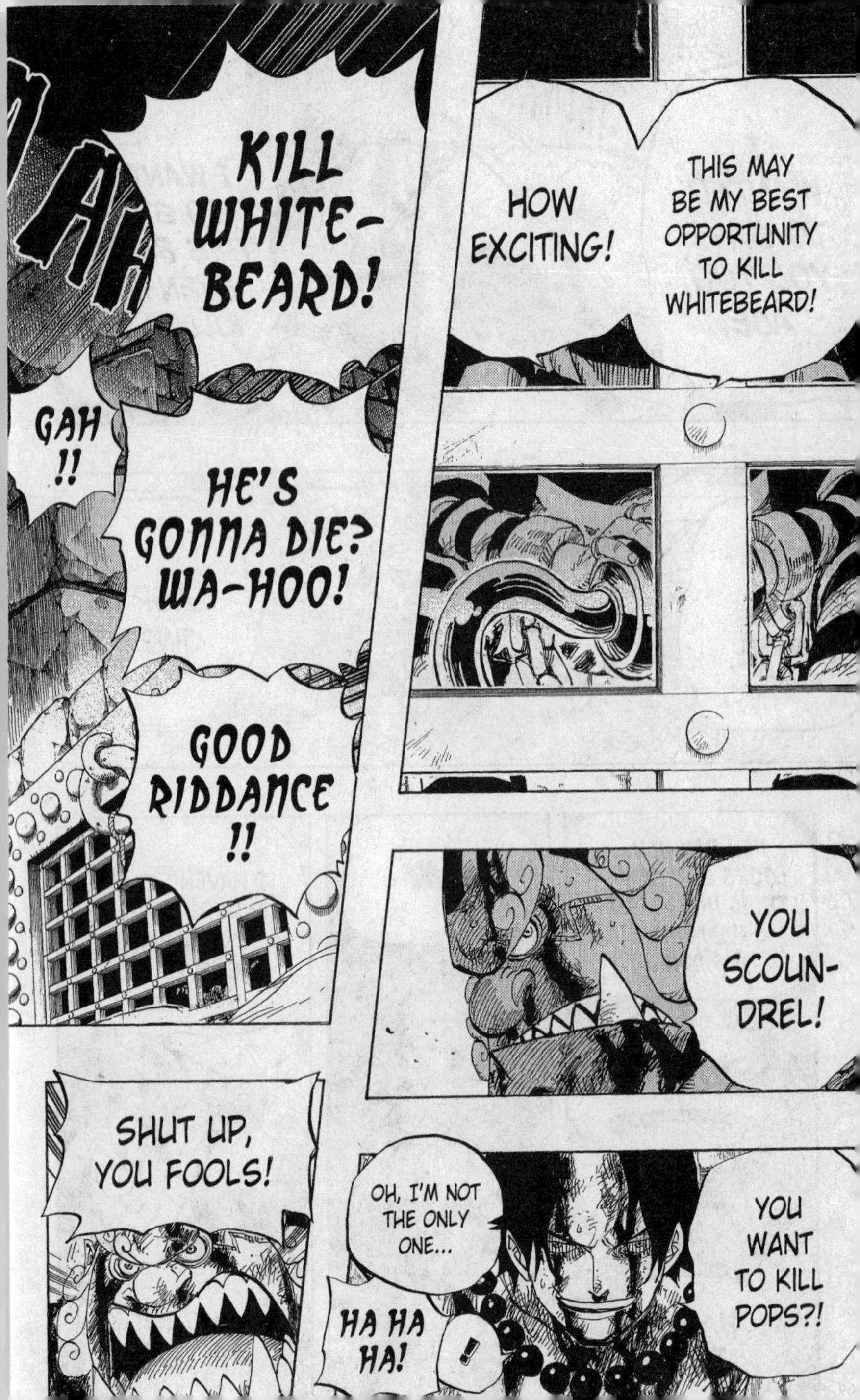
THIS MAY BE MY BEST OPPORTUNITY TO KILL WHITEBEARD!
HOW EXCITING!
YOU SCOUN-DREL!
KILL WHITE-BEARD!
GAH !!
HE'S GONNA DIE? WA-HOO!
GOOD RIDDANCE !!
YOU WANT TO KILL POPS?!
OH, I'M NOT THE ONLY ONE...
!
HA HA HA!
SHUT UP, YOU FOOLS!

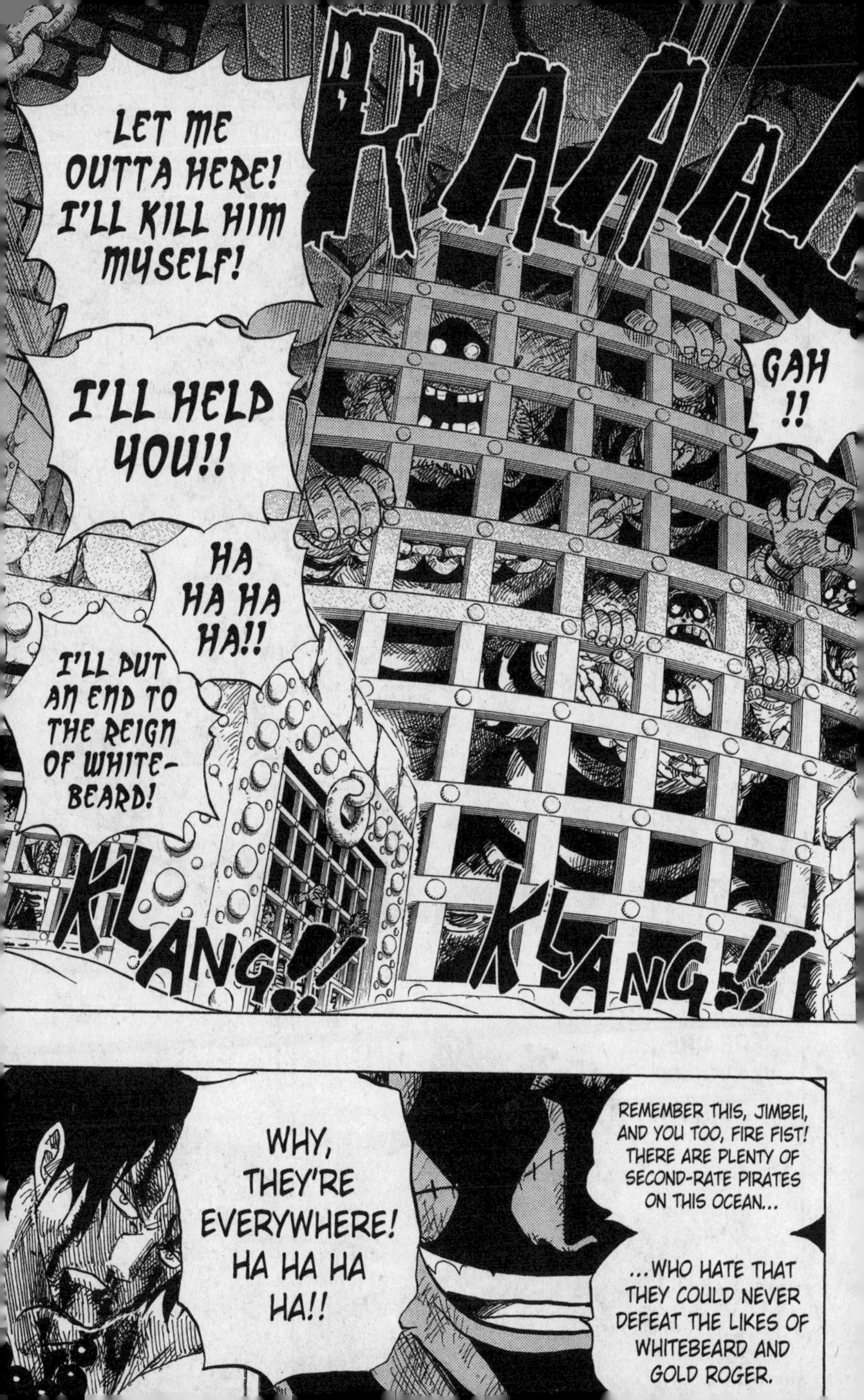
RAAA
LET ME OUTTA HERE! I'LL KILL HIM MYSELF!
GAH!!
I'LL HELP YOU!!
HA HA HA HA!!
I'LL PUT AN END TO THE REIGN OF WHITE-BEARD!
KLANG!!
KLANG!!
REMEMBER THIS, JIMBEI, AND YOU TOO, FIRE FIST! THERE ARE PLENTY OF SECOND-RATE PIRATES ON THIS OCEAN...
...WHO HATE THAT THEY COULD NEVER DEFEAT THE LIKES OF WHITEBEARD AND GOLD ROGER.
WHY, THEY'RE EVERYWHERE! HA HA HA HA!!

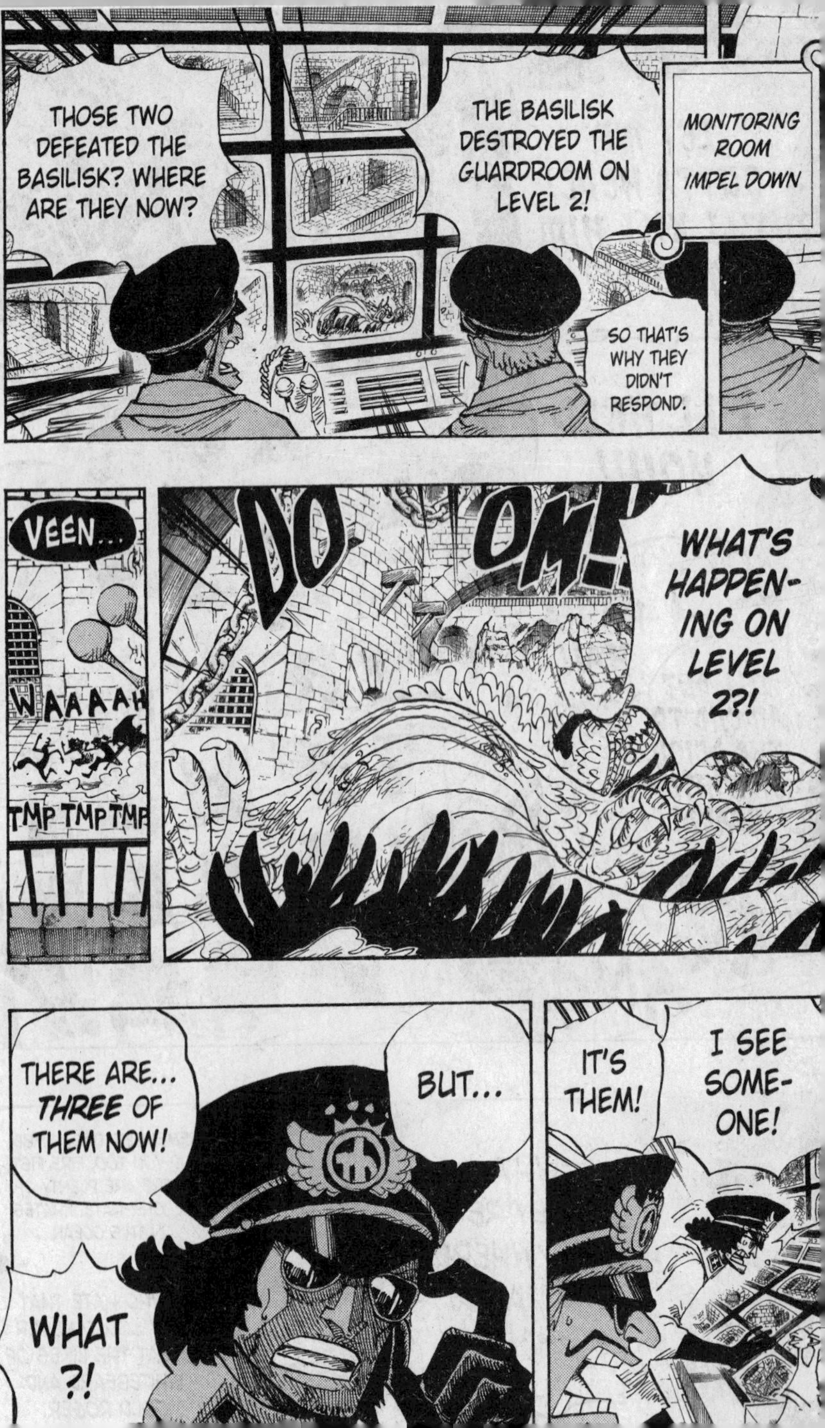

MONITORING ROOM IMPEL DOWN
THE BASILISK DESTROYED THE GUARDROOM ON LEVEL 2!
SO THAT'S WHY THEY DIDN'T RESPOND.
THOSE TWO DEFEATED THE BASILISK? WHERE ARE THEY NOW?
WHAT'S HAPPENING ON LEVEL 2?!
DO...OM!!
VEEN...
WAAAAH
TMP TMP TMP
I SEE SOMEONE!
IT'S THEM!
BUT...
THERE ARE... *THREE* OF THEM NOW!
WHAT ?!

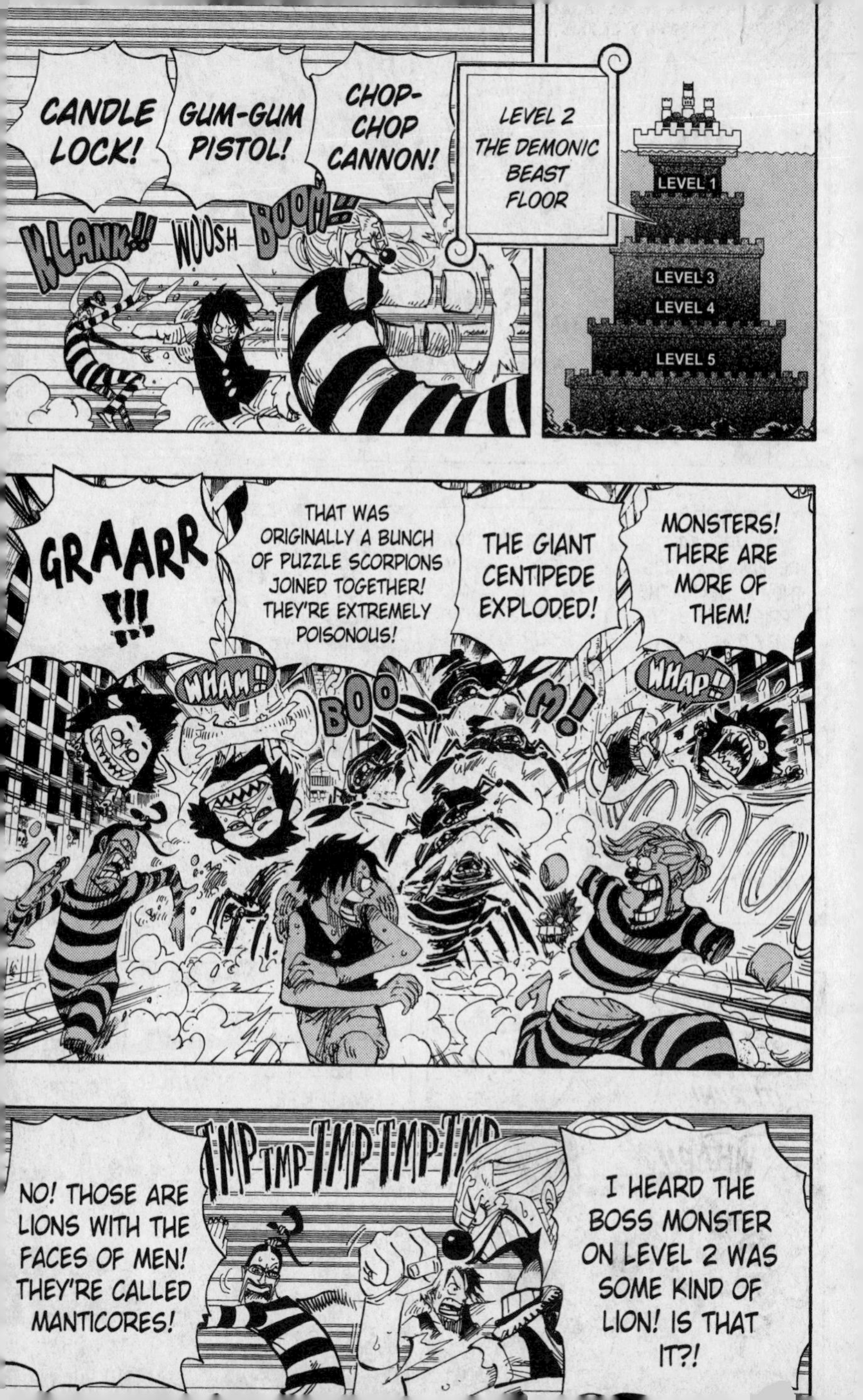
LEVEL 2 THE DEMONIC BEAST FLOOR
LEVEL 1
LEVEL 3
LEVEL 4
LEVEL 5
CHOP-CHOP CANNON!
GUM-GUM PISTOL!
CANDLE LOCK!
BOOM!!
WOOSH
KLANK!!
MONSTERS! THERE ARE MORE OF THEM!
THE GIANT CENTIPEDE EXPLODED!
THAT WAS ORIGINALLY A BUNCH OF PUZZLE SCORPIONS JOINED TOGETHER! THEY'RE EXTREMELY POISONOUS!
GRAARR!!!
WHAP!!
BOOM!
WHAM!!
TMP TMP TMP TMP TMP
I HEARD THE BOSS MONSTER ON LEVEL 2 WAS SOME KIND OF LION! IS THAT IT?!
NO! THOSE ARE LIONS WITH THE FACES OF MEN! THEY'RE CALLED MANTICORES!

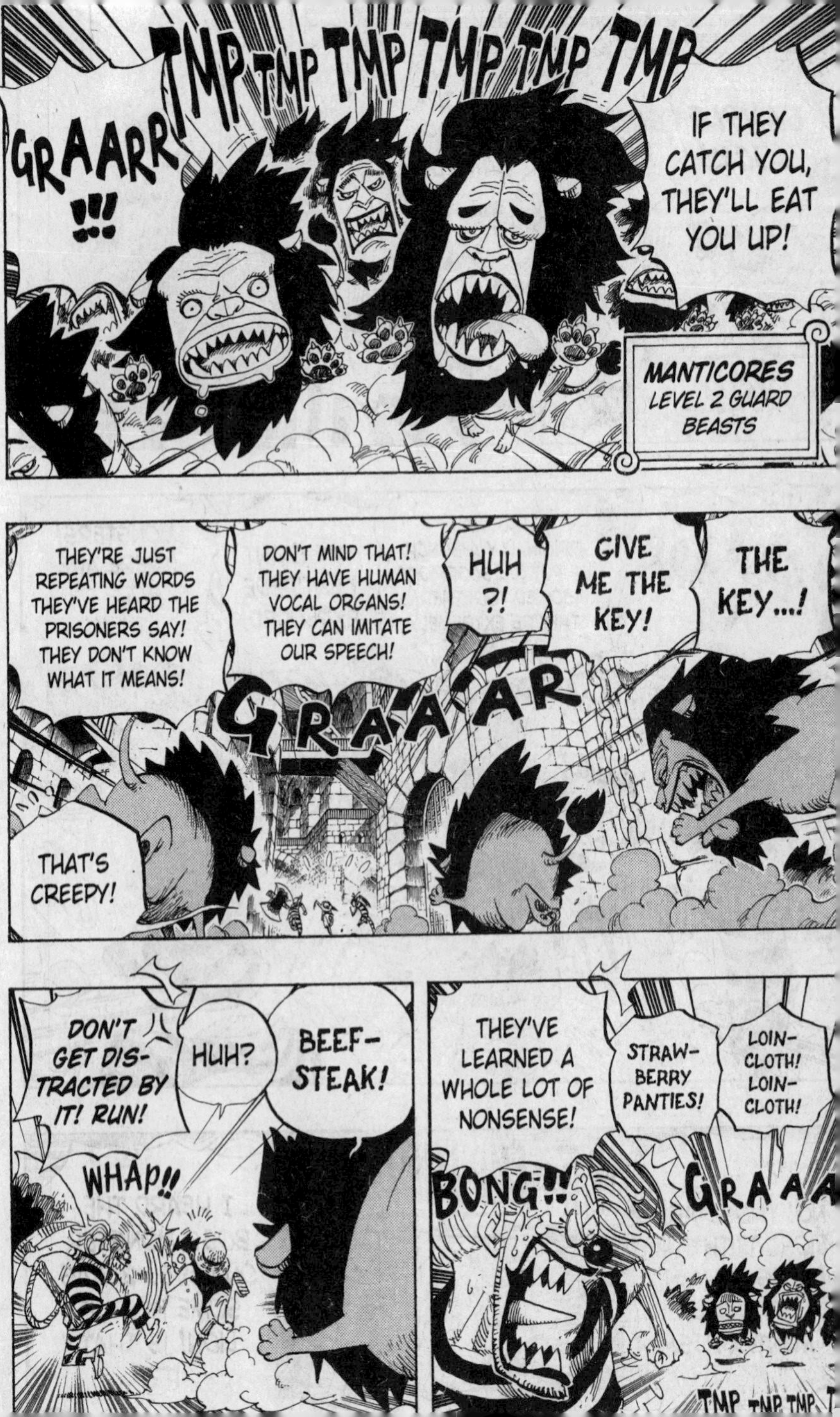
IF THEY CATCH YOU, THEY'LL EAT YOU UP!
MANTICORES LEVEL 2 GUARD BEASTS
TMP TMP TMP TMP TMP TMP
GRAARR!!!
THE KEY...!
GIVE ME THE KEY!
HUH ?!
DON'T MIND THAT! THEY HAVE HUMAN VOCAL ORGANS! THEY CAN IMITATE OUR SPEECH!
THEY'RE JUST REPEATING WORDS THEY'VE HEARD THE PRISONERS SAY! THEY DON'T KNOW WHAT IT MEANS!
GRAAAR
THAT'S CREEPY!
LOIN-CLOTH! LOIN-CLOTH!
STRAW-BERRY PANTIES!
THEY'VE LEARNED A WHOLE LOT OF NONSENSE!
GRAAA
BONG!!
TMP TMP TMP
BEEF-STEAK!
HUH?
DON'T GET DIS-TRACTED BY IT! RUN!
WHAP!!

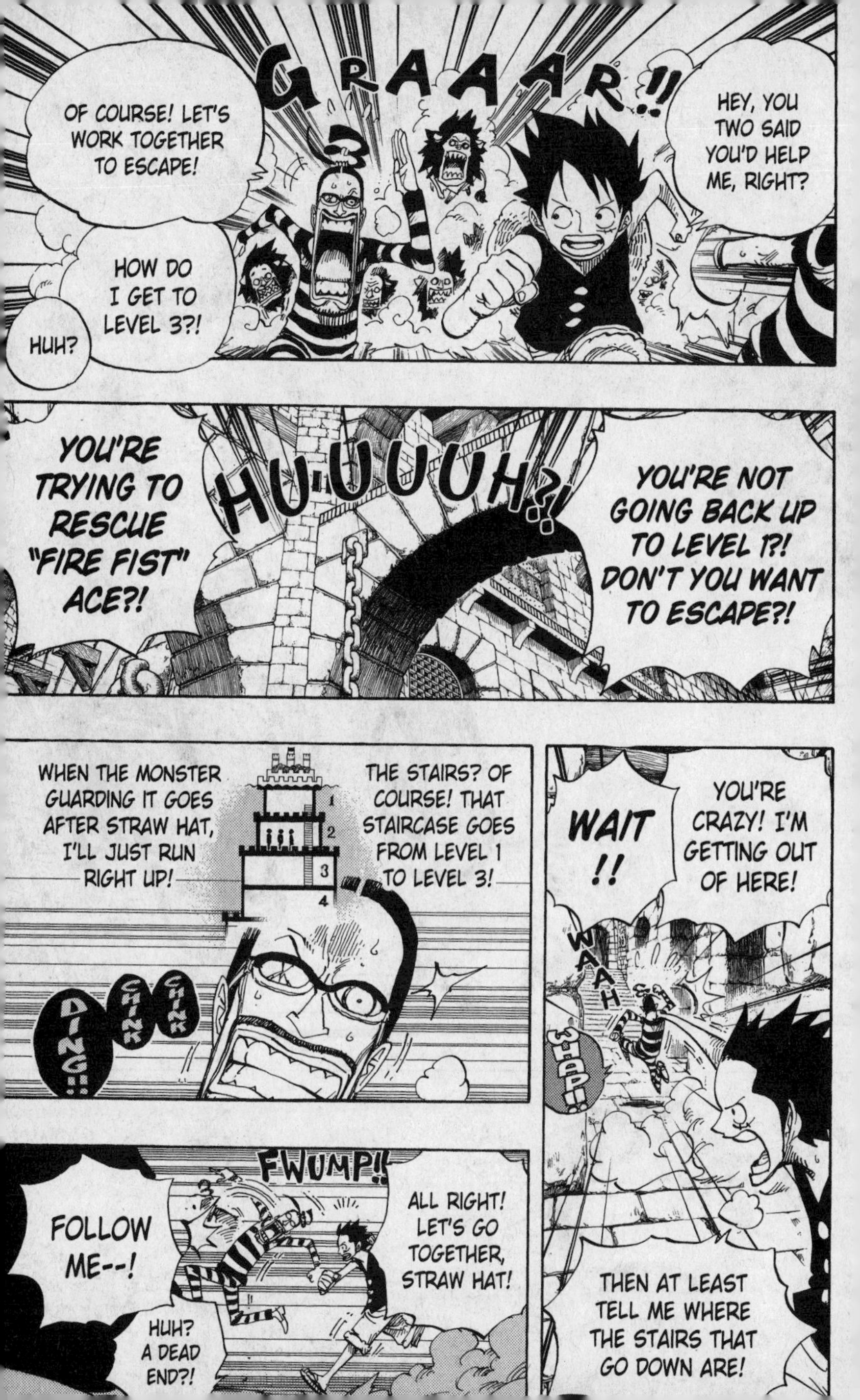
HEY, YOU TWO SAID YOU'D HELP ME, RIGHT?
GRAAAAR!!
OF COURSE! LET'S WORK TOGETHER TO ESCAPE!
HOW DO I GET TO LEVEL 3?!
HUH?
YOU'RE NOT GOING BACK UP TO LEVEL 1?! DON'T YOU WANT TO ESCAPE?!
HUUUUH?!
YOU'RE TRYING TO RESCUE "FIRE FIST" ACE?!
YOU'RE CRAZY! I'M GETTING OUT OF HERE!
WAIT!!
WAAAH
SHAP!!
THEN AT LEAST TELL ME WHERE THE STAIRS THAT GO DOWN ARE!
THE STAIRS? OF COURSE! THAT STAIRCASE GOES FROM LEVEL 1 TO LEVEL 3!
1
2
3
4
WHEN THE MONSTER GUARDING IT GOES AFTER STRAW HAT, I'LL JUST RUN RIGHT UP!
CHINK
CHINK
DING!!
ALL RIGHT! LET'S GO TOGETHER, STRAW HAT!
FWUMP!!
FOLLOW ME--!
HUH? A DEAD END?!

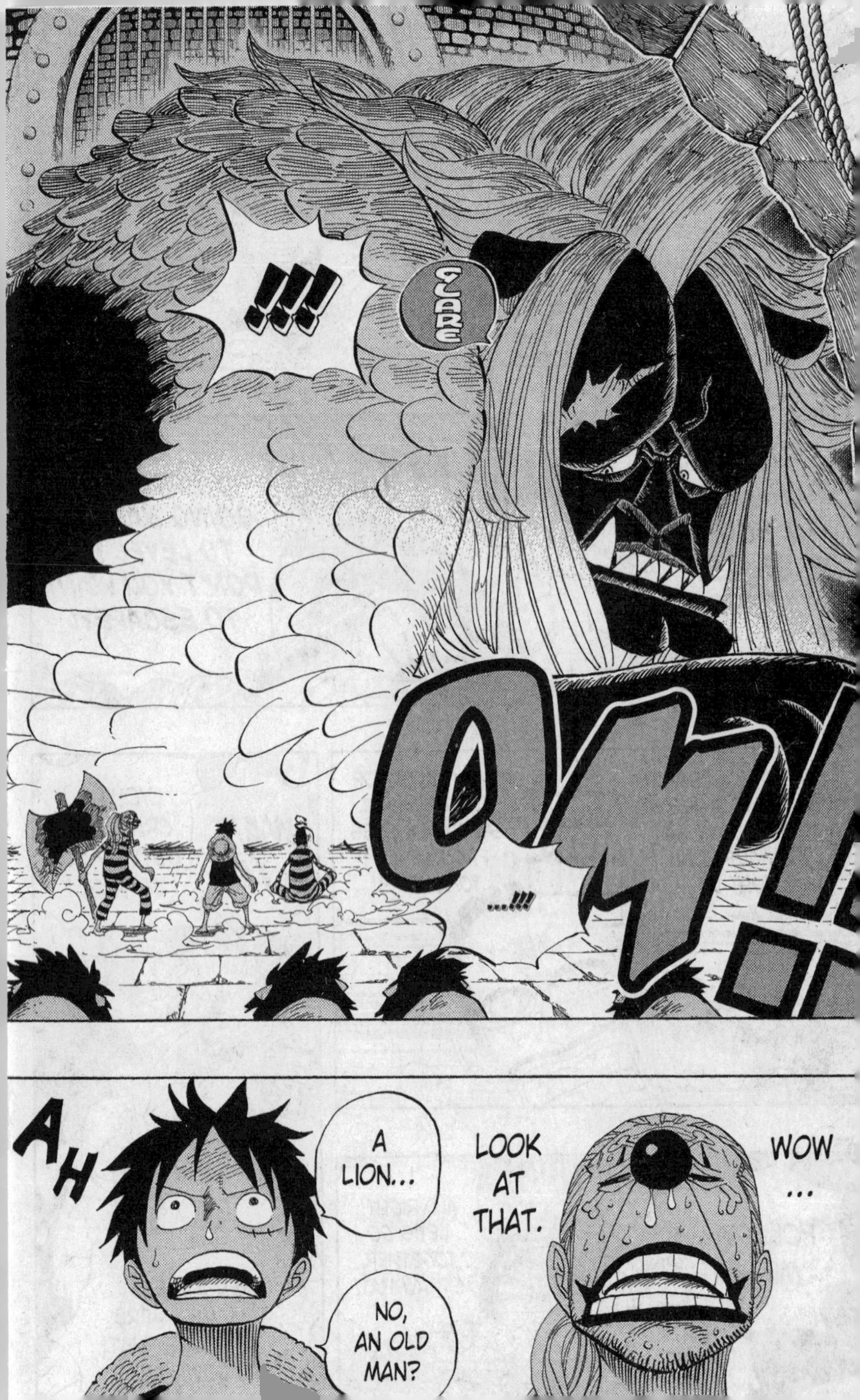
GLARE
!!!
OH!!
...!!!
WOW ...
LOOK AT THAT.
A LION...
NO, AN OLD MAN?
AH

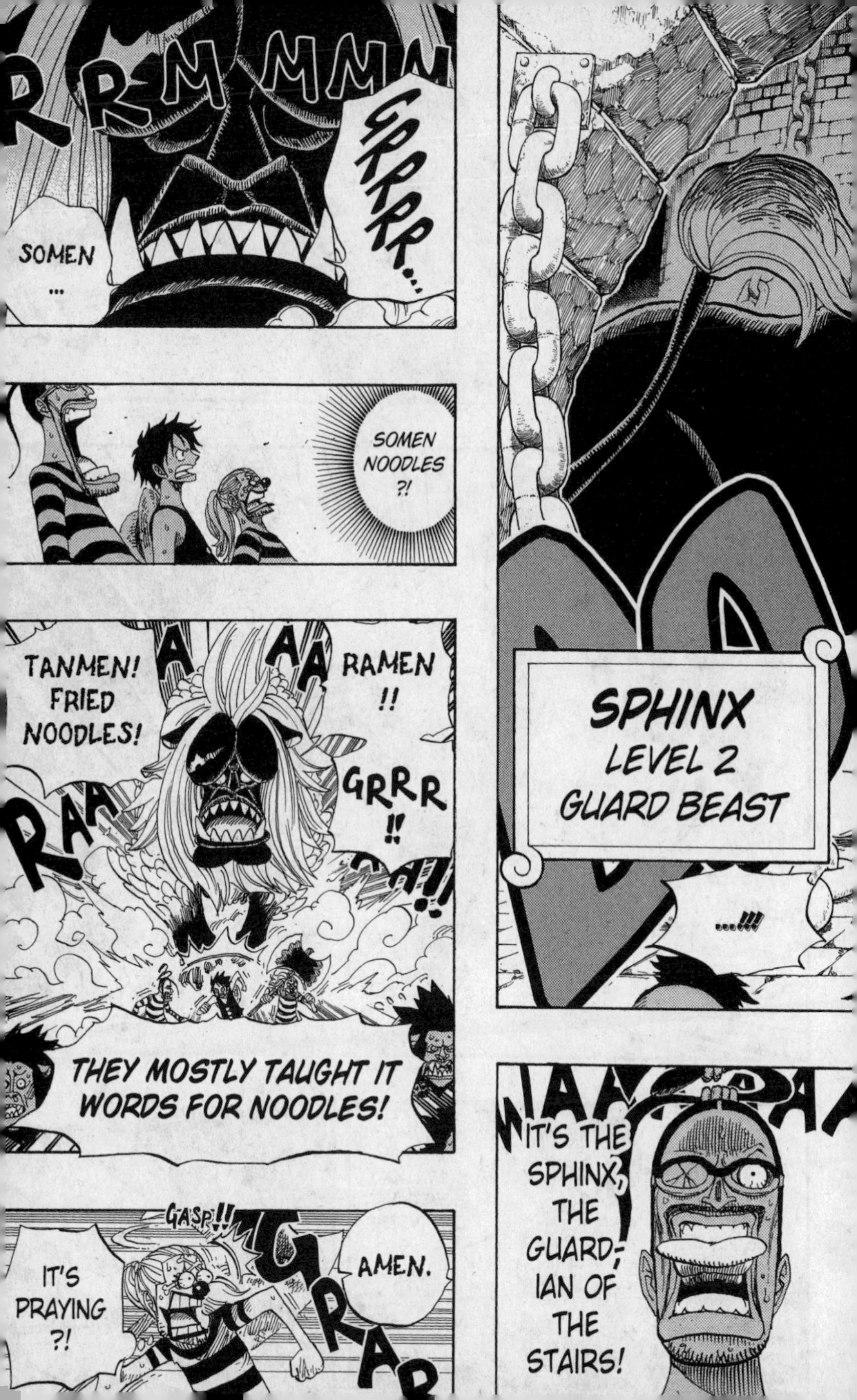
SPHINX
LEVEL 2
GUARD BEAST
...!!!
IT'S THE SPHINX, THE GUARDIAN OF THE STAIRS!
GRRRRR...
RRMMMMM
SOMEN ...
SOMEN NOODLES ?!
RAMEN !!
TANMEN! FRIED NOODLES!
GRRR !!
THEY MOSTLY TAUGHT IT WORDS FOR NOODLES!
AMEN.
GASP!!
IT'S PRAYING ?!

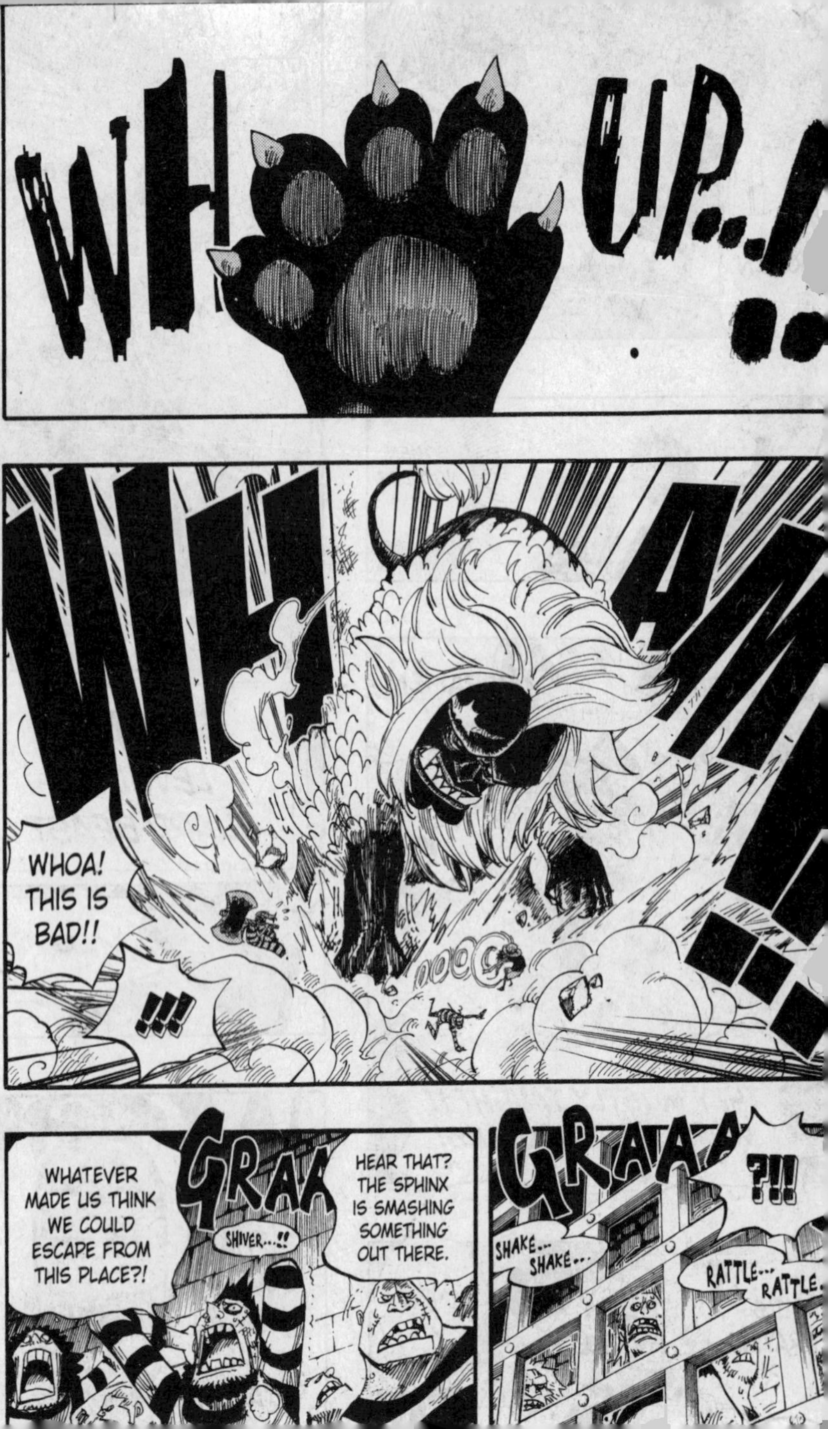
WH UP..!!
WHAM!!
WHOA! THIS IS BAD!!
!!!
GRAAA
?!!
RATTLE... RATTLE.
SHAKE... SHAKE...
HEAR THAT? THE SPHINX IS SMASHING SOMETHING OUT THERE.
GRAA
SHIVER...!!
WHATEVER MADE US THINK WE COULD ESCAPE FROM THIS PLACE?!

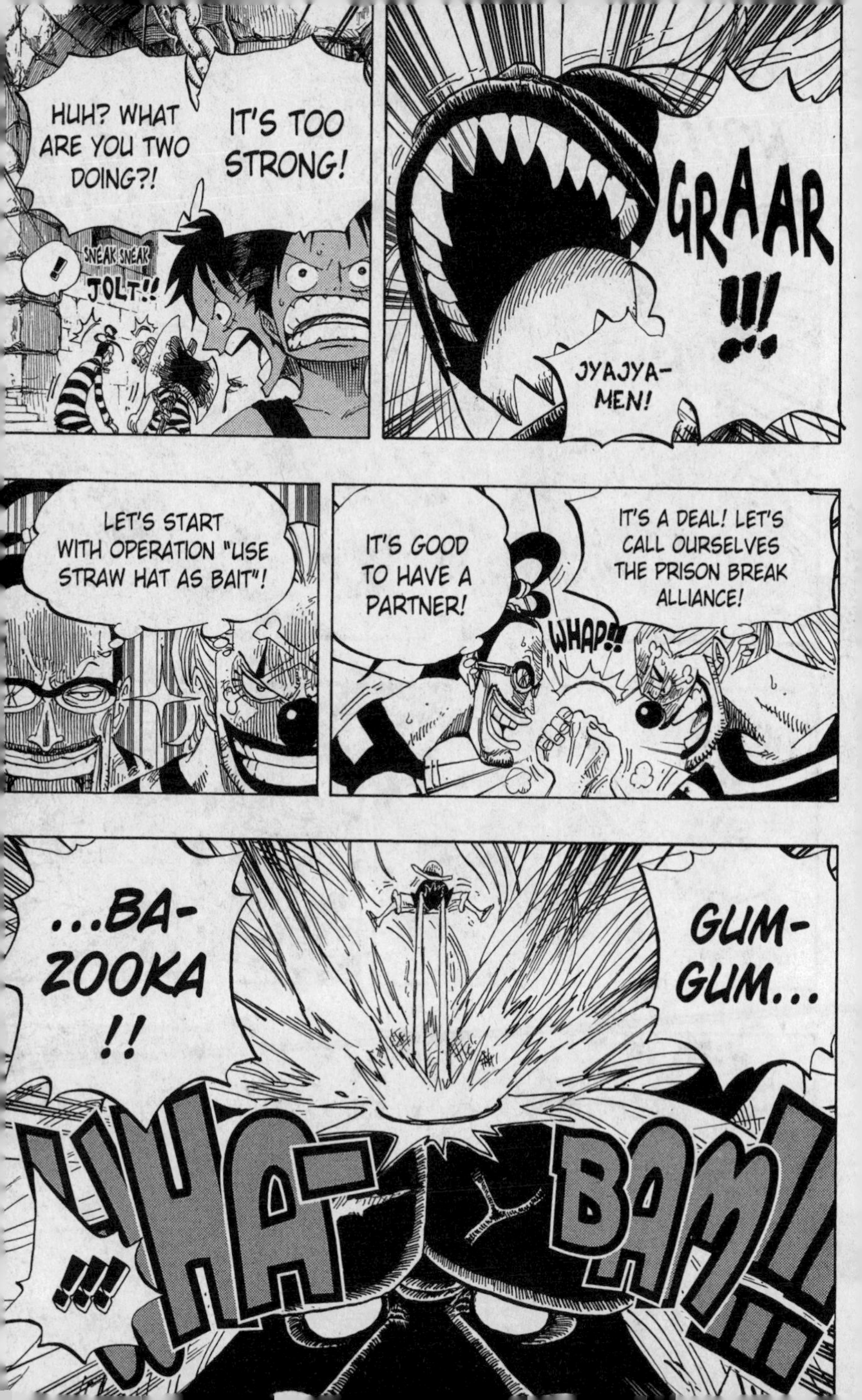
GRAAR!!!
JYAJYA-MEN!
IT'S TOO STRONG!
HUH? WHAT ARE YOU TWO DOING?!
!
SNEAK SNEAK
JOLT!!
IT'S A DEAL! LET'S CALL OURSELVES THE PRISON BREAK ALLIANCE!
IT'S GOOD TO HAVE A PARTNER!
WHAP!!
LET'S START WITH OPERATION "USE STRAW HAT AS BAIT"!
GUM-GUM...
...BA-ZOOKA!!
!!! WHA-BAM!!

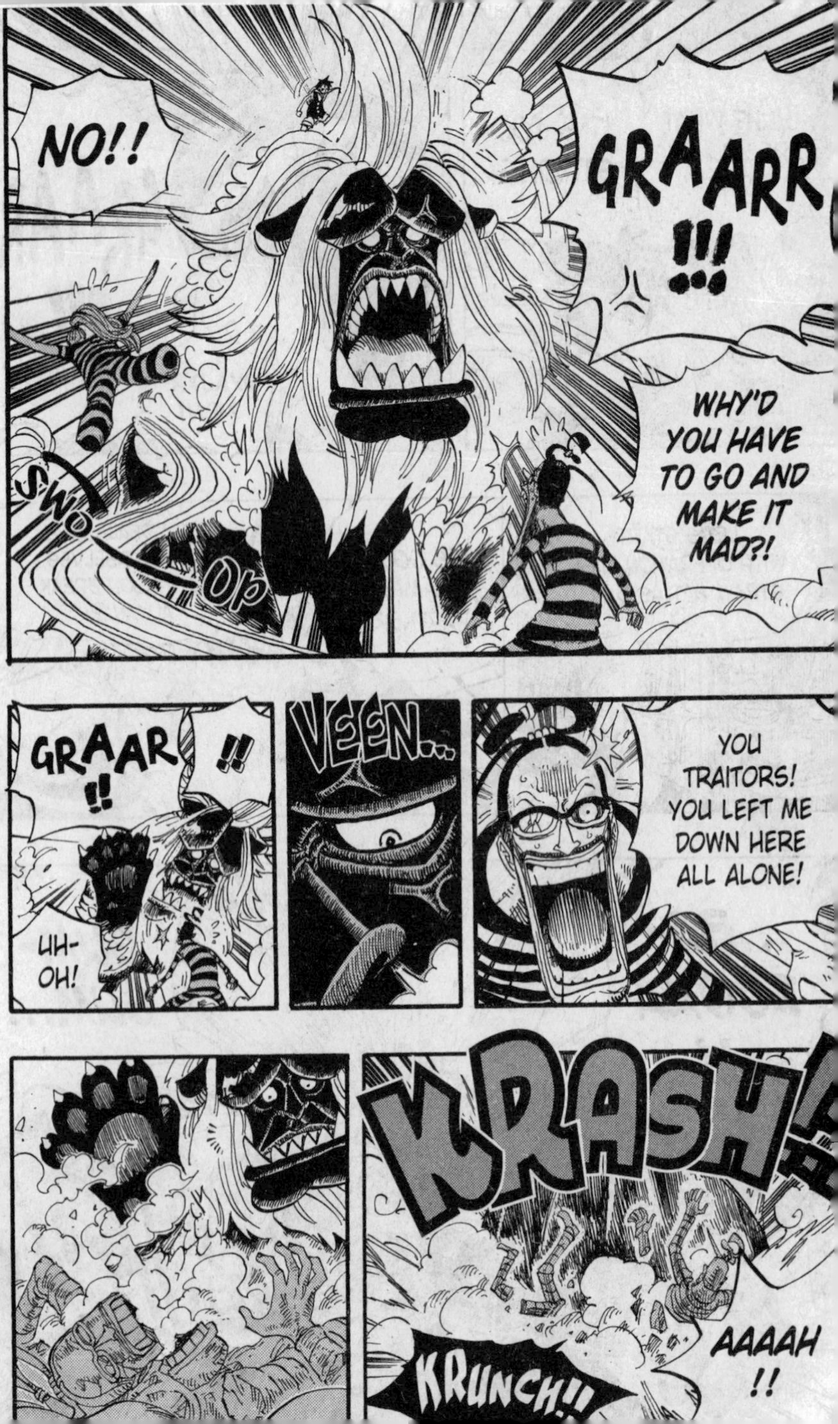
GRAARR!!!
NO!!
WHY'D YOU HAVE TO GO AND MAKE IT MAD?!
SWOOP
YOU TRAITORS! YOU LEFT ME DOWN HERE ALL ALONE!
VEEN...
GRAAR!! !!
UH-OH!
KRASH!!
AAAAH!!
KRUNCH!!

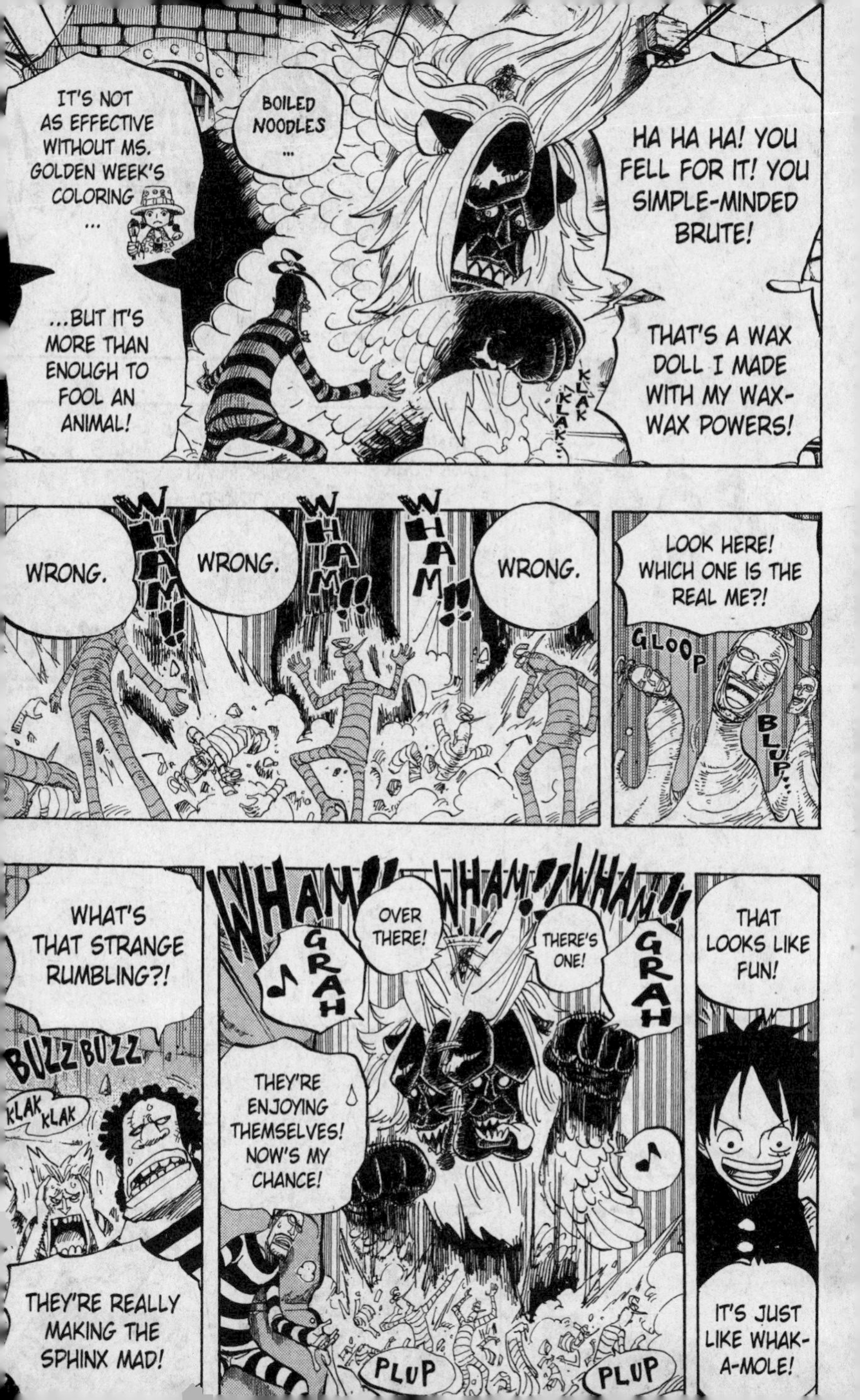
HA HA HA! YOU FELL FOR IT! YOU SIMPLE-MINDED BRUTE!
THAT'S A WAX DOLL I MADE WITH MY WAX-WAX POWERS!
KLAK KLAK
KLAK...
BOILED NOODLES ...
IT'S NOT AS EFFECTIVE WITHOUT MS. GOLDEN WEEK'S COLORING ...
...BUT IT'S MORE THAN ENOUGH TO FOOL AN ANIMAL!
LOOK HERE! WHICH ONE IS THE REAL ME?!
GLOOP
BLUP...
WRONG.
WHAM!!
WHAM!!
WRONG.
WHAM!!
WRONG.
THAT LOOKS LIKE FUN!
IT'S JUST LIKE WHAK-A-MOLE!
WHAM!! WHAM!! WHAM!!
GRAH
THERE'S ONE!
OVER THERE!
GRAH
THEY'RE ENJOYING THEMSELVES! NOW'S MY CHANCE!
PLUP
PLUP
WHAT'S THAT STRANGE RUMBLING?!
BUZZ BUZZ
KLAK KLAK
THEY'RE REALLY MAKING THE SPHINX MAD!

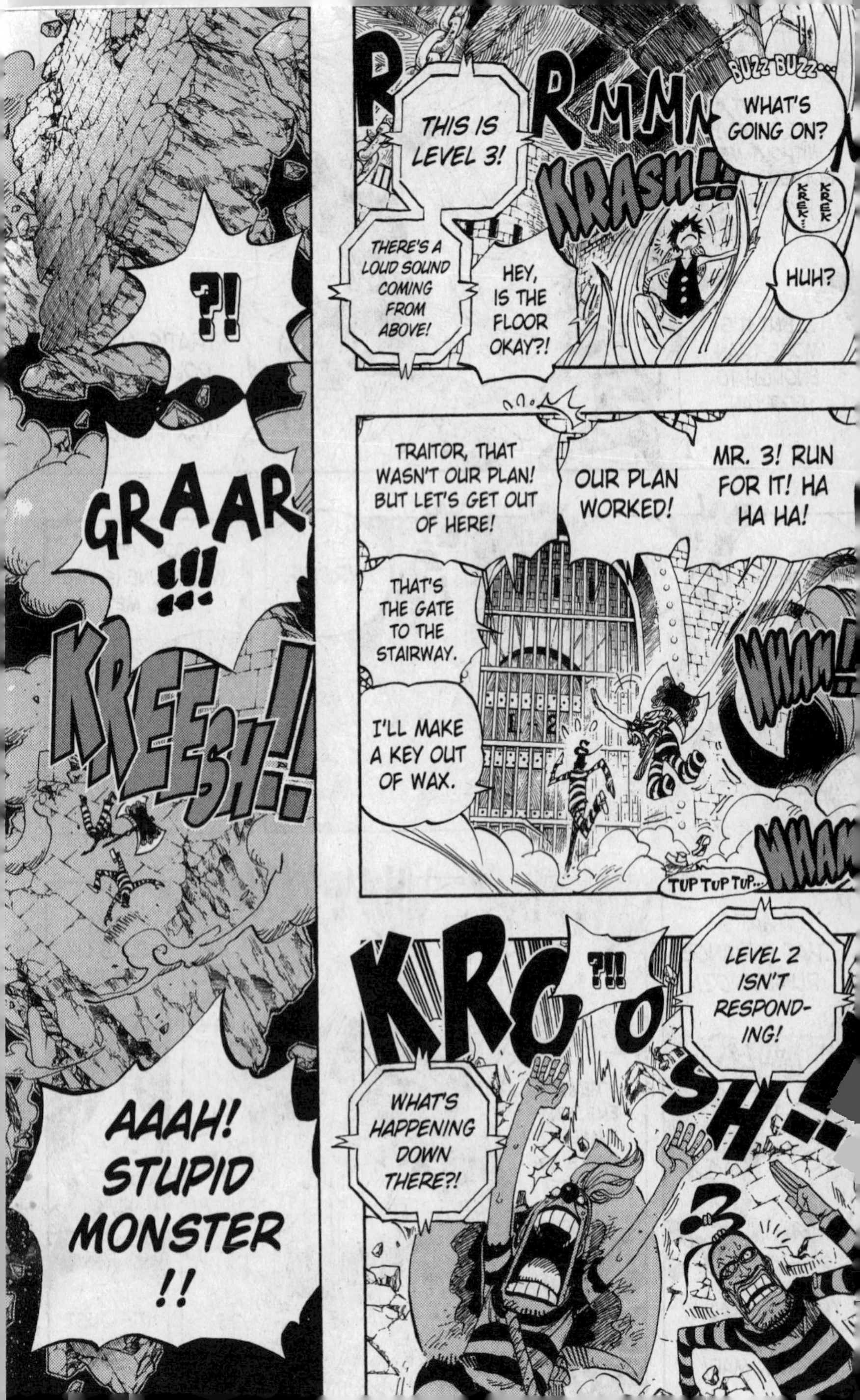
BUZZ BUZZ...
WHAT'S GOING ON?
KREK KREK...
HUH?
R R MMMN
KRASH!!
THIS IS LEVEL 3!
HEY, IS THE FLOOR OKAY?!
THERE'S A LOUD SOUND COMING FROM ABOVE!
MR. 3! RUN FOR IT! HA HA HA!
OUR PLAN WORKED!
TRAITOR, THAT WASN'T OUR PLAN! BUT LET'S GET OUT OF HERE!
WHAM!!
THAT'S THE GATE TO THE STAIRWAY.
I'LL MAKE A KEY OUT OF WAX.
WHAM
TUP TUP TUP...
LEVEL 2 ISN'T RESPOND-ING!
KROOSH!!
?!!
WHAT'S HAPPENING DOWN THERE?!
?!
GRAAR!!!
KREESH!!
AAAH! STUPID MONSTER!!

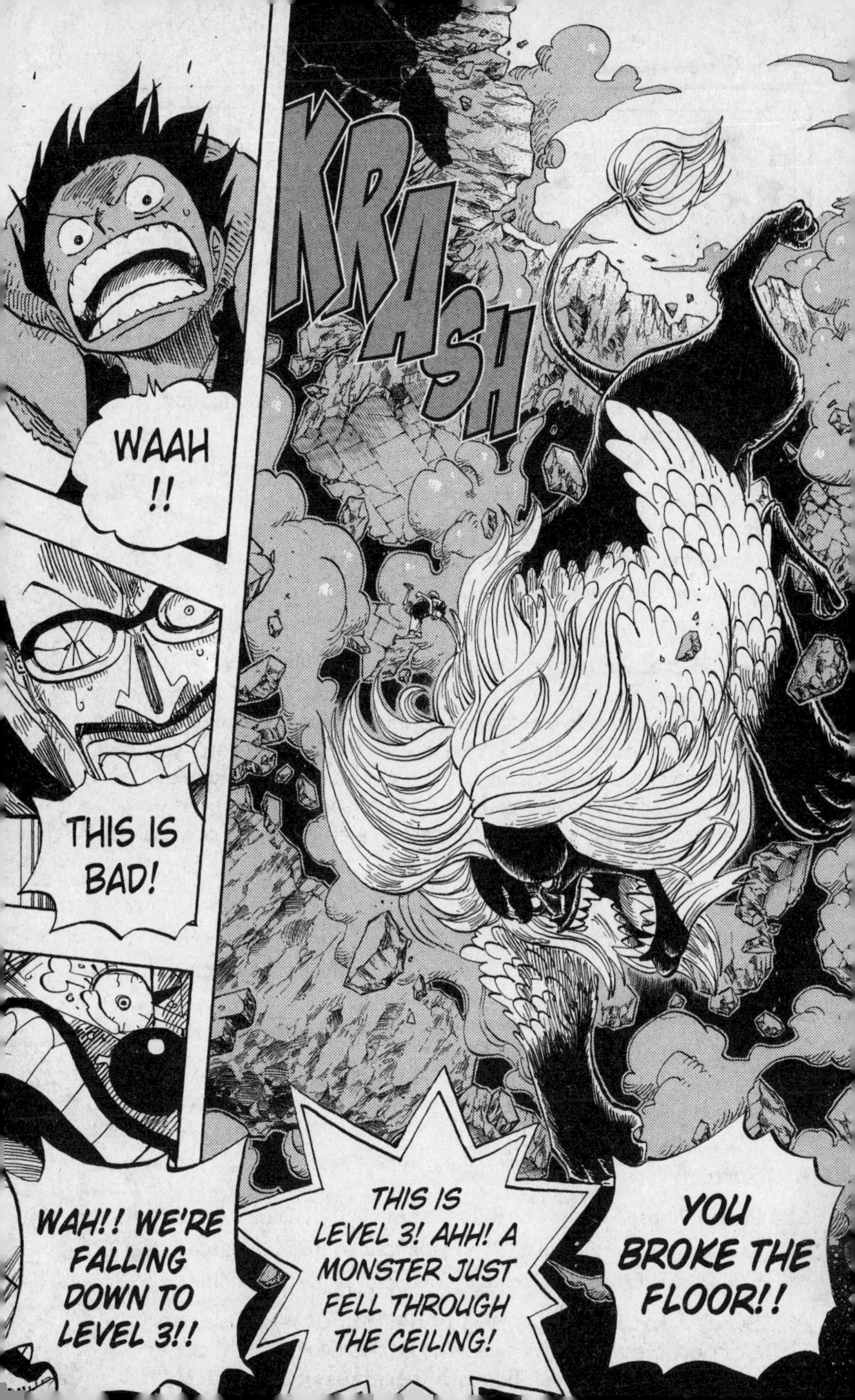
KRASH
YOU BROKE THE FLOOR!!
THIS IS LEVEL 3! AHH! A MONSTER JUST FELL THROUGH THE CEILING!
WAAH !!
THIS IS BAD!
WAH!! WE'RE FALLING DOWN TO LEVEL 3!!

SBS Question Corner

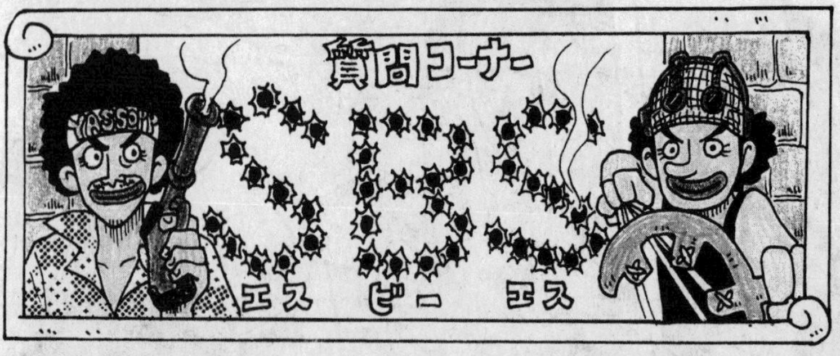
質問コーナー
SBS
エス ビー エス

(Skeleton Yukichi, Iwate)

Q: Hello, Mr. Oda. I just made a discovery about Nami's fighting technique during her battle with Kalifa. Do you remember "Mirage Tempo, Fata Morgana?" According to a book, it said something about the end of the famous witch Morgana. Isn't it something about the mirages that appear in the waters off of Italy? I don't really understand, so please explain. --Rail

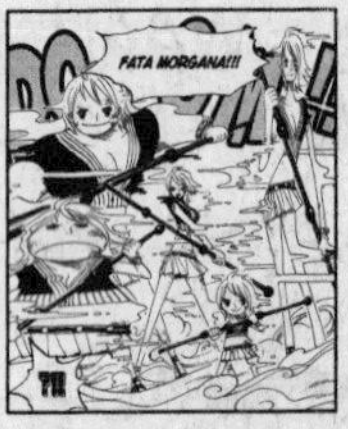
FATA MORGANA!!!

A: Yes. There are lots of theories about this. Mirages that are seen near Sicily, Italy, are called "Fata Morgana," as in the fairy of illusion. In European legend, there is a witch called Morgana. I don't really know the details either, but you said the book calls it the end of the witch. I've read somewhere that the mirages are caused by Morgana, but either way, the local people who saw the "mirages" blamed them on the doings of the witch.

Q: I became the mother of "Sanji"! (Sanji = three children in Japanese)

--Mother of Three

A: Oh. Congratulations.

Q: Make Hancock's birthday September 2, please. Since September is the 9th month (9 ="Ku" in Japanese) and 2 sounds like "Ja" in Japanese!

--Sun

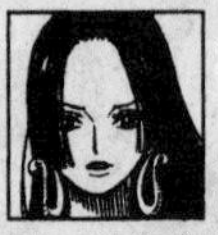

A: Sure.

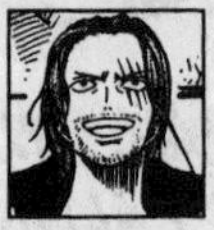

Q: Please choose Shanks's birthday already! "Sha" sounds like "3" and "ks" sounds like "9" in Japanese, so make it March 9! Please, Odacchi! Decide it now! Please! --Pudding

A: Sure. Whatever. Okay, this is the end of the Question Corner. Starting on page 166 is the Question Corner of the voice actors! This is a weird way to end this!

Chapter 530:
FROM ONE HELL TO ANOTHER

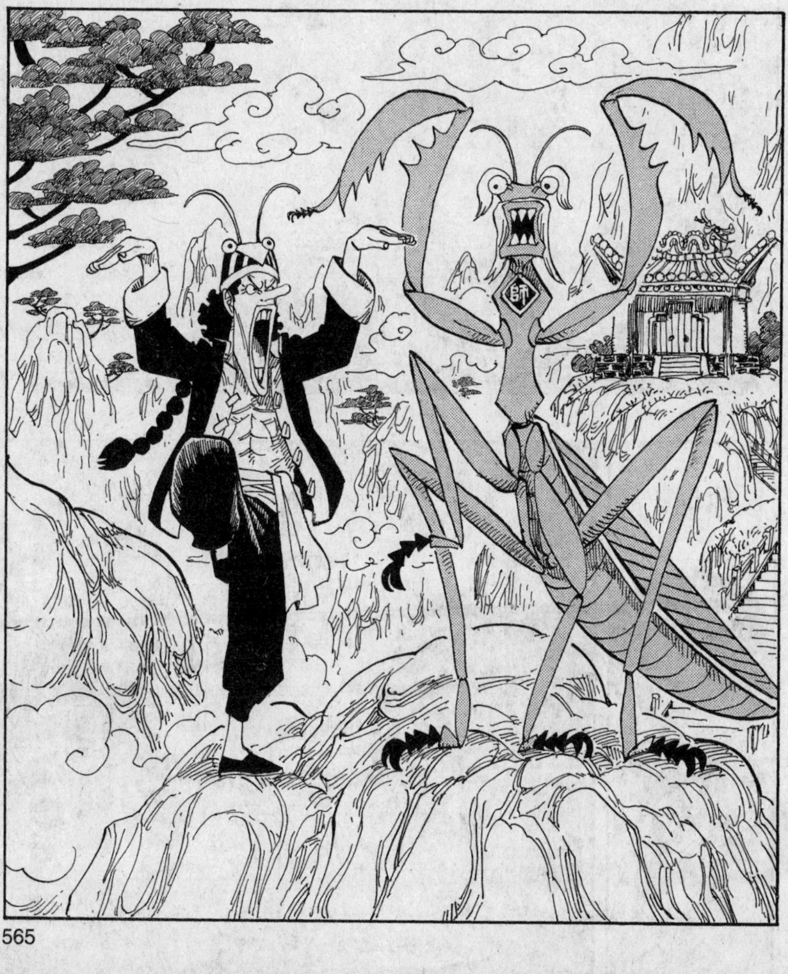

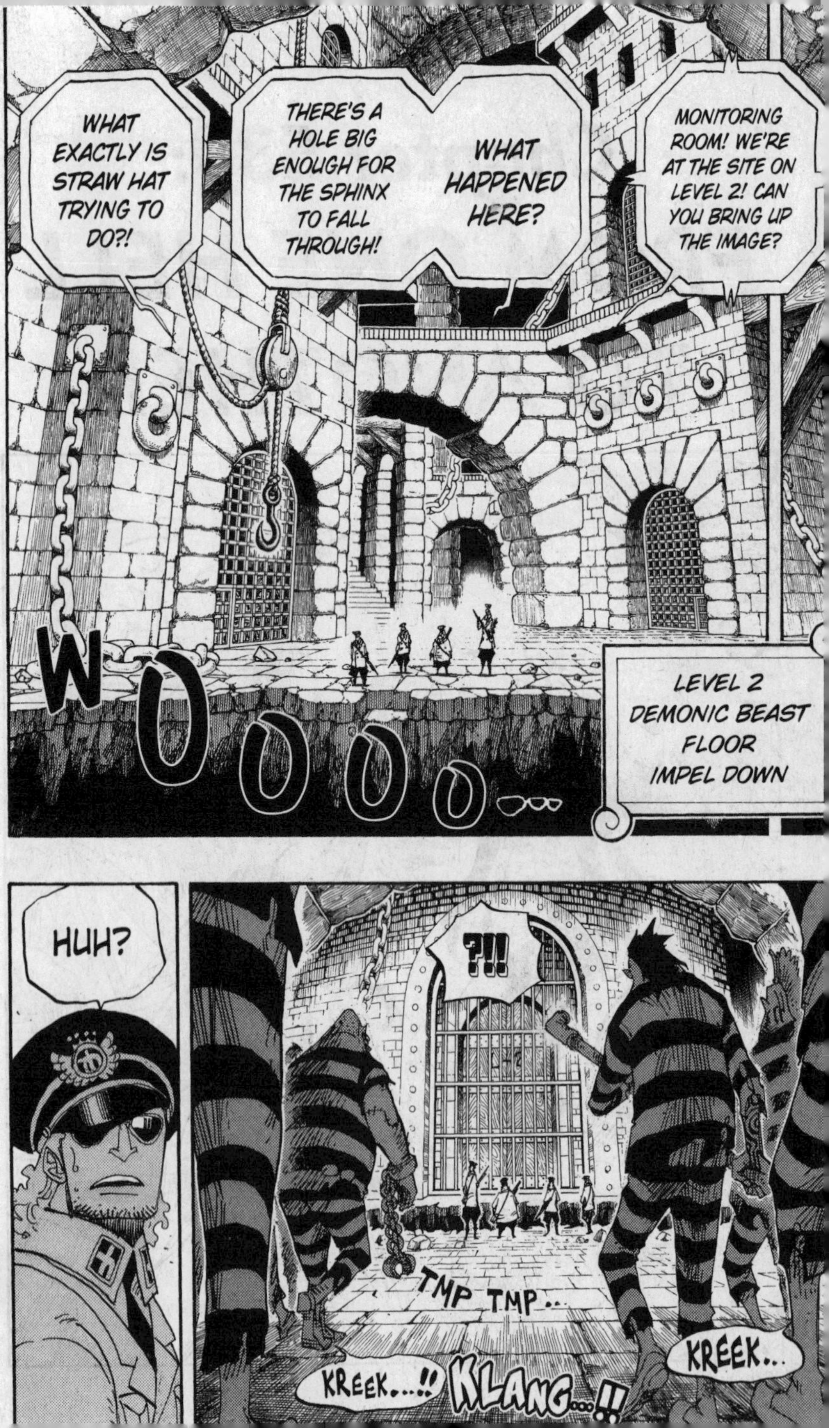
MONITORING ROOM! WE'RE AT THE SITE ON LEVEL 2! CAN YOU BRING UP THE IMAGE?
WHAT HAPPENED HERE?
THERE'S A HOLE BIG ENOUGH FOR THE SPHINX TO FALL THROUGH!
WHAT EXACTLY IS STRAW HAT TRYING TO DO?!
LEVEL 2 DEMONIC BEAST FLOOR IMPEL DOWN
WOOOO...
?!!
TMP TMP...
KREEK...
KLANG...!!
KREEK...!!
HUH?

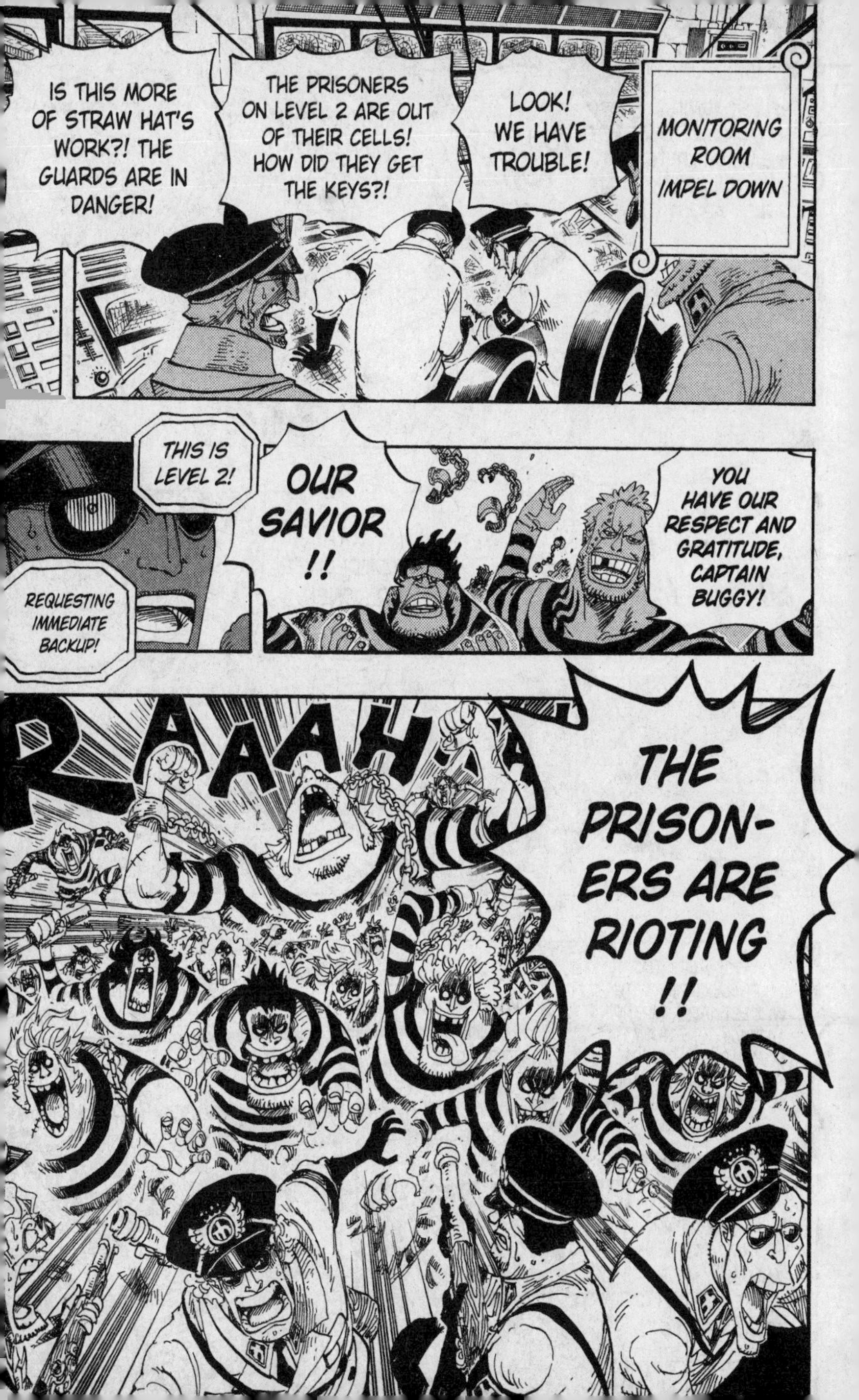
MONITORING ROOM IMPEL DOWN
LOOK! WE HAVE TROUBLE!
THE PRISONERS ON LEVEL 2 ARE OUT OF THEIR CELLS! HOW DID THEY GET THE KEYS?!
IS THIS MORE OF STRAW HAT'S WORK?! THE GUARDS ARE IN DANGER!
YOU HAVE OUR RESPECT AND GRATITUDE, CAPTAIN BUGGY!
OUR SAVIOR !!
THIS IS LEVEL 2!
REQUESTING IMMEDIATE BACKUP!
THE PRISON-ERS ARE RIOTING !!

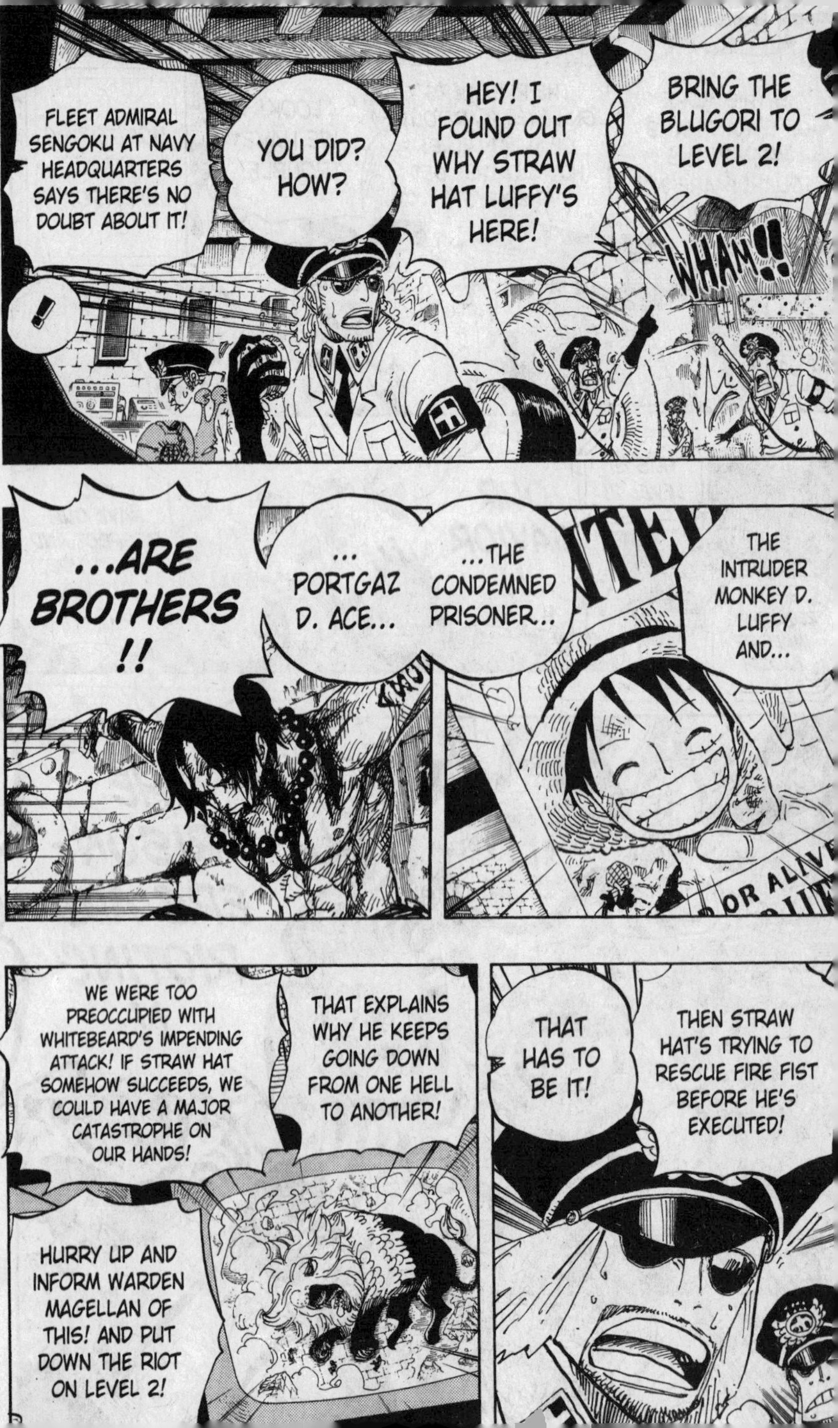
BRING THE BLUGORI TO LEVEL 2!
WHAM!!
HEY! I FOUND OUT WHY STRAW HAT LUFFY'S HERE!
YOU DID? HOW?
FLEET ADMIRAL SENGOKU AT NAVY HEADQUARTERS SAYS THERE'S NO DOUBT ABOUT IT!
!
THE INTRUDER MONKEY D. LUFFY AND...
...THE CONDEMNED PRISONER...
... PORTGAZ D. ACE...
...ARE BROTHERS !!
OR ALIVE
THEN STRAW HAT'S TRYING TO RESCUE FIRE FIST BEFORE HE'S EXECUTED!
THAT HAS TO BE IT!
THAT EXPLAINS WHY HE KEEPS GOING DOWN FROM ONE HELL TO ANOTHER!
WE WERE TOO PREOCCUPIED WITH WHITEBEARD'S IMPENDING ATTACK! IF STRAW HAT SOMEHOW SUCCEEDS, WE COULD HAVE A MAJOR CATASTROPHE ON OUR HANDS!
HURRY UP AND INFORM WARDEN MAGELLAN OF THIS! AND PUT DOWN THE RIOT ON LEVEL 2!

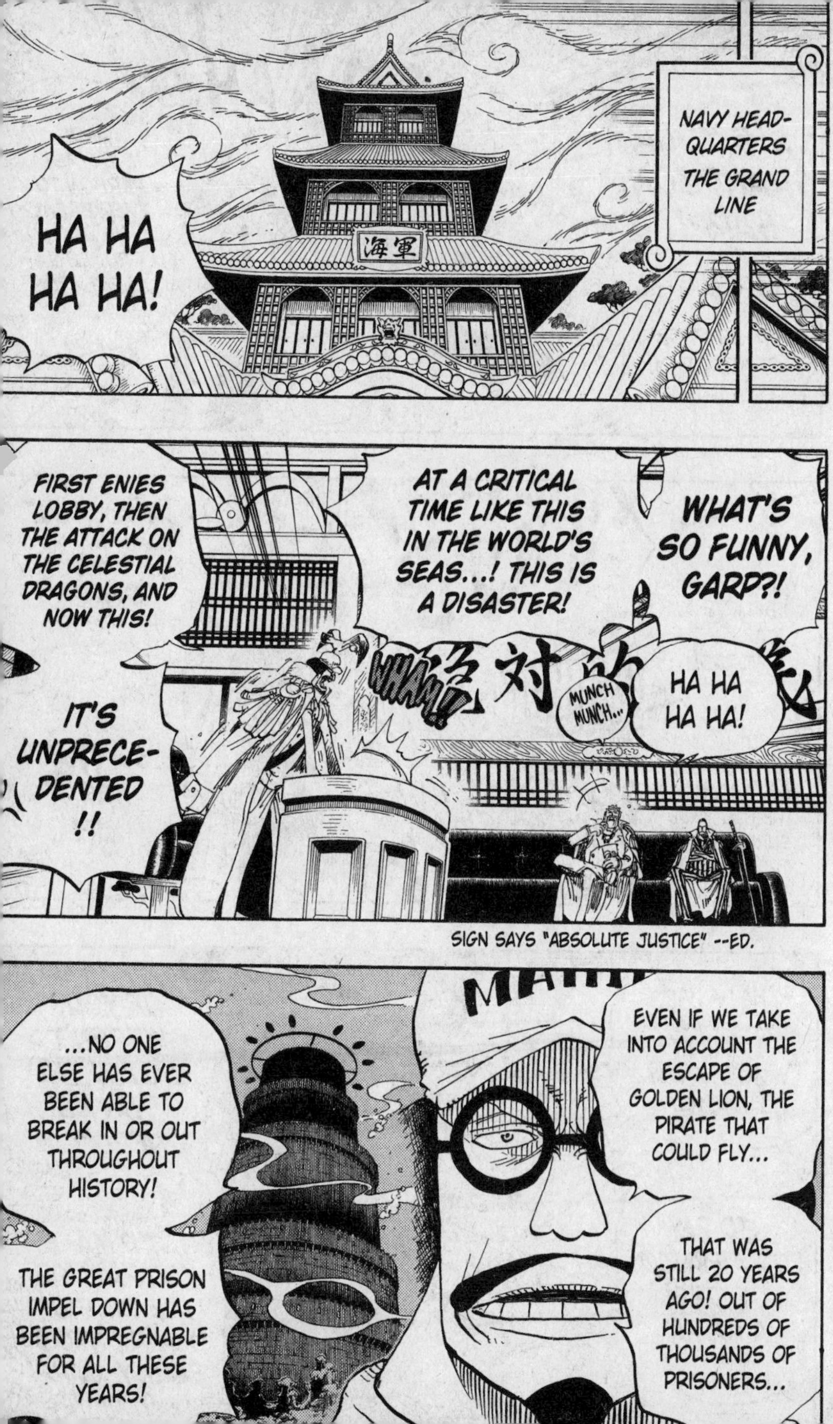
NAVY HEAD-QUARTERS THE GRAND LINE
HA HA HA HA!
WHAT'S SO FUNNY, GARP?!
AT A CRITICAL TIME LIKE THIS IN THE WORLD'S SEAS...! THIS IS A DISASTER!
FIRST ENIES LOBBY, THEN THE ATTACK ON THE CELESTIAL DRAGONS, AND NOW THIS!
WHAM!!
HA HA HA HA!
MUNCH MUNCH...
IT'S UNPRECE-DENTED!!
SIGN SAYS "ABSOLUTE JUSTICE" --ED.
EVEN IF WE TAKE INTO ACCOUNT THE ESCAPE OF GOLDEN LION, THE PIRATE THAT COULD FLY...
THAT WAS STILL 20 YEARS AGO! OUT OF HUNDREDS OF THOUSANDS OF PRISONERS...
...NO ONE ELSE HAS EVER BEEN ABLE TO BREAK IN OR OUT THROUGHOUT HISTORY!
THE GREAT PRISON IMPEL DOWN HAS BEEN IMPREGNABLE FOR ALL THESE YEARS!

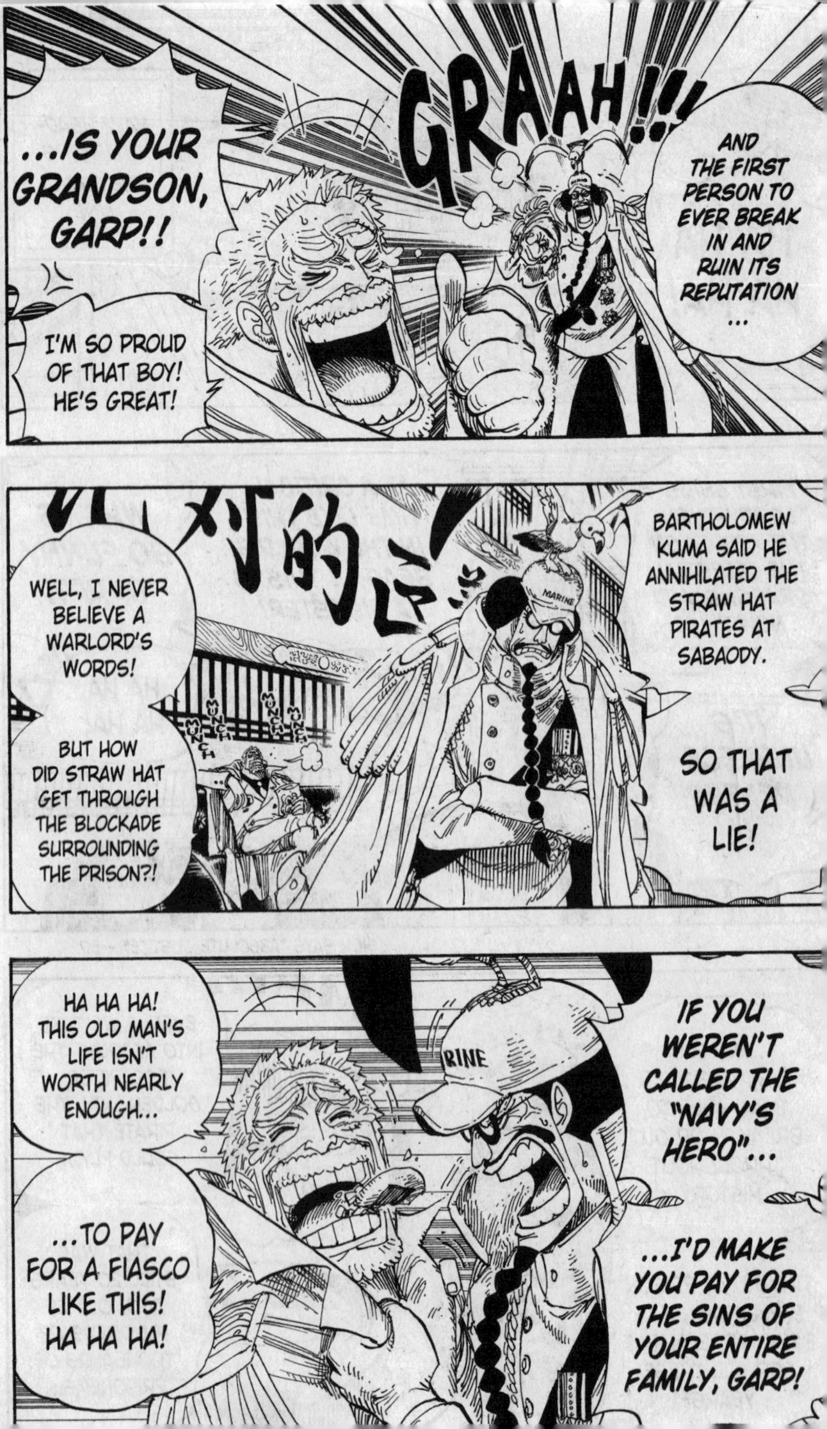
AND THE FIRST PERSON TO EVER BREAK IN AND RUIN ITS REPUTATION...
GRAAH!!!
...IS YOUR GRANDSON, GARP!!
I'M SO PROUD OF THAT BOY! HE'S GREAT!
BARTHOLOMEW KUMA SAID HE ANNIHILATED THE STRAW HAT PIRATES AT SABAODY.
SO THAT WAS A LIE!
WELL, I NEVER BELIEVE A WARLORD'S WORDS!
BUT HOW DID STRAW HAT GET THROUGH THE BLOCKADE SURROUNDING THE PRISON?!
MUNCH MUNCH MUNCH MUNCH
IF YOU WEREN'T CALLED THE "NAVY'S HERO"...
...I'D MAKE YOU PAY FOR THE SINS OF YOUR ENTIRE FAMILY, GARP!
HA HA HA! THIS OLD MAN'S LIFE ISN'T WORTH NEARLY ENOUGH...
...TO PAY FOR A FIASCO LIKE THIS! HA HA HA!

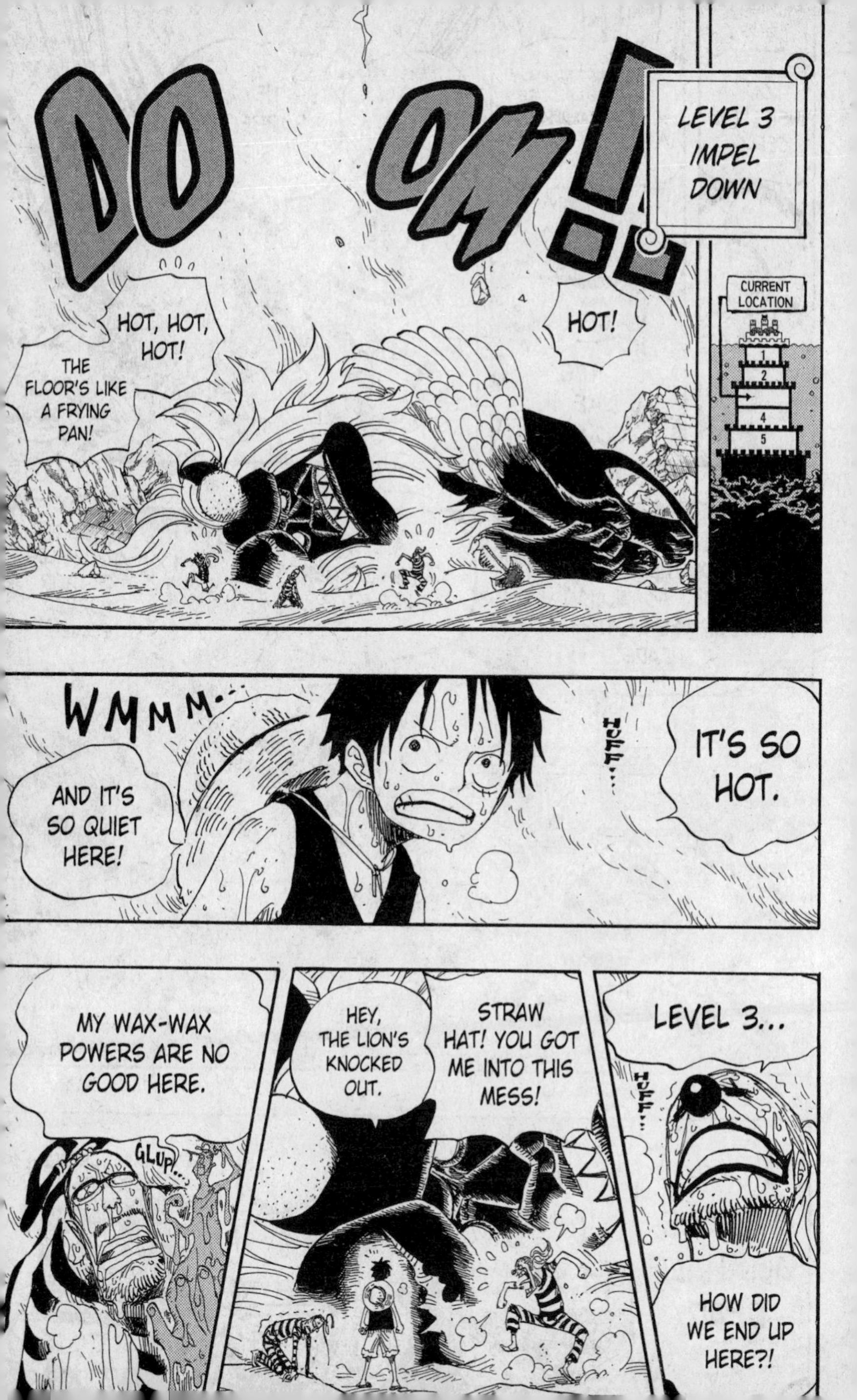
LEVEL 3 IMPEL DOWN
CURRENT LOCATION
1
2
4
5
DOOM!!
HOT!
HOT, HOT, HOT!
THE FLOOR'S LIKE A FRYING PAN!
IT'S SO HOT.
HUFF...
WMMM...
AND IT'S SO QUIET HERE!
LEVEL 3...
HUFF...
HOW DID WE END UP HERE?!
STRAW HAT! YOU GOT ME INTO THIS MESS!
HEY, THE LION'S KNOCKED OUT.
MY WAX-WAX POWERS ARE NO GOOD HERE.
GLUP...

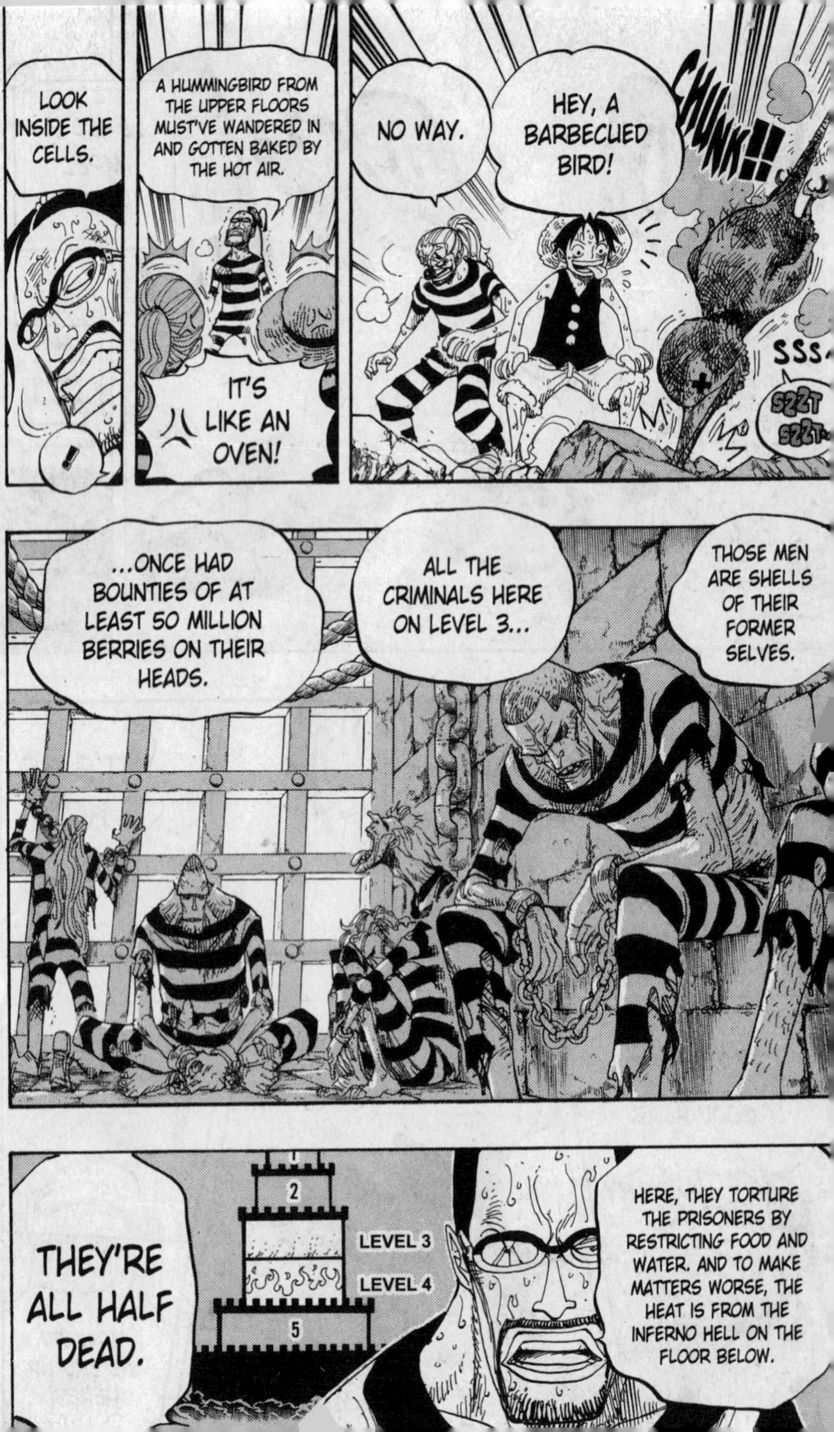
CHUNK!!
HEY, A BARBECUED BIRD!
NO WAY.
SSS
SZZT
SZZT
A HUMMINGBIRD FROM THE UPPER FLOORS MUST'VE WANDERED IN AND GOTTEN BAKED BY THE HOT AIR.
IT'S LIKE AN OVEN!
LOOK INSIDE THE CELLS.
!
THOSE MEN ARE SHELLS OF THEIR FORMER SELVES.
ALL THE CRIMINALS HERE ON LEVEL 3...
...ONCE HAD BOUNTIES OF AT LEAST 50 MILLION BERRIES ON THEIR HEADS.
HERE, THEY TORTURE THE PRISONERS BY RESTRICTING FOOD AND WATER. AND TO MAKE MATTERS WORSE, THE HEAT IS FROM THE INFERNO HELL ON THE FLOOR BELOW.
2
LEVEL 3
LEVEL 4
5
THEY'RE ALL HALF DEAD.

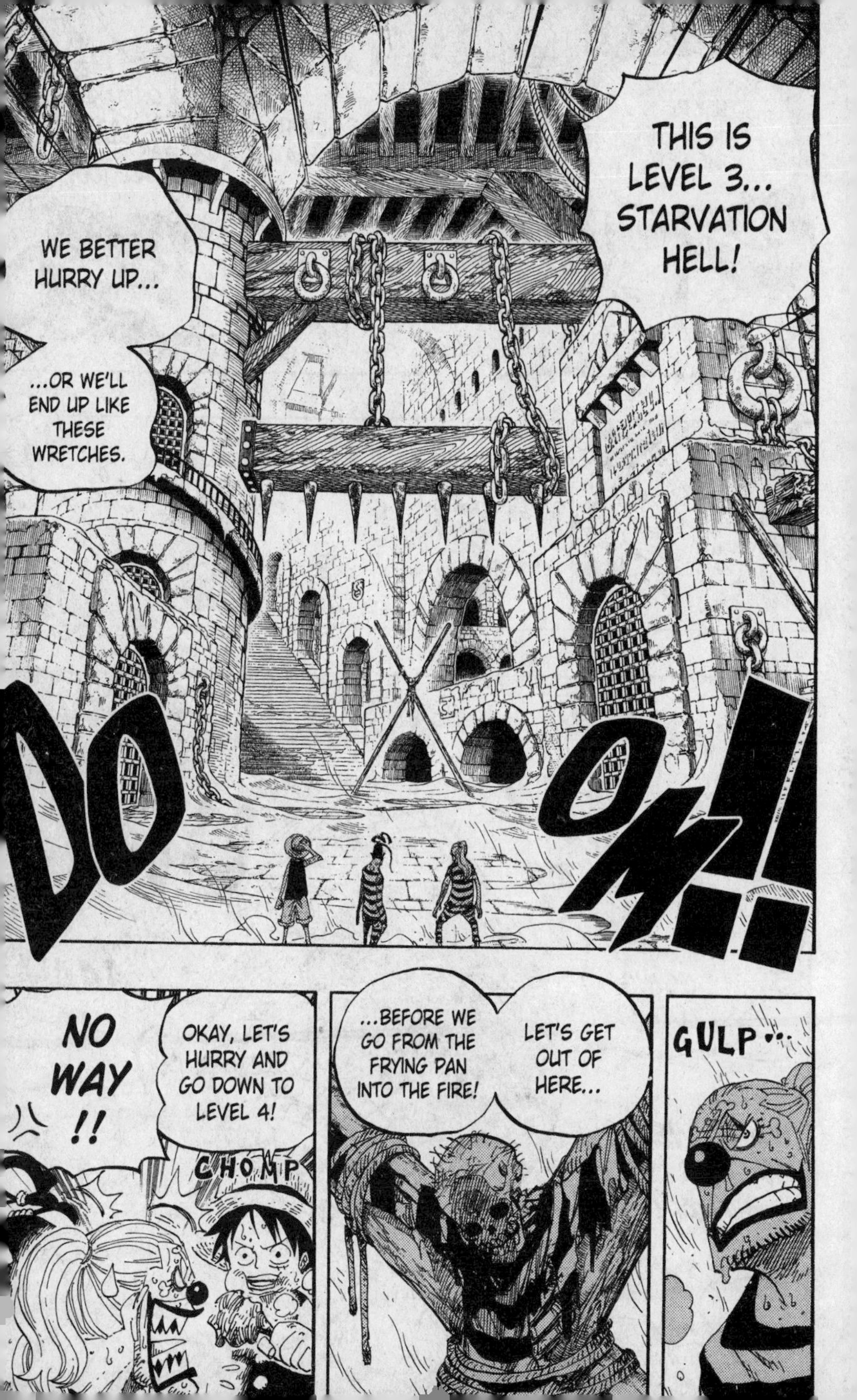
THIS IS LEVEL 3... STARVATION HELL!
WE BETTER HURRY UP...
...OR WE'LL END UP LIKE THESE WRETCHES.
DO ON!!
GULP...
LET'S GET OUT OF HERE...
...BEFORE WE GO FROM THE FRYING PAN INTO THE FIRE!
OKAY, LET'S HURRY AND GO DOWN TO LEVEL 4!
CHOMP
NO WAY!!

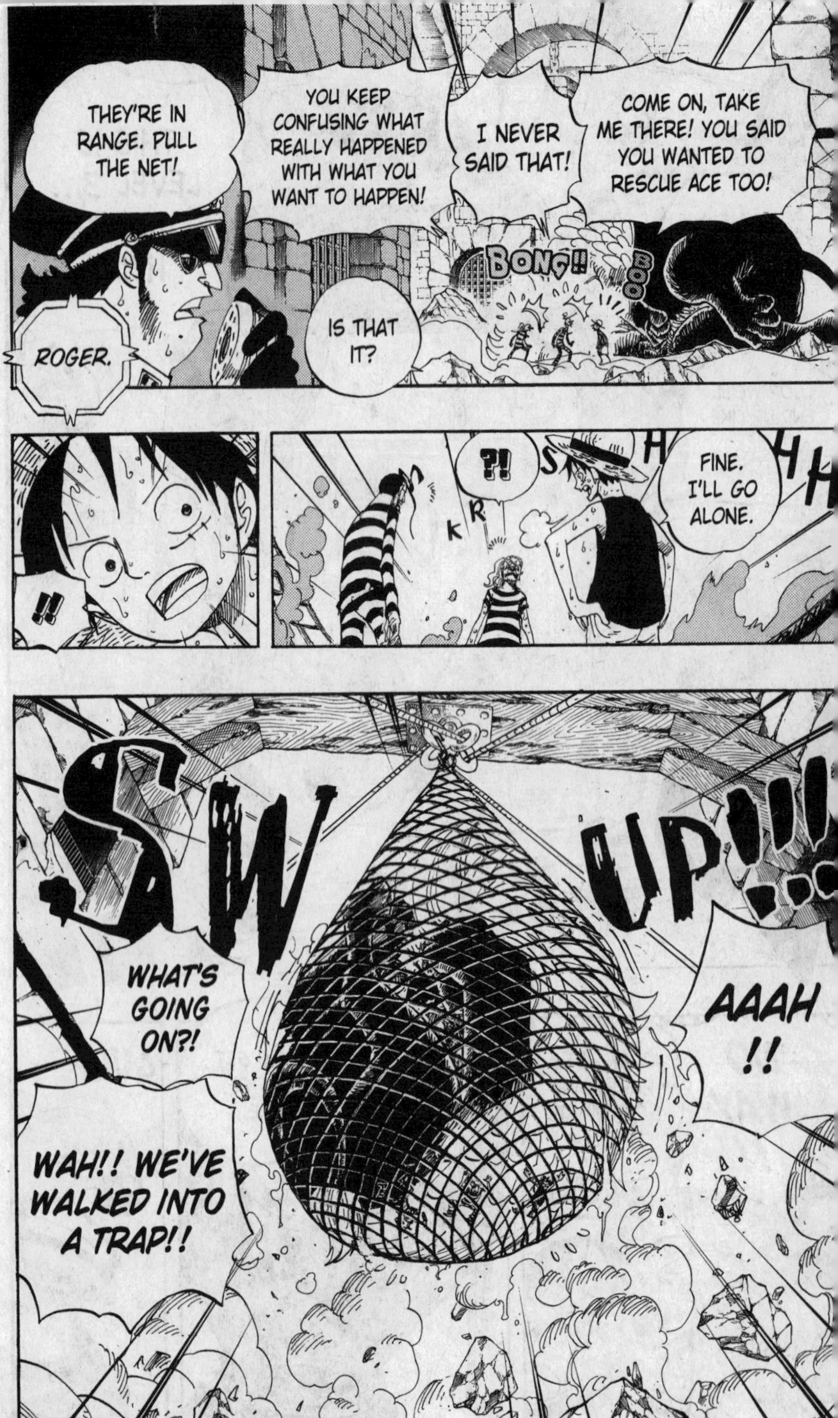

COME ON, TAKE ME THERE! YOU SAID YOU WANTED TO RESCUE ACE TOO!
BOO
I NEVER SAID THAT!
BONG!!
YOU KEEP CONFUSING WHAT REALLY HAPPENED WITH WHAT YOU WANT TO HAPPEN!
IS THAT IT?
THEY'RE IN RANGE. PULL THE NET!
ROGER.
FINE. I'LL GO ALONE.
?!
!!
SWUP!!!
AAAH!!
WHAT'S GOING ON?!
WAH!! WE'VE WALKED INTO A TRAP!!

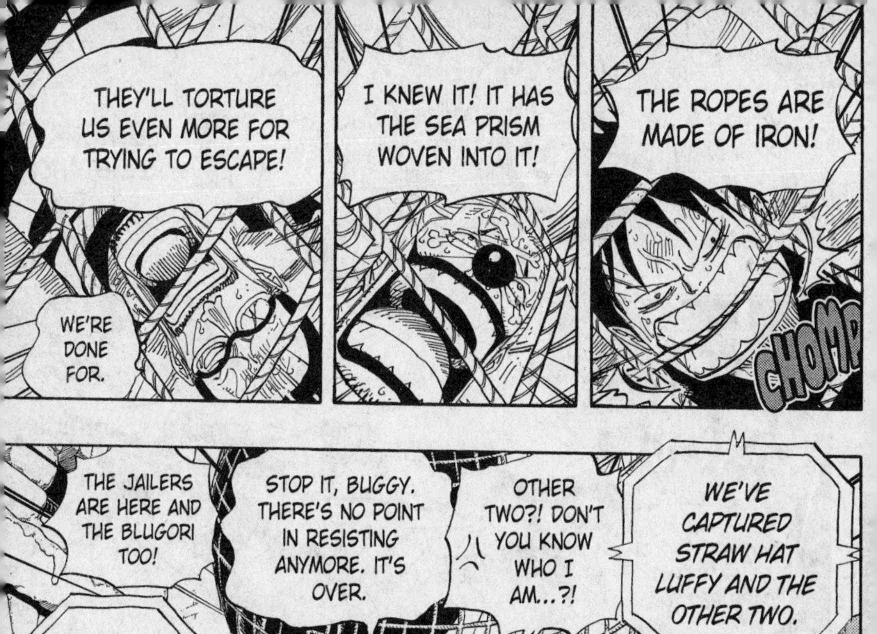
THE ROPES ARE MADE OF IRON!
CHOMP
I KNEW IT! IT HAS THE SEA PRISM WOVEN INTO IT!
THEY'LL TORTURE US EVEN MORE FOR TRYING TO ESCAPE!
WE'RE DONE FOR.
WE'VE CAPTURED STRAW HAT LUFFY AND THE OTHER TWO.
OTHER TWO?! DON'T YOU KNOW WHO I AM...?!
STOP IT, BUGGY. THERE'S NO POINT IN RESISTING ANYMORE. IT'S OVER.
THE JAILERS ARE HERE AND THE BLUGORI TOO!
LET ME OUT OF THIS NET!
PUT THE SEA PRISM CUFFS ON THEM!
ROGER.
SHF SHF SHF SHF

"SARU" MEANS "MONKEY" IN JAPANESE. --ED.

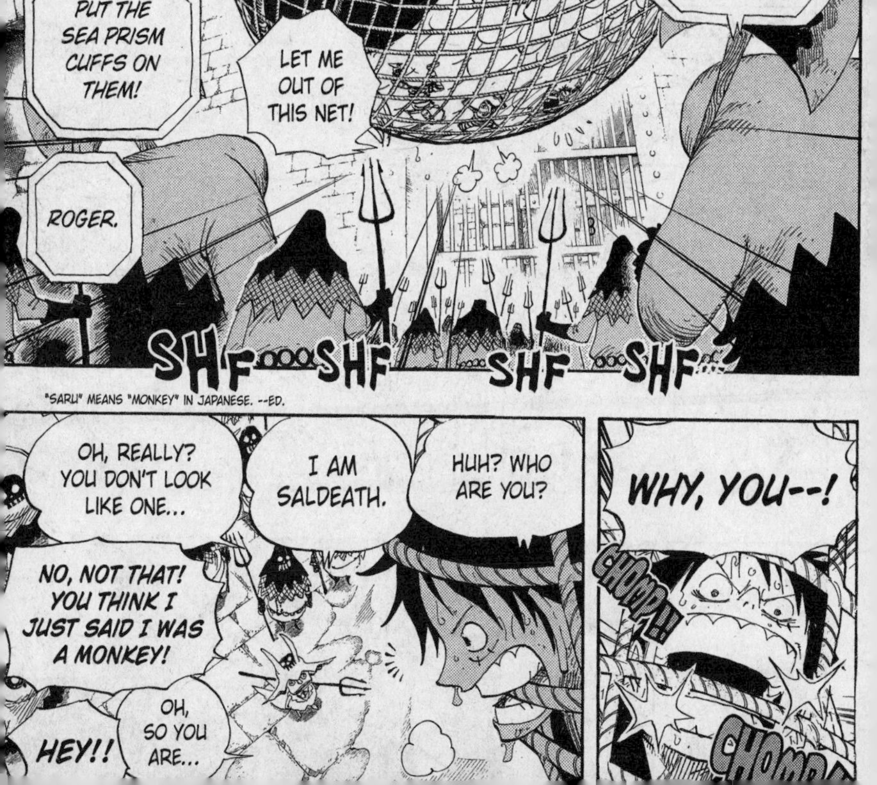
WHY, YOU--!
CHOMP!!
CHOMP
HUH? WHO ARE YOU?
I AM SALDEATH.
OH, REALLY? YOU DON'T LOOK LIKE ONE...
NO, NOT THAT! YOU THINK I JUST SAID I WAS A MONKEY!
OH, SO YOU ARE...
HEY!!

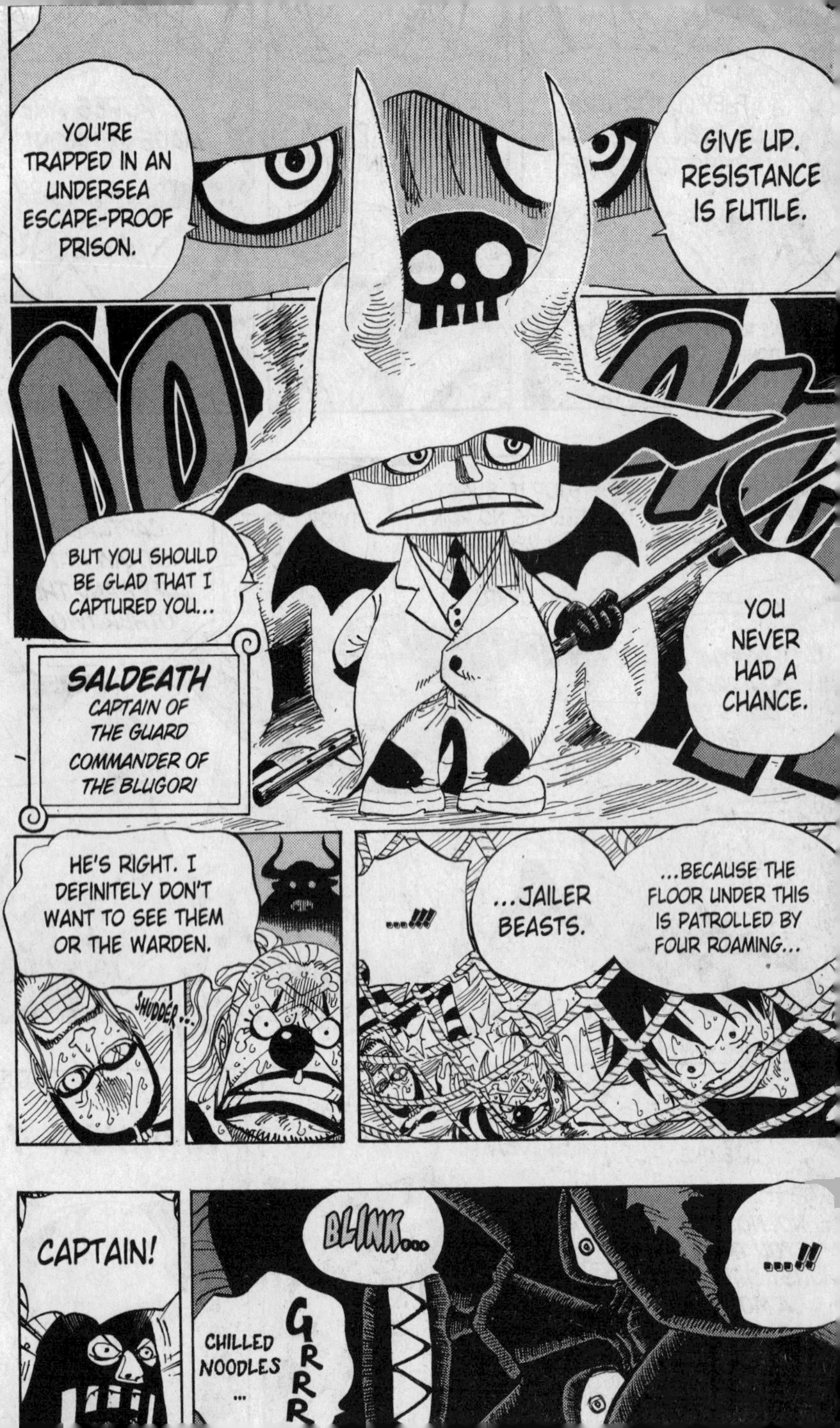
GIVE UP. RESISTANCE IS FUTILE.
YOU'RE TRAPPED IN AN UNDERSEA ESCAPE-PROOF PRISON.
DO
YOU NEVER HAD A CHANCE.
BUT YOU SHOULD BE GLAD THAT I CAPTURED YOU...
SALDEATH
CAPTAIN OF THE GUARD COMMANDER OF THE BLUGORI
...BECAUSE THE FLOOR UNDER THIS IS PATROLLED BY FOUR ROAMING...
...JAILER BEASTS.
...!!!
HE'S RIGHT. I DEFINITELY DON'T WANT TO SEE THEM OR THE WARDEN.
SHUDDER...
...!!
BLINK...
GRRR
CHILLED NOODLES ...
CAPTAIN!

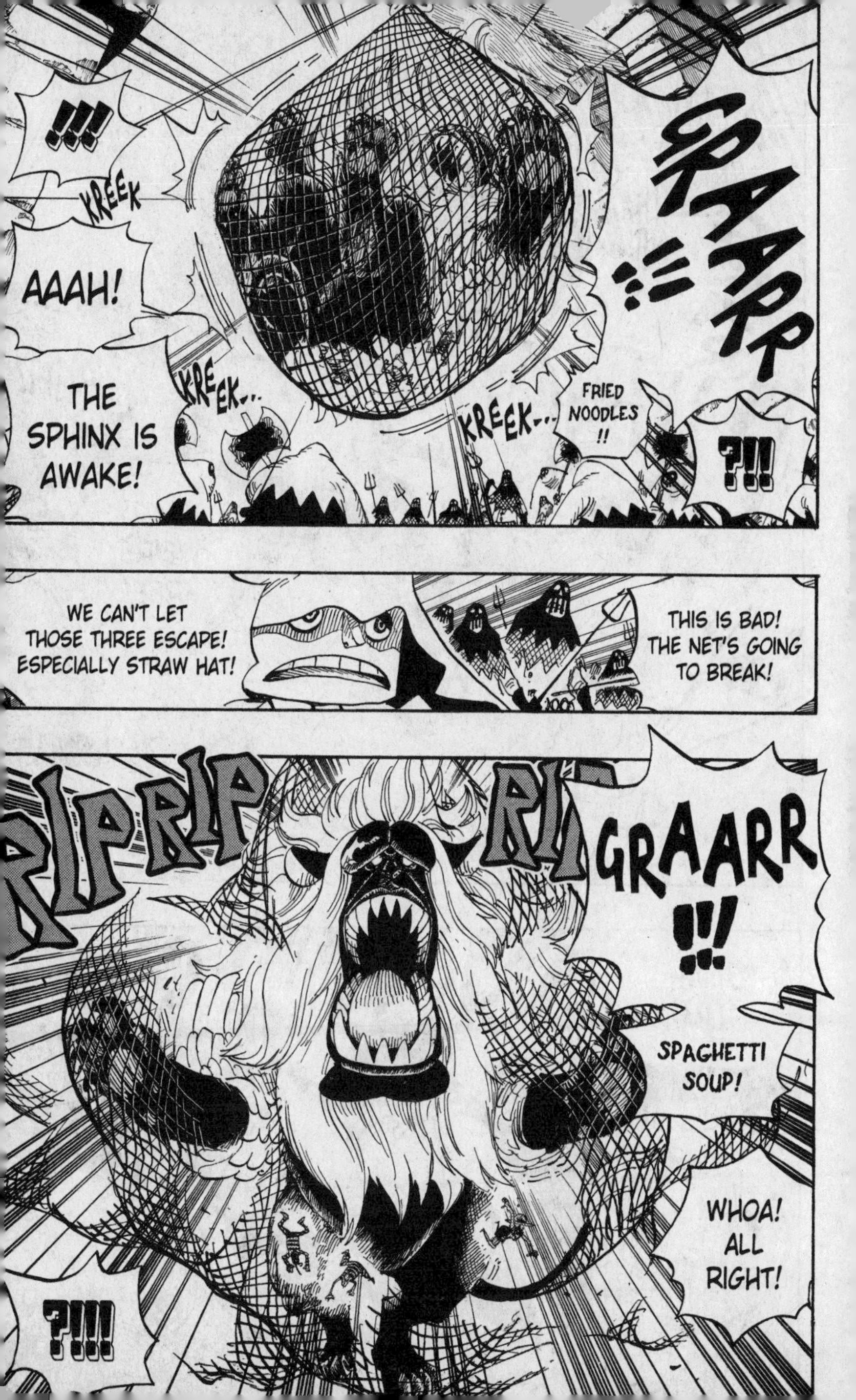
GRAARR
?!!
FRIED NOODLES !!
KREEK...
!!!
KREEK
AAAH!
KREEK...
THE SPHINX IS AWAKE!
THIS IS BAD! THE NET'S GOING TO BREAK!
WE CAN'T LET THOSE THREE ESCAPE! ESPECIALLY STRAW HAT!
GRAARR !!!
RIPRIPRI
SPAGHETTI SOUP!
WHOA! ALL RIGHT!
?!!!

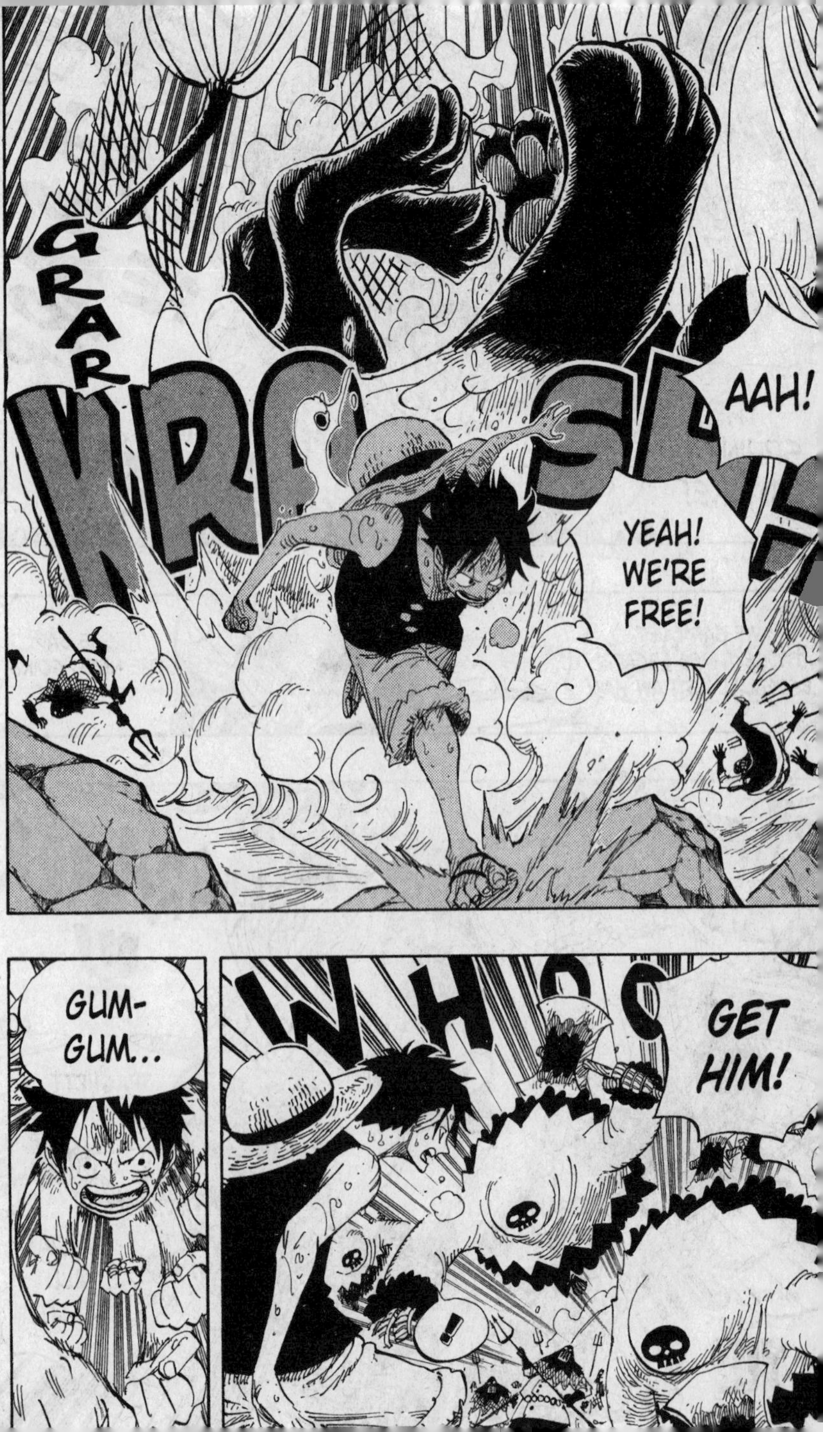
AAH!
YEAH! WE'RE FREE!
GRAR
GET HIM!
!
GUM-GUM...

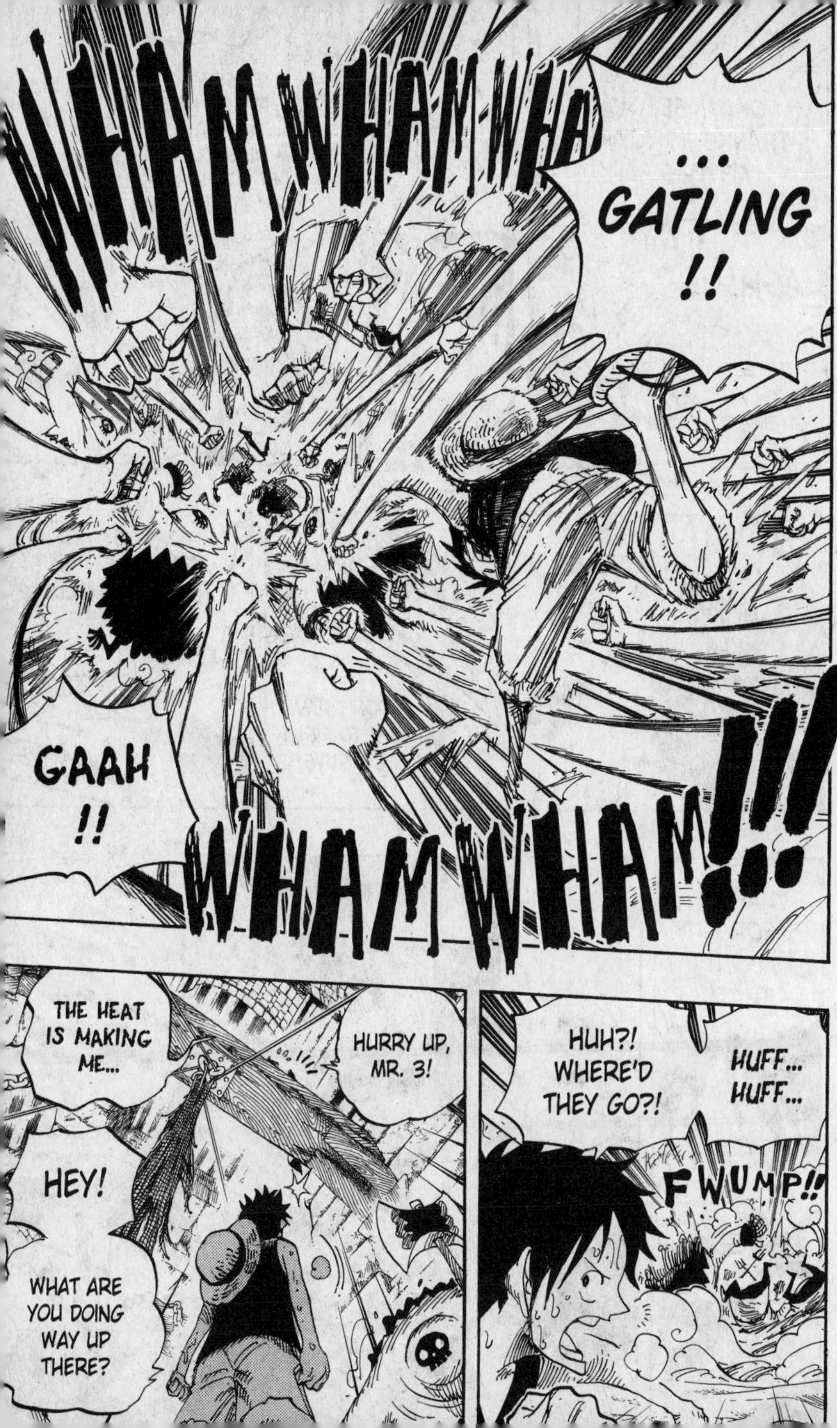
... GATLING !!
WHAM WHAM WHA
GAAH !!
WHAM WHAM!!!
HUFF... HUFF...
HUH?! WHERE'D THEY GO?!
FWUMP!!
HURRY UP, MR. 3!
THE HEAT IS MAKING ME...
HEY!
WHAT ARE YOU DOING WAY UP THERE?

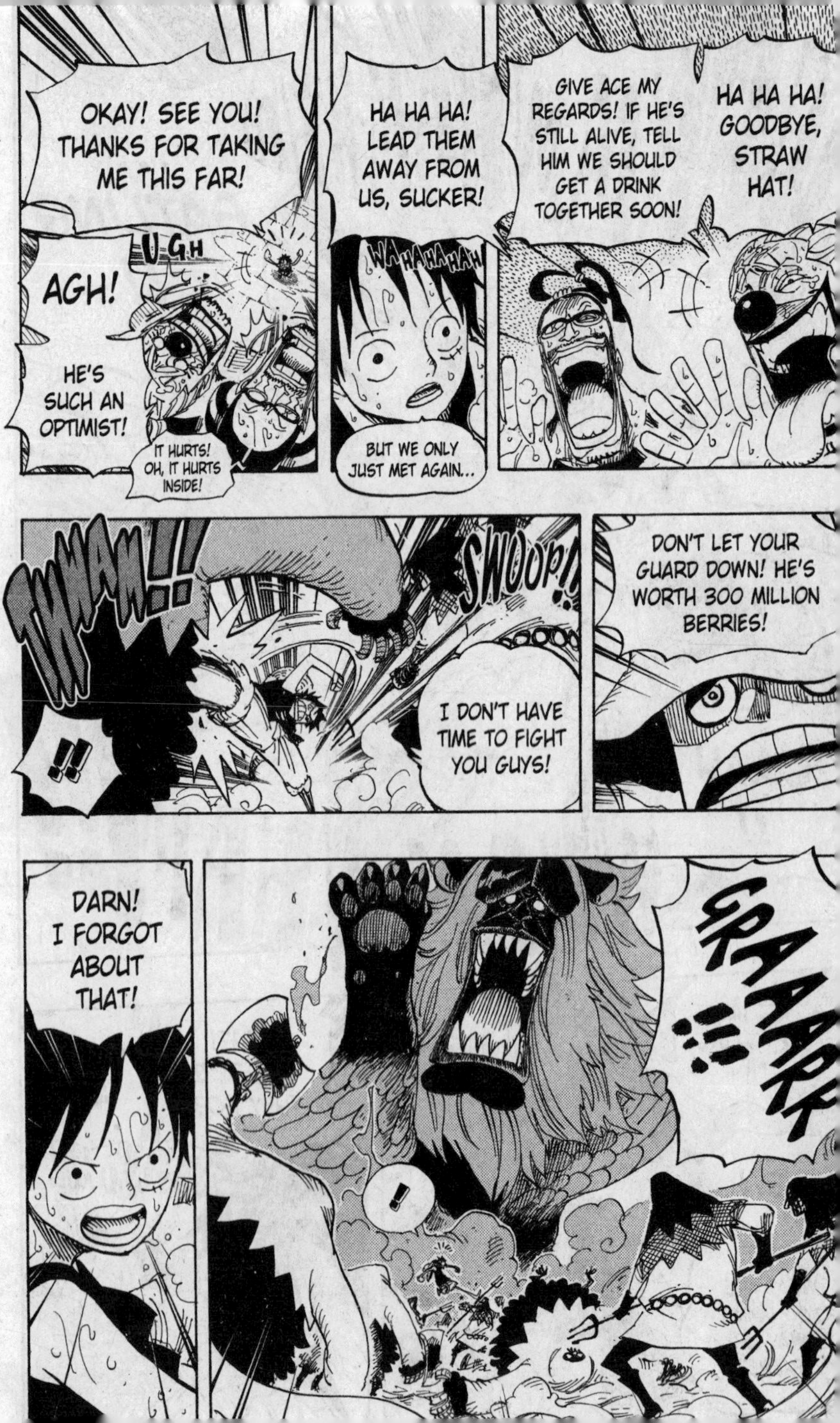
HA HA HA! GOODBYE, STRAW HAT!
GIVE ACE MY REGARDS! IF HE'S STILL ALIVE, TELL HIM WE SHOULD GET A DRINK TOGETHER SOON!
HA HA HA! LEAD THEM AWAY FROM US, SUCKER!
WAHAHAHAH
BUT WE ONLY JUST MET AGAIN...
OKAY! SEE YOU! THANKS FOR TAKING ME THIS FAR!
UGH
AGH!
HE'S SUCH AN OPTIMIST!
IT HURTS! OH, IT HURTS INSIDE!
DON'T LET YOUR GUARD DOWN! HE'S WORTH 300 MILLION BERRIES!
SWOOP!!
THWAM!!
I DON'T HAVE TIME TO FIGHT YOU GUYS!
!!
GRAAARR
!
DARN! I FORGOT ABOUT THAT!

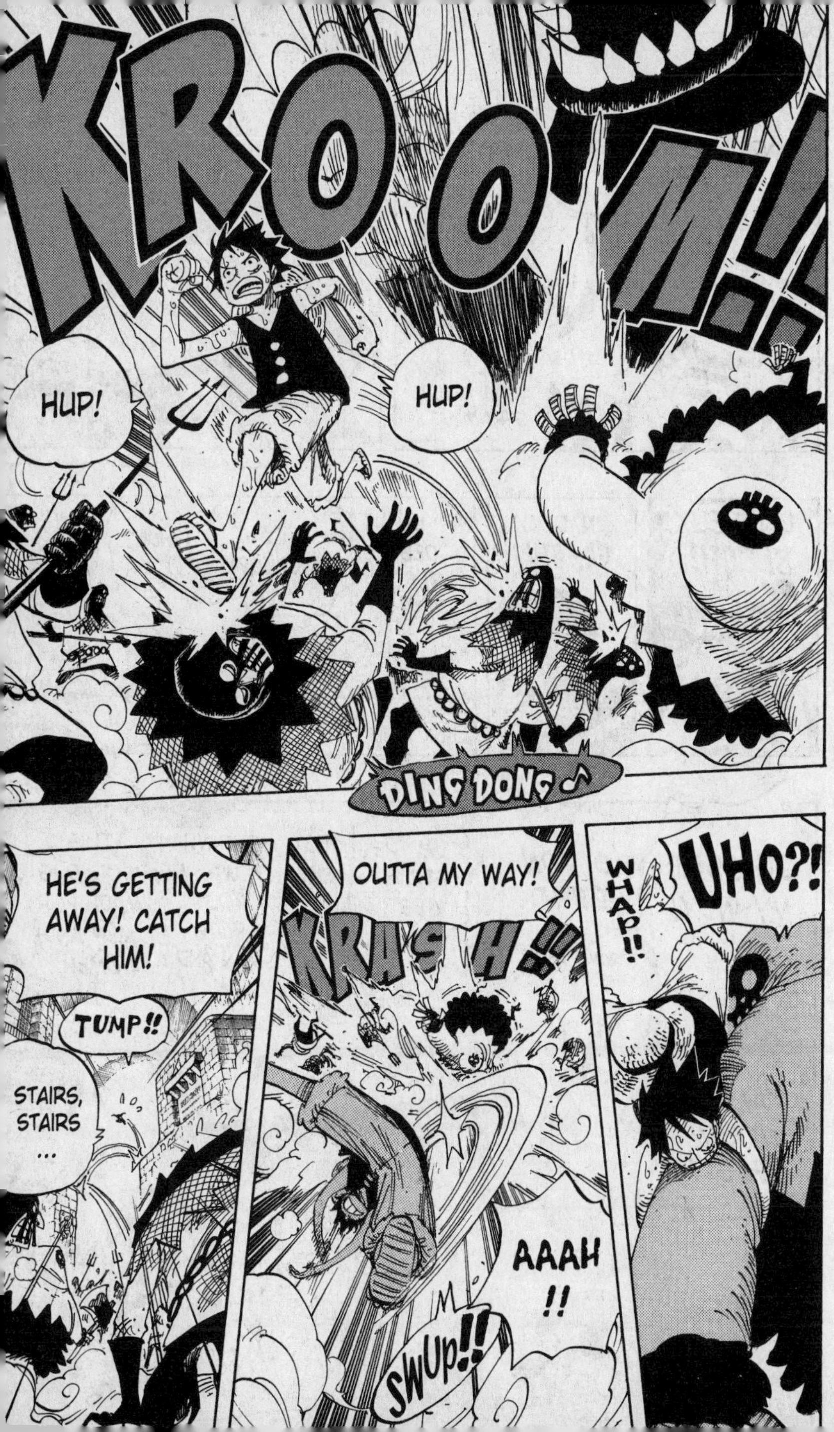
KROOM!!
HUP!
HUP!
DING DONG ♪
UHO?!
WHAP!!
OUTTA MY WAY!
KRASH!!
AAAH!!
SWUP!!
HE'S GETTING AWAY! CATCH HIM!
TUMP!!
STAIRS, STAIRS ...

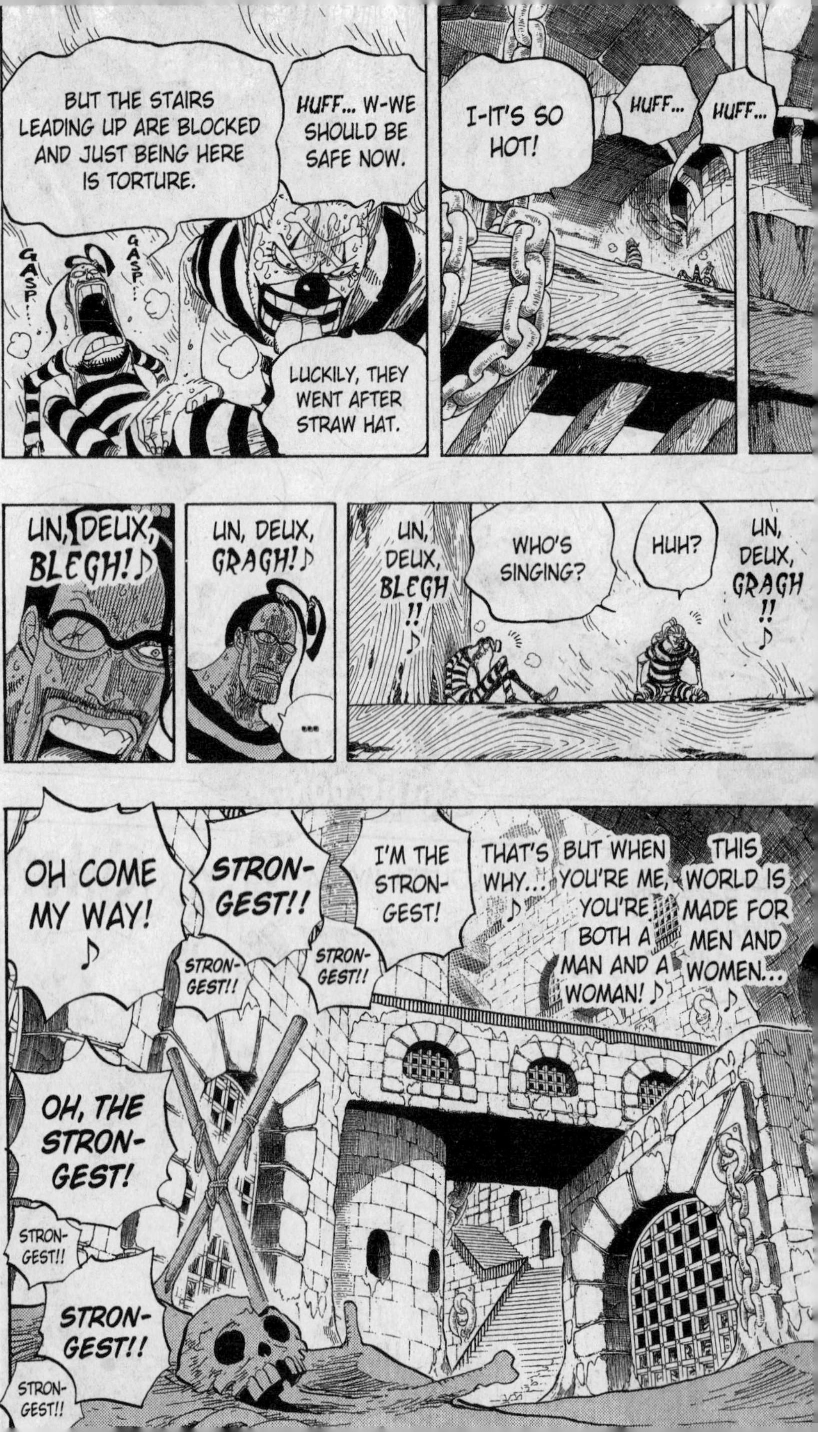
HUFF...
HUFF...
I-IT'S SO HOT!
HUFF... W-WE SHOULD BE SAFE NOW.
BUT THE STAIRS LEADING UP ARE BLOCKED AND JUST BEING HERE IS TORTURE.
GASP...
GASP...
LUCKILY, THEY WENT AFTER STRAW HAT.
UN, DEUX, GRAGH!! ♪
HUH?
WHO'S SINGING?
UN, DEUX, BLEGH!! ♪
UN, DEUX, GRAGH! ♪
...
UN, DEUX, BLEGH! ♪
THIS WORLD IS MADE FOR MEN AND WOMEN... ♪
BUT WHEN YOU'RE ME, YOU'RE BOTH A MAN AND A WOMAN! ♪
THAT'S WHY... ♪
I'M THE STRON-GEST!
STRON-GEST!!
STRON-GEST!!
STRON-GEST!!
OH COME MY WAY! ♪
OH, THE STRON-GEST!
STRON-GEST!!
STRON-GEST!!
STRON-GEST!!

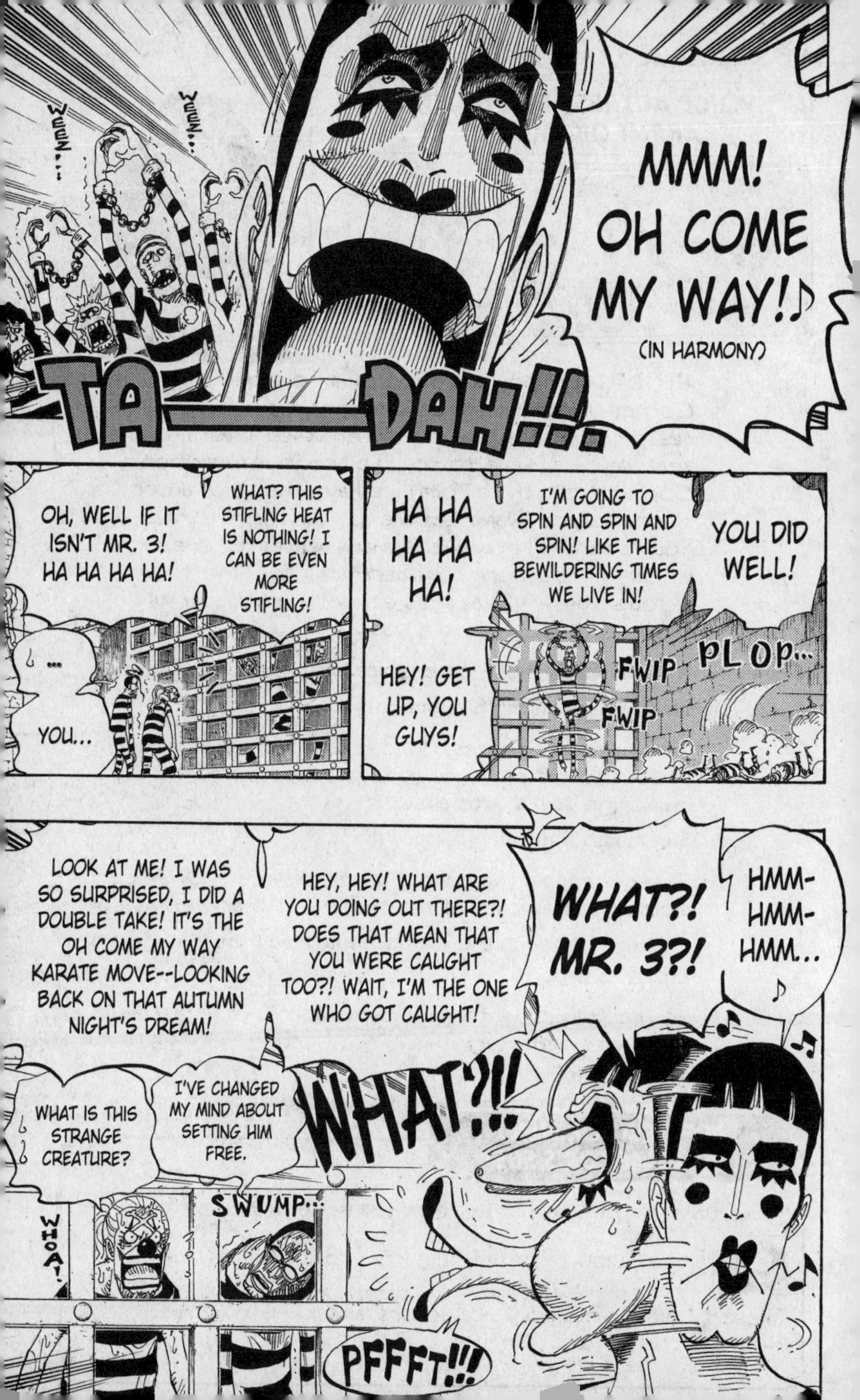
MMM! OH COME MY WAY!♪
(IN HARMONY)
TA——DAH!!!
WEEN...
WEEN...
YOU DID WELL!
I'M GOING TO SPIN AND SPIN AND SPIN! LIKE THE BEWILDERING TIMES WE LIVE IN!
HA HA HA HA HA!
PLOP...
FWIP
FWIP
HEY! GET UP, YOU GUYS!
WHAT? THIS STIFLING HEAT IS NOTHING! I CAN BE EVEN MORE STIFLING!
OH, WELL IF IT ISN'T MR. 3! HA HA HA HA!
...
YOU...
HMM-HMM-HMM...♪
WHAT?! MR. 3?!
HEY, HEY! WHAT ARE YOU DOING OUT THERE?! DOES THAT MEAN THAT YOU WERE CAUGHT TOO?! WAIT, I'M THE ONE WHO GOT CAUGHT!
LOOK AT ME! I WAS SO SURPRISED, I DID A DOUBLE TAKE! IT'S THE OH COME MY WAY KARATE MOVE--LOOKING BACK ON THAT AUTUMN NIGHT'S DREAM!
WHAT?!!
I'VE CHANGED MY MIND ABOUT SETTING HIM FREE.
WHAT IS THIS STRANGE CREATURE?
SWUMP...
WHOA!
PFFFT!!!

SBS Question Corner

VOICE ACTRESS FOR NAMI, AKEMI OKAMURA!

(Tomofuni Kawakami, Tottori)

 HDYD?! (How do you do?) This is now the third Question Corner for the voice actors! It always ends up being a really nice read, But all the other voice actors complain Because they'll have to top the previous Question Corner! Now then. Today we have the voice actor for the navigator, Nami! Let me say this first to the readers. You're sending in way too many perverted questions! Can you be a little more considerate since I have to go through them?! Okay, let's go on! Our wonderful lady Akemi Okamura is in the house!

Oda(O): Here is Okamura! Please gracefully introduce yourself!

Akemi(A): Hello. This is Akemi Okamura, always with a smile.

O: Good intro! ♪♪ Yes, I love it when you guys take this seriously. By the way, do you know what SBS stands for? I'm hoping for a cute answer.

A: Sure thing. (S)tupidity (B)ashed (S)illy. ♡

O: That's scary! ♫ I introduced you as a sweet lady! Are you going to disappoint all the readers who are young boys?!

A: Oh, that wasn't good? Okay, one more time then. (S)illy (B)oys (S)lapped. ♡

O: You're still going to beat them, aren't you?! ♫ Whatever! Okay, let's just start this.

A: Sure thing. ♡

The Question Corner with Okamura continued on page 206! ☞

PREVIEW FOR NEXT VOICE ACTOR'S SBS

Next time and the one after that will be with these two!

Usopp (Kappei Yamaguchi)   Sanji (Hiroaki Hirata)

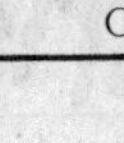

These two are veteran voice actors, and you know exactly how they are!

Chapter 531:
LEVEL 3: STARVATION HELL

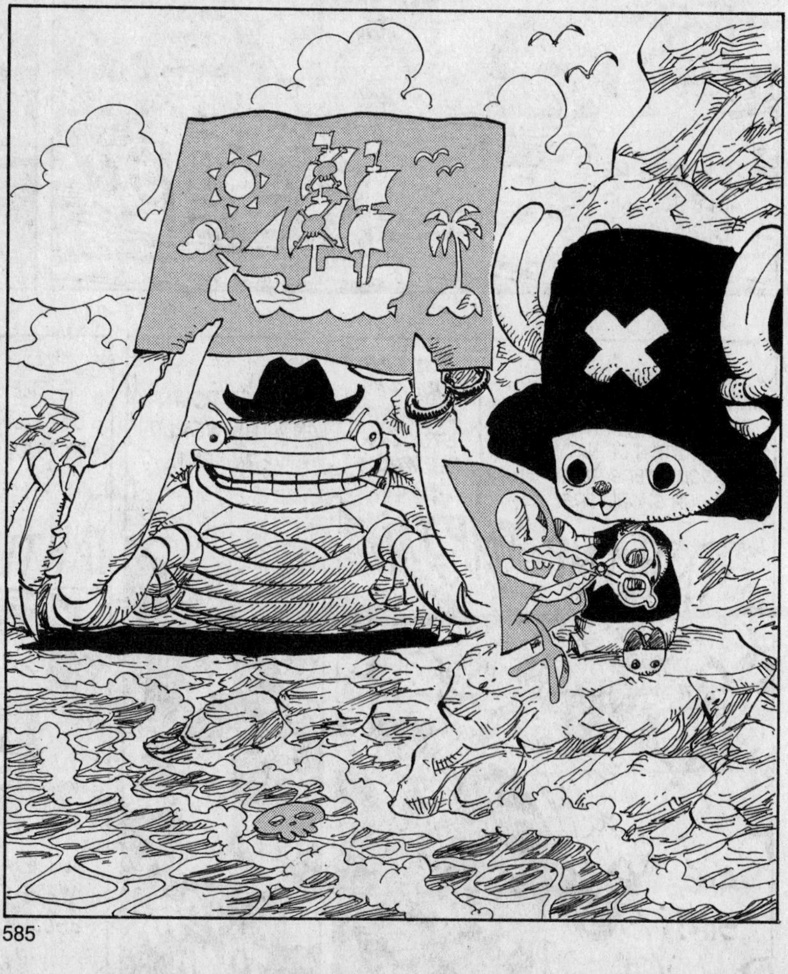

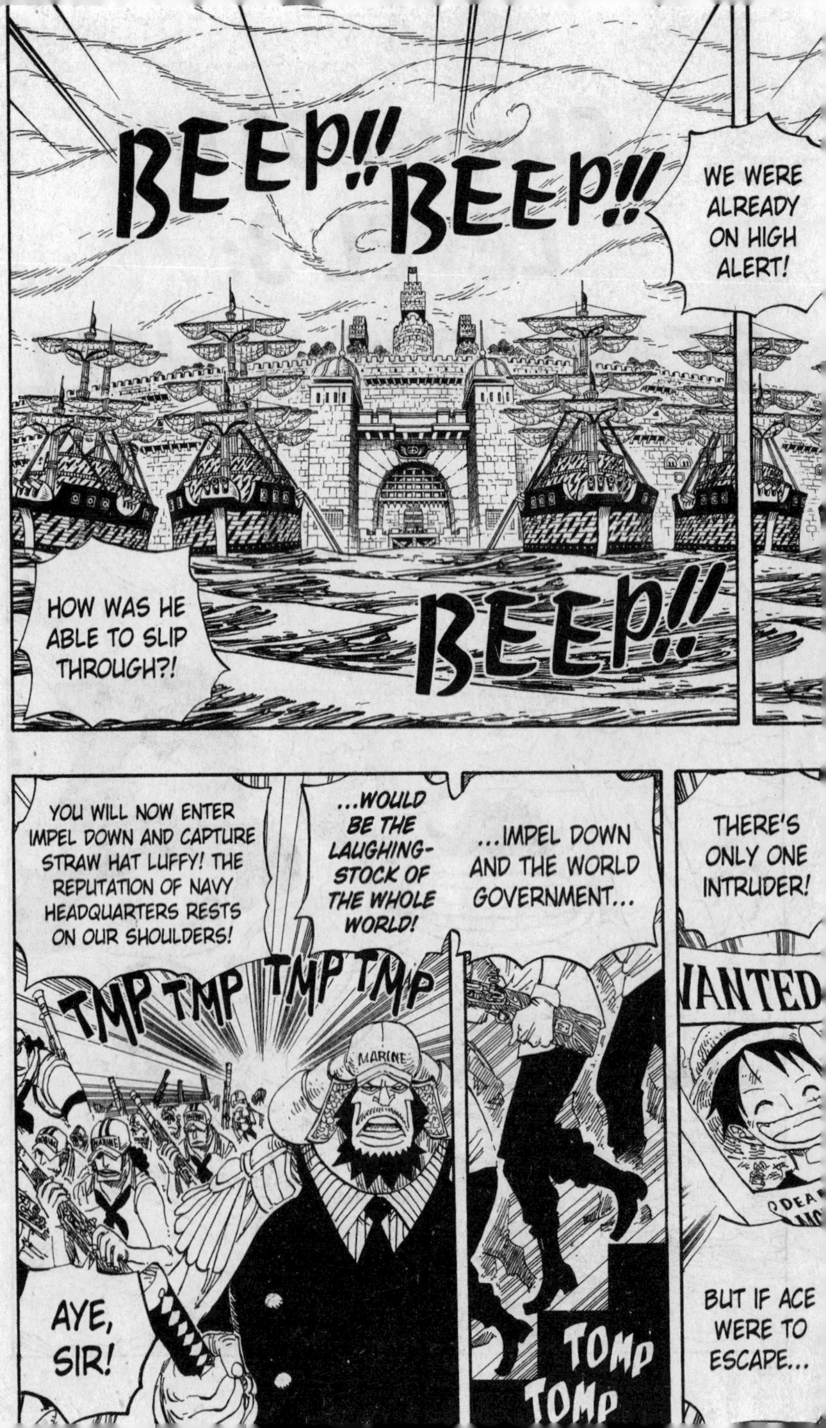
WE WERE ALREADY ON HIGH ALERT!
BEEP!! BEEP!!
BEEP!!
HOW WAS HE ABLE TO SLIP THROUGH?!
THERE'S ONLY ONE INTRUDER!
BUT IF ACE WERE TO ESCAPE...
...IMPEL DOWN AND THE WORLD GOVERNMENT...
...WOULD BE THE LAUGHING-STOCK OF THE WHOLE WORLD!
TOMP TOMP
YOU WILL NOW ENTER IMPEL DOWN AND CAPTURE STRAW HAT LUFFY! THE REPUTATION OF NAVY HEADQUARTERS RESTS ON OUR SHOULDERS!
TMP TMP TMP TMP
MARINE
AYE, SIR!

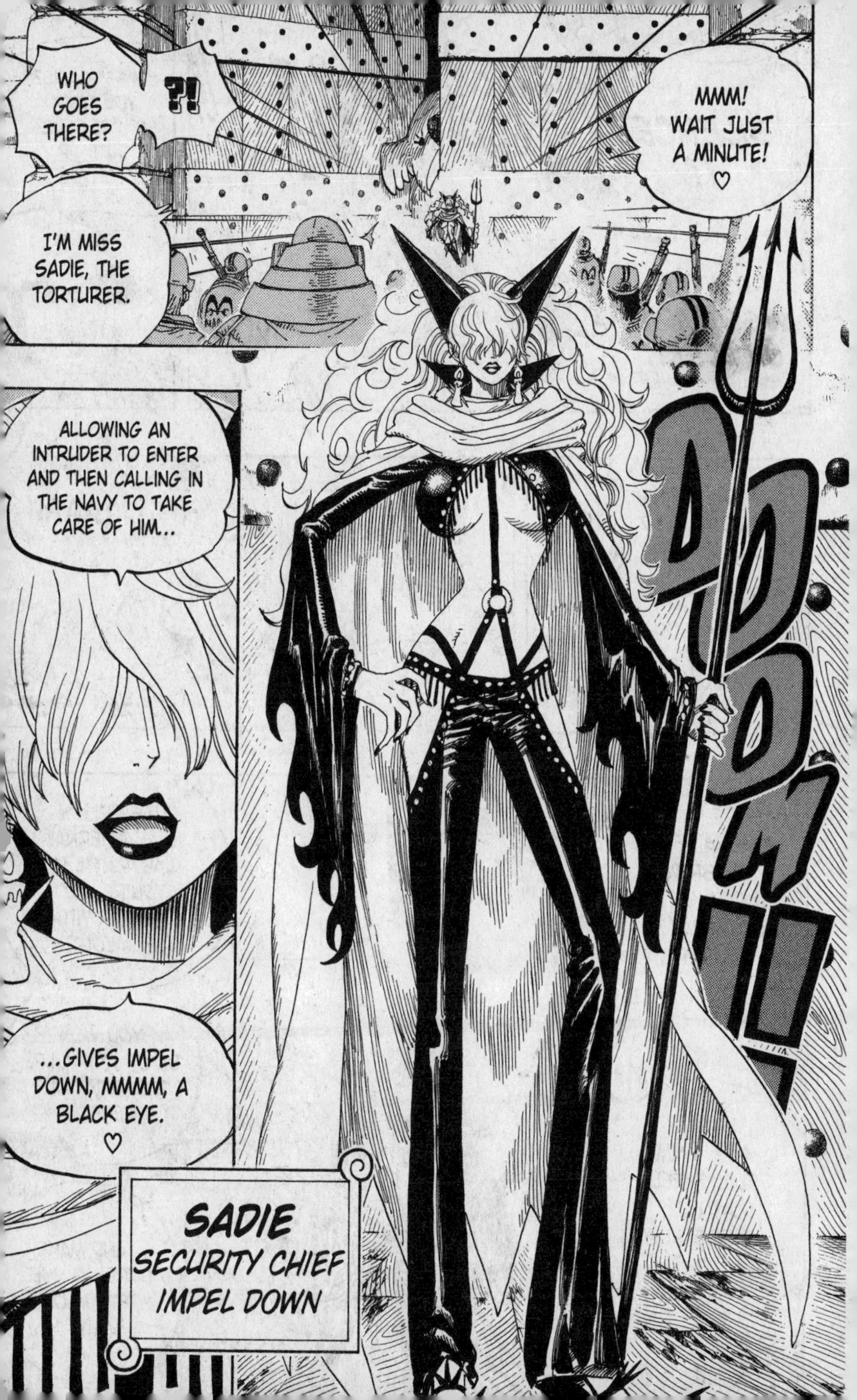
MMM! WAIT JUST A MINUTE! ♡
WHO GOES THERE?
?!
I'M MISS SADIE, THE TORTURER.
DOOM!!
SADIE
SECURITY CHIEF
IMPEL DOWN
ALLOWING AN INTRUDER TO ENTER AND THEN CALLING IN THE NAVY TO TAKE CARE OF HIM...
...GIVES IMPEL DOWN, MMMM, A BLACK EYE. ♡

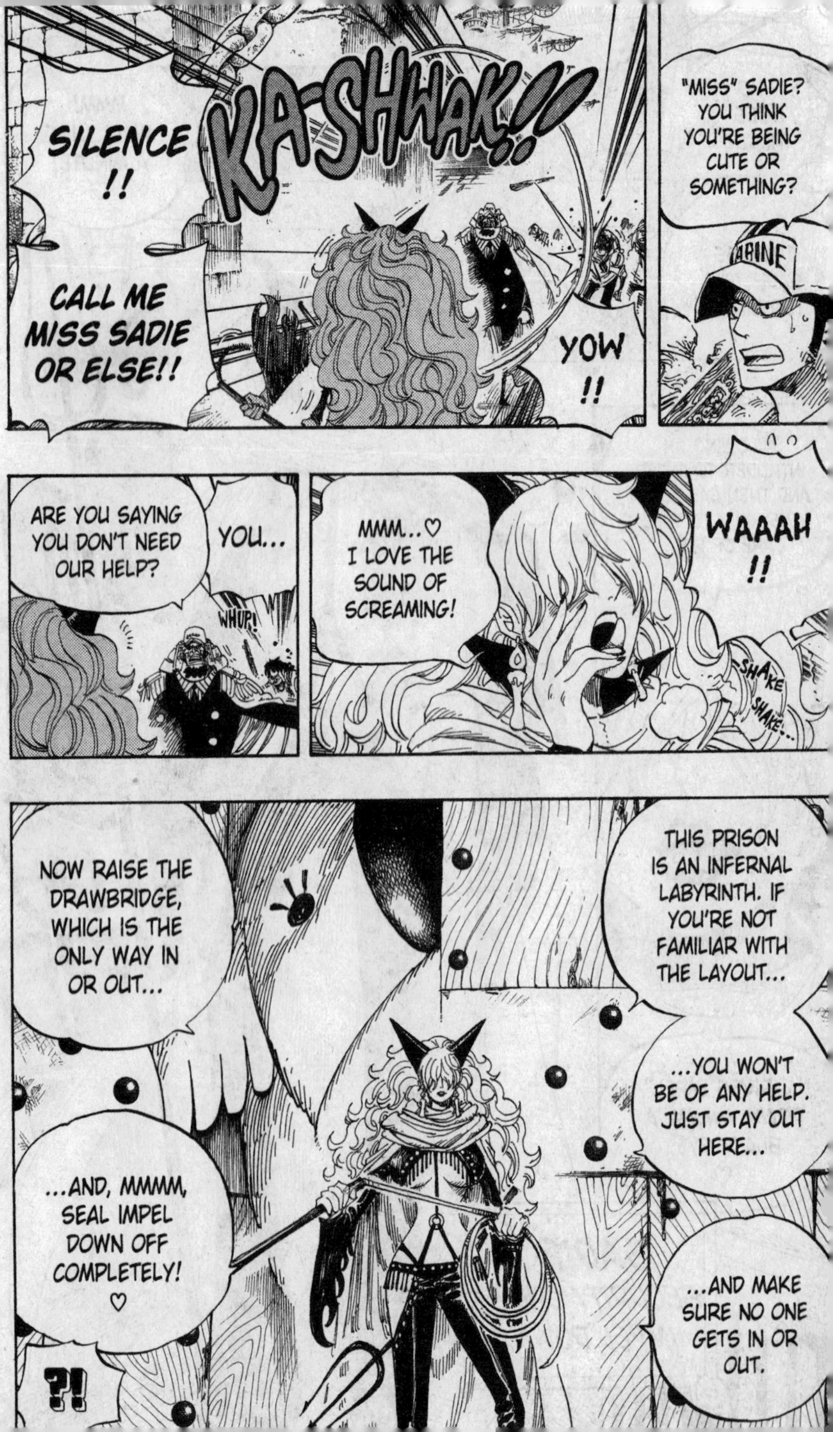
"MISS" SADIE? YOU THINK YOU'RE BEING CUTE OR SOMETHING?
KA-SHWAK!!
YOW!!
SILENCE!!
CALL ME MISS SADIE OR ELSE!!
WAAAH!!
MMM..♡ I LOVE THE SOUND OF SCREAMING!
SHAKE SHAKE...
YOU...
ARE YOU SAYING YOU DON'T NEED OUR HELP?
WHUP!
THIS PRISON IS AN INFERNAL LABYRINTH. IF YOU'RE NOT FAMILIAR WITH THE LAYOUT...
...YOU WON'T BE OF ANY HELP. JUST STAY OUT HERE...
...AND MAKE SURE NO ONE GETS IN OR OUT.
NOW RAISE THE DRAWBRIDGE, WHICH IS THE ONLY WAY IN OR OUT...
...AND, MMMM, SEAL IMPEL DOWN OFF COMPLETELY! ♡
?!

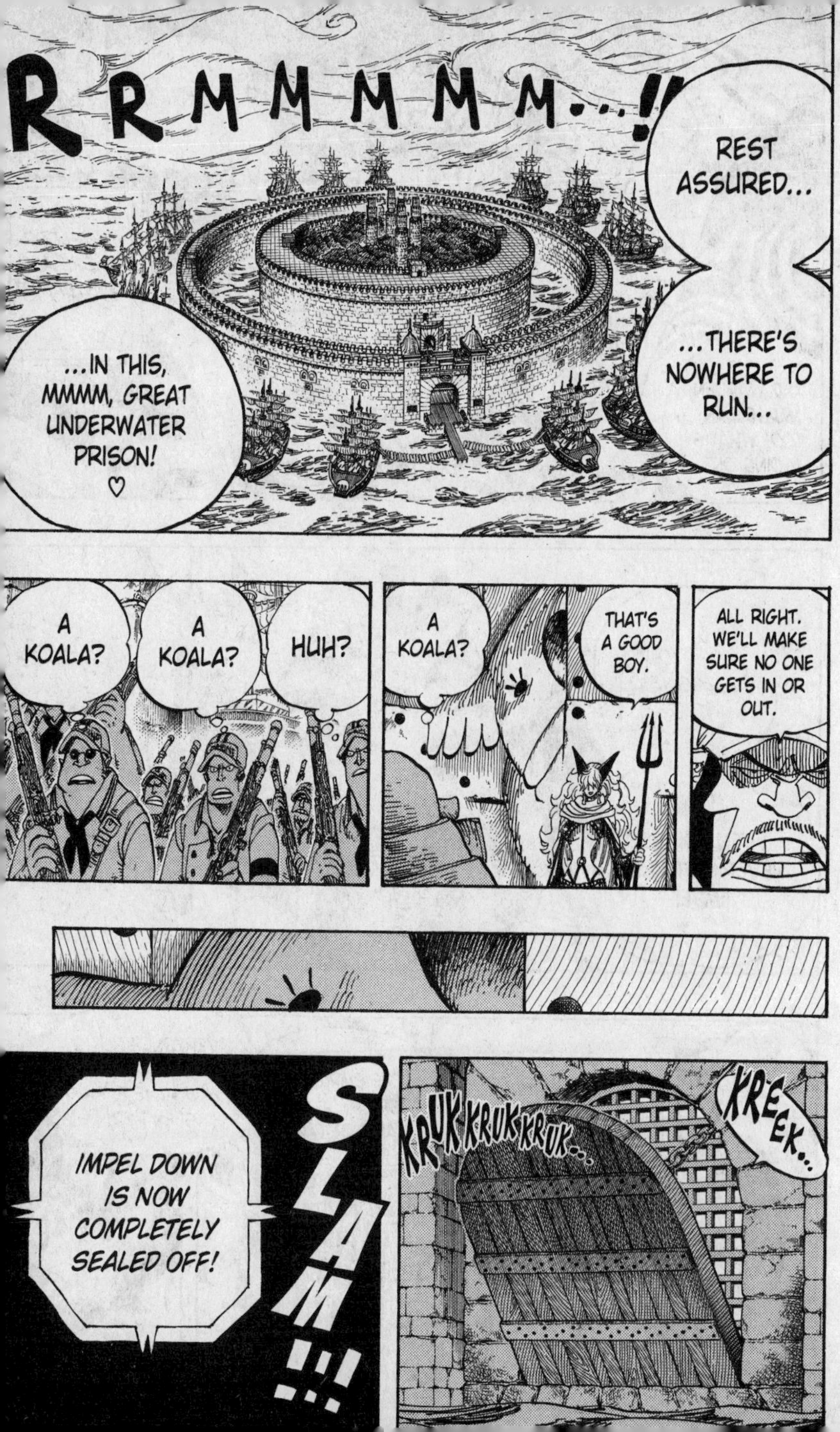
RRMMMMMM...!!
REST ASSURED...
...THERE'S NOWHERE TO RUN...
...IN THIS, MMMM, GREAT UNDERWATER PRISON! ♡
ALL RIGHT. WE'LL MAKE SURE NO ONE GETS IN OR OUT.
THAT'S A GOOD BOY.
A KOALA?
HUH?
A KOALA?
A KOALA?
KREEK...
KRUK KRUK KRUK...
SLAM!!!
IMPEL DOWN IS NOW COMPLETELY SEALED OFF!

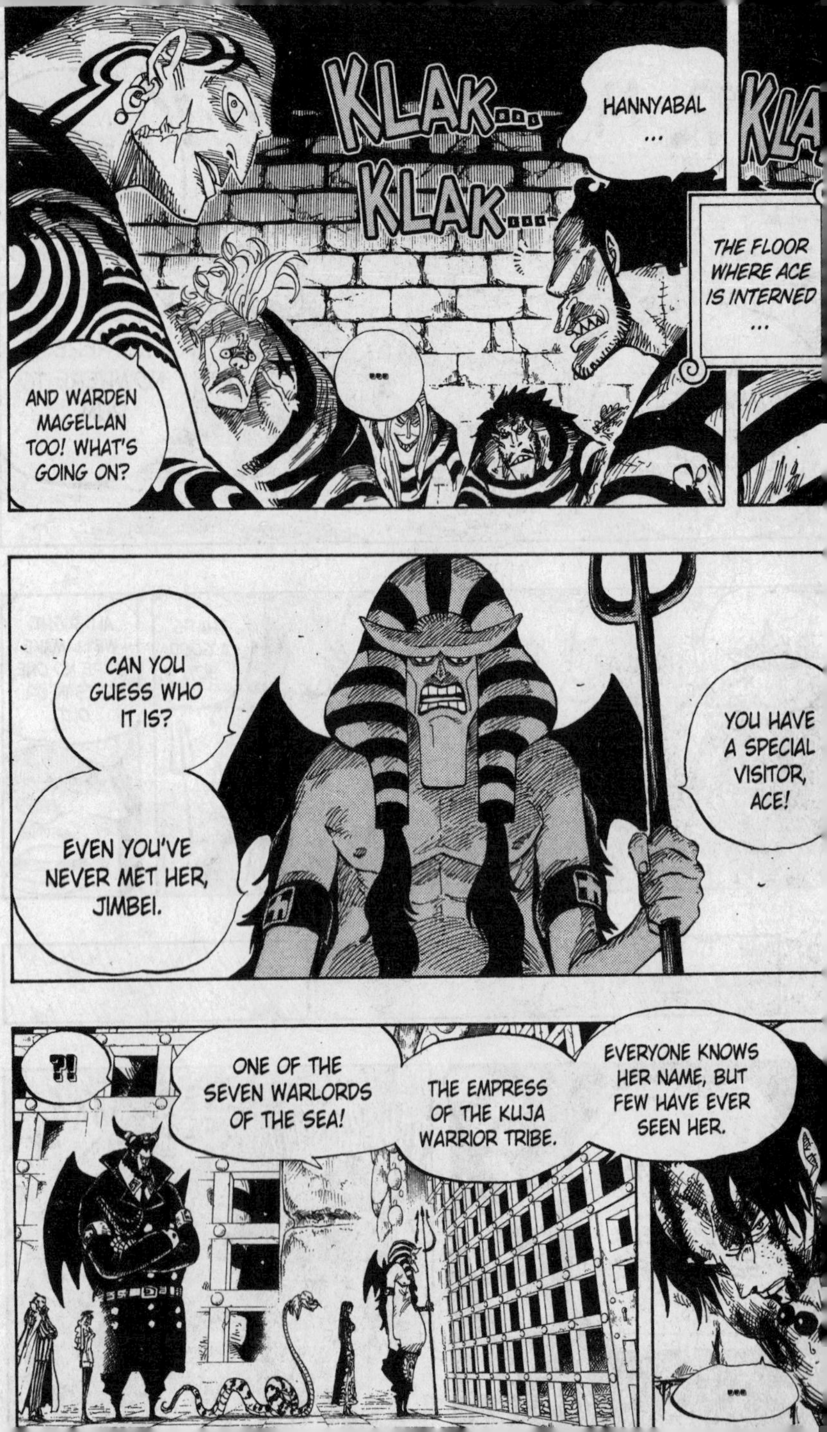
KLA
THE FLOOR WHERE ACE IS INTERNED ...
KLAK... KLAK...
HANNYABAL ...
...
AND WARDEN MAGELLAN TOO! WHAT'S GOING ON?
YOU HAVE A SPECIAL VISITOR, ACE!
CAN YOU GUESS WHO IT IS?
EVEN YOU'VE NEVER MET HER, JIMBEI.
EVERYONE KNOWS HER NAME, BUT FEW HAVE EVER SEEN HER.
THE EMPRESS OF THE KUJA WARRIOR TRIBE.
ONE OF THE SEVEN WARLORDS OF THE SEA!
?!
...

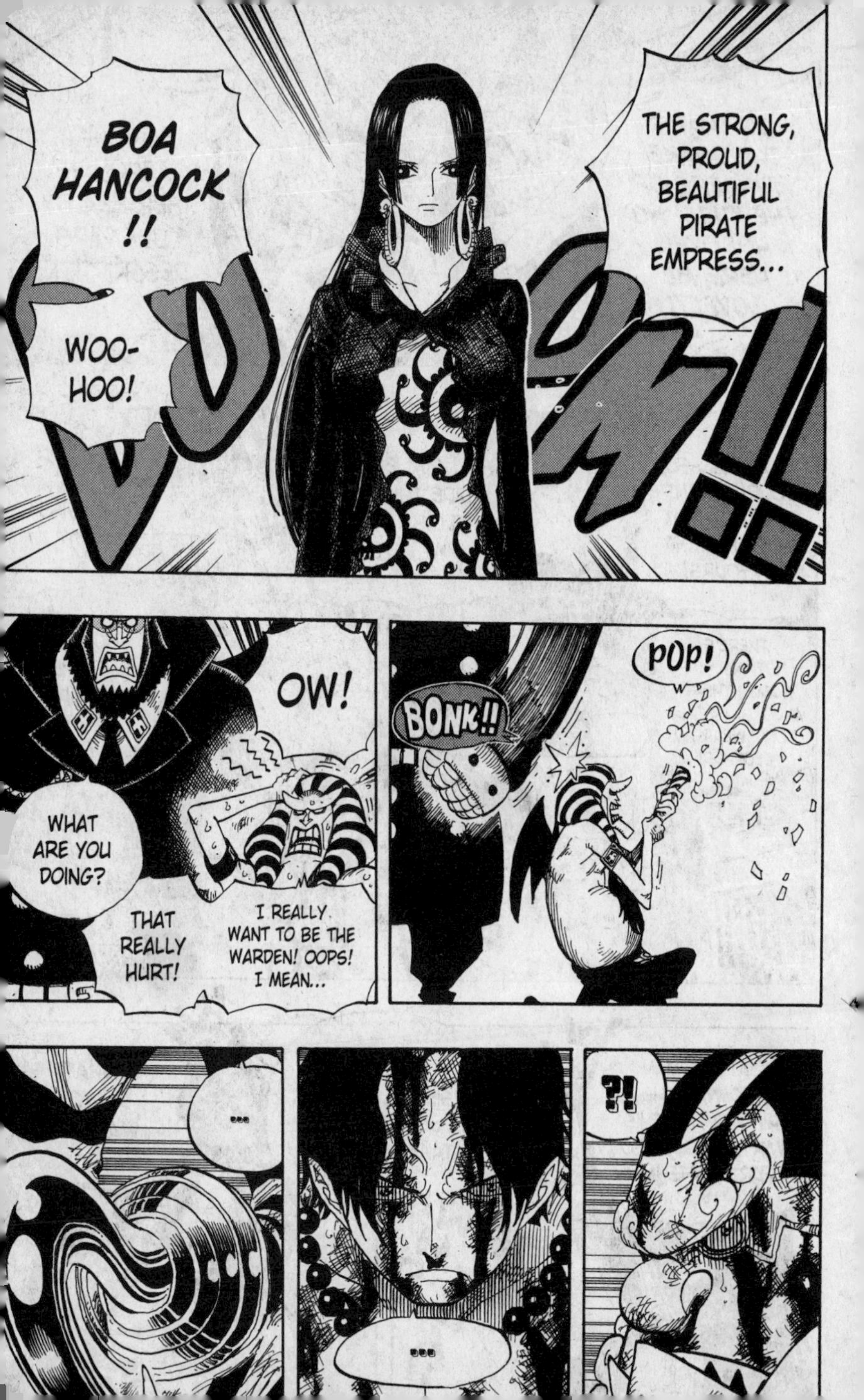

THE STRONG, PROUD, BEAUTIFUL PIRATE EMPRESS...
BOA HANCOCK!!
WOO-HOO!
POP!
BONK!!
OW!
I REALLY WANT TO BE THE WARDEN! OOPS! I MEAN...
THAT REALLY HURT!
WHAT ARE YOU DOING?
?!
...
...

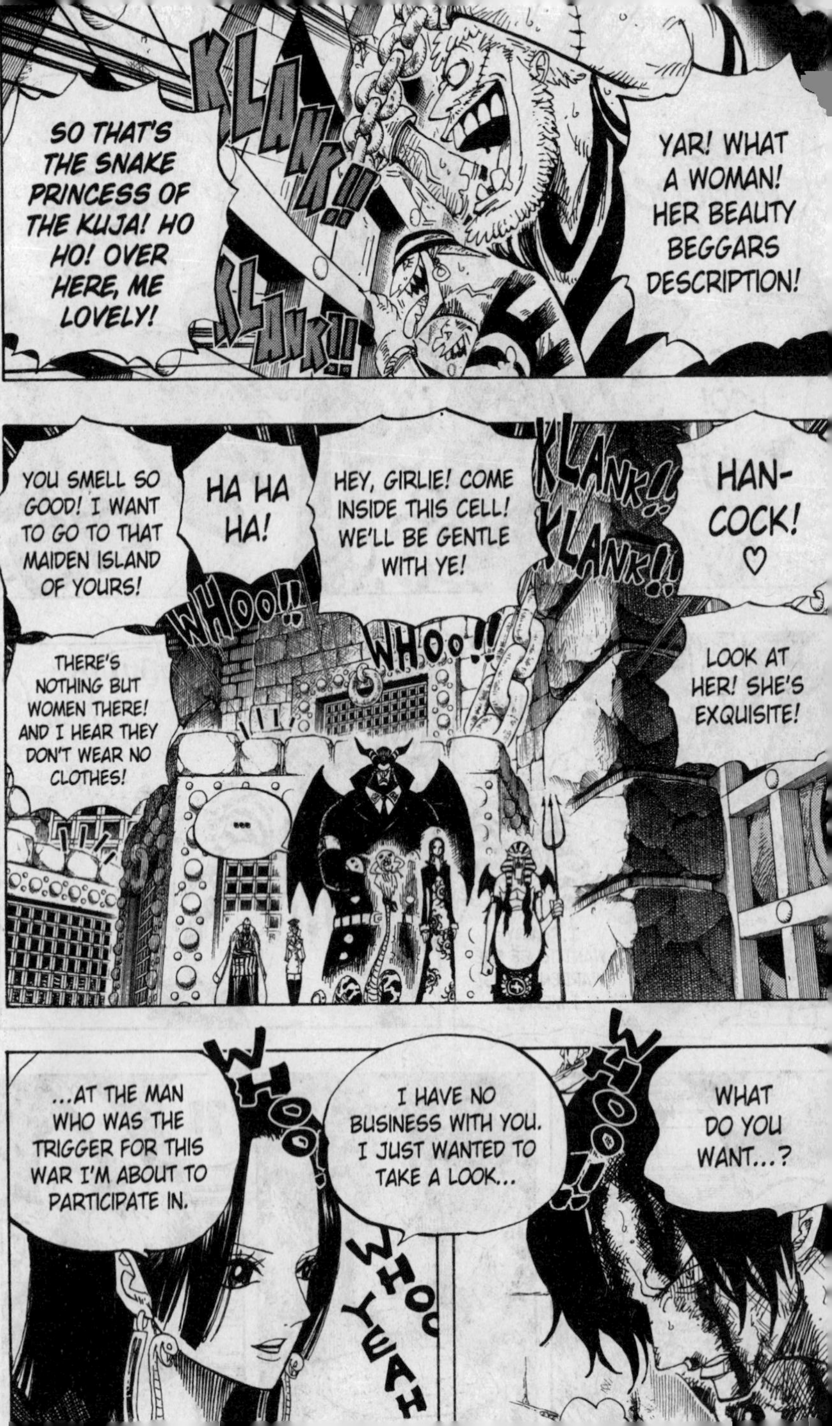
YAR! WHAT A WOMAN! HER BEAUTY BEGGARS DESCRIPTION!
KLANK!!
SLANK!!
SO THAT'S THE SNAKE PRINCESS OF THE KUJA! HO HO! OVER HERE, ME LOVELY!
HAN-COCK! ♡
KLANK!!
KLANK!!
LOOK AT HER! SHE'S EXQUISITE!
HEY, GIRLIE! COME INSIDE THIS CELL! WE'LL BE GENTLE WITH YE!
WHOO!!
HA HA HA!
YOU SMELL SO GOOD! I WANT TO GO TO THAT MAIDEN ISLAND OF YOURS!
WHOO!!
THERE'S NOTHING BUT WOMEN THERE! AND I HEAR THEY DON'T WEAR NO CLOTHES!
...
WHAT DO YOU WANT...?
WHOO!!
I HAVE NO BUSINESS WITH YOU. I JUST WANTED TO TAKE A LOOK...
WHOO!!
WHOO
YEAH
...AT THE MAN WHO WAS THE TRIGGER FOR THIS WAR I'M ABOUT TO PARTICIPATE IN.

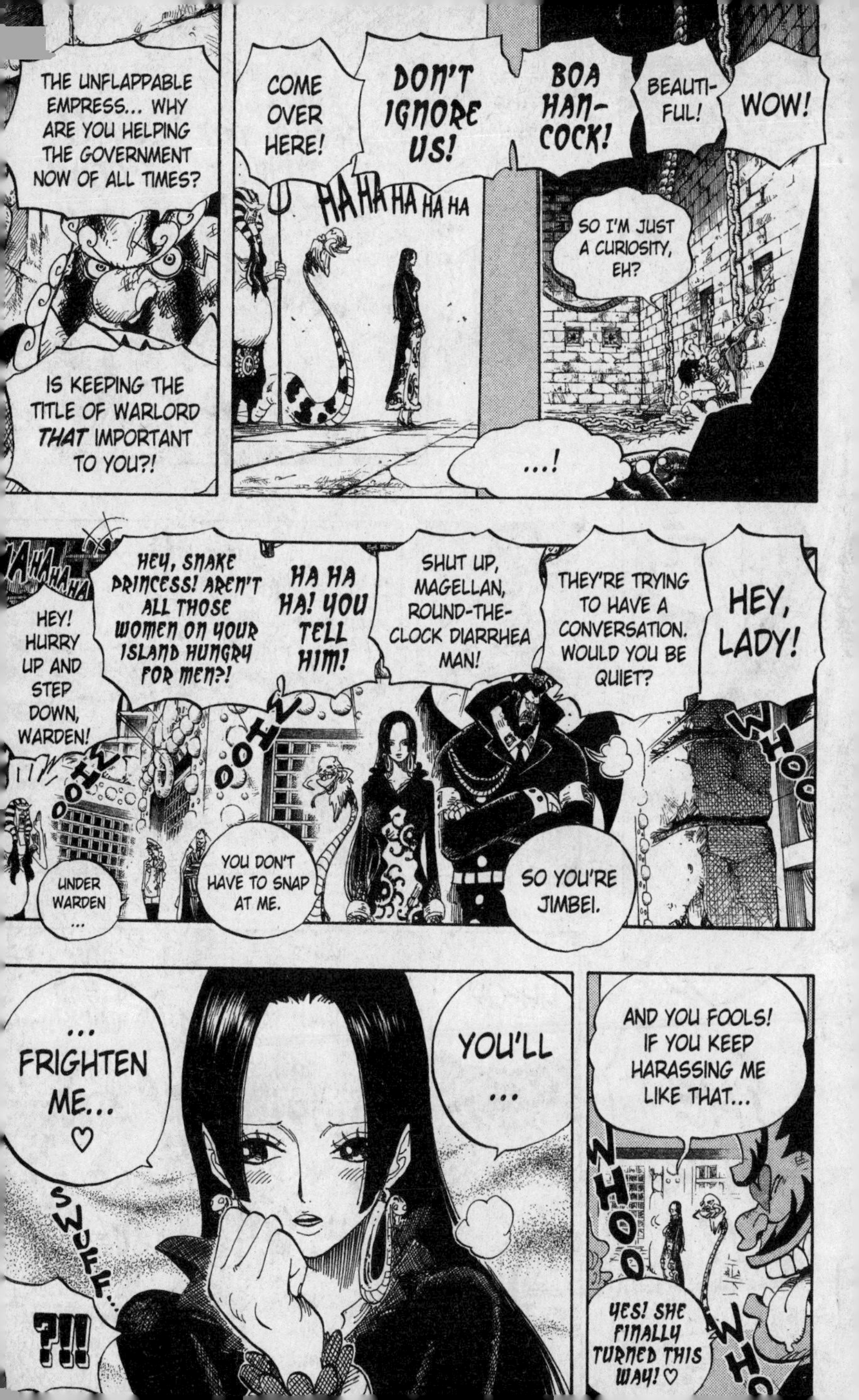
WOW!
BEAUTIFUL!
BOA HANCOCK!
DON'T IGNORE US!
COME OVER HERE!
HAHA HA HA HA
SO I'M JUST A CURIOSITY, EH?
...!
THE UNFLAPPABLE EMPRESS... WHY ARE YOU HELPING THE GOVERNMENT NOW OF ALL TIMES?
IS KEEPING THE TITLE OF WARLORD *THAT* IMPORTANT TO YOU?!
HEY, LADY!
THEY'RE TRYING TO HAVE A CONVERSATION. WOULD YOU BE QUIET?
SHUT UP, MAGELLAN, ROUND-THE-CLOCK DIARRHEA MAN!
HA HA HA! YOU TELL HIM!
HEY, SNAKE PRINCESS! AREN'T ALL THOSE WOMEN ON YOUR ISLAND HUNGRY FOR MEN?!
HAHAHAHA
HEY! HURRY UP AND STEP DOWN, WARDEN!
WHOO
WHOO
WHOO
SO YOU'RE JIMBEI.
YOU DON'T HAVE TO SNAP AT ME.
UNDER WARDEN ...
AND YOU FOOLS! IF YOU KEEP HARASSING ME LIKE THAT...
WHOO
YES! SHE FINALLY TURNED THIS WAY! ♡
WHO
YOU'LL ...
... FRIGHTEN ME... ♡
SWUFF...
?!!

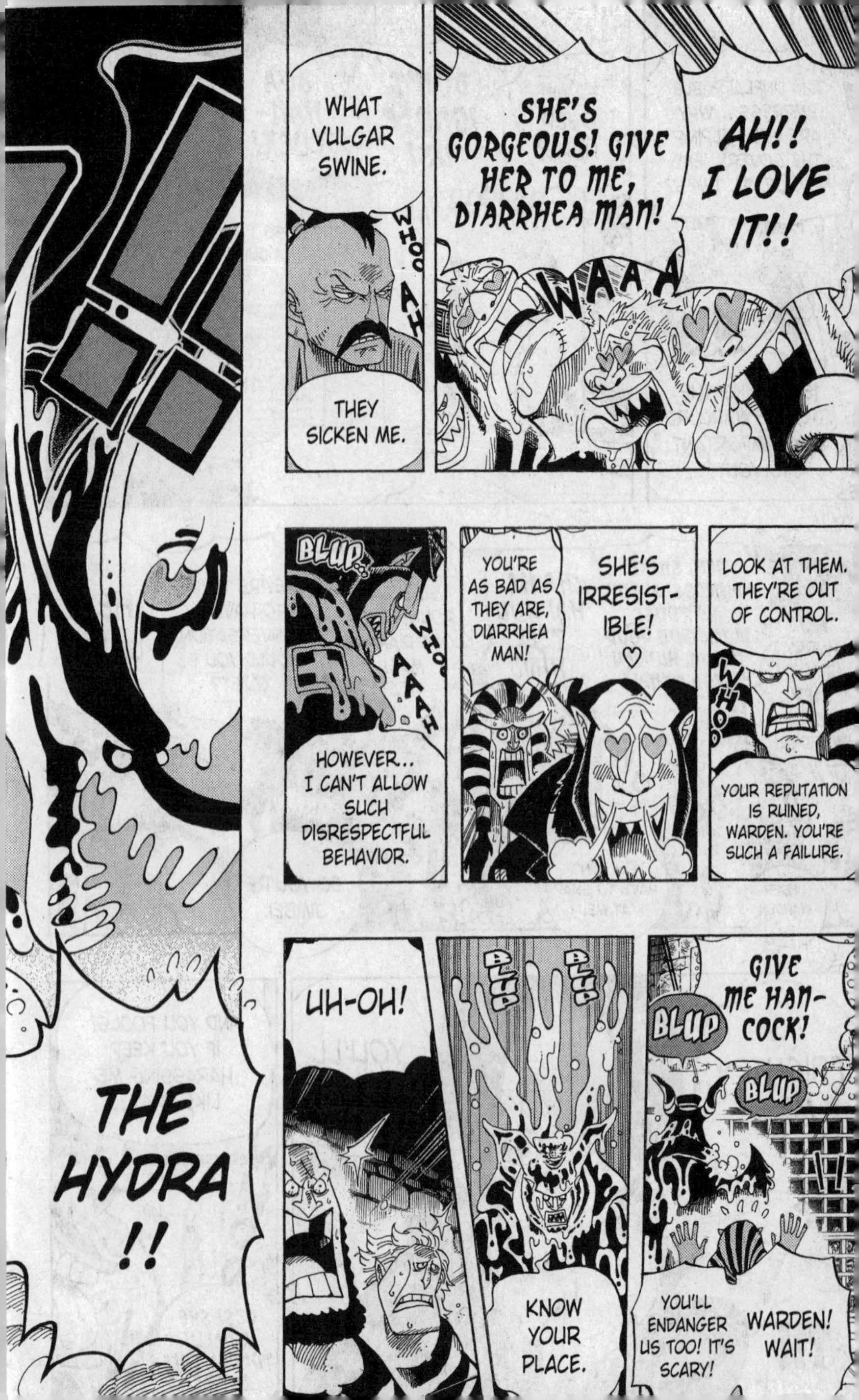
AH!! I LOVE IT!!
SHE'S GORGEOUS! GIVE HER TO ME, DIARRHEA MAN!
WAAA
WHAT VULGAR SWINE.
WHOOAH
THEY SICKEN ME.
LOOK AT THEM. THEY'RE OUT OF CONTROL.
WHOO
YOUR REPUTATION IS RUINED, WARDEN. YOU'RE SUCH A FAILURE.
SHE'S IRRESIST-IBLE! ♥
YOU'RE AS BAD AS THEY ARE, DIARRHEA MAN!
BLUP
WHOOAAAAH
HOWEVER... I CAN'T ALLOW SUCH DISRESPECTFUL BEHAVIOR.
GIVE ME HAN-COCK!
BLUP
BLUP
WARDEN! WAIT!
YOU'LL ENDANGER US TOO! IT'S SCARY!
BLUP
BLUP
KNOW YOUR PLACE.
UH-OH!
THE HYDRA!!

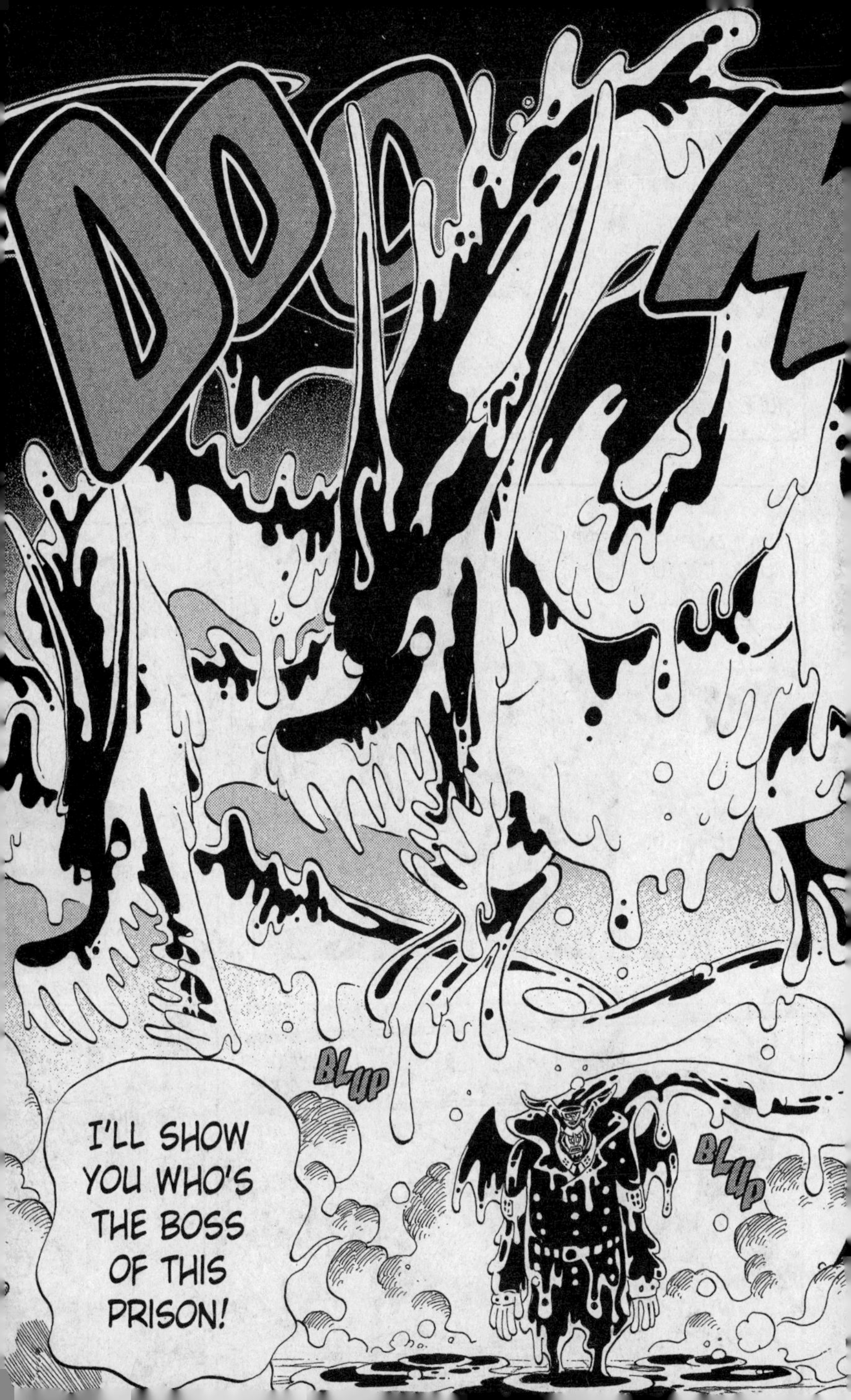
DOOM
BLUP
BLUP
I'LL SHOW YOU WHO'S THE BOSS OF THIS PRISON!

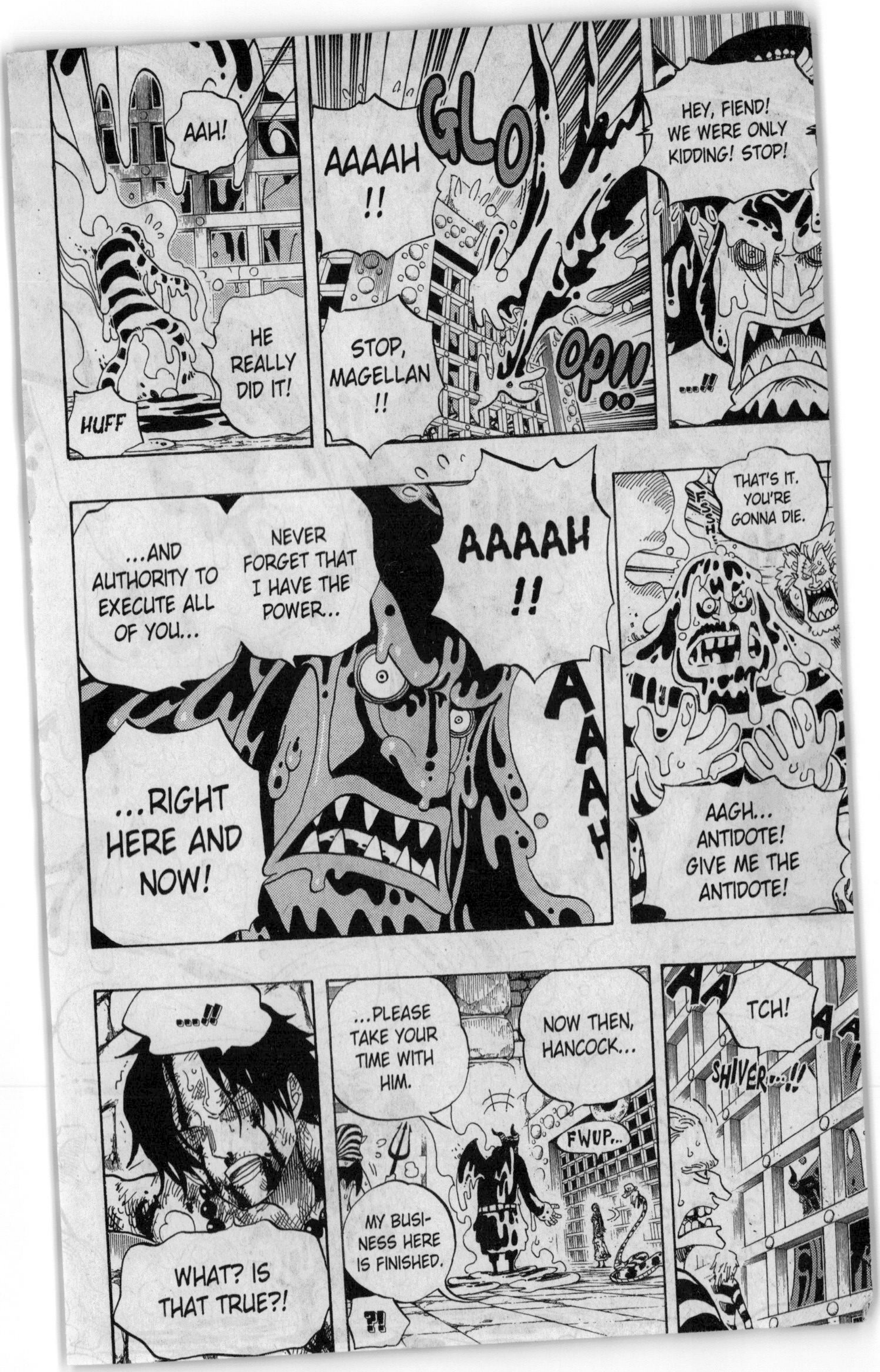
HEY, FIEND! WE WERE ONLY KIDDING! STOP!
...!!
GLOOP!!
AAAAH !!
STOP, MAGELLAN !!
AAH!
HE REALLY DID IT!
HUFF
FSSH
THAT'S IT. YOU'RE GONNA DIE.
AAGH... ANTIDOTE! GIVE ME THE ANTIDOTE!
AAAAH !!
AAAAH
NEVER FORGET THAT I HAVE THE POWER...
...AND AUTHORITY TO EXECUTE ALL OF YOU...
...RIGHT HERE AND NOW!
AAA
TCH!
SHIVER...!!
NOW THEN, HANCOCK...
...PLEASE TAKE YOUR TIME WITH HIM.
FWUP..
MY BUSINESS HERE IS FINISHED.
?!
...!!
WHAT? IS THAT TRUE?!

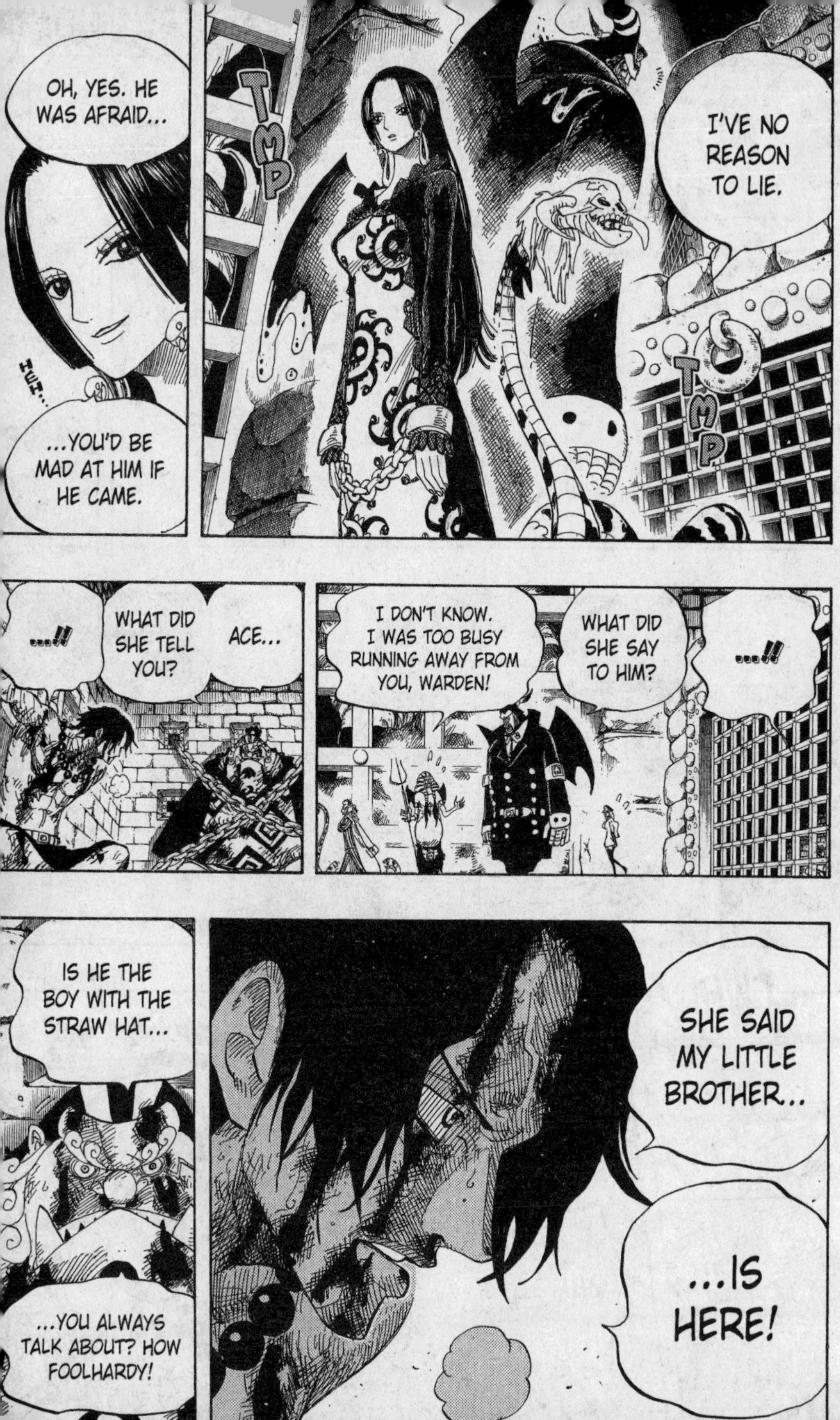
I'VE NO REASON TO LIE.
TMP
TMP
OH, YES. HE WAS AFRAID...
HEH...
...YOU'D BE MAD AT HIM IF HE CAME.
...!!
WHAT DID SHE SAY TO HIM?
I DON'T KNOW. I WAS TOO BUSY RUNNING AWAY FROM YOU, WARDEN!
ACE...
WHAT DID SHE TELL YOU?
...!!
SHE SAID MY LITTLE BROTHER...
...IS HERE!
IS HE THE BOY WITH THE STRAW HAT...
...YOU ALWAYS TALK ABOUT? HOW FOOLHARDY!

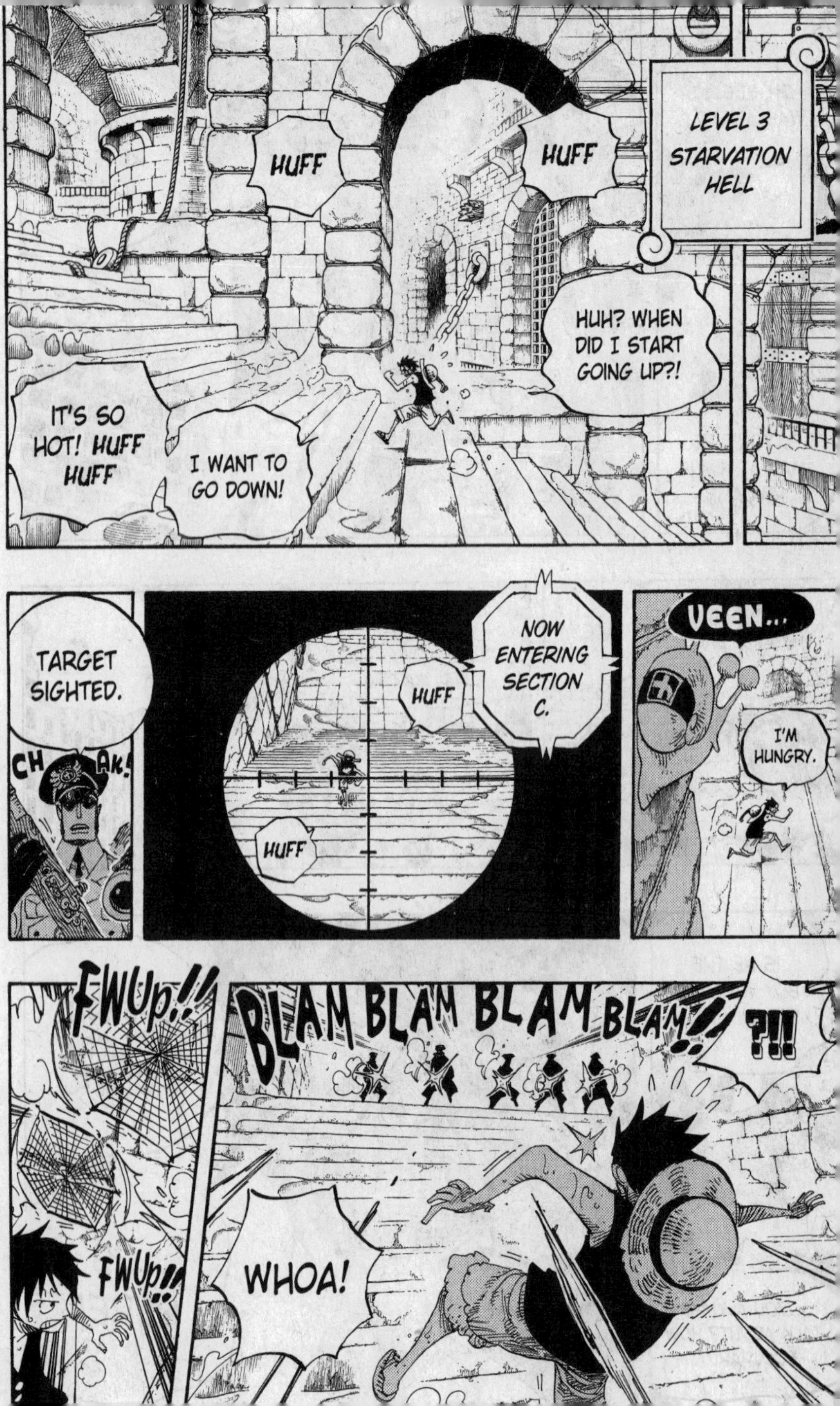
LEVEL 3
STARVATION
HELL
HUFF
HUFF
HUH? WHEN DID I START GOING UP?!
I WANT TO GO DOWN!
IT'S SO HOT! HUFF HUFF
VEEN...
I'M HUNGRY.
NOW ENTERING SECTION C.
HUFF
HUFF
TARGET SIGHTED.
BLAM BLAM BLAM BLAM!!
?!!
WHOA!
FWUp!!
FWUp!!

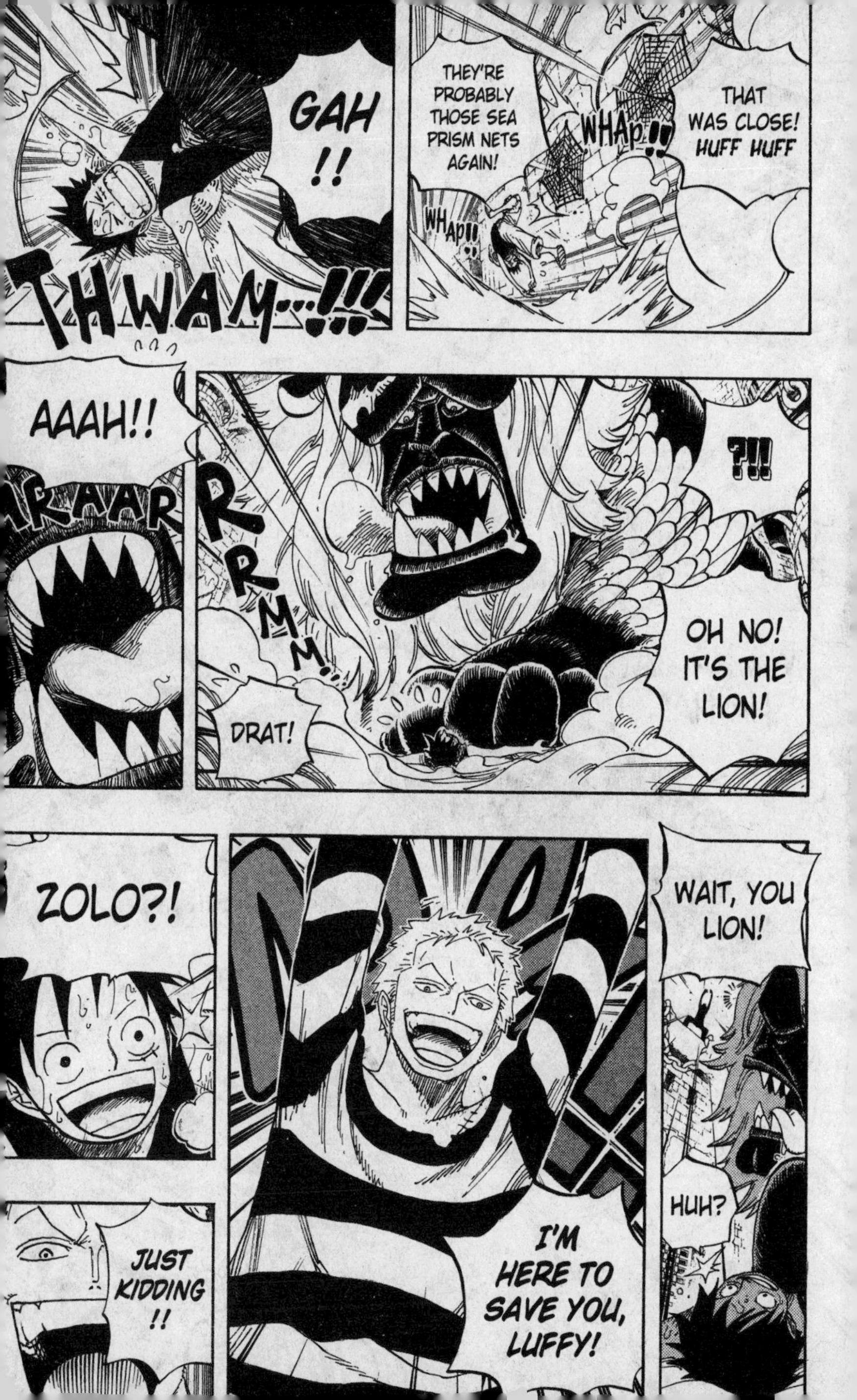
THAT WAS CLOSE! HUFF HUFF
WHAp!!
THEY'RE PROBABLY THOSE SEA PRISM NETS AGAIN!
WHAp!!
GAH !!
THWAM...!!!
?!!
OH NO! IT'S THE LION!
RRRMM...
DRAT!
AAAH!!
RAAAR
WAIT, YOU LION!
HUH?
I'M HERE TO SAVE YOU, LUFFY!
ZOLO?!
JUST KIDDING !!

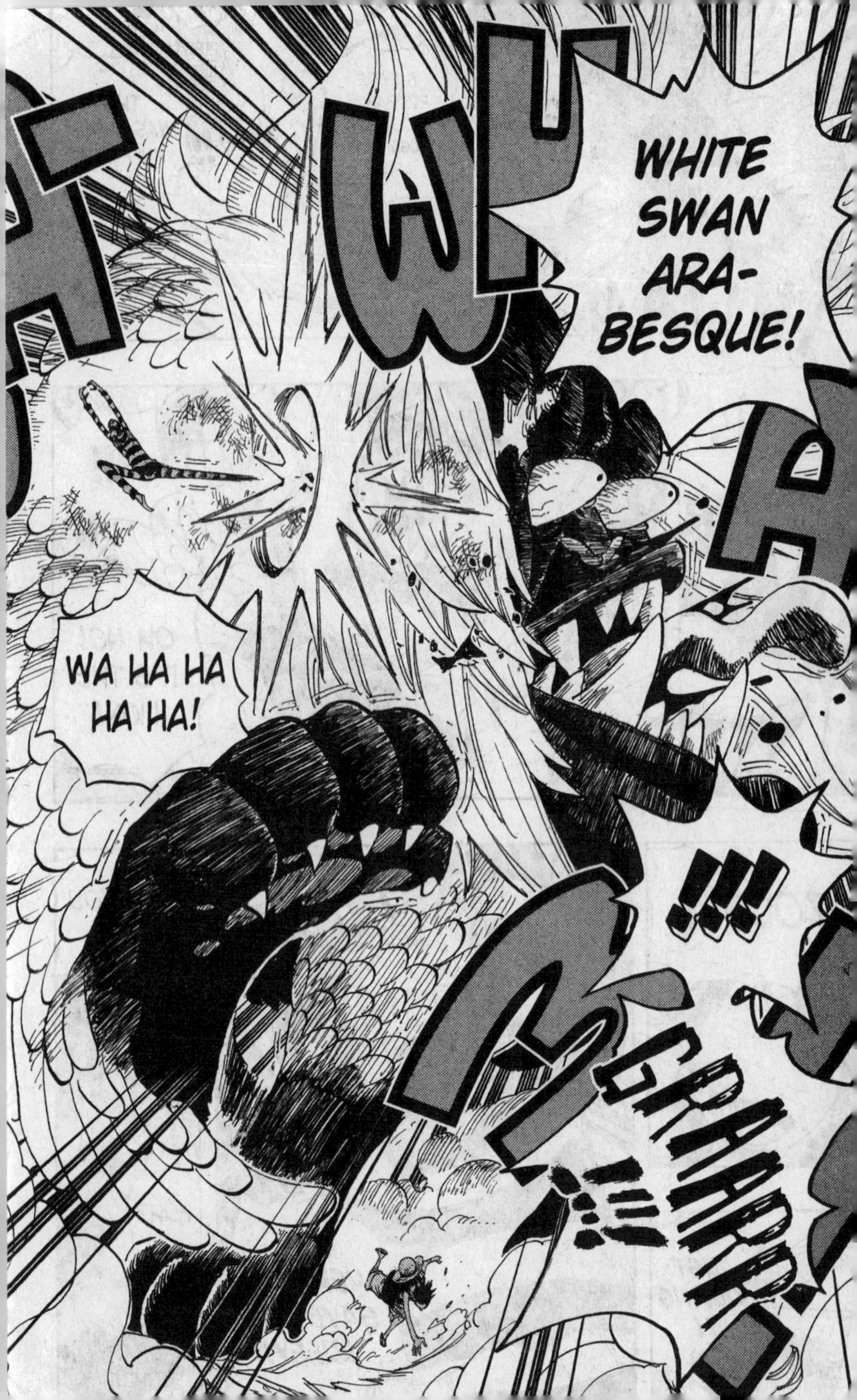
WHITE SWAN ARA-BESQUE!
WA HA HA HA HA!
!!!
GRAHRR!!

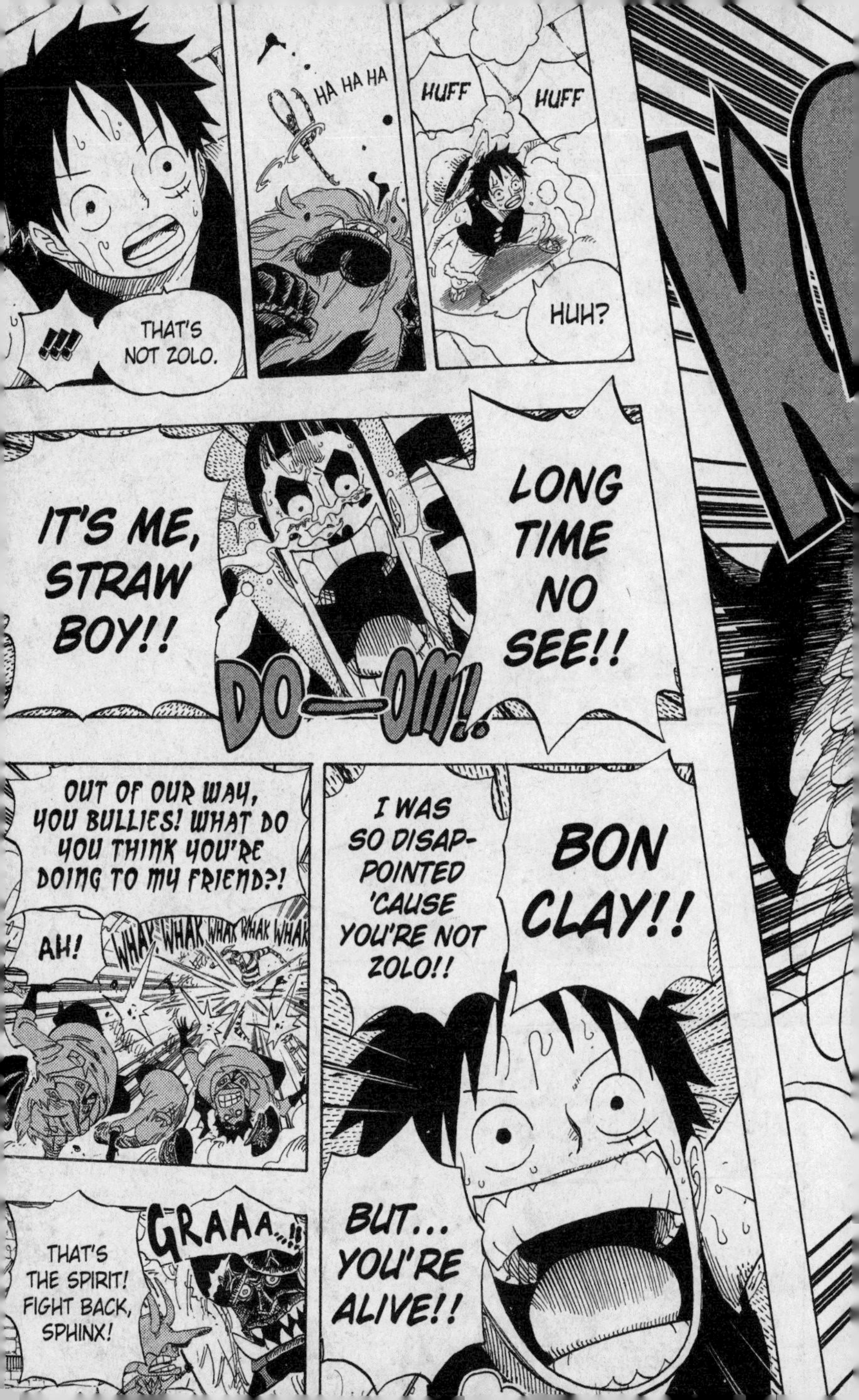
HUFF
HUFF
HUH?
HA HA HA
!!!
THAT'S NOT ZOLO.
LONG TIME NO SEE!!
IT'S ME, STRAW BOY!!
DO-OM!..
BON CLAY!!
I WAS SO DISAP-POINTED 'CAUSE YOU'RE NOT ZOLO!!
BUT... YOU'RE ALIVE!!
OUT OF OUR WAY, YOU BULLIES! WHAT DO YOU THINK YOU'RE DOING TO MY FRIEND?!
WHAK WHAK WHAK WHAK WHAK
AH!
GRAAA..!!
THAT'S THE SPIRIT! FIGHT BACK, SPHINX!

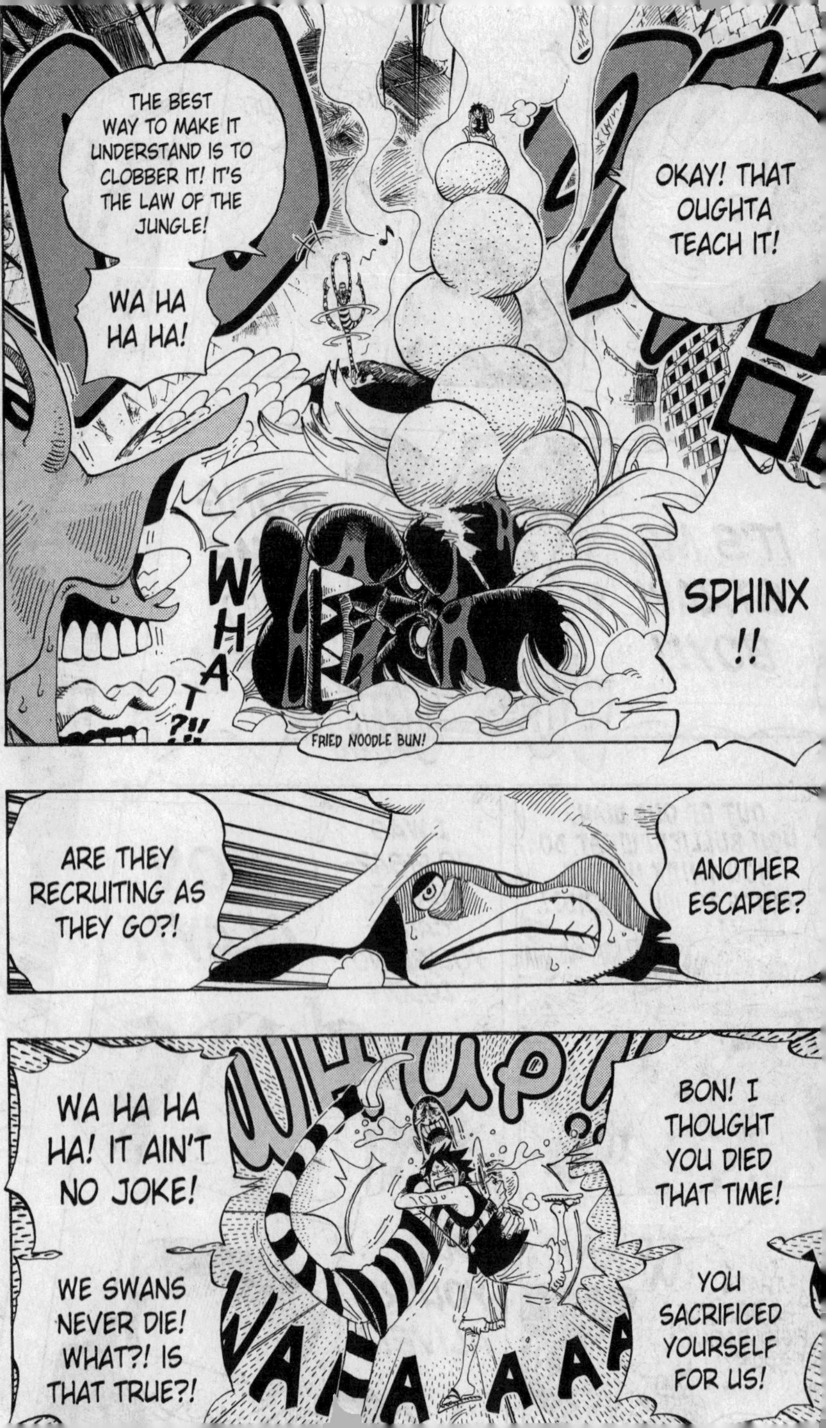
OKAY! THAT OUGHTA TEACH IT!
SPHINX!!
THE BEST WAY TO MAKE IT UNDERSTAND IS TO CLOBBER IT! IT'S THE LAW OF THE JUNGLE!
WA HA HA HA!
WHAT?!!
FRIED NOODLE BUN!
ANOTHER ESCAPEE?
ARE THEY RECRUITING AS THEY GO?!
WHUP!
BON! I THOUGHT YOU DIED THAT TIME!
YOU SACRIFICED YOURSELF FOR US!
WA HA HA HA! IT AIN'T NO JOKE!
WE SWANS NEVER DIE! WHAT?! IS THAT TRUE?!

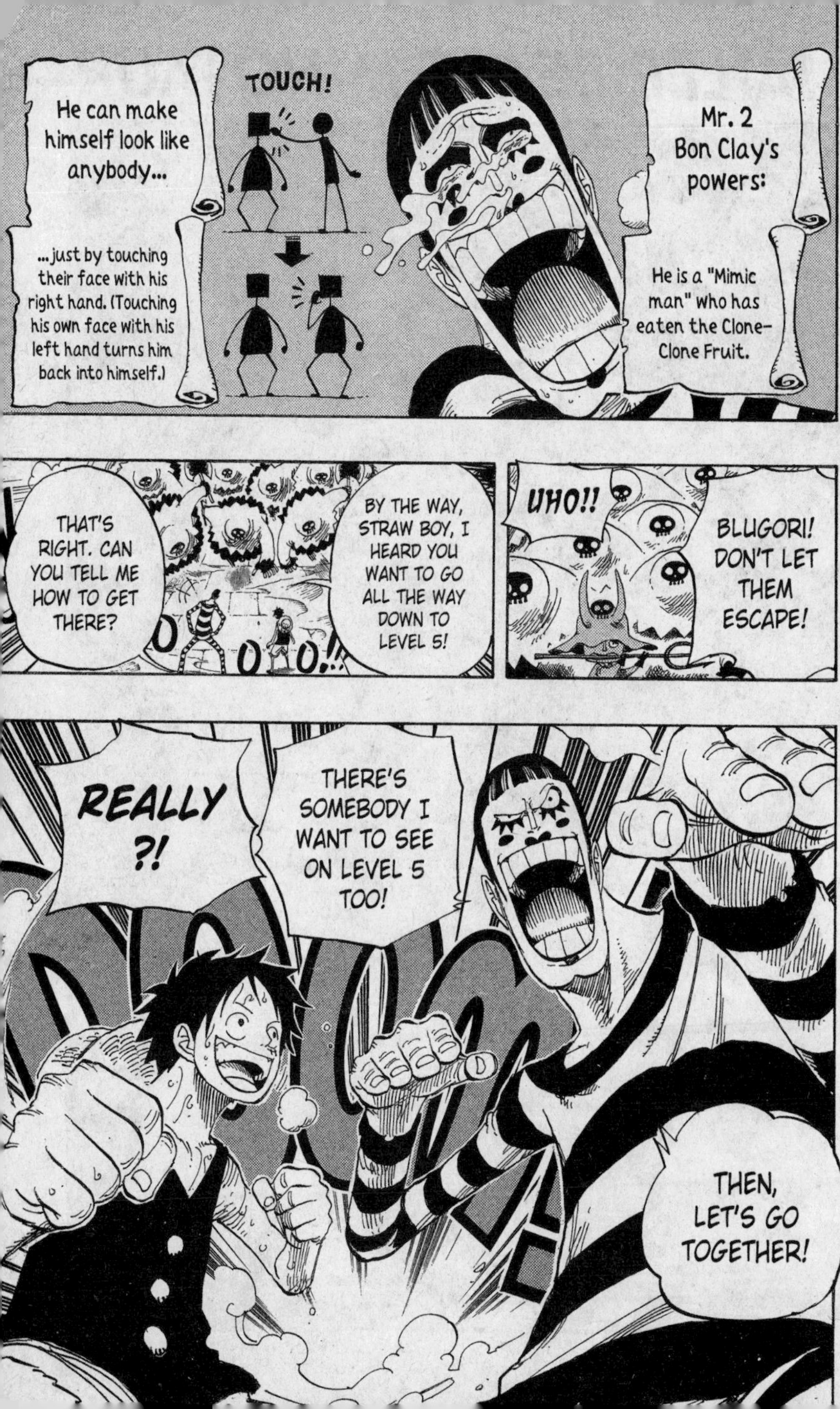
Mr. 2 Bon Clay's powers:
He is a "Mimic man" who has eaten the Clone-Clone Fruit.
TOUCH!
He can make himself look like anybody...
...just by touching their face with his right hand. (Touching his own face with his left hand turns him back into himself.)
UHO!!
BLUGORI! DON'T LET THEM ESCAPE!
BY THE WAY, STRAW BOY, I HEARD YOU WANT TO GO ALL THE WAY DOWN TO LEVEL 5!
THAT'S RIGHT. CAN YOU TELL ME HOW TO GET THERE?
THEN, LET'S GO TOGETHER!
THERE'S SOMEBODY I WANT TO SEE ON LEVEL 5 TOO!
REALLY ?!

JAILER BEAST MINOTAUR

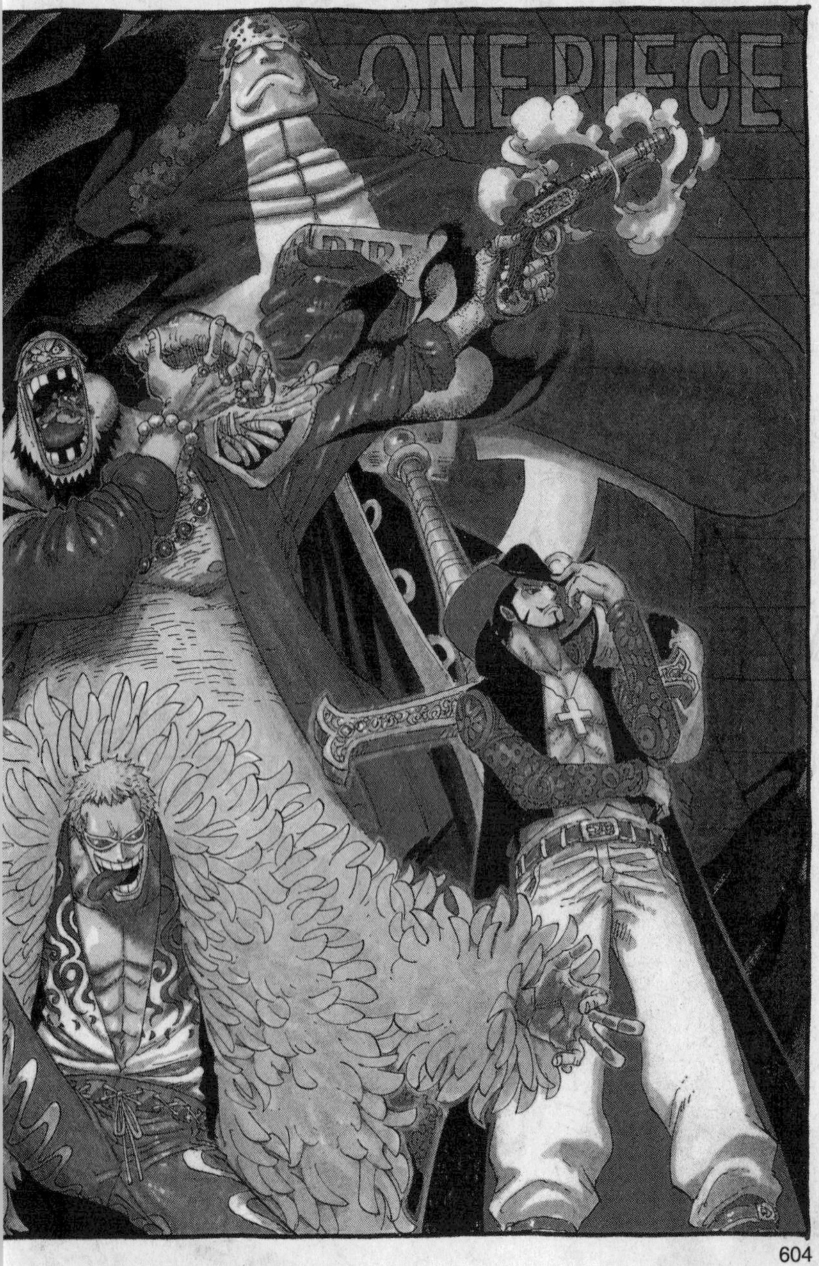
ONE PIECE

Chapter 532:

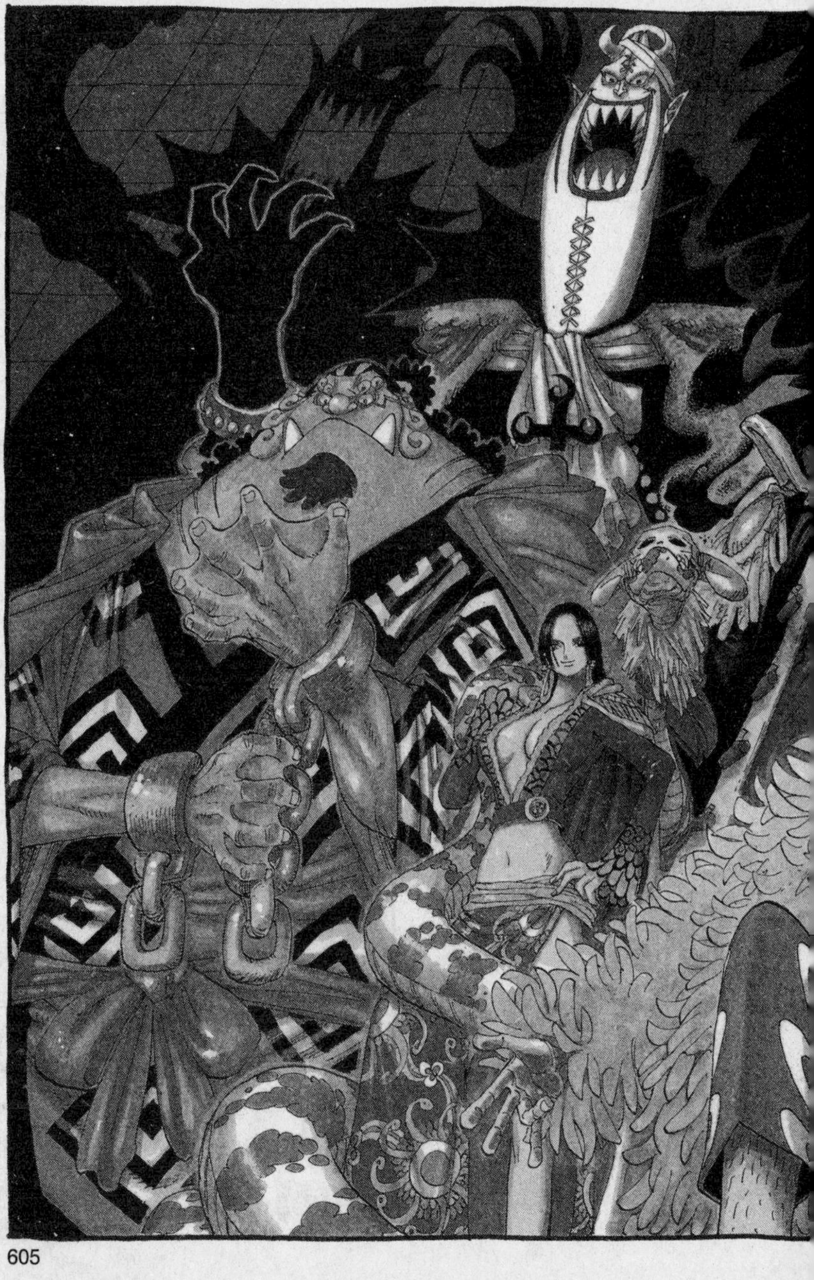

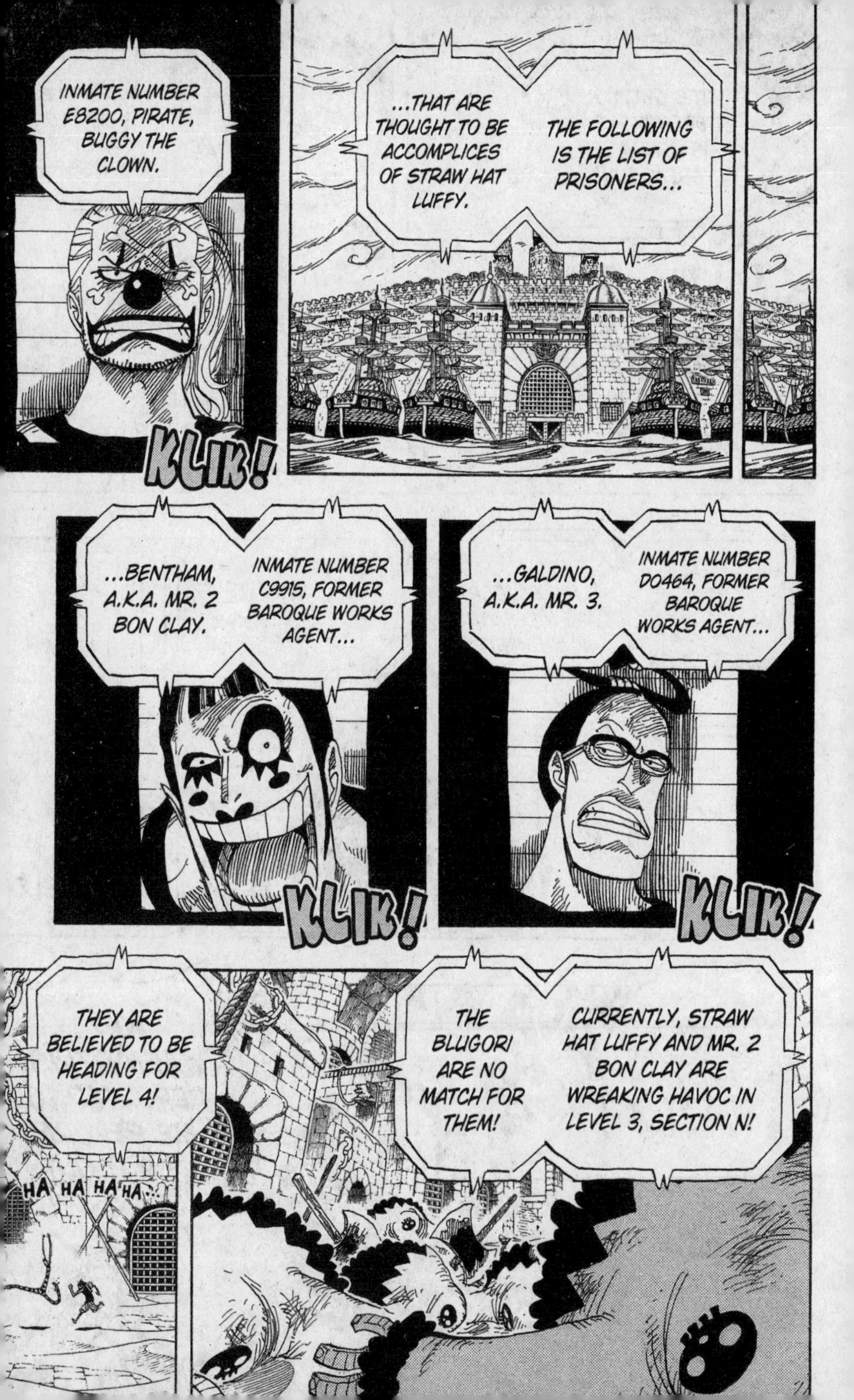
THE FOLLOWING IS THE LIST OF PRISONERS...
...THAT ARE THOUGHT TO BE ACCOMPLICES OF STRAW HAT LUFFY.
INMATE NUMBER E8200, PIRATE, BUGGY THE CLOWN.
KLIK!
INMATE NUMBER D0464, FORMER BAROQUE WORKS AGENT...
...GALDINO, A.K.A. MR. 3.
KLIK!
INMATE NUMBER C9915, FORMER BAROQUE WORKS AGENT...
...BENTHAM, A.K.A. MR. 2 BON CLAY.
KLIK!
CURRENTLY, STRAW HAT LUFFY AND MR. 2 BON CLAY ARE WREAKING HAVOC IN LEVEL 3, SECTION N!
THE BLUGORI ARE NO MATCH FOR THEM!
THEY ARE BELIEVED TO BE HEADING FOR LEVEL 4!
HA HA HA HA...

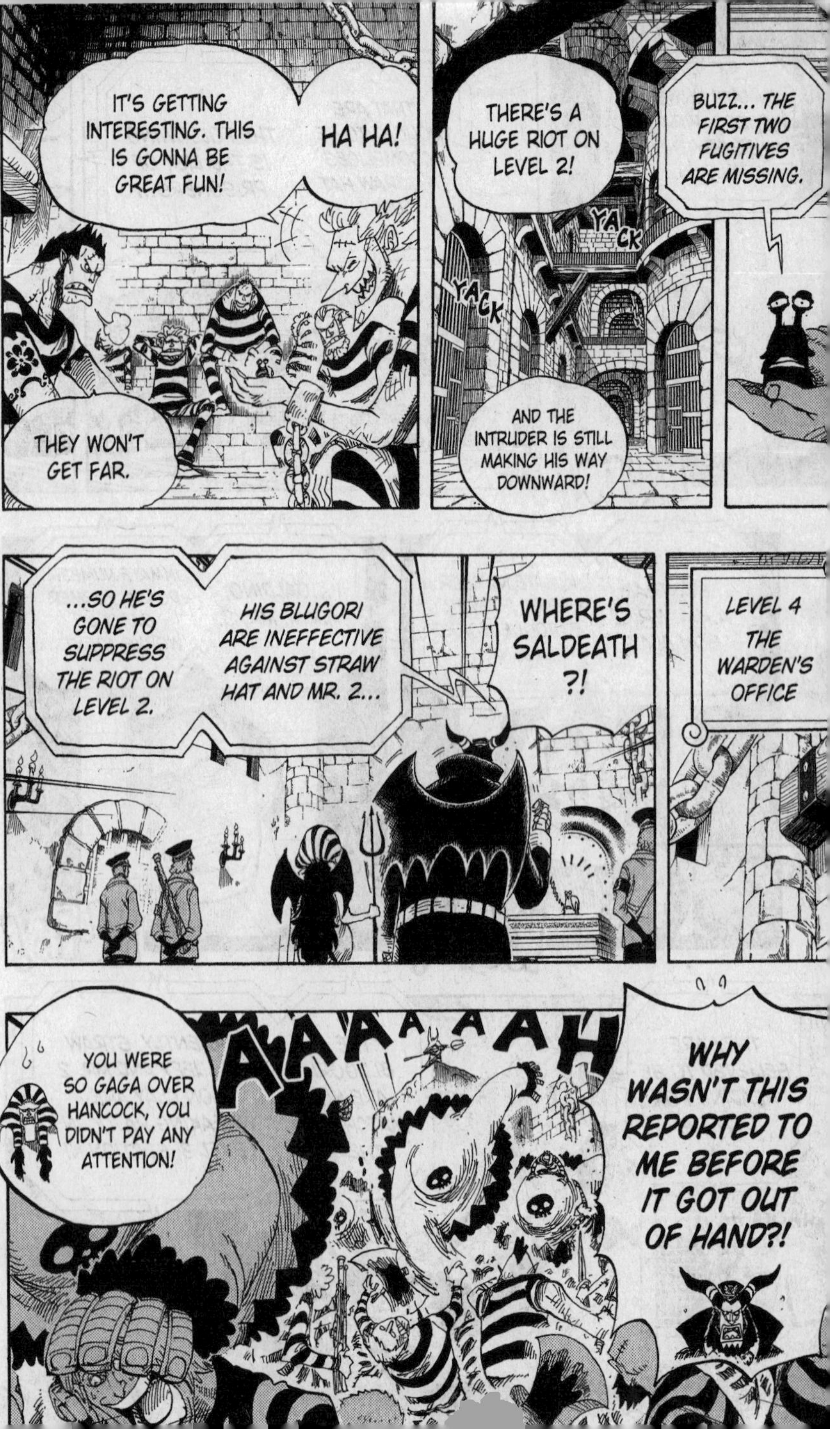
BUZZ... THE FIRST TWO FUGITIVES ARE MISSING.
THERE'S A HUGE RIOT ON LEVEL 2!
YACK
YACK
AND THE INTRUDER IS STILL MAKING HIS WAY DOWNWARD!
HA HA!
IT'S GETTING INTERESTING. THIS IS GONNA BE GREAT FUN!
THEY WON'T GET FAR.
LEVEL 4 THE WARDEN'S OFFICE
WHERE'S SALDEATH ?!
HIS BLUGORI ARE INEFFECTIVE AGAINST STRAW HAT AND MR. 2...
...SO HE'S GONE TO SUPPRESS THE RIOT ON LEVEL 2.
WHY WASN'T THIS REPORTED TO ME BEFORE IT GOT OUT OF HAND?!
AAAAAAH
YOU WERE SO GAGA OVER HANCOCK, YOU DIDN'T PAY ANY ATTENTION!

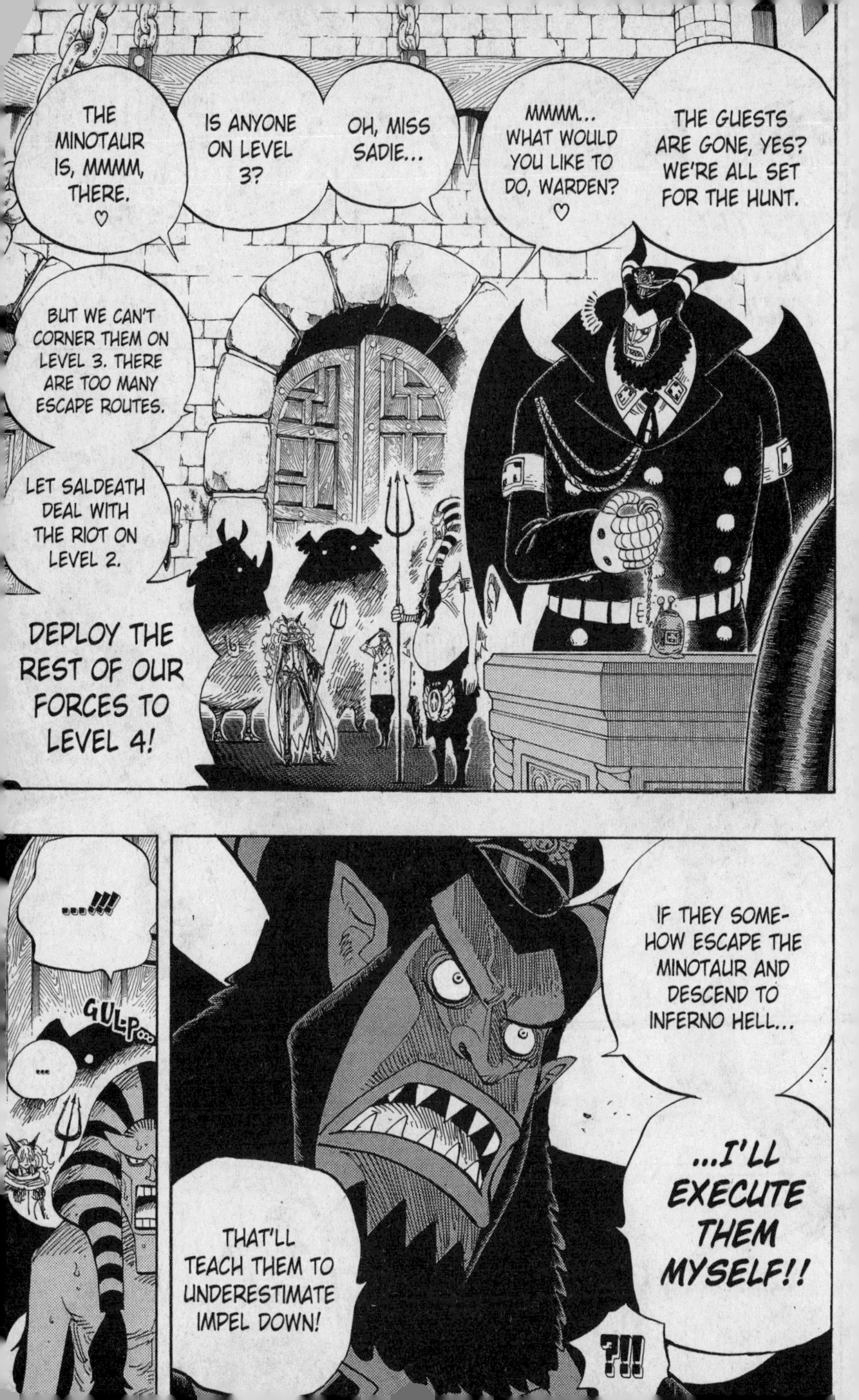
THE GUESTS ARE GONE, YES? WE'RE ALL SET FOR THE HUNT.
MMMM... WHAT WOULD YOU LIKE TO DO, WARDEN? ♡
OH, MISS SADIE...
IS ANYONE ON LEVEL 3?
THE MINOTAUR IS, MMMM, THERE. ♡
BUT WE CAN'T CORNER THEM ON LEVEL 3. THERE ARE TOO MANY ESCAPE ROUTES.
LET SALDEATH DEAL WITH THE RIOT ON LEVEL 2.
DEPLOY THE REST OF OUR FORCES TO LEVEL 4!
IF THEY SOME-HOW ESCAPE THE MINOTAUR AND DESCEND TO INFERNO HELL...
...I'LL EXECUTE THEM MYSELF!!
THAT'LL TEACH THEM TO UNDERESTIMATE IMPEL DOWN!
?!!
...!!!
GULP...
...

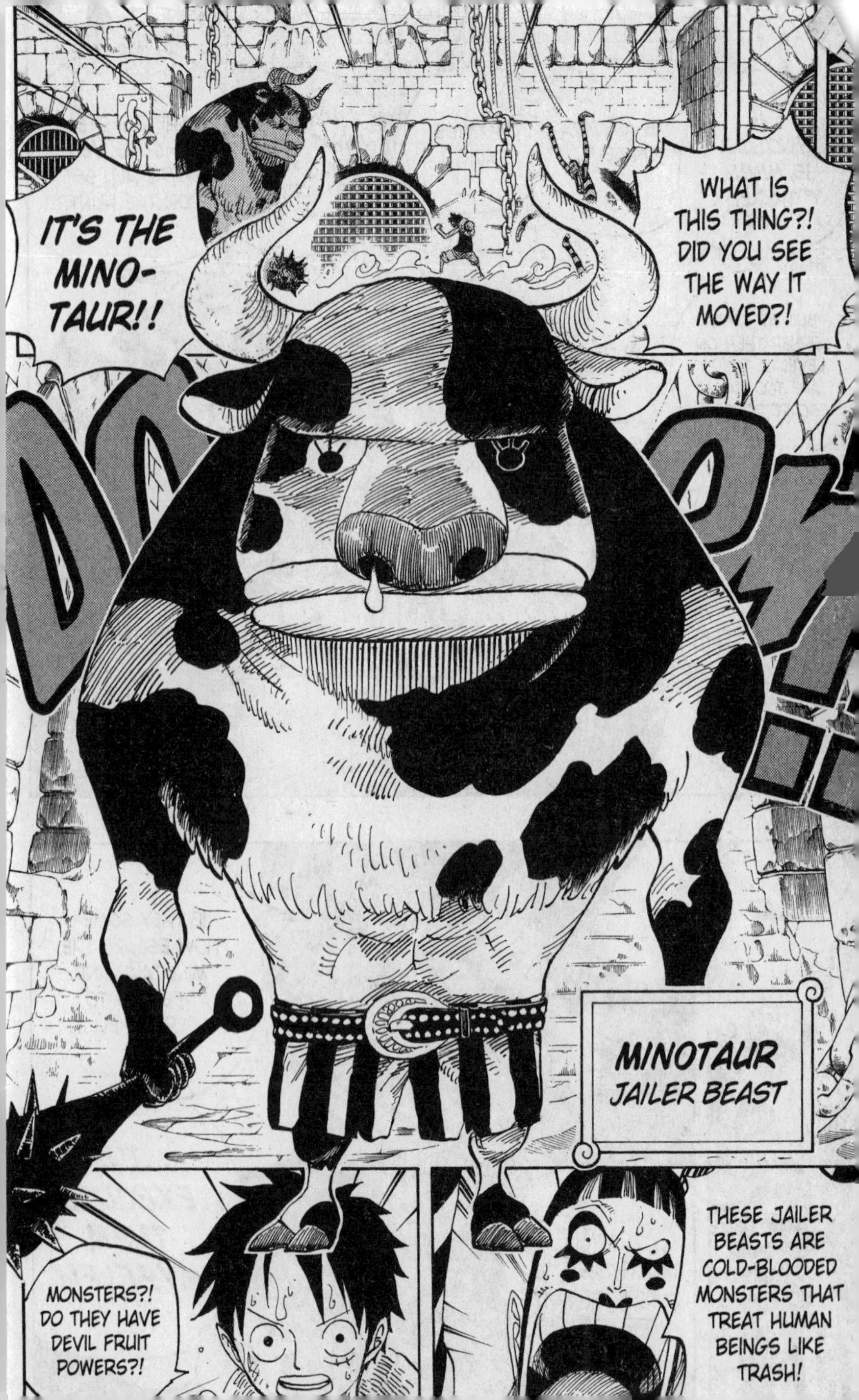
WHAT IS THIS THING?! DID YOU SEE THE WAY IT MOVED?!
IT'S THE MINO-TAUR!!
MINOTAUR JAILER BEAST
THESE JAILER BEASTS ARE COLD-BLOODED MONSTERS THAT TREAT HUMAN BEINGS LIKE TRASH!
MONSTERS?! DO THEY HAVE DEVIL FRUIT POWERS?!

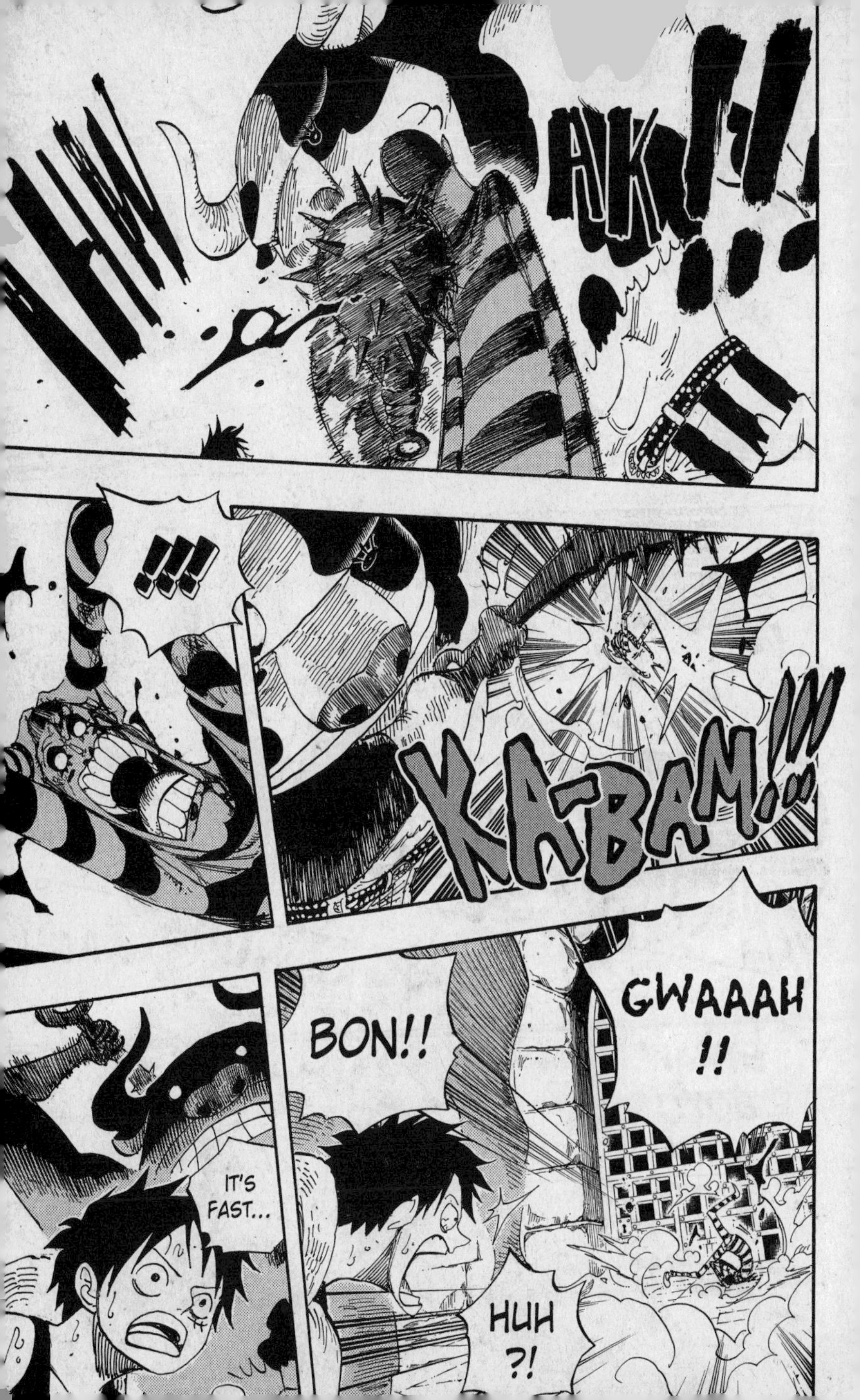
AK!!
KA-BAM!!!
!!!
GWAAAH !!
BON!!
HUH ?!
IT'S FAST...

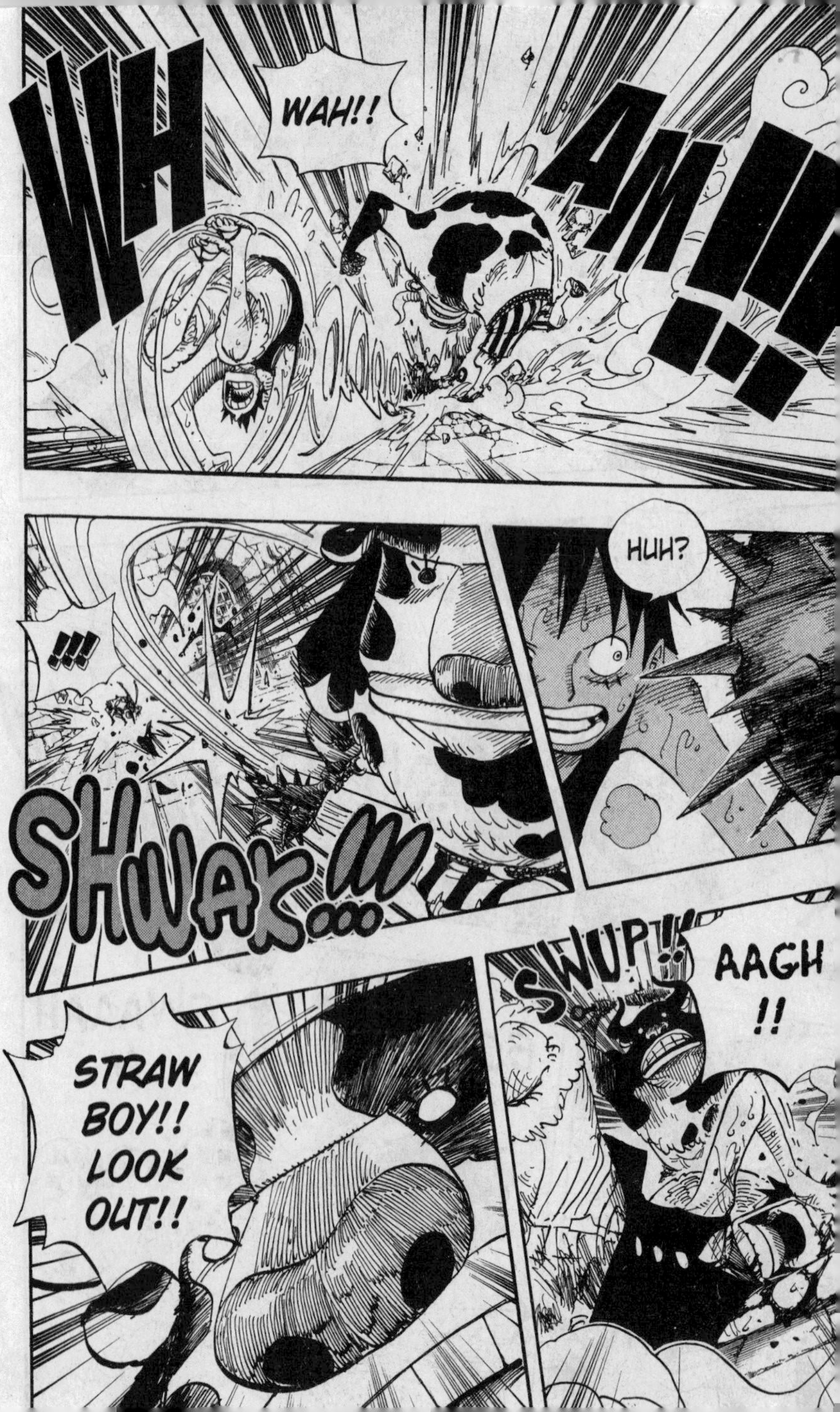
WAH!!
WHAM!!!
HUH?
!!!
SHWAK...!!!
AAGH !!
SWUP!!
STRAW BOY!! LOOK OUT!!

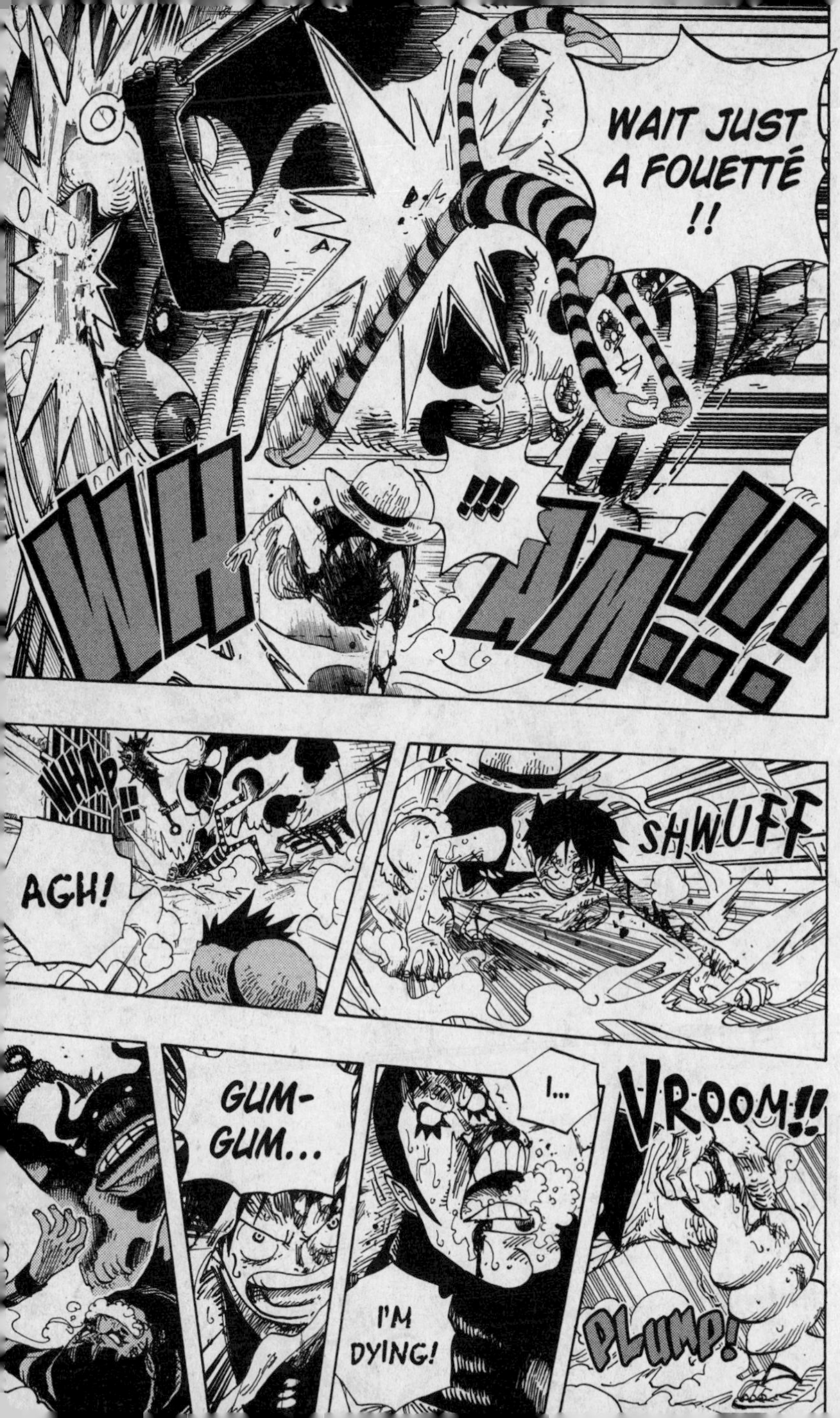
WAIT JUST A FOUETTÉ !!
!!!
WHAM...!!
SHWUFF
WHAP!!
AGH!
VROOM!!
PLUMP!
I...
I'M DYING!
GUM-GUM...

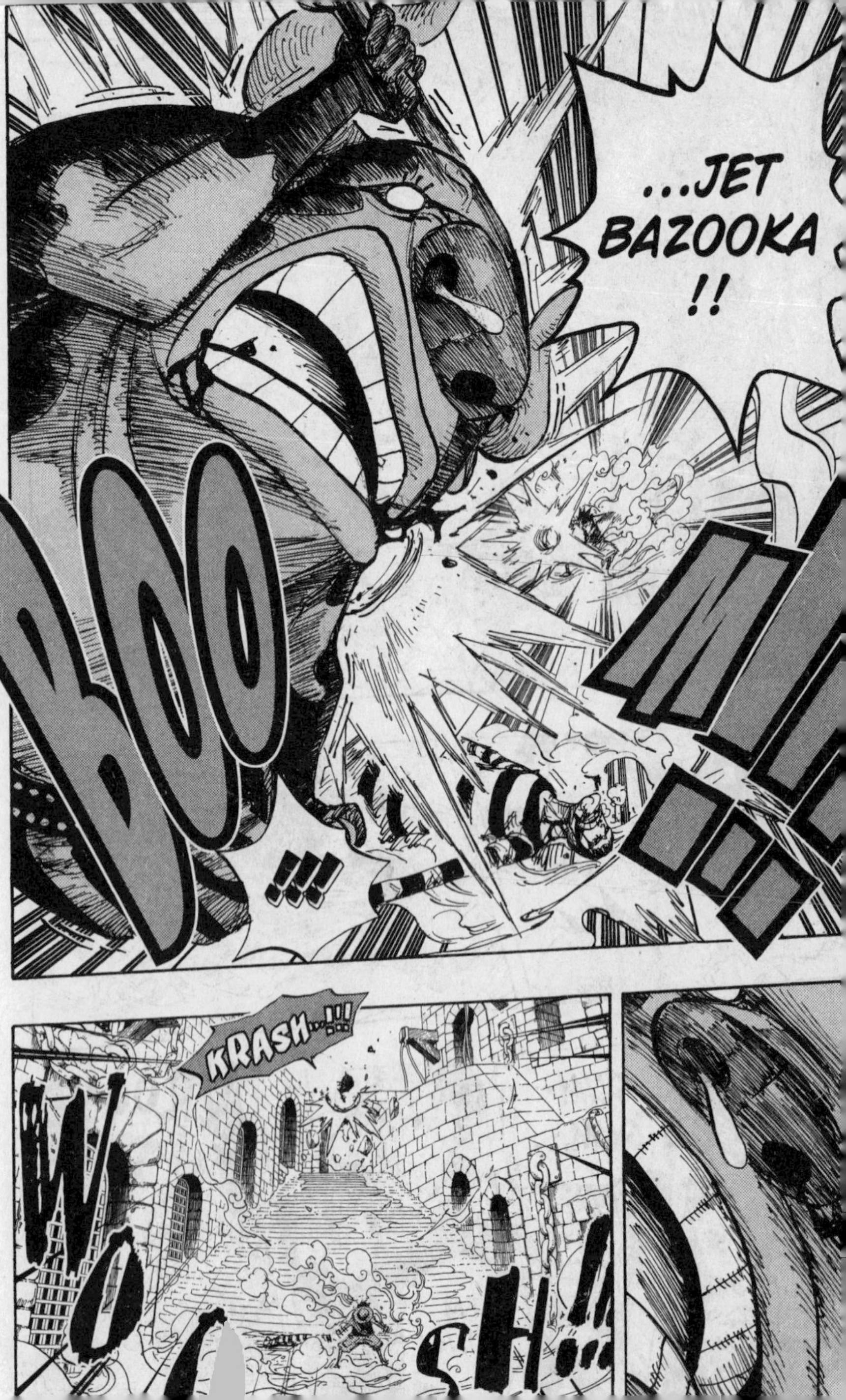
...JET BAZOOKA !!
BOOOM!!!
KRASH...!!!
WOOSH...!!

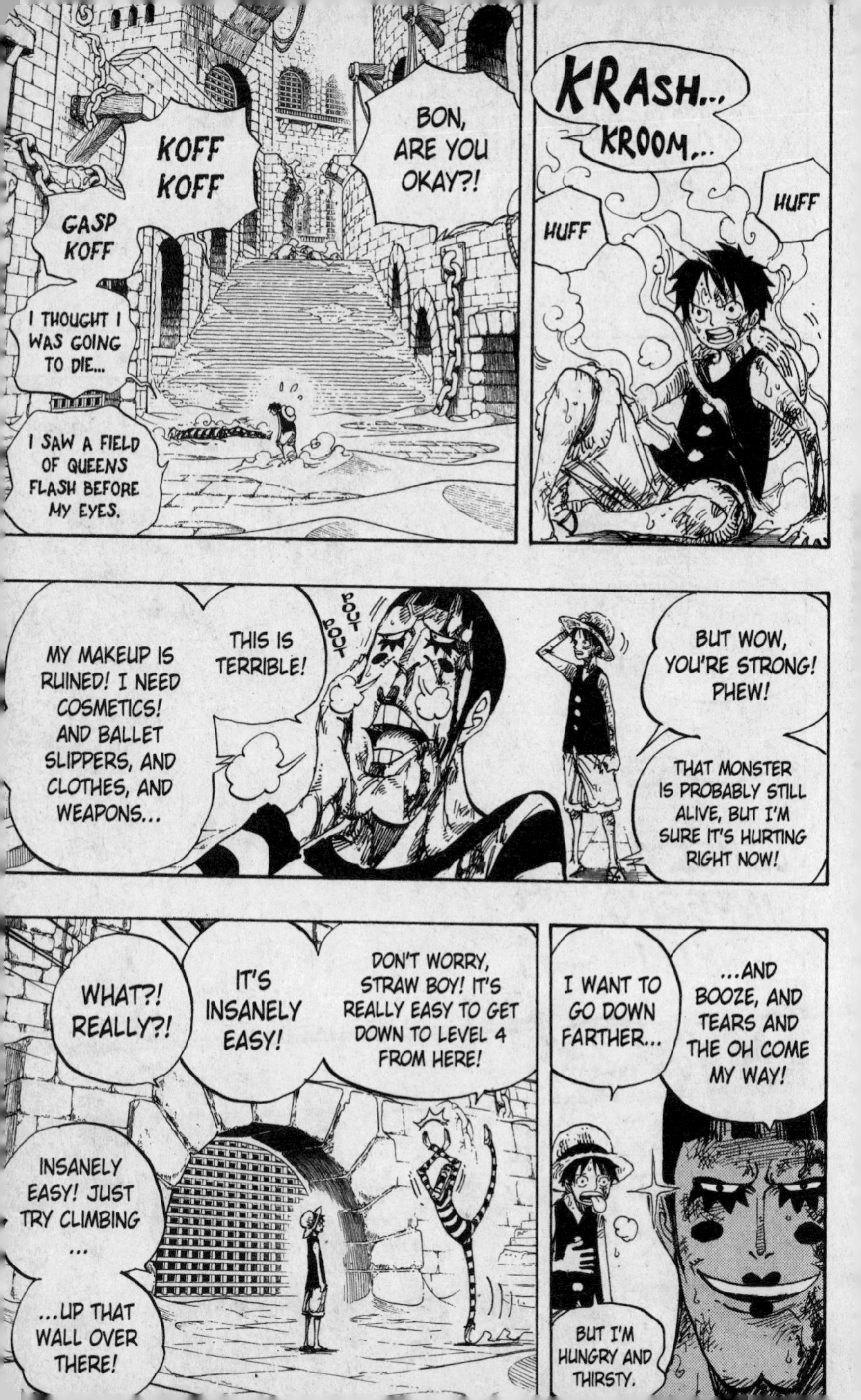
KRASH...
KROOM...
HUFF
HUFF
BON, ARE YOU OKAY?!
KOFF KOFF
GASP KOFF
I THOUGHT I WAS GOING TO DIE...
I SAW A FIELD OF QUEENS FLASH BEFORE MY EYES.
BUT WOW, YOU'RE STRONG! PHEW!
THAT MONSTER IS PROBABLY STILL ALIVE, BUT I'M SURE IT'S HURTING RIGHT NOW!
POUT POUT
THIS IS TERRIBLE!
MY MAKEUP IS RUINED! I NEED COSMETICS! AND BALLET SLIPPERS, AND CLOTHES, AND WEAPONS...
...AND BOOZE, AND TEARS AND THE OH COME MY WAY!
I WANT TO GO DOWN FARTHER...
BUT I'M HUNGRY AND THIRSTY.
DON'T WORRY, STRAW BOY! IT'S REALLY EASY TO GET DOWN TO LEVEL 4 FROM HERE!
IT'S INSANELY EASY!
WHAT?! REALLY?!
INSANELY EASY! JUST TRY CLIMBING ...
...UP THAT WALL OVER THERE!

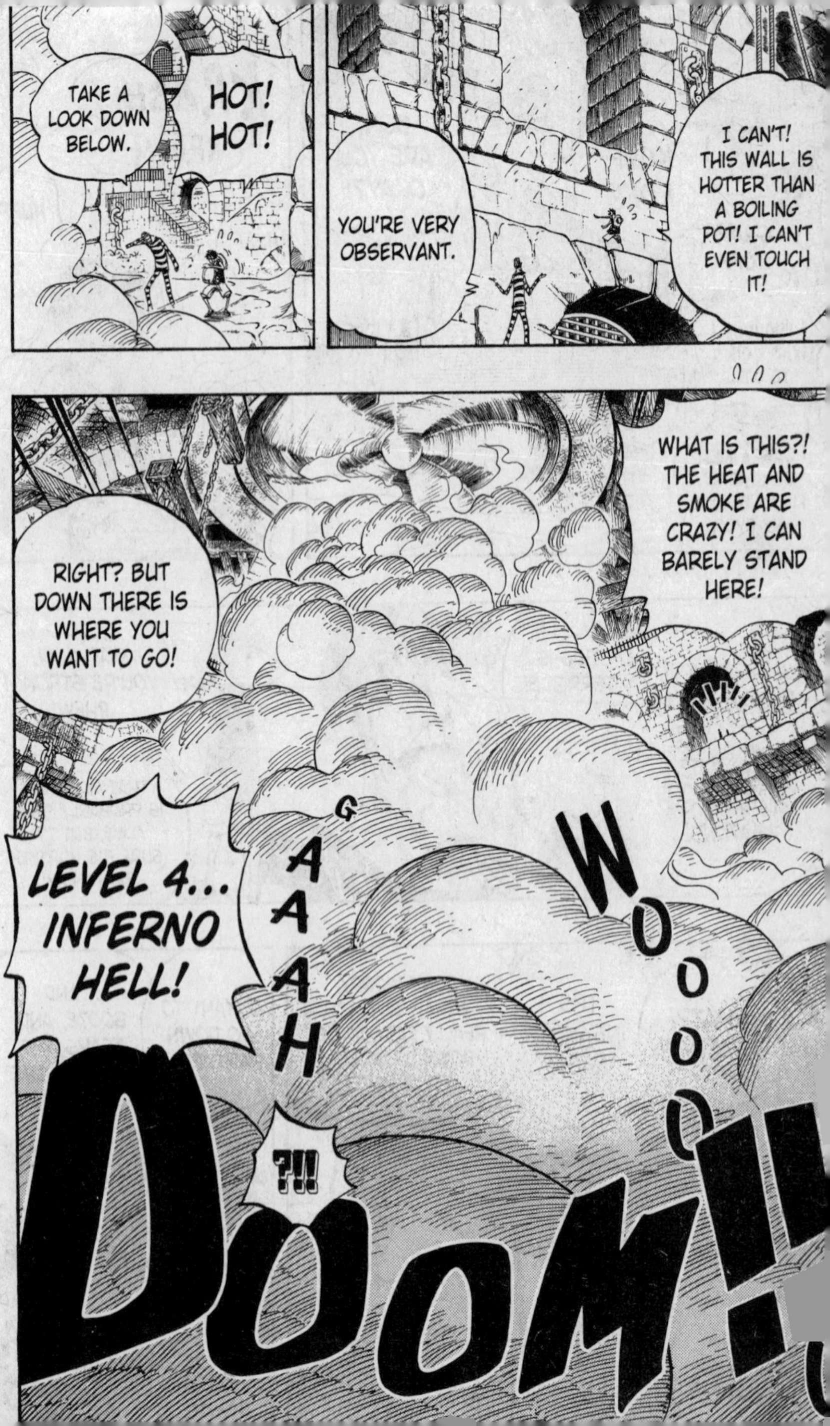
I CAN'T! THIS WALL IS HOTTER THAN A BOILING POT! I CAN'T EVEN TOUCH IT!
YOU'RE VERY OBSERVANT.
HOT! HOT!
TAKE A LOOK DOWN BELOW.
WHAT IS THIS?! THE HEAT AND SMOKE ARE CRAZY! I CAN BARELY STAND HERE!
RIGHT? BUT DOWN THERE IS WHERE YOU WANT TO GO!
WOOOO
GAAAH
?!!
LEVEL 4... INFERNO HELL!
DOOM!!

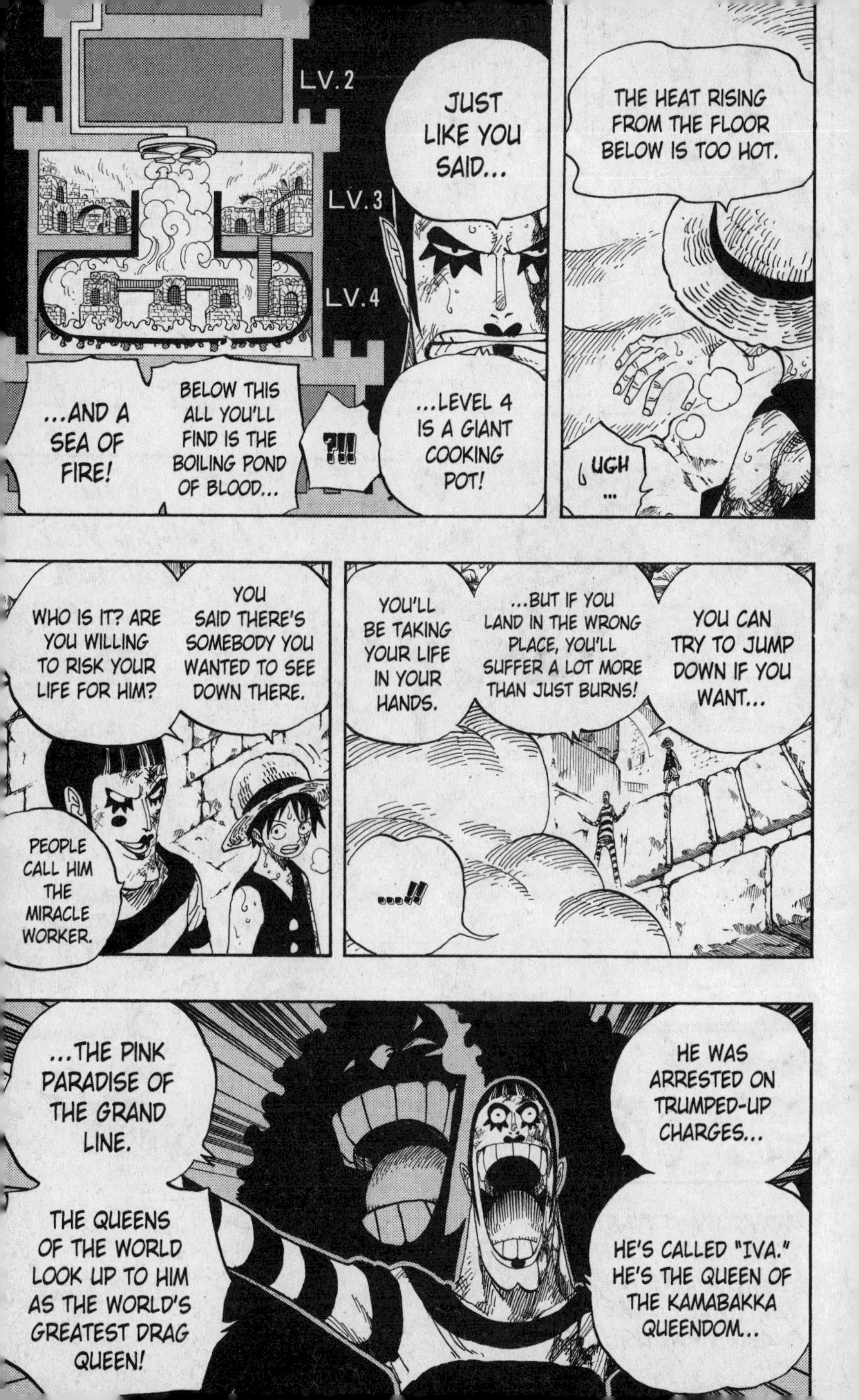
THE HEAT RISING FROM THE FLOOR BELOW IS TOO HOT.
UGH ...
JUST LIKE YOU SAID...
...LEVEL 4 IS A GIANT COOKING POT!
LV. 2
LV. 3
LV. 4
?!!
BELOW THIS ALL YOU'LL FIND IS THE BOILING POND OF BLOOD...
...AND A SEA OF FIRE!
YOU CAN TRY TO JUMP DOWN IF YOU WANT...
...BUT IF YOU LAND IN THE WRONG PLACE, YOU'LL SUFFER A LOT MORE THAN JUST BURNS!
YOU'LL BE TAKING YOUR LIFE IN YOUR HANDS.
...!!
YOU SAID THERE'S SOMEBODY YOU WANTED TO SEE DOWN THERE.
WHO IS IT? ARE YOU WILLING TO RISK YOUR LIFE FOR HIM?
PEOPLE CALL HIM THE MIRACLE WORKER.
HE WAS ARRESTED ON TRUMPED-UP CHARGES...
HE'S CALLED "IVA." HE'S THE QUEEN OF THE KAMABAKKA QUEENDOM...
...THE PINK PARADISE OF THE GRAND LINE.
THE QUEENS OF THE WORLD LOOK UP TO HIM AS THE WORLD'S GREATEST DRAG QUEEN!

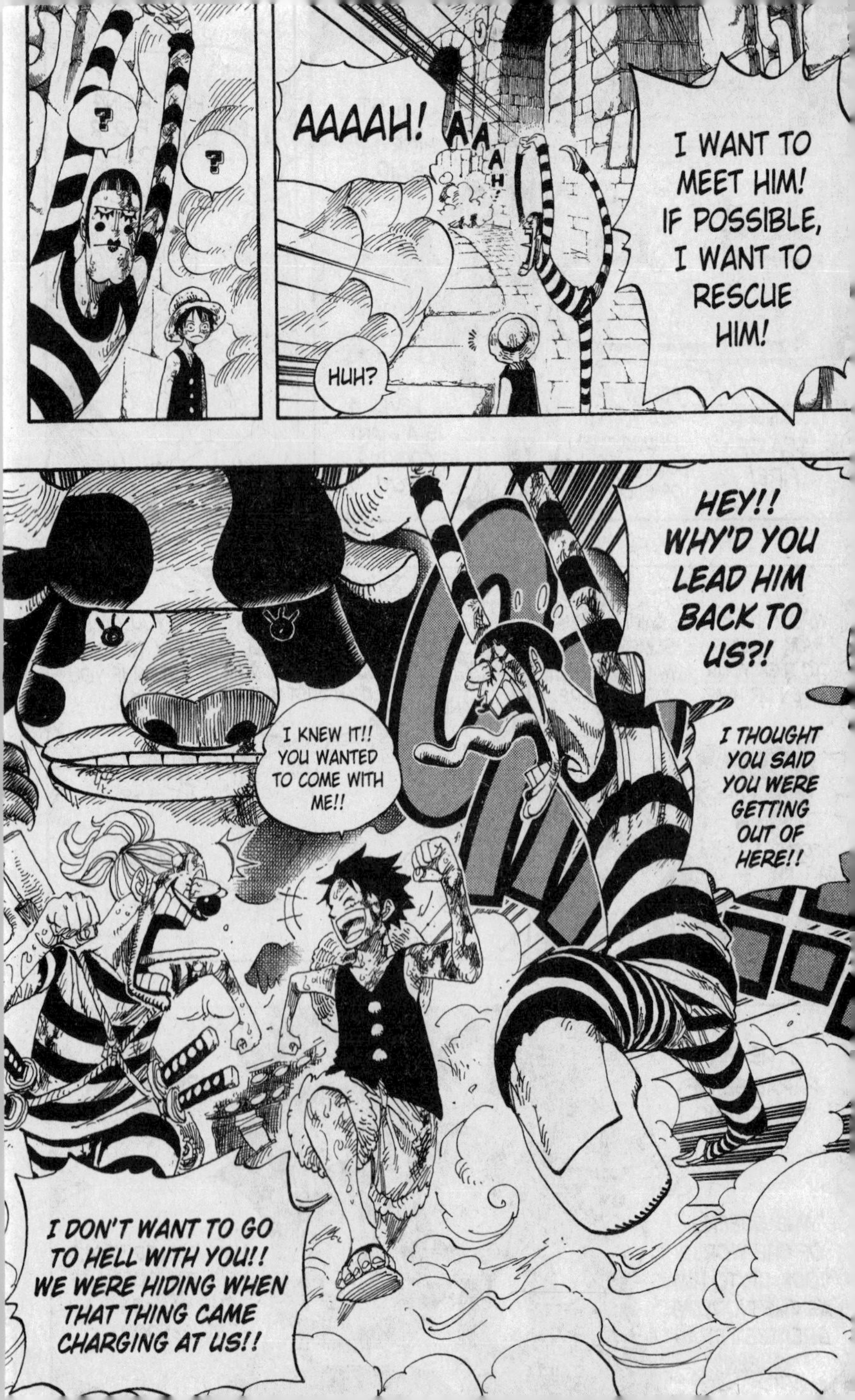
I WANT TO MEET HIM! IF POSSIBLE, I WANT TO RESCUE HIM!
AAAAH!
AAAH!
HUH?
?
?
HEY!! WHY'D YOU LEAD HIM BACK TO US?!
I THOUGHT YOU SAID YOU WERE GETTING OUT OF HERE!!
I KNEW IT!! YOU WANTED TO COME WITH ME!!
I DON'T WANT TO GO TO HELL WITH YOU!! WE WERE HIDING WHEN THAT THING CAME CHARGING AT US!!

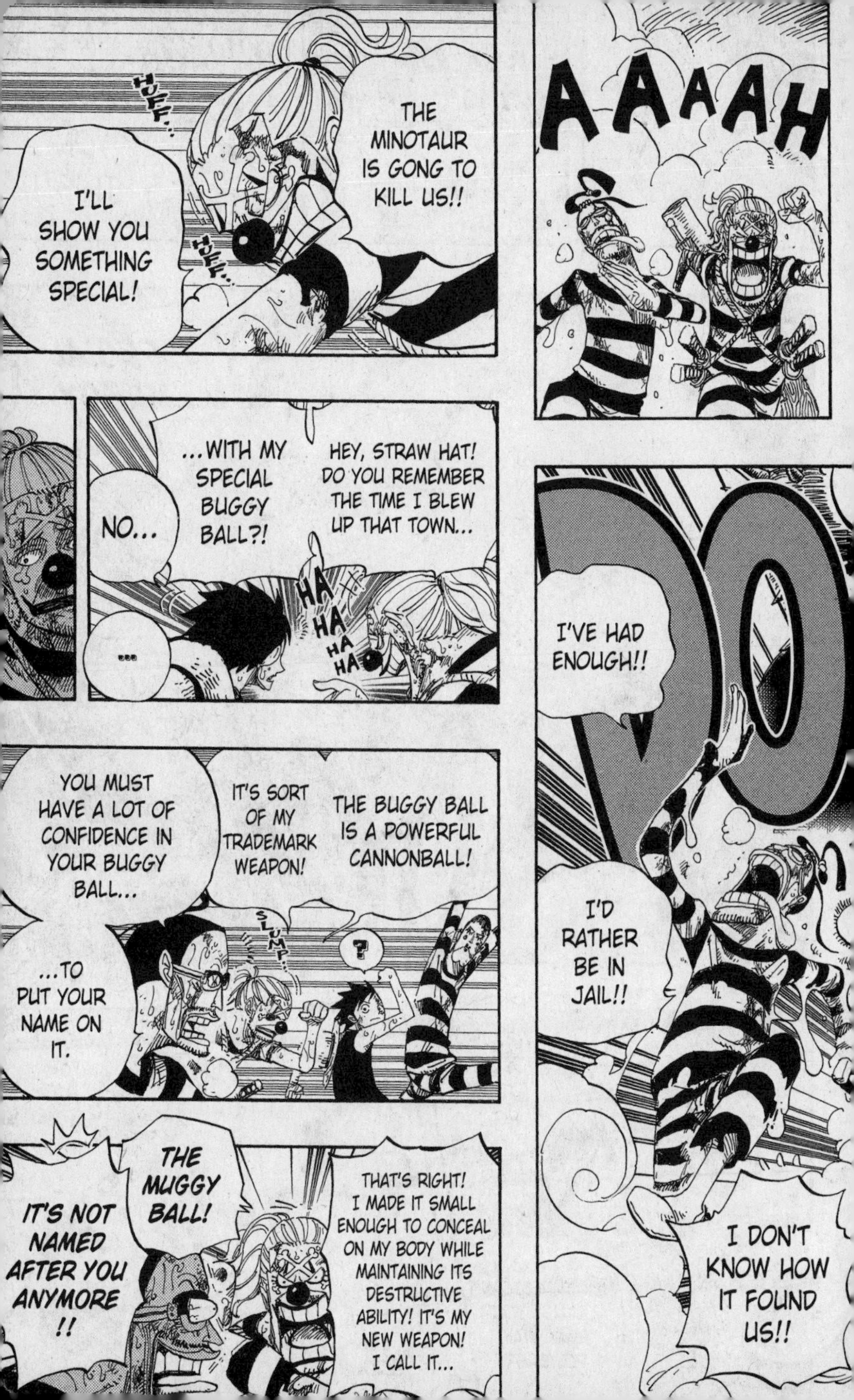
AAAAH
I'VE HAD ENOUGH!!
I'D RATHER BE IN JAIL!!
I DON'T KNOW HOW IT FOUND US!!
HUFF...
HUFF...
THE MINOTAUR IS GONG TO KILL US!!
I'LL SHOW YOU SOMETHING SPECIAL!
HEY, STRAW HAT! DO YOU REMEMBER THE TIME I BLEW UP THAT TOWN...
...WITH MY SPECIAL BUGGY BALL?!
HA HA HA HA
NO...
...
THE BUGGY BALL IS A POWERFUL CANNONBALL!
IT'S SORT OF MY TRADEMARK WEAPON!
YOU MUST HAVE A LOT OF CONFIDENCE IN YOUR BUGGY BALL...
SLUMP...
?
...TO PUT YOUR NAME ON IT.
THAT'S RIGHT! I MADE IT SMALL ENOUGH TO CONCEAL ON MY BODY WHILE MAINTAINING ITS DESTRUCTIVE ABILITY! IT'S MY NEW WEAPON! I CALL IT...
THE MUGGY BALL!
IT'S NOT NAMED AFTER YOU ANYMORE!!

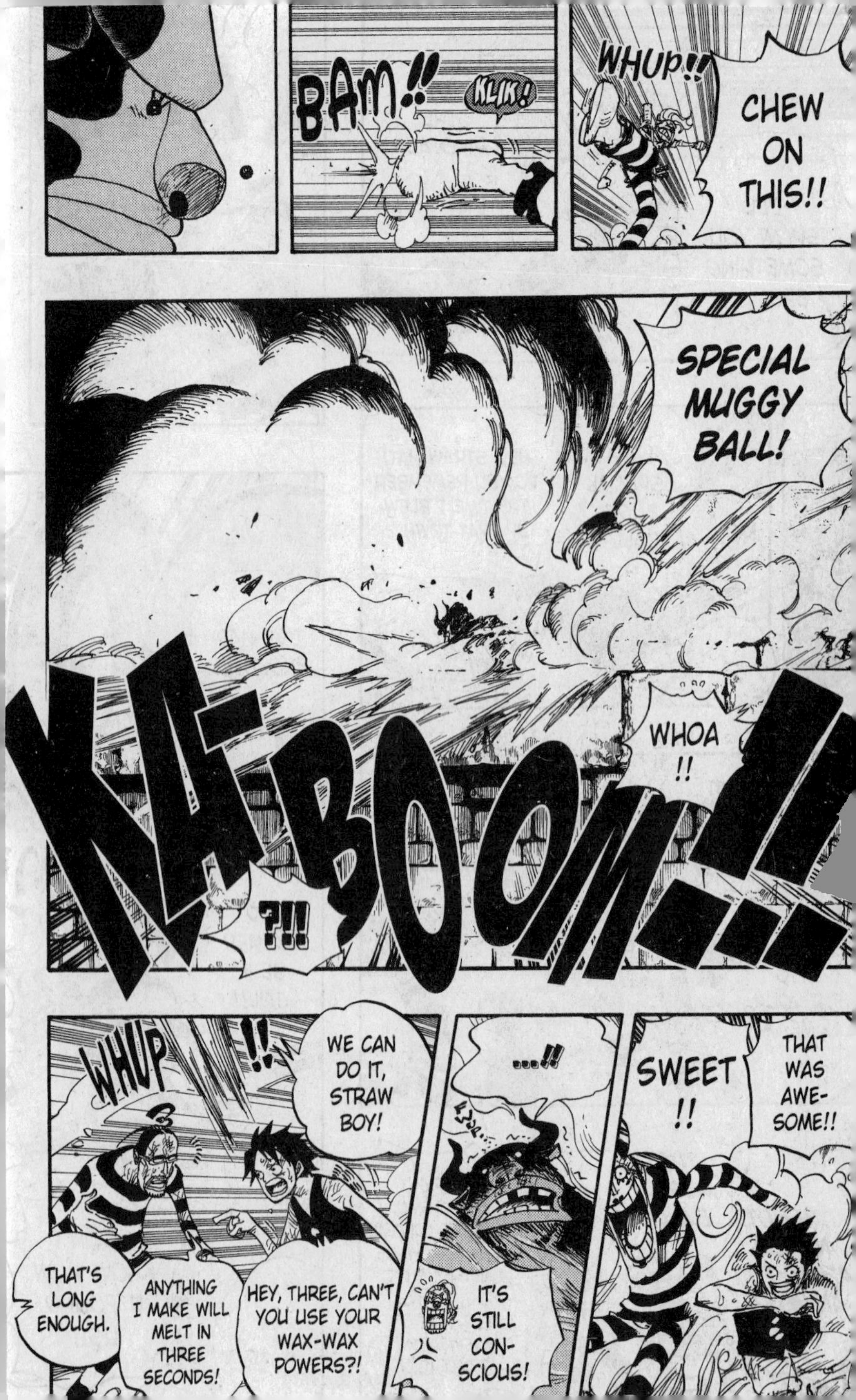
WHUP!!
CHEW ON THIS!!
BAM!!
KLIK!
SPECIAL MUGGY BALL!
WHOA !!
KA-BOOM...!!
?!!
THAT WAS AWE-SOME!!
SWEET !!
...!!
IT'S STILL CON-SCIOUS!
WHUP
!!
WE CAN DO IT, STRAW BOY!
HEY, THREE, CAN'T YOU USE YOUR WAX-WAX POWERS?!
ANYTHING I MAKE WILL MELT IN THREE SECONDS!
THAT'S LONG ENOUGH.

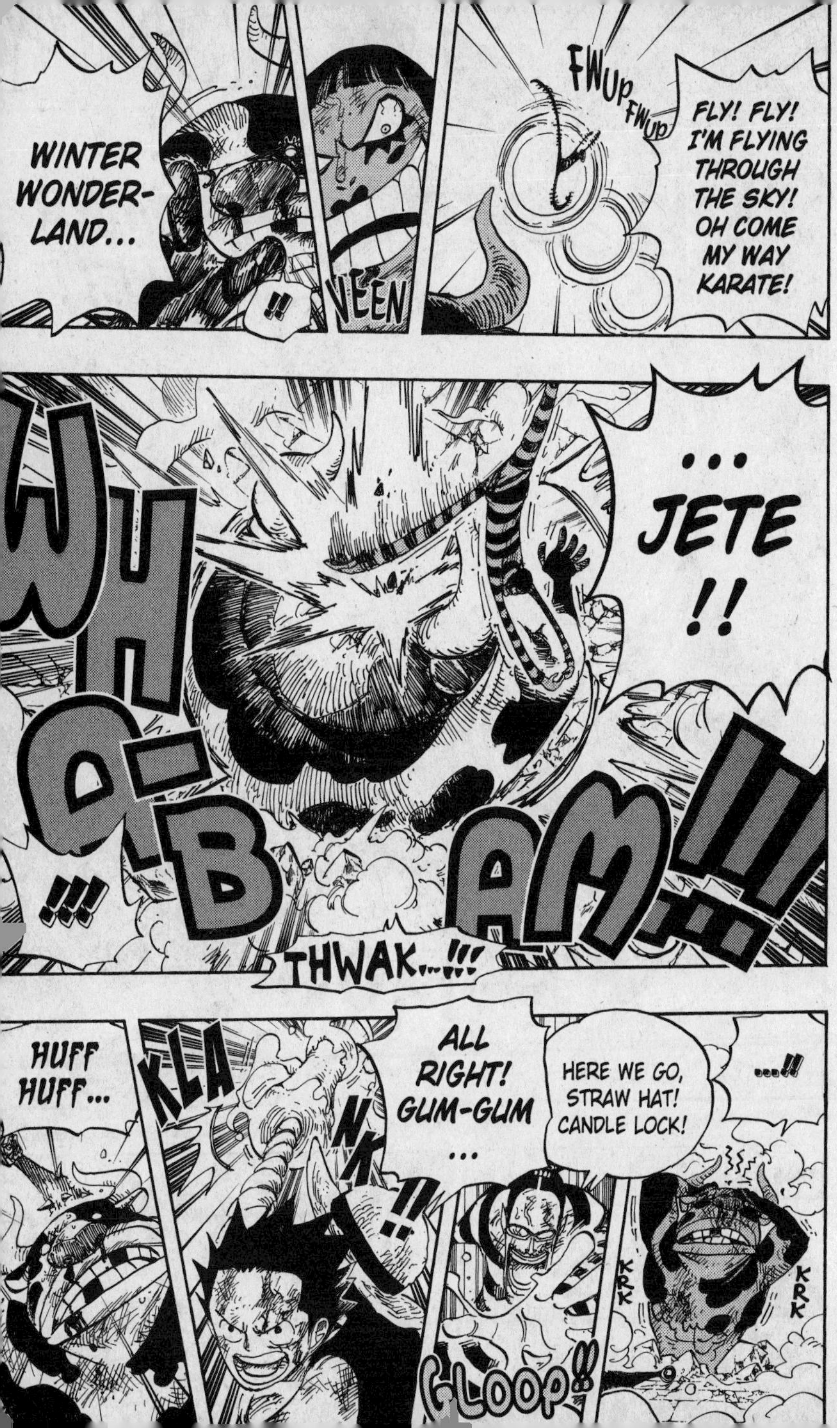
FWUP FWUP
FLY! FLY! I'M FLYING THROUGH THE SKY! OH COME MY WAY KARATE!
VEEN
!!
WINTER WONDER-LAND...
...JETE!!
WHA-BAM!!!
THWAK...!!!
...!!
KRK
KRK
HERE WE GO, STRAW HAT! CANDLE LOCK!
GLOOP!!
ALL RIGHT! GUM-GUM ...
KLANK!!
HUFF HUFF...

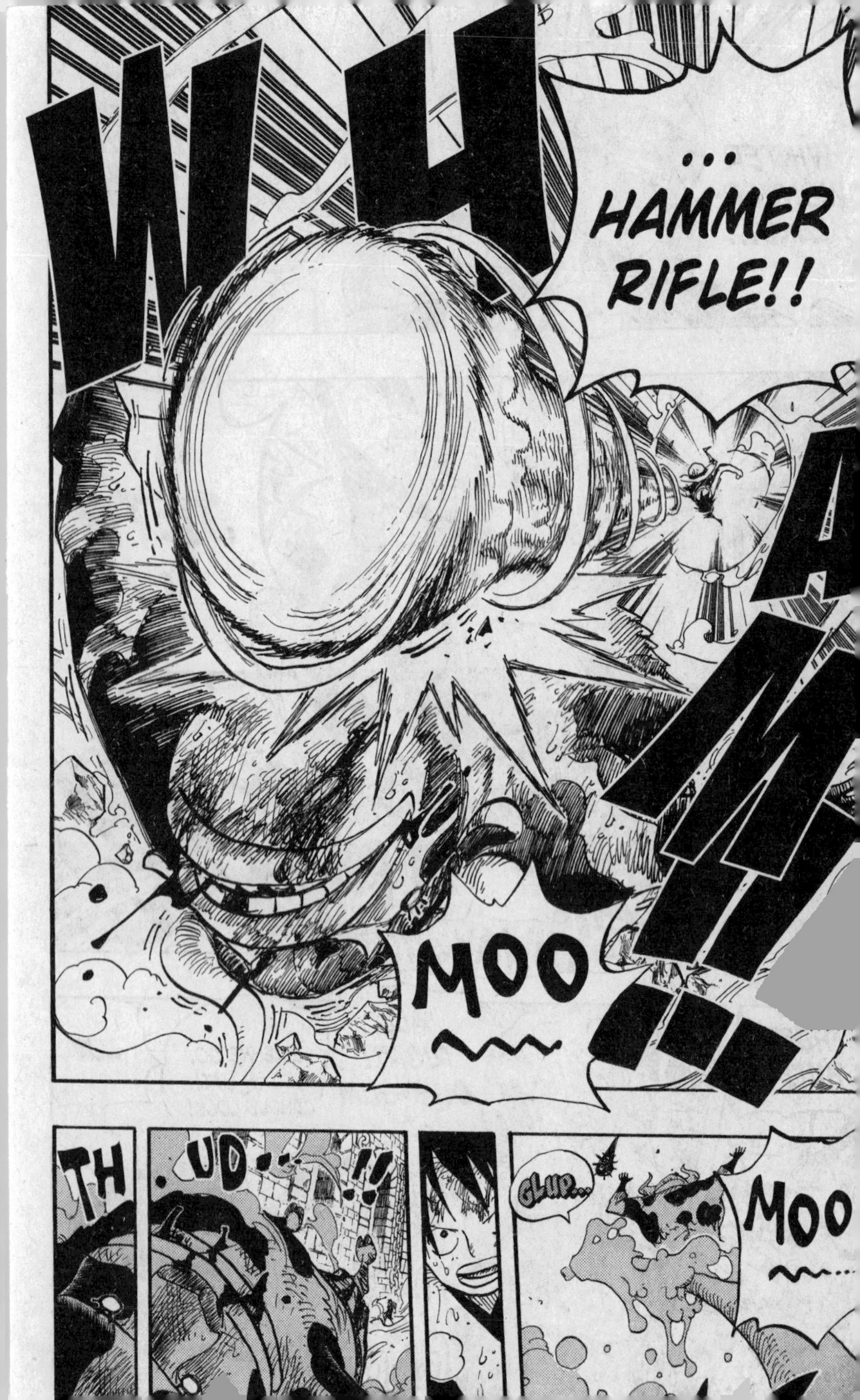
... HAMMER RIFLE!!
MOO ~~~
MOO ~~~
GLUP...
UD...!!
TH

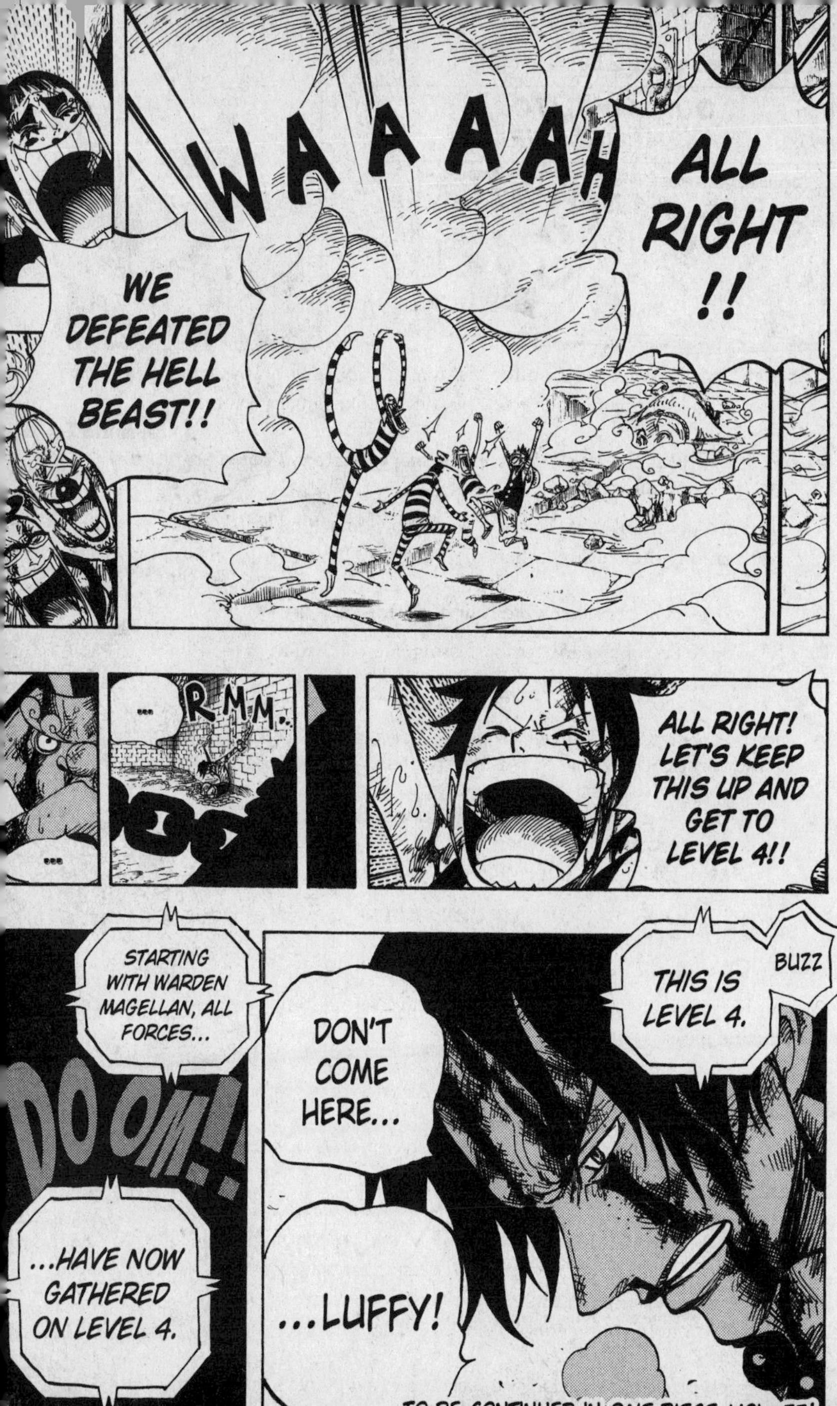
ALL RIGHT!!
WAAAAH
WE DEFEATED THE HELL BEAST!!
ALL RIGHT! LET'S KEEP THIS UP AND GET TO LEVEL 4!!
...
RMM..
...
BUZZ
THIS IS LEVEL 4.
DON'T COME HERE...
...LUFFY!
STARTING WITH WARDEN MAGELLAN, ALL FORCES...
DOOM!!
...HAVE NOW GATHERED ON LEVEL 4.

TO BE CONTINUED IN ONE PIECE, VOL. 55!

SBS Question Corner

OUR NAVIGATOR, AKEMI OKAMURA!

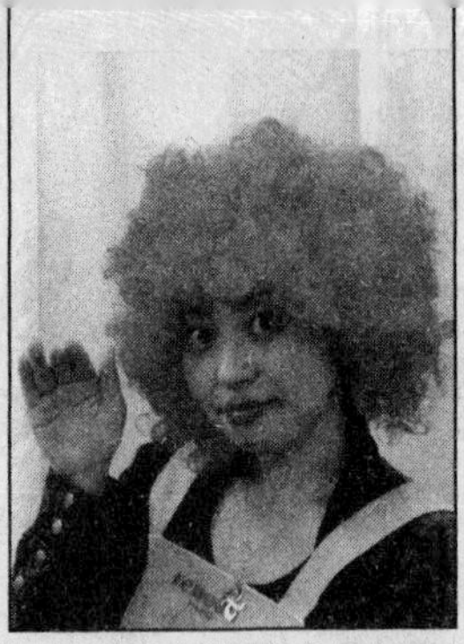

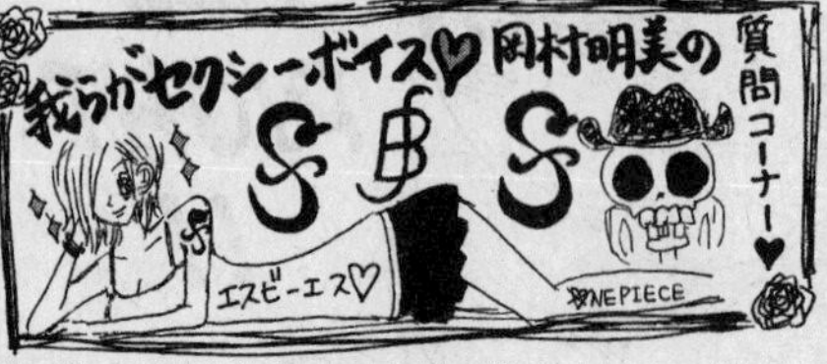

我らがセクシーボイス♡岡村明美の
SBS
質問コーナー♥
エスビーエス♡
ONE PIECE

(Shimauma, Ehime)

Reader(R): I have a question for Ms. Akemi! ♪ Nami is always taking good care of her tangerine trees, but do you like tangerines too?

--Kaorin

Akemi(A): I love them. ♡ I sit in my warm kotatsu table and eat them all winter.

R: I have a question! What's your type? Who would you like to go out with among the crew members of the Straw Hats?

--TMT

A: All of them combined. The thing called Gargon. ➡

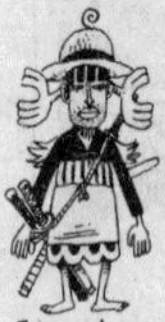

From volume 33, Gargon

R: Has there even been an…embarrassing line you had to say? If so, which one?

--Windy

A: In the script, the captain (Mayumi Tanaka) rewrote my line that says "Thunderbolt--Tempo." The "te" part in "Tempo" was rewritten with a "chi." That was so embarrassing when I screamed it out! [Note: replacing the "te" with the "chi" turns the word "tempo" into the word for male parts.]

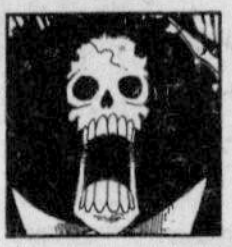

R: To Akemi Okamura on the Question Corner.

May I look at your underwear? --Corbuckle

A: No!

R: I always go on spending sprees. Can you give me some advice? In the voice of Nami, please.

--Hiromu

A: I'll lend you money. ♡ Only 30 percent interest! ♪

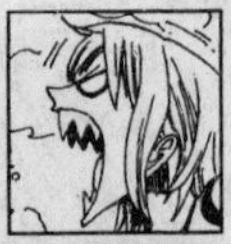

R: What does it mean to believe?

--Umeboshi Chazuke

A: Beats me!

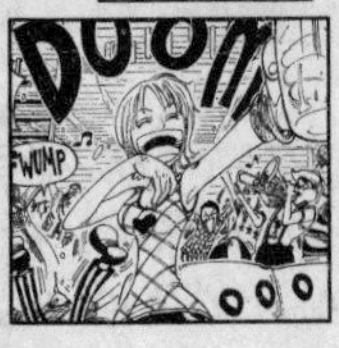

DOON
WUMP

R: Hello! My friend told me of the time he saw you on stage at Jump Festa. During that event, you said that you always go drinking after recording. If that's true, does that mean you hold your alcohol well? Like Nami?

--Aino

A: We often go out to party with the cast and staff of *One Piece*. We don't just go drinking. It's a party! ♥

R: Hello, Okamura! I have a question. In the previous Question Corner and the one before that, Tanaka and Nakai both said that they go for "realism" when they do their acts. Do you do the same? If you do, how did you go about doing it during the "Happiness Punch" part...? Ahem. Never mind. Forget I said that.

--Nami Fan Club Member No. 73

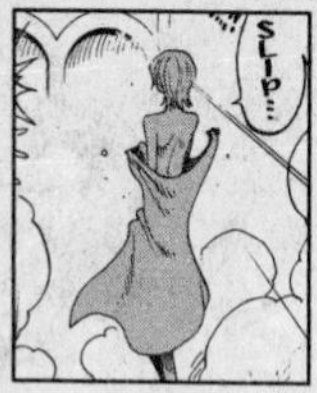
SLIP...

A: Of course I go for "realism," too! On that day, I didn't wear my underwea... What are you making me say?!

R: I have a question for Nami on the Question Corner. Nami often smacks the other crew members, but do you actually do it to the other voice actors? For realism? Also, why don't you smack Chopper too much? Because he's cute?

--Raccoon Dog

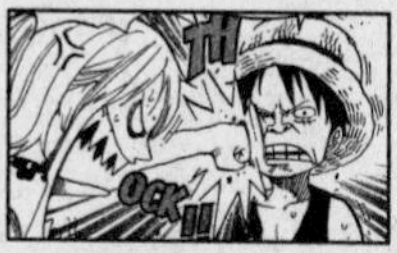
TH
OCK!!

A: Of course I go for realism too! Chopper is played by someone who's a much higher senior member of the agency! (Behind-the-scenes circumstances♡)

R: Please draw a picture of your character! (Don't use any reference materials!☆)

--Tokoyan

A: ➡

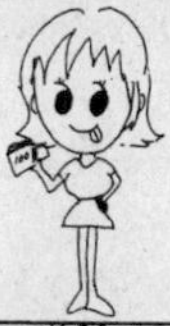

R: I have a question for Nami (Akemi Okamura). Nami always acts uninterested, but does she actually like gentlemen characters like Sanji?

--Blonde Winding Eyebrows Thick-Lips

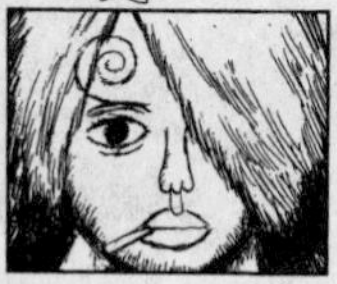

A: What? Sanji? A gentleman? I thought he was a cook.

R: During Thriller Bark, Nami was the only one who wasn't hit by the Negative Hollow. All right! Have the same be done to you like Nakai! "Take this! Negative Hollow!"

--Mayonnaise Black

A: Ugh... I'm sorry I'm so beautiful...

Oda: That's not negative! Okay. It's time, Okamura. The last question is a bit dangerous, so just brush it off.

R: Hello, Okamura. I often watch *One Piece* with my family members. So here's my question. If you were to take a trip, where would you want to go? (In Kuma's voice) Pop!

--Sou-kun

A: Noooo! (Somewhere warm, has a beach, has great food, has a pretty sky, has a hot spring, and a place where I can relax!)

Oda: You have way too many requests! Oh, there she goes. Goodbye, Okamura. And thank you! Now then! Look forward to the next Voice Actor Question Corner!

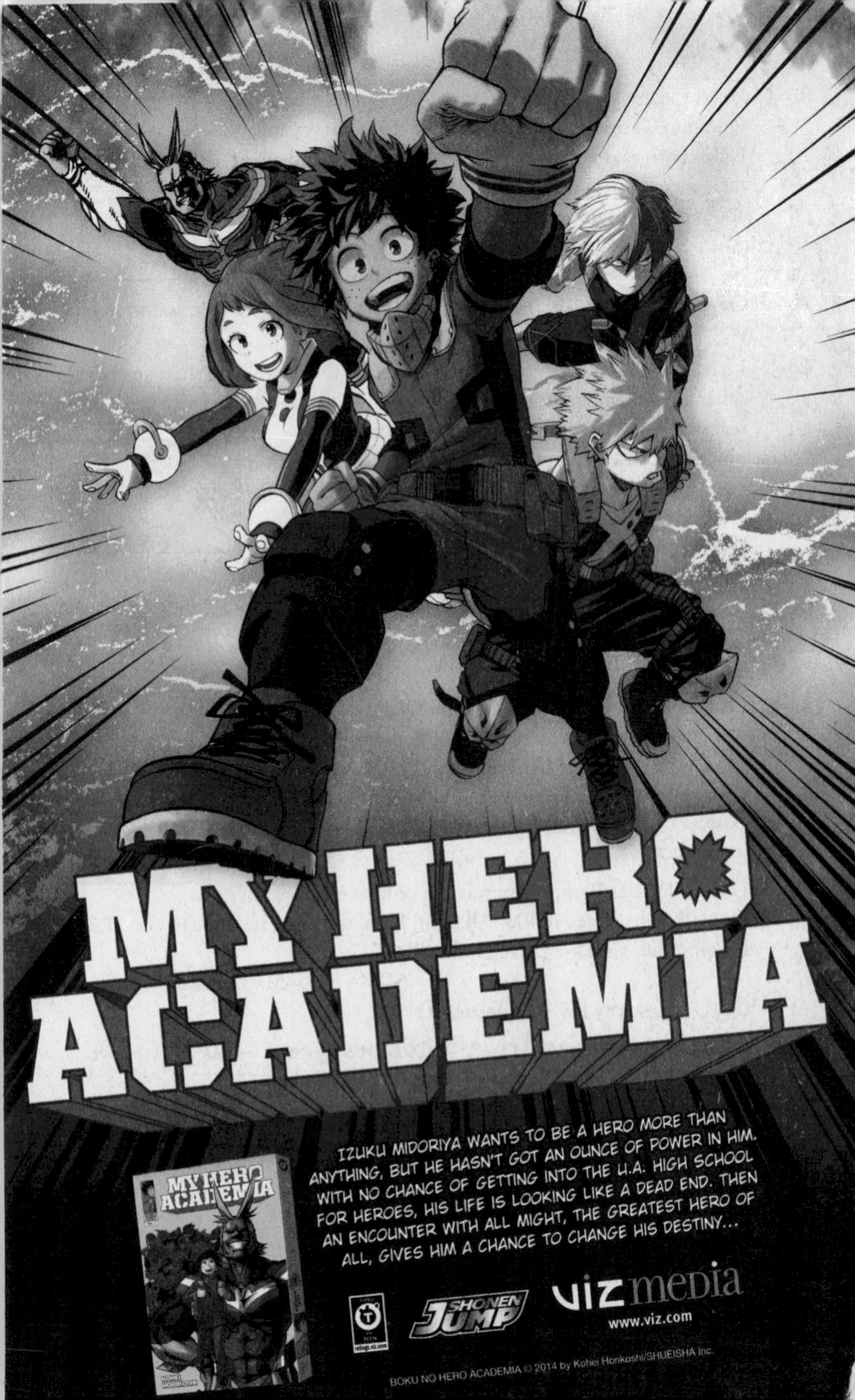
MY HERO ACADEMIA
IZUKU MIDORIYA WANTS TO BE A HERO MORE THAN ANYTHING, BUT HE HASN'T GOT AN OUNCE OF POWER IN HIM. WITH NO CHANCE OF GETTING INTO THE U.A. HIGH SCHOOL FOR HEROES, HIS LIFE IS LOOKING LIKE A DEAD END. THEN AN ENCOUNTER WITH ALL MIGHT, THE GREATEST HERO OF ALL, GIVES HIM A CHANCE TO CHANGE HIS DESTINY...
MY HERO ACADEMIA
KOHEI HORIKOSHI
TEEN
ratings.viz.com
SHONEN JUMP
VIZ media
www.viz.com
BOKU NO HERO ACADEMIA © 2014 by Kohei Horikoshi/SHUEISHA Inc.

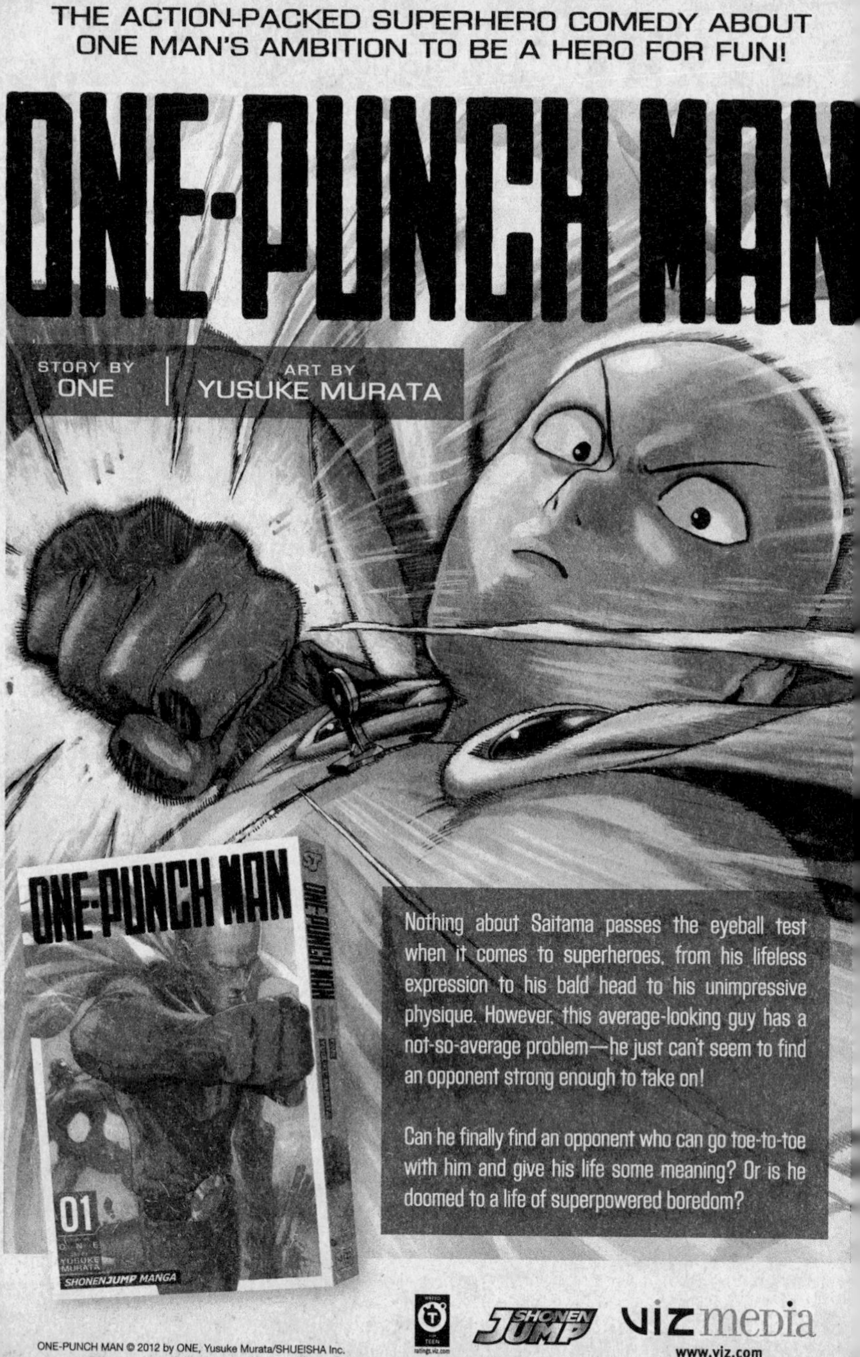
THE ACTION-PACKED SUPERHERO COMEDY ABOUT ONE MAN'S AMBITION TO BE A HERO FOR FUN!
ONE-PUNCH MAN
STORY BY ONE
ART BY YUSUKE MURATA
ONE-PUNCH MAN
01
ONE
YUSUKE MURATA
SHONENJUMP MANGA
Nothing about Saitama passes the eyeball test when it comes to superheroes, from his lifeless expression to his bald head to his unimpressive physique. However, this average-looking guy has a not-so-average problem—he just can't seem to find an opponent strong enough to take on!
Can he finally find an opponent who can go toe-to-toe with him and give his life some meaning? Or is he doomed to a life of superpowered boredom?
TEEN
ratings.viz.com
SHONEN JUMP
viz media
www.viz.com
ONE-PUNCH MAN © 2012 by ONE, Yusuke Murata/SHUEISHA Inc.

IN A SAVAGE WORLD RULED BY THE PURSUIT OF THE MOST DELICIOUS FOODS, IT'S EITHER EAT OR BE EATEN!

"The most bizarrely entertaining manga out there on comic shelves. *Toriko* is a great series. If you're looking for a weirdly fun book or a fighting manga with a bizarre take, this is the story for you to read."

—ComicAttack.com

Story and Art by Mitsutoshi Shimabukuro

In an era where the world's gone crazy for increasingly bizarre gourmet foods, only Gourmet Hunter Toriko can hunt down the ferocious ingredients that supply the world's best restaurants. Join Toriko as he tracks and defeats the tastiest and most dangerous animals with his bare hands.

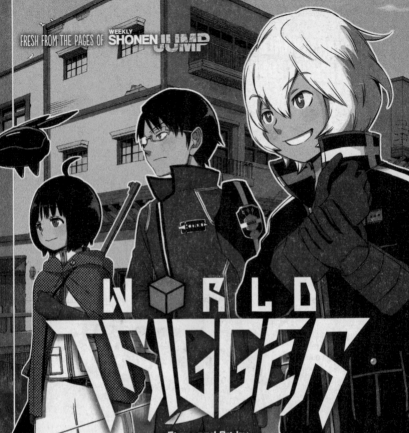

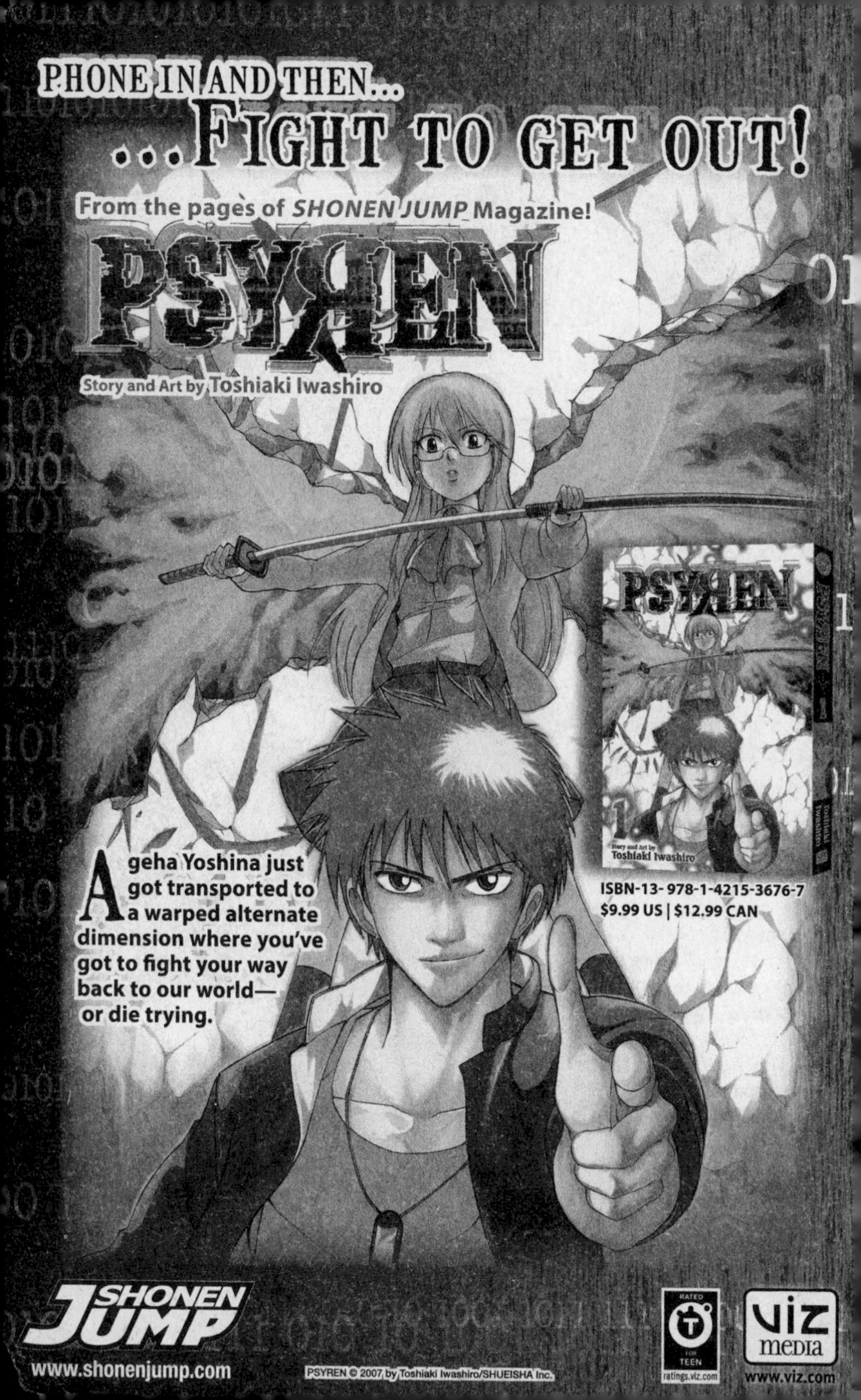
PHONE IN AND THEN...
...FIGHT TO GET OUT!
From the pages of SHONEN JUMP Magazine!
PSYREN
Story and Art by Toshiaki Iwashiro
PSYREN
1
Story and Art by Toshiaki Iwashiro
ISBN-13- 978-1-4215-3676-7
$9.99 US | $12.99 CAN
Ageha Yoshina just got transported to a warped alternate dimension where you've got to fight your way back to our world— or die trying.
SHONEN JUMP
www.shonenjump.com
PSYREN © 2007 by Toshiaki Iwashiro/SHUEISHA Inc.
RATED T FOR TEEN
ratings.viz.com
VIZ media
www.viz.com

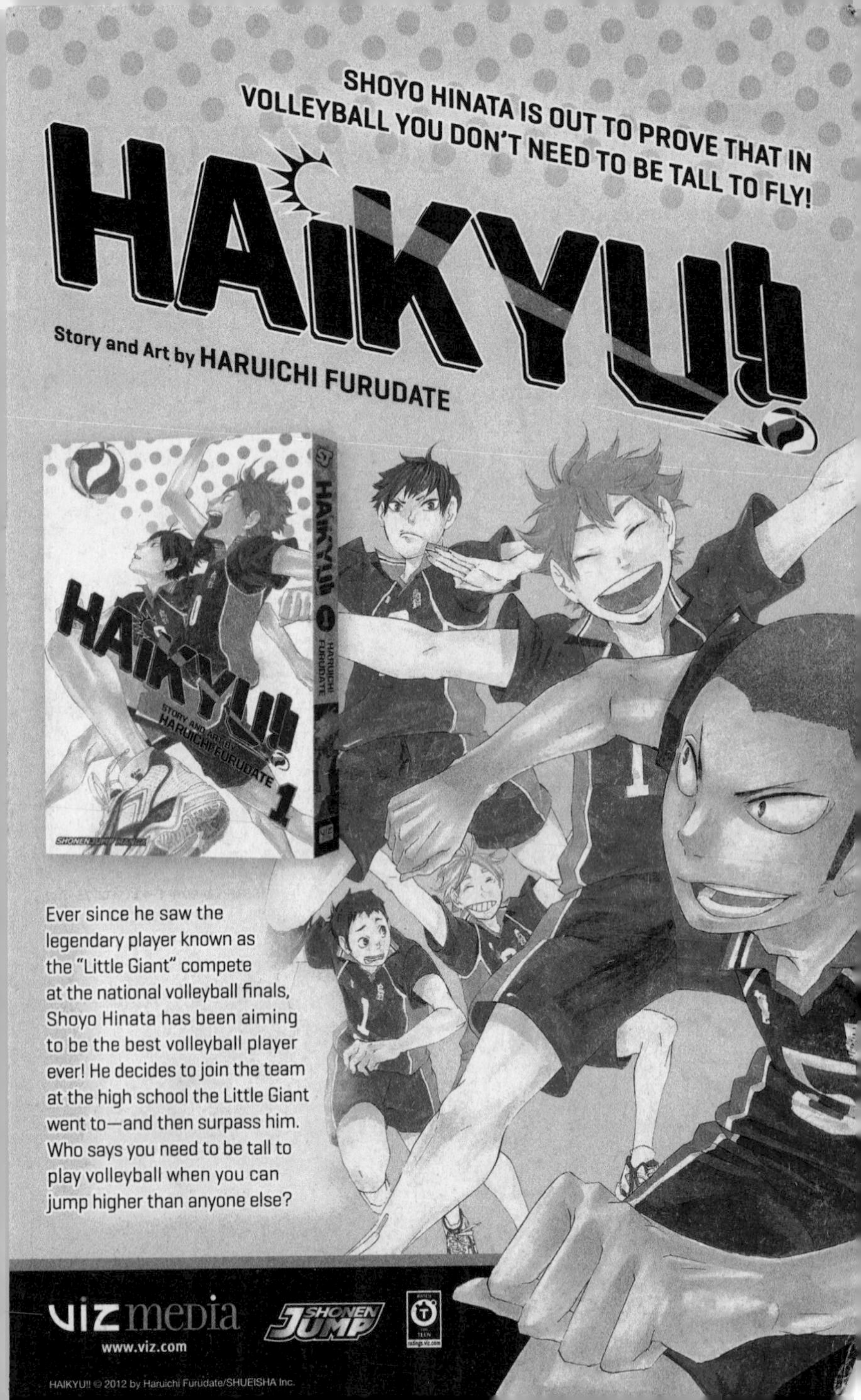
SHOYO HINATA IS OUT TO PROVE THAT IN VOLLEYBALL YOU DON'T NEED TO BE TALL TO FLY!
HAIKYU!!
Story and Art by HARUICHI FURUDATE
HAIKYU!! STORY AND ART BY HARUICHI FURUDATE 1
SHONEN JUMP MANGA
Ever since he saw the legendary player known as the "Little Giant" compete at the national volleyball finals, Shoyo Hinata has been aiming to be the best volleyball player ever! He decides to join the team at the high school the Little Giant went to—and then surpass him. Who says you need to be tall to play volleyball when you can jump higher than anyone else?
viz media
www.viz.com
SHONEN JUMP
RATED T TEEN ratings.viz.com
HAIKYU!! © 2012 by Haruichi Furudate/SHUEISHA Inc.

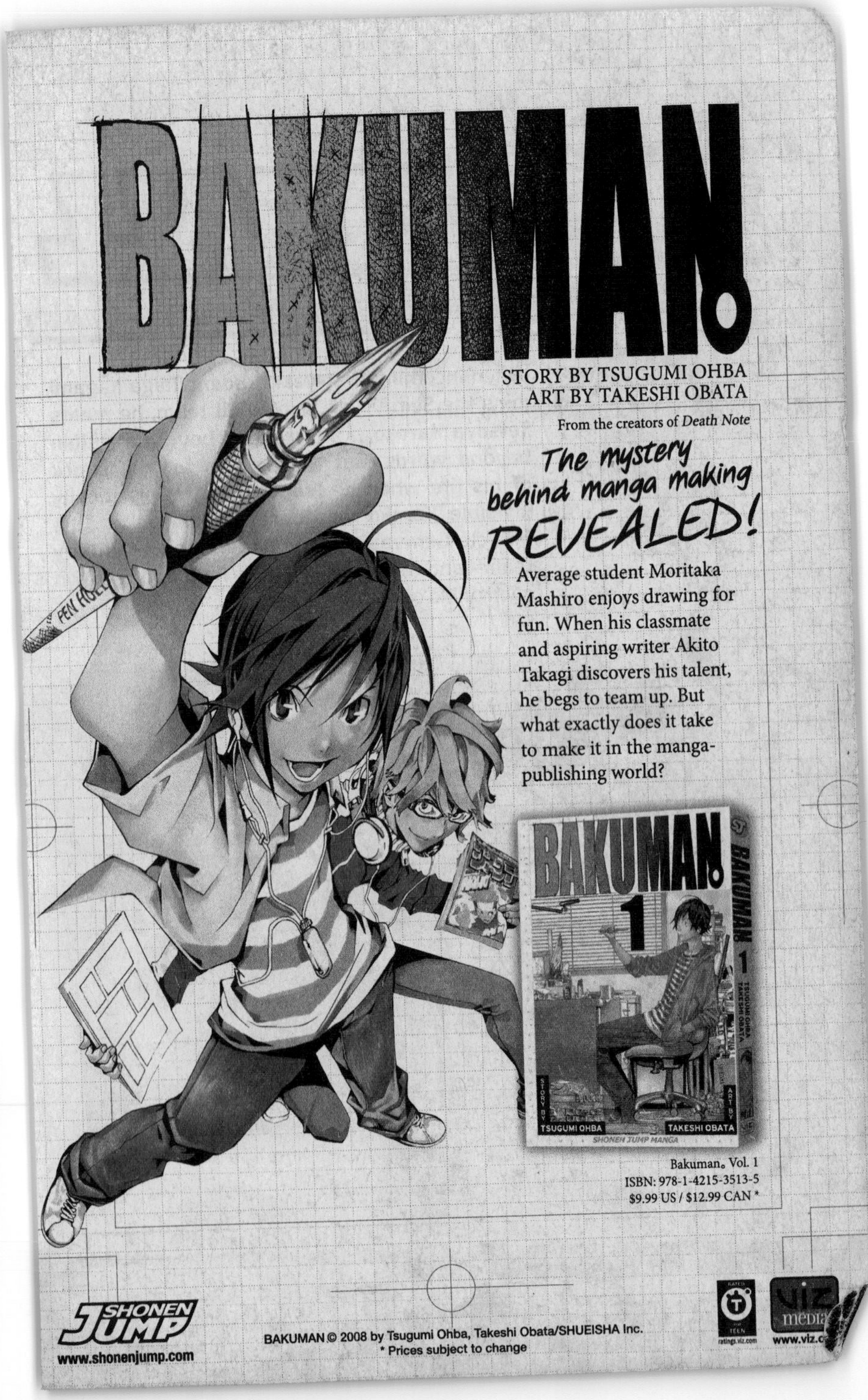
BAKUMAN。
STORY BY TSUGUMI OHBA
ART BY TAKESHI OBATA
From the creators of Death Note
The mystery behind manga making REVEALED!
Average student Moritaka Mashiro enjoys drawing for fun. When his classmate and aspiring writer Akito Takagi discovers his talent, he begs to team up. But what exactly does it take to make it in the manga-publishing world?
BAKUMAN。 1
STORY BY TSUGUMI OHBA
ART BY TAKESHI OBATA
SHONEN JUMP MANGA
Bakuman。 Vol. 1
ISBN: 978-1-4215-3513-5
$9.99 US / $12.99 CAN *
SHONEN JUMP
www.shonenjump.com
BAKUMAN © 2008 by Tsugumi Ohba, Takeshi Obata/SHUEISHA Inc.
* Prices subject to change
RATED T TEEN
ratings.viz.com
VIZ media
www.viz.com

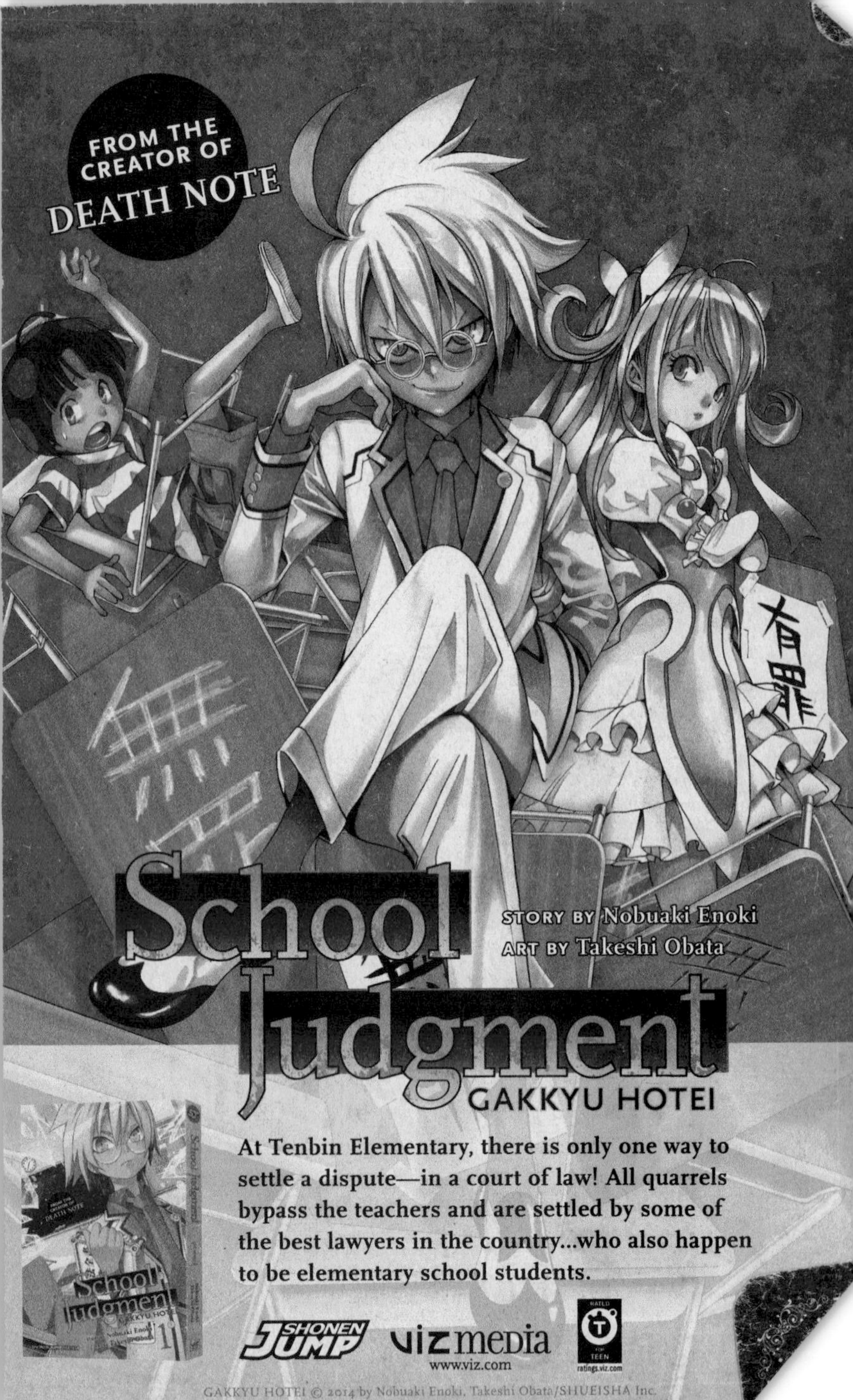
FROM THE CREATOR OF DEATH NOTE
School Judgment
STORY BY Nobuaki Enoki
ART BY Takeshi Obata
GAKKYU HOTEI
At Tenbin Elementary, there is only one way to settle a dispute—in a court of law! All quarrels bypass the teachers and are settled by some of the best lawyers in the country...who also happen to be elementary school students.
SHONEN JUMP
VIZ media
www.viz.com
RATED T FOR TEEN
ratings.viz.com
GAKKYU HOTEI © 2014 by Nobuaki Enoki, Takeshi Obata/SHUEISHA Inc.